URBAN PLANNING LAW

AUSTRALIA
The Law Book Company Ltd.
Sydney : Melbourne : Brisbane

CANADA AND U.S.A
The Carswell Company Ltd.
Agincourt, Ontario

INDIA
N. M. Tripathi Private Ltd.
Bombay
and
Eastern Law House Private Ltd.
Calcutta and Delhi
M.P.P. House
Bangalore

ISRAEL
Steimatzky's Agency Ltd.
Jerusalem : Tel Aviv : Haifa

MALAYSIA : SINGAPORE : BRUNEI
Malayan Law Journal (Pte.) Ltd.
Singapore

NEW ZEALAND
Sweet & Maxwell (N.Z.) Ltd.
Auckland

PAKISTAN
Pakistan Law House
Karachi

URBAN PLANNING LAW

By

MALCOLM GRANT, LL.M.

Barrister, New Zealand
Lecturer in Law, University of Southampton

LONDON
SWEET & MAXWELL
1982

Published in 1982 by
Sweet and Maxwell Limited of
11 New Fetter Lane, London
Computerset by Promenade Graphics Limited, Cheltenham
Printed and bound in Great Britain by
Robert Hartnoll Limited, Bodmin, Cornwall

British Library Cataloguing in Publication Data

Grant, Malcolm
  Urban planning law.
  1. City planning and redevelopment law—England
  I. Title
  344.206'45   KD1125

  ISBN 0-421-24120-9

PREFACE

A new book on planning law requires special justification. With this text I have aimed to bridge two gaps: first, the gap between the existing introductory planning law books and the all-embracing *Encyclopedia of Planning Law and Practice*; and, secondly, the gap between the law and the practice of land-use planning. The breadth of that latter gap is nowhere better illustrated than by Patrick McAuslan's two excellent books, *Land, Law and Planning* (Wiedenfeld and Nicolson, 1975) and *The Ideologies of Planning Law* (Pergamon Press, 1980). Planning law in itself tells us remarkably little about land-use planning as a regulatory system, and I have tried therefore to set the system of controls in its broader functional context. At the same time, I have consciously adopted a style more expositive than theoretical, in an attempt to provide a basic working tool for all those coming into contact with the planning machine. But I have avoided simple reproduction of the legislation, which readers will find in updated and amended form in the *Encyclopedia* and in my *Planning Law Handbook* (Sweet and Maxwell, 1981).

The aims of the book are ambitious, no doubt over-ambitious. When I started writing it in 1978, they seemed more logical and more attainable than they do today. In those days the first structure plans were only starting to filter through the system, the community land scheme was at its (limited) peak, and there was no hint of the great mass of new legislation and the many policy changes which were about to erupt following the change in government in 1979. Unpredictability became the only constant factor in planning law, and there were times when I wondered whether there was a causal link between my completion of a draft section of manuscript on a topic and the Secretary of State's announcement of proposals for immediate fundamental changes. Repeated rewriting is a valuable discipline, but it has stretched the patience and resources both of my secretary for the past nine years, Mrs Beryl Johnstone (whose tireless efforts have conferred on the book such limited intelligibility as it may have, and whose choice of early and well deserved retirement she loyally maintains to be due to other factors); and of my publishers, to whom I owe a special debt for their courage in commissioning the book and for their unfailing encouragement, enthusiasm and efficiency thereafter. I am also grateful to them for allowing me to draw from material that I have written in the past for the *Journal of Planning and Environment Law* and *Current Law Statutes*, and for entrusting me in 1981–1982 with the task of revising the *Encyclopedia of Planning Law and Practice*, which broadened my knowledge of the detail of planning law enormously (though it has led inevitably to some similarities in approach between the *Encyclopedia* and this book).

My list of other debts is unusually long. Many different people have helped me, often unwittingly, in supplying information, in challenging ideas and in pointing me in new directions. In particular, I acknowledge the contribution that has been made by my students over the years on the planning law course at Southampton University, and those on the joint LL.M.–M.Sc. course in planning and environmental control at University

College London. I owe a very great debt to Jeffrey Jowell, both for allowing me to share the teaching of the London seminars with him for the past three years and for his unrivalled understanding of the British planning system. I am deeply grateful also to those colleagues and friends who have read all or part of the draft manuscript at different stages—Alison Clarke, Charles Cross, Malcolm Forster, and Michael Purdue: to them goes all the credit and none of the blame for what follows. Also to the Law Faculty at Southampton University, for their positive and highly professional approach to legal education, and their continued willingness to devote time and facilities to legal research in an era of recession. A period of sabbatical leave in 1979 gave me the opportunity to lay the basis of the book; and I have had unfailing and expert assistance from Joan Hoyle and Diana Marshalsay of the University Library, and access to the superb Ford Collection of Parliamentary Papers. Grateful acknowledgment must also be made to J. McAuslan and the *Estates Gazette*, to R. H. Best and *The Planner*, and to *Town and Country Planning*, for permitting me to cite the material appearing in the tables on pp. 26, 306 and 505 respectively; also to the Controller of Her Majesty's Stationery Office for kind permission to use the various extracts from Government and Departmental Publications that appear in this book. The Department of the Environment, the Welsh Office and the Land Authority for Wales have provided the utmost cooperation in answering my queries and in forwarding material to me.

Finally, the quartet whose sacrifice has been the greatest and whose support has meant the most: my wife, Chris, and our three children Nicky, Joanna and Tom. My dedication of the book to them is no more than an insignificant symbol of my great debt.

The manuscript was completed at the end of 1981, but the generous flexibility of my publishers has meant that I have been able to incorporate subsequent changes in the law as the book has progressed through the various printing stages. So far as possible the law is stated as at October 1, 1982.

MALCOLM GRANT

The University,
Southampton.
October 1, 1982.

TABLE OF CONTENTS

TABLE OF CASES

TABLE OF STATUTES

TABLE OF STATUTORY INSTRUMENTS

TABLE OF CIRCULARS

LIST OF TABLES

LIST OF ABBREVIATIONS

A.M.A.A.A. 1979	– Ancient Monuments and Archaeological Areas Act 1979
A.O.N.B.	– Area of Outstanding Natural Beauty
A.P.R.	– Town and Country Planning (Determination by Appointed Persons) (Inquiries Procedure) Rules 1974 (S.I. 1974 No. 420)
B.C.	– Borough Council
C.A.	– Court of Appeal
C.B.C.	– County Borough Council
C.C.	– County Council or City Council
C.L.J.	– Cambridge Law Journal
C.L.R.	– Commonwealth Law Reports (Aust)
C.O.P.A.	– Control of Pollution Act 1974
D.C.	– District Council
D.C.P.N.	– Development Control Policy Notes
D.O.E.	– Department of the Environment
D.R.R.G.	– Domestic Rate Relief Grant
E.G.	– Estates Gazette
E.I.P.R.	– Town and Country Planning (Enforcement) (Inquiries Procedure) Rules 1981 (S.I. 1981 No. 1743)
G.D.O.	– Town and Country Planning General Development Order 1977 (S.I. 1977 No. 289)
G.I.A.	– General Improvement Area
G.L.C.	– Greater London Council
G.L.D.P.	– Greater London Development Plan
H.A.A.	– Housing Action Area
H.C. Deb.	– House of Commons Debates
H.L.	– House of Lords
H.L. Deb.	– House of Lords Debates
H.M.S.O.	– Her Majesty's Stationery Office
I.D.C.	– Industrial Development Certificate
I.D.P.	– Initial Development Plan
I.I.A.	– Industrial and Commercial Improvement Area
I.P.R.	– Town and Country Planning (Inquiries Procedure) Rules 1974 (S.I. 1974 No. 419)
I.R.C.	– Inland Revenue Commissioners
J.P.L.	– Journal of Planning and Environment Law
L.A.W.	– Land Authority for Wales
L.B.C.	– London Borough Council
L.C.A. 1961	– Land Compensation Act 1961
L.C.A. 1973	– Land Compensation Act 1973
L.G.A.	– Local Government Act 1972/1974

L.G.P.(A).A. 1981   – Local Government and Planning (Amendment) Act
                   1981
L.G.P.L.A. 1980   – Local Government, Planning and Land Act 1980
L.P.A.   – Local Planning Authority
M.A.F.F.   – Ministry of Agriculture, Fisheries and Food
M.B.C.   – Metropolitan Borough Council
M.H.L.G.   – Ministry of Housing and Local Government
m.p.d.   – ministerial planning decision
M.T.C.P.   – Ministry of Town and Country Planning
N.P.A.C.A. 1949   – National Parks and Access to the Countryside Act
                   1949
O.C.P.U.   – Outer Circle Policy Unit
O.D.P.   – Office Development Permit
O.J.L.   – Official Journal of the European Communities —
                   Legislation series
O.P.C.S.   – Office of Population Censuses and Surveys
P.A.G.   – Planning Advisory Group
P. & C.R.   – Property and Compensation Reports
Plans Regulations   – Town and Country Planning (Structure and Local
                   Plans) Regulations 1982 (S.I. 1982 No. 555)
R.D.C.   – Rural District Council
R.L.B.C.   – Royal London Borough Council
R.S.C.   – Rules of the Supreme Court
R.S.G.   – Rate Support Grant
S.A.U.S.   – School for Advanced Urban Studies (University of
                   Bristol)
S.D.O.   – Special Development Order
S.I.   – Statutory Instrument
S.O.S.E.   – Secretary of State for the Environment
S.S.S.I.   – Site of Special Scientific Interest
T.C.P.   – Town and Country Planning
T.C.P.A. 1932   – Town and Country Planning Act 1932
T.C.P.A. 1947   – Town and Country Planning Act 1947
T.C.P.A. 1971   – Town and Country Planning Act 1971
T.C.P.(A.)A 1972   – Town and Country Planning (Amendment) Act 1972
T.C.P.(M.).A. 1981 – Town and Country Planning (Minerals) Act 1981
U.C.O.   – Use Classes Order
U.D.C.   – Urban Development Corporation *or* Urban District
                   Council
W.A.   – Water Authority
W.C.A. 1981   – Wildlife and Countryside Act 1981
W.O.   – Welsh Office

CHAPTER 1

INTRODUCTION

A. Planning in modern Britain

1. Introduction

Of all the regulatory machinery that has been established in post-war Britain, none has proved so persistently controversial as the land use planning system. It is variously accused by its critics of being too rigid (and, equally vociferously, of being too flexible), too restrictive (or too permissive), too adventurous (or too conventional) and too comprehensive (or too narrow). It is blamed for a variety of evils ranging from national economic decline to teenage crime, and the list includes the many adverse changes in post-war urban conditions such as urban motorways, tower blocks, inner city deprivation, vacant land, the destruction of historic buildings and the loss of good agricultural land to urban development.

The list is long, and the criticisms are difficult to counter if it is true that these ills were ever within the power of planners to overcome. The reality is, however, that the planning system has wielded comparatively little by way of real power and resources to direct or influence the pattern of urban change. Apart from the isolated instances of large scale and planning-based public enterprise such as the new towns, British land-use planning is still primarily a system of response to change, a system of guidance and regulation of a predominantly private development market; and, above all, it is a political system. Planning law establishes the framework for power through which planning control over land use is exercised, but the policies which are pursued in the name of planning and the choices which are made between competing alternatives for development are the product of a variety of largely unregulated influences and pressures, some of them powerful, others weak. Planning law prescribes the procedures—it sets the battle lines—for the resolution of conflict over land use between the interests of private property and the prevailing "public" or "community" interest. It is neither a static nor a neutral system of rules, and the balance which it sets between private and public interest, and between the different institutions representing the public interest, is constantly changing.

The clearest example of change is the legislative programme of the past two years, which has thrown up in quick succession the Local Government, Planning and Land Act 1980, the Town and Country Planning (Minerals) Act 1981 and the Local Government and Planning (Amendment) Act 1981, together with a host of new subordinate legislation and administrative circulars. These measures collectively represent something more than merely the carrying out of running repairs to increase the efficiency and effectiveness of the planning machine; nor may they be expected overnight to silence the critics of planning. As McAuslan has pointed out,

"Lawyers, planners, politicians and laymen tend to stress a different ideology and argue for changes or reforms in the law or new laws in terms of the ideology they espouse and the resultant cacophony, first translated into law and then continued in its administration and interpretation, leads to confusion and disarray."[1]

But what McAuslan identifies as confusion and disarray in modern planning is in reality the normal working state of a healthy political institution, responding and adjusting to changing pressures; and much of the undoubted disenchantment which attaches to the post-war performance of planning is due to the overly ambitious promises which invariably attach to each new reform, as well as to the fact that the successes of a primarily regulatory system inevitably fall to be assessed in primarily negative terms. Without planning and the controls on urban growth that have guided post-war development, there is little prospect that the pre-war pattern of sprawl into the countryside and extensive ribbon development would have diminished, nor that the congestion and squalor of the inner cities would have been eased. That the physical scars of post-war urban Britain have now largely disappeared is a tribute in itself to the way planning has operated; though it must not be allowed to disguise the fact that many social and economic problems remain, and that unsympathetic new development has too often scarred the cities afresh.

2. The Roots of Modern Planning Law

Modern land use planning is entirely the product of statutory legislation. The common law regulated private rights, but recognised no supervening public or governmental interest in the private use of land. Land use regulation was instead a product primarily of tenure, and restrictions on use and new building were imposed as conditions upon which the land was held from the superior landlord. A limited extension of that doctrine emerged in the mid-nineteenth century as the break-up of the large estates and the spread of freehold ownership loosened the traditional controls, and made it necessary to allow the enforcement of similar restrictive conditions between the freehold owners of adjacent land. The leading case in the development of this doctrine was *Tulk* v. *Moxhay*,[2] where the defendants had purchased the open gardens of London's Leicester Square with knowledge of a covenant against development entered into by the former owners, and now asserted a right to build there. They had, after all, no contractual nexus with the original owners who now sought to enforce the covenant. But despite this, the Court refused to contemplate that a subsequent purchaser might violate such a condition imposed by a prior vendor, for "If that were so, it would be impossible for an owner of land to sell part of it without incurring the risk of rendering what he retains worthless." And further, the value of the land would be affected by whether there existed an unrestricted right to build, and

> " . . . nothing could be more inequitable than that the original purchaser should be able to sell the property the next day for a greater price, in consideration of the assignee being allowed to escape from the liability which he had himself undertaken."[3]

---

[1] Patrick McAuslan, *The Ideologies of Planning Law* (Pergamon Press, 1980) p.2.
[2] (1849) 2 PL. 774 (41 E.R. 1143).
[3] *Ibid.* per Lord Cottenham L.C.

Thus was born the doctrine of enforceability of restrictive covenants between freehold owners, a device which continues today to provide a powerful means both of regulating development of land upon its subdivision, and also, through a further extension to the doctrine, of exerting continuing control between purchasers of the various plots of development schemes.[4]

The other relevant limb of the common law was that of nuisance. The courts came to insist that the full right of enjoyment and exploitation of land which the common law recognised as a benefit of ownership, was nonetheless subject to some limitation in order to preserve the enjoyment and exploitation rights of adjoining occupiers. Many of the early rulings in nuisance dealt with the everyday problems of an essentially rural society, such as the diversion of streams, failure to repair bridges, the stopping up of rights of way across meadows, interference with markets and fairs and damage caused by pigeons. But by the late-eighteenth century an urban element was clearly discernible in cases dealing with adjoining dwellings and industrial nuisances in towns. Hence

> "If I have a house by prescription upon my soil, and another erects a *new house* upon his own soil next adjoining, so near to my house that it *stops the light of my house*, this is a nuisance to my house; for the light is of great comfort and profit to men."

And the second edition of *Viners Abridgement*,[5] which appeared in 1793, lists a variety of actionable urban nuisances, including bawdy houses,[6] bowling alleys, common gaming houses, playhouses (though only where drawing together such number of coaches or people as prove generally inconvenient to the places adjacent); and brewhouses and chandleries, although some dispute remained between the judges as to whether a man should be punished for erecting anything necessary for his lawful trade, notwithstanding that there was no necessity to carry on that trade within the town itself.[7] There is nothing new about the conflict between industry and amenity.

Nuisance and tenure then were the instruments of the common law, but they proved increasingly inadequate to deal with the problems of an increasingly urban and industrial society, particularly as the industrial revolution led to the massive influx of population from the country to the cities. There is some support for the view that the fault lay not with the instruments of the common law, but in the failure by the judiciary to develop and adapt them to changing social needs, and there is a continuing debate today as to the unfulfilled potential of private law remedies in land

---

[4] For a study of the role of restrictive covenants as private land use regulators, see Patrick McAuslan, *Land, Law and Planning* (Wiedenfeld and Nicolson, 1975), Chap. 3.

[5] *Viners Abridgement* (2nd ed.), Vol.XV1, pp. 19–47.

[6] "Not only in respect of its endangering the public peace by drawing together dissolute and debauched persons, but also in respect of its apparent tendency to corrupt the manners of both sexes by such an open profession of lewdness." Hawk. Pl. C. 196.

[7] The editors of the 5th edition of *Bacon's Abridgement* (1798) thought it "the better opinion" that such enterprises would still be common nuisances where "set up in such inconvenient parts of a town, that they cannot but greatly incommode the neighbourhood": Vol. V, p.151.

use and environmental regulation.[8] The argument is that governmental intervention in a private market inevitably creates diseconomies and distortive externalities, which would disappear if a system of private rights could be developed which could give landowners the right to "negotiate or obtain an acceptable compensation for any external diseconomy imposed upon them."[9] But it is an approach which focuses upon one part only of the planning function; and whilst some shift in balance between private right and public regulation might well relieve public planning of some of the pressure imposed on it by localised land use disputes, the weakness in the general line of argument lies in the assumption that private land ownership interests should be the final arbiter of environmental standards, and that the regulation of those standards should be a matter purely for bargaining and trading like any other market commodity.

Whatever the scope of the debate today, it was clear to the social reformers of the nineteenth century that the *laissez-faire* ideology of the common law was unlikely to offer any relief to the overcrowding, congestion and disease of the Victorian cities, and certainly not at the suit of those who lacked resources and property rights. The law of nuisance, moreover, offered no means of overcoming established nuisances in order to improve badly polluted and unhealthy urban areas. It was primarily a means of preserving the status quo, and "what would be a nuisance in Belgrave Square would not necessarily be so in Bermondsey"[10] was the philosophy by which the judges were guided. New laws were necessary, but Parliamentary legislation offered the only realistic possibility for reform. Between the early steps of the enabling Public Health legislation of the mid-nineteenth century and the complex interventionist legislation of today there lies more than a century of experiment, evolution and change. The most dramatic reform, in terms both of purpose and effect, was undoubtedly that of the Town and Country Planning Act 1947, which substantially strengthened the control by the state over the use and development of privately owned land, and which provided the basic framework through which planning is still undertaken today. In the words of one contemporary writer,

> "Here at last was an Act which seemed likely to touch something that no previous Acts had touched—the landowner's pocket."[11]

But much of the content of the 1947 Act was more a consolidation and refinement of earlier measures than a revolutionary departure from them, and despite reforms in procedure and methodology, and the ever-shifting balance between private property and state power, there is a continuity of purpose and ideology which links directly the nineteenth century measures with contemporary planning.

The evolutionary, gradualist, development of planning legislation over the past century has been well surveyed by a number of writers, and there is no

---

[8] For an intelligent analysis of the debate see B.J.Pearce, "Property Rights v. Development Control" (1981) Vol.52 *Town Planning Review* 45; and "Instruments for Land Policy" (1980) Vol.3 *Urban Law and Policy* 115. A more vociferous anti-interventionist approach is contained in D.R. Denman, *The Place of Property* (Geographical Publications Ltd., 1978).

[9] B.J. Pearce, "Property Rights v Development Control" *op.cit.* p.54.

[10] *Sturges* v. *Bridgman* (1879) 11 Ch.D. 852 at 865.

[11] William Wood, *Planning and the Law* (Percival Marshall & Co. 1949) p.3.

intention to duplicate their work here.[12] A step by step account of legislative development tells part only of a more complex history of planning in action, and the remainder of this chapter is therefore devoted not to a conventional history, but to an examination of the development of three central themes. First, there is the political structure of the planning system, and its implications for the formulation of planning policy; second, the question of land values and the interaction between planning and the market, and third, the problems of law and policy, and the uneasy balance which has to be struck in planning between rules and discretion, and between flexibility and certainty. They are themes which themselves interweave, but the implications of each can be seen clearly throughout the history of planning, and they continue to underly its operations today. They are not themes which are unique to planning law, however; indeed, in general terms they arise in every area of governmental intervention in the modern economy. Further historical material has been included as necessary in later chapters in order to explain the development of individual ideas and legislative responses.

B. The Political Context

1. *Introduction*

When Mr. Lewis Silkin M.P. introduced his Town and Country Planning Bill to the House of Commons on January 29, 1947, he described it as "long, technical and complex, and naturally, in some respects, controversial."[13] In the 30 years since then the length, technicality and complexity of the legislation have all grown at an alarming rate. The 1947 Act, after all, had no more than 120 sections and 11 Schedules; but by 1971 the total had risen to 295 sections and 25 Schedules, with a further boost being offered by the 197 sections and 34 schedules (though not all relating to planning) of the Local Government, Planning and Land Act 1980.

And the controversy which greeted the 1947 Bill has refused to go away. Land use planning remains a highly disputatious issue in British society, both at an ideological level (witnessed by the abrupt changes and reversals in land policy pursued by governments of different political persuasions) and at a local level. There are daily reports of conflicts between developers and planning authorities, between groups and individual members of the public and planning authorities, between the planning authorities themselves, and between planning authorities and central government. If the planning system is so heated and volatile as the evidence suggests it is, how can it possibly achieve the aims and objectives of effective land use planning? And what, for that matter, are those aims and objectives? If there is any clear consensus about the purpose of planning, how can there be such scope for conflict?

Answers to these questions are not easy to find. Certainly, they cannot be found in the legislation. The Act carefully avoids any definition of "planning," or of its aims or objectives: "planning," from a reading of the

[12] See, in particular, W. Ashworth, *The Genesis of Modern British Town Planning* (Routledge and Kegan Paul, 1954); G.E. Cherry, *The Evolution of British Town Planning* (Leonard Hill Books, 1974) and J.B. Cullingworth, *Peacetime History of Environmental Planning* (H.M.S.O., 1978–1980), Vols. I–IV.
[13] *Hansard*, H.C. Deb., Vol.432, col.1137 (January 30, 1947).

Act as a whole, is to do with whatever central government and the local planning authorities decide it is to do with. To that proposition, the courts will add the rider, " . . . so long as they act reasonably, taking into account relevant or 'material' considerations and disregarding those that are irrelevant." But we are still no nearer an answer: the issue of what may be relevant or material can be answered only in relation to what the purpose of planning is perceived to be, and by whom.

But at least the Act offers a clue. It places the administration of British land use planning entirely in the hands of politicians. It is thus deliberately established as a process of political decision making, through local government agencies under the general supervision of central government. It is "political" in the broadest sense of the word, involving the making of policy and accepting responsibility for its implementation through the accountability of the democratic process. The planning system, then, is created as an instrument of government, as a means of restricting private land use rights in the interests of the community as a whole. That does not imply that ballot box accountability should be the only measure of political choice, and that the powers conferred may be used for whatever ends those who are exercising them deem popular or expedient. It does mean, however, that the objectives sought for planning and the values applied in decision making have ultimately no greater rationality than the degree of public support which they command. It is a system of politically based decision making which operates within a series of constraints laid down by law.

The Act sets out to achieve a balance between political freedom and legal control, and the balance is established in a variety of ways. First, and most important, there is a diffusion of planning power. There is no clear chain of planning command stretching downwards from central government, through county councils to district councils. Instead, there is a network of relationships, some legal, others political and yet others financial. Developers and others aggrieved by decisions taken at a local level have wide rights of objection and appeal to central government in the form of the Secretary of State, and there is in turn a general right of appeal to the High Court on questions of law from his decisions.

Second, the Act emphasises the importance of long term policy making. It requires that the local planning authorities should prepare development plans (split, since 1968, between *structure plans* prepared by county councils, and *local plans* which are generally prepared by districts, though may be prepared by counties), and that these should guide them in their general decision making. But there is a delicate balance: authorities retain the right to depart from their prepared plans where they see fit, but subject to various legal and political safeguards and balances. And as with other functions under the Act, the safeguards are in practice roughly related to the importance of the decisions. In some cases the responsible authority will be obliged to consult with, or refer the application for decision to, another authority; or they may be directed by the other authority as to how they should determine the matter, or they may have it taken out of their hands altogether by the Secretary of State "calling-in" the matter for his own decision.

Planning, then, is in Britain an overtly political function. But the scope of the political power is closely circumscribed through a network of institutional relationships. In some instances, they are hidden: conflict between the objectives of different departments of an authority, or between its officers and members, for example, is very often resolved internally and a united front presented to the public. Other relationships are clear and well defined. The right of appeal to the Secretary of State, for example, is preserved and defined in the Act itself and there is a well understood allocation of responsibility. But in many other instances there is the vagueness and ambiguity of relationship which so characterises British government systems, and it is this which gives the planning system its particular flavour. There is, for example, the question of the balance of power between central and local government, and the strength of each to press for its own planning objectives against the opposition of the other. A major reason why planning decisions are perennially controversial is that they so often involve far more than the task, difficult enough in itself, of balancing private right against the "public interest." The power system is so structured that more than one view of the "public interest" frequently emerges, such as when adjoining planning authorities disagree about urban expansion proposals, or the county council take a different view from the district on the desirability of further settlement in the country-side. The division of power between authorities almost institutionalises inter-authority conflict, and that has been roundly criticised in the past as wasteful of resources and inducive of delay. But it highlights, for our present purposes, the way in which democratic accountability can pull in different directions at different tiers in the system, and it brings out the elusiveness of any general consensus as to the objectives of land use planning. Additionally there are the "public interest" arguments advanced by non-governmental bodies, such as environmental interest groups pressing for new approaches and policies from the government agencies, and exerting influence through publicity, education, research, and protest.

In a system structured like this there can be no straightforward rule book of principles by which controversial issues may be settled, and it is the function of planning law not to prescribe the substance but to lay down the procedures through which the conflicting views may be presented and assessed.

2. The Evolvement of Contemporary Planning Policy

There was not always this apparent lack of consensus. To Lewis Silkin in 1947, the objects of town and country planning were "becoming increasingly understood and accepted."[14] They were primarily, he suggested, "to secure a proper balance between the competing demands for land, so that all the land of the country is used in the best interests of the whole people."[15] He pointed to the projects that needed urgent implementation in post-war Britain: the rebuilding of blitzed areas, population dispersal out of the overcrowded cities, the re-equipment of industry and the building of new communications networks. And he stressed the need to maintain a balance between the competing demands for land between agriculture and develop-

---

[14] *Hansard*, H.C. Deb., Vol.432, col.947 (January 29, 1947).
[15] *Ibid.* col.947; and see too his comments in 1941 when he proclaimed himself to be struck by the "remarkable unanimity" in the House of Lords as to what planning should do: *Hansard*, H.C. Deb., Vol.370, col.213 (March 19, 1941).

ment, the need to contain urban sprawl and to conserve villages and areas of beautiful countryside.

They were objectives that few would quarrel with, and it was a clearer statement than any that had accompanied the earlier Acts of 1909 and 1932. But, as Donnison has recently pointed out, Silkin had succeeded skilfully in drawing together a wide range of support which cut across political party boundaries for each of his objectives, and had succeeded in disguising the potential conflicts between them and the substantial reallocation of wealth and resources in society that was implicit in the programmes he envisaged:

> "Silkin had temporarily united one of the most contentious parliaments in British history with a vision of the liberal dream shared by the coalition of interests supporting the idea of town planning—a dream expressed [by Silkin] in a mixture of phrases . . . which stemmed directly from the utilitarian and utopian roots of the liberal tradition."[16]

Parliamentary debates on the 1947 Act were not of course without controversy or bitterness, but the energy of the Conservative Opposition was directed mainly towards the Bill's financial provisions, which proposed the nationalisation of development values in land. By contrast with those measures, the objectives of planning and even the nationalisation of the right to develop land paled in significance, and the use by the Government of a "guillotine" motion on debates prevented lengthy discussion. A lone voice was that of the Shadow Minister, Mr. W.S. Morrison, who suggested that the new powers were too vague and too ambiguous. He complained that "in increasing the elasticity of the Government's planning powers the Bill goes too far in that it renders the future destiny of man too uncertain and makes it liable to so many unpredictable vicissitudes."[17] The case for broader and untrammelled governmental powers was based largely upon the need to have the flexibility to cope with "unpredictable vicissitudes," but the absence from the legislation of specific criteria and desiderata did not mean that the government were proceeding in an intellectual vacuum and without clear policies. The 1947 Act was, in policy terms at least, a continuation and development of a liberal political tradition stretching back to the preceding century.

(a) The two strands of early planning philosophy

The concern of modern planning with issues of amenity, controlled urban growth and the general physical welfare of citizens is based upon two separately evolving strands of urban philosophy—the public health movement and the garden city movement—each prompted initially by the overcrowded and disease-ridden conditions of the industrial slums, and each offering alternative responses.

The public health movement of the second half of the nineteenth century offered the first direct challenge to the strength of nineteenth century private landlordism in urban areas. It was a challenge to the sanctity of the landlord's proprietary and contractual rights to use his property to his

[16] D. Donnison and P.Soto, *The Good City* (Heinemann, 1980) p.6.
[17] *Hansard*, H.C. Deb., Vol. 432, col.991 (January 29, 1947).

maximum financial advantage, and it involved acceptance of the proposition that the health of the community, or a part of the community, was a matter calling for government protection. It was unsurprising that progress was slow. It was not simply a matter of conferring interventionist powers upon local authorities, but also of persuading them to exercise them. Where authorities themselves sought powers under private legislation, by promoting their own Town Improvement Acts, they were all the more likely to be prepared to use them. But much of the early public legislation, like Ernest Chadwick's Public Health Act of 1848, was purely permissive in character. The 1848 Act was the first general Act on public health, and it made provision for, *inter alia*, the registration of common lodging houses, prohibition on the letting of basement rooms as dwellings, and requirements as to water supply, drains and the provision of water closets in new dwellings.

From those tentative beginnings there developed gradually a broader acceptance of the idea that general legislation should be used as a means of bringing about changes in urban conditions, but progress was inevitably slow, and the scope of the ensuing legislation was narrow. It was concerned with health, nuisances and sanitation, but not with general housing standards, amenity, landscaping or aesthetics.

Those, however, were central issues in the other strand of planning philosophy which emerged with its greatest coherence in the garden city movement. There had been a number of experiments by enlightened Victorian employers in providing decent housing settlements for their workforces, notably at Bourneville and Port Sunlight. To the social reformers who followed, particularly Ebenezer Howard, the only effective solution to the problems of the Victorian cities was to build on these experiments, by directing attention away from the old cities and starting afresh with new planned cities in the countryside. Howard's was a visionary approach: these were to be garden cities, aesthetically attractive and spaciously laid out, yet each with its own economic base and adequate local employment.[18] They would offer a dramatically different way of life to the urban workers, but their creation would involve neither the use of compulsory powers against recalcitrant landlords, nor charity. The cities could be economically self-sufficient, and their assets communally managed.

Indeed, until 1946, the garden city ideal had no legislative or other state backing at all, yet Howard and the movement which developed behind him succeeded through private enterprise and private capital in developing Letchworth and Welwyn Garden Cities. Neither was a great financial success in the early years, but the model of attractive residential layouts and designs was quickly seized upon by other private developers and "garden city" and "garden suburb" became fashionable labels for prestigious developments. But Howard's ideas of self-sufficiency and economic self-containment were lost. The lack of any statutory backing meant that the prospect of establishing further completely new towns was bleak, and instead the "garden suburb," with its economic dependence on an existing

---

[18] Howard's most influential work was *Tomorrow: A Peaceful Path to Real Reform* published in 1898 and reissued subsequently as *Garden Cities of Tomorrow* (Faber and Faber, 1965).

city, alone flourished often exacerbating the very problems of over-grown urban areas which Howard had been anxious to prevent.[19]

But Howard's notion of the role of planning in urban development was to have its effect upon government thinking. The Housing, Town Planning, etc, Act 1909 and the successive Town and Country Planning Acts of 1919 and 1932 all attempted (through provisions which were successively strengthened) to extend the physical planning ideals of Howard and others to new urban development in and near existing settlements. But while the legislation clearly had some impact upon the layout and servicing of new development, implementation was for the most part voluntary and dogged by clumsy procedural requirements; and its failure to contain and control growth was demonstrated dramatically by the urban sprawl which ate up thousands of acres of agricultural land every year during the 1930s.

(b) The objectives of the post-war system

The 1947 Act, together with the New Towns Act of 1946, at last provided the machinery through which the two earlier strands could be drawn together and developed further. They gave government support to the original garden city ideal, and new towns were seen as an important planning tool in dealing with the overcrowding in the old cities and dispersing the urban population to a better working and living environment. But the legislation was also interventionist. It allowed an authority to vet all applications for urban development of all kinds so that, for the future, developers could be held to the needs of the community. Finally there were broad powers to deal with the inherited defects in the urban fabric and the mistakes of the past: to acquire land compulsorily and redevelop it, and to require the discontinuance of any undesirable existing use of land.

In terms of macro-planning, at least, there may perhaps have been uncertainty but there was no vacuum in government policy. The general thinking behind the policies of population dispersal, new town development and urban containment had been generated during the war by a series of distinguished committees, and their reports heavily influenced government thinking for many years thereafter.

The groundwork had been laid first by the Report of the Barlow Commission, (the Royal Commission on the Distribution of the Industrial Population),[20] whose *Report* drew attention to the continued congestion of the old industrial cities, and pointed to the high mortality rates which continued to exist there despite the action taken under the successive Public Health Acts. They accepted the evidence of the Registrar General that the most important factors involved were:

"(1) the crowding together of houses;
(2) the crowding together of people into houses too small for them;
(3) the apparent aggravation by urban conditions of other adverse effects of economic pressure upon the standard of living and environment; and

---

[19] See further the classic study of the new town movement, Osborn and Whittick's *New Towns* (Leonard Hill, 1977), Chap. 5; and as to current new policy, see *post* p.503.
[20] Cmd. 6513 (1940).

(4) the production of smoke from factories and homes which reduces the effective sunshine."[21]

And they proposed physical, spatially based remedies: further redevelopment within the congested areas and decentralisation and dispersal of industry and population away from them.[22] Secondly, the Reith Committee on New Towns, in its three reports produced rapidly in 1946,[23] filled in the gaps in the dispersal proposals, by giving detailed consideration to the preparation of a large scale new towns programme.

The Scott Committee on Land Utilisation in Rural Areas, which reported in 1941,[24] placed the emphasis upon proper use of agricultural land, and was anxious to see the establishment of containment policies to prevent urban sprawl and the loss of villages, along with amenity policies to protect the appearance of the countryside. Importantly, they wanted to see a planning system which would allow "*all* considerations affecting land use [to] be taken into account in land planning"; and they urged that agricultural land should not be handed over to urban development unless the developer had first been able to establish a clear case in the national interest for it.[25]

3. *Political consensus and conflict*

Throughout the war-time Reports and the debates on the 1947 Act there ran the assumption that a "proper" balance could in fact be achieved in land use decision making between the competing forces. There were some clearly identifiable social evils which needed to be overcome, and the legislation existed to promote the "best" solution. Those evils, the policies needed to rectify them and thus the objectives for which the planning system should aim, were far more obvious to all then than they are today. This extract from the Simon Report in 1944 reflects the prevailing mood:

"With a building force of 1¼ million workers it should be possible (on the one condition that prices are maintained at a reasonable level) in a single generation to build a good home for every family at a rent or a price it can afford, and to erect all the necessary concomitant buildings, so planned that father can get easily to factory, club and public house, the mother and children to shop, school and clinic, and the whole family to libraries and places of amusement, to parks, playing fields and open country."[26]

And planning was the machinery of reform, the means to a better post-war life. In the words of W.A. Robson, writing in 1941, the havoc which had been wrought by the war would be almost unbearable to those who had to

---

[21] *Ibid*. para.123.

[22] *Ibid* Chap. VI.

[23] The Committee produced two interim reports (Cmd. 6759 and Cmd. 6794). Their final report (Cmd 6794) was produced only nine months after the setting up of the Committee.

[24] Cmd. 6386

[25] *Ibid*. paras. 232–233.

[26] *Report of the Central Council for Works and Buildings to the Minister of Works on the Placing and Management of Building Contracts*: (H.M.S.O., 1944), p. 1.

live among it "were they not aided by a vision of a fairer habitation in days to come." He continued,

> "It is impossible to over-estimate the value of the vision, vague and unsubstantial though it doubtless is, as an aid to the maintenance of public morale. And every vision implies a plan. Indeed, a vision is a kind of plan, or at least it is the stuff of which plans are made. Without vision there can be no planning of any sort."[27]

Time, and, paradoxically, the successes of planning itself over the past 30 years, have obscured the objectives, have evened out the old distinctions between "good" and "bad" urban environments; whilst the apparent failures of planning have undermined the planners' confidence in preparing new policies, and particularly discouraged planning enterprise on the grand scale of the earlier dispersal and comprehensive development programmes.

Most significantly, the political consensus of the late 1940's has gone. It is even uncertain how long it lasted in any recognisable form. It is unlikely, for example, that it had been fully appreciated that achievement of the Act's planning objectives was about to involve quite a radical intervention by the State in matters concerning private property, and that it also necessarily called for a more equal distribution of resources between the old divided classes of British society. The brave new world would need to be financed by public spending, and that in turn would need to be recouped from taxation.

As the programmes got under way it was not only ideological splits that became apparent, but also parochial conflicts and disputes between town and country interests. The new towns programme offered a clear example of an ideal which found almost universal theoretical support, but in practice encountered huge local opposition. It often meant that existing towns and rural villages were suddenly to be engulfed by urban development, transforming the lives of those already living there. The legislation made it clear that the resultant conflict between local and national interests was for the Minister to resolve, and that the touchstone of his decision was to be largely the political rationality of democratic accountability. A firm determination on his part to pursue his dispersal policy meant that objectors' rights, whatever the Act provided, were often weak indeed. And the courts, faced with broad discretionary legislation, were quite unwilling to intervene.

When Mr. Silkin went to Stevenage in 1946 to address a public meeting on the proposal to proceed with a new town there, (which had been proposed in the Greater London Plan of 1944 and accepted as being a matter of first priority by the Reith Committee),[28] he met with a barrage of opposition, as the following extracts from a contemporary report of the meeting demonstrate:

> "I want to carry out a daring exercise in town planning—(*Jeers*). It is no good you jeering: it is going to be done—(*Applause and boos*). (Cries of "Dictator")." . . . "The project will go forward. It will do so more smoothly and more successfully with your cooperation. Stevenage will

---

[27] *The War and the Planning Outlook*, (Faber and Faber, 1941), p.8.
[28] *First Interim Report* Cmd. 6759, para.16.

in a short time become world famous—(*Laughter*). . . . While I will
consult as far as possible all the local authorities, at the end, if people are
fractious and unreasonable, I shall have to carry out my duty—(*Voice*:
Gestapo!).”[29]

Did those comments show such a firm determination on the part of the
Minister so as to disable him from exercising subsequently his formal
functions, under the New Towns Act 1946, of taking local objections into
account following a local public inquiry, before confirming the necessary
designation order? That question went to the courts, and eventually to the
House of Lords, who thought not. They declined to accept that any judicial
or quasi-judicial duty fell on the Minister by reason of his having to consider
objections. His function was purely administrative, and his only duty was to
“consider” the report of the inquiry.[30]

Thus the “public interest,” as interpreted by central government,
prevailed, but the consequence was that the right of the objectors to oppose
designation was rendered nugatory, so strong was government political
commitment to it. Indeed, it has only recently been revealed that the
objectors had in fact successfully convinced the Inspector at the inquiry that
their objections were “inescapable,” and that he had made the rather curious
recommendation to Mr. Silkin that “the Stevenage project might well be
held up until a safer example of the new town principle can be advanced as
the first under the Act.”[31] The Minister had overruled him. But the
inspector’s report was not published, and nor, significantly, was it made
generally known that his recommendations had not been followed by the
Minister.

The Stevenage case and others like it were a foretaste of the great planning
conflicts which were to come, but it was an era when the issues tended to be
relatively clear cut. There was no serious dispute that the new towns policy
was in itself a “good” and a popular planning policy: it was the question of
location which was controversial, and it was a political question whether
national or local considerations should prevail. In the prevailing climate,
local objection had little chance of success.

Once the most serious urban problems of the immediate post-war era had
been mitigated, so necessarily the focus of planning shifted. The period
which followed was one of self-doubt and questioning. The limitations and
weaknesses of the planning system were becoming apparent, and many of
the grand designs for the renewal of towns, especially town centres, had
resulted in bleak, unattractive development, including high rise housing,
badly designed and poorly serviced housing estates and elaborate urban
highways schemes. Other policies had perhaps succeeded too well. The
green belts, for example, had become sacrosanct in the public imagination
and embedded in property prices, allowing little by way of redesign by the
planning authorities to accommodate further growth. And the desolation,
economic decay and emptiness of the old inner cities attested to the success
of dispersal and overspill policies, and the failure to attract new growth.

---

[29] As reported in *Franklin v. Minister of Town and Country Planning* [1948] A.C. 87.
[30] *Franklin v. Minister of Town and Country Planning* [1948] A.C. 87.
[31] For a full account, see J.B. Cullingworth’s *Peacetime History of Environmental Planning*,
Vol. III: *New Towns Policy*. (H.M.S.O., 1979), pp. 29–30.

The Report of a working group established by the Royal Town Planning Institute, published in 1976, identified the early 1970's as the time when the general consensus on planning objectives began to dissolve.[32] The Report identified six major elements or influences in the transition: the influence of the ecological movement, and its serious questioning of the unlimited growth assumptions of post-war governments; the growth of social planning, which emphasised community rather than physical form; the voluntary conservation movement which fought against comprehensive urban change; a concern, on the part of planners, for the redistributive effects of planning policy and the realisation that the system had very often operated mainly in favour of powerful interest groups; the world economic crisis, (and, more recently, the industrial slump and rising unemployment of the late 1970s); and finally, disillusionment that post-war government policies had failed to produce the ideal society which had been held out as their primary objective.

These are all intangible, speculative influences in themselves and there is no general agreement as to their effects on public or professional attitudes to planning. But taken together they represent a questioning of long accepted assumptions. They place a more critical, and certainly a more cynical, interpretation on the motives underlying planning policy and the nature of its administration; and they pose the question not only of whether legal and institutional change is necessary, but whether any such change can any longer be expected to regenerate the visionary ideals of planning.

The Report's observations have been further borne out by events since 1976. In particular, the Windscale inquiry, the Vale of Belvoir inquiry, the renewed search for a site for a third London airport and the disruption of motorway inquiries have all demonstrated substantial public dissatisfaction going beyond the local impact of particular proposals, and questioning the long term assumptions, particularly in energy and transportation matters, underlying government thinking. They are issues which arise in a planning context, not solely because of their relevance to the question of the need for the development under consideration, but because the planning system provides a forum for public objection and debate which is absent from the other departments of government. The vulnerability of long–held policy assumptions leads to a danger that decisions will be taken increasingly on an ad hoc basis, balancing the political pressures applied by competing public and private interest groups, and relying—as in the case of economic policy generally—upon democratic accountability as the ultimate justification both for policies and for day to day decisions. If that is a danger in the case of decisions involving a high element of national policy, then it is equally a danger at local level; and in either case it is the antithesis of the long term view which it is the purpose of planning to consider.

4. *The development plan as a policy instrument*

It was clearly not the assumption in 1947 that political accountability on a case by case basis should be the main or only safeguard of the local planning system's rational operation. The instrument of policy making was to be the

---

[32] *Planning and the Future* R.T.P.I. (1976), pp. 9–12

development plan, and authorities were required to prepare formal plans, incorporating their planning policies for the area. When approved by the Minister, the plan would guide the authority's decision-making, particularly in development control. True, it was not to be the only factor. They could also have regard to "any other material considerations," and there might well be such considerations in respect of a particular application which would bias the authority away from their plan. But the intention had always been that any departures from the plan would be closely supervised by the Minister. It was through the development plan that the planning objectives for each area were to be settled, and the plans approval machinery gave the Minister the opportunity to consider local views and to resolve major issues of controversy, and to iron out arbitrary, biased and baseless policies.

It was, however, the inability of this approval machinery to function swiftly and efficiently that led to a significant change in emphasis in practice. The lengthy delays in plan approval that occurred in the 1950s, and the further delays in processing the subsequent amendments necessary to keep pace with the unexpected urban growth over the period, meant that the formal plans grew further and further apart from reality. The power to take into account "other material considerations" became of increasingly practical significance as authorities were forced to release land for development without it first having been allocated in the formal plan. In recognition of the changing pressures on authorities, central government controls over plan departures were gradually relaxed. The "other material consideration" was often simple necessity: the need to bring land into development, especially for housing and industry to satisfy a large and legitimate demand. But the process symbolised a significant switch from reliance upon formal plans, containing a series of decisions which incorporated both consensus ideals and decisions imposed by the Minister, to a more ad hoc and potentially volatile system.

The introduction of a new system of statutory plans in 1968 was intended in part to restore the balance, but even the new streamlined procedures failed to overcome the delays, with the result that the dominance of statutory forward planning has not in practice been reasserted. The ability of local planning authorities to prepare and adopt local plans without ministerial approval has in turn raised new questions as to the "proper" scope of planning policy. In the past (and still in the case of structure plans) the minister could be relied upon to reject policies which went beyond central government's conception of the role and scope of planning. But now that central supervision is less direct there is already a diversity of policy content in different local plans, including experimentation with social planning and policies based upon raw ideology and untested hypotheses.

To the lawyer the question is not so much whether such policies are "proper" policies, but whether they fall within the powers conferred by the Act. As with the meaning of "material considerations" (and it is significant that litigation concerned with that phrase has mushroomed in the past 10 years) the Act itself does nothing more than hint at the answer. There is a common core of agreement as to the legitimacy of planning's concern with, for example, the layout of buildings and the preservation of amenity. But beyond the established boundaries there is a penumbra of uncertainty and ambiguity which has allowed and accommodated the many changes in philosophy and objectives since 1947.

The objectives of planning and the choices to be made between competing strategies for achieving them, are matters for political decision. The choices, once made, may require fresh parliamentary or delegated legislation for their implementation, or they may be able to be pursued within the confines of existing laws. Those laws impose a system of controls and safeguards over political action, in the interests of balancing central and local political interests, public objection and private rights. Their purpose is thus to confine political freedom, but within a fluid and often deliberately ambiguous structure of relationships.

C. Planning control and the urban land market: the problem of land values

1. *The nature of the urban land market*[33]

The primary rationale for any land-use planning control is the perceived failure of the market to achieve socially acceptable land allocation and development. The main mechanism of the market in the unplanned city is the pricing system, which in theory achieves an economically efficient allocation of uses to sites. Land has a value for development to an intending purchaser in accordance with its likely profitability, which is in turn determined by the likely demand for the completed development, or, in the case of industrial premises, for the goods to be manufactured therein. Changes in land use occur as the value of a site for development or redevelopment exceeds its value for its present use. As the city spreads out, land which was formerly agricultural and had a value related to its agricultural productivity, comes to acquire an additional, enhanced, value for urban development. The extent of the increment in value depends both upon the likely profitability of the development, and its timing. Land suitable now (or "ripe") for development will fetch a higher price than land whose development is unlikely for some years, where the current use value may be enhanced only marginally by an element of prospective development value, or "hope" value.

The urban land market has a number of characteristics which distinguish it from markets in other commodities. There is a finite stock of land overall, which can be added to in real terms only by reclamation, though it may to some extent be capable of more efficient use by redevelopment at higher densities. Fixed supply against rising demand means that land prices are bound to remain buoyant over the long term, despite cyclical fluctuations. Economic crises like that occasioned by the oil crisis of 1973 have tended to have a severe short term effect on land values, but without impeding longer term recovery. In a period of sluggish or diminishing demand there remains the consolation that land itself, as opposed to buildings, does not depreciate in value as other goods generally do. Except in the case of destructive development like minerals extraction, its value is not destroyed; and its value for redevelopment remains as buildings deteriorate and depreciate.

---

[33] See generally, B. Goodall, *The Economics of Urban Areas* (Pergamon Press, 1972); H. Darin-Drabkin, *Land Policy and Urban Growth* (Pergamon Press, 1977); N. Lichfield and H. Darin-Drabkin, *Land Policy in Planning* (George Allen and Unwin, 1980); and N. Lichfield, "Land Values and Planning" (1979) 2 Urban Law & Policy 111.

Perhaps the most important determinant of value in the unregulated land market is location. Land is a fixed-location commodity, and its value is heavily dependent upon its spatial relationship with other sites. Demand for land located in the central business district of a city typically exceeds by a substantial margin the demand for land on the city perimeter. Value is determined therefore not merely in terms of the suitability of the particular site to the particular use, but in terms of its association with other sites; and that influence may be positive or negative. The value of a development site may be enhanced by the development of adjoining land, for example, but not if it is put to use as a sewage farm or a public convenience. These are the "externalities" of the land pricing system, the costs and benefits which arise from the actions of one landowner but which are endured or enjoyed by another. Some costs are recoverable through the common law actions for nuisance, but the available remedies do not extend to all costs and there is no provision at all between private owners for recoupment of benefit.

Public sector development is equally creative of externalities, and by its nature the effects are frequently dramatic. Investment in new physical infrastructure such as roads and sewers in a development area, and in social infrastructure such as schools and health clinics, enhances the value of development land in the area by increasing the attractiveness of the area to prospective purchasers of dwellings. Conversely, obtrusive and polluting public schemes like motorways and sewage treatment plants will depress values of adjoining property.

2. The effects of planning regulation

The externality effects of land use are complex and difficult to evaluate. They influence, but by no means determine, land values; and there is no scientifically fixed scale of economic effect. The price of development land in general terms is dictated by the price which is attainable for the completed development; that is, it is a residual value, the amount the developer can afford to pay after deducting development costs and profits from anticipated selling price. The selling price in turn depends not solely upon the locational attractions of the site, but upon a variety of interrelated factors, including in the case of the residential market, availability of mortgage finance and overall demand for housing.

Ignoring specific local distortions, therefore, the general distribution of land values in a town is typically concentrated at the centre and diminishes towards the outer boundaries and beyond. Without planning control, the town's growth can be expected in theory to occur evenly around its circumference as it spreads out into the surrounding countryside, assuming the land all to be equally capable of development. The consequence is a roughly even distribution of development value; with values of agricultural land steadily rising as the town grows. In reality, the pattern is bound to be uneven, and often distorted by demand for sites adjoining main roads (and hence ribbon development) or other specific locational attractions.

The general pattern is clearly upset by planning regulation, however. Planning controls may halt the outward spread of a settlement altogether, or concentrate growth upon one sector alone of the town's circumference. Zoning controls, growth area allocations and green belt restrictions all distort the distribution of value. Assuming demand to remain constant, (which need not necessarily be the case), it is now concentrated upon the sites available for development in planning terms. Their value is enhanced; and the value of the land formerly available is reduced.

The expanding city example demonstrates the potential impact of growth controls, but similar consequences arise from positive planning action, such as new town development, where development value attaches to agricultural land by reason entirely of the proposal to create a new urban centre there. The converse case is that of selective restrictive controls, such as those for the preservation of historic buildings, where development value for site redevelopment may be destroyed or substantially diminished by administrative decision.

Planning can thus be seen as a powerful force in the urban land market, redistributing value in a manner which is largely independent of the actions of the individual landowners. Planning regulation does not destroy the market, which simply reacts to controls in a largely predictable way; but it does distort the market, and those distortions in turn are liable to affect the quality and flexibility of planning. Although planning regulation gives the impression of being above the market and of being guided only by the dictates of planning objectives, the financial consequences of decisions are in reality never far from the forefront. Land prices often form a sufficiently high proportion of overall development costs to make them critical in assessing the viability of a project.

3. Compensation, betterment and recoupment

It is a sensible proposition that a planning system which is capable of wreaking such an arbitrary redistribution of value is in need of a balancing mechanism. There is no obvious greater justification for permitting the retention by one landowner of large profits accruing solely from the decision or investment of a public authority, than for depriving another equally arbitrarily of value paid by him for his land. It is true that profit and risk respectively are inherent in any investment in a capitalist economy, and that externalities between private landowners in an unregulated system are only to a limited extent balanced through private law. But the impact and purpose of planning policy is distinctly different from private interactions, and the more effectively it operates the more extreme is its effect on the private market. In short, it effects a redistribution which is neither deserved nor earned, and which is largely inequitable.

Where the effect of planning control is to destroy value completely, it has never been in doubt that in principle that loss should be compensated. The physical taking of property by government by way of compulsory purchase has always in Britain been subject to a liability to pay compensation, and that obligation is enshrined in the American and other Federal Constitutions, couched in terms of a prohibition against the "taking" of property without "just" compensation.[34] But where control depresses but does not destroy value, the obligation to compensate is less clear-cut. The premise,

---

[34] For a detailed comparative study, see D.Hagman and D. Misczynski (Eds.) *Windfalls for Wipeouts* (Chicago: American Society of Planning Officials 1978).

though not always clearly articulated, is that the state should not always be required to compensate for intervention affecting private property. The debate in the United States centres around the "taking" issue; that is, how far planning control may go by way of uncompensated regulation or "police power" until it reaches the point of "taking" the property of landowners. The formula of the Fifth Amendment has been taken by the United States Supreme Court to be a guarantee against Government "forcing some people alone to bear public burdens which, in all fairness and justice, should be borne by the public as a whole,"[35] but that has not prevented them from upholding zoning controls[36] and even selective building preservation ordinances.[37]

The constitutional limitation does not arise in Britain, given the sovereignty of Parliament, and significant regulatory legislation has been possible in the areas of housing, public health and planning without compensation. As Lord Radcliffe pointed out in *Belfast Corporation* v. *O.D.Cars Ltd.*,[38] the powers taken in the interests of public health and amenity in the nineteenth century alone went well beyond the American idea of the police power, but no question of compensation arose.

But with the emergence of the more comprehensive land-use controls of the twentieth century, compensation became a fundamental feature of the legislation and a guarantee against investment losses for landowners. The early legislation imposed such a financial liability upon local authorities as to impede seriously any effective planning, but the 1947 Act adopted the once and for all solution of nationalising all development values in land. Even although later legislation lifted the 100 per cent. development charge and effectively restored development values, the present code of compensation is based still upon the concept of state ownership of development rights, so that the refusal of planning permission for development is not generally compensatable. The compensation provisions of the present legislation are analysed in Chapter 15.

The issue of "betterment"—or the increase in private land values attributable to public investment or regulation of other land—and the extent to which it should be regarded as recoverable by the state, has proved highly controversial and deeply politically divisive. Every post-war Government has upon election almost immediately set about dismantling the land policies of its predecessors. In broad ideological terms the debate is clear-cut. It is a question of whether the market should be left to absorb beneficial externalities of whatever source; or whether the enhanced values caused by public sector activity should be recouped in whole or in part (and if so, how much) by the state. At one extreme the argument is for an unregulated market, whilst at the other it is for full recoupment machinery, and, taken to its logical extreme, for the nationalisation of land.

---

[35] *Armstrong* v. *United States* 364 U.S.40 (1960). The classic case is that of *Pennsylvania Coal Co.* v. *Mahon* 260 U.S.393 (1922) where a state statute which forbade coal mining except in certain circumstances and rendered it commercially unpracticable to exploit mining rights which had been reserved by the plaintiff on a sale of the surface rights of his land, was held to amount to a "taking."

[36] See, *e.g. Euclid* v. *Amber Realty Co.* 272 U.S. 365 (1926).

[37] *Penn Central Transport Co.* v. *New York City* 438 U.S. 104 (1978).

[38] [1960] A.C. 490 at 523.

The problem is not one of principle alone, but also of practice. "Betterment," as understood by the Uthwatt Committee, is a narrow concept of value enhanced only by public sector activity "whether positive, e.g. by the execution of public works or improvements, or negative, e.g. by the imposition of restrictions on other land."[39] Such a formulation would exclude increases in the current use value of a site, and increases deriving from other causes, such as private sector activity on other land, general inflation, owners' improvements and urban growth generally. The market value of a site to a purchaser might be enhanced by any of these factors, but the degree of their respective influence is incapable of separate analysis. Even in a steady land market, the valuation exercise of distinguishing elements of value is inherently subjective; but with the range of variables affecting development values in the modern urban land market the exercise is pure guesswork. For this reason alone, machinery established in different countries for recoupment of betterment has tended to have a broader sweep, ranging from that which attaches by way of tax or levy to all land value increase, to that which attaches solely to "development value," that is, the difference between the market value of land and its value for its current use.

Throughout the debates in this country betterment and compensation have been treated as quite separate issues despite the obvious links between them. But there has been maintained a close link between betterment and positive planning, particularly through schemes involving the public ownership of development land which is seen as conferring upon public agencies the dual benefits of planning control over land release, and profit from enhanced values as a consequence of original acquisition at reduced value, perhaps no greater than current use value. Short of public acquisition, though, there is a range of instruments through which ad hoc recoupment of value may occur, including developers' financial contributions to the provision by a public agency of physical infrastructure such as roads and sewers necessary to allow development to proceed, and the provision of other facilities of public benefit as part of the development. Betterment policy need not be purely an instrument for revenue raising, and it may in theory be designed so as economically to encourage socially desirable development. It has also had, in some manifestations, the more complex objective of holding down land price levels generally.

Betterment policy therefore encompasses a variety of techniques and objectives, as the history of British experience demonstrates.

4. Betterment recoupment in practise

(a) The pre-war machinery

The collection of betterment first became an issue in Britain long before statutory planning, in the context of private land value increases attributable to public expenditure on improvements to adjoining land. The building of the Thames Embankment in London in the late nineteenth century was a case in point, because its effect was to increase substantially the value of

---

[39] Final Report of the Expert Committee on Compensation and Betterment Cmd. 6386, para. 260, (1942).

adjoining houses. In 1894 a Select Committee of the House of Lords was appointed to examine the betterment issue, and reported that in their view:

> "The principle of betterment, in other words, the principle that persons whose property has clearly been increased in market value should specially contribute to the cost of the improvement, is not in itself unjust, and such persons can equitably be required to do so."[40]

The difficulty in practice, the Committee predicted, would be that of making any accurate and fair valuation.

Their fears were borne out by subsequent experience of the 1932 Town and Country Planning Act, which had adopted the principle that there should be recovered from landowners not only increases due to public works, but also what might be called "planning" increases, that is, increases in value caused by "the coming into operation of any provision contained in a scheme" made under the Act.[41] Authorities were legally permitted to recover 75 per cent. of the amount of increase, but the valuation problems were insurmountable. It quickly proved "quite impossible to establish the amount by which one piece of land has increased in value as a direct consequence of a restriction imposed on another and not from other causes."[42] There was, however, a direct liability under the Act to compensate for planning restrictions, but with inadequate funds flowing in under the betterment machinery to pay the compensation authorities were unable to plan effectively. Instead, they tended either to leave the Act alone, or they turned to compensation avoidance devices. For example, since compensation was not generally payable in respect of controls imposed over the density of new development, many authorities set about their chief objective of preserving good agricultural land from development not by prohibiting development altogether (which would have required compensation) but, paradoxically, by allocating it for development at extremely low densities, requiring perhaps five, ten, or even 50 acres per house. The effect was as good as an outright prohibition, because it reduced development potential to an uneconomic level; although it was a device of dubious legality, and it led to a huge artificial over-allocation of land for development.[43]

(b) The Uthwatt Proposals

Both the Scott Report[44] and the Barlow Report[45] identified the resolution of the betterment/compensation issue as the key to effective planning. The Barlow Committee were sufficiently concerned to recommend the Govern-

---

[40] *Report from the Select Committee of the House of Lords on Town Improvement (Betterment)* H.C. 292 (1894).

[41] T.C.P.A. 1932, s.21(1).

[42] *Town and Country Planning Bill 1947: Explanatory Memorandum* Cmd. 7006, para.22. (1947).

[43] *Report of the Committee on Land Utilisation in Rural Areas* Cmd. 6378, para.143. The Barlow Commission's report contained an estimate that by 1937 enough land had been zoned in draft schemes for residential development to house a population of 291 millions: Cmd. 6153, para.241.

[44] Cmd. 6378, para.223.

[45] Cmd. 6153, Ch.IX.

ment to set up a body of experts to examine the question further,[46] and this recommendation was implemented in 1941 with the appointment of the Uthwatt Committee. It was held out as a non-political exercise. The Committee, headed by a High Court judge, were asked to "make an objective analysis of the subject of the payment of compensation and recovery of betterment in respect of public control of the use of land," and to advise, *inter alia*, on "possible means of stabilising the value of land required for development or redevelopment."

The Committee's terms of reference were thus in fact a clear invitation to them to consider the practicability of adopting far-reaching provisions for better recoupment. These were problems which, in the words of the Minister, "go right to the root of our economic life."[47] The Committee obliged. They rejected the general nationalisation of land as an answer, though agreeing that it would present a logical solution to the problem presented to them to examine. They thought it impracticable, at least in the short term.[48] But they supported limited nationalisation. They recommended, first, that the rights of development in all land lying outside built-up areas should be vested immediately in the State, subject to payment of fair compensation. The land itself would then be acquired by the State as and when it was needed for development. Such arrangements would deal with the problems of "shifting value" and "floating value" which had arisen from the compensation provisions of the 1932 Act, because the values could be fixed and the compensation paid as at one fixed date, ignoring any subsequent increases due to increased development demand.[49]

Second, so far as already developed areas were concerned, the Committee recommended the conferment on local authorities of broader compulsory purchase powers, though they found difficulty in justifying a compensation base below market value.[50] Third, they were in favour of annual site value rating as a continuing means of taxing increases in land values. This latter recommendation was one which they believed could stand on its own, whether the other recommendations were accepted or not.[51]

(c) The financial scheme of the 1947 Act

The Uthwatt proposals were not accepted in full by either the wartime coalition,[52] nor the post-war Labour government. But their influence upon

---

[46] Cmd. 6378, para.250.

[47] *Hansard* H.C. Deb., Vol. 370, col. 186 (March 19, 1941).

[48] Cmd. 6386, paras. 46–47. The Committee was, however, divided over a proposal for converting freehold ownerships to long-term leaseholds with the reversion vested in the state: Chap.X.

[49] In the Committee's view, implementation of the 1932 Act had been hindered by the liability of authorities to compensate for values which (1) had not been lost at all but had shifted to other sites where development was to be permitted under the scheme (or "shifting values"); or (2) were purely speculative in the sense that valuations for compensation purposes were assuming a higher level of development probability on a site by site basis than was true overall, by including each time a speculative element (or "floating value").

[50] Cmd. 6386, para.50.

[51] *Ibid.* paras. 51–52.

[52] See further, *The Control of Land Use* Cmd. 6537 (1944) in which the Government argued that the Uthwatt proposals would be inequitable as between owners of developed and undeveloped land, would be administratively complex and would be harsh on those whose established land investments would be lost.

the radical scheme of the 1947 Act was clear. The Act imposed first a general prohibition against any development without permission, and adopted the general principle that no compensation should have to be paid for refusal of permission except in certain limited cases. Instead, landowners were left with a claim against a "global sum" of £300m. in respect of any loss of development value caused by the Act. A scheme for distribution of the fund was to have been effected by mid-1953. Second, a development charge was imposed, (in practice set at 100 per cent.)[53] upon development value accruing to land by virtue of planning permission or otherwise. The intention was that the existence of the charge would result in market transactions taking place at current use value, since any sum paid in excess of that amount would be payable by way of charge to the Central Land Board. Finally, it was expected that the Central Land Board would themselves play a highly interventionist role, through compulsory purchase, in bringing land onto the market, prompted in their acquisitions by requests from individual developers for particular sites.[54]

No radical reformation in the market in fact occurred, and the Central Land Board's own conclusion after two years' experience was that "Evidence suggests that sales at or near existing use value are more the exception than the rule."[55] Four reasons for the scheme's ineffectiveness have been advanced. The first was that the Conservative Opposition had pledged the repeal of the Act, or at least of its financial provisions. That meant that landowners had no incentive to bring land forward, rather the reverse. From their point of view, there was a strong possibility of a change in government within 10 years, and there was little risk in awaiting the outcome rather than selling on an artificially depressed market. And so the pledge to repeal became self-fulfilling. The charge had to be repealed, it was argued, because it had kept land from the market.

The second reason was that the exercise by the Central Land Board of its powers of compulsory purchase was challenged in the courts in a case which went eventually to the House of Lords.[56] The landowners sought to challenge the use of compulsory purchase powers by the Board for the purpose of discouraging private sales of land at prices in excess of existing use value. The Board's submissions were upheld throughout, but the fact of the challenge was to prove inhibitive in their use of the powers between 1949 and 1952, preventing them from bringing land onto the market when landowners proved unwilling.

Thirdly, demand for building land was affected not so much by planning controls as by the severe licensing restrictions retained by the Government

---

[53] Under the Town and Country Planning (Development Charge) Regulations 1948 (S.I. 1948 No. 1189), which set the charge at 100 per cent. of the "additional value . . . of the land due to planning permission"; but this could be reduced by the Central Land Board so as to comply with the "Governing Principle": *i.e.* "to secure that land can be freely and readily bought and sold or otherwise disposed of in the open market at a price neither greater nor less than its value for its existing use" (Regulations, Schedule).

[54] *Town and Country Planning Bill 1947 : Explanatory Memorandum* Cmd. 7006, para.34.

[55] *Report of the Central Land Board for the Financial Year 1949–50* H.C.148, para.32, (1950). Subsequent reports noted no change: see *Reports for 1950–51* H.C. 258 (1951) and 1951–52 H.C. 242 (1952).

[56] *Earl Fitzwilliam's Wentworth Estate Co.Ltd.* v. *M.H.L.G.* [1952] A.C. 362.

over private house building. The Board had from the outset determined not to collect the scarcity value attributable to the possession of a building licence, and were thus powerless to intervene except by way of exhortation and advice.

Finally, the scheme was complex and little understood by those affected by it. Purchasers were sometimes tricked into paying development value to their vendors, only to find themselves liable to pay it again to the Central Land Board. One such transaction subsequently prompted the widely publicised suicide of its victim, a Mr. Pilgrim, and a consequent public disaffection with the charge. Even Labour spokesmen in the House of Commons were forced eventually to concede that the charge had proved highly unpopular with the public, had fallen heavily on "small" people and was commonly resented.[57]

And so the Conservatives' pledged repeal was carried out upon their return to power in 1952. The Town and Country Planning Act 1953 abolished development charges as from November 18, 1952 and froze claims against the £300m. fund. Further legislation in the following year remodelled and limited the scheme for payments from the fund, and provided for the dissolution of the Central Land Board.[58] The effect of these changes was to restore a free market in development land, with increases in development value subject to no levy and in some cases not even to any direct taxation. There remained one important exception, however. Compensation for acquisition by public authorities remained pegged at existing use values, so that there developed a dual market in which prices grew steadily further apart. It meant that local authorities could acquire their land cheaply, but their inability to pay market values necessarily involved unfair discrimination between landowners. Compulsory purchase was understandably fiercely resisted, and the Franks Committee in 1957 observed that the structure of the market was the major cause of public dissatisfaction with the whole procedure of compulsory purchase.[59] The anomaly was rectified in 1959, when the Town and Country Planning Act of that year restored market value as the basis for compensation assessment, except in the most extreme and identifiable instances of public sector enhancement of private land values such as the new towns, comprehensive development areas and town development schemes.

The logic of the Conservative reforms is hard to appreciate. As the economists Lichfield and Darin-Drabkin point out,

" . . . the most astonishing feature is that the government should have been willing to pay out up to £300 m.—quite a sizable sum in those days—without any compensating income by way of development

---

[57] See, e.g. the second reading debate on the Town and Country Planning Bill 1952: *Hansard* H.C. Deb., Vol. 508, col.1108 *et seq.* (December 1, 1952). In the words of one member, it "became about as popular with the public as Lord Montgomery's memoirs have been with some of the generals" *Hansard* H.C. Deb., Vol. 595, col.584 (November 13, 1958).

[58] T.C.P.A. 1954, which eventually gave effect to the proposals of the Government outlined in their White Paper, Cmd. 8699 (1952). As to the present scope of compensation liability under the surviving provision, see *post*, Chap. 15.

[59] *Report of the Committee on Administrative Tribunals and Enquiries* Cmd. 218 (H.M.S.O., 1957) para. 278.

charges from those clearly able to pay from increased land value on planning permission. And with hindsight, what a bad business deal it was, considering what happened to land values thereafter."[60]

No machinery existed for the recoupment of betterment, save through the somewhat peripheral demands of the tax system. Traders in land were taxed on their net profits in the normal way through income tax and, in the case of companies, through profits tax and from 1965, corporation tax. But these were not land policy measures and their impact could be minimised by good management; and land prices and profits continued to rise steadily and substantially. The only specifically land-related tax to emerge over the fifteen years following the 1952 reforms was the short-term speculative gains tax announced in 1962, designed to catch, among others, "the man who buys land in the hope of a quick speculative profit through a sale to a genuine developer."[61] The Chancellor stressed that the objective was not so much to raise revenue as to ensure an equitable balance between taxpayers, and to ensure similar treatment of traders and non-traders in land. These measures were extended under the Labour Government in 1965 which introduced an additional capital gains tax set at 30 per cent. of realised gains, and which introduced a new corporation tax on companies, applicable both to income and capital gains.

Neither of these measures was seen as having any particular relationship to land policy and planning, however. As opposed to the development charge, whose primary purpose was to hold land prices down by taking development values out of the market completely, the taxes could be expected only to push prices upwards by reducing the incentive for landowners to release their land. Further, they attached to all land value increases, including increases in current use value and other increases unrelated to public sector activity. It was partly in recognition of these factors that the Labour Government again in 1967 brought forward machinery for collecting betterment coupled with new positive planning powers vested in a centralised land agency, the Land Commission. The betterment levy was intended "to secure that a substantial part of the development value created by the community returns to the community and that the burden of the cost of land for essential services is reduced."[62] The levy was set initially at a rate of 40 per cent. of the development value in land, with the intention that it should rise over the long term; and a highly sophisticated (and complex) system of assessment was established. It was an attempt to return to the principles of the 1947 Act, but avoiding the mistakes of the earlier experiment. The levy was set at a rate which would not immediately dry up the land supply; increases in the rate would be incremental; the levy was normally payable by the vendor and could not be passed on, and there were broader powers of compulsory purchase for land assembly.

But the Commission itself was a new, centralised body which took time to become established and to forge links with the local planning authorities. In

[60] *Land Policy in Planning*: (George Allen and Unwin, 1980) p. 144.
[61] *Hansard* Vol. 657 H.C. Debs. col. 979 (April 9, 1962).
[62] *Land Commission* Cmd. 2771 (1965) para. 7.

the event, it had only three years in existence, and much of the first year was taken up with establishment problems. One of the very first acts of the newly returned Conservative Government in 1970 was to announce the repeal of the 1967 Act,[63] and the short time it remained in operation makes it impossible to attempt any detailed analysis of the scheme. It achieved little over the three years, and it signally failed to hold down land prices. Even the Commission's limited land purchases (2,800 acres were acquired over the period) introduced a new force into the market which, coupled with their slow turnaround of sites, raised demand overall; and the prospect of the betterment levy's repeal inhibited the amount of land being brought forward voluntarily. The consequence was an acute land shortage and high prices,[64] particularly in areas of high demand.

The pattern of increase of residential land prices over the period for London and two county areas is demonstrated by Table 1, which shows a doubling of prices over the period 1967–70 for some regions; and which also demonstrates the dramatic longer term land value increase.

Table 1

Regional Price Changes 1962–73

Residential Land

Price per acre (£)

	1962	1963	1964	1965	1966	1967	1968	1969	1970	1971	1972	1973
London 0–20 miles	11,100	13,771	16,500	17,500	18,545	17,800	32,650	35,300	37,325	57,000	88,888	99,310
London 21–40 miles	7,100	8,228	10,800	11,800	11,220	12,900	18,000	17,000	20,800	40,000	60,571	48,400
Hampshire	3,062	5,460	7,550	8,000	9,600	10,690	13,700	20,784	17,132	24,240	47,839	48,000
York	2,520	2,630	3,733	4,800	4,348	3,100	5,000	6,666	6,600	5,576	13,362	20,288

Source: adapted from J. McAuslan, "Residential Land Prices 1962–1974" (1975) 234 E.G. 348.

These were problems which might have been ironed out over a longer period, given the necessary financial and political support. But the latter in particular was absent. The Ministry of Housing and Local Government was not firmly committed to the scheme, and Richard Crossman believed it to have been a mistake from the outset. Local authorities, for their part, saw the Land Commission as an unwarranted invasion upon their own territory. So far as land assembly was concerned they had adequate statutory powers already and a detailed local knowledge of planning needs and priorities.

---

[63] Land Commission (Dissolution) Act 1971, effective as from July 22, 1970.
[64] For a detailed study, see P. Hall, *The Containment of Urban England* (George Allen and Unwin, 1973) Vol. 2, pp. 224–225.

What they lacked was finance, and there was bitterness that the Ministry had cut back on loan sanctions for local authority land acquisition programmes in favour of the centralised scheme.[65]

(d) The property boom

The years that followed the repeal of the Land Commission were boom years in property speculation and development. Land values rose dramatically above the levels, already high, established by the end of the 1960's. The abolition of the betterment levy coincided with the deliberate slackening of government control over credit, and money poured into the property market, particularly in commercial and industrial property, rather than into the re-financing and re-equipping of industry which the Government had intended. The residential market was also overheated, as Table 1 demonstrates, and house prices increased dramatically. Land supply for development still fell far short of demand, and government efforts came to be concentrated upon persuading authorities both to release more land through the planning system and to bring land themselves onto the market through compulsory purchase and resale to developers if necessary.[66]

Profits from private land transactions did not go untaxed, however. The proceeds of speculative transactions were still taxable as income in the hands of individuals receiving them, at the usual rates of up to 75 per cent. But where land which had been held as an investment was sold the gains were taxed as capital gains at the rate of 30 per cent. There were reports of huge profits going untaxed, including windfall gains of a size that even the Government found "offensive." In consequence, proposals were introduced in December 1973 for greatly increased taxation by means of a development gains tax. The reason for singling out land transactions for special treatment, according to the (Conservative) Chancellor of the Exchequer, was that "an owner can quite fortuitously make huge windfall gains simply as a result of decisions made by planning authorities acting on behalf of the community as a whole."[67]

That statement, above all others, hinted that the great political divide between the two major parties on land policy had narrowed substantially; and this impression was strengthened when it fell to the new Labour Government, which came to power a little over two months later, to bring forward the necessary legislation introducing the tax. But the tax itself still did not meet Labour's aim of stabilised land prices and greater public sector intervention and control in the land market.

(e) The Community Land Scheme

The Community Land Act was heralded by a White Paper in 1974 which held out two aims for the scheme:

---

[65] Despite the dissolution of the Commission and the repeal of the levy, assessment and collection of outstanding levy is still being undertaken, though the amounts collected are in danger of being overtaken by the administrative costs involved, with an estimate for 1980–81 of £82,228 levy and interest, against costs of £64,000: for figures see *Hansard* Vol. 974 H.C.Deb., col. 211 (November 21, 1979) and Vol. 3 H.C.Deb. col. 131 (April 14, 1981).

[66] See, *e.g.* D.O.E. Circulars 102/72 and 122/73.

[67] *Hansard* Vol. 866 H.C.Deb. cols. 956–957.

"a. to enable the community to control the development of land in accordance with its needs and priorities; and
b. to restore to the community the increase in value of land arising from its efforts."[68]

The first aim was to be achieved through a programme of gradually increasing public sector intervention in the land market. In the first phase of the scheme local authorities were given broad powers to acquire, not only by agreement but also compulsorily, any land in their area which in their opinion was suitable for development. The idea was that they should undertake a rolling programme of acquisition and disposal. Although finance would need to be borrowed in the first instance, the scheme was intended to become eventually self-financing. Further acquisitions would be financed from disposals, with the authority benefiting from any increases in development values and also from the discount they enjoyed when purchasing by reason of being exempt from liability to the new development land tax.

The tax itself was to be an integral part of the scheme. It has survived the repeal of the Community Land Act, and its main provisions are discussed further below. It is a tax upon realised development value in land, but it differs from the earlier taxes in that it was a completely new system based on development values rather than market values and it was designed for a long-term objective of holding land prices down to current use values. But it attaches to more than "betterment" in the original, Uthwatt, sense of the word, in that it is levied against all increases in development value however caused, subject to various exceptions and exemptions.

The rate at the time of introduction of the tax was 80 per cent. on the aggregate development values realised by any person in any financial year, though there was an exemption in respect of the first £10,000 and an interim reduced rate of 66 and two-thirds per cent. in respect of the next £150,000. The intention under the Labour Government was that the rate of tax would eventually be increased, ultimately to 100 per cent., as part of the community land scheme's strategy to transfer development values in land from private to public ownership. Then in the second phase of the scheme authorities were to have near monopoly powers in the acquisition and disposal of development land, and, except on small sites, no development would be permitted save on land which had passed through an authority's hands. An authority would then be able to buy the land at current use value, and sell it at market value, in a market in which it was the monopoly vendor.

Like the schemes of 1947 and 1967 the community land scheme combined fiscal and planning measures, but it reinforced the planning influence by conferring powers directly on local planning authorities (except in Wales)[69] rather than on a centralised body. It had short-term aims similar to those of the 1967 scheme, principally land supply and site assembly, but long-term

---

[68] *Land* Cmd. 5730, para.16.
[69] In Wales implementation of the scheme was by a special authority, the Land Authority for Wales, which proved significantly more successful than the English and Scottish authorities in both planning and commercial terms, and survived the repeal of the Community Land Act 1975 though in restructured form. See further *post*, p.521.

aims more akin to the 1947 scheme in attempting to hold land values down to current use value. The difference was that under the long-term community land scheme, development values were neither to be taxed (except in purely private sector transactions of which, presumably, few of significance would remain) nor to be destroyed; instead, they were to be exploited by local authorities through their land acquisitions and disposals.

But the scheme suffered from three major problems.[70] First, the Conservative Opposition had from the outset pledged themselves to its repeal. Since implementation of the second phase of the scheme was over 11 years away on even the most optimistic of assessments, and since no post-war Labour Government had ever survived for more that six years, the repeal pledge made the long-term aims appear quite illusory, and it also dogged implementation of the first phase. In the mingled metaphors of a Labour member of the House of Lords opposing the repeal of the scheme by the Local Government Planning and Land Act 1980, the pledge to repeal meant "that from the very first moment the whole scheme was being dragged backwards and was walking along with a limp the whole time, and had really very little chance of getting off the ground."[71]

Secondly, implementation of the scheme coincided with major cutbacks in public expenditure from 1976 onwards. The community land scheme survived the first round of cuts at the end of 1976, but suffered in subsequent rounds because it was a comparatively painless sacrifice for authorities to make. Unlike other areas of expenditure like education and housing, there was limited political support and little by way of standing financial commitment at risk. Expenditure cuts were disguised initially as postponements of full implementation, but by 1978 it was clear that profitability would not be achieved for many years.

Thirdly, except in Wales, there was heavy-handed administration of the scheme on the part of central government. An administrative structure had been established to regulate central/local government interaction, but it was designed to cope with the high levels of expenditure that had been anticipated originally, and it proved an expensive and cumbersome machine for the small scale of activity which actually transpired. It was the ultimate irony that, in each of the three main years the scheme was extant, expenditure by local authorities fell far short not only of the original forecasts, but also of even the reduced allocations allowed by central government. The figures are contained in Table 2, and they illustrate how limited was the actual impact of the scheme, especially when set against an annual land take valued at around £1,300m. at 1976 prices. On a rough estimate, less than 2 per cent. of the annual land take was acquired over the life of the scheme.

Financing of the scheme was designed so as to throw no burden upon the rates, and interest charges and administration costs were to be rolled up and financed from further borrowing in the short term until the scheme became

---

[70] For more detailed analysis, see Grant, "The Community Land Act: An Overview" [1976] J.P.L. 614 at 675 and 732; "Community Land?" [1978] J.P.L. 669, and "Britain's Community Land Act: A Post-Mortem" (1979) 2 *Urban Law and Policy* 359; and S. Barrett *et.al.*, *The Implementation of the Community Land Scheme* Bristol: S.A.U.S (1979).

[71] *Hansard* H.L. Deb., Vol. 414 col., 384 (October 28, 1980).

Table 2

Capital Expenditure: Great Britain (£m)

	1976–77	1977–78	1978–79	1979–80
Forecast expenditure 1976[1]	31.3	76.7	102	102
Actual allocation[2]	31.3	38	64	54
Actual expenditure[3]	14.75	14.20	25	13

Sources: [1] Cmnd. 6393
         [2] Successive annual expenditure White Papers, Cmnd. 6721, 7049, 7439
         [3] Parliamentary written answers: for details see [1978] J.P.L. 669; and *Hansard* Vol. 3 H.C. Deb. cols. 180–182; 198–199 (April 15, 1981).

self-financing. This inevitably placed a premium on achieving commercial profitability in the early years, yet authorities paradoxically were urged not to intervene in respect of those sites which were likely to be brought forward for early development by the private sector, often the most commercially attractive. It also placed pressure on them to seek out sites which offered the most attractive benefits from the development land tax concessions available to authorities—more often to be found on green field sites and the urban fringe than in the inner cities where the planning need for intervention was greatest.

A number of authorities—some for purely ideological reasons—resolved not to implement the scheme at all, but even their administrative costs in meeting the minimum procedural requirements under the Act came to appreciable sums without a penny spent on land. Any appraisal of the success of the scheme in financial terms is difficult because up-to-date national accounts have not been maintained of transactions and landholdings since the termination of the scheme in 1979,[72] no estimate is available of the capital value of land retained by authorities or sold since then (or of the opportunity costs of their continued ownership), and no figures are available for the cost of the development land tax concessions involved specifically in community land acquisitions over the implementation period. But between March 1979 and March 1980 the accounts for England showed an increase in accumulated deficit from £33m to £56m, and a drop in surplus realised during the year from £0.68m to £0.15m.[73]

The Community Land Act was repealed by the Local Government, Planning and Land Act 1980, except that in Wales the special Land Authority for Wales which had been established under the Act has been preserved. Local planning authorities in England and Wales are still able to

[72] For detailed information on the earlier years, see *Community Land Act Statistics 1977–78 Actuals* London: C.I.P.F.A. (1979).
[73] *Community Land Act 1975. Account 1978–1979* H.C. 652 (H.M.S.O., 1980); and *Account 1979–1980* H.C. 235 (H.M.S.O., 1981).

acquire land for "planning purposes," but the scope of their powers is now much more closely confined and acquisitions are no longer supported by a separate specific allocation of loan sanction.

(f) Development Land Tax

Development land tax remains, but the rate of charge has been reduced to 60 per cent., and the personal exemption raised to £50,000 per year.[74] It thus continues as a mechanism for recovering "betterment" so far as it encompasses a proportion of increase in development values, but its original long-term planning purpose has been lost. It is a complex tax, and a discussion of its detailed provisions is well beyond the scope of this book. But a general understanding of its purpose and scope is useful.

Development land tax is payable by the owner of an interest in land on any development value accruing to him upon the disposal of his interest. It does not, therefore, become payable simply because planning permission may have been granted (though there is a "deemed disposal" immediately before "material" development actually commences);[75] nor is it payable in respect of all or any increases in value of land. It is a tax on increases in development values, but not on increases in current use values.

The person disposing of an interest will often already have paid an element of development value when purchasing it himself, and the Act is concerned only with increases in development value during his ownership. There are therefore three alternative bases from which the calculation of the realised development value (against which the tax is levied) can be made. They are[76]:

Base A, which is the aggregate of:
  (a) the cost of acquisition of the interest in question;
  (b) any expenditure on "relevant" improvements;
  (c) any increase in current use value from the time of acquisition or April 6, 1965 whichever is the later; and
  (d) certain special additions.
Base B, which is the aggregate of:
  (a) 115 per cent. of the current use value of the interest at the time of disposal; and
  (b) any expenditure on *relevant* improvements.
Base C, which is 115 per cent. of the aggregate of:
  (a) the cost of acquisition of the interest; and
  (b) any expenditure on *any* improvements.

The realised development value is the difference between the highest figure reached on the alternative bases, and the net proceeds of the disposal of the interest in question. Thus a landowner who has already paid some development value when acquiring his interest, and disposes of it within a year or two of acquisition, will probably find Base A or Base C most

---

[74] Finance (No.2) Act 1979, s.24.
[75] Development Land Tax Act 1976, s.2.
[76] *Ibid.,* s.5, as amended by Finance Act 1980, s.116(1) raising from 110 per cent. to 115 per cent. the aggregate values for Bases B and C. For disposal of land held as stock in trade for residential development after March 9, 1981 the figure is raised to 150 per cent.: Finance Act 1981, s.129.

beneficial; whilst one who has held the interest for many years, or has acquired it by way of gift or bequest will prefer Base B.

Although no detailed study of the impact of the tax has been completed, the prospect that it may inhibit the bringing forward of land for development, or the commencement of the development itself, seems to be diminished by two factors. First, the principle of the tax has been apparently adopted by the two main political parties, though subject to different views as to its most appropriate level, and there is presumably therefore no incentive now to withhold land simply in the hope of future reductions. Secondly, there is provision for deferred payment of the tax in some cases, such as new industrial buildings,[77] so that payment may be postponed until the next disposal of the site.

Although the tax is clearly closely related to land development and planning, its administration is completely separate from the planning system. It is a fiscal measure, not an instrument of land policy. It is also true that the tax has become one of only marginal fiscal significance, and its original take has been greatly reduced by the new concessions mentioned above. Table 3 shows the assessments to development land tax in its first two years, and the actual receipts (which appear to be still some distance behind assessments).

Table 3

Development Land Tax: Assessments and receipts 1976–81 (£m)

	Assessments[1]	Net Receipts[2]
1976/77	19.567	1.1
77/78	27.408	6.8
78/79	—	13.1
79/80	—	26.3
80/81	—	26.0

Sources: [1] *Inland Revenue Statistics 1980* H.M.S.O. (1980)
            [2] *CSO Financial Statistics No. 229* H.M.S.O. (1981)

The level of future receipts can be expected to fluctuate according to the state of the development market, and to be enhanced somewhat as the significance decreases of certain special additions available in respect of sites acquired before 1965, but overall the income product of the tax is insignificant. Its function as a betterment recoupment device is now little more than symbolic.

Local authorities have now lost their former valuable right to purchase development land net of the tax, which was a privilege capable of conferring a substantial financial benefit, and the change has re-asserted the centralised

---

[77] *Ibid.* s.19, which exempts industrial development from the deemed disposals provisions, and exempts sale and lease-back arrangements and now, lease and lease-back arrangements (Finance Act 1980, s.116(3)). There is also a general exemption in respect of land in enterprise zones (Finance Act 1980, s.110) and in respect of works extending existing buildings by up to one–third (Sched.4 to 1976 Act, as amended by Finance Act 1981, s.133).

nature of the tax. It does not hold down land prices for planning authorities, and there is no direct link or transference between the revenue raised under the tax and expenditure by local authorities on planning and land. Further, the effect of taking away the broad positive planning powers of the Community Land Act and replacing them with more restrictive provisions has been to reduce the role of planning to a largely regulatory function and to reassert private sector initiative as the primary means for plan implementation.

5. *The Implications of Land Values for Planning and Development*

Holding down land prices is not a primary objective of the planning system as it now stands, and indeed one of the effects of planning generally has been to raise land costs by restricting the availability of land for development to a level below that which the market, particularly in housing, could absorb. As Hall points out, post-war planning has had outstanding success in physical terms in its containment of urban growth, but its fiscal failures are witnessed by the huge inflation which has occurred, an "inflation in land and property prices, at least since the late 1950's, on a scale never before witnessed in British history."[78]

There has, however, been surprisingly little research into the variables affecting land prices or the impact of development values on prices for completed developments. In housebuilding the general impression is that the proportion of land costs to final prices runs at around 20 per cent., but with substantial regional variations and with cyclical fluctuations according to development pressures. In the South East the average is probably between 25 and 30 per cent., whilst 14 per cent. is the average in Wales.[79] Within London the range is between 30 and 40 per cent. In the case of commercial development, the Government's own estimate is that land costs in outer London make up around 50 per cent. of the total, whilst in central London the average proportion rises to 75 per cent.[80]

Price levels of between £40,000 and £100,000 per acre for residential sites were reached in 1980, depending upon location, suitability and availability of permission and services.[81] Those figures represent between 15 and 30 times the value of the land for ordinary agricultural use, and the multiplier is far higher in the case of commercial and industrial land. These disparities place a substantial strain upon planning; and the further current use and market values grow apart, the greater the impact.

First, it leads to inequalities between landowners. The planning system is capable of conferring substantial gains on some whilst denying them to others, in accordance with a logic which has no market basis. From the landowner's point of view it is an arbitrary decision which results in his

---

[78] *Containment of Urban England*, vol.2, p.394.

[79] Estimates drawn from the consultants' study on *Housing Land Availability in the South East* (H.M.S.O., 1975), p.41, and the Nationwide Building Society *Occasional Bulletin No.144.*

[80] *Hansard* H.C. Deb., Vol. 896 col.560 (July 31, 1975). In real terms commmercial land values exceed residential values by a substantial factor. Darin–Drabkin's study of land values in 20 major world cities showed a ratio of residential to commercial values ranging from 1:4 (Madrid) to 1:75 (Munich): *Land Policy and Urban Growth* (Pergamon Press, 1977), p. 92.

[81] See generally, "Residential Market in 1980" (1981) 257 E.G 351.

neighbour's land being allocated for highly profitable development whilst his is not, or which leads to off-site infrastructure being put in to the benefit of other land, but not his. The fact that the logic of planning is necessarily discriminatory is of little consolation if there exists no substantial financial readjustment to mitigate the disparities. And so there are inevitably pressures on the system for equal treatment of adjoining or comparable sites, resulting in a very common reluctance on the part of planning authorities to permit development on a particular site, otherwise unobjectionable, for fear of creating a precedent which might lead to pressures for further harmful allocations of similar sites.

Second, there is a problem of provision of off-site infrastructure servicing new development. Traditionally it has been the function of public sector agencies to provide and pay for (subject in some instances to contributions from developers) such facilities as roads, sewerage and sewage treatment, water supply, public open space and the range of so-called "social" infrastructure such as community and recreation, educational, social services and similar facilities. There are two land value related problems here. The first is that the public agencies very often must pay prices for land on which to provide the facilities which reflect the potential of the land for profitable development, and not simply for the service function which it is actually to provide. In some cases this may be "double value," reflecting the worth of the very services themselves to development land in the area. Second, whilst it is true that through development land tax the State is able to recoup some of the cost, and that the occupiers of the new development will contribute through payment of rates to servicing the borrowing charges incurred, the financial relationships are indirect and intangible. Cutbacks in public expenditure have inevitably affected infrastructure programmes and resulted in a slowing down of development. Where this has occurred it has become common for developers to make substantial voluntary capital contributions towards infrastructure costs, and their ability to do so is closely related to anticipated resulting increases in land values. For some authorities this has become a standard practice in large development schemes and it is a potential source of recoupment of betterment; but the process is still rudimentary and the rules governing it remain unclear. Again, its effects are liable to be arbitrary, and discriminatory between large scale and small scale developers, and between those whose development and contributions provide the key to opening up an area, and those who follow and enjoy the benefits.

Third, the structure of the land market often means that dealing in land is as profitable an operation as actually carrying out development. The fact that land has been allocated for development by no means guarantees that it will be immediately released for that purpose, because greater long term profits may be made by postponing release as development values rise. The land supply process is frequently inefficient, and in times of peak demand developers have found their development profits matched, if not exceeded by, increases in the value of land held by them for future projects.[82]

---

[82] See further *Housing Land Availability in the South East*, (H.M.S.O., 1975), pp.44–49; and S. Markowski, "Thoughts on Land Speculation" in *Urban Economics 1977* (A. Evans ed., C.E.S. Conference Series, 1979), Vol. 2, p.393.

Fourth, high prices for development land inevitably affect the economics of any proposed development, with pressures on planning authorities to accept reduced standards or higher densities to make a scheme viable. In theory such pressures should not arise because the price paid for a site will reflect the developer's profit estimate both in light of the likely market for the completed development and in light of the known planning constraints. It is a residual valuation, in the sense that the value of the land to the developer is the value of the final development less the costs (including profits) of carrying it out. But fluctuations in the land market and unforeseen planning demands may seriously disturb the original assumptions. Nonetheless, it is obvious that foreseeable planning requirements will affect residual site valuations, and it is curious therefore that, in legal analysis, questions of validity and "reasonableness" of planning standards have been assessed largely in an economic vacuum.[83]

Finally there are particular problems in respect of sites for which no readily assessable market value exists. Vacant land in inner urban areas is an obvious example. Local authority efforts to stimulate redevelopment have been hampered by unrealistically high book valuations recorded by the owners, frequently themselves public sector agencies, which makes voluntary sale unlikely;[84]; and by the fact that development value assumptions built into the compensation code for compulsory purchase frequently raise compensation costs for sites where there is little evidence of any private market activity at all. Paradoxically, should the authority succeed in stimulating regeneration, their success will be reflected in the increased cost to them of future sites acquired, except in the limited case where their efforts constitute a "scheme" under the compensation provisions in which case betterment resulting from its implementation can be ignored in subsequent acquisitions. Under the 1980 Act, the "scheme" provisions have been specifically extended to urban development areas,[85] but it has otherwise proved difficult for authorities to establish a case for holding down values.

These are but some of the interactions between planning and the development land market, but they serve to demonstrate that development values are an important factor in planning and a substantial influence in decision making. Failure to achieve an equitable and enduring land policy is one of the greatest weaknesses of the British planning system, and it accounts for many of the shortfalls in the implementation of post-war land use policy.

D. Law, discretion and the planning system

1. *The nature of planning legislation*

One final question which demands attention is that of the role of law in modern urban planning. Parliamentary legislation is clearly the cornerstone of the system, and practically all the new planning initiatives regularly

---

[83] See further *post*, p.342.
[84] For a detailed account see *Land Values and Planning in the Inner Areas. Report of the RTPI Working Party* (R.T.P.I., 1978), Chap. 3.
[85] L.G.P.L.A. 1980, s.145; and see further *post*, p.539.

promoted by central government have required fresh legislation and new rules. New legislation has become almost a symbol of government commitment to a new policy. And as new laws are more readily enacted than old ones repealed, there has been a steady build-up of statutory powers. Planning law is a subject which has for the most part been unsympathetically handled by the parliamentary draftsmen and their departmental advisors, so that the resultant mass of legislation is highly technical and poorly integrated. It lacks any overall coherence, and comprehending and interpreting it is a difficult enough task for the professional, let alone the laymen. The paradox is that this is an administrative system which is perhaps more than any other reliant on general public support, yet which in an era of public participation evinces every sign of slipping farther and farther away from popular intelligibility.

Some of the factors that have led to this situation are apparent enough, including the procedures through which Parliamentary business is conducted, and the heavy reliance which is placed upon subordinate legislation. There is, for example, often little consistency in the choices made between Parliamentary legislation on the one hand, and statutory regulations, orders and rules on the other as the machinery for detailed law making. In theory, subordinate legislation offers a more flexible instrument for prescribing matters of detail, but that has not in practice prevented the primary legislation from becoming overburdened with detail and susceptible to regular revision and amendment; and, conversely, the provisions of much of the subordinate legislation, like the Use Classes Order and General Development Order, have proved remarkably enduring.

There are substantive as well as mechanical reasons, however. New legislation is the first weapon in implementing new policies because often it is only through legislation that established legal relationships can be changed. To a large extent it is the relationship between private sector and public sector which is affected. There has been a steady strengthening of local planning authority powers over the past twenty years, with a consequent diminution of private sector freedom. Legislation is the necessary means of bringing private choice under State control in the interests of the good of the wider community. But the general pattern has been for each new power conferred to be supported by further new administrative machinery governing applications, decision making and appeals. Assimilation through revision of existing procedures has proved generally a less attractive legislative course than introducing completely new systems as a package of reforms, and the result is piecemeal regulation.

But providing for regulation of private sector activity is no longer the primary obsession of planning legislation. An increasing proportion of new rules are concerned with relationships within the pubic sector. Some of this is the result of the creation in 1974 of the two-tier local government system, and the conferment of overlapping powers on district and county councils. But there is also the growth of the public sector and the proliferation of its agencies, whose land use activities affect, and are themselves affected by, the planning system. And then there is the local/central government relationship. Recent legislation has increasingly involved the imposition of new policies on often unwilling authorities, and has had to be comprehensively structured to ensure its implementation. The Housing Finance Act 1972, the Community Land Act 1975 and the Local Government, Planning and Land

Act 1980 are all examples. Regulation of public sector relations has become a major facet of planning and environmental legislation, and although the 1980 Act has brought about some minor relaxations of central controls over authorities, its main impact has been in strengthening centralised government at the expense of local autonomy.

Law is required to coordinate the public sector in planning, both because of the diffusion of power, which has already been touched upon, and because of the conflict of planning objectives that exists between the different public sector agencies. This results in some unusual uses of legislation. Provisions are frequently designed with a view to excluding litigation, intended rather to establish or reinforce a primarily political relationship or to impose a largely symbolic duty. Thus the Community Land Act contained a provision which required local authorities to have regard to "the desirability of bringing development land into public ownership" when exercising their functions under the Act. But a number of authorities found that proposition ideologically offensive. Could they be said to have been in breach of the duty, having had regard to the desirability of a policy of public ownership and having rejected it? The 1980 Act contains a further largely symbolic duty, requiring local planning authorities when determining planning applications "to seek the achievement of the general objectives of the structure plan for the time being in force in their area." The meaning is obscure and legal enforcement unlikely, but it serves as a general political crutch for the structure plan in decision making. It is a policy statement, and its appearance in the Act rather than in a circular is intended to underline its importance.

The quest for uniformity between local planning authorities is also a theme of much planning legislation, more particularly subordinate legislation. The Regulations governing structure plans and local plans, for example, prescribe in surprising detail the form and style of the documents to be prepared by authorities, belying the promise of flexibility and broad local discretion that lay behind the enabling primary legislation in 1968. Actual adherence to plans, however, is primarily a matter between central and local government. The rules can be upheld by the Secretary of State's intervention in modifying a structure plan, or calling in a local plan for his own decision. The duty on authorities to comply with the requirements of the Regulations is owed primarily to the Secretary of State, in pursuance of his coordinating and supervisory role in planning, and so it is curious that subordinate legislation rather than ministerial circular should have been chosen as the basis for it.

2. Law and policy: certainty and discretion

Planning law, like most administrative systems, functions largely through statutory discretion. Wherever statutory duties are imposed on authorities they tend to be either of a detailed procedural nature, such as the procedures governing the handling of planning applications, or so broad as to be generally unenforceable. The main language of the legislation is that of discretion. Planning authorities have freedom as to what may go into their plans, whether to grant planning permissions, whether to take enforcement action, and so on. From the language of the Act the discretion often appears unconfined: by virtue of section 29(1) of the 1971 Act, for example, an authority may "grant planning permission, either unconditionally or subject to such conditions as they think fit; or . . . may refuse permission." But the potential scope of the discretion is confined both by the administrative structures through which the powers are exercised, and by the power of the courts to review for unlawful exercise of discretion. There are procedural safeguards within the administrative system, including appeals, consultations and so on; and there is also the influence of established relationships and understandings between public agencies.

So far as the substance of planning decisions is concerned, discretion is inevitably constrained substantially by policy. Policy informs the exercise of discretion. It acts as the link between planning objectives and individual decisions. It promotes consistent handling of applications. Policies may be structured in some detail and be intended to be applied rigidly, as in the case of green belt protection. Or they may be loose, informal, perhaps unsubstantiated assumptions and of little aid other than as a general guide. Decision making often involves the balancing of several policies, and statutory discretion in planning is exercised against a background of policies from different sources, of differing status and designed to secure different and sometimes conflicting objectives.

The statutory development plan is the most formal policy source, and in 1947 the intention was that all the decision making by local authorities would be tied closely to policies approved in the plan. But that balance has shifted over the years, less in law than in practice, with a consequent broadening of *de facto* discretion in the hands of authorities. It means that planning decisions are often less predictable, less consistent and less rigid than before. There is greater flexibility, and more scope for intelligent and purposive handling of applications. The structuring of discretion and the control of its misuse are central themes in contemporary administrative law, and the planning system offers a good example of a complex administrative structure with a wide range of direct and indirect measures designed to contain and confine the broad discretions notionally conferred by the Act, whilst at the same time attempting to promote flexibility in responding to urban problems. This dichotomy underlies and explains the structure of the laws which are examined in the subsequent chapters of this book.

Chapter 2

THE ADMINISTRATION OF PLANNING

A. Introduction

It is paradoxical that although the administration of land-use planning in Britain is a matter primarily for local authorities, the system as a whole is highly centralised. This is due to the fact that the local authorities all derive their powers from the same central legislation, and, unlike the situation in federally governed countries, a number of supervisory powers are conferred on a central figure, the Secretary of State for the Environment or, in Wales, the Secretary of State for Wales. There is thus a common machinery for local decision making, and a central coordinating and adjudicative agency. But there is, within that framework, considerable scope for variation between local planning authorities in the way they carry out their functions, and particularly in how they formulate and implement their policies. Detailed administration is not a centrally directed affair: it is a matter for local accountability.

Precisely where the balance should be struck between local accountability and central supervision is an issue perennially debated. The planning Acts prescribe certain basic legal requirements: the Secretary of State's approval is necessary to the validity of a structure plan, for example, and it is to him that disappointed applicants for planning permission may appeal. Yet, as always in matters of power and influence, the legal provisions alone tell us little about the true relationship. That is part of the broader picture of central/local government relations which are governed by numerous variable factors, of which, undoubtedly, the most important is finance. The new Local Government, Planning and Land Act 1980 has made significant changes in the way British local government is financed, and has conferred upon central government new discretionary powers in the allocation and withholding of resources. The effect is necessarily a shifting overall in the balance formerly established (albeit precariously) between central and local government. But the changes are impossible to measure or quantify. There is a symbolic dimension to the legislation and only through practical experience will it be possible to assess its influence.

So far as land-use planning is concerned, the overall balance, and the relationship between planning authorities themselves (especially the two tiers of county and district) is a matter which has a highly significant influence upon policy making. Sometimes it is clear and direct. A new Minister may choose to pursue a policy of substantial land release for private housebuilding. There is a variety of means by which he can do so within existing legislation: by modifying submitted structure plans, for example, or by overruling on appeal decisions by local authorities not to grant planning permission. These direct mechanisms also act as a backcloth for indirect influence. Policy statements by the Minister may be sufficient to trigger off a change of course by local planning authorities; or authorities may be persuaded by private negotiation, rational argument or through common ideological sympathies.

The central/local relationship is clearly never a static affair. Nor is it the only important statute-based relationship in planning. There are similar problems of coordination and control between the individual planning authorities themselves; and in their relationships with other public bodies such as water authorities and the energy supply industries, and with the large scale public sector development agencies like airport and docks authorities and the nationalised transport operators.

And so there emerges the picture of a system where effective power is far more diffuse than a cursory reading of the 1971 Act might suggest. Even in the prescribed central/local relationship there are few clear chains of command or control, and central government's intervention against planning authorities is largely a discretionary matter. Because of the diversity of public agencies and relationships there is no single mouthpiece for the "public interest," which might provide a yardstick against which the effect on private rights could be balanced in decision making. Instead, there is a complex network of interlocking agencies and influences, not always pressing in the same directions. Effective land-use control, perhaps more than any other government service, is dependent on coordination between the various public sector agencies, but coordination implies a two-way relationship. The planner is by no means the master, and it is this ambiguity and diffusion of power that above all gives British planning its distinctive character. It is a pragmatic and flexible system. Statutory development plans offer planners a means of drawing together the strands, but they do not represent a unilateral imposition of policy nor even a long term commitment on the part of the public agencies involved.

These relationships need to be examined in greater depth, but it is first necessary to understand the structure and responsibilities of the central and local agencies engaged in land-use planning.

B. Central Government

1. *The early Ministries*

The centralisation of British planning came with the 1947 Act. The years since 1909 had seen increasing central intervention in planning, which had originally been a purely optional arrangement for local authorities; but there had been little attempt, beyond issuing sets of model clauses for local planning schemes, at standardising local practice, let alone at piecing together any national policy. The Second World War, however, ushered in a new era of centralised administration and national economic planning, and the old objections to central government intervention had been pushed to one side in the interests of military success. And so it was unsurprising that the idea of a centrally run system became readily accepted as the necessary basis for post-war planning. In 1943 a brief Act was passed to authorise the appointment of a Minister of Town and Country Planning, with the duty of "securing consistency and continuity in the framing and execution of a national policy with respect to the use and development of land throughout England and Wales."[1] But it did not go very far: the Government resisted pressure for the establishment of a centralised development agency, and the

---

[1] Minister of Town and Country Planning Act 1943, s.1.

Act conferred upon the Minister no new executive powers. There was no immediate way in which he could hope to undertake what had been described as the "very difficult task to secure consistency with 750 different planning authorities in England and Wales, each concerned to merely to plan its own area in the way which suits its rateable value best."[2] The main task facing the Minister was therefore that of designing and securing Parliamentary endorsement of the framework and powers necessary to impose centralised supervision.

The Ministry of Town and Country Planning oversaw the passage of the 1947 Act and supervised its early implementation, but the Ministry itself survived as a separate entity only until 1951, when there began the trend towards integration of land use planning with other central government activity that has continued since. The proponents of integration have pointed to the benefits of coordination of related central functions, and to the impact of land-use planning upon other governmental activity. But the degree of functional integration which has been achieved simply through departmental reorganisation has proved illusory in practice, and there has always been the danger that "integration" of the planning function implies its subjugation to the development demands of the other departments.

The first step came in January 1951 with the setting up of a Ministry of Local Government and Planning,[3] but upon the return of a Conservative government ten months later, housing was also transferred to the Ministry (from the Ministry of Health), and the title "Planning" was dropped from its title.[4] The new Ministry of Housing and Local Government survived in much the same form for the next nineteen years, responsible primarily for the functions of land use planning, housing, the new towns, public health and local government.[5]

In Wales there was initially a separate office of the English ministry, but in 1965 the Welsh Office was established as a means of regional administration, and planning and local government functions for the Principality were transferred to it.[6]

Reform of the Ministry of Housing and Local Government was under way in the final years of the Labour Government in the late sixties. Integrationist reforms had been urged by the Maud Commission on local government reform, and the case for amalgamation of the ministries of Transport and Housing and Local Government were accepted by the Government, largely on the basis that there was a need for integration of highways and transportation planning with physical land use planning. A Secretary of State for Local Government and Regional Planning was appointed with the task initially of coordinating the work of the two

---

[2] *Hansard*, H.C.Deb., Vol. 386, col. 449 (January 26, 1943), *per* Mr. L. Silkin M.P.
[3] The Transfer of Functions (Minister of Health and Minister of Local Government and Planning) (Nos. 1 and 2) Orders 1951 (S.Is 1951 Nos. 142 and 753)
[4] Minister of Local Government and Planning (Change of Style and Title) Order 1951.
[5] For a detailed study of the Ministry, see E. Sharp, *The Ministry of Housing and Local Government* (George Allen and Unwin, 1969). Richard Crossman's *Diaries of a Cabinet Minister*, Vol. 1 (1975) offer an alternative and more revealing account.
[6] Secretary of State for Wales and Minister of Land and Natural Resources Order 1965 (S.I. 1965 No. 319).

ministries with a view to their eventual amalgamation.[7] The Secretary of State also took over responsibility from the Department of Economic Affairs for the Government's regional policy (not only because of the obvious links between regional economic and regional physical planning, but also because the Department was being axed); and he was instructed to give urgent attention to the problems of environmental pollution.

2. The Department of the Environment

Those reforms were swiftly overtaken by events. The incoming Conservative government a few months later undertook the full integration of the two ministries, but combining them with the Ministry of Buildings and Public Works under a new Department of the Environment.[8] Its creation was part of a trend towards new 'hyper" departments in Whitehall, and it was to be presided over by a Secretary of State, aided by three second-tier Ministers and four Parliamentary Under-Secretaries. The new Department employed over 70,000 staff, and its gross expenditure (including rate support grants to local authorities) accounted for about 12 per cent of all public expenditure. Integration of the work of the former Ministries was achieved by re-allocating staff and physically moving them into new premises, and by establishing new internal management and committee structures.[9]

But in 1976 the decision was made to split the Department once more, and a separate Department of Transport emerged to assume responsibility for all matters affecting inland surface transport.[10] The Department has since been down-graded to ministry status, then brought back to departmental status.[11] It has functions relating to highways, road traffic, road and rail transport, ports, docks and harbours. Inevitably many of the advantages that had come from the central integration of land-use planning and transportation were lost as a result of the changes, which were undertaken more for political than for functional reasons, but some continuity was retained by preserving common services including personnel, legal and research services; and by establishing joint committees between the two Departments. Further, planning decisions on the construction of new motorways and trunk roads are shared by the two Secretaries of State.

The Department of the Environment retains general central responsibility

---

[7] *Hansard,* H.C. Deb., Vol. 788, cols. 32–34 (October 13, 1969).

[8] The Department was formerly established by the Secretary of State for the Environment Order 1970 (S.I. 1970 No. 1681). Some puzzlement has been expressed that one of the Department's responsibilities was for sport, leading to the happy suggestion that it was brought in by mistake because it formed part of the word "transport." The truth, more prosaic but no more rational, is that it had formerly been the responsibility of one of the new ministers when he had been in the Department of Education, and had transferred with him.

[9] For a detailed account, see P. Draper, *The Creation of the D.O.E.* London (HMSO 1977). A more critical stance is taken by Painter in "Policy Coordination in the Department of the Environment, 1970–1976" (1980) 59 Public Administration 135, who finds little evidence of real integration of transport and planning, and instead a "highly competitive arena" in which directorates "found more reason to fight stubbornly for their point of view" than when the ministries were separate.

[10] The Secretary of State for Transport Order 1976 (S.I. 1976 No. 1775).

[11] The Minister of Transport Order 1979 (No. 571); Transfer of Functions (Transport) Order 1981 (S.I. 1981 No. 238).

for planning, housing and the administration and financing of local government. And it has a broad supplementary environmental brief, which encompasses supervision of the water authorities and many (but not all) controls over environmental pollution. An off-shoot of the Department, the Property Services Agency, bears responsibility for arranging accommodation for government departments. And there is a variety of Committees, Boards, Groups and Commissions associated with the Department, some of which have been set up specifically to provide specialist advice on particular aspects of the Department's work. Some, like the Environmental Board and the Regional Economic Planning Councils have already become casualties of the recent drive to abolish so-called "Quangos," but those which have so far survived include many with planning related functions, such as the Royal Commission on Environmental Pollution, the Advisory Group on Property Development, the Royal Commission on Historical Monuments, the Historic Buildings Council, the Ancient Monuments Board, the Countryside Commission, the Nature Conservancy Council, the Noise Advisory Council and the National Water Council. Some have statutory powers and independent responsibilities; others are non-statutory and have only advisory functions.

Within the Department, the administration is presently split between six main divisions: (1) Planning, New Towns and Inner Areas; (2) Local Government; (3) Planning (London and South East), Regional Organisation, Conservation, Sport, Recreation and Rural Affairs; (4) Environmental Protection; (5) Housing and (6) Finance. It is the first of these that has primary responsibility for land-use planning, including development planning, development control, land availability and land economy.[12]

The work of the Department has been progressively decentralised since 1972, and some directorates (including the planning inspectorate) are physically located outside London. Further, much of the Department's liaison with local authorities is through eight regional offices maintained jointly with the Department of Transport, though these arrangements are presently under review.

3. The Secretary of State

The office of Secretary of State is something of a constitutional anomaly. Historically, and still in theory, Britain had but one Secretary of State. But in reality today the title is held by several senior cabinet ministers, each of whom is the political head of a government department. The 1971 Act, however, pays homage to the theory. It contains no general definition of the "Secretary of State," and no general provisions acknowledging the existence of any specific Environment Secretary.[13] It refers only to "the Secretary of

---

[12] Details of the Department's internal arrangement of functions are contained in the annual *Civil Service Year Book* London (HMSO); and in the *Management Information Service for Ministers* (MINIS) published by the Department in 1980.

[13] There are two exceptions where ministerial definitions are necessary: in T.C.P.A. 1971, ss. 113 and 224, authorising compulsory purchase on behalf of the Crown, and defining the "appropriate minister" for the purpose of joint approval of development by statutory undertakers, respectively.

State," and theoretically the powers could be exercised by any of Her Majesty's Secretaries of State.[14] In Wales most of the functions are carried out by the Secretary of State for Wales, and the form of the Act is thus a convenient shorthand. But in practice the allocation of functions between the Secretaries of State is by convention a matter for the Royal Prerogative, and it is the Secretary of State for the Environment Order 1970, made under prerogative powers, which creates the title and allocates the functions.

The Secretary of State is a "corporation sole,"[15] which is a constitutional arrangement conferring an independent legal status upon the office, and ensuring a continuity of power and liability which allows the business of administration to continue uninterrupted by changes in ministerial appointments.

The Secretary of State is a government minister and a member of Cabinet. For legal and constitutional purposes, he and his Department are one and the same thing. The Department acts in his name, and he alone is accountable to Parliament for the Department's administration. There are presently two junior Ministers in the Department: the Minister for Local Government and Environmental Services and the Minister for Housing and Construction Industries. They are assisted in turn by five Parliamentary Under-Secretaries of State, one of whom is normally the Government's environment spokesman in the House of Lords.

4. *The Planning Inspectorate*

Planning inspectors are the quasi-judicial arm of the Department. Their functions are to hear appeals and objections on behalf of the Secretary of State over a large range of environmental issues. Planning inspectors are employed in the examination in public of structure plans; they preside at public local inquiries in respect of local plans (though reporting usually to the local planning authority and not the Secretary of State); and they are responsible for planning and enforcement appeals and other related matters. The title "inspector" has no statutory meaning or status. The inspector is, in statutory terms, a "person appointed" by the Secretary of State to hear representations or objections on matters before the Secretary of State for decision. Usually the person is appointed from amongst the salaried members of the Department's inspectorate,[16] but appointments of outsiders is not uncommon. This is particularly so in technical and in controversial cases where some particular expertise and an appearance of independence

---

[14] By virtue of the Interpretation Act 1978, s.5 and Sched.1, "Secretary of State" means simply "any of Her Majesty's Principal Secretaries of State." See also D.O.E. Circular 121/72, para. 6. Reallocation of functions between ministries and departments may be undertaken by orders made under the Ministers of the Crown Act 1975, s.1.

[15] Secretary of State for the Environment Order 1970 (No. 1681), art.3 (2).

[16] Recent examples include the Windscale inquiry, where the inspector was a High Court judge, and the airport inquiries for the Fourth Terminal Building at Heathrow and the Stanstead inquiry for the proposed third London airport. In highway inquiries it has now been decided to ask the Lord Chancellor to nominate inspectors. There is some discussion of the status and appointment of outside inspectors in *Edwards (Inspector of Taxes)* v. *Clinch* [1980] 3 All E.R. 278 (C.A.); [1981] 3 All E.R. 543 (H.L.).

from the Department may be needed to confer credibility on the process in the eyes of objectors.[17]

Traditionally, the inspector's role was in each case to conduct a local inquiry and prepare a report, upon which the Secretary of State's decision would be based. But there have been some substantial changes in the past fifteen years. The great bulk of ordinary planning appeals are now determined following an exchange of written representations between the parties rather than following an inquiry; and jurisdiction has now been transferred to inspectors themselves to determine the great majority of appeals without reporting at all to the Secretary of State.[18]

There are many critics of the Department's decision making structures who have pointed to the possible conflicts of function and interest that are inherent in the employment of "judicial" officers directly by the Department. The conflict may be trivial or non-existent where the issues at stake are primarily matters of dispute between individuals and planning authorities; but where the Department's own interests are involved the independence of the inspectorate is no longer visibly guaranteed. The controversy hinges on the proper definition of the inspector's role. In the eyes of the Department he is still primarily an administrative officer whose function is to assemble the factual basis for policy decisions. But the alternative and opposing view is that he is effectively a planning judge, and the increased powers that have been conferred upon inspectors since 1960 have strengthened this view. The Franks Committee, whose recommendations led to these reforms, found neither the "administrative" nor the "judicial" analysis satisfactory in itself and sought to find a "reasonable balance between them."[19] Part of their prescription was that the Inspectorate should be granted its independence, and that it should be placed under the control of the Lord Chancellor. The Committee accepted that it might be no more than a change of name, but argued that "the appearance is what matters" and the change would "do much to allay public misgiving."[20]

But change has been consistently opposed by successive Governments, and the Inspectorate remains within the Department.[21] One reason is to ensure that inspectors are kept in touch with Departmental policy. In terms of decision making though, their relationship is necessarily at "arm's length": the Department's officers have no power to interfere with an inspector's report or decision, though they do sometimes in practice point out errors and invite the inspector to amend his report.[22] The status of the Inspectorate remains therefore ambiguous. Whilst they remain within the

---

[17] For a background study, see Wraith and Lamb's work, *Public Inquiries as an Instrument of Government* (George Allen and Unwin, 1971), 181.

[18] See further, *post*, p.568.

[19] *Report of the Committee on Administrative Tribunals and Inquiries*, Cmnd.218 (1957), para.276.

[20] *Ibid;* para. 303.

[21] George Dobry Q.C. in his final report (para. 11.49) and more recently the Prime Minister (*Hansard*, H.C. Deb., Vol. 972 col 1) have insisted that transfer of the inspectorate from the Department is unnecessary, and have maintained the view that its function is administrative rather than judicial.

[22] *Post*, p.571.

Department, they are by no means involved in its executive functions and the "administrative" classification is fast losing credibility as increasing powers are conferred on inspectors to determine appeals themselves.

C. Local Government

1. *Distribution of planning responsibility before 1974*

The 1947 Act vested responsibility for local planning outside London in the county councils and county borough councils. The county boroughs were the councils of the cities and certain large towns, and the way in which functions were allocated meant that within the geographical area of each county there were often several planning authorities: the county boroughs with responsibility for the large urban areas, and the county council with responsibility for the remainder. Each was a unitary authority, and there was no geographical overlap in responsibility. There was, however, provision for delegation of some development control functions by county councils to the urban and rural district councils within their area. The larger of these (with populations over 60,000) could insist upon delegation[23]; in the case of the smaller authorities delegation might be required by the Minister, but otherwise it was a matter for the county's discretion.

The responsibility for development plan preparation remained with the county councils and county boroughs, but the interests of the two types of authority were frequently opposed, and the allocation of planning responsibility meant that conflict between adjoining authorities was often impossible to resolve at a local level. County and city interests pushed in different directions: the county boroughs' needs for expansion were dependent upon the county councils' willingness through their development plans to release land. Each authority was accountable to a quite different electorate, (a fact often reflected in the different political composition of the councils, which did little in itself to enhance relations) and it was commonplace for conflicts to have to be resolved by the Ministry either in the course of examining and approving the development plans, or on appeals against the refusal of planning permissions. The problems experienced by the city of Birmingham in the late 1950s provide the most celebrated example of inter-authority conflict. Overspill difficulties arose there after the approval of the early development plans, and conflicts were brought to a head in 1959 with Birmingham City's attempt to obtain permission to develop an area of approximately two square miles at Wythall to house 54,000 people.[24] The application was opposed by the two authorities in whose areas the land was, the Borough of Solihull and the Bromsgrove Rural District Council, and after a long running public inquiry Birmingham lost the battle.[25]

---

[23] Originally under T.C.P.A. 1947, s.34 and the T.C.P. (Authorisation of Delegation) Regulations 1947 (S.I. 1947 No. 2499) which authorised delegation by agreement; and later the T.C.P. (Authorisation of Delegation) Regulations 1959 (S.I. 1959 No. 1915) which made it mandatory.

[24] For a more detailed account, see Hall (Ed.) *The Containment of Urban England* (George Allen and Unwin 1973), Chap. 10, Vol. 1.

[25] See further, Joyce Long, *The Wythall Inquiry* (Estates Gazette Ltd. 1961).

Important changes had been made in London's local government in 1965, when the London Government Act 1963 came into effect, creating a new federal style Greater London Council, and 33 London Boroughs. The allocation of responsibilities between the two tiers was on a functional rather than a geographical basis. The G.L.C. was given a strategic planning role, and a responsibility for services, such as transport and education, affecting the whole of the Greater London area. Other services are the responsibility of the Boroughs, and there is joint responsibility in certain matters including housing.

The Redcliffe Maud Commission, which had been established in 1966 to study the workings of local government outside London, rejected the two-tier model as a basis for general reform. The majority view of the Commission was that unitary authorities should be established in the case of "coherent areas which made good units for planning and transportation and also combined a population of about 250,000 to 1,000,000."[26] They favoured a two-tier system in the larger metropolitan areas however, because they wished to provide for a strategic, coordinating body, and for an authority capable of operating sufficiently closely with the general public. The larger the area to be covered, the less likely were those two aims to be achieved by a unitary authority.

2. The reorganisation of local government

The Committee's recommendations found some sympathy with the then Labour Government. But the Conservative Government which came into power in the General Election of 1970 were less happy with the proposed solution. They favoured instead a universal two-tier structure, and after much debate effect was given to that choice by the Local Government Act 1972. The Act, which took effect from April 1, 1974, preserved the county councils (though with many boundary and functional changes) and it created a second tier of district councils. Functions were to be split between the two tiers according to assumptions as to the optimum size for efficient delivery of services. In six metropolitan areas (Greater Manchester, Merseyside, South Yorkshire, Tyne and Wear, West Midlands and West Yorkshire) the county councils were given a limited strategic role concerned with strategic planning, highways, traffic and parking, police and fire service. But the 39 new non-metropolitan or "shire" counties were given further responsibilities—for education, personal social services, libraries and youth employment—which in the metropolitan areas went to the metropolitan district councils. That left a list of "local" matters which were to be the responsibility of all 296 non-metropolitan and 36 metropolitan district councils, including housing, local planning, environmental health and slum clearance. Finally the provision of facilities such as parks and playing fields, baths, off-street parking, and museums and art galleries were left for local arrangement between the new counties and districts.

The effect of the reform was that some aspects of county-level government were strengthened, mainly at the expense of the old county

---

[26] *Report of the Royal Commission on Local Government in England,* Cmnd. 4040 (1969), para. 277.

boroughs whose status and influence was reduced by the reform; whilst in other respects the counties lost powers. There was both a geographical and a functional redistribution of power, and it was particularly noticeable in the shire counties. Some mitigation of the effects of the changes was possible: the new Act made provision for authorities to rearrange the statutory allocation of functions by agreement,[27] and some new district councils were able to continue to exercise their old "county borough" functions in a new guise as agents of the new counties.

Planning was a function which proved especially difficult to split. The scope of modern planning is such that it continually raises issues ranging from the strategically important to the local and trivial, often without any clear divisions. There needed to be an arrangement which could overcome the parochial conflicts of the past by providing a level of government which represented within it all the affected factions; and yet which could offer easy access to the public and provide the local responsiveness and accountability necessary in the new era of public participation.

3. *Planning after reorganisation*

(a) Forward planning

The role of structure planning was one which clearly fell to the new county councils to perform because of its strategic nature. But the preparation of local plans raised different issues. The thinking behind the new system of structure plans and local plans, which had been introduced by the 1968 Act, had always been that they would be prepared by the same authority. The local plan would be the next step in the refinement of their policy once the general strategy had been settled and approved.

But the split between structure plan and local plan offered an attractive means of splitting forward planning between the new authorities, and the argument that this arrangement would allow flexible planning by district councils within parameters set by the structure plan won the day. The 1972 Act enshrined the general principle that the preparation of local plans should be primarily a matter for district councils,[28] but that allocation of responsibility and the timetabling of local plan preparation should be settled by agreement between the authorities and recorded in a statutory development plan scheme. Disagreement could be resolved by the Secretary of State. Additionally (or alternatively) the county might reserve in its structure plan the exclusive power to prepare local plans. This course would allow the issue of plan preparation to be considered alongside the strategy itself, and the proposals could of course be modified or rejected by the Secretary of State.[29]

But the division in responsibility has placed unanticipated strains upon the plans system. Structure plans assumed a new function as documents prescribing the power relationships in planning between the two tiers of local government. The more the plan ventured into matters of detail the less discretion it left to the district councils, and substantial modifications have

---

[27] L.G.A. 1972, s.101.
[28] T.C.P.A. 1971, s. 10C(1), added by L.G.A. 1972, s.183(2).
[29] See generally *post*, Chap. 3.

had to be made by successive Secretaries of State to almost all of the first round of structure plans deleting overly detailed policies.

Conversely, the broader the discretion left by the structure plan, the greater the scope for district authorities to disturb the plan's possibly unwelcome principles whilst purporting to implement them. The local plan needed to be in "general conformity" with the structure plan, which meant in practice that only where there was a clear breach in principle between the two would a county be justified in withholding its certificate of conformity. And so the relationship between structure planning and local planning has often proved uncertain and tenuous, far from the expectations that were raised when the split development plans system was introduced.

(b) Development control

The 1972 Act also attempted to ensure a comparable strategic/local split in development control. Primary responsibility for handling and determining planning applications vested in district councils. But applications which in their view involved "county matters" had to be forwarded to the county council for determination. There was an additional safeguard from the county's point of view, in that the county could require that copies of *all* applications should be forwarded to them, and they had power to issue a direction to the district authority as to how they should decide.

The statutory list of county matters was broadly cast so as to include all minerals and related applications, and other applications involving development which might be in conflict with the county's structure plan, local plans and even any non-statutory policies adopted by them and notified to the districts. In many areas the arrangements worked smoothly enough, albeit with some delay and duplication of effort, and many counties were able to agree upon detailed development control schemes with the districts, effecting a more precise reallocation of responsibility than the Act prescribed. But in other areas the division of responsibility led also to frequent conflict between authorities, with the counties seeking to assert planning dominance, while the districts sought independence.

4. *Planning after the 1980 Act*

Problems with the post-reorganisation structure were not confined solely to planning, but the conflicts were perhaps sharper and more apparent in this area. Proposals were prepared by the Labour Government in 1978 which sought further limited reorganisation, or "organic change," which would have "restored" to the main old county boroughs their former broad powers in education, social services and planning,[30] and would have altered the distribution of highways and transportation functions. With the exception of planning, however, the proposals found no favour with the incoming Conservative administration in 1979, whose affinity lay far more closely with the counties, particularly the shire counties, than with the urban areas.

But the need for some reorganisation of planning functions was widely accepted, particularly because of the delays that the two-tier structure had

[30] The proposals were advanced in a white paper, *Organic Change*, Cmnd. 7457 (1979).

led to. The 1980 Act has now substantially altered the balance of planning power in favour of district authorities generally, and has gone further than the "organic change" proposals. The details of the new arrangements are examined in subsequent chapters, but the general principles of the changes are that district councils have been given power in certain circumstances to adopt or alter local plans in advance of any necessary approval or alteration to the relevant structure plan. Certification by the county of general conformity with the structure plan (or their refusal to certify) may now follow rather than precede adoption of the plan by the district authority. Similarly, the new enterprise zones are to be matters of district council responsibility, and it will be for the county to review their structure plan following, rather than ahead of, the adoption of an enterprise zone scheme.

Second, the new Act takes away the former broad county powers in development control. Their functions are now limited to development involving mineral extraction[31] and waste disposal matters, though there is a new duty upon district councils to consult with the county in cases prescribed by the Act, many of which are taken directly from the old "county matters" definition. The power of decision now rests with the districts, however. District councils are also enjoined in their development control functions to seek to achieve the "general objectives" of the structure plan for the area,[32] in recognition that the county's power to secure structure plan compliance directly has been lost. Their power to direct the refusal of an application has been repealed. If the views of the county, given in response to consultation, do not prevail with the district authority, the county's chief weapon will now be to make representations to the Secretary of State with a view to his "calling-in" the application for his own decision.

The danger of the new arrangements is that they leave county authorities with a strategic planning function, but without the legal machinery to supervise its implementation. The prospect therefore is that strategic planning may become an empty ritual, with its coordinating role sacrificed to the principle of district council independence. In an era of economic recession that is perhaps less alarming than it might have been in a period of rapid growth, but that prospect is not an explicit nor an underlying reason for the changes brought about by the 1980 Act. The argument for reform has been efficiency and manpower savings, rather than functional rationalisation.

5. Corporate planning in local government

"Planning" is an ambiguous expression, because it is often used on its own as a description not only of land-use planning, but also of economic planning, development planning and management planning. Corporate planning falls into the last category, and it refers to the management of a corporate entity as a whole in accordance with overall objectives. British local government had traditionally been run through a variety of committees serviced by individual departments, often with little coordination of activity.

---

[31] The powers in this respect are strengthened by the Town and Country Planning (Minerals) Act 1981, which creates "mineral planning authorities." Outside London the function will be undertaken by the county planning authorities.
[32] L.G.P.L.A. 1980, s.86(3).

First steps towards a more business-like structure came with the publication in 1967 of the Redcliff Maud Committee's Report on *Management of Local Government*,[33] which urged that authorities should move towards a broader approach, and should coordinate their activities through management committees. The committees' functions would be "to formulate the principal objectives of the authority and to present them together with plans to attain them to the council for consideration," and generally to review, monitor, supervise, coordinate the work of the authority and take a variety of executive decisions.[34] The purpose of the proposals was to streamline and modernise management, and in particular to reduce the amount of detailed administration painstakingly undertaken by elected members in committees. Greater responsibility was to be given to officers in the day to day running of an authority's affairs.

These themes were taken further by the Bains Committee, set up in 1971 to advise on possible management structures for the new local authorities which were to follow reorganisation in 1974. Their recommendations proved highly influential, and the great majority of new authorities adopted them, perhaps too readily and with too little adjustment to cater for local needs. The committee urged a "wide ranging corporate outlook,"[35] with central corporate roles being played by a members' committee (the Policy and Resources Committee) and by a management team of principal officers, led by a Chief Executive. The Chief Executive was to have no specific departmental responsibilities, but instead have a coordinative role.

Efficient management requires a concentration rather than a diffusion of power, and it is a valid criticism of corporate management in local government that it has often disenfranchised ordinary members of the authority in favour of a central group, or elite, of members and officers.[36] The balance has often shifted too far towards professionalism and away from democratic responsiveness, and some authorities have since abolished both management teams and chief executives, ostensibly often as part of expenditure cutbacks but also with a view to redressing the concentration of power.

The relationship between corporate planning and land-use planning is direct, although the two functions are quite separate in law and in practice. Corporate planning is an instrument of management and is entirely a non-statutory process. Plans are not submitted to the Secretary of State for approval, and apart from the Bains Report which was commissioned jointly by the Department and the local authority associations, there has been no formal advice on the subject given by central government. But corporate planning ties in with land-use planning because of the resource control in terms of capital spending programmes which it facilitates. The implementation of land-use plans is never dependent purely upon private sector activity.

---

[33] HMSO 1967.
[34] Vol. 1, para. 162.
[35] *The New Local Authorities. Management and Structure* (Chairman M.A. Bains)(HMSO, 1972), para. 2.11.
[36] For a detailed critique see C. Cockburn, *The Local State. Management of Cities and People.* (Pluto Press, 1977), and P. McAuslan, *The Ideologies of Planning Law* (Pergamon Press, 1980), pp. 238–244.

It involves public sector commitments to social and physical infrastructure and, in many cases, positive intervention in the land market to ensure availability of sites. Corporate planning allows some coordination between the land-use plans of an authority and its capital spending plans; as well as coordination with the corporate plans of other public authorities. In theory, corporate planning facilitates land-use planning because it allows development decisions to be taken on an economically realistic footing, but in practice there are inevitably difficulties in resolving conflicting priorities and in securing long-term coordination, especially given the different time spans of the two exercises. A structure plan may be prepared against a proposed capital programme for implementation which has lost its validity by the time the plan is approved. The Secretary of State has generally resisted efforts to build corporate commitments, advocative policies or development timing specifications into structure plans, so that it is often the corporate plan of the implementing authority which dictates the pace of implementation of its land-use plans.

6. The financing of local government

The financing of local government has always been a highly controversial issue, and the conflict over resource allocation has become more bitter following the Local Government, Planning and Land Act 1980. The effects of the new centralised spending controls are likely to be felt less by planning than by other services that have high capital expenditure, but there are important implications nonetheless both for general planning services and for programmes of positive planning. Financing arrangements are of crucial importance in the interaction between central and local government, and to a large extent determine the character of the relationship. The more closely central government is able to control local expenditure, the more closely local government is forced into fulfilling an agency role, subordinate to and dependent upon central government. Greater financial freedom, on the other hand, permits greater local influence and control over the carrying out of functions, and full local accountability for expenditure would require the abolition of central controls over both the spending and the raising of money by local government. It was this consideration which led the Layfield Committee in 1976 to urge that a local income tax should be introduced as "the only serious candidate for a new source of local revenue that could give a substantial yield and at the same time maintain or enhance accountability."[37]

Central government has maintained and strengthened controls over local expenditure for three main reasons, however. First, a proportion of around 60 per cent. of local government revenue comes from central government by way of grant aid. The remainder is raised from rates levied on properties in the authority's area, and to a small extent, from fees and charges levied for certain services. This financial balance gives central government a stake in local expenditure, and the means to dictate how it shall be applied.

---

[37] *Local Government Finance: Report of the Committee of Inquiry*, Cmnd. 6453, pp 190–191; and for a detailed study of the problem see Foster, Jackson and Perlman, *Local Government Finance in a Unitary State* (George Allen and Unwin, 1980).

Second, there has been the effect of general economic policy. Capital works undertaken by authorities are financed largely out of borrowing, and the loans incurred are serviced from the authority's revenue. Local authority borrowing is a substantial proportion of the overall public sector borrowing requirement. Monetary policies of both Labour and, more visibly, Conservative administrations in recent years have sought to control public sector borrowing and to curtail the growth of the money supply, and this has involved the establishment of close control over capital expenditure by local authorities. Close control similarly has been exercised over revenue expenditure which has as a result fallen in real terms since 1974–75. But it is still a sizable proportion of gross public sector expenditure. For 1980–81, the Government estimated that total local authority expenditure would run at around one third the figure anticipated for central government expenditure.[38] Capital expenditure on town and country planning, including local assistance to industry, has been hard hit by expenditure costs, with the allocation falling substantially from £159m. in 1975–76 to £64m. in 1979–80.[39]

The third reason for central government overview of local expenditure has been the increasing wish to see value for money, and the pressure exerted on central government, particularly by industries, to curb over-spending by local authorities. Extravagant development schemes and wasteful policies have undoubtedly been pursued by some authorities in the past and the wish to restrain waste is understandable, but the great danger is that central controls to curb authorities must almost inevitably be selective and arbitrary, and politically discriminatory. Cost effectiveness is not a purely economic issue in policy implementation. Socialist policies which are heavily dependent upon public sector intervention and subsidies are understandably more expensive for local authorities to pursue than are non-interventionist Conservative policies, and the expense is compounded by the fact that Labour groups have consistently had political control in many of the inner city areas where service needs are high and so too are the costs in providing them.

These considerations have led to the setting up of an elaborate and complex new system of financial controls by the Local Government, Planning and Land Act 1980, and further legislation to curb expenditure is presently proposed.

(a) Revenue financing

The annual revenue of local authorities is made up of approximately 60 per cent. government grant aid, which is distributed by means of a number of specific revenue and supplementary grants, together with a rate support grant, comprising block grant and domestic rate relief grant. The specific grants are related to expenditure on matters such as police and magistrates' courts, and to such planning-related subjects as the urban programme, open space and derelict land, clean air, urban development, improvement grants

[38] *The Government's Expenditure Plans 1980–81 to 1983–84,* Cmnd. 7841 (1980) Table 1.1.
[39] *Ibid;* Table 2.8.1.

and area improvement grants and slum clearance. Supplementary grants are paid in respect of transport and the national parks.

The rate support grant is calculated annually, and is based upon a national estimate of local authorities' "relevant" expenditure, set for 1981–82 at £17,338m. for England.[40] From the total exchequer contribution of around 60 per cent. (59.1 per cent. in 1981–82) there is deducted the sum payable by way of specific and supplementary grants. The remainder is the amount payable as rate support grant. Part of that (approximately 7 per cent. in 1981–82) is paid separately as domestic rate relief grant, which is not paid to county authorities.[41] The remainder is distributed as block grant between authorities, according to a complex formula which takes into account their total estimated expenditure, (calculated on the basis of a variety of indicators for each authority, embracing population, physical features of the area, social and environmental problems, differences in the costs of providing services and special requirements of particular services)[42] the gross rateable value of their area and their "grant related poundage," a figure determined by the Secretary of State and based upon a given expenditure ratio which may, but need not, take into account the population figure for the area.[43] The grant is set therefore on a generalised rather than a particularised basis, and the level of rates actually set by the authority to finance their own estimates of expenditure remains a matter for them, subject to the overspending controls discussed below.

The same principles for distribution of the rate support grant must be applied to all authorities, though there is nothing to prevent the principles themselves from incorporating discriminatory biases. The criteria may, for example, deliberately lean in favour of authorities in rural areas or those with large populations, but the general principle is to give authorities sufficient grant to put them in a position where they can provide similar standards of service for a similar rate in the pound. Some discrimination is now deliberately built in, however, to control overspending. First, grant calculations are no longer based upon past spending figures (a practice which was seen as bolstering high spending authorities), but instead on indicators of need. Second, the block grant system allows the Government to limit their contribution to authorities whose actual expenditure exceeds a specified level, set at a threshold point of, for 1981–82,[44] 10 per cent. above their prescribed grant related expenditure. Authorities who choose to breach the threshold must levy higher rates to meet the excess. Third, the Act went so far as to authorise the retrospective reduction of grant for the financial year 1980–81, where the Secretary of State believed any authority to be guilty of "overspending"—a concept to be measured in this case by the extent to which their level of rates exceeded a "notional uniform rate," being

---

[40] Details are contained in Loc. ' Government Finance (England): Rate Support Grant Report (England) 1980 (HMSO 1980).
[41] With two exceptions, D.R.R.G. has been set at the same level of 18½p. in the pound for the past six years.
[42] Details are contained in the R.S.G. Report (op. cit.), Annex J.
[43] L.G.P.L.A. 1980, s.55.
[44] R.S.G. Report (op.cit.), para.33.

a notional amount thought by the Secretary of State to be adequate to finance the spending needs of authorities.[45]

(b) Controls over capital expenditure

In past years central control over local authority capital expenditure has attached primarily to borrowing. Loan sanction was required before an authority could borrow, and sanction was allocated in two main ways. Certain proposals which involved national policy, such as education and housing, fell within the "key" sector and required individual approval, (though certain supportive and preliminary expenditure was authorised without specific consent under the "subsidiary" sector); the remainder fell within the "locally determined schemes" sector, where an annual block borrowing sanction was allocated between authorities according to a national formula, leaving each to determine its own expenditure priorities.[46] The community land scheme involved key sector sanctions, but for the most part capital expenditure for planning purposes has had to compete with other local projects against the locally determined schemes allocation.

The 1980 Act has replaced those controls with a new system of cash limits, and (except for law and order services) loan sanction will be given each year to each authority for borrowing up to a prescribed total amount.[47] The amount is fixed following consideration of submitted expenditure programmes on housing, education, personal social services, transport and other services,[48] but it is not tied into the individual programmes. The Act allows authorities freedom to aggregate the allocations and to select priorities for expenditure, though there is power for the Secretary of State to direct that some part of the aggregate should be spent only upon a specified project of national or regional importance[49] Separate subsidiary allocations will be made for such projects, which will in each case require the approval of the appropriate minister.

There are changes, too, in the treatment of capital received by authorities from the sale of assets and other sources. This may be applied to any purpose, irrespective of the function from which it arises, except in the case of housing capital receipts where special arrangements have been made.[50] Capital receipts swell the cash limits even where the capital received has been applied to repayment of debt incurred in the original acquisition of the asset

[45] L.G.P.L.A. 1980, s.48. Authorities have an entitlement to rate support grant, which may be withdrawn by the Secretary of State only after hearing their representations: *R. v. S.O.S.E, ex parte Brent L.B.C.* [1982] 2 W.L.R. 693
[46] Details were contained in the D.O.E. Circular 86/74, as amended and updated by 66/76.
[47] L.G.P.L.A. 1980, Pt. VIII.
[48] Details from D.O.E. *Administrative Memorandum* (Sept. 1980) and D.O.E. Circular 14/81, *Capital Programmes.*
[49] L.G.P.L.A. 1980, s. 73.
[50] The sums to be treated as net capital assets are prescribed by L.G.P.L.A. 1980, s. 75 and by Sched. 2 of the Local Government (Prescribed Expenditure) Regulations 1981 (No. 348) (as amended by S.I. 1982 No. 302), and include not only receipts from the sale of land and disposal of assets but also such other payments as contributions under s.52 agreements and highways agreements, and gifts and bequests.

concerned, but any additional expenditure justified by the receipt would then need to be financed from a different source, and no further borrowing for the purpose is permitted.

Overspending is controlled generally through reductions in allocation for the following year; but there is a special power for the Secretary of State, where he is satisfied that an authority has not kept within the expenditure limits or are unlikely to do so, to prohibit the limits from being exceeded without his consent.[51] It would then be *ultra vires* for an authority to make a payment or enter into a contract in contravention of the direction,[52] and although that will not invalidate the transaction itself[53] it will render those responsible in the authority to surcharge.

So far as planning is concerned, the effect of the changes is to create a notionally broader discretion for authorities. Land acquisition for planning purposes, for example, is no longer confined to financing from the locally determined schemes allocation, and authorities are able to set their own expenditure priorities across the broad range of their activities. But the general availability of capital is tightly restricted under the cash limit controls, and "planning purposes" expenditure will often be given a low priority by authorities. The controls also inhibit the positive planning initiatives which authorities increasingly believe to be necessary to stimulate local economic growth. The Act requires that where an authority take a lease of land they should be deemed, for accounting purposes, to have paid full freehold value.[54] The purpose is to discourage avoidance of the expenditure controls by authorities resorting to leasing instead of freehold acquisition, or to sale and leaseback schemes as an alternative to borrowing. But it effectively discourages all leasing arrangements, including the valuable head-leasing arrangement used as a means of underwriting new development.

7. Parish, town and community councils[55]

Discussion so far has focused on the larger units of local government, but it would not be complete without bringing in the smaller local bodies. There are around 10,000 civil parishes in England and 900 equivalent "communities" in Wales, of which some 7,000 and 750 respectively have established elected councils. Any of these councils may resolve to call itself a town council, but its general powers remain the same.

Parish councils have limited statutory powers, and those most relevant to planning include the right to be consulted by the district council on planning applications for their areas,[56] and the right to appear at any subsequent planning inquiry in support of their representations.[57] They have power also

---

[51] L.G.P.L.A. 1980, s. 78(1). At the time of going to press, the Local Government Finance (No. 2) Bill was under consideration in the House, and contained proposals for further restricting local authority expenditure by, *inter alia* abolishing the power to levy supplementary rates and supplementary precept.

[52] *Ibid.* s. 79(2).

[53] *Ibid.* s. 79(3).

[54] *Ibid.* s. 80(4).

[55] For a detailed study, see C. Arnold-Baker, *Local Council Administration* (Longcross Press 1975).

[56] T.C.P. General Development Order 1977, art. 17; and see further *post*, p.230.

[57] T.C.P. (Inquiries Procedure) Rules 1974 (No. 419), r. 7(1)(iii).

to acquire,[58] appropriate[59] and dispose[60] of land. Acquisition may be undertaken for the purposes of any of their functions[61] such as the provision of recreation space and amenities but there is no direct power of compulsory purchase. If the local council are unable to acquire by agreement, the district council may be able to exercise compulsory powers on their behalf, but only following a complex procedure which involves a preliminary local inquiry held by the district council before making any compulsory purchase order.[62] If an order then is made, and objected to by the landowner or other statutory objector, there will be a second inquiry on behalf of the Secretary of State prior to the confirmation or rejection of the order.

Appropriation and disposal of land is governed by rules similar to those applicable to district and county councils.[63]

Although their powers are limited and their resources slender, parish and community councils are capable of playing an important role in planning, influencing decisions primarily through the consultations process backed up by lobbying, publicity and the application of other pressures to the principal statutory agencies.

8. Local legislation

Although planning and local government legislation applies evenly across the country, some local variation is possible through local Acts promoted by individual authorities. Special powers have been taken by many authorities for specific large scale schemes, such as town centre redevelopment proposals and large construction works. But much local legislation also includes local variations and extensions of general statutory powers. Examples include extended planning agreement and public/private sector partnership powers; curbs on roadside trading; special powers to impose conditions on planning permissions requiring, for example, the provision of walkways in new development, and, more recently, powers to promote economic regeneration including provisions for financial aid to industry.

Local legislation is expensive to promote and it results in confusing local differences. It was therefore intended with the passage of the Local Government Act 1972 that local Acts should be overhauled and their provisions replaced, so far as expedient, by general enabling legislation. Accordingly, the Act provided that all existing local legislation should cease to have effect by the end of 1979 (later extended to the end of 1980)[64] in the case of metropolitan counties, and the end of 1984 elsewhere.[65] Some of the

---

[58] L.G.A. 1972, ss. 124 and 125.

[59] *Ibid.* s. 126.

[60] *Ibid.* s. 127.

[61] *Ibid.* s. 124. Acquisition is also authorised for "the benefit, improvement or development of their area," but there is no compulsory power exercisable by the district council in such cases: s.125(1)(a).

[62] *Ibid.* s.125. by subs. (5) the district council and the Secretary of State are obliged to "have regard to the extent of land held in the neighbourhood by any owner and to the convenience of other property belonging to the same owner and shall, so far as practicable, avoid taking an undue or inconvenient quantity of land from any owner."

[63] *Post*, pp.512–518, 520.

[64] The Metropolitan Counties (Local Statutory Provisions) Order 1979 (S.I. 1979 No. 969).

[65] L.G.A. 1972, s. 262(9).

old legislation has now been re-enacted in general form in the 1972 Act itself and in the Local Government (Miscellaneous Provisions) Acts of 1976 and 1982.

Authorities may still promote fresh local legislation, and this has been used recently in attempts, largely unsuccessful, to gain wider planning powers over certain types of development (Kensington and Chelsea Corporation Bill 1977) and for municipal trading (City of Birmingham Bill 1977). The test case with post-reorganisation Bills came with the County of South Glamorgan Bill in 1976, where the select committee of the House which examined it asserted a basic rule that there should be a burden of proof on authorities to establish a case based on compelling local need for change in the general law.[66] Only limited variations have since passed that test, and although various powers for local economic initiatives have been approved the Department of the Environment has been anxious to oppose any substantial broadening of powers under local legislation.

D. The Relationship between Central and Local Government

1. *The nature of the relationship*

The nature of the relationship between central and local government is a highly significant factor in land-use policy, because it determines the relative balance of national, regional and local influences in policy making. It also bears upon the true allocations of power in decision making. Whilst primary power is vested in the local planning authorities there are also a number of supervisory and reserve powers vested in the Secretary of State. Their purpose is twofold.

First, they provide the machinery through which the Secretary of State may comply with his statutory duty of "securing consistency and continuity in the framing and execution of a national policy."[67] Despite their own broad statutory discretions, local planning authorities can be brought into line with national policy when the occasion demands. One celebrated instance occurred in Scotland in the 1950's when the development plan which had been prepared for the city of St. Andrews failed to make adequate provision, in the Minister's view, for the expansion of the university.[68] He directed the authority to amend the plan, but they refused. He then proceeded, using reserve powers, to make his own amendments, which were later approved in modified form following a public inquiry. Instances of outright conflict like this are rare, however, because the existence of the reserve powers creates a working relationship in which local planning authorities are generally subordinated to central government, and where there is benefit to both sides in resolving disputes behind the scenes through consultation, persuasion and indirect influence.

Second, the Secretary of State is the major source of redress within the system for aggrieved citizens. Formal rights of appeal exist to him against

---

[66] *Special Report from the Select Committee (on Re-commitment) of the House of Lords on the County of South Glamorgan Bill*, H.C. 347 (1975–76).

[67] Minister of Town and Country Planning Act 1943, s.1.

[68] Details of the dispute may be found in the Annual Reports of the Director of Health for Scotland for 1956–57 (Cmnd. 140, p.91) 1957–58 (Cmnd. 385, p. 93) and 1958–59 (Cmnd. 697, p. 81).

adverse decisions by local planning authorities, and informal access is equally important. Representations from members of the public frequently succeed in persuading the Secretary of State to take a decision out of the hands of a local planning authority by calling it in for his own decision, or he may choose to institute proceedings for the revocation of a permission which he believes ought not to have been granted, or to intervene by taking enforcement action himself against unauthorised development where a local authority have refused to act.

The most characteristic feature of central/local relations in planning, as in other matters, is its imprecision. It is impossible to describe local planning authorities either as agents for central government, or as independent bodies. Central government supervises them, directs them, offers them advice, consults with them and so on, but there is no clear chain of command and few discrete allocations of split responsibility. In part this is due to the complex structure of the two systems. Even to talk in terms of central and local government is to use unrealistic abstractions:

> "Central government is, in fact, a federation of separate departments with their own Ministers and their own policies. The aims of the Treasury and of the DOE in its capacity as the "Department of Local Government" often cut across those of the spending or service departments. They in turn compete with each other for scarce resources. The development of an interdepartmental view about a local authority service is a rare achievement. . . . Much the same is true of local authorities. They are made up of officers and elected members whose interests and objectives on particular issues may differ. Separate committees, chief officers and departments may equally be pursuing their own ends."[69]

It could be added, too, that there exist different relationships not only in different services, but also within services. Planning, for example, encompasses a multiplicity of functions each with differing central/local implications.

It is also true, though, that imprecision and confusion serve the purposes of central government well. It offers a fluid and flexible arrangement for the use of influence. The absence of precise demarcations increases discretion, and since it is central government which has the reserve powers, it is their discretion which is broadened. Authorities will seek clarification, interpretation and advice rather than proceed on a course which might lead to subsequent central intervention. In the eyes of the Layfield Committee on Local Government Finance, confusion over responsibility for financing local government and for controls over spending was the major cause of dissatisfaction with the financing system. They concluded that there is "at present no coherent system,"[70] and that misunderstandings had arisen between central and local government which only a clear demarcation of responsibility could dispel.

---

[69] Report of the Central Policy Review Staff. *Relations Between Central Government and Local Authorities* (HMSO 1977), p.21.
[70] *Local Government Finance*, Cmnd. 6453, p. 49.

But that idea found little sympathy with the government, whose response is worth setting down in detail:

> "The Government accept that the dividing line between central and local responsibilities is not always clear. There are many reasons for this. The central/local relationship is changing all the time because national economic and social priorities can alter substantially even within quite short periods. . . . Any formal definition of central and local responsibilities would lack the advantages of flexibility and rapidity of response to new circumstances. It would be likely to break down under the pressure of events. . . . It is unrealistic to envisage developing a middle way which reduces the whole relationship between central and local government to a simply defined form of allocation of responsibilities. Rather the Government see the duties and responsibilities involved in the provision of local public services as being shared on a partnership basis between central and local government."[71]

The partnership theory is far from new, but it is equally far from offering a comprehensive explanation of present arrangements. Local authorities effectively have discretion in providing services only within the limits prescribed by central government policy. To the extent that they have that discretion, their function is not purely one of agency. But nor does it constitute a partnership, with the joint freedom and responsibility the expression implies, with central government. In short, analogies with other relationships are unhelpful and misleading. The central/local relationship is an amalgam of individual balances of power, pragmatically arrived at and struck in terms of finance, statutory relationships and convention. It has no entrenched constitutional significance, and it is susceptible to whatever legislative rearrangement the majority Parliamentary party may be able to find support for. Local authorities are not without bargaining power in seeking increased resources and extended functions, especially through their collective associations and their sympathisers in both Houses of Parliament, but their effective strength against a central administration intent on centralising power is limited. The Local Government, Planning and Land Act 1980 is evidence enough of that, and, at the time of going to press, further legislation had been proposed by the Government to restrict local authority autonomy in increasing rate revenue beyond a level to be prescribed by central government.

In land-use planning the relationship is as imprecise as in other areas of activity with the possible exception of the quasi-judicial work of the Department. Much of the decision making on planning appeals involves little by way of policy, and is processed according to fairly precise rules. But in plan making and implementation, and in the more difficult development control work, government policy and local objectives are balanced through a complex structure of inputs and influences. To many authorities it is not the *fact* of central governmnt intervention in planning so much as its *extent* and *quality* which is objectionable. Ministerial scrutiny and approval of development plans, for example, has been a notoriously time-consuming

---

[71] *Local Government Finance (Comments on the Layfield Report)*, Cmnd. 6813 (1977), paras. 2.8–2.9. For a detailed review of the legal basis of central-local relations, see M. J. Elliott, *The Role of Law in Central-Local Relations* S.S.R.C. (1981).

process; and although the introduction of structure planning and local planning in 1968 was intended to reduce central involvement and boost local autonomy within the centrally approved framework of the structure plan, that objective is still frustrated by lengthy delays in approval, and by continued central involvement in issues of detail.[72]

2. Communication of Government Policy

Central government's communication of policy objectives to local authorities is done in two main formal ways, although there is a background of informal communication and personal networks which add their own flavour to the relationship.[73]

First, there is legislation, which includes not only parliamentary Acts but also subordinate legislation and directions issued to authorities. All are formal measures with legal effects. Second, there are purely advisory instruments, such as circulars, ministerial statements, white papers, policy notes and the like. Their purpose is generally to guide authorities in the exercise of discretionary powers, but they have no standing in law and no direct legal effect.

(a) Preliminary consultations

Although all the above policy instruments are issued from Parliament and central government, it would be wrong to assume that their formulation is entirely a unilateral process. It has become customary for central government to undertake extensive consultation with local authorities and other interested groups before making any significant changes. Through the consultative process authorities have succeeded frequently in altering at least the form, and sometimes the substance of the Government's proposed reforms. Hostile reactions against the capital expenditure controls initially proposed under the 1980 Act, for example, led to substantial revisions being made by the Department.[74] In the case of proposed new policy circulars it is now also common for a draft to be distributed for consultation, before the final version is agreed upon. The new circular on development control which was issued late in 1980 emerged from the consultation process significantly amended.[75]

Government action in planning is subject therefore to informal and political constraints, and policy reforms may be difficult to achieve without some measure of agreement from local authorities. They and other environmental interest groups are capable of mustering sufficient parliamentary support to influence and even force changes in government legislation (as happened in the Lords and in Standing Committee in the Commons on

---

[72] See further *post*, Chap. 3.

[73] Thus Dame Evelyn Sharp's account, in *The Ministry of Housing and Local Government* (George Allen and Unwin 1969), p. 32: "Many local government officers make it their business to know their way around the Ministry, whom to go to in order to find out how such and such a proposal is likely to fare, or why something seems to have stuck. Some will just drop in to find out what is cooking."

[74] See, *e.g.* D.O.E. Consultation Paper, *Capital Expenditure Controls. Response to Local Government Comments* (1980).

[75] The draft version is published at [1980] J.P.L.663.

the Local Government, Planning and Land Bill) and to block unwelcome changes in subordinate legislation (as occurred in 1977 when amendments to the General Development Order which would have reduced the scope of planning control were rejected in the House of Lords).[76]

Pressure is often applied by individual authorities who fear that their interests may be particularly affected by proposed changes, but much of the Government's consultative work is done through four local authority associations: the Association of Metropolitan Authorities, the Association of County Councils, the Association of District Councils and the London Boroughs Association. Although their primary function is to represent their constituent authorities' viewpoint, there are obvious difficulties in ascertaining precisely what views their members hold. In the words of one study, they are "essentially voluntary bodies neither mandated by their members nor able to guarantee their members' support for the line they take. Sometimes they find it hard to develop views at all."[77] The political composition of the executive of each Association depends on the political control of its member authorities, and this factor coupled with the concern of each authority with its own sector of local government, frequently determines the line taken in consultations.

(b) The legislative instruments

Much of the detail of planning administration is reserved by the 1971 Act to be dealt with by subordinate legislation. This sub-legislative power is exercised by the Secretary of State generally by way of statutory instrument,[78] and in the case of regulations and some orders [79] the instrument must be laid before the House and is subject to negative resolution procedure, *i.e.* it may be annulled by a resolution of either House of Parliament. In some few cases Parliamentary scrutiny is firmer, and the instrument does not have effect except where approved by resolution of each House.[80]

A sub-legislative device which is widely used in planning and which avoids the formalities of statutory instruments, is the power conferred on the Secretary of State to issue *directions* to local planning authorities. He may, for example, direct that certain planning applications be referred to him for decision, and such a direction may be given to authorities generally or individually, and relate to a particular application or to a class of applications.[81] Similarly, he has power to direct the scope of the demolition controls over buildings in conservation areas,[82] the circumstances in which

---

[76] *Hansard,* H.L. Deb., Vol. 387, cols. 1793–1822 (December 8, 1977).

[77] *Relations Between Central Government and Local Authorities* (Report by the Central Policy Review Staff)(HMSO 1977), para. 10.2.

[78] T.C.P.A. 1971, s. 287(2). The procedure for publication and laying instruments before the House (where necessary) is governed by the Statutory Instruments Act 1946.

[79] T.C.P.A. 1971, s. 287(4) and (5). Some orders, although made by statutory instrument, need not be laid before the House including the Use Classes Order and amendments to it. As to the making of procedural rules, see the Tribunals and Inquiries Act 1971, ss. 10, 11 and 16.

[80] See, *e.g.* T.C.P.A. 1971, s. 287(7): designation of areas for office development controls.

[81] T.C.P.A. 1971, s. 35(1) and (2); and *cf.* the broad powers to make directions formulating the procedures for authorities' forward planning functions and for requiring them to supply information to the Secretary of State: s. 18(3).

[82] *Ibid.* s. 277A (4)–(6).

departures may be made from the development plan[83] and the consultations to be undertaken by authorities before granting planning permission.[84] Where directions are issued on an individual basis their legal status is presumably the same as any other statutory decision[85]; but general directions are better classified as delegated legislation.

Directions intended to be of general application are issued in or accompanying circulars from the Department, but despite their less formal style they have direct legal effect.[86] In the case of applications called in by direction of the Secretary of State, for example, the local planning authority lose jurisdiction to determine the application and are unable to issue a valid decision. In other cases the power of direction has been used to introduce a time limit or other requirement to an otherwise open-ended statutory duty, such as that to prepare a structure plan and submit it for approval[87] or to consider whether to designate conservation areas. It thereby converts the duty into one more readily enforceable by an action for mandamus.

(c) Circulars and policy notes

There is a whole range of informal routes through which government policy and advice is communicated to local planning authorities. Best known are government circulars, many of which are published by the Stationery Office; and advice of lesser significance is regularly communicated by way of circular letters, administrative memoranda, advice notes, planning bulletins, policy notes and even by asking the local authority associations to relay material to their members. There is nothing fixed or pre-ordained about these methods, and to the outsider the choice between them often appears quite arbitrary. Most of the important policy behind the Community Land Act's implementation, for example, was communicated by means of a series of highly informal and unpublished *Guidance Notes for Local Authorities.* The advice in the early notes was subsequently consolidated and reprinted in published circulars, but once the scheme was under way *Guidance Notes* alone were used for running it, for amending orders made under it, and even for winding it up.

Circulars and the like may have no direct legal effect, but they play an important function in regulating the central/local relationship and many of their provisions are capable of enforcement through the administrative machinery because they tie in with central government decision making. Advice on the form and content of structure plans, for example, if ignored by the county planning authority, may nonetheless be implemented by means of Secretary of State's modifications to their submitted plan. Central policy on development control similarly may be reasserted in decisions on

---

[83] G.D.O. 1977, art. 14.
[84] *Ibid.* Art. 15(4). Note too the power under art. 12 for local highway authorities to issue directions to planning authorities, discussed further, *post*, p.232.
[85] Except that they are not (other than in the case of directions issued under T.C.P.A. 1971, s.38) protected by the privative clauses which preclude judicial review of other action by the Secretary of State save in prescribed circumstances: *post* p. 642.
[86] Whether or not published: see, *e.g. Blackpool Corporation* v. *Locker* [1948] 1 Q.B. 349, where there was strong criticism by the Court of Appeal of the authority's refusal, endorsed by the minister, to disclose the terms of a sub-legislative circular under which they sought to exercise a requisitioning power; but no doubt existed as to the legal effect of its provisions.
[87] T.C.P.A. 1971, s. 7(1).

appeal, by calling in applications or ultimately even by use of reserve powers. And even when enforcement is not possible or is remote, the influence of policy advice may still be substantial as providing a yardstick by which an authority's decision making is liable to be measured by outside bodies and by other public agencies, and by giving support to particular arguments or groups inside or outside the authority. An example is the sentence in D.O.E. Circular 23/77 which requires authorities to "set an example" to other owners in their treatment of their own listed buildings,[88] which has greatly strengthened the conservation cause against local authorities who neglect their buildings. It provides a basis for requests for central government intervention, and it places a hurdle in front of authorities seeking listed building consent from the Secretary of State.

Policy advice is not the same thing as a legal rule, however, and there is often little indication of the status of the advice and the degree to which authorities are expected to comply with it: " . . . circulars variously advise, warn, hope, urge, encourage, ask, recommend and so on."[89] The status and effect of policies change often incrementally, such as with a change in government or on the appointment of a new minister, the introduction of new measures or simply the passage of time. Seldom does this lead to radical change. It is more a matter of a shift in emphasis, though the consequences are as a result often indefinable and vague.

There is a recent circular on development control, for example, which is in some respects at odds with the long established *Development Control Policy Notes* (or, perhaps more significantly, it has a different tone), and whilst the *Notes* remain Government policy until they are withdrawn their status is somewhat shaken by the new circular. Its provisions can be expected to be applied strictly by the Secretary of State who prepared it, but not necessarily by any successor of his.

The continuing importance of a circular is highly dependent upon the degree of support and adherence it is found to command in practice. If the Secretary of State and the inspectorate are seen to be applying its terms rigorously, then the greater its influence upon authorities is likely to be. It is a matter of inference and suggestion. Circulars have sometimes followed some distance behind the changes in policy they record, which may already have influenced ministerial decision making. This was the case in the land release exercise of the early 1970s, when detailed policy advice came to authorities some two years after its adoption in general terms by central government.

In short, communication of planning policy to local authorities is muddled and confused, and this adds to the complexity of the central/local relationship. Although some heed has been paid to the recommendation in the *Dobry Report*[90] in 1975 that obsolete circulars should be cancelled and extant advice consolidated "without delay," progress has been surprisingly slow and formal statements of central government's planning policy are presently spread through well over 100 circulars, supplemented by a range of other materials.

---

[88] *Historic Buildings and Conservation Areas—Policy and Procedure*, para. 65.
[89] *Relations between Central Government and Local Authorities (op. cit.)*, para. 6.2
[90] *Review of the Development Control System* (HMSO 1975), para. 8.43.

3. *The influence of Government policy in local planning*

Government policy does not bind local planning authorities directly, although it guides their use of discretionary powers. The guidance is frequently ignored or explicitly rejected by authorities, who may feel that it is patronising, irrelevant to local circumstances or the result of an inadequate understanding by central government of the nature of local planning. In asserting their right to disregard central policy and to order their own affairs, local authorities have found, surprisingly, considerable central government sympathy.

The Expenditure Committee of the House of Commons in 1977 conducted, through its Environment Sub-Committee, a detailed study of planning procedures and they concluded that the central/local policy relationship went to the heart of the operation of the planning system.[91] On the one hand, developers pressed for more vigorous intervention by the Department "to compel the planning authorities both to operate more efficiently and to implement central government's planning policies,"[92] and they wanted sanctions to be applied against unwilling authorities. On the other hand, the Department emphasised the fact that planning powers were conferred upon local authorities by legislation and not delegated by the Department; and that the Department's role was necessarily limited.[93]

The Committee recommended *inter alia* that a small number of planning assessors should be appointed to advise authorities and monitor their performance, and that inefficiency should be penalised by being made an additional reason for the award of costs on appeal. But the Government found strong opposition from local authorities to the first recommendation, and they rejected the second because its effect "would be to make a marked change in the relationship between central and local government. The Secretaries of State would be reluctant to do this without overwhelming evidence in support of such a change."[94]

The Committee then took the unusual step of hearing further evidence and issuing a response to the Government's white paper, in which they reasserted the need for independent assessors and argued that in light of the adverse local authority reaction, they would need to be centrally appointed and accountable.[95] But no Government reaction followed, and the proposal has gone no further. The traditional relationship has been preserved, and the only apparent influence on it of the Dobry Report and the Expenditure Committee's Reports has been the programme of revision and consolidation of some of the circulars, and perhaps a general raising of the consciousness of authorities to the problems caused to developers and the general public by

---

[91] *Eighth Report from the Expenditure Committee,*Session 1976–1977 *Planning Procedures,* Vol. 1, para. 60.

[92] *Ibid.* para. 58.

[93] *Ibid.* para. 59.

[94] *Planning Procedures,* Cmnd. 7056 (1978), para. 14. In a later memorandum to the Committee the Department of the Environment explained that imposing penalties would "make local authorities accountable to central government for the exercise of functions in a way not envisaged in the legislation. It would, moreover, be resented and would inhibit the co-operation which is essential if the development control machinery is to be made more effective through joint action:" Minutes of Evidence, *Eleventh Report from the Expenditure Committee,* Session 1977–78, p.3.

inefficient conduct and inadvertent failure to observe central policy. The national, centralised policy context of planning remains loose, but the major changes made by central government in the recent past have instead been in the direction of releasing planning controls altogether in some cases. Relaxation of the General Development Order, enterprise zones and proposals for planning by special development order, are all examples of a new approach that involves centralised dismantling of local controls.

E. The European Dimension

The influence of the agencies of the European Economic Community has come to be felt increasingly in Britain's land use and environmental policy since membership in 1972, and proposals currently before the Commission can be expected to take the European dimension much further over the coming years. The foundation of the Community's involvement is notionally the objective contained in Article 2 of the Treaty of Rome, of promoting the harmonious development of economic activities between member states, but in practice the Commission's environmental programme has extended far beyond issues of direct economic harmonisation. The link is clear enough in the case of measures intended to achieve common standards in industrial pollution, not only because of the extra-territorial impact of much pollution but also in terms of securing fair competition between firms in different Member States. Uncontrolled emission in one country may be seen as a form of indirect subsidy to industrialists there, in the form of an exploited natural resource, unavailable in countries where emission is controlled. But the economic link is less obvious in the case of measures for the preservation of wildlife and their habitats.

These latter policies are pursued as "contributing to harmonious economic development," and in fulfilment of two primary objectives:

> "(1) to ensure sound management of natural resources—which are economic assets of increasing importance and common to all mankind now and in the future—and
> (ii) to bring qualitative aspects into the planning and organisation of economic and social development."[95]

But there has had to be some reliance upon the supplementary powers conferred by Article 235 of the Treaty, which allows the Council, acting unanimously on a Commission proposal and after consulting the Assembly, to take "appropriate measures" on such issues as they think fit. The broad scope of the environmental brief is thus based on a wide view of the Community's interest in the impact of environmental issues on existing policies in such areas as commerce, agriculture and fisheries.

The Community's environmental programme dates from 1972, when a meeting of Heads of State resolved that the Community should be empowered to undertake an environmental role, and in 1973 the Council of Ministers adopted an environmental action programme[96] which has subse-

---

[95] *Progress made in connection with the Environmental Action Programme and Assessment of the work done to implement it.* Com. 80.222 (1980), p.1.
[96] *Declaration of the Council on the Programme of Action of the European Communities on the Environment* O.J. 1973, C.112.1 (December 20, 1973).

quently been updated from time to time. It is concerned primarily with the protection of the natural environment, and with securing controls over water and atmospheric pollution. But it has also the stated objective of ensuring "that more account is taken of environmental aspects in town planning and land use."[97] The Commission's Draft Directive on environmental impact analysis has been their first major challenge to established planning procedures, and it has had a mixed reception in Britain.[98] It will, if adopted, require that any approval of major development projects by either private or public sector agencies should be preceded by a detailed analysis of the likely environmental impact.

A more specifically urban bias is discernible in the study undertaken by the Community since 1978 into the problems of urban growth. It is a programme largely of research and information exchange, but it has extremely broad objectives, including a proposal

" . . . to study the effects of economic integration and of Community policy on the cities and to take action under its existing powers and resources to reduce negative effects and to multiply positive effects."[99]

It lays the basis for future European intervention in urban development by way both of monetary aid and regulation.

To date the impact of measures actually adopted by the Community has been felt in Britain in three main areas:

(1) A number of directives have been issued under the environmental programme. They are listed in Table 3. Directives, unlike Community Regulations, have no direct effect in Member States. They are prepared initially in draft form by the Commission for discussion and comment, then forwarded in final form to the Council of Ministers for adoption. Once adopted, the general rule is that they need to be implemented in Member States through new legislation, though existing legislation may suffice if its powers are broad enough. There has been considerable variation between States in implementing environmental directives. Only three had complied with the obligation in respect of the eight directives that were required to be embodied in national law by 1980, and two Member States had still to undertake any implementation at that date. British enthusiasm for the environmental programme has been tempered by the belief that environmental measures already in force in this country go beyond Community requirements in some respects, and also by a difference in philosophy. British planning and pollution controls are based to a large extent upon discretion and flexible standards, and the Community's quest for uniformity is seen as unnecessary and wasteful. Rigid formulae in practice need to be qualified by detailed exemptions and to make provision for discretionary variation, so uniformity can easily become illusory.

---

[97] *Progress made in connection with the Environmental Action Programme and Assessment of the work done to implement it:* Com. 80.222 (1980), p.29.
[98] *Post*, p.433.
[99] *Ibid.* para. IV. 5 And see also the D.O.E. report, *Urban Renaissance* (HMSO 1980) prepared under this programme.

Table 4

European Community Directives under the Environmental Action Programme

75/440EEC	Directive concerning the quality required of surface water intended for the abstraction of drinking water in the Member States. In force from June 18, 1977 [O.J. L. 194, July 25, 1975].
75/442/EEC	Directive on waste. [O.J. L. 194 26].
76/160/EEC	Directive concerning the quality of bathing water. In force from December 10, 1977 [O.J. L. 31, February 2, 1976].
76/464/EEC	Directive on pollution caused by certain dangerous substances discharged into the aquatic environment of the Community. In force from May 4, 1978 [O.J. L. 129, May 18, 1976].
78/176/EEC	Directive on waste from the titanium dioxide industry. In force from February 20, 1979 [O.J. L. 54].
78/319/EEC	Directive on toxic and dangerous waste. In force from March 22, 1980 [O.J. L. 84, March 31, 1978].
78/659/EEC	Directive on the quality of fresh waters needing protection or improvement in order to support fish life. In force from July 20, 1980 [O.J. L. 222, August 14, 1978].
79/869/EEC	Directive concerning the methods of measurement and frequencies of sampling and analysis of surface water intended for the abstraction of drinking water in the Member States. In force from October 9, 1981 [O.J. L. 281, October 29, 1979].
79/923/EEC	Directive on the quality required of shellfish waters. In force from October 30, 1981 [O.J. L. 281, November 11, 1979].
80/68/EEC	Directive on the protection of ground water against pollution caused by certain dangerous substances. In force from December 19, 1981 [O.J. L. 20, Janaury 1, 1980].

(2) Under the Information Agreement signed in 1973 Member States undertook to send to the Commission all their draft national environmental legislation before adoption. The Commission lacks any power to overrule the proposals, but it may ask that adoption be postponed and instead propose comparable Community-wide measures for adoption by the Council of Ministers.

(3) The European Regional Development Fund, which was established in

1975 under the reserve powers of Article 235,[1] has made substantial contributions to large scale infrastructure projects in Britain, intended to promote new development in economically depressed area. Over £566m. was committed in aid up to 1980.[2] The impact of the contributions is diminished by the Government's insistence that the aid should count against existing loan sanction and expenditure allocations of the recipient authorities,[3] so that it does not therefore extend the capital resources of an authority. Its effect, however, is to lessen the overall debt liability on new infrastructure development, and that in itself helps underwrite new infrastructure projects in the regions.

F. The Role of the Major Public Sector Agencies

1. The Public Sector in Development

Britain's mixed economy rests to a large extent on the activities of a variety of agencies established to provide public services and facilities. Their activities have an impact upon physical planning policy not only because of the scale of resources they command and the type of development they undertake, but also of the purpose of the development. There are, for example, the major infrastructure agencies, including the water authorities and harbour boards; the transport agencies such as the nationalised railways, bus operators, airports and road transport agencies, and the energy supply industry including the National Coal Board and the gas and electricity supply authorities. There is an interaction at two levels with the planning system. The agencies are responsible for the provision of the services which are necessary to sustain many planning policies, particularly urban growth strategies and policies for the regeneration of inner city areas or economically depressed areas.

There is an obvious need, therefore, for co-ordination of objectives and for joint long term planning. At another level there is the problem of exerting effective planning control over large scale public sector development, which by virtue of its size, environmental impact and location tends to raise problems seldom encountered with private sector development. The search for a site for London's third airport, the Windscale Inquiry and the Vale of Belvoir are recent examples. In some cases, such as the Vale of Belvoir, the location is fixed and predetermined, and the balance to be struck is one between the demands of a coal based energy programme and environmental preservation; whilst in others, such as the third London airport, the location is the main issue. The planning process has developed into the main decision-making forum because it offers the means for broader questions of energy or transportation policy to be assessed against longer term conservation objectives.

Decisions on major projects like these represent the tip of an iceberg in public sector development, where there has evolved an elaborate network of relationships between government departments, local authorities and the

---

[1] Council Regulation 724/75.
[2] Hansard, H.C. Deb. Vol. 1000, col. 396 (March 12, 1981).
[3] See now D.O.E. Circular 14/81, para. 13.

public agencies involved. The agencies are consulted directly by local planning authorities as part of the forward planning process, and, although there is frequently subsequent agreement between them on broad priorities, the agencies may appear at a public local inquiry or at the examination in public of a structure plan to pursue an objection. They are also able to influence central government policy directly through the ministries and departments to which they are accountable.

In development control there are also requirements upon local planning authorities to consult certain agencies affected by proposed development, but in practice consultation is often far more broadly spread and may be on a continuing basis between the authority and an agency closely affected by development, such as the regional water authority. Control over the public sector's own development depends upon the constitutional status of the agency involved. There is a rich variety. Some bodies in the public sector are under the direct control of the Crown and have no independent status; others are independent corporations subject to "arms' length" ministerial supervision, whilst others include local authorities themselves and hybrid agencies such as British Nuclear Fuels Ltd., which is a wholly owned subsidiary of the UK Atomic Energy Authority.

For the purposes of planning control, distinctions are drawn between the development proposals of (1) the Crown and government departments; (2) statutory undertakers; (3) local planning authorities and (4) other bodies. The detailed procedures are examined in Chapter 5, but the essence of the distinctions is that all development in the first category is exempt from planning control, though governed by informal procedures involving consultation with planning authorities. Some development by statutory undertakers, and, to a lesser extent by other agencies, is also exempt from control by reasons of the broad deemed permissions granted under the General Development Order. Local planning authorities obtain deemed permission under their own auspices by passing two resolutions, but otherwise observing procedures comparable to those for ordinary applications, and they have otherwise no special status except when acting as a statutory undertaker.

An important qualification, however, is that in practice the lines of demarcation are not as clear cut as the above summary suggests. To a large extent the rules relating to Crown development and local planning authority proposals are based simply on constitutional expedience, and the procedures followed make allowance for publicity and the consideration of representations from the public and other agencies in a manner roughly similar to that for private sector development.

Two groups within the public sector have a special relationship with planning authorities, and their functions call for further comment. These are the statutory undertakers and the water authorities.

2. The Statutory Undertakers

The funereal title enjoyed by agencies falling within this category derives from the fact that they each have specific statutory backing for the undertaking they carry on. It is a functional classification. "Statutory undertakers" are those with statutory authority to carry on:

" . . . any railway, light railway, tramway, road transport, water transport, canal, inland navigation, dock, harbour, pier or lighthouse undertaking, or any undertaking for the supply of electricity, gas, hydraulic power or water."[4]

That is the definition for the purposes of planning legislation, and it is extended on an ad hoc basis by other legislation to include the British Airports Authority in respect of aerodromes owned by them,[5] and also, for certain purposes, the Post Office[6] and Civil Aviation Authority.[7] It is, however, a flexible classification, and some agencies are statutory undertakers for the purposes of some legislation but not for other. The Local Government, Planning and Land Act 1980, for example, defines different categories for different purposes of the legislation, and it excludes from the requirements of Part X (which require registers to be drawn up of un-used or under-used publicly owned land) those agencies whose undertaking is merely ancillary to the main purpose of their business.[8]

The bodies included in the general category are for the most part publicly owned, but the regular transference of undertakings between the public and private sectors (under schemes of nationalisation and privatisation) has left a few anomalies. The Felixstowe Dock and Railway Company and the Mersey Dock and Harbour Board, for example, both enjoy statutory undertaker status though privately owned. Statutory authority is not, of course, confined to the public sector, and it is only as a result of the assumption by the state of direct responsibility for most public service undertakings since the second World War that the majority of statutory undertakings are now publicly owned. Many important public corporations do not enjoy statutory undertaker status at all, though falling wholly within the public sector, such as the Housing Corporation, British Shipbuilders and the National Coal Board.

The statutory undertakers' privileges under planning legislation do not extend to all their development, nor to all their land. Permission is deemed to be granted only for certain types of development carried out on "operational land," which is defined by the 1971 Act as being:

"(a) land which is used for the purposes of carrying on their undertaking; and
(b) land in which an interest is held for that purpose, not being land which, in respect of its nature and situation, is comparable rather with land in general than with land which is used, or in which interests are held, for the purpose of the carrying on of statutory undertakings."[9]

The called-for comparison between "land in general" an land "for the purposes of carrying on statutory undertakings" is one of the most

---

[4] T.C.P.A. 1971, s. 290(1).
[5] Airports Authority Act 1975, s. 19; although the status does not extend to airports to which the Authority have not yet gained title: *British Airports Authority* v. *Secretary of State for Scotland* [1980] J.P.L. 260.
[6] Post Office Act 1969, s.76.
[7] Civil Aviation Act 1982, s.19(2) and Sched. 2.
[8] L.G.P.L.A. 1980, s. 93 and Sched. 16.
[9] T.C.P.A. 1971, s. 222.

awkwardly constructed formulae in modern legislation, but it suggests that a distinction be drawn between "works" premises and other separate premises such as offices and showrooms located in a town centre.[10] The latter will not be covered by the special immunity conferred by the legislation, and the deemed permissions of the General Development Order take the general distinctions further by referring only to specific types of "works" related operations.

There may be special standing under other provisions, however. Local planning authorities and new town and urban development corporations, for example, all have some limited statutory undertaker status, as well as special status for their development in their areas by reason of being planning authority for certain purposes.

3. The Water Authorities

The 10 regional water authorities came into being in 1974,[11] and their birth was timed to coincide with local government reform. The functions they took over had previously been distributed between no fewer than 1600 different agencies, including local authorities, joint water boards, water companies, joint sewerage boards and river and drainage boards. There had been a great variety between them in terms of objectives, costs and performance and comparatively little co-ordination; and rationalisation had been mooted for many years.

The new authorities were established on a regional basis in order to co-ordinate the interlocking functions, but their boundaries were based not on existing political boundaries but on natural watersheds. Within their areas, their functions include primary responsibility for all water matters, including supply (although the statutory water companies retained their local water supply functions where they existed before 1974), sewerage and sewage treatment, land drainage, control of river pollution and water quality, fisheries, water conservation and water recreation. Responsibility for formulating a national policy for water in England and Wales rests jointly with the Secretary of State and the Minister of Agriculture, Fisheries and Food. Overseeing the execution of the policy by the authorities is a matter for the Secretary of State, except for land drainage and fisheries which are matters for the Minister.[12] The National Water Council has an advisory role. Either minister may issue directions "of a general character"[13] to the authorities as to the exercise of their functions, and the relationship thereby established between them and central government is thus akin to the "arms' length" relationship of the nationalised industries. But the financing of water authority functions, which directly affects their role in servicing new development and in maintaining and improving services, is now closely controlled by central government.

There are four main elements to the financial structure. First, authorities

---

[10] See further, R. v. Minister of Fuel and Power, ex. p. Warwickshire C.C. [1957] 1 W.L.R. 861.
[11] Under the Water Act 1973.
[12] Ibid. s. 1.
[13] Ibid. s. 5(1) and (2).

are under a statutory duty to at least cover their outgoings on revenue expenditure account, taking one year with another.[14] At the same time, they have been required, by April 1, 1981, to implement a non-discriminatory charging system for their services so as not to "show undue preference to, or discriminate unfairly against, any class of person."[15] Secondly, capital expenditure for each year is subject to an overall ceiling set by central government on the basis of five year rolling programmes submitted by the authorities. Thirdly, there has also been established an external financing limit which restricts the amount of net additional borrowing and total leasing by an authority in any financial year. Finally, since 1981 authorities have been expected to achieve a financial perfomance measured in terms of a percentage rate of return on net assets valued under current cost accounting procedures.[16] The purpose of that requirement is to ensure that there is a limit to the extent that additional costs may be passed on to consumers through increased charges,[17] and it does not apply to land drainage functions where costs are subject to contributions from benefited landowners by way of rates precept.

The consequence of close financial control has been that capital investment has been reduced substantially in recent years. Not only has that meant that water quality improvement programmes have been set back and that there has been a lengthy delay in bringing into force the new control provisions under Part II of the Control of Pollution Act 1974, but also the capacity of the authorities to meet the demands of urban growth has been severely limited. There are two alternatives available where funds are inadequate to meet demand, other than merely deferring the works. The first is to cast a greater proportion of the burden on to private developers. In certain circumstances developers can already be required to contribute to costs of connecting the development to existing sewerage and water supply, but the code is arbitrary in its distribution of costs between different developers and limited in its effects.[18] The second alternative is to place an unofficial embargo on new development by seeking to persuade planning authorities to resist proposals in areas where existing capacity is inadequate.

Local administration of water functions is primarily a matter for the water authorities, but there is in practice a diffusion of responsibility. The authorities may, for example, enter into "arrangements" with local authorities for the latter to discharge sewerage functions in their own areas.[19] The arrangements amount to neither an agency nor to the full delegation of responsibility, but they allow the local authority to determine their own priorities through the preparation and submission of an annual programme. Financial responsibility rests with the water authority, however, and programmes are subject to their approval.

[14] *Ibid.* s. 29.
[15] *Ibid.* s. 30(5), as amended by the Water Charges Act 1976.
[16] This requirement is imposed under s. 29(2) of the Act which allows the Secretary of State to direct authorities to secure a minimum rate of return on the value of their assets or otherwise as he thinks fit.
[17] For a detailed study of the operational context of the water authorities from the point of view of cost effectiveness, see the *Report of the Monopolies and Mergers Commission on the Severn-Trent Water Authority* (HMSO 1981) H.C. 339.
[18] Post, p.380.
[19] Water Act 1973, s.15.

In land drainage matters the allocation of responsibility reflects the agricultural bias of the function. Although the water authority exercise a general supervision, they are required to arrange for the discharge of all their functions (except for certain financial responsibilites) by their regional land drainage committees.[20] The authority have again a curious "arms' length" relationship with their own committee, retaining financial controls and a power to issue directions in respect of functions "likely to affect materially the authority's management of water for purposes other than land drainage."[21]

---

[20] Land Drainage Act 1976, s.1(1).
[21] *Ibid.* s. 1(2).

CHAPTER 3

DEVELOPMENT PLANS

A. Introduction

The development plan is the central policy document in the British planning system. Development planning is the machinery through which decisions are made and recorded as to the policies and proposals to be pursued for the future. The plan thereafter acts as a guide for, and a constraint upon, authorities in exercising their powers of control over new development, and co-ordinates future investment and development activity in both the public and the private sector.

In the early years of post-war planning the development plan was intended to be a comparatively detailed and precise document, indicating the manner in which the local planning authority proposed that land in their area should be used. Following central government scrutiny- and approval, the planning authority would be tied closely to its policies. The "old style" plans were physical plans, based upon fairly precise site allocation and designations.

But the system proved too rigid, and substantial reforms came in 1968, with the introduction of a two-tier system. The purpose of the reforms was to encourage greater flexibility by separating issues of strategic policy (such as the most practicable means of accommodating substantial new urban growth) from matters of local detail. Decisions relating to the former are now to be recorded in *structure plans*, whilst the detailed policies are set out in *local plans*. Following local government reorganisation in 1974, responsibility for the preparation of structure plans outside London lies with county planning authorities, whilst responsibility for local planning rests primarily with the district planning authority. A comparable division of responsibility exists within the Greater London area, between the G.L.C. and the London boroughs. Central government interest is primarily in the structure plans. Local plans do not normally require central government approval.

Changeover to the new system has been proceeding gradually since 1968, but progress has been slow. Although a majority of the country's structure plans have now been prepared and approved,[1] comparatively few local plans have yet appeared, largely because until recently their formal preparation had to await approval of the structure plan and delays at that level held back the whole programme. Local plans may take any one of three different forms. The commonest in practice will be a *district plan*, resembling in many ways the old style development plan and prepared for specific districts. But there is also provision for *action area plans*, prepared for areas (which until recently had first to be identified in the structure plan) intended for substantial change within a 10–year period; and *subject plans*, dealing with planning issues not tied to specific sites, such as recreation or mineral extraction.

The old style development plan remains in force pending approval of the

[1] A table of approved plans is contained in Appendix A.

75

new plans, and is thus successively supplanted by the two elements of the new development plan: first by the structure plan whose provisions, once approved, thereafter prevail; then by the district and other local plans as their provisions supersede those of the old plan. Once there is both a structure plan and a local plan for any area, the provisions of the old style plan will normally be superseded altogether.

The development plan is a statutory document. Its preparation is required and governed by legislation, and its provisions remain in force, however outdated, until formally altered or superseded. But in practice its provisions are supplemented by a range of non-statutory plans and policies, prepared by individual planning authorities. Non-statutory devices are almost always the result of the inability of the statutory planning mechanism to adapt as readily to change as authorities would wish, and whilst the status of the policies and the authority's commitment to them are both often uncertain, there exist some common examples whose influence in practice is greater than that of the approved development plan itself. Examples include interim green belt policies, town centre plans, village envelope policies and, importantly, draft statutory plans still in the course of preparation. All are of significance in development control.

This range of plans is further supplemented by non-physical plans prepared from time to time by authorities. Corporate plans, and transportation policy programmes and other budgetary programmes may have few specific land use implications, but nonetheless bear directly upon the content and pace of implementation of the physical plans.

Finally, there are some other relevant plans, not statutory in the sense of requiring observance of statutorily prescribed procedures in their preparation and approval, but prepared nonetheless under the umbrella of other land use related legislation, such as the master plans for new town development and management plans for national parks.

Plan preparation, and the status of prepared plans, are thus in practice considerably more complex matters than a cursory glance at Part II of the Town and Country Planning Act 1971 might suggest; and before turning to examine its provisions it is useful to have some understanding of the rationale and evolution of plan making.

1. The rationale of forward planning[2]

Planning is a process of rational decision making. Its central assumption is that the consequences of planned action are likely to prove more beneficial than those of unplanned action. Plan based action ought over a longer term to increase efficiency in the use of resources and lead to a more consistent and co-ordinated pattern of behaviour than short term decision making. But plan making alone can never be enough. Success in achieving the plan's goals is largely dependent upon the strength of influence of the plan over the

---

[2] There exist a number of books dealing with planning theory, though comparatively few touch upon the particular problems of pursuing a theoretical ideal within a statutory framework and through political agencies. The following are useful further reading: A. Faludi (ed.), *A Reader in Planning Theory* (Pergamon, 1973), A. Faludi, *Planning Theory* (Hutchinson, 1974) and M.J. Bruton, *The Spirit and Purpose of Planning* (Hutchinson, 1975).

course of events; that is, upon power to achieve and control change in accordance with the plan's objectives.

In the case of land use planning the power is limited. In formal terms it is limited to the control over new development exerted through decisions made on planning applications, and to the ordering of public sector investment in positive planning, including the construction of major infrastructure works. But the development plan is capable of having an influence which goes beyond this, moulding private sector investment and expectations and influencing decisions relating to social provision and even economic growth.

The plan then may influence, but it cannot control events. Its provisions are necessarily based upon assumptions and predictions. The rate of future population growth, the extent of future private car ownership, possible employment patterns and prospects and changes in other interrelated factors may be guessed at with greater or lesser degrees of certainty and rationality, and policies devised. Things may change swiftly and unpredictably, as a consequence of international decisions or technological development for example. For the plan to enjoy the long term stability envisaged by the legislation it needs adequate flexibility. Various techniques have been employed to secure flexibility within an overall strategy. A plan's policies may be cast in open-ended terms, so as to indicate how population growth to predicted levels might be accommodated, but not tied to any specific target date. Or the plan may provide for alternative policies in anticipation of different types of change that might occur during the plan period. Policies are often expressed in broad terms, reserving an interpretative power for when a more precise ruling may be needed. But failing internal flexibility, the only response to material change in external events over which the planner has no control, is to change the plan. To continue to implement it solely for the sake of plan adherence is usually to depart altogether from the original objectives.

British forward planning theory is still generally based on the so-called "rational comprehensive" model, and although various alternative decision models have been debated in the technical press, reliance on the rational comprehensive model is virtually dictated by the legislative and institutional context of forward planning. It typically involves six main stages:

(1) a survey of the existing conditions
(2) the determination of a set of goals for change
(3) the selection of alternative possible courses of action to achieve the goals
(4) an evaluation of those alternatives and selection of the preferred alternative
(5) implementation of the selected alternative
(6) monitoring the implementation and revising the plan if necessary.

It can be seen that an essential element of the model is the adaptive process based upon monitoring, and that it envisages a continuous process. But in translating the model into the format of statutory planning much of its logic has been lost. The formalities and delay surrounding plan preparation, and the complexity of processes of urban change have long precluded effective monitoring and speedy revision. Successful implementation may be precluded by factors which subsequent revision may do little to alleviate, such as political opposition to growth plans exerted by adjoining authorities.

The statutory procedures have themselves proved a source of inflexibility even following the 1968 reforms, particularly in structure planning where a range of provisions safeguard central government's interests; and there is a serious view that the time has come to abandon the statutory system in favour of an arrangement which would leave it to the local planning authorities to adopt and apply such plans, as and when, and following such procedures, as they themselves may determine. Such a change could of course lead to a development control system based upon largely ad hoc (and potentially arbitrary) response to development initiative, and there is a fear that "flexibility" is already too often used as a shorthand for political expediency. But a shift away from statutory planning could equally encourage more effective monitoring and revision of adopted plans, with beneficial results. In only one other area of public administration is policy making so closely regulated by legislation, and that is under the Education Act 1944. But the reality is that the old education development plans were abandoned by the 1960s because of their inflexibility in the face of rapid population change, and have not since been revived.[3]

The achievement of a suitable balance between certainty and flexibility in planning has been a central goal ever since the 1947 Act, but planning is so volatile a process, both politically and in terms of response to unanticipated change, that no ideal solution is likely ever to emerge. The political dimension is significant, not just because planning is concerned with achieving a measure of state control over private land use decisions, but also because the plans have themselves become critically important in determining the boundaries of planning power between public sector authorities, particularly as between central government and local government and between the two tiers of local government. The function of plans is not therefore simply that of providing a present rule system for dictating future decisions, but rather as a means of moulding and guiding future decisions and the public agencies responsible for them and constraining them, co-ordinating them, towards the plan's objectives.

2. The historical background to development planning

The requirement under the 1947 Act that planning authorities should prepare comprehensive development plans, which they then might apply with some flexibility in development control, represented a radical departure from the earlier planning system. Under pre-war legislation the primary planning tool was the planning scheme, which was simply an extension into the public arena of the model of the private building scheme. The private scheme was, and remains today, a system of restrictive covenants imposed upon purchasers of sites upon the subdivision of land for development.

[3] The Education Minister had power to make orders to impose upon local education authorities duties to secure that effect would be given to the education plan, but none were ever made: see further, Hansard, H.C. Deb., Vol. 604, col. 103 (April 29, 1959); and Wood v. Ealing L.B.C. [1967] Ch. 364.

Provided certain legal preconditions are met,[4] the covenants are thereafter enforceable not only in contract between vendor and purchaser, but also between different purchasers of the various sites on a new estate, and similarly, between their successors in title in perpetuity. The building schemes normally allow for detailed aesthetic control over the development and its future use, restraining non-residential use on a housing estate, for example, and forbidding new building or alterations without prior consent. As such, they have proved a valuable source of private planning law.[5]

The statutory planning scheme under the Acts of 1909, 1919 and 1932 built upon that idea, except that the statutory schemes were to be prepared and enforced by the local authority. The schemes had direct legal effect, and the *Model Clauses* eventually issued by the Ministry of Health under the 1932 Act provided for control over a range of matters, including land reservation in new development, land zoning on a basis which allowed certain types of building to proceed in different zones with or without the authority's consent or to be prohibited altogether, and provision for open spaces, water supply and so on.[6]

But the schemes did not succeed. Five major defects emerged in practice, and they were defects which the 1947 legislation was designed specifically to overcome. They call for further comment, because they pose legal and institutional problems which in some respects continue to dog land use planning still.

(a) Preparation of schemes was voluntary, and progress slow

Although the powers were introduced in 1909, by 1919 only three schemes had been prepared in the whole of England and Wales. An initial disincentive had been the limited applicability of scheme-based planning: under the 1909 Act a scheme could only be made for "any land which is in course of development or appears likely to be used for building purposes" or for necessary neighbouring lands.[7] But in 1932 the scope was extended and authorities were authorised to include existing built-up areas where public improvement or other development was expected, and undeveloped land comprising objects or places of natural interest or beauty.[8] And the 1919 Act had made it obligatory for urban authorities with a population of 20,000 or more to complete planning schemes by the beginning of 1926; a period later extended to 1929.[9] But even by then comparatively few schemes had become operative. By 1933 approved planning schemes covered less than one quarter of a million acres.[10] There was a clear imbalance between legislative ambition and practical achievement.

---

[4] That is, that the two parties involved have each derived title from or under a common vendor who had first laid out the whole site in lots and sold them subject to restrictions intended to be for the benefit of all: for a detailed account see Preston and Newson, *Restrictive Covenants* (Sweet & Maxwell, 7th ed., 1982), Chap.2.

[5] A theme which is further examined by McAuslan, *Land Law and Planning* (1975), Chap. 4.

[6] *Town and Country Planning. Model Clauses for Use in the Preparation of Schemes* (1935).

[7] Housing, Town Planning, etc., Act 1909, s.54.

[8] T.C.P.A. 1932, s.1.

[9] Housing and Town Planning Act 1919, s.46.

[10] There is a detailed study of pre-war planning contained in the *Report of the Committee on Qualifications of Planners* Cmd. 8059 (1950) (*The Schuster Report*), Chap. 1.

(b) Schemes were local, unrelated and not scientifically prepared

In short, schemes were systems for continuing control, rather than plans for the future. They were seldom based upon any comprehensive analysis of present needs or probable future requirements. They concentrated upon controlling the physical aspects of new development, not upon promoting the wider needs of the towns or their residents, let alone any regional or national objectives. And they were negative and restrictive; not positive nor innovative.

(c) The contents of schemes were heavily influenced by liability to pay compensation

In many instances the planning authority could find themselves liable to compensate a landowner whose property was adversely affected by a scheme's restrictions. The consequence was that the schemes were necessarily cautious. The early philosophy was that planning would be a consensual rather than an imposed process, designed " . . . to secure agreement, by conference, by co-ordinating the varying and conflicting interests, and, in the case of an objectionable owner, to buy him out or to exchange his land for some other piece or to make arrangements which will be suitable to everybody."[11] Where no agreement was forthcoming, authorities were deterred from restricting development for fear of the expense and the planning scheme became quite inadequate as an instrument for containing urban growth. If anything, the reluctance of authorities to impose the available restraints acted as a spur to developers, and the rate of land taken for urban development reached a peak in the 1930s that has never been exceeded before or since.[12] Yet by 1937, with still less than one half the country covered by draft or operative schemes, there was already sufficient land allocated for housing to accommodate the astonishing figure of 350 million people.[13]

(d) The procedure for central approval of schemes was slow and cumbersome

As the Schuster Report explained:

"The Act of 1909 placed no obligation on local authorities to make schemes and the consent of the Local Government Board was necessary before one could be started. A scheme then required the approval of the Board, and if there were then objections it had to be laid before Parliament before it became effective. These requirements were dropped in 1919, but reimposed in 1932 with the difference that all the

---

[11] Mr. John Burns M.P., Chairman of the Local Government Board speaking in the course of the second reading debate on the 1909 Act: H.C. Deb., Vol. 188 col. 964–5 (May 12, 1908).
[12] See further *post*, p.306.
[13] H.C.Deb., Vol. 432, col. 978, *per* Mr. Lewis Silkin M.P. introducing the second reading debate on the 1947 Act (January 29, 1947). The primary reason for the great over-allocation was the ploy, widely adopted, of allocating land for development at very low densities (for which no compensation was payable) rather than prohibiting development outright which carried compensation liability: see further *ante*, p.21.

schemes, whether or not there were objections, had to be laid before Parliament."[14]

Direct Parliamentary supervision necessarily meant that approval was slow, even where the planning authority had simply adapted the Ministry's own Model Clauses to its own area. It also meant that once approved, the scheme could be amended only with great difficulty. Its terms could be rigid and perpetual.

(e) There was only limited central government supervision

The role of the Ministry under the 1932 Act was not a positive role. It had quasi-judicial powers designed to secure fair play to landowners, but no effective powers of initiative nor of financial assistance to authorities.[15] These defects were partly overcome under wartime legislation. The Minister of Town and Country Planning Act 1943, the Town and Country Planning (Interim Development) Act 1943 and the Town and Country Planning Act 1944 led to a strengthening of central government's influence and extended authorities' own powers of control, but at the expense of formal forward planning. The planning schemes were pushed into the background in favour of the more flexible discretionary system of interim development control which was to become the model for post-war development control.

3. Development plans after the 1947 Act

The form of the new development plans was intended to overcome all the shortfalls of the old schemes. The new plan would be mandatory, comprehensive and flexible. It would have no direct legal effect and no directly compensatable financial implications so far as the planning authority were concerned.[16] And it would be preceded by and based upon a detailed survey of the area. The report of the survey was to be submitted to the Minister with the plan, and a fresh survey undertaken at least once every five years following approval of the plan.[17] These arrangements bore the air of impressive efficiency and the hallmarks of a scientific approach to planning. Authorities had a new role, and strong ministerial backing. Yet over the ensuing 20 years the procedures and the plans themselves came in for increasing criticism, suggesting that the ills of the 1932 system had by no means been overcome.

First, the form of the new development plans was closely prescribed by the Act and by regulations.[18] They were to have a map base, on a scale of six inches to the mile for town maps (prepared by county boroughs and London), and of one inch to the mile for counties, where additional town maps could also be prepared for urban areas.[19] The system was one of fairly

---

[14] Cmd. 8059, para. 20
[15] For a detailed critique of these problems, see the *Final Report of the Expert Committee on Compensation and Betterment*, Cmd. 6386, paras. 12–15 (1942).
[16] Compensation claims in respect of planning restriction could instead be lodged against a centrally administered fund of £300m.
[17] T.C.P.A. 1947, s.6(1).
[18] Town and Country Planning (Development Plan) Regulations 1948 (S.I. 1948 No. 1767).
[19] *Ibid.* reg.6.

precise site designation and allocation, particularly within urban areas. A town map would show the boundaries of areas of comprehensive development (the details of which would then be set out in detail on a map on an even greater scale of $\frac{1}{2500}$),[20] together with the areas for industrial use; the principal business, civic, cultural or other special uses for the town as a whole; residential areas including the proposed densities, and the location of shopping centres.[21] Additionally, the map was required to show the location of principal roads, parking places, railway and water transport facilities, and schools and other educational institutions and their playing fields.[22] Then there were the specially protected areas such as green belts, areas of great landscape value or of scientific or historic value, and areas to be held for central and local government purposes.[23] The maps were accompanied by a written statement, summarising the plan's proposals and explaining the details, such as those of the use zone allocations and the plan's programming.[24] This tendency to great detail and precision was to lead to increasing criticism, not only that the "broad brush" intention of the legislation had been lost, but that the certainty which precise designations and allocations offered was too often spurious, and particularly so given the slow response of the planning system to the rapid rate of change in the real world.

Secondly, preparation of the new development plans ran into difficulty from the outset. The planning authorities varied greatly in size, and many lacked the resources and the expertise to undertake the new task. At one extreme, London County Council were able to engage some 200 planning staff, whilst, at the other Canterbury County Borough had "approximately 2½."[25] Few staff were specifically trained in planning. The great majority of the new senior planners came to the task having first qualified in engineering (especially in the urban authorities), architecture or surveying,[26] and the plans not unnaturally reflected their professional preoccupation with techniques of measurement and design rather than the social and economic requirements of the area. And many of the strategic decisions that the new planning structure called for were fraught with political conflict. The key to a densely populated county borough's plans would often necessarily be a policy of expansion or overspill into the territory of another, not always welcoming, authority. Patient negotiation and compromise at political level were needed before a viable plan could emerge, and disputes inevitably carried over into the formal approval stages casting the Minister in the role of political arbitrator. An additional handicap in attempting any basic "scientific" analysis was the absence of any reliable data. No population census had been taken since 1931, and the War had substantially changed the balance of population in a way which caught all levels of government unawares.

[20] *Ibid.* reg.7.
[21] *Ibid.* Sched. 1, Part I.
[22] *Ibid.*
[23] *Ibid.* Sched. 1, Part III.
[24] *Ibid.* regs. 12 and 13.
[25] *Schuster Report*, Cmd. 8059, para. 87.
[26] *Ibid*, paras. 83–86.

The Act had required that all plans should be submitted for ministerial approval within three years of the coming into force of the 1947 Act; that is, by July 1951.[27] But the time limit proved hopelessly ambitious, and had to be extended in the great majority of cases. Only 22 out of 148 planning authorities managed to meet the deadline, and although the bulk of the remaining plans were submitted over the following two years it was not until 1957 that the final two plans were submitted for England and Wales.[28] At the end of the same year the Department of Health for Scotland reported that some 15 out of the 57 local planning authorities there (mainly the highland and border counties) had still to submit any plans.[29] Indeed, one of them, Sutherland County Council, sturdily succeeded in never actually submitting a development plan; whilst two others, Banff and Argyll, rushed to submit their first old style plans a matter of months before the 1968 Act abandoned the old machinery in favour of structure plans and local plans.

Pending the preparation and approval of a statutory plan, authorities were still able to exercise control over undesirable development. The Act required, for that interim period, that instead of having regard to the provisions of the plan, they should have regard instead to the policies "likely" to be included in such a plan.[30] Once a plan was approved, they were fairly closely tied to its provisions. There was therefore, paradoxically, a greater degree of discretion in development control for authorities who had no formal plan, (and this was doubtless a factor inhibiting enthusiasm for speedy plan preparation in some cases); though the absence of such a plan necessarily made interventionist planning difficult, and left policies more vulnerable to reversal by the Secretary of State in individual planning appeals.

Delays in plan preparation by the local authorities were, however, to prove a minor problem compared with the substantial delays that occurred in obtaining central government approval. The task simply proved too great for the resources available within the Ministry of Housing and Local Government. Table 5 demonstrates the extent of the time lag in the handling of the first round of plans by the Ministry.

Some of the delay was caused by the hearing of objections at public local inquiries. Of the first 55 plans approved, only nine went through without an inquiry. The Middlesex County plan attracted no fewer than 7,000 objectors, and the inquiry into the London plan took 153 days and employed four inspectors.[31]

The approval machinery became even more clogged by the late 1950s as local authorities, in compliance with their duty under section 6 of the 1947 Act, carried out fresh surveys and submitted review plans for approval. They were urged by the Ministry to be cautious,[32] and not to seek to extend the validity period of the original plan. The review was to be an exercise in gap filling, rather of radical revision. Further, many authorities were anxious to

[27] T.C.P.A. 1947, s.5.
[28] *M.H.L.G. Annual Report 1950–1954* (Cmd. 9559), p. 61.
[29] *Annual Report of the Department of Health for Scotland, 1958,* Cmnd. 385, pp.92–93.
[30] T.C.P.A. 1947, s.36.
[31] *M.H.L.G. Annual Report 1950–1954,* Cmd. 9559, p.61.
[32] *M.H.L.G. Annual Report 1955,* Cmd. 9876, p.42.

Table 5

Progress in Plan Preparation and Approval 1947–60

Year	Plans submitted	Plans approved
1948	1	0
1949	0	0
1950	4	0
1951	55	3
1952	63	10
1953	22	20
1954	3	22
1955	2	25
1956	0	17
1957	2	13
1958	0	18
1959	0	13
1960	0	8

Source: MHLG Annual Reports 1954–60.

secure amendments and additions to existing plans. In particular, the designation of comprehensive development areas became increasingly urgent as the basis for town centre redevelopment schemes, which were rapidly growing in popularity. By 1959, 243 plan alterations had been submitted to the English Ministry; and 1960 alone saw the submission of a further 213.[33]

The Ministry's reaction to this snowballing of development plans activity was one of disengagement. Authorities were discouraged from using the machinery of the Act, and steered instead towards the use of non-statutory policies, particularly for town centre and village plans, which would fill policy gaps on an interim basis, pending full review of the statutory plan. For some authorities, statutory planning effectively stopped in the 1950s and non-statutory machinery has been relied upon as required up to the time of preparation of the new structure plans and local plans over the past few years. The other reaction by the Ministry was to set up, somewhat belatedly, a committee known as the Planning Advisory Group, to suggest possible reforms to the development planning system.

4. *The Planning Advisory Group*

The Advisory Group approached their review of the system with four objectives, not all of them readily compatible. They sought

(1) "to ensure that the planning system serves its purpose satisfactorily both as an instrument of planning policy and as a means of public participation in the planning process;

(2) to improve the technical quality of development plans and to

---

[33] *M.H.L.G. Annual Report 1960,* Cmnd. 1435, Appendix XIV, Table A.

strengthen their policy content, so that they provide an adequate framework for future development and redevelopment, and a sound basis for development control;

(3) to get the level of responsibility right, so that only matters of general policy and major objectives are submitted for Ministerial approval, and matters of local land use are settled locally in the light of these considerations;

(4) to simplify planning administration."[34]

The objectives were thus weighted in favour of continuing with a system of detailed forward planning, but with shifting responsibility for supervision of the detail away from central government. To achieve this the Group proposed a split in plan preparation between "structure" plans, which would be "primarily statements of policy illustrated where necessary with sketch maps and diagrams and accompanied by a diagrammatic or 'structure' map designed to clarify the basic physical structure of the area and its transport system;"[35] and local plans "which will serve as a guide to development control and a basis for the more positive aspects of environmental planning."[36] Only the former would be submitted for Ministerial approval, and they would then provide the framework for detailed planning.

It was essentially a streamlining exercise, and the Group's recommendations were readily accepted by the Government with the comment that "since the number of plans requiring ministerial approval will be reduced and their content will be far less detailed, a substantial speeding up in the process of approval should be achieved."[37] The reforms were introduced in the Town and Country Planning Act 1968, and the provisions subsequently consolidated and re-enacted as Part II of the Act of 1971.

But one of the fundamental assumptions of the Advisory Group—that the plans would be the responsibility of unitary planning authorities—was thrown over by local government reform in 1974. The splitting of planning responsibility between the two new tiers of local government has inevitably placed new pressures on the forward planning process, particularly in the use of plans as instruments in the demarcation battle between county and district interests. The Act of 1980 has achieved some re-allocation of power in a way which may yet prove to undermine the role of structure planning, and the reforms are considered subsequently in this chapter.

B. Structure Plans

1. *The transition to structure planning*

The structure plan is now the central document in strategic land use decision making. The new system was introduced only gradually, on a county by

---

[34] P.A.G. Report, *The Future of Development Plans*, para. 1.1.
[35] *Ibid.* para. 1.36.
[36] *Ibid.* para. 1.41.
[37] *Town and Country Planning*, Cmnd. 3333, para. 4(1) (1967).

county basis, following the passage of the 1968 Act, because the Government were anxious not to impose the new function on ill-equipped authorities, especially at a time when a general reform of local government was under serious consideration.[38] Perhaps, too, it was deemed sensible to avoid having an avalanche of plans again submerging the Ministry. But since 1974 a duty to prepare and submit structure plans has been imposed upon all county authorities in England and Wales.[39] The great majority have now been examined and approved and the process of preparing and approving alterations to approved plans is now also well under way: Appendix A sets out the present position.

The procedures governing the preparation and approval of plans and alterations to plans, and their style and content, are prescribed partly by Part II of the Act and partly by the Town and Country Planning (Structure and Local Plans) Regulations 1982.[40] These are supplemented by a detailed and regularly updated D.O.E. Circular (currently No. 4/79) and a range of technical and advisory departmental publications. For the most part the procedures governing initial plan preparation extend equally to proposals for the making of subsequent alterations to the plan, and that is the context in which in the future they will be of most significance. It used to be the rule that approved plans could never be repealed, except where it was proposed to replace separate plans for two or more parts of an area with a new single plan. Complete repeal and replacement is now possible, following the Act of 1980, but it will be rare except in the case of consolidation of part-area plans because it suggests the abandonment of the whole strategy of the approved plan. For the most part, therefore, changes will be introduced by way of formal alterations.

There are some differences in London's forward planning history and present arrangements which require brief comment. The statutory old-style development plan for the Greater London area, known as "the initial development plan for Greater London" is the product of all the development plans, operative before London's local government reorganisation on March 31st 1965, and relating to any part of the new Greater London area.[41] The strategic decisions of those plans have now been supplanted by the Greater London Development Plan, whose preparation was required by the London Government Act 1963,[42] and which was finally approved in 1976.[43] Though prepared largely before the advent of structure plans, it is similar in

---

[38] See further, Cmnd. 3333, para. 21.

[39] By virtue of T.C.P.A. 1971, s.7(1) and the Town and Country Planning Act 1971 (Commencement No. 27)(Rest of England) Order 1974 (S.I. 1974 No. 1069), which brought into force Part II of the 1971 Act, except ss. 9(4) and 18–21, for the whole of England excepting those areas where commencement orders had already been made.

[40] S.I. 1982 No. 555 (hereafter "the Plans Regulations"). These regulations superseded the 1974 Regulations (S.I. 1974 No. 1486) from May 26, 1982.

[41] London Government Act 1963, s.25(2).

[42] *Ibid.* s.25(3).

[43] The approved version of the plan was published by the G.L.C. in 1976. For the background to approval, see further the *Report of the Panel of Inquiry into the G.L.D.P.* (2 vols., H.M.S.O., 1973) and the *Statement by the Rt.Hon. Geoffrey Rippon Q.C., M.P.* (H.M.S.O., 1973).

its concentration upon strategic issues, and is deemed by the Act to be the structure plan for Greater London.[44]

The remaining provisions of the initial development plan remain in force, but are gradually being replaced as local plans are adopted for individual parts of the area.[45]

2. Structure plans and their preparation

In brief, a structure plan is a written statement formulating the local planning authority's policy and general proposals in respect of the development and other use of land in the plan area, and containing such other matters as may be prescribed or directed by the Secretary of State.[46] The written statement is illustrated by "such diagram or diagrams as may be prescribed," and these form part of the plan.[47] Then there is an explanatory memorandum (formerly a "written justification"), which summarises the reasons for the policies and general proposals contained in the written statement and generally states their effect. The written justification for structure plans prepared before the 1980 Act actually forms part of the plan, but the new explanatory memorandum does not.[48]

The duty to prepare structure plans falls upon the county planning authority,[49] and although the legislation allows some flexibility for schemes of joint preparation[50] and for the making of arrangements for the function to be carried out by other authorities,[51] the main pattern in practice has been one of individual county preparation and submission. A structure plan may be prepared for the whole of the authority's area, or, with the consent or at the direction of the Secretary of State, for part.[52] A choice to prepare part-area plans is usually made on the basis of geographical or political convenience. In some areas the county authorities have inherited part-area plans prepared and submitted before local government reform in 1974, and which they will consolidate in a replacement plan in due course.

Further, the county formerly could, with the consent (or at the direction) of the Secretary of State, prepare separate *urban* structure plans for parts of their area which were already urbanised, or which it was proposed should become urban. The purpose of this provision was to enable special attention

---

[44] T.C.P.A. 1971, s.19, Sched.4, para.5.

[45] *Ibid.* Sched.5, para.8(5).

[46] T.C.P.A. 1971, s.7(1A); added by L.G.P.L.A. 1980, Sched.14, para. 2(*a*).

[47] *Ibid.* s. 7(6); amended by L.G.P.L.A. 1980, Sched. 14, para. 2(*c*)

[48] *Ibid.* s. 7(6A); added by L.G.P.L.A. 1980, Sched. 14, para. 2(*d*). An attempt had been made to make the old written justification non-statutory in the Town and Country Planning (Structure and Local Plans)(Amendment) Regulations 1979 (S.I. 1979 No. 1738), but the Regulations could not defeat the provisions of s. 7(6) of the 1971 Act which required any "descriptive matter" to be treated as part of the plan.

[49] Subject to a default power vested in the Secretary of State: T.C.P.A. 1971, s.17; Plans Regulations 1982, reg. 45. Any structure plan submitted for approval before April 1, 1974 is now deemed to have been submitted by the new county planning authority for the area to which it relates: Town and Country Planning (Development Plans) Order 1974, (S.I. 1974 No. 460), art.6.

[50] T.C.P.A. 1971, s.10A; L.G.A. 1972, s.101(5), and Sched. 16, paras. 8–14 which prescribe the procedure for joint plans.

[51] L.G.A. 1972, s.101.

[52] T.C.P.A. 1971, s.7(7).

to be directed to the problems of larger urban areas in counties, particularly where substantial and complex change was proposed. But it was repealed by the 1982 Regulations in respect of any structure plans not submitted for approval before those Regulations came into force.[53]

The legislation formerly made provision for the designation of "action areas" in structure plans. These are successors to the comprehensive development area designations of the old style plans, and they are areas selected for comprehensive treatment by development, redevelopment or improvement. The action area designation was a first step and not a separate plan in itself, and implementation of the proposals follows the preparation of a detailed local plan, known as an "action area plan," for the specific area.[54] Because of the time scales involved in preparing and approving structure plans, the requirement of prior designation of action areas proved hopelessly cumbersome and has now been lifted by the Act of 1980.[55]

The statutory procedures for structure plan preparation fall into eight main stages:

(a) the carrying out of a survey of the area to be covered by the plan;

(b) the formulation of policy alternatives based upon the survey;

(c) a public participation exercise following publication of the survey report;

(d) submission of a draft plan;

(e) a study of some or all of the objections to the plan at an "examination in public;"

(f) publication of the Secretary of State's proposed modifications, if any, to the plan; and the consideration by him of consequent objections;

(g) the Secretary of State's decision approving or rejecting the plan; and

(h) continued monitoring by the authority of the plan's implementation and the assumptions upon which its policies were based with a view to the preparation of proposals for alteration.

Each of these stages must now be examined in greater detail.

(a) The survey stage

The information base for structure planning is prescribed by section 6 of the 1971 Act. The authority are required to survey their area, examining the matters which may be expected to affect the development of that area or the planning of its development. The survey is to be continuous, in that all the matters are required to be kept under review even once the statutory report

---

[53] Plans Regulations 1982, reg. 46. If there should be any contradiction between a separate part of an existing structure plan prepared under this procedure, and the rest of the plan the provisions of the separate part prevail: Plans Regulations, reg. 46(5).
[54] *Post*, p. 116.
[55] L.G.P.L.A. 1980, Sched. 14, para. 2(b).

of survey has been prepared. And the scope of the required survey is comprehensive. The matters to be examined and kept under review must include:

(a) "the principal physical and economic characteristics of the area of the authority (including the principal purposes for which land is used) and, so far as they may be expected to affect that area, of any neighbouring areas;

(b) the size, composition and distribution of the population of that area (whether resident or otherwise);

(c) without prejudice to paragraph (a) of this subsection, the communications, transport system and traffic of that area and, so far as they may be expected to affect that area, of any neighbouring areas;

(d) any considerations not mentioned in any of the preceding paragraphs which may be expected to affect any matters so mentioned;

(e) such other matters as may be prescribed or as the Secretary of State may in a particular case direct;

(f) any changes already projected in any of the matters mentioned in any of the preceding paragraphs and the effect which those changes are likely to have on the development of that area or the planning of such development."[56]

No further matters have been prescribed under paragraph (e). As with the old-style development plans, the focus is primarily upon land use and development, and this impression is borne out by the Act's prescription that the structure plan shall be a written statement "formulating the local planning authority's policy and general proposals in respect of the development and other use of land in that area (including measures for the improvement of the physical environment and the management of traffic)."[57] But the general scope of the provisions is deliberately cast broader, so as to give effect to the Government's wish to secure an integration of land use planning, transport and investment "in order to meet our economic and social objectives."[58]

The report of survey does not legally form part of the plan, and following the Act of 1980 no longer needs to be submitted to the Secretary of State with the draft structure plan or alteration. Instead, it operates as its information base, and authorities are required simply to secure that the

---

[56] *Ibid.* s. 6(3). Compliance with the duties imposed by paras. (a) and (c) must include consultation with the neighbouring authorities: s. 6(4). The actual report of the survey is reduced in significance by the 1980 Act which removes the former requirement that it should be submitted to the Secretary of State with the plan, and that publicity should be given to its contents.

[57] *Ibid.* s. 7(1A).

[58] Cmnd. 3333, para. 16. But exactly how far the plan itself should stray from purely physical land use considerations has proved a controversial issue, and is examined more fully *post* p. 93.

plan's policies and proposals are justified by the results of their survey and by any other information which they may obtain.[59] The extent to which they have been successful is liable to be examined at the subsequent examination in public, and the plan is expected by the Secretary of State to summarize the relevant survey information so as to indicate the basis on which its policies were formulated.[60]

There are various sources of survey information. Authorities generally maintain their own data bases on matters close to their everyday functions, such as details of site allocations in outstanding (*i.e.* unimplemented) planning permissions, building completions, rateable values and traffic flow data, and these information or "intelligence" banks have been substantially built up in recent years by most counties. There is also a variety of local and national information collated centrally, including census and employment data. The available raw information is then supplemented by authorities' own surveys. Not all of this need be detailed statistical information. Expert forecasts, surveys of community attitudes, correspondence, meetings and observations may all be relied upon to produce so-called "soft" data, which social scientists are satisfied may be of relevance despite the often unsystematic basis of its collation.[61]

The purpose of the survey is more than to provide simply a summary of an existing state of affairs. It is to provide the basis for the prediction exercise upon which the plan or alteration is to be based.[62] Absolutely accurate forecast of future change is, of course, impossible. But there are lesser degrees of accuracy, degrees of foreseeability or probability, upon which decisions may still be based with some reliability. The longer the period in respect of which the forecast is to be made, and the less knowledge of, and control exercised by the planner over, the factors involved, then the less accurate are likely to be the forecasts. Given the comparatively limited control of the planning system over such vital matters as human reproduction and rises in oil prices, for example, forecasting in planning is often largely intuitive. There is still comparatively little understanding of the complex nature of urban form and of the likely impact of land use changes upon other forms of human activity. Much forecasting is therefore necessarily reliant upon the use of past information, the discernment of past trends, and their projection, on the basis of present information, into the future.

Two closely related factors have been accepted as being of central importance to structure planners: future population trends and future employment in the plan area. But population prediction has proved

[59] T.C.P.A. 1971, s. 7(4).

[60] D.O.E. Circular 4/79, *Memorandum* para. 2.9. But see also the criticism in D.O.E. Circular 23/81 of "over elaborate" work being undertaken at survey stage, and the request that authorities should keep new survey work to a minimum.

[61] For a more detailed study, see William Solesbury, *Policy in Urban Planning* (Pergamon Press, 1974), Chap. 3.

[62] The power which originally existed, for the Secretary of State to direct the period of time over which the estimates should be made, was repealed by the L.G.P.L.A. 1980, Sched. 14, para. 2. As Solesbury (*op.cit.* p. 101) points out, an authority may wish to use different bases for different projections, relating population growth, for example, to the key census years of 1971, 1981, 1991 and beyond.

particularly hazardous in the past. The early post-war development plans failed to anticipate the great increase in rate of population growth that was to take place in the ensuing decade; and, equally, many of the present structure plans have made excessive allowance for population increase. Population change and movement is influenced by many different social, political and economic factors, including the planning system itself, and the relations between them are largely unknown. Projections of likely change are based on assumptions as to future migration, fertility and mortality but they represent no more than an informed guess of future trends. And whilst it is true that "there is a considerable amount of inertia in population change,"[63] it is the changes at the margin with which planning is primarily concerned. Further, as the Office of Population Censuses and Surveys are at pains to point out, there are liable to be significant local and regional variations in the reliability of projections. The London Boroughs, for example, particularly those in central London, experience high migration rates which make prediction substantially less reliable than in areas of more stable population.[64]

The inherent unreliability of population projections over even comparatively short terms is most graphically demonstrated by the experience of the past 15 years. In 1968 it was anticipated that England's population would grow to 53.1 million by 1991, an increase of around 316,000 per annum. But the mid-1977 prediction was for 47 million by 1991, only 47,000 per annum.[65] The new structure plans which followed the 1968 Act were based upon the early predictions and were conceived on assumptions of large scale growth. Many were revised significantly during the approval process, but remain over-ambitious in light of the most recent projections. Those projections may, of course, prove to be as wide of the mark as the 1968 figures, and it is necessary to continue to regard all structure plan population predictions with great caution, at least until their conformity with the 1981 census is established.

It is not only the size but also the make-up of the local population which carries planning implications, particularly in terms of planning for new housing development, employment, sheltered accommodation, recreational facilities, education and so on; and county authorities have continued to justify growth policies by reference to the demand generated by the continuing trend towards smaller household size and new employment.

Population figures are, of course, only one of the many variables affecting plan implementation. An attempt has been made over the past 15 years to achieve greater accuracy in prediction through a closer examination of the relationships between various urban systems, or activities. The reasoning is that change in one existing system or variable is dependent upon a combination of changes in other variables.[66] The exercise of measuring the degree of dependence is mathematical, and techniques involving functional

---

[63] O.P.C.S., *Population projectors 1977–1991* (London, H.M.S.O. 1980), p.2.
[64] *Ibid.* pp. 2–3.
[65] *Ibid.* pp. 8–9.
[66] For an influential study of systems analysis, see J.B. McLoughlin, *Urban and Regional Planning* (Faber and Faber, 1969).

analysis have evolved for the expression of varieties of urban relationships in
the form of abstract mathematical models. These techniques have proved
valuable analytical tools, but as the Department's own material
acknowledges,[67] they cannot replace the more intuitive methods. Even the
most complex model is liable to provide only a superficial analogue of the
real world, so complex are the real interrelationships, and it offers only a
part of the picture. Intuitive judgement will always be needed for
interpreting and if necessary adjusting the projections so as to make them
useful in plan making. Their danger, perhaps, is that their use may tend to
disguise the inherent unreliability of the long term forecasting that plan
making presently requires; but their merit is in drawing out ideas of basic
rationality in decision making, and in ensuring that political choice is made
with some understanding of the possible alternatives.

(b) Policy formulation

(i) The law

The Act makes it clear that the heart of structure planning is to be found in
the authority's *policy* and *general proposals* contained in the written
statement. There is no statutory definition of the two terms, and in practice
there is some overlap. A "policy" is generally understood to be a general
statement intended to guide a continuing process of decision making in
pursuit of an objective or aim of the plan. A "general proposal," on the other
hand, is generally understood as meaning a chosen course of action in
respect of some particular area.[68] It may, for example, be a decision to allow
expansion of a particular village, or to restrain the further outward growth of
a city.

The legislation now requires that "each and every policy and general
proposal" in the plan should be justified by reasons given in the explanatory
memorandum, which should also state its relationship to expected development and other use of land in neighbouring areas where relevant.[69] In
formulating their policies and proposals authorities are also required to have
regard:

(a) "to current policies with respect to the economic planning and
    development of the region as a whole;

(b) to the resources likely to be available for the carrying out of the
    proposals of the structure plan; and

(c) to such other matters as the Secretary of State may direct them to
    take into account."[70]

The 1974 Plans Regulations additionally imposed a further general

---

[67] *Using Predictive Models for Structure Plans* (D.O.E. 1973), para. 2.18.
[68] The definitions adopted in the text have been adapted from those contained in the *Manual on Form and Content* (H.M.S.O. 1971), p.97.
[69] T.C.P.A. 1971, s. 7(6A).
[70] *Ibid.* s. 7(4). The regional context is examined further below.

requirement on all authorities to ensure that policy in their plans should relate to such of the following matters as they think appropriate:

- (i) "Distribution of population and employment.
- (ii) Housing.
- (iii) Industry and commerce.
- (iv) Transportation.
- (v) Shopping.
- (vi) Education.
- (vii) Other social and community services.
- (viii) Recreation and leisure.
- (ix) Conservation, townscape and landscape.
- (x) Utility services.
- (xi) Any other relevant matters."[71]

It was a particularly clumsy way of prescribing issues. Although expressed in terms of a duty, the obligation to consider these matters was remarkably loose: policy need relate only to such of them as the authority thought "appropriate" and they could bring in any other "relevant" matters, so that it is difficult to understand why this complex legislative structure was thought a better vehicle than a departmental circular for such an advisory function. It was therefore abandoned in the 1982 Regulations, and instead the authority are required by Regulation 9 to include in the explanatory memorandum such indications as they may think appropriate of the regard they have had to:

"(*a*) current national and regional policies;

(*b*) social considerations;

(*c*) the resources likely to be available for carrying out the policy and general proposals formulated in the structure plan."

(ii) *The physical planning limitation*

Planning under the Acts of 1947 and 1962 was in practice confined to physical planning, preoccupied with the location, arrangement and appearance of buildings and the containment of growth. Only gradually did the social consequences of planning policy come to be understood, particularly through the reaction that set in against the "positive planning" achievements of the 1960s: the widespread slum clearance, high rise building and urban road schemes. The Planning Advisory Group were impressed by the need to broaden the scope of planning, the 1968 Act was drafted broadly to encourage this, and authorities have been enjoined both to take account of existing social policies and to examine the social impact of their own policies, as, for example, between different groups in the population.[72] But in practice the Secretary of State has limited the extent to which structure plans themselves should attempt to influence or dictate broader social policy. The

---

[71] Plans Regulations, reg. 9 and Sched. 1, Part I.
[72] D.O.E. Circular 4/79, *Memorandum*, para. 2.37.

view is that as the formal influence of structure plans is confined to changes in land use patterns, policies and general proposals should not extend beyond that. The clearest statement of this limitation appeared in the Notice of Approval of the West Bromwich Structure Plan in 1978:

> "Structure plans are about land and the use made of it. The planning policies in support of the chosen plan strategy should provide guidance on future decisions regarding the development and other use of land (including measures for the improvement of the physical environment and the management of traffic) but only in strategic terms. Policies should not, therefore, include expressions of intent to consult with or make requests of other bodies or to take administrative action unrelated to the use of land, for example in the fields of education or social services or for the provision, allocation or management of public sector housing."[73]

This is a narrow interpretation of the statutory phrase "development and other use of land" and the Secretary of State's interpretation imposes a significant restraint upon planning's sphere of influence. There is little doubt that it was open to him to take a broader view,[74] but a broader interpretation would give rise to practical difficulties in implementation, given the limited practical ability of a structure plan to influence policy making in areas not involving land use change. In particular, the fact that responsibility for public sector housing now rests with district councils limits the extent to which the structure plan can fulfil any corporate planning function involving housing, which might have been possible had a unitary local government structure been adopted. What is left is a purely advocative role, and even in the case of other social functions of the non-metropolitan county authorities, such as education and personal social services, policies cannot actually be made in the structure plan, though they may be influenced by it. Similarly, the further structure plan policies stray away from land use issues, the more difficult they become to employ in development control. Their implementation falls outside the planning legislation, and their impact on county/district consultation arrangements poses serious demarcation problems.

The physical planning restraint extends only to the policies and general proposals of the plan, however. The report of survey and the explanatory memorandum will normally contain an analysis of the social material on which the policies and proposals are based, and in some cases the Secretary of State has relegated material to the status of "written justification" using his powers of modification. The result is that an ambiguous category of quasi-policy and social objectives continues to appear in the approved document and may still influence subsequent decision making.[75]

---

[73] Notice of Approval (May 17, 1978), para. 7.1.

[74] He might, for example, have chosen to exercise his power under s. 7(3)(c) to prescribe social policies as "other matters" to be contained in the plan.

[75] See further Jowell and Noble, "Planning as Social Engineering" *Urban Law and Policy* 3 (1980) 293.

(iii) *The strategic policy limitation*

Structure plan policy is intended to be strategic only, leaving matters of detail to be dealt with in local plans. For this reason the plans have no detailed, ordnance based map, but only a diagram illustrating general locations where change is proposed. But the distinction between strategy and detail is by no means easy to draw in practice. It is a distinction of degree rather than of principle and it is a distinction which has assumed political connotations in many areas, following the allocation of responsibility for the two tiers of development plan between the two newly created tiers of local government. This has meant that structure plan decisions now have the additional function of defining the respective spheres of planning influence of the two local government tiers: the structure plan acts as a net cast across district authorities' planning freedom. Not only are they obliged to ensure that their local plans comply with the structure plan,[76] but the structure plan also guides their development control decisions. Indeed, until 1980, an application for planning permission which conflicted with or prejudiced the implementation of any "fundamental" provision of the structure plan, was deemed a county matter and it was altogether outside the district authority's jurisdiction to grant permission.[77] The more detailed the provisions of the structure plan, the greater the county's invasion of district authority territory, and this remains the case after 1980 although now the district authorities have power to handle such applications subject to consultation with the county, and the influence of the structure plan may well be weaker as a result.

Central government has recognised the danger of structure plans being used for ulterior demarcation purposes and has become increasingly insistent that authorities should confine their plans to issues of "key structural importance."[78] The Department have pointed to the delay which is likely to result from preoccupation with detail, and there has been no hesitation in using the Secretary of State's modification power to delete matters of detail, particularly detailed statements of development control policy, from submitted plans.

(iv) *Regional planning and the policy hierarchy*

The requirement that authorities should have regard to "current policies with respect to the economic planning and development of the region as a whole"[79] was introduced in an attempt formally to tie physical planning in with regional planning, which had developed on a non-statutory basis through the 1960s. The idea was that regional planning offered a wider view, which made it possible to analyse overall population and settlement patterns and to examine more readily any activities and developments that might have an impact reaching beyond the area of individual county authorities.

---

[76] T.C.P.A. 1971, s. 14(2), and see *post*, p. 119.
[77] By virtue of the Local Government Act 1972, Sched. 16, para. 32(*d*) repealed as from November 13, 1980 by L.G.P.L.A. 1980, s. 62(3): see further *post* p. 223.
[78] D.O.E. Circular 4/79, *Memorandum* para. 2.10.
[79] T.C.P.A. 1971, s. 7(4).

The main impetus to regional planning came in the early 1960s with a series of Government sponsored regional studies, and the process was reinforced with the setting-up in 1965 of the Regional Economic Planning Councils. Their functions included the production of regional economic strategies, and they had a clear interest therefore in strengthening regional physical planning policy. A tripartite pattern of regional policy making emerged in most regions, based upon consultations between the Councils, the local authorities in the region and central government.[80] In most cases a regional report was first prepared by a joint planning team drawn from the local authorities and the regional council. It was then submitted to central government and published. A period of appraisal followed, during which the report was assessed by the Department of the Environment and measured against national policy and in the light of comments submitted by the public. A formal response was then issued, and the response, read with the report, constituted the approved strategy.[81]

The procedure was completely non-statutory, and there were serious criticisms of the vagueness and ambiguity of both report and response in some instances, of the lengthy delays in appraisal, and of the absence of any formal participation or objection machinery. When in 1979 the incoming government announced the abolition of the regional economic planning councils, it was clear that regional planning could not continue as it had done. In July of that year the Government took the further step of announcing that it intended not to be bound by the existing strategies, though account would continue to be taken of them in the approval of structure plans pending the issuance in due course of new or amended regional guidance for structure planning purposes.[82] No general guidance has yet been issued[83] and the published strategies, though of uncertain status and dating rapidly, continue to provide a limited regional framework.

Adherence to the Government's regional policy in structure plans has been ensured through the approval process, and the Secretary of State has

---

[80] The tripartite approach was extended to plans for the North West, East Anglia and the North; while in the case of the West Midlands the plan was prepared largely by the local authorities, and in the Southwest and in Yorkshire and Humberside, by the economic planning councils. For a detailed account, see A.G. Powell, "Strategies for the English Regions" (1978) 49 *Town Planning Review* 5.

[81] A less formal process is envisaged for the preparation of regional recreational strategies by Regional Councils for Sport and Recreation, although these too will be relevant in structure plan preparation: see further, D.O.E. Circular 73/77.

[82] H.C. Deb., Vol. 970, col. *230*; although a subsequent reply that such regional guidance would be given "as and when necessary" indicates that a more ad hoc approach may be employed: H.C. Deb., Vol. 982, col. *687*.

[83] This may be compared with the practice of the Scottish Development Department since 1976 of issuing a series of *National Planning Guidelines* setting an overall strategy on a number of themes, including coastal planning, large industrial sites, aggregates, petrochemical industry and rural conservation. The *Guidelines* offer positive guidance to authorities and, importantly, offer the basis for strategic control through being integrated with the "calling-in" systems. See further: Diamond *et al*, "The Uses of Strategic Planning" (1979) 50 *Town Planning Review* 18.

indicated in the past that a very clear case would need to be shown to justify any departure.[84]

Authorities have similarly been held to other governmental policies. At one level the purpose is simply to ensure uniform treatment of issues. Amendments have been made to submitted plans, to ensure that common policy statements conform to a national norm; for example, that green belt policies should be the same from area to area. At the substantive level, national policy is brought in through the statutory pre-plan consultations with affected government departments,[85] in addition to the informal talks which regularly take place between the authority and officials of the Department of Environment during the course of preparation of a plan.[86] Further, representatives of government departments frequently appear at the examination in public to advance their departments' policies, or at least to safeguard the Department's interest. But, importantly, government policy is not regarded as a matter for debate at the examination in public. The Secretary of State's decision inevitably reflects current government policy, and although the modification procedures offer a limited means for challenge, government policy remains paramount.

The hierarchy of policy influence is complex, and it works primarily downwards. The detail of an area's future development might well have been processed progressively (or worse, contemporaneously), through regional strategy, sub-regional study, structure plan and local plan—with perhaps other non-statutory documents as well. But the pressure is not entirely one way. Not only are district authorities left with some considerable freedom by virtue of the strategic level of the structure plan, but they are also required to be consulted in the course of its preparation along with other appropriate authorities and bodies.[87] And it is to be expected that much of the pressure for future alteration to approved structure plans will come from district level following their experience with implementation.

(v) *Methodology in policy formulation*

Policy is the stuff of politics, and policy making is primarily a political process. It involves the selection of preferred courses of action in pursuance of goals or aims, and there are no fixed or ordained standards. Choices may have to be made between selected, and often highly controversial, alternatives: between policies of restraint or growth, encouragement of public or private modes of transport, or between conservation or redevelop-

---

[84] See, *e.g.* Notice of Approval of Staffordshire Structure Plan (April 11, 1978), para. 7.4, where the population growth forecasts of the three Staffordshire structure plans taken together exceeded by a substantial amount the figures contained in the sub-regional strategy. The Secretary of State proceeded to modify the plan, though recognizing that there was necessarily a great deal of uncertainty in the forecasts.

[85] Authorities have been asked to consult at an early stage any government department or public body carrying out responsibilities which may be affected by the plan, and to maintain consultation as a continuing process: D.O.E. Circular 4/79, *Memorandum*, paras. 2.53–2.54.

[86] The extensive scope of private consultation and liaison between the Department and authorities is examined in detail in Roberts, *The Reform of Planning Law* (Macmillan, 1976), Chap. 9.

[87] Plans Regulations, reg. 6.

ment for example. These are political decisions, and electoral popularity, and hence direct accountability, may depend upon which course is chosen.

But that is not to say that policy choice in planning must be wholly intuitive, or that it need be rational in terms only of political criteria. The birth of structure planning coincided with the development of a variety of new and sophisticated techniques designed to bring a greater degree of rationality to policy making. Mathematical modelling was developed as an aid to analysis and prediction, and proved useful also as a means of evaluating possible alternative policy choices.[88] Management theory similarly has been adapted to the decision processes involved in plan preparation, and used to emphasise the necessary linkages between different inputs to the process, as well as formalising the relationships between the successive stages of the rational comprehensive model. In particular it stressed the necessity for rigorous analysis of alternatives and continuous monitoring. Evaluation of alternative strategies could be considered rationally against common agreed criteria, such as their effectiveness in meeting the plan's aims, the availability of resources, their distributional effects and their flexibility in response to uncertainty.[89] Availability of resources for implementation is a particularly important factor. Authorities are required by the Act to have regard to it,[90] and severe cutbacks in public expenditure in recent years have meant that authorities have had to trim down policies calling for extensive public sector investment.

But this does not mean that policy evaluation is purely an exercise in pursuing cost effectiveness. Social and environmental benefits can rarely if ever be balanced rationally against financial costs, despite the development of complex techniques of cost benefit analysis in this field. Indeed the complexity of analysis too readily disguises the subjectivity and bias of the evaluative criteria, and it is a serious criticism that the techniques that have evolved for the study of existing human systems are still so rudimentary as to make realistic forecasting and control impossible, certainly over a long term, and they constitute a fragile and dangerous basis for policy choice.[91] The ultimate choice must always be political. A policy may be deemed worth pursuing notwithstanding its cost because it brings strongly desired social benefits, or because an alternative course is strongly opposed by the public, perhaps in the course of the participation exercise, or by other local authorities.

To emphasise political accountability is not to assert that policy making need not rise above the intuitive or the irrational. Methodology aimed at achieving greater rationality can at least ensure that explicit choices are made

---

[88] Detailed analysis is beyond the scope of this book, but valuable information is contained in P.W.J. Batey and M.J. Breheny, "Methods in Strategic Planning" (1978) 48 *Town Planning Review* 259–273, 502–518; Richard Barras (ed.), "Current Issues in Structure Planning" (C.E.S. Policy Series No.4, 1978) and earlier C.E.S. Research Paper No. 20 (1975) *Aspects of Structure Planning in Britain*.

[89] See further, D.O.E. *Structure Plan Note* 8/72; and the D.O.E.'s two booklet study, *Management Networks. A Study for Structure Plans* (H.M.S.O., 1971).

[90] T.C.P.A. 1971, s. 7(4).

[91] For a detailed critique and alternative approach see Stanley Openshaw and P.T. Whitehead, "Decision-making in local plans" (1977) 44 *Town Planning Review* 29.

with a fuller understanding of likely consequences and the merits of possible alternatives. And where a policy is selected for its political merits, that choice ought to be made openly and explicitly. The danger otherwise is, as the Committee of Inquiry into the *Greater London Development Plan* observed in 1973, that the choice may be represented as the inevitable logical consequence of the technical information.[92] The Committee went on to urge that the "reasoned justification" (now the explanatory memorandum) for structure plan policies should indicate where a choice was preferred on political grounds, but in practice this has rarely happened. Many structure plans still explain comparatively little of the reasoning behind policy choices, let alone the respective influences of technical evaluation and political preference. If any trend can be observed, it is that less reliance has been placed in the more recent plans upon technical evaluation, and that the era of methodological imperialism has given way to a more obviously political and conflictual approach.

(c) Public participation

(i) *the law*

There is a statutory duty to secure that adequate publicity is given in the area to the matters the authority propose to include in the plan (or alteration), and to the proposed content of the explanatory memorandum relating to each matter.[93] Further, the planning authority must secure that "persons who may be expected to desire an opportunity of making representations to the authority with respect to those matters" are not only made aware of their entitlement to do so, but are also given an adequate opportunity.[94] A period of six weeks is prescribed from the time the authority publicise their draft proposals, in which representations may be made,[95] and all representations duly made must be considered by the authority.[96] The wording of the general duty is imprecise, but there is machinery for its supervision. The authority are required to forward a statement to the Secretary of State not only of the steps taken by the authority to comply with the duty, but also giving particulars of "the authority's consultations with, and consideration of the views of, other persons with respect to those matters."[97] The Secretary of State has insisted that the authority's draft proposals and policies be published in full, and that where they have put forward specific alternatives for comment, they should indicate their own preferences.[98] If not satisfied as to the adequacy of the authority's efforts, the Secretary of State must remit the plan for further publicity or participation.[99] That power has not, to date, been exercised,

---

[92] *Report of the Committee of Inquiry* (H.M.S.O., 1973), para. 2.17 (*c*).
[93] T.C.P.A. 1971, s. 8(1)(*a*) as substituted by L.G.P.L.A. 1980, Sched. 14, para. 3(*a*). The 1980 Act has lifted the former duty to give publicity to the report of survey.
[94] *Ibid.* s. 8(1)(*b*) and (*c*).
[95] Plans Regulations 1982, reg. 5. Under the 1974 Regulations, the six week period was prescribed as a minimum.
[96] T.C.P.A. 1971, s. 8(1).
[97] *Ibid.* s. 8(3).
[98] D.O.E. Circular 4/79, *Memorandum*, para. 2.48.
[99] T.C.P.A. 1971, s. 8(4).

partly because not even the Department of Environment are very clear as to
how the adequacy of participation might be judged, or what criteria could be
used to assess its success. In the words of the Department's chief planner,
"At the end of the day, it amounts to the faith of the individual in how the
system as a whole should operate, rather than that a particular procedure
should be gone through."[1] The remitting power has been kept very much in
reserve, and there has therefore in practice been a wide range of variation in
the action taken by authorities.

The provisions are intended to encourage an early phase of public
participation, in order to overcome the disadvantages of the old style plan
procedure where public objection was invited to the completed document,
and subsequently considered at a public inquiry in an adversarial atmosphere. A similar objection procedure remains as a second phase in structure
plan participation, except that the right to pursue objections at inquiry has
now been lost. The inquiry has been replaced by a wide ranging examination
in public of selected key issues, which is discussed below.

(ii) *participation in practice*

Public participation in governmental decision making is an idea which has
attracted increasing interest over the past 15 years, particularly in the context
of local government. A wish to encourage greater participation in planning
was an important factor underlying the reforms recommended by the
Planning Advisory Group, and it was specifically acknowledged in the
Government's subsequent white paper.[2] But because the idea was thought to
be experimental, and its effects perhaps unpredictable, the Government
chose to refrain from imposing a detailed legislative framework. Instead, a
committee was established under the chairmanship of the late Arthur
Skeffington, then Parliamentary Undersecretary to the Minister of Housing
and Local Government. The Skeffington Committee's Report was to prove
influential in thinking on participation over the ensuing decade, particularly
because of its optimism that participation could contribute substantially to
plan preparation. The Committee argued that:

> "People should be able to say what kind of community they want and
> how it should develop: and should be able to do so in a way that is
> positive and first-hand. It matters to us all that we should know that we
> can influence the shape of our community so that the towns and villages
> in which we live, work, learn and relax may reflect our best aspirations.
> This becomes all the more vital where the demands of a complex society
> occasion massive changes; changes which in some areas may completely
> alter the character of a town, a neighbourhood or a rural area. The pace,
> intensity and scale of change will inevitably bring bewilderment and
> frustration if people affected think it is to be imposed without respect
> for their views. This leads all too easily to alienation between the
> authority and people."[3]

---

[1] Mr. W. Burns, in evidence to the House of Commons Expenditure Committee (Environment
Sub-Committee) June 23, 1976 (H.C. 395–11, p.73).

[2] Cmnd. 3333, para. 16.

[3] *People and Planning (Report of the Committee on Public Participation in Planning)*
(H.M.S.O., 1969), para. 8.

The Committee urged that authorities should concentrate upon ensuring effective publicity for their proposals and attracting participation through public meetings, exhibitions, films and press conferences.[4] Their Report went on to stress the importance of securing continuing participation from an early stage in policy making, and urged that authorities should appoint community development officers to stimulate interest among people not already members of organisations, the so-called "non-joiners," or "silent majority," and to pass their views on to the authority.[5]

Although there has been comparatively little systematic and comprehensive research into participation in practice,[6] the evidence suggests that performance has fallen some way short of the Skeffington ideal, and that for some authorities the statutorily prescribed participation stage has amounted to little more than an unenthusiastic public relations exercise. Partly this has been because the intended scope of participation has never been made clear. The new procedures were certainly not intended to supplant local elective democracy in favour of a fully participative system. Their purpose was to extend the opportunity for the exercise of influence by citizens, not to achieve any transfer of power. Effective publicity (not necessarily public relations) is an essential legal and practical requirement. But encouraging an intelligent and representative response, and reacting to it intelligently, is far more difficult. The false assumption underlying the Skeffington proposals is that participation could proceed on a consensual basis, involving little more than the absorption of public input by the authority which would then be reflected in amendments to the draft plan. It is a vision of an orderly process of influence through information gathering, not a system designed to assess and cope with pressure and political hostility. And, as the authors of a subsequent research study have pointed out, the Act itself

> "seems to be based on the assumption that the public consists of rational individuals who know what they want, and that a consensus view can be achieved between them. The role of the local authority is to provide a channel for them to express their views. Once expressed, it is assumed that the planners will hear their views, understand them and incorporate them into the policy making process."[7]

The Act offers no independent procedure for the settlement of conflict until the examination in public is reached, and there is a procedural vagueness at this earlier stage which both allows authorities to avoid potential con-

---

[4] *Ibid.* Chaps. V and VI.

[5] *Ibid.* paras. 80–90.

[6] There is, however, a valuable bibliography of research in *Structure Plans. List B: The Literature and Debate on Structure Plans and Structure Planning* (D.O.E. 1976); and see A. Barker, *Public Participation in Britain: A Classified Bibliography* (Bedford Square Press, 1979). Also, the Department's Linked Research Programme into Public Participation in Structure Planning has resulted in a series of research papers, whose contents are referred to further below.

[7] M. Drake *et al, Aspects of Structure Planning in Britain* (London: C.E.S. Research Paper 20, 1975), p. 173. This view is further developed by Damer and Hague in "Public Participation in Planning: A Review" (1971) 42 *Town Planning Review* 217, who also highlight the extent to which such a model of participation is liable to manipulation by professional planners.

troversy and supports the view of structure planning as a remote and imprecise process, not readily susceptible to participation. It may be that local plans will prove a better vehicle for participation, but if so it is to be expected that many an indirect challenge will at that stage be attempted against approved structure plan proposals, even though none may have been made to the structure plan itself.

A further factor which has limited the effectiveness of participation programmes has been the remoteness and complexity of structure planning in practice. The issues involved are seldom immediate and compelling, and any attempt to present them to the general public in readily intelligible form necessarily requires that the authority select and simplify the proposals and supporting information, leading often to a carefully structured series of choices for comment. Postal questionnaires and other methods of social survey have been used to test public opinion, but the dangers of too close a reliance upon the results of even the most carefully structured survey are clear enough.[8] Qualitative input is difficult for an authority to handle, and their problems have been exacerbated by low public response rates to survey material, and poor attendances at public meetings.[9] Working with already organised groups, such as amenity societies, housebuilding representatives and farming interests, has generally proved from the planners' viewpoint a more fruitful and organised source of opinion and expertise; and it is also a useful means of assessing in advance the strength and quality of interest group objections to the draft, and of considering how best to meet them (if at all) before the examination in public.

There are many important and fundamental issues raised by participation in structure planning which have proved too sensitive and too difficult to deal with by means of legislation or even by circular. Perhaps the most obvious is that participation is necessarily confined to existing residents in the plan area. The feedback from existing residents has tended, increasingly in the past few years, to be opposed to growth and to major change. In response, authorities have tended to devise restrictive policies, particularly for green belt preservation and extension and restraints on village expansion. Similarly, many have attempted to restrict changes to a scale no greater than that necessary to meet the needs of established residents. But an effective local participation programme along those lines excludes and disenfranchises those who might wish or need to move to the area, and makes it difficult for an authority to take a broader view of future needs. It is no real compensation that participation by national groups such as the housebuilding industry and developers' organisations provides some balance, because their objectives are substantially different.

Some disenchantment with the idea of participation has been inevitable,

---

[8] For a useful study, see N. Boaden and R. Walker, *Sample Surveys and Public Participation* (Linked Research Project, I.R.P. 10, 1976), and N. Boaden *et al*, "Public Participation in Planning within a Representative Local Democracy," *Policy and Politics*, (1979), Vol. 7, p.55.

[9] A study of experience in Cheshire showed that audiences at public meetings there tended to be predominantly middle class, middle aged, male long term residents, but concluded that despite an average attendance of 58.4 persons per meeting the exercise was worthwhile: M. Goldsmith and P. Saunders, *Participation through Public Meetings: the Case in Cheshire* (Linked Research Project, I.R.P. 9, 1969.)

given the limitations to the type of exercise envisaged by the architects of the 1968 legislation. But even so, the abrupt change in policy announced by the Department in 1981 was remarkable. Earlier exhortation to authorities to regard the statutory requirements as basic minimum steps and to encourage full participation, has been superseded by advice that the requirements are now considered "adequate."[10] Authorities are now warned that further work should not be necessary, and should be undertaken only where they are satisfied that the work and delay it entails is clearly justified. The implication is that ministerial intervention on the grounds of inadequacy in the publicity given to plan proposals is unlikely, and that a ritualistic observance of the formalities prescribed by the Act will suffice.

(d) Preparation and submission of a draft plan

(i) *Form and content of submitted plans*

No structure plan or alteration has any legal effect until approved by the Secretary of State, although it may be used as a guide in development control in the interim period and effectively phased in as its provisions become clearer in the course of preparation. It is not uncommon, for example, for planning applications to be turned down as premature pending the preparation and approval of the plan, or as liable to frustrate the implementation of a plan under preparation.

The Secretary of State's supervision is exercised over both the content of the plan and its form. So far as the Act is concerned, a structure plan is simply a written statement whose primary function is to formulate the authority's policy and general proposals in respect of the development and other use of land in the plan area. It is accompanied by an explanatory memorandum and it includes a key diagram indicating in broad terms the location of its strategic proposals. The use of a map base is forbidden,[11] so as to avoid disputes at the strategic level over precise boundaries and site designations. The Department's *Manual of Form and Content*[12] provides authorities with model policy statements and diagrams, but its contents are advisory only and there has in practice been a great deal of variation in style between the submitted plans, and the Secretary of State's formal powers of modification have frequently been used to establish a degree of conformity.

(ii) *The submission of the plan*

Submission of the plan or alteration to the Secretary of State for approval must be accompanied by a copy of the authority's statement on public participation.[13] The plan, together with that statement and the explanatory memorandum, must then be placed on deposit for public inspection[14]; and a formal notice of the plan's submission must be advertised indicating the

---

[10] D.O.E. Circular 23/81, para. 16.
[11] Plans Regulations 1982, reg. 8(3).
[12] *Development Plans. A Manual on Form and Content* (H.M.S.O., 1970).
[13] T.C.P.A. 1971, s. 8(3).
[14] *Ibid.* s. 8(2).

right to make objections to the plan.[15] Objections (opposing the plan) and representations (supporting it) may be made in any manner, but a recommended form has been devised by the Department for the purpose.[16]

This is the second, and more formal, phase of public participation. There is no restriction on the persons or bodies who may forward objections or representations to the Secretary of State. Objections and representations must, however, be lodged within the prescribed time[17]; and there is no duty on the Secretary of State to consider any which appear to him to be in substance objections or representations with respect to action to be taken under certain other prescribed legislation which itself makes provision for consideration and hearing of objections.[18] That provision, significantly, excludes objections to major new road schemes (though county roads remain) even although plan strategy may be dependent upon their approval. But the exclusion is discretionary and not automatic, and the Secretary of State will often find it difficult to exclude such objections altogether, particularly at such a general level of policy making.

3. The approval process

(a) Preliminary consideration by the Secretary of State

A submitted plan (or alteration) may be returned to the authority, rejected, or approved by the Secretary of State. Alternatively, it may at any time following submission and before approval, be withdrawn by the authority. In that case it is to be treated as having never been submitted.[19]

A submitted plan (or alteration) must be returned to the authority where the Secretary of State is not satisfied that the publicity and participation requirements of section 8 have been fulfilled. The authority will in that event be directed to take further specified steps to comply with the section and to resubmit, for which a time limit may be imposed.[20]

A plan (or alteration) may also be rejected outright on grounds other than that of inadequate publicity or participation. The power to reject is cast in broad terms,[21] although reasons must be given.[22] It has never been exercised, and outright rejection must be regarded as a longstop control applicable only

---

[15] Plan Regulations 1982, reg. 16; Sched., Form 1.

[16] D.O.E. Circular 4/79, *Memorandum*, Annex C.

[17] A period of six weeks must be allowed: Plan Regulations 1982, Sched., Form 1. In practice, however, late objections have been regularly admitted: indeed, in some cases, the Department have themselves invited objections from selected organisations after the end of the prescribed period.

[18] T.C.P.A. 1971, s. 16 (as amended by the Highways Act 1980, Sched. 24, para. 20 (*a*)) The prescribed matters include trunk road orders, special road schemes and ancillary orders; schemes for bridge or tunnel construction as part of a maintainable highway; orders authorising diversion of a navigable watercourse; supplementary orders relating to trunk roads, classified roads or special roads, and designation of sites of new towns.

[19] T.C.P.A. 1971, s. 10B(1). Withdrawal of a plan may be useful where the county wish to amend it to take into account objections lodged following submission. In practice, however, authorities have tended instead to draft their own modifications to the plan, and have presented them at the examination in public and invited the Secretary of State to adopt them.

[20] *Ibid.* s. 8(4).

[21] *Ibid.* s. 9(1).

[22] *Ibid.* s. 9(8).

where a plan or alteration as submitted has defects so severe that they could not be remedied by Secretary of State's modifications.

Where the Secretary of State decides against outright rejection of the plan or alteration, he is obliged to give consideration to objections to the plan and to cause an examination in public to be held before determining whether to approve it, with or without modifications or reservations, or to reject it.[23] An examination need no longer be held into proposals for the alteration or repeal and replacement of a plan, provided the Secretary of State is satisfied that no issues arise requiring examination.[24]

(b) The examination in public

When structure planning was first introduced, the legislation made no changes in the traditional machinery for hearing objections, the public local inquiry. But an amendment passed in 1972, before any of the early plans had reached approval stage, replaced the inquiry with a new procedure. The new examination in public is intended to investigate, "by way of a probing discussion,"[25] those matters arising from the plan which the Secretary of State selects as calling for further examination. For this purpose a panel is appointed by him.[26] The procedure is closely controlled by the Secretary of State, and the former right of objectors to be heard in support of their objections is now lost. Whilst the Secretary of State is obliged to consider all objections which have been duly made,[27] the only objectors who may appear at the examination in public to advance their arguments are those to whom he or the chairman of the Panel, in their discretion, extend an invitation to do so. Procedure at the examination is governed only by a non-statutory code,[28] and the Secretary of State is not bound by the Panel's recommendations: indeed, there is no formal requirement that he should even have regard to their report.[29] Hence the procedure lacks any solid legal framework. The Act is carefully worded to avoid judicial review. The Secretary of State may take into account "any matters which he thinks are relevant,"[30] his reasons for his final decision are to be given in "such statement as he thinks appropriate,"[31] and he is relieved from any obligation to consult with or consider the views of any local authority or other person.[32]

---

[23] *Ibid.* s. 9(3); as inserted by T.C.P. (Amendment) Act 1972, s. 3(1).

[24] *Ibid.* s. 10(8), as inserted by L.G.P.L.A. 1980, Sched. 14, para. 5.

[25] *Structure Plans. The Examination in Public* D.O.E. 1973, para. 1.3.

[26] The examination could, under s.9(3)(*b*), be conducted by a single person, but a panel of three is normal practice for England. In Scotland, examinations have been conducted by a single Reporter, or planning inspector. It is not uncommon for one panel to examine two or more plans, either concurrently (as in the West Midlands and in Teeside) or consecutively (as in Mid and North East Hampshire).

[27] T.C.P.A. 1971, s. 9(3)(*a*).

[28] The Code is set out in *Structure Plans. The Examination in Public* D.O.E. 1973, and is based upon the views expressed in Parliament when the 1972 amending legislation was debated. For convenience the whole booklet is hereafter referred to as the *Code*, though strictly only Chapter 3 of it qualifies for that title.

[29] Though see further *post*, pp. 108–109.

[30] T.C.P.A. 1971, s. 9(2).

[31] *Ibid.* s. 9(8). The reasons must still be adequate and intelligible, and deal with the substantive points raised: *Bradley (E.H.) and Sons Ltd.* v. *S.O.S.E. The Times*, August 4, 1982.

[32] *Ibid.* s. 9(7).

The changes are based upon three assumptions.[33] First, that the traditional public inquiry is best suited to an examination of detailed, site based objections, and seldom suitable as a means of examining strategic policy issues. Second, it was thought that detailed objections could now be safely confined to the local plan public inquiries, and that to permit them to be pursued at structure plan level would lead to unnecessary duplication. Third, there was the question of delay. The format of the examination in public is clearly far more readily manageable than that of the inquiry. The selected topics, the sequence of their examination, the time allotted to each and the participants permitted to contribute to each discussion can all be determined in advance and incorporated into a binding programme. The avoidance of delay was clearly the most compelling of the three arguments, for the proposals for the new procedure were introduced at a time when the mammoth G.L.D.P. inquiry was drawing to a close, having consumed some 237 hearing days spread over 22 months in hearing over 28,000 separate objections. The Panel's Report was critical of the public inquiry procedure and welcomed the idea of examinations in public for the future, warning that without the reform " . . . it will be very difficult to avoid an entrenched defensive presentation of a structure plan over a long period against many objectors."[34] By way of contrast to the old public inquiries, the average examination in public has been confined to between three and six weeks. In management terms therefore the procedure has been a great success, but serious doubts exist as to its effectiveness, and as to whether it does offer advantages over the local inquiry as a means of concentrating arguments and of allowing for detailed, searching consideration of objections and alternatives. The reform has deliberately destroyed the former rights of objectors and has diminished their influence upon decision making.

(i) *Selection of issues, Panel and participants*

The *Code* indicates that the examination will not normally be concerned with all the key strategic issues—population, employment, growth constraints, resources and so on—but only with those selected because their treatment in the plan clashes with national or regional policy or with neighbouring local authorities' plans; or where there are internal inconsistencies or substantial and unresolved controversy.[35] An important function of the examination is then clearly that of policy reconciliation and co-ordination as well as airing controversial proposals.

The Panel comprises an independent chairman (in practice commonly a barrister or retired senior civil servant), a planning inspector and a person with "recent experience in a government office in the region."[36] The participants in the examination are selected by the Secretary of State,

---

[33] See further the *Code*, paras. 2.9–2.13.
[34] *Report of the Panel of Inquiry into the G.L.D.P.* (H.M.S.O., 1973), para. 2.16.
[35] *Code*, para. 3.13. A list of selected matters is published promptly following the closing date for objections, and representations invited upon it. A final list is published subsequently: *Code*, paras. 3.34–3.39.
[36] *Ibid.* paras. 3.6–3.9 as amended in 1978. Assessors may also be appointed to the Panel where expert knowledge in a specialist field is essential.

although the chairman has power to invite additional participants. Those selected may not necessarily have objected to the plan. Conversely, the lodging of an objection is no guarantee of an invitation to participate. The Secretary of State has regularly used his power to recruit non-objectors to the examination, and as many as a quarter of the participants have been selected through this route in some cases.[37] The structure planning authority will be represented at all sessions, and other local and statutory authorities will be invited to participate in the discussion of topics of relevance to them, together, where appropriate, with representatives of any government departments affected.[38]

The special position of the Department of Environment is reflected by its representation on the Panel, and also by its practice of privately briefing the Panel before and during the examination on background issues. There is in this latter procedure a distinct risk of prejudicing the Panel's independence, and the members of at least one Panel have declined to become involved in it.[39]

(ii) The conduct of the examination

The procedure is still experimental, and assessments of its value can be little more than tentative at this stage.[40] The examination is in essence a meeting rather than a hearing. Its most marked difference from the public local inquiry lies in the relationship between Panel and participants. The Panel, largely through the chairman, control the proceedings closely. Provision is made for a preliminary meeting of Panel and participants, at which detailed arrangements and procedures can be discussed and finalised.[41] The general submissions of participants will have been submitted in writing in advance, distributed to other participants, and taken as read by the Panel.[42] At the examination itself attention tends therefore to be focused by the Panel upon particular issues by means of introductory statements by the chairman and participants, and through the Panel's questioning of participants. Little initiative is left with participants themselves. In particu-

---

[37] See further J. Dunlop, "Examination in Public of Structure Plans" [1976] J.P.L. 75 at 77; and C. Veilba, *Survey of Those Taking Part in Two Structure Plan Examinations in Public* (University of Birmingham, 1976), Table 2.8, p.11.

[38] *Code,* para. 3.55. The Departments, it seems, are intended to fulfil the passive role of explaining their views on the plan and giving information. But it is a serious criticism that the *Code* makes no provision for the submission in advance of written statements by them, or for questioning: see further L. Bridges, "The Structure Plan Examination in Public" *Urban Law and Policy,* (1979), Vol. 2, 241 at 258.

[39] In the case of the South Yorkshire Plan: see further R. Darke, "Public Participation and State Power: the Case of South Yorkshire" *Policy and Politics,* (1979), Vol. 7, 337 at 343.

[40] There have been a number of studies published of individual examinations, some more highly impressionistic than others, and the comments that follow in the text are based upon a general consensus that appears from them: see, in addition to those referred to in the three preceding footnotes, L. Bridges and C. Veilba, *Structure Plan Examinations in Public: A Descriptive Analysis* (University of Birmingham, 1976) (Staffordshire and Leicestershire); L. Bridges, "The Approval of Structure Plans—the Staffordshire Case" [1978] J.P.L. 599; A. Samuels, "Structure Plan Examination in Public" [1975] J.P.L. 125 (South Hampshire) and W. Hampton and R. Walker, "The Teeside/Cleveland Examination in Public" in *Local Government Studies* (N.S.) (1976), Vol. 2, p.27.

[41] *Code,* para. 3.42.

[42] *Ibid.* para. 3.51.

lar, there is no power to cross-examine other participants. The procedure militates indeed against any interaction between participants. Disputes between the views of experts over technical issues, such as forecasts and reliability of survey data, are expected to be resolved instead by private side-room or lunch-time discussions.[43] Legal representation is neither encouraged nor discouraged, but it is a tacit assumption that it is unnecessary because of the lack of opportunity for any display of forensic skills. McAuslan argues convincingly that the balance has shifted, not in favour of participation, but in favour of the administrative machine:

> "The impression is given that what is aimed for is a high-level graduate seminar in which all the students are equal in status and ability and the tutors are paragons of all educational qualities. In practice, reality is different. Formality and rules aided the property-owner and his principle [sic] professional adviser, the lawyer; informality and lack of rules aids the planner and the public authority, participators losing out each time."[44]

It has proved a common complaint that using discussion rather than questioning as the basic procedure has led to superficiality of treatment of the issues; that participants have been too readily able to avoid being drawn on the legitimate arguments raised by other participants, and have been able to hide behind technical jargon and unexamined assumptions. These are defects which weaken the suitability of the examination as a vehicle for public participation except through well-equipped groups, and this has already created difficulties when more general public opinion has come to be expressed once the approved policies have filtered down to local plan and development control level. But policy making at this level is certainly not a quasi-judicial process; if anything, it is quasi-legislative, and the adoption of a model based on discussion and debate recognises this distinction. At the same time, however, the examination falls short of the standards of other similar legislative models, particularly the Select Committees of the House of Commons, because there is no overall independence in the Panel and no general willingness to undertake, or to allow to be undertaken, any vigorous inquisition of participants.

(c) The Panel's Report

The Report of the Panel is made to the Secretary of State. As a matter of practice it is not published until preliminary decisions have been made on the plan, and its publication normally coincides with the publication by the Secretary of State of his proposed modifications to the plan. In form, the Reports have tended to adopt the subject arrangement of the examination itself, and have presented a summary of each discussion followed by the Panel's conclusions and recommendations. They are generally brief, particularly in comparison with Inspectors' reports on the old style plans.

The Report is not binding upon the Secretary of State, and Panels' recommendations have been rejected by him in many instances. Further, the

---

[43] *Ibid.* para. 3.56.
[44] *The Ideologies of Planning Law* (Pergamon Press, 1980), pp. 42–43.

Report, though not the examination itself, is non-statutory. Its recommendations are therefore persuasive only, and although as a matter of law it is at least impliedly incumbent upon the Secretary of State to consider them, given that the examination is a requisite stage in the approval process, no reasons need be given for their rejection. The Secretary of State's decision may, indeed, be based upon issues neither canvassed at the examination nor included in the Panel's Report. There is an assurance in the *Code*, however, that new information likely to influence such a decision will first normally be published and an opportunity provided for written comments to be made.[45] The requirement that any proposed modifications to the plan be published first in draft form allows some further consideration in some cases, though not in cases where the Secretary of State's decision has been to reject amendments put forward by the Panel and to uphold the plan.

(d) Reservations and modifications

The Secretary of State may decide, in light of the Panel's report, to reject the plan.[46] Such a course is highly unlikely at this stage. Fundamental defects in a plan will normally have been apparent much earlier, and less significant defects may be overcome through modifications. Alternatively, the Secretary of State may approve the plan unconditionally. That course is theoretically less unlikely, but it has yet to occur in practice. The normal course is for approval to be subject to modifications or reservations by the Secretary of State, or for a plan to be approved "in part," and these alternative courses require further explanation.

(i) *Reservations*

The Act fails to define the scope of "reservations," but in practice the power has been interpreted as allowing the Secretary of State to reserve his approval of some part of the plan when approving the rest. The consequence is that those provisions remain unapproved, but not rejected. This may occur, for example, where there are issues which are unlikely to be resolved within a reasonable time, and are delaying approval of the plan as a whole. The normal course has been to accompany the decision with a direction to the planning authority to submit fresh proposals in respect of the reserved matters.[47] These then constitute a proposed alteration to the approved plan, and are required to be processed again through the plan preparation procedures.[48] In approving the structure plan for Stoke-on-Trent, for example, the Secretary of State directed that fresh proposals on transportation should be submitted to him within two years of approval of the plan.[49] But there are obvious problems in following such a course. It cuts across the

---

[45] *Ibid.* para. 3.59.
[46] The general powers of the Secretary of State, as provided by T.C.P.A. 1971, s. 9(1), are simply to " ... approve it (in whole or in part and with or without modifications or reservations) or reject it."
[47] See further D.O.E. Circular 4/79, *Memorandum*, para. 2.70.
[48] See further, *post* p. 112.
[49] *Notice of Approval*, April 11, 1978, para. 9.4.

basic structure planning concept of devising a coherent, interlocking strategy for the whole plan area, and may lead to substantial further delay in plan approval.[50] It also leaves the "reserved" policies in an ambiguous state. They have not been rejected, and may continue to be used as a guide in development control pending preparation and submission of fresh proposals, particularly in the rejection of potentially conflicting development proposals.

(ii) *Approval in part*

Approval of a plan in part implies rejection of the remainder, unless it is the subject of a reservation or modification. Rejected policies clearly lack even informal status for the purposes of development control.

(iii) *Modifications*

The power to modify submitted plans has been widely used. Unlike the above two courses, it is governed by a special procedure. Except where he is satisfied that a modification will not materially affect the content of the plan, the Secretary of State is required first to notify the planning authority of his proposed modifications, and copies are then required to be served by them on such persons as the Secretary of State may direct.[51] There is power to lodge objections to the proposals (not limited to persons who may have been served with copies); and all duly made objections must be considered.[52] In many cases modifications have been suggested to the Panel conducting the examination in public by the planning authority as a means of overcoming objections and may have been discussed and generally agreed by the participants. But in other instances the reaction to the proposals may be such as to warrant the re-convening of the examination; and this would clearly be appropriate where the modifications included new proposals which had not been subject to public participation. There is no legal obligation to re-open, however, and the Secretary of State may instead seek to obtain a comprehensive picture of official and public opinion using his broad consultative powers under section 9(7).

The effect of the objections received by the Secretary of State may be to persuade him not to proceed with one or more of his proposed modifications. In that case he may proceed directly to approval of the plan; and similarly if he decides to proceed with his proposed modifications. If, however, he seeks to amend his proposed modifications, it will be necessary for the new proposals in turn to be published, and for objections to them to be considered. The effect of the Regulations is that no modifications may be made, apart from those deemed immaterial, unless they have first been notified under the prescribed procedures.[53]

---

[50] These points are illustrated by Bridges in the context of the Staffordshire plan: [1978] J.P.L. 599.

[51] Plans Regulations 1982, reg. 21.

[52] *Ibid.* reg. 21(1)(a).

[53] Second sets of modifications have been issued on a few occasions, including both the Peak District National Park Plan, and the Derbyshire Structure Plan, where the first proposed modifications drew a hostile response.

The scope of the power to make modifications has proved particularly controversial in practice. It has been used in practically every instance for some straightforward and some technical purposes: to ensure that policies and proposals are clearly distinguished in the plan from the remaining material, for example, to delete non-structural and detailed matters, and to reduce the rigidity of proposed policies by inserting expressions such as "normally" and "except in exceptional circumstances." More importantly, perhaps, the power has been used for a range of substantive purposes, such as to keep plans within the regional strategy and to revise controversial policies.

In the past the Secretary of State has taken a particularly narrow view of the scope of the power, insisting that it should be exercised only in respect of formal policies, general proposals and the key diagram. The remaining contents of the plan including the written justification have been regarded as outside the modification power. In practice it has led to absurd results, including a refusal to modify a chapter of the Staffordshire Plan setting out the regional context, notwithstanding that it was based on out-of-date material; and similarly, in the case of the Suffolk Structure Plan, a refusal to modify the reasoned justification for policies whilst modifying the policies themselves. Approved plans may therefore contain conflicting and illogical material: a table of figures may remain after the policies they supported have been deleted, or cross-references may be lost altogether. It is difficult to imagine that so strained an interpretation could have been correct under the Act as it stood, but it is confirmed by the 1980 amendments which divorce the written justification (now the explanatory memorandum) from the plan. This change at least avoids for the future the confusion that has arisen in the past when the modification power has been exercised so as to reduce submitted policies and general proposals to the status of "written justification material," thereby consigning them to an ambiguous policy limbo. The explanatory memorandum is now outside the Secretary of State's purview, and may presumably be subsequently amended by the planning authority if necessary so as to accord with the structure plan as approved.

(e) Plan approval and effect

The formal Notice of Approval of the plan is normally communicated by letter to the plan authority. The Notice, together with its modifications and reservations, in effect becomes part of the plan: the Act requires that the plan and the Notice be read together.[54] Legal challenge to the plan is confined to proceedings commenced within a six week period running from the date of publication of the Notice of Approval,[55] and thus provision is normally made in the Notice[56] to bring the plan formally into operation at the end of that period. In the past this has had to be achieved by the promulgation of two statutory instruments in each case, one to substitute the new plan as the statutory "development plan" for the purposes of the planning and

---

[54] T.C.P.A. 1971, s.20(1).
[55] *Ibid.* s. 242. See further, *post*, p. 133.
[56] Pursuant to T.C.P.A. 1971, s. 18(4).

highways Acts and for land valuation, and the second to repeal the transitional provisions of the 1971 Act which had retained power to make and amend old style plans. The procedure has been streamlined by the 1980 Act, and the changes mentioned above now occur automatically upon the date of coming into operation of the new plan.[57] The consequence is that thereafter the phrase "development plan" for the purpose of planning and associated legislation becomes the structure plan read together with the old style development plan. In case of conflict, the provisions of the structure plan prevail.[58] The old plan continues in force in this supplementary role until supplanted by approved local plans, when it will cease to have effect except to the extent that the Secretary of State may direct.[59] Once the structure plan for an area has become operative any amendment, or repeal and replacement, simply becomes operative on the date provided in the Notice of Approval, and no consequential amendments are necessary.

4. *Alteration and replacement of structure plans*

Continuity is an essential legal requirement of a statutory plan because of the variety of functions required of it. For this reason the legislation originally provided that approved structure plans should be unrepealable. Policy change, no matter how fundamental, was to be achieved through formal alteration of the plan rather than through its repeal and replacement. The 1980 Bill initially offered a narrow exception to the rule by allowing authorities to repeal a number of part-area plans and consolidate their policies in a single replacement structure plan, but the provision was subsequently broadened to allow complete repeal and replacement of any structure plan.[60] The legislation leaves to planning authorities' discretion the frequency and need for plan alteration and replacement, abandoning the idea of quinquennial review which was required in the case of old style development plans. Informally, however, five years is retained as a general guide to the timing of plan review, though more frequent submission of alterations is encouraged where necessary[61] and there is in any event a duty to review the plan and submit any necessary alterations to accommodate the designation or modification of an enterprise zone.[62] In the case of a joint

---

[57] T.C.P.A. 1971, s. 21(1) as inserted by L.G.P.L.A. 1980, Sched. 14, para. 12: the effect of the provisions is that s. 20 and para. 1 of Sched. 23 to the 1971 Act come into operation in the plan area (redefining the development plan); and Sched. 6 and Part I of Sched. 5 (transitional old style plan provisions) cease to have effect.

[58] *Ibid.* Sched. 7, para. 3 (as inserted by L.G.P.L.A. 1980, Sched. 14, para. 14).

[59] Under T.C.P.A. 1971, Sched. 7, paras. 5A, 5B and 5C (added by L.G.P.L.A. 1980, Sched. 14, para. 15(1)).

[60] T.C.P.A. 1971, s. 10(2) as substituted by L.G.P.L.A. 1980, Sched. 14, para. 5.

[61] D.O.E. Circular 4/79, *Memorandum*, para. 2.4. It is predictable that pressure for alterations will often come from the districts, who are obliged to ensure that their local plans generally conform to the structure plan and will normally therefore need to have the structure plan altered before they can take any fresh initiative at local plan level, although new expedited procedures now allow the two to be processed simultaneously in certain cases: see further *post*, p. 120. More recent advice from the Department, in D.O.E. Circular 23/81, para. 7 has urged that unnecessary work be eliminated and that alterations be confined to occasions where they are clearly necessary.

[62] L.G.P.L.A. 1980, Sched. 32, para. 23; and see as to enterprise zones generally, *post*, p. 544.

plan any of the authorities by whom it was prepared may submit proposals for alterations affecting their area[63]; and in every case there is a reserve power for the Secretary of State to require proposals to be submitted.[64] There is a continuing statutory duty to keep "under review" the matters included in the report of survey,[65] which implies a monitoring programme but leaves its scope to the authority.[66]

The Act requires that proposals for the alteration of structure plans should follow the same approval procedures as the plans themselves. The publicity provisions of section 8 of the Act apply equally, and the submitted proposals need also to be accompanied by an explanatory memorandum summarising the authority's reasons justifying the proposed alterations or justifying the repeal and replacement.[67] Similarly, the Secretary of State is bound to follow the same approval procedure, but with the important exception that there is no obligation to hold an examination in public where he is satisfied that no matters requiring one arise from the proposed alterations or replacement structure plan.[68] The 1980 Act has made special provision for a problem which had apparently not been foreseen earlier, which is that policy changes made to the structure plan will in turn affect local plans for the area. A local plan which formerly complied with the structure plan may no longer do so once an alteration has been approved. It is now the duty of the structure plan authority upon approval to review the existing local plans and to draw up a list of those which do, and those which do not, any longer comply generally with structure plan policy.[69] In the event of any policy conflict, only the provisions of local plans in the first list will prevail over structure plan policy, and those in the second list will be subordinate to the structure plan.[70]

The provisions of an approved structure plan may be overridden in individual development control decisions, provided the appropriate consultation and "departure"[71] procedures are complied with, where necessary, since the plan is designed as a guide rather than a rule-book for decisions. It will often therefore be a matter of judgement for an authority and for the Secretary of State whether to sanction an application as a departure from the plan, or to insist that the plan should first be altered. The latter procedure is better suited to substantial and controversial projects (and for this reason it might be expected that the power to dispense with an examination in public would rarely be used), but the former procedure may be dictated even in

---

[3] L.G.A. 1972, Sched. 16, para. 9(1) as inserted by L.G.P.L.A. 1980, Sched. 14, para. 17.
[4] T.C.P.A. 1971, s. 10(1).
[5] T.C.P.A. 1971, s. 6(1).
[6] See further D.O.E. Circular 4/79, *Memorandum*, para. 2.4. Many of the approved plans set out details of the authority's proposed monitoring exercise.
[7] T.C.P.A. 1971, s. 10(4), added by L.G.P.L.A. 1980, Sched. 14, para. 5. The explanatory memorandum in each case is required also to state the relationship of the proposals to relevant proposals for land in neighbouring areas (s. 10(5)), to contain any information on which the proposals are based, and it may contain such illustrative material as the authority think appropriate (s. 10(6)).
[8] *Ibid.* s. 10(8), added by L.G.P.L.A. 1980, Sched. 14, para. 5.
[9] T.C.P.A. 1971, s. 15B (inserted by L.G.P.L.A. 1980, s. 88(1)).
[0] *Ibid.* s. 14(8), added by L.G.P.L.A. 1980, Sched. 14, para. 10(*d*).
[1] *Post*, pp. 221, 233.

controversial cases by considerations of urgency. At least the power of the
Secretary of State to call in a departure application means that in cases where
the power is exercised comparable central government supervision exists, the
major distinction being that the issues will then be aired at a public local
inquiry rather than an examination in public.

5. *Structure planning: an interim assessment*

Even after more than a decade of experience in structure planning it is
difficult to offer a balanced assessment of what has been achieved. Partly this
is due to the delays that have occurred in plan preparation and approval,
perhaps the most conspicuous shortcoming of the reformed system, which
have meant that approved plans have yet to have any substantial impact.
Delay in plan preparation by the county authorities is a product not simply
of local government reform, which did indeed hold back structure plan
programmes, but also of a lack of commitment on the part of many of the
authorities to the idea of the new plans. Structure plans were widely seen as
strategies for growth, and counties anticipating low growth accordingly gave
them low priority. Local government reform also often led to new conflicts
in plan preparation between the interests of the new districts and the county,
which increased the time needed for consultation and negotiation. Public
participation programmes, too, have proved time consuming, particularly
where they have succeeded in engaging public interest but failed in satisfying
it.

But for many years the most spectacular delays occurred in the processes
of central government scrutiny. The visible parts of that process, the
examination in public and the publication of draft modifications, were
regularly completed within brief periods of time; but the secret processes of
central government that preceded and followed those steps too often spread
over several years, with a paralysing effect on policy. It is true that the
incoming Government in 1979 was able to achieve a more rapid turnover of
plans, but the image of dilatoriness has proved difficult to dispel, and is
likely to inhibit authorities from submitting the range of alterations that will
be necessary to maintain the plans as contemporary documents. Even high
level strategic planning cannot hope to retain validity over a lengthy period.

Perhaps no accurate assessment of structure planning can be attempted
until the new plans have been fully tested, in terms both of their internal
flexibility and the ease with which alterations can be made, and of their
impact upon the local planning decisions through which they will be
implemented. But experience already has led to the widespread impression
that the whole concept of structure planning is of tenuous validity,
particularly in an era of low growth; and, more significantly perhaps, that
whatever validity it did have has been destroyed by the complexity of the
rules and regulations confining the planning authorities' flexibility and
discretion in plan preparation. The end product of the 1968 reforms has been
an unnecessarily cumbersome forward planning structure, in which neither
central government involvement nor obsession with detail have been
substantially diminished. The institutional problems of the old-style
plans—and, before them, the planning schemes—have not been overcome.
The technical quality of the plans, particularly the early plans, was not high,
and the strategic framework established by them has not fully succeeded in

providing a positive, forward looking basis for local planning. The role of structure plans has now been diminished for development control purposes by the 1980 Act's conferment of greater autonomy on district councils, and effective non-statutory supplementation can no longer be made to bind district planning authorities.[72]

The reality of structure planning has failed to match the early rhetoric. The plans have achieved some co-ordination of public sector policy but have not provided the firm lead that had been promised. Attempts to advance the role of the structure plan as an overall corporate, or even inter-corporate plan, have failed because of the different planning timescales for different public sector activities, and particularly the uncertainty in recent years of long term investment planning. Implementing a growth area strategy, for example, is still more closely dependent upon the scale of the water authority's annual capital programme than phasing provisions of the plan. The new procedures have failed to speed up forward planning, and the experience of the past twelve years must cause serious questioning of the viability of long term strategic planning given the present institutional constraints.

On the merit side, the introduction of structure planning has at least initiated a serious examination of planning strategy in county areas, and has provided the first opportunity for any comprehensive review and public debate that has been enjoyed in some counties for many years. This is no insignificant achievement. It has prompted a re-examination of received assumptions, and a reformulation of policies. Further, whilst there has been widespread criticism of the means prescribed for structure plan preparation and of the general concept of structure planning, there is no denying the importance of the approved plans themselves, and the significance for the areas concerned of the decisions taken in the plans. Shortcomings in the medium do not necessarily affect the seriousness and the implications of the decisions involved, even although events in the real world have led to a scaling down of many of the early plans' growth proposals. Some policies, including those of constraint and conservation, are more enduring and the choices made at structure plan level in the pursuit of these objectives may be expected to have long term effect.

C. Local Plans

1. *Introduction*

Local plans are the workhorses of the reformed planning system. They are statutory plans, intended to develop and refine the policies of the structure plan, and to elaborate in detail how they will relate to individual areas and sites. In terms of both content and purpose, then, they bear a resemblance to the old style development plans. They provide a detailed basis for development control and for the co-ordination of development and other land use. But they are prepared on a more selective basis than the comprehensive coverage of county areas that was required of the old plans.

---

[72] *Post*, p. 223.

The main documents are a proposals map (on an ordnance survey base) and a written statement. It is not a zoning system as such, but more a mix of general policies for the whole area, and specific proposals confined to identified areas of land. The plans include land allocations for future development and indicate the criteria against which applications for planning permission will be assessed.

The most important features distinguishing the new local plans from the old system are that authorities have discretion as to the type and scope of plan to prepare, and that there is only limited central government supervision. For the most part the local planning authorities, including both county and district councils, prepare the plans, invite participation, consider objections and adopt the plans themselves. Safeguards against erratic conduct exist in the form of a "calling in" power vested in the Secretary of State, a requirement that the plan should conform generally with the structure plan for the area, and a requirement that objections to the plan should be heard by an independent inspector at a public local inquiry.

2. Types of local plan

The 1974 Plans Regulations provided for three types of local plan, and although the 1982 Regulations are not as specific, it is likely that the three main models will continue. The procedures for the preparation of each are the same, but their intended functions are different.

(a) District plans:

District plans are general plans, in the sense that they are based upon a "comprehensive consideration of matters affecting the development and other use of land"[73] in the plan area. They thus most closely resemble the old style plans.

(b) Action area plans

These are prepared in respect of areas selected for a programme of development, redevelopment or improvement. The areas had formerly to be first identified in the structure plan, but following the 1980 Act planning authorities are free to make their own selection. They are comprehensive plans, but for comparatively small areas, and in a sense they are the reincarnation of the old comprehensive development areas, although with the added benefit of being largely free from ministerial supervision and subject to slightly more stringent timing requirements. It was formerly a precondition for the identification of an action area that the *commencement* of a programme of comprehensive treatment, in accordance with an action area plan, should occur within 10 years of the submission of the structure plan, but now the time limit is 10 years from the date of the placing on deposit of the action area plan itself.[74] No attempt has been made to

---

[73] Plans Regulations 1974, reg. 15(1).
[74] Plans Regulations 1982, reg. 14. General advice on the selection of areas for action area treatment is contained in D.O.E. Circular 4/79, *Memorandum*, paras. 2.31–2.35.

prescribe a period in which the treatment must be *completed*, although the adequacy of resources to carry through the programme will clearly be a central issue in plan preparation and approval. A major advantage of using an action area plan in preference to a district plan lies in its implications for land valuation for public sector acquisitions. The valuation rules allow any increase in value in the area attributable to the programme of development or redevelopment itself to be ignored.[75]

(c) Subject plans

Subject plans deal with selected issues and are thus not comprehensive. It is to be expected that they will frequently be prepared either by counties or jointly by district authorities, to examine subjects of more than purely local concern, such as recreation policies, mineral extraction or green belts.

3. *Development plan schemes*

The general presumption is that preparation of local plans should be the function of district planning authorities.[76] But the counties also have local planning powers, and thus it is necessary for some co-ordination between the two tiers. Outside London this is achieved through the medium of a development plan scheme, prepared by the county in consultation with the district authorities,[77] which is in essence a plans programme. The scheme is a statutory document, and its contents may be amended by the Secretary of State if a district authority make representations that they are dissatisfied with the county's proposals.[78] The scheme contains a description of the title, nature, area and scope of each proposed local plan, and provides a programme for their preparation. Some may be prepared solely by a district or solely by the county; others may be the subject of joint arrangements.[79] The county may retain a reserve power, and indeed this may be included in the structure plan itself.[80] There is a duty to keep the scheme under review and to amend it if the county think fit.[81] In practice, an annual review has become common in order, too often, to cope with unexpected delays (or "slippage") in plan preparation and approval. There has also been a drastic reduction in the numbers of proposed plans, from the 3,500[82] or more anticipated in the first round of English development plan schemes proposed to start by 1980, to a more realistic estimate of 1,650 by 1979.[83] There are no

---

[75] By reason of Land Compensation Act 1961, s.6 and Sched. 1 (as amended by T.C.P.A. 1971, s.291 and Sched. 23, Part I).

[76] T.C.P.A. 1971, s.10C(1); except in the national parks, where the local planning function is with the county: L.G.A. 1972, s.182(4).

[77] *Ibid.* s. 10C(2).

[78] *Ibid.* s. 100(6), as amended by L.G.P.L.A. 1980, Sched. 14, para. 6.

[79] The special procedures for joint local planning are prescribed by L.G.A. 1972, Sched. 16, paras. 10–14; and for London see also T.C.P.A. 1971, Sched. 4, para. 7A.

[80] *Ibid.* s. 10C(5).

[81] *Ibid.* s. 10C(2).

[82] R. Mabey and L. Craig, "Development Plan Schemes" *The Planner* 1976, p.70.

[83] [1980] J.P.L. 361. Of these, the schemes envisaged that 130 would be action area plans, 200 subject plans and the remaining 1,320 district plans.

statutory time requirements. Authorities are free to concentrate upon priority areas and are under no obligation to prepare plans for all of their area. They must, however, "consider and thereafter keep under review"[84] the desirability of preparing a local plan. Curiously, as soon as they consider it "desirable" to do so, they become subject to a statutory duty to prepare the desired plan.[85]

In London the allocation of responsibility is slightly different. The boroughs have the function of preparing all local plans, except in respect of any action area identified in the G.L.D.P. as a "G.L.C. action area."[86]

4. Local plan preparation

The procedures for local plan preparation closely resemble those for structure plans. There are the same two main phases, of preparation and approval. Whilst each will be examined in more detail in the following pages, it is convenient first to summarise them here.

Preparation of a local plan need not await structure plan approval. It may be commenced at any time, though since it will be necessary to ensure that the plan will conform generally to the structure plan (or to any proposed alterations to it) there is a limit to what can be done in advance. There is no obligation to conduct a fresh survey, though the authority may find it necessary to do so to supplement the structure plan survey.[87] When the policies and proposals have been prepared, they must be publicised and an opportunity provided for the making of representations by the public.

The second phase is deliberately more formal. It commences when the draft plan is placed on deposit; that is, when copies are made available for inspection by and sale to members of the public, and a copy is forwarded to the Secretary of State. Until the Act of 1980 this phase could not normally commence until the structure plan had been approved, but earlier deposit is now possible. A period follows in which objections may be lodged to the plan, and representations made in support of it. The authority may be able to overcome objections by negotiation, but if any remain outstanding there must be a public local inquiry. The Inspector reports, not to the Secretary of State but to the authority themselves. Should they decide in light of his report to modify the plan, their modifications must first be advertised and comment invited. Following the consideration of any further objections the plan may be adopted, with or without modification. It then assumes the status of being part of the statutory development plan.

Full responsibility for local planning therefore rests with the authority themselves, subject to the requirement of structure plan conformity (considered further below); and subject also to the general vigilance maintained by the Secretary of State who retains power to call in a local plan for his own decision.

---

[84] T.C.P.A. 1971, s. 11(2).
[85] Ibid.
[86] T.C.P.A. 1971, Sched. 4, para. 8.
[87] Ibid. s. 11(9A).

5. *The structure plan framework*

It is a key concept in the two tier planning system that local plans should conform with the policies and proposals of the structure plan for the area. The primary purpose of local plans is to crystallize and refine the selected strategies, and to offer a detailed local interpretation of the broad policies so as to act "as a positive brief for developers, public and private, setting the standards and objectives for future development."[88] These purposes have always been clear enough, but they have had to be specifically underpinned in the legislation in order to maintain the hierarchy in the face of very real pressures in practice. There has been a need to bind district councils to the discipline of their county's structure plan, as well as to bind the counties to their own plans and to any modifications introduced by the Secretary of State.

The legislation therefore requires "general conformity" between local plans and structure plans, and insists that the authority should ensure that their local plan so conforms, both when they are formulating proposals[89] and when they come to adopt the plan.[90] "General conformity" is an admittedly vague test, and there is room for a high degree of subjectivity in its application. A broad interpretation is hinted at by the government's advice that the phrase should be interpreted as embracing "does not conflict with" the structure plan.[91] Where the plan is prepared by the county authority, they are the sole judges of general conformity, subject to the Secretary of State's calling-in power.[92] But in the case of district councils, the plan must be submitted to the county for certification as being in general conformity to the structure plan, before it may be placed upon deposit.[93] The certificate must be issued within one month of the district's request for a certificate (or such longer period as may have been agreed), or the matter referred to the Secretary of State for determination.[94] That, in the view of the Secretary of State, should be a procedure of the last resort.[95]

"General conformity," as the legislation was originally cast, was always to be measured in terms of the approved structure plan. An authority could proceed with the preparation of a local plan whilst the structure plan was still unapproved, but they could not initiate the second phase by placing the local plan on deposit until the structure plan had final approval. That requirement proved too rigid, and it became clear, particularly in the inner cities, that delay in structure plan approval was causing unnecessary uncertainty and delay in local planning. Authorities could, of course,

---

[88] *The Future of Development Plans* (H.M.S.O., 1965), para. 5.3.
[89] T.C.P.A. 1971, s. 11(9).
[90] *Ibid.* s. 14(2).
[91] D.O.E. Circular 4/79, *Memorandum*, para. 3.62.
[92] Under T.C.P.A. 1971, s. 14(6), which allows the Secretary of State, by direction to the county, to reserve the question of conformity in any case for his own determination.
[93] T.C.P.A. 1971, ss. 12(2) and 14(2),(5) and (7).
[94] *Ibid.* s. 14(5).
[95] D.O.E. Circular 4/79, *Memorandum*, para. 3.62. The emphasis in official advice is on conciliation and agreement, and there is a suggestion in the *Memorandum* that non-statutory development plan briefs, prepared by the county and explaining the thinking behind structure plan policies, might ease co-ordination: para. 3.29.

prepare their local plans and use them on a non-statutory basis whilst awaiting the structure plan decision, but their status remained uncertain.

The 1980 Act therefore extended to all authorities the power, which had already been given to Scottish[96] and to inner city English and Welsh authorities,[97] to adopt local plans in advance of structure plan approval.[98] A direction must first be made by the Secretary of State, and there is still a requirement of general conformity with the unapproved structure plan: before adopting the local plan the authority must make such modifications as may be necessary to make it conform to the structure plan as it stands for the time being.[99] There is no need for a district authority to obtain a certificate of conformity from the county, and enforcement is instead exercisable through the Secretary of State's calling-in power.

The new provisions come too late for the majority of authorities, given that the bulk of structure plans have now been approved. But they extend also to unapproved alterations to structure plans, and it is here that they will play a significant part in the future. The general rule remains that the Secretary of State's approval of alterations is a precondition to the placing on deposit of a local plan, or an alteration to a local plan, intended to carry through the structure plan alteration. But the Secretary of State may now direct that the local plan should proceed as if the structure plan alterations had been approved by him, provided there is general conformity between the two.[1] And he may ensure that conformity when making the direction, by requiring modifications to be made to the local plan to bring it into line.[2] But the apparent inability to use that modification power at any time other than when the original direction is given means that its use in practice must be limited to cases where the proposed alterations have received general approval, or where no changes are expected which would cut across the local plan.

The two-tier hierarchy of forward planning, though pure in concept, has cast up a great many problems in practice. Of particular significance has been the conflict between the need to continue to secure general conformity with the structure plan, and the need to have regard to public objections and representations to the local plan which may, directly or indirectly, be opposed to the structure plan strategy. The structure plan *Code of Procedure* offers reassurances that objections which straddle structure plans and local plans and which are lodged at structure plan level will be carefully handled,[3] but no corresponding provision is made at local plan level. Such objections may validly be made, and the Inspector and the authority must consider them. They may find room for movement within the structure plan

---

[96] Town and Country Planning (Scotland) Act 1977, s.2.
[97] Inner Urban Areas Act 1978, s. 12 (which is superseded by the new provisions: L.G.P.L.A. 1980, s. 64(3)).
[98] T.C.P.A. 1971, s. 15A, as inserted by L.G.P.L.A. 1980, s. 88.
[99] *Ibid.* s. 15A(5).
[1] *Ibid.* s. 15A(6) and (7).
[2] *Ibid.* s. 15A(8). Subs. (7) imposes a duty upon the Secretary of State to consult every planning authority affected before making any direction under the section.
[3] *Code*, paras. 4.5—4.11.

framework, or an opportunity for compromise through the scaling down of development proposals. For example, in his report on the Fareham Western Wards Action Area Plan in 1978, the Inspector, observing that objectors had attacked the structure plan growth proposals "with verve and ingenuity" held that the *issue* of growth could not be challenged because of its structure plan basis, but that the *rate and scale* of growth might be reviewed. He took the view that the exact figures of houses and jobs, and the timing envisaged in the structure plan did not need to be incorporated into the action area plan.[4] He recommended a reduction by one-third of the proposed number of houses, on the grounds that this would meet many objections, cause less local disruption and allow for adequate infrastructure to be provided.[5]

That report does not, of course, constitute a binding precedent, but it does highlight the scope which exists for a review of strategic issues at local plan level. The Inspector's interpretation of the structure plan's flexibility does not, however, bind the local planning authority, who remain under the duty to secure general conformity as at the time of adoption; and Inspectors have been instructed to seek to ensure that their recommendations could be implemented without disturbing the general conformity of the plan with the structure plan.[6]

6. *The first phase: preparation of the plan*

A local plan comprises a written statement and a proposals map.[7] The written statement contains proposals (but not, significantly, policies) for the development and other use of land in the plan area,[8] and these are required to be set out as to be readily distinguishable from the other contents of the plan.[9] The written statement is required also to include a reasoned justification for the proposals,[10] but the Regulations no longer require that it should contain such indication as the authority think appropriate of a range of matters, which formerly included *inter alia,* social policies and considerations, likely available resources for implementation and development control criteria.[11] Finally, the Secretary of State has suggested[12] that the statement should include a short introductory guide to the plan, with any necessary indexing and listing of contents, as well as of the accompanying diagrams, illustrations and descriptive matter which, unlike the new explanatory memorandum for structure plans, legally form part of the plan.[13]

Consultation with other public authorities for the area is mandatory, but

[4] *Report of Public Inquiry into Objections,* February 1978 (Hampshire C.C.), p.11.
[5] *Ibid.* p. 12.
[6] D.O.E. Circular 4/79, *Memorandum,* para. 3.73.
[7] T.C.P.A. 1971, s. 11(3).
[8] *Ibid.* s. 11(3)(*a*), which also makes provision for plans containing proposals for "any description of development or other use of land," thus authorising subject plans. As with structure planning, the formula includes "such measures as the authority think fit for the improvement of the physical environment and the management of traffic."
[9] Plans Regulations 1982, reg. 12(1).
[10] Plans Regulations 1982, reg. 12(2).
[11] It is anticipated that advice will instead be offered by way of circular.
[12] D.O.E. Circular 4/79, *Memorandum,* para. 3.42.
[13] T.C.P.A. 1971, s. 11(5). The proposals map is required to be on an Ordnance Survey base: Plans Regulations 1982, reg. 13(1).

there is no specified stage in the preparation process when it must occur. The intention is that it should be a continuing process as the plan proposals are pieced together.

Public participation is more formalised, however, although it is open to an authority to conduct a continuing participative programme and it is likely that many local plans because of their specificity will excite and promote extensive participation. Proposals for radical change at a detailed level can be expected to lead to hostility and conflict and it may be tempting for authorities to resort to extensive public relations programmes to ease their progress. So far as the legislation is concerned, the requirement is that the authority should, during this phase, publicise their proposals together with any relevant survey material, and make people aware of their opportunity to make representations, for which an "adequate opportunity" must be allowed.[14] But the Department envisage that this should occur at a comparatively late stage in plan preparation, that is, when they have prepared all their proposals for development and other use of land.[15] They may indicate alternative choices for public comment, but are advised to indicate their own preference. Where they decide to change the plan, they are expected to undertake further participation only where the changes are substantial or controversial.[16] There will still be an opportunity for formal objections to be made and considered during the plan approval process.

Authorities have, within that statutory framework, broad discretion as to how they run their participation programmes. They are obliged to inform the Secretary of State of the steps they have taken under the Act,[17] and if he is not satisfied of their adequacy he may require that adoption should not proceed until further action has been taken.[18] The scope and style of effective participation are, however, without definition; as with structure planning, there are no agreed criteria by which effectiveness itself may be measured.[19] All is dependent upon the lessons learned from experience, upon the enthusiasm of the authority themselves, and upon the level of response they may be able to achieve.

7. Phase two: deposited plans, objections and representations

The approval phase is initiated by the placing of the plan on deposit for public inspection.[20] Copies of the plan are also forwarded to the Secretary of State (together with the public participation statement) and to the other relevant planning authority for the plan area.[21] Each deposited copy must be accompanied by a statement of the time within which objections may be made, which must be six weeks.[22] As with structure plans, representations in

---

[14] *Ibid.* s. 12(1).
[15] D.O.E. Circular 4/79, *Memorandum*, para. 3.50.
[16] *Ibid.*
[17] T.C.P.A. 1971, s. 12(3).
[18] *Ibid.* s. 12(4) and (5).
[19] But see, for an intelligent discussion of the issues, S. Loew, *Local Planning* (Pembridge Press, 1979), Chap. 4; and M.J. Bruton, "Public Participation, Local Planning and Conflicts of Interest" (1980) 8 *Policy and Politics* 423.
[20] T.C.P.A. 1971, s. 12(2).
[21] *Ibid.* s. 12(2).
[22] Plans Regulations 1982, Sched., Form 7.

support of the plan are also encouraged, though there is no statutory basis for these.[23] There is thus no formal duty to consider representations, and the Inspector has discretion whether to permit representations to be pursued at the inquiry.

8. Consideration of objections: the public local inquiry

All objections which have been made within the prescribed time must be "considered" by the authority,[24] except where they relate to action proposed to be taken under other prescribed legislation, such as schemes under the Highways Act 1980 or the New Towns Act 1981.[25] There are no other restrictions upon either the content or the form of objections (although a standard form for objections is recommended in the relevant circular),[26] and it is thus not competent for an authority unilaterally to reject an objection on the grounds, for example, of its irrelevance or capriciousness unless it could not be said to be an objection to the plan at all. It is, however, an opportunity to object to the plan itself, and thus offers only a limited means of introducing alternatives to the plan's proposals. Alternative proposals will be considered at an inquiry only insofar as they may relate to a possible modification of the plan.[27]

One of the purposes of the reform of the forward planning system was to confer greater autonomy on local planning authorities, and to allow them the power not only to prepare local plans but also to approve them. But there is a clear conflict of interest inherent in a scheme which allows them to be the sole judge of the merits of objections to their own plan, and adequate safeguards against unfair and arbitrary conduct have had to be devised. The Secretary of State's power to call in a plan for his own decision is one, and it is likely to be used most often in instances of sharp conflict and substantial controversy.[28] But in most cases the most significant safeguard is that, for the purpose of considering validly made objections, the authority are required to arrange for the holding of a public local inquiry.[29] Objections may of course be resolved without recourse to inquiry, by negotiation and compromise. Significantly, of the first 29 local plans to be adopted, public inquiries were held into only 16. But where valid objections are not withdrawn, an inquiry will be necessary.

The public local inquiry is only a limited safeguard, however, because of the loose relationship which exists between forward planning and other functions of the authority concerned. Decisions may be taken under other

---

[23] The word "representations" is employed in the Act only in the context of the public participation exercise required in the first phase of plan preparation: see, e.g. T.C.P.A. 1971, ss. 12(1), 16 and 18(1)(c).

[24] T.C.P.A. 1971, s. 14(1).

[25] Ibid. s. 18(1). The matters are the same as those prescribed in respect of structure plans (ante, p. 104, note 18.)

[26] D.O.E. Circular 4/79, Memorandum, Annex E.

[27] See further, Local Plans: Public Local Inquiries (H.M.S.O., 1977), para. 3.5.

[28] See further, post, p. 128.

[29] T.C.P.A. 1971, s. 13(1). The Act provides for a local inquiry or other hearing of objections, but the Plans Regulations make it clear that a public local inquiry will always be necessary: reg. 31.

powers which have the effect of strengthening the authority's case and pre-empting objections, such as the demolition before the local plan inquiry, of property owned by them in an area proposed for redevelopment, despite objections favouring rehabilitation of existing buildings. In the case of development control, it is clear that the flexibility that authorities enjoy to have regard to all "material considerations" prevails over proposals in a draft plan or objections to them. It would be a curious result, for example, if by putting proposals in the form of a draft local plan and inviting objections, the authority were in a worse position in development control than if no draft plan had been prepared. Conversely, even if it were an approved plan, they would be under no direct legal obligation to adhere to it. But a reasonable balance between giving proper consideration to objections under forward planning, and retaining discretion in development control, may be hard to maintain. An example of the potential conflict is *R. v. City of London Corporation, ex parte Allan*,[30] where the plaintiffs argued that their formal objections to a district plan prepared by the Corporation would be pre-empted before the inquiry if the Corporation proceeded, as they proposed to do, to grant planning permission for a development which included a road proposal bisecting the area. The developers had put in a tempting planning gain offer: they were prepared to carry out the necessary major road improvements at their own expense, and the Corporation were anxious to proceed. The Court declined to issue an order of prohibition to prevent them from granting permission, holding that the two functions of forward planning and development control should be regarded as independent, and that the Corporation could not be said to be giving permission in circumstances in which no reasonable authority could conclude that it should grant permission.

A local plan inquiry is conducted by an Inspector appointed by the Secretary of State, and not only must his report be considered by the authority, but they are also required to consider each recommendation separately and to give reasons for their decisions.[31] Thus although they are not obliged to accept each recommendation, they may not arbitrarily reject any. The inquiry is therefore a critical exercise in the plan approval procedure, and deserves closer analysis.

(a) The background to local plan inquiries

Objections to old style development plans were examined at public local inquiries, and it was unsurprising that the same procedure should have been retained for the new local plans, notwithstanding that it had been supplanted in the case of structure plans by the examination in public. The introduction of the examination in public enabled the Secretary of State to strengthen the

---

[30] (1980) 79 L.G.R. 223; followed in *Davies v. Hammersmith L.B.C.* [1981] J.P.L. 682, where the Court of Appeal rejected a submission that an authority should override an objection only in circumstances of real urgent necessity, but accepted that it might be perverse or unreasonable to act deliberately in order to pre-empt the plan.
[31] Plans Regulations 1982, reg. 29(1). The authority are required by the Regulations to prepare a formal statement of their decisions and reasons and to make it available for inspection together with the Inspector's report.

traditional Government view that plan reviewing procedures existed primarily to inform the Minister, and to allow him to come to a decision based upon a comprehensive study of all relevant factors and the conflicting opinions. But the local plan inquiry has inherited from the old development plan inquiries the ambiguity of function that encompasses both political and quasi-judicial elements, with the further consideration that it is now the local authority, the centrally interested "party" in the quasi-judicial sense, rather than the Minister to whom the Inspector's report is to be addressed.

The legislation confers rights of objection and, by implication, the right to appear at the inquiry to pursue an objection[32] This in turn creates expectations that where an objection is upheld by the Inspector the plan should be modified accordingly. But the local authority retain the ultimate power to accept or reject the Inspector's recommendations, even though this may involve that they reassert the arguments advanced on their own behalf at the inquiry but rejected by the Inspector. Outright conflict such as that may be avoided by the calling in of the plan for ministerial approval, and the existence of that power arguably itself alters the balance of function by underwriting objectors' rights. But it by no means resolves all the problems of conflict of interest and ambiguity of function which underly the inquiry and the post-inquiry procedure.

Uncertainty as to the function of local plan inquiries has also been fostered by the Government's failure to prescribe any procedural rules, notwithstanding an express statutory power to do so. Instead, a non-statutory code has been prepared. The *Code*[33] is detailed, but its provisions are explanatory rather than regulatory, and its informal status precludes legal challenge for procedural breach in respect of any departures the Inspector may choose to make from it.

(b) Pre-inquiry procedure

It is usual for every effort to be made to programme the inquiry so that it will progress smoothly, and the Inspector is assisted in this by a programme officer.[34] A provisional timetable is prepared once it has been ascertained how many objectors wish to appear or be represented at the inquiry, and this informs objectors of the order in which they are likely to be heard. There will often also be an informal procedural meeting some time before the inquiry opens to settle the final details of the programme and to agree procedures for dealing with technical evidence.[35]

Formal notice of the inquiry must be given at least six weeks beforehand, both by general advertisement and by individual notification to objectors.[36]

---

[32] Such a right is not expressly conferred but is implicit from the purpose of the inquiry. So far as supporting representations and late objections are concerned, however, the Inspector has discretion whether to permit appearance at the inquiry.

[33] *Local Plans: Public Local Inquiries* (H.M.S.O., 1977). Only Section 3 of the booklet constitutes the actual code of procedure, but for the sake of convenience the whole booklet is hereafter referred to as the *Code*. It is a significant precedent perhaps, that no procedural regulations were ever made for the conduct of inquiries into the old development plans.

[34] *Code*, para. 3.22.

[35] *Ibid.* para. 3.21.

[36] Plans Regulations 1982, reg. 28.

(c) Inquiry procedure

In the absence of any formal rules, inquiry procedure is a matter primarily for the Inspector's discretion. But it is subject generally to the rules of natural justice, and the *Code* offers the reassurance that inquiries will be conducted "in accordance with well established principles of openness and fairness," and that subject to the need to maintain order and avoid time wasting, "everyone may put their [sic] case in their own way."[37]

The *Code* envisages that the inquiry will proceed from issue to issue, and that in each instance there will first be a statement of the objector's submission, in the course of which the objector may call witnesses to whom "questions may be put."[38] Next, the planning authority will respond to the objection or to a group of objections relating to the same issue, and again there may be supporting evidence and the questioning of witnesses. Finally, the objector has a right of reply.

It can be seen that the recommended procedures are based firmly in the adversarial tradition of courtroom practice, and that no attempt has been made to emulate the probing discussion of the examination in public. Not surprisingly, perhaps, members of the Inspectorate have tended in practice to draw upon their experiene in the conduct of planning appeals and have maintained a formal approach to procedure, in one instance even though both the authority and the objectors had agreed to dispense with legal representation and to pursue as informal a procedure as possible.[39] The Inspector is appointed by the Secretary of State rather than the authority,[40] and his status is thus more visibly independent of the final decision making process than is the case in most other inquiries. But it is an independence which brings with it the quasi-judicial traditions of the Inspectorate, which, applied rigorously in interpretation of the *Code,* may allow comparatively little debate, informal interchange or cross-fertilisation of ideas. It is a procedure which may, therefore, allow some inquiries to be dominated and almost directed by highly experienced counsel employed by the authority and some objectors, yet not be sufficiently responsive to the less articulate objector. These inequalities are inherent in the planning process and throw up difficulties for any procedure, but it is doubtful whether the present procedures offer sufficient flexibility to accommodate the variety of expectations participants may have. There is the further danger of a compartmentalised consideration of individual issues, all of which relate closely to each other and require to be viewed in that broader perspective, although intelligent programming can go some way to avoid the problem.

[37] *Code,* para. 3.28.
[38] *Ibid.* para. 3.40. Surprisingly, the *Code* fails to indicate by whom the questions may be put, *i.e.* how far there will be a right of cross-examination. The general assurance of openness and fairness would seem to require that on each objection the authority and the objector should be entitled to question each other's witnesses, but cross-examination by other objectors will be a matter for the Inspector's discretion.
[39] See further, A.P. Lavers, "Inquiries without lawyers" [1979] J.P.L. 518, and M.J. Bruton *et al,* "Local Plans: Public Local Inquiries" [1980] J.P.L. 374.
[40] T.C.P.A. 1971, s. 13(1). Power to make the appointment may be extended to planning authorities themselves by regulations, but no provision has yet been made for this.

(d) The Inspector's report

There are two main functions served by the Inspector's report. The first is that of summarising the evidence and submissions presented at the inquiry. The *Code* indicates that the Inspector will also deal with objections lodged to the plan, but not pursued at the inquiry.[41] Secondly, the report contains the Inspector's recommendations to the planning authority. The recommendations will relate to the authority's next function, which is to consider whether to abandon the plan, or to adopt it with or without modifications. Normally, therefore, the recommendations will point to specific modifications which might be made by the authority. The Inspector's report does not, of course, bind the authority. Subject to their duty to consider each recommendation and to give reasons for their decision, they may reject his recommendations. But it would be simplistic to suggest that the planning authority retain a broad discretion in the matter. The wording of an Inspector's report may be such that rejection of his recommendations will be hazardous, certainly politically and possibly also legally. In practice the wording of the recommendations is critical, not the least because it forms the basis for the Secretary of State's decision whether to call in a plan for his own consideration. If an authority determine to override a recommendation where the Inspector has suggested, for example, that upon the most careful examination of all the evidence and arguments he can find no good planning reasons at all in support of a proposal in the plan, or that a policy goes far beyond what any reasonable planning authority might have thought necessary to control a particular problem, then they may find the matter removed from their jurisdiction.

(e) Modifications to the plan

No modifications, no matter how minor, may be made to a local plan after it has been deposited, except in accordance with the prescribed procedures. The formal process starts after consideration by the authority of the Inspector's report, although they may well have suggested modifications to him before or in the course of the inquiry which may in turn be endorsed or reflected in the report. Modifications could originally be made only so as to take account of objections and matters arising from them, but the power has now been extended so as to allow the authority also to take account of other "material" considerations.[42] Where formal modification is proposed, the authority are required first to prepare a list for publication of the proposed modifications giving their reasons for them and to notify objectors.[43] Objections may be made by any person, and must be considered by the authority.[44] They are required also to decide whether those objections should be the subject of a further public local inquiry,[45] and that is a choice

---

[41] *Code*, para. 3.45.
[42] T.C.P.A. 1971, s. 14(1), as amended by L.G.P.L.A. 1980, Sched. 14, para. 10.
[43] Plans Regulations 1982, reg. 31(1).
[44] *Ibid.* reg. 31(1)(*c*).
[45] *Ibid.* reg. 31(1)(*d*). The Secretary of State may direct a further inquiry in any case, but he has indicated that an inquiry need be held only where matters have arisen which were not in issue at all at the first inquiry, or perhaps where the authority are disposed to withdraw or alter a modification, particularly where it was proposed in the first place in order to meet an objection: D.O.E. Circular 4/79, *Memorandum*, para. 3.75.

which would need to be made in light of the extent to which the objections raised significant new matters not already examined at the first inquiry. The objections may persuade the authority to abandon a proposed modification; but should they decide to propose an alternative modification instead, the procedures would again require to be followed. The power enjoyed by the Secretary of State to make immaterial modifications to structure plans without following the formal procedures was extended to local plan modification by the 1982 Regulations.

9. The adoption of local plans

Adoption is the final stage. It is the formal step by which the authority give effect to their approval of the plan, with or without modification. They must first publish notice of their intention to adopt, both by general advertisement and by individual notification to objectors (and "other such persons as they think fit").[46] A certificate of their compliance with those requirements must be forwarded to the Secretary of State, and adoption may then take place, provided that 28 days have elapsed from the time the certificate was sent and the Secretary of State has not notified them of his intention to intervene.[47] A special safeguard has been introduced by the 1980 Act for objections lodged by the Minister of Agriculture, Fisheries and Food, which will usually relate to the taking of good quality agricultural land for urban development. If the authority do not propose to modify the plan to take account of the objection the Secretary of State is obliged to intervene and take over the approval of the plan unless he is satisfied that the Minister no longer objects.[48] The rationale for the provisions is clear enough, but they breach further the doctrine of local responsibility for local planning and are an unwelcome precedent.

Adoption is by resolution of the authority, and must again be notified.[49] Upon the adoption of the plan, so much of the old development plan as related to the plan area shall cease to have effect, unless the Secretary of State otherwise directs.[50] Such a direction would normally be appropriate only in the case of a subject plan, since district and action area plans will provide comprehensive policy coverage for their area.

A local plan may be abandoned by the authority at any time before adoption, but once the plan has been deposited it is necessary that formal notice be given of the abandonment.[51]

---

[46] *Ibid.* reg. 32(1).
[47] *Ibid.* reg. 32(2).
[48] T.C.P.A. 1971, s. 14(1A), inserted by L.G.P.L.A. 1980, Sched. 14, para. 10.
[49] Plans Regulations 1982, reg. 33. By virtue of T.C.P.A. 1971, s. 18(4), the plan will become operative on a date prescribed in the resolution of adoption.
[50] T.C.P.A. 1971, Sched. 7, paras. 5A, 5B and 5C as inserted by L.G.P.L.A. 1980, Sched. 14, para. 15. The new provisions are badly designed, because they hinge on the date of adoption rather than the operative date for the new plan. The operative date would normally be postponed to more than six weeks following the date of adoption, to allow for challenge in the High Court within the six-week period, but now there will be an hiatus in the development plan unless the operative date coincides with the date of adoption.
[51] Plans Regulations 1982, reg. 33.

10. *The Secretary of State's supervision*

The fundamental rule is that the functions of preparation and adoption of local plans are vested primarily in the local planning authority concerned. But a form of central government supervision, at arm's length, is maintained over the whole local planning process. Two copies of each local plan must be sent to the Secretary of State at the time it is placed on deposit,[52] and there is power for him, at any time from then until the plan is adopted, to "call-in" the plan; that is, to direct that it shall have no effect unless approved by him.[53] The general policy is that the power will be exercised in limited circumstances, and even then normally only once the inquiry has been held and the authority's reactions to the Inspector's recommendations are known.[54] But there is now the additional requirement, mentioned above, that calling-in should automatically occur in the case of any outstanding objection by the Minister of Agriculture, Fisheries and Food. It does not oblige the Secretary of State to give effect to the Minister's objection (and indeed his decision would be challengeable if that were his automatic response),[55] but it presumably imposes a greater burden upon authorities to establish the case for allocating agricultural land, or whatever other proposal to which the Minister objects.

The Plans Regulations therefore have been designed to strengthen the Secretary of State's position at the post-inquiry stage, by requiring that the authority give him not less than 28 days' notice of their intention to adopt the plan.[56] He may then delay the adoption, by directing that it should not proceed until he notifies the authority that he has decided not to call-in the plan for his own approval.[57] Calling-in might be appropriate where the plan raised matters of national or regional significance, or where it has given rise to substantial controversy.[58] Although there is no specific statutory provision, it will always be open to dissatisfied objectors to make representations to the Secretary of State in an attempt to persuade him to call in a plan, particularly since the procedure constitutes an important safeguard against arbitrary and unfair behaviour by authorities.

Calling-in has the effect of depriving the authority of their power to *adopt* the plan. It vests instead a power of approval in the Secretary of State, who may *approve* it, with or without modifications, or reject it.[59] His discretion is broad. He must hold an inquiry into objections, but only if one has not already been held at the instance of the authority, and he may undertake consultations and take into account any matters he thinks relevant.[60] Should he propose to modify the plan, the formal procedures of advertisement, notification and consideration of objections must be observed.[61] Any

---

[52] T.C.P.A. 1971, s. 13(2).
[53] *Ibid.* s. 14(3).
[54] D.O.E. Circular 4/79, *Memorandum*, para. 3.78.
[55] See *e.g. Lavender (H) & Son Ltd.* v. *M.H.L.G.* [1970] 3 All E.R. 871.
[56] Reg. 32(2).
[57] *Ibid.*
[58] See further D.O.E. Circular 4/79, *Memorandum*, para. 3.79.
[59] T.C.P.A. 1971, s. 14(4)(*a*).
[60] *Ibid.* s. 14(4)(*b*), (*c*), (*d*) and (*e*).
[61] Plans Regulations 1982, reg. 34.

modification introduced by him is reinforced for development control purposes by the Development Plans Direction, which requires that he be notified of any planning application which the authority do not propose to refuse which would conflict with or prejudice the implementation of the modification.[62]

There is a further range of subsidiary powers and controls vested in the Secretary of State. Some, such as the appointment of inspectors for local inquiries, supervision of the adequacy of an authority's efforts in public participation and the certification of conformity with the structure plan have already been mentioned. A further important supplementary power conferred by the Act allows the Secretary of State to direct any particular authority, or authorities generally, to supply him with information required for the carrying out of his functions, and to prescribe procedures for them to observe in the carrying out of their functions.[63] Finally, there is the default power under which the Secretary of State may himself undertake to prepare or adopt a local plan, or authorise another local authority to do so where he is satisfied, after holding a local inquiry, that the designated authority have failed to take the necessary steps within a reasonable period.[64]

11. *Alterations to operative plans*

There are no formal requirements for regular monitoring and review of local plans, but the planning authority who adopted a plan may at any time make proposals for its alteration, repeal or replacement.[65] These procedures are quite independent of the development plan scheme. But any new proposals must still conform generally to the approved structure plan; and therefore, except where concurrent adoption is authorised by the Secretary of State,[66] local plan alterations will need to be preceded by the approval of any necessary structure plan alterations. The procedures to be followed for adoption or approval of local plan alterations, repeal or replacement are otherwise the same as for the adoption or approval of an original plan.[67]

What may be involved in a plan alteration is clear enough: any amendment, whether by way of alteration, addition to or deletion of the proposals or other part of the plan must constitute an alteration. But there is no guidance given as to the circumstances in which repeal and replacement powers might be used. Presumably repeal without replacement would be undesirable in the case of district plans and action area plans because of the policy void which would ensue, but that objection need not apply in the case of a subject plan. Repeal coupled with replacement would be a useful course

---

[62] See further, *post,* p. 234.
[63] T.C.P.A. 1971, s. 18(3).
[64] *Ibid.* s.17.
[65] T.C.P.A. 1971, s. 15. With the consent of the Secretary of State they may also make proposals in respect of any local plan approved by him, and he may in any case issue a direction to prepare proposals. There is no right to propose alterations to a plan adopted by the other planning authority for the area, (county or district as the case may be) but arrangements may be made by agreement under the Local Government Act 1972, s. 101 for that purpose.
[66] See further *ante,* p. 120.
[67] T.C.P.A. 1971, s. 15(3); Plans Regulations 1982, reg. 41.

in drawing together a number of past local plans into a new single comprehensive plan. But in general the presumption must be that a local plan should have continuing effect, and that changes will be made normally by means of alteration to the operative plan.

12. *Resolution of conflicts and contradictions*

Despite the requirement of general conformity, there may still be contradictions between structure plans and local plans, between different local plans (such, for example, as a district plan and a subject plan) and even between different parts of the same plan. The rules for resolving conflicts and contradictions are straightforward.

First, they provide that generally the provisions of a local plan shall prevail over those of the structure plan in case of conflict.[68] There is now an exception, however, in the case of local plans which no longer conform with the structure plan when it has been altered or replaced. There is a duty on the county to prepare and send to the Secretary of State within one month of his approval of the plan or alteration, lists of the local plans which in their opinion continue to conform and those which do not.[69] The provisions of local plans on the conforming list continue to prevail for all purposes over the structure plan, but those on the non-conforming list do not.[70] The legislation does not make them subordinate to the structure plan, but merely takes away their priority until they have been altered so as to comply. For the interim period no rules for resolving conflict are prescribed, and the efficiency of monitoring and revision is likely to be seriously impeded by policy confusion between the two tiers of forward planning.

Second, as between two or more local plans, the more recently adopted prevails.[71] Third, the written statement of a structure plan or local plan prevails over any other document forming part of the plan, such as the key diagram or map.[72] And finally, both structure plan and local plan provisions prevail over any surviving provisions in the old development plan.[73]

13. *London*

The preceding pages relate specifically to local planning outside the Greater London area, but for the most part identical procedures govern local planning within London. They are, however, prescribed by separate provisions contained in Schedule 4 to the 1971 Act, and in the Town and Country Planning (Local Plans for Greater London) Regulations 1974.[74] The major distinction is that, apart from their reserve powers at the direction of the Secretary of State,[75] plan preparation by the G.L.C. is confined to

---

[68] *Ibid.* s. 14(8), added by L.G.P.L.A. 1980, Sched. 14, para. 10(*d*).
[69] *Ibid.* s. 15B, added by L.G.P.L.A. 1980, s. 88.
[70] *Ibid.* s. 14(8).
[71] Plans Regulations 1982, reg. 45.
[72] *Ibid.* regs. 43 and 44.
[73] T.C.P.A. 1971, Sched. 7, para. 3 as amended by L.G.P.L.A. 1980, Sched. 14, para. 14.
[74] S.I. 1974 No. 1481. The Regulations mirror, with a few modifications, the local planning provisions of the Plans Regulations.
[75] T.C.P.A. 1971, Sched. 4, para. 10.

G.L.C. action areas as defined in the approved Greater London Development Plan.[76] All other plans are the responsibility of the London boroughs,[77] and there is therefore no provision for any development plan scheme. The 1980 Act has introduced, with effect from a date to be appointed, provisions requiring local plans to be certified by the G.L.C. as being in general conformity with the G.L.D.P. before adoption,[78] and has extended the conforming and non-conforming categorisation of local plans to cover alterations made to the G.L.D.P.[79] Otherwise the prescribed procedures are as for authorities outside London, with only some minor amendments necessary to deal with consultation between authorities and with action areas straddling borough boundaries.[80]

14. Development plans registers

Approved plans are public documents, and the authority concerned with preparation are therefore required to maintain copies for public inspection free of charge, and to provide printed copies for sale at a reasonable charge.[81] Both county and district authorities are also required to maintain a public register containing brief particulars of any structure or local plans placed upon deposit for public inspection, as well as of operative plans and of any deposited proposals for the alteration, repeal or replacement of any operative plans.[82] It is also required that an index map for each authority's area be prepared, showing the boundaries of operative plans.[83] The requirements do not extend to any surviving old style development plans, but the Secretary of State has asked that appropriate references be made where necessary to maintain a comprehensive register.[84]

A national register is required to be maintained by the Secretary of State showing the areas for which, and the dates upon which, various provisions of Part II of the 1971 Act have come into effect consequent upon approval or adoption of structure plans and local plans.[85]

D. Challenging the validity of statutory plans

1. Introduction

Structure plans and local plans are prepared and approved by public authorities exercising statutory powers. Their provisions are therefore liable to be challenged in the courts, on the grounds that those powers may have

---

[76] *Ibid.* paras. 8 and 9.
[77] *Ibid.* para. 8(3)(*a*).
[78] *Ibid.* paras. 7A and 12(2).
[79] *Ibid.* para. 7B. The Act has also, by repealing para. 6 of the Schedule, removed the power for the boroughs to propose alterations for action areas for the G.L.D.P.
[80] *Ibid.* para. 9(1)(*b*).
[81] Plans Regulations 1982, regs. 37 and 38.
[82] *Ibid.* reg. 39.
[83] *Ibid.* reg. 39(2).
[84] D.O.E. Circular 4/79, *Memorandum*, para. 4.2.
[85] T.C.P.A. 1971, s. 21(7B) as inserted by L.G.P.L.A. 1980, Sched. 10, para. 6.

been exceeded, that is, that the local planning authority or the Secretary of State may have acted *ultra vires*. It was the intention behind the original Planning Bill in 1947 that the normal rules of judicial review should be left to apply without restriction. This was thought to pose little risk because it was generally assumed that the powers conferred upon the Minister were so broad that, as one Member put it, "it would take seven league boots to step outside the limits the Minister has set for himself."[86] But restrictions upon challenge in the courts were later added to the Bill in response to an Opposition amendment, and remain substantially the same today.[87] They are modelled on a formula first used in the Public Works Facilities Act 1930, which has since become a favourite of the Parliamentary draftsmen. The effect of the provisions is to preclude any challenge to a plan (or any alteration, repeal or replacement) otherwise than by way of an application to the High Court under section 244 of the 1971 Act, and to confine the period within which such an application may be made, the grounds upon which it may be made and the persons who may apply.

2. The six-week rule

Application may be made under section 244 only within the period of six weeks running from the date of publication of the first notice of approval or adoption of the plan.[88] The period is short but the restriction is absolute. It applies even where an applicant's ground of challenge is based upon some vitiating act of the authority, such as bad faith or fraud, which has only come to light after the expiry of the six-week period.[89] The courts have resisted the temptation to allow exceptions based on the doctrine of *Anisminic Ltd.* v. *Foreign Compensation Commission*,[90] where the House of Lords ruled that a clause which purported to oust altogether the supervisory jurisdiction of the courts was not effective in the case of decisions which were found to be outside the power of the determining body, and therefore nullities from the outset. Instead they have accepted the need to achieve administrative certainty, in cases involving the public interest, where the validity of subsequent decisions and actions may also be at stake.[91] After six weeks, the public interest prevails over all else, and the aggrieved applicant is left to such other legal or political remedies as may be available.

The six-week rule not only prevents post-approval challenge, however, because section 242 encompasses any questioning of validity "whether before or after the plan, alteration, repeal or replacement has been approved

---

[86] H.C. Deb. Vol. 437, col. 1336 (May 13, 1947), *per* Mr. W.S. Morrison M.P.

[87] Originally T.C.P.A. 1947, s. 11(2) and (3); see now T.C.P.A. 1971, ss. 242 and 244.

[88] T.C.P.A. 1971, s.244(1).

[89] See, *e.g. R.* v. *S.O.S.E., ex parte Ostler* [1977] Q.B. 122 (decided on a comparable provision in the Highways Act 1959, Sched. 2, para. 2) where the applicant alleged that there had been a secret agreement between officers of the Department of Transport and another objector which he could not have known of within the statutory six-week period.

[90] [1969] 2 A.C. 147.

[91] See, *e.g. Smith* v. *East Elloe R.D.C.* [1956] A.C. 736, followed in *Routh* v. *Reading Corporation* (1970) 217 E.G. 1337), *Hamilton* v. *Secretary of State for Scotland* 1972 S.L.T. 233; and *R.* v. *S.O.S.E., ex parte Ostler* [1977] Q.B. 122, particularly at 136 *per Lord Denning M.R.*

or adopted." The scope of that prohibition is less clear. On a broad interpretation any action which attempted to secure compliance with the Act or Regulations in the course of plan preparation and approval is prohibited, on the grounds that any breach would go to the validity of the plan. That would mean that no immediate legal remedy would be available against an authority who failed to arrange a local public inquiry to consider objections to a local plan, for example, or an Inspector who refused to hear relevant objections to the plan. If it were really the intention of the legislature to postpone any challenge, even indirect challenge, until after the approval or adoption of the plan, then the section is liable to lead to uncertainty and waste because a decision to quash in whole or in part requires that the authority and the Department retrace their steps and lose a year or more in remedying the breach. No court would lightly make a ruling which brought about that result, and the consequence is that the burden upon the aggrieved applicant is likely to be substantially greater than if he were permitted to bring proceedings earlier. It is true that there is, particularly in local planning, the political safeguard of the Secretary of State's largely independent supervision of local authority performance, but the exercise of his power of intervention is governed by quite different considerations, and has no value for any "aggrieved" person whose dispute is with the Secretary of State himself.

These are factors which indicate that a narrower interpretation of the section would be fairer to aggrieved applicants. That would involve confining it to direct challenges to the validity of the contents of unadopted or unapproved plans, and distinguishing actions seeking to ensure compliance with the prescribed procedures.

3. Persons aggrieved

The right of challenge preserved by the Act is available only to persons "aggrieved" by a plan, on the ground either that it is outside the powers conferred by Part II of the 1971 Act, or that there has been procedural irregularity in its approval or adoption.[92] The courts have for years wrestled with the "person aggrieved" formula. The traditional view was that the expression included only persons possessing legal rights which might be infringed by the action complained of,[93] but that approach was clearly out of place in the context of a planning system designed to secure participation in decision making by any or all members of the public irrespective of their property ownership. There has therefore been a deliberate broadening of interpretation,[94] with the consequence that the expression is likely now, in the context of development planning, to include all statutory objectors (in respect both of objections lodged to a deposited or submitted plan and to any modifications) as well as any other persons permitted at the Inspector's

---

[92] T.C.P.A. 1971, s. 244(1).
[93] See e.g. Buxton v. M.H.L.G. [1960] 3 All E.R. 408; discussed further post, p. 618.
[94] Led particularly by Lord Denning in Attorney General of the Gambia v. N'Jie [1961] A.C. 617, and Maurice v. London C.C. [1964] 2 Q.B. 362.

discretion to appear at a local plan inquiry.[95] Presumably, too, the category would include persons selected to participate in an examination in public, and although breach of the non-statutory *Code* would not in itself constitute a procedural breach it may well be the yardstick by which natural justice requirements should be assessed. Whether persons whose involvement had not extended beyond the early public participation phase would be included would depend upon the closeness or remoteness of their interest in the issue under challenge. Similarly in the case of one who asserts that his property rights were adversely affected by the plan but who has not exercised any rights of objection or representation, particularly if the breach (a failure to advertise properly, for example) is the reason for his non-participation.

The position of local planning authorities themselves is unclear. An authority might well wish to challenge the validity of a plan adopted by the other-tier authority or a neighbouring authority, or to challenge the manner of the Secretary of State's intervention in their own plan. In the former case the aggrieved authority may well qualify as a statutory consultee, but in the latter case there has been a ruling in the context of planning enforcement, that the authority will not automatically be a person aggrieved.[96] The policy arguments for not extending that decision to development plan challenge are strong, not only because it was swiftly reversed by legislation in the case of enforcement,[97] but also because the context is quite different. An unlawful modification made to a structure plan by the Secretary of State, for example, might well impose an additional financial burden upon an authority or affect their own land holdings in a way not possible in the case of the quashing of an enforcement notice. But it is a significant consideration that the express rights of challenge now conferred upon authorities in the case of enforcement and other decisions[98] of the Secretary of State were not at the same time extended to development plan challenges.

4. The grounds of challenge

A plan may be challenged on two grounds. First, that it is not within the powers conferred by Part II of the 1971 Act. Part II is particularly notable for the breadth and the degree of subjectivity of the discretionary power it confers upon authorities and upon the Secretary of State, and there must be a heavy burden on any applicant attempting to establish that the limits had been exceeded. A particular policy or proposal might still be unlawful, however, as importing non-planning considerations; and the Secretary of

---

[95] Applying by analogy *Turner* v. *S.O.S.E.* (1973) 28 P. & C.R. 123, where Ackner J. at 132–139 approved such a formulation in the case of ordinary planning inquiries; and see *Easter Ross Land Use Committee* v. *Secretary of State for Scotland* 1970 S.C. 182 where the standing of a voluntary organisation challenging a development plan amendment appears to have been assumed.

[96] In *Ealing Corporation* v. *Jones* [1959] 1 Q.B. 384, where the Divisional Court took the view that where no financial or legal burden was placed upon the authority by the decision (made in that case by magistrates quashing an enforcement notice), they could not claim to be aggrieved; and if Parliament had intended local planning authorities to have had a right of appeal, it could have been specifically given to them.

[97] In the Caravan Sites and Control of Development Act 1960, s.35; now T.C.P.A. 1971, s. 246.

[98] See *e.g.* T.C.P.A. 1971, ss. 245(2) (other orders, decisions and directions), 246 (enforcement) and 247 (appeals under s. 53).

State has also regularly used his modification powers to guard against authorities incorporating blanket policies which might be interpreted as fettering their development control discretion. That may be a wise precautionary measure, but legal challenge to a potentially fettering policy under section 244 would be mistimed, because the development plan does not itself fetter subsequent decision making. Only if it were in fact rigidly applied, to the exclusion of other material considerations, could discretion be regarded as fettered.

The second ground of challenge is that any requirement of Part II or of any regulations made thereunder has not been complied with in relation to the approval or adoption of the plan. "Approval or adoption" must refer to all the steps of plan preparation, and not simply final formal requirements, particularly if all challenge is precluded until final approval or adoption of a plan.

Not every procedural irregularity need affect the validity of the plan. The scope for challenge has been substantially diminished in practice by the Government's decision to rely upon informal codes of procedure instead of statutory regulations. And the connection is otherwise at best indirect. The court may find a requirement contained in the legislation to be directory rather than mandatory, and permit some deviation from it.[99] The more drastic the likely consequences of invalidity, the less likely is the court to lean towards an interpretation which would bring them about. The only remedy available under section 244 is the quashing of the plan, in whole or in part, coupled with a power to make an interim suspensory order; and these are weighty sanctions to be applied in any but the most serious instances of procedural breach. These considerations are further reinforced by the requirement of the section that the court may only quash for procedural irregularity where the breach has substantially prejudiced the applicant.[1]

It follows that the courts will be unwilling to imply any further restrictions into the legislation beyond those expressly prescribed. Thus when in 1955 Cambridge City Council sought to challenge the validity of the county's old-style development plan on the ground that it had not been formally *approved* by the county before submission to the Minister, the court had little difficulty in declining to imply such a requirement into the legislation: the county's resolution to *submit* the plan was all the Act required, and that was sufficient.[2] It would be wrong, however, to suggest that the legislation provides a comprehensive procedural code in all respects. In particular, in the absence of statutory procedures governing the examination in public and local public inquiry, the courts will wish to ensure that some basic norms of fairness or natural justice are observed. How far

---

[99] There are no fixed criteria by which such a choice is governed, save that a general balance may need to be struck between the extent of the breach, the sanction available and the prejudice suffered by the applicant. In practice therefore the test may overlap with the requirement of s. 244 that an applicant should show substantial prejudice before the court may quash for procedural irregularity.

[1] T.C.P.A. 1971, s. 244(2)(*b*). The scope of the right of challenge is discussed in *Bradley (E.H.) and Sons Ltd.* v. *S.O.S.E.* The Times, August 4, 1982.

[2] *Cambridge City Council* v. *M.H.L.G. The Times* January 25, 1955; and see *Annual Report of the Ministry of Housing and Local Government 1950–1954*, Cmd. 8724, p.62.

they might be prepared to go is uncertain, but the *Codes* offer at least a starting point in assessing the requirements of natural justice and fairness in plan preparation and approval.

5. *Procedure for challenge*

The section precludes all challenge other than by way of statutory application. The correct procedure is by way of originating motion,[3] and there is a right of appeal to the Court of Appeal.[4] There is power for the court by interim order to suspend the operation of the plan, either generally or in so far as it affects any property of the applicant, until the final determination of the proceedings; and upon that final determination the court may similarly quash the plan generally or in so far as it affects the applicant's property.[5] The latter course is curious in the case of any modern plan, and quite inapplicable to a structure plan except in the most exceptional case. Where the landowner's holding is sufficiently substantial for it to be identified in the plan, any order quashing that part of the plan is liable to interfere substantially with the whole strategy.

E. Non-statutory planning

1. *Introduction*

The statutory procedures governing the preparation and approval of development plans are complex, and the whole process has long been plagued by uncertainty and delay, which even the 1968 reforms have failed to dispel. The plans have not proved to be easily adaptable to cope with rapid change in the real world. It is not surprising therefore that planning authorities have often instead chosen to bypass the statutory machinery by preparing so-called "informal" or "non-statutory" plans. These have taken a variety of different forms, ranging from straightforward policy resolutions of the planning committee through to highly sophisticated map based plans for large scale land release and major development. The only common factor is that these are statements of planning policy which lack any statutory backing. Their only strength comes from the breadth of the discretion enjoyed by authorities in determining applications for planning permission. Section 29 of the 1971 Act requires that authorities should "have regard" to the provisions of the statutory plan so far as material to a planning application, but it does not oblige them to adhere unflinchingly to it. They must also take into account any other material considerations, such as some particular feature of the site itself, for example. A statement of policy adopted by the authority may equally be a material consideration for the purposes of the section.

This does not, however, mean that an authority may simply abandon an

---

[3] Rules of the Supreme Court, Ord. 55(3). Under R.S.C. Ord. 94(1) the jurisdiction is exercisable by a single judge of the Queen's Bench Division.

[4] R.S.C. Ord. 59; since the proceedings are by way of statutory application rather than statutory appeal, they fall outside the Judicature Act 1925, s. 31(1)(*f*) and leave is not required for appeal to the Court of Appeal.

[5] T.C.P.A. 1971, s. 244(2).

approved plan which has become politically inconvenient or outmoded in favour of non-statutory planning. There are two important safeguards. The first is that any application which constitutes a departure from the approved plan must be advertised and in some cases notified to the Secretary of State before permission may be granted, even though it may be in compliance with a subsequent non-statutory plan.[6] The second safeguard exists in the appeal system. Where the authority have refused permission in reliance upon a non-statutory plan, there is no guarantee that the Secretary of State will, on appeal by the applicant, accord any weight at all to the authority's plan. The question of the status which may be afforded an informal plan or policy is governed not by law but by administrative practice. That practice has emerged in the course of the historical development of non-statutory planning, a process in which central government played an important role. The topic has been sadly neglected in the standard planning and planning law texts, yet non-statutory planning has played a highly significant part in British planning practice over the past 20 years; it therefore requires more detailed examination.

2. The historical background

Post-war forward planning was necessarily non-statutory in its early years. Although comprehensive control of development had been introduced in 1948, there were to be no approved plans to which "regard" might be had for many years. In that interim period authorities instead had a very general discretion to have regard to any directions given by the Minister as to provisions to be included in their plan (in fact a rarely used power), and, subject to them, "to the provisions which in their opinion will be required to be so included for securing the proper planning" of their area.[7] As a matter of practical necessity draft development plans thus enjoyed a semi-formal status. Before the draft plan was published the authority had very broad discretion indeed, which became progressively narrower as the plan progressed through the approval stages. Once it was approved the authority had little freedom to depart from it. The procedures governing departures were tightly drawn, and there was in those days little practical scope for non-statutory planning.[8]

But over the following 20 years the balance altered significantly. The courts had been determined to emphasise the broad discretion enjoyed by authorities to take into account considerations outside their development plans,[9] and both local and central government came gradually to accept that non-statutory planning offered at least an interim solution to the problem of delays in statutory plan approval.

The first step was taken in 1955 when the Government suddenly decided

---

[6] See further post, p. 233.
[7] T.C.P.A. 1947, s. 36.
[8] The "departure" criteria were initially prescribed by the Town and Country Planning (Development Plans) Direction 1954, whose terms were later successively relaxed to make allowance for the weaknesses of the statutory plans: see further post, p. 279.
[9] See, e.g. Simpson v. Edinburgh Corporation 1960 S.C. 313.

that the containment of urban sprawl should be a high priority. They urged authorities to consider designating green belts around the large conurbations,[10] hoping to build upon the success of the London green belt which had been first established some years earlier. So urgent was the need to contain growth, authorities were requested not only to submit green belt proposals as formal development plan amendments, but also to submit sketch plans to the Minister as soon as possible indicating the boundaries of the proposed belt, and to start applying the principles in development control immediately, on an interim basis. Formal amendment proposals could be submitted later following a detailed survey. The implication was that the Minister would in general be prepared to lend his support to an authority's sketch plan proposals on appeal, even although they imposed stricter restraints than those contained in the development plan and even although, as often happened in practice, substantial delays might have occurred in the submission and approval of a formal amendment. These "interim" or "unapproved" green belts quickly became a popular device for urban containment, and although they lacked the full status of approved plans they tended to be applied by authorities with the same rigour. Nor did it seem to alarm authorities or the courts that the unapproved status might continue indefinitely. In one case, *Hodgkinsons (Ringway) Ltd. v. Bucklow R.D.C.,*[11] the fact that the submission of a formal amendment to the development plan some 10 years earlier had still to be rewarded by the holding of a public inquiry into it did not affect the right of the authority to continue to rely upon it in development control.

But at least the intention had been that this should be purely an interim device, to be incorporated by formal amendment into the statutory system. But that was not the assumption behind the Ministry's next move. The most pressing problem of the late fifties and early sixties was urban renewal. There was great pressure for town centre redevelopment and for new office and retail development, and the comprehensive development area machinery of the 1947 Act was the prescribed planning base, but proposals were too often frustrated by delays in processing the necessary development plan amendments. In 1963 the Ministry suggested that authorities should instead prepare informal Town Centre Maps as a basis for their proposals, and offered the all-important undertaking that, provided such a Map had been made available for public examination or discussion it "would be fully taken into account" by the Minister in any matter which came to him for decision.[12] There was no need to submit the proposals for approval: that could await the next review of the statutory plan. It was, in the words of one critic, "an unspoken admission that the Development Plan machinery had broken down through delay and that, since town centre plans were in many areas the most urgent planning problems, the system should be by-passed."[13] Although the informal map system effectively destroyed the

[10] M.H.L.G. Circular 42/55; followed up by Circular 50/57. As to green belt policy generally, see *post*, p. 307.

[11] (1972) 225 E.G. 2105.

[12] *Town Centres. Approach to Renewal* H.M.S.O. 1963, and M.H.L.G. Circular 38/62. By 1965 authorities were being urged not to submit any further statutory town maps for towns with populations below 10,000, but instead to keep such plans informal: M.H.L.G. Circular 58/65.

[13] Lewis Keeble, *Principles and Practice of Town and Country Planning* (4th ed., 1969), p. 39.

rights of formal objection which otherwise would have been enjoyed by affected persons, the Ministry through its regional officers strongly advocated its use and eventually simply refused to permit submission of any further statutory supplementary town maps for approval.[14] Moreover, although properties could quickly be blighted by Town Centre Plans, the blight notice provisions introduced by the Town and Country Planning Act 1959[15] and re-enacted in 1962[16] extended only to designations in statutory plans. Even by 1968 when non-statutory planning had become widespread, new legislation failed to extend the benefits of the blight notice procedures,[17] although altorities were urged by circular to make discretionary payments in such cases.[18] Statutory recognition of blight by non-statutory plans was withheld until 1973.[19]

Preservation of the undeveloped coast was another planning policy considered by the Ministry to be sufficiently important to be pursued outside formal development plans. The Minister himself had intended that close control should be exerted through the "calling-in" procedures, but his officials warned of the additional administrative load this would cast upon the Ministry.[20] And so a circular was issued instead, urging maritime authorities to prepare "forthwith" informal policies for coasts and indicating again that they would be taken into account in ministerial decision making.[21] The Minister, said the Circular, would be "glad" to receive copies (but not as amendments to the development plan). Formal inclusion in the statutory plan could await the next review. The circular also contained surprisingly detailed instructions as to form and content, and significantly, compliance with the terms of the circular was reinforced by a requirement that authorities should submit annual returns of refusals and consents.

Next, in 1967, came the "village envelope" policy, under which authorities were urged to adopt informal plans for small towns and villages with the purpose of strengthening their power to resist pressures for expansion.[22] On this occasion authorities were, however, carefully advised that applications should not be refused solely on the grounds of conflict with informal policy and that the Minister would be bound on appeal to satisfy himself that informal policies were soundly based before taking them into account. The reason for this caveat was that these were to be policies which were not intended ever to be submitted to the Minister, save on an ad hoc basis for consideration in planning appeals. And even then, as the Court of Appeal was later to rule, the way in which they might be applied raised no

---

[14] See further J.A.G. Griffiths, *Government Departments and Local Authorities* (1965), p. 312; and H. Brown, "Town Maps or Town Centre Maps?" [1965] J.P.L. 413.
[15] T.C.P.A. 1959, Part IV. As to planning blight, see further *post*, p. 665.
[16] T.C.P.A. 1962, s. 138.
[17] T.C.P.A. 1968, s. 33, where entitlement was, however, extended in respect of property blighted by structure and local plans.
[18] M.H.L.G. Circular 46/70, paras. 6 and 7.
[19] Land Compensation Act 1973, Part V.
[20] See R.H.S. Crossman, *The Diaries of a Cabinet Minister* (Hamish Hamilton, 1976), Vol. 1, p. 212.
[21] M.H.L.G. Circular 7/66.
[22] *Planning Bulletin No. 8: Settlement in the Countryside. A Planning Method* (H.M.S.O., 1967), paras. 25–28; and M.H.L.G. Circular 72/67, paras. 3 and 4.

issue of law but was a matter purely of planning policy within the Minister's discretion.[23]

The reforms advocated by the Planning Advisory Group in 1965 had spelled the end of the old-style statutory plans, and their implementation in the 1968 Act was accompanied by new provisions requiring authorities to obtain ministerial consent before submitting any further amendments to their old development plans.[24] Such consent, they were advised, would be granted only where amendments were "essential to the achievement of the proper planning of the area concerned."[25] Official discouragement from following the old statutory procedures thus combined with a general inability to pursue the new. Substantial delays were to occur before the approval of any structure plans or local plans. Non-statutory planning was the only policy instrument available to fill the gap, particularly in the early years of the 1970s when great pressure was brought on authorities in growth areas to release more land for development. Non-statutory policies for land release provided a more rational basis for decision making than one of purely ad hoc response to individual planning applications, and gave authorities some basis for resisting unwanted land releases on appeal.

Ironically, but perhaps inevitably, limited statutory recognition came at last to non-statutory planning in the extension of blight notice availability and also through the Local Government Act 1972. For some years after local government reorganisation county authorities were able to safeguard matters of county concern through the adoption of informal policy resolutions which upon notification to district authorities had effect as defining supplementary "county matters" for development control purposes[26]; and non-statutory plans were also specifically permitted to provide planning backing in limited circumstances for compulsory purchase under the Community Land Act 1975.[27] Both provisions, however, have now been repealed by the Act of 1980.

3. Non-statutory planning and the reformed statutory system

Throughout its history the function of non-statutory planning has been as a temporary expedient. It has allowed authorities the opportunity to maintain the up-to-date plans and policies otherwise denied them by the delays and rigidity of the Act and Regulations. It is tempting therefore to assume that the reformed statutory system, if successful, will no longer require non-statutory supplementation. The new plans were intended, after all, to be both comprehensive and flexible.

In the short term, however, many of the old non-statutory policies will survive. It will still be many years before all are supplanted by the new plans. Further, it is widely recognised that the new plans themselves may be employed in development control on a "non-statutory" basis whilst still in the course of adoption or approval. This offers a useful safeguarding device.

[23] *Luke* v. *M.H.L.G.* [1968] 1 Q.B. 172.
[24] T.C.P.A. 1968, Sched. 10, para. 1.
[25] M.H.L.G. Circular 66/68, para. 6.
[26] Under the Local Government Act 1972, Sched. 16, para. 32.
[27] Community Land Act 1975, Sched. 4, para. 3.

Applications may be refused on the basis of prematurity or as conflicting with the draft plan, or granted as being in accordance with the draft plan. But a balance needs to be struck, particularly in the latter case, between observing the draft plan as it stands and yet fulfilling the statutory duty to consider objections to it. The Secretary of State is prepared to regard provisions of draft structure plans as material considerations provided they conform generally to the matters publicised as proposals for inclusion, and have been the subject of a resolution by the local planning authority.[28] Local plans in draft form will also be taken into account, with the weight to be placed on them increasing as they progress through the stages of adoption or approval.[29]

The scope for further non-statutory planning once structure plans and local plans for an area have been approved is less clear. Once a district plan has been adopted, it is arguable that all pre-existing non-statutory plans must be regarded as having lapsed because district plans were, under the 1974 Plans Regulations, required to be based upon a "comprehensive" survey of the area,[30] which suggests that their statutory proposals and policies should themselves be comprehensive. As a matter of law, however, it does not follow that an old non-statutory plan is incapable of continuing to be a "material consideration." The real test of their effectiveness is the extent to which the Secretary of State is prepared to continue to have regard to them on appeal, and his view is that any informal plan not treated as a draft local plan must be treated as having lapsed.[31] It would be a curious result if the old-style statutory plan is automatically supplanted by the adoption of a new plan, but the authority continued to place weight on old non-statutory plans.

Some authorities have attempted to tie in new non-statutory policies with their new formal plans, so as to permit easy amendment for the future. That is a course which the Panel rejected in the case of the Greater London Development Plan as "inappropriate,"[32] and the Secretary of State has taken a similar line in respect of structure plans, using his powers of modification to delete such matter from the plans. There is a particular difficulty in the case of local plans if non-statutory material is published together with the statutory material, for it may then be thought to be illustrative or descriptive matter which must be "treated as forming part of the plan."[33] In the case of structure plans, the new explanatory memorandum has a separate existence from the plan and may become a vehicle for non-statutory supplementation of policies and proposals in the plan. But under the 1982 Plans Regulations (reg. 38), authorities are required to print their structure plans and local plans in the form approved or adopted and to exclude any material not forming part of the plan; so that any non-statutory supplementation may no longer appear in the same document.

Finally, it is necessary to consider the validity of non-statutory plans and

---

[28] D.O.E. Circular 4/79, *Memorandum*, para. 4.3.
[29] *Ibid.* para. 4.4.
[30] Plans Regulations 1974, reg. 15(1). The 1982 Regulations impose no specific duty.
[31] D.O.E. Circular 4/79, *Memorandum*, para. 4.6.
[32] *Report of the Panel of Inquiry* Vol. 1, p. 607. The G.L.C. had sought to incorporate a non-statutory "high buildings map" into the plan.
[33] T.C.P.A. 1971, s. 11(5).

policies prepared after the approval of structure plans and local plans for an authority's area. It is clear that there can be no legal objection to such plans. Informal plans and policies may lawfully constitute material considerations in development control, equally as much as precedent, site considerations and so on. Some authorities have already resorted to annual non-statutory updating of their structure plans, which is a simple and efficient means of recording changes based upon monitoring.[34] But central government's view is that non-statutory forms are now inappropriate for land use plans, and that their use should be confined to supplementary material such as design guides and development briefs.[35] The clear implication is that more extensive experiments with non-statutory policy making will be ignored in ministerial decision making unless presented in the form of a draft statutory plan. But there is room for a variety of interpretation as to what may be a land use policy to be pursued through a statutory plan, and "supplementary" material; and it is likely that the interests of expediency will continue to be served through non-statutory mechanisms, and that policies pursued in this form will be sufficiently justifiable on their merits alone to be upheld on appeal. Thus, an authority who resolve to resist any further non-retail uses in a shopping area, for example, will not be penalised on appeal for having expressed the policy simply by way of resolution rather than in a draft statutory plan or alteration made for the purpose, if the factors upon which the policy is based are themselves material considerations in considering an application involving further non-retail encroachment. But these considerations will be accorded no greater status merely by reason of their adoption as "policy" by the authority.

4. Status of non-statutory plans

Non-statutory plans have in the past taken a variety of forms and fulfilled a variety of purposes. Their flexibility stems of course from the fact that no statutory provisions attempt to prescribe their form, contents or approval procedure; nor can legislation proscribe their use without a radical change in the scope of development control discretion. But that lack of discipline creates very real dangers. On the one hand, the plans may be used to override the formal planning process and to deny the public the procedural safeguards which exist in statutory planning. On the other hand, an informal plan may readily enough be ignored by an authority whenever convenient, and allowed to lapse when regarded as no longer of value. Hence, the description "bottom-drawer" plan, and McLoughlin's charge that it is difficult for the public to know just what degree of backing they have: "their very ambiguity can be used by less scrupulous authorities to make bottom-drawer plans seem all things to all men."[36]

---

[34] For a discussion of East Sussex County Council's experiments in non-statutory updating, see M. Parker, "Structure planning—its future role" *Surveyor*, February 2, 1978, p. 8.

[35] D.O.E. Circular 4/79, *Memorandum*, para. 4.7. Provided the supplementary guidance is in conformity with the statutory plan, has been made the subject of a council resolution and is kept publicly available, the Secretary of State will be prepared to take it into account in decision making.

[36] J.B. McLoughlin, *Control and Urban Planning* (Faber, 1973), p. 125.

The primary safeguards against abuse remain the fact that it is the statutory plan against which departure applications need to be measured[37]; and that the Secretary of State will always be anxious to review an informal plan's background before giving it any weight in decision making. But abuse may, and does, exist in some contexts where these safeguards are absent or avoidable. It has become the practice, for example, for some highways authorities to maintain non-statutory road widening safeguarding schemes. The schemes, which indicate where road widening is proposed in the future, are deliberately not adopted by resolution so as not to form any basis for blight notice proceedings. For the same reason they have been withheld from district authorities anxious to incorporate them into their local plans. But when a planning application is received for land indicated as required for possible road widening, the highways authority will seek to have the building set back to the road widening line, an arrangement which the applicant may be prepared to accept without appeal if offered a greater density on the reduced site to compensate. But the consequence is that the appearance of the street gradually changes as various redevelopments proceed, without any public consideration of the policy. The policy remains non-statutory and unpublicised purely for financial reasons, although, ironically, it also avoids blighting of the property affected. Financial expedience is no substitute for open planning, but the use of this mechanism is practically immune from challenge.

[37] Though in 1973 the Secretary of State went so far as to announce that the availability of informal planning backing might make it unnecessary for him to call in a series of departure applications: see D.O.E. Circular 122/73, Annex A, para. 7.

CHAPTER 4

DEVELOPMENT AND ITS CONTROL

A. Introduction

Development control is the business end of the British planning system. Statutory plans in themselves have no direct legal impact upon land development, and perhaps the most striking feature of the post–1947 planning system is the independence of forward planning and development control. Unlike the zoning scheme systems commonly found in North America and many Commonwealth countries, where permission is conferred or witheld by the scheme itself and development control has a subordinate role in dealing with departure applications and conditional uses, British development control is comprehensive. The general rule is that building operations and changes in land use may only lawfully be undertaken where planning permission has been granted. The consequence is that each application for permission is able to be judged on its merits, and according not only to the physical criteria such as height, bulk and density which might be prescribed by a zoning scheme, but also less tangible criteria including the likely aesthetic, economic and social consequences of the development and its suitability for the particular site.

This is finely tuned control, in which the function of the statutory plans is one of guidance rather than prescription. The plan is always a "material consideration" in development control, but adherence to it is not prescribed by law. It is instead loosely underpinned by administrative practice and political interaction. This legal distinction between forward planning and development control is reflected in planning practice. It is a long standing (and still valid) criticism of the internal organisation of local authority planning departments that there is often little communication between the two branches, resulting in plans which bear little understanding of the difficulties of implementation through development control; and, equally, development control decisions which go against the carefully formulated policies of the plan. One explanation is that for some years development control has had to proceed in many areas without any up to date development plans at all, and that the business of local plan preparation is at last drawing together the two branches again. But the 1980 Act, with its reduction in the scope of county authority development control power, has served to increase the gap between strategic planning and development control for the future.

Development control is clearly an important means for securing plan implementation, although in the case of policies for growth and change it is positive intervention and public sector investment in infrastructure which play the dominant part in securing realisation of the proposals. Equally, it is wrong to see development control simply as the tool for plan implementation. The scope of activity controlled often goes well beyond that covered in any detail by approved plans, and a high proportion of applications for planning permission concern matters of only limited interest to those engaged in forward planning, such as minor house extensions and small scale use changes. The excessive concern of development control with issues of detail compared with its apparent impotence in the face of large scale development pressures has led to frequent charges that it is petty, bureaucratic, slow, inflexible and unresponsive. But there is a genuine dilemma in trying to design a control system with sufficient flexibility to cope with the great variety of issues thrown up by urban development, yet which is objectively fair in its application. This dilemma is particularly apparent at the boundaries of the development control jurisdiction. Most applications involving minor development raise no issues of planning significance when viewed individually, but their cumulative effects may be substantial. The prevailing philosophy since 1947 therefore has been to cast the net of development control broadly and to accept that many minor applications may be caught by it. It is not as unpopular a strategy as might be thought. Attempts by the Labour Government in 1977 to relax controls led to such fierce opposition that they were defeated in the House of Lords, and a renewed attempt by the Conservative Government in 1981 succeeded only after concessions had been made in respect of environmentally sensitive areas.

The reasons for the changes were twofold: there was first the ideological aim of reducing the scope of state interference in private enterprise, and secondly the practical aim of speeding up the planning process by reducing the number of planning applications. Applications for planning permission have been running at over 400,000 per annum for England and Wales over the past few years, although there was an increase of more than 50 per cent. during the boom years of 1972–74. Table 6 gives a breakdown by subject-matter of the development control workload in 1978–79, though it tells us little about the respective proportions of environmentally "significant" and "insignificant" applications and clearly views differ as to how such a distinction could be drawn. Although a significantly high proportion of applications were granted, it does not follow that the control process was purely a formality in those instances. By bringing development within the ambit of control there is provided a basis for negotiated modification of development proposals and for the imposition of conditions over the carrying out and subsequent use of the development.

Evidence to the House of Commons Expenditure Committee in 1977, and to George Dobry Q.C. in 1975 in the course of his review of development control, was sharply divided on where the limits to development control should be drawn. The Expenditure Committee accepted that concentration on too much minor development was clogging up the system and recommended a broadening of the exemptions from control conferred by the General Development Order.[1] Dobry, on the other hand, saw the solution in terms of retaining the broad scope of control but streamlining its management by dividing applications into two categories, and providing an expedited procedure for "Class A" applications, which would include all those which complied with an up to date development plan and all simple or minor applications where there were no significant objections.[2] But his

---

[1] *Planning Procedures; Eighth Report of the Expenditure Committee* (H.M.S.O., 1977), paras. 88–90.
[2] *Review of the Development Control System*, Final Report by George Dobry Q.C. (H.M.S.O., 1975).

Table 6

Planning Applications Decisions by Class of Development

Class of development	1978/79		
	Total decisions	Permissions granted	
		Number	%
A Building, engineering and other operations of which:	420,251	367,216	87
Residential	97,269	71,891	74
Industrial, storage and warehousing	23,846	21,202	89
Offices	8,431	7,416	88
Retail distribution and servicing	19,358	16,675	86
Mineral working	540	441	82
All other classes of building and other operations	270,807	249,591	92
B Changes of use	48,039	37,521	78
All classes of development	468,290	404,737	86

Source: Development Control Statistics 1978–79 D.O.E. 1980

recommendation, (together with the great majority of others in his report), found no favour with the Department of the Environment, and it is true that it would have introduced a cumbersome management system.

An important issue in drawing the boundary to control is the question of cost. The Expenditure Committee estimated the total cost of land use planning in England and Wales in 1976 as £113.5 million, of which around £38 million represented local authorities' development control costs.[3] The average cost per application was therefore something over £70, although authorities varied substantially in their estimates of attributable costs. Processing minor applications might be expected to cost well below the average, but the annual costs are still significant. They have to some extent been shifted to the private sector by the introduction of charges for planning applications from April 1, 1981, but that does not affect the overall issue of the cost effectiveness of a control system which is in some respects unnecessarily broad and in others unnecessarily restricted.

The heart of the problem lies in the way development is defined and the

---

[3] Op. cit. paras. 18 and 19. A detailed breakdown appears in the survey conducted for the Committee by Professor H.W.E. Davies, reproduced in Vol. III of the Appendices to the Report. The Local Government Financial Statistics England and Wales 1978–79 (H.M.S.O., 1981) indicate a cost of nearly £130 million by 1979, but the information is based upon different assumptions from the Davies survey.

sharp distinction between the legal definition and its planning implications. It is a definition couched in physically objective terms rather than in terms of environmental impact. Development is brought within control because of its type rather than its effects, and although some sifting of categories of development according to their likely effect is achieved by the exemptions provisions of the subordinate legislation, it is at best a crude reallocation.

B. The Concept of Development

1. *The scheme of the legislation*

In practical terms the first question is always to establish whether the activity concerned constitutes "development" as defined by the Act of 1971, and then to consider whether it is exempt from planning control either under the Use Classes Order (which deems certain use changes not to involve development) or the General Development Order (which grants "deemed" permission for a variety of cases). The first part of this chapter examines the general principles of interpretation of the definition and the function of the subordinate legislation, and there follows a brief analysis of the scope of control in respect of different classes of development. The deemed permissions under the General Development Order, and the Use Classes Order, are reproduced in Appendices B and C at the rear of the book. Subsequent chapters deal with the procedures for development control, the tools through which control is exerted and the decision making process.

The legal basis for development control stems from the simple requirement of the Act that planning permission be obtained for the carrying out of development.[4] Thus the way in which "development" is defined itself defines the scope of control. But obtaining a clear picture of what the word means is no easy matter. The scheme of the legislation is complex. It starts by first offering a very broad definition[5]:

> "In this Act, except where the context otherwise requires, "development", subject to the following provisions of this section, means the carrying out of building, engineering, mining or other operations in, on, over or under land, or the making of a material change in the use of any buildings or other land."

Then the Act goes on specifically to bring certain specific types of activity within the definition (in a series of provisions somewhat ironically introduced as being "for the avoidance of doubt")[6]; and specifically to exclude from control other defined activities.[7] Next, through subordinate

---

[4] T.C.P.A. 1971, s. 23(1).
[5] T.C.P.A. 1971, s. 22(1). The definition was drawn mainly from the Town and Country Planning Act 1932, s. 52, but extended to include a wider range of operational development, and at the same time restricted to "material" changes in use. The geographical scope of planning control is limited to the land mass of the British Isles, and the cordon has been tightly drawn by the Scottish courts at the high water mark: see *Argyle and Bute D.C.* v. *Secretary of State for Scotland* 1977 S.L.T. 33.
[6] T.C.P.A. 1971, s. 22(3).
[7] T.C.P.A. 1971, s. 22(2).

legislation and a variety of administrative devices, control is relaxed or strengthened in respect of different types of development, for different types of property, for different geographical areas and for different types of developers. The principal relaxations of control are brought about by two statutory instruments, the General Development Order[8] and the Use Classes Order,[9] but even in respect of these there may be modifications in respect of any particular site by virtue of some earlier planning permission,[10] or by virtue of some special direction[11] or special development order.[12] And finally, the Act contains special forms of control aimed at the preservation of buildings of special interest[13] and those located in conservation areas,[14] for tree preservation,[15] and for detailed control of caravan sites[16] and advertisements.[17]

The result is that to discover the impact of planning control upon a wide range of land use activity requires an understanding of an awkward mix of broadly conceptual provisions and some highly technical modifications. The definition proceeds "empirically rather than logically",[18] and the lack of overall conceptual cohesion has made it difficult to develop broad approaches to interpretation.[19]

2. The statutory definition

There are two distinct limbs to the statutory definition. First, there is the so-called "operational development" limb: the carrying out of building, engineering, mining or other operations in, on, over or under land, and where the common theme is that of the making of some physical change. The second limb extends to material changes in the use to which land is put, notwithstanding that such changes may result in no visible change in the appearance of a property. A dwellinghouse may be converted to office use without any physical changes, yet the conversion may have important planning implications. The distinction between the two limbs runs throughout the Act, and it is further reflected in the subordinate legislation. It has therefore become an important factor in interpretation,[20] not the least

---

[8] Town and Country Planning General Development Order 1977 (S.I. 1977 No. 289): *post*, p. 178 and Appendix B.
[9] Town and Country Planning (Use Classes) Order 1972 (S.I. 1972 No. 1385): *post*, p. 184, and Appendix C.
[10] See further *post*, p. 181.
[11] Under art. 4 of the General Development Order: *post*, p. 179.
[12] See further *post*, p. 183.
[13] *Post*, p. 462.
[14] *Post*, p. 475.
[15] *Post*, p. 456.
[16] Under the Caravan Sites and Control of Development Act 1960 and T.C.P.A. 1971, s. 29(5).
[17] *Post*, p. 483.
[18] *Coleshill and District Investment Co. Ltd.* v. *M.H.L.G.* [1969] 2 All E.R. 525 at 537 *per* Lord Wilberforce.
[19] Hence the comment of Donovan J. in *Fyson* v. *Bucks C.C.* [1958] 1 W.L.R. 634 at 637, that problems under the Act "would become even more difficult than they are already, and perhaps insoluble, if each time a construction had to be sought which would resolve all discord into song."
[20] See, *e.g. Parke* v. *S.O.S.E.* [1978] 1 W.L.R. 1308.

because different consequences flow from the categorisation of an activity. Enforcement power is more limited in the case of operational development, for example; and similarly although permission to carry out building operations generally carries with it the right to make any necessary change in use,[21] the converse is not true.[22] Some activities straddle the boundary, either because they involve elements of each or because they defy ready classification. Into the latter category falls such an activity as tipping waste materials on land: it may be undertaken simply for their disposal, and thus involve a change in use of the land[23]; or it may be an integral part of an engineering operation intended to enhance an existing use of land, such as to level out a field to allow more intensive cropping.[24] The land use implications may be identical in each case, and the determining factor is the intention underlying the activity.

Although the definition is wide and *prima facie* capable of extending to most land-related activity, there are two significant limitations. The most fundamental is that it is directed only to land use *changes*: the right to continue to use land or buildings in their present state and for their existing purposes remains unaffected by it. Development control is control over change, and although intervention against existing uses is possible under other powers in the Act it carries with it liability to pay compensation. That has in practice proved a sufficient deterrent to intervention in all but exceptional cases, and the consequence is that planning control has achieved comparatively little improvement in the impact of long established development.

The second limitation, which has been touched upon already, is that the definition is concerned with activity rather than impact. Impact is perhaps too intangible a concept to form the basis of a general working definition, although the Act does toy with it in other contexts by exempting, for example, "works . . . which do not materially affect the external appearance of the building",[25] and punishing unauthorised works which affect the "character" of a listed building.[26] But so far as the general definition is concerned there is a mismatch between the scope of the definition and its planning implications, and this gives rise in practice to intensive litigation over issues which to the casual observer seem trivial indeed. Why for example, should a county have decided to use the full weight of their enforcement powers against a small scale model railway and model houses in a model village on the grounds that they were unauthorised "development"?[27] And what could have possessed another authority to demand the removal of an offending development consisting of nothing more than twelve small metal pegs driven into the ground and connected by two thin strands of nylon rope?[28] The answer in each case is that the external

---

[21] T.C.P.A. 1971, s. 33 (2).
[22] So that "use" is defined by the Act as not including "the use of land for the carrying out of any building or other operations thereon": T.C.P.A. 1971, s. 290(1).
[23] See *e.g. Bilboe* v. *S.O.S.E.* (1980) 39 P. & C.R. 495.
[24] See *e.g. Northavon D.C.* v. *S.O.S.E.* (1980) 39 P. & C.R. 332.
[25] T.C.P.A. 1971, s. 22(2) *(a)*.
[26] *Ibid.* s. 55(1).
[27] *Buckinghamshire C.C.* v. *Callingham* (1952) 2 P. & C.R. 400.
[28] [1977] J.P.L. 122.

effects of the physical activities were potentially far more damaging than the development viewed in isolation, and the fact of the development was being used as the key for bringing the externalities within control. In the case of the model village the fear was that of attracting large numbers of visitors to the site; and in the second case the physical development was a step towards the sub-division of agricultural land into leisure plots, again liable to attract visitors and traffic as well as detracting from the appearance of unspoilt countryside.

Interpretation of the definition therefore takes place against the background of these two limitations, and they have influenced significantly the course of interpretation. It is an open textured definition, and in the words of Lord Wilberforce:

> " 'Development' is a key word in the planner's vocabulary but it is one whose meaning has evolved and is still evolving. It is impossible to ascribe to it any certain dictionary meaning, and difficult to analyse it accurately from the statutory definition."[29]

A significant feature of the evolution of interpretation has been the influence of the decision-making structure itself. The vagueness of the language means that in the absence of any more precise refinement of principle its application in individual cases is liable to depend upon the subjective assessment of the decision maker. Under planning legislation the primary decisions are taken by the Secretary of State, and comparatively rarely do questions involving the definition go to the courts in the first instance.

The scope for direct judicial determination has been whittled down by statute, and for the most part questions arise in the courts only upon appeal from the Secretary of State—to whom in turn the issue may have come upon appeal from a local authority determination or enforcement notice, or (rarely) by calling-in. Appeals to the High Court, unlike those to the Secretary of State, are confined to issues of law. And the scope for judicial rationalisation and development of principle has been limited by a characteristic reluctance on the part of the judges to intrude upon a sphere of decision-making reserved primarily for a government minister. Judicial jurisdiction is thus confined largely to supervision; and the principles governing this process are derived from public rather than private law. The courts' role is thus not one primarily of determining the rights of subjects vis-a-vis the local planning authority, but of ascertaining whether the Secretary of State has gone wrong in law. The distinction between issues of law and issues of fact is notoriously difficult to draw,[30] but the courts have shown little hesitation in confining the scope of their review in this context. The issues are "emphatically" not those of such complexity requiring legal skills for their resolution,[31] and the judges will not therefore normally

---

[29] *Coleshill and District Investment Co. Ltd.* v. *M.H.L.G.* [1969] 2 All E.R. 525 at 536.

[30] For a detailed analysis see S.A. de Smith, *Judicial Review of Administrative Action* (4th ed. 1980) pp. 126–151.

[31] *Coleshill and District Investment Co. Ltd.* v. *M.H.L.G.* [1969] 2 All E.R. 525 at 534 *per* Lord Upjohn, applying the following analysis of Denning L.J. in *British Launders' Research Association* v. *Central Middlesex Assessment Committee and Hendon Rating Authority* [1949] 1 K.B. 462 at 472: "Primary facts are facts which are observed by witnesses and proved by oral testimony or facts proved by the production of a thing itself, such as original documents. Their determination is essentially a matter of fact for the tribunal of fact, and the

substitute their inferences from the primary facts for those drawn by the Secretary of State, unless there was no evidence to support the findings of primary facts, the conclusions drawn by him could not reasonably be drawn from the primary facts, or he has gone so far beyond a reasonable interpretation of the Act as to render his decision wrong in law.[32]

It is this special relationship between the courts and the Secretary of State which lends an unusual character to the evolution of the definition of development. The Divisional Court has played a particularly influental role under the leadership in the 1960s of Lord Parker C.J. and in the 1970s under Lord Widgery C.J.[33] Each has consistently reiterated that interpretation of the section is primarily a matter of fact and degree for the responsible minister. The consequence is that the general pattern in the evolution of interpretative principles to meet the facts of new cases has been one of minsterial initiative, followed by judicial confirmation or occasional check or reformulation of principles. Hence, the application of the planning power to such instances as intensification of use, abandonment of use, the "planning unit" and demolition[34] has been left largely to the minister to determine, to the point where it is now said that it is only in "exceptional" cases that the court intervenes on appeal.[35]

Thus it is an area where, although nominally concerned with interpretation of a legal provision, there is a need to examine closely ministerial policy in interpretation. This is available to some limited extent from circulars, particularly Circular No. 67 published in 1949, (though recently cancelled) and from published ministerial decisions. For some years the decisions were collected and published officially by the ministry, but with one exception[36]

---

only question of law that can arise from them is whether there was any evidence to support the finding. The conclusions from primary facts are, however, inferences deduced by a process of reasoning from them. If, and in so far as, those conclusions can as well be drawn by a layman (properly instructed on the law) as by a lawyer, they are conclusions of fact for a tribunal of fact: and the only question of law which can arise on them are whether there was a proper direction in point of law; and whether the conclusion is one which could reasonably be drawn from the primary facts."

[32] Thus, the court may take the view that a different result may have ensued if it had taken the initial decision, but that nonetheless no error of law is evident: see, *e.g. Bendles Motors Ltd.* v. *Bristol Corporation* [1963] 1 W.L.R. 247 at 251–252, *per*Lord Parker C.J., and *Coleshill and District Investment Co. Ltd.* v. *M.H.L.G.* [1969] 2 All E.R. 525 at 538, *per* Lord Wilberforce, and 534, *per* Lord Upjohn.

[33] Both Lord Parker and Lord Widgery had served as junior Treasury counsel before their elevation to the bench, and Lord Widgery had had particular experience of planning cases in that role, with further experience as a regular member of Lord Parker's Divisional Court for some years.

[34] *Post*, p. 158, and see particularly the approach of the House of Lords in *Coleshill and District Investment Co. Ltd.* v. *M.H.L.G.* [1969] 2 All E.R. 525, where at 538 Lord Wilberforce said of the minister's policy advice on the matter that "it has no legal status but it acquired vitality and strength when, through the years, it passed as it certainly did, into planning practice and textbooks," observing too that the advice had been acted on in decisions and that no change in the statutory formula had been made in subsequent re-enactments.

[35] *Snook* v. *S.O.S.E.* (1975) 33 P. & C.R. 1 at 6, *per* Bridge J.; *Hilliard* v. *S.O.S.E.* [1978] J.P.L. 839 at 841 *per* Shaw L.J. delivering the judgment of the Court of Appeal.

[36] A volume of *Selected Enforcement and Allied Appeals* was published in 1977, (hereafter *Enforcement Appeals*). Otherwise the main sources of published decisions are the *Journal of Planning and Environment Law* (J.P.L.), the *Estates Gazette* and the series *Planning Appeals* published by Ambit Publications.

that practice has now ceased, and reports of decisions are generally available only in the pages of various professional and trade journals. These rulings have no formal binding effect, and there have been instances where the Secretary of State's interpretation has varied over the years. Moreover the decisions tend to avoid the enunciation of general principles and the detailed interpretative analysis that a lawyer might expect from a judicial decision. But they are nevertheless of important persuasive value. The consequence of over 30 years of judicial and ministerial interpretation is that there has now emerged a superstructure of interpretative principle: some principles are tentative, others tested and confirmed. We now turn to examine them in detail.

3. Operational development

Under this limb of the definition it is the "carrying out of building, engineering, mining and other operations in, on, over or under land" which is brought within the scope of planning control. The underlying theme of this grouping of activities is that of physical change: they each deal with positive indentifiable acts of a constructive (or in the case of mining, destructive) character, with visible results. Given this overall theme, it has often proved unnecessary to distinguish in practice between each of the described operations: simply to identify some operaton resulting in physical change will be sufficient. But various distinctions are drawn in the Act itself and in the subordinate legislation affecting the incidence of control, and detailed analysis is therefore necessary.

(a) Building operations

A "building" is further defined by the Act for general development control purposes as including "any structure or erection, and any part of a building, as so defined, but does not include plant or machinery comprised in a building."[37] "Building operations" also receives an extended definition, as including "rebuilding operations, structural alterations of or addition to buildings, and other operations normally undertaken by a person carrying on business as a builder."[38] Vague though it is, that final phrase offers perhaps the clearest indication of general principle in the definition. The courts tended initially to be guided in their interpretation of the section by the property lawyer's distinction between fixtures passing with the freehold upon sale of land, and chattels: although no clear single test existed, the usual approach was to examine the degree and purpose of the annexation of the object to the land,[39] and to distinguish between the placing of a chattel and the erection of a more permanent structure. But more recently the question has been posed in slightly different form. It is first necessary to ask whether what has been done has resulted in the erection of a "building": if so, then the court "should want a great deal of persuading that the erection of it had

---

[37] T.C.P.A. 1971, s. 280(1).
[38] Ibid.
[39] Cheshire C.C. v. Woodward [1962] 2 Q.B. 126. The fixtures/chattels test was not rigidly applied in ministerial determination however: see further W.A. Leach, "Building Operations and Buildings" [1969] J.P.L. 368.

not amounted to a building or other operation."[40] In construing the meaning of "building" under the Act, the Divisional Court has in *Barvis Ltd. v. Secretary of State for the Environment*[41] placed reliance upon a passage in the judgment of Jenkins J. in *Cardiff Rating Authority v. Guest Keen Baldwin's Iron & Steel Co. Ltd.*,[42] where the comparable words "structure or in the nature of a structure" in the context of rating legislation were considered. It was accepted that no single universal test applied, but three primary factors are identified by that judgment as being relevant:

(i) *Size*

The expressions "building" and "structure" suggest something sizeable: "I think of such size that they either have been in fact, or would normally be, built or constructed on the hereditament as opposed to being brought onto the hereditament already made."[43] A "building" may still be comparatively small however: thus the Divisional Court has, albeit with some reluctance, accepted that the erection of further small model buildings and a model railway in an existing model village constituted development.[44] And comparatively minor operations such as the erection of a carport with a cardboard roof covered in roofing felt and canvas tarpaulin sides,[45] and the fixing of striped blinds outside the windows of a building,[46] have been held by the minister to constitute development. But where the operations are quite insignificant they may be regarded as *de minimis*, and outside control.[47]

(ii) *Permanence*

A building, structure or erection normally also denotes the making of a physical change of some permanence. For example, it might be something which once installed would normally remain, and only be removed by a process of demolition or dismantling.[48] Thus the Divisional Court has declined to find any error in a ruling that a battery of fairground swing

---

[40] *Barvis Ltd. v. S.O.S.E.* (1971) 22 P. & C.R. 710. Lord Parker C.J., who gave the leading judgment in the *Cheshire* case, was also a member of the Divisional Court in *Barvis*, where the leading judgment was delivered by Bridge J.

[41] *Ibid.*, p. 716.

[42] [1949] 1 K.B. 385. The case had been cited to the Divisional Court in the *Cheshire* case, but not relied upon in the judgment of Lord Parker C.J.

[43] *Cardiff Rating Authority v. Guest Keen Baldwin's Iron and Steel Co. Ltd.* [1949] 1 K.B. 385 at 402.

[44] *Bucks C.C. v. Callingham* [1952] 1 All E.R. 1166. The buildings were constructed on a scale of one inch to the foot, on a concrete foundation.

[45] *Enforcement Appeals*, p. 35. And similarly a carport on wheels standing on a concrete base has been held to be a "structure": [1967] J.P.L. 552.

[46] *Enforcement Appeals*, p. 40; but cf. *Kensington and Chelsea R.L.B.C. v. C.G. Hotels* (1980) 41 P. & C.R. 40.

[47] The maxim, *de minimis non curat lex* (the law does not take account of very small or trivial matters) has been used broadly to allow an area of tolerance in control. It may mean no more, however, than a reinforcement of the view that trivial works do not constitute operations within the Act: see, *e.g.* [1977] J.P.L. 122.

[48] *Cardiff Rating Authority v. Guest Keen Baldwin's Iron & Steel Co. Ltd.* [1948] 1 K.B. 385, *supra.*

boats, capable of being lifted and taken away complete by six men, or dismantled in about one hour,[49] did not constitute development. Lord Parker C.J. expressed the view that "the building or erection to constitute development must be of some permanent character to which the word "demolition" can be more aptly applied than it can be to something which can be carried off by a few men intact".[50]

(iii) *Physical attachment*

Slightly less weight appears to have been placed upon the degree of physical attachment to the land under this test than is usual in fixture/chattel cases. It is said to be a relevant consideration, but of itself inconclusive. In general terms the tendency has been to exclude from control objects not affixed to the land, such as free-standing residential caravans.[51] In the *Cheshire* case the Divisional Court had declined to interfere with the finding of the minister that no development had occurred when a wheeled coal hopper and conveyor some sixteen to twenty feet high had been brought onto the appeal site.[52] But in the *Barvis*[53] case itself the Divisional Court had no hesitation in upholding a ministerial ruling that development had occurred with the erection of a tower crane some 89 feet high with a lifting jib 120 feet long, which ran along rails 120 feet long permanently fixed to precast concrete beams. The very size of the crane was sufficient to convince the Court that it was a "structure or erection" under the Act. And the minister has been prepared to hold that the erection of a tent, of about 30 feet x 14 feet x 10½ feet used for storage, constitutes operational development.[54]

It follows that the fact that an object is capable of limited motion on site, does not conclusively prevent a finding that it is a structure or erection, although the ease with which it may be moved both on site and away from the site may also be a function of its size and its degree of annexation, and go to the question of intended permanence.

The Act specifically excludes from control the "carrying out of works for the maintenance, improvement or other alteration of any building, being works which affect only the interior of the building or which do not materially affect the external appearance of the building."[55] The exemption falls short of conferring unlimited rights to rebuild dilapidated or destroyed buildings[56]; but the dividing line between alteration and rebuilding is always

---

[49] *James v. Brecon C.C.* (1963) 15 P. & C.R. 20.
[50] *Ibid.* at 24.
[51] Although their use may involve a material change in use: for examples of the general approach see [1975] J.P.L. 104 (m.p.d.); [1975] J.P.L. 586 (m.p.d.); and compare [1975] J.P.L. 368 (erection of "portacabins" involving development) and [1977] J.P.L. 47 (chicken "verandahs" 51 feet high but not affixed, involving development).
[52] [1962] 2 Q.B. 126.
[53] (1971) 22 P. & C.R. 710. An extended extract from the minister's decision in that case is reprinted in *Enforcement Appeals*, pp. 38–39.
[54] [1969] J.P.L. 592.
[55] T.C.P.A. 1971, s. 22(2)(a). The subsection is derived from the Town and Country Planning (General Interim Development) Order 1933, art. 4. The exemption now excludes, however, works for alteration of a building by providing additional space therein below ground.
[56] The refusal of permission to rebuild may, however, render an authority financially liable: see, as to purchase notice procedure, *post*, p. 653.

a matter of degree. The replacement of all four walls together with the laying of a new concrete floor has been held to constitute development,[57] even where the necessity for more extensive works was not apparent when a programme of repairs was commenced.[58]

(b) Engineering operations

Less guidance is available as to the extent of "engineering operations": the expression does however include "the formation or laying out of means of access to highways,"[59] and "means of access" includes "any means of access, whether private or public, for vehicles or for foot passengers, and includes a street."[60] But highway authority works for the maintenance or improvement of roads do not constitute development,[61] and nor do works carried out by local authorities and statutory undertakers for the purpose of inspection, repair or renewal of sewers, pipes, cables or other apparatus.[62]

Again the question of scale may be relevant, but the matter is one of degree. Thus " . . . a little job of shifting a few cubic yards of soil with a digger and a lorry is not, in my judgment, an operation of a kind which could ever be dignified with the title of an engineering operation"[63]; but, on the other hand, the removal of large soil and rubble embankments could well be.[64]

Other types of activity held to fall within the definition include the drilling of exploratory bores,[65] the tipping of soil and rubble for the

---

[57] *Enforcement Appeals*, p. 35; and *cf. Larkin* v. *Basildon D.C.* [1980] J.P.L. 407, where the rebuilding of four walls of a dwelling was held not to constitute simply "enlargement, improvement or alteration" under Sched. I, Class I of the General Development Order.

[58] *Street* v. *Essex C.C.* (1965) E.G. 537.

[59] T.C.P.A. 1971, s. 290(1). "Highway" is also given an extended definition, covering not only carriageways but also bridle-paths and foot-paths, though excluding private rights of way: s. 290(1), and Highways Act 1980, ss. 328 and 329. And "means of access" extends to "any means of access, whether private or public, for vehicles or for foot passengers, and includes a street": T.C.P.A. 1971, s. 290(1). "Development" in laying out an access still requires some engineering development, and not simply the removal of an existing fence: [1981] J.P.L. 380 (m.p.d.)

[60] T.C.P.A. 1971, s. 290(1).

[61] *Ibid.* s.22 (2)(b). The exception is limited to existing roads, and to works carried out within their boundaries. Neither maintenance nor improvement is defined by the Act, but reference to the Highways Act 1980 suggests that they might be given a broad interpretation. A similar exemption is conferred by the General Development Order Sched. I, Class IX for works by any person on unadopted streets and private ways.

[62] *Ibid.* s. 22(2)(b). The works may extend to the breaking-up of any street or other land; but see further controls under the Public Utilities Street Works Act 1950.

[63] *Coleshill and District Investment Co. Ltd.* v. *M.H.L.G.* [1968] 1 All E.R. 62 at 65, *per* Widgery J. But both the Court of Appeal [1968] 1 All E.R. 945 (and the House of Lords [1969] 2 All E.R. 525) disagreed with the description of the facts, Lord Pearson however observing (at 542) that if he were able to agree with it, he would also agree that such works were not an engineering operation.

[64] *Coleshill and District Investment Co. Ltd.* v. *M.H.L.G.* [1969] 2 All E.R. 525, upholding the minister's original determination.

[65] [1975] J.P.L. 609; and see Report of Stevens Committee, *Planning Control over Mineral Working* (H.M.S.O., 1976), Chap. 13. Such an operation is likely in many cases to be temporary or *de minimis*: see further D.O.E. Circular 58/78, Report of the Committee on Planning Control over Mineral Working.

purposes of agricultural improvement,[66] and earth moving and building a green, earth mounds and bunkers as parts of a scheme for golf course improvement.[67]

(c) Mining operations

"Mining operations" as such receives no statutory definition, but "minerals" is exhaustively defined as including "all minerals and substances in or under land of a kind ordinarily worked for removal by underground or surface working, except that it does not include peat cut for purposes other than sale."[68] "Mining operations" is however defined in almost identical fashion by the Town and Country (Minerals) Regulations 1971 [69] and by the General Development Order,[70] as "the mining and working of minerals[71] in, on, or under land, whether by surface or underground working"; and the Town and Country Planning (Minerals) Act 1981 has added a further activity, "the removal of material of any description from a mineral-working deposit."[72]

In terms of general principle, the extraction of minerals is substantially different from building and engineering operations. Although defined by the Act as an "operation", mining generally bears more resemblance to activities covered by the "use" limb of the definition, (from which the statutory definition expressly excludes it)[73] to the extent that it is a continuing activity, frequently over a very long term, and an end in itself. And unlike the other types of operation, by removing and processing minerals, which are part of the land, mining operations actually destroy land: their general effect is destructive rather than constructive.[74] The possibility of unlawful mining operations escaping planning control by virtue of the "four year rule"[75] has been narrowed by a Court of Appeal ruling rejecting the notion of mining as a continuous user, and insisting that for the purposes of development control, each shovelful is a mining operation constituting development.[76]

But weaknesses in the control system led, amongst other considerations, to the recommendation by the Stevens Committee on Planning Control over Mineral Working[77] that there should be established a "special regime" for

---

[66] And hence within the scope of exemption under Class VI of the Schedule to the General Development Order: see *Northavon D.C.* v. *S.O.S.E.*(1980) 39 P. & C.R. 332.

[67] *Enforcement Appeals*, p. 50.

[68] T.C.P.A. 1971, s. 290(1)

[69] S.I. 1971 No. 756, reg. 1(3). By virtue of the special statutory power in s. 264 of the 1971 Act, the regulations may modify or adapt certain provisions of the Act.

[70] art. 2(1)

[71] Excluding, in the case of the Minerals Regulations, excepted minerals, such as those mined in connection with agricultural use and those vested in the National Coal Board: reg. 1 (3)(a) and (b). These rights are preserved by the Act itself in s. 264(4).

[72] T.C.P.A. 1971, s. 22 (3A), added by T.C.P.(M).A. 1981, s. 1.

[73] T.C.P.A. 1971, s. 290(1). See also Town and Country Planning (Minerals) Regulations 1971, reg. 3.

[74] Hence the difficulty experienced by Lord Pearson in his opinion in the *Coleshill* case, in detecting any common characteristic in the three specific heads of operational development which might aid in interpreting the residual category of "other operations": [1969] 2 All E.R. 525 at 543–544.

[75] *Post*, pp. 389–391.

[76] *Thomas David (Porthcawl) Ltd.* v. *Penybont R.D.C.* [1971] 1 W.L.R. 1526.

[77] *Planning Control over Mineral Working* (H.M.S.O., 1976), Chap. 3.

planning control over mining, with fresh definition of "mining operations"[78] and a special procedure for mineral applications and permissions. The "special regime" recommendation has been rejected by the government,[79] but substantial amendments have now been made to the 1971 Act by the Town and Country Planning (Minerals) Act 1981, and their effect is analysed in a separate section of this book.[80]

(d) "Other operations"

It is unclear what type of activity is brought within control by virtue of this part of the definition, and it has rarely been relied upon in practice. The courts have rejected an approach to interpretation based upon the *eiusdem generis* rule,[81] which would have limited the expression to operations of the same class or "genus" as building, engineering and mining operations. It proved impossible to identify any such class or genus beyond the very general notion of physical change. But a limiting interpretation has nonetheless emerged, based upon the reluctance of the courts to permit the breadth of control, which a literal interpretation of the phrase might otherwise allow, to extend to matters of no possible planning relevance: mowing grass, draining septic tanks or cleaning windows, for example. And so the phrase is to be read as taking meaning from the other more precise operation definitions, but in a less rigid sense than that inherent in the *eiusdem generis* rule.[82] From this it may be deduced that an "other operation" should be such as might alter the physical characteristics of land, sufficiently substantially to be beyond the *de minimis* principle and in such a manner as to be within the general contemplation of planning legislation. In practice the breadth of exemption afforded by the General Development Order to various minor works renders the scope of "other operations" largely theoretical, although there remains the power of authorities to exclude certain of the exemptions of the Order by directions under Article 4 or by conditions on a planning permission.[83]

(e) Demolition

Except in the case of listed buildings and buildings in a conservation area,

---

[78] So as to extend control to the mining and working of minerals from a deposit of mineral waste: see now s. 22 (3A), note 72, *supra*.

[79] D.O.E. Circular 58/78 (W.O. 103/78) *Report of the Committee on Planning Control over Mineral Working*, p. 5.

[80] *Post*, pp. 487–498.

[81] *Coleshill and District Investment Co. Ltd.* v. *M.H.L.G.* [1969] 2 All E.R. 525 at 532 (*per* Lord Wilberforce, brusquely rejecting the minister's suggestion that the genus might be "development" itself as "a process . . . of levitation by intellectual boot strap"; and at 543 (*per* Lord Pearson). A similar approach had been taken in the Scottish case of *Ross* v. *Aberdeen C.C.* 1955. S.C. (Sh. Subs.) 65 at 68.

[82] Adopting instead the doctrine of *noscitur a sociis*: see, in the *Coleshill* case (*supra*) the opinions of Lord Morris (at 529), Lord Wilberforce (at 537) and Lord Pearson (at 543).

[83] And there are instances where exemptions conferred by the Order extend only to certain types of operation: thus the agricultural development exemption of Class VI extends to building and engineering, but not "other" operations, on which see the decision cited at note 66, *ante*. The General Development Order 1977, Sched. 1, Class II.3 specifically authorises "the painting of the exterior of any building. . . . "; but it is dubious whether that falls within the definition of development in any event.

the legislation imposes no clear prohibition against demolition. There may, however, be some cases where the nature of the work falls within the general definition of development. A particular demolition undertaking may constitute so large or complex a project, for example, as to constitute an engineering operation.[84] Or demolition may form the first part of a rebuilding operation,[85] or in the case of partial demolition it may amount to a building operation making a material change in the external appearance of the building and therefore not exempted by section 22.[86] But beyond this there is little agreement as to the extent to which demolition falls within control, and both the courts[87] and the ministry have shown remarkable reluctance to clarify the position.

There are further practical problems. The enforcement machinery is designed primarily to achieve the remedying of any breaches of control, and large scale demolition clearly poses remedial difficulties. A "stop" notice[88] might be served to prevent further unauthorised development, but uncertainty as to the extent to which demolition constitutes development coupled with the requirement to compensate for wrongful use of this procedure, involves that authorities are necessarily reluctant to invoke it.

Reform aimed at bringing demolition generally within control was strongly advocated in 1974 by George Dobry Q.C. in a special Interim Report,[89] but his recommendations were not accepted. The minister continues to take the view[90] that demolition by itself does not generally constitute development.[91] It is perverse that an operation which may have such serious land use implications, especially in urban areas, should remain uncontrolled; but the introduction of any control would need to be accompanied by measures requiring at least minimum maintenance to be undertaken.

4. Material Change of Use

The concept of material change of use has a beguiling simplicity. In the parliamentary debates on the 1947 Act, one distinguished lawyer commented that he thought it eminently reasonable and satisfactory: "It lays down what each one of us using commonsense would say that development

---

[84] As in the *Coleshill* case, where the House of Lords declined to overturn a ministerial finding that removal of an embankment of rubble and soil which had been protecting the blast walls of some disused explosives stores and magazines constituted an engineering operation.

[85] See, e.g. *London C.C.* v. *Marks and Spencer Ltd.* [1953] A.C. 535 at 541; but compare *Iddenden* v. *S.O.S.E.* [1972] 3 All E.R. 883, where the demolition of Nissen huts was held not to constitute development, nor to form part of an unauthorised rebuilding operation.

[86] *Ante*, p. 155. In *City of Glasgow D.C.* v. *Secretary of State for Scotland* 1982 S.L.T. 28 the Court of Session held that the demolition of the upper storeys of a tenement block constituted development, but that planning permission was not required where the work had been carried out under a warrant granted under building regulation controls entitling the authority to enter the property and carry out the demolition if the owners had failed to do so.

[87] See *e.g. Coleshill and District Investment Co. Ltd.* v. *M.H.L.G.* [1969] 2 All E.R. 525.

[88] *Post*, p. 423.

[89] *Control of Demolition* (H.M.S.O., 1974).

[90] First adopted in M.T.C.P. Circular 67 of 1949, para. 4(i).

[91] See, e.g. [1976] J.P.L. 53 (m.p.d.) Note, however, the requirement under the Public Health Act 1961, s. 29, that notice be given to the local authority of any intended demolition (with certain exceptions), and the powers of the authority to require the carrying out of supplementary works including the shoring up of adjacent buildings, sealing of sewers and the removal of rubbish.

was."[92] But commonsense has proved too frail a guide for case by case analysis, and the concept of material change of use has proved peculiarly difficult to apply in practice. Land uses tend to start, grow, decline, change, intertwine and separate in a way which defies simple analysis. The remarkable vagueness of the statutory formula has led to the development of a body of detailed principles by the Secretary of State and some highly conceptual doctrine from the courts, in an attempt to achieve some degree of consistency and certainty in its application.

There is a simple process of comparison suggested by the formula. The new or proposed use is compared with the old. If the two are different, there is a change of use. If the two are materially different, there is a material change in use. Thus the key to the definition lies in two interlocking concepts: the notion of an "existing" use (and the extent of rights enjoyable with it), and the notion of "materiality" in assessing the degree of change. But before considering each of these elements, it is necessary to grapple with some semantic difficulties. In practice the question has often developed into one of how land uses may be described for the purpose of comparison. If the application of the definition is to be a matter entirely of fact and degree for subjective assessment, then the problem of labelling different land uses is of marginal significance. But the achievement of some degree of rationalisation and consistency in determinations under the section requires the establishment of some common language of land use description. It is a requirement reinforced by the insistence of the enforcement machinery, through which so many of the borderline diputes are fought, that the alleged breach of control be "specified."[93] But establishing, and distinguishing between, different categories of land use with any precision has proved a difficult proposition, partly because of the vagueness of the Act itself, and partly because of the reluctance of the courts to establish more specific rules. There is, as a result, some limited cohesion in analysis, but also much semantic confusion.

(a) The Use Description: Specific or General?

Language is hierarchical. A use description may be very general, or quite specific. The Act offers no guidance as to which level of the hierarchy to select for analysis. The more abstract the appropriate use descriptions in any particular case, the less likely is it that a finding of material change of use will follow. At one level of land use description there are such broad categories as agricultural, residential, industrial and commercial. If material change of use were held to occur only when a change was made from one of these categories to another, the impact of this limb of control would be comparatively limited. But within the category of "residential" use there are numerous sub-categories of use description in everyday language, such as "house," "private dwelling-house," "hotel," "hostel," or "agricultural dwelling." If regard were not had to these, and if "residential" were to be treated as the appropriate use description, a change such as that from private

[92] H.C. Deb., Vol. 437, col. 1562 (May 14, 1947) *per* Mr. Quentin Hogg M.P. (later Lord Hailsham, Lord Chancellor). However, Mr. J.S.C. Reid M.P., who later became a Lord of Appeal in Ordinary was more cautious. Of material change of use, he said "Nobody knows what that means": *Standing Committee on Scottish Bills* (1946–47) col. 1266 (April 29, 1947).
[93] T.C.P.A. 1971, s. 87(6).

dwelling-house to hotel could not be regarded as a material change of use, since each use falls within the general classification. On the other hand, if the appropriate descriptions were "private dwelling-house" and "hotel" respectively, then a finding of material change would follow.

At issue is the scope of the planning power. Is it the intention of the legislation that control should extend as far as changes in ownership of a site, for example, through use descriptions as specific as "agricultural labourer's dwelling," or "middle class residence for occupation by husband and wife and two children"? And should control extend to the detailed nature of industrial processes carried on in a factory, or the nature of goods sold in a shop? No systematic attempt has ever been made to classify land uses precisely in such a way as to provide a ready reckoner for applying the definition.[94] Instead there has developed a body of interpretative principle based upon general indications in the Act itself, upon the wording of the subordinate legislation, and ultimately upon minsterial and judicial perceptions of the sort of activity which ought to be controlled by planning. An examination of the way in which the test has developed in the context of residential accommodation illustrates the effect of these various influences.

The initiative came first from the minister. In an early circular he indicated that the choice of label would be an important part of analysis, and that his primary concentration would be upon broad use descriptions, although changes falling within those categories might also in certain circumstances be material:

"A change in *kind* will always be material—*e.g.* from house to shop or from shop to factory. A change in the *degree* of an existing use may be material but only if it is very marked. For example, the fact that lodgers are taken privately in a family dwelling house would not in the minister's view constitute a material change in itself so long as the use of the house remains substantially that of a private residence. On the other hand, the change from a private residence with lodgers to a declared guest house, boarding house or private hotel would be 'material'."[95]

By a "change in kind" therefore the Minister meant a change between two categories defined at a comparatively high level of abstraction. A change from agricultural to industrial, or residential to commercial will always be material. For practical purposes it is often unnecessary to go any further than that. The Act itself draws a high level of abstraction in the case of agricultural uses, for example, and the Use Classes Order does the same for "office" and (with some exceptions) "shop" uses. In none of those cases is it necessary to look beyond the abstract label.

In cases where those exceptions do not apply, however, the Minister's advice clearly envisaged that closer enquiry was possible, and that more precise labels might be used, provided recognition was extended to what

---

[94] And the difficulties encountered in establishing a common land use description pattern for the purpose of collating data for monitoring change demonstrate the complexity. A joint governmental study team reported in 1976 that it had examined no less than 21 different classification systems currently in use, and found great differences between them. They advocated the adoption of a standard classification system based on 2,500 land use names, and ordered into a hierarchy of four tiers: *National Land Use Classification* (H.M.S.O., 1976), and D.O.E. Circular 16/76.

[95] M.T.C.P. Circular No. 67 of 1949, para. 4(iii).

have since come to be known as "ancillary" or "incidental" uses[96]: the right
to carry out a range of activity, such as the taking in of lodgers, which is
closely related to the primary use, or "predominant" use, of the site as a
whole. Again, of course, the scope of permissible ancillary uses depends
upon how broadly or narrowly the predominant use is defined. The Act
offered some clues in the case of residential accommodation, by referring
twice to the use-description of "dwelling-house." Buildings or land within
the curtilage of a dwelling-house may be used for any purpose incidental to
the enjoyment of the dwelling-house as such,[97] and further, conversion of
one dwelling-house into two or more is declared ("for the avoidance of
doubt") to involve a material change in use.[98]

So it was not surprising then when the minister's selection of more precise
use descriptions than simply "residential" was subsequently upheld by the
Divisional Court, although, curiously, in a case where the minister had failed
to follow his own advice.[99] And the Court was prepared to go further. The
minister had quashed an enforcement notice alleging material change of use
from "single dwelling-house" to "house-let-in-lodgings" on the ground that
the property remained residential. Lord Parker C.J. thought "that it would
be very odd if one could not go further than merely determine that because it
is residential that is an end of the matter."[1] He turned for guidance to the
Use Classes Order, and accepted that the point of many of the Order's
specific exemptions would be lost if it were found that the minister could not
in any event choose a more specific use description.[2]

The courts have proceeded from that basis in numerous subsequent cases,
although drawing upon somewhat variable criteria. Thus they have upheld
minsterial distinctions between such specific use descriptions as "private
dwelling-house," "staff hostel,"[3] "lodging-house"[4] (or "house-let-in-
lodgings"),[5] "students' hostel,"[6] "bed-sitting rooms"[7] and "hotel."[8] Further, the description "multiple paying occupation" has emerged as distinct
from "private dwelling-house" to describe accommodation occupied by
persons other than a family.[9] But equally they have upheld a finding that no

---

[96] *Post*, p. 168.
[97] T.C.P.A. 1971, s. 22(3)(a).
[98] T.C.P.A. 1971, s. 22(2)(d).
[99] *Birmingham Corporation* v. *Habib Ullah* [1964] 1 Q.B. 178.
[1] *Ibid.*
[2] The Lord Chief Justice's fondness for employing subordinate legislation as a guide for
interpreting the authorising Act had been criticised by the Court of Appeal in an earlier
planning case, *Stephens* v. *Cuckfield R.D.C.* [1960] 2 Q.B. 373 at 381 (though compare *Britt*
v. *Buckinghamshire C.C.* [1964] 1 Q.B. at 93 *per* Pearson L.J.). In essence it involves that the
minister's interpretation of the Act as revealed in his subordinate legislation becomes the
determining factor in the courts' interpretation of the Act itself. Whatever the legalities, the
result has been a pragmatic marriage of concept between the Act and its subordinate
legislation; but for a robust rejection of this approach see *Crowborough Parish Council* v.
S.O.S.E. [1981] J.P.L. 281.
[3] *Clarke* v. *M.H.L.G.* (1966) 18 P. & C.R. 82.
[4] *Hammersmith L.B.C.* v. *S.O.S.E.* (1975) 73 L.G.R. 288.
[5] *Birmingham Corporation* v. *Habib Ullah* [1964] 1 Q.B. 178 at 190, *per* Lord Parker C.J.,
Borg v. *Khan* (1965) 17 P. & C.R. 144.
[6] *Mornford Investments Ltd.* v. *M.H.L.G.* [1970] 2 All E.R. 253.
[7] *Mayflower Cambridge Ltd.* v. *S.O.S.E.* (1975) 30 P. & C.R. 28, where differences in
transience of residents was used to distinguish bed-sitting room use from use as a hotel.
[8] *Mornford Investments Ltd.* v. *M.H.L.G.* [1970] 2 All E.R. 253.
[9] See, *e.g. Duffy* v. *Pilling* (1977) 33 P. & C.R. 85, *Lipson* v. *S.O.S.E.* (1976) 33 P. & C.R. 95.

change in character occurred when a "private dwelling" came to be used as a "holiday house" by its owner, who also made it available to members of his staff and on a limited basis to rent paying family groups.[10] It is not, of course, purely a question of labelling. Descriptive language may be inadequate to describe a change; and, conversely, the mere fact that different labels can readily be attached to the old and the new use does not necessarily mean that the change has been "material". But the choice of labels is of practical importance as establishing a common language for identifying the scope of activity to which control extends.

These examples may convey the impression that the meaning of the concept has become precisely defined in practice over the years. And in many cases this is true. But there remain a number of borderline issues—some involving complex issues of multiple use where overall assessment may never be more than impressionistic; and others where the courts' insistence upon broad ministerial discretion has often obscured the scope for straightforward and precise analysis. This has been a particular feature of the judicial approach to the word "material" in the definition.

(b) Materiality: size or impact?

The Minister initially interpreted "material" as meaning "substantial," in the sense that "a proposed change of use constitutes development only if the new use is *substantially* different from the old."[11] But he offered no criteria by which this might be measured, otherwise than to indicate that "comparison with the previous use of the land or building in question is the governing factor and the effect of a proposal on a surrounding neighbourhood is not relevant to the issue."[12] It was thus an attempt to distinguish between the initial *legal* issue of whether permission was required under the Act, and the *planning* issue of whether permission ought actually to be granted. But assessment of materiality by such limited criteria is difficult. In borderline cases both the minister and the courts have been guided by subjective assessments of the types of activity which the Act might be expected to control: assessments in which predictions in general terms of the likely planning impact of a proposal must necessarily play a part. It is true that the scale of change is a relevant factor, and the boundaries of materiality in that sense have in practice been set through reliance upon the lawyer's concept of *de minimis*, to exclude from control activities thought to be unimportant by reason of their small scale[13] or infrequent occurrence.[14]

---

[10] *Blackpool B.C.* v. *S.O.S.E.* [1980] J.P.L. 527.

[11] M.T.C.P. Circular No. 67, para. 4(iii) (emphasis in the original).

[12] *Ibid.* para. 4(ii).

[13] The maxim in full is *de minimis non curat lex*, or, "the law has no regard to trivial matters." The relationship between *de minimis* and materiality is ill-defined. They are not exclusive descriptions of use change: there may be changes which are neither material nor *de minimis* (see, *e.g.* [1978] J.P.L. 568 (m.p.d.) where the appellant was advised that although his activities had not yet involved development, any further changes by way of intensification would involve development). The courts have avoided the semantic possibilities of the distinctions by leaving it to the minister: see, *e.g. Williams* v. *M.H.L.G.* (1967) 18 P. & C.R. 514 at 518, *per* Widgery J.; *London Borough of Bromley* v. *Hoeltschi* [1978] J.P.L. 45; and see *Kwik Save Discount Group Ltd.* v. *S.O.S.E.* [1981] J.P.L. 198, where the use of premises of 20,000 square feet for a period of one month offering five cars for sale was held to be purely a token use and *de minimis* thus precluding the company from exercising the right under the Use Classes Order to change the use to use as a discount store.

[14] See *e.g.* [1978] J.P.L. 201 (m.p.d.): one instance of cutting up old motor vehicle bodies.

But the courts have overturned the minister's early advice. To them the word "material" carried the sense of "material for planning purposes", having regard in particular to the possible effects of a development proposal upon local amenity.[15] As a guide to general interpretation such an approach is clearly helpful: it enables the courts to have regard to whether the change proposed is of the sort likely to have been within the contemplation of the legislature. There are still other limits of course: it has been held as a widely accepted truth that planning has no concern with the characteristics of individual people, the number of their children or how well behaved they may be,[16] (no matter what detrimental effect may result to the local amenities). But in assessing planning impact in less personal terms, one judge has been prepared to go so far as to suggest that the proposals be measured against the specific planning implications of each proposal, employing such guides as the development plan for an area or any other declared policy of the planning authority.[17] It is implicit in such an approach that planning policy and legality become irretrievably intertwined, and that the scope of control as a result might vary substantially between different parts of the country. A change of use might be thought to be material in a rural area, but not in town. This extreme approach has not found subsequent endorsement.

But the general approach of assessing likely environmental impact as a guide to the intended scope of planning control has had substantial influence. It has gone hand in hand with the insistence by the courts on the degree of discretion enjoyed by the Secretary of State, for materiality in planning terms must necessarily be a matter for ministerial rather than judicial determination. Thus the Divisional Court was swift to reject in the early 1960s attempts by counsel to establish *a priori* criteria for distinguishing between general and specific use descriptions: between, for example, changes from general kinds of use and changes of method or systems of user.[18] These were matters for the Minister. And in the assessment of materiality, the Minister was entitled to look to general planning implications. Thus in *Williams* v. *Minister of Housing and Local Government*[19] the Minister had declared that the sale of imported produce from a nursery garden, which had an established use for the sale of produce grown on the land, involved a material change of use. In upholding that decision, the Divisional Court accepted the distinction:

" . . . because there is clearly, from a planning point of view, a significant difference in character between a use which involves selling the produce of the land itself, and a use which involves importing goods from elsewhere for sale. All sorts of planning considerations may arise which render one activity appropriate and desirable in a neighbourhood and the other activity quite unsuitable."[20]

[15] *Devonshire C.C.* v. *Allens Caravans (Estates) Ltd.* (1962) 14 P. & C.R. 440 at 441, *per* Lord Parker C.J.; *East Barnet U.D.C.* v. *British Transport Commission* [1962] 2 Q.B. 484 at 490, *per* Lord Parker C.J.

[16] *Birmingham Corporation* v. *Habib Ullah* [1964] 1 Q.B. 178 at 188, *per* Lord Parker C.J.

[17] *Wilson* v. *West Sussex C.C.* [1963] 2 Q.B. 764 at 785, *per* Diplock L.J.; and *cf.* views of Danckwerts L.J. at 781.

[18] See, *e.g. Hidderley* v. *Warwickshire C.C.* (1963) 14 P. & C.R. 134 at 136, *per* Lord Parker C.J.; *Gray* v. *Oxfordshire C.C.* (1963) 15 P. & C.R. 1 at 3, *per* Lord Parker C.J.

[19] (1967) 18 P. & C.R. 514.

[20] *Ibid.* at 518 *per* Widgery J. And compare *Ross* v. *Aberdeen C.C.* (1955) S.L.T. (Sh.Ct.) 55, and [1972] J.P.L. 219 (m.p.d.).

Of course, a use may still be materially different in "character" (itself a concept entirely of ministerial creation[21] though derived from the 1932 Act[22] and now legitimized by judicial acceptance)[23] even although on the specific facts it has no necessary immediate offsite impact. A house may be converted to warehouse use without any observable detrimental effect on local amenities. But it is the potential impact which will be relevant; the extent to which the new use might then be exploited without the need for planning permission.

But some boundaries have been drawn to the Secretary of State's discretion in assessing materiality from a planning point of view. A mere change in the personality of the user, it is said, cannot amount to a change which is material,[24] (though in the case of an ancillary use it may result in the severance of the link with the primary use and the creation of a new planning unit). And similarly, if there are no planning implications and no change in "character": the goods sold in a shop may change, for example, but according to one judge it would be difficult "to see how or why such a change can be material from any point of view which could legitimately be taken by planning authority."[25] But in other cases, particularly involving storage, offsite implications have proved an influential guide. Thus it has been held that a change in the purpose for which goods are stored on a site cannot be material if both the level and proportion of offsite activity and the general planning implications remain identical.[26] But the storage of different goods with different impact considerations may involve a material change,[27] as may a change in the ownership or source of supply of goods stored or sold where the effect is greatly to increase "the volume of traffic, business or activity on the land."[28]

Guiding principles are not yet clearly established. The courts have tended to take different approaches in different cases, and their reluctance to intervene on appeal has inhibited the development of overall concepts.

(c) Intensification of use

The evolvement of the doctrine of intensification of use illustrates both the semantic difficulties of applying the whole definition, and the influence of the courts' perception of materiality. The conclusive endorsement by the Court of Appeal in 1977 of the view that intensification might constitute material change of use,[29] was based primarily upon judicial acceptance of a pattern of ministerial practice,[30] which had in turn followed certain *obiter*

---

[21] Stated first in Circular No. 67, para. 4(iii).
[22] T.C.P.A. 1932, s. 21 (12): "For the purposes of this section a change of use of property shall not be deemed to have occurred if the character of the new use is similar to that of the previous use."
[23] See *e.g. Devonshire C.C.* v. *Horton* (1962) 14 P. & C.R. 444 at 447, *per* Lord Parker C.J.
[24] *Lewis* v. *S.O.S.E.* (1971) 23 P. & C.R. 125 at 128, *per* Lord Widgery C.J.
[25] *Marshall* v. *Nottingham Corpn.* [1960] 1 W.L.R. 707 at 717, *per* Glyn-Jones J.
[26] *Snook* v. *S.O.S.E.* (1975) 33 P. & C.R. 1 at 5 and 6, *per* Bridge L.J.
[27] See, *e.g.* [1976] J.P.L. 248 (m.p.d.) (change from storage of coal and coke to storage of cars, held to involve material change).
[28] *Costa Chrysanthou* v. *S.O.S.E.* [1976] J.P.L. 371 at 372, *per* Lord Widgery C.J. (although the decision itself dealt with extension of an ancillary use beyond the point where it could any longer be said to be ancillary).
[29] In *Brooks and Burton Ltd.* v. *S.O.S.E.* [1978] 1 All E.R. 733.
[30] *Ibid.* at 744.

dicta of Lord Evershed M.R. in the Court of Appeal in 1959.[31] In rejecting counsel's submission that mere intensity of user or occupation could never be a relevant planning consideration, Lord Evershed based an opposing, though necessarily inconclusive, argument on two grounds: first, that changes in intensity of use might have significant external planning impact, perhaps leading to "a substantial increase in the burden of services which a local authority has to supply."[32] Secondly, he pointed to the possible change in "character" of a use which might follow intensification. If the Kennington Oval Cricket Ground were used so as to provide continuously a great number of pitches in contemporaneous use, he argued, it no doubt "would remain a cricket ground but it would be a cricket ground substantially changed."[33]

In that argument lies the key to understanding the doctrine of intensification. If an appropriate and distinct word existed to describe the changed cricket ground—if it now fell into a different recognised use category—then no question of intensification would have arisen. Thus in Circular 67 of 1949 the minister hinted at the notion of intensification when he referred to changes in the "degree" of existing use, giving as examples the change from private residence to guest-house, lodging-house or hotel. Because of the subsequent establishment of each of those categories as appropriate use descriptions, intensification no longer is an issue in that context. Its gradual development as a separate doctrine obscures the fact that intensification is simply an extension of the use comparison process: it is nothing more than a recognition by the Secretary of State and the courts that for the purpose of drawing material distinctions between former and future uses, issues of scale and site are relevant notwithstanding that they may be difficult to translate into appropriate use descriptions. It sounds more scientific to allege that a use has been intensified, than to allege that a little use has developed into a big use.[34]

It follows, then, that for those instances for which the Use Classes Order prescribes general use descriptions, intensification of the use cannot amount to development unless its result is to take the use outside the general category altogether.[35]

The notion of intensification has also been applied in analysis of the growth of ancillary uses,[36] but there is danger here of obscuring the primary rule by regarding intensification as an independent doctrine. The true rule is

---

[31] In *Guildford R.D.C.* v. *Fortescue* [1959] 2 Q.B. 112 at 125. And there had been subsequent judicial comment, though often inconclusive, favouring the view that intensification might amount to material change of use: see *e.g. James* v. *Secretary of State for Wales* [1966] 1 W.L.R. 135 at 143, *per* Lord Denning M.R., and 150, *per* Russell L.J.; *Esdell Caravan Parks Ltd.* v. *Hemel Hempstead R.D.C.* [1966] 1 Q.B. 895 at 921, *per* Lord Denning M.R.; *Brooks* v. *Gloucestershire C.C.* (1967) 66 L.G.R. 386 at 391, *per* Lord Widgery C.J.; but compare *Glamorgan C.C.* v. *Carter* [1963] 1 W.L.R. 1 at 5, *per* Salmon J.

[32] *Guildford R.D.C.* v. *Fortescue* [1959] 2 Q.B. 112, 125.

[33] *Ibid.*

[34] See now *Royal London Borough of Kensington and Chelsea* v. *S.O.S.E.* [1981] J.P.L. 50 for an analysis along these lines, and acceptance that intensification *per se* is insufficient to constitute development.

[35] As in *Brooks and Burton* v. *S.O.S.E.* [1978] 1 All E.R. 733.

[36] See, *e.g. Hilliard* v. *S.O.S.E.* (1978) 34 P. & C.R. 223, (and at [1977] J.P.L. 123 m.p.d.). And see [1978] J.P.L. 270 and 395 (m.p.d.)

that uses ancillary to the primary use of land may be exploited without permission, provided exploitation does not proceed past the point where it can be said that the use has lost its ancillary link. Intensification of the ancillary use *may* lead to that result, but it need not.

There has been no attempt to establish a doctrine of disintensification, and even the complete abandonment of a use does not constitute development notwithstanding that a reduction in the level of activity may itself have significant planning implications. The reason lies in the reluctance of the courts to permit a controlling power to become a coercive power, for the consequence of such a doctrine would be that a planning authority might require a land user to increase the scale of loss-making or uneconomic activity or business.

(d) Multiple use and the planning unit

The difficulties which arise in applying the definition to sites where a variety of activity is undertaken have led to the establishment of a number of doctrinal refinements. To some extent the initial difficulty is still that of use description. A general use description such as "industrial" might extend to cover all the activities on one site, so that it would not be seen as involving multiple use at all. The selection of narrower use descriptions within the "industrial" designation, on the other hand, might lead to the identification of numerous individual uses, such as (in the colourful language of the Use Classes Order) "blood boiler" or "bone burner" or "bone grinder."[37]

The pattern in interpretation has been to adapt different analyses according to the degree of relationship between the uses. Thus there will be some instances where there is a primary, or predominant use of the site as a whole which can be conveniently identified and labelled, and to which all the activities taking place on the site are related in the sense of being "ancillary" or "incidental". Thus, having established "private dwelling-house" as an appropriate use description, the normal activities of the occupiers such as bathing, laundering, cooking and recreation will not be regarded in themselves as separate uses: the site will not be regarded as being in multiple use at all.

But where the activities are not related in this way, different considerations apply. Different, yet unrelated, uses may take place contemporaneously over the entire site, or they may be separated not only functionally, but also physically, or by time.

Before turning to consider the rules applicable to each of these situation, it is necessary to consider the "planning unit": a tool of analysis which has developed in an attempt to achieve some degree of evenness and consistency in applying the definition to instances of multiple use. It had largely been assumed in the first 20 or so years of comprehensive planning control that in general terms the "building or other land" referred to in the definition of material change of use meant the whole of the site in the occupation of its present user.[38] The materiality of any change in use would need to be

---

[37] Schedule, Class IX (Special Industrial Group E).
[38] See, *e.g.* M.T.C.P. Circular No. 67/49, para. 4(iii), (although impliedly recognising a distinction between ancillary and non-ancillary activities); *East Barnet U.D.C.* v. *British Transport Commission* [1962] 2 Q.B. 484; *Vickers Armstrong Ltd.* v. *Central Land Board*

measured against the character of the whole. But strict adherence to that rule could lead to the undesirable conclusion that planning control would differ in respect of two identical developments, simply because of the size or other characteristics of the site occupied by each developer. In some instances this result might flow as the result of one change of use being protected as being ancillary to the primary use of the site, but in other cases there could be no logical justification for any distinction. If it were the character of the whole site which was at issue, it might be difficult to argue that, for example, the placing and use of a residential caravan on a corner of a 10 acre field involved a material change; although had the actual site of the caravan first been sold to its occupier, the use change of that piece of land must necessarily have been material.[39]

The doctrine of the "planning unit" has developed in recent years[40] to enable such anomalies to be overcome. The doctrine simply reduces the significance in calculating the materiality of land use change, of the size of any individual land-holding, by authorising the Secretary of State notionally to slice up sites in one occupation for analysis, so as to concentrate upon the smaller physical unit where change has actually occurred or is proposed. Thus, where a residential caravan is placed in a 10 acre field, planning control need not depend upon any actual severance in ownership, or occupation: the same effect can be achieved by selecting the actual site of the caravan as the planning unit.

But the ability to select smaller planning units is limited:

(1) by the need to continue to protect genuine ancillary uses; and
(2) by the need for some degree of physical separation between the different land uses. There is no scope for the doctrine where separate uses are undertaken over the site as a whole, although horizontal as well as vertical separation may suffice: the planning unit is capable of being three dimensional, as in the case of a multi-storey building or an outdoor storage or tipping use.

Against this background it is now possible to analyse the four categories of multiple use, and the extent of the planning unit doctrine.

(i) Predominant use and the ancillary umbrella

In many cases it is possible to isolate one use description which adequately describes the overall on-site activity, such as "private dwelling-house," "retail shop," "hotel," "farm" and so on. That description may in any given case describe the sum of a number of "incidental" or "ancillary"[41] uses of

---

(1958) 9 P. & C.R. 33; G. Percy Trentham Ltd. v. Gloucestershire C.C. (1966) 18 P. & C.R 225; Brazil Concrete Ltd. v. Amersham R.D.C. (1967) 18 P. & C.R. 396; Shephard v. Buckinghamshire C.C. (1966) 18 P. & C.R. 419; T.A. Miller Ltd. v. M.H.L.G. [1968] 1 W.L.R. 992 at 996.

[39] The example in the text (which is based on the assumption that no operational development was involved) gave rise to some animated correspondence in the Journal of Planning Law in 1959 which demonstrated the uncertainty of approach at that time: [1959] J.P.L. 221–223 and 383–384. See further Mellows (1963) 27 Conv. 197.

[40] The leading case is Burdle v. S.O.S.E. [1972] 1 W.L.R. 1207, where at 1212 Bridge J. formulated the criteria, discussed further below, governing the selection of the planning unit.

[41] The word "ancillary" is broadly used, although it does not appear in the Act. "Incidental" uses are preserved under the Use Classes Order, art. 3(2) (which preserves the right to exploit

quite different character: the "hotel" use, for example, describes a variety of different activities such as uses for retail sales, storage, car parking, restaurant, paying accommodation, conference facilities, entertainment, staff accommodation and offices. But planning control focuses simply upon the primary use description, permitting fluctuation in the level of ancillary activity and the initiation of new ancillary uses or the abandonment of old without permission. The planning unit in this instance is the whole unit of occupation devoted to the primary use,[42] with the consequence that only where there has been a material change in the character of that use is planning control involved.

But there are limits. A subordinate use may develop in such a manner as to become no longer ancillary. A solicitor who has customarily worked in the evening at home now starts to work from home during the day as well. The point may come where either the office use excludes the domestic use of that part of the dwelling, bringing the case into category (ii) below and leading to a subdivision in the initial planning unit, because "some smaller unit can then be recognised as the site of activities which amount in substance to a separate use both physically and functionally."[43] Alternatively, there may still be a material change if the extent of the use means that the character of the use of the whole unit can be said to have changed: perhaps to a dual use as private dwelling-house and solicitor's office, and falling within category (iii) below.[44] In the case of dwelling-houses, the courts have been reluctant to pursue the first alternative, however, and have preferred to look at overall change rather than split the unit.[45]

Much decision-making in this area necessarily involves the forming of value judgments as to the type and scope of ancillary activities ordinarily regarded as incidental to particular use descriptions. It involves the making of two determinations, first as to the level of abstraction at which the primary use is to be defined, and second as to the types of ancillary uses normally found in such cases. It can produce some odd results: for example, the keeping and ritual slaughtering of chickens in shop premises is apparently not to be regarded as incidental to the use of a "retail shop", notwithstanding that it be in accordance with Moslem law and carried out in premises situated in a largely Moslem neighbourhood.[46] Similarly, limited

---

any "use which is ordinarily incidental to and included in any use specified in the Schedule"); and by section 22(2)(d) of the Act, permitting any "purpose incidental to the enjoyment of [a] dwelling house as such". But the minister and the courts have not limited the concept of ancillary rights to those specific contexts.

[42] *Burdle* v. *S.O.S.E.* [1972] 1 W.L.R. 1207 at 1212, *per* Bridge J.

[43] *Ibid.*

[44] The use of domestic premises by professional people has not always been easily resolved: the minister's advice in Circular 67/49, para. 4(iii) appeared to accept the full-time use by, for example, a dentist or doctor, of one or two rooms in his house for purposes of consultation with patients as not involving material change of use, presumably as ancillary uses; though drawing the line at use of the same house "to provide suites for consulting rooms or a dental clinic." For a discussion of subsequent ministerial decisions, see P.T. Adams, "The Medium and the Massage (or Circular Reasoning)" [1978] J.P.L. 685; and compare the business use case of *Cook* v. *Secretary of State for Wales* (1971) 220 E.G. 1433 (*post*, note 55).

[45] See, *e.g. Brooks* v. *Gloucestershire C.C.* (1967) 19 P. & C.R. 90; *Williams* v. *M.H.L.G.* (1967) 18 P. & C.R. 514 and *Wood* v. *S.O.S.E.* (1973) 25 P. & C.R. 303 where Lord Widgery at 309 thought it could "rarely if ever be right to dissect a single dwelling house. . . . "

[46] *Hussain* v. *S.O.S.E.* (1971) 23 P. & C.R. 330; followed in *Ahmed* v. *Birmingham C.C.* (1972) 224 E.G. 689 (in respect of rival premises directly opposite those of Mr. Hussain). The

sale of farm produce from a farm is regarded as an ancillary activity, but it may lose that status if produce imported from outside is sold,[47] or if the use involves processing of a type or on a scale beyond that ordinarily found on farms.[48] A lairage erected on a farm is capable of being used as ancillary to the keeping of livestock on the farm, but loses ancillary protection if its purpose is that of accommodating other livestock awaiting shipment outside the United Kingdom.[49] A residential caravan parked in the curtilage of a dwelling-house may be regarded as devoted to an ancillary use so long as it is not used as a separate dwelling[50]; and similarly the parking of a private car in the curtilage will normally be ancillary, but not the parking of a heavy commercial lorry or van.[51] The "ancillary" protection in the case of a domestic garage will permit repairs to a private car, but the protection is lost if cars belonging to others come to be repaired, on a commercial scale.[52] It is important to note that this may be the case despite the general rule of *Lewis* v. *Secretary of State*[53] that in assessing change in the *primary* use of land, the mere identity of the owner of goods or vehicles being repaired would not be relevant. Ancillary protection in the case of a domestic garage, by comparison, is limited largely to private repair work: ownership of goods or vehicles repaired may be an influential factor in determining whether the activity goes beyond ancillary status.

Change is often gradual. Activities once regarded as ancillary may only slowly or erratically grow in scale to the point where they can no longer be regarded as ancillary. If they are physically concentrated in a recognisably separate area, then it may be possible to select that area as the planning unit, and to determine that its use has materially changed.[54] Alternatively the growth of the ancillary use may have been such that the use of the whole has converted from a single primary use to a composite use (category (ii) below);

subjectivity of ancillary use protection is also illustrated by *Emma Hotels Ltd.* v. *S.O.S.E.* [1981] J.P.L. 283 where the question was whether the use of an area of a private hotel as a bar open to non-residents was incidental to the primary hotel use. The Secretary of State thought not, and maintained that view after his determination was set aside by the Divisional Court; who thereupon set aside his second determination.

[47] See *e.g.* *Wood* v. *S.O.S.E.* [1973] 1 W.L.R. 707 at 709 *per* Lord Widgery C.J.; *Lloyd-Jones* v. *M.H.L.G.* (1967) 204 E.G. 1200; *Bromley L.B.C.* v. *Hoeltschi (George) & Son Ltd.* (1977) 244 E.G. 49. And *cf. Williams* v. *M.H.L.G.* (1967) 65 L.G.R. 495 (sale of imported produce from shop ancillary to nursery garden use).

[48] See *e.g.* ministerial decisions at [1974] J.P.L. 165, [1975] J.P.L. 369 and [1978] J.P.L. 792, instances where the sale of meat from farms was held not to be an ancillary use, having regard to the associated processing and storage uses. And compare extent of agricultural operational development exemption in Class VI, Sched. 1 to the General Development Order, discussed at [1974] J.P.L. 483, [1977] J.P.L. 392 (sale of livestock ancillary, but not meat derived from it) [1977] J.P.L. 47 and [1978] J.P.L. 795.

[49] *Warnock* v. *S.O.S.E.* [1980] J.P.L. 590.

[50] See, *e.g.* ministerial determinations at [1975] J.P.L. 104, [1976] J.P.L. 586 (no material change); and compare [1978] J.P.L. 489 (material change where caravan capable of fully independent use).

[51] See, *e.g.* ministerial determination at [1977] J.P.L. 397 and [1978] J.P.L. 789 (lorries); [1976] J.P.L. 529 (van).

[52] See, *e.g. Peake* v. *Secretary of State for Wales* (1971) 70 L.G.R. 98 (repairs to own private car growing into full-time commercial occupation); and m.p.d. [1978] J.P.L. 201 (material change when repairs carried out on four vehicles raced as a hobby).

[53] (1971) 221 E.G. 1493, *ante*, p. 165.

[54] Applying the test of Bridge J. in *Burdle* v. *S.O.S.E.* [1972] 1 W.L.R. 1207 at 1212.

or further, to the point where the former ancillary use has become the primary use.[55]

Ancillary uses are purely parasitic. The protection is lost therefore if the primary use disappears,[56] or the ancillary link is severed.[57] This would occur if, for example, the land upon which the ancillary activity was carried out were to be sold or to become occupied by somebody with no links with the primary use. Conversely, a pre-existing unauthorised use may become authorised by the merger of two planning units in which it becomes ancillary to a lawful primary use.[58]

(ii) *Composite use*

This category includes the case of two or more separate uses being carried on without clear physical separation, on a particular site. Each use right carries with it the right to enjoy ancillary uses, and excessive exploitation of them may amount to a material change of the whole in accordance with the principles discussed under heading (i) above. But the relationship between the principal uses is more complex. In the absence of physical separation it will not prove possible to select a smaller planning unit, and changes occurring must be measured for materiality against the site as a whole. Thus some fluctuation in the level of user will be possible within the scope of existing use right protection, and further, cessation altogether of one principal use will not amount to development.[59] But there may be a material change if one component use absorbs the entire site to the exclusion of the other.[60]

(iii) *Dual use*

The category of dual use covers the situation where there is geographical separation of separate uses. Thus a site may have existing use rights on one half for the storage of scrap-metal and on the other half for the sale of motor cars, with no ancillary link. In such a case it would be usual to regard each half as a separate planning unit,[61] and the site is then treated for the purposes of analysis no longer as a case of multiple use, but as two sites with different single primary uses. Such a result may also follow where a site which had formerly one primary use has a building erected upon it, with permission. The result may be a new chapter in the planning history of the site, superseding the established use rights attaching to that part of it.[62]

---

[55] Compare *e.g. Jones* v. *S.O.S.E.* (1974) 232 E.G. 453, where a former haulage business with an ancillary trailer making use, had changed solely to trailer making: a material change of use; *Decorative and Caravan Paints Ltd.* v. *M.H.L.G.* (1970) 214 E.G. 1355 (warehouse use changed to shop use following increase in retail sales); *Cook* v. *Secretary of State for Wales* (1971) 220 E.G. 1433 (taxi proprietor's house used as centre for his business: enough evidence upon which to base a finding of material change use).

[56] But not if the use is composite rather than ancillary: *Wipperman* v. *Barking L.B.C.* (1965) 17 P. & C.R. 225 at 229, *per* Widgery J.

[57] See, *e.g. David W. Barling Ltd.* v. *S.O.S.E.* [1980] J.P.L. 594 (on-site storage use of building materials in connection with housing development, lost once the dwellings were completed.)

[58] See, *e.g. T.L.G. Building Materials* v. *S.O.S.E.* (1980) 41 P. & C.R. 243.

[59] *Wipperman* v. *Barking L.B.C.* (1965) 17 P. & C.R. 225 at 230.

[60] *Burdle* v. *S.O.S.E.* [1972] 1 W.L.R. 1207 at 1212 *per* Bridge J.

[61] *Ibid.*

[62] See further *post,* p. 175.

(iv) *Recurrent or seasonal uses*

Given that an existing use right is not necessarily abandoned simply because its enjoyment ceases temporarily, no material change of use will occur where enjoyment of a use is intermittent, (inevitable in outdoor uses dependent upon British climatic conditions), even although there may be lengthy periods when the use is suspended.[63] But the Divisional Court was initially hesitant to find that land might have two or more active existing uses separated, not physically, but in time.[64] Their doubts were dispelled in 1968 when the Court of Appeal in *Webber* v. *Minister of Housing and Local Government*[65] ruled that the "purpose" for which land was "normally used", in the terms of the Act, could include two seasonal uses, such as the existing use of a field for camping in the summer months, and the grazing of cattle in the winter.

(v) *Subdivision of the planning unit*

Subdivision of the planning unit does not necessarily mean that there has been a material change in use. The splitting of a shop or an office into two or more separately occupied units, for example, would not normally involve development because each unit remains a "shop" or "office" as the case may be, though different considerations may apply where the high level abstractions maintained by the Use Classes Order do not apply. In the case of residential subdivision for example, the subdivision of a dwelling-house is specifically caught by the Act, and the courts have been prepared also to uphold a finding of material change in the splitting of occupation between a house in large grounds and its ancillary lodge.[66]

5. *Existing and established uses*

(a) Lawfulness and immunity

Development control is concerned only with changes in use, and it follows that the right to continue to use land for its existing use is unaffected. But it is necessary to enquire as to the status of the existing use, since if it has been commenced in breach of planning control then it may be actionable under enforcement procedures, together with any other changes made subsequently in purported reliance upon, for example, the exemptions of the Act or the Use Classes Order.

The starting point is to consider whether an existing use is lawful or unlawful. Lawfulness stems from two sources. The use may be authorised by express or deemed planning permission, or it may be exempt from the

---

[63] See, *e.g. Fyson* v. *Buckinghamshire C.C.* [1958] 1 W.L.R. 634 and *Hawes* v. *Thornton Cleveleys U.D.C.* (1965) 17 P. & C.R. 22.

[64] See, *e.g. Hawes* v. *Thornton Cleveleys U.D.C.* (1965) 17 P. & C.R. 22 at 28, *per* Widgery J., but compare *Washington U.D.C.* v. *Gray* (1958) 10 P. & C.R. 264 at 267, *per* Lord Parker C.J.

[65] [1968] 1 W.L.R. 29. In the Divisional Court, Widgery J. had observed that such an approach might be just and sensible, but felt unable to adopt it on his interpretation of the Act: (1967) 18 P. & C.R. 491 at 495.

[66] *Wakelin* v. *S.O.S.E.* (1978) 77 L.G.R. 101. p. 186.

requirement of planning permission by reason of having been commenced before the introduction of comprehensive planning control. The scheme of the 1947 legislation was such that "for planning purposes every plot of land is stamped, as it were, with a hallmark of permission to use it after the coming into force of the Act for the purpose for which it had last been used before the Act came into force."[67] The governing factor therefore is the pre-1948 use of the site, and various supplementary provisions extend the scope of protection to intermittent uses[68] and for the resurrection of "normal" uses where in 1948[69] land was occupied for or devoted to temporary use.[70] All these uses remain lawful, and have a status generally equivalent to a use expressly permitted by a grant of permission, subject to the doctrine that a use may be abandoned or extinguished, which is considered further below.

There is a further category, however, of uses which though unlawful have immunity from enforcement action. This hybrid class arises because enforcement is possible only against unlawful use change which has occurred since 1963.[71] Any change occurring before then is now immune, and therefore "established"; and its immunity may be certified by the issuance of an established use certificate by the planning authority.[72] This constitutes conclusive proof in subsequent enforcement proceedings of the existence of immunity, but it does not confer any status of lawfulness upon the use, which means that established uses are a limited class of existing use: not all the benefits attaching to other existing uses extend to them, and the benefit of immunity may be lost. If, for example, a subsequent unauthorised change of use is made and an enforcement notice served in respect of it, there is a right then to revert to the former lawful use of the land, but not if it is no more than an established use.[73] Nor is there such a reversion right where a temporary permission for development has been implemented and expired.[74] In each case, the right to continue the former, established use is lost, and the site may as a result have no authorised use at all.

For the most part, advantage may be taken of the exemptions conferred by the Use Classes Order and General Development Order on the basis of no

---

[67] *Marshall* v. *Nottingham Corporation* [1960] 1 W.L.R. 707 at 713, *per* Glyn-Jones J.
[68] See now T.C.P.A. 1971, s. 22(3); *Washington U.D.C.* v. *Gray* (1958) 10 P. & C.R. 264.
[69] On the first appointed day of the 1947 legislation, July 1, 1948.
[70] T.C.P.A. 1971, s. 23(2) and (4). And see *Kingdon* v. *M.H.L.G.* (1967) 18 P. & C.R. 507, where the right to resume normal use was held to have been lost following 20 years exploitation of the "temporary" use. The rights under s. 23(2)(3) and (4) are all now subject to the "normal" use having been resumed by December 6, 1968.
[71] T.C.P.A. 1971, s. 87. Instances of operational development, breach of condition or limitation, and change of use to single dwelling-house are however subject to the rule that enforcement proceedings be instituted within four years of the breach. See further, *post*, p. 389.
[72] T.C.P.A. 1971, ss. 94 and 95. Such certificates are also issuable in respect of non-compliance since the beginning of 1964 with conditions attached to a permission, and in respect of changes of use since that time not requiring permission. See further, *post*, p. 390.
[73] T.C.P.A. 1971, s. 23(9): *L.T.S.S. Print and Supply Services Ltd.* v. *Hackney L.B.C.* [1976] 1 Q.B. 663.
[74] T.C.P.A. 1971, s. 23(5) and (6); and *cf. Bolivian and General Tin Trust Ltd.* v. *S.O.S.E.* [1972] 1 W.L.R. 1481 (refusal to grant established use certificate where use had continued from 1964–1969 under the terms of a temporary planning permission).

more than an *established* use, but there is a specific exemption in the case of industrial development.[75]

(b) Loss of use rights

There is, not surprisingly, a tension between the continuance of existing use rights, and comprehensive planning control. The greater the scope for exploitation of the existing rights, the narrower the scope of control. And there is some conceptual difficulty, in particular, in reconciling existing use rights with specific planning permission. Is the existing use to be regarded as something forever sacred, or may it be lost through the implementation of a subsequent permission or even simply through underuse? The legislation leaves the relationship ill-defined, and the courts have of necessity had to reconcile a number of conflicting factors in determining the extent to which existing use rights should prevail or give way in the cause of administrative workability.

On the other hand they have been particularly astute to ensure that existing use rights should not be inadvertently lost in enforcement proceedings. They have required the Secretary of State and local authorities to pay particular regard to the need to draft or amend enforcement notices so as to preserve existing user rights: for example, to ensure that a requirement to cease a particular unauthorised use does not go so far as to make it illegal to continue with the specified activity as an ancillary right.[76] But in other circumstances they have been prepared to acknowledge that existing use rights may disappear, and three main categories of case have emerged.

(i) *By the grant of planning permission*

It is now clear that existing use rights may be abrogated in appropriate cases by the imposition of an appropriate condition on a planning permission. The courts have not been deterred by the argument that the formal statutory procedure for achieving the same ends, the making of a discontinuance order, is accompanied by a requirement to compensate: provided the condition is otherwise reasonable and fairly relates to the permitted development, its effect upon existing rights in no way affects its validity.[77]

And tentative steps have been made towards recognising that existing use rights may be lost when a new permission is implemented, even without such a condition: the purchasers of new dwellings built on land formerly used as a refuse tip would not expect to be able to continue that use in their gardens without permission. But where the limits are to be drawn is less

---

[75] General Development Order, Schedule, Class VIII.

[76] The leading case is *Mansi* v. *Elstree R.D.C.* (1964) 16 P. & C.R. 153: for a full discussion see *post*, p. 420.

[77] *Prosser* v. *M.H.L.G.* (1968) 67 L.G.R. 109; *Kingston L.B.C.* v. *S.O.S.E.* [1973] 1 W.L.R. 1549 (distinguishing both *Hartnell* v. *M.H.L.G.* [1965] A.C. 1134 and *Allnatt London Properties Ltd.* v. *Middlesex C.C.* (1964) 62 L.G.R. 304); *Leighton and Newman Ltd.* v. *S.O.S.E.* (1976) 32 P. & C.R. 1 at 9–10 and *A.I. & P. (Stratford) Ltd.* v. *Tower Hamlets L.B.C.* (1975) 237 E.G. 415 condition restricting use of existing accommodation from general to solely ancillary purposes.

clear. Where a new building has been erected in accordance with planning permission, covering the whole site, the result may be, following the Divisional Court decision in *Petticoat Lane Rentals Ltd.* v. *Secretary of State for the Environment*,[78] that a new "planning unit" emerges with no planning history, and a "nil" existing use. The use to which the building itself may be put may be specified by the planning permission. If not, the permission is to be construed as including permission to use the building for the purpose for which it was designed:[79] and "designed" for those purposes means "intended", rather than "architecturally designed".[80] But in *Jennings Motors Ltd.* v. *Secretary of State for the Environment*,[81] the Court of Appeal rejected the argument that replacement of an old building with a new building automatically had the effect of extinguishing the old use. It is one of the factors to be taken into account in determining whether there has been a change of so radical a character as to constitute a "break in the planning history" or a new "planning unit." Lord Denning M.R. preferred the former expression, but Oliver L.J. (with whom Watkins L.J. agreed) thought the distinction between the two to be largely semantic, and preferred to employ the "planning unit" concept in this broader context as including the right to continue the existing use of land.

It is therefore a matter of fact and degree in each case. A permission may be for a building which covers only part of a site,[82] or may be granted only for a change of use. In each case much will depend upon the interpretation of the permission, and upon an understanding of the site it was intended to cover. Thus, in the case of a building over part only of the site, the correct inference may be that the building was for a use ancillary to the existing use of the remainder of the site; or alternatively that the remainder of the site was intended to be used as a "curtilage" for the building, thereby excluding exercise of former use rights.[83] Cases dealing with the implementation of inconsistent planning permission suggest that in borderline instances the courts might be unhappy to accept that existing use rights would be lost simply as a consequence of implementing a permission, provided the two are capable of physical co-existence, and can otherwise be undertaken consistently.[84] If upon implementation of the permission the existing use

---

[78] [1971] 1 W.L.R. 1112. The land had been formerly used as an open market, and the new building was supported on pillars with an open car-parking area at ground floor level. Enforcement proceedings were instituted when the market use resumed in the car-park.

[79] T.C.P.A. 1971, s. 33(2).

[80] *Wilson* v. *West Sussex C.C.* [1963] 2 Q.B. 764.

[81] [1982] 1 All E.R. 471. The Divisional Court, whose decision was overturned by the Court of Appeal had followed their unreported decision in *Ashton* v. *S.O.S.E.* (April 9, 1973), though expressing doubt as to whether it was correctly decided. The Court of Appeal took the view that *Ashton* was probably not wrongly decided on the facts, since the new building there covered over 90 per cent. of the available site, but that the court had wrongly accepted that a new building would automatically cancel existing use rights.

[82] In the *Petticoat Lane* case Bridge J. and Lord Parker C.J. (at 1118) both reserved the question as to whether, in the absence of an express condition, user rights on land which remained open would be affected.

[83] *Cf. Pilkington* v. *S.O.S.E.* [1973] 1 W.L.R. 1527 at 1531–1532 *per* Lord Widgery C.J; *Joyce Shopfitters Ltd.* v. *S.O.S.E.* [1976] J.P.L. 236.

[84] *Pilkington* v. *S.O.S.E.* [1973] 1 W.L.R. 1527; *Thomas Langley Group Ltd.* v. *Warwick D.C.* (1974) 73 L.G.R. 171.

rights cease to be exercised, however, there may be a strong inference that they have been abandoned, following the principles discussed below.

In other words, if the implementation of the new permission is such as to change radically the use of the land, then it may be assumed that the old rights have been lost. The most obvious case is where a building has been erected, because there is then a clear physical symbol of the change; but there is no reason why the doctrine should not extend equally to cases of change of use. In the words of Lord Lane, in *Newbury District Council* v. *Secretary of State for the Environment*, "it is not the reason for the break in planning history which is important. It is the existence of the break itself, whatever the reasons for it may have been."[85]

If there is no break, there can be no loss of existing use rights. If the new permission ties in closely with existing activities on the site, for example, there will be no break involved in its implementation. It follows, therefore, that a permission granted in circumstances where it was strictly unnecessary, because the right conferred by it already existed, cannot destroy that right. The consequence then is that any conditions imposed on the permission are unenforceable in the face of a subsisting existing use right. In the *Newbury* case, for example, planning permission had been granted in 1962 for a storage use, which the House of Lords held to have been already permitted under the Use Classes Order. The fact that permission had been applied for and granted did not, they held, constitute a break in the planning history of the site (and nor did it amount to a waiver by the owners of their existing rights), so that a condition imposed upon the permission requiring the demolition of the buildings at the end of 10 years was unenforceable.

(ii) *By abandonment*

Despite a hesitant start,[86] there has emerged a doctrine that existing use rights may be lost by having been abandoned,[87] even where the right has been conferred by an express grant of planning permission.[88] It is a principle based upon analogy with the property lawyer's rules relating to abandonment of proprietary rights,[89] qualified by a pragmatic interpretation of the concept of material change of use. First, the courts have insisted that the mere cessation of a land use is not a material change and is therefore a matter falling outside planning control:[90] to hold otherwise would be to confer

---

[85] [1980] 1 All E.R. 731 at 760.

[86] In *Fyson* v. *Buckinghamshire C.C.* [1958] 1 W.L.R. 634, where land had been left unused from 1949, Donovan J. in the Divisional Court expressed the view that there clearly had been no material change when an earlier storage use was resumed in 1956, and refused to upset the decision of the justices that no development had occurred.

[87] See now *Hartley* v. *M.H.L.G.* [1970] 1 Q.B. 413, *Draco* v. *Oxfordshire C.C.* (1972) 224 E.G. 1037; *Ratcliffe* v. *S.O.S.E.* [1975] J.P.L. 728; *Maddern* v. *S.O.S.E.* [1980] J.P.L. 676 *Nicholls* v. *S.O.S.E.* [1981] J.P.L. 890; *Balco Transport Services Ltd.* v. *S.O.S.E.* [1982] J.P.L. 177.

[88] *Maddern* v. *S.O.S.E.* [1980] J.P.L. 676.

[89] See, *e.g. Slough Estates Ltd.* v. *Slough B.C.* (1967) 19 P. & C.R. 326 at 357–358, *per* Megarry J.; but compare the approach of the Court of Appeal at [1969] 2 Ch. 305, where it was held that rights arising under a planning permission granted in 1945 had been abandoned when in 1955 the plaintiff company had applied for and been awarded compensation. On further appeal, the House of Lords reserved their views on the abandonment issue: [1971] A.C. 958 at 971.

[90] *Hartley* v. *M.H.L.G.* [1970] 1 Q.B. 413 at 422, *per* Widgery L.J.

upon planning authorities the power to require, through the enforcement machinery, the continuance of unprofitable uses in perpetuity. That is too extensive a power to be read into provisions aimed primarily at controlling use changes rather than maintaining the level of their intensity.

Thus the focus of the abandonment doctrine is upon the next stage, where the use which has ceased is recommenced. If the use had ceased with no intention to resume it, the inference may be drawn that it has been abandoned, that in consequence the site has been left with a "nil" use, and that permission will therefore be required before the earlier use may be recommenced. The inference may be drawn from direct or indirect evidence of intention.[91] There is clearly no abandonment if a use is by its nature intermittent or recurrent; but in other cases the influential factors are liable to be the circumstances surrounding the cessation of the use, and the length of period of non-use.[92]

(iii) By demolition

It is tempting to assume that the demolition of a building must necessarily involve the destruction of the existing use rights formerly enjoyed with it; but the courts have declined to make a clear ruling.[93] Demolition may, of course, signal abandonment. Or it may render further enjoyment of the rights physically impossible without the grant of new permission for rebuilding. Further, there are statutory rights to enjoy ancillary uses which attach solely to buildings: the use of the curtilage to a dwelling-house for example.[94] These would necessarily be lost if the building disappeared.

But in other cases the use enjoyed with a building may correspond to the use of the rest of the land: for example, goods may be stored on a particular site both in the open and within a building, with the result that even if the building use were lost upon demolition, continued use of its old site for

---

[91] The earlier view of Lord Widgery C.J. was that "I do not think it within the scheme of the Act of 1947 to make the intentions of the landowner a material factor when deciding whether development has taken place and, if so, whether permission for the development was required": *Britt* v. *Buckinghamshire C.C.* (1962) 60 L.G.R. 430 at 434. But that clearly no longer holds sway. In *Hartley* Lord Denning M.R. at 420 suggested an objective test on intention, based upon the drawing of inferences from the fact of land having "remained unused for a considerable time, in such circumstances that a reasonable man might conclude that the previous use had been abandoned." But the judgment of Widgery L.J. perhaps suggested that a more subjective approach might be possible, when at p. 421 he spoke of use having "ceased with no intention to resume it at any particular time." In *Nicholls* v. *S.O.S.E.* [1981] J.P.L. 890 the court accepted that evidence of intention might be relevant, but that it might come both from direct evidence and from the conduct of the owner or occupier. The latter may well contradict the former, and entitle the Secretary of State to reject the direct evidence.

[92] But *cf.* ministerial determinations at [1978] J.P.L. 651 and [1978] J.P.L. 653, (where no material change of use although dwelling-houses out of use for 35 years and 23 years respectively and [1977] J.P.L. 326 (material change where dwelling had been rendered uninhabitable).

[93] See, *e.g. Ashton* v. *S.O.S.E.* April 9, 1973 (Unreported, but noticed in S.E.A.A., p. 25). From *Jennings Motors Ltd.* v. *S.O.S.E.* [1982] 1 All E.R. 471 it is now clear that demolition will not automatically extinguish existing rights, but may constitute a change of so radical a character as to amount to the creation of a new planning unit.

[94] T.C.P.A. 1971, s. 22(2)(*d*) and *cf.* Class I, Schedule to General Development Order 1977.

storage might not necessarily result in any material change in the use of the site as a whole.

(c) Discontinuance and surrender of use rights

Use rights may be compulsorily extinguished by the use of discontinuance proceedings under section 51 of the 1971 Act,[95] but the requirement to compensate for use of the power means that it is comparatively rarely employed. Alternatively, rights may be surrendered in a section 52 agreement, often as part of an arrangement with the authority conferring upon them that benefit as a planning gain in return for a permission for further development.

C. The General Development Order

The full text of the Schedule to the current general development order is reproduced in Appendix B, and details of some of its exemptions are analysed later in this Chapter. In addition to supplementing some of the procedural provisions of the Act, the Order itself grants permission for a wide range of development. The principal categories of so-called "permitted development" include: householder and other minor works, temporary land uses, agricultural and forestry development, industrial development, and certain development by local authorities and statutory undertakers. There are varying rationale for the exemptions. In some cases it is the wish to avoid too detailed control; perhaps even to promote (as with agriculture) the activity so far as possible. In other cases, exemptions are based upon the public accountability of the developer, such as local authorities themselves and other statutory bodies.

The power to achieve these exemptions through delegated legislation was conferred as a means of ensuring flexibility: orders might be modified with experience, without the need for further legislation. But although there have been some five new general development orders and 14 amendments since 1948, the scope of the exemptions has changed comparatively little, except perhaps for the further tolerances granted in 1981. The general trend has been towards a broadening of the scope of permitted development, and one reason why the trend has not been towards greater restriction is that the permission granted by the Order is directly comparable with permission expressly granted by a planning authority, and its modification by a subsequent Order is compensatable.[96] The new General Development Order Amendment 1981 increases the scope of permitted development for so-called householder development by increasing from 10 to 15 per cent the permitted tolerance for the works of improvement and extension, and it confers similar benefits for industrial development. But proposals for reducing the scope of planning intervention have always proved controversial, and they are subject to annulment by resolution in either House of Parliament.[97] The Labour Government, indeed, were forced to withdraw

---

[95] *Post*, p. 454.
[96] T.C.P.A. 1971, s. 165(1)*(b)*.
[97] T.C.P.A. 1971, s. 287(5). Orders are required to be made by statutory instrument, (s. 287(4)) and by virtue of the Statutory Instruments Act 1946, s. 5(1) must be laid before Parliament after being made. Either House may then within a period of 40 days, resolve that the Order be annulled.

similar proposals in 1977 following a spirited battle in the House of Lords,[98] and the present Government bowed to conservationist pressure in 1981 by retaining tighter controls through a special development order, in national parks, conservation areas and areas of outstanding natural beauty.

1. Withdrawal of the permission

In addition to ministerial amendment, the permission granted by the Order may be withdrawn in two main ways: by a direction under article 4 of the Order, or by a valid condition imposed upon a planning permission. It may also be effectively withdrawn by a covenant in a section 52 agreement.

(a) Article 4 Directions

The Order confers power upon the Secretary of State or appropriate planning authority[99] to withdraw some or all of the general permission by making an order under article 4, where satisfied that it is "expedient" that development within the Order should not be carried out. A direction under article 4 may be in general terms, withdrawing permission for all or any development of all or any of the classes of permitted development in any particular area specified in the direction,[1] or it may be simply a preemptive prohibition in respect of some particular development.[2] In each case notice of the direction must be served upon owners and occupiers of every part of the land affected, but in the former case there is power to dispense with the individual service requirement where it would be impracticable.[3]

In most cases approval of the Secretary of State is required before a direction may take effect, although no formal machinery exists for public local inquiry, and approval or rejection is based instead upon a statement of the authority's reasons for their proposed direction.[4] But in 1978 power was conferred upon local planning authorities to make directions limited to the exclusion of Clauses I–IV of the Schedule to the Order, where in their

---

[98] Town and Country Planning General Development (Amendment) Order 1977 (S.I. 1977 No. 1781). (Revoked by S.I. 1977 No. 2085). The Order was debated in the Lords, and although the formal annulment procedure was not used, the Government complied with a motion calling for the Order's withdrawal: H.L. Deb., Vol. 387, cols. 1793–1821 (December 7, 1977).

[99] Either the county or the district planning authority may make an Article 4 direction in relation to a conservation area, but otherwise responsibility vests in the authority which would have the function of granting or refusing planning permission on any application necessitated by the direction: art. 4(10) (as amended by S.I. 1980 No. 1946). The other authority must be notified: art. 4(11) (as amended); D.O.E. Circular 43/74, para. 6.

[1] art. 4(1)(a). Specific authority for art. 4 exists in T.C.P.A. 1971, s. 24(5)(b).

[2] art. 4(1)(b). For a discussion of the distinction between the two categories, see *Speedworth Ltd.* v. *S.O.S.E.* (1972) 71 L.G.R. 123, and *Thanet D.C.* v. *Ninedrive Ltd.* [1978] 1 All E.R. 703 at 711, per Walton J.: " . . . the planning authority may either ban all or any development or ban a specific development, that is to say, it can either sweep the board clean or be as extremely selective as it chooses."

[3] " . . . having regard to the number of persons interested in the land as owners or occupiers, or the difficulty of identifying and locating such persons": G.D.O., art. 4(6).

[4] The administrative requirements for submission and approval are set out in Appendix D to D.O.E. Circular 12/73; and see Circular Letter of 30.1.74 issued by the Department of the Environment.

opinion the development would be prejudicial to the proper planning of their area or constitute a threat to the amenities of their area.[5] Such a direction will remain in force for no longer than six months unless approved by the Secretary of State.[6] Approved directions remain in force indefinitely, surviving fresh general development orders,[7] until cancelled by the authority which made them.[8]

The use of the article 4 direction is in practice limited by the twin restraints of finance and administrative practice. A direction is of no effect against development which has already occurred within the terms of the General Development Order,[9] and compensation is payable for the restrictions it imposes upon future development if planning permission is subsequently refused or granted subject to conditions other than those previously imposed by the Order.[10] Compensation entitlement is not limited to persons owning an interest in the land, but extends also to a contractual right of use which is affected by the direction.[11] And ministerial advice on the use of article 4 directions has been cautious: the view is that the exemptions of the Order should be withdrawn only in exceptional circumstances, and that it would rarely be justifiable unless there is a real and specific threat.[12] Even the fact that an area is a conservation area is not in itself sufficient to justify the making of a direction: a special need must be clearly shown, and "unless there are obvious and immediate reasons for it, a direction should not be made until it is clear that there will not be adequate public co-operation in the improvement of the area."[13]

(b) Conditions on a planning permission

It is likely that some or all of the benefits of the General Development Order may be excluded in an appropriate case by a condition imposed upon a planning permission, but in the absence of a specific High Court ruling the position remains uncertain. The Act makes no express provision for this, and

---

[5] Now G.D.O. 1977, art. 4(3)(b). A direction may be made without any ministerial approval in the case of listed buildings, so long as certain works of statutory undertakers (defined in art. 4(9)) remain unaffected.

[6] art. 4(3)(1). Conversely, the Secretary of State may disallow a direction within the six-month period: art. 4(4). It is not possible to maintain control without central government approval by using successive six-monthly directions: art. 4(3)(ii).

[7] See e.g. art. 4(8) as to saving for directions made under G.D.O. 1963.

[8] art. 4(7).

[9] Cole v. Somerset C.C. [1957] 1 Q.B. 23. The ruling causes difficulties in the case of permissions which have been only partly implemented (though it is presumably possible to withdraw permission for any further extension even though part of the tolerance under Class I of the Order has been used up), and the temporary permission under Class IV which allows use for up to 28 days in any calendar year. Because it is a new permission every year, it can presumably be withdrawn at the commencement of a year despite implementation in previous years; and it would be sensible that it should be able to be withdrawn premanently, without any need of annual Directions.

[10] T.C.P.A. 1971, s. 165. There is no fee payable for a planning application for development for when permission has been withdrawn under art. 4; see further post, p. 212.

[11] Pennine Raceway Ltd. v. Kirklees D.C. (1982) 263 E.G. 721 (C.A.).

[12] D.O.E. Circular 12/73, para. 2.

[13] D.O.E. Circular 23/77, para. 41. For the criteria applicable to approval of directions covering wide areas of land, see M.H.L.G. Circular 39/67, para. 5.

it is a theme thought by many to be central to the legislation that, without the consent of the landowner, existing rights may be abrogated, and existing permissions revoked, only upon the payment of compensation. Moreover, one possible legal basis for such a condition, contained in article 3 of the General Development Order (that nothing in the Order should operate so as to permit development contrary to an express condition imposed in a planning permission) has been construed narrowly so as to confine it to permissions in existence before the coming into effect of the applicable provisions of the Order.[14] But against that view is the fact that there has been a judicial trend in recent years towards enlargement of the power to impose conditions limiting existing or future use rights, notwithstanding that had other statutory powers been used, compensation would have been payable.[15] Moreover, a condition need not operate against the consent of the landowner: the developer retains the choice, limited though it may be, of not implementing the permission and thereby rejecting the condition.[16] Such persuasive considerations appear to have influenced the Secretary of State, and conditions excluding certain specified permitted development rights have been imposed by him in appeal cases.[17] Alternatively, where the consent of the landowner is forthcoming, a section 52 agreement may be employed.

2. Permitted development and specific permissions

It was initially quite clear that the making of an application for express permission was not to be taken as an admission that permission was actually needed for a proposed development[18]; nor that the grant of permission precluded the developer from relying instead on the General Development Order.[19] If deemed permission already existed, conditions imposed on the express permission would be unenforceable. But this doctrine came to be doubted, particularly by Lord Denning M.R. who insisted that developers should not be allowed to "blow hot and cold," and that, having applied for and obtained permission, should abide by its terms.[20] In *Newbury District Council* v. *Secretary of State for the Environment*[21] the House of Lords

---

[14] *East Barnet U.D.C.* v. *British Transport Commission* [1962] 2 Q.B. 484 at 498, *per* Lord Parker C.J. The Divisional Court held that no application for permission had in fact been necessary, and that a condition imposing a time limit upon the development, despite art. 3, could not be deemed for the future to exclude the very provisions which permitted the development.

[15] See *e.g. Westminster Bank* v. *M.H.L.G.* [1971] A.C. 508; *City of London Corporation* v. *S.O.S.E.* (1973) 23 P. & C.R. 169; *Kingston-upon-Thames Royal London Borough* v. *S.O.S.E.* [1973] 1 W.L.R. 1549 (differing from *Allnatt London Properties Ltd.* v. *Middlesex C.C.* (1964) 62 L.G.R. 304); and *Peak Park Joint Planning Board* v. *S.O.S.E.* [1980] J.P.L. 114.

[16] For a contrary view, see J.E. Alder, "Planning Conditions and Existing Rights" (1972) 36 Conv. (N.S.) 421; "The effect of a Planning Condition upon Existing Rights" [1973] J.P.L. 701, and *Development Control* (1979), p. 105.

[17] See *e.g.* [1976] J.P.L. 253, [1977] J.P.L. 56. And see *Essex Construction Co. Ltd.* v. *East Ham B.C.* (1963) 61 L.G.R. 452 at 458, *per* Lord Parker C.J.

[18] *Mounsdon* v. *Weymouth and Melcombe B.C.* [1960] 1 Q.B. 645 at 655–656.

[19] *East Barnet U.D.C.* v. *British Transport Commission* [1962] 2 Q.B. 484 at 497–499, *per* Lord Parker C.J.

[20] *Newbury D.C.* v. *S.O.S.E.* [1978] 1 W.L.R. 1241 at 1250.

[21] [1981] A.C. 578.

unanimously rejected that view, holding that pre-existing use rights could always be asserted in the face of subsequent permission, except where the effect of the implementation of the permission was to create a new planning unit. The consequence is that it would be rare indeed for deemed permission to be excluded by nothing more than the grant of express permission.

3. Conditions and limitations

Confusion arises in the operation of the Order from the means used to define the scope of permissions granted under it. Not only are there conditions imposed in many cases, but permissions are also governed by "limitations." Conditions imposed by the Order are directly comparable with conditions imposed on an express grant of consent, and enforcement action may be taken where their terms are breached. Limitations, on the other hand, are the means through which the tolerances or limits of permitted development are defined, such as the right to use land for temporary uses for up to 28 days, or the right to extend a dwelling house by up to 15 per cent. of its original capacity. It has been possible since 1959 for enforcement action to be taken also in respect of breach of any "limitation" attaching to a permission,[22] but it is a limited power which gives rise to practical difficulties. If the 15 per cent. tolerance is exceeded by a few cubic metres, for example, are the authority limited to requiring simply that the excess be removed (and, if so, how?); or may they regard the whole extension as unauthorised because of the excess, and require its demolition? The latter course, though on the face of it draconian, has in the past been the only realistic method of applying the enforcement code in cases of breach, because there would otherwise have needed to be piecemeal demolition and rebuilding. And so "limitation" in the Order has not been interpreted as identical to "limitation" in the enforcement code, and the courts have insisted that development carried out in excess of any limitation is to be regarded as wholly, rather than partly, unauthorised.[23]

Although in *Garland* v. *Minister of Housing and Local Government*, Lord Denning M.R. thought that a "trifling excess" might be a different matter,[24] and Widgery L.J. confined his remarks to development "substantially different"[25] from that described in the Order, the scale of non-compliance in fact made no difference to the practical problems of enforcement which underlie the decision. A minor deviation may, as with an express permission, be ignored as *de minimis*, but beyond that point the question is one of principle rather than degree. The objection of principle does not arise, however, in cases where the damage is easily prevented for the future; such as where the breach is one of having exceeded the yearly allocation of 28 days for temporary uses of land.[26] Only in such a case, though, is it possible

---

[22] T.C.P.A. 1971, s. 87(2); and see also s. 243 (5) which allows breach of condition or limitation to be alleged interchangeably.

[23] See *e.g. Miller-Mead* v. *M.H.L.G.* [1963] 2 Q.B. 196; *Garland* v. *M.H.L.G.* (1968) 20 P. & C.R. 93 and *Rochdale M.B.C.* v. *Simmonds* [1981] J.P.L. 191. See also cases involving the express grant of permission: *Copeland B.C.* v. *S.O.S.E.* (1976) 31 P. & C.R. 93 and *Kerrier D.C.* v. *S.O.S.E.* [1981] J.P.L. 193.

[24] (1968) 20 P. & C.R. 93 at 102.

[25] *Ibid.* at 104.

[26] It was in respect of this particular limitation that changes were made in 1959 following the decision in *Cater* v. *Essex C.C.* [1960] 1 Q.B. 424.

to regard the development as authorised up to the point of infringement, rather than unauthorised *ab initio*.

Changes introduced by the Local Government and Planning (Amendment) Act 1981, however, confer greater flexibility on authorities in enforcement, and allow them to require, as an alternative to demolition, that steps be taken to make the development comply with the terms of any planning permission. This flexibility makes the identification of the breach less critical than before, though it does not alter the pre-existing case law.

In addition to the specific limitations defining each permission in the Schedule to the Order, there is a general highways limitation applicable to most of the permitted classes, which excludes any development requiring or involving works of access to trunk or classified road, or which "creates an obstruction to the view of persons using any highway used by vehicular traffic at or near any bend, corner, junction or intersection so as to be likely to cause danger to such persons."[27]

4. *Special Development Orders*

The Act[28] also authorises special development orders, whose effect is limited to the land or descriptions of land specified by the Order. By this means, permission has been granted for development within the designated areas of new towns,[29] for atomic energy development[30] and for ironstone areas[31]; the scope of the General Development Order has been limited within environmentally sensitive areas[32]; and a special condition has been imposed enabling authorities to control the design and external appearance (but not the siting) of permitted agricultural and forestry buildings in certain designated special landscape areas.[33] The making of a development order has been held to be a purely administrative and not a judicial act,[34] and this

---

[27] G.D.O., art. 3(3).

[28] T.C.P.A. 1971, s. 24(3).

[29] Town and Country Planning (New Towns) Special Development Order 1977 S.I. 1977 No. 665, Town and Country Planning (New Towns in Rural Wales) Special Development Order 1977 S.I. 1977 No. 815. Permission is granted by these orders for development in accordance with proposals approved by the Secretary of State, and similar provision is now made in respect of the two urban development areas by the Town and Country Planning (Merseyside Urban Development Area) Special Development Order 1981 (S.I. 1981 No. 560), art. 3, and the Town and Country Planning (London Docklands Urban Development Area) Special Development Order 1980 (S.I. 1980 No. 1080), art.3.

[30] Town and Country Planning (Atomic Energy Establishments Special Development) Order 1954, S.I. 1954 No. 982 (as amended by S.I. 1957 No. 806 and S.I. 1961 No. 1295); Town and Country Planning (Windscale and Calder Works) Special Development Order 1978, S.I. No. 523.

[31] Town and Country Planning (Ironstone Areas Special Development) Order 1950, S.I. 1950 No. 1177.

[32] Town and Country Planning (National Parks, Areas of Outstanding Natural Beauty and Conservation Areas) Special Development Order 1981, S.I. 1981 No. 246.

[33] Town and Country Planning (Landscape Areas Special Development) Order 1950, S.I. 1950 No. 729. Broadly speaking the Order covers most of three national parks: the Peak Park, the Lakes and Snowdonia, although the boundaries do not coincide exactly. No action has yet been taken on the recommendation by the Sandford Committee in 1974 (*Report of the National Parks Policies Review Committee* (H.M.S.O., 1974) that there should also be siting control over the whole of every national park.

[34] *Essex C.C.* v. *M.H.L.G.* (1967) 18 P. & C.R. 532.

allows it to be used as an alternative to the granting of permission upon appeal, in cases where the Secretary of State may wish to override the Inquiries Procedure Rules. In the case of the recent application for the reprocessing of nuclear fuels at Windscale, for example, the Secretary of State wished to test Parliamentary opinion before acting upon the recommendation of the Inspector who conducted the inquiry. He therefore refused permission on the application, but proceeded instead to grant it by special order, subject to Parliamentary approval.[35]

D. The Use Classes Order

The full text of the Use Classes Order 1972 is reproduced in Appendix C. The effect of section 22 (2) (f) of the 1971 Act, under which the Order is made, is to enable the Secretary of State to exclude from the Act's definition of development, changes of use falling within classes described in the Order. The Order prescribes some classes simply by setting a highly abstract use description, such as "office" and "shop," but in other cases the interchangeable uses are very much more closely defined, down to the level of "bone grinder" and "breeder of maggots from putrescible animal matter" in the special industrial category. The broad classes give considerable freedom for use change and for the intensification of existing uses within each class.

In practice, use of the Order is governed by three main principles:

(1) It is the predominant use of the planning unit, and not merely some ancillary use, against which the impact of the Order is to be assessed.[36] In some of the classes the exemption is confined to a "building," such as certain industrial buildings (Classes III and IV) and certain buildings for religious purposes (Class XIII); but the wider planning unit is brought in under Article 2 (3) which allows references to "building" to include "land occupied therewith and used for the same purposes." This does not require that there should be any ancillary dependent link between the building and the land occupied with it, and provided the same purpose is pursued on each the whole is capable of being regarded as a single building for the purposes of the Order.[37]

(2) The Order operates to exclude certain types of use change from control, not to define itself the types of use which involve development.[38] Change from one use to another in the same class involves no development, but it does not follow that development will necessarily occur if a change is made to a use in another class. And the Order itself provides that the fact

---

[35] See the debate reported at Hansard, H.C. Deb., Vol. 950, cols. 111–179 (May 15, 1978). Similarly, in respect of the proposal to site the third London airport at Stansted in Essex, see *Essex C.C.* v. *M.H.L.G.* (1967) 18 P. & C.R. 531, where the plaintiff authority failed in its attempt to have the special development order quashed.

[36] *Vickers Armstrong Ltd.* v. *Central Land Board* (1958) 9 P. & C.R. 33; *G. Percy Trentham Ltd.* v. *Gloucestershire C.C.* [1966] 1 W.L.R. 506; *Brazil Concrete Ltd.* v. *Amersham R.D.C.* (1967) 18 P. & C.R. 396; and *cf. Shepherd* v. *Buckinghamshire C.C.* (1966) 18 P. & C.R. 419 where the predominant former use was held to be as an office, notwithstanding that it had been of a specialised military nature and accompanied by some ancillary residential use.

[37] *Brooks and Burton Ltd.* v. *S.O.S.E.* [1978] 1 All E.R. 733.

[38] *Rann* v. *S.O.S.E.* (1980) 40 P. & C.R. 113.

that a use which is ordinarily incidental to a particular predominant use, but appears as a different use in the Order, does not prevent it from being enjoyed as an incidental use.[39] This is particularly important given the detailed level at which some of the uses are defined. But there is no doubt that the design of the Order has had a persuasive influence upon the way the courts have interpreted the statutory formula of "material change of use" itself, and that they would be reluctant to allow interpretations which would ignore the conceptual framework employed in the Order.

(3) The courts have insisted that the Order should be interpreted restrictively, in the sense that the specified classes should not be stretched to accommodate activities which do not clearly fall within them: a sculptor's studio[40] and a motor vehicle hire business,[41] for example, have both been held to be outside the general industrial category of "making or manufacturing of articles in the course of trade or business," and thus *sui generis*.

In the main, the classifications have been selected by reference to the similarities in likely planning or environmental implications of the uses. Thus it is assumed that the use of a building as offices for one purpose is unlikely to differ significantly from its use as offices for any other purposes. There may be occasions when this assumption does not hold true, however, and where there may be a special case for allowing a particular user without wishing to extend the whole range of Use Classes Order exemptions. In such a case a condition excluding the benefits of the Order in whole or in part would be justifiable.[42] The ability to switch between permitted uses otherwise may mean that a new building can rapidly come to be used for a purpose quite different from that for which permission was granted. In *Kwik Save Discount Group Ltd.* v. *Secretary of State for Wales*[43] permission had been granted for a self service petrol station and car showroom. The plaintiffs acquired the site before the buildings had been occupied and wished to use them immediately for use as a retail store. In order to claim the benefit of the Order they first used the premises for one month as a car showroom, offering five cars for sale. The Court of Appeal upheld the Secretary of State's ruling that the use was minimal, and insufficient to establish a starting point for exploitation of the Order.

E. The Impact of Control on different categories of development

So far, the discussion has been at the level of general principles. It is necessary now to turn to examine the way in which different types of development are affected by both the general definition and the variable exemptions conferred by the subordinate legislation.

---

[39] U.C.O., art. 3(3).
[40] *Tessier* v. *S.O.S.E.* (1975) 31 P. & C.R. 161.
[41] *Farm Facilities Ltd.* v. *S.O.S.E.* [1981] J.P.L. 42.
[42] See further M.H.L.G. Circular 5/68, para. 23 (and model condition in Appendix, para. 7); *City of London Corporation* v. *S.O.S.E.* (1971) 23 P. & C.R. 169 (where a condition that premises should be used as an employment agency and for no other purpose was upheld). An unequivocal condition to that effect is required: *Carpet Decor (Guildford) Ltd.* v. *S.O.S.E.* [1981] J.P.L. 806.
[43] [1981] J.P.L. 198.

1. *Residential and householder development*

(a) Changes in use

Changes of use into and out of the general residential category are clearly material and within the scope of control, but it is clear that many changes within the category are also caught. In the case of an ordinary dwellinghouse there are three main classes of change: those protected by the ancillary umbrella, those resulting in the creation of more than one separate dwellinghouse and those involving a change in "character".

Into the first class falls the situation where a householder takes in guests or lodgers whilst retaining the primary use of the house as a private dwelling. There is no material change in use unless the ancillary use expands to the point where it becomes the dominant use. The second class is that of the subdivision of a dwellinghouse ("the use as two or more separate dwellinghouses of any building previously used as a single dwellinghouse") which is specifically deemed by the Act to involve a material change in use.[44] The words "separate dwellinghouses" imply a degree of severance and individual self-sufficiency, which might be evidenced by physical separation (such as separate facilities, access or services for each unit) and legal separation (such as separate letting arrangements for each unit).[45] In some cases there may be a material change without any internal alteration at all[46]; but conversion of a house to bed-sitting rooms, or group sharing of a house, would not normally satisfy the statutory test. They would often, however, fall within the third class, as involving a change in the character of the residential use. It will generally constitute such a change if a private dwelling has become a house let in lodgings or has been put into some other form of multiple paying occupation. It is the departure from the norm of family group occupation which is the critical factor, but beyond that the matter is very much one of fact and degree for the Secretary of State.

The Use Classes Order confers some degree of flexibility in the case of premises already lawfully used as commercial residential premises, by allowing under Class XI, use change between "use as a boarding or guest house, or an hotel providing sleeping accommodation."[49] Another class,

---

[44] T.C.P.A. 1971, ss. 22(3)(*a*). "Building," by virtue of s. 290(1), includes any part of a building, so that the subdivision of a flat would fall within s. 22(3)(*a*). Note that use changes falling under this head have a four year limitation period for enforcement purposes: s. 87(4)(*c*); and enforcement is possible against each part as well as against the whole: s. 22(3)(*a*).

[45] The test is different from but overlaps with that for determining whether a separate planning unit has emerged. There may be a separate planning unit without there actually being separate dwellinghouses; but there would not necessarily be a material change in the use of the unit. Further, in the absence of any provision in the Act deeming the converse (the change from separate dwellinghouses into a single dwelling) to constitute development, the ordinary rules suggest that it is not unless somehow the "character" of the use is also changed.

[46] *Wakelin* v. *S.O.S.E.* (1978) 77 L.G.R. 101 where the Court of Appeal upheld a finding of material change where there was a proposal to sever the occupational link between a large house and its ancillary lodge; and *Rann* v. *S.O.S.E.* (1980) 40 P. & C.R. 113.

[49] Schedule, Class XI. A students' hostel does not fall within the Class (*Mornford Investments Ltd.* v. *M.H.L.G.* (1970) 21 P. & C.R. 609); nor, any longer, does a residential club (see, *e.g.* *English Speaking Union of the Commonwealth* v. *Westminster L.B.C.* (1973) 26 P. & C.R. 575), nor a building with permission for bed-sitting rooms (*Mayflower Cambridge Ltd.* v. *S.O.S.E.* (1975) 30 P. & C.R. 28, where Lord Widgery C.J. said "the essence of a hotel is that it takes transient passengers," whereas a bed-sitting room "is where somebody remains for a long time").

Class XII, permits use changes between "use as a residential or boarding school or a residential college." Finally there is the institutional care class, Class XIV, which permits "use as a home or institution providing for the boarding, care and maintenance of children, old people or persons under a disability, a convalescent home, a nursing home, a sanatorium or a hospital."

Change from a use within a class to a use of another class, or a use outside the Order altogether, does not of itself involve development, and it is still necessary to inquire whether there has been a change in character of use. There is also some overlap. A use may combine the provision of a hotel type accommodation (Class XI) with institutional care (Class XIV), as in *Rann* v. *Secretary of State for the Environment*[50] where premises with permission for guest-house use came to be used for providing holiday accommodation for mentally handicapped children. The High Court set aside the Secretary of State's ruling that this was an institutional use involving care and supervision and thus within Class XIV, emphasising instead the temporary, transient nature of the children's stay which qualified the use for inclusion in Class XI.

(b) Incidental uses

The doctrine of ancillary or incidental use is given statutory effect in the case of dwellinghouse use, where the Act deems as not involving development "the use of any buildings or other land within the curtilage of a dwellinghouse for any purpose incidental to the enjoyment of the dwellinghouse as such."[51] The curtilage has been defined as follows: "the ground which is used for the comfortable enjoyment of a house or other building . . . although it has not been marked off or enclosed in any way. It is enough that it serves the purpose of the house or building in some necessary or reasonably useful way."[52] In the case of the majority of urban homes, the whole site will normally be the curtilage, but in rural areas the boundaries are often notional rather than real. The statutory exemption supplements rather than supplants the general ancillary use doctrine, however, and it is important to accept that simply because an ancillary use is outside the curtilage, it does not mean that it is incapable of ancillary protection as part of the planning unit. The curtilage will often coincide with the planning unit, but it may not necessarily do so.

Uses incidental to dwellinghouse enjoyment cover a wide range, and include the provision of additional living accommodation in outbuildings and caravans (provided no separate unit is created, which would involve the severance of the ancillary link),[53] and the accommodation of hobbies such as the stabling of a horse[54] and the parking and repair of private motor vehicles up to a "normal" incidental level of activity.[55]

---

[50] (1980) 40 P. & C.R. 113; and see, as to uses incidental to uses within Class XI, *Emma Hotels Ltd.* v. *S.O.S.E.* (1980) 41 P & C.R. 255.

[51] T.C.P.A., s. 22 (2)(d).

[52] *Sinclair-Lockhart's Trustees* v. *Central Land Board* (1950) 1 P. & C.R. 195.

[53] See *e.g.* ministerial decisions at [1975] J.P.L. 104, [1979] J.P.L. 124 (use for extra bedspace only) and *cf.* [1976] J.P.L. 586, [1978] J.P.L. 489 (separate dwelling).

[54] See, *e.g.* [1978] J.P.L. 128.

[55] See, *e.g.* [1978] J.P.L. 201: repairs of own vehicles held to be within s. 22; but does not cover 4 vehicles used for racing hobby because of extent of additional repair work.

(c) Operational and "householder" development

Dwellinghouses fall within the usual exemptions for the carrying out of works "for the maintenance, improvement or alteration of any building, being works which affect only the interior of the building or which do not materially affect the external appearance of the building,"[56] but there are further specific exceptions provided by the General Development Order. These have been amended in 1981, and a different regime has been established for dwellings situated in conservation areas, national parks and areas of outstanding natural beauty, hereafter "the special areas." The general rules permit five types of householder development:[57]

(i) *The enlargement, improvement or other alteration of a dwellinghouse*

This exemption is available only in the case of existing dwellinghouses,[58] not including flats,[59] and it falls short of authorising works of complete rebuilding.[60] It is subject to limitations as to volume, height and location.

(a) Volume. Enlargement is permitted up to 70 cubic metres or 15 per cent. (whichever is the greater) of the original dwellinghouse (or 50 cubic metres or 10 per cent. in the case of a terrace house, or dwellinghouses in the special areas), subject in all cases to an upper limit of 115 cubic metres. Calculations are to be based on external measurement, and the exemption is once and for all. A dwelling extended under the permission or even under an express permission cannot then subsequently be re-extended, and the calculations are always to be made against the cubic capacity of the "original" dwellinghouse, being the building as it existed on July 1, 1948; or if built after that date, as so built. Further, outbuildings are brought into the calculation: the erection of a stable or loose box anywhere within the curtilage is to be treated as dwellinghouse enlargement; and so also the erection of a garage or coach-house if any part of it lies within a distance of five metres from any part of the dwellinghouse.[61] Otherwise it is permitted in its own right as an incidental building under (iii) below, and the purpose of the five metre rule is to discourage infilling between houses and outbuildings. The five metre limit does not apply in the special areas,

---

[56] T.C.P.A. 1971, s. 22(2)(a): the exemption does not extend to works for making good war damage, or works begun after December 5, 1968 for building alterations for providing additional space below ground.

[57] The exemptions and limitations are prescribed by article 3 and Class I of Schedule 1 to the General Development Order 1977 as amended by the 1981 Amendment Order (S.I. 1981 No. 245); and as modified by the Special Development Order (S.I. 1981, No. 246). There is a limited summary of the changes in Annex A to D.O.E. Circular 9/81.

[58] And not therefore a building used substantially for non-residential purposes: *Scurlock* v. *Secretary of State for Wales* (1977) 33 P. & C.R. 202.

[59] Defined in G.D.O. art. 2 as "a separate and self contained set of premises constructed for use for the purpose of a dwelling and forming part of a building from some other part of which it is divided horizontally."

[60] See, *e.g. Sainty* v. *M.H.L.G.* (1964) 15 P. & C.R. 432; *Larkin* v. *Basildon D.C.* [1980] J.P.L. 407.

[61] Conversely, an existing garage or coach-house may be brought into the calculation for dwellinghouse alteration, enlargement or improvement if the effect of the works will be to bring the dwelling within the five metre zone.

however, where any such building anywhere in the curtilage must be included in the calculation.[62]

(b) Height. The height of the enlarged, approved or altered dwellinghouse may not exceed the height of the highest part of the roof of the original dwelling, as measured from the ground level[63]; and no part lying nearer than two metres to the curtilage boundary may have a height exceeding four metres, except in the case of insertion or alteration of a window or of alterations to the original roof.

(c) Location. No part of the alterations may extend beyond the forwardmost part of any wall of the original dwellinghouse which fronts on a highway.[64] Any works which bring the altered dwellinghouse within five metres of any existing garage or coach-house have the result of deeming them to form part of the altered, enlarged or improved dwellinghouse for the purpose of calculating its new cubic capacity.[65] Finally, there is an overall limit to plot coverage: the area of ground covered by buildings within the curtilage excluding the original dwellinghouse may not exceed 50 per cent. of the total curtilage, again excluding the ground area of the original dwellinghouse.

(ii) *The erection or construction of a porch*

This is a minor exemption under Class I.2 permitting the construction or erection of a porch outside an external door limited to two metres in area, three metres in height and no nearer than two metres to any curtilage boundary fronting on a highway.

(iii) *Buildings and enclosures for incidental purposes*

This category of development, under Class I.3, which has now been extended to include garages and coach-houses (except in the special areas), permits the "erection, construction or placing, and the maintenance, improvement or other alteration" of any building or enclosure[66] in the curtilage required for a purpose incidental to the enjoyment of the dwellinghouse as such.[67] There are no volume limitations and the permission can therefore be implemented without affecting the dwellinghouse extension tolerances under Class I.1, provided a five metre distance is maintained between the two. Limitations do however restrict forward projection and

---

[62] S.D.O., art. 3.
[63] By art. 2(1B) "ground level" is now taken to be the level of the surface of the ground immediately adjacent to the building, or where it is not uniform, the highest part adjacent to the building.
[64] Note also the general highways limitation in art. 3(3) which prohibits any development "which requires or involves the formation, laying out or material widening of a means of access to an existing highway which is a trunk or classified road, or creates an obstruction to the view of persons using any highway used by vehicular traffic at or near any bend, corner, junction or intersection so as to be likely to cause danger to such persons."
[65] Not applicable in the special areas. S.D.O., art. 3.
[66] Except for a dwelling, stable or loose box.
[67] Including "the keeping of poultry, bees, pet animals, birds or other livestock for the domestic needs or personal enjoyment of the occupants of the dwellinghouse."

the total area of curtilage which may be covered (both as for Class I.1 above) and height (four metres for a ridged roof, otherwise three metres).

(iv) *Construction of hardstanding for vehicle*

This exemption permits construction of a hardstanding within the curtilage for vehicles "for a purpose incidental to the enjoyment of the dwellinghouse as such."[68] It does not, therefore, extend to the parking of commercial vehicles, nor to non-incidental use of domestic vehicles; and it is subject to the general prohibition on laying out of access to certain types of highway.[69]

(v) *Oil storage tanks*

This is a more recent addition to category of permitted development. The permission is limited by the forward projection rule (as for Class I.1 above) and to tanks no more than three metres above ground level and of no more than 3,500 litre capacity.[70]

2. *Minor development*

There is a general permission under Class II of the General Development Order for the painting of the exterior of buildings; for the making of an access to the highway (except to classified or trunk roads) required in connection with permitted development other than under Class II itself, and for the "erection or construction of gates, fences, walls or other means of enclosure" and their maintenance, improvement and alteration. There is an overall height limit of two metres, or one metre when abutting on a highway.[71] The Divisional Court have construed the permission considerably more narrowly than is suggested by a straightforward reading of it, by insisting that only a wall having the function of enclosure will qualify.[72]

3. *Office development*

The office use of any premises as ancillary to the primary use of the planning unit does not constitute development, but change in the primary use from residential or industrial to office use will normally constitute a material change.

Where the permitted use of premises is for office use, the Use Classes Order confers a broad exemption from control for subsequent use change, allowing use as an office for any purpose[73] and defining "office" broadly.[74]

---

[68] G.D.O., Sched. 1 Class I.4.

[69] *Ante*, note 64.

[70] G.D.O., Sched. 1, Class I.6.

[71] The planning authority are entitled to require the removal of the whole of a fence where the height limit is exceeded: *Rochdale M.B.C.* v. *Simmonds* [1981] J.P.L. 191.

[72] *Prengate Properties Ltd.* v. *S.O.S.E.* (1973) 25 P. & C.R. 311; and *cf. Ewen Developments Ltd.* v. *S.O.S.E.* [1980] J.P.L. 404 where the court declined to overturn an inspector's conclusion that embankments constructed to enclose a caravan site were not permitted by the Order.

[73] Schedule, Class II.

[74] So as to include banks, and premises used for an estate agency, building society and

This means that the identity and the business of the office user is rendered irrelevant for planning purposes, and that intensification of use which might otherwise require permission is also permitted, provided the use is still that of an "office." The exemption may be excluded, in appropriate cases, by a condition imposed on the permission allowing the use,[75] so making any change of use even within the Order a breach of condition and enforceable as such.

4. Shops

A similarly abstract level of use description is set for shopping uses under Class I of the Use Classes Order, but there are five exceptions involving uses whose planning implications are such that it is deemed necessary to retain some control.[76] Change from any of those five specific categories to use as an ordinary shop is permitted,[77] but not the reverse. This does not mean that such a change will always be material.

"Shop" is broadly defined as including any building wherein the primary purpose is the selling of goods by retail, and the definition is extended to include hairdressers, post offices and undertakers.[78] But there are several uses expressly excluded from the definition including restaurants and "offices."

A retail use may also arise as a use ancillary to the primary use of land, and the courts have been prepared to recognise this in the case of sale of produce from a farm,[79] for example, or as ancillary to a primary warehousing use. But they have resisted attempts to exploit the scope of Class X of the Use Classes Order, which permits "use as a wholesale warehouse or repository for any purpose," so as to allow uncontrolled change from warehouse to supermarket.[80]

5. Industrial development

Exemptions from development control for industry are conferred by both the General Development and the Use Classes Orders. The starting point is the definition of industrial process contained in the General Development Order, which forms also the basis for the definition of "industrial building" in the General Development Order. The definition includes the carrying on

---

employment agency, but not a post office or betting office. The distinction presumably is that the latter two bear closer resemblance to shops than to ordinary commerical offices, whilst the others fall on the other side of the line.

[75] *City of London Corporation* v. *S.O.S.E.* (1971) 23 P. & C.R. 169.

[76] The categories, looking somewhat dated now, are: (i) a shop for the sale of hot food; (ii) a tripe shop; (iii) a shop for the sale of pet animals or birds; (iv) a cats-meat shop and (v) a shop for the sale of motor vehicles.

[77] G.D.O., Sched., Class III(b).

[78] U.C.O., art. 2(2).

[79] See, *e.g. Wood* v. *S.O.S.E.* [1973] 1 W.L.R. 707; and *cf. Williams* v. *M.H.L.G.* (1967) 65 L.G.R. 495.

[80] See *e.g. L.T.S.S. Print and Supply Services Ltd.* v. *Hackney L.B.C.* [1976] Q.B. 663 (change to primary use for retail sale of furniture); *Decorative and Caravan Paints Ltd.* v. *M.H.L.G.* (1970) 214 E.G. 1355, (change from wholesale to retail sales) and *Monomart (Warehouses) Ltd.* v. *S.O.S.E.* (1970) 34 P. & C.R. 305 (change from "builders' merchants' warehouse" to "do-it-yourself supermarket").

of any process for or incidental to the making of any article (broadly defined as including an article of any description including a ship or a vessel), the carrying out of various other operations on "articles" and the getting, dressing or treatment of minerals.[81] The process in each case must be one carried on "in the course of trade or business other than agriculture."

The definition is broad, and has been given suitably broad interpretation by the courts, so as to include horticultural activities involving the sorting, grading and dispatch of plant bulbs[82]; and even the cooking of school meals.[83]

(a) Industrial use change

For the purposes of the Use Classes Order industrial buildings (being buildings used for the carrying on of industrial processes) are divided into three primary classes: light, general and special. The "general" category is purely residual, and includes all industrial buildings not falling into the other two. "Light industrial buildings" are defined in surprisingly subjective terms as those "in which the processes carried on or the machinery installed are such as could be carried on or installed in any residential area without detriment to the amenity of that area by reason of noise, vibration, smell, fumes, smoke, soot, ash, dust or grit."[84] It is a definition couched in terms of actual and potential environmental impact, and it limits the category to virtually emission-free uses. Any change within the class is permitted by the General Development Order.[85]

The special industrial building class is further subdivided into five groups, Groups A–E, ordered roughly in ascending order of adverse environmental impact and ranging from the mildly offensive to the downright disgusting.[86] Use change to another use in the same group is authorised by the Order, though it does not follow that changes to a use contained in another group necessarily constitute development. Further, where there is a group of buildings used as parts of a single undertaking and used for two or more of the seven classes of industrial uses, those particular two or more classes may be treated as a single class, provided the area occupied in the group by either general or special industrial buildings is not substantially increased thereby.[87]

(b) Industrial operational development

Permission is granted under Class VIII of the General Development Order for a range of operational development by industrial undertakers

---

[81] U.C.O., art. 2(2).

[82] *Horwitz* v. *Rowson* [1960] 1 W.L.R. 803.

[83] *Rael-Brook Ltd.* v. *M.H.L.G.* [1967] 2 Q.B. 65, where the Divisional Court ruled that neither the making of profit nor any commercial activity was essential to "a trade or business," but were concerned nonetheless to draw a broad distinction between amateur and professional users.

[84] U.C.O., art. 2(2).

[85] G.D.O., Sched., Class III(*a*).

[86] Thus much of the argument at first instance in *Western Fish Products Ltd.* v. *Penwith D.C.* concerned the scope of "putrescibility" under Class IX of the Order; and Walton J.'s ruling (unreported) that "putrescible," meaning "liable to rot or become putride," ought not to be limited to what happens in the course of manufacture, was upheld by the Court of Appeal.

[87] U.C.O., art. 3(2).

(undertakers by whom an industrial process is carried on), including (i) the construction of private highways and footpaths, railways, sewers and other apparatus; (ii) the installation of plant and machinery not exceeding 15 metres in height and (iii) the extension or alteration of buildings so long as the original height is not exceeded and the cubic content not exceeded by more than 20 per cent.,[88] nor the aggregate floor space by more than 750 square metres.[89] The limits were raised in 1981 in an attempt by the Government to ease controls over industrial expansion. Limitations restrict the permission to operations, in the case of (ii) and (iii) above, which do not materially affect the external appearance of the premises; and in the case of (iii), restrict development any closer than 5 metres to the curtilage boundary and limit the permission to cases not requiring an industrial development certificate under the Act.

Most importantly, the permission is not available unless the existing use of the land is lawful, and not merely immune from enforcement.[90]

6. Agriculture and forestry

The exemptions from control conferred upon agriculture and forestry are the broadest of all, and they stem from the consistent post-war policy of promoting agricultural development. But conflict has arisen in recent years between the demands of an increasingly mechanised and industrialised farming community, and those who fear that the traditional rural landscape is being irretrievably damaged and that rare fauna and flora are being destroyed by changing farming patterns. Debates in the House in 1981 on the Wildlife and Countryside Bill showed how strong is the support for increasing the scope of planning control over agriculture and forestry, and that Bill contains certain selective protective mechanisms, such as proposals for extending the effect of the designation of sites of special scientific interest.

(a) Agricultural use changes

But so far as planning control is concerned, broad exemptions are conferred by the Act and by the General Development Order. The Act provides that the "use of any land for the purposes of agriculture or forestry (including afforestation) and the use for any of those purposes of any building occupied together with land so used" is not to be taken as involving the development of the land.[91] But it is not the use of land, but the making of a material change in its use, which constitutes development, and the section is ambiguous. The ambiguity has been resolved by a broad interpretation, extending the exemption to cover changes to agriculture use from other uses.[92]

The statutory exemption sets a high level use description which allows changes to occur between different methods of agriculture and forestry

---

[88] Or 10 per cent. in the special areas: S.D.O., art. 3(c).
[89] Or 500 square metres in the special areas: S.D.O. art. 3(c).
[90] Ante, pp. 172–174; and see Brooks and Burton Ltd. v. S.O.S.E. [1978] 1 All E.R. 733 at 745.
[91] T.C.P.A. 1971, s. 22(2)(e).
[92] McKellan v. M.H.L.G. (1966) 188 E.G. 683.

without control. "Agriculture" also has an extended definition,[93] but numerous problems have arisen at the borderline. The wish to prevent the breaking up of existing farms into smaller units, particularly leisure gardens and allotments, for example, has led the Secretary of State to rule that material change may flow from the greater intensity of use, the consequent changes in appearance of the land, and the increased numbers of people visiting it; but this approach has now been rejected by the Divisional Court.[94] The effect of their ruling is to re-emphasise the breadth of the agricultural use-description. Provided the primary purpose may be said to be "agricultural" then changes in character are irrelevant. Hence, they held, the subdivision of agricultural land into allotments would not involve development, because of their continuing primary horticultural use.

The "breeding and keeping of livestock" is included in the definition, but it has been restrictively interpreted by the courts to cover only livestock kept for agricultural purposes,[95] thus exluding uses such as a stud farm or riding school, and the breeding of cats and dogs for use in research.[96] There is, however, a supplementary limb to the definition which authorises the "use of land as grazing land," and the keeping of non-agricultural livestock whose food comes primarily from grazing is therefore protected under this head.[97] The main question is whether the predominant use of the land is for grazing, or for some other purpose.

(b) Operational development for agricultural purposes

Under Class VI of the General Development Order further exemption from control is extended to operational development, but the exemption is limited to agricultural land of more than one acre comprised in an agricultural unit. The Order authorises the carrying out of "building or engineering operations requisite for the use of that land for the purposes of agriculture (other than the placing on land of structures not designed for those purposes or the provision and alteration of dwellings)," subject to limitations as to the maximum ground area covered, height, and adjacency to any trunk or classified road. Mineral operations relating to agriculture are similarly permitted, but the Order makes no mention of the "other operations" included in the Act's definition of development. This must almost certainly be an oversight, because the omission leads to absurd results. For example, an operation of such scale as to amount to an "engineering" operation may be protected by the Order; but conducted on a smaller and less obtrusive scale it may require planning permission.

[93] It is defined by T.C.P.A. 1971, s. 290(1) as including "horticulture, fruit growing, seed growing, dairy farming, the breeding and keeping of livestock (including any creature kept for the production of food, wool, skins or fur, or for the purpose of its use in the farming of land), the use of land as grazing land, meadow land, osier land, market gardens and nursery grounds and the use of land for woodlands where "that use is ancillary to the farming of the land for other agricultural purposes, and 'agricultural' shall be construed accordingly."
[94] *Crowborough Parish Council* v. *S.O.S.E.* [1981] J.P.L. 281.
[95] *Belmont Farm Ltd.* v. *M.H.L.G.* (1962) 13 P. & C.R. 417 (building used for breeding and training horses for show jumping). Livestock includes fish: [1980] J.P.L. 480 (m.p.d.) despite the more restrictive rulings in rating law; see *e.g. Cresswell* v. *B.O.C. Ltd.* [1980] 3 All E.R. 443.
[96] *Minister of Agriculture, Fisheries and Food* v. *Appleton* [1970] 1 Q.B. 221, where the Divisional Court followed the *Belmont* case.
[97] See, *e.g. Sykes* v. *S.O.S.E.* [1981] J.P.L. 285.

Whether a particular building or engineering operation may be "requisite" for the use of land for agricultural purposes raises questions of balancing need, intention and purpose. It is not presumably the intention to require a farmer to demonstrate economic necessity to justify exploitation of the permission, and provided the purpose for which works are carried out is in fact agricultural, the question of whether they are "requisite" must be one largely for his own subjective assessment. Intention also comes into it, however, as demonstrating whether the primary purpose of the works is agricultural or not. Thus the tipping of waste materials on agricultural land may be carried out as part of an engineering operation with the primary intention of increasing its productivity by making it easier to crop[98]; or it may be done primarily to dispose of the material, and thus involve a change from agricultural use to use for tipping.[99]

[98] *Northavon D.C.* v. *S.O.S.E.* (1980) 39 P. & C.R. 332.
[99] *Bilboe* v. *S.O.S.E.* (1980) 39 P. & C.R. 495.

CHAPTER 5

THE MACHINERY OF DEVELOPMENT CONTROL

A. Introduction

Development control has become the central process of the British land use planning system, and its importance is reflected in the increasing complexity of the procedures which govern it. The basic procedure is simple. An application for planning permission is made to the local planning authority. It is examined by them against the background of the current development plan, and permission granted or refused. There is a right of appeal to the Secretary of State against refusal, against any conditions which may be imposed upon the grant of permission and against a failure by the authority to issue a decision within the prescribed time.

But onto this simple structure there has been grafted a variety of technical rules. Some have the purpose of reinforcing the split in responsibility for development control between district councils and county councils, and others lay the basis for the overall supervisory jurisdiction of the Secretary of State. Other rules are designed to ensure that the authority have before them a wide range of information before any decision is made.

One important function of many of the rules is to secure coordination between public sector agencies, and the development control process is consciously and increasingly used as the focal point for drawing together a wide range of government policy. The relationships are complex, but there are three main categories. First, there are central government's powers of veto. In the case of applications involving industrial development, private hospitals, oil refineries (and formerly office development), the validity of the planning application and the competence of the authority to handle it depend upon prior approval, in the form of certification having been obtained from the government department responsible (although the industrial development control is presently suspended). Their powers are not necessarily exercised on planning grounds at all: the development control system merely provides a convenient administrative structure through which to intervene.

Second, there are several powers of "direction," used primarily as a back-up to support the statutory allocations of decision making responsibility between central government and the two tiers of local government. A district council, for example, may be directed by the local highway authority to determine an application in a certain manner; or they may be directed by the Secretary of State to refer it to him for decision. The power for county planning authorities to direct the refusal by districts of certain applications has now been repealed, and the county/district relationship remodelled.

Third, there are the consultation provisions, and here there is a complex network of relationships. The general pattern is that there is an obligation upon the authority to notify the application to different public agencies who will be allowed an opportunity to comment before any decision is taken. The rules govern consultation between the two tiers of local government, as well as consultation with central departments and statutory undertakers.

Some general points need to be made before turning to more detailed analysis of the rules. First, their effect is primarily procedural. They are designed to ensure that an authority has before it a sufficient basis of information and opinion before coming to a decision; but apart from those instances where a power of veto rests elsewhere, the rules do not directly inhibit substantive decision making. Authorities have a broad discretion, only loosely constrained by the development plan, to grant or refuse planning permission. Further, the procedural requirements go largely to preliminary, and at times peripheral, matters. The internal decision structures and procedures of each authority are to a large extent their own design. The consequence is that in practice there is a wide variation in approach between different local authorities, though operating within the same legal framework.

Second, the basic rules convey an impression of clear cut decision making which is not always the case in practice, particularly on more complex development proposals. The application will often have been preceded by lengthy private negotiations between the developer and planning officers, resulting already in tentative commitments. The rules still govern the procedure following the making of an application, but often more as a backcloth to a process of negotiated decision making, than establishing the basis for a completely independent assessment of the proposals.

Third, although the rules are often specific and clear in their requirements, they are seldom accompanied by an indication of what consequences may follow if they are breached. Instances of non-compliance are not uncommon; sometimes they are deliberate, but more often the result of inadvertence, misinterpretation or misunderstanding. At one extreme there lies corruption on the part of officers and councillors to which the British planning system because of its flexibility is dangerously susceptible; whilst at the other extreme, there are the simple mistakes which the complexity of the system renders inevitable. In the absence of any better administrative law remedy, the most obvious consequence is that the action taken, such as the granting of a planning permission, is void or voidable if the rules are breached. But this is a consequence the courts have often been reluctant to insist upon. They have instead attempted to strike a pragmatic balance between rule enforcement and flexibility in development control, and have found no difficulty in holding, for example, that an apparently mandatory statutory requirement should be regarded as purely directory if too literal an interpretation would otherwise cause unnecessary rigidity. But no clear interpretative doctrines have emerged, and further development is often hampered by the limited ability of third parties either to discover whether irregularities have occurred or to challenge erratic conduct in the courts. It is an area, however, where the investigative jurisdiction of the local government ombudsmen is starting to have an effect, and authorities are less likely today to brush aside procedural formalities affecting the rights of applicants and third parties.

B. Planning Applications

The planning application is the trigger for development control. There is a variety of special applications which may be made under the Act, including applications for listed building consent, tree felling and advertisement consents, which are examined elsewhere in this book. The main categories of general planning applications are those for full planning permission, for outline planning permission, for the discharge of a planning condition or limitation and for a determination under section 53 as to whether planning permission is actually required.

1. Applications for full planning permission

There is no nationally prescribed form for applications, although a model form has been issued by the Department[1] and local planning authorities have in practice adopted it with some variations. Applications are governed by the General Development Order, which requires that they should be made on the form issued by the authority, should include the particulars required by the form and should be accompanied by a site plan (sufficient to identify the land to which the application relates) and such other plans and drawings as are necessary to describe the development.[2] If the authority require any further information, they may direct the applicant to supply it[3], and they may also require the production of evidence to verify the particulars of any information supplied.[4] No sanction is imposed for failure to comply with a direction, and the validity of the application does not turn upon it. But the authority may decline to issue a determination, or refuse permission, and leave the applicant to his right of appeal.

More than one application may be made for permission,[5] whether successively or as a means of presenting alternative schemes to the authority; although the introduction of fees for applications can be expected to reduce the popularity of this practice.[6]

It is a fundamental principle, and symbolic of planning's indifference to patterns of private land ownership, that the applicant need not be the owner of all or any of the land affected by the application,[7] though it will be necessary to notify other owners.[8] It is possible, therefore, for a prospective purchaser to test the development potential of land before entering a binding contract for its acquisition,[9] though since only the applicant and not the

---

[1] In D.O.E. Circular 23/72.

[2] G.D.O. art. 5(1).

[3] *Ibid.*

[4] *Ibid.* art. 5(4).

[5] *Heron Corporation Ltd.* v. *Manchester C.C.* [1978] 1 W.L.R. 937 at 947, *per* Bridge L.J.

[6] There is, however, a 75 per cent. discount for second applications submitted within 28 days of the first: Town and Country Planning (Fees for Applications and Deemed Applications) Regulations 1981, Sched. 1, para. 2.

[7] There is a suggestion in *Ayles* v. *Romsey and Stockbridge R.D.C.* (1944) 42 L.G.R. 210 (under the 1932 Act) and *Hanily* v. *M.H.L.G.* [1952] 2 Q.B. 444 at 451, *per* Parker J., that the power to apply may be limited to a person "who genuinely hopes to acquire the interest in the land," but there is no further authority to back such an implied limitation, and it would be extremely difficult to give it practical effect. The Irish Supreme Court, however, interpreting similar provisions have been prepared to insist that the power to apply for permission should not be available to an individual with no proprietary rights and with the purpose solely of advancing some personal motive: *Frescati Estates Ltd.* v. *Walker* 1975 I.R. 177.

[8] *Post*, p. 214.

[9] The act of seeking permission will not in itself amount to part performance in the absence of a written memorandum evidencing the contract unless referable to the existence of an agreement: *New Hart Builders Ltd.* v. *Brindley* (1974) 237 E.G. 959.

landowner will have the right of appeal it may be more convenient, and also more expeditious, for the applicant to apply as agent for the owner.[10] All planning applications are made to the district authority,[11] who are required to acknowledge the application[12] and to notify the applicant if it is forwarded to the county planning authority for determination.[13] If either authority form the view that an application is invalid by reason of failure to comply with any of the statutory requirements, they must notify that view to the applicant as well.[14]

2. Applications for outline planning permission

A change to the General Development Order in 1950 first brought in this procedure, which allows an applicant to seek approval in principle to development, before being put to the expense of preparing detailed plans. Although the procedure is now recognised indirectly in the primary legislation, it has never been completely satisfactorily designed. Reliance upon planning conditions to achieve the purpose has proved cumbersome and confusing, particularly as successive amendments to the General Development Order have come to regulate the procedure more closely. The general principle is that on an outline application, nothing more is required than a site plan and a verbal description of the proposed development.[15] Permission may then be granted, but subject to a condition requiring the subsequent approval of the authority to certain specified "reserved matters" before development may commence. Alternatively, the authority may within one month from receipt of the application require the submission of further details on all or any of the reserved matters, to the point, if thought necessary, of converting it to an application for full permission.[16] The applicant has a right of appeal against such a requirement, and although the power of authorities is broad they have been exhorted by the Department to use it sparingly and "only if the information is indispensable in reaching a decision."[17] Even in conservation areas, where an authority may be anxious to see detailed plans before conceding the principle of the development, straightforward outline procedures are not to be discarded automatically.[18]

This means that an outline application may contain only a very general

---

[10] But see *English* v. *Dedham Vale Properties Ltd.* [1978] 1 W.L.R. 93 as to the unauthorised use of the vendor's name on a planning application.

[11] L.G.A. 1972, Sched. 16, para. 15(3); G.D.O. art. 7(1). Application is also made to the district in respect of land in a National Park (*ibid.*, Sched. 16, para. 16), but for land in the two urban development areas is required to be made direct to the urban development corporations: Town and Country Planning (Merseyside Urban Development Area) Special Development Order 1981 (S.I. 1981 No. 560), art. 10; Town and Country Planning (London Docklands Urban Development Area) Special Development Order 1981 (S.I. 1981 No. 1082), art. 10.

[12] G.D.O., art. 7(3).

[13] *Ibid.* art. 7(4).

[14] *Ibid.* art. 7(5).

[15] *Ibid.* art. 6(2).

[16] *Ibid.*

[17] D.O.E. Circular 22/80, para. 9. The details thus obtained become part of the application even although the authority proceed to refuse permission on other grounds; and may therefore form the basis for the grant of full permission on appeal: *Hammersmith and Fulham L.B.C.* v. *S.O.S.E.* [1980] J.P.L. 750.

[18] D.O.E. Circular 23/77, para. 38.

description of the development proposed, such as "the erection of five small factory units," or "residential development at a density not exceeding ten dwellings to the acre." Where the purpose is one to which the land is already allocated in a local plan, broad proposals like this are more likely to be acceptable to the authority than where an exception is sought to existing policies for the area. Further information supplied at the direction of the authority will, unless accepted by them as purely illustrative (as to which, see further below) have the effect of limiting the outline permission; and planning conditions may also be imposed by the authority on the outline permission to limit its scope.

(a) The limitation to erection of buildings

Outline applications may be made only "for the erection of a building,"[19] and hence the procedure does not extend to engineering or mining operations, or to other operations involving building works other than the erection of a building. Nor does it extend to applications for material changes of use, although any use change and any other form of operational development may doubtless be authorised under outline procedures so long as it is ancillary or incidental to the primary development consisting of the erection of a building. The reasons for this limitation are far from clear, and it does not exist in Scotland.[20] The option is now open, however, for an authority of their own initiative to reserve matters on any detailed application for their subsequent approval by means of an appropriate condition (discussed under heading 4 below), and this procedure offers them greater flexibility in non-outline cases. From the applicant's viewpoint, however, it differs from outline procedure in that he enjoys no right to seek such a permission and is required still to submit a detailed application.

(b) "Reserved matters"

"Reserved matters" are defined by the General Development Order as meaning "any of the following matters relating to the building to which the planning permission or the application relates which are relevant to the proposal and in respect of which details have not been given in the application, namely: (a) siting, (b) design, (c) external appearance, (d) means of access (e) the landscaping of the site."[21] The definition was not introduced

---

[19] Which by virtue of G.D.O., art. 2., does not include plant or machinery.
[20] The Town and Country Planning (General Development) (Scotland) Order 1975 (S.I. 1975 No. 679) art. 5 allows an outline application to be made for any development. Careful consideration was given by the Stevens Committee to the case for extending outline procedures to minerals applications, but they concluded that in the special circumstances governing minerals extraction it would prove inflexible for both operators and planning authorities: *Planning Control over Mineral Working* (H.M.S.O., 1976), Chap. 7.
[21] G.D.O., art. 2(1). "Landscaping" is also defined, as "the treatment of land (other than buildings) being the site or part of the site in respect of which an outline planning permission is granted, for the purpose of enhancing or protecting the amenities of the site and the area in which it is situated and includes screening by fences, walls or other means, planting of trees, hedges, shrubs or grass, formation of banks, terraces or other earthworks, laying out of gardens or courts, and other amenity features."

until 1969, and its purpose originally was to restrict the range of matters which could be reserved for subsequent approval.

It now seems clear, however, that an authority may also reserve matters other than these for subsequent approval in appropriate cases, by imposing a suitable condition whether on an outline or a full permission; and the application for subsequent approval then falls within category (4) below (applications for consent, approval or agreement) rather than category (3).

It often happens, also, that an application is hybrid, in the sense that it contains details of some, but not all, of the reserved matters. In some cases the detailed material may be included with the application purely for illustrative purposes, and not as part of it. If the authority regard it as part of the application and fail to reserve the matter for subsequent approval, the applicant may find himself held to details which he had not intended to be binding. George Dobry's[22] recommendation that the range of applications be extended to include "outline," "illustrative," "detailed" and "guideline" might have gone some way to overcoming this problem though increasing the complexity of the system; but it has not been implemented and the only safeguard is for the applicant to distinguish clearly between illustrative and detailed material.

The converse, which also causes difficulties, is where the authority are prepared to grant outline permission on a hybrid application, but wish to reserve their approval of detailed material submitted with it. The Department's view is that where details have been given, the matter cannot be a "reserved matter" within the definition of the General Development Order.[23] An appropriate course would be to amend the application by agreement, or where necessary to invite the applicant to submit a revised application; but an alternative and swifter method would be to impose a separate condition requiring subsequent approval of the matter or some part of it, not as a prescribed "reserved matter," but as an ordinary planning condition.[24] Again, application for subsequent approval would not be for approval of "reserved matters" under category (3) below, but under category (4). This seems, however, an unnecessarily complex means of dealing with a simple problem, and a better solution would be a complete reformulation of the General Development Order's procedures so as to allow an authority to approve or reject details when granting outline permission, and to integrate the two forms of "outline" conditions.

3. Applications for approval of reserved matters

The outline permission is itself the planning permission for all purposes of the Act,[25] and the application for approval of reserved matters is a subsidiary procedure undertaken within the parameters set by the outline permission. Outline applications are often made with no immediate intention to proceed with the development, often as a method of providing a basis for land

---

[22] *Final Report,* pp. 75–78.
[23] M.H.L.G. Circular 12/69, *Memorandum*, para. 2.
[24] See, *e.g. Sutton L.B.C.* v. *S.O.S.E.* (1975) 29 P. & C.R. 350 where the authority, on an application for full permission, had reserved approval of "the type and treatment of materials" to be used on the exterior of the building.
[25] *Hargreaves Transport Ltd.* v. *Lynch* [1969] 1 All E.R. 455.

valuation by testing the authority's reaction in principle to development of the site, and perhaps as a preliminary step in the disposal of the site to a developer.[26] In the absence of detailed and up-to-date development plans this has become an increasingly common use of the procedure. But it places a strain on the subsequent procedures, because although in theory the submission and approval of a reserved matter application should involve nothing more than the filling of gaps left by the outline permission, the issues are often hotly contested. On the applicant's side, subsequent changes in site ownership and market conditions are liable to lead to attempts to revise and extend the scope of the outline approval; while the planning authority may be equally anxious to try to limit its scope, and by no means remain still convinced that approval should have been given at all.

(a) Time limits for applications

An important step towards minimising the conflict has been the introduction of time limits for the submission of applications for the approval of reserved matters. Since 1968, legislation has reinforced the former practice of many authorities in requiring that application for approval should be made within three years (or such other period as the authority may specify) of the grant of outline permission.[27] If permission is actually granted without such a condition being imposed, it is nonetheless deemed to be granted subject to it. The power for the authority to vary the time period allows them to specify separate periods in relation to separate parts of the development[28] to make allowance for phased implementation.

The time limit is imposed by way of condition rather than by general statutory prescription, and the applicant may appeal against the time specified.[29] But breach of the condition is treated differently from breach of other conditions. It is not a matter for enforcement by the authority. Instead, the Act provides that an application for approval of reserved matters made beyond the specified time "shall be treated as not made in accordance with the terms of the permission."[30] The permission therefore is no longer capable of lawful implementation and, effectively, lapses.

The statutory time limits extend only to "reserved matters" as defined by the General Development Order,[31] and do not therefore affect applications for approval of other matters reserved by the authority. They may wish to leave this open, so as to be able to exert continuing control over an activity; or they may impose an express time-limiting condition.

---

[26] For an interesting background study, see the D.O.E. Consultants' Report, *Housing Land Availability in the South East* (H.M.S.O., 1975), pp 26–27.

[27] T.C.P.A. 1971, s. 42(2). In *Sievers* v. *Bromley L.B.C.* [1980] J.P.L. 520 the application had been lodged on the third anniversary of the granting of outline permission rather than the day before (which was a Sunday) which would have brought it within the three year period. The Court held the lateness, if any, to be *de minimis* and issued mandamus to require the authority to consider it.

[28] T.C.P.A. 1971, s. 42(5).

[29] *Ibid.* s. 43(6).

[30] *Ibid.* s. 43(7)(*b*). It may still be treated as a fresh application for full permission, if the authority so elect, and determined accordingly: see note 32, below.

[31] Because s. 42(1) adopts the Order's definition of "outline planning permission," though it does not directly adopt the restrictive definition of "reserved matters."

(b) Procedures for applications

Application for approval of reserved matters is not itself a planning application, although it is usually (and sometimes confusingly)[32] made on the same form. There is therefore no need for compliance with the notification and certification provisions of the Act,[33] but there is provision for the calling-in of applications and for appeals against refusal of approval.[34] The application must include such particulars, and be accompanied by such plans and drawings, as are necessary to deal with the matters reserved.[35] Because of the pre-existing approval in principle, consideration of reserved matters is characteristically a matter for negotiated settlement between applicant and the authority's officers; and some authorities have been prepared to delegate the function of approval completely.

(c) Successive applications

The essence of negotiations over reserved matters is flexibility, and the courts have interpreted the procedures broadly. They have refused to rule, for example, that the applicant is limited to one application. Further applications may be lodged under the same outline permission, provided they are within the time limit,[36] whether they follow an earlier refusal or offer an alternative to a scheme already approved.[37] Similarly, it is possible for separate applications to be made for piecemeal approval of reserved matters for separate parts of a development,[38] or for different reserved matters.[39] But it would be possible for the authority in either case to withhold permission on planning grounds; if they took the view, for example, that siting ought not to be considered separately from external design, or in the absence of a layout plan for the whole development.

Amendment to submitted applications can also be permitted on a more flexible basis than with applications for full permission, because the principle of the development has been settled. The application for approval is not a planning application, and amendment rather than resubmission is the more

---

[32] See, e.g. *Cardiff Corporation* v. *Secretary of State for Wales* (1971) 22 P. & C.R. 718, where, however, the Court was prepared to construe an application for full planning permission as one made for reserved approval; *Inverclyde D.C.* v. *Secretary of State for Scotland* 1982 S.L.T. 200, where the House of Lords was prepared to interpret an application for reserved matters as a fresh application for planning permission where it departed from the outline permission; and *Thomas Langley Group Ltd.* v. *Leamington Spa R.B.C.* (1974) 29 P. & C.R. 358.

[33] *R.* v. *Bradford-on-Avon U.D.C., ex parte Boulton* [1964] 1 W.L.R. 1136.

[34] T.C.P.A. 1971, ss. 35 and 36. It is anomalous, however, that there is no provision for further appeal to the High Court against the Secretary of State's decision on a called-in application: T.C.P.A. 1971, s. 242(3)(a) and *Turner* v. *S.O.S.E.* (1973) 28 P. & C.R. 123. As to the availability of judicial review in such a case, see *post*, p. 623.

[35] G.D.O., art. 6(1). This requirement is directory, and the validity of the application is not therefore affected by a failure to supply all the necessary information at the time of the application: *Inverclyde D.C.* v. *Secretary of State for Scotland* 1982 S.L.T. 200.

[36] And note that separate time limits may be prescribed by the outline permission for a phased approval of reserved matters: T.C.P.A. 1971, s. 42(5).

[37] *Heron Corporation Ltd.* v. *Manchester City Council* [1978] 1 W.L.R. 937.

[38] *R.* v. *S.O.S.E., ex parte Percy Bilton Industrial Properties Ltd.* (1975) 31 P. & C.R. 154; although the question of whether phased approval might be insisted upon by either party was expressly left open.

[39] *Heron Corporation Ltd.* v. *Manchester City Council* [1978] 1 W.L.R. 937.

convenient method of accommodating changes until the point is reached where there may be a departure from the outline permission.[40]

(d) The scope of reserved approval

The scheme of outline permission requires that the principal features of the development should be settled at outline stage. No significant departure from them may therefore be sought under the guise of the reserved approval procedure. If material revisions are sought the proper course is for a fresh application to be made for planning permission, and to undertake again any necessary notification and publication. The borderline between principle and detail is often difficult to draw, particularly when the outline permission has been granted in general terms on the basis of sketchy information submitted in support of the original application. In practice, the distinction has been drawn in terms of planning implications, and the best test in borderline cases is to ask whether the revision is sufficiently important to warrant re-submission.

Some cases have shown an obvious discrepancy between the two stages. In *Calcaria Construction Co. Ltd.* v. *Secretary of State for the Environment*,[41] for example, outline permission had been granted for a warehouse, and the court had little hesitation in upholding the Secretary of State's rejection of detailed proposals in which the development had become an out-of-town supermarket surrounded by a car-park for 992 cars. Similarly, there has been held to be a departure from the outline permission where a scheme approved in outline for residential development of three five-storey blocks with garages, had changed to four four-storey blocks at detailed stage, with different parking and access arrangements.[42] Although the number of residential units remained the same, the revised scheme was thought by the planning authority to be liable to prejudice the development of nearby sites. In contrast, where an amendment has been made without off-site implications, such as the re-positioning of a private road, it would be unlikely to involve a departure from the outline permission.[43] In some cases it will be possible for the authority to overcome a departure from the terms of the outline permission by granting part approval only on the reserved matters application.[44]

Conversely, the grant of outline permission is a commitment on the part of the planning authority, and it follows that they have no power to revoke it except in accordance with the statutory procedures, or to reject detailed plans on grounds other than those expressly reserved,[45] or on grounds

---

[40] *Inverclyde D.C.* v. *Secretary of State for Scotland* 1982 S.L.T. 200, where the House of Lords held (on the corresponding provisions of the Scottish legislation) that an application lodged within the prescribed time might still be amended after that time provided the amendment did not alter the whole character of the application, and did not bring in other reserved matters in respect of which an application should have been made in time. Authorities are exhorted by the Secretary of State to allow amendments, and not to deal at length with matters of detail: D.O.E. Circular 22/80, para. 8.

[41] (1974) 27 P. & C.R. 435.

[42] *Shemara* v. *Luton Corporation* (1967) 18 P. & C.R. 520.

[43] As in *Hamilton* v. *West Sussex C.C.* [1958] 2 Q.B. 286.

[44] See, *e.g. Inverclyde D.C.* v. *Secretary of State for Scotland* 1982 S.L.T. 200.

[45] As in *Hamilton* v. *West Sussex C.C.* [1958] 2 Q.B. 286. But if a new means of access, not sought at outline stage and therefore not reserved by the outline permission, is proposed in detailed plans, this would be a departure from the outline entitling the authority to refuse to approve the plans: *Chalgray Ltd.* v. *S.O.S.E.* (1976) 33 P. & C.R. 10.

already implicitly conceded by the outline permission. It is too late at detailed stages, for example, to maintain that the development would be premature, or would involve undesirable "urbanisation."[46]

(e) Conditional reserved approval

Whether reserved matters may be approved subject to conditions is a matter of some doubt. There is no statutory power to impose conditions, the relevant sections of the Act being confined to conditions on planning permissions[47]; and even if the necessary power were specifically reserved by a condition on the outline permission, breach of a condition imposed on approval of reserved matters would not be a breach of planning control for which enforcement action could be taken. There is curiously, though, a right of appeal reserved by the Act against conditional approval of details.[48] The matter has expressly been left open by the High Court[49]; but despite the fact that ministerial advice and practice clearly assume there to be a power,[50] the legal justification must still be regarded as tenuous.

4. Applications for consent, approval or agreement

Planning authorities have for some time made use of conditions requiring their subsequent consent, approval or agreement to some specified aspect of the development. This flexibility has proved useful, especially in cases of change of use where the ordinary outline procedures are unavailable. Unless the matter was a "reserved matter," however, there remained some doubt as to such conditions' validity. There was an argument that the condition might be too uncertain, as reserving a future discretion to be exercised against unknown criteria; that use of such conditions conflicted with the duty to "determine" applications within eight weeks because matters were necessarily left undetermined, and also that such a condition was capable, in the absence of any right of appeal against refusal or failure by the authority to issue any decision, of working manifestly unreasonably. But the courts, albeit without any detailed analysis of these issues, were in due course prepared to recognise and uphold such conditions,[51] and the 1980 Act has now introduced a general right of appeal against the refusal, conditional

---

[46] *Lewis Thirkwell Ltd.* v. *S.O.S.E.* [1978] J.P.L. 844.

[47] See, *e.g. Chelmsford Corporation* v. *S.O.S.E.* (1971) 22 P. & C.R. 880, where the court declined to hold that reserving the "layout" of the development for later approval empowered the authority to decide whether walls or fences for decorative purposes, and to protect privacy, should be provided. The General Development Order has since been amended to allow authorities to reserve "landscaping" for subsequent approval; and the word has deliberately been defined (art. 2(1)) in broad terms as meaning "the treatment of land . . . for the purpose of enhancing or protecting the amenities of the site and the area in which it is situated and includes screening by fences, walls or other means, planting of trees, hedges, shrubs or grass, formation of banks, terraces or other earthworks, laying out of gardens or courts, and other amenity features."

[48] T.C.P.A. 1971, s. 36(1).

[49] *Chelmsford Corporation* v. *S.O.S.E.* (1971) 33 P. & C.R. 880 at 887.

[50] See, *e.g.* M.H.L.G. Circular 5/68, para. 22.

[51] See, *e.g. Sutton L.B.C.* v. *S.O.S.E.* (1975) 29 P. & C.R. 350; *Roberts* v. *Vale Royal D.C.* (1977) 242 E.G. 811 and *Bilboe* v. *S.O.S.E.* [1979] J.P.L. 100; reversed on other grounds, (1980) 39 P. & C.R. 495.

grant or failure to decide on any application for "consent, agreement or approval . . . required by a condition imposed on a grant of planning permission."[52]

There is thus now statutory acknowledgement of the practice, but it remains a different procedure from that governing outline permissions. It is a condition unilaterally imposed by the authority whilst an outline permission is sought as such by the applicant. It may, however, be imposed upon either an outline application (in respect of matters other than the "reserved matters" as defined by the General Development Order) or on a full permission granted pursuant to a full application. The range of matters which may be covered by such a condition is not constrained either by legislation or by the fact that full details may have been submitted with the application. The authority may wish to retain discretionary rather than prescriptive control over future activities on the site, or to exercise a dispensing power through conditions such as "The applicant shall not, except with the prior consent of the authority" carry out certain prescribed activities. Or they may wish to settle a detailed scheme with the applicant for the carrying out of some aspect of the development, such as is commonly employed in the case of landscaping requirements.

An advantage of the use of such conditions is that applications made for the consent, approval or agreement of the authority do not, unlike applications for the approval of reserved matters, require the payment of any fee by the applicant. One unfortunate limitation to the new timelimit and appeals provisions, however, is that the procedures do not regulate applications made under conditions imposed in an enforcement notice, despite the ruling in *Murfitt* v. *Secretary of State for the Environment*[53] that a "scheme approval" arrangement could validly be employed as a means of specifying the steps required by the authority to remedy a breach of planning control. Although the validity of such an arrangement is not affected by the omission, its inclusion in the new procedures would make it easier to implement.

5. *Applications for extensions of permission*

There is a simplified procedure under the General Development Order for the extension of the life of a planning permission where development has not commenced, but nor has the permission lapsed. In such a case a detailed application is unnecessary, provided there is a written application giving the authority sufficient information to enable identification of the subsisting permission. Further information may, however, be sought by the authority. It is, however, an application for permission and it is necessary for the usual notification and publicity procedures to be undertaken again.

There is, of course, no obligation upon the authority to renew permission, but when the simplified procedure was introduced the Minister advised authorities that permission for renewal should be refused only where

"(a) there has been some material change of planning circumstances since the permission was granted (*e.g.*, a change in planning policy for the area or in relevant highway considerations);

[52] T.C.P.A. 1971, s. 36(1); as amended by L.G.P.L.A. 1980, Sched. 15, para. 4(2).
[53] (1980) 40 P. & C.R. 254.

(b) continued failure to implement the development will contribute unacceptably to uncertainty about the future pattern of development; or

(c) the application is premature because the permission still has a reasonable time to run."[54]

In *Peak Park Joint Planning Board* v. *Secretary of State for the Environment*,[55] Sir Douglas Frank Q.C. (sitting as a Deputy Judge of the High Court) rejected that advice on two grounds. First, the former permission had actually expired by the time the application for renewal came on appeal to the Secretary of State; and second, the advice was "not a planning policy consideration" but "some form of administrative policy unrelated to planning" and *ultra vires*. With respect, both grounds are unsatisfactory. As to the first, the application for renewal had been correctly lodged under the special procedures *before* the expiry of the permission, and the terms of the circular were therefore clearly relevant. It cannot be right that the relevance of the advice should depend solely upon the timing of the subsequent decision making by the authority or the Secretary of State. As to the second point, there can be no doubt that the past planning history of a site is capable of being a relevant consideration in determining a planning application for the future; and that the achievement of consistency in decision making, which is what the policy is primarily directed to, is equally a relevant factor. In requiring the authority to justify the refusal of renewal of permission the Secretary of State is no less pursuing a planning policy than in requiring an applicant to make out adequate justification for development in a green belt, or in urging authorities always to grant planning permission except where there were clear grounds for refusal. The rejection of the advice in the circular was, however, strictly *obiter;* and the persuasive influence of the court's views has been substantially weakened by the criticism directed to it in the subsequent case of *South Oxfordshire District Council* v. *Secretary of State for the Environment*.[56]

There is no need to seek renewal of a permission where development has commenced under it, and given that the carrying out of comparatively minor works may amount to the "beginning" of development,[57] this may prove a more convenient and cheaper[58] method of keeping a permission alive. It is of course possible only where the permission is full; or, if outline, where details have been approved.

6. *Applications for retrospective approval of contravening development*

An application for planning permission may relate to development carried out before the date of the application.[59] The development may have been carried out entirely without permission; or in accordance with a permission

---

[54] M.H.L.G. Circular 17/69, para. 8.
[55] [1979] J.P.L. 618.
[56] [1981] J.P.L. 359 at 360, per Woolf J.
[57] *Post*, pp. 357–358.
[58] A fee is payable for applications under the simplified procedures as for ordinary applications.
[59] T.C.P.A. 1971, s. 32(1).

granted only for a limited period, or in breach of a condition imposed on a previous permission. Permission may be granted retrospectively, and may authorise the retention of buildings or works carried out, or the continuance of any use of land.

Authorities frequently invite applications under these provisions as a means of regularising breaches of planning control and for enabling them to impose conditions as necessary upon their future use, as an alternative to undertaking enforcement action. Applications are ordinary planning applications, and retrospective approval may be sought for existing development as part of an application for new development.

7. *Applications for the discharge or variation of conditions or limitations*

There is a curious hiatus in the Act, in that no special provision is made for applications for the discharge or variation of conditions or limitations on subsisting permissions. If the condition or limitation has already been breached, then retrospective approval may be sought, under the provisions discussed above. But if the change is still prospective, it may be that it does not itself constitute "development" for which permission may be sought though it would be a "breach of planning control" against which enforcement action could be taken if no permission were obtained.[60] An "hours of working" condition imposed upon a factory development in a residential area is an example of such a situation. It is common practice, however, for variation or discharge of a condition to be sought by means of an application for planning permission in the normal way.

8. *Applications for determination whether planning permission required*

Given the complexity of the statutory definition of development, it is not surprising that there exists a procedure under section 53 of the 1971 Act for clarifying its impact in particular cases. Any person proposing to carry out any operations or change in use of land may apply to the local planning authority for a determination of two questions: whether the proposals involve development; and, if so, whether permission is required under the Act, having regard to the deemed permissions available under the General Development Order. The great value of the procedure before 1953 was that it gave developers the opportunity to investigate their liability to development charge before seeking planning permission.[61] It is possible that there may be a resurgence in its popularity following the imposition of fees for planning applications, because whilst there is no fee payable for an application for a section 53 determination, the fee payable on an application for development potentially within the General Development Order will in some cases be substantial.

The principal benefit of the procedure, however, is as a guarantee against

---

[60] There is specific power for the Secretary of State, in an enforcement appeal, to vary or discharge any condition or limitation: T.C.P.A. 1971, s. 88B (added by the Schedule to L.G.P.(A). A 1981).

[61] "Now that the charge has gone, owners are not concerned whether or not development is involved provided they can get permission to do what they want:" *Report of the Ministry of Housing and Local Government 1950/51—1954* (Cmd. 9559), p. 77.

enforcement proceedings. Although no effect is prescribed by the Act for a favourable determination, it is said by the courts to be as good as an unconditional planning permission.[62] It is, as a statutory decision, binding on the authority and irrevocable by them, even where subsequent changes in the law may have altered the basis upon which it was given.[63]

(a) The procedure for applications

The application procedure is less formal than is the case with ordinary planning applications. There are no prescribed forms, but a written application including a description of the proposals and a site plan is required; together with, in the case of a proposal relating to the carrying out of operations, such plans and drawings as are necessary to show the nature of the operations, and in the case of proposed use change, a full description of present and proposed uses.[64] The applicant may be directed to supply any further information.

During the 1960s the courts attempted to develop a form of protection for applicants who acted in reliance upon the informal statements of planning authorities and their officers, by extending the scope of the section 53 procedure to cover the common situation where an applicant for planning permission was assured informally that no permission was required. In *Wells* v. *Minister of Housing and Local Government*[65] the Court of Appeal held that an application for planning permission might itself be regarded as containing an invitation (which the authority would be at liberty to reject) to determine under section 53 that permission was not required. Further, an opinion expressed in correspondence might constitute a binding determination,[66] and one judge was even prepared to accept that a purely oral assurance by telephone by a planning officer might suffice.[67]

But the trend towards informality has been curtailed. Amendments made to the General Development Order in 1969 increased significantly the degree of procedural formality required, by insisting upon the provision by applicants of more information than formerly, and allowing the rejection of applications for failure to provide information.[68] It thus became more

---

[62] *Wells* v. *M.H.L.G.* (1967) 65 L.G.R. 43 at 50, *per* Widgery J., and 53, *per* Salmon L.J. (Div.Ct.); [1967] 1 W.L.R. 1000 at 1007–8, *per* Lord Denning M.R. (C.A.).

[63] *English-Speaking Union of the Commonwealth* v. *City of Westminster L.B.C.* (1973) 26 P. & C.R. 575.

[64] G.D.O. 1977, art. 6(2). Appeal lies to the Secretary of State against an unfavourable decision, and upon the failure of the authority to issue a decision within the prescribed time (T.C.P.A., ss. 53(2); 37); and there is a further appeal to the High Court (s. 247). Applications under section 53 may also be called in for decision by the Secretary of State.

[65] [1967] 1 W.L.R. 1000 at 1007, *per* Lord Denning M.R. and 1010, *per* Davies L.J. But *cf.* the strong dissenting judgment of Russell L.J., at 1015, attacking this approach as stemming "in large measure from a natural indignation that a practice, which seems to have grown up since the system in this form was introduced in 1947, should operate merely as a trap for the unwary landowner."

[66] *English-Speaking Union of the Commonwealth* v. *City of Westminster L.B.C.* (1973) 26 P. & C.R. 575.

[67] *Lever (Finance) Ltd.* v. *Westminster Corporation* [1971] 1 Q.B. 222 and 234 *per* Sachs L.J.; disapproved by the Court of Appeal in *Western Fish Products Ltd.* v. *Penwith D.C.* [1981] 2 All E.R. 204.

[68] Town and Country Planning General Development (Amendment) Order 1969 (S.I. 1969 No. 276), art. 2(c).

difficult to assert that an authority might be taken to have waived the procedural formalities of the Order when issuing an informal assurance, and it was arguable that the earlier cases no longer represented the law. But in 1978 the Court of Appeal, in *Western Fish Products Ltd.* v. *Penwith District Council,*[69] though without considering the effect of the amendments to the Order, ruled reluctantly that they were bound by the earlier decisions, at least to the extent of accepting that an application for planning permission impliedly contained an invitation for section 53 determination. In some, but by no means all, cases the similarity between the two types of application is likely to be so close that any waiver of formalities by the authority is comparatively trivial, and in some cases the only practical distinction is the wording of the specific request. Further, section 53 clearly envisages the making of an express application under that section as part of an application for planning permission.

The Court of Appeal were emphatic that only a formal request for a determination or an application for planning permission would suffice, but they failed to consider the decision in *English Speaking Union of the Commonwealth* v. *City of Westminster London Borough Council*[70] where Pennycuick V.-C. had been happy to construe a section 53 determination from an exchange of letters. It may be that the case must be taken now to be overruled by the *Western Fish Products* decision, but there is a possible point of distinction in that, whilst the correspondence involved there nowhere referred in terms to section 53, it nonetheless described clearly the site, its history and the proposed development, and contained a formally expressed request for a ruling by the authority, which was answered in unequivocal terms. It was arguably capable therefore, of satisfying the procedural requirements of a section 53 determination without more, although neither of the parties may have intended it at the time.

(b) The scope of section 53

The potential usefulness of section 53 procedure is in practice limited by the narrow wording of the section and the restrictive interpretation it has had in the courts. The section refers to "proposals," and the procedure is not therefore available to test the lawfulness of operations or change of use already carried out. Nor may it be used to examine background questions, such as the validity or interpretation of a planning permission affecting the site.[71] The questions which can be put under section 53 are, first, whether the proposals involve "development;" and second, whether permission is required for them or is deemed to be granted under the General Development Order. The inability of the planning authority to go beyond these issues and look at the whole planning history of the site means that their decision may be given on the basis of false assumptions. The fact that the *existing* use of the land may be unlawful,[72] for example, or that valid

---

[69] [1981] 2 All E.R. 204; and see further *post*, p. 396.
[70] (1973) 26 P. & C.R. 575.
[71] *Edgwarebury Park Investments Ltd.* M.H.L.G. [1963] 2 Q.B. 408; *East Suffolk C.C.* v. *S.O.S.E.* (1972) 70 L.G.R. 595.
[72] See, *e.g. Enforcement and Allied Appeals* (H.M.S.O., 1975), p. 78.

permission already exists for the proposals,[73] are both deemed irrelevant. Further, a particularly narrow ministerial interpretation of the section has held that once it is found that the proposals in fact involve no change in use, let alone any material change, the determining authority lack any jurisdiction to make a formal determination.[74]

Finally, the benefits of the procedure are limited to the person who actually proposes to carry out the operations or change in use. There is, therefore, no right to use the procedure for quite hypothetical ends, or to test the lawfulness of some other person's proposals.[75]

The more irksome of these restrictions have been partially overcome by the readiness of the Secretary of State to offer informal opinions in cases falling strictly outside his jurisdiction,[76] but reform of the procedures to increase their general value is overdue.

For issues falling outside the section the only other possible administrative machinery for determination is through an application for planning permission, through enforcement proceedings, or through the use of the established use certificate procedures.[77] Where no suitable administrative machinery exists, the courts have indicated their willingness to assume jurisdiction in declaratory proceedings to determine such matters as the validity[78] and interpretation[79] of planning permissions, the scope of an enforcement notice[80] and the interpretation of exemptions offered by the Orders.[81] But the extent to which the High Court may be prepared to assume such jurisdiction in cases falling within section 53 is uncertain. Initially there was thought to be no formal barrier to jurisdiction,[82] but in 1959 there was introduced a right of appeal direct to the Divisional Court from ministerial determinations.[83] Under this procedure, if the Court believes the decision to be erroneous in law, it may not set it aside or vary it, but must remit it to the Minister for rehearing and redetermination by him.[84] In light of these provisions and in view of the courts' repeated emphasis of the significance of ministerial expertise in these types of

---

[73] *Ibid.* p. 75.

[74] *Ibid.* pp. 79–80.

[75] *Ibid.* p. 76.

[76] *Ibid.* pp. 75–76; and see also at p. 74, where a subsequent appeal to the High Court against the determination was dismissed: *East Suffolk C.C.* v. *S.O.S.E.* (1972) 70 L.G.R. 595.

[77] *Post,* p. 390.

[78] In *Edgwarebury Park Investments Ltd.* v. *M.H.L.G.* [1963] 2 Q.B. 408 at 417, *per* Lord Parker L.J.

[79] *Edmunds* v. *Cardiganshire C.C.* (1969) 113 S.J. 406.

[80] See, *e.g. St. Hermans Estate Co. Ltd.* v. *Havant and Waterlooville U.D.C.* (1970) 69 L.G.R. 286.

[81] *British Paper and Board Industry Research Association* v. *London Borough of Croydon* (1969) 210 E.G. 461. Similar issues may also be litigated in private actions between, for example, vendor and purchaser or landlord and tenant: see, *e.g. Horwitz* v. *Rowson* [1960] 1 W.L.R. 803.

[82] *Pyx Granite Co. Ltd.* v. *M.H.L.G.* [1958] 1 Q.B. 554 (C.A.) (although *cf.* the powerful dissenting judgement of Hodson L.J. at 574–575); [1960] A.C. 260 (H.L.).

[83] By the Tribunals and Inquiries Act 1958, s. 9(1), as extended by the Town and Country Planning Act 1959, s. 32, implementing the recommendation of the Franks Committee (Cmnd. 218, 1957, para. 107). See now T.C.P.A. 1971, s. 247.

[84] R.S.C. Ord. 94, R.12.

decisions,[85] it is possible that they may decline to issue a declaration in such a case.

C. Fees for planning applications

The introduction in 1981[86] of a system of charging for planning applications is likely to lead to some significant changes over the long term in the relationship between applicants and local planning authorities. The fees are primarily a revenue raising device, and as such the structure of the system is progressive, in the economic sense, to the extent that the level of fee is set generally in accordance with the scale of the development. It bears only an indirect relationship to the likely costs to the authority of handling the application. The fees have been set at a level likely to recoup between one-half and two-thirds of the costs to authorities of administering development control, though additional staff costs in respect of assessment and collection need to be set off against the total.

The introduction of fees destroys the tradition of development control as an entirely State funded public service, and it can be expected to inhibit the making of applications, potentially increasing the extent of minor, and even substantial, infringement of planning control. Although for large scale development the fees form a minute proportion of development costs, developers nonetheless can be expected to be less willing to submit alternative schemes; and there will be renewed pressure from developers to iron out difficulties in pre-application negotiations with planning officers. The fees are probably not allowable expenditure against corporation tax.[87]

1. Applicability and exemptions

Fees are payable for all planning applications, (including applications both for outline permission and for the approval of reserved matters) except for (a) applications for determinations under section 53; (b) applications for consent, approval or agreement other than "reserved matters"; and (c) applications under section 32 for permission to retain buildings or works or continue a use beyond the life of a temporary planning permission.[88] The regulations exempt, however, applications for providing special facilities or access for a dwellinghouse in which there lives a disabled person[89]; and applications made necessary only because of the withdrawal of deemed permission under the General Development Order by way of an article 4 Direction or a planning permission.[90]

---

[85] Cf. Square Meals Frozen Foods Ltd. v. Dunstable Corporation [1974] 1 W.L.R. 59 at 65 per Lord Denning M.R. and 67, per Scarman L.J.

[86] Under the Town and Country Planning (Fees for Applications and Deemed Applications) Regulations 1981, (No. 369), as amended by S.I. 1982 No. 716; made under L.G.P.L.A. 1980, s. 87. The Regulations were effective from April 1, 1981, and the rates were increased by 10 per cent., and other amendments made by the 1982 Regulations with effect from June 1, 1982. There is an explanatory memorandum on the Regulations in D.O.E. Circular 9/81, Annex B.

[87] In that they are, like other expenditure incurred in the obtaining of planning permission, a lump sum payment of a capital and not a revenue nature: see further E.C.C. Quarries Ltd. v. Watkis [1977] 1 W.L.R. 1386.

[88] Fees Regulations, reg. 6.

[89] Ibid. reg. 4.

[90] Ibid. reg. 5. As to article 4 Directions, see ante, p. 179.

2. Scale of fees

The scale of fees prescribed by the Regulations is printed in Appendix D. The amounts there specified are, however, reduced in certain cases.

(a) Fees for approval of reserved matters

There is a distinction drawn between reserved matters applications involving design and external appearance of the buildings (for which a fee is payable as on an application for full permission); and applications for other reserved matters, where there is a flat rate fee of £44.

(b) Duplicate applications

The practice of many developers of submitting duplicate applications (in order to facilitate appeal on one against failure to determine within the prescribed period whilst still negotiating in the other), is recognised by the Regulations, which prescribe a 25 per cent. fee for the second application provided it is lodged within 28 days of the first.[91] There is no discount for further alternative applications.

(c) Successive applications

The Regulations make favourable provision for revised applications by allowing a second application to be made without fee, within 12 months of the making of the first application if that has been withdrawn, or of the refusal of permission by the authority or the Secretary of State.[92] The exemption does not extend to cases where permission has been granted on the first application and the developer now seeks approval to an amended scheme, though he may of course withdraw the original application at any time before the notification to him of the grant of permission if he proposes to make amendments to it.

(d) Sports and recreational organisations

A special exemption limits to £44 the fee payable in respect of applications relating to playing fields for use by non-profit making sports and recreational clubs, societies and other organisations.[93]

3. Disputes procedures

There are no procedures prescribed for the resolution of disputes between planning authority and applicant as to the liability to, and the extent of, the fees. The applicant's remedies are either to seek a declaratory ruling from the High Court; or to appeal to the Secretary of State against the failure by the authority to issue a decision within the prescribed period. The Secretary of

---

[91] *Ibid.* Sched. 1, para. 2. The application must be lodged by or for the same applicant, and relate to the same site and the same development (or reserved matters).
[92] *Ibid.* reg. 7. The application must relate to the same site, be made on behalf of the same applicant, and relate to development of the "same character or description."
[93] *Ibid.* Sched. 1, para. 3.

State's jurisdiction in such a case will depend upon whether the prescribed fee has in fact been paid, and so a ruling from him will be necessary as a preliminary issue.

4. Effect of payment and non-payment

The validity of a planning application is not dependent upon the payment of the fee, but the time within which the authority must issue a decision now commences at the time when a valid application, accompanied by the prescribed fee, is received by them.[94] This means that they may decline to proceed with an application; but if they do proceed, the validity of any decision reached is untainted by the lack of a fee, which would still presumably be recoverable by them by civil action.

5. Fees for deemed applications

Fees are payable on the deemed application for planning permission which forms part of an enforcement appeal, and similarly on established use certificate appeals and called-in cases. The fees are assessed in the same way, but are payable to the Secretary of State and must be refunded by him (though without interest) if the appellant succeeds on grounds other than those relating to planning merits, or if the Secretary of State declines jurisdiction or dismisses or allows the appeal for failure by the appellant or local planning authority to comply with the prescribed procedural requirements.

D. Ownership Certificates

There was a belief underlying the 1947 Act that effective planning required the subordination of private land ownership to the greater public good, and in line with that philosophy there was originally no requirement upon applicants for planning permission to notify the owners of the land affected. With the restoration of development values in land in the early 1950s, however, the opportunity and incentive for sharp practice in the land market at the expense of vendors unaware of the development potential of their land grew rapidly. And so, acting upon a recommendation of the Franks Committee,[95] Parliament in 1959 introduced a requirement that owners should be notified of all planning applications affecting their land.

The burden of notification rests with the applicant, and the authority have no jurisdiction to entertain a planning application unless it is accompanied by an ownership certificate in one of four alternative prescribed[96] forms, certifying that no person other than the applicant owned[97] any of the land to

---

[94] G.D.O., art. 7(6A)(added by S.I. 1980 No. 1949). Time ceases to run, by virtue of art. 7(6C) if the cheque by which the fee was paid is later dishonoured.

[95] *Report of the Committee on Administrative Tribunals and Enquiries,* Cmnd. 218 (H.M.S.O., 1957), para. 384.

[96] G.D.O. 1977, art. 9 and Sched. 4.

[97] By virtue of T.C.P.A. 1971, s. 27(7) (as amended by the L.G.P.L.A. 1980, Sched. 15, para. 3), "owner" now means "a person who is for the time being the estate owner in respect of the fee simple in the land or is entitled to a tenancy of the land granted or extended for a term of years certain of which not less than seven years remain unexpired." There is a separate obligation to notify agricultural tenants: see note 99 below.

which the application relates at the time 21 days prior to the application, or that he has notified the actual owners or been unable to ascertain who some, or all of them are.[98] There is a separate obligation to certify either that none of the land is in an agricultural holding, or that if it is the tenant has been notified.[99]

The submission of a certificate is a condition precedent to the authority's proceeding with the application,[1] but they are not obliged to establish for themselves the accuracy of its contents.[2] This does not mean that the way is open therefore for prospective purchasers to present false certificates, or to purport to act on behalf of the present owners without first obtaining their consent. Deliberate or reckless misstatement in a certificate is an offence[3]; and unauthorised agency may breach the fiduciary relationship between vendor and purchaser and render the purchaser liable to account for excess profits realised through the non-disclosure of the planning application.[4]

E. Nationally controlled Development

Planning control is employed in three classes of case as a device to enforce central government policy. In the case of certain applications relating to industrial development, the provision of private health care facilities and the construction of oil refineries, there is the additional requirement that a certificate should be obtained from the relevant Minister before the application may be entertained by the planning authority, although the provisions relating to industrial development are presently suspended. Without it, the application is "of no effect." A similar requirement was introduced in respect of office development in London and the south-east area in 1965,[5] and though intended always to operate as a temporary measure its effect was successively extended[6] until its termination in 1979.[7] Termination was not unexpected, because there had been a growing belief that external pressures upon London office employment had developed to the point where voluntary decentralisation would continue, and that new development could therefore again be satisfactorily controlled by individual planning authorities, albeit subject to central supervision through the

---

[98] In such a case the certificate must also state that notice of the application has also been advertised in a local newspaper: T.C.P.A. 1971, s. 27(2).
[99] T.C.P.A. 1971, s. 27(3). The particular justification in this case is that the grant of planning permission may destroy the tenant's statutory security of tenure: Agricultural Holdings (Notice to Quit) Act 1977, s. 2(3).
[1] T.C.P.A. 1971, s. 27(1).
[2] R. v. Bradford-on-Avon U.D.C., ex parte Boulton [1964] 1 W.L.R. 1136.
[3] T.C.P.A. 1971, s. 27(5); and cf. the appeal decision at [1977] J.P.L. 680 where an applicant was held to be unable to avoid compliance with a condition which had been imposed in reliance upon his false statement as to ownership.
[4] English v. Dedham Vale Properties Ltd. [1978] 1 W.L.R. 93.
[5] Under Mr. George Brown's Control of Office and Industrial Development Act 1965, implementing the Labour Government's ban on office development announced in Offices—A Statement by Her Majesty's Government (H.M.S.O., 1963).
[6] Most recently by the Control of Office Development Act 1977, s. 1.
[7] Control of Office Development (Cessation) Order 1979 (S.I. No. 908), effective as from August 6, 1979.

calling-in power.[8] The control over office development was primarily a planning policy, administered by the Secretary of State for the Environment.

Industrial development controls were first relaxed, and later suspended, since the Conservative government came to office in 1979, and the health facilities provisions have been substantially revised by the Health Services Act 1980.

1. Industrial development certificates

(a) Introduction

Controls over industrial development are exercised in the name of regional economic policy, and the planning system is simply a ready-made structure onto which the certification procedure has been grafted. Although regional policy is an important feature of strategic physical planning, its implementation through industrial development certificates operates quite independently from development control. The purpose is to steer industry to the economically depressed areas, by refusing to permit new development in the more prosperous regions. This negative control is backed up by a variety of positive financial incentives including grants, subsidies and taxation reliefs designed to attract industry to the designated development areas, supplemented by the special benefits now available in the new enterprise zones. It is at best a crudely structured re-location programme, and there is of course no guarantee that a firm whose establishment or expansion is prevented in the area of their choice will in fact move to a designated area.

A study conducted by the Department of Industry in 1975 analysed the subsequent action taken by firms who had been refused an industrial development certificate over the period 1958–71, and found that only 18 per cent. had actually moved to a location favoured by the Government, while 50 per cent. had developed in the area originally chosen or some other non-preferred area. The details of the Study are set out in Table 7.

The policy evolved in an era when there were labour shortages in the south-east and a strong wish to defuse pressure for further expansion in that region; but changing employment patterns and rising unemployment over the past 10 years have shaken that thinking, and the cost effectiveness of the whole of the regional industrial strategy has come to be seriously questioned.[9] One consequence is that the scheme has been administered in recent years with "decreasing severity"[10] to the point where the House of Commons Public Accounts Committee has concluded that it does "not play

---

[8] See further *Office Location Review* (H.M.S.O., 1976), and for a critical review of the policy, Wehrmann, "A Policy in Search of an Objective" (1978) 56 *Public Administration* 425.

[9] Notably in the Second Report from the House of Commons Expenditure Committee on Regional Development Incentives (1973–74; H.C. 85)(H.M.S.O., 1974).

[10] Evidence of the Permanent Secretary to the Department of Industry to the House of Commons Committee of Public Accounts, March 4, 1981 (Appendix to the Committee's Fifth Report, 1980–81). A further relaxation announced on August 7, 1980 (H.C. Deb., Vol. 990, col. 293) meant that certificates would be freely available to both local authorities and private developers to allow industrial estates to be developed with individual factory units of up to 50,000 square feet, subject to conditions restricting occupancy to firms not moving from assisted areas, and to a total of 50,000 square feet for each firm.

Table 7
Impact of Industrial Development Certificates

Action taken by firm	No. of cases	% of total cases analysed
1. Moved to location favoured by Government		
(a) assisted area	122	9
(b) overspill/new town	71	5
(c) other	58	4
	(251)	(18)
2. Developed in area originally chosen or in some other non-preferred area		
(a) in existing premises	340	25
(b) by building	343	25
	(683)	(50)
3. Rationalisation/reorganisation	84	6
4. Abandoned	176	13
5. Firm closed before taking action	29	2
6. Developed abroad	7	1
7. Miscellaneous	25	2
8. Insufficient information	114	8
Totals	1,369	100

Source: adapted from Appendix to the Fifth Report from the Committee of Public Accounts 1980–81 (H.C. 206) (H.M.S.O. 1981).

any significant part in regional policies at the present time."[11]

(b) Exemptions

Since 1979, industrial development certificates have not been required at all in any of the development areas, special development areas or intermediate areas and the exemption limit was raised in that year for the remaining areas from 15,000 square feet (12,500 in the south-east) to 50,000 square feet.[12] But with effect from January 9, 1982, the requirements have been suspended by the Town and Country Planning (Industrial Development Certificates)(Prescribed Classes of Building) Regulations 1981,[13] which remove all classes of building from the requirements of the Act.

(c) Certificates, restrictions and conditions

The scheme is administered by the Department of Industry, and the general statutory duty of the Secretary of State is to satisfy himself that the

[11] Fifth Report, 1980–81; para. 13.
[12] T.C.P. (Industrial Development Certificates) Regulations 1979 (S.I. 1979 No. 838); T.C.P. (Industrial Development Certificates: Exemptions) Order 1979 (S.I. 1979 No. 839).
[13] S.I.1981 No. 1826.

development can be carried out consistently with the "proper" distribution of industry.[14] In practice the principal factors taken into account have been the extent to which the development could be considered to be mobile as to its location (and particularly whether it can be carried out in a development area), and the extent to which it is compatible with the needs and resources, especially in employment terms, of the locality proposed.

The control is exercised without any provision for hearings or appeals, and is based instead upon discussion and negotiation. Actual refusals of certificates have been rare (lower than one per cent. for the past four years,[15]) though the figures do not indicate the numbers of applications not pursued following informal contact with the Department.

Control continued to be exerted following the issuance of a certificate through restrictions and conditions. *Restrictions* were used generally to limit the time in which a planning application based on the certificate may be made, and the firm by which it may be made.[16] *Conditions* were imposed as the Secretary of State considered appropriate having regard to the proper distribution of industry,[17] and these were incorporated into the planning permission, if not by the planning authority then automatically by statutory implication.[18] With the suspension of control, any restrictions imposed are presently ineffective; but any conditions already imposed on planning permissions remain in effect. Enforcement is through the planning enforcement machinery, except that there is no power to challenge the validity of the conditions on the ground that they fall outside the planning authority's power,[19] nor to appeal against them.[20] Nor is compensation payable for the refusal of a certificate, or for the imposition of any restriction or condition.

2. Health Services

The system of controls introduced by the Health Services Act 1976 was intended to restrain private sector hospital development where it would to a significant extent either interfere with the statutory duties of the Secretary of State for Health and Social Services, or disadvantage national health patients.[21] Those criteria remain, but the Health Services Act 1980 has relaxed the extent of the controls.

The legislation provides that an application for planning permission in respect of "controlled works" shall be of no effect unless accompanied by a certificate issued by the Secretary of State,[22] and there are supplementary penal provisions to restrain unlawful development.[23] The controls are directed only to premises which have, or will have, facilities for one or more

---

[14] T.C.P.A., s. 67(1).
[15] For details, see the Annual Report (for 1979–80) by the Secretary of State for Industry under the Industry Act 1972 (H.C. 772)(H.M.S.O., 1980), Appendix 8.
[16] T.C.P.A. 1971, s. 70(1).
[17] *Ibid.* s. 70(2).
[18] *Ibid.* s. 70(5) and (6).
[19] *Ibid.* s. 70(4).
[20] *Ibid.* s. 71(2).
[21] Health Services Act 1976, s. 13(2).
[22] *Ibid.* s. 15(2).
[23] *Ibid.* s. 18(1) and (2).

of five specialised services, (a) the carrying out of surgical procedures under general anaesthesia, (b) obstetrics, (c) radiotherapy, (d) haemodialysis or peritoneal dialysis or (e) pathology or diagnostic radiology.[24] Further in such cases, premises are "controlled" only if they either have 120 or more beds or are situated in a designated area.[25] "Controlled works," for which a certificate is required, are works (subject to limited exceptions) for the construction of controlled premises; or for the construction of a "controlled extension" to controlled premises or for converting any premises into controlled premises.

It is a control exercisable purely in terms of health care management[26] and not a planning-related control; and the Secretary of State for the Environment has also exhorted planning authorities for their part not to be influenced by the fact that a proposal may be for the provision of private health care facilities, or may in their view prejudice the National Health Service.[27]

3. Oil Refineries

Similar procedures were introduced in respect of oil refinery development in 1975, designed to underwrite national petroleum policy by requiring the authorisation of the Secretary of State for Energy before the making of any application for planning permission for constructing or extending a refinery, or converting existing plant into a refinery.[28] The authorisation procedure enables him to maintain a national policy on refinery capacity and its general location, and allows a decision to be made at the overall policy level before detailed land-use planning[29] questions arise. The issuance of a certificate by no means pre-empts the planning process, although the need for refinery facilities in accordance with national energy policy will always be a highly influential policy issue.

F. Publicity for Planning Applications

1. The purpose of publicity

Development control is undertaken by elected and politically accountable authorities, whose usual sensitivity to public opinion is enhanced in planning matters by the special provision made for public participation. How communities should grow and how urban change should be controlled, are issues on which public opinion is liable today to be forcefully expressed and carefully taken into account in decision making.

---

[24] *Ibid.* s. 12(2); as amended by the 1980 Act, s. 12(1).

[25] *Ibid.*

[26] The criteria for decision making are prescribed by the Health Services Act 1976, s. 13(2) and (3), amended by the 1980 Act, s. 15 and Sched. 3, para. 2. There is provision under s. 17 of the 1976 Act, for appeal on a point of law to the High Court by the applicant; and also, if a certificate is granted, by any other person appearing and being heard at any hearing held by the Secretary of State.

[27] D.O.E. Circular 2/81, Appendix E, para. 11.

[28] Petroleum and Submarine Pipe-lines Act 1975, s. 36. For general guidance on the Act, see D.O.E. Circular 20/76, *Memorandum.*

[29] For an analysis of the relationship between national energy policy and local planning policy within the planning appeals system, see *Kent C.C. v. S.O.S.E.* (1976) 33 P. & C.R. 70.

Publicity for planning applications is the starting point for participation in development control, and it is a reflection on the ambivalence of the British planning system generally to participation that formal publicity requirements are minimal and not always effective. There are two arguments advanced against extending them further. First, there is the fear of over-burdening the planning machine by placing too many formalities in the path of decision making. Secondly, there is continuing doubt about the value and quality of public input in development control; and particularly the extent of influence of self-interested pressure groups, and of immediate neighbours concerned only with neighbourhood amenity and the possible impact on their property values of new development nearby. There is an underlying belief still in the distinction between public and private interest, of which only the former should concern public land-use decisions. The argument spills over to the issue of how far planning authorities should be answerable in the courts, for irregularities in procedure, to members of the public, interest groups and adjoining landowners. The traditional view is reflected in this observation by Salmon J. in *Buxton* v. *Minister of Housing and Local Government*[30]:

> "The scheme of the town and country planning legislation, in my judgement, is to restrict development for the benefit of the public at large and not to confer new rights on any individual members of the public, whether they live close to or far from the proposed development."

The distinction, unfortunately, is not as sharp as the comment suggests; and as confidence in the ideal of some overriding concept of public interest has come to ebb in recent years, so too have the judges come more to accept the political reality of planning control.

2. The statutory requirements

Publicity is only legally required at all for planning applications in three cases[31]; (1) for applications involving a departure from the development plan; (2) those involving "unneighbourly" development, and (3) applications for development in conservation areas or affecting listed buildings. But authorities have been asked to arrange additional publicity, at their discretion, for a variety of further cases.

In the three cases where publicity is legally required, the application must be advertised in a newspaper circulating in the locality,[32] and in the latter two cases there is an additional requirement to provide a site notice so as to

---

[30] [1961] 1 Q.B. 278 at 283.

[31] See generally T.C.P.A. 1971, s. 26(7) (unneighbourly development); s. 28(3) (conservation areas and listed buildings); and Town and Country Planning (Development Plans)(England) Direction 1981, para. 2 (departures from the development plan). There are separate Directions for Wales (1981) and London (1978).

[32] Provided the newspaper chosen does circulate in the general locality and adequate public notice has in consequence been given, this will suffice. The courts will not insist on exhaustive coverage: see, *e.g. Wilson* v. *S.O.S.E.* [1973] 1 W.R.L. 1083; *McMeechan* v. *S.O.S.E.* (1974) 232 E.G. 201.

draw the proposals to the attention of neighbours and passers-by.[33] There is a form prescribed for each,[34] but the nature of the form itself is perhaps the single most inhibitive factor in the effort to achieve effective notification. It is drafted in a formal way calculated to enthral experienced conveyancers, rather than to communicate readily to ordinary members of the public; and typically it gives only the most general description of the character of development proposed. Full details are available only at the offices of the planning authority.

The obligation to undertake the publicity requirements rests with the applicant in the case of unneighbourly development, and must be undertaken before submission of the application[35]; but otherwise the task falls to the planning authority themselves, following receipt of the application. A period of 21 days must be allowed from the date of publication for the receipt of representations, which must then in all cases be taken into account in determining the application.

Failure to carry out the requirements of advertisement need not necessarily invalidate any subsequent grant of planning permission. In the case of unneighbourly development it is the existence of the applicant's certificate accompanying the application, rather than its accuracy, which sets the authority's jurisdiction.[36] Again, in the case of development plan departures, it is arguable that the requirements are purely procedural and do not restrict the authority's jurisdiction to grant permission departing from the plan.[37] But for listed building and conservation area cases the requirements are on their face mandatory, and they are used in the legislation to set the basis of jurisdiction of the authority. Their power to determine the application arises only after 21 days have elapsed from publication, and thus cannot arise unless there has been publication.[38]

(a) Departures from the development plan

It is clear that development plans are not intended to operate as unalterable blueprints for the future, and that authorities need not adhere to them closely. But it would undermine public participation in development planning and weaken the Secretary of State's supervisory role, if there were to be no prior notification of an authority's intention to override an approved plan. Departure applications are therefore governed by a Direction issued by the Secretary of State, requiring newspaper advertisement of any

---

[33] A site notice must be left in position for not less than seven days. In the case of unneighbourly development the obligation is on the developer, and it is a requirement that the notice be "sited and displayed in such a way as to be easily visible and legible by [sic] members of the public without going on the land:" T.C.P.A. 1971, s. 26(4). The obligation may be avoided if the applicant has no rights of access to the land, but only if he had unsuccessfully taken reasonable steps to acquire the rights. In the case of conservation area and listed building development the obligation is on the authority, and the requirement is simply to display the notice "on or near the land:" T.C.P.A. 1971, s. 28(2).

[34] G.D.O. Sched. 3. For applications affecting conservation areas and listed buildings the contents of the notice are prescribed by T.C.P.A. 1971, s. 28(2).

[35] T.C.P.A. 1971, s. 26.

[36] Cf. R. v. Bradford-on-Avon U.D.C., ex parte Boulton [1964] 1 W.L.R. 1136 (ownership certificate).

[37] Post, p. 235.

[38] T.C.P.A. 1971, s. 28(3); and cf. Steeples v. Derbyshire C.C. [1981] J.P.L. 582.

application which the authority do not propose to refuse and which consists of or includes any development which in the opinion of the authority responsible for determining the application, would "conflict with or prejudice the implementation of any development plan in force in the area in which the land to which the application relates is situated."[39] Any representations made within 21 days of advertisement are to be taken into account by the authority in determining the application. In some cases, it is necessary also to notify the Secretary of State with a view to his calling in the application for decision[40]; and it is in any event open to members of the public on any application to make representations to the Secretary of State seeking a call-in.

There is no obligation to advertise an application which the authority propose to refuse, nor one for which they propose to grant permission subject to such conditions as will, in their opinion, secure that (if they are observed) there will be no conflict with the plan.[41] And, curiously, there is no obligation to advertise an application as a departure application if it has already been advertised "in pursuance of other planning requirements."[42] Thus an application advertised by the applicant as involving unneighbourly development, for example, need not be re-advertised by the planning authority under the Direction, though it clearly would be good practice to do so because the purpose underlying the publicity is different.

No site notice is required in plan departure cases, but the Secretary of State has urged their use on a discretionary basis.[43]

(b) "Unneighbourly" development

Site notice and newspaper advertisements are prerequisites to the making of applications for certain prescribed categories of development which are liable to give rise to injury to neighbourhood amenity. The prescribed classes include[44] buildings over 20 metres high, and groupings of developments liable to offend because of noxious emissions (such as sewage works, slaughter-houses, knackers' yards, tipping, scrap yards, minerals extraction and poultry works); those where there may be problems of traffic and noise (including casinos, funfairs, bingo halls, theatres, cinemas, music halls, dance halls, skating rinks, swimming pools, gymnasia and motor racing) and other assorted cases (including Turkish baths and cemeteries).

(c) Development affecting listed buildings and conservation areas

The planning authority are required to publicise applications by advertisement and site notice, where in their opinion the development would affect

---

[39] T.C.P. (Development Plans)(England) Direction 1981 (published as Appendix D to D.O.E. Circular 2/81), para. 2; T.C.P. (Development Plans)(Wales) Direction 1981, para. 2 and T.C.P. (Development Plans)(London) Direction 1978, para. 2.
[40] See further *post*, pp. 233–236.
[41] para. 7 of the England and Wales Directions; para. 8 of the London Direction.
[42] para. 3.
[43] D.O.E. Circular 71/73, paras. 7 and 18.
[44] The full list appears in G.D.O., art. 8 (*post*, Appendix B). The Secretary of State has urged that publicity also be given on a discretionary basis to other development which may have a substantial effect on a neighbourhood, such as those likely to cause activity and noise in a quiet area, or at unusual hours: D.O.E. Circular 71/73, para. 7.

either the character or appearance of a conservation area, or the setting of a listed building.[45] Applications for listed building consent need to be publicised in the same way.[46]

G. "County matter" Applications

1. *Introduction*

With the reform of local government outside London in 1974, the planning function was split between the new county authorities and the new district authorities. Although all applications were made to the district authority in the first instance, they were obliged to forward to the county for determination those applications which in their opinion related to "county matters" as defined by the Local Government Act 1972. There was a back-up power for the county authority to issue to the district a direction as to how any other application might be determined where it appeared to them to "substantially and adversely affect their interests as local planning authority."[47]

The definition of "county matters" included two comparatively discrete areas of jurisdiction, in respect of applications involving mineral matters, and the development of land straddling national park boundaries. In those cases the county had full powers of determination. There was a further area of county jurisdiction which was far less clearly defined, however, and where the duty on the district to forward the application to the county arose only where they did not themselves propose to refuse permission. This was in the case of applications which involved conflict with county planning policy. The categories of application were defined by the Act in highly subjective terms, as including applications involving development which would (a) "conflict with, or prejudice the implementation of, fundamental provisions of" a structure plan or old style development plan (or "fundamental proposals" for a structure plan or its alteration or submitted amendments to an old style plan); or (b) "would be inconsistent in any respect" with (i) the provisions of a local plan prepared by the county planning authority (or publicised proposals for such a plan, or alterations); or (ii) any non-statutory policy statement adopted by the county and notified to the district; or (iii) any county development proposal notified to the district.[48]

The subjectivity of the definition, the fact that it was for the district to interpret it, the right preserved for the county to receive copies of all applications (unless they otherwise directed) and their power to intervene by way of direction all meant that county/district conflict over development control powers was inevitable, particularly in areas where there already existed political differences between the two tiers. Conflict was diminished in many areas by the joint production of non-statutory development control

---

[45] T.C.P.A., s. 28(1).
[46] Town and Country Planning (Listed Buildings and Buildings in Conservation Areas) Regulations 1977, reg. 4.
[47] L.G.A. 1972, Sched. 16, para. 19.
[48] *Ibid.* Sched. 16, para. 32.

schemes which allowed more precise definitions to be agreed and which established machinery, such as joint county/district committees, for dispute resolution.[49]

But unproductive conflict remained. By October1975 nearly 20 per cent. of English counties had still to agree development control schemes, and a further 89 per cent. were still insisting that copies of all applications should be forwarded to them.[50] The proportion of applications classified as "county matters" varied enormously. In 1975–76, some 14 per cent. of districts had no county matter applications at all; whilst at the other extreme some districts found that over 20 per cent. of their applications related to county matters.[51]

The main consequence of the conflict was delay and uncertainty, and legislative action was proposed by the Labour Government in early 1979, as part of their package of proposals for "organic change" in local government, to confer full development control powers on the larger city district councils.[52] The Local Government, Planning and Land Act 1980 has introduced a different arrangement, however, under which the county/district arrangement is reorganised in all areas and the scope of county involvement substantially diminished.

The scheme of the 1980 Act is to confine "county matters" to applications involving minerals development, waste disposal and development within, or straddling the boundaries of, a national park. But on a variety of other applications involving policy conflict, the districts are still obliged to consult with the county before determining the application. The former county power to issue directions to the district has gone, but there is a new provision designed to strengthen the role of the structure plan in development control.

2. County matters after the 1980 Act: outside London

The three main areas of jurisdiction remaining as county matters are:

(a) Minerals applications

The new Act gives an extended definition of minerals applications which extends not only to the mining and working of minerals itself, but to a range of ancillary and related development including processing and related manufacturing processes, disposal of mineral waste and the transportation of aggregates.[53] The Town and Country Planning (Minerals) Act 1981 further designates counties as "mineral planning authorities" and extends the range of their minerals planning functions.[54]

---

[49] Advocated by central government in D.O.E. Circular 74/73, Annex 2.
[50] D. Beardmore, "An uneasy partnership in development control" *The Planner* (1976), Vol. 62, p. 73.
[51] Figures drawn from Professor Davies' survey for the House of Commons Expenditure Committee, published in Vol.III of their *Eighth Report, 1976–77*.
[52] *Organic Change in Local Government*, Cmnd. 7457 (H.M.S.O., 1979).
[53] L.G.A. 1972, Sched. 16, para. 32(*a*)—(*d*).
[54] *Post*, p. 487.

(b) National park development

Development within national parks is a matter for county authorities by reason of their being the sole local planning authority for the area (except for functions relating to tree preservation and replacement, and waste land where the districts have concurrent powers).[55] Development on sites straddling the boundary, on the other hand, is a "county matter."[56] In either case, any application is made first to the district council for forwarding to the county for determination.

(c) Waste disposal

Waste disposal applications have been added to the "county matters" list by regulations made under the 1972 Act, but they do not extend to Wales.[57] The matters covered are

"(a) the use of land for the carrying out of operations in or on land for the deposit of refuse or waste materials;

(b) the erection of any building, plant or machinery designed to be used wholly or mainly for purposes of treating, storing, processing or disposing of refuse or waste materials."

Responsibility for these applications ties in with counties' functions as waste disposal authorities under Part I of the Control of Pollution Act 1974.[58]

3. Handling county matter applications

Application is made to the district authority, who are obliged to send it to the county "as soon as may be and in any case not later than seven days after they have received it."[59] The decision as to whether an application does relate to a county matter rests with the district, and further criteria and machinery for resolving disputes have been agreed in some county areas since the new Act. It is open to the authorities to agree to vary the allocation prescribed by the Act, and to give legal effect to the re-allocation as an arrangement for the discharge of their functions by another authority under section 101 of the 1972 Act. The validity of a permission or determination may not be questioned on the grounds that it has been given by the wrong planning authority,[60] and the purpose of that provision "is obviously to protect the public from being affected by demarcation disputes between district and county."[61] But the courts have held that the protection does not extend to a case where the decision is otherwise invalid, and in particular

---

[55] L.G.A. 1972, s. 182(4)—(6); Sched. 16, para. 16.

[56] *Ibid.* Sched. 16, para. 32(*e*).

[57] Town and Country Planning (Prescription of County Matters) Regulations 1980 (S.I. 1980 No. 2010).

[58] *Post*, p. 437. In Wales, the district authorities are disposal authorities under the 1974 Act.

[59] A formula which provoked vigorous debate in the Commons, the Government taking the view against a sceptical Opposition that "as soon as may be" implied a period substantially shorter than seven days: H.C. Deb., Vol. 992, col. 350 (November 11, 1980).

[60] L.G.A. 1972, Sched. 16, para. 51.

[61] *Co-operative Retail Services Ltd.* v. *Taff Ely B.C.* (1979) 39 P. & C.R. 223 at 253, *per* Browne L.J.

where the district, having formed the opinion that an application does relate to a county matter, nonetheless purport to determine it without reference to the county.[62]

Before determining a county matter application, the county are required to consult with the district authority.[63] It is not only applications for planning permission which must be forwarded to the county as relating to county matters, but also applications under section 53 for determination of whether planning permission is required and applications for established use certificates.[64] Applications for approval of reserved matters, or of other matters prescribed by a planning condition, do not appear on the list. Reserved matter applications need still to be made to the district authority[65] but power to determine them will have been normally reserved by the county to themselves in the original condition, though they may make arrangements under section 101 of the 1972 Act for the district to assume responsibility for them. Other applications for consent, approval or agreement required by a condition imposed by the county may be made directly to the county. The duty to consult with the district extends to reserved matters applications,[66] but not to the other applications.

4. The allocation of functions in London

The division of planning responsibilities in London between the Greater London Council and the Boroughs dates back to the London reforms of 1965, and because of this history it follows a different pattern. The allocation is prescribed by Regulations, and the trend in recent years has been towards increasing disengagement by the G.L.C. The Marshall Inquiry on Greater London reported in 1978 that there were still shortcomings in the system giving rise to problems of detail, duplication and delay.[67] The Report recommended that development control should become a matter entirely for the London boroughs, with three exceptions relating to G.L.C. action areas, the G.L.C.'s own development and applications involving substantial departures from the Greater London Development Plan (G.L.D.P.) or the Initial Development Plan (I.D.P.)(where it had not been superseded by a local plan).

But the new Regulations made in 1980 went only part of the way advocated by Marshall. The G.L.C. are now the local planning authority in respect only of the Covent Garden Action Area and for mineral extraction on sites exceeding two hectares,[68] although applications are still made to the Boroughs in the first instance.

[62] Attorney-General ex. rel. Co-operative Retail Services Ltd.v. Taff Ely. B.C. (1981) 42 P. & C.R. 1 (H.L.) upholding the Court of Appeal ruling, 39 P. & C.R. 223.
[63] G.D.O., art. 16(1); L.G.A. 1972, Sched. 16, para. 16(2) (land in national parks).
[64] L.G.A. 1972, Sched. 16, para. 15(1).
[65] G.D.O., art. 7(1).
[66] Ibid. art. 16(1)(d).
[67] Report of the Marshall Inquiry on Greater London G.L.C. 1978.
[68] Town and Country Planning (Local Planning Authorities in Greater London) Regulations 1980 (S.I. 1980 No. 443), reg. 3. The G.L.C. also retain the function in respect of their own development proposals under the Town and Country Planning General Regulations 1976 (S.I. 1976 No. 1419) (see further Attorney-General, ex. rel. Turley v. G.L.C. (1976) 239 E.G. 893), but only for development in respect of which they are the local planning authority under the 1980 Regulations.

Applications must also be referred to the G.L.C., however, if they relate to development in any of a number of prescribed classes, which include large scale development; certain development near any Category A metropolitan road; non-agricultural development in the green belt and the demolition or material alteration of a listed building.[69] In the case of applications referred under these provisions the G.L.C. has power to direct the borough to refuse permission or grant it subject to conditions, but their discretion is confined by reference to certain limited criteria prescribed by the Regulations.[70]

Finally, applications must also be referred to the G.L.C. if the borough consider that permission should be granted, but the application in their opinion relates to matters which would conflict with, or prejudice the implementation of any provision of the G.L.D.P., any "fundamental" provision of the I.D.P. still in force or any provision of a local plan inserted by the Secretary of State by way of modification.[71] The G.L.C. may direct refusal, or direct that permission be granted subject to protective conditions; but they must refer the matter on to the Secretary of State if of the opinion that the application ought to be granted and that conditions will not prevent the plan conflict or prejudice.[72]

H. County/district consultations

1. *Consultations outside London*

Consultation is an important function in the determination of planning applications, because of the ability through the development control system to coordinate the land use policies and requirements of the many public sector agencies whose interests are liable to be affected by development. It has assumed a new importance following the 1980 Act, because consultation has been substituted for the old distribution of power between counties and districts. Districts now have the function of determining all applications other than those relating to county matters, but are required first to consult with the county authority in certain cases. These include some of the matters which were formerly county matters, though the wording of the definitions has changed.

Consultation is required in three main categories of application for planning permission.[73] The first is applications involving conflict with policy; that is, where the proposed development "would materially conflict with or prejudice the implementation" (i) of any policy or general proposal contained in an approved or submitted structure plan (or proposals for a structure plan or alteration); or (ii) of any fundamental provision of an old style development plan still in force; or (iii) any proposal in a county local

---

[69] *Ibid.* reg. 4. The list no longer includes proposals for buildings exceeding a certain height, which under the 1978 Regulations were referable to the G.L.C.
[70] *Ibid.* reg. 5.
[71] *Ibid.* reg. 6.
[72] *Ibid.* regs. 7 and 8.
[73] But not for approval of reserved matters, or approval of any other details or section 53 determinations.

plan or alteration whether or not adopted or approved (provided the matter has received publicity under section 12 of the 1971 Act).[74]

The second category of applications are those relating to development of land "which would, by reason of its scale or nature or the location of the land, be of major importance for the implementation of the approved structure plan."[75]

Third, there is the "safeguarding" category. Here consultation is required where the site is one which the county have notified to the district as having minerals or (in England) waste disposal potential, or as being proposed for development by themselves; and the consultation requirement extends to development of any land which would prejudice such a proposed use.[76]

In all cases the duty to consult now arises whether or not the district propose to grant permission.

A non-statutory *Code of Practice* prepared by the local authority associations and the Department of the Environment urges authorities to interpret the categories broadly so as to confine consultation "to proposals that are significant in regard to local conditions"[77] and to the objectives of the structure plan. The *Code* suggests that a "technical or relatively insignificant conflict with the structure plan would be insufficient to justify consultation,"[78] though it would need to be borne in mind in reaching a decision. The county have power to waive consultation on any application or class of applications,[79] and there is thus the basis for agreeing individual working arrangements between authorities.

2. The machinery of consultation

Where consultation with the county is required, the district may not proceed to determine the application until after 28 days from the date the county have been notified and sent a copy, or such longer period as may be agreed in writing by the district.[80] Earlier determination is possible if the county respond earlier with their representations, or indicating that they do not wish to make any.[81] Because the district's power to determine is limited by reference to the time following consultation, it follows that they lack power to make any valid determination where consultation is required unless they do actually consult. No longer are the categories of development prescribed in the purely subjective manner which formerly might have prevented a court from reviewing a district's decision,[82] and the validity of a planning

---

[74] L.G.A. 1972 Sched. 16, para. 19(2)(*a*) (as inserted by L.G.P.L.A. 1980, s. 86(2)). The category thus includes unapproved statutory plans, but there is no longer the power to safeguard policies in non-statutory plans.

[75] *Ibid.* para. 19(2)(*b*).

[76] *Ibid.* paras. 19(2)(*c*)—(*g*).

[77] *Code of Practice for Consultations* (reproduced as Appendix B to D.O.E. Circular 2/81), para. 6.

[78] *Ibid.* para. 9.

[79] L.G.A. 1972, Sched. 16, para. 19(3) and (4).

[80] G.D.O., art. 15A (added by S.I. 1980 No. 1949).

[81] L.G.A. 1972, Sched. 16, para. 19(6).

[82] See, *e.g. Co-operative Retail Services Ltd.* v. *Taff Ely B.C.* (1979) 39 P & C.R. 223 at 244, *per* Ormrod L.J., and 249, *per* Browne L.J.

permission or refusal issued by a district is now closely dependent upon whether consultation has been undertaken as required.

Representations received from the county must be taken into account in determining the application,[83] but they have no direct legal force. They are a material consideration, and they may be given effect in the determination,[84] or may be overridden in favour of other considerations. There is a prospect that districts may well use their new powers to assert their independence of county planning policy, and particularly of structure plans, and treat the consultation process as little more than a necessary ritual. The role of the structure plan is therefore especially safeguarded by a new provision requiring authorities to "seek the achievement" of its "general objectives;"[85] and there are further safeguards in the form of the Secretary of State's power to call in applications for his own determination,[86] or to order the revocation of a permission and allow the compensation bill to rest with the athority concerned.[87]

3. The London provisions

The 1980 Act envisages a new regime for consultation in London, to be established through an amendment to the General Development Order.[88] No amendment had been made at the time of going to press, and the arrangements discussed *ante* at p. 226 remain in force.

I. Other consultations

1. Mandatory consultations

There is a further duty, on all authorities before granting permission, to consult on applications affecting the policies or spheres of interest of a variety of public agencies. The list includes local planning authorities for other areas, the Secretary of State for Transport, the Theatres Trust, the National Coal Board, the Minister of Agriculture, Fisheries and Food, the local highway authority, the Nature Conservancy Council and the regional water authority.[89] The range of cases does not extend to every matter which may affect the body concerned, not only because of the administrative complexity which might ensue but also because the extensive consultations undertaken in the preparation of development plans will already have achieved some measure of policy co-ordination. Thus consultation with the Agriculture Minister on loss of agricultural land to urban development, for example, is necessary only in cases not in accordance with the development

---

[83] *Ibid.* para. 19(7).
[84] In which case the county may be required to justify them if the matter goes on appeal, under the Inquiries Procedure Rules: *post*, pp. 579–580.
[85] L.G.P.L.A. 1980, s. 86(3).
[86] *Post*, p. 233.
[87] *Post*, p. 270.
[88] T.C.P.A. 1971, Sched. 3, para. 7B (added by L.G.P.L.A. 1980, s. 86(7)).
[89] G.D.O., art. 15. Detailed provisions governing agriculture consultations are contained in D.O.E. Circular 75/76; and consultation is also required, on applications for permission for caravan site use, with the site licensing authority: T.C.P.A. 1971, s. 29(5).

plan, and then only where an area of more than 10 acres is involved. Similarly, consultation with water authorities is required, not in their service capacity as providers of the physical infrastructure which may be necessary for the development to proceed, but in their capacity as guardians of water quality. Water authorities are in practice widely consulted on infrastructure capacity, however, and working arrangements for consultation supplementary to those prescribed by the Order operate in most districts.

The categories of prescribed consultations are supplemented by a power for the Secretary of State to give directions as to additional consultations to be undertaken by authorities,[90] and two general Directions are presently operative.

On applications involving a change from use as a dwelling, there is a requirement that the housing authority be consulted (which in almost all cases now is the authority determining the application).[91] Secondly, the Town and Country Planning (Aerodromes) Direction 1981 requires consultation with the Secretary of State for Defence or the Civil Aviation Authority, as the case may be, in respect of applications involving development of land adjoining a civil or military aerodrome for which a safeguarding map has been furnished to the authority.[92] Consultation was formerly required also with the Secretary of State for Trade and Industry before granting permission for development of land within public safety zones at aerodromes, but from January 1, 1982, responsibility passed to the Civil Aviation Authority for day to day administration, and separate consultation is no longer required. In the designated public safety zones at the major aerodromes, it is Government policy that there should be no significant increase in the number of people living, working or congregating.

2. Parish councils

Special provisions govern parish council consultation, which tends in practice to provide a fruitful basis for public participation. Parish and community councils are entitled to be informed of every application for permission or approval of reserved matters arising in their area if they so notify the district authority.[93] They may waive the right, or confine their interest to some classes of application. The requirement is simply to "notify" the parish council,[94] but in practice many authorities are prepared also to forward copies of applications and plans to provide a reasonable opportunity for informed comment.

3. The machinery of statutory consultation

The period allowed under the General Development Order for consultations

---

[90] Ibid. art. 15(4).
[91] T.C.P. (Housing Accommodation) Direction 1952. There has as yet been no revision of the Direction to take local government reform into account.
[92] Issued with D.O.E. Circular 39/81 (W.O. 62/81), which cancelled the earlier 1972 Direction as from January 1, 1982.
[93] L.G.A. 1972, Sched. 16, para. 20.
[94] G.D.O., art. 17.

is only 14 days[95] and the authority are required only to have regard to such representations as are received within the period, though late representations may still qualify as a material consideration in reaching a decision. This fact underlies the *Code of Practice*[96] published in 1980 by the National Development Control Forum, in which the local authority associations and the bodies regularly consulted on planning applications have agreed, on an entirely non-statutory basis, to a maximum consultation period in practice of 28 days.

The *Code* provides that where a local planning authority undertake consultation they will notify the consultee within seven days of receiving the application, and intimate that the application will not be determined within a 28 day period following notification. Extended time may be allowed, but the parties to the *Code* have agreed that it should be sought only in exceptional circumstances.

The *Code* does not extend to parish council consultations, though it is likely to become the standardised model in practice for all consultations; and its success in securing the main objective of streamlining the practical operation of the consultation process is to be closely monitored.

4. *Discretionary consultation*

Authorities regularly undertake broader consultation than the minimum prescribed by the General Development Order. It is common practice to consult with neighbours, and with local amenity groups on relevant applications, for example, and authorities have been especially requested to consult with the Health and Safety Executive's Factory Inspectorate in respect of applications involving the use or storage of hazardous materials.[97] Other bodies also commonly consulted include the Countryside Commission, the National Trust and the Council for the Protection of Rural England.

The gathering of information and opinion through consultation has become an essential part of development control, and the representations obtained are "material considerations" in determining applications. It is arguable, therefore, that in failing to consult with some person or group whose interests may be closely affected by an application, the authority have failed to have regard to a material consideration. The courts have not been prepared to go so far, however, and have preserved a broad discretion for authorities in the matter.[98]

J. Notification and Direction Procedures

In all the consultation arrangements discussed above the planning authority retain full responsibility for the final decision. They may decide in accordance with the representations they receive, in which case the consultee (if a government department or another local authority) may subsequently be called upon to justify their representations at a public inquiry.[99] Or they may override the representations.

[95] *Ibid.* art. 15(5); 17(3) (parish councils).
[96] Reproduced at [1980] J.P.L. 492.
[97] D.O.E. Circular 1/72 (W.O. 3/72).
[98] *R. v. Sheffield C.C., ex parte Mansfield* (1978) 37 P. & C.R. 1.
[99] *Post,* pp. 579–580.

In two particular cases, however, the relationship is not simply that of consultation, but of direction. The local highway authority and the Secretary of State for Transport may each issue directions restricting the grant of permission, and the Secretary of State for the Environment may direct that a planning application be referred to him, or "called in," for determination.

1. *Highways Directions: the local highway authority*

Authorities outside London are required to send copies of all planning applications to the county council as local highway authority. There is power then for the highway authority to issue directions restricting the grant of permission for development involving either the formation, laying out or alteration of any means of access to a classified road or proposed road; or any other development which appears to the highway authority "to be likely to result in a material increase in the volume of traffic entering or leaving such a classified or proposed road, to prejudice the improvement or construction of such a road or to result in a material change in the character of traffic entering, leaving or using such a road."[1] The implication is, therefore, that the power is conferred to regulate development in the interests of road safety and to safeguard future road construction or improvement. The power authorises directions either for refusal of permission or the imposition of conditions. In the interests of road safety the power to impose conditions is used primarily to regulate access, particularly by requiring the construction of visibility splays to ensure adequate sight lines for traffic emerging from the site. The requirements tend to be standardised, and arrangements have been made through development control schemes in many areas for the local planning authority to act as agent for the highway authority in imposing them.

An important distinction with highways consultations is that the power of the planning authority to determine an application is suspended until either a direction is made, or notification is given that none is proposed.[2] Highways authorities have collectively agreed to observe the spirit of the non-statutory code and act within 28 days, but the restriction on planning authorities remains.

Consultation is also required with local highway authorities where the development includes the laying out or construction of any new street,[3] and although there is no power of direction in this case, it allows details relating to construction standards and dedication to be regulated through planning control or by an agreement under the Highways Act 1980.[4]

2. *Highways directions: the Secretary of State*

The Secretary of State's responsibility is for trunk roads and motorways, and

---

[1] G.D.O. art. 12.
[2] *Ibid.* art. 12(2).
[3] G.D.O., art. 13(1).
[4] *Post*, p. 382.

notification[5] to him is required of applications for permission for the formation, laying out or alteration of any means of access to such highways; or for any other development within 67 metres of the middle line of an existing or proposed highway.[6]

The planning authority are denied jurisdiction until a direction is received from the Secretary of State restricting the grant of permission, or notification that no direction is proposed[7]; although the overall time limit for determining the application remains the same. The Secretary of State may, alternatively, call the matter in for his own decision, and has indicated that he will do so in cases of applications involving residential development of thirty or more dwellings where a future trunk road line may be prejudiced.[8]

3. Calling-in of applications for ministerial determination

The power of the Secretary of State to intervene directly in planning authority decision making is broad. He may issue directions to authorities restricting the grant of permission,[9] and he may deprive them of jurisdiction altogether by directing that an application or class of applications should be referred to him for decision.[10] The most common use of the power in practice is in respect of applications involving departure from the development plan.

(a) Development plan departures

There has been a significant, though gradual, change since 1947 in the function of the development plan. The plan was intended originally to constrain authorities closely in their exercise of development control powers; but as plans became increasingly out of date, so development control became of increasing importance as a policy making function in its own right and not simply a mechanical step in the plan implementation process. Authorities have been held to their plans, however, by means of a series of development plan Directions issued by central government. Their provisions have gradually been relaxed, but the new county/district arrangements of the 1980 Act have given the procedure fresh significance. The requirements of the Direction are that departure applications should be advertised, and in the more substantial cases should be notified to the Secretary of State. The purpose is to provide him with the means to supervise plan compliance and to call in applications for his own

---

[5] The power is exercised by the Regional Controller (Roads and Transportation). For detailed procedures, see D.O.E. Circular 12/73, Annex A. The Government announced in early 1982 that they proposed to reform these powers, and to retain a power of direction only in the limited circumstances set out in the *Consultation Paper* issued by the Department of Transport in 1981.

[6] G.D.O., art. 11(2). The significance of 67 metres is "lost in the mists of time," according to a memorandum submitted by the Department to the House of Commons Expenditure Committee, though it appeared first as 220 feet in the Restriction of Ribbon Development Act 1935 and has been preserved through subsequent legislation: *Eighth Report*, (1975–76), Vol.III, p.756.

[7] G.D.O., art. 11(2).

[8] D.O.E. Circular 132/72.

[9] G.D.O., art. 10.

[10] T.C.P.A. 1971, s. 35.

determination as necessary. The observance by district councils of the provisions of the county's structure plan is likely to be closely scrutinised under this procedure for the future.

Applications outside London need be notified to the Secretary of State only where they:

"(a) would materially conflict with or prejudice the implementation of any of the policies or general proposals of the structure plan in force in the area or with a fundamental provision of an old development plan insofar as it is in force in the area; or

(b) would conflict with or prejudice the implementation of any provision of a local plan introduced by way of modification by the Secretary of State when approving the plan."[11]

The Direction does not, therefore, extend to non-compliance with local plans except where, and to the extent that, there has been ministerial involvement; and also where the proposal is made by the planning authority themselves.[12] Nor is there any requirement to notify if the authority propose to refuse pemission or grant it subject to conditions which will prevent the conflict or the prejudice to implementation.[13] Copies of any representations made by the county authority (or, as the case may be, recommendations made by the district), and any objections received as a result of the advertisement, must be forwarded along with the notification,[14] and these will bring to the Secretary of State's attention any inter-authority conflict or public controversy over the application.

Calling-in is not the automatic response to departure applications, however. Past practice has been highly selective, and calling-in will still occur only where issues of more than local importance are involved.[15] It is a pre-emptive power, designed as a means of preventing the local planning authority from granting permission without a wider review of the issues. Often the called-in applications raise issues of national political significance, and the Secretary of State is liable to be pressed to intervene by members of Parliament, interest groups and individuals.

---

[11] T.C.P. (Development Plans)(England) Direction 1981, para. 4; T.C.P. (Development Plans)(Wales) Direction 1981, para. 4. Except for minor drafting variations, the two Directives are identical. For London, under the T.C.P. (Development Plans)(Greater London) Direction 1978 and the T.C.P. (Local Planning Authorities in Greater London) Regulations 1980, reg. 6, the test is whether the application relates to a matter which in the opinion of the authority would conflict with or prejudice the implementation of the G.L.D.P., or a fundamental provision of the I.D.P. or any provision of a local plan inserted by way of modification by the Secretary of State. Departure applications from the Boroughs go to the G.L.C. in the first instance, for forwarding to the Secretary of State if of the opinion that the development can properly be permitted.

[12] For development by planning authorities the test is more broadly cast to include development which "would conflict with or prejudice the implementation of the provisions of any development plan:" para. 8. As to the handling of development proposals of local planning authorities, see further post, p. 237.

[13] Ibid. para. 7.

[14] Op.cit. para. 4.

[15] See further, D.O.E. Circular 2/81, paras. 10–18. Under the pre-1975 rules around 0.2 per cent. of all applications were notified to the Secretary of State, and of these fewer than 10 per cent. were actually called in.

(b) Non-compliance with the Direction

The Direction permits the granting of permission by the authority if no direction has been received from the Secretary of State within 21 days from their notification to him. But it nowhere prescribes the converse: that authorities should be without jurisdiction to determine applications within that time or without observing the procedures at all. Although it lays down a procedure for handling departure applications, it does not impose it as a matter of law, and it leaves intact the broad discretion of authorities to depart from their plans under section 29 of the 1971 Act. The fault lies in the wording of section 31(1)(*b*) of the 1971 Act, and article 14 of the General Development Order. Article 14 purports to authorise authorities to depart from the development plan "in such cases and subject to such conditions as may be prescribed by directions given by the Secretary of State." That is clearly incapable of overriding or restricting the broad discretion to depart from the plan conferred by the Act itself, and the consequence is that the Direction cannot be regarded as restricting the jurisdiction of authorities in determining applications.[16] Only when a further Direction is issued actually calling in the application or restricting the power of the authority to grant it, is their jurisdiction affected. Non-compliance with the Development Plans Direction, therefore, would not of itself render any determination void.

(c) Other calling-in cases

The calling-in power is not confined to departure applications, but is a flexible device which may be used to bring applications before the Secretary of State for a variety of reasons. He may use it, for example, as a means of examining the planning backing for a compulsory purchase order at the same time as hearing objections to the confirmation of the order itself, or for examining competing applications for the same site, or where there is a serious and otherwise unavoidable conflict of interest on the part of the planning authority.[17] It has also been used in respect of types of development which, even though not departing from the development plan, the Secretary of State is anxious to supervise. Out-of-town shopping centre and hypermarket applications have been treated in this way since the early 1970s, and authorities are still requested (though not directed) to notify the Secretary of State of proposals of over 100,000 square feet gross floor area outside existing city, town or district centres, with a view to calling in.[18]

---

[16] *Simpson* v. *Edinburgh Corporation* 1960. S.C.313 at 319. This view was endorsed by the majority in the Court of Appeal in *Co-operative Retail Services Ltd.* v. *Taff-Ely B.C.* (1979) 39 P. & C.R. 223 (*per* Ormrod L.J. at 245–246 and Browne L.J. at 253–254), who took the view that the county authority retained jurisdiction to determine an application, notwithstanding their failure to notify the Secretary of State because of the prior wrongful determination of the application by the district.

[17] D.O.E. Circulars 71/76 (W.O. 98/76); and 96/77 (W.O. 154/77).

[18] See, *e.g.* *Glacier Metal Co. Ltd.* v. *Hillingdon L.B.C.* (1975) 239 E.G. 573 where the authority, having already refused permission on an application, then sought, in partnership with the developer, permission for another site in circumstances which would have required overturning the first decision.

(d) Consequences of calling in

Called-in applications are treated in a similar way to planning appeals. There is provision for a local public inquiry, unless it is waived by the parties with the agreement of the Secretary of State, and the procedure is governed by the Inquiries Procedure Rules. The Rules are modified, however, to cast more broadly the scope of third party participation at the inquiry,[19] and to impose on the Secretary of State a duty to provide a statement before the inquiry of the reasons for calling in the application and of any points which seem to him to be relevant to his consideration of it.[20]

K. Development by Government Departments

The Crown is not bound by planning legislation, and there is therefore no legal obligation upon government departments to obtain planning permission for their development.[21] It would be a straightforward matter to bring development by government departments under the 1971 Act, but there is understandably some reluctance to extend to local government the statutory power to control the activities of central government. Government departments are substantial land developers, however, responsible often for schemes on a scale and of a type well beyond the capacity of the private sector; and it would make nonsense of general planning controls if they could simply be overridden in cases of governmental development. There has therefore been established a non-statutory convention under which government departments have agreed to consult local planning authorities before undertaking development which would, but for the exemption, require permission. The simplest method of informal co-ordination would have been for the departments to participate through the normal procedures and subject to the usual rules, save those relating to enforcement. But that course has not been followed. Instead, there is an elaborate set of shadow procedures, through which the constitutional niceties are carefully preserved.[22] A planning application becomes a Notice of Intention to Develop (which may be submitted in detailed or outline form) and the planning authority, instead of issuing their decision, are required instead to make representations to the department concerned. County authorities are involved on applications relating to county matters, and the usual consultation rules apply.

---

[19] The category includes persons from whom representations have been received following re-notification of owners and re-advertisement of "unneighbourly" development: T.C.P. (Inquiries Procedure) Rules 1974, r.3.

[20] *Ibid.* r.6; and see generally *post,* Chap. 11.

[21] *Ministry of Agriculture, Fisheries and Food* v. *Jenkins* [1963] 2 Q.B. 317. Some modifications are made to that general rule by T.C.P.A. 1971, ss. 266–268 but the provisions expressly prohibit action by local planning authorities against Crown land. By s. 266(7) "Crown land" means land in which there is a Crown interest or Duchy interest, and "Crown interest" means an interest belonging to Her Majesty in right of the Crown, or belonging to a government department, or held in trust for Her Majesty for the purposes of a government department.

[22] The details of the agreed conventions are set out in D.O.E. Circular 7/77, as amended by D.O.E. Circular 2/81, Appendix C, to take account of the new county/district arrangements. The Crown Estates Commissioners and the Duchies of Lancaster and Cornwall have agreed to use the procedures.

There is, of course, no appeal against an authority's objections to the development, but the developing department if they still wish to proceed, "will bring the matter to the attention" of the Department of the Environment. Disputes may then be resolved by the Department by way of written representations or informal meetings; or there may be a non-statutory public local inquiry.

There are three important variants on the standard planning procedures. First, the departments do not consult in respect of development involving national security. Second, if no representations are made by the authority within the eight week period following submission of the Notice of Intention to Develop, they are taken to have no objections to the development proceeding. This rule is thus the converse of that governing ordinary planning applications. Thirdly, there is provision for "special urgency" applications where the eight week period is reduced to 14 working days. The normal publicity arrangements do not apply in these cases, and to be able to work to this time-scale, authorities would normally require to have made suitable delegation arrangements. Departments have agreed to use the procedure in as few cases as possible.

There is no enforcement procedure, and the whole scheme rests upon responsible government, political accountability and the informal settlement of disputes. The immunity of the Crown does not, however, extend to other persons having an interest, such as a lease, over Crown land[23]; and nor does it extend to governmental bodies established on a wholly independent basis.[24]

L. Development by local planning authorities

1. *Introduction*

The control of development proposed by local planning authorities themselves poses grave difficulties for the planning system. There is an attractive argument that authorities are themselves best qualified to assess their own proposals, in the same way as they deal with those coming from the private sector. But there is a clear danger of conflict of interest. It is a legitimate fear, for example, that pressure will be exerted within an authority for a more generous application of planning standards than a private developer could hope for, particularly when expensive environmental requirements need to be assessed against a background of public expenditure constraint. The fact that the dual function of developer and controller are merged in the one authority means that conflict between the two roles is internalised; a position reinforced by the obvious inability of the authority themselves to appeal against a decision taken in their name and to have the issued aired at a public inquiry. Some authorities have experimented with non-statutory hearings in such cases in order to ensure that public opinion is

---

[23] Although enforcement action may not be commenced without prior consent on behalf of the Crown: T.C.P.A. 1971, s. 266(2); and see *Moulton Builders* v. *Westminster City Council* (1975) 30 P. & C.R. 182.

[24] Immunity is, however, claimed in respect of land held by Health Authorities, Industrial Estates Corporations and the Receiver for the Metropolitan Police District: D.O.E. Circular 7/77, para. 2.

fully considered, but it is rare for a proposal to be defeated once the procedures have been set in motion.

It is true that planning authorities are not in practice the unitary corporations which they are deemed in law to be, and that internal policy conflicts between departments are not uncommon. But the ability of planning staff, and even the planning committee, to hold out against unwelcome development proposals of other departments is substantially weaker than in the case of private sector proposals where there is an arm's length relationship with the developer. Local authorities are political agencies, and there is a pragmatism in local politics which is liable to result in the compromise of good planning.

These fears are not purely academic. Nor are they necessarily concerned with only a comparatively small proportion of development activity. In addition to being sizable consumers of land for their statutory functions, many authorities have traded extensively and competitively in development land in the past decade; and many also have engaged in commercial and industrial development projects through partnership arrangements with private developers.

2. Deemed permission under the General Regulations

The need for independent supervision of planning authorities' own development has been recognised since 1947. The rules initially were tightly drawn. Details of all development proposals were required to be submitted to the Minister to enable him to exercise supervision through the call-in power.[25] But this scheme was abandoned within three years as being too cumbersome, and there followed an arrangement under which planning authorities' development was simply deemed automatically to have the benefit of planning permission granted by the Minister.[26] That model survives today, but it has been subjected over the years to a number of procedural limitations intended to bring it more closely into line with the procedures for private sector applications. Permission is still deemed to be granted by the Secretary of State for development upon the authority passing a resolution to carry it out; or, if it is to be carried out by somebody else, a resolution authorising the carrying out. Such a resolution may now only be passed, however, if it has been preceded by a resolution to seek permission for the carrying out of the development. This initial resolution is treated as comparable to a planning application, and it is required to be notified, publicised and consulted over in a similar, though not identical, manner.

The procedure is prescribed by the Town and Country Planning General Regulations 1976[27], which have the effect of modifying the usual development control provisions of the 1971 Act in relation to the land of, and development in their areas by, local planning authorities.[28] The procedures

[25] T.C.P. (Development by Local Planning Authorities) Regulations 1948, reg. 2.
[26] T.C.P. (Development by Local Planning Authorities) Regulations 1951, reg. 2.
[27] T.C.P. General Regulations 1976 (S.I. 1976 No. 1419).
[28] By virtue of T.C.P.A. 1971, s. 270 and Sched. 21, Pt. V. The wording of the section is ambiguous, but it has been held to have the effect of applying only those sections as are mentioned in the Schedule to the land or development of local planning authorities, subject to the amendments of the Regulations, and excluding the remainder: *Steeples* v. *Derbyshire C.C.* [1981] J.P.L. 582.

are available in only two situations, however, and the wording of the Regulations is critical since it is arguable that they prescribe an exclusive code for the authorisation of development by local planning authorities.[29] In no case do the procedures extend to works for the alteration or extension of a listed building, for which application is required to be made to the Secretary of State.[30] The Regulations extend to all local planning authorities, including urban development corporations where they have been constituted local planning authority, although they extend to the Greater London Council only where they are the local planning authority in respect of the development.[31]

(a) Development to be carried out by the authority

Permission may be sought under regulation 4 of the General Regulations where the authority require a permission for development which they propose to carry out themselves. It is a personal permission which enures for the benefit only of the authority, but it may be sought in respect of any land in their area whether or not already vested in them.[32] The procedure is therefore clearly intended for use in connection with development for statutory purposes where the authority will retain future ownership. It is not available, therefore, where the intention is that the fee simple or a long lease should be conveyed to a private developer, although the alternative procedure below may then be available. Further, the requirement that the planning authority should themselves propose to carry out the development limits the value of the procedure in any case involving private/public sector partnership. In *Sunbell Properties Ltd.* v. *Dorset County Council*[33] the plaintiffs sought and obtained an interim injunction preventing reliance by the County on regulation 4 where they proposed to develop a travel interchange complex in partnership with private developers. On the basis of a concession by the County that regulation 4 would not extend to a scheme under which a commercial developer was to take a share in the profits (as opposed to acting purely as a contractor), Browne-Wilkinson J. granted the injunction. There was an arguable case that the scheme was not a development of the whole site by the County alone. It was, however, a decision taken in interlocutory proceedings and it places so restrictive a gloss upon the Regulations that it may not be followed for the future, at least in a case where the authority themselves intend to maintain full control over the carrying out of the development, and to retain a freehold or leasehold interest in the land.

---

[29] *Post*, p. 241.
[30] T.C.P. General Regulations 1976, reg. 7; which requires that the authority lodge an ordinary application with themselves, which is then deemed to have been referred to the Secretary of State under T.C.P.A. 1971, s. 35.
[31] Reg. 3, as amended by S.I. 1981, No. 558.
[32] T.C.P. General Regulations 1976, reg. 4(1) and (7). Under reg. 6 the powers may be exercised by officers where appropriate arrangements have been made under L.G.A. 1972, s. 101 and it is common for the first step at least to be taken by an officer, giving written notice to the authority that he intends to seek permission. If the authority wish to develop land outside their area, an ordinary application to the competent planning authority for that area would be necessary.
[33] (1979) 253 E.G. 1123.

A further limitation which was suggested in the *Sunbell* case was that the words "development which they propose to carry out" in regulation 4 implied that the proposals should be firm, at least to the extent that their financing should have been considered. That again is a limitation which would need not to be taken too far, given the present uncertain base for longer term capital programming by local authorities, but it emphasises the unsuitability of the regulation 4 procedure for purely speculative proposals.

(b) Development not to be carried out by the authority

This alternative procedure, which is available only in respect of land vested in an authority, applies where they seek to obtain permission for development which they do not themselves propose to carry out. The procedure, contained in regulation 5, was designed originally to facilitate the participation by planning authorities in the land market under the Community Land Act 1975. The permission in this case runs with the land, and the authority's ability to bring land onto the market with outline permission already granted for development was to have been the primary means for promoting positive planning.

The procedure is similar to that under regulation 4 and involves the passing of two resolutions, but the second, which authorises the carrying out of the development, may also contain conditions and is treated as if it were a planning permission granted on an application.[34]

3. *Procedures for deemed permission*

Although the procedures have come to resemble the procedures for private sector applications, there are some significant distinctions. First, the passing of the initial resolution constitutes the first formal step in the procedure, and neither notification nor publicity requirements come into force until after that time.[35] They are imposed not by the Act, but by the Regulations, though to similar effect apart from timing. There is a further special requirement that a copy of the resolution should be placed in the register of planning applications, and a period of 21 days must then elapse before the passing of the second resolution.[36]

Second, the fact that permission is deemed to be granted by the Secretary of State has several consequences. It means that there can be no appeal to the Secretary of State, even by a purchaser of the land from the authority wishing to challenge any condition imposed. It also means that there is no power for the local highway authority to issue directions on highways matters,[37] though the Secretary of State's power in respect of trunk roads is preserved in the Regulations.[38] Moreover, the procedures confer autonomy upon both county and district authorities. The county need not lodge an

---

[34] T.C.P. General Regulations, reg. 5(6).

[35] See further *Steeples* v. *Derbyshire C.C.* [1981] J.P.L. 582.

[36] T.C.P. General Regulations reg. 4(4)(e); 5(2). Because the power of the authority to pass the second resolution is governed by this requirement, failure to comply with it may render their second resolution void: *Steeples* v. *Derbyshire C.C.* [1981] J.P.L. 582.

[37] Because under the General Development Order, art. 12(1), the power is limited to cases of grant of planning permission by local planning authorities.

[38] *Op. cit.* reg. 11.

application with the district; nor need the district refer any proposal of theirs to the county even where it relates to a county matter.[39] Each must, however, consult with the other before proceeding to pass the second resolution.[40]

Third, compliance with the development plan is more carefully supervised than in the case of private sector applications. The Secretary of State must be notified of proposals which conflict with, not necessarily "materially," or prejudice the implementation of, *any* development plan.[41]

4. *The exclusivity of the Regulations*

The Regulations limit the ability of local planning authorities to obtain planning permission where either the land is vested in them, or they propose to carry out the development themselves. It follows that they have no power to make speculative proposals in respect of land not owned by them, and there is doubt as to the flexibility of the Regulations in their application to local authority/private enterprise partnership schemes. The question arises of how far it is possible for the Regulations to be circumvented by the making of an ordinary application to the planning authority, whether by the authority themselves, by their development partners or by any other person. Given that an applicant need normally have no proprietary interest in the land to which his application relates, provided the owners are notified of the application, there is no immediate bar to a third party seeking permission by way of an ordinary application in respect of land vested in the local planning authority. It is a device which has frequently been used in the past by amenity societies and others to force the consideration by the authority of alternative proposals for the site.

The Act, however, provides that its provisions relating to the making of applications for permission shall have effect in relation to the land of, and development by, local planning authorities subject to the modifications made by the Regulations.[42] Those modifications preclude the making of ordinary applications wherever an authority either "require a permission for development they propose to carry out," or "seek to obtain permission for development" for land in their area vested in them. In each of those cases, therefore, the Regulations provide an exclusive code, and an authority would have no jurisdiction to entertain an ordinary planning application. A private application unrelated to any proposal of the authority would not, however, be excluded, because the Regulations do not purport to cover such a case. The position is less clear where authority and developer are proposing to develop in partnership. If the land is already vested in the authority, it is likely that the Regulations again must be taken as prescribing the exclusive procedure to the extent that the authority as well as the developer are seeking to obtain permission, though much may depend upon the terms of the partnership arrangements. For land not vested in the authority, an ordinary application by the developer would be the proper course.

---

[39] See *e.g. Attorney-General (ex. rel. Turley)* v. *G.L.C.* (1976) 239 E.G. 893.
[40] T.C.P. General Regulations, reg. 10(2).
[41] T.C.P. Development Plans (England) Direction 1981, para. 8. Identical provision is made by para. 8 of the Wales Direction, and by para. 9 of the London Direction.
[42] T.C.P.A. 1971, s. 270; and *cf.* T.C.P. General Regulations 1976, reg. 3.

Perhaps the guiding principle in drawing the boundaries to the special procedures should be that of ensuring adequate supervision in cases raising conflicts of interest, of not allowing the conflict to be disguised by too readily permitting the authority to take refuge behind a private sector application, and bearing in mind the closer scrutiny exerted through the Development Plans Direction over plan compliance in cases dealt with under the Regulations.

5. *The problem of conflict of interest*

There is a problem of conflict of interest in any matter where the planning authority are both planner and developer, but it is liable to become acute in cases where there is a pre-existing partnership agreement. There is a danger that the authority may so commit themselves contractually to the developer as to fetter their discretion in determining the planning application. An example occurred in the recent important case of *Steeples* v. *Derbyshire C.C.*[43] where the defendant authority had entered into an agreement with a development company which bound them, *inter alia*, to "take all reasonable steps to obtain the grant of outline planning permission." Failure to obtain permission gave the developers the right to determine the agreement, and to claim £117,000 liquidated damages from the authority if they had failed to use their "best endeavours" to obtain permission. The plaintiff alleged that the authority had thereby fettered, or at least had given the appearance of having fettered, their statutory discretion. In the High Court, Webster J. upheld the submission, holding that a reasonable man would think that there was a reasonable likelihood that the provisions of the contract "had had a material and significant effect on the Planning Committee's decision to grant the permission." And he emphasised that "in operating the procedures under regulations 4 and 5 the planning authority must be particularly scrupulous to ensure that its decision is seen to be fair, particularly when it is at all controversial."

M. Development by statutory undertakers

Statutory undertakers[44] enjoy substantial exemptions from development control, and their special position in the planning system reflects both their quasi-public status and the supervisory jurisdiction exerted by the "appropriate Minister" for the purpose of the undertaking. Exemptions are conferred by the Act itself,[45] and by the General Development Order.[46] For

---

[43] [1981] J.P.L. 582; and *cf.* the decision of the New Zealand Court of Appeal in *Lower Hutt C.C.* v. *Bank* [1974] 1 N.Z.L.R. 545 where, at 550, commenting on the authority's duty in respect of objections lodged to road stopping proposals, the Court said, "We think that the state of impartiality which is required is the capacity in a council to preserve a freedom, notwithstanding earlier investigations and decisions, to approach their duty of inquiring into and disposing of the objections without a closed mind, so that if considerations advanced by the objectors bring them to a different frame of mind they can, and will go back on their proposals."

[44] For the statutory definition, see *ante*, p. 70.

[45] T.C.P.A. 1971, s. 22(2)(*c*): maintenance work on existing apparatus.

[46] G.D.O., Classes XVIII—XX.

some categories of permitted development the benefits extend only to "operational land," that is, land actually used or held for the purpose of carrying on the undertaking as opposed to land held for investment purposes or used for ancillary activities.[47]

For development requiring permission, the normal practice is for application to be made to, and to be processed by, the local planning authority in the usual way, except that in some cases appeal lies from an unfavourable decision to the Secretary of State and the "appropriate Minister"[48] jointly.[49]

There is, however, a limited procedure for obtaining deemed permission, which arises in the case of development for which authorisation of a government department is statutorily required. The Department may, when granting the authorisation, also direct that planning permission for the permission be deemed to be granted.[50] The permission would normally be subject to conditions, enforceable in the usual way by the local planning authority. It is, however, a procedure which by-passes the usual planning procedures, often in respect of development which because of its scale or type may have a seriously adverse local environmental impact, and in practice its use has come to be limited to certain operations of energy undertakers. The normal course in other cases is for an application to be submitted to the local planning authority.[51]

The scope of the permitted development exemptions means that there is often no formal opportunity for public discussion of significant proposals by statutory undertakers, and so an informal code of practice has been agreed which urges undertakers to consult with planning authorities in important cases.[52] The powers of the authority are limited, however, to discussing with the undertaker how the proposals might be improved or amended to overcome planning objections. It is therefore a relationship of negotiation rather than control, but against the background of the authority's power to seek to limit the scope of the exemptions through an article 4 Direction.[53]

---

[47] Or, as the Act defines it, "not being land which, in respect of its nature and situation, is comparable rather with land in general than with land which is used, or in which interests are held, for the purpose of the carrying on of statutory undertakings:" T.C.P.A. 1971, s. 222; and see further qualifications introduced by s. 223.

[48] As defined by T.C.P.A. 1971, s. 224.

[49] T.C.P.A. 1971, s. 225(1).

[50] T.C.P.A. 1971, s. 40; and cf. Opencast Coal Act 1958, s. 2.

[51] 965 H.C. Deb., col. 322 (March 29, 1979).

[52] D.O.E. Circular 71/73, paras. 25–30.

[53] Ante, p. 179. The power is excluded in the case of development under Class XII where the authorising Act or Order was passed after July 1, 1948.

CHAPTER 6

DECISION MAKING IN DEVELOPMENT CONTROL

A. Preliminary

1. *Introduction*

The preceding chapters have dealt with the question of what constitutes development requiring planning permission, and the preliminary steps required to obtain it. This chapter concentrates upon the procedures governing the handling and consideration of applications by local planning authorities, whilst the next chapter deals with the policy input to development control.

The most striking characteristic of both the consideration of applications and the policy input is that they are comparatively little regulated by legal rules. Planning authorities exercise their functions against a backcloth of broad statutory discretion. The keynote is flexibility, and the legislation imposes few constraints upon either the internal procedures or organisation of authorities, or the criteria by which they may be guided in decision making. Many of the rules are open ended. There is no attempt in the legislation to define the scope of development control or the objectives of the process. The Act envisages that decisions will be taken in "planning" terms, by which is meant that authorities will be guided by the provisions of the development plan, the representations received from the organisations and persons notified and consulted on the application and any other "material" considerations. But the balance to be struck between competing considerations is a matter for the authority themselves, subject to the overall supervision of the Secretary of State through the "calling in" procedures and the appeals system, and through his various reserve powers.

Development control is not, therefore, structured as a mechanical, rules dominated process. It is a discretionary system of regulation, intended not simply to operate through fixed and predetermined standards, but to be purposive. It is designed to allow objectives to be pursued and not simply rules obeyed, and to allow objectives and policies to be changed to keep pace with changing social and political demands.

So much for the legislative structure. The reality is somewhat different, because local authorities exercise their powers, not in a vacuum, but in a complex legal and political context which has its own systems of safeguards, influences and accountability. The freedom of movement which authorities actually enjoy is in practice constrained by pressures and publicity, by policies and past commitments, understandings and the like. Despite the apparent flexibility of discretion, there is strong pressure to act consistently, to treat like cases similarly and to adhere to policies. The result is that control is influenced to a greater extent than is sometimes realised by sets of rules, policies, criteria and standards. Many will appear in the development plan, particularly if it is up to date; but many more will not. They may not be set down anywhere, but have emerged simply from a pattern of past decision making. The more common examples are examined in the following chapter.

Similarly in procedural terms, the formalities prescribed by the 1971 Act and its subordinate legislation, in particular the General Development Order, are intended to secure that decisions shall not be made without there having been an adequate opportunity for consultation and comment. But they are reinforced by the institutional constraints on local government decision making, and by rules relating to the management structure of the authority, the disclosure of interests by members and officers and other similar constraints.

2. The Receipt of Planning Applications

The early steps to be taken by a local planning authority upon the receipt of a planning application are largely mechanical. The application is scrutinised to check that it is accompanied by any necessary certificates, such as the ownership certificate under section 26 or an industrial development certificate if required. The fee payable for the application is also checked, and where the authority are satisfied that the application and fee are generally in order they are required to send an acknowledgement to the applicant, "as soon as may be."[1] The acknowledgement may reserve the right subsequently to determine that the application is invalid. If the authority do form the opinion that it is invalid, they are required to notify the applicant of that decision.[2]

The defects which may render an application invalid are various. The most obvious is breach of requirements which are fundamental to the jurisdiction of the authority to entertain the application at all, such a preliminary certificate. Payment of a fee does not go to jurisdiction in the same way, and although it is required to be paid at the time the application is made, it is by way of being a collateral requirement. The sanction for non-payment is not the invalidity of the application, but the fact that time does not begin to run against the authority until the fee is paid.[3] There is therefore no duty upon them to determine the application until then, and no right of appeal in default. If a cheque received in payment of the fee is later dishonoured, time ceases to run against the authority until the fee is paid.[4]

A more troublesome problem for all authorities is applications which are wrongly completed, and which contain errors, often in the accompanying plans, which give a false impression of the proposed development. The plans may show a neighbouring dwelling to be further away from the site than is actually the case, or the application may contain an erroneous description of the site or its ownership. Defective applications are a major cause of delay in development control, and to require the authority to check every detail before determining an application is to impose a very heavy burden on them. The defects are often insufficiently serious to render an application invalid, but they may still if undetected lead to the granting of a permission which would not otherwise have been granted. The Commission for Local

---

[1] Town and Country Planning General Development Order 1977 (S.I. 1977 No. 289) (hereafter G.D.O.), art. 7(3); Sched.2,Pt.I.
[2] *Ibid.* art.7(5).
[3] Town and Country Planning (Fees for Applications and Deemed Applications) Regulations 1981 (S.I. 1981 No 369), reg.3; G.D.O., art. 7(6A).
[4] G.D.O., art. 7(6C).

Administration have recently taken the view that, although primary responsibility for ensuring the accuracy of an application rests with the applicant, the authority are not themselves without responsibility, and "the citizen might question the value of a planning service that could not protect him from the approval of plans that were grossly inaccurate."[5] The Commission have indicated, therefore, that a finding of maladministration is likely against an authority who fail to detect a gross error in a planning application, upon a complaint by a citizen suffering as a result.

The proper course in dealing with a defective application which is not invalid is to seek further information[6] and to seek its amendment by the applicant (although if substantial amendment is required, it may be necessary for the application to be resubmitted,[7]) and, if necessary, to require the applicant to submit such evidence as is reasonably necessary to verify any particulars of information in the application.[8]

Where the application relates to a "county matter," the authority are obliged to send on to the county all the relevant documents[9] (or, in London, transmit the application to the Greater London Council where it relates to development in respect of which they are the local planning authority).[10] Notification of the reference of the application as a county matter is required to be given to the applicant.[11]

3. The Planning Register

The purpose of the planning register, which each local planning authority is required to maintain, is to provide a publicly accessible record of pending applications and decisions made on applications. The register is kept in two parts. First, there is a register of pending applications, including applications for approval of reserved matters, together with copies of plans and drawings submitted in relation thereto. Entries relating to applications are required to be made within 14 days of their receipt by the authority.[12] The entry remains in the register until the application is finally disposed of, which means that it may not be removed until either the application (or an appeal against the authority's decision on it) has been withdrawn, or the authority have given a decision and the time for appeal to the Secretary of State has expired (or, if an appeal has been lodged, the time for further appeal to the court).[13]

Part II of the register contains details of all applications for planning permission (whether pending or determined), including not only the application and plans and drawings, but also any decisions of the authority

---

[5] Commission for Local Administration, *Annual Report 1979/80*, p.11.

[6] Under G.D.O., art. 5(1).

[7] See generally *Inverclyde D.C.* v. *Secretary of State for Scotland* 1982 S.L.T. 200; and *ante*, p. 20.

[8] G.D.O., art.5(4).

[9] *Ibid.* art. 7(4).

[10] *Ibid.* art. 7(2).

[11] *Ibid.* art. 7(4).

[12] T.C.P.A. 1971, s.34; G.D.O. art. 21(7). Similarly, the entry of any direction, decision or approval is required to be made within 14 days of its being given or made.

[13] G.D.O., art. 21(9). But in the case of local planning authorities' own development details must remain in Part I until the development is completed: T.C.P. General Regulations, 1976, reg. 4(9).

or the Secretary of State and the date of any subsequent approvals given in relation to the application. That last category extends to applications for approval of reserved matters, and also applications for consent, approval or agreement required by a condition on the permission concerned.[14] Similarly, if planning permission is granted by the Secretary of State on the deemed application for permission resulting from an enforcement or established use certificate appeal, details of that permission are required to be entered in the register.

The requirements of the General Development Order relating to registers are specific and detailed. Each register is to contain an index for enabling a person to trace any entry in it, and registers are to be kept physically at the offices of the district authority (and although the county are required to "keep" a register its physical location must be at the district offices) except in relation to development in any National Park. In London, the register is to be kept at the offices of the Common Council or London borough. The register may be split geographically, however, and parts maintained at a place within the area for which the part is kept.[15]

Finally, the register is required to be available for public inspection at "all reasonable hours."[16] Whilst complying generally with the spirit of the Order and maintaining files of applications to which the public are permitted access, a number of authorities have failed in the past to comply strictly with the detailed requirements and to keep the register in two distinct parts. A common practice has been for a single file to be opened on each application, and to be moved from one filing cabinet to another once the determination of the authority has been made. But such an arrangement is not the "register" required by the Act.[17] It may be sufficient compliance for ordinary planning applications, because entry of the application into the register is not expressly made a pre-requisite to the validity of the authority's determination. But in the case of a local planning authority's own development proposals, regulations require that a resolution granting permission may be passed only after 21 days have elapsed from the entry being made in Part I of the register.[18] Unless a proper entry is made, therefore, the authority are without power to pass the resolution.

B. Determining Planning Applications.

1.*Planning Committees and Sub-committees*

Although all planning decisions are formally made in the name of the local planning authority itself, it is common for the function to be delegated largely to a committee of the authority. The authority may also establish

---

[14] *Ibid.* art.21(2). Applications for s. 53 determinations are required to be kept in a separate register (art. 21(4)), which also includes applications for established use certificates: art. 22(11). A separate register is required for applications for consent to display advertisements, under the T.C.P. (Control of Advertisements) Regulations 1969 (S.I. 1969 No. 1532), reg.31.
[15] *Ibid.* art. 21(1), (5) and (8).
[16] T.C.P.A. 1971, s.34(3).
[17] *Steeples* v. *Derbyshire C.C.* [1981] J.P.L. 582.
[18] T.C.P. General Regulations 1976 (S.I. 1977 No. 1419), regs.3(3) and 5(3).

sub-committees and delegate functions to officers.[19] And the planning committee may also, unless otherwise directed by the authority, delegate to a sub-committee or officer.[20] Delegation deprives the delegating body of none of their powers,[21] however, and they may exercise a parallel jurisdiction and even pre-empt, if they wish, the exercise of power by the delegatee.

Members of committees are appointed by the authority, and there is power to co-opt up to one third of the membership from persons who are not members of the authority.[22] Sub-committees are appointed by committees, and there is no statutory limit on the proportion of outside members.[23]

Committees are traditionally the workhorses of local government administration, and as the scope of local government has expanded, so has grown the pressure for more widespread delegation to committees and officers in the interests of efficient management. The legislative backing is now cast in the broadest terms. The word "delegation" has been replaced in the Local Government Act 1972 by the looser expression "arrangements for the discharge of functions,"[24] and the former statutory requirements relating specifically to the constitution of planning committees have been dropped. Gone too is the requirement that delegation should be to named officers only, and "arrangements for the discharge of functions" implies that formal instruments of delegation are unnecessary to establish the necessary chain of authorisation. Authorities are thus able to piece together the management structure that best suits their requirements, and there is now a great deal of variation between authorities in practice.

The common pattern is for there to be a main committee concerned with planning, and often also with at least one other related statutory function such as housing, estates, development, transportation or highways; and for there to be a number of sub-committees responsible for different functions, such as local plans and development control. In large urban authorities the main committee may be concerned solely with policy and strategic issues, and the bulk of development control decision making will be entrusted to the relevant sub-committee and the chief planning officer. Several approaches have emerged since local government reorganisation to apportioning responsibility between the main committee and sub-committees. In some authorities there is a geographical division, with special area sub-committees dealing solely with applications arising in their designated area; whilst others have a functional division with the sub-committee dealing only with applications of a certain type or below a certain size. Sub-committees may have full powers to determine applications, or they may be limited to recommending to the main committee. There may be a

---

[19] The powers are conferred by the L.G.A. 1972. s.101; and the committee structure of local authorities is generally regulated by standing orders made by the authority.

[20] L.G.A. 1972, s.101(2). A sub-committee may also, in turn, delegate to an officer of the authority any function which they have power to discharge, unless otherwise directed by the authority or the main committee. Decision making by officers is discussed *post,* p. 256.

[21] L.G.A. 1972, s. 101(4), although the saving clause does not extend to delegation by a sub-committee.

[22] L.G.A. 1972, 102(1),(2) and (3). Except in the case of advisory committees, co-opted membership is not common, although it offers a means of broadening the expertise and local knowledge of the committee.

[23] L.G.A. 1972, s.102(2).

[24] *Ibid.* s.101(1).

combination of the two. Some authorities, for example, require applications to be referred upwards where the sub-committee's decision is against the recommendation of the planning officer, or there has been a tied vote, or a minority of members have formally requested that it should be referred. Decisions of the main committee may in turn be able to be referred to a meeting of the full council.

Inter-authority arrangements are also expressly authorised by the Act,[25] and a variety of forms exist. A county and district, for example, may agree upon a reallocation of the statutory distribution of functions between them so that one is authorised to discharge certain functions of the other[26]; or they may set up a joint committee to exercise jurisdiction in cases of disputed jurisdiction or those raising matters of mutual interest.[27]

Committees are also commonly established on a non-statutory basis, exercising an investigative or advisory function but with no statutory functions to exercise. Some are ad hoc, such as viewing sub-committees dispatched to examine a particular site and report back, and working parties set up to examine a specific project. Others are standing committees, including advisory panels with special expertise in architecture, conservation, minerals extraction or archaeology, for example.[28]

The formal committees and their inter-relationships, functions and meetings are regulated through standing orders approved by each authority, subject to which each committee is free to regulate its own procedures.[29]

2. Consideration of Planning Applications

(a) The officers' report

The administrative work involved in processing planning applications is a matter generally for the professional planning staff, subject to the overview of the responsible committee. The usual arrangement is that the officers carry out the preliminary functions of receiving, acknowledging and registering planning applications, carrying out the necessary notifications and consultation and dispatching "county matter" applications and advising and negotiating with developers. Members will be notified at an early stage of any important applications, and their guidance sought in difficult cases; and they often play a part informally in negotiations with developers or by way of intervention on behalf of objectors. The Chairman of the committee typically has a consultative role, and may even be involved on a day-by-day advisory basis in the administration. But in general the preliminary work is undertaken by officers, and the results reported to the committee.

The officers' report is not a statutory document—indeed, it may be purely

[25] *Ibid.* s.101(1) and (3). Where the function is to be exercised by another authority, subs.(3) authorises its discharge by a committee, sub-committee or officer of that authority.
[26] Such arrangements have been common in the past to deal with "county matters," where the county may wish to arrange for certain applications to be dealt with by the district rather than to be referred in the normal way.
[27] The setting up of joint committees is authorised by L.G.A. 1972, s.101(5), and their expenses are to be defrayed by the authorities: s.103.
[28] Advisory committees are appointed under L.G.A. 1972, s.102(4), and they are empowered in turn to appoint one or more sub-committees to advise them in respect of any matter.
[29] L.G.A. 1972, s.106. Certain aspects of procedure are also regulated by Sched.12 to that Act: see further *post*, p. 251.

oral—but it is liable to fulfil some important statutory functions. The legislation requires that the authority should take into account the representations received by them in response to advertisements and consultation, but the scale and range of response frequently makes it difficult for committee members to read all the representations for themselves before the meeting, let alone for them to be set out in full in the officers' report or read aloud at the meeting. On a controversial application an authority may receive hundreds, perhaps thousands of letters; and such is the nature of politics, the members are liable to be as interested in the quantity as in the quality of objection. In short, expedience demands that they make arrangements for the discharge of their function of taking representations into account, and the officers' report is the usual machinery through which there is carried out a preliminary sifting and summarising of representations. Even if there is no express delegation to them of the function of "taking account" of but discarding immaterial representations, it is nonetheless a usual and accepted "arrangement" through which the statutory duty is discharged.[30] In some authorities the practice is bolstered by the deposit of copies of all representations in the members' room, and whether or not they are examined by the members this practice no doubt increases substantially the burden of proof on an objector who asserts that his views have been overlooked.

The officers' recommendations need not be accepted by the members. Theirs is the ultimate responsibility for decision-making, and they may take a different view of the information presented to them, interpret their policies differently, or act upon new information or views arising in the course of debate. Full judicial endorsement of this freedom of movement is to be found in the judgment of Thesiger J. in *Cardiff Corporation v. Secretary of State for Wales*[31]:

> "In this case one finds that the local planning authority, which of course, consists of elected persons, quite legitimately referred back a committee decision for further consideration, considered a petition from certain members of the public, had advice from the city planning officer different from that given by the city engineer and had on at least one occasion to decide the matter by a narrow majority vote."

He went on to criticise the "rather odd question" raised by the Welsh Office of why permission had been granted against the recommendation of the city planning officer:

> "Apparently these offices sometimes forget that local planning authorities consist of democratically elected members, and the members are, in my view, in practice constantly considering what their voters want and may, on dealing with any question, deal with it in accordance with what

---

[30] The courts have been prepared to take a broad approach in upholding the validity of the discharge by officers of statutory functions under such informal arrangements: see *e.g.* the rating cases of *Bar Hill Developments Ltd. v. South Cambridgeshire D.C.* (1979) 252 E.G. 915; *B. Kettle Ltd. v. Newcastle-under-Lyme B.C.* (1979) 77 L.G.R. 700 and *Provident Mutual Life Assurance Association v. Derby C.C.* [1981] 1 W.L.R. 173 (H.L.).
[31] (1971) 22 P.& C.R. 718 at 722–723.

they think will be satisfactory to those whose votes they have solicited in the past and intend to solicit in the future."[32]

In short, development control is a function, like other local authority functions, for which members are politically accountable. Responsible discharge of their functions no doubt requires that officers' recommendations will not be rejected arbitrarily. There is a continuing relationship between members and officers which would be damaged if this were so, and a number of authorities have built into their standing orders certain safeguards which require that decisions be referred upwards to the main committee or full council if it is proposed to go against the officers' advice. There is the further consideration that a decision taken against officers' advice tends to be difficult to defend upon appeal, because the conflict between officers and members may be brought out and exploited by the appellant in cross-examination.

(b) Admission of press and public to meetings

Meetings of the full council and its committees are required to be open to the press and public, except where the body resolve to exclude them for the whole or part of the proceedings on the grounds that "publicity would be prejudicial to the public interest by reason of the confidential nature of the business to be transacted or for other special reasons stated in the resolution and arising from the nature of that business or of the proceedings."[33] Whether exclusion is sought for reasons of confidentiality or other reasons, therefore, the overriding requirement is still that publicity would be prejudicial to the public interest.[34] But the test is couched in highly subjective terms, and practice varies considerably between authorities. Some take the view that all development control decisions should be taken privately and invoke the confidentiality clause automatically. The justification is that publicity would in their view be prejudicial to the public interest in that it might inhibit debate and prevent officers from contributing fully, and that personal matters might need to be considered. Other authorities pursue the principle of open government, and not only admit the press and public to all meetings (but subject to clear and agreed exceptions in respect of certain types of confidential business), but also advertise widely the date and place of meetings so as to encourage attendance. The statutory minimum notice is three days, to be posted at the authority's offices,[35] but the period is almost always exceeded substantially.

There are, of course, occasions when publicity would clearly be prejudicial in planning matters. Advance intimation of a proposal to serve a

---

[32] *Ibid.* at 726.

[33] Public Bodies (Admission to Meetings) Act 1960, s.1, as applied also to meetings of committees by L.G.A. 1972, s.100.

[34] And see *Peachy Property Corporation Ltd.* v. *Paddington B.C.* (1964) 108 S.J. 499. S. 1(3) of the 1960 Act, however, expressly authorises the authority to treat the need to receive or consider recommendations or advice from sources other than members, committees or sub-committees of the body as a special reason why publicity would be prejudicial without regard to the subject or purport of the recommendations or advice.

[35] Public Bodies (Admission to Meetings) Act 1960, s.1(4)(*a*); L.G.A. 1972, Sched.12, para.4(2): but if the meeting is actually convened on shorter notice than this, public notice may be given at the time it is convened.

building preservation notice or a tree preservation order, for example, is tantamount to an invitation to the owner to take swift destructive action; and publicity given to reports of confidential negotiations with developers or of potential legal proceedings is likely to weaken the authority's hand in the matter. But the general trend in planning administration over the past 15 years, endorsed by central government and by Parliament, has been towards greater openness as an aid to public participation; and use of the exclusion powers in cases other than those where there are such special circumstances—however easily it may be able to be justified in law because of the subjectivity of the formula—runs counter to that trend and to the spirit of the Local Government Act 1972, in extending the public access provisions to committee meetings.

The open meeting requirements do not extend to meetings of subcommittees, and there was a fear at one time that authorities might be tempted to avoid compliance by simply placing matters in the hands of sub-committees rather than committees. But the fear has not altogether been borne out. The Government's advice has been that:

" . . . meetings of sub-committees should be treated in the same way as other meetings, particularly where they have delegated powers. If decisions affecting the public are to be taken, the public ought to know what is decided and why; the status of the body taking the decisions is irrelevant. . . . If it is decided, on cogent grounds, that a sub-committee should not transact its business in public, it becomes the more important that, to the maximum extent permitted by the nature of the matter involved, its reports to the parent committee or council should be fully explanatory and should be available to the public and the press."[36]

In practice, many authorities follow the advice closely and apply the admission rules equally to sub-committee meetings. But the rules do not apply, of course, to meetings of party groups; and where there is prior agreement between members of the majority group on the preferred course of action, the decision of the committee or sub-committee may have been effectively pre-empted in closed meeting.[37]

(c) Natural justice in decision-making

It is a generally accepted proposition that the rules of natural justice do not require local planning authorities to hold a hearing in determining applications, but it is a proposition which owes more to history and expedience than to principle. Ever since 1947 the pattern has been for the function of development control to be carried out by local authorities in the same way as any other committee function, informally and through debate rather than through adversarial proceedings; and the practice has never been challenged in the courts. It received some indirect endorsement in 1952 in *Hanily* v. *Minister of Local Government and Planning*[38] when Parker J.

[36] D.O.E. Circular 45/75, paras. 12 and 13.
[37] See further *post*, pp. 286–289.
[38] [1952] 2 Q.B. 444,452. Different legislation has led Commonwealth courts to different conclusions, however: see, *e.g. Denton* v. *Auckland C.C.* [1969] N.Z.L.R. 256, where the legislation expressly conferred a right to a "hearing" by the committee and the applicant was

declined to imply any additional requirements of pre-decision notification, and implicitly rejected the natural justice rules as inapplicable. There matters have remained, untouched either by the development of natural justice doctrine in other areas of administrative law or by the changes in character and consequence of the decisions now falling to be taken by local authorities. The informality of the procedure has now become so deeply embedded in practice that it would be difficult indeed to move to a more formal model. As Megarry J. observed in *Gaiman* v. *National Association for Mental Health*,[39] thousands of planning applications are refused every year without any hearing, "yet I know of no suggestion that local planning authorities are thereby universally acting in contravention of the principles of natural justice."

The applicant's safeguard against mishandling of the application is his right of appeal to the Secretary of State, where a right to a hearing is guaranteed by statute and it is clear that the natural justice rules apply in full. But the contrast between "first instance" and appellate procedure could scarcely be more marked. Applications determined in a matter of minutes by the planning committee may later consume days of hearing on appeal. The planning committee is bound by no rules of evidence and may meet and determine applications in conditions of secrecy, giving the applicant and objectors no prospect of correcting or challenging prejudicial or inaccurate statements made by the other, or by the officers or members. It is an expedient method for conducting administrative business, and across a broad range of decision making it works remarkably well. The great bulk of applications coming through the system makes it impossible to provide for hearing rights in every case without quite radical changes in planning administration, and there is no guarantee that the quality of decisions would thereby be improved.

Whilst natural justice may not require that there be any "hearing" of applications, there is still a basic standard of procedural fairness which the courts require of those exercising administrative statutory functions. There may be occasions, for example, when conflicting applications are to be considered for development where the authority are resolved to grant one only (such, for example, as an out of town hypermarket) where a high standard of care in recording, reporting and assessing the competing claims may be required; and equally where the authority are considering their own development proposals and are necessarily acting as judges in their own cause.[40]

The basic model of committee decision making is frequently sup-

---

held to be entitled to be supplied with a copy of the planning officer's report to the committee.

[39] [1971] Ch.317.

[40] See *e.g. Steeples* v. *Derbyshire C.C.* [1981] J.P.L.582, where the authority's contractual obligation to use their best endeavours to obtain planning permission was held to be a factor indicating a real likelihood that they had acted unfairly in determining their own application. And although the rules of natural justice may not be strictly applicable, the courts may still intervene to ensure that in dealing with conflicting interests the authority acts fairly between them: see, *e.g. Hoggard* v. *Worsborough U.D.C.* [1962] 1 All E.R. 468; *R.* v. *Liverpool Corporation, ex parte Liverpool Taxi Fleet Operators' Association* [1972] 2 Q.B. 299, particularly at 308, *per* Lord Denning M.R. and at 310, *per* Roskill L.J.

plemented in practice to accommodate the requirements of good administration, and to ensure the maximum input of information and opinion. Officers frequently undertake discussion and negotiation with applicants before the matter goes to committee, often even before there is an application. The committee too may invite the applicant to discuss his proposals with them, or to join them in a site visit to get a better understanding of the likely impact of the development. There may also be informal meetings with objectors, and some authorities have gone so far as arrange non-statutory hearings at which evidence is presented and cross-examination undertaken. There has long been pressure from developers and amenity groups for more widespread use of these arrangements, and for more direct access to the planning committee than is commonly provided. But the procedures remain non-statutory, and they are designed primarily for the benefit of the authority rather than to satisfy any sense of procedural obligation to the parties.

It remains true, therefore, that the informality of the system and the broad discretionary power of local planning authorities together raise important problems of discretionary justice. The developer's right of appeal affords him a remedy, but it is not shared by third parties, for whom rights of direct access to the courts by way of application for judicial review are only now coming to be established.[41] Some evidence of the extent of public dissatisfaction with the administration of planning control is provided by the number of complaints received by the Commissioners for Local Administration. Ever since the Commissioners started their investigations, they have received more complaints about planning control than about any other area of local authority activity. Table 8, taken from the Commission's *Annual Report* for the year ended March 31, 1981 demonstrates the range of complaints received.

The Commissioners have been prepared to find maladministration on these complaints not only in instances of non-compliance with statutory requirements, such as failure to take into account statutory representations, but also in breaches of informal codes of practice and internal rules of management of authorities. If, for example, it is the practice of the authority to consult with immediate neighbours on all applications, then failure to do so may be maladministration. Other examples include instances where planning committees have acted on inadequate, inaccurate or misleading officers' reports or other information[42]; where officers have mishandled or misrepresented objections,[43] or have otherwise failed to follow good administrative practice, such as policing developers' compliance with approved plans,[44] checking submitted plans carefully against the actual site,[45] or pointing out to members any discrepancies between outline and detailed applications.[46]

[41] See further *post*, pp. 626–629.
[42] See, *e.g.* reports of investigations in [1976] J.P.L. 442. [1977] J.P.L. 252 (inadequate reports); [1977] J.P.L. 39 (and subsequent ruling [1977] J.P.L. 594) (inaccurate reports); and [1975] J.P.L. 546, [1977] J.P.L. 380, [1978] J.P.L. 120 and 263 (misleading reports).
[43] [1978] J.P.L. 189.
[44] [1976] J.P.L. 438.
[45] [1976] J.P.L. 179, 764; and see further *ante*, p. 246.
[46] [1976] J.P.L. 244.

Table 8
Range of Complaints Received by Commissioners for Local Administration
Planning

— failure to take into account, when granting planning permission, that an extension would effectively block a window in the house of a neighbour, who had not been consulted about the development;

— failure to consult neighbours about planning applications when Council policy was that neighbours should be consulted;

— failure to take proper account of objections to proposals for developments;

— inadequate inspection of the site of an application and failure to appreciate the importance of site levels;

— basing a decision not to take enforcement action on incorrect advice;

— unreasonable delay in taking agreed enforcement action;

— the giving of misleading information about a planning application;

— regarding substantial changes to a planning application only as an amendment which an officer could determine;

— delays in determining planning applications;

— failure in communication between the different sections of a Planning Department;

— allowing development to proceed in contravention of the Building Regulations.

Source: Commission for Local Administration, *Annual Report*, year ended March 31, 1981.

The Commissioners' jurisdiction thus complements that of the courts, and despite the caveat that they should not investigate where alternative remedies are available,[47] there is some overlap of function. The applicant's right of appeal generally precludes investigation at his instance of local authority action, but the potential remedies of third parties in the courts for procedural irregularities have not been taken by the Commissioners as preclusive of jurisdiction. The major difference is that the validity of the decision is not at issue with the Commissioners, and the remedies which they may pursue on behalf of a complainant are limited.[48] The effects of

[47] Local Government Act 1974, s. 26(6), which retains jurisdiction for the Commissioners, however, where satisfied that in the particular circumstances it is not reasonable to expect the complainant to pursue his alternative remedy.

[48] Perhaps the most significant potential remedy lies in the payment of compensation by the authority at the recommendation of the Commissioner, and this has occurred in a number of planning cases where third parties have been adversely affected by planning decisions: see, e.g. the report at [1981] J.P.L. 600. But payments are still at the discretion of the authority, and were formerly on an *ex gratia* basis and subject therefore to the approval of the Secretary of State under L.G.A. 1972, s. 161. The Local Government Act 1978 then conferred specific power on authorities to pay compensation, but the power is limited to cases where the Commissioner has made his report, and does not therefore authorise payment at once by an authority who accept responsibility whilst the investigation is still in progress. A report by Justice has recommended that this complex procedure be simplified by giving authorities express power to make such payments where the ombudsman certifies that he is satisfied that the payment is in respect of a complaint which would fall within his jurisdiction to investigate: *The Local Ombudsmen* (Justice, 1980) para.112.

their intervention overall have been mixed. They have on occasion spurred authorities to review their management structures and procedures for handling applications; but at the same time it is true that if an authority have no internal rules for such matters as additional non-statutory consultation, they cannot be found guilty of maladministration for failing to abide by them; and there have therefore been instances of retreat by authorities from enlightened administrative arrangements for the cynical purpose of avoiding investigation.[49]

3. Decision Making by Officers

It has been legally possible since 1968 for authorities to delegate decision making powers to officers, and the original provisions have now been assimilated into the broader authorisation of the 1972 Act to "arrange for the discharge of functions" by officers.[50] Delegation has become widespread, especially in the large urban areas where the sheer volume of applications makes it impossible for members to participate intelligently in every decision. It permits decisions to be taken more swiftly, particularly where committee meetings are infrequent, and it has been consistently urged by a central government as a practice which can speed up the planning machine and free members to concentrate upon the more important applications and upon general policy.[51] A common pattern is for decisions on householder and similar minor applications to be delegated completely, and other categories of application to be delegated subject to a power of veto by the committee. A committee may also wish to approve an application in principle but reserve some detail to be approved by the officers before permission is issued.

But where power is delegated in matters going beyond these, requiring more than fairly mechanical determination in accordance with clearly understood criteria, there is a very real danger that democratic accountability is diluted. In such a perennially contentious area as planning this constitutes a legitimate objection, and it is one which has led a number of authorities still to resist the call to delegate. Resistance has come too from officers, reluctant to undertake and to accept responsibility for an important statutory function.

Any decision taken by an officer in accordance with arrangements made by the authority is in law the decision of the authority.[52] The applicant need

---

[49] A remarkable response to the Commissioners' findings of maladministration came in 1979 when the Association of District Councils actually advised its members, not on how to improve their administration of planning, but on how to avoid unfavourable investigation by not adopting standards for publicity and consultation, and instead authorising officers to make informal consultations entirely at their own discretion. The Commission expressed their regret at this approach: see further their *Annual Report of 1979/80*; and the editorial comment at [1980] J.P.L. 557.

[50] L.G.A. 1972, s. 101(1).

[51] See, *e.g. Report of the Committee on the Management of Local Government* (Chairman Sir John Maud) (H.M.S.O., 1967), Vol. 1, pp. 16–20 and Chap. 3; *Management Study on Development Control* (H.M.S.O., 1967), pp. 9–10; D.O.E. Circular 142/73, para. 7(ii); *Dobry Report*, paras. 7.175 – 7.179; D.O.E. Circular 9/76, para. 2(iv); D.O.E. Circular 22/80, para. 6.

[52] This was formerly specifically stated (T.C.P.A. 1968, s. 64(5)) but today flows directly from the new statutory formula: the authority are said to be discharging their function "through" the officer: Local Government Act 1972, s. 101.

not, as a general rule, check to satisfy himself that the officer in fact had the necessary authority. Although a permission which is issued by mistake,[53] or is a forgery, or is outside the authority of the issuing officer or of the planning authority themselves[54] will be a nullity, it may nonetheless be given effect through the doctrine of estoppel. There will need to be, however, some evidence to justify the applicant in assuming that the officer's actions would bind the authority, and the type and scale of development is a material factor. The courts might not readily accept that an applicant could simply assume that a planning officer would have power to grant or amend permission for the redevelopment of Picadilly Circus, for example.[55] There would need also to be some detrimental reliance upon the permission, if only because the permission might otherwise be set aside without injustice; but the scope of this requirement remains uncertain. Substantial commencement of development would no doubt suffice, but preliminary steps which may readily be reversed, such as arranging finance or ordering machinery may not.[56]

Short of an actual grant of permission or any other statutory decision, representations made by an officer will rarely be binding upon his authority. In negotiations with applicants he has no power to commit the authority to a decision which falls to be taken by the members, and the courts have been anxious to restrict the applicability of the estoppel rules to local planning authorities in order to ensure that they should not be held unwittingly to some chance remark ventured in the course of negotiations.[57]

4. Delegation to Individual Members

There is no statutory power to arrange for any functions of an authority to be discharged by a member of the authority acting individually. Arrangements may be made only through committees and sub-committees, and the accepted rule is that a committee must include more than one person. Its powers are exercisable under the 1972 Act only through meetings, and an individual cannot "meet" with himself.[58] This limitation imposes an important safeguard against arbitrary arrogation of power by dominant politicians, but it restricts the ability of committee chairmen to act urgently between meetings when the necessity arises. An amendment was moved in the Third Reading of the Local Government, Planning and Land Bill in the

---

[53] As in *Norfolk C.C.* v. *S.O.S.E.* [1973] 1 W.L.R. 1400 (permission issued by mistake when the committee's decision had been to refuse it).

[54] *Co-operative Retail Services Ltd.* v. *Taff-Ely B.C.* (1979) 39 P. & C.R. 223 upheld by the House of Lords.

[55] *Western Fish Products Ltd.* v. *Penwith D.C.* [1981] 2 All E.R. 204, where the Court of Appeal were anxious to narrow Lord Denning's dictum in *Lever (Finance) Ltd.* v. *Westminster C.C.* [1971] 1 Q.B. 222 at 231 that persons dealing with officers are entitled to assume that all necessary resolutions have been passed. See further the discussion of estoppel in the context of enforcement of planning control, *post*, pp. 393–400.

[56] See, *e.g. Norfolk C.C.* v. *S.O.S.E.* [1973] 1 W.L.R. 1400 (contract for machinery capable of being cancelled).

[57] See further *Brooks and Burton Ltd.* v. *S.O.S.E.* (1978) 35 P.& C.R. 27 at p.40, *per* Lord Widgery C.J., cited with approval by the Court of Appeal in the *Western Fish Products* case note 55, *supra* at 221–22).

[58] See, *e.g. Re London Flats Ltd.* [1969] 1 W.L.R. 711.

Commons which would have conferred a general power to delegate to individual members, but the Government were satisfied that no need existed and the amendment was rejected.[59] Urgent business can if necessary be undertaken through a special urgency sub-committee, or by arranging for the planning officer to take urgent action in consultation with the planning committee chairman. Alternatively, the chairman may be authorised to act on behalf of the committee, subject to ratification at the next meeting. Provided his action is taken on behalf of the committee and is action which is within their own powers, upon ratification by them it becomes valid as from the time it was taken.[60] If not ratified, it has no validity.

5. Declaration of Pecuniary or Other Interest

Land use planning is an area of modern government which is particularly susceptible to corrupt practice. The combination of broad discretion and the large sums at stake has proved irresistible to a number of members and officers. The Redcliffe-Maud Report on Conduct in Local Government in 1974, itself prompted by the notorious Poulson affair, identified the three areas of local government activity where they believed conflicts of interest might have "especially damaging consequences" as being the award of contracts, the planning and control of land use, and participation (including participation as a landowner) in comprehensive development and redevelopment.[61] That view was expressly endorsed two years later by the Royal Commission on Standards of Conduct in Public Life, who added an important rider:

> "Without making the slightest excuse for anybody, we nevertheless feel that the conditions created by Parliament in the field of planning law and in urban and housing development have put greater strain than has generally been realised upon our system of locally elected councils, whose members may enter public life with little preparation and may find themselves handling matters on a financial scale quite beyond their experience in private life. The power to make decisions which lead to large capital gains or business profits has led to obvious temptations on both sides."[62]

Regular conflict of interest is inevitable in the case of committees made up of professionals with local property interests, including solicitors, surveyors, estate agents and builders. One way of overcoming it is by excluding such persons from membership, but the result is that there is thereby also

---

[59] Hansard H.C. Deb., Vol.988, cols 1431–1432 (July 15, 1980).
[60] Firth v. Staines [1897] 2 Q.B. 70; R. v. Chapman, ex parte Arlidge [1918] 2 K.B. 298 (chairman of public health committee appointed to act on urgent matters over the vacation, subject to subsequent ratification). There can be no power to ratify if the act itself is outside the powers of the authority itself: Ashbury Carriage Co. v. Rich (1875) L.R. 7 H.L.653, applied by Lord Denning M.R. in Co-operative Retail Services Ltd. v. Taff-Ely B.C. (1980) 39 P. & C.R. 223 at 238–39 (expressing doubt also whether a resolution "confirming" the action of the Clerk could be said to have ratified it).
[61] Conduct in Local Government, Report of the Prime Minister's Committee on Local Government Rules of Conduct, Cmnd. 5636, para.70 (1974).
[62] Cmnd. 6524, para.38.

excluded the benefit of their knowledge and experience of local development conditions.

The law therefore imposes no general prohibition, but instead places a disability from participating in particular decisions on members who have any pecuniary interest, and imposes a duty on them to disclose the interest.[63] The duty extends to "any pecuniary interest, direct or indirect, in any contract, proposed contract or other matter,"[64] except where it is "so remote or insignificant that it cannot reasonably be regarded as likely to influence a member in the consideration or discussion of, or in voting on, any question with respect to that contract or matter."[65] A pecuniary interest is not only one owned directly, but includes also any interest held by a company or other body of which the person or a nominee of his is a member, or held by any partner or employer of his.[66] In the case of married persons living together, the interests of each are deemed to be interests of the other if known to the other.[67]

Where a direct or indirect pecuniary interest is held by a member, he is obliged as soon as practicable after the commencement of a meeting at which he is present and at which the contract or other matter to which the interest relates is the subject of consideration, to disclose the fact.[68] He is permitted neither to take part in the discussion, nor to vote on any question with respect to it. It is common for the standing orders of local authorities to go further than this, and to insist that the member be excluded for the meeting whilst the matter is under consideration unless formally invited by resolution to remain.[69] It is possible, but not mandatory, for a member to give a general declaration relating to interests held by him which is then entered in a register available for inspection by any member of the authority.[70] Although such a declaration lifts the requirement of making ad hoc declarations of interest, it does not remove the disqualification from participating in the decision.

Breach of the statutory requirements is an offence,[71] and the participation of a member holding a pecuniary interest in a planning decision is capable of rendering the decision void. The leading case is a decision under the Town

---

[63] L.G.A. 1972, s. 94(1). The obligation does not extend, however, to an interest held "as a ratepayer or inhabitant of the area or as an ordinary consumer of water, or to an interest in any matter relating to the terms on which the right to participate in any service, including the supply of goods, is offered to the public": s. 97(4).

[64] L.G.A. 1972, s. 94(1).

[65] *Ibid.* s. 97(5). There is also power for the Secretary of State to remove any disability in any case where the proportion of members disabled would otherwise be so great as to impede the transaction of business, or where it appears to be in the interests of the inhabitants of the area that the disability should be removed: s.97(1).

[66] *Ibid.* s. 95(1); where the indirect interest arises from beneficial ownership of shares the disability does not operate (although the duty to disclose still does) if the shareholding is small: s. 97(6).

[67] L.G.A. 1972, s. 95(3).

[68] *Ibid.* s. 94(1). The disability is extended to meetings of committees and sub-committees by s. 105.

[69] Such a requirement is expressly authorised by L.G.A. 1972, s.94(4).

[70] L.G.A. 1972, s. 96.

[71] *Ibid.* s. 94(2): it is a defence for the member to prove that he did not know that the contract or other matter in which he had an interest was the subject of consideration at the meeting. A prosecution under the section may be brought only by or on behalf of the Director of Public Prosecutions.

and Country Planning Act 1925, *R. v. Hendon Rural District Council, ex parte Chorley*[72] where the authority had by resolution granted permission for development which did not comply with the allocations of the town scheme for the area. A member of the authority's Plans and Highways Committee, which passed the resolution, was the sole member of a firm of estate agents who were acting for the vendors of the property, and had negotiated a contract conditional upon the granting of the permission. But he failed to declare his interest and participated in the decision.[73] The court had no hesitation in quashing the resolution on the grounds that the member was biased or held such an interest as to disqualify him. The relevance of the decision to development control following the 1947 Act was for some time in doubt, because it was thought that the court's classification of the function as "quasi-judicial" was inappropriate to the more administrative nature of the post-1947 function; and also because of doubts as to the *locus standi* of the applicant (as a neighbour) to seek certiorari. Those doubts have now been set to rest, and it is clear that certiorari will go to decisions of local planning authorities.[74]

Whilst the statutory provisions extend only to pecuniary interests, it is clear that the impression of bias may be given by the participation in a decision by a member having some other interest in the matter under consideration. A personal or business relationship, for example, may make it difficult to separate his personal feelings from his duties as a councillor; and, in recognition of this, advice issued by central government in the form of a national Code of Conduct stresses the importance of recognising the influence of "kinship, friendship, membership of an association, society or trade union, trusteeship and many other kinds of relationship."[75] The *Code* suggests that members should ask themselves whether others would think the interest sufficiently close to influence someone in their position, and to treat the interest as if it were a pecuniary one unless they are in no doubt that it is not sufficiently close. But the category is potentially very broad, and the test suggested is not easy to apply in practice. It relies upon the judgment of individual members, and it is based upon relationships rather than actual feelings. In some cases the member may have strong personal feelings against rather than in favour of the applicant. It also raises the difficulty of distinguishing between the appearance of personal bias as a result of the relationship, and broader political accountability. A member may be opposed to an application, for example, because of his membership of a voluntary organisation which has objected to it. Provided that objection, if pursued by him, is made on planning grounds and not for the advancement of personal interest, then there can be no obvious harm in his relationship.

But the line is difficult to draw, and it is likely that a personal relationship

---

[72] [1933] 2 K.B. 696.
[73] The decision had been taken unanimously and without discussion, but the member's presence on the committee was sufficient participation.
[74] See *e.g. R. v. Hillingdon L.B.C., ex parte Royco Homes Ltd.* [1974] Q.B.720; and see further *post*, pp. 624–626.
[75] *National Code of Local Government Conduct* (issued as an Annex to D.O.E. Circular 94/75), para. 3.The *Code* is based closely on a draft prepared by the Prime Minister's Committee on Local Government Rules of Conduct, and its terms were agreed between the Government and the local authority associations.

which is sufficiently close to give the impression of bias on the part of a member is capable of rendering a decision void. Further, the Commission for Local Administration have taken a firm line in declaring breaches of the *Code of Conduct* to constitute maladministration, whether or not the *Code* has actually been adopted by the authority concerned.[76] They have rejected the argument that the requirements are by their nature impossible for the authority to police internally and so avoid a finding of maladministration, and have thereby imposed a heavy burden on authorities and their members to observe scrupulously the terms of the *Code*.

The rules are not applied by the Act to officers as strictly as they are to members, partly because of the ability of the authority to regulate officers' conduct more closely through the terms of their employment. The 1972 Act requires that an officer should give written notice to the authority of any pecuniary interest he has in a contract which has been, or is proposed to be, entered into by them.[77] But it does not extend to any "other matter," such as a planning application, although officers are forbidden to accept any fee or reward other than their proper remuneration.[78] But again, the Local Government Commissioners have been ready to find maladministration in cases where too close a relationship may have been thought to give an appearance of bias,[79] and many authorities make provision in their standing orders requiring officers who may be directly or indirectly interested in a planning application to disclose their interest immediately upon its submission and to play no part in the processing of it.

6. *Time Limits for Decisions*

The General Development Order requires that notification of an authority's decision on a planning application should be given to the applicant within eight weeks of the receipt by them of a valid application, or within such longer period as may have been agreed upon in writing by the applicant and the relevant authority.[80] But the requirement has in the past been interpreted more as a general guide than as an established rule. The period has never been extended (indeed, it has been slightly diminished[81]) to take account of the new demands imposed on development control, such as the split between county and district responsibility and the broader arrangements for publicity and consultation. As a result, long delays in processing applications became common, particularly as authorities attempted to cope with the large increase in numbers of applications during the boom years of 1972–75.

---

[76] See further the Commission's *Annual Report for the year ending March 31, 1981*, p.6; and [1979] J.P.L. 115 (maladministration found when a relative spoke against a planning application without disclosing an interest.)
[77] L.G.A. 1972, s.117(1): "pecuniary interest" carries the same definition as in the case of a member of an authority.
[78] *Ibid.* s. 117(2).
[79] See, *e.g.* [1976] J.P.L. 320.
[80] G.D.O., art.7(6). It extends to applications for planning permission, for approval of reserved matters and (by implication from T.C.P.A. 1971, s.37) to applications for approval, consent or agreement of the authority required by a condition imposed on a planning permission.
[81] The period was originally two months, but was changed to eight weeks to bring it in line with the requirements of the Community Land Act 1975, by the G.D.O. (Amendment) Order 1976 (S.I. 1976 No. 301).

Those delays led in turn to increased pressure from central government for a more efficient management approach by local authorities, and to the appointment of Mr. George Dobry Q.C. in 1974 to undertake a review of the whole development control system. Dobry's main recommendation was that applications should be divided into two categories: "Class A" applications, which would include all applications of a simple nature, those complying with the provisions of the development plan and development only just exceeding the tolerances of the General Development Order; and "Class B" applications which would include all other applications.[82] The purpose was to allow applications in Class A to be disposed of quickly, and permission would be deemed to be granted unless either a decision was notified within 42 days, or the application was transferred to Class B within 28 days.

But the recommendation found no favour with the Government.[83] It was thought to add an additional measure of procedural complexity to development control, and such a sub-division was already possible on an internal and non-statutory basis within authorities. The Government also pointed to the fall in applications experienced after Dobry had been appointed, and saw in this some relief from the congestion which had led to earlier delays. But their expectations were not fulfilled. By the year 1976–77, only 16 per cent. of district planning authorities had succeeded in processing 80 per cent. or more of their applications within the statutory period, and only 75 per cent. of all authorities managed to process more than half their applications in that period.[84] Not unexpectedly, given the duplication of effort and the complexity and impact of referred applications, the county performance was substantially worse: none achieved the 80 per cent. rate, and only 16 per cent. succeeded in processing 50 per cent. of applications within the prescribed time.

There has been a dramatic improvement in more recent years, however. In the first quarter of 1981, no fewer than 69 per cent. of all applications were determined within the eight week period, and a further 20 per cent. were determined within 13 weeks.[85] The reasons for the improvement are varied. Decision making has been made easier as a firmer planning base has come to be established through local plans, the county/district arrangements have been reformed, the building industry has been in recession and more applications have been for extensions to dwellings than for major new projects, the tolerances of the General Development Order have been extended (although difficulties in interpreting it have multiplied) and there has generally been a greater sense of urgency on the part of authorities.

The eight-week period is directory rather than mandatory, and a decision

---

[82] *Review of the Development Control System: Final Report by Mr George Dobry Q.C.* (H.M.S.O., 1975), Chap.7.
[83] The Government's response to the Dobry Report is contained in D.O.E. Circular 113/75 (since cancelled).
[84] The figures are taken from the survey carried out by Professor H.W.E. Davies for the House of Commons Expenditure Committee in 1977:
[85] [1981] J.P.L. 783. The figures are now published quarterly by the Department of the Environment, and they show still a wide range of variation between authorities. Some few authorities still process fewer than 20 *per cent.* of applications within the prescribed time.

issued late without the agreement of the applicant is nonetheless valid, at any rate if it has been accepted and acted upon.[86] Lateness does not, therefore, entitle an applicant subsequently to avoid a condition imposed in such a decision. The period may, of course, be extended by written agreement at any time (except where an appeal has already been lodged to the Secretary of State),[87] but central government advice urges that this should not be an automatic, perfunctory or routine matter: "the applicant ought to be given a proper explanation, including information about consultations with other bodies, and some indication as to when a decision is likely to be given."[88]

The remedy for non-compliance by an authority with the time limit is that the applicant has a right of appeal, as if his application had been refused at the end of the period prescribed or agreed.[89]

C. Planning Permission

1. *What Constitutes a Grant of Planning Permission*

It is remarkable that the question of what constitutes the grant of a planning permission should have remained an open question for so long, given that so much depends upon the answer. There are two competing possibilities. One is that permission is granted at the time the authority or its committee resolve to grant it. The other is that it is the notification to the applicant which constitutes the grant. The Act itself gives no clear guidance. The resolution of the authority or its committee is clearly the decision to grant permission, and that decision is then required to be notified to the applicant.[90] And the time of the decision itself is taken, for certain compensation purposes, to be the time that it is made by the authority.[91] But under other provisions, it is the notification of the decision which has legal effect. Time for appeal from a decision runs from the date of notification.[92] Other provisions of the Act are neutral, such as those regulating the life of planning permission which refer only to the time of "grant" of permission.[93] The problem has been recognised for some years. The Management Study Team on Development Control in 1967 recommended that the date of the issue of the decision notice should be made the date of decision,[94] and more recently, in the first draft of the Local Government, Planning and Land Bill, an amendment was proposed with the same effect, to require authorities to give the applicant "a decision in writing on his application."

But the proposed amendment did not find its way into the revised version

---

[86] *James* v. *M.H.L.G.* [1966] 1 W.L.R. 135 (C.A.), approved by the House of Lords, *sub. nom.* *James* v. *Secretary of State for Wales* [1966] 3 All E.R. 964.

[87] G.D.O., art.7(6).

[88] D.O.E. Circular 22/80, para.7.

[89] T.C.P.A. 1971, s. 37.

[90] G.D.O. 1977, art. 7(6).

[91] T.C.P.A. 1971, s. 290(4).

[92] G.D.O. 1977, art. 20(1).

[93] T.C.P.A. 1971, ss.41 and 42. For a detailed study of the competing arguments, see Garner [1972] J.P.L. 193, and Albery, "What and When is a Planning Permission?" (1974) 90 L.Q.R. 351: both authors take the view that it is the resolution rather than the notification which is the grant.

[94] *Report of the Management Study Team on Development Control* M.H.L.G. 1967, p.23.

of the Bill, and it is necessary still to consider the approach taken by the courts in interpreting the present provisions of the Act. Although the consensus of judicial opinion is also, on the face of it, in favour of treating the notification rather than the resolution as the "grant" of permission, there is not yet a clear and unequivocal ruling to that effect.

In *R. v. Yeovil Corporation, ex parte Trustees of Elim Pentecostal Church, Yeovil*[95] the Divisional Court held that planning permission had not been granted when the committee had resolved to grant it subject to the Town Clerk being satisfied as to car parking arrangements. The Court accepted as "entirely right" the view expressed by Lord Denning M.R. in *Slough Estates Ltd.* v. *Slough Borough Council (No.2)*[96] that:

> "The grant is not made when the county council resolve to give permission. It is only made when their clerk, on their authority, issues the permission to the applicant."

But the decision in the *Slough Estates* case rested not on the interpretation of the 1971 Act, but on the provisions of the Town and Country Planning (General Interim Development) Order 1945, which required that the grant or refusal of permission to develop land should be in writing. The different wording of the General Development Order—that the authority should give "notice to the applicant of their decision or determination"—implies that it may have been intended that the issuing of the notification was to be a purely administrative act following the grant of permission. This distinction between the legislation was not brought to the attention of the Divisional Court,[97] and their ruling cannot therefore be regarded as conclusive of the matter.

The question arose again at first instance in *Co-operative Retail Services Ltd.* v. *Taff-Ely Borough Council*,[98] where Sir Douglas Frank Q.C. (sitting as a deputy Judge of the High Court) thought the provisions of the 1971 Act to be inconclusive in themselves, but that they pointed to the notification rather than the resolution as constituting the grant of permission, because it would be unfair if time were to run against the applicant without knowledge or the means of knowledge of a decision where time is of the essence (such as for the submission of reserved matters for approval). The point was not taken further in either the Court of Appeal (which overturned the decision on other grounds) or the House of Lords, because the view was there taken that the authority had lacked the jurisdiction to determine the application at all once they had come to the opinion that it related to a "county matter."[99]

Despite the overruling of the first instance judgment, Sir Douglas Frank's analysis is one which is likely to be accepted for the future. To hold that it is the notification rather than the resolution which constitutes the grant of permission means that the applicant is not prejudiced subsequently by any delay on the part of the authority in issuing the notification, and it also accords with the position where arrangements have been made for the

---

[95] (1971) 70 L.G.R. 142.
[96] [1969] 2 Ch. 305 at 315.
[97] Although it had been carefully stressed by Megarry J. at first instance in the *Slough Estates* case: (1967) 19 P. & C.R. 326 at 339.
[98] (1978) 38 P. & C.R. 156.
[99] See further (1979) 39 P. & C.R. 223 (C.A.); (1980) 42 P. & C.R.1 (H.L.).

determination of applications by an officer. In that case, the grant of permission is simply the one-step process of issuing the notification.[1] This approach also allows the authority to resolve to grant permission in principle but to hold back the formal notification pending agreement or approval by the officers on some point of detail; and, if agreement has not been reached (or even if it has) to subsequently change their minds.[2] Such an arrangement is in essence an arrangement for the discharge of the function of granting permission by an officer of the authority, and that is an arrangement which may be rescinded or pre-empted by the authority or committee at any time before it is exercised by the officer.[3]

2.Notification of the Decision

Notification of the authority's decision must be accompanied by a statement of reasons, whether for refusing the application or for imposing conditions on a grant of permission.[4] Further, where the decision has been taken pursuant to a direction by the Secretary of State, the local highway authority or the county planning authority, or a view expressed by a government department, details of the direction or opinion must be given.[5] The Minister has urged authorities to make the statement full enough to give the applicant an adequate understanding of their reasons, and to offer something more than such vagaries as "the development would be detrimental to amenity" or "contrary to the development plan."[6] But practice varies substantially. Many authorities have lists of standard reasons (and standard conditions) which are often identified by number only in the officers' recommendations to committee, and which are issued automatically with the decision if the recommendations are followed by the committee, irrespective of the matters raised in the debate on the application.

A failure to give adequate, or indeed any reasons, does not make a refusal of permission void, nor render a condition unenforceable[7] ; although the duty to supply reasons is enforceable by mandamus.[8] Nor are the authority on appeal confined in argument to the reasons given for refusal or for the imposition of a condition appealed against.[9]

Where reasons are given the courts will normally accept them as giving a faithful indication of the factors taken into account by the authority, unless they are challenged for lack of bona fides or on the ground that there is no

---

[1] This was expressly provided in the delegation provisions of the 1968 Act (s.64(1)), but its successor, s.4 of the 1971 Act was repealed by the L.G.A. 1972 in favour of the broader provisions of s.101 of that Act.
[2] As in the *Yeovil* case (*supra*), where the authority had granted permission subject to evidence being provided as to arrangements for car parking; and were held to be entitled later to refuse permission altogether.
[3] See further *ante*, p. 256.
[4] G.D.O., art. 7(7)(a).
[5] *Ibid.*
[6] M.H.L.G. Circular 9/58, para.8.
[7] *Brayhead (Ascot) Ltd.* v. *Berkshire C.C.* [1964] 2 Q.B. 303.
[8] *Ibid.* at 313.
[9] See further *post*, p. 578.

evidence to support them.[10] But where no reasons are given, the court is entitled to ascertain them by extrinsic evidence, looking at all the circumstances surrounding the grant of permission.[11]

3. *The Scope of Planning Permission*

The grant of planning permission necessarily relates back to the application which triggered off the authority's decision making. Thus, although the contents of the application may be amended by the applicant at any time before the decision is made[12] (provided the result is not so substantially different as to amount to a fresh application), the authority are, as a general rule, without power unilaterally to achieve any major alteration by the permission itself.[13]

But the general rule is too inflexible, and there are some exceptions. First, the authority may grant less than the applicant has sought, by deleting part of the site shown in the submitted plan from the scope of the permission, for example, or by dealing separately with different divisible elements of the application.[14] Secondly, permission may extend to development beyond that sought by the application, where it is incidental or ancillary to that applied for. Such a power is clearly envisaged in the power to require approval of reserved matters on an outline application, whereby the authority may seek the carrying out of landscaping works and the making up of a means of access, although neither matter has been specified in the application. Further conditions may be imposed to ensure that ancillary works required by the authority are carried out, or at least that land is reserved for them[15]; and a condition imposed for this purpose of requiring works to be carried out is effective to grant planning permission for them.[16] But if the authority should wish to see non-ancillary works or development carried out as well, the correct course would be for a fresh application incorporating them to be submitted for determination.

---

[10] *R.K.T. Investments Ltd.* v. *Hackney L.B.C.* (1978) 36 P.& C.R. 442. In *Western Fish Products Ltd.* v. *Penwith D.C.* (1978) 38 P.& C.R 7 the Court of Appeal were prepared to look at the authority's resolution where the grounds for refusal of permission differed from those given in the notice of refusal, but they did so by concession of the parties.

[11] *Ibid*, at 445–46.

[12] *Britannia (Cheltenham) Ltd.* v. *S.O.S.E.* [1978] J.P.L. 554 at 556.

[13] See, *e.g. Richmond–upon–Thames L.B.C.* v. *S.O.S.E.* (1972) 224 E.G. 1555; *Glacier Metal Co.Ltd.* v. *Hillingdon L.B.C.* [1976] J.P.L. 165, *Kent C.C.* v. *S.O.S.E.* (1976) 33 P. & C.R. 70.

[14] See, *e.g. Kent C.C.* v. *S.O.S.E.* (1976) 33 P. & C.R. 70 (deletion of proposed means of access); *Dudley B.C.* v. *S.O.S.E.* [1981] J.P.L. 181 (part-permission granted on enforcement appeal by Secretary of State). In *Bernard Wheatcroft Ltd.* v. *S.O.S.E.* [1982] J.P.L. 37, Forbes J. rejected the "severability" test proposed in the *Kent* case in favour of a test based on whether the effect of the conditional permission would be to allow development which was in substance not that which was applied for. The main criteria in applying that formula should be whether the development would be so changed that to grant permission for it would be to deprive those who should have been consulted on it of an opportunity to make representations.

[15] *Britannia (Cheltenham) Ltd.* v. *S.O.S.E.* [1978] J.P.S. 554. reversed on different grounds by the Court of Appeal: [1979] J.P.L. 534.

[16] *R.* v. *Derbyshire C.C., ex parte North Derbyshire D.C.* (1979) 77 L.G.R. 389.

4. *Interpreting Planning Permissions*

The general rule in the interpretation of planning permissions is that regard may be had only to the permission itself, including the reasons given by the authority. Background information, such as correspondence between the applicant and the authority or representations made by third parties may be an invaluable aid to construction as indicating the purpose of any condition introduced by the authority, but the general rule precludes access to it on the ground that, as the permission runs with the land, purchasers must be able to rely on what appears on the face of the document. The process of interpretation of planning permission is not comparable to the interpretation of contracts; and the intention of the parties is not the true test in interpreting a document with third party implications.[17]

But there are exceptions. First, where the validity of a permission is being questioned, rather than simply its interpretation, the courts have shown no hesitation in going behind the permission itself and looking at all the background circumstances, so as to establish that the permission was not issued by mistake[18] or without any authority.[19] Second, it is common for the permission itself to incorporate by reference the application and the accompanying plan. A common formula is that "Permission is hereby granted for development in accordance with the plan and application submitted to the council, subject to the following conditions . . . ." In such a case the application and plan are used as a means of defining the scope of the permission, and may be relied upon in interpreting the permission itself.[20] But that formula does not extend to correspondence, officers' reports or other matters taken into account by the authority, although a letter from the applicant which explains the plan submitted by him and which is therefore "inextricably attached" to it may be thereby incorporated.[21]

5. *Implementation of permission*

(a) non-compliance with submitted plans

Awkward problems are liable to arise in practice where development has proceeded otherwise than in strict accordance with the details approved by the planning authority. The courts have permitted a degree of latitude, and have indicated that in order to permit developers to cope with unforeseen difficulties, permissions should be interpreted as covering the work included in the detailed plans together with any immaterial variations.[22] If the

---

[17] *R.* v. *S.O.S.E., ex parte Reinisch* (1971) 22 P. & C.R. 1022.

[18] *Norfolk C. C.* v. *S.O.S.E.* [1973] 3 All E.R. 673.

[19] *Co-operative Retail Services Ltd.* v. *Taff-Ely B.C.* (1978) 38 P. & C.R. 156; (1979) 39 P.& C.R. 223 (C.A.); (1980) 42 P.& C.R. 1.

[20] See, *e.g. Kent* v. *Guildford R.D.C.* (1959) 11 P.& C.R. 255; *Wilson* v. *West Sussex C.C.* [1963] 2 Q.B. 764 (although Willmer L.J. at 777 expressed misgivings at the "very unfortunate practice" of incorporating correspondence which might not be accessible to subsequent purchasers); *Slough Estates Ltd.* v. *Slough B.C. (No.2)* [1969] 2 Ch.305, and *cf. Ames (L.A.H.) Ltd.* v. *North Bedfordshire B.C.* [1980] J.P.L. 183 (planning condition not able to be construed by reference to a section 52 agreement so as to extend the life of the permission).

[21] *Edmunds* v. *Secretary of State for Wales* [1981] J.P.L. 52.

[22] *Lever Finance Ltd.* v. *Westminster (City) L.B.C.* [1971] 1 Q.B. 220.

authority wish to ensure closer compliance it will be open to them to impose a condition to that effect.[23]

Where an unauthorised material variation has been made, the authority are entitled to regard the whole of the development which has been carried out as unauthorised, and not simply the particular variation.[24] They have the power to take enforcement action against the whole development as a breach of planning control, although they may choose instead to under-enforce, and to concentrate instead on the unauthorised variation.[25]

Failure to carry out a development in accordance with the approved plans does not, however, involve that a permission has not been "implemented." The commencement of the development will in itself have normally been sufficient to keep the permission alive under the provisions governing the lapse of permission; and to rule that a permission had not been implemented by the applicant in carrying out materially different development would allow him to ignore the conditions imposed by it. Thus in *Kerrier District Council* v. *Secretary of State for the Environment*[26] permission had been granted for the erection of a bungalow, subject to a condition limiting occupation of it to agricultural employees. The design of the dwelling differed materially from that approved, but the four year period during which enforcement action could have been taken by the authority had expired. The purchasers of the dwelling then maintained that the occupancy condition was ineffective, because the permission had not been implemented. The Divisional Court rejected the argument, ruling that "implementation" was not a term of art in this context, and that having relied on the permission to build the house, the occupiers should be bound by the condition, particularly if it was their own fault that the permission had not been complied with.

(b) failure to complete the development

Failure to complete the development is a particular instance of failure to comply strictly with submitted plans. At one time it was thought that the different elements comprised in a permission might be readily divisible, and the document regarded as authorising each one individually.[27] But that view has had a rather cool reception subsequently. It is clearly inapplicable in the case of a single building operation, where, it has been pointed out it would mean that the "eccentric land developer could produce most extraordinary results . . . he could leave holes in the walls of his house; he could leave half the roof off; he could do all sorts of eccentric things of that kind."[28] Thus, as

---

[23] Thus: "The development hereby permitted shall not be carried out otherwise than in complete accordance with the approved plans and specifications" (M.H.L.G. Circular 5/68, Appendix).

[24] *Garland.* v. *M.H.L.G.* (1968) 20 P. & C.R. 98 (development exceeding limits of General Development Order held not authorised at all by the Order); *Copeland B.C.* v. *S.O.S.E.* (1976) 31 P.& C.R. 403.

[25] See further *post*, p. 412.

[26] [1981] J.P.L. 193.

[27] *Lucas (F.) & Sons Ltd.* v. *Dorking and Horley R.D.C.* (1964) 17 P. & C.R.111.

[28] *Copeland B.C.* v. *S.O.S.E.*(1976) 31 P. & C.R. 403 at 407, *per* Lord Widgery C.J. Although the *Lucas* case was not referred to in the judgment, it has been referred to as an "exceptional" case by Lord Widgery himself in *Pilkington* v. *S.O.S.E.* [1973] 1 W.L.R. 1527 at 1533; a view shared by the Court of Appeal in *Hoveringham Gravels Ltd.* v. *Chiltern D.C.* (1977) 35 P. & C.R. 295 at 302.

with unauthorised variation, an incomplete building may be regarded as not permitted at all by the permission. But the earlier view has still not been expressly overruled, and the question of severability of elements, (such as different buildings or facilities in a permission for an estate development) remains open. It is open to authority and developer to agree to piecemeal approval of detailed plans and hence to piecemeal or phased implementation. Conversely, the authority may wish to tie in provision of facilities, or ensure completion of all, or at least some part, of the development, by means of a condition prohibiting the occupation of the buildings before completion of the specified development.

There is no express power, however, to require a developer to complete a development. Enforcement is aimed at remedying any breach of planning control, and in the case of unauthorised incomplete development the authority's powers are limited to requiring the demolition and removal of whatever development has been undertaken. Even then there are difficulties. If work on the development has not actually stopped there can be no question of breach of control: it is the cessation of development, rather than the development itself, which is the breach.

There is a supplementary power, designed partially to overcome this difficulty, for an authority to serve a "completion notice" in respect of development which has been commenced within the time limits prescribed by the permission, but remains uncompleted.[29] Where the authority are of the opinion that the development will not be completed within a reasonable time, the procedure allows them to specify a time for completion (being not less than 12 months) following which the permission will be invalid except so far as it authorises any development already carried out. The notice has no effect until confirmed by the Secretary of State.[30]

The procedure is of very limited effectiveness. Its main usefulness is where only token steps have been taken to ensure the commencement of development before the prescribed date, but it offers little remedy in the common instances where the development is well under way but there are no funds available to complete it; or where the profitable parts of the development have been completed but not the remainder. Thus an authority may wish, in the case of large scale or particularly speculative development, to make further detailed provision for phasing and completion, through conditions or planning agreements.

(c) Conflicting permissions

There may be more than one permission in force over the same site at any time. A landowner, the Divisional Court have held, is entitled to make any number of applications, even though the proposed development may be quite different in each case; and the authority must deal with them separately, ignoring their mutual inconsistency.[31] The consequence is that the landowner will be able to select which permission to implement: but he

---

[29] T.C.P.A. 1971, s.44.
[30] Ibid. s.44(3)(b). Further, if the recipient of the notice so requires within 28 days of service, the Secretary of State is obliged to arrange for an inquiry before confirming the notice: s.44(4).
[31] Pilkington v. S.O.S.E. [1973] 1 W.L.R. 1527 at 1531.

will not be able to implement more than one where the two are incompatible.[32] Implementation may be physically impossible, or the permissions may be simply inconsistent: for example, two permissions each authorising the erection of a dwelling on a site, and each showing one acre of land to be occupied with the house, cannot be read together as authorising two houses on the same one acre site.[33]

6. Revocation or Modification of Planning Permission

Planning permission enures for the benefit of land. It may not be unilaterally revoked or withdrawn by the planning authority,[34] except in accordance with special procedures. And compensation is payable.[35] The power to revoke or modify is conferred in broad terms. If it appears to the authority, having regard to the development plan and to any other material considerations, that it is "expedient" to revoke or modify a permission, they may prepare an order to that effect for confirmation by the Secretary of State.[36] But the power is rarely used. The need to compensate is a strong inhibiting factor, and so is the accepted view that strong justification is required, because:

" . . . people ought to be able to count on public authorities standing by their decisions. The justification for a revocation order is either that the planning authority were seriously at fault in granting the permission, or else circumstances have changed radically since the permission was given."[37]

Authorities may be understandably reluctant to admit to serious error and to accept the financial consequences, but there have been instances where the Minister has been prepared to initiate the revocation of permissions acting under reserve powers, whilst leaving the burden of compensation with the local planning authority. That course has been proposed by the Secretary of State recently as a means of correcting district authorities who may be tempted to take advantage of the new county/district arrangements by

---

[32] *Pilkington* v. *S.O.S.E. (supra)* endorsed by the Court of Appeal in *Hoveringham Gravels Ltd.* v. *Chiltern D.C.* (1977) 35 P. & C.R. 295.

[33] *Ellis* v. *Worcestershire C.C.* (1961) 12 P. & C.R. 178 (L.T.), followed by the Divisional Court in the *Pilkington* decision.

[34] *R.* v. *S.O.S.E., ex parte Reinisch* (1971) 22 P. & C.R. 1022 at 1025.

[35] T.C.P.A. 1971, s.164: compensation may be payable for expenditure incurred in carrying out work rendered abortive, and for other loss or damage directly attributable to the revocation or modification.

[36] *Ibid.* s.45(1). The power may be exercised only up until the time any permitted operational development is completed (and may not in any event affect operations already carried out), or any change of use has been instituted: s.45(4). The Scottish Court of Session has ruled that the relevant time under the corresponding provisions of the Scottish legislation is the time the order is made by the local planning authority, and not the date of its confirmation: *Caledonian Terminal Investments Ltd.* v. *Edinburgh Corporation* 1970 S.C. 271.Where the s.45 procedure is no longer possible, the authority may still be able to act under s.51 (discontinuance orders).

[37] *Report of the M.H.L.G. 1955* (Cmd. 9876), p.62.

granting permissions which conflict substantially with the structure plan for their areas.[38]

Modification of minerals permissions is also proposed under the Town and Country Planning (Minerals) Act 1981, as a means of imposing requirements as to the restoration and aftercare of sites used for minerals workings. Compensation in these cases is to be governed by special provisions, which are designed to cast a proportion of the cost restoration and aftercare onto the extraction industry itself.[39]

Even where revocation or modification is unopposed, not only by the owner or occupier but by any person likely to be affected, there is a formal procedure to be followed; although the Secretary of State's confirmation may not be necessary.[40] An alternative course would be for an agreement to be concluded under section 52 of the 1971 Act, under which the owner would covenant not to carry out the permitted development or some part of it. Modification of a permission may also arise upon the grant of a further permission for the site, whether by broadening the original permission (by discharging or varying a condition, for example) or by restricting an existing use of the land.[41]

D. Civil Liability for Exercise of Development Control Functions

1. The Evolution of a Doctrine of Liability

The normal remedy available to a citizen aggrieved by an unlawful decision of a local authority is to seek to have it set aside. "Unlawful" in this context means "unauthorised," and a decision which is not authorised by the legislation conferring the function on the authority is invalid. It may be a decision relating to a matter over which the authority have no jurisdiction. Or it may be a decision on a matter where they have jurisdiction, but where in coming to the decision they have committed some error of law. The power of the courts to intervene is a supervisory power, and their review of decisions is indirect. They have no power to review the merits of the decision, unless such a power is conferred by statute in relation to any given function; and they are therefore limited to reviewing the manner in which a discretionary power has been exercised rather than its outcome. Provided the authority have exercised their discretion within the limits set by Parliament and the courts, they have discretion to decide either "rightly" or "wrongly"; and that is the essence of discretionary power.

The existence of this "public law" remedy does not, however, exempt local authorities from liability under principles of private law. They have power to enter into contracts, for example, and may be liable for breach. And in carrying on their operations they may be liable in negligence to persons to whom they owe a duty of care and who are harmed by their

---

[38] Two documented instances are the revocation of an outline permission granted for residential development in 20 acres by Bradford C.C. (*Report of M.H.L.G. 1958*, Cmnd. 737, p.91); and an outline permission granted by Bristol C.C. for hotel development in the Avon Gorge (V. Moore in [1971] *Public Law* 7).

[39] See further *post*, p. 496.

[40] T.C.P.A. 1971, s.46.

[41] See further *ante*, p. 174.

actions. A duty of care may arise, for example, from their ownership of premises or land, or from their activities as a supplier of services. Where the element of policy, or discretion, in relation to an activity is small or non-existent, there is no obvious reason for applying any different standard of care from that arising in the case of a private individual. To do so would be to confer a different remedy upon an injured plaintiff according to whether he had been struck by a local authority bus or a privately owned bus.

But as the element of policy in a function increases, the problem of determining the scope of a duty of care becomes more complex. Discretionary powers are conferred by statute upon public bodies and not upon individuals, and so the possibility of making an arbitrary distinction between identical acts does not arise. The question which does arise is the broader policy issue of the extent to which public bodies should be rendered liable in civil law for their execution of policy through discretionary powers.

For some years there was assumed to be a distinction between the carrying out by an authority of a statutory duty and the exercise of a statutory power. The former was capable of giving rise to liability in tort, and the latter not, unless the exercise of the power involved some positive act creating some fresh or additional damage.[42] But more recently the courts have accepted that liability should be determined according to broader principles. In *Anns* v. *London Borough of Merton*[43] the House of Lords finally set aside the old distinctions, and ruled that the fact that an act had been performed in the exercise of a statutory power did not exclude the possibility that it might be in breach of a common law duty of care.

This case raises the possibility, therefore, that civil liability may attach to the exercise of development control functions by local planning authorities and by the Secretary of State. But it falls a considerable way short of establishing any general entitlement, and the possible limitations to any such right of action need to be considered with care.

2. The Existence of a Duty of Care

The first question to ask is whether any duty of care is capable of arising in relation to development control. In *Anns* v. *London Borough of Merton* Lord Wilberforce proposed that the question should be approached in two stages.[44] First, it was necessary to ask whether, as between the alleged wrongdoer and the person who suffered damage there is a sufficient relationship of "proximity or neighbourhood" such that, in the reasonable contemplation of the former, carelessness on his part may be likely to cause damage to the latter. In that case, a prima facie duty of care exists. The second question, if the first is answered affirmatively, is whether there are

---

[42] A view based largely on the House of Lords decision in *East Suffolk Rivers Catchment Board* v. *Kent* [1941] A.C. 74.

[43] [1978] A.C. 728; the decision effectively affirms the Court of Appeal decision in *Dutton* v. *Bognor Regis United Building Co. Ltd.* [1972]. 1 Q.B. 373, although for different reasons.

[44] *Ibid.* p. 751. In formulating this approach to the question, Lord Wilberforce relied upon the evolvement of principle through the three landmark negligence cases, *Donoghue* v. *Stevenson* [1932] A.C. 562; *Hedley Byrne & Co. Ltd.. v. Heller and Partners Ltd.* [1964] A.C. 465 and *Home Office* v. *Dorset Yacht Co. Ltd.* [1970] A.C. 1004.

any considerations which ought to negative, or to reduce or limit the scope of the duty or the class of persons to whom it is owed or the damages to which a breach of it may give rise.

In that case the House of Lords found that a duty of care did exist in the exercise by an authority of their functions under the Public Health Act 1936 and byelaws made under the Act, of inspecting the foundations of new buildings to ensure that they complied with the requirements of the byelaws. The duty would arise if the council had not properly exercised their discretion as to whether to inspect, or having inspected had acted otherwise than in bona fide exercise of discretion under the Act and had failed to take reasonable care to ensure that the byelaws were complied with.

Exercise of development control functions, however, is not closely analogous to exercise of building control functions. The decision whether or not to grant permission is taken under very broad discretionary powers, and there is no continuing obligation to police compliance with approved plans except in relation to the equally broad discretion as to whether to take enforcement action. But there may well be occasions where carelessness in the exercise of the powers may cause damage, such as a notification of permission negligently issued where the authority have in fact resolved to refuse it. It is possible therefore that a duty of care may arise, at least to applicants and perhaps to third parties as well. And although the Privy Council in *Dunlop* v. *Woollahra Municipal Council*[45] felt "considerable doubt" whether the plaintiff there was owed a duty by the council to take reasonable care to ascertain whether a resolution passed by them would be within their statutory powers, they did not exclude the possibility that a duty of some description might arise in the exercise of the powers. As Lord Wilberforce stressed in the *Anns* case, the greater the element of discretion, the more difficult it will be to superimpose a duty of care. Conversely, the more "operational" the function, the easier it would be to establish a duty. This distinction implies that although a broad immunity may attach to decision making on a planning application, it will not extend to the more operational aspects of development control work, such as the notification of the authority's decision, or the making of a negligent misstatement by a planning officer as to the existence of a permission.

3. *Limits to the Duty of Care*

Assuming that a duty of care may be *ex facie* capable of arising in connection with the exercise of development control functions, the second question which arises under Lord Wilberforce's formulation is whether any limitation ought to be imposed to reduce the scope of the duty, the persons to whom it is owed or the damages payable. The most significant limitation arises from the inter-relationship between questions of validity under public law principles of the action taken and questions of civil liability. The reason is that, if a decision is taken within the discretion of the authority and is valid, it is taken within the ambit of a statutory authorisation. The courts have

---

[45] [1981] 1 All E.R. 1202 and see *Lyons* v. *F. W. Booth (Contractors) Ltd.* (1982) 262 E.G. 981, where the High Court (on the basis of a concession by counsel and without detailed analysis) held the nature and scope of the duty under the 1971 Act to be similar to that under the Building Regulations.

proved unwilling to find that an exercise of power authorised by Parliament may nonetheless be actionable at common law, and it is clear therefore that any duty of care which may arise under the *Anns* doctrine is limited to cases where the action or decision is outside the scope of the discretion conferred on the authority. Lord Wilberforce in the *Anns* case stated:

> " . . . there may be room, once one is outside the area of legitimate discretion or policy, for a duty of care at common law. It is irrelevant to the existence of this duty of care whether what is created by the statute is a duty or a power: the duty of care may exist in either case. The difference between the two lies in this, that, in the case of a power, liability cannot exist unless the act complained of lies outside the ambit of the power."[46]

It is a pre-condition, therefore, to civil liability, that the act complained of should have been invalid.[47] There remains the question of liability in the case of decisions or other action which is protected from challenge under public law principles by reason of the preclusive clauses contained in the 1971 Act. Unless challenge is made within a prescribed period from the time the action is taken, usually six weeks, its validity may not be questioned in any proceedings whatsoever.[48] It remains to be seen whether the courts would baulk at permitting action to proceed under a common law duty of care when the validity of the decision itself was protected in so broad a manner; or whether they might take the alternative course of moulding a remedy for those unable to challenge the decision itself, where the grounds of the action have only come to light after the limited period for challenge under the Act has expired. The court might still investigate the question of whether the decision was within the legitimate area of the statutory discretion for the purpose of the common law action, without questioning its validity; and such a remedy would doubtless overcome much of the potential injustice caused by the preclusive clauses.[49]

4. Breach of the Duty

Although a duty of care arises only where the action complained of falls outside the ambit of power of the authority, it does not follow that because a decision is *ultra vires* the duty is thereby automatically breached. It is still necessary to show that the authority acted negligently in taking the decision, and invalidity in itself is not conclusive evidence of negligence. In *Dunlop* v.

---

[46] [1978] A.C. 728; and *cf. Home Office* v. *Dorset Yacht Club* (*op. cit.*) at 1031, Lord Reid and at 1068, *per* Lord Diplock.

[47] See further *Welbridge Holdings Ltd.* v. *Metropolitan Corporation of Greater Winnipeg* (1970) 22 D.L.R. (3d) 470, where Laskin C.J. maintained that " . . . the risk of loss from the exercise of legislative or adjudicative authority is a general public risk and not one for which compensation can be supported on the basis of a private duty of care"; and *Tokaro Properties Ltd.* v. *Rowling* [1978] 2 N.Z.L.R. 314, where the New Zealand Supreme Court were prepared to accept as "arguable" that a duty of care might arise between a Minister and a company directly affected by his invalid exercise of power, but that negligence would need to be established.

[48] See further *post*, p. 642.

[49] As in *R.* v. *Secretary of State for the Environment, ex parte Ostler* [1977] Q.B.122, where the Court of Appeal chose the course indicated by administrative convenience and construed the six week limit as absolute, notwithstanding that the alleged vitiating defect had not come to the knowledge of the applicant until some time later. See further *post*, p. 643.

Woollahra Municipal Council[50] the plaintiff had succeeded in an earlier action in having set aside two resolutions passed by the council imposing planning restrictions on his land. One was a building line restriction; and the other, a height restriction prohibiting any building exceeding three storeys . He then sought damages in respect of the interest and charges incurred by him in holding the land over the period between the passing of the resolutions and the making of a fresh application for permission following the quashing by the court of the resolutions. The grounds upon which the resolutions had been quashed were that, in the case of the building line, prior notice had not been given to the plaintiff of the council's intention to pass the resolution; and, in the case of the height restriction, that it was outside the powers conferred by the relevant planning ordinance. The judge in that action had rejected the plaintiff's claim that the council had not acted bona fide in passing the resolutions.

The Privy Council upheld the trial judge's finding that there had been no negligence on the part of the council. They had taken advice from their solicitors before passing the resolutions, and the issues at the first trial had been evenly balanced. To have answered it in the way their solicitors had at any time before that judgment was given could not amount to negligence.

But on the question whether there was negligence in the council's failure to afford the plaintiff a hearing before exercising a power affecting him or his property, their Lordships also maintained that there was no negligence because the person complaining of the failure was in as good a position as the authority to know that the exercise of the power was void, and that he could ignore the resolution.[51] As a reason for negativing the possibility of negligence, that ground must be treated with some caution. It means, in effect, that the more careless the conduct of the authority, the more likely they may be to avoid liability, because the plaintiff is the more likely to be able to disregard their decision. It imposes upon him the risk of so doing. And it is not a ground which extends to protect the council against action by third parties, such as a successor in title, who may have no knowledge of the defect in the decision until it subsequently comes to light. Nor does it extend to any defect not known to the plaintiff. A decision may be set aside at the suit of a third party, for example, causing financial loss to the plaintiff, at the least over the period between the time of the decision of the planning authority and the making of the challenge. Or a third party may have lost the right of challenge under the preclusive clauses. Where the planning authority's decision is one which has had the effect of conferring a benefit on the plaintiff, such as a planning permission, different considerations may apply from those where, as in the *Dunlop* case, the effect of the decision is to impose a restriction upon him.

The doctrine of liability for the negligent exercise of statutory powers is one which is still evolving, and the course of its future development is impossible to predict. But at least the prospect is that an authority may be liable, although it will be an exceptional case where liability can be established in development control.

---

[50] [1981] 1 All E.R. 1202.
[51] *Ibid.* at 1209–1210.

5. *The Beaudesert Principle*

An alternative approach to liability for the unauthorised exercise of statutory powers, outside any requirement of negligence, was suggested by the ruling of the Australian High Court in 1965 in *Beaudesert Shire Council* v. *Smith*[52] that:

> " . . . independently of trespass, negligence or nuisance but by an action for damages upon the case, a person who suffers harm or loss as the inevitable consequence of the unlawful, intentional and positive acts of another is entitled to recover damages from that other."

On the face of it, the doctrine therein enunciated affords a basis for challenging unauthorised official action, which, for want of statutory authority, may be categorised as "unlawful." But the doctrine itself has been doubted, and it has not been applied in any subsequent case. The Australian and New Zealand[53] courts, and the Privy Council in *Dunlop* v. *Woollahra Municipal Council*,[54] have instead interpreted "unlawful" as meaning "forbidden by law," rather than merely "unauthorised," and have thus rejected the argument that an invalid act or decision by a statutory authority may in itself give rise to a cause of action for damages.

6. *Malicious Exercise of Power*

Malice, or bad faith, in the exercise of power is an abuse of power capable of giving rise to civil liability.[55] But it is an allegation which it is notoriously difficult to prove; and the mere making of a decision without malice and without knowledge of its invalidity is not an abuse of power capable of sustaining action under this head.[56]

---

[52] (1966) 120 C.L.R. 145 (Aust. H.Ct.).
[53] See, *e.g. Kitano* v. *The Commonwealth* (1973) 129 C.L.R. 151; *Tokaro Properties Ltd. Rowling* [1978] 2 N.Z.L.R. 314.
[54] [1981] 1 All E.R. 1202.
[55] See, *e.g. Roncarelli* v. *Duplessis* (1959) 16 D.L.R.(2d) 689; and for a detailed study, see J. McBride, "Damages as a Remedy for Unlawful Administrative Action" (1979) 38 C.L.J. 323.
[56] *Dunlop* v. *Woollahra Municipal Council* [1981] 1 All E.R. 1202 at 1210.

CHAPTER 7

DISCRETION, POLICIES AND STANDARDS IN DEVELOPMENT
CONTROL

A. The Discretionary Basis of Control

1. *The Statutory Discretion*

Development control is a regulatory administrative function, and its basis is
discretion. Local planning authorities have a choice whether or not to grant
planning permission, and the power to name the terms on which they will
grant it. It is a process of political choice undertaken by accountable public
bodies, and their breadth of discretion is expressly preserved by the Act of
1971. The key section is section 29(1), which establishes the legal basis for
decision making in development control:

" . . . where an application is made to a local planning authority for
planning permission, that authority, in dealing with the application,
shall have regard to the provisions of the development plan, so far as
material to the application, and to any other material considerations,
and—

(a) . . . may grant planning permission, either unconditionally or
subject to such conditions as they think fit; or
(b) may refuse planning permission."

Decisions, then, are to be guided (but not dictated) by the provisions of the
development plan, and by "any other material considerations." And, so
guided, authorities may impose "such conditions as they think fit."

It is, on the face of it, one of the least fettered discretions in the whole
British administrative system, especially bearing in mind the potential
distributional effects of planning decisions. It is worth recalling that the
machinery was designed originally in the financial context of the 1947 Act,
which sought to eliminate development values in land and thereby remove
financial pressure from planning authorities. Whether so broad a discretion
would have otherwise been conferred, or would be today if the system were
being designed afresh, is a matter for some conjecture.

But the section cannot be viewed in a vacuum, and, placed in its true legal
and political context, the discretionary power can be seen to be governed by
a variety of interacting constraints. These include, first, the various statutory
restraints, such as the county/district relationship, the developer's right of
appeal to the Secretary of State, and his power to call in applications for
determination. Then there is the supervision exercised by the courts, to
whom falls the task of setting the practical boundaries to the statutory
concept of "material" considerations, and who have insisted in accordance
with familiar administrative law doctrine that "any other material considerations" means *all* material considerations, and the exclusion of all irrelevant
considerations. Further, planning conditions may not be distributed as
freely as the section suggests, at the whim of the authority, but only in
pursuit of legitimate "planning" objectives. Decision making by local

planning authorities is admittedly more insulated from judicial review than that by the Secretary of State,[1] and authorities and developers for reasons of their own often accept arrangements which would undoubtedly be struck down were they challenged in the courts; but the principles of judicial review are still of general application.

Finally, there are the constraints of the internal structure and the political framework of local government, as reinforced by the consultation and notification requirements of the Act. Decision making is designed as an open, accountable process in which due regard is given to each application in the light of representations made by the public and other agencies consulted, to the advice of the authority's professional staff and to the adopted policies and objectives of the authority. The statutory discretion is thus an invitation to make a reasonable political choice between competing alternatives, none of which may be obviously categorisable as "right" or "wrong" by any objective criteria.

It is, as was shown in the preceding chapter, an imperfect system. Authorities may act on the basis of inadequate information and hidden prejudice, and their assessment of the long-term and short-term advantages and disadvantages of a proposed development can often be no more than purely speculative.

The way in which development control is structured can be seen as subjecting it to three main influences or ideologies by which the choices available in decision making are moulded.[2] There is first the political influence of the elected members, influenced not only by their party allegiance, if any, but also by their personal knowledge of the area and its inhabitants, and by pressure from individuals, interest groups and the Press. Then there is the professional ideology of the planning staff, with a preference for technical, "rational" solutions and for placing long-term objectives above short-term pragmatic responses. Finally, the legal structure of the control processes brings its own ideological assumptions, with pressures for adherence to more judicialised models of decision making, and for remaining distanced from the market, treating competing developers even-handedly and applying policies in rule-like fashion to secure consistency and visible fairness.

There are substantial areas of overlap between the three, but areas of conflict as well and an interaction which clearly moulds the nature of decisions taken. In the view of one writer, it is this split ideology which above all else is to blame for the malaise of the British planning system; and that "the problems stem largely from unrealities and incompatibilities in the way the system itself is constructed."[3] It has been "stretched to breaking point over the years in trying to embrace diverse and mutually contradictory

---

[1] See further post, Chap. 14.
[2] Comparatively little research has been carried out into the influences and pressure exerted upon the control process in practice, but some helpful description and analysis may be found in: J.B.McLoughlin, Control and Urban Planning (Faber, 1973), Chaps. 5–7; D.E. Regan, "The Pathology of British Land Use Planning" in Local Government Studies, April 1978, p.3; M.L. Harrison, "Development Control: The Influence of Political, Legal and Ideological Factors," in Town Planning Review, (1972), Vol.43 No. 3, p.254, and "Social Policy and Normative Theories of Town Planning" in Urban Law and Policy (1978), Vol.1, p.77.
[3] Regan, op cit., p.3.

elements."[4] But the argument is overstated and unconvincing, and in the final analysis goes to the proportions rather than the components of the ideological mix. It is less the split ideology than the relative strength of planning professionalism against the other two which he criticises, and that strength has, in the evolution of recent years, generally been on the decline. It has been overtaken by the emergence of a more vigorous political contest in planning, with conflict not only between the ideologies of the main party groups, but also between the different styles of democracy represented by the elective and participative models.

2. The Role of the Development Plan

The legal relationship between forward planning and development control is loose. The provisions of the development plan are a consideration which must be taken into account "so far as material" to the application. But there may be "other material considerations" affecting the application such as to persuade an authority that the plan should not prevail. On the face of section 29, a development plan is not a necessary precondition of decision making at all.[5]

This broad discretion is however qualified by the appeals provisions and by the special procedure for departure applications, and it is the way the departures procedure has evolved since 1947 which has been the main influence on the degree of plan compliance in practice. The clear ministerial intention at the outset of comprehensive development control was that authorities should be held closely to their approved plans, and that was the practice:

" . . . it was all simple, short, definable and greatly to the point; it didn't wander out and about, over and across imponderable fields touching all manner of indefinable things. Basically the planning decision was motivated by the fact that the development was (or was not) development in an area marked on the development plan for the sort of development which it was proposed to carry out. When this was the case then *prima facie* the answer was to grant the application to develop."[6]

The plan departure rules were originally drawn tightly, but in 1954 some tentative steps were taken to relax them, and more have followed. The Minister was firm in his advice to authorities that it would be a "cardinal mistake" if as a result of the relaxation they showed "any tendency to minimise the importance of the Plan in favour of short-term considerations."[7]

But three further factors have since combined to reduce the

---

[4] *Ibid* p.18.
[5] Thus in the hiatus years of control before development plans had been approved, authorities exercised the same statutory discretion, except that they were required instead to have regard to any ministerial directions as to the provisions to be included in their plan, and to their own proposed provisions for "securing the proper planning" of the area: T.C.P.A. 1947, s.36.
[6] Sir Desmond Heap, *The Land and the Development* (Stevens 1975), pp.42–43
[7] M.H.L.G. Circular 45/54, para.6.

dominance of the statutory plan in development control. First, the early plans were slow to materialise, and with their inaccurate population projections were quickly out of date. Formal revision proved equally slow and cumbersome, and as the initial land allocations came to be used up, many authorities had no choice but to use development control as the primary land release mechanism. The process is not fully documented, but it has been estimated by the Department of the Environment that probably over one-half the green field housing development in London took place on land not formally allocated in the Initial Development Plan.[8]

Second, there was a growing realisation of the limitations to the purely physical land use planning assumptions that underlay the old plans, and authorities sought to cast their nets more widely in control so as to encompass a broader social and economic perspective. Finally, the courts proved reluctant to undertake detailed supervision of plan compliance. They dismissed unhesitatingly the ministerial interpretation of the Act—that authorities were able to depart from their plans only in accordance with the departure rules—and reasserted instead the broad scope of section 29. The plain meaning of the section was that "the planning authority are to consider all the material considerations, of which the development plan is one."[9]

Despite the comparative freedom now available to authorities, the development plan necessarily remains a highly persuasive factor in control.[10] It would be arbitrary conduct for an authority to reject provisions agreed upon following full public participation unless the reasons were quite compelling, but the pressures for plan compliance are more political than legal. For this reason it is becoming an increasingly common problem for there to be policy change following change in political control of authorities without any reformulation of the statutory plan. A political group may, for example, have fought the election on an anti–growth pledge, directly opposed to a statutory plan recently adopted by the authority. The statutory discretion allows them substantial room thereafter for manoeuvre in frustrating implementation of the policy. The developer may appeal to the Secretary of State against an arbitrary refusal of permission and seek an order for costs against the authority,[11] and these procedures secure some continuity in policy. But it remains true that a statutory plan offers no

---

[8] *Eleventh Report from the Expenditure Committee* Session 1977–78, para.16.

[9] *Simpson* v. *Edinburgh Corporation* 1960 S.C. 313, at *per* Lord Guest; *Enfield L.B.C.* v. *S.O.S.E.* (1974) 233 E.G. 53 and *Niarchos (London) Ltd.* v. *S.O.S.E.* (1977) 35 P. & C.R. 259, and *cf. Evans* v. *London C.C.* (1960) 12 P. & C.R. 172 (Cty.Ct.) where an action seeking damages for an alleged failure to have regard to the plan's provisions was dismissed.

[10] It is impossible to draw any general picture of the influence overall of development plans in practice, but research done by J.B. McLoughlin found that the case-workers interviewed held the plan to be the most important factor in making a recommendation, followed by "local policies, the site and its surroundings, 'experience and common sense,' and personal judgment and philosophy":*Control and Urban Planning* Faber, 1973, pp.99–100. But a study of the first batch of local plans, conducted by the Building Research Establishment, has found that a high proportion of subsequent development control applications (ranging from 24 to 65 per cent.) were not covered by any specific policy in the plan (Kingsbury, *Local Plans: increasing their usefulness for development control* B.R.E. 1982) and concluded that the fault lay with the plans in not anticipating common control problems. Between 2 and 17 per cent. of decisions taken on the applications were in "apparent contradiction" with the plan.

[11] Departure from clear policy without adequate justification may be a ground for the award of costs on appeal against an authority under M.H.L.G. Circular 73/65: see further *post*, p. 600.

long–term guarantee of commitment, especially if its policies are politically controversial.

It is in the areas of policy-making and policy change that the effects of the loose relationship between statutory plan and control are most marked. The relationship is continuous, not static. It is not a two-stage system of policy formulation through plans, followed by implementation through development control, but more a continuing interaction. The policies contained in an emerging local plan, even in its early stages, must be taken into account in development control to avoid the taking of decisions which may frustrate the plan altogether. Equally, an application which accords with the draft plan may nonetheless be objectionable if to grant it would undermine objections to the plan, or if the proposed development is dependent upon approval of the strategy of the plan as a whole. It is a common and legitimate objection that an application may prejudice a draft plan or be premature in relation to the policy making process.

The question is one of balance rather than law, however, and the courts have declined to intervene even in cases where the exercise by an authority of their development control power or other statutory functions clearly prejudges the issue still at large in the preparation of statutory planning policy. There are two related arguments, both based upon section 29. First, if the provisions of an approved plan are no more than a consideration in development control, then *a fortiori* the provisions of a draft plan and the submissions of objectors to it can carry no greater weight. Second, if in the absence of a draft plan there could be no legal objection to pursuing the policies concerned as "other material considerations," their inclusion in a draft plan should not place any disability on the authority.

There has thus emerged a doctrine of clear separation of power between forward planning and development control, illustrated most dramatically by *R. v. City of London Corporation, ex parte Allan*.[12] The authority there had prepared a draft plan which contained a proposal for the construction of a road which would bisect an area of the City, and which had attracted a number of objections. Before the holding of an inquiry into objections to the plan, the Corporation received a planning application for the redevelopment of the area, which included an offer from the developers to construct the road at no cost to the Corporation. They proposed to grant permission notwithstanding the awaited plan inquiry, and the court declined to issue an order of prohibition preventing them. They had taken the draft plan and the objections into account, and their decision was not so unreasonable that no reasonable planning authority could have taken it.

An attempt to qualify this doctrine failed in a later case, *Davies v. London Borough of Hammersmith*[13] where the applicants sought an injunction to prevent the demolition by the authority of certain property belonging to them whose fate was under consideration in the draft plan. The Court of Appeal rejected the submission that only in cases of "real, urgent necessity"

---

[12] (1980) 79 L.G.R. 223 (*sub nom Allan* v. *Corporation of the City of London* [1981] J.P.L. 685).

[13] [1981] J.P.L. 682; and *cf. Attorney-General, ex rel. Rivers Moore* v. *Portsmouth C.C.* (1978) 76 L.G.R. 643 (demolition of properties in clearance area prior to approval of compulsory purchase order in respect of other properties in the area).

should an authority override an objection, and insisted that provided the objections were considered by the authority, it did not follow that their decision was perverse or unreasonable simply if it went against the objections.

It would be a different matter, of course, if it could be shown that an authority were motivated by the desire to pre-empt objections to a plan, but identifying the true motivation in local authority decision making is seldom easy. What the members and officers may in fact have taken into account is not always confined to what the records may indicate to have been before them. The present law thus maintains a functional independence between local authority powers which reasserts the breadth of section 29, but it is at the expense of the statutory right of objection at the stage of policy formulation through statutory plans. There is a serious risk of pragmatic pursuit of short-term objectives by authorities, particularly at the instance of developers able to offer attractive planning gains, and if the value of the forward planning system is not to be undermined there is a need for a more positive use of the Secretary of State's powers to call in decisions or to direct the refusal of permission pending approval of the plan.

Freedom to depart from a plan does not necessarily confer sole interpretative power on the authority concerned. Only by interpreting the plan correctly can an authority be said to have had regard to it, and interpretation thus becomes a question of law upon which decisions may be reviewed.[14]

3. Other Material Considerations

In addition to the development plan, authorities are to have regard to "any other material considerations." "Material" means "relevant to the application," and the only considerations which are relevant are planning considerations: permissions are not (at least in legal theory), to be granted or refused according to a toss of a coin, the colour of an applicant's hair or the size of any financial inducement offered to members of the planning committee. But beyond such extravagantly extraneous considerations, the definition of materiality is difficult to draw. The more widely it is defined, the broader are the powers exercisable by planning authorities in development control. Planning legislation has never offered any precise guidelines, and ideas as to what might be proper planning considerations have been left to be formulated by the minister and local planning authorities within their discretions, subject to overall supervision by the courts.

The early view of the Act was that the discretion was comparatively narrow; and that the phrase covered simply "considerations of amenity and aesthetics and all the details of a sound code of planning standards."[15]

---

[14] *Niarchos (London) Ltd.* v. *S.O.S.E.* (1977) 35 P. & C.R. 259 at 264–65; *Moldene Ltd* v. *S.O.S.E.* [1979] J.P.L. 176; and *Bell and Colvill Ltd.* v. *S.O.S.E.* [1980] J.P.L. 52. If the Secretary of State proposes to override his Inspector's interpretation of plan policies, there may be fresh questions of fact requiring the matter to be referred back to the parties: *Pyrford Properties Ltd.* v. *S.O.S.E.* (1977) 36 P. & C.R. 28.

[15] William Wood, *Planning and the Law* (1949), p.66: these would be matters, he argued, for which "the more detailed operative scheme of the 1932 Act system made provision under such heads as space about buildings, number of buildings in the area, size, height, design and external appearance of buildings."

Certainly there is clear agreement today as to the materiality of a core of basic factors, building upon that "amenity and aesthetics" basis. Thus an application may be for development in accordance with statutory plan allocations, but be rejected justifiably because of the physical unsuitability of the site, or the noise or smell likely to come from the development. Or objection may be made to the proposed design or landscaping, the likely effect upon the neighbourhood, public safety, or traffic flows. In some cases the objections can be overcome by a few amendments to the application, or by conditions imposed upon the permission. In other cases they may prove to be an insurmountable obstacle to development of the proposed type, or at the proposed time—or even to any development at all on the particular site.[16] A dissatisfied developer may appeal. But provided the policy issues taken into account by the local planning authority or the Secretary of State are "material" and adequate the courts will not intervene.[17]

There has been strong pressure, however, to extend the concept of material considerations beyond aesthetic and amenity considerations; and beyond purely physical, land use planning ideas. The argument is that it is artificial and distortive to separate land use planning from the whole range of human activity that it affects, and particularly other government efforts in the areas of housing, social and public services and economic policy.[18] This approach reflects also the movement away from the early concept of planning as a rational, technocratic exercise based upon technical end-state plans, to the concept of the nineteen-sixties and since of planning as a continuing process of urban management, more flexible and politically responsive. It is an approach which rejects the physical determinism of early planning theory, and places it in a broader context of government. It brings in the problems of the reallocative function of planning, of employment and the local economy, of housing conditions and racial and social integration. These are issues which today clearly relate to the policy making side of planning, but the question of how far they may influence site-by-site development control decisions is more problematical.

In legal terms the starting point in analysis of section 29 is the very broad interpretation offered by Cooke J. in *Stringer* v. *Minister of Housing and Local Government*,[19] that:

"In principle, it seems to me that any consideration which relates to the use and development of land is capable of being a planning consideration. Whether a particular consideration falling within that broad class is material in any given case will depend on the circumstances."

The test offers support for a broad view of "material considerations," and hence of the planning power itself. It is a reasonable guess that it draws the

---

[16] Although where the land has become incapable of reasonably beneficial use in its existing state, the owner may have rights under T.C.P.A. 1971, s.180 to require its purchase by the local authority; see further *post*, p. 653.

[17] "This is planning policy and nothing else. The courts have no authority to interfere with the way the Minister carries it out": *Lord Luke of Pavenham* v. *M.H.L.G.* [1968] 1 Q.B. 172 at 192 *per* Lord Denning M.R.

[18] There has been no detailed central government guidance on the formula, but *Development Control Policy Note No.1* (1969), paras. 13–17 offers a general discussion.

[19] [1971] 1 All E.R. 65 at 77.

boundaries very much more broadly than might have been the case had the courts been called upon to offer a definitive test in the early years of planning legislation. But it places the emphasis upon the individual circumstance of each application, and there is little that has yet emerged in the way of overall guidelines. There can therefore be no exhaustive list of material considerations; and nor is it desirable that there should be. There is no discernible need to confine authorities too closely in making political choices between competing pressures and values, and legal constraints are liable to prove highly artificial. To categorise issues too rigidly as being material or immaterial is to introduce meaningless formality into decision making. There are five main areas where the courts have been asked to strike a balance, however, which indicate significant trends in judicial thinking on the issue and are considered further below. Numerous other instances where disputes have arisen in practice are considered within the broader study of development control policy contained in the next section of this chapter.

(a) The public interest/private right dimension

Planning is a public activity. The legislation deliberately subjects the traditional freedoms of landowners, to develop their own land as they wished, to controls based upon public interest. The courts were not initially prepared to interpret the Act as conferring any new rights upon individual members of the public. The provisions, they maintained, "have been passed to give rights to the public only, and not to any particular class of the public."[20]

But the sharp divide between public and private interest in planning has become more blurred, and judicial support can now be found for the argument that the "public interest" is not an immutable and separate ideal, but the sum of a variety of private interests. There is thus no objection in principle to using planning powers to protect private interests, even to an extent going well beyond normal common law protection. In the *Stringer* case, for example, the court upheld the planning authority's policy of restraining development within an area of several square miles of Jodrell Bank telescope, so as to minimise interference to it. And in *R.M.C. Management Services Ltd.* v. *Secretary of State for the Environment*[21] the same reasoning was employed in upholding the rejection of an application for permission to construct a ready-mixed concrete plant on a site close to four high-precision engineering plants, which all required specially clean air. There was a public planning ground for the decision, in that the proposed use was incompatible with the existing uses of adjoining land, and the fact that the existing plants thereby gained a benefit from the decision was irrelevant.

The effect of such a line of reasoning is of considerable economic significance, because it can mean that the true costs of carrying on and protecting a particularly sensitive use of land, are not borne by the individual user alone but imposed upon adjoining owners. To achieve through the

---

[20] *Gregory* v. *Camden L.B.C.* [1966] 2 All E.R. 196 at 202, *per* Paull J.; and *cf. Buxton* v. *M.H.L.G.* [1961] 1 Q.B. 278 at 283, *per* Salmon J.; though there is now a less rigid approach, see *post*, p. 619.

[21] (1972) 222 E.G. 1593.

market the protection conferred by planning control would involve sensitive users in the expense of acquiring title to, or covenants over, the surrounding land, so as to create a "cordon sanitaire." The use of planning control subjects the land to similar restrictions, but imposes the costs upon the present owners.

Similar consequences, though on a smaller scale, follow in the case of householder development with the protection which planning controls confer against existing owners losing their view, light or privacy from new development or extensions on adjoining land. The broad issue is still the environmental quality of the neighbourhood overall, but it tends to be assessed in terms of impact upon individual sites.

(b) "Exclusive code" restrictions

A further restriction which the courts have been urged to impose has been to divorce planning from other areas of government activity carried on by different local authority or government departments, and through different statutory powers. It is essentially a different path towards confining planning to an amenities-based role. And this too has been largely unsuccessful: the courts have taken the view that whatever other specific legislation may exist, the planning Acts are of more general, overall applicability.[22] Thus the Court of Appeal has declined, for example, to draw lines of demarcation between "site" considerations under caravan legislation, and "planning" considerations under planning legislation. Lord Denning M.R. argued that there were inevitable overlaps between the two: that issues relating to sewage disposal, educational facilities and traffic considerations, for example, raised implications under each head.[23] And more recently the Court of Appeal in *Clyde & Co.* v. *Secretary of State for the Environment*[23a] has upheld housing need as a material consideration, in connection with an application to change from residential to office use, notwithstanding that it was a need for public sector housing and that the use of Housing Act powers might be needed to bring the premises into use for housing purposes.

But although the courts have declined to prescribe precise compartments, their decisions do not support the proposition that every housing, educational or public health consideration is necessarily also a planning consideration. It might still be a misuse of the planning power, for example, to attempt to pursue objectives related purely to educational policy through planning decisions, such as to refuse permission for a school solely on the ground that it proposed to adopt a particular educational method or a discriminatory form of student selection. Similarly, it would not be a lawful

---

[22] An early contrary dictum was expressed in the Court of Appeal by Pearce L.J. in *Fawcett Properties Ltd.* v. *Buckinghamshire C.C.* [1959] Ch. 543 at 578; when he suggested that a planning authority would be acting beyond their powers if they were to take into account housing, public health or social considerations other than town planning; but the authority cited, *Pilling* v. *Abergele U.D.C* [1950] 1 K.B. 636 dealt with the distinguishable converse: the taking into account of amenity considerations in exercising powers under the Public Health Act 1936.

[23] *Esdell Caravan Parks Ltd.* v. *Hemel Hempstead R.D.C.* [1966] 1 Q.B. 895; and compare similar rejections of the exclusive code arguments in *Maurice* v. *London C.C.* [1964] 2 Q.B. 362 and *Allnatt (London Properties) Ltd.* v. *Middlesex C.C.* (1964) 15 P. & C.R. 288.

[23a] [1977] 1 W.L.R. 926.

planning decision to reject an application for a betting-shop or a casino purely on moral grounds, though the question of the environmental impact of the development on the area could be taken into account under both Betting and Gaming legislation and planning legislation.[24] The risk is that any substantial overlap may become counter-productive, and that conflicting requirements may be imposed by the different agencies involved. Planning control is often not the best machinery for regulating the post-development use of land, and an authority may properly choose not to attempt to regulate through planning matters which can be better controlled and monitored under other powers whether by itself or by another body.[25]

A particular variant of the "exclusive code" argument has arisen where the use of the planning power to control development has deprived the applicant of compensation which would have been payable if another statutory power had been used. Permission may have been refused, for example, because the site was needed eventually for development or redevelopment by a public authority, to preserve an ancient monument[26] or for a highways widening or improvement scheme. The House of Lords[27] has upheld this practice of site reservation through the planning power, and has even gone so far as to hold that it would not be an excess of power for authorities to use the power of refusal under section 29 in preference to other powers, purely from a desire to save public money.[28] Certainly there is no requirement that authorities should choose to use only the code which would permit a claim to be made for compensation.

(c) Political considerations

The materiality of "political" considerations in development control has been the subject of confused debate for some time. Political influence is sometimes assumed to be absent from development control decision making, as witness the evidence given on behalf of the Department of the Environment to the House of Commons Expenditure Committee in 1976:

"I think I should say at the outset that we have no evidence that planning decisions are sometimes taken for political reasons. But this is not surprising because if such evidence existed, the decisions would be

---

[24] Cf. *Development Control Policy Note No.1*, para.13; and *Ladbroke (Rentals) Ltd.* v. *S.O.S.E.* [1981] J.P.L.427.

[25] Provided they have correctly understood the scope of other powers: see, *e.g. Harwich Harbour Conservancy Board* v. *S.O.S.E.* [1974] J.P.L. 724. A particular example of overlap is that between planning and pollution controls, as to which see *post*, Chap. 10.

[26] *Hoveringham Gravels Ltd.* v. *S.O.S.E.* [1975] Q.B. 754, where the Court of Appeal held the protection of an ancient monument to be a "material consideration" and a proper use of s.29, notwithstanding the further powers under other legislation.

[27] *Westminster Bank Ltd.* v. *M.H.L.G.* [1971] A.C.508. The Secretary of State appears to have interpreted the decision narrowly, however, and has declined to allow authorities to reduce their own compensation costs by refusing permission for land which they wish to acquire themselves for the same development: [1974] J.P.L. 167.

[28] *Ibid.* at 530, *per* Lord Reid (in whose opinion the majority concurred). Indeed, the Minister of Transport and Civil Aviation had in 1954 requested authorities no longer to use the statutory powers but to rely instead on planning control; and refused any longer to contribute to compensation payments: Circular Letter No.696, (1954). An authority may render themselves liable to blight notice or purchase notice procedure, however (see further *post*, Chap. 15, and some prefer to operate entirely non-statutory road widening schemes as a basis for bargaining with developers.

open to challenge in the Courts. This is because it is settled law that a local planning authority must base their decision on relevant planning considerations only."[29]

It is a surprising statement, not only because it is contrary to the general understanding of how local authorities are presently operating, but also because of the assumptions it makes as to the availability of judicial remedies. As to the first point, the statement of Lord Gisborough during the Committee stage of the Town and Country Planning (Minerals) Bill in 1981 is more realistic:

"Planning decisions should be taken for planning reasons, but all who have been in local government know that there are occasions when planning decisions are taken for blatantly political reasons. This can happen on either side: I am not blaming one party or the other."[30]

If it is not an uncommon practice, and if political considerations are "pre-eminently extraneous"[31] in the exercise of discretionary power, then why has it not then been challenged in the courts? There are doubtless many obvious practical reasons, including the difficulties of proving such an allegation and of obtaining *locus standi* (in the case of objectors to an application) or persuading the court that no better alternative remedy exists by way of administrative appeal (in the case of an aggrieved applicant for permission).[32]

But there is also the theoretical problem of defining the "proper" role of politics in planning. Planning is, after all, a political process vested in accountable agencies and requiring choices to be made between competing alternative values. It is not a process purely of rational choice following technically objective assessment, but one in which the touchstone of rationality is often little more than public opinion and political accountability. It is clearly not a "pre-eminently extraneous" consideration for a local planning authority to be influenced by public opposition in their area, either to a general policy or a particular development. The legislation specifically requires public representations to be taken into account in a range of cases, and elected members must remain aware that unpopular decisions carry the prospect of unpopularity at the ballot-box at the next local election. Local elections may be won or lost on planning issues, particularly over the contest between urban growth and conservation policies.

The broad political context in which local planning authorities operate is thus a fact of life, and "political considerations" in this more general sense underly much of the policy making and decisions of most authorities. Similarly, a Secretary of State who seeks to fulfil a manifesto pledge of revitalising the housing market by bringing more land forward for development, may be actuated by political considerations in his ideological

---

[29] Supplementary Memorandum by the Department of the Environment (N.P.108) *Planning Procedures,* Vol.III, p.752
[30] Hansard, H.L. Debs., Vol.417, col.491 (February 16, 1981)
[31] *R. v. Board of Education* [1910] 2 K.B. 165 at 181, *per* Farwell L.J.; *Padfield* v. *Minister of Agriculture, Fisheries and Food* [1968] A.C. 997 at 1058, *per* Lord Upjohn.
[32] See generally *post*, Chap.14.

attachment to the private market, yet still be within the powers of planning legislation.

When objection is taken to politics in planning, therefore, it is objection more to the effects of party political organisation and irrelevant ideological adherence than to ideas of broader democratic accountability. It is also an objection to applying in individual cases the criteria which might legitimately guide policy making at a more general level. These objections call for closer scrutiny.

(i) Party political organisation

The party politicisation of local authorities has spread substantially since local government reorganisation in 1974. Many more authorities now have an identifiable ruling group, who typically will meet privately in caucus at regular intervals to formulate policy and organise business. The danger for local democracy is the ease with which caucus organisation can be used to pre-empt discussion and genuine consideration of issues at council meetings. Group members may be subject to formal or informal pressures to follow the agreed party line on an issue. The Labour Party's Model Standing Orders for labour groups on local authorities, for example, provides for the withdrawal of the Group whip from members who violate the provisions, and forbids the submission or moving of resolutions by individual members without prior Group approval, or speaking or voting in opposition to Group decisions.[33]

Caucus organisation in general has given rise to serious concern, particularly in view of the undermining of the democratic structure that may ensue. The Royal Commission on Standards of Conduct in Public Life[34] observed in 1976 that:

> "In our view, it is natural that a majority party should consider issues of major policy in its own caucus meetings. It is essential in the public interest, however, that policy questions are adequately debated at meetings of the local authority itself, where decisions can be democratically made. Furthermore, most of a local authority's business is of an executive nature and does not involve major policy. . . . We have reason to believe that in too many local authorities, decisions are taken in the majority party caucus on matters that are not of a politically controversial nature."

Caucus organisation may be a convenient forum for discussing issues of major policy, such as levels of overall expenditure or general growth strategy for an area, but in matters involving the exercise of an administrative discretion, such as in determining planning applications, it may effectively pre-empt the decision. Resorting to the majority party whip in development control would be to fetter the discretion of the authority, and there are no doubt occasions when group pressures short of formal whipping may have

---

[33] *The Labour Party: Model Standing Orders for Labour Groups on Local Authorities* (reproduced in M. Minogue, *Documents on Contemporary British Government* (C.U.P., 1977, Vol.II, p.157)

[34] Cmnd.6524, para.245.

the same effect. The danger is particularly apparent in cases involving development by the authority themselves where there may already have been caucus discussion and strong party commitment to a project well before the making of the detailed application.

(ii) *Irrelevant political considerations*

Planning may be a process of political choice, but it does not follow that all political considerations are necessarily relevant to it. Some must be regarded as pre-eminently extraneous, including considerations of personal political advantage, political horsetrading between parties and the desire to avoid political embarrassment.[35] Others are no doubt relevant at a policy making level but not at an executive level because they are not directly planning considerations. Thus the majority group in an authority may have strong views on the redistribution of wealth, on the organisation of the health services, on social mix and so on, which may inform their corporate objectives for the authority and influence their planning strategy. But ideological commitment is not in itself planning policy, and its direct influence in development control may lead either to extraneous considerations being brought to bear on planning issues, or to a fettering of discretion.

But given the nature of political interaction, it is often a question of degree rather than of principle. A planning committee who reject an application for the construction of a private hospital solely because they are opposed to any undermining of the national health service have no doubt wrongly closed their eyes to the planning implications. But if the site is one where they would normally not allow development to occur except where the applicant could show special need for the development, it would be more difficult to categorise as unlawful the fact that they might require a higher level of proof than an authority whose members were sympathetic to private medicine.

Finally, there is the category of considerations which are doubtless land-use related but politically determined. The majority group may have come to power on a pledge to restrain further office development or further urban encroachment into their rural area, to promote development as a means of stimulating the local economy or to promote more vigorous conservation policies. Provided there is no fetter on discretion—such as an outright ban on office development, for example—these are no doubt perfectly legitimate planning considerations to be taken into account in development control.

The categorisations drawn above are necessarily simplistic because of the subjectivity of the issues. An anti-office policy, for example, may be based equally firmly upon an anti-speculative ideology as upon a conservationist stance. And the real influences on decision making can seldom be so clearly identified and categorised. Finally, the political context of local authority decision making is dampened by the supervisory and politically ambiguous role of the Secretary of State. A decision on political considerations may still need to be justified on technical grounds on appeal, and the status of the

---

[35] It was specifically this type of consideration which Lord Upjohn in *Padfield* v. *Minister of Agriculture, Fisheries and Food*, *ante*, thought to be extraneous.

consideration will also be important. It may be fully worked out as a policy on the way to being incorporated in a formal plan; or it may be no more than a momentary whim.

(d) Planning and the market

It has sometimes been urged that planning authorities should operate in an economic vacuum. The basis for the argument is the assumption that only by preserving a position of adjudicative remoteness from the market can the integrity of planning principles be made to prevail over market dictates. Stated so broadly, the proposition is clearly unrealistic. There is a complex, two-way relationship between market forces and planning regulation, and authorities who ignore or misunderstand market pressures may find that development fails to take place following the grant of permission, or that it proceeds in a different way than envisaged by them. The implementation of plans is dependent upon an intelligent understanding of market response, and in an era when many authorities are anxious to promote development, particularly employment generating development, planning and market have in practice come closer together. Whether financial and economic questions may be "material considerations" in development control has exercised the courts on several recent occasions,[36] but their analysis has proved disappointingly artificial, largely because the question has been framed so widely. It is possible, in fact, to isolate four main issues.

(i) the developers' resources

It has often been asserted that authorities should have no regard to the expense or the financing of the particular development. The view is based upon the argument that the choice of whether to implement a planning permission or not is a matter entirely for the developer, and the risks are his to bear. Thus, it is said, planners have no "paternalistic or avuncular jurisdiction" to protect developers from their follies or restrain the eccentric millionaire who chooses to pursue an unusually expensive project.[37]

To convert this sensible dictum into a universal rule, however, is to overstate the case. The authority cannot always close their eyes to the issue of cost because of the danger, not simply that the development will not be built at all (in which case the outstanding permission can be taken care of through the provisions dealing with time-expired permissions provided no works have commenced) but that it will be only half built before financial difficulties force a stop. Or it may be completed, but remain unoccupied, unlettable perhaps at a rent necessary to cover costs. There is a strong case for arguing that to accept the resources and intentions of the prospective developer as relevant considerations in instances where such dangers clearly exist is a necessary safeguard. But except in the most absurd cases, financial

---

[36] The authorities are reviewed in M. Purdue, "The Economics of Development" [1979] J.P.L. 146 and M. Loughlin, "Planning Control and the Property Market" (1980) 3 *Urban Law and Policy* 1.

[37] *J. Murphy and Sons Ltd.* v. *S.O.S.E.* (1973) 1 W.L.R. 560 at 565, *per* Ackner J., though later qualified by him in *Hambledon and Chiddingfold Parish Councils* v. *S.O.S.E.* [1976] J.P.L. 502 to the extent that he "may have stated the general proposition, which I still think is correct, too widely"; *Walters* v. *Secretary of State for Wales* [1979] J.P.L. 170.

assessment at permission stage may well be arbitrary. The property market has proved particularly volatile over the past 20 years, and profitability prediction in marginal cases is liable to be hazardous. And it is difficult, except in the case of personal permissions, to see how the specific resources of individual developers should be a relevant issue when the land, and with it the benefit of any permission granted, may be resold at any time—at a price reflecting the value of the permission.

Equally problematical is the converse case, which is that of the developer who seeks the relaxation of normal planning requirements so as to render his proposed development economically viable. The issue is clearly a material consideration to an authority anxious to ensure that development will actually take place. It is often a consideration implicit in any event in adopted planning policies, such as those requiring the retention of an existing use or the provision of some amenity "wherever reasonable."[38] The choice between demolishing or rehabilitating a listed building is a specific example of a case where financial considerations require to be weighed in with planning considerations.[39] It may not be the business of the authority to guarantee the developer's profit by setting their planning standards at a level to match his resources, but it is implicit in their function that they should have regard to the prospect of the permission actually being implemented.

The relationship between planning controls and development viability is neither simple nor direct, however. A substantial component in the cost of any development is the price of the land, which is influenced by the potential of the site for development and thus by the planning system itself. This means that to a large extent planning requirements can be taken into account in land purchase and the costs spread back to the vendor as a reduction in the development value otherwise accruing to him. In an ideal market there would be a steady supply of land for the development permitted by the authority, at a price which would allow developers to meet the requisite standards, and no questions of economic viability need arise in development control. But neither market nor planning system conform to the ideal, and planning standards are increasingly frequently regarded as matters for negotiation between developer and authority, in a financial context.

(ii) *the authority's resources*

The financial resources of the planning authority and of other public agencies are clearly capable of being a material consideration where a

---

[38] See, *e.g.Niarchos (London) Ltd* v. *S.O.S.E.* (1977) 35 P. & C.R. 259, where the relevant initial development plan provision stating " . . . the Council will not permit any further extension of temporary planning permissions for commercial or office purposes in respect of any property which is reasonably capable of adaptation or conversion for residential purposes" was held to require an examination of the costs of such adaptation or conversion. A somewhat broader principle was, however, drawn from the decision by Sir Douglas Frank in *Brighton B.C.* v. *S.O.S.E.* [1979] J.P.L. 173. As to "deemed" materiality generally, see *post*, p. 294.

[39] See *e.g. Kent Messenger Ltd.* v. *S.O.S.E.* [1976] J.P.L. 372, *Richmond–Upon–Thames L.B.C.* v. *S.O.S.E.* [1979] J.P.L. 175; and *cf. Eckersley* v. *S.O.S.E.* (1977) 76 L.G.R. 245 (comparison between costs of redevelopment and rehabilitation in compulsory acquisition procedure under Housing Act 1957); *Sovmots Investments Ltd.* v. *S.O.S.E.* [1977] Q.B. 411 (high unit costs of housing a relevant factor in Housing Act compulsory purchase).

planning decision is likely to affect them. The fact that a refusal of permission may lead to the service of a purchase notice, or to a claim for Eighth Schedule compensation, is a matter which has long influenced planning decisions, and the Act even makes express provision for decisions to be reviewed where a compensation claim has been lodged.[40] The influence of the compensation threat is perhaps most marked in the case of buildings that have been destroyed, and where there will be pressure on the authority to permit rebuilding notwithstanding planning objections because of the cost of refusing permission.

Another relevant financial factor is the cost of providing services to a new development. One of the objectives of containing urban expansion is to make more efficient use of publicly funded infrastructure, and the costs to the authority themselves or to the other relevant agencies of accommodating a new development may be a factor in opposing a development, or at least in postponing it as "premature" until the necessary works can be funded.[41]

(iii) protection and competition

A quite different aspect of the economics of development is the question of the impact of a new development on established trading markets. We may accept that it would be a misuse of the planning power specifically to promote or prevent competition between individual traders.[42] But at a more generalised level the question does assume significance. The competition created by a new retailing outlet may be quite substantial in planning terms. A new out-of-town superstore, for example, may draw trade away from existing town centres, causing shop closures, general economic deterioration and a loss of services to town centre dwellers who lack the necessary mobility to take advantage of the new competition.[43] Empty and derelict premises may result from an over-supply of development, leading to pressures on the authority for permission for more profitable users.

The issue of competition and the existing state of supply of a commodity or service often arises in the context of restraint policies which require the developer to make out a case for the grant of permission, in terms of demand. It is thus not a direct regulation of competition, but the policy may have that indirect effect at least within the restraint area. Similarly, an authority may wish to act to prevent or promote the development of a concentration of specific traders, or to prevent the loss of further retail space in a town centre to banks, building societies and estate agents. Their efforts no doubt serve to sustain the position of existing traders, but the primary objective is to achieve a desired mix.

(iv) planning gain

"Planning gain" is an imprecise expression which has emerged in planning practice in recent years. In its most general sense it encompasses the process

---

[40] T.C.P.A. 1971, ss. 38 and 39; and see further post, p. 652.
[41] See further, post, p. 377.
[42] See, e.g. D.O.E. Circular 96/77 and accompanying Policy Note (No.13), Large New Stores, para.2
[43] See e.g. J.Sainsbury Ltd. v. S.O.S.E. [1978] J.P.L. 378; and cf. D.O.E. Circular 71/76, Large New Stores particularly decision No.9.

of balancing the likely beneficial and detrimental effects of a proposed development. Hence, although a proposed use may not be in accordance with general policy and may not be the best possible for the site, it may nonetheless be a substantial improvement upon the present use, and to be encouraged for the planning gain that might result. Thus an authority may be anxious to promote residential development in an area, yet be prepared to accept a non-residential use on a particular site if it was likely to be the only effective means of terminating the site's existing offensive use. Or they might be prepared to balance a planning "loss" on a site (from residential to office use) against a planning "gain" through conversion of the applicant's existing premises elsewhere in the district from offices to residential. These are legitimate planning considerations; provided, perhaps, that the planning power is used to persuade rather than coerce.[44]

But a more specific and more controversial approach to planning gain has flowed from this. Authorities have sought specific benefits from developers: the provision of residential accommodation in a commercial development, for example, or the building of community facilities such as a swimming pool or public hall. Although characterised as a "planning" gain, the true effect is often that of a financial gain to the local authority who are thereby relieved of the cost of providing the facilities themselves. Hence assessment of "gain" frequently involves authorities in general financial considerations, because the greater the likely profitability of the scheme, the greater the ability of the developer to adapt his proposals to achieve planning gains. For the most part the bartering which lies behind such arrangements is done secretly and informally[45] and the requirements are expressed, not as conditions upon a permission (for there will often be doubts as to their legitimacy),[46] but in contractual arrangements between authority and developer.[47]

There is a narrow line between requiring developers to improve their development proposals before granting permission, and the open pursuit of a community share in development profitability under the guise of "other material considerations." In the extreme case the pursuit of gain, or the acceptance of an offer of gain from a developer as an inducement to grant permission, must amount to an irrelevant or improper consideration, for it attaches an unauthorised purchase price to the grant of planning permission.[48] Where the inducement or gain has no planning significance, it follows that it may not be a "material consideration." But where the trade-off is couched specifically in planning terms it is more difficult to condemn it on these grounds, no matter how speculative or indirect the assumed gain may be.

---

[44] See e.g. R.T.K. Investments Ltd. v. Hackney L.B.C. [1979] J.P.L. 234; (1978) 35 P. & C.R. 442 at 446–7.

[45] J. Jowell, "Bargaining in Development Control" [1977] J.P.L. 414.

[46] See further post pp. 334–351.

[47] See further, post, pp. 360–374.

[48] Thus, "the Secretary of State wishes to make it clear that in his view the conferring of financial benefits on the local planning authority (or the avoidance of financial disadvantage to them) cannot be a material consideration in dealing with a planning application"; m.p.d. [1975] J.P.L. 424 at 426.

The case of *Brighton Borough Council* v. *Secretary of State for the Environment*[49] provides an example of how narrow the distinction may be. A school sought permission to develop an unused area of one of their playing-fields as a housing estate. The proposal was contrary to the development plan and rejected on amenity grounds by the authority. On appeal the decision to grant permission was influenced by the desire of the school to realise sufficient profit from the sale of the site to allow them to refurbish the main school buildings, which were Grade 2 listed buildings situated in a conservation area. The court held that this was a planning benefit, rather than a financial benefit, which the Secretary of State was entitled to take into account. Nor, apparently, did it matter that there had been no firm costings, and no guarantee or undertaking that the money would be used in this way. It was sufficient that there was:

> "the possibility that, by granting planning permission, there would thereby result a planning benefit in the maintenance and refurbishment of an important listed building."[50]

Presumably, then, the issue would have been different had the school proposed instead to use the money for purely educational purposes, such as to establish a scholarship scheme or to hold fees down. But the relationship between the housing development and the refurbishment was tenuous at best, and a subsequent change of mind on the part of the school could not have been challenged by the planning authority.

The practice of planning gain may offer a pragmatic means of overcoming seemingly intractable planning problems, but it is clearly capable of abuse both by developers and planning authorities. In extreme forms, it involves the sacrifice of good planning to financial benefit, and of long–term objectives to ad hoc gains. But it has become widespread nevertheless, particularly in areas of high development pressure, and finding a means of restraining it has now become an issue of high priority. That planning gain, whether direct or resulting indirectly from financial gain, is capable of amounting to a "material consideration" is an issue of principle which is now unlikely to be disturbed; but the mechanisms through which it is usually secured, including planning agreements, may well be open to review.

(e) "Deemed" materiality

Although the concept of "material considerations" remains imprecise, there are sometimes factors by which a politically accountable authority might wish to be influenced which are clearly outside the scope of planning, and many more whose materiality is doubtful. But the provisions of the development plan are always matters to which authorities—including the Secretary of State—must have regard, and thus, to the extent that they may be material to any given application, are considerations which must be taken into account. Moreover, unless their validity has been challenged successfully in an action commenced within six weeks of the approval or adoption of the statutory plan, they achieve a status of deemed validity.[51] Some

---

[49] (1978) 39 P. & C.R. 46
[50] *Ibid.* at 51, *per* Sir Douglas Frank Q.C.
[51] T.C.P.A., ss.242 and 244; although in *Webb* v. *M.H.L.G.* [1965] 2 All E.R. 193 the Court of Appeal (Lord Denning dissenting) were prepared to permit indirect questioning of the validity of a Coast Protection Scheme, notwithstanding a comparable privative provision.

authorities have already taken advantage of the greater freedom offered them by the new local plans system to incorporate policies whose legitimacy might otherwise have been questionable, such as policies insisting upon the payment of infrastructure contributions as a prerequisite to the grant of permission or incorporating broadly defined criteria of social need.

Legitimacy may also be bestowed less directly, by inference from the statutory plan. Thus, as was discussed in the preceding section, a plan requiring that regard should be had to "reasonable" alternative uses may necessarily require comparisons based upon otherwise irrelevant issues of financial viability.[52]

There is little doubt that even in extreme cases the approved development plan policies must stand as a matter of law and be taken into account in development control, even although challenge to their validity might have succeeded if commenced in time. It would be open, however, to the Secretary of State on appeal to depart from the approved policy; and if necessary to exercise his call-in powers over local plans to exclude such policies before approval or to require amendment to be made to a plan already adopted.

B. Policy in Development Control

1. *The Policy Context*

Development control is carried out in a broad policy context. It is neither a process of ad hoc response to planning applications, nor simply of mechanical application of development plan rules. The discretionary basis of control is a deliberate attempt to align decisions with objectives, and the machinery which links the two is policy. "Policy" is a conveniently flexible concept which is capable of encompassing not only that which an authority may have formally adopted and labelled as "policy," whether in a statutory plan or otherwise, but also the less tangible factors like ideologies, past commitments, rules of thumb, future aspirations, pressures for consistency and political accountability which set the operational context of governmental work. This is "policy" or "public policy," of which specific policy statements are only one manifestation. Policy making is more an evolutionary than a revolutionary process, and often not even a process of conscious change. And policy considerations, even when adapted into specific policies, often overlap and conflict. The balancing of competing planning policies and the weight to be attached to each is a matter for judgement, and a matter not of law but of government.

Section 29 has therefore been interpreted widely to allow broad scope to planning authorities, particularly in looking to policy considerations outside their development plans, but there are three important limitations. First, as discussed above, the "policy" consideration must qualify as a "material" consideration; second, in the case at least of specific development plan policies, the authority must interpret the policies properly; and third, resort to policy must not be permitted to fetter discretion.

The third rule is in a sense a restatement of section 29, because the

---

[52] *Niarchos (London) Ltd.* v. *S.O S.E.* (1977) 35. P. & C.R. 259; and *post*, p. 291.

requirement to have regard to "any other material considerations" is at once a prohibition against rigid adherence to development plan policy. Even in cases where the development plan itself categorically provides for a certain decision to be taken without exceptions, section 29 requires that it be assessed still against other considerations. But it is also a more general rule of administrative law, that an authority exercising a statutory discretion are entitled to formulate and apply policy to guide the discretion, but not to bind it.[53] The rule offers a guarantee against the mechanical rubber-stamping of decisions, but it is a procedural rather than a substantive safeguard.

The issues arose in the *Stringer* case, because of the undertaking given by the planning authority to Manchester University that they would "discourage development within the limits of their powers" in the area of the Jodrell Bank telescope.[54] This, in the opinion of the Court, had led to their regard to other considerations being purely perfunctory and thus not within section 29. Since the agreement had been signed it had been their practice not to override Jodrell Bank objections. It had not, however, fettered the Minister's discretion because he had not failed to weigh the appellant's submissions against the policy; or, at least, he had not dismissed those submissions out of hand.[55]

2. Sources of Policy

Discretionary decision making is a fluid process, and the various factors which influence the weight which may be attached to any one policy are largely intangible and unquantifiable. A particular policy may be favoured because it is recently formulated, or has been adhered to firmly in the past, or attracts a high degree of political commitment. There is, however, a mix of types of policy and sources of policy in common use, and the status of any policy depends to some extent both on the way it is designed and upon its source. Two main models are discussed in the final two sections of this chapter: the so-called "presumptive" policies which operate by setting rules and casting the burden upon the authority or the developer to show that the rule should not apply; and the quantitative standards, adopted by authorities as a guide to regulating development in a comparatively precise way.

But also relevant is the source of policy. The policy context is set not only by the development plan but also by central government, through local authority non-statutory means and through input from other public agencies.

(a) Secretary of State's policy

The Secretary of State for the Environment's duty "to secure consistency

---

[53] See generally, *R.* v. *Port of London Authority, ex parte Kynoch Ltd.* [1919] 1 K.B. 176; *R.* v. *Flintshire C.C. County Licensing (Stage Plays) Committee, ex part Barrett* (1957) 1 Q.B. 350.
[54] [1971] 1 All E.R. 65; and *cf. Lavender* v. *M.H.L.G.* [1970] 1 W.L.R. 1231.
[55] *Cf. Rugby School Governors* v. *S.O.S.E.* (1974) 234 E.G. 371 where strict adherence to an administrative policy, (not to consider any application in advance of a master plan having been drawn up for the whole estate by the applicants) was held not to have fettered the minister's discretion, since it had been agreed originally with the applicants, and the Inspector having considered all the facts thought the application should not be treated exceptionally.

and continuity"[56] in land use policy gives legal backing to the injection of ministerial policy into development control. The policy filters through to local authorities in two main ways. First, it is a central element in regional planning, and is reflected in approved structure plans and carried through into local plans. Secondly, there is often a high policy content in government circulars, and in planning appeal decisions, which is carried through into development control.

In 1969 an attempt was made to systematise central government policy in development control through the publication of a series of *Development Control Policy Notes*.[57] Although the *Notes* were accompanied by a warning that "they should not be interpreted as set formulae for settling planning applications and appeals without regard to the circumstances of individual cases or to any special expression of policy for particular areas contained in the development plan,"[58] the specific terms in which many of the policies are cast makes it difficult for them to be overriden. For example, as part of their policy governing development in the open countryside the *Notes* stress that "new houses will not normally be permitted unless there is a special need in the particular case," and that "inside the green belts as defined in the development plans, permission will not be given, except in very special circumstances, for the construction of new buildings or for the change of use of existing buildings for purposes other than agriculture, recreation or other uses appropriate to a rural area."[59]

The result is that there exists a national presumption against non-agricultural development in the countryside, and it is a presumption upon which authorities may lawfully rely until a case rebutting the presumption has been established.[60] Except so far as they build upon policies already incorporated into the development plan, the *Notes* are not site specific, nor even regionally differentiating.[61] There have been additions to the series since 1969, but the *Notes* are not comprehensive and statements of government policy are by no means confined to them: government policies on planning issues are still announced through statements on regional strategies and reviews, circulars, appeal decisions, white papers, statements in the House and other common forms of government communication.

---

[56] Minister of Town and Country Planning Act 1944, s.1.

[57] The original *Notes* were issued under cover of M.H.L.G. Circular 23/69, and they deal respectively with: (1) general principles, (2) development in residential areas, (3) industrial and commercial development, (4) development in rural areas, (5) development in town centres, (6) road safety and traffic requirements, (7) preservation of historic buildings and areas, (8) caravan sites, (9) petrol filling stations and motels, (10) design. Subsequent *Notes* have been issued in respect of (11) amusement centres (1969), (12) hotels and motels (1972), (13) large new stores (1972, revised in 1977), (14) warehouses (1975) and (15) hostels and homes (1975).

[58] M.H.L.G. Circular 23/69, para.2.

[59] D.C.P.N. 4, paras.3 and 4.

[60] *Vale Estates (Acton) Ltd.*v. *S.O.S.E.* (1970) 69 L.G.R. 543; and *cf. Shepperton Builders Ltd.* v. *S.O.S.E.* [1979] J.P.L. 102.

[61] In Scotland a different approach has been adopted by the Scottish Office, with the publication of a series of national planning guidelines which include general policies and also broad land use allocations on the basis of a diagrammatic map. Authorities are informed that the "proper use" of areas noted on the map "is regarded as a matter of national importance, and this implies a general presumption in favour of the [land-use] characteristic indicated": *S.D.D. National Planning Guidelines*, para.3.

Ministerial policy is not legally binding upon local planning authorities. It is simply a "material consideration." Nor is its application a matter for the courts, provided those charged with decision making remain within the prescribed legal parameters. But it does not follow that central government is therefore powerless to impose policy change upon local planning authorities; or that the courts play no role in its review.

This is strikingly demonstrated by the attempt by central government in the early 1970s to persuade local authorities to release more land for residential development. The strategy involved a centrally directed reversal of development plan policies in relation to "white" land; that is, land unallocated in the plans, and in respect of which no major change of use had been anticipated during the plan period. Through a series of circulars[62] the Secretary of State made it clear that "white" land within growth areas (as defined by strategic plans prepared by the Government) was thereafter to carry a strong general presumption in favour of housing. And in those parts of an area which were clear candidates for inclusion in specific growth area plans, the presumption was to be overridden only if there were "exceptionally compelling planning objections" to the development.[63] Even outside growth areas "white" land was to be regarded as suitable for housing, providing its development represented a natural and compatible extension of existing development.[64] Finally, there was a call for release of limited areas of metropolitan green belt land where ready availability of services meant that development could start quickly, the areas to be identified through local authority co–operation.[65]

The detailed criteria and presumptions remained in force until 1980, and provided a detailed set of ground rules for handling residential applications. Authorities who were reluctant to release land found that it would often be released instead by the Secretary of State on appeal.[66] And in the case of release of green belt land the courts were to decline to restrict the Secretary of State's power, rejecting the argument that the terms of the White Paper bound him, as a matter of natural justice, to consult with local authorities through the South East Standing Conference in preparing a programme of land release.[67] But the precision with which the policies were defined has meant that they have dictated the terms upon which appeals have been fought, and the battle of the circulars has thus inevitably spilled over into the courts. It was held that there would be, or might lead to, an error of law, for example, for an Inspector to apply the wrong presumption[68]; or to fail to tie

---

[62] Principally D.O.E. Circular 122/73, which had been preceded by D.O.E. Circulars 10/70 and 102/72, each pressing for release of more residential land.
[63] D.O.E. Circular 122/73, Annex A, para.4.
[64] *Ibid* para. 5.
[65] *Widening the Choice: the Next Steps in Housing,* Cmnd. 5280, paras. 13–16 (1973). The Government requested the Standing Conference on London and South East Regional Planning, with the authorities concerned, to identify the most suitable areas. Releases of green belt land were to be matched by improvements and extensions elsewhere.
[66] Thus by January 1975, of the 2,000 acres sought by the Government, only 950 had been identified by authorities but a further 740 acres had been released on appeal, against the wishes of the authorities concerned: *Hansard,* H.C. Deb., Vol.885, cols. 346–47 (January 31, 1975).
[67] *Enfield L.B.C.* v. *S.O.S.E.* (1974) 233 E.G. 53.
[68] *George Wimpey & Co. Ltd.* v. *S.O.S.E.* (1979) 250 E.G. 242, although on the facts no error of law was found to have occurred.

his report in adequately with the presumptions[69]; or for the Secretary of State to attempt to alter the emphasis of the presumptions when differing from his Inspector,[70] or to fail to give any reason for rejecting the strong presumption of the circulars when differing from his Inspector.[71]

The cases demonstrate how closely local authorities, and even the Secretary of State, may be bound by precise central government policy statements; and how little room there may be, as a matter of law, for manoeuvre, short of casting aside the policy altogether. But they also illustrate the ability of central government to disturb local policy by superimposing national objectives, reinforced through the appeals system.

(b) policy of other government departments

There is a clear relationship between land use policy and the policies of many government departments. In certain matters affecting highways and agriculture, there are formal requirements for consultation imposed upon the authority handling the application[72]; and an outstanding objection by another department to an application is often a ground for it to be "called-in." But the relevant policy of any government department may still be a material consideration even although not formally fed into the decision making process. Even on appeal, the Secretary of State is entitled to take into account the views of another Government Department without allowing the parties an opportunity to comment upon them.[73] And the particular strength of government policy is further preserved by provisions which allow witnesses to be called to explain government policy at an inquiry, but prohibit cross-examination directed to any discussion of its merits.[74] But an important limitation upon too close a degree of governmental integration is that such policy necessarily remains simply a "material consideration": where it is relied upon without consideration of the merits of individual applications, the authority or the Secretary of State may be held to have fettered their discretion, or even to have unlawfully delegated their function to the other department.[75]

(c) local authority non-statutory policies

There has been a vacuum created by the failure of the statutory development plans system to adapt readily to rapid change. Many authorities have attempted to fill the gap by preparing non-statutory plans, which may be prepared with a view to submission for ministerial approval at the time of the next formal plan review—or possibly with no intention at all of securing statutory approval. Non-statutory plans have in the past proved

---

[69] *Link Homes Ltd* v. *S.O.S.E.* [1977] J.P.L. 310: as a matter of construction the Inspector's decision could be tied in adequately with the presumptions.
[70] *French Kier Developments Ltd.* v. *S.O.S.E.* [1977]1 All E.R. 296.
[71] *French Kier Developments Ltd.* v. *S.O.S.E. and Surrey Heath D.C.* [1977] J.P.L. 311; but *cf.* *Hope* v. *S.O.S.E.* [1979] J.P.L. 104 where Inspector's conclusions based on para. 5 of Annex A to D.O.E. Circular 122/73 were upheld by the court.
[72] General Development Order 1977, arts.11, 15.
[73] *Kent C.C.* v. *S.O.S.E.* (1976) 33 P. & C.R. 70.
[74] Inquiries Procedure Rules 1974,R. 8.
[75] *Lavender (H) and Son Ltd.* v. *M.H.L.G.* [1970] 3 All E.R. 871.

a useful method of informal policy co-ordination and updating, and their provisions may be taken into account as "other material considerations" in development control. The practice developed largely at the instance of central government, and the background has been described earlier in this book.[76]

So far as the courts are concerned, non-statutory planning has proved unexceptionable. They have expressed no misgivings in instances where the Minister has been guided, for example, by outline development plan proposals[77] or green belt proposals[78] (even in one case where submission to the Minister ten years previously had yet to be followed by a public inquiry).[79] But non-statutory policy enjoys no special evidentiary status. An interim development control policy, for example, has been held to be a document which could give no basis for a Secretary of State's decision when at the inquiry the local planning authority had been unable to explain where the document came from, had called no evidence about it, and had conceded that the figures it contained relating to land supply conflicted with those presented by the county authority at an earlier inquiry.[80]

In the absence of any procedural framework governing the preparation of non-statutory plans, establishing its authenticity may be a particular problem. So far as influence upon appeal decisions is concerned, it has been made clear that there are some minimum requirements. The Secretary of State will continue to take non-statutory "supplementary planning guidance" into account, provided it has been prepared in consultation with the public, has been made the subject of a council resolution and is kept publicly available. Similarly, the provisions of draft statutory local plans are regarded as "material considerations" in development control, provided they are in accordance with structure plan proposals and have been the subject of a council resolution.[81] And their influence is likely to be stronger the further the plan has progressed through the various stages towards final adoption.

Despite the reform of the foward planning system, non-statutory policies continue to play an important role in practice, and they have even, paradoxically, received statutory recognition.[82] So long as forward planning continues to be characterised by delay and rigidity, the freedom offered by the broad discretion of section 29 to rely upon non-statutory policies will continue to be exploited. Already, informal plans have been used as a way of updating structure plans, on an annual or biennial basis; and as a way of supplying contemporaneous supplementary material for statutory plans. But the safeguards which are carefully maintained in the case of statutory plans

[76] *Ante*, pp. 137–144.

[77] *Fawcett Properties Ltd.* v. *Buckinghamshire C.C.* [1961] A.C. 636.

[78] *Myton Ltd.* v. *M.H.L.G.* (1963) 61 L.G.R. 1690.

[79] *Hodgkinsons (Ringway) Ltd.* v. *Bucklow R.D.C.* (1972) 225 E.G. 2105.

[80] *French Kier Developments Ltd.* v. *S.O.S.E.* [1977] 1 All E.R. 296.

[81] D.O.E. Circular 4/79; Annex, para.4.7. So far as Inspectors are concerned, the pedigree and authenticity of the plan or policy are of particular importance, to ensure that it is genuinely representative of council policy: C.F. Allan, "The Inspector's Criteria" in *Planning Inquiry Practice* (Sweet & Maxwell, 1974), p.4.

[82] Thus, in its definition of "county matters," the Local Government Act 1972 originally included "any statement of planning policy adopted by the county planning authority"; (Sched.16, para.32 *(d)* (iv) repealed by the L.G.P.L.A. 1980); and in 1973 Parliament belatedly recognised the potentially blighting effect of non-statutory plans in the Land Compensation Act 1973, ss. 68 and 71.

are absent, and the Secretary of State's overview through the appeals system is important.

Two particular types of non-statutory planning documents, design guides and development briefs, have emerged in recent years and have attained some popularity in practice. The purpose of design guides has been to set out for prospective developers the planning authority's general standards and design criteria for particular types of development. The documents tend to contain not only a statement of standards required by the authority in respect of such matters as roads, access, car-parking and spacing of buildings (all discussed in the final section of this Chapter) but also pointers to better design with sample sketches and elevations. These attempts to guide architectural standards have proved controversial, and a survey carried out on behalf of the Department of the Environment in 1976 showed that the streamlining of development control which had been sought through preparation of the guides had not been achieved.[83] The reasons were uncertain, but two alternative theories emerged. One was that the authorities who had prepared the guides had done so because they tended generally to be more critical of design and remained anxious to secure improvements, whilst the other possible explanation was that design guides had not significantly improved the quality of applications.

Development briefs, or design briefs, unlike the design guides tend to be site-specific documents, prepared on an ad hoc basis with the objective of translating existing policies and standards into more specific requirements for individual sites. Their purpose is usually therefore promotional, and their use is most common in the case of publicly owned land being released for development.[84] Development briefs are often used to set the terms for disposal of the site, and developers invited to compete in terms of design or purchase price, or both. Although frequently accompanied by a grant of outline permission, the briefs have no statutory or contractual force in themselves, and enforcement of their terms is therefore dependent upon their being translated into an appropriate legal relationship such as conditional planning permission, statutory agreement or, in the case of leasehold disposal, the terms of the headlease.

(d) precedent

The processes of formal policy making, through the preparation of plans and other documents, consultations and public participation impose a discipline upon the planning process. But policy may equally emerge from a course of dealing or a series of decisions taken by an authority, in the sense of committing the authority, in the interests of consistency at least, to take a similar line in respect of subsequent comparable applications. This precedent effect of planning decisions is well known, and it is particularly acute in the context of development control because of the incremental effect of detrimental development. One, two or even three houses in a rural area may have little impact and be unobjectionable, but one hundred may transform its character completely. There is seldom any obvious point at which to

[83] *Design Guidance Survey* London: D.O.E. (1976).
[84] Advice on the use of briefs in this context is contained in "Development Advice Note No.1" in *Development Briefs* (H.M.S.O., 1975).

draw the line, and to grant permission for the one or two without special justification may lead to irresistible pressure on the authority to unlock the whole area for development. This is particularly likely where no clear plans have been drawn up for the area. The pressures which may flow from the grant of permission in these circumstances have been recognised both in the courts[85] and by the Minister as a material consideration, as a possible side-effect affecting the whole of a locality, and thus as a ground for withholding planning permission. The Minister's advice (contained in a circular since cancelled) was that it should be a factor only in borderline cases, and that:

" . . . where, apart from the question of precedent, there are good reasons for allowing an applicant to carry out development, the fact that the granting of permission in this case may lead to other applications being made should not be accepted as a sufficient reason for refusal".[86]

C. Presumptive Policies

The policies which guide discretion in development control fall roughly into two separate categories. First, there are the *presumptive* policies—those which create a presumption either in favour of or against the granting of planning permission. The best known are no doubt the various constraint policies; through which development has been prevented or restricted in designated areas. These are, by and large, policies of general principle; some of them of general application, and others tied to specific designated areas.

The second group are those policies which impose *quantitative standards.* They tend to be policies of detail, expressed in mathematical terms, and their purpose is that of regulating development for which permission is to be granted, rather than for restricting development. The two groups overlap to some extent, and quantitative standards have at times been employed for the ulterior purpose of preventing development (as, for example, with the very low density standards imposed by a number of planning schemes made under the 1932 Act).

In both cases, the source of policies is mixed. Some derive from approved plans, others from central government advice and research publications, whilst others are entirely local and non-statutory.

1. *The Presumption in Favour of Permission*

There is a general presumption in central government policy in favour of planning permission being granted, which goes back as far as 1949[87] and which has been regularly reasserted in recent years as concern has grown with the operation of the development control system. It has doubtless had some effect, in that permission is granted by local planning authorities on over 80 per cent. of all applications. But it is by no means an unqualified

---

[85] *Collis Radio Ltd.* v. *S.O.S.E.* (1975) 29 P. & C.R. 390.
[86] M.T.C.P. Circular 69/49, para. 7.
[87] M.T.C.P. Circular 69/49, para.5, where the advice was more tentatively expressed than in later circulars, as applying to cases where "no serious issue is involved" and no "sufficient" reason could be found for refusing permission.

presumption. In the most recent statement of it, the Department has emphasised that the presumption is subordinate to constraint policies, and that its purpose is to encourage authorities to overcome minor objections and afford developers the benefit of doubt in borderline cases[88]:

"Local planning authorities are asked therefore to pay greater regard to time and efficiency; to adopt a more positive attitude to planning applications; and always to grant planning permission, having regard to all material considerations, unless there are sound and clear cut reasons for refusal. ... The Government's concern for positive attitudes and efficiency in development control does not mean that their attitude to conservation is in any way weakened: in particular, they remain committed to the need to conserve and improve the countryside, natural habitats and areas of architectural, natural, historical or scientific interest and listed buildings."

Breach of an established constraint policy may therefore amount to a "clear cut reason" for refusing permission, but otherwise the effect of the presumption is to place upon authorities a burden of proof at planning inquiries to establish good reasons for refusal. The existence of a constraint policy is an influence rather than a guarantee; and it is still open to the developer to persuade the Secretary of State that the policy itself is unsound, or that the development proposal would not breach it or frustrate its objectives.

The device of imposing presumptive policies has also been used by central government as a means of putting pressure on authorities in ensuring adequate land supply for housing development. Unless the authority can point to an identified five–year supply of sites, there is now a presumption in favour "of granting permission for housing except where there are clear planning objections which in the circumstances of the case outweigh the need to make the land available for housing."[89] And if they contemplate refusing permission instead on the ground that the development would overload existing sewerage facilities, they are warned that "they must be prepared to support their decision on appeal by specific evidence of overload."[90]

A less obvious form of centralised policy influence has been the request to give priority to the handling of certain categories of planning application. Initially, it was applications for housing which were to be processed with urgency, then housing and industrial applications; but from 1980 the request is that authorities "pick out for priority handling those applications which in their judgement will contribute most to national and local economic activity."[91] Although it is not in terms a request to lean in favour of granting permission, it carries the strong implication that the priority requested should carry over to the substantive issues raised by the application.

---

[88] D.O.E. Circular 22/80, paras. 3 and 4.
[89] *Ibid.* Annex, para.3.
[90] *Ibid.* Annex. para. 11.
[91] *Ibid.*

2. Constraint Policies

The constraint policies of British planning are probably its most conspicuously successful achievement. Presumptions against development or limiting development in the prescribed areas tie in happily with a negative controlling system. Urban growth has been successfully contained and areas of beautiful countryside have been conserved at little cost to the public purse, and at great benefit in terms of infrastructure investment; and constraint policies remain today amongst the most valuable weapons in the planner's armoury. A list of current policy restraints appears in Table 9. and it can be seen that all are based upon area or site designation. Not all are specifically planning controls, but all are relevant in development control. Those which are relevant in terms of urban growth are discussed in this chapter, whilst the site-specific amenity controls such as listed buildings and tree preservation orders are examined in Chapter 12.

There is now almost one half of the land surface of England and Wales designated as an area to which one or more formal development constraints are applicable, as Table 9 demonstrates.

Table 9

Major restraints on development 1966–70

	England and Wales	(thousand acres)
I.	Urban Area 1970	4,330
II.	Policy restraints	
	1. National Parks	3,366
	2. Forest Parks	167
	3. National Nature Reserves	77
	4. Areas of outstanding Natural Beauty	2,746
	5. Green belts: statutory	1,211
	non-statutory	2,445
	6. Areas of high landscape value	5,974
	7. Deduction for overlap between categories	−583
	Total conservation restraints	15,403
III.	Physical restraint in high land	
	Land over 800′ not included in II above	1,246
	Total actual and potential restraints	20,979
	Total area	37,343

Source: adapted from Long Term Population Distribution in Great Britain—A Study (H.M.S.O., 1971, Table 4.7).

To those figures there must also now be added the areas designated as sites of special scientific interest which occupy no less than 9 per cent. of the surface land area (although there is some overlap with other designations), and upon which some further protection has been conferred by the Wildlife and Countryside Act 1981. Further, the figures for the most part include only specific statutory designations. If all the planning restraint policies contained in development plans or implemented on a non-statutory basis by authorities were included, the proportion of land affected would be very much higher.

Restraint policies therefore provide the main starting point in development control decisions raising issues of location and land release. Through them the ground rules are laid for new urban development outside existing settlements: the policies and their objectives are well understood, and the battle takes place on the scope of the exceptions. They differ from other policies in one important respect, which is that they tend automatically to become more restrictive over the years without any conscious change on the part of the planning authority, because the rate of development has often exceeded new land release. Indeed, the more successful a restraint policy in holding back ad hoc development, the more difficult it becomes to allow for planned expansion.

Different designations have different objectives, and the purpose in each case is to single out the area concerned for special attention, to strengthen the authority's hand in control, to concentrate resources and to achieve a degree of priority for the objective concerned. Some designations have their origin in the planning process and their legal backing in the 1971 Act, either directly or through statutory plans; others have been established under other legislation and may be designated or administered by other agencies, but still have planning implications. This range of differing powers, designations, programmes and agencies is often confusing and unnecessarily complex, and its very existence is a recognition of the comparative weakness of the planning system to order priorities and resist undesirable development without external support.

3. The General Justification for Constraint

Much of the pressure for introduction of comprehensive planning control stemmed from a fear of unrestrained urban sprawl. There was a recognised need to contain urban growth: to prevent unsightly and inefficient ribbon development along roads, to prevent the coalescence of towns and cities as they expanded further and further towards each other, and to slow down the rate of loss of good agricultural land to urban development. These were all trends which the schemes under the Planning Acts of 1925 and 1932 had seemed powerless to reverse. Indeed, the decade 1929–39 was a period of unprecedented urban expansion as speculative builders took advantage of cheap land costs at the urban fringe, the upturn in the economy following the depression and improvements in vital communications networks, particularly the suburban railways.

The annual rate of loss of agricultural land to urban development ran at around 9,000 hectares in England and Wales between 1922–26, but soared to over 25,000 hectares during the period 1931–39. As Table 10 shows, despite intense development activity, the average annual post-war conversion rate has been held to around 16,000 hectares (with a further 1,700 hectares in Scotland where figures have been available only since 1960).[92]

[92] Detailed figures of agricultural land use change may be found in R.H. Best and J.T. Coppock's classic work, *The Changing Use of Land in Britain* (Faber, 1962). For more recent studies see Best, *The Planner* (1976), p.16; Countryside Review Committee Report, Food Production in the Countryside (H.M.S.O., 1978); and annual series of *Agricultural Statistics* published by H.M.S.O.

Table 10

Annual Average net Losses of Agricultural Land to Urban Use

Period	England and Wales '000 hectares	Scotland '000 hectares	Britain '000 hectares
1922–26	9.1		
1926–31	21.1		
1931–36	25.1		
1936–39	25.1		Figures not
1939–45	5.3		available
1945–50	17.5		
1950–55	15.5		
1955–60	14.0		
1960–65	15.3	2.5	17.8
1965–70	16.8	2.8	19.6
1970–74	15.4	2.0	17.4

Source: R. H. Best, "Agricultural Land Loss—myth or reality?" (1977) *The Planner* p. 15.

Containment has been pursued as a deliberate policy, although it has been aided by unintended factors such as the failure of the forward planning system to react swiftly to upward revisions in population projections, the influence of rural and preservationist pressures and the impact of soaring land prices.[93] Growth policies have been formulated with containment firmly in mind. The common pattern has been to concentrate upon incremental but controlled expansion of existing towns and larger settlements, supplemented by schemes of more dramatic expansion under the Town Development Act[94] to accommodate overspill from the major conurbations, and the creation of whole new communities as new towns.[95] And there has been acceptance of the need for higher residential densities in urban development to reduce the land take. With the phasing out of further new towns and town development schemes, the bulk of future development can be expected to take place within and around existing towns, both through schemes of infill and redevelopment and through limited expansion within limits set by existing and proposed employment capacity and social and physical infrastructure. There is currently a programme intended to bring vacant urban land into development, and various public bodies are required now to maintain registers of land owned by them but not required for their immediate purposes.[96] Large tracts of land are capable of being brought into development through the registers (coupled with the Secretary of State's power to direct disposal), but many require expensive infrastructure and site clearance works to be undertaken before development can commence.

[93] For a comprehensive analysis, see Peter Hall, *The Containment of Urban England* (George Allen & Unwin Ltd., 1973).
[94] *Post* p. 506.
[95] *Post* p. 503.
[96] *Post* p. 518.

4. *Green Belts*

The green belts have proved a major influence in limiting urban growth. The idea can be traced back at least as far as Ebenezer Howard's proposals for garden cities, but as a tool of contemporary planning it derives from Sir Raymond Unwin's proposals in 1933 for restraining development on the outskirts of London.[97] He recommended that a girdle of open space be preserved around the existing boundaries, and that it be maintained primarily for recreation. In 1938 the Green Belt (London and Home Counties) Act was passed, and conferred powers on local authorities to control development in the designated area by buying up areas of land and by accepting covenants by landowners against development.[98] Professor Abercrombie's Greater London Plan of 1944 built on the idea by directing overspill development to satellite towns to be established beyond the green belt.[99]

The legislative backing has given the metropolitan green belt special status, and ministerial approval is required for development of sites protected under the 1938 Act[1] But green belts were not originally intended to be used as a containment device in other parts of the country. The assumption was that with comprehensive development control unnecessary encroachment upon agricultural land could be prevented, and development channelled along precise development plan allocations. But it soon became clear that some strengthening of policy was necessary in the era of rapid growth that followed the scrapping of building licence controls in the early 1950s.

London authorities had built upon the pre-war base in their early development plans, by defining an area of between 7 and 10 miles deep around the capital in which no further expansion would be permitted, except to round-off existing settlements. But other authorities had made no comparable provision, and in the now classic Circular No.42 of 1955, the government urged them to consider establishing green belts wherever desirable, and as quickly as possible.[2] No matter that the development plan regulations made no provision for them: they could be declared and implemented immediately as interim or informal policies. The Circular suggested that Sketch Plans indicating the approximate boundaries of the proposed green belts should be submitted to the Ministry, but that development constraints should be applied on a provisional basis in advance

---

[97] *Second Report of the Greater London Regional Planning Committee, 1933.*

[98] The *Municipal Yearbook 1979* records current ownership by local authorities of over 10,000 acres of green belt land for public open space, and over 30,000 acres held for preservation from building.

[99] For a detailed history, see D. Thomas, *London's Green Belt* (Faber, 1970) and D.R. Mandelker, *Green Belts and Urban Growth* (University of Wisconsin Press, 1962) and [1960] *Public Law* 256.

[1] Green Belt (London and Home Counties) Act 1938, s. 10; but see *Lovelock v. Minister of Transport* (1980) 40 P. & C.R. 226.

[2] The circular, issued in August 1955, had been heralded by a ministerial statement in April that year, (H.C. Deb., Vol.540, col. 45) emphasising the urgent need for green belt restraints around provincial centres. A second circular, No. 50/57, gave detailed advice on the form of submission of green belt proposals. See further *ante* pp. 138–139.

of submitting any formal development plan amendments. Formal approval of green belts in fact took many years. None at all had been approved when, seven years after the Circular, the Ministry issued a special advisory booklet on green belts,[3] and it transpired that the Ministry much preferred to maintain interim status rather than process proposals through to formal approval. Once formally approved, the designation implied a more or less permanent restriction on development, and because of the support it enjoyed was very difficult to modify subsequently.[4] An "interim" proposal, even though many years old, offered greater flexibility. It could be taken into account in decision making,[5] but overridden more readily.

The 1955 Circular indicated the criteria by which applications for development in green belts should be assessed, and a subsequent circular urged that in the interests of national uniformity these be carried through directly to development plans without amendment.[6] That has remained the general rule with the new structure plans as well, and the purpose has been both to provide a common formula to avoid disputes between adjoining authorities, and to secure that proposals not within the criteria should be treated as plan departure applications.

The presumption against non-agricultural or non-recreational development in green belt areas is strong, and the terms of the circular are backed up by the Development Control Policy Notes which warn that permission will not be given except in very special circumstances, and that special care will be taken to prevent breaches along the inner edge.[7] The terms of the 1955 circular are that:

> "5. Inside a Green Belt, . . . approval should not be given, except in very special circumstances for the construction of new buildings or for the change of use of existing buildings for purposes other than agriculture, sports, cemeteries, institutions standing in extensive grounds, or other uses appropriate to a rural area.
>
> 6. Apart from a strictly limited amount of 'infilling' or 'rounding off' (within boundaries to be defined in Town Maps) existing towns and villages inside a Green Belt should not be allowed to expand further. Even within the urban areas thus defined, every effort should be made to prevent any further building for industrial or commercial purposes; since this, if allowed, would lead to a demand for more labour, which in turn would create a need for the development of additional land for housing."

Those criteria continue in force today, but the role played by green belts is controversial. The purposes of green belt control were suggested by the Circular to be:

> "(a) to check the further growth of a built-up area; or

---

[3] *The Green Belts* (H.M.S.O., 1962).
[4] A view expressed by the Ministry to the Council on Tribunals in 1968: see further, the Council's *Annual Report for 1968*, p.18.
[5] See, *e.g.Hodgkinsons (Ringway) Ltd.* v. *Bucklow R.D.C.* (1972) 225 E.G. 2105.
[6] M.H.L.G. Circular 50/57, para.10(*b*).
[7] *Policy Note No.4*, para.4.

(b) to prevent neighbouring towns from merging into one another; or

(c) to preserve the special character of a town."[8]

But the areas were not therefore simply restricted solely to agricultural use. They offered a convenient means of keeping "stretches of unspoilt country within easy reach of town-dwellers," and recreational facilities were to be a permitted land use.

But resolving the conflicts between the needs of undisturbed agricultural use and those of recreation and easy urban access has not proved easy; and future patterns in green belt preservation, extent and function have already led to many county/district disputes in plan preparation. Too rigidly drawn boundaries may act to the economic disadvantage of the town, increasing land values and placing increased demands upon surrounding villages and road networks; yet the rigidity of the constraint is the very factor which has made green belts so effective in containing development. Green belts have assumed enormous political and emotional significance, and there is inevitably fierce resistance to proposed changes in boundaries.

Government policy in allowing or encouraging green belt release for development has been to insist upon equivalent reinstatement of protected areas elsewhere[9]; but only at times of exceptional need for housing land has green belt land release been generally countenanced, otherwise than in the context of statutory plans. In some instances the initiative for revision has come from the structure plan authorities, in others it has come from the Secretary of State, as in the case of the Hertfordshire Structure Plan, proposing modifications to the plan.

5. White Land

"White land" is a term of no legal significance: it simply means land not allocated for development by an old-style development plan, particularly those pockets of land between a town and the inside edge of its green belt which were not intended for development within the plan period.[10] Failure to update the plans swiftly meant however, that much white land was released for development without ever having been allocated in a statutory plan, as plan departures; and by the early 1970s, in growth areas at least, the old presumption had been reversed. Central government unilaterally introduced a presumption in favour of housing development on white land, which could only be overridden by "exceptionally compelling planning objections to the development."[11] Even outside growth areas, white land had nevertheless to be generally regarded as suitable for housing provided the development represented "a natural extension of existing development and is compatible with its size, character, location and setting."[12]

[8] *Ibid.*, para.3.

[9] See *e.g. Widening the Choice: Next Steps in Housing* Cmnd.5280 (1973). Current government policy on the Metropolitan Green Belt is for detailed review in the context of structure plans, with special justification required for extension to a depth greater than 12–15 miles: see further, *Government Statement on Strategic Plan for the South East*, (H.M.S.O., 1978), pp.13–14.

[10] See, *e.g.* M.H.L.G. Circular 50/57.

[11] D.O.E. Circular 122/73; Annex A, para.4.

[12] *Ibid.*, para.5. For a discussion of the legal battles fought over the terms of the circular, see *ante*, p. 298.

The white land presumptions were gradually overtaken by the fresh allocations made in structure plans and local plans, and were eventually superseded in 1980 by the more generalised development presumptions of Circular 22/80.[13]

6. Development in the Countryside

Development in the open countryside is subject to similar, but less rigid, restrictions as in the green belt. The general principle has been that, except in the case of completely new settlements, development should be restricted to that necessary to sustain agricultural productivity, and that it should be concentrated upon existing towns and villages.[14] The purpose of the control is to conserve rural amenity, and it has the back-up of a loose statutory duty imposed upon all Ministers and public bodies to "have regard to the desirability of conserving the natural beauty and amenity of the countryside."[15] Creeping suburbanisation and sporadic development are the evils to be avoided, and development pressure of this sort can generally be resisted through control based on statutory or non-statutory plan policies; but there is provision for strengthened controls in certain areas and for heightened awareness through special designations.

Five of the special amenity designations which have direct planning consequences deserve further comment.

(a) Areas of outstanding natural beauty

This designation is at the instance of the Countryside Commission, acting under the National Parks and Access to the Countryside Act 1949,[16] and designation orders are subject to confirmation by the Secretary of State. Designation attracts special grant-aid for local authorities, and it confers additional powers on them and upon the Countryside Commission. The Commission are required to be consulted upon development plan proposals affecting the area,[17] and the designation is in practice carried through into the plans and supported by appropriate planning policies. There is no requirement that the Commission be consulted on planning applications in the area, but they have specific power to advise authorities if consulted.[18] Table 11 sets out the location and area of the designations which have been made and confirmed to date.

(b) Sites of special scientific interest

This designation is at the instance of the Nature Conservancy Council, and the only step formerly involved was that the Council were obliged to

---

[13] *Ante*, p. 303.
[14] See *e.g. Development Control Policy Note No.4*. The Note offers detailed guidance as to the criteria by which applications for agricultural dwellings should be determined. Most other agricultural development is outside the scope of planning control by virtue of General Development Order Sched.1, Class VI. Guidance on expansion of existing towns and villages is contained in *Settlement in the Countryside*, Planning Bulletin No.8 (H.M.S.O., 1967) which recommended the use of non-statutory plans to guide decision making.
[15] Countryside Act 1968, s.11.
[16] N.P.A.C.A. 1949, s.87.
[17] *Ibid*. s.9.
[18] *Ibid*. s.6(4) as applied by s.88.

Table 11

Areas of Outstanding Natural Beauty as at
September 30, 1980

Area	Date of confirmation of order	Area in sq km
Gower	10 December 1956	189
Quantock Hills	1 January 1957	99
Lleyn	28 May 1957	155
Northumberland Coast	21 March 1958	129
Surrey Hills	8 May 1958	414
Cannock Chase	16 September 1958	68
Shropshire Hills	11 March 1959	777
Dorset	29 July 1959	1,036
Malvern Hills	22 October 1959	104
Cornwall	25 November 1959	932
North Devon	25 May 1960	171
South Devon	2 August 1960	332
East Hampshire	26 September 1962	391
East Devon	20 September 1963	267
Isle of Wight	20 September 1963	189
Chichester Harbour	4 February 1964	75
Forest of Bowland	10 February 1964	803
Solway Coast	12 December 1964	107
Chilterns	16 December 1965	800
Sussex Downs	7 April 1966	981
Cotswolds	19 August 1966	1,507
Anglesey	13 November 1967	215
South Hampshire Coast	18 December 1967	78
Norfolk Coast	8 April 1968	450
Kent Downs	23 July 1968	845
Suffolk Coast and Heaths	4 March 1970	391
Dedham Vale	20 May 1970	57
Extension	21 August 1978	15
Wye Valley	13 December 1971	325
North Wessex Downs	1 December 1972	1,738
Mendip Hills	1 December 1972	202
Arnside and Silverdale	15 December 1972	75
Lincolnshire Wolds	17 April 1973	560
Scilly Isles	18 February 1976	16
		14,493

Source: Annual Report of the Countryside Commission 1979–80, Appendix 6.

notify the local planning authority for the area that they were of the opinion that the land was "of special interest by reason of its flora, fauna, or geological or physiographical features." There was no obligation to notify the landowner of the designation, and some owners and occupiers of S.S.S.I.s remained unaware of it. The Wildlife and Countryside Act 1981 remodelled the designation procedure, and the Council are now required to give prior notification to the planning authority, every owner and occupier of the land and the Secretary of State; and to consider any representations or objections before making a formal designation.[19] The planning authority are

[19] Wildlife and Countryside Act 1981, s.28 (formerly N.P.A.C.A. 1949, s.23: designations made under the earlier legislation remain in force by virtue of W.C.A. 1981, s.28(*b*)).

thereafter obliged to consult with the Council in respect of any proposals for development of the land, except where the Council dispense with the requirement.[20] Authorities have also been requested to consult on any development within the vicinity of designated sites which may affect the site.[21] Development within the catchment area of a designated wetland, for example, may have a serious impact upon the scientific value of the site.

Conflict between agricultural requirements and nature conservation has proved an obstacle to the success of these arrangements in the past. Most agricultural operations are permitted development under Class VI of the General Development Order, and the value of a site is therefore capable of being destroyed without any planning application being required. The deemed permission is capable of being withdrawn under article 4 of the Order, and there is power also for the Council to enter into management agreements with owners under which financial support can be given towards conservation. But these measures have not prevented destructive development. Even where an article 4 Direction is in force, enforcement is through the usual machinery which means that there is no penal sanction available until after "development" has occurred. The damage done is often irremediable, and the enforcement machinery is therefore of little use.

The Wildlife and Countryside Act 1981 has now introduced further protection, by requiring that the designation of an S.S.S.I. should be accompanied by notification to owners and occupiers of the particular features of the site which are of special interest and of any operations appearing to the Council to be likely to damage them. Those operations may thereafter be carried out lawfully only following notification to the Council, who may give consent or offer to enter into a management agreement. But the arrangments are suspensory rather than prohibitive, and the Council have no power to prevent the works going ahead if no agreement has been reached within three months. The Act also strengthens these controls in certain cases, by authorising the Secretary of State, in consultation with the Council, to make orders affecting the most valuable sites.[22] The power is limited to two categories of sites, which either are of special interest and for which protection is sought "for the purpose of securing the survival in Great Britain of any kind of animal or plant or of complying with an international obligation"; or for sites of special scientific interest which are of national importance.[23] The order makes it an offence to carry out such operations as are specified in it, being operations which appear to the Secretary of State to be likely to destroy or damage the flora, fauna, or geological or physiographical features by reason of which the land falls into the two categories above. The prohibition is qualified in two ways. First, it is a reasonable excuse excluding liability that the operation was authorised by an express (but not deemed) planning permission or was an emergency operation notified to the Council as soon as practicable. Secondly, there are provisions under which notification of the proposal to carry out an operation may be given to the Council. The prohibition contained in the order is then lifted if the Council consent to the operation, if it is carried out

---

[20] General Development Order 1977, art.15(1)(g).
[21] D.O.E. Circular 108/77 *Nature Conservation and Planning*, para.12.
[22] W.C.A. 1981, s.29 and Sched.11.
[23] *Ibid.* s.29(1).

in accordance with a management agreement or if three months have expired from notification without the Council offering to enter into a management agreement or making a compulsory purchase order.[24]

Under the new provisions it is thus now possible to convert the general policy designation into one having direct and specific effect in controlling a range of operations, in circumstances where the planning system alone offered only broad protection.

(c) Nature reserves

The nature reserve designation affords additional protection for areas in the interests of nature conservancy. National nature reserves are established by the Nature Conservancy Council as sites of national or international importance.[25] The sites are either owned or leased by the Council, or are managed through agreements with the owners. For the purposes of planning control the land is deemed to be Crown Land.[26]

Local nature reserves are established by local authorities in consultation with the Council, and may be protected and regulated through direct ownership or management agreement, and through byelaws made by the authority.[27]

(d) Areas of great landscape, scientific or historic value

This designation has its origins in the 1948 Development Plans Regulations which required that authorities should indicate such areas in their plans where appropriate.[28] The requirement has not been carried through to the reformed plans system, and authorities have greater flexibility to adapt earlier policies and designations to present needs.

(e) Coastal conservation areas

These designations were established originally in 1966 on a non-statutory basis with a view to providing an immediate means of safeguarding unspoilt stretches of coastline.[29] Some were later incorporated into statutory plans, but the remainder stayed in non-statutory form. The protective policies which followed were, in the view of the Countryside Commission in 1970, too vague to be really effective.[30] They recommended the designation of 34 separate areas of unspoilt coastline as "heritage coasts," where local planning authorities would be expected to restrict development more severely than elsewhere on the coast.

Coastal protection is now generally based upon appropriate policies formulated in the new structure plans and local plans, building on the earlier non-statutory designations.

---

[24] *Ibid.* s.29(5)—(7).
[25] N.P.A.C.A. 1949, Pt.III.
[26] Nature Conservancy Council Act 1973, Sched.3, para.15.
[27] N.P.A.C.A. 1949, s.21.
[28] T.C.P. (Development Plans) Regulations 1948, Sched.1, Pt.III.
[29] M.H.L.G. Circular 7/66.
[30] *The Planning of the Coastline* (H.M.S.O., 1970) and *The Coastal Heritage* (H.M.S.O., 1970).

7. Agricultural Land Conservation Policies

The annual rate of loss of good agricultural land to urban development, although held down by constraint policies, continues to give rise to serious concern. And this despite the fact that increases in agricultural productivity through mechanisation and improved techniques have more than made up for the impact of the urban land-take. The quality and extent of land taken has always been a particularly important factor; and the government policy is currently twofold: "to ensure that, as far as possible, land of a higher agricultural quality is not taken for development where land of a lower quality is available"; and to ensure that "the amount of land taken is no greater than is reasonably required for carrying out the development in accordance with proper standards."[31] The policy is imprecise, but it is backed up by two important factors: the land classification system operated by the Ministry of Agriculture, Fisheries and Food, and the Ministry's input through the development control consultation procedures. These have now been further reinforced by the Ministry's right to pursue objections to local plans, preventing adoption by the authority without the authorisation of the Secretary of State.[32]

(a) The agricultural land classifications

Five gradings are recognised by the Ministry[33]:

Grade 1: land of exceptional quality, comprising around 2.8 per cent. of the total.

Grade 2: land which is versatile and high yielding. It comprises 14.6 per cent. of the total.

Grade 3: land with moderate physical limitations, comprising about 50 per cent. of the total.

Grade 4: land with moderately severe physical limitations, comprising 19.7 per cent. of the total.

Grade 5: land of very restricted agricultural potential. It comprises 14 per cent. of the total.

Development of land within Grades 1 and 2 is not normally acceptable to the Ministry, except where there is no reasonable alternative. Development of land in Grades 4 and 5 would seldom attract any agricultural objection. But Grade 3 is so broad a classification that the Ministry's standard is of little practical assistance. The land, comprising as it does 50 per cent. of the total, is not inferior quality and the agriculture/development balance can only be struck satisfactorily on the basis of individual assessment. Proposals were announced in 1981 for a review of the classifications, but were limited to a relabelling rather than a comprehensive revision of the system.[34] The purpose was to remove the impression that Grade 3 land was third class for agricultural purposes by redesignating Grades 1, 2 and 3 as 1A, 1B and 1C respectively. But there was to be no subdivision of grade 3 (or 1C), and thus

[31] D.O.E. Circular 75/76, *Development Involving Agricultural Land*, para.3.

[32] T.C.P.A. 1971, s.14(1A); *ante* p. 128.

[33] Details drawn from D.O.E. Circular 75/76 and the Countryside Review Committee's Discussion Paper *Food Production in the Countryside* (H.M.S.O. 1978.)

[34] Hansard, H.C. Deb., Vol.3, col.31 (May 5, 1981).

no means of identifying more readily the better quality land within the category.

(b) Ministry consultation

The classifications are reinforced by the requirement that planning authorities consult with M.A.F.F. in the preparation of development plans, where many strategic issues involving urban/rural conflict may need to be resolved. The reasoned justification section of the plan is required to indicate the regard had by the authority to agriculture and to the protection of good agricultural land[35]; and a sustained objection by the M.A.F.F. would in practice be difficult to overcome, particularly with the new entrenchment conferred by the Act of 1980.

Authorities are also required to consult the Ministry in development control, in connection with applications for non-agricultural development involving 10 acres or more of agricultural land where the development does not accord with the plan; and also where the immediate loss is less than 10 acres, but more may follow.[36] If the Ministry object to the proposal and the objection remains unresolved, the Secretary of State for the Environment would normally call the application in for decision.[37]

8. Balancing Constraints and Land Supply

The effect of rigidly applied constraint policies, often backed up by strong local anti-growth pressure, has led increasingly to charges that authorities have failed to meet the land demands of the housebuilding industry. The danger is not only of resultant long–term damage to an already vulnerable and cyclical industry, but of higher house prices and pressure for increased densities in residential development. Larger housebuilding firms have had the ability to hold large stocks of land long–term, representing five or more years supply, as a buffer against short–term supply problems.[38] But smaller firms have lacked that capacity, and by 1978 the Government had been persuaded that increased taxation of development values had reduced land banking capacity generally.[39]

These charges have all focused attention upon planning authority responsibility in land supply, and upon the techniques by which demand and availability might be measured. The general duty which planning authorities always had, to take into account development pressures in the preparation of development plans and to maintain general supervision of the rate of land release through development control, has been sharpened and re-defined. By 1970 the Department of the Environment was urging authorities to assume a positive role in land supply and to release urgently a five-year supply of housing land.[40] That requirement was re-emphasised on

---

[35] D.O.E. Circular 4/79, para.2.24.
[36] General Development Order 1977, art.15(1)(i).
[37] H.C.Deb., Vol. 964, col.627 (March 21, 1979).
[38] Useful studies of the housebuilding industry and land supply include Roy Drewett, "The Developers: Decision Process" in Hall's *Containment of Urban England*, Vol.2, P.163; and the Consultants' Study, *Housing Land Availability in the South East* (H.M.S.O., 1975).
[39] *Memorandum*, D.O.E. Circular 44/78, para.15.
[40] D.O.E. Circular 10/70, para. 6.

numerous subsequent occasions during the peak years of land demand; and the land supply function of authorities later became a central feature of the Community Land Act. The intention was that the planning authorities should gradually assume dominance in the development land market as their land trading activity increased; and the Act specifically required them to have special regard to the land needs of the building industry, or persons already living in their area and of those wishing to live in the area.[41]

Constraint policies in particular have led to a reluctance to over-allocate land for development, and the resultant tight balance between demand and supply has highlighted the gap between the allocation of sites and their actual availability for development. Authorities have tended to define land availability in planning terms, pointing to such indicators as plan allocations and outstanding planning permissions[42]; but developers have insisted that actual availability is dependent upon a wider variety of factors, including planning delays, the owner's willingness to sell, limiting site constraints, the size of the site and the availability of services. A consultants' study published in 1975 of land availability in the South East supported their case, indicating that there existed only an indirect, tenuous relationship between the two states of land availability.[43] That view has been supported by further studies.[44]

The Secretary of State has also urged local planning authorities to undertake their own residential land availability studies, in co-ordination with the housebuilding industry.[45] The authority's input is seen as involving the preparation of a list of sites available for development in planning terms, and a quantitative statement of their housing policies or requirements. Representatives of the building industry would then carry out their own assessment of availability, and produce a study for discussion with the authority. The purpose of these arrangements is to bridge the gap between planning availability and market availability, and the Secretary of State has been sufficiently convinced of the value of the exercise as to take reserve powers in the 1980 Act to direct authorities to participate in land availability assessments.[46]

But beyond improved consultative machinery, there is scope still for a more efficient approach to land supply, particularly if new development does come to be concentrated on sites within the boundaries of existing

---

[41] Community Land Act 1975, Sched.6, para 1.
[42] This was the basis for quantification which had been adopted in the D.O.E. Circular 102/72 in which planning authorities in the Midlands and South East were requested to file returns of sites in their areas considered available and likely to come forward for development within five years.
[43] *Housing Land Availability in the South East* (H.M.S.O.,1975).
[44] See, e.g. *Study of the Availability of Private Housebuilding Land in Greater Manchester—1978–81* (D.O.E., 1979)and *Land Authority for Wales: Land Policy Statement 1978*. In one study of 1,000 sites conducted between 1975 and 1977, however, researchers were able to conclude that in the market conditions prevailing at the time, the stock of outstanding permissions in mid-1975 proved to be about 70 per cent. accurate as an indicator of real availability, in the sense that it had proved possible to start development within two years: *Land Availability: A Study of Land with Residential Planning Permission* (D.O.E., 1978). For a critique, see A. Hooper, "Land for Private Housebuilding" [1980] J.P.L. 795.
[45] D.O.E. Circular 9/80. The Appendix to the Circular contains a suggested simplified methodology for land availability studies.
[46] L.G.P.L.A. 1980, s.116.

urban areas, through, for example, closer co–ordination between planning and site servicing, and through readier use of statutory (including compulsory) powers to bring land on to the market or to overcome particular site difficulties, such as access or "ransom" ownership of key parts of a site. In industrial and commercial development land supply has not proved so great a difficulty, at least in overall terms, given the readiness of authorities to make sites available as a means of attracting industry and employment to an area. The greater problems have been experienced with expansion on existing sites in developed areas.

D. Quantitative Standards

1. *Introduction*

The use of quantitative standards in decision making is little researched, but their influence is clearly substantial. Their effect is not that of directing where, and what type, of development should occur, but more of setting the physical limits of the development. The shape, bulk, location, spacing, height and physical services of the new development are in practice regulated through a variety of standards employed by local planning authorities. These are controls of the details of development rather than the principle, though they may well have the effect of preventing it from proceeding.

Quantitative standards are more obviously the tools of zoning oriented planning systems, where the plan or zoning scheme itself defines the development permitted in each zone and is thus required to prescribe the applicable standards in precise legislative terms. In the British comprehensive system the opportunity exists for a more flexible approach, but there remains a considerable degree of uniformity between authorities in the nature of the standards they adopt, and a surprising rigidity in their application. Practice varies, however, in the way standards are adopted by authorities and in the extent to which their existence and scope is made public. In some cases the standards are incorporated into the development plan, more particularly the new local plans. They may contain provisions regulating such matters as densities and plot ratios, and off-street parking. But standards are also frequently adopted on a non-statutory basis, as "supplementary planning guidance." The Secretary of State has accepted this practice in the case of requirements too detailed or too liable to frequent change to be included in a local plan, and has undertaken to take them into account in appeals, provided the material has been prepared in consultation with the public (there is characteristically no guidance as to the extent of this requirement), has been the subject of a council resolution (and something more, therefore, than a planning officer's rule of thumb) and is kept publicly available.[47]

How often these requirements are met in practice is uncertain.

---

[47] D.O.E. Circular 4/79, Annex, para.4.7. Early research on the new local plans indicates that authorities have tended to neglect quantitative standards in drafting the plans, and have preferred to continue to rely on supplementary guidance: *Building Research Establishment Information Paper 1/82.*

Table 12
Publication of Planning Standards

Design Groups	Percentages of responding authorities		
	Published standards or policies	Unpublished standards or policies agreed internally	No pre-determined standards
	per cent.	per cent.	per cent.
General site planning (includes density, layout, mix, open space)	18	38	44
Roads and parking	67	29	3
Detailed design and landscaping (includes height and massing of buildings, daylight and sunlight, type of materials, sound insulation, trees)	13	25	61
All topics	24	30	46

Source: *Design Guidance Survey* D.O.E. 1976, based on postal reponses from 284 districts, London boroughs and new towns (67 per cent. of total).

As Table 12 shows, many authorities do not even publish their stand-dards when they have been agreed, let alone undertake consultation in preparing them. One explanation, (which is also relevant to the numbers of authorities claiming to have no predetermined standards at all) is that a highly significant influence on standards in some areas of control is central government guidance. Many of the standards suggested by central govern-ment are applied routinely by local planning authorities, and although not necessarily constituting departmental policy, are liable nonetheless to be upheld on appeal without there having been any formal adoption by the authority. In the case of standards for design and layout of estate roads the department's advisory criteria have recently been translated into maximum standards, by an announcement that the Secretary of State and the Minister of Transport "are not prepared to support any planning or highway authority requiring standards which are higher" than those prescribed.[48] There is therefore little point in an authority adopting more demanding standards for their areas, whether through non-statutory means or in statutory plans, even although they may take the view that the national standards are unsuitable.

Reliance upon standards in development control is thus a hidden but highly influential factor in decision making. Their effect is felt at the stage of negotiation of detailed approval following the grant of outline permission,

[48] D.O.E. Circular 22/80, para. 13; see further *post*, p. 328.

because they tend to affect issues of siting buildings, external appearance, means of access, car-parking and landscaping; but developers will often wish to obtain a comprehensive statement of requirements at pre-application stage. The subject matter of the standards means that they are capable of moulding the appearance of completed development to quite a marked degree if applied rigidly, and that uniformity of style—whether aesthetically desirable or not—may result. As was the case with bye-law housing, standards intended to prescribe a minimum below which development should not fall, too readily become an upper limit beyond which aspiration will not rise. A rigidly standardised urban environment is bound to be architecturally sterile, regular and monotonous. Why, then, are they used, and on what assumptions?

The custom of viewing standards as relating purely to matters of detail has meant that they are rarely reviewed and their true impact rarely assessed. A research report from the Department of the Environment in 1976, *The Value of Standards for the External Residential Environment*[49] pointed to the substantial variation in practice between authorities in their use of standards, but found that most authorities regarded at least some standards essential to development control and some saw them as "not only indispensable but the main tools of control." But the importance attached to standards in general and certain standards in particular was influenced by a variety of factors, including the wish not to reject the views of the Engineer or Surveyor on road widths, for example; or thoughtless habit, in the sense that some standards had been applied for so long that they were now taken completely for granted.

But perhaps the most significant function of standards, not touched on in the *Research Report*, is that they set a base-line for negotiations with developers. The development controller need not justify on each application the need for off-street car-parking or for adequate sight-lines for traffic safety. He need do no more than point to his standards, and leave it to the developer to justify any departure from them. The standards also have implications for land valuation for development. Permitted densities and open space requirements, for example, will influence the price the developer is prepared to pay for the land. But the consequence of this is that where an authority subsequently propose to seek different requirements from the normal, they may expect pressure from the developer for trade-offs against other standards so as to retain the economic viability of the development. The developer may seek a higher density of housing development, for example, in return for increased open space requirements. In this interaction lies the true significance of standards, and the reason for authorities' reluctance to operate them with greater flexibility. Regardless of the objectives secured by the standards, developers and their architects may be reluctant to challenge them through the appeals system. There is pressure for them to comply in the interests in maintaining a good relationship with the planning authority, and avoiding high land holding charges pending the outcome of appeal proceedings where prospects of success may be uncertain.[50]

Standards, then, are policy tools of uncertain effect. Their function as generalised measures of a desired urban environment is overtaken in practice

[49] D.O.E. 1976.
[50] See further, *Design Guidance Survey* (D.O.E., 1976), para.2.36.

by their prescriptive effect. They are not the best means to achieve imaginative development, but they are a useful way of setting the ground rules and for countering bad design. It is the interaction between developer, land market and planning authority which turns them into something more than principles for achieving general consistency, and into rules of specific application.

Quite different considerations underly the formulation and application of the different standards in common use, and it is not always easy to trace their origins or the assumptions underlying them. The main standards systems may now be examined.

2. Density Standards

(a) The purpose of density standards

The use of density standards in controlling development is widespread, though they are almost always confined to residential development. Commercial and industrial development tends instead to be regulated through locational and height controls, and no equivalent density standards can be readily formulated. The historical roots of density controls lie in the concern of the early planners with reducing overcrowding in the inner cities. High density was equated with squalor and disease, and it became a priority of policy to reduce densities. But density and quality of urban life are in reality less directly related than this. Overcrowding is a concept measured in terms of persons per dwelling, whilst density is the ratio of persons (or dwellings) per unit of land. More dwellings per unit of land raises residential density but does not result in residential overcrowding. Density is not, therefore, a measure of urban quality. As Jane Jacobs has argued, a high concentration of population is one of the necessary conditions for flourishing city diversity.[51] Nor are density differences necessarily descriptive of different types of development: in particular, high–rise development does not necessarily follow from high densities.

Density standards in practice reflect a variety of different concerns. Pressure for higher urban densities is prompted by a concern to conserve agricultural land and to make more efficient use of under-used urban sites. It is also prompted by high land values—again as leading to a more efficient use—although in this case the arguments are less convincing because the relationship works both ways. Land values are the product not only of location but of development potential, and within the middle range of residential densities for an area, the higher the density the greater the development potential and the higher the site value. As a general rule, developers will wish to build at the highest densities for which there is a market demand.

Densities may therefore be set on a maximum or minimum basis, according to the direction in which the economic pressures are likely to push the developer. They also vary substantially according to the type and location of the development, but the reasons for the variation are seldom clearly articulated. Little is understood about human needs for space,[52] and

---

[51] *The Death and Life of Great American Cities* (Jonathan Cape, 1962), p.205.
[52] For a detailed critique, see L.A. Stein, "The Relevance of Density Controls" (1978) 1 *Urban Law and Policy* 51.

standards tend to be informed less by research and analysis of consumer preference than by unsubstantiated beliefs as to housing mix and historical patterns. Professor Abercrombie's early development plan for London,[53] for example, based its net zoning policy on historical patterns of densities, with high densities at the centre, falling, through 10 concentric rings, to lower densities beyond, thereby reinforcing rather than disturbing, the existing pattern of land value distribution. The earlier standards tended to be expressed as averages, leaving the levels to be raised or lowered on a site by site basis, but retaining a general overall control on the type of development in each density zone. But the result was that standards became minima, and that conforming rather than variable densities became the norm. More recent practice has been to promote a variety of densities in new development, particularly on larger sites, by specifying an overall average density and seeking a spread in different housing forms. The control has thus become an instrument for ensuring a mix of unit densities, with a view to achieving a social mix of population between families (low density with gardens), elderly persons (higher density, low rise) and persons without families (high density, high rise).

The controls give authorities a mechanism through which to regulate housing development in very general terms, but they do not in themselves regulate design or bulk. The Department's Research Study found that "there is nothing in the way of housing environment benefit that can be gained by the imposition of a density standard which could not be better achieved by designing directly for the benefit."[54] Designing for a benefit is too subjective an ideal for everyday development control, however, and the ultimate value to planners of density controls is that they give a firm, quantified, starting point for negotiations on design and layout.

(b) Types of density standard

Density standards are expressed in five main alternative forms, and local planning authorities vary in which they select. The forms are

"1. *Persons per acre or hectare* (for development control purposes this may have to be turned into accommodation per acre or hectare by applying a hypothetical occupancy rate).
2. *Dwellings per acre or hectare.*
3. *Habitable rooms per acre or hectare* ("habitable room" is an ambiguous term in practice. A kitchen may or may not be a habitable room. Bedrooms of certain dimensions are habitable rooms, but a small room in use as a bedroom is not a habitable room if its dimensions are below a certain level).
4. *Bedspaces per acre or hectare* (bedrooms are counted as double or single according to their dimensions).
5. *Floor space in square metres per hectare* (used by quantity surveyors to establish building possibilities and costs, but not much use in development control)."[55]

[53] *Greater London Plan* (H.M.S.O., 1944), Chap.8.
[54] *The Value of Standards for the External Residential Environment* para. 5.14.
[55] *Ibid.* para. 5.17.

Each method has certain advantages and disadvantages, but the major distinction is in terms of indicating the total housing capacity of a site. The measure of dwellings per acre provides a useful measure for assessing the total needs for roads and services for the development, but tells nothing of its population capacity. Bedspace capacity is the most accurate measure of that; and the measure of persons per acre is a useful indication of actual occupancy in the case of existing development for the purposes of measuring needs for other services, such as shops and schools, though it has little value as a control standard. The measurements may also be assessed on alternative bases, either as a *net* density which excludes land being used for shops, schools, and open space (but not normally local roads and incidental local space); or a *gross* density which includes all the land.

Statutory plans are the most common source of density standards, and local plan level is the most appropriate for the details to be settled. Structure plans have sometimes set general parameters, and in the case of the Greater London Development Plan general density standards were added by the Secretary of State after the Panel had concluded that the question "was too important to be left to the widely differing opinions of individual boroughs."[56] But the Secretary of State wished to go further and make special provision for lower density family housing in London, and the Plan now urges that densities on schemes for predominantly family housing should not exceed 85 habitable rooms per acre. In areas outside London circumstances are different, and density controls are seen as being largely the prerogative of local plans. "Broad density policies" may be acceptable in structure plans[57] (though to what purpose is unclear), but will be more closely defined in local plans. There is a trend also to breaking down overall policies by providing for standards to be set site by site through development briefs, as part of a package of measures prescribing the terms upon which development is to be carried out. It is a method which typically is more effective for growth areas, or where the land is in the ownership of the authority and is being offered for sale on the terms of the brief.

In the absence of a development brief the density standards for a particular site are usually (but not inevitably) settled in the outline permission. Permission is commonly sought for residential development at a particular density, and even if no density is specified it would be usual for the authority to limit it in the outline permission.

(c) Central government policy on densities

In central government thinking the level of overall densities for residential development has since 1947 been influenced largely by the need to contain urban sprawl and to conserve agricultural land, and successive Ministries have exhorted local authorities to allow higher densities and resist the trend towards low density suburbanisation. In a booklet published by the

---

[56] *G.L.D.P. Notice of Approval* para. 6.3. The Panel attached particular importance to density control overall, because of their "intangible feeling" that high densities themselves were part of the reason for the declining quality of life in London, and also because with all their limitations "density controls are the only existing measure by which some assurance of proper environmental standards can be assured in residential development": *G.L.D.P. Report of the Panel of Inquiry*, (H.M.S.O., 1973), para.6.73.

[57] D.O.E. Circular 4/79, Annex, para.2.25.

Ministry of Housing and Local Government in 1952, planners were urged to follow a general line of investigation "to try to define the first *essential* needs that must be met in a residential area, then to ascertain the *least* amount of land necessary to satisfy those needs, leaving for further consideration the relaxations that may be desirable in the way of more generous spacing."[58]

That theme was reinforced 10 years later in a planning bulletin issued by the Ministry, *Residential Areas: Higher Densities*,[59] which sought to demonstrate that higher densities could be achieved with low rise accommodation, and, if necessary, with tower blocks. The same theme underlay the *Development Control Policy Notes*[60] published by the Ministry in 1969. By the 1970s the emphasis had shifted to housing need, and the need to build smaller and lower priced houses to meet the demands of the increasing number of smaller households and of first–time house buyers. Authorities were this time urged to raise their minimum density standards to levels "significantly higher than the low figures which have been widely used in suburban development in the past"[61]; and developers were assured that the Secretary of State would be sympathetic, in dealing with appeals, "towards proposals for densities above the low levels commonly used at present, if these provide a good environment."[62] Two years later, authorities were again urged to make special provision, this time for the needs of small households, by allowing higher densities than would be normal for families.[63]

The reform of the forward planning system has given authorities an opportunity to review their density policies and to give effect to them in statutory plans. How far that review has altered established practices is difficult to assess, but the relative insulation of the local plans process from the detailed overview of the Secretary of State means that comparatively low density standards have been adopted by some authorities without central intervention. More recent policy advice from central government implicitly recognises this, but stresses the need to take into account the character and surroundings of the site, the design and layout of the development and its marketing possibilities as well as "any density policies for the area as a whole." The circular goes on to single out two types of development for which higher densities may be necessary: low cost starter homes, which may only be able to be built at higher than conventional densities, and small development and infill sites for which "general density requirements cannot be a reliable guide."[64]

3. *Plot Ratio Controls*

Plot ratio controls are the equivalent for commercial development purposes of density controls, and are expressed in terms of building bulk rather than population or employment densities. They prescribe an overall ratio of permitted floor space to site area in terms of a straightforward formula. A

[58] *The Density of Residential Areas* (H.M.S.O., 1952), para.5.
[59] Planning Bulletin No.2 (H.M.S.O., 1962).
[60] Note No.2, para.2.
[61] D.O.E. Circular 122/73, Annex A, para 21.
[62] *Widening the Choice: First Steps in Housing*, Cmnd.5280. (H.M.S.O. 1973). para.17.
[63] D.O.E. Circular 24/75 (Housing Needs and Action), para. 18.
[64] D.O.E. Circular 22/80 (Development Control) Annex A, para. 12.

plot ratio of 2:1 represents a two-storey building covering the whole site; but it equally describes a four-storey building covering half the site or an eight-storey building covering one quarter. The standards were designed originally to get away from former strict height controls and to have a more flexible system to control building bulk, to space out higher buildings and to preserve daylighting and ventilation for adjoining buildings.[65] They give authorities a basis from which to resist concentrated high–rise building, and from which to establish a more regular pattern of densities. But there is nothing pre-ordained about the actual ratios selected in practice, and the choice of multiplier depends on whether the planning authority wish to retain, reduce or increase existing density. Ratio standards therefore vary between cities, and Sim has found a range from around 5.5:1 in parts of the City of London to 2.25:1 in Cambridge, designed to preserve the city's skyline; with an average of around 3.5:1 adopted by such cities as Leeds and Glasgow.[66] Graduated ratios are favoured by some cities.

Effectiveness of the controls was undermined for some years by the provisions of the Third Schedule to the 1947 Act, which for the purposes of calculating liability to development charge, deemed the "enlargement, improvement or other alteration" of a building up to 10 per cent. of its original capacity to be part of its existing use. The developer still required planning permission, but if it were refused, the authority could face a compensation bill. Because the Act was expressed in terms of cubic capacity rather than floor area, it proved possible through modern building methods to keep within the 10 per cent. rule whilst expanding floor area by up to 40 per cent. That prospective capacity in turn enhanced the development value of the land, and thus the price an authority might have to pay if permission were refused. Until the rule was modified in 1963, the choice for local authorities was to grant permission for development and redevelopment which breached their plot ratio standards, or face the financial consequences.

Of all the standards controls, plot densities appear to be the most arbitrary in operation, and the most liable to provide the basis for negotiation towards ulterior ends between developer and planning authority. Their effect has been to establish the "right" to a certain density of development, and to push up building heights as other demands are made for surface level uses. The standard sets a minimum so far as developers are concerned, and financial pressures are too powerful for authorities to tinker with levels in the interests of variations and flexibility. Instead, they tend to manipulate the controls in the interests of financial expedience. A developer may, for example, be permitted to add a further storey to his proposed building in return for moving it back from the site frontage in order to accommodate a future road-widening scheme; or in return for providing public facilities such as pedestrian walkways or for vesting part of the site in the authority for their own statutory functions. The frequency of such deals is unknown, and only one instance—the Centre Point development in London—is well

---

[65] Plot ratio controls emerged originally as "floor space ratios" in the Ministry of Town and Country Planning's *Advisory Handbook on the Redevelopment of Central Areas* (H.M.S.O., 1947), which described them as "the simplest method by which Planning Authorities can determine, compare and control the density or distribution of building accommodation within areas of land of any size."

[66] D. Sim, "Effects and Effectiveness of Plot Ratio Controls" (1981) *Planning Outlook* 23.

documented.[67] In that case the developers agreed to acquire land wanted by the G.L.C. for road improvement and adjoining the development site, and to vest it in the authority in return for an undertaking that it could still be taken into account in calculating the plot ratio for the remaining site. The actual plot ratio achieved on the site has been estimated as around 10:1.[68] Deals of this sort reflect not only the essential arbitrariness of the standards, but also the disparity between property values and planning objectives.

That is reflected too in the effects observed in Sim's study of Glasgow, that a density limit once imposed immediately becomes a ceiling. There is pressure for the redevelopment of existing low density buildings so as to exploit the site's capacity as defined by the plot ratio, whether or not the building has come to the end of its economic life. But existing high density buildings tended not to be redeveloped, except in the case of Victorian purpose built office accommodation of grand design but wasteful space. In Glasgow, too, the controls were applied with some flexibility and trade-offs accepted against them. Over 40 per cent. of the new buildings in the area erected since 1947 exceeded the prescribed ratio.

4. Sunlight and Daylight

Designing buildings to ensure maximum benefit of sunlight and daylight is an important architectural priority, and it is reinforced and extended by the planning system. New buildings, especially in areas of high density development, need to be skilfully designed and located if they are to achieve maximum natural lighting and yet not to deprive other buildings of light.

The common law recognised no general right to light for existing buildings against new development except where such a right had been acquired by prescriptive uses over a lengthy period ("ancient lights"), eventually set by the Prescription Act 1832 as 20 years. Where that test was satisfied, the common law applied a highly subjective and uncertain test by which the extent of the entitlement could be measured:

" . . . generally speaking an owner of ancient lights is entitled to sufficient light according to the ordinary notions of mankind for the comfortable use and enjoyment of his house as a dwelling house, if it is a dwelling house, or for the beneficial use and occupation of the house if it is a warehouse, a shop or other place of business."[69]

But the common law right is of course a purely private right, which may be bought out[70] and which offers only limited public benefit. The rationale for

---

[67] See further O. Marriott, *The Property Boom* (1967), Chap. 4; and S. L. Elkin, *Politics and Land Use Planning*, (C.U.P., 1974), pp.64–70.

[68] Marriott, *ante.*, p.114.

[69] *Colls* v. *Home and Colonial Stores Ltd.* [1904] A.C. 179 at 208. For a more recent example of the extent of the doctrine see *Allen* v. *Greenwood* [1980] Ch. 119 where the obstruction of light to a private greenhouse was held to amount to an interference with the owner's rights to light.

[70] On the marketability of ancient lights, Lord MacNaghten in *Colls* v. *Home and Colonial Stores Ltd.*, *ante*, at 193 observed: "Often a person who is engaged in a large building scheme has to pay money right and left in order to avoid litigation. . . . there is quite as much oppression on the part of those who invoke the assistance of the Court to protect some ancient lights, which they have never before considered of any great value, as there is on the part of those who are improving the neighbourhood by the erection of buildings that must necessarily to some extent interfere with the light of adjoining premises."

exercising supplementary control through planning is simply that of achieving a better urban environment; and the view that "Of all that has to be done to make cities good to live in, nothing is more fundamental than letting in the sun and keeping open the sky."[71]

Planning practice in assessing the daylight and sunlight requirements and implications of new development is guided by standards prepared and recommended by the Department of the Environment. The "planning aim" of the standards is stated to be "To ensure good conditions in the local environment *considered broadly* with enough sunlight and daylight on and between the faces of the building blocks for good interior and exterior conditions."[72]

The primary purpose of the standards is to achieve adequate sunlighting and daylighting for the new building itself, and the criteria recommended for the spacing of building blocks on site are expressed in terms of sunlight angles against the sides of the proposed development. The standards are expressed in precise, quantified terms, and calculations are aided by special, protractor-like measuring indicators. The mathematical exactitude of the exercise tends to obscure the assumptions that have gone into its design, and it sets sharp boundaries which lack any real validity except as the results of applying generalised and unsubstantiated assumptions about the needs of residents and occupants to a particular site irrespective of the characteristics of the site. Applying the standards also protects the light of existing buildings to some extent because of the direct lighting relationship between buildings, and the spacing requirements of the indicators. But whether such protection should be given any further consideration is said to depend upon "the functional efficiency, value and likely life of the building in question, and in particular whether it is listed as being of historic or architectural value"; and also relevant (though equally unmeasurable) is whether the other building is itself a good neighbour and not a dominant consumer of sunlight and daylight.[73]

These are flexible criteria, and the basic quantitative standards themselves are purely advisory. But they are capable of having a significant effect upon the shape and location of new buildings, though not perhaps as marked as that of their predecessors, the bye-law daylight controls based upon building angles, which in London (under the London Building Acts) produced the characteristic tiered "wedding cake" effect. The impact of the new standards is reinforced by the plot ratio controls, because where the daylight and sunlight indicators show that part only of a site is suitable for development, the developer's response is to exploit the plot ratio potential on that part by building high rise. In the case of the new National Westminster Bank building in the City, daylight and sunlight indicators not only dictated the height of the building (eventually 52 floors instead of the 9 floors originally proposed by the Bank, on a 5.5:1 plot ratio) but also its triangular shape because of the angles drawn by the indicators.[74]

---

[71] *Sunlight and Daylight* (H.M.S.O., 1971), Foreword.
[72] *Ibid.*para.2.3.
[73] *Ibid.*para.6.4.
[74] A damning account of the impact of the controls on the building's design appeared in *The Sunday Times Magazine*, March 14, 1979.

The standards are widely applied in practice to development where daylighting and sunlighting adequacy is in issue, but they overlap also with standards for the spacing of buildings to preserve privacy and view. An authority may still insist upon wider spacing than may be indicated by the sunlight/daylight standards, and the Department of Environment *Research Report* found that

" . . . the common run of development control practice still sticks to the traditional 70 or so feet test for the mass of face-to-face and back-to-back road frontage housing for which applications are still being made. We got the impression that development controllers tend to regard this as the only safe and understood spacing rule for the commonplace 'builder's lay out' in which environmental design initiative is absent. It remains one of the most universal and high priority requirements of much current practice."[75]

The daylight/sunlight indicators and spacing standards are intended to guide the lay-out of decent urban development. But like the other planning standards, their "guidance" status rapidly converts to "rules" status in the effort to resist unimaginative and exploitative development. But they are at least genuine guides to quality control.

5. *Roads and Streets*

There is an overlap in responsibility for roads between local planning authority and local highway authority, and although various standards are commonly enforced through the planning system, they mainly originate from the highway authority. The highway authority's influence has legal backing in two forms. First, there is the statutory relationship between the two authorities secured through the consultation and direction provisions of the General Development Order.[76] The highways authority are required to be consulted in cases involving the "formation, laying out or alteration of any means of access" to a highway (other than a trunk road, where responsibility lies with the Secretary of State). The highways authority may respond to each such application individually by issuing a direction, or a notification that they do not propose to issue one (without which the planning authority are unable to proceed); they may issue a *general* direction expressed in terms of design standards; or they may arrange for the planning authority to exercise the function on their behalf in accordance with prescribed standards. Many highway authorities have simply issued codes of practice, retaining power to grant waivers in special cases. The guiding factor in setting standards for new access to highways is safety, and the requirements of the highway authority are generally directed to the location of the junction, and to ensuring adequate visibility splays (or "sight lines") for emerging traffic.

Second, in the case of new streets to be constructed on-site by the developer, the highways authority has the power to insist that they be made

---

[75] *The Value of Standards for the External Residential Environment*, para.8.22. The Report goes on to condemn this approach as permitting "neither of a sense of urban enclosure in front of, nor adequate privacy behind, the dwelling."

[76] *Ante*, p. 232. The arrangements are presently under review.

up to satisfactory standards and comply with their standard design criteria before agreeing to adopt them and maintain them thereafter at public expense. These standards may be imposed through planning conditions or by special agreements between developer and highway authority.[77] In new residential development roads account for between 15 and 30 per cent. (depending on residential densities) of the total area of development, and their design, layout and landscaping are therefore highly significant.

Detailed county standards are therefore common, and this background explains both why road standards are published by more than two-thirds of district-level authorities (see Table 12), and also why they are regarded as being among the least flexible in practice. The division in responsibility can mean that roads requirements are insisted upon by the county highway engineer regardless of district planning policy; and that district council officers have little choice but to apply them. Conflict between the two tiers may take months to resolve, ultimately perhaps by the county's highways and transportation committee. The Department of the Environment *Research Report* found that:

> " . . . road standards are strictly adhered to and have a very high priority. . . . While the standards are promulgated as "recommended," they are often treated as a minima by highway authorities. They are unquestioningly assumed to be beneficial environmentally and to contribute positively to safety."[78]

The Secretaries of State have now acted in the case of residential development in an attempt to hold highway authorities to the standards recommended by central government in the Department's Design Bulletin No.32, *Residential Roads and Footpaths*, by announcing that they will not support "any planning or highway authority requiring standards which are higher than those which would result from applying principles set out in [the] Design Bulletin,"[79] and requesting authorities not to circumvent this ruling in their use of adoption agreements. The effect is to set the *Bulletin* standards not just as a norm, but as maxima; but whether highway authorities will in practice change their present policies is doubtful.

There is, however, increasing technical support for the view that high specification roads with broad carriageways, lengthy sight lines and wide pavements may actually militate against road safety by encouraging higher vehicle speeds.[80] Road standards were originally set with the firm objectives of safety and allowing the free flow of traffic at a reasonable speed. The latter objective has tended to dominate, as engineers came to attach more importance to the technical aspects of design speed than to notions of environmental quality. The Department's *Design Bulletin* goes some way towards restoring a balance, by moving from the "hard" standards of the earlier departmental advice contained in *Roads in Urban Areas*[81] and *Layout*

---

[77] Highways Act 1980, s.38 (formerly Highways Act 1959, s.40); see further *post*, p. 382.
[78] D.O.E. *Research Report, ante* note 75, para.17.17.
[79] D.O.E. Circular 22/80, Annex A, para. 13.
[80] See, *e.g.* J.M. McCluskey, "Roads for People" (1977) *Highway Engineer* 12; and the D.O.E. *Research Report, ante* note 75, Chap.17.
[81] H.M.S.O. (1967).

of Roads in Rural Areas,[82] each of which specified recommended carriageway widths and sight line measurements; to a softer approach which analyses the implications of, for example, dropping from a recommended maximum carriageway width of 5.5 metres in residential layouts, to a recommended minimum of 3 metres, and leaves it to authorities to apply the analysis to individual sites. The *Bulletin* also places greater emphasis on environmental design.

The summary of common carriageway width standards contained in Table 13 needs therefore to be read in the context of the more flexible approach urged in the *Design Bulletin* and the specifications are also liable to be affected in practice by particular requirements of local services such as refuse vehicles and emergency services.

Visibility splays are another matter to which comparatively precise standards need to be applied in practice. Uncontrolled junctions between access roads and through roads are to be designed to ensure clear visibility for emerging and through traffic over an area whose parameters are set in relation to the speed limit and traffic volume on the through road, with greater distances typically required in rural areas.[83] Achieving the standards creates problems in some cases because the land required may not be in the ownership of the applicant, and may need to be acquired by him (and usually, after completion of the works, offered for adoption by the highway authorities) before planning permission is granted.[84]

Table 13

Common Carriageway Width Standards

Carriageway widths	
(a) *residential areas*	
Local distributor roads	6.75m.
Access roads	
principal access	5.5m.
service road	5m.
access road (cars only)	4m.
footpath	2m.
(b) *industrial areas*	7.30m. (wider on certain local distributor roads)
(c) *principal business areas*	6.75–7.30m.

[82] H.M.S.O. 1968.
[83] For details of national standards, see *Residential Roads and Footpaths,* p.38; *Roads in Urban Areas,* p.50; *Layout of Roads in Rural Areas* Chap. 4.
[84] See further *post,* pp. 340–342.

6. *Parking*

Parking standards are adopted by many authorities, but there is considerable variation in the way they are defined and applied. The earlier policies of making ample provision for off-street parking to accommodate peak demands has now been reversed in the case of authorities wishing to restrict private motor-car use in urban areas; and instead of specifiying minimum requirements some have moved to imposing maximum standards. Parking standards need therefore to be established against the transportation policies for the area and against planning policies. As a general rule, however, planning authorities remain convinced of the need to make some provision for off-street parking, particularly in new residential development and in cases where a new building or change of use is likely to generate vehicle movements. The general basis of standards is a crude ratio of car spaces to dwellings, varying in practice from under 1:1 for old people's estates to 3:1 for some private developments. Typical standards for other development include one space per bedroom for hotels and guesthouses (more if there are public facilities), and one per unit of gross floor area in the case of office development. In dense urban areas where there is high use of public transport the requirements may be as low as 1:1,000 square metres, but in less dense areas it often rises to as high as 1:20 square metres.

The standards are liable to create particular problems in the case of redevelopment and refurbishment of sites or buildings in high density areas, because of the lack of ground-level space. The requirements may of course be waived by the authority, or they may be commuted by the payment of money in lieu. The theory is that the developer should be able to off-load on to the authority the burden of meeting the parking requirements for the site elsewhere in the area, subject to his contributing to their costs in so doing. The advantage to the authority of such a scheme is that they are able to meet parking demand more flexibly and retain control over it, and the developer for his part is able to shake off a physical restraint on development.

But schemes for commuted car-parking payments have in practice often been badly managed, and have as a result become entangled with planning gain and confused with the purchase of planning permissions (discussed in Chapter 9 *post*). Contributions made by developers to parking funds have not always been used for parking; and the delicate balance sought by the courts and central government (the developer may not be *required* to contribute, but may do so *voluntarily*) has hindered a more open and realistic relationship. The Secretary of State has insisted that no planning decision should turn upon the readiness of a developer to contribute towards the costs of off-street parking to be incurred by the authority, and a planning condition which imposed such a requirement would be unlawful.[85] But permission may, of course, be refused altogether on the grounds that on-site parking standards have not been met, an objection which evaporates if the developer is prepared to meet the authority's contribution requirements. The issues are thus primarily economic rather than ethical or doctrinal, but present practice remains confused.

[85] See further *post*, pp. 343–345.

7. Open Space

Standards of open space provision in new development, where they exist, are probably the most variable of all planning standards. There are no national guidelines, and there is a variety of different types of open space which may be required, including common amenity space, private open space, landscaping areas and children's play areas. The extent of local provision tends also to hinge on the division of financial responsibility between public sector and private sector,[86] and precise standards are sometimes avoided in statutory plans in order to allow flexibility in negotiations with developers. The following extract from a recently approved local plan illustrates the tendency:

> "Developers are expected to provide and lay out local open space (amenity open space and children's play spaces) as part of their development to the satisfaction of the local planning authority. Arrangements for the maintenance of local open space should be agreed with the District Council. Major open space (sports grounds and parkland) will be provided by the district and parish councils. [The] District Council will expect developers to make contributions towards the provision of these major open spaces identified in the plan."

The general standards adopted by one county council and carried through into the local plans for their area are set out in Table 14, and give a general indication of the level of provision expected by a growth area authority.

The first two categories would usually serve such a large catchment area that a developer would be required to contribute to them only in the case of a large development scheme. Standards applicable to suburban development in growth areas on green field sites do not translate readily to inner urban areas, where the guiding considerations will be the adequacy of existing open space and scale and location of the development.

Design and maintenance are important issues in providing open space. As to the former, it is a common criticism that open space design tends often to take second place to housing design, and to "consist of remnants which are the randomly located waste products of spacing requirements connected with provision of dwellings and vehicle space."[87] Maintenance, too, creates difficulties. Unless a management scheme can be devised between the occupants of the new accommodation,[88] the maintenance burden must fall on the local authority. Attempts to impose any continuing liability on the developer are rarely satisfactory. Open-ended requirements by way of planning conditions are in practice unenforceable, and planning agreements are avoidable by the simple expedient of transferring the site to an assetless company. The only satisfactory method is for arrangements to be made for the land to be dedicated to and adopted by the local authority under the Open Spaces Act 1906, usually accompanied by a capitalised contribution by

---

[86] See further post, p. 347.
[87] The Value of Standards for the External Residential Environment para. 16.6.
[88] The major barrier to such schemes in practice has been the unenforceability of positive covenants between freeholders; but an alternative is to employ rent charges instead (expressly saved by the Rent Charges Act 1977): for a precedent see the Precedents for the Conveyancer, Vol. 2, p.9577.

Table 14

Common Open Space Standards

Minimum open space provision per 1,000 population: Hampshire County Council.	
Urban parks	0.4 ha.
Sports grounds	1.0 ha.
Amenity open space	1.4 ha.
(including	
children's play spaces	0.2 ha.
children's "kickabout" areas	0.8 ha.
landscaped amenity areas	0.4 ha.)

Source: Totton District Plan, Hants County Council, 1980.

the developer towards future maintenance costs. Management of open space which remains in the developer's ownership but is maintained by the authority, is also a matter of some difficulty, and authorities have come to seek bye-law making powers under local legislation that will extend to privately owned amenity land and regulate its use.[89]

---

[89] See, *e.g.* Tyne and Wear Act 1980, s.5.

CHAPTER 8

THE TOOLS OF PLANNING CONTROL: CONDITIONS AND AGREEMENTS

A. Introduction

The power to impose conditions and to enter into agreements brings an important measure of flexibility into development control. The authority's response to a planning application is not limited simply to "yes" or "no": it may be "yes, subject to conditions." But in practice, the two powers have proved highly controversial, for reasons which are largely economic. At the heart of the controversy lies the question of the distribution of the external costs of development, and particularly the allocation of costs between the private and the public sectors. Most planning conditions impose costs on the developer. Some costs are direct and involve an increase in development costs, such as in the case of a landscaping condition, or one which requires that the building be finished in particular materials more expensive than those proposed by the developer. Other costs are less direct, and may be reflected in the land value of the site. An hours-of-working condition, for example, may reduce the value of the completed development by limiting the number of purchasers or tenants willing to accept it, or by restricting the potential productivity of the unit. Similarly, a condition imposed on a permission for the erection of a dwelling house, limiting its occupancy to a person employed in agriculture or a person having some local employment or residential qualification, may be expected to limit the value of the completed development significantly.

As a general rule, the power to impose planning conditions carries no compensation liability. The costs imposed on developers are not recoverable from the planning authority. But if the authority were to attempt to intervene against an existing use of land, imposing conditions by way of a discontinuance order, the full cost would fall on them. The difference is that an application for planning permission is a voluntary act. A permission granted subject to unwelcome conditions need not be implemented. But conditions imposed under discontinuance procedures are involuntary and binding.

There are two important and interrelated consequences of this economic relationship. The first arises from the traditional allocation of functions between developers and public authorities for the servicing of new development. In modern Britain, the provision of general services is a function primarily of public agencies. The off-site physical services required for a new housing estate, for example, are provided by the water authorities (water supply, sewerage and sewage disposal), the highways authority (new off-site roads or alterations to existing roads required to accommodate the development) and the district or county authority (parks and amenities). In some cases the developer may be required to make a contribution to the capital costs involved, but the rules are arbitrary and ill-defined. They frequently impose a high cost upon the first developer whose development unlocks the area, but not upon subsequent developers. There is no overall rational system of infrastructure contributions, and as government expenditure cuts have become more stringent in recent years the capacity of public agencies to provide the necessary services has diminished. If the site cannot be serviced, planning permission may be refused. The development is "premature," until the expenditure programmes of the agencies can accommodate the investment required. But developers have often found it financially advantageous to bring forward the development by contributing all or part of the infrastructure costs. The traditional allocation of functions has thus been superseded in some areas by a pragmatic reallocation.

The second consequence is that there is an economic imbalance between the use of the regulatory power to achieve environmental improvements, and the use of the discontinuance power involving compensation liability. Planning authorities have sought to use conditions and agreements, when granting permission for new development, as a means of securing control over existing uses on the same site. It is a practice which achieves largely fortuitous improvements in circumstances which would otherwise involve compensation.

There are two competing theories which underly analysis of the power to impose conditions and to enter into planning agreements. The first, which we may call the *privilege theory*, holds that planning permission for development is a privilege rather than an entitlement, and that developers may be called upon to bear all the social costs occasioned by the development. They need not implement the permission if the terms are disadvantageous. It is a theory which ties closely in with the views that development control may be deployed as an indirect means of recouping enhanced developed values arising from the grant of permission, and it has some reinforcement from the apparent willingness of developers to meet additional costs imposed in this way as the price of obtaining permission.

The second theory, which we may call the *private property theory*, holds that planning control is an interference with established proprietary rights, and that applicants are entitled to planning permission in the absence of cogent reasons to the contrary. The powers should be interpreted in such a way as not to deprive an applicant of any compensation entitlement, and not as to disturb private rights of ownership. Planning losses should be compensated, and financial gains recouped only through the national taxation system.

The approach of the courts has wavered between the two but the overall trend has been in favour of the latter theory; and this has meant that in practice authorities have turned increasingly towards the use of planning agreements and a process based notionally on consensus, albeit against the backcloth of regulation. Planning agreements provide a means of passing public costs onto the private sector, and are not only broader in scope than conditions, but less susceptible to challenge.

B. Planning Conditions

1. *The statutory discretion*

Section 29 of the 1971 Act confers a broad discretion on local planning authorities to attach "such conditions as they think fit" to the grant of planning permission. It is governed by the overall requirement that they should have regard to the provisions of the development plan and to any other material considerations,[1] but is otherwise unlimited. But it has been consistently accepted that some limitation must necessarily be implied, and the fundamental priciple is that the power is conferred only for "planning" purposes. It has in practice been narrowly construed. Thus in 1932 the Minister of Health took care to caution local planning authorities that they should not use the power as a means of charging developers a fee in respect of the services of the clerk to the council in connection with handling planning applications, but should instead bear the costs themselves by raising his salary for the additional duties.[2] And his successor, the Minister of Town and Country Planning, had no hesitation in quashing on appeal conditions which would have required developers to enter into planning agreements conceding rights beyond the ambit of planning legislation,[3] requiring the payment of an annual sum as security for the fulfilment of conditions[4] or requiring that land should be conveyed to the authority.[5]

But not until the late 1950s did the matter come to the courts for consideration, and it is significant that the terms in which they came to define the implied limitations to the power were strongly influenced by past ministerial practice and rulings.[6]

The most recent reformulation of the test was undertaken in the House of Lords in *Newbury District Council* v. *Secretary of State for the Environment*,[7] where it was held that there were three limbs to the implied restriction on section 29. First, that a condition must be imposed for a "planning purpose," and not for an ulterior purpose. Secondly, that the condition must fairly and reasonably relate to the development permitted by the planning permission. Thirdly, that the condition should not be so unreasonable that no reasonable planning authority properly advised could have imposed it.

A condition which breaches any of these tests is invalid, but invalidity is not the only route through which a condition may be struck down. The developer may additionally appeal to the Secretary of State on the merits of the condition, and there is broad power for him to modify or discharge a condition against broad planning criteria.[8] But where the condition is, in his opinion, invalid under the *Newbury* formulae, he will be obliged to set it aside; and he may be obliged to regard the entire permission as invalid, if the invalid condition cannot readily be severed from it. The invalidity rules therefore govern the Secretary of State's jurisdiction on appeal, and in practice most challenges to the validity of conditions are made through the statutory appeals system, either directly or in the course of an enforcement appeal.

The criteria adopted by the Secretary of State in reviewing conditions imposed by local planning authorities incorporate questions both of validity and of merits. The test applied[9] is to ask whether the condition is:

---

[1] See further the analysis of this formula, *ante*, p. 282.
[2] *Fourteenth Annual Report of the Minister of Health 1932-33*, Cmd.4372, p.129.
[3] See, *e.g. Bulletin of Selected Planning Appeals* No.I/18.
[4] *Bulletin of Selected Planning Appeals* No.III/16.
[5] *Bulletin of Selected Planning Appeals* No. II/17.
[6] See, *e.g.* the judgement of Lord Denning in *Pyx Granite Ltd.* v. *M.H.L.G.*[1958] 1 Q.B.554.
[7] [1981] A.C. 578.
[8] T.C.P.A. 1971, s.36(3); and *c.f.* s.88B(1) (enforcement appeals).
[9] M.H.L.G. Circular 5/68, para. 6.

"(a) necessary
(b) relevant to planning
(c) relevant to the development to be permitted
(d) enforceable
(e) precise
(f) reasonable"

Both (b) and (c) are aspects of the *Newbury* formula, and (f) is a more broadly expressed version of the third head of validity under the *Newbury* formula. The Secretary of State is prepared to review a condition which is in his opinion unreasonable on the merits, and not merely where it is arbitrary or manifestly unreasonable. The distinction is important, because in the former case he may discharge or modify the condition on appeal, or substitute a fresh condition for it; but in the latter case he may have to regard the condition as invalid. Ground (a) of the Secretary of State's criteria is perhaps also based upon a more broadly expressed concept of reasonableness, and the question posed by it is:

" . . . whether, without the condition, permission for the proposed development would have to be refused. If the answer to that question is "No", the condition needs some special justification. It is not enough to say that a condition will do no harm. If it is to be right to impose it, it ought to do some good."[10]

The question of enforceability, under ground (d), raises a similar point, because there can be little justification for imposing an unenforceable condition. Enforceability is also relevant to the requirement of precision, because a condition may be so vague as to be unenforceable, such as a requirement to improve an access "if the growth of traffic makes it desirable." But precision also goes to validity, and it is discussed further below.[11]

The *Newbury* formulae are couched in terms of general principle, and their application often calls for highly subjective judgement. At their heart lies the judicial concept of reasonableness: planning authorities should act "reasonably", and if they do, the conditions they impose will themselves be "reasonable."[12] The test is doctrinal rather than economic, and it is no justification for the imposition of any condition that the developer is in a sufficiently strong financial position to be able to accept without hardship the burden cast upon him. Although there is an underlying implication of economic judgement, particularly in the case of unreasonableness (the fact that a condition substantially prevents the profitable development of a site may be evidence of manifest unreasonableness), it is not a case of simple economic assessment.

The three heads of the *Newbury* formula need now to be examined in greater detail.

[10] *Ibid.*para.7. It is an issue going to validity in the sense that it cannot be "expedient" to impose an unnecessary condition: see, *e.g. British Airports Authority* v. *Secretary of State for Scotland* [1980] J.P.L. 260 at 263.
[11] *Post,* p. 348.
[12] See, *e.g. Fawcett Properties Ltd.* v.*Buckinghamshire C.C.* [1961] A.C. 636 at 679 *per* Lord Denning.

2. *Conditions must fulfil some planning purpose*

The basis of this limitation is the fact that the power is conferred in legislation regulating town and country planning and that, more particularly, the planning authority are required, in exercising it, to have regard to the development plan and to any other material considerations. It matters not that a condition may also fulfil some other purpose, provided it has a planning basis. But if the purpose in imposing it is solely or primarily to pursue some non-planning objective, it will be invalid. Thus in *R. v. Hillingdon London Borough Council, ex parte Royco Homes Ltd.*[13] the authority had imposed conditions, on a grant of planning permission for residential development, requiring that the dwellings should first be occupied by persons on the local authority's housing waiting list, and should thereafter for a period of 10 years be rented to persons enjoying security of tenure under the Rent Acts. The Divisional Court readily accepted the argument that the purpose of the conditions was to relieve the local authority of part of its burden as housing authority to provide homes for the homeless. In the words of Bridge J., it was "difficult to see how any authority could go further towards unburdening themselves and placing on the shoulders of the applicant the duty to provide housing accommodation which Parliament has said in Part V of the Housing Act 1957 shall be performed by the local authority in the various ways in which it can be performed under that Part of that Act, all of them requiring acquisition of the land by the local authority."[14]

But the decision raises a number of questions. There is first the question of what is a legitimate "planning" purpose, and at what point does a purpose stray so far from planning as to be "ulterior"? Simply to pursue a "housing" objective would not in itself necessarily take a condition outside the powers of the planning Acts, because land use planning is centrally concerned with the issues of adequacy and quality of housing accommodation. The primary objection in the *Royco* case was therefore not that the housing motive was ulterior, but that the purpose was to shift a financial burden from the authority to the developer, and that that was an ulterior purpose. That might have been a valid criticism had the council in fact proposed to *require* the developer to assume such a burden, but it is interesting to note that, on the background facts of the case, which were not apparently brought to the attention of the Court, the economic question arose in a quite different form. The authority had been negotiating for the acquisition of the land in order to build council housing on it themselves, and a compulsory purchase order had been made but not confirmed.[15] The purpose of imposing the conditions was so as not to prejudice the confirmation of the order, nor to prejudice the authority's own proposals in the event of the developer commencing work before the order had been confirmed. Doubtless, too, for valuation purposes the authority's liability to pay compensation would have been increased by the granting of a full permission, but not by one subject to conditions limiting the use to that which the authority themselves proposed for the site. Under the *privilege* theory the condition would have been regarded as unobjectionable.

[13] [1974] 1 Q.B. 720.
[14] *Ibid.* p. 733.
[15] The background is set out at [1974] J.P.L. 470.

The second question which arises is the relationship between adopted planning policies and the conditions imposed by authorities. It is clear that the policies contained in a development plan may be relied upon to justify, as satisfying a "planning" consideration, a condition which might otherwise require special justification. Indeed, Lord Scarman in the *Newbury* case insisted that the condition "must fairly and reasonably relate to the provisions of the development plan and to planning considerations affecting the land."[16] So far as it suggests that in every case there should be development plan justification for a condition that formulation no doubt goes too far, and a condition may be properly imposed in pursuit of some material planning consideration which nowhere appears in the development plan: not every item of relevant planning policy is expected to be recorded in the formal plans. But there remains the question of how far the formal plan may be taken as being conclusive as to material planning policy. If, for example, the local plan adopted by the London Borough of Hillingdon had included a policy statement to the effect that the authority desired to ensure that a balanced housing policy of private renting, council housing and owner-occupation would be pursued in their area, and that they proposed to require that there be a mix of tenures in all new housing development, would a condition reflecting those aims be invalid? The validity of the policy itself is protected by the preclusive clause[17] unless challenged within six weeks of the plan's approval or adoption. It is a "planning" policy, but its effect is again to cast some of the burden of implementation onto the private sector. It is not invalid on that ground alone, and it may be that its formal inclusion in the approved plan is sufficient to accord it the stamp of materiality for planning purposes.

3. The condition should fairly and reasonably relate to the permitted development

This limitation is similarly directed to ensuring that the power is not exercised for extraneous motives, by insisting that it be directed only to the development which is the subject of the planning permission.

The starting point of the modern law on this limitation is the judgement of Lord Denning in *Pyx Granite Co. Ltd.* v. *Minister of Housing and Local Government*, where he ruled that:

" . . . conditions, to be valid, must fairly and reasonably relate to the permitted development. The planning authority are not at liberty to use their powers for an ulterior object, however desirable that object may seem to them to be in the public interest."[18]

But there has been some dispute as to how closely conditions should be required to relate to the actual development authorised by the permission. Lord Denning himself has subsequently stressed that the test was not to be

---

[16] [1981] A.C. 578 at 618.
[17] T.C.P.A. 1971, ss.242, 244: see further *post*, p. 642.
[18] [1958] 1 Q.B. 554 at 572. The question was not considered in the House of Lords: [1960] A.C. 260, but the formula was subsequently approved in the House of Lords in *Fawcett Properties Ltd.* v. *Buckinghamshire C.C.* [1961] A.C. 636 at 674, 679, 685; in *Mixnam' Properties Ltd.* v. *Chertsey U.D.C.* [1965] A.C. 735 at 751, 761 and in the *Newbury* case.

too narrowly construed,[19] and it has come to be accepted that a condition may "fairly and reasonably" relate, even although it is imposed in respect of other parts of the site or even other sites under the applicant's control. Thus, the courts have upheld conditions restricting not only the use and occupation of buildings authorised by the permission, but also of other buildings on the site: conditions requiring, for example, that the use of existing on-site office accommodation be restricted for the future to purely ancillary office use[20]; that noise levels, working hours and noxious emissions from the whole of a factory be restricted as a condition upon permission to erect an extension[21]; and that land shown as allocated for car-parking on drawings submitted as part of an application to reconstruct a railway station, should be actually used for that purpose and no other.[22]

The *Newbury* case itself, however, has now drawn the limitation more narrowly. In that case the applicants had obtained planning permission in 1962 for the use of two aircraft hangers, which had been erected on a wartime airfield, for warehousing purposes. The permission was in effect a temporary permission for 10 years and a condition attached to it required that the buildings be removed at the end of 1972. The condition was intended to promote the authority's development plan policies, which referred to problems arising from the use of buildings on sites relinquished by government departments, whose location in open countryside made them unsuitable for employment use, and stated that the authority therefore proposed to seek their removal.

Reversing the Court of Appeal decision, the House of Lords held that no planning permission had in fact been required in 1962 because of the existing use of the building at that time, and that the applicants were not prevented from relying on that point now, despite having acted on the permission and not having challenged the condition at the time. But the House also ruled the condition to be invalid, accepting the view of the Secretary of State that the purpose of the condition was to restore the area as a whole rather than to meet any planning need arising from the actual change of use for which permission had been sought. They declined to go as far as the Ministry circular, which had insisted categorically that a condition requiring the removal of a building could reasonably be imposed only where the need for removal springs directly from the fact that a new building is to be erected.[23] There might be cases in which a removal condition would be appropriate on a permission for the change of use of a building, but the Secretary of State had committed no error in law in finding that this was not such a case.

But the effect of the ruling is to tighten up the requirment that a condition should "relate" to the permitted development, and it limits the ability of the

[19] In *Newbury D.C.* v. *S.O.S.E.* [1978] 1 W.L.R. 1241 at 1248; and Lawton L.J. observed, at p. 1252, that "what Lord Denning said [in *Pyx Granite*] must not be construed as if they were statutory words."
[20] *A.I. & P (Stratford) Ltd.* v. *Tower Hamlets L.B.C.* (1975) 237 E.G. 415.
[21] *Penwith D.C.* v. *S.O.S.E.* (1977) 34 P. & C.R. 269. And compare *Pyx Granite Co. Ltd.* v. *M.H.L.G.(supra)* where conditions restricting working hours and requiring the eventual removal of screening and crushing machinery already installed at another site were upheld.
[22] *Kingston-upon-Thames Royal L.B.C.* v. *S.O.S.E.* [1974] 1 All E.R. 193.
[23] M.H.L.G. Circular 5/68, para. 9.

planning authority to achieve environmental improvements in respect of the site as a whole.

Two particular instances of the general rule call for comment. They raise the question of how far the requirement that the condition should relate to the permitted development (or, for that matter, either of the other two heads of the *Newbury* formula) requires that the power should be limited to the terms of the planning application, and to the land which is the subject of the application.

(a) The terms of the planning application

It is clear that the power to impose conditions may not be used so as to alter radically the nature of the development sought by the planning application. It would not be open to an authority, for example, to grant an application for office development but attach a condition requiring the building to be used solely for residential purposes. The ground of objection in such a case is not that the condition does not relate to the permitted development, but that it has unilaterally redefined the development for which approval was sought. But it is equally clear that conditions may be used to modify the developer's proposals, and to inject new elements into the development of a less fundamental nature; so as, for example, to reduce the proposed residential densities on an outline application,[24] or to require tree planting,[25] off-street car parking[26] or suitable visibility splays,[27] or to delete a proposed means of access.[28] Provided that in each case the requirement is one which does relate fairly and reasonably to the permitted development, it is no objection that strays beyond the terms of the actual application.

Similarly, a condition may be used to scale down the applicant's proposals, by granting permission in respect of part only of the development for which approval is sought; or in respect of part only of the land to which the application relates. The test is not whether the application is capable of being split up into readily severable components, but whether the effect of such a condition would be to grant permission for development so substantially different from that originally proposed that to grant it would be to deprive those who should have been consulted on the changed development of that opportunity.[29]

(b) Conditions relating to land outside the application site

The proposition has emerged that, to be valid, a condition should relate either to land included in the application, or to other land within the

---

[24] As to the general matters which may be reserved by condition on an outline approval, see *ante.*, p. 200.

[25] There is a statutory duty upon authorities to ensure whenever appropriate that conditions are imposed to secure the preservation or planting of trees: T.C.P.A. 1971, s.59(*a*).

[26] See, *e.g. Richmond-upon-Thames Royal L.B.C.* v. *S.O.S.E.* [1974] 1 All E.R.193.

[27] See, *e.g. Hildenborough Village Preservation Association* v. *S.O.S.E.* [1978] J.P.L. 708.

[28] See, *e.g. Kent C.C.* v. *S.O.S.E.* (1976) 33 P. & C.R. 70.

[29] *Wheatcroft* v. *S.O.S.E.* [1982] J.P.L. 37; qualifying *Kent C.C.* v. *S.O.S.E.* (1976) 33 P. & C.R.70.

applicant's control.[30] The latter requirement is based upon section 30(1)(a) of the 1971 Act, which expressly authorises conditions:

> "for regulating the development or use of any land under the control of the applicant (whether or not it is land in respect of which the application was made) or requiring the carrying out of work on such land, so far as it appears to the local planning authority to be expedient for the purposes of or in connection with the development authorised by the permission."

The proviso to the subsection thus gives legislative effect to the requirement of relationship between condition and permitted development, and it has been interpreted narrowly by the Secretary of State. He has insisted that there should be some close physical connection between the application site and the other land under the applicant's control, rather than a less direct economic or social link. For example, he accepts that the power may be used to have an existing service station dismantled when permission is granted for a new one across the road or next door; but not to require the closure of another service station on the other side of town or even a few streets away.[31] And the courts have similarly expressed misgivings about the use of this power to achieve balanced planning gains, by requiring the cessation of activity on one site in return for permission to undertake it elsewhere.[32] The condition might not in such a case have a sufficiently close relationship to the development authorised by the permission.

The express power to impose conditions in respect of other land under the applicant's control is conferred "without prejudice to the generality"[33] of section 29, and it is arguable therefore that the general power to impose conditions is not limited to instances where the land is under the control of the applicant. The question of control clearly does not extend to land which is within the application, because the applicant may have no present interest in the application land at all. But it appears to have become accepted that there is no power to impose conditions in respect of land which is neither within the application, nor under the applicant's control. The need for such conditions commonly arises in cases of access, where the authority may wish

---

[30] See, e.g. *Hayns* v. *S.O.S.E.* [1977] J.P.L. 663; *Hildenborough Village Preservation Association* v. *S.O.S.E.* [1978] J.P.L. 708 (although condition enforceable in the special circumstances: see further *post*, p. 352; *George Wimpey & Co. Ltd* v. *New Forest D.C.* (1979) 250 E.G. 249; *Peak Park Joint Planning Board* v. *S.O.S.E.* [1980] J.P.L. 114. Prior to these recent decisions, the rule had been followed in Scotland (see, e.g. *Birnie* v. *Banff C.C.* 1954 S.L.T. 9) and in ministerial practice in England: see e.g. m.p.d. [1967] J.P.L. 615 and 617.

[31] M.H.L.G. Circular 5/68, para. 9 and cf. *Kember* v. *S.O.S.E.* [1982] J.P.L. 383 (occupancy condition imposed in respect of existing cottage, but not for purpose directly related to the permitted development of new farm house).

[32] See, e.g. *Pyx Granite Co. Ltd.* v. *M.H.L.G.* [1958] 1 Q.B. 554 at 573, *per* Lord Denning, citing with approval a ministerial decision to the effect that such a condition would be an attempt to suppress an existing development by depriving the applicants of their right to continue using their existing factory, and that such suppression could only be achieved through a discontinuance order. That view was not dissented from by Lord Widgery C.J. in *Kingston Royal L.B.C.* (*supra*), but his Lordship was careful to confine the principle, disapproving the reasoning of Glyn-Jones J. in *Allnatt (London) Properties Ltd.* v. *Middlesex C.C.* (1964) 15 P. & C.R. 288 which had assumed that a condition would be void simply if its effect was to deprive the applicant of existing use rights without compensation. And cf. *R.T.K. Investments Ltd.* v. *Hackney L.B.C.* (1978) 36 P. & C.R. 442.

[33] T.C.P.A. 1971, s.30(1).

to require visibility splays to be constructed which would require the acquisition by the developer of portions of neighbouring land; or to insist upon the construction of an access road or a footpath linking the site with a highway or other land, and passing over land not under the applicant's control.

The doctrine has been questioned,[34] and the justification is said to be that unless the other land is under the applicant's control, he will be unable to comply with the condition[35]; or, more pragmatically, that it may prove difficult to enforce against him, particularly if it has not been expressed as a pre-condition to commencing work on the remainder of the development. But that argument is out of line with the general scheme of the Act that the impact of planning ought not to be confined by details of individual site ownership, and it will always be possible for the applicant to attempt to acquire the necessary control through negotiation with the owner (as he must do in respect of land within the application of which he is not the owner). And if the condition is suitably worded, the permission may not lawfully be implemented until he succeeds.

The more compelling justification for the rule is that the imposition of a condition is equivalent to the grant of planning permission for the works required to be carried out or the change of use required by it.[36] To allow conditions to be imposed in respect of land over which the applicant has control means that permission may effectively be granted without any application in respect of that site. To allow that to occur where the land is outside not only the application but also the applicant's control would mean that permission would effectively be granted without any of the normal safeguards of notification to owners and, where necessary, publicity.

There are therefore strong policy grounds for reading into the power a limitation that it should be exercisable only in respect of land contained in the application or within the applicant's control. It is a matter primarily then for the planning authority to determine whether the degree of control enjoyed by the applicant is sufficient to satisfy them that the condition can be complied with, without more[37]; or whether a fresh application, bringing in the other land, should be required.

4. The condition should not be manifestly unreasonable

"Unreasonableness" in this context means not simply the opposite of "reasonableness," but such manifest arbitrariness, injustice or partiality in a condition that a court must conclude that Parliament could never have intended to give authority to impose it.[38] Put another way, the "condition must be so unreasonable that no reasonable planning authority could have

---

[34] *George Wimpey & Co. Ltd.* v. *New Forest D.C.* (1979) 250 E.G. 249 at 250, *per* Sir Douglas Frank Q.C.

[35] See, *e.g. Hayns* v. *S.O.S.E.* [1977] J.P.L. 663.

[36] *R.* v. *Derbyshire C.C., ex parte North East Derbyshire D.C.* (1979) 77 L.G.R. 389.

[37] *George Wimpey and Co. Ltd.* v. *New Forest D.C.* (1979) 250 E.G. 249. "Control" does not imply full ownership, and for some conditions a contractual licence or other informal arrangement may suffice.

[38] See, *e.g. Mixnam's Properties Ltd.* v. *Chertsey U.D.C.* (1964) 1 Q.B. 214, at 237, *per* Diplock L.J.

imposed it."[39] The test clearly overlaps with the other two. A condition may be manifestly unreasonable because it bears no relation at all to "planning" purposes, nor to the permitted development. But there may be cases where both the first tests are satisfied, but the condition is still unreasonable. An example is in the case of a condition requiring the applicant to make up a road and permit access along it to the occupiers of adjoining land.[40] It may be in pursuit of a legitimate planning purpose of unlocking another area for development, and it may relate sufficiently to the permitted development itself. But the burden it imposes upon the applicant may be such that the condition is manifestly unreasonable. This assessment, again, is not purely economic. The doctrine has emerged that a condition may be invalid as unreasonable if it requires the applicant to give up or contribute money, land or other rights to the authority, or if it otherwise interferes with his proprietary interests. The question is one of principle, rather than of quantum, and its inflexibility in the context of land development has led authorities and developers to alternative forms of relationship, primarily through planning agreements.

Five specific instances of the operation of the "unreasonableness" principle call for further consideration.

(a) Conditions seeking developers' contributions

It is a clear rule that a planning condition may not lawfully require the payment of money to the authority or other consideration, although the extent of the doctrine has never been fully analysed in the courts.[41] The basis of the rule has not so far been the test of unreasonableness at all, but two separate other principles. The first is the practice of statutory interpretation drawn from the Bill of Rights that Parliament should not be taken to have intended to authorise taxation by public bodies unless the power has been conferred in clear terms.[42] It would, for example, be possible for Parliament to legislate to allow authorities to charge for granting permission, and fees for planning applications have now been introduced, but in the absence of an express power such conditions will be unlawful. The second strand of authority for the doctrine is the strong judicial antipathy to the selling of licences and permissions by public authorities: notwithstanding that a large unearned increment may pass to the successful applicant they have declined to imply into a general power to impose conditions a further power for the authority to divert some profit to public benefit.

Thus in the licensing case of *R. v. Bowman*,[43] licensing justices had

---

[39] *Kingston-upon-Thames Royal L.B.C.* v. *S.O.S.E.* [1974] 1 All E.R. 193 at 196, *per* Lord Widgery C.J.

[40] See, *e.g. Hall and Co. Ltd.* v. *Shoreham-by-Sea U.D.C.* [1964] 1 W.L.R. 240.

[41] It has, however, figured prominently in ministerial decision making: see, *e.g. Bulletin of Selected Planning Appeals*, nos. II/17, III/16, III/18. The Canadian courts have regularly struck down requirements for developers' contributions where unauthorised by statute, and have allowed developers to recover payments made by them under "practical compulsion": see *cf. Eadie* v. *Brentford* [1967] S.C.R. 573; *Severson* v. *Qualicum Beach* [1980] 3 W.W.R. 375; *Qualicum Beach* v. *Glidurray Holdings Ltd.* [1982] 1 W.W.R. 718.

[42] The leading cases are *Attorney-General* v. *Wilts United Dairies Ltd.* (1921) 37 T.L.R. 884 (affirmed by the House of Lords: (1922) 91 L.J.K.B. 897) (milk price equalisation levy) and *Liverpool Corporation* v. *Maiden (Arthur) Ltd.* [1938] 4 All E.R. 200 (fee sought unlawfully for licences to erect advertisements).

[43] [1898] 1 Q.B. 663.

granted a licence to the applicant on condition that he surrender his existing licences, and that he pay the sum of £1,000 to the justices which would then be used by them in reducing the rates in the borough. This the court refused to countenance, and Wills J. commented:

> "The justices had no more right to require the payment of money for public purposes than to require that it should be paid into their own pockets. If the attachment of such a condition were allowed to pass without objection there would soon grow up a system of putting licences up to auction—a system which would be eminently mischievous and would open the door to the gravest abuse. No doubt the justices were acting in perfect bona fides and in the interests of the public. But their conduct was nonetheless illegal."

The motive for the condition was, in the words of Darling J., that the justices had approached the case "with preconceived theories as to the proper distribution of the unearned increment of value arising from the grant of a licence." No doubt the principle applies directly by analogy to the power to attach conditions to a planning permission, at least to the extent that an authority's intention is simply to share in the enhancement of value attributable to the grant of permission.

But the rigidity of the rule, if interpreted too widely, inhibits even the unobjectionable and beneficial financial relationships between authorities and developers; and there is a case for arguing that the process would be more open, flexible and accountable if express conditions could be imposed relating to financial arrangements involved directly in the permitted development.[44] There are often aspects of land development which bring the developer and the authority into a financial relationship. A common example has been where a developer has been unable to meet the authority's requirements for the development on his site, such as for car parking or public open space. The authority have no power to grant permission conditional upon the developer contributing towards their costs in providing substitute facilities off-site, notwithstanding his willingness to do so. So that in practice such arrangements have had to be made under alternative legal relationships.[45] Encouraged by government advice[46] many authorities have allowed developers to commute car-parking requirements by making monetary contributions to a central fund.[47] But, except in

---

[44] The Australian courts have been willing to recognise financial conditions provided they can be shown to relate to work which would otherwise have to be done by the applicant and tie in closely with the permitted development: see, e.g. Woolworths Properties Ltd. v. Ku-ring-gai Municipal Council (1964) 10 L.G.R.A. 177, Gillott v. Hornsby Shire Council (1964) 10 L.G.R.A. 285, Twenty Seven Properties Ltd. v. Noarlunga Corporation (1975) 11 S.A.S.R. 188.

[45] Normally either simply contract, or statutory agreement: see further post, p. 359.

[46] Particularly in Planning Bulletin No. 7: Parking in Town Centres (1965) paras. 102-105. A subsequent circular (M.H.L.G. Circular No. 54/67) had to be issued rather hastily to emphasise that contributions should only be negotiated in respect of sites where parking conditions could be validly imposed, and not for sites where on-site parking was in any event impracticable.

[47] The decision in County and District Properties Ltd. v. Horsham U.D.C. (1970) 215 E.G. 1399 casts some doubt upon the custom of some authorities to categorise contributions as "gifts." There, the developer was held entitled to claim a refund of his contribution upon the failure of the authority to use it to provide off-site parking facilities.

London,[48] there is no legislative backing for the exercise and no independent means of resolving disputes as to quantum.[49] And there remains a faint aura of impropriety about the exercise. Authorities are advised not to indicate to developers that the success of their application may turn upon their willingness to contribute.[50] Yet this ability to overcome some legitimate planning objection to an application has often been welcomed by developers, and has proved financially attractive when set against possible land holding costs likely to be induced by otherwise inevitable development delays. A review of the distribution of the burden of the social costs of major new development and the establishment of legally backed means for its assessment and use is long overdue.

The objection to financial conditions is based primarily upon notions of taxation and the sale of permissions, rather than upon any view that the developer should not be required to expend money beyond that envisaged by the application. It does not therefore render invalid conditions requiring the carrying out of works which necessarily require capital expenditure, provided the condition satisfies the other heads of validity.[51] So that although a developer may not be required by condition to provide and maintain public open space, for example, where the submitted plans indicate that open space will be provided there would be no objection on the grounds of validity to a condition requiring its upkeep and maintenance.[52] The New Zealand Supreme Court has even been prepared to sanction a condition requiring direct off-site capital expenditure, in the form of an obligation to purchase neighbouring objectors' lands if so required by them within three years of starting manufacturing operations in the permitted development.[53] But the approach of the English authorities has tended to be more restrictive.

(b) Conditions interfering with private land ownership

The main instance in which conditions have been held invalid for unreasonableness has been where they have been seen as not simply restricting the use of a site, but going so far as to interfere with ownership. Two leading cases illustrate the approach adopted by the courts. In *Hall and*

---

[48] Where the Greater London Council (General Powers) Act 1973, s.24 authorises the authorities at the request of the developer, to enter into an agreement providing for payment towards the cost to them of providing public car parks. There is a broad discretion for the authority to determine an appropriate amount, and the agreement is registrable against the land and thus binding upon successive owners. Similar powers are also conferred by the County of Kent Act 1981, s.6.

[49] The problem has been overcome in New Zealand by legislation which prescribes standards for assessment of quantum, and allows reference to an appeal tribunal in case of dispute: Town and Country Planning Act (N.Z.) 1977, s.79.

[50] M.H.L.G. Circular 54/67, paras. 4 and 5; *Development Control Policy Notes* No.5, para.9.

[51] T.C.P.A. 1971, s.30(1).

[52] The major difficulty is enforcement, particularly if the development company is put into liquidation. For this reason an authority will often prefer to accept a dedication of the land coupled perhaps with a commuted maintenance contribution.

[53] *Lange* v. *Town and Country Planning Appeal Board (No.2)* [1967] N.Z.L.R. 898.

Co. Ltd. v. *Shoreham-by-Sea U.D.C.*[54] the Court of Appeal struck down as unreasonable a condition which required the developers to construct an ancillary road at their own expense which would be available also for use as a means of access to adjoining properties. It did not require dedication of the road to the public, but the Court held that this was its actual effect, and that in the absence of any provision for compensation the condition was unreasonable and void. It did not matter, therefore, that the condition did, as the Court found, fairly and reasonably relate to the permitted development, or that the object it sought to attain was in their view perfectly reasonable. They would, apparently, have been prepared to uphold the condition had its effect been merely that of granting rights of passage to the occupiers of immediately adjoining land, rather than to the public at large.

That ruling was followed closely by the Divisional Court in 1974 in *R.* v. *Hillingdon L.B.C., ex parte Royco Homes Ltd.*[55] where, it will be recalled, conditions imposed upon a permission for residential development required the developers to comply with municipal housing standards, and to allocate the dwellings to persons selected from the authority's housing waiting list with occupancy for the first ten years limited solely to tenants enjoying Rent Act protection. The conditions were held unreasonable, in that they required the applicants "to take on at their own expense a significant part of the duty of the council as a housing authority,"[56] just as in *Hall's* case the condition had required the developer in effect to assume the function of a highway authority.

But the distinctions are less clear cut than the cases suggest. There are two central principles. The first is the argument which clearly influenced the Court of Appeal in the *Hall* case: that an authority ought not to be permitted to achieve, through a condition, ends in respect of which other statutory powers made provision for compensation.[57] But much of the force of that argument has been lost following its rejection by a unanimous House of Lords in the context of refusal of planning permission[58]; and by the Divisional Court in the context of conditions restricting existing use rights.[59] Perhaps, then, the only surviving principle justifying the "reasonableness" test as a separate test is that of unlawful taxation: that just as a condition may not lawfully require a financial contribution from a landowner, nor may it require a comparable non-monetary benefit such as the gift of land, or the provision of a public road or other facility which would otherwise need to be provided and paid for by the authority.

[54] [1964] 1 W.L.R. 240, followed in *M. J. Shanley Ltd.* v. *S.O.S.E.* [1982] J.P.L. 380 (condition requiring provision of land for public open space invalid); and *cf. Attorney-General, ex rel. Lamb* v. *Maidstone R.D.C.* (1973) 226 E.G. 805 (access condition imposed on caravan site licence *ultra vires*).

[55] [1974] 1 Q.B. 720.

[56] *Ibid.* p.732, *per* Lord Widgery C.J. Bridge L.J. at 739 relied similarly upon the *Hall* principle, observing that the council had done everything possible to unburden themselves and place their own statutory duty as housing authority upon the shoulders of the applicants.

[57] [1964] 1 W.L.R. 240 at 250-251, *per* Willmer L.J., 256, *per* Harman L.J., 260-261, *per* Pearson L.J.

[58] *Westminster Bank Ltd.* v. *M.H.L.G.* [1971] A.C. 508.

[59] *Kingston-upon-Thames Royal L.B.C.* v. *S.O.S.E.* [1974] 1 All E.R. 193. Willmer L.J. in the *Hall* case himself acknowledged the similarity between the condition in question and other restrictions on land use, preferring to base his judgement instead upon the "alternative code" approach: [1964] 1 W.L.R. 240 at 248, 250-251.

This was the distinction drawn by the High Court in the subsequent case of *Britannia (Cheltenham) Ltd.* v. *Secretary of State for the Environment*,[60] a decision which demonstrates how finely the line may need to be drawn. The conditions in question required the developer to provide play areas and public open space as part of a scheme of residential development, and to maintain them until they were adopted by the authority. But there was no requirement that the developer should dedicate the land to the public, and it was thus possible to distinguish the *Hall* case on the ground that in the absence of such a requirement the developer was at liberty to exclude people from using the facilities. It is difficult to imagine a more artificial distinction. Public access and enjoyment were the obvious aims of the conditions, particularly in the case of the children's play areas. And adoption of the land by the authority in these circumstances, even at a nil consideration, is almost inevitably a benefit rather than a detriment to the developer because he is then relieved of any maintenance obligation.

In large scale development schemes in the modern world the restrictions imposed by the courts upon the uses to which conditional permission may be put, have often meant simply that requirements not able to be reflected as conditions have had to be negotiated behind the permission. The willingness of developers to contribute has too often been at odds with the limitations imposed upon the statutory machinery. But it is worth considering how far the normal statutory relationship of development control can be used to accommodate the land and amenity requirements of authorities.

First, it is clear that the developer must provide necessary on-site infrastructure such as estate roads and sewers. An authority would be justified in refusing to grant permission unless satisfied that adequate provision for these can be made; and following the grant of outline permission the details may be regulated under conditions relating to access and layout.[61] Construction standards and maintenance of estate roads may then be governed by a condition, but the preferred method is to avoid the complex machinery of the private street works code by entering into an agreement under section 38 of the Highways Act 1980 (formerly section 40 of the Highways Act 1959.).[62] Similarly, provided proposals for other facilities such as public open space and play areas are included in the application, the authority may by condition validly require their provision, equipping, landscaping and maintenance. Again, though, the developer may

---

[60] [1978] J.P.L. 554. An appeal by the Secretary of State to the Court of Appeal failed, but on a different ground: *sub.nom. Robert Hitchens Builders Ltd.* v. *S.O.S.E.* [1979] J.P.L. 534. The reluctance of the judge at first instance (Sir Douglas Frank Q.C.) to strike down the conditions might well have been influenced by the unusual background. The conditions had been agreed to between the authority and the developer and submitted to the Secretary of State for approval in settlement of an outstanding appeal. But the Secretary of State felt that they went beyond his power, and rejected the appeal. The developers appealed to the High Court, forcing the Secretary of State to argue in favour of an implied restriction upon his powers.

[61] *Ante*, p. 200.

[62] This permits the developer to undertake to carry out the necessary road works in lieu of making a contribution under the private street works code (Highways Act 1980, s. 219 (4)(*d*)). Upon satisfactory completion (and a bond is often required as a guarantee: see *National Employers' Mutual General Insurance Association Ltd.* v. *Herne Bay U.D.C.* (1972) 70 L.G.R. 542) the road is dedicated to the public and becomes maintainable at public expense.

find it preferable to dedicate the land to public use and to place the maintenance burden on the shoulders of the authority, perhaps contributing a capital sum as commuted payment towards the cost.[63]

If the proposal is not included in the application, the authority may choose either to reject the application, or by condition reserve part of the site either for some general facility such as open space, or for some specific future development such as a shopping centre[64] or a school, or perhaps to allow a road to be linked with roads to be provided for future development of adjoining land.[65] Such a restriction does not, of course, vest the land in the authority, nor does it necessarily hold its value down. At one time it meant that the authority might be forced itself to purchase the land under the inverse compulsory purchase procedure,[66] but the obligation of the Secretary of State to confirm a notice served in those circumstances has now been lifted.[67]

But where the developer and the authority choose to undertake arrangements involving the conveyance of land, or financial contributions, or the provision of off-site facilities on land not under the control of the applicant, they are forced beyond planning permission to other legal relationships.

(c) Uncertain conditions

It has been judicially accepted that a planning condition may be so uncertain as to be invalid,[68] and the doctrine is probably best regarded as part of the unreasonableness rule. The condition may be viewed as manifestly unreasonable, in that it purports to impose on the applicant an obligation the extent of which cannot be ascertained.

But the courts have stressed that only in extreme cases of unintelligibility should a condition be struck down on this ground.[69] Uncertainty has long been a test of validity of local authority byelaws[70]; but its application in the planning context is restricted both by the reluctance of the courts to admit to defeat in interpretation, and by their willingness to assume that authorities

---

[63] Machinery exists in the form of the statutory agreements, or under the Open Spaces Act 1906.

[64] *Britannia (Cheltenham) Ltd.* v. *S.O.S.E.* [1978] J.P.L. 554.

[65] The question of validity of such a condition was canvassed in *Tarmac Properties Ltd.* v. *Secretary of State for Wales* (1976) 33 P. & C.R. 103 and appeared to be conceded by the respondent; but it was found unnecessary to consider the matter in the judgement. The Court of Appeal in the *Hall* case appeared to accept it as a valid alternative.

[66] *Adams and Wade Ltd.* v. *M.H.L.G.* (1965) 18 P. & C.R. 60.

[67] T.C.P.A. 1971, s. 184, provided the permission containing the condition was granted on an application "which contemplated (expressly or by necessary implication)" that the land should not be otherwise developed or should be laid out or preserved: s.184(2)(b). See further as to purchase notice procedures, Chap. 15, *post*.

[68] *Fawcett Properties Ltd.* v. *Buckinghamshire C.C.* [1961] A.C. 636; *Mixnam's Properties Ltd.* v. *Chertsey U.D.C.* [1965] A.C. 735; *David Lowe and Sons Ltd.* v. *Burgh of Musselburgh* 1974 S.L.T. 5 (Scottish Court of Session); *M. J. Shanley Ltd* v. *S.O.S.E.* [1982] J.P.L. 380.

[69] See, *e.g. Bizony* v. *S.O.S.E.* [1976] J.P.L. 306.

[70] See, *e.g. Nash* v. *Finlay* (1901) 85 L.T.682; *Attorney-General* v. *Denby* [1925] Ch.596 (but *cf. Martin* v. *Clarke* (1893) 62 L.J.M.C. 178).

will act reasonably in their interpretation[71] and enforcement[72] of uncertain conditions.

A particular variant of the uncertainty argument arises when a condition reserves a matter for subsequent agreement, determination or direction. For example, many of the Ministry's model conditions require works to be carried out "to the satisfaction of the local planning authority"[73]; and it is arguable that they impose an obligation which, at the time of the granting of permission, is quite uncertain.

But that argument has been rejected by the courts,[74] and the objection has now been largely overcome by the 1980 Act, which conferred a right of appeal to the Secretary of State against the refusal of, or conditions imposed upon, any consent, approval or agreement of the planning authority required by a planning condition.[75]

(d) Occupancy conditions

Conditions which restrict the occupancy of the completed development have long raised questions of validity, on the grounds both that the personality or personal characteristics of occupiers cannot be a matter of valid planning concern, and that such a condition is necessarily unreasonable in its effects. The first argument was effectively disposed of by the House of Lords in *Fawcett Properties Ltd.* v. *Buckinghamshire County Council*,[76] where they upheld a condition restricting the occupancy of a dwelling to persons whose employment is or was in agriculture, forestry or some associated industry. The purpose of the condition was to further the policy adopted by the authority of not permitting the erection of houses in the area so as to preserve the amenities of the green belt, unless required in connection with the use of adjoining land for agriculture or similar purposes. The second argument, of manifest unreasonableness, is also destroyed by the *Fawcett* case as a general proposition, but there would no doubt be cases in which to use an occupancy condition would be arbitrary and unjustified.

A special form of occupancy condition which authorities have sought to impose in recent years has been that which limits occupancy to those with some "local" connection, expressed in terms of residence or employment. Such conditions have been used occasionally in connection with commercial and industrial development in the past,[77] but their extension to residential

---

[71] Thus the courts have been prepared to accept that uncertainty in an outline condition may readily be resolved at detailed stage, and should not therefore be regarded as invalidatory: *Britannia (Cheltenham) Ltd.* v. *S.O.S.E.* [1978] J.P.L. 554.

[72] Applying the doctrine of *Kruse* v. *Johnson* [1898] 2 Q.B. 91: see, *e.g. Fawcett Properties Ltd.* v. *Buckinghamshire C.C. (supra)* at 671, *per* Lord Denning; *Hall and Co. Ltd.* v. *Shoreham-by-sea U.D.C.* [1964] 1 W.L.R. 240.

[73] M.H.L.G. Circular 5/68, Annex of model conditions.

[74] *Hall and Co.Ltd.* v. *Shoreham-by-Sea U.D.C.* [1964] 1 W.L.R. 240 at 245; and *cf. Roberts* v. *Vale Royal D.C.* [1977] J.P.L. 369. The courts of Australia and New Zealand have expressly accepted such conditions as valid: see, *e.g. Weigall Constructions Pty. Ltd.* v. *Melbourne and Metropolitan Board of Works* [1972] V.R. 781, *Turner* v. *Allison* [1971] N.Z.L.R. 833.

[75] See further *ante*, p. 205.

[76] [1961] A.C. 636. Agricultural occupancy conditions may now be suspended in certain cases to provide security of tenure: Rent (Agriculture) Act 1977, s. 33. See also *M. J. Shanley Ltd.* v. *S.O.S.E.* [1982] J.P.L. 380 where the court held invalid a proposed condition requiring that local people be given the first opportunity to buy the houses to be developed.

[77] See, *e.g.* M.H.L.G. Circular 5/68, para. 24; and *Pyrford Properties Ltd.* v. *S.O.S.E.* (1977) 244 E.G. 383.

development is controversial. The purpose of the conditions is clear enough, in that they are imposed usually where the authority are anxious to restrict growth in a locality, but wish to ensure that there is sufficient new development to meet the needs of existing communities. There is also a wish in some areas to ensure that new houses are not taken up largely as second homes, to be left empty for much of the year; or as commuter houses, changing the character of villages and pushing prices up beyond levels that the local community can afford to pay.

The purpose of such conditions, assuming them to be valid, is to create a two-tier market in property; but the prices of "local" houses would not necessarily be held down, because demand from existing local residents may still be sufficient to balance price levels. The Panel conducting the examination in public of the Mid-Hampshire Structure Plan in 1979 concluded that for this reason a "locals only" policy ought not to be included in the plan, and urged instead that provision be made for local needs through small scale local authority and housing association schemes.[78] But the Panel recognised that if such a policy were adopted in the plan, this would in itself support the validity of conditions based upon it. Without adopted policies to support "local" conditions, a number of authorities have resorted instead to planning agreements as a means of exerting control.

(e) Conditions for purposes for which compensation is otherwise payable

One test of reasonableness may be to ask whether the condition achieves a purpose for which compensation is otherwise payable, either under planning legislation or under other related provisions. At one time it was accepted by the Minister that the power to impose conditions should be narrowly construed, and that there was no power to limit or restrict existing use rights on the land except by way of discontinuance order, carrying compensation liability. To deprive the owner of those rights without compensation, where an alternative procedure existed which would have required it, was thought to be sufficiently unreasonable to render a condition invalid.[79]

But that doctrine has been largely superseded by two judicial decisions. First, in *Westminster Bank Ltd.* v. *Beverley Borough Council*,[80] the House of Lords upheld a decision by the Minister refusing planning permission for development on the ground that the land might be required in the future for a road widening scheme. Had such a restriction been formally imposed by way of the imposition of an improvement line under the Highways Acts, the owners would have been entitled to compensation. But the House of Lords declined to rule that achieving the same end under planning legislation, "even if the sole reason for the authority proceeding in the way it did had been the desire to save public money,"[81] rendered the decision unreasonable. Parliament had chosen to set up two ways of preventing development which would interfere with schemes for street widening, one of which

---

[78] *Report of the Panel* Hants.C.C. (1979), paras. 2.20—2.31.
[79] The view was based partly on *M.H.L G.* v. *Hartnell* [1965] A.C. 1134, which dealt with the special case where an obligation to obtain permission had been imposed upon caravan site operators by legislation; and *Allnatt London Properties Ltd.* v. *Middlesex C.C.* (1964) 15 P. & C.R. 288.
[80] [1971] A.C. 508.
[81] *Ibid.* at 530, *per* Lord Reid.

involved compensation and the other of which did not. But the legislation expressed no preference for the use of either, and imposed no limits on their use; and there was nothing in the legislation to indicate that Parliament disapproved of an authority shifting the burden to the applicant rather than bearing it themselves.

Secondly, in *Kingston-upon-Thames Royal London Borough Council* v. *Secretary of State for the Environment*[82] the Divisional Court unequivocally rejected the proposition that a condition which restricted existing use rights without the payment of compensation was invalid. Provided it related sufficiently closely to the development permitted under the permission, the fact that it might restrict some existing activity was irrelevant.

5. *Estoppel as a validating factor*

The rules restricting the scope of the power to impose conditions operate as a valuable safeguard against arbitrary or unfair conduct by authorities. But they are also liable to prove artificial and unnecessarily restrictive in the context of large scale development and positive planning. The issues are too complex to be left simply to the formal procedures of application and decision. The arrangements must be negotiated, and the parties are fully entitled to agree to a variety of terms, including obligations which may not be enforceable as planning conditions.

The artificiality of rules which require that a planning condition be struck down notwithstanding the developer's willingness to accept it have become apparent, but short of the parties entering into other legal relationships to secure enforcement, there has been no means of reconciliation. The planning agreement route offers a solution where the matter is settled at local level, but it is not available to the Secretary of State on appeal. The parties may submit an executed agreement before or after the inquiry, but in the absence of such a document the Secretary of State may be obliged to dismiss the appeal if satisfactory implementation of the development is dependent upon requirements which cannot validly be expressed as conditions, notwithstanding the willingness of the developer to accept them.

The Scottish courts pointed the way to one possible solution in 1971, where at a public inquiry into proposed extensions to the main runway at Glasgow Airport, the appellants, Glasgow Corporation, had given undertakings that if permission were granted they would take certain specified steps to monitor and keep down noise levels, and if necessary seek powers to make sound insulation grants to owners of affected dwellings. The Secretary of State's decision to rely upon the undertakings without attempting to express them as conditions (which he thought to be impracticable), and to grant permission was upheld by the Court of Session.[83] The undertakings were clearly a material consideration to which the Secretary of State had been able to have regard to the extent that they were of value, and bearing in

---

[82] [1974] 1 All E.R. 193; followed in *Peak Park Joint Planning Board* v. *S.O.S.E.* [1980] J.P.L. 114; and in *British Airports Authority* v. *Secretary of State for Scotland* [1980] J.P.L. 262, where however a condition seeking to control aircraft noise imposed on permission for extension to the airport, was discharged because the matter was dealt with already by a condition on the original permission.

[83] *Bearsdon Town Council* v. *Glasgow Corporation* 1971 S.C. 274.

mind that, in the case of a responsible local authority, legal enforcement might be less significant than susceptibility to political pressure.[84]

In a recent English case, however, a different and more far-reaching approach has been adopted. In *Hildenborough Village Preservation Association* v. *Secretary of State for the Environment*[85] an undertaking had been given by the appellants at the inquiry that if permission were granted they would purchase any land necessary to provide visibility splays to the authority's satisfaction and carry out the necessary work. Permission was granted, subject to a condition reflecting the terms of the undertaking. It was therefore of questionable validity in that it related to land neither within the application nor under the present control of the applicant. The Scottish decision was not apparently cited to the court, but similar reasoning was adopted, and built upon. It was held that the condition should stand and was enforceable because the developers would be estopped from denying its validity in enforcement proceedings because of its relationship to their undertaking, in reliance upon which the Secretary of State had acted in imposing the condition.

The decision bristles with difficulties, not the least because it involves a conscious extension of the doctrine of promissory estoppel into an area where no contractual relationship exists.[86] Further, enforcement of the undertaking, or the condition imposed in reliance upon it, is on the basis of a personal rather than a proprietary right. No remedy would exist against a purchaser, and the Secretary of State in choosing to rely upon this method of validation must be prepared to accept that risk. A condition imposed as a once and for all obligation at the outset of, or during the course of, operational development, might pose less of a risk than one imposing a long term, continuing obligation. But the mechanism offers only a clumsy, makeshift, means of enforcement; and in view of the clear antipathy expressed recently by both the House of Lords[87] and the Court of Appeal[88] to any extension of estoppel in planning law, there can be little room for any further development of the doctrine.

6. *Severance of invalid conditions*

Whenever a condition is held to be invalid, the next question is invariably whether its invalidity affects the validity of the permission as a whole or whether the two may be severed and the permission allowed to stand. The test adopted by the courts is whether the condition goes to the root of the permission, or whether it deals with some ulterior, collateral or trivial

---

[84] That was a consideration in the forefront of the authority's submissions to the Court, although the Court itself regarded enforceability as a secondary matter provided the Secretary of State was under no misapprehension about it.

[85] [1978] J.P.L. 708.

[86] In reliance upon the statement of Donaldson J. in *Durham Fancy Goods* v. *Michael Jackson* [1968] 2 All E.R. 987 at 991 that a pre-existing legal relationship between the parties which could in certain circumstances give rise to liabilities and penalties would suffice, and that the relationship need not be contractual. The New Zealand Supreme Court has doubted whether such a relationship exists between applicant and planning authority: *Attorney-General* v. *Codnor* [1973] 1 N.Z.L.R. 545.

[87] In *Newbury D.C.* v. *S.O.S.E.* [1980] A.C. 578.

[88] *Western Fish Products Ltd.* v. *Penwith D.C.* (1977) 39 P. & C.R.7.

matter.[89] Severance is a function to be approached with caution, for it requires a subjective judgement as to whether the permission would have been likely to be granted without the condition.[90] A condition relating not at all to the permitted development may be severed readily enough, but one challenged successfully for unreasonableness, for example, will often be difficult to sever.[91] Further, if the challenge is by way of statutory appeal from the decision of the Secretary of State, the function of the Court is confined to upholding or quashing his decision as a whole.[92] The decision whether to issue an amended permission or to refuse consent altogether is then a matter for the Secretary of State.

7. Machinery for challenging validity

The validity of a planning condition imposed by a local planning authority may be challenged by the developer by way of appeal to the Secretary of State. His jurisdiction is not confined merely to the issue of validity, and he may review not only the condition complained of but also the permission itself. An alternative means of challenge is by way of application to the High Court for judicial review seeking an order of certiorari[93]; although the Divisional Court has indicated that this course ought to be pursued only where a decision is liable to be upset because on its face it was clearly made without jurisdiction or in consequence of an error of law.[94] In other cases the statutory appeal to the Secretary of State will normally offer a better alternative remedy and certiorari may be withheld. An alternative means of bringing the matter before the High Court is by way of proceedings for a declaration, which may be brought also as an application for judicial review.[95] Either the planning authority or the developer may commence such an action, and in the past no objection has been raised to actions being commenced several years after the date the condition was imposed.[96] Alternatively, the developer may raise the validity of a condition as a ground

---

[89] Kent C.C. v. Kingsway Investments Ltd. [1971] A.C. 72 at 90, per Lord Reid, 102, per Lord Morris and 113, per Lord Upjohn. But an indication of the practical difficulties which may arise in applying the test is given by the fact that only by a majority of 3 to 2 did their Lordships rule that the condition in question was inseverable, and the question split the Court of Appeal 2:1: [1969] 2 Q.B. 332. In Turner v. Allison [1971] N.Z.L.R. 833 the New Zealand Court of Appeal followed Lord Morris's formulation of the severance test, but reserved the question of whether a test more favourable to severance might not be adopted in the future.

[90] Kent C.C. v. Kingsway Investments Ltd. [1971] A.C.72 at 90, per Lord Reid.

[91] As in Hall & Co. Ltd. v. Shoreham-by-Sea U.D.C. [1964] 1 W.L.R. 240 and R. v. Hillingdon L.B.C., ex parte Royco Homes Ltd. [1974] Q.B. 720. Australian courts have applied the same principles: see, e.g. Spurling v. Development Underwriting (Victoria) Pty. Ltd. [1973] V.R.1; Twenty Seven Properties Ltd. v. Noarlunga Corporation (1975) 11 S.A.S.R. 188.

[92] T.C.P.A. 1971, s. 245(4).

[93] Under Order 53 of the Rules of the Supreme Court; see further post, p. 624.

[94] R. v. Hillingdon L.B.C., ex parte Royco Homes Ltd. [1974] Q.B. 720 at 729 per Lord Widgery C.J.

[95] R.S.C. Ord. 53, r.1(2).

[96] See, e.g. Manning v. S.O.S.E. [1976] J.P.L. 634 (declaration granted for interpretation of condition notwithstanding that several years had elapsed); Hall & Co. Ltd. v. Shoreham-by-Sea U.D.C. [1964] 1 W.L.R. 240 (18 months delay in challenging validity). But as to the powers of the court on application for judicial review where it considers there has been undue delay, see R.S.C. Ord. 53, r.4(1).

for resisting enforcement action taken by the planning authority and pursue the issue on appeal to the Secretary of State[97] and further to the High Court.

Conditions imposed by the Secretary of State are protected by the preclusive provisions, however, and no challenge may be made to their validity except by way of statutory application to the High Court by the developer or any other "person aggrieved,"[98] or by the local authority, within six weeks of the date of the decision.[99]

8. Enforcement

(a) The enforcement machinery

Enforcement of planning conditions is through the normal enforcement procedures discussed in Chapter 9. Their aim is to provide an opportunity to remedy any breach of control rather than to impose direct criminal sanctions, and this places demands upon the wording of conditions. Thus a condition may be unenforceable, or practically so, if it is designed to prevent some irremediable action, such as the felling of a particular tree or the demolition of a particular building or landmark. Equally, a condition requiring works to be performed, or other positive action taken, will be unenforceable if no time is prescribed for compliance, since it cannot be said at what point it has been breached. The most flexible form of time limitation is one which ties in with some event in the development itself: requiring, for example, that estate roads be completed before any dwellings constructed are occupied. But the fact that a condition may be unenforceable or difficult to enforce does not render it *ultra vires*.[1]

(b) The necessity for implementation of the permission

It is axiomatic that a developer is not bound by any condition unless the permission is implemented. If it is not implemented, the permission and its conditions lapse under the relevant statutory provisions. There has been some conflict of judicial opinion as to whether a developer may be bound by conditions attached to a permission which was not in fact necessary, perhaps because the activity undertaken did not constitute development, or was already permitted. Two early decisions of the Divisional Court[2] rejected the idea that the terms of an unnecessary permission should thereafter govern a development. But Lord Denning, in *Newbury District Council* v. *Secretary of State for the Environment*[3] was prepared to go some distance in the other direction, arguing that a developer ought not to be permitted to "blow hot

---

[97] There is no power for the Secretary of State to actually quash the original permission where he finds a condition *ultra vires* on an enforcement appeal and takes the view that it is inseverable: see, *e.g.* m.p.d. at [1977] J.P.L. 742.

[98] As to which see *post*, p. 618. Third parties who have participated in the appeal may be able to challenge conditions under this head: see, *e.g. Hildenborough Village Preservation Association* v. *S.O.S.E.* [1978] J.P.L. 708.

[99] T.C.P.A. 1971, ss. 242(1)(e) and (3)(b); 245(1) and (2).

[1] *Bizony* v. *S.O.S.E.* [1976] J.P.L. 306; *Peak Park Joint Planning Board* v. *S.O.S.E.* [1980] J.P.L. 114 at 118.

[2] *Mounsdon* v. *Weymouth and Melcombe B.C.* [1960] 1 Q.B. 645; *East Barnet U.D.C.* v. *British Transport Commission* [1962] 2Q.B. 484.

[3] [1980] 2 W.L.R. 379.

and cold": having applied for and accepted the benefit of a permission without objection, he might not come back later and assert that he was free from its burdens.[4] This broad view failed to find acceptance with his brother judges, and on appeal it was expressly rejected by the House of Lords.

There is only one exception, *viz*, where a new planning unit or a new physical unit has been created, and the former use rights are no longer applicable.[5] In other instances, the implementation of a necessary permission must be a prerequisite to the enforcement of its conditions.

But the Divisional Court has rejected the proposition that only the carrying out of authorised development is sufficient to bring a planning condition into play.[6] Development may be undertaken in ostensible implementation of a permission, but later be found to be unauthorised for want of compliance with the approved plans. The defect may only come to light after the expiry of the four-year enforcement period for operational development, and to hold conditions regulating use or occupancy thereafter ineffective would be to relieve a defaulting developer of obligations which would be binding against an authorised development. It is a distinction based more on pragmatism than principle, but the need for it arises directly from the artificiality of the rule that non-compliance with approved plans renders the whole development unauthorised and not merely that part of it which is in breach.

(c) The necessity for the condition to be express

There is no doctrine of implied conditions in planning law[7] and the courts, although ready to be generous in interpretation,[8] have shown a reluctance to build upon the actual language employed in order to give effect to the unexpressed intentions of the planning authority.[9]

But a particular problem arises in the context of "limitations," since breach of either a "condition" or a "limitation" on a permission is a breach of planning control, in respect of which enforcement action may be commenced. There is no express power for planning authorities to impose "limitations" as opposed to conditions, although such a power exists for the

---

[4] [1978] 1 W.L.R. 1240 at 1250. Such an approach had been expressly left open by the Divisional Court in *Brayhead (Ascot) Ltd.* v. *Berkshire C.C.* [1964] 2 Q.B. 303 at 315; but had found some support in *Prossor* v. *M.H.L.G.* (1968) 67 L.G.R. 109 and further support from Lord Denning M.R. in *Gray* v. *M.H.L.G.* (1969) 68 L.G.R. 15, at 18.
[5] As in *Prossor* v. *M.H.L.G. (supra)* and *Gray* v. *M.H.L.G. (supra)*.
[6] *Kerrier D.C.* v. *S.O.S.E.* [1981] J.P.L. 193.
[7] *Trustees of Walton-on-Thames Charities* v. *Walton and Weybridge U.D.C.* (1970) 68 L.G.R. 488 at 497.
[8] Thus a condition is not to be interpreted *contra proferentes* the planning authority (*Crisp from the Fens Ltd.* v. *Rutland C.C.* (1950) 1 P. & C.R. 48); nor are its terms "to be scrutinized in the same way as the words used by a Parliamentary draftsman": *Hall & Co. Ltd.* v. *Shoreham-by-Sea U.D.C.* [1964] 1 W.L.R. 240 at 245, *per* Willmer L.J.
[9] See, *e.g. Sutton L.B.C.* v. *S.O.S.E.* (1975) 73 L.G.R. 349, where the Divisional Court refused to imply into a condition governing the type and treatment of exterior materials to be used on a building, a further condition as to the standard of workmanship required in their application. It was held in *Lucas (F.) and Sons Ltd.* v. *Dorking and Horley R.D.C.* (1964) 62 L.G.R. 491 that no condition could be implied requiring the whole of a permission to be implemented, but this doctrine is now suspect: see further *ante*, p. 268.

Secretary of State when granting permission by Development Order.[10] Although the legislation which introduced breach of "limitation" as a basis for enforcement was clearly designed solely to catch development order limitations,[11] that restriction was lost in the consolidating Act of 1962 and there is no reference to it at all in the Act of 1971.

The most common example of a limited permission is where permission is stated to be granted for a particular sort of building or use, but without any actual condition being imposed to formally restrict the use: for example, a permission for an agricultural dwelling house. Section 33(2) of the 1971 Act allows authorities to specify the use to which the building may be put, and if no purpose is specified, "the permission shall be construed as including permission to use the building for the purpose for which it is designed." In a number of cases the courts have referred to such an express "specification" under the section as a "limitation," but, without consideration of the scope of the enforcement power, have held simply that the test of breach of control is whether a material change of use would result from using the building otherwise than in accordance with the limitation.[12] The limitation thus has a functional significance in restricting the scope of the permitted development. But the accepted view at present is that only express conditions may be enforced as such and that that is a desirable principle[13]; but the matter is capable of being reviewed by the courts in the future.

9. Special conditions

(a) Personal permission

The general rule is that planning permission runs with the land, [14] and that its benefits are therefore available to any subsequent purchasers or successors in title to the owner. But an authority may choose to grant a personal permission only, usually by condition restricting enjoyment to a named person. The power is employed normally in circumstances where permission might not otherwise have been granted, but there are "strong compassionate or other personal grounds."[15] Deemed permission for

---

[10] T.C.P.A. 1971, s.24(4).

[11] Post, p. 389.

[12] Wilson v. West Sussex C.C. [1963] 2 Q.B. 764, a decision based upon the pre-1962 legislation, followed in Trinder v. Sevenoaks R.D.C. (1967) 204 E.G. 803 and East Suffolk C.C. v. S.O.S.E. (1972) 70 L.G.R. 595, although there is a suggestion in the Lands Tribunal decision in Williamson & Stevens v. Cambridgeshire C.C. (1977) 34 P. & C.R. 117 that a limitation might be specifically enforceable. The better view is that the effect of a limitation is to restrict the use to which the development may be put upon its completion, but that once that has been established the limitation does not prevent the making of any change of use which would not otherwise require permission: Kwik Save Discount Group Ltd. v. S.O.S.E. [1981] J.P.L. 806; Waverley D.C. v. S.O.S.E. [1982] J.P.L. 105.

[13] Trustees of Walton-on-Thames Charities v. Walton and Weybridge U.D.C. (1970) 68 L.G.R. 488; Carpet Decor (Guildford) Ltd. v. S.O.S.E. [1981] J.P.L. 806.

[14] T.C.P.A. 1971, s.33(1).

[15] Memorandum, M.H.L.G. Circular 5/68, para. 36. The Circular stresses that such a condition would scarcely ever be justified in the case of permission to erect a permanent building: but cf. Federated Homes Ltd. v. Mill Lodge Properties Ltd. [1980] 1 All E.R. 371, where personal permission had been granted for a development of 1,250 dwellings and ancillary buildings, apparently because it was tied in with a phasing agreement enforceable only against the applicants.

development by local planning authorities themselves is always personal, although there is power for them to acquire normal permission in respect of land for disposal for development by others.[16]

(b) Temporary permission

The granting of temporary permission is achieved by imposing a condition under section 30(1)(*b*), requiring the removal of any buildings or works authorised by the permission, or the discontinuance of any use of land so authorised, at the end of a stated period, together with the carrying out of any works needed at that time for reinstatement of the land.[17] The statutory formula authorises the demolition of buildings and removal of works only where they have been erected under the terms of the permission, and the *Newbury* case indicates that only in an exceptional case would the courts uphold as valid a condition imposing such a requirement on a permission authorising only the change of use of existing buildings, even where the authority's policy had development plan backing and was known to the applicants when they purchased the property.[18]

(c) Expiry of unimplemented permissions

All permissions are granted, whether expressly or by statutory implication, subject to conditions requiring development to commence within five years from the date of grant, or such other period as the planning authority may direct.[19] In the case of outline permissions, the requirement is that application for approval of reserved matters should be made within three years of the grant, and that the development should have commenced not later than five years from the date of grant or two years from the final approval of reserved matters, whichever date is later.[20] Other periods may be substituted by the authority.[21] The fact that these conditions are imposed or supported by statute does not prevent an appeal being made against them to the Secretary of State.[22]

The requirement that development should have commenced within the specified period does not necessarily call for any substantial works to have begun: development is taken to have commenced on the earliest date on which any of the operations specified by the Act began to be carried out, such as construction work for building erection, trench digging for the foundations, pipe-laying, road construction or material change in use of the

[16] *Ante*, p. 240.
[17] T.C.P.A. 1971, s.30(1)(*b*). The result of such a condition is that the permission is then statutorily recognised as "planning permission granted for a limited period": s.30(2).
[18] *Newbury D.C.* v. *S.O.S.E.* [1980] A.C. 578; and *cf. Agricultural Enterprises Ltd.* v. *Amersham R.D.C.* (1967) 202 E.G. 1223.
[19] T.C.P.A. 1971, s.41. Although such conditions now have statutory backing, the House of Lords has been prepared to uphold comparable conditions imposed under the general power: *Kingsway Investments Ltd.* v. *Kent C.C.* [1971] A.C. 72.
[20] *Ibid.* s.42(2).
[21] *Ibid.* s.42(3).
[22] *Ibid.* s.43(6).

land.[23] Even if one permission relates to several parcels of land, commencement on just one parcel will suffice.[24] Token commencement consisting of nothing more than the digging of trenches will suffice to keep a permission alive, even although there may be no intention to proceed to develop immediately and they are subsequently filled in.[25] But the pattern of the trenches should at least conform to the design of the development authorised by the permission.[26]

The effect of failure to comply with the conditions is that development carried out after the specified date is unauthorised, or, as the case may be, late application for approval of reserved matters is treated as not made in accordance with the terms of the permission.[27] Application may, of course, be made for a renewal of permission; and provided it is lodged before expiry of the old permission and sufficiently identifies it, there is no need to provide the usual plans and descriptions.[28] There is no guarantee that permission will be renewed, although it would normally be difficult to refuse renewal unless there had been a change in planning policy affecting the area or uncertainty as to the development of the site was having undesirable side effects elsewhere.

(d) Special office and industrial conditions

Conditions imposed by the appropriate Secretary of State on industrial development certificates or office development permits are carried over to the subsequent grant of planning permission, although no appeal exists against them in the normal way to the Secretary of State.[29] In the case of office development, however, authorities were permitted to attach to their decision a certificate to the effect that the Secretary of State's conditions would have in any event been imposed by the authority.[30] Upon the expiry of the special system of office control such conditions continued in force.[31]

10. Registration of conditions

Planning conditions attached to deemed permissions, and those attached to permissions granted before August 1, 1977, are not registrable as local land

---

[23] *Ibid.* s.43(1). In *Spackman* v. *S.O.S.E.* [1977] 1 W.L.R. 257 the construction of a soakaway and trenches, and of a private driveway were held to amount to specified operations in the case of a permission for the erection of a single dwelling house; and in *United Refineries Ltd.* v. *Essex C.C.* [1978] J.P.L. 110 the court held that development had "commenced" for the purposes of a non-statutory condition, with the building of an access road, notwithstanding its small significance when set against the estimated £15,000,000 capital cost of the total oil refinery development. This liberal interpretation of the requirements was carried to its extreme in *Malvern Hills D.C.* v. *S.O.S.E.* (1982) 262 E.G. 1190, where a majority in the Court of Appeal held that the pegging out of the lines of a new estate road was sufficient to constitute an "operation" in the course of laying out the road.

[24] *R.* v. *S.O.S.E., ex parte Percy Bilton Industrial Properties Ltd.* (1976) 31 P. & C.R. 154.

[25] *High Peak B.C.* v. *S.O.S.E.* [1981] J.P.L. 366.

[26] *South Oxfordshire D.C.* v. *S.O.S.E.* [1981] J.P.L. 359.

[27] T.C.P.A. 1971, s.43(7). In the case of a commencement condition imposed otherwise than under ss. 41 or 42 in respect of permission for building or other operations a similar provision exists in T.C.P.A. 1971, s.30(3).

[28] General Development Order, art.5(3); and see *ante*, p. 206.

[29] T.C.P.A. 1971, ss.71, 82.

[30] *Ibid.* s.82(3).

[31] *Ibid.* s.82(6).

charges.[32] But conditions imposed upon any permission granted by a local planning authority or the Secretary of State since that time are registrable if they impose any prohibition or restriction on the use of the land, and a duty falls upon the local authority to ensure registration.[33] The consequence of failure to register is not that the condition is unenforceable, but that a purchaser who suffers any loss by reason that a search of the register before he purchased failed to reveal the existence of the condition may claim compensation against the registering authority.[34] Conditions will also appear in the special planning register required by the 1971 Act, as part of the recorded decision of the authority.[35]

C. Planning by Agreement

The use of planning agreements as a means of overcoming many of the restrictions of the development control machinery has become increasingly widespread in the last ten years. Agreements can be used to impose obligations beyond those possible through normal procedures, and their consensual basis reflects the negotiated background to much modern planning control. But there are major objections to the phenomenon, and its rise is highly controversial. There is the fear, for example, that authorities may have engaged in the sale of planning permission, prescribing conditions of little relevance to the proposed development but of great financial benefit to the authority. There is the fact that the developer's willingness to agree to onerous terms is likely to be greatest in circumstances where planning controls are most rigid; not simply because of a realisation that something substantial might be needed to induce the authority to relax their policies, but because of the vast potential difference between the value of the land with no permission and no apparent prospect of it, and its value with permission for development. This *quid pro quo* approach to planning may lead to thoroughly bad development, because the less likely the prospect of permission under established plans and policies, the greater the increment in land value if permission is actually granted. An area of park land in a city centre, for example, may have a negative value in its existing use because of the maintenance burden attaching to it; but with planning permission for office development its value would soar. That is no doubt an extreme example, but it indicates the strength of the economic forces underlying negotiated planning control.

Those forces have always been there, although they have been strengthened since the early 1960s as development value in land has grown at an unprecedented rate, and as the imbalance between private development profits and local planning authority's financial resources to intervene positively in development has increased. But planning control and development profit are uneasy partners. The control of land use is a system of regulation imposed upon the private market, which has a distorting

---

[32] Local Land Charges Act 1975, ss. 1 and 2(*e*). The register formerly contained details only of conditions imposed by local planning authorities, and these were cleared from the register on the coming into force of the new Act on August 1, 1977. Planning charges are registered in Part 3 of the register: Local Land Charges Rules 1977 (S.I. 1977 No. 985).

[33] *Ibid.* s.5.

[34] *Ibid.* s.10.

[35] T.C.P.A. 1971, s.31; General Development Order 1977, art. 21.

influence upon the distribution of land value only because it pursues different ends from those of the market. Planning gain, in the sense of trade-offs between development values and planning permissions, brings the two closer together in a way which ultimately subjects planning decisions further and further to market criteria. This was the view taken by the Department of Environment's Property Advisory Group in 1981, in a special report on planning gain, when they insisted that:

" . . . as soon as a system of accepting public benefits is established which goes beyond the strict consideration of the planning merits of a proposed development, the entire system of development control becomes subtly distorted, and may fall into disrepute. Developers may come forward with schemes to which no conceivable planning objection could be raised, but be left with the impression that if they are not prepared to offer up some wholly extraneous planning gain, their application may receive a less sympathetic or less speedy consideration; there might have to be an appeal against a deemed, if not an actual, refusal of permission, which will cause expense and delay; and in the end, in order to overcome purely political difficulties which could not in any way be explained in technical, planning or legal terms, the developer may simply give way, and pay up."[36]

The machinery through which planning gain is pursued may be the normal development control machinery discussed above, either by way of conditions imposed on the grant of permission or through negotiations leading to the submission and approval of an application in accordance with the authority's wishes; but it is more commonly through agreements, particularly the statutory agreements for which provision is made under section 52 of the 1971 Act, and section 126 of the Housing Act 1974 (now superseded by s. 33 of the Local Government (Miscellaneous Provisions) Act 1982). The advantage of these arrangements, from the point of view of the authority, is that they are consensual rather than imposed, and that they are largely insulated from review by either the Secretary of State or the courts. It is this which has above all else fostered the growth of planning gain as a device in contemporary planning, and the machinery of the statutory agreements demands further analysis.

1. Contract

The simplest machinery is contract. The transaction is governed only by the rules of contract, and by the implied limits to the contracting power of the local authority. There is no specific statutory authorisation, but such contracts clearly fall within the broad terms of section 111 of the Local Government Act 1972, which authorises authorities to do "anything (whether or not involving the expenditure, borrowing or lending of money or the acquisition or disposal of any property or rights) which is calculated to facilitate, or is conducive or incidental to, the discharge of any of their functions." The courts have been prepared to interpret the section

[36] *Planning Gain* (H.M.S.O., 1981), para.6.02.

broadly,[37] and contract may therefore be used in a wide range of planning contexts.[38] It may not, however, be used so as to fetter the authority's future discretion: an undertaking by the authority to grant permission in the future, or to refuse permission to neighbouring landowners,[39] would be invalid.

But the major limitation upon simple contract arises from the rules of contract law itself. First, the doctrine of privity of contract involves that any obligation entered into by the developer is personal only, and does not run with the land so as to bind purchasers.[40] That may be of little concern in the case of "once and for all" obligations, such as the making of a capital contribution to infrastructure costs or the conveyance of land before permission is granted. But it seriously restricts enforcement of continuing obligations. Second, the doctrine of consideration requires that some consideration should have flowed from the authority to support the promise of the developer. The grant of permission is probably not itself consideration,[41] and something further will be necessary before the agreement will be enforceable. But at common law the problem of lack of consideration may be avoided in the case of documents under seal. The device supports a subsequent action for an injunction to restrain breaches of covenant and for damages (although it is often the case that a public authority, acting in the public interest, has suffered no pecuniary loss itself as a result of the developer's breach); but not an action for the equitable remedy of specific performance.[42] Moreover, in the absence of consideration, a financial or other contribution may fall to be considered as a "gift" to the authority. This may be the case where land is dedicated to some public purpose under specific statutory powers, but it is more difficult so to characterise a straightforward financial or other contribution. The result may be that acceptance of a benefit, otherwise than through contract, may be beyond the powers of an authority; and that it is therefore subsequently recoverable by the developer or, if he has gone into liquidation, by the receiver. Thus in *County and District Properties Ltd.* v. *Horsham Urban District Council*[43] the developers had contributed substantial sums to the authority for the purpose of overcoming on-site parking difficulties. The idea was that the authority themselves would make the necessary additional provision, in off-street car parks to be constructed, to accommodate the demand generated by the development. But when planning permission was still not forthcoming, the developers sought a refund, and the authority

---

[37] *R.* v. *G.L.C., ex parte Burgess* (1978) 77 L.G.R. 74 (upholding closed-shop agreement in G.L.C.).

[38] In *Lewis Jones* v. *Secretary of State for Wales* (1974) 72 L.G.R. 583 the Court of Appeal upheld a partnership agreement for the redevelopment of central Cardiff, as falling within the earlier (and slightly narrower) powers of the Local Government Act 1933.

[39] *Stringer* v. *M.H.L.G.* [1971] 1 All E.R. 65.

[40] See, *e.g. London C.C.* v. *Allen* [1914] 3 K.B. 642, where the authority had attempted by covenant to reserve land in a new development for future street extensions; but was held unable to enforce against a subsequent purchaser.

[41] The precise issue remains open, but the general approach of the courts has been to decline to regard benefit flowing from the exercise of a statutory discretion as consideration, except in unusual circumstances: see, *e.g. Glasbrook Bros. Ltd.* v. *Glamorgan C.C.* [1925] A.C. 270.

[42] *Kekewich* v. *Manning* (1851) 1 De G.M. & G. 176.

[43] (1970) 215 E.G. 1399.

maintained that the money had been accepted as a "gift." To this argument, Paull J. responded:

> "To describe such a sum of money as a gift was . . . a complete misuse of the word "gift" and a misunderstanding of the council's power under section 268 [now section 139 of the Local Government Act 1972]. That section contemplated a charitable gift by a charitably minded person to benefit a district. It did not mean money paid as an inducement for the favourable consideration of a project which, if granted, would put large sums of money into the donor's pockets. The last thing in the plaintiff's mind was charity. This was a final desperate attempt to get detailed development plans passed by the council."

That analysis holds true whether or not planning permission is granted unless the grant of permission amounts to consideration converting the transaction from "gift" to contract. But it does not affect an arrangement under which a contribution is made other than to the authority themselves, such as for the purpose of rehabilitating a privately owned listed building on the site.

2. Proprietary relationships

Both the contractual limitations may be overcome where the obligation is assumed as part of a proprietary relationship, such as lease or mortgage, or as a restrictive covenant between adjoining freehold landowners. Privity of contract is replaced by privity of estate, allowing the obligation to be enforced against subsequent purchasers. A leasehold relationship between authority and developer is common in large scale developments, and is suited particularly to partnership arrangements,[44] where rent review clauses offer a basis for equity sharing. But it is dependent upon either the authority having freehold ownership of the site, or the developer being willing to enter into a sale and leaseback arrangement with the authority.

3. Statutory planning agreements: historical background

The power to enter into formal agreements for planning purposes, now contained in section 52 of the 1971 Act and supplemented by section 126 of the Housing Act 1974 (which has in turn been superseded by s. 33 of the Local Government (Miscellaneous Provisions) Act 1982), allows authorities to accept contractual undertakings from developers in proprietary form. Provided the terms of the agreement satisfy the statutory criteria, they are registrable against the land and enforceable against successors in title. The authority need have no proprietary interest in the land at all, and their powers to enforce are conferred by statute rather than property relationship.

Planning agreements are as old as public land-use planning itself. The power first appeared in the Housing, Town Planning etc Act 1909,[45] and it reflected the limited interventionist powers conferred by that Act and the extent to which its implementation was dependent upon consensus and upon the voluntary agreement of landowners. The Town and Country Planning

[44] See further *post*, p. 524.
[45] Sched. 4, para. 13.

Act 1932 similarly made provision, under section 34, for planning agreements; and again their consensual basis proved an attractive method of securing planning objectives. Landowners proved willing to subject their land to planning restrictions, whether permanently or for a specified period, and the Inland Revenue Board provided a further incentive when they agreed to recognise the restrictions as diminishing the valuation of land for death duty purposes.[46] The agreements initially required no ministerial approval, but by scheduling them to a planning scheme prepared and approved under the Act, the authority and the landowner could confer statutory effect on the agreement and override the provisions of the scheme.

The Ministry's view was that planning agreements were a matter for local negotiation, and that there was no need for any detailed central supervision of their terms; but they recognised the danger that agreements could be used to secure non-planning ends, and urged authorities to confine their use to incorporating conditions which could otherwise be imposed on planning permissions.[47] But disquiet with the way in which agreements were being used by local planning authorities led eventually to central government assuming supervisory control over them.[48]

Concern about the use and misuse of planning agreements was voiced also in the Parliamentary debates on the 1947 Act. The Government had proposed initially to override all the agreements entered into under section 34. The Parliamentary Secretary to the Ministry of Town and Country Planning cited instances where the (apparently common) arrangement of an owner accepting restrictions over part of his land in return for the right to develop another part had led to bad development.[49] One was a case where the owner had agreed to preserve an existing golf course in return for rights to build on the fringe of it, and the result had been a long line of unattractive ribbon development along the side of the course.

But eventually the Government accepted that past agreements should be preserved,[50] and that power to enter into further agreements should be retained. They insisted, however, that each agreement should require ministerial approval before taking effect, and the Ministry's criteria were strict:

> "For an agreement to be appropriate, it should be clear not only that it is a possible way of securing the desired result, but also that it is the best and most convenient way."[51]

The ministerial control was removed in 1969,[52] however, pursuant to a recommendation by the Management Team on Development Control[53]; and local planning authorities gradually came to resort increasingly to the

---

[46] *Eighteenth Annual Report of the Ministry of Health 1936-37*, Cmd. 5516, para.144.
[47] *Twentieth Annual Report of the Ministry of Health 1938-39*, Cmd. 6089, para 112, where the Ministry insisted that to attempt to force the applicant into an agreement where the authority had no power to impose an express condition was an abuse of their powers.
[48] T.C.P. (Interim Development) Act 1943, s.10.
[49] *Official Report, Standing Committee D* (Session 1946-47, Vol. III) col. 205 (March 4, 1947).
[50] See now T.C.P.A. 1971, Sched. 24, para. 88, which preserves the old agreements, subject to modification or discharge either by the Secretary of State, or by an arbitrator at the instance of the landowner.
[51] *Report of the Ministry of Housing and Local Government 1957*, Cmnd. 419, p. 8l.
[52] T.C.P.A. 1968, Sched. 9. para. 19.
[53] H.M.S.O. 1967, p.22.

statutory power. It was not that ministerial consent had been refused often in the past,[54] but simply the requirement that it be obtained, which had formerly inhibited authorities in their use of the powers; but with ministerial supervision lifted there were few obvious constraints upon the use of section 52 agreements.

The agreements offered a limited basis for partnership arrangements with developers, and also a more flexible means through which local planning authorities could regulate the phasing of development and the provision of infrastructure. These functions assumed greater significance in the boom era of property development of the late 1960s and early 1970s, when authorities were being urged to play a more positive role in land supply and facilitating residential development. The Working Party on Local Authority/Private Enterprise Partnership Schemes in 1972 acknowledged the value of planning agreements and urged the Government to introduce broader powers allowing authorities to enforce positive as well as negative covenants in their agreements,[55] and effect was given to the recommendation in 1974.[56] A number of authorities had already taken special powers under local Acts for that purpose.

The consequence of increased reliance by authorities on planning agreements as an instrument in development control was that the traditional regulatory model of control in many cases was superseded by a consensual, negotiated model. Detailed research carried out by Professor Jowell in the mid-1970s indicated that many authorities were consciously using agreements as a means of broadening the scope of planning control, and that agreements were being used to achieve gains which went beyond those which could lawfully be achieved through planning conditions.[57]

4. The machinery of section 52 agreements

(a) The scope of the section

Section 52 of the 1971 Act permits authorities to enter into an agreement "for the purpose of restricting or regulating the development or use" of land in their area, and it provides that "any such agreement may contain such incidental and consequential provisions (including provisions of a financial character) as appear to the local planning authority to be necessary or expedient for the purposes of the agreement."[58] The limitations of privity of contract are overcome by a provision which deems the authority to be possessed of adjacent land, and deems the agreement to have been expressed to be made for the benefit of such land. The purpose of these arrangements is to place the authority in the same position as a landowner entitled to enforce a restrictive covenant against an adjoining landowner. But the device is awkward, and doubts remain as to the permitted scope of section 52 agreements. A broad interpretation of the "deeming" provision is simply

---

[54] Few agreements were ever refused by the Ministry, and then usually on technical rather than policy grounds: Jowell, "Bargaining in Development Control" [1977] J.P.L. 414 at 416.
[55] *Report of Working Party on Local Authority/Private Enterprise Partnership Schemes* (H.M.S.O., 1972), p.13.
[56] Housing Act 1974, s. 126; *post*, p. 373.
[57] "Bargaining in Development Control" [1977] J.P.L. 414.
[58] T.C.P.A. 1971, s.52(l).

that it gives the authority the necessary status to enforce all the terms of an agreement against successors in title.

If that is the case, there would be no need for the courts to import further rules governing enforcement of restrictive covenants; such as to insist, for example, that the obligations should be restrictive rather than positive, or that they should be capable of benefiting adjoining land rather than merely conferring some broad public benefit.[59] The broad terms of section 52(1) suggest that such restrictions are inapplicable, and that provided the main purpose of the agreement is the restriction or regulation of land development or use, it may include consequential positive terms and need show no benefit to immediately adjoining land.

Terms going beyond the scope of section 52 are not necessarily invalid. They may still be enforceable in contract between the original parties. But the benefit conferred by section 52 of enforceability against third parties will not extend to them.

(b) Agreement or contract?

The precise legal status of a section 52 agreement is the subject of some dispute. The section speaks of "agreement" rather than "contract," and the implication is that an arrangement falling short of an actual enforceable contract may suffice. The point is of some significance, because it raises the question of the consideration which an authority may be able to provide to support the undertakings offered by the landowner. If there need be no contract, there need be no consideration; and the authority may enforce the obligations against the covenantor without more.

Provided enforceability against the original covenantor is established, consideration is irrelevant to the issue of enforceability against a successor in title to the original covenantor. The Act permits enforcement against "persons deriving title under" the original covenantor "as if the local planning authority were possessed of adjacent land and as if the agreement had been expressed to be made for the benefit of such land."[60] The effect of these "deeming" provisions is to establish a quasi-proprietary relationship between the planning authority and successors of the covenantor. The authority are deemed to have a property right to secure the observance by successors of obligations under the agreement; and the right is effectively an interest in the land subject to the agreement. The pre-requisite to enforcement against successors in title is that they should have taken title with notice of the obligations; and that is secured through the registration of agreements under the Local Land Charges Act 1975.

Enforcement against the original covenantor, however, raises different questions; and these in turn raise some fundamental issues as the whole relationship between the local planning authority and the developer. If we assume for the moment that some form of consideration is needed to support the landowner's covenants, there are three main possibilities.

---

[59] In *Gee* v. *National Trust* (1965) 17 P. & C.R. 6 at p.10 Lord Denning M.R. in the Court of Appeal accepted a broad approach to the interpretation of a closely comparable provision of the National Trust Act 1937; but Davies and Salmon L.JJ. reserved their opinions on the point.

[60] T.C.P.A. 1971, s.52(2).

(i) **Nominal consideration:** it is common practice for authorities to import some nominal consideration into their agreements, which may be intended never to be actually paid. It is thus a fictitious device, but no doubt effective.[61] So too, for most purposes, if the agreement is executed under seal.

(ii) **Actual consideration:** an agreement may incorporate some real contractual undertaking by the planning authority, such as to provide some amenity or service for the land.

(iii) **Planning permission as consideration:** this is at first sight an attractive proposition, because the reality behind most section 52 agreements is that the planning permission is the *quid pro quo* offered by the authority for the developer's obligations. But there is the objection that in granting or refusing planning permission, an authority are exercising a statutory function; and that it would be wrong to import private law principles into this public law arena.[62] In particular, an agreement ordinarily ought not to purport to bind the authority to grant permission in the future or to restrict them in their exercise of statutory powers. It has now been accepted, however, that for an authority to enter into a section 52 agreement is itself an exercise of a statutory discretion, and that an agreement may therefore lawfully fetter the future exercise of other discretionary powers except where they are exercised in accordance with the provisions of the development plan.[63] This line of argument therefore lends some support to the idea that the authority's consideration may indeed flow from the grant of permission or the fettering of discretion. But it is not satisfactory as a comprehensive answer. An agreement may be entirely voluntary on the landowner's part, or at least not be backed by the prospect of permission.

In short, there are serious difficulties in the way of implying into section 52 a requirement that agreements under the section should be supported by consideration. There is no compelling role for the doctrine of consideration in this context, and no obvious reason for attempting to mould a public law power into a private law format.[64]

Where an authority do assume obligations under an agreement, enforcement by the original covenantee is in contract. Although the section makes no provision for enforcement by his successors in title, the benefit of any covenant entered into by the authority runs with the land, both at common law and under section 78 of the Law of Property Act 1925, providing the

---

[61] See, *e.g. Midland Bank Trust Co. Ltd.* v. *Green* [1981] 1 All E.R. 153 where the House of Lords accepted that a "nominal" consideration, as referring to "a sum or consideration which can be mentioned as consideration but is not necessarily paid" (at 159, *per* Lord Wilberforce) was nonetheless sufficient to amount to "valuable" consideration under the Land Charges Act 1925.

[62] In the only reported case of enforcement of a planning agreement, the covenantor's breach was apparently regarded by the Court as contractual, but the case relates not to section 52 but to a local Act power authorising the acceptance and enforcement by the authority of any "undertaking" given by the developer: *Beaconsfield D.C.* v. *Gams* (1974) 234 E.G. 749 (see the corrected report at (1976) 237 E.G. 657).

[63] *Royal Borough of Windsor and Maidenhead* v. *Brandrose Investments Ltd.*[1981] 1 W.L.R. 423; *post*, p. 368.

[64] For a useful analysis of the competing arguments, see Loughlin, "Planning Gain: Law, Policy and Practice" 1 *Oxford Journal of Legal Studies* 61 at 78–86.

covenant is one which "touches or concerns" the land, and it was the intention of the parties that it should run.[65]

(c) Validity of terms and the fettering of discretion

Although section 52 agreements have been widely used in practice to impose terms which would not be valid if imposed as planning conditions, doubt has remained as to whether the power is subject to the same implied limitations as the power to impose conditions. The language of the section is broad; but so too is the power to impose conditions, and the view of central government on the planning agreement powers of the 1932 Act was that both were subject to the same limitations.[66]

But there are compelling arguments against that position in relation to section 52. The power is conferred in the 1971 Act as an "additional" power of control, and to limit its function to that already fulfilled by the planning condition power would be to restrict it to the point where it offered no additional benefits except more efficient enforcement. Further, the section itself specifically authorises terms of a financial character, which go beyond those which may be imposed by way of condition.

Perhaps the strongest point of distinction, however, is that planning agreements are consensual, and are based upon negotiated agreement rather than imposed obligation. If the developer is prepared to agree to terms restricting or regulating the development or use of his land, can he subsequently be heard to complain that they were unreasonable, or even that they did not relate fairly and reasonably to the permitted development? An agreement may be entered into when there is no application for planning permission at all, but where the developer is prepared to agree to some restriction upon the development of his land for other reasons. Nor, in order for the agreement to have been based on consensus, is it necessary to maintain the pretence that the developer should have been under no pressure to accept its terms.

This view of the section, and of the breadth of the powers conferred by it, were confirmed in the High Court in the first instance judgement of Walton J. in *Western Fish Products Ltd.* v. *Penwith District Council*,[67] although the Court of Appeal found it unnecessary to pronounce upon them. Walton J. accepted first that:

" . . . the purpose of an agreement under section 52 is that it will enable the local planning authority to control matters which it might otherwise have no power to control by the imposition of conditions on any planning permission. In the present case, for example, it might enable the factory to be controlled with a view to minimising any possible nuisance, whereas it would be clearly impossible to impose restrictions on the working of the factory as part of a planning condition."

---

[65] *Smith and Snipes Hall Farm Ltd.* v. *River Douglas Catchment Board* [1949] 2 K.B. 500. The absence of any mutuality in the section itself suggested to Lord Greene M.R. in *Ransom & Luck Ltd.* v. *Surbiton B.C.* [1949] Ch.180, 196 that consideration was not intended to be an element of agreements under s.34 of the 1932 Act, but the question was left open by the court.

[66] See further *ante*, footnote 47.

[67] (1977) unreported.

Counsel for the plaintiffs had suggested that an agreement was lawful only where the developer entered into it completely voluntarily, but the Judge rejected the submission as:

" . . . a wholly unrealistic approach to the matter. Left to themselves, few if any developers would ever enter into such [an] agreement which must, in the nature of things, be disadvantageous to them. The sanction—mostly unspoken, but sometimes stated in no uncertain terms—is that if there is no section 52 agreement there will be no planning permission. . . . from the first to the last this involves no illegal action on the part of the Defendant Council."

But one important limitation remains, which is that an authority may not, as a general rule, enter into a contractual arrangement which has the effect of fettering the future exercise of a statutory discretion. Subsection (3) of section 52 acknowledges the rule, by providing that nothing in the section, or in any agreement made under it, should be construed as restricting the exercise of any powers conferred by the Act. In its original form in the 1947 Bill, that prohibition was absolute. But opposition members argued that, as it stood, the section offered no security to landowners that the authorities would keep their side of the bargain, and not simply override agreements under their statutory powers.[68] An amendment was therefore introduced, which added the words "so long as the powers are exercised in accordance with the provisions of the development plan." Although the subsection as finally enacted proceeds by way of a double negative, its intended effect must be to confer on authorities the power to restrict the future exercise of a statutory power, except where the power is to be exercised in accordance with the development plan.

But it must be remembered that the provision was designed to relate to the detailed land use plans which it was envisaged would be made under the 1947 Act, and that it was anticipated that authorities would be required to comply closely with the plans in practice.[69] The effect of an agreement containing provisions which were authorised by the subsection was therefore more to enforce the provisions of the adopted plan, and to require the authority to gain approval to a formal amendment to the plan before overriding the agreement, than to impose any fetter on a broad discretion such as that enjoyed by authorities in development control today. Moreover, the plans were themselves to be sufficiently precise for it to be possible to ascertain what exercise of power would, and what would not, be in accordance with the plan. But in the case of the modern, flexible, structure plans and local plans, such an assessment may often cause difficulties.

These problems were largely overlooked in *Royal Borough of Windsor and Maidenhead* v. *Brandrose Investments Ltd,*[70] where the authority had entered into an agreement under the section which implicitly accepted that premises belonging to the developers would be demolished. The authority

---

[68] *Hansard,* H.C. Deb., Vol. 439, col. 1835 (July 7, 1947); the objection was made in the course of proceedings on the identical provisions of the T.C.P. (Scotland) Bill, and the amendment was carried through to the English provisions.

[69] See further *ante,* pp. 279–280.

[70] [1981] 1 W.L.R. 1083.

then extended their existing conservation area so that those premises came within it, and maintained that listed building consent should accordingly be obtained before demolition was undertaken. That submission was rejected by the court, and it was held that it was an implied and enforceable term of the agreement that the authority would do nothing to impede the demolition of the premises. The decision is unsatisfactory overall for two reasons. First, the Secretary of State had already granted a general consent to the demolition of buildings in a conservation area where such demolition was required by section 52 agreement, but the terms of his direction were not apparently brought to the attention of the court.[71] Secondly, the court found that there was no development plan in force for the area; and that must necessarily have been an erronous conclusion. Even if there were no structure plan or local plan yet in force, an old-style development plan must have been in existence for the area, and its terms may well have been of relevance. And would the fetter on discretion have been effective if there were an adopted policy in general terms, not site-specific, which committed the authority to furthering the objectives of conservation in their area by, *inter alia*, exercise of their powers to declare and extend conservation areas?

Perhaps the most significant part of the ruling, however, is the judge's acceptance of the proposition that an agreement under section 52 was not governed at all by the usual rules relating to the fetter of discretionary powers, because the authority's participation in the agreement in itself constituted the exercise of a discretionary power, and was thus something more than merely a contractual fetter.[72] If that view is correct, then it follows that an agreement under section 52 may enable an authority to undertake to grant planning permission, or to withhold enforcement action, at any time in the future, and that the only constraint will be the "development plan," a document no longer designed to fulfil such a role.

The principal constraint upon terms contained in a section 52 agreement is therefore simply that their primary purpose should be to restrict or regulate the development or use of the land to which the agreement relates. They should therefore be primarily restrictive or regulatory in nature as opposed to positive, in the sense of requiring works to be carried out. And they should relate to the site itself, though not necessarily to any permitted development. The purpose may be to restrict development on another, unrelated, part of the site from that upon which development is being undertaken. But this does not restrict all the terms of the agreement to these purposes. It may contain incidental and consequential provisions, which may be positive in nature, and which may seek to govern the off-site effects of the development, such as a lorry-routing scheme. There is no warrant for reading into the section any limitation which would make validity dependent upon the need for the agreement in planning terms, so as to require the authority to demonstrate that without the agreement permission would not have been granted for development. Such an approach would necessarily confuse policy and legality.

The validity of the terms of an agreement may be questioned as a defence

---

[71] D.O.E. Circular 23/77, para. 71.
[72] Following *Dowty Boulton Paul* v. *Wolverhampton Corporation* [1971] 1 W.L.R. 204.

to proceedings brought for their enforcement,[73] and although it is likely that the courts would intervene at an earlier stage to prevent the improper use of the machinery,[74] challenge by third parties to deals between authorities and developers under these mechanisms is complicated not only by problems of *locus standi* but also by lack of public information as to the negotiations leading up to the formal agreement.

The courts' assistance may be sought in connection with the interpretation of a concluded agreement, by way of an action for declaration.[75]

(d) The interest bound by the agreement

The section authorises only agreements entered into with persons "interested in land" in the authority's area. "Interested" does not necessarily mean owning an interest (in the legal sense) in the land. It has been suggested that a purely contractual right may suffice,[75a] but there would be no power to enforce against successors unless and until an alienable interest was required. Freehold ownership is not necessary, but a covenant entered into by the owner of any lesser interest may be of limited value to the authority. An applicant whose interest was no more than that of a prospective purchaser under an option to purchase or even an agreement of sale would be able to bind only his limited interest and not the freehold, until he actually acquired title to it.

Similarly, a lessee may enter into an agreement under the section, but its effects will be limited to the leasehold estate owned by him. The freehold estate could be bound only by the person having power to do so, who may of course, join in the agreement. Otherwise, the terms of the agreement will be limited to the leasehold estate, although binding upon purchasers of that estate and other persons, such as sub-tenants, deriving title "directly or indirectly" under the original covenantor.[76] It means also that tenants' covenants are limited in time to the life of the estate, and that they will determine upon the expiry of the lease or its earlier surrender or forfeiture.

Terms of agreements are registrable as land charges,[77] but they need not appear in the public planning register maintained by the local planning authority and are frequently, perhaps too readily, regarded as confidential documents. But it would be difficult for an authority to refuse any *bona fide* request under the Local Land Charges Rules for a search to be undertaken in the register in respect of any land subject to an agreement, and the terms of agreements may therefore be more readily available to public scrutiny than is commonly supposed.

[73] Enforcement is also dependent upon the terms of the agreement having been expressed with sufficient clarity and certainty to provide a basis for an injunction: see, *e.g. National Trust* v. *Midlands Electricity Board* [1952] 1 All E.R. 298 (no act to be done which would injure, prejudice or destroy the natural aspect and condition of the land: held to be too vague to be enforceable).

[74] See, *e.g. Attorney-General* v. *Barnes Corporation and Ranelagh Club Ltd.* [1939] Ch. 110 at 128, *per* Luxmoore J.; and see also *R.* v. *Barnes B.C., ex parte Conlan* [1938] 3 All E.R. 226 (right of councillor to inspect documents relating to the pending litigation in the first case) and *Ranelagh Club Ltd.* v. *Central Land Board* (1958) 9 P. & C.R. 462 (agreement held not to have constituted nor incorporated any grant of planning permission).

[75] See, *e.g. Crittenden (Warren Park) Ltd.* v. *Surrey C.C.* [1966] 1 W.L.R.25.

[75a] *Pennine Raceway Ltd* v. *Kirklees M.D.C.* (1982) 263 E.G. 721 at 722, *per* Eveleigh L.J.

[76] See further the definition of "deriving title" in T.C.P.A. 1971, s.290(7).

[77] Local Land Charges Act 1975, s.1(1)(*b*)(ii).

(e) Variation and extinguishment

The life of an agreement may be expressly limited to a specified period, but otherwise its terms remain effective in perpetuity. They are not extinguished by the subsequent grant of planning permission, whether by the Secretary of State or by the local planning authority; and they therefore provide the planning authority with a more secure means of control over development than planning conditions, which may be appealed against to the Secretary of State. The terms of an agreement may be varied if both parties are prepared to agree to variation, and the most convenient method is usually through entering into a second agreement under the section modifying or extinguishing the terms of the first. Alternatively, the original agreement may make provision for its discharge in certain circumstances, whether by arbitration or on the occurrence of some event such as the granting of planning permission for development prohibited by the agreement. There may be provision for compensation in such a case, where necessary to allow the authority to acquire elsewhere the benefit lost by discharging the agreement.

The means through which unilateral challenge to the terms of an agreement may be made by the landowner, is by way of application to the Lands Tribunal under section 84 of the Law of Property Act 1925. Under that provision, the Tribunal has broad powers, substantially widened by amendments made in 1969,[78] to discharge or modify any "restriction arising under covenant or otherwise as to the user" of any freehold land "or the building thereon." The grounds upon which the jurisdiction may be exercised are

(a) that the restriction ought to be deemed obsolete, by reason of changes in the property or the neighbourhood, or other material circumstances;

(b) that the continued existence of the restriction would impede some reasonable public or private user of the land, without securing any practical benefits of substantial value or advantage to the persons entitled to the benefit of the covenant (or the covenant is contrary to the public interest) and that money would be adequate compensation for any loss or disadvantage suffered;

(c) that the proposed discharge or modification has the consent of the persons entitled to enjoy the benefit of the restriction and who are capable of consenting;

(d) that the proposed discharge or modification would not injure the persons entitled to the benefit of the restriction.

It had always been assumed that the Lands Tribunal's jurisdiction extended to restrictive covenants contained in section 52 agreements,[79] but that it would be used sparingly and most commonly on the first of the above grounds. But in *Re Beecham's Application*,[80] the first case to come before the Tribunal involving a planning agreement, the Tribunal took a broad

---

[78] Under the Law of Property Act 1969, s.28.
[79] See, *e.g. Gee v. National Trust* [1966] 1 W.L.R. 170, where the Tribunal's jurisdiction in respect of covenants under closely similar provisions of the National Trusts Acts had been accepted.
[80] [1981] J.P.L. 55.

approach, and discharged a restriction on the fourth ground. It was a surprising course to take, not the least because the covenant was only 10 years old, and the applicants were the original covenantors. But, curiously, the Tribunal stressed the fact that the council did not in fact own any land capable of being benefited by the covenant; and that was one of five factors deemed relevant to the exercise of discretion. But it is an objection common to practically every section 52 agreement. The deeming of the authority to be the owner of adjacent land is nothing more than a legal device to secure enforceability against successors in title, and if the authority were in fact owners of adjoining land the mechanisms of section 52 would be unnecessary. The essence of the statutory agreement is not that it is necessarily of benefit to any particular piece of land or locality, but that it serves a broader planning purpose desired by the authority. Once this background is established, it becomes difficult to assess how ground (d) may intelligently be applied to a section 52 agreement. It is designed for covenants which secure private advantage, not planning ends.

Most important of the other factors identified by the Tribunal were the fact that substantial development had taken place in the area since the date of the agreement (but not so, in the Tribunal's opinion, as to render the restriction obsolete under ground (a)); and that planning permission for the proposed development had been granted by the Secretary of State. The latter is a particularly persuasive factor, but it by no means follows that because the development is favoured by the Secretary of State, the local planning authority would not be injured by the discharge of the restriction. It may still fulfil an important planning role, by securing, for example, an area of open space; and the Secretary of State's decision may have been based upon the reasoning that the advantages of the proposed use would outweigh the advantages of the retention of the land in its present state. In that case, ground (b) might be thought to be a better ground upon which discharge might be granted, which not only requires the Tribunal to strike a balance between some proposed reasonable user of the land and the practical benefits secured by the restriction, but which might also provide a basis for the award of compensation to the authority to place them in a position to acquire replacement open space land.

The central defect lies in the criteria themselves. They were designed for ordinary restrictive covenants, and are unable to be applied easily or logically to agreements with a broader purpose. And the jurisdiction of the Tribunal is limited to covenants of a purely restrictive nature. It does not, therefore, extend to any positive covenants contained in a section 52 agreement as incidental to the primary restrictive covenants; and neither does it extend to positive covenants contained in an instrument under the Housing Act 1974, the Local Government (Miscellaneous Provisions) Act 1982, or one made under local Act powers. These exceptions are anomalous, and demonstrate further the need for reconsideration of the Tribunal's jurisdiction and role.

(f) Section 52 and development land tax

The entering into a section 52 agreement by a landowner is capable of amounting to the disposal or part disposal of an interest in his land,[81] and the

---

[81] Development Land Tax Act 1976, s. 46, which defines an interest in land as including "any right in or over land or affecting the use or disposition of land."

transaction may thus render any consideration or increased value resulting to retained land from it liable to development land tax. But it would be a rare case in which the provisions operated in this way to impose any liability, because such enhancement of value as might accrue normally results from the grant of planning permission for the development to which the agreement relates, and is thus taxable in itself upon the subsequent disposal of the land or the commencement of any "material" development on it.[82]

A section 52 agreement usually has the effect in itself of diminishing the value of land, by subjecting it to some restriction or liability. Thus the cost of controls under section 52 is to some extent borne by the Exchequer, because of the diminished gain accruing to development land tax. And any expenditure on relevant improvements required under an agreement may be expressly set off for tax purposes,[83] as may any diminution in value suffered by other land subject to an agreement entered into as part of the arrangement for the granting of planning permission.[84]

5. Section 126 of the Housing Act 1974

Following the recommendations in 1972 of the Sheaf Committee[85] and the pressures exerted upon planning by the property boom of the early 1970s, the Government introduced, in 1974, legislation permitting authorities to enter into and enforce agreements containing positive covenants.[86]

The section allowed an authority to become a party to "an instrument under seal" (thereby dispensing with any requirement of consideration) with a person having an interest in land in their area; and provided the instrument was executed for the purpose of securing the carrying out of works on that land or of facilitating the development of that land (or of other land in which that person has an interest), any positive covenants contained in it were enforcable against successors in title.[87] Although conferred by a Housing Act, the power was of general application, and was available to district and county councils, and to London Boroughs and Special Planning Boards.[88]

The strength of the section lay in the additional enforcement powers offered by it. In the event of breach of covenant, an authority might enter upon the land and carry out the works themselves, recovering the cost from the covenantor.[89]

But the section did not integrate easily with section 52, nor with the various Local Act powers. The enforcement powers of section 126, for

[82] Ibid. ss. 1(2); 2(1).
[83] Ibid. s.5.
[84] Ibid. Sched. 3, para. 6.
[85] Report of the Working Party on Local Authority/Private Enterprise Partnership Schemes, (1972) para. 53.
[86] The provision had been introduced originally in the Housing and Planning Bill, which lapsed with the change in Government in February 1974; but it was reintroduced and became part of the Housing Bill of the new government.
[87] Housing Act 1974, s.126(1). To be enforceable the covenant should be expressed to be one to which the section applies: s.126(2)(c).
[88] Ibid. s. 126(7), as amended by Local Government (Miscellaneous Provisions) Act 1976, s.43.
[89] Ibid. s.126(3). There is a preliminary procedure requiring not less than 21 days' notice of intention to be given to any person with an interest in the land and against whom a covenant is enforceable: s.126(4). This special means of enforcement is without prejudice to any other method.

example, extended only to positive covenants and not to negative terms, even although they would often be in the same agreement and might even appear in the same individual covenant.

6. *The new power: Section 33 of the Local Government (Miscellaneous Provisions) Act 1982*

Section 126 is superseded by the Act of 1982, which allows local authorities to become parties to instruments under seal for a range of purposes wider than section 126. They include securing the carrying out of works or facilitating the development or regulating the use of land. But the reforms achieved by the new section are largely technical. Enforceability against successors in title is still possible only in the case of positive covenants ("being a covenant to carry out any works or do any other thing on or in relation to that land"); and purely restrictive covenants are enforceable only against the original covenantor, unless falling also within section 52 of the 1971 Act.

D. Controlling Planning Gain

Planning agreements offer a flexible alternative to the more conventional forms of planning control, but there has been increasing concern in recent years about the abuse made of this flexibility by some authorities. Agreements may be used to impose obligations going well beyond those which may be sought through planning permissions and conditions, and to shield the deals from public scrutiny and external review. As the nature of the obligations imposed extends further and further away from the planning requirements of the particular development, it becomes difficult to resist the conclusion that the power is being used by the authority for an ulterior purpose—usually the purpose of securing the best possible "price" for the planning permission being granted by them. But although all would agree that blatant abuse of power should not be permitted, opinions vary widely as to the point at which the line should be drawn in determining what are the "proper" limits to section 52 agreements and less formal arrangements through which gains may be secured, and as to the best means of regulating the system.

The Property Advisory Group's Report to the Secretary of State in 1981 struggled with the former problem, and came to the view that planning gain should have no place in planning control, except in certain special cases.[90] It represented a victory for the *private property* theory of planning regulation. But their Report failed to grasp the economic forces from which planning gain arises, and failed therefore to give full consideration to how the phenomenon might be brought under control.

Five guidelines were recommended by the Group, but they recommended no procedural or substantive changes, and took the view that even the guidelines ought not to be translated into a formal code of practice. The guidelines set out in the Report are as follows:

> "(1) When a local authority receives an application for planning permission, it should be considered on its merits, and as a whole.

[90] *Planning Gain* (H.M.S.O., 1981).

(2) If the proposal is one to which no legitimate planning objection can be raised, the authority should grant permission.

(3) If there are objections to the proposal which can be overcome by the imposition of valid planning conditions, permission should be granted subject to those conditions.

(4) If there are objections to the proposal which, but for some technical legal objection, could be overcome by the imposition of a valid planning condition, the local authority should be willing to grant permission subject to the developer's entering into an agreement, under section 52 of the 1971 Act or other powers,which will overcome the legitimate planning objection.

(5) If the application is a "mixed" application which contains a number of elements, some of which are, by themselves objectionable, but others of which promote positive planning advantages, the separate elements should be looked at individually as well as collectively so that, in the final result, the decision on the application, which must be a decision on the application as a whole, will achieve a just balance which cannot be characterised as the mere 'sale' of development rights."[91]

The guidelines are vague and difficult to apply intelligently in practice. It appears from other paragraphs in the Report, for example, that a "technical legal objection" which would vitiate a condition (under (4) above) might well be an objection of some importance, such as the objection to a condition requiring the payment by a developer of financial contributions to the authority.[92] Secondly, the Report tends to see decision-making in development control in black and white terms, and this is the case particularly with guideline (5). It is seldom a matter of technical planning assessment of the individual elements of an overall development scheme, but more a matter of policy, politics and compromise. The authority may have a policy against certain types of development in specified parts of their areas, or against development above a specified height or density; but nonetheless be prepared to admit as exceptions to the general policy, proposals which offer other advantages which may tip the balance. The other advantage may be nothing more than skilful design (not, incidentally, a "planning gain" within the terms of the Report), or it may be some public advantage such as open space or play facilities. The Report tends too readily to turn to the judicial model of development control, and to overlook the realities of consensual control and the element of bargaining between authority and developer which is not purely a product of planning gain. Similarly, the Report fails to identify clearly the scope of developers' obligations in providing necessary services for their development, and the point at which the obligation becomes more "public" in nature, and passes to the public utilities and statutory agencies. Much of that which is sometimes identified as "gain" is simply the inevitable result of a development system which so clumsily allocates liability for the provision of physical services.

Perhaps the most important criticism of the Report, however, is its failure to look at the mechanisms of planning gain, and to assume that the use, or abuse, of planning agreements is likely to be brought under control by no more than a policy statement by central government. But the process is one

[91] *Ibid.* para. 9.01.
[92] See, *e.g.* para. 4.02.

which is almost entirely outside the purview of central government. Developers, indeed, are frequently prepared to accept additional obligations in an agreement because of the time which it would otherwise take to bring an appeal on the merits of the development to the Secretary of State against a refusal of permission by the authority. And, as the Report correctly emphasises, the pressure for planning gain comes often from developers themselves, anxious to sell a scheme to the authority. Neither the developer nor the authority are likely to press the other to observe the guidelines, and the extent to which third party views may be heard is dependent upon the extent to which the authority are prepared to involve third parties, and upon the willingness of the Secretary of State to "call-in" an application where there is a prospect of planning gain going beyond the guidelines. And so some analysis of the existing machinery and how it might be adapted to allow closer view of the deals reached between developers and authorities is called for. Three courses that have been suggested require further comment:

Broaden the scope of planning conditions: one approach to reform might be to broaden expressly the power to impose planning conditions so as to overcome the "technical" objections referred to in the Group's Report. Such a broadened power might include power to require the payment of money to, or the vesting of land in, the authority; or power to direct the nature of occupancy of some or all of the completed development or the facilities to be provided with it. The developer would then have the normal right of appeal against the condition, and the Secretary of State's policies about the circumstances in which the powers might properly be used could be made effective.

Arbitration: an alternative is to introduce a system of arbitration to assess the "fairness" of the burden imposed under an agreement upon a developer.[93] But it is unclear by what criteria the arbitrator might be guided; and the prospect of arbitration would prove a strong incentive for developers to participate in planning gain arrangements as a means towards a permission, and then to seek arbitration subsequently to rearrange the agreement into more favourable terms.

Development plan policies: the use of development plans, and particularly the new local plans, as a means of both publicising and legitimising planning gain arrangements was barely touched upon by the Group's Report, but it is an important new development. If the criteria by which an authority propose to assess development proposals in an area include planning gain matters, such as securing better provision of open space and seeking contributions towards off-site infrastructure, then there is clear advantage in expressing those policies in the formal plan. It means that they may be the subject of public debate, and of challenge at a public local inquiry or by way of application to quash the plan in the courts. It also means that developers acquiring sites in the area are aware of the authority's requirements, and that they may be taken into account in their assessment of the price they can afford to pay for the land. Thus, the cost of meeting the requirements is passed back to the landowner and operates as a factor diminishing the enhancement of development value which would attach to the land if it were

---

[93] This course finds favour with Suddards, in "Section 52 Agreements: A Case for new Legislation?" [1979] J.P.L. 661.

assumed that all necessary services would be put in and funded by public authorities.

There is also the argument that, except where challenge has been made to such a policy within six weeks of the approval or adoption of the plan, the validity of the policy is unchallengeable.[94] It may therefore lawfully support a refusal of permission to a developer unwilling to meet the requirements, or an agreement entered into in accordance with the plan. The only comment of the Group on this practice was that "the drafting of such plans requires the very greatest care,"[95] without indicating the way in which that care was to be directed; and the guidelines are of limited assistance in a case where there is no "black and white" answer under planning principles, but a development plan statement drafted with consensual, compromise planning very much in mind.

Planning gain is the product of market forces influencing a regulatory system of decision-making which had long been believed to be above the market; and unless reform is made in either the working of the market or in the legal machinery through which planning gains are secured, the phenomenon is likely to become more widespread. But one matter which ought to be distinguished more clearly than it has in the past from planning gain, is the question of infrastructure. It is paradoxical that public agencies should be subject to a duty to provide physical services required in connection with new development, yet be deprived of the funds to finance the necessary works because of expenditure cut-backs, and thus have to seek to persuade planning authorities to defer proposals in their areas so as not to stretch resources.

Contributions by developers are usually the only means of bringing works forward, and this practice has grown significantly in recent years. This the Property Advisory Group's Report would characterise as planning gain, but only because the contributions could not validly be required by a condition imposed on a planning permission. Three particular cases, highways, water and sewerage, crop up in practically every development of any size, and particularly in growth areas; and an examination of the statutory allocation of liability between the private and public sector provides a useful background to understanding the distinction between infrastructure contributions and planning gain in the broader sense.

E. Infrastructure

1. *Introduction*

The word "infrastructure" has slowly crept into the planner's vocabulary, originally in the narrower sense as describing the physical services upon which new development is dependent, such as roads and streets, drains and sewers and water supply. But it has been given an extended meaning in more recent years as including the whole range of services and facilities affected by new development, such as education, health care, social services, recreational facilities and other amenities. Major new development inevitably has

---

[94] By virtue of T.C.P.A. 1971, ss.242, 244.
[95] *Planning Gain, op. cit.*, para. 5.03.

implications for services, and one of the important reasons underlying the introduction of planning control, and the restriction of ribbon development in particular, was the need to use services more efficiently in locating new development, and to coordinate the construction of new development with the provision of new infrastructure. Thus the adequacy of existing infrastructure and the ease with which it may be extended are necessarily highly persuasive factors in land release for new development; and, equally, absence of services has long been a justifiable basis for rejection of a planning application, even on allocated land, on the grounds that the application is premature until services will be available.[96]

This relationship between planning and services is sensible, but there is a risk that planning choices may come to be dictated by the capital programmes of public agencies, particularly the water authorities, over which the planning authority has no formal control. Alternatively, planning decisions may have sudden, unanticipated implications for the expenditure programmes of other agencies, but in no formal legal sense are the relationships tied in with each other: they remain ambiguous, and dependent upon close working co-operation.

A further issue is the distribution of function and cost of providing services, between the public sector, private developer and ultimate consumer. The equations are necessarily complex, because of the problems in identifying and distinguishing the various financial inputs and the extent to which they are absorbed or passed on by each group. The traditional distinction has been that the developer has met the cost of providing physical infrastructure needed on-site, such as estate roads and sewerage up to the boundary of the site; and that off-site provision has been the function of the public agencies concerned. Its funding has also been primarily their responsibility, the assumption being that the burden of servicing the capital borrowing involved should be shared between all the ratepayers of the district (or, in the case of water services since the establishment of the water authorities, between all the water consumers of the region). But that principle has become increasingly vulnerable. Authorities have sought to share the burden with developers: in some instances have been authorised to require financial contributions, and in other cases have been prepared to accept voluntary contributions in order to accelerate provision or adapt existing programmes.

It is a curious feature of British land development that no fixed national code exists governing cost distribution. The Government announced in 1975 that it believed that "the developer should be required to pay for those publicly provided services which make the development feasible,"[97] and that early legislation would follow. But it did not, and the arrangements which remain are necessarily uncertain and often dependent upon persuasion and negotiation in individual cases. Developers' costs need not necessarily be passed on to house purchasers. Where requirements are known with certainty in advance of site acquisition they will affect the price paid for the

---

[96] The government has taken the view that at times the objection may have been too easily relied on by local authorities as a means of restraining growth; and during the early 1970s urged them to take positive steps towards overcoming lack of capacity by, for example, entering into financial arrangements with developers: see, *e.g.* D.O.E. Circulars 10/72, 122/73.

[97] *Widening the Choice: The Next Steps in Housing,* Cmnd. 5280, para. 24.

site, and thus the advantage of clear code is that it might act as an informal tax on development values with an equitable and more flexible local distribution of benefit.[98]

But even in the absence of clear principles there has been a marked shift in responsibility in the past 15 years. Inflated development value in land has been a major factor. Authorities have been anxious to avoid the inequities of paying "double value" for land needed for the provision by them of infrastructure: that is, a value which is not only enhanced by the permission granted by them for the development, but which also reflects the value in market terms of the services they propose to provide. The better the services to be provided by an authority, the more they may have to pay for the sites on which to provide them. And so pressure has been brought to bear upon developers to make the necessary sites available at lower values or even to vest them in the authority at a nominal consideration, and to underwrite other infrastructure costs as well.

2. *Water supply and sewerage*

(a) The requisitioning power

Since 1974 the water authorities have been responsible for water services, and so far as new development is concerned the relevant duties are twofold: to provide a water supply[99] and to provide sewerage and sewage disposal facilities.[1] In each case the duty is enforceable through a requisitioning procedure, whereby the authority may be required to provide a public sewer for domestic purposes for the drainage of new buildings,[2] or to lay any necessary water mains (together with any necessary service reservoirs) for domestic purposes to such point as will enable the buildings to be connected at reasonable cost.[3] Where the requisitioning power is used, the developer may be required to contribute to the cost to the extent of the annual difference between one eighth of the capital cost, and the income from actual charges levied on the premises, over a period of twelve years. The authority may require a deposit to be paid as security; or alternatively the developer may agree to capitalise the anticipated expenditure and pay a single lump sum instead.[4]

[98] This point was taken by the R.I.C.S. in a working paper in 1974, *The Land Problem—a Fresh Approach,* where it was argued that there should be a national scheme whereby developers made cash contributions towards notional (rather than actual) off-site costs, and supplied free of charge land needed for public purposes such as schools, open space and recreation facilities.

[99] The general duty is imposed by Water Act 1973, s.11; and its application to new development prescribed by Water Act 1945, s.37 (as amended by the 1973 Act).

[1] The general duty, to provide "such public sewers as may be necessary for effectually draining their area and to make ... provision ... for effectually dealing with the contents of their sewers" is imposed by Water Act 1973, s.14.

[2] Water Act 1973, s.16.

[3] Water Act 1945, s.37.

[4] Details of the requisitioning powers are contained in Water Act 1973, s.16 and Water Act 1945, s.37. The scheme of the legislation is to distinguish between existing buildings, whose owners or occupiers need to pay no contribution towards off-site costs in the case of water supply, and only limited contributions for sewerage, from developers: see *Royco Homes Ltd. v. Southern Water Authority* (1978) 77 L.G.R.133. But the distinction is not particularly clear and the government has accepted that amendment may be needed: *The Water Industry in England and Wales: The Next Steps*, Cmnd. 6876, pp.21–22.

When the requisitioning power was extended to sewerage in 1974, it was widely believed to have ended the justification for rejection of development proposals through development control. It was argued that the new provisions enabled the developer to overcome sewerage problems unilaterally. But the courts have rejected that approach, declining to place an interpretation on the Act which would make for an inefficient and uneconomic use of water authorities' resources.[5] They have been able to reassert the dominance of planning control by insisting that the requisitioning power may be exercised only once planning permission has been granted for the development, so that the private sewer to which the authority are required to connect can be lawfully constructed. Thus the planning authority may continue to take into account existing capacity and capital expenditure plans, through consultations with the water authority in land release plan preparation and on individual planning applications.[6] But the water authority has no power of veto.

(b) Cost apportionment

There is a surprising gap in the requisitioning provisions in that no means exists for apportioning the costs of new infrastructure between the developers of different sites where more than one is likely to benefit. Sensible engineering practice dictates that the authority should anticipate future demand and provide for a greater capacity, when it appears likely that development of adjoining sites will take place in the future. But as the provisions stand the initial developer may be required to find a higher proportion of the cost. In the case of water mains the Act requires developers' contributions only where what is supplied is a "necessary" mains; that is, a mains laid for the sole purpose of supplying the development.[7] Although its size may be increased to take account of potential customers along its route, it will no longer be a "necessary" mains if built to accommodate extensions beyond the developer's site.[8]

In practice water authorities agree to an apportionment of cost between the developer and themselves, but the initial developer may still often expect to contribute more handsomely than subsequent adjoining developers from whom no contribution may lawfully be demanded in respect of the work already done.

(c) Public adoption of sewers

The duty of the water authority is to connect up to the private sewer constructed on-site by the developer.[9] But the developer will normally wish

[5] *George Wimpey & Co. Ltd.* v. *S.O.S.E.* (1978) 250 E.G. 241.
[6] Under General Development Order 1977, art. 15(f) the planning authority are obliged to consult with the water authority where the development includes(*inter alia*) the carrying out of building or other operations (with limited exceptions).
[7] Water Act 1945, s.37.
[8] *Royco Homes Ltd.* v. *Southern Water Authority* (1978) 77 L.G.R. 133; *Cherwell D.C..* v. *Thames Water Authority* [1975] 1 W.L.R. 448.
[9] Water Act 1973, s.16. The water authority's discretion under s.16 as to the manner and place of communication of the public sewer with the private sewer provided by the developer still requires that they provide a "communicating" sewer, and not merely bring it to a point they think appropriate: *William Leech (Midlands) Ltd.* v. *Severn Trent W.A.* The Times, May 22, 1981. It should be emphasised that the requisitioning procedure applies only to the situation where off-site works are needed. Where a public sewer already exists the land owner has a right to have his sewers connected to it provided he has rights by virtue or ownership or easements to have his sewer pass through the intervening land: Public Health Act 1936, s.34.

to pass on responsibility for maintenance of on-site sewers to the water authority, and this is achieved normally through an adoption agreement whereby the authority agree to adopt at some future date a sewer constructed in accordance with the terms of the agreement.[10]

3. *Highways*

(a) Highways input in development control

The requirements that the highway authority be consulted on certain planning applications, and their power to direct the planning authority in their handling of applications, means that questions of access to highways and development affecting their use are regulated through planning control.

This structure permits the highway authority to prevent permission being granted, at least at local level, until their highways objections may be overcome. Where the objection is to the means and nature of access it will often be possible through negotiation to secure, through amendment to the submitted plans, a satisfactory alternative. The developer may, for example, be asked to provide access to a different existing road, or at another point, or to provide improved sight lines or a different junction layout. But there will be occasions when the highways objection can be overcome only by major works of highways improvement or the provision of new off-site roads. This must generally await capital allocation under the highway authority's expenditure programme, and there is no power for the developer to requisition new roads. But there is a power for highway authorities to agree with developers to accept contributions towards the cost of proposed highways works, in order to bring them forward, for example, or to modify or add to them.[11] The highway authority may enter into such an agreement only where "they are satisfied that it will be of benefit to the public," but quite how the public benefit should be established is nowhere explained, and the limitation appears designed as a largely unspecific brake upon unrestrained use of the power. Notwithstanding this, the power is widely used as a basis for securing contributions by developers to the off-site works undertaken by the highway authority in connection with new development. The authority may agree, for example, to construct a new spine road to which the development will have access; or to instal traffic controls at a junction where traffic generated by the new development will join an existing road. As with water supply, however, there is no power to impose uniform contribution requirements on all developers benefiting from the works, and it is the initial developer whose proposals will unlock the area who is required to bear the main burden.

(b) On-site roads

In some cases developers may not wish their new estate roads to become public highways. But in housing development public adoption is usually

---

[10] Public Health Act 1936, s.18. The declaration of adoption is made under s.17.
[11] Highways Act 1980, s.278; formerly s.60 of the Highways Act 1971.

important, and there are two main means of securing it.[12] The most common today is by way of an agreement under section 38 of the Highways Act 1980,[13] which allows the developer to undertake the construction (or to meet the cost of construction) of the roads to the highway authority's standards, in return for an agreement that the authority will at some specified date adopt them and extinguish the developer's maintenance duty. The agreement is usually supported by a bond; without it the house purchasers might be required to contribute to the cost of making up the roads if the developer defaulted, notwithstanding that they had paid a purchase price reflecting the developer's obligation to do the work at his own expense.

The second method is under Part IX of the Highways Act 1980, whereby the highway authority may insist that no development should commence until the developer has paid or secured a sum required for making up the street.[14] After the carrying out of street works in a private street, the highway authority may then adopt the street and maintain it at public expense except if the owner of the street (or the majority in number of the owners) object.[15]

---

[12] The topic of new streets, private streets and street charges generally is one of some complexity, and beyond the scope of this book. Any examination of the impact of new street bye-laws has been deliberately omitted, because of the temporary nature of the power. Byelaws made under s.157 of the Highways Act 1959 or s.186 of the Highways Act 1980 are limited to expire after 10 years or such longer period as may be allowed by the Secretary of State (Act of 1980, s.186(8)). There has been constant urging by central government to local authorities to abandon them altogether in favour of the methods discussed in the text (see, e.g. D.O.E. Circulars 79/74, 94/77 and D.O.E. Circular No. Roads 25/74).

[13] Formerly s.40 of the Highways Act 1959.

[14] The "advance payments" code is of general application, and there is therefore special exemption from its provisions where an adoption agreement has been concluded under s. 38 of the 1980 Act: Highways Act 1980, s.219(4)(d).

[15] Highways Act 1980, s.228.

CHAPTER 9

THE ENFORCEMENT OF PLANNING CONTROL

A. Introduction

Enforcement has always been the weak link in the chain of planning control. Breach of planning control is not in itself an offence. Instead, the legislation provides for a buffer between breach and prosecution, in the form of an enforcement notice, served by the planning authority. Its purpose is remedial rather than punitive, and a power of prosecution exists only in respect of failure to observe the requirements of the notice. There is a right of appeal to the Secretary of State against an enforcement notice, and from there, on a point of law to the High Court.

On the face of it the procedure is elegantly simple. The whole process is undertaken against a consideration of the planning merits of the unauthorised development, and permission may be granted for it instead of action taken against it. But in practice it has proved by far the most technical and complex area of all planning law. There are two main reasons. The first is that the effect of an enforcement notice is suspended pending the outcome of any appeal. There is therefore clear advantage to be had to an appellant to appeal, even on purely technical and unmeritorious grounds, and to protract proceedings for as long as possible. In that ambition he has been further aided over the years by lengthy delays in the handling of appeals by the Department of the Environment.

The second reason is that the detailed statutory procedures have been clumsily assembled and attempts at reform have been piecemeal. The resulting gaps and ambiguities have left broad scope for ingenious legal argument, and the courts have at times been prepared to accept unrealistically fine distinctions, particularly in their review of the validity of enforcement notices. For them, the nearest analogy was, for some years, the criminal charge. If the authority got the charge wrong in their notice, the developer deserved to be "acquitted." But planning authorities have never had anything like the investigative resources or powers of the police, especially in the case of the old urban and rural district councils who carried much of the enforcement burden in the years up to 1974. The true facts might be known only to the developer himself, and he often had a clear interest in suppressing them; yet the authority misdrafted an enforcement notice at their peril.

Clumsy procedures are not necessarily ineffective procedures, however. The knowledge that the system can usually be made to work eventually is generally sufficient to discourage landowners from undertaking extensive building development without permission. The risk of being forced to demolish and losing their investment altogether is too great. But the greatest practical difficulties arise in cases of change of use. Change is often gradual and difficult to detect. In many cases there is great profit to be made, particularly at the urban fringe where pressure for cheap industrial sites provides strong incentive for unauthorised changes from agricultural use. There is a dilemma here for the designers of any effective enforcement system. The safeguards that are essential to prevent arbitrary dispossession from homes and businesses, are bound, if too broadly cast, to encourage unmeritorious exploitation, and particularly so where gross imbalances in land values offer strong financial incentives.

These have been perennial problems, and the background deserves further study. The 1947 Act originally offered two lines of defence to the recipient of an enforcement notice. He might make an application for planning permission or lodge an appeal against the notice to the local justices. Or he could do both. In either case the effect of the notice would be suspended until the outcome of proceedings, which could extend as far in the first case as an appeal to the Minister, and in the second to successive further appeals through the hierarchy of the courts, starting with the local magistrates and progressing gradually even as far as the House of Lords. Further, the courts rapidly became embroiled in questions not of the merits, but of the validity of enforcement notices. Their role was cast as that of defenders of citizens against legislation that encroached upon private rights, and their response was to "insist upon strict and rigid adherence to formalities."[1] In a series of robust decisions, they proceeded to assert that the validity of a notice could be challenged in the course of an appeal to the justices,[2] by way of declaratory proceedings in the High Court (whether the plaintiff had already taken advantage of the statutory remedies[3] or had simply ignored the notice[4]) and by way of defence to any subsequent prosecution.[5] In the words of Harman L.J., "instead of trying to make things simpler, lawyers succeeded day by day in making it more difficult and less comprehensible."[6] By 1957 the courts themselves were inviting legislative reform to overcome "the difficulties which have arisen in the application of this somewhat obscure Act."[7]

The weaknesses of the system were most startlingly demonstrated by the boom in unauthorised caravan sites in the 1950s brought about by the perennial housing shortage. By 1959 there were reported to be no fewer than 3,000 sites operating in England alone in contravention of the Act.[8] Site operators were prepared to exploit the system, to accept comparatively low fines once a notice had become effective as a form of licence fee, and simply move to a fresh site when the pressure became too great. Authorities turned to civil remedies to bolster their statutory powers, only often to find great practical difficulties in enforcing injunctions against the whole communities of caravan dwellers who had become established on the site whilst the legal

---

[1] *East Riding C.C.* v. *Park Estate (Bridlington) Ltd.* [1957] A.C. 223 at 233, *per* Viscount Simonds.

[2] See, *e.g. Eastbourne Corporation* v. *Fortes Ice Cream Parlour (1955) Ltd.* [1959] 2 Q.B. 92; *Guildford R.D.C.* v. *Fortescue* [1959] 2 Q.B. 112 (jurisdiction of justices to inquire into accuracy of allegations contained in a notice); *Francis* v. *Yiewsley and West Drayton U.D.C.* [1958] 1 Q.B. 478; *Cater* v. *Essex C.C.* [1960] 1 Q.B. 424 and *Britt* v. *Bucks C.C.* (1962) 60 L.G.R. 430 (effect upon validity of false recitals of fact).

[3] *Swallow and Pearson Ltd.* v. *Middlesex C.C.* (1953) 3 P. & C.R. 314; *Mounsdon* v. *Weymouth & Melcombe B.C.* [1960] 1 Q.B. 645.

[4] *Francis* v. *Yiewsley & West Drayton U.D.C.* [1958] 1 Q.B. 478.

[5] *Mead* v. *Chelmsford R.D.C.* [1953] 1 Q.B. 32.

[6] In *Britt* v. *Bucks C.C.* [1964] 1 Q.B. 77 at 87; and *cf. James* v. *M.H.L.G.* [1966] 1 W.L.R. 135 at 141, *per* Lord Denning M.R.

[7] *Norris* v. *Edmonton Corporation* [1957] 2 Q.B. 564 at 567–68, *per* Lord Goddard C.J.

[8] *Caravans as Homes.* Report by Sir John Arton Wilson, Cmnd. 872 (1959), paras. 193–216.

battle dragged on. It was the violence that erupted in the course of one such attempted eviction in Egham[9] in 1958 which led to the preparation of a special Report[10] pinpointing the inadequacies of the Act, and to legislative reform the following year.

The intention behind the Caravan Sites and Control of Development Act 1960 was to provide for a unified procedure, whereby the sole remedy available to the recipient of an enforcement notice would be his appeal to the Minister. The Minister was given power to review the notice in a broad planning context, with additional special powers to amend notices so as to rid them of technical defects. Access to the courts was retained by means of an appeal on point of law from the Minister's decision.

The Act succeeded in restoring some semblance of order, but it failed to solve all the problems. The comprehensive code that was intended to govern all challenges to notices by channelling them to the Minister in the first instance was defective. The grounds of appeal failed to incorporate all the grounds upon which the courts had formerly been prepared to review the validity of enforcement notices, and the courts in turn were reluctant to set aside the earlier case law that had evolved on the technicalities governing the drafting of valid notices. It soon became clear that a notice might still be so defective as to be a nullity, and could therefore be ignored by a recipient (albeit at his own risk) despite the new appeals procedure.[11] There was to continue to be an uneasy co-existence of statutory appeal to the Minister and judicial review, notwithstanding that the Act had turned the balance in favour of the former.

Further, the problems of delay in the handling of appeals worsened to the extent where the right of appeal conferred nothing less than a licence to continue with the unauthorised activity for at least a further year and very often longer. By 1968 it was necessary to introduce a new "stop notice" procedure, which allowed immediately effective enforcement in certain cases, subject to a liability to compensate in the event of the wrongful use of the powers.[12] The range of cases to which the procedure extends was widened in 1977.

In 1981 there was passed the Local Government and Planning (Amendment) Act, which brought about a further series of reforms in enforcement procedures. But the reforms do little to counter the technicalities and the shortfalls of the enforcement procedures. Instead of being directed to the central question of the validity of enforcement notices, the reforms for the most part are confined to peripheral points of procedure. The Act was a private Member's measure, although based on a package of reforms which appeared first in the Government's first draft of the Local Government, Planning and Land Bill 1980, but which were dropped from the Bill when the second version was introduced. Parliamentary scrutiny of the Act was perfunctory, and the opportunity to clarify and extend its provisions was lost.

---

[9] Following the grant of the injunction in *Attorney-General* v. *Smith* [1958] 2 Q.B. 173.
[10] *Caravans as Homes, supra,* note 8.
[11] *Miller-Mead* v. *M.H.L.G.* [1963] 2 Q.B. 196 at 226, *per* Upjohn L.J.; 238, *per* Diplock L.J.
[12] See further *post*, p. 425.

B. Preliminary

1. The Power to Enforce Planning Control

Power to commence enforcement action outside London is vested primarily in district authorities, who are under a duty to consult the county where a "county matter" is involved.[13] County authorities may also of their own volition take action in a case where they are of the opinion that a county matter is involved[14]; and, following the coming into force of the Town and Country Planning (Minerals) Act 1981, they have exclusive enforcement powers in relation to minerals matters.[15] The two urban development corporations also have exclusive jurisdiction in their areas.[16] In London the power vests in the boroughs, except in the urban development area and in the prescribed classes of Greater London Council jurisdiction.[17] The Secretary of State has reserve powers to issue an enforcement notice if it appears to him, after consultation with the local planning authority, to be expedient to do so.[18] The Crown, being outside planning control, is immune from enforcement; and the consent of the Crown Commissioners is necessary before enforcement action may be taken against tenants of Crown land.[19]

The enforcement of planning control is entirely discretionary. No systematic research has ever been attempted to determine the extent to which planning control is breached from day to day, but it is obvious that the great majority of minor infringements, and a good number of substantial ones as well, are never brought to the attention of authorities. Some authorities employ expert full-time enforcement staff, but most are largely dependent for their initial information upon complaints from neighbours and the general public. The discretionary nature of enforcement means that there is no duty to proceed even where clear evidence of breach exists.

The authority simply may issue and serve a notice under section 87 of the 1971 Act, "if they consider it expedient to do so having regard to the provisions of the development plan and to any other material considerations."[20] "Expedience" is a highly subjective matter, and a decision not to proceed will be unchallengeable in the courts, unless perhaps it could

---

[13] Local Government Act 1972, Sched. 16, para. 24(1) and (2).

[14] *Ibid.* para. 24(3). It is no ground for challenging the validity of a notice that it has been served by the wrong authority: para. 51(2).

[15] *Ibid.* para. 4, inserted by Town and Country Planning (Minerals) Act 1981, s. 2(4).

[16] Merseyside Development Corporation (Planning Functions) Order 1981 (S.I. 1981 No. 561) art. 3(b), Sched. 1; London Docklands Development Corporation (Planning Functions) Order 1981 (S.I. 1981 No. 1081), art. 3(b), Sched. 1.

[17] T.C.P.A. 1971, s. 290(1), Sched. 3, para. 2(1); Town and Country Planning (Local Authorities in Greater London) Regulations 1978, reg. 3.

[18] T.C.P.A. 1971, s. 276(5).

[19] *Ibid.* s. 266(2) and (3); and see *Molton Builders Ltd.* v. *Westminster C.C.* (1975) 30 P. & C.R. 182: no derogation from grant of tenancy for Commissioners to consent to service of enforcement notice.

[20] *Ibid.* s. 87(1). Authorities are now required also to specify in the notice the reasons why they consider it expedient to take enforcement action: Town and Country Planning (Enforcement Notices and Appeals) Regulations 1981 (No. 1742), reg. 3.

be shown to have been taken arbitrarily or capriciously.[21] The references in the section to the development plan and other material considerations imply that an authority must also consider the planning consequences of the unauthorised development, and that this should be the measure of "expedience." Enforcement action should not be taken simply because there has been a breach. This is reinforced by the fact that it is a ground of appeal against a notice that planning permission should be granted, and on average over one-half of all successful appeals every year succeed on this ground. The Secretary of State has therefore urged authorities (in D.O.E. Circular 22/80) to limit enforcement action, and to undertake it:

> " . . . only where planning reasons clearly warrant such action, and there is no alternative to enforcement proceedings. Where the activity involved is one which would not give rise to insuperable planning objections if it were carried out somewhere else, then the planning authority should do all it can to help in finding suitable alternative premises before initiating enforcement action."

In the case of small businesses, authorities were further requested to explore the possibility of reaching a compromise, and to use enforcement as a "last resort," making every effort to help find a suitable alternative site and timetabling enforcement to allow the firm to acquire and move to other suitable premises without unreasonably disrupting the business.

The advice has no direct legal effect, but it provides an indication of the course likely to be adopted by the Secretary of State on appeal in borderline cases. And it imposes a further burden on authorities in taking any action against unauthorised development. If they decide not to enforce in any particular instance, the development does not thereby become authorised. Their decision is not the equivalent of a grant of permission, and the matter may be subsequently reviewed. But there is a four year limit to enforceability in the case of most operational development, and the opportunity to take action may be lost altogether. Thereafter the development is immune from enforcement, almost as if it had permission, but without there having been any of the normal publicity and other safeguards surrounding the grant of express permission, and without an opportunity for the authority to impose conditions. It is common practice, therefore, to invite developers to seek express permission as an alternative to enforcement, often with a view to authorising the development through the normal procedures and subject to any necessary conditions.[22]

"Expedience," however, is not a matter entirely of planning merits. The authority may decide not to proceed, for example, because they are satisfied that the breach will come to an end of its own accord, or that other statutory

---

[21] See, *e.g. Swindon Corporation* v. *Pearce and Pugh* [1948] 2 K.B. 301, *Perry* v. *Stanborough (Developments) Ltd.* (1977) 244 E.G. 551. The matter is however within the jurisdiction of the Local Government Commissioners, at least so far as reviewing the actions of the authority in dealing with third party complaints and assembling information upon which to come to a decision: see further *ante,* pp. 254–256.

[22] George Dobry Q.C. in his *Final Report* (1975) recommended that authorities should be empowered to offer to grant planning permission before resorting to enforcement action (para.12.4); but that has now been translated by the Town and Country Planning (Enforcement Notices and Appeals) Regulations 1981 (S.I. 1981 No. 1742), reg. 6, into a requirement that they respond to an appeal against an enforcement notice with a statement of whether they would be prepared to grant permission, and if so, on what terms.

measures, such as compulsory purchase, could more effectively deal with the problem.[23] Or they may take the view that enforcement would be unwarranted given the scale of the breach, or too burdensome given the likely prospects of long term success. That latter view stretches "expedience" some distance, but it is a matter for the discretion of the authority. Enforcement converts soft policies into hard rules, and there is sometimes a reluctance on the part of authorities, now reinforced by the shift in central government policy, to pursue enforcement vigorously. But the consequence is likely to be an uneven and unfair application of the rules, with damaging long term effects.

2. The breach of planning control

There are two limbs to the statutory definition of breach of planning control. There is a breach, for the purposes of enforcement, involved (1) in the carrying out of development without the grant of necessary planning permission, or (2) if any conditions or limitations subject to which permission was granted have not been complied with.[24] As we shall see, the validity of the enforcement notice is dependent upon selecting the right breach. It is not, however, dependent upon the authority being "satisfied" that there has been a breach, so long as it "appears" to them that a breach has occurred. Failure to investigate whether there is any likelihood of deemed permission under the General Development Order will not therefore invalidate their action,[25] although it may result in fruitless proceedings. However, the statutory machinery for obtaining information from the developer by means of an information requisition[26] or entry as of right onto the land,[27] is available only before the notice is served, so that as a matter of practice the authority will normally need to undertake all their detailed factual investigation before proceeding.

If it transpires on appeal that the unauthorised development is in fact within the terms of a deemed or express permission, or that it is immune from enforcement, then the Secretary of State is obliged to quash the notice. But if no appeal is lodged, the effect of the enforcement notice will be to destroy the existing entitlement. The argument that planning permission existed for the development, or that it was immune, are both grounds of appeal to the Secretary of State and thus beyond the jurisdiction of the

[23] See, e.g. Perry v. Stanborough (Development) Ltd. (1977) 244 E.G. 551 where the authority had refused to enforce a condition requiring the construction of an access to an adjoining site, preferring to leave the matter for resolution between the neighbouring developers.
[24] T.C.P.A. 1971, s. 87(2).
[25] Tidswell v. S.O.S.E. (1976) 34 P. & C.R. 152.
[26] T.C.P.A. 1971, s. 284 confers power to require detailed information, from the occupier or person in receipt of rent from premises, relating to his own interest in the premises and that of any other persons known to him to be interested; the purpose (and its date of commencement) for which the premises are being used; details of other persons known to him to have used the premises for those purposes; and the time when any activities being carried out on the premises began. There is an additional power conferred by s. 16 of the Local Government (Miscellaneous Provisions) Act 1976 which allows an authority to require a speedier response (14 days instead of 21) and is exercisable at any time; but it is more restricted as to the information which may be required.
[27] T.C.P.A. 1971, s. 280 confers a general right of entry for the purposes of surveying any land in connection with, inter alia, "any proposal . . . to . . . serve any . . . notice under . . . Part V" of the Act.

courts to entertain[28]; and in the case of development protected by an established use certificate, the Act is clear that the certificate is conclusive only for the purposes of an enforcement appeal to the Secretary of State.[29] The prohibition contained in an enforcement notice gives way to a grant of planning permission made after the notice was served,[30] but not to a prior permission. The only limit to this important distinction is in the extreme case, where the prior authorisation of the development must have been so obvious to the authority that it could not possibly have "appeared" to them that there was a breach of planning control.

The power to enforce against breach of a condition is clear enough, but breach of a "limitation" is ambiguous. The distinction is technical and unnecessary, but the only express power conferred by the Act to impose limitations on the grant of permission is in the case of development orders, including the General Development Order, made by the Secretary of State.[31] When power to enforce for breach of limitation was first introduced in 1959 it was confined to development order limitations,[32] but that distinction was lost in subsequent re-enactments. Nonetheless, it is doubtful whether limitations attaching to the grant of express permission, such as a permission for "an agricultural dwelling" are directly enforceable. The better view is that where the restriction is not imposed expressly by a condition, it will still be necessary to prove unauthorised development by way of material change of use.[33]

But even in the case of development order limitations, the expression is difficult to apply. A breach of control may arise where the tolerances of the development order are exceeded, but constituting so substantial a departure from the terms of the deemed permission as to be unauthorised altogether. The distinction between development in breach of a limitation, and development which is completely unauthorised, is centrally important, because the courts have insisted that the correct breach be identified by the enforcement notice[34]; and, of course, the steps which the authority may require to be taken were formerly limited to those required to remedy the breach. The courts have preferred, therefore, to take the view that it is the whole development, rather than merely the excess, which is unauthorised. If "breach of limitation" has any independent effect as defining a breach of planning control, it is probably only in the context of minor and clearly severable excess over development order limitations.

3. Development immune from enforcement

Immunity was originally conferred upon all unauthorised development which had escaped enforcement action for four years. But difficulties in policing contraventions, particularly in the case of gradual changes of use, led in 1968 to a distinction being drawn. The four year rule was retained for

[28] As a result of the preclusive provisions of T.C.P.A. 1971, s. 243: *post*, p. 642.
[29] T.C.P.A. 1971, s. 94(7)
[30] *Ibid.* s. 92.
[31] T.C.P.A. 1971, s. 24(4) and (6).
[32] It was introduced by T.C.P.A. 1959, s. 38 in order to overcome the decision in *Cater* v. *Essex C.C.* [1960] 1 Q.B. 424.
[33] See further *ante*, pp. 355–356.
[34] See further *post*, p. 404.

unauthorised operational development, but lifted in the case of material changes of use except for changes to use as a single dwelling house. The 1981 Act extended the four year rule also to breaches of conditions relating to changes to dwelling house use,[35] and the list of breaches now subject to the four year rule is:

"(a) the carrying out without planning permission of building, engineering, mining or other operations in, on, over or under land; or

(b) the failure to comply with any condition or limitation which relates to the carrying out of such operations and subject to which planning permission was granted for the development of that land; or

(c) the making without planning permission of a change of use of any building to use as a single dwelling-house; or

(d) the failure to comply with a condition which prohibits or has the effect of preventing a change of use of a building to use as a single dwelling-house."[36]

All other material change of use has lost the four year immunity, with the consequence that only breaches occurring more than four years before the beginning of 1964, (that is, four years before the 1968 legislation) are now immune.[37] Such a use is now an "established use," and its immunity may be verified and guaranteed by the issuance of an established use certificate by the planning authority upon application.[38] There was formerly a disparity between the enforcement provisions, which allow an appeal to be based on the ground that the change of use occurred before 1964, and the established use certificate requirement that the breach should have *continued* since then. The Secretary of State had interpreted the latter requirement as excluding the grant of a certificate where any break in continuity had occurred[39]; but has now revised that opinion so as to include any use instituted before 1964 which has not since been abandoned or superseded,[40] and thereby brought the two provisions into line.

In order to be able to apply the time limitations properly it is necessary to be able to pinpoint the date when the breach occurred. In the case of material change of use this is often difficult. Change may have been gradual, or there may have been a slow intensification of the former use. The only effective test in such cases is to compare the present use with the pre-1964 use and to assess whether there has been material change.[41] An enforcement notice may not extinguish the immune pre-1964 use: it may do no more than require reversion to that former level of activity.[42]

---

[35] Thereby giving legislative effect to the decision of the Divisional Court in *Backer* v. *S.O.S.E.* [1981] J.P.L. 357.

[36] T.C.P.A. 1971, s. 87(4). In the case of extraction of minerals an enforcement notice may be served for breach of condition or limitation at any time within four years after the non-compliance has come to the knowledge of the local planning authority: T.C.P.A. 1971, s. 264 and Sched. 21; Town and Country Planning (Minerals) Regulations 1971, reg.4.

[37] *Ibid.* s. 87(1).

[38] *Ibid.* ss. 94, 95.

[39] See, e.g. [1979] J.P.L. 780.

[40] [1981] J.P.L. 449.

[41] *Cheshire C.C.* v. *S.O.S.E.* (1971) 222 E.G. 35.

[42] *Post,* p. 420.

Where the alleged breach is one involving operational development, the right to commence enforcement action arises once any act of unauthorised development has occurred. But the four year limitation period does not begin to run until the date of the substantial completion of the operation, whether it is a once and for all project like the erection of a building,[43] or a continuing operation such as the extraction of minerals.[44]

It follows, then, that the immunity in respect of development undertaken more than four years before does not extend to individual components of the overall development, if the substantial completion of the development is still within the period.[45] A similar consequence ensues in the case of acts of operational development which have been undertaken as incidental to the making of a material change of use, but through a different route. The power of the authority to require through their enforcement notice that the land be restored to its condition prior to the making of the change in use allows them to require the undoing of any incidental operational development, irrespective of any immunity it may enjoy in itself.[46]

Breach of planning control involving breaches of conditions or limitations is split also between change of use and operational development. Where the relevant condition is one which has been imposed on a permission for operational development, or is one which prevents change to use as a single dwelling-house, the four year rule applies; otherwise the pre-1964 period is applicable. It is not necessary that the breach should have been continuous for the relevant period in order to gain immunity. Once it has been established that breach occurred before the commencement of the period, it is irrelevant that there have been further subsequent breaches or, conversely, that there may have been significant periods without any breach.[47]

4. The Issuance and Service of Enforcement Notices

There are two steps to the instituting of enforcement action. An enforcement notice is first issued by the authority and copies of it are then served by them, not later than 28 days after having been issued, and not later than 28 days before it is to take effect.[48] The requirement that a notice be "issued" was introduced by the 1981 Act, and is intended to overcome the difficulty in the past, where notices were drafted so as to come into effect at the end of a specified period following service, and the effect of serving different recipients at different times meant that different requirements might be imposed under what purported to be the same notice.[49] What is required in "issuing" a notice is that the authority should prepare a properly authorised

---

[43] See, e.g. [1972] J.P.L. 385 (appeal decision).

[44] *Thomas David (Porthcawl) Ltd.* v. *Penybont R.D.C.* [1972] 1 W.L.R. 1526, though note Lord Denning's insistence that mining operations should be regarded as *sui generis* (at 1531). The tipping of waste materials is not a continuous operation but a change in use: *Bilboe* v. *S.O.S.E.* [1980] J.P.L. 330.

[45] *Ewen Developments Ltd.* v. *S.O.S.E.* [1980] J.P.L. 404.

[46] *Burn* v. *S.O.S.E.* (1971) 219 E.G. 586; *Murfitt* v. *S.O.S.E.* [1980] J.P.L. 598 (requirement that hardcore laid for storage of vehicles, be removed though it had been laid more than four years earlier); *Perkins* v. *S.O.S.E.* [1981] J.P.L. 755.

[47] *Bilboe* v. *S.O.S.E.* [1980] J.P.L. 330; (1980) 39 P. & C.R. 495.

[48] T.C.P.A. 1971, s. 87(5).

[49] See, e.g. *Bambury* v. *Hounslow L.B.C.* [1966] 2 Q.B. 204; *Stevens* v. *Bromley L.B.C.* [1972] 1 Ch. 400.

document and retain it in their records[50]; and there is a further obligation to enter details of the notice in the special register of enforcement and stop notices.[51]

Copies of the enforcement notice must be served upon the owner (including the owner of any leasehold interest) and on the occupier of the land to which it relates; and it must also be served upon any other person having an interest in the land.[52] That requirement is sufficiently broadly cast as to include both legal and equitable ownership of interests such as easements and mortgages, though not a person who is simply otherwise "interested" in the colloquial sense.[53] Persons having an interest in the land need be served only when their interest is, in the opinion of the authority, materially affected by the notice. Any occupier, however, must on the face of it be served, even though he has no interest as such: he may, for example, be in occupation as a licensee or as a squatter. But the courts have had in the past to strike an awkward balance between, on the one hand, protecting the interests of insecure occupants such as caravan dwellers, whose homes may be dependent upon the outcome of enforcement proceedings and who should therefore be notified of the issuance of a notice; and on the other hand securing that the primary culprits, such as the site owners, should not be able to evade enforcement on the technical ground that service has not been effected on all concerned, or has been effected at different times so as to render the notice a nullity. It appears from the case law that an "occupier" need have no interest such as a tenancy, but should nonetheless have some contractual or other right of something more than a purely transient nature.[54] Since the 1981 Act, occupiers have a right of appeal only if they have an interest in the land, but their right to be notified of enforcement action remains unaltered.[55]

Changes introduced by the 1968 Act, moreover, ensure that inadequacy of service should not necessarily affect the validity of a notice. It is now a ground of appeal to the Secretary of State that a notice has not been served in accordance with the Act,[56] and any person lodging an appeal (on whatever ground) cannot be heard in any subsequent proceedings to complain of ineffective service.[57] Further, the Secretary of State need not quash the

---

[50] D.O.E. Circular 26/81, Annex para. 3.

[51] T.C.P.A. 1971, s. 92A; G.D.O. 1977, art. 21A (inserted by S.I. 1981 No. 1569).

[52] T.C.P.A. 1971, s. 87(5).

[53] *Stevens* v. *Bromley L.B.C.* [1972] Ch. 400 at 410, *per* Salmon L.J.

[54] *Ibid.* at 411, where Salmon L.J. at 412 and Edmund Davies L.J. at 414 both expressed doubt about Lord Denning's assertion in *Munnich* v. *Godstone R.D.C.* [1966] 1 W.L.R. 427 at 436 that "caravan-dwellers . . . are never to be regarded as occupiers unless they are granted a tenancy." It is clear from *Stevens* that at least a licensee whose occupation is substantial in time and scale must be an "occupier." But not, perhaps, a squatter: see, *e.g. Woodcock* v. *South West Electricity Board* [1975] 1 W.L.R. 983. Curiously, s. 284 of the 1971 Act which enables the authority to require information refers only to persons with "interests" or those who have used the land for the purpose being investigated, and obtaining adequate details of occupiers may be a difficult task. By posting an adequate site notice it may be possible to establish that notice has been given to all, and that there has been no substantial prejudice: see, *e.g.* appeal decision at [1979] J.P.L. 403. Alternatively the notice may be served by post addressed to "The Occupier:" T.C.P.A. 1971, s. 283(2), and see *Hammersmith L.B.C.* v. *Winner Investments Ltd.* (1968) 20 P. & C.R. 971.

[55] T.C.P.A. 1971, s. 88(1).

[56] T.C.P.A. 1971, s. 88(2)(*f*).

[57] *Ibid.* s. 110(2).

notice for ineffective service if he is satisfied that neither the appellant nor any other person who ought to have been served has been substantially prejudiced.[58] That is something upon which he will need some evidence, but it need not be particularly heavy: in one case the Divisional Court held that failure to serve a landlord with copies of notices served on his tenants could be disregarded where he had been served with a different notice for the whole site, because one of the first things he should have done was "to go down to the individual tenants and see what they were up to."[59] Once a notice takes effect, whether or not following an appeal, the issue of service is thereafter closed save as a limited defence in prosecution proceedings.[60]

5. Multiple Notices and Multiple Breaches

It is possible for an authority to serve alternative notices in respect of the same alleged breach.[61] In the case of multiple breaches they may either include all the breaches in the one notice[62] or issue separate notices. The latter course may raise difficulties in change of use cases, however, if the notices relate to different parts of the site. If the site as a whole is the correct planning unit the artificial subdivision may result in over-enforcement and create problems in reconciling the notices against the planning unit.[63]

6. Estoppel

It has frequently been asserted that the power to take enforcement action may be lost through estoppel, but the scope of the doctrine is far from clear. The most common situation in which the matter arises is where a prospective developer has been assured by the planning authority that no permission is required for his proposals, only to be threatened later with enforcement action when he has implemented them. Such inconsistency smacks of incompetence and unfairness. But whether estoppel, or some other remedy, is the most satisfactory way to ensure fairness, is a complex question.

(a) Estoppel in private law

In similar disputes between private individuals the courts have been prepared to hold parties to their representations even when unsupported by consideration flowing from the other party, relying upon the doctrine of estoppel. But even in private law the scope of the doctrine is uncertain. There is currently a clear split in judicial opinion. On the one hand there are those judges, led by Lord Denning, who believe the doctrine to be flexible

---

[58] *Ibid.* s. 88A(3).
[59] *Skinner* v. *S.O.S.E.* [1978] J.P.L. 842.
[60] T.C.P.A. 1971, s. 243(2).
[61] *Britt* v. *Buckinghamshire C.C.* (1962) 60 L.G.R. 430, *Holtby* v. *Stretford B.C.* (1964) 189 E.G. 517, *Edwick* v. *Sunbury on Thames U.D.C.* (1964) 62 L.G.R. 504.
[62] *Ormston* v. *Horsham R.D.C.* (1965) 63 L.G.R. 293: five different acts of development alleged in one notice.
[63] See, *e.g. de Mulder* v. *S.O.S.E.* [1974] Q.B. 792 at 801 where Lord Widgery C.J. thought reconstruction of three notices by the Secretary of State might be possible but would require a bold man. The practice of splitting up areas by separate notices was "fraught with difficulty."

and based entirely on judicial perceptions of conscionability. In the words of Lord Denning:

> "Estoppel is not a rule of evidence. It is not a cause of action. It is a principle of justice and of equity. It comes to this: when a man, by his words or conduct, has led another to believe in a particular state of affairs, he will not be allowed to go back on it when it would be unjust or inequitable for him to do so."[64]

But other judges deny the scope for evolution, and prefer the dictum (characteristically overstated) of Harman L.J. that:

> "Equitable principles are, I think, perhaps rather too often bandied about in common law courts as though the Chancellor still had only the length of his own foot to measure when coming to a conclusion. Since the time of Lord Eldon the system of equity for good or evil has been a very precise one, and equitable jurisdiction is exercised only on well known principles."[65]

The "well known principles" in the case of estoppel are less than crystal clear, but *Halsbury*[66] describes four main accepted categories: estoppel by record (or *res judicata*); estoppel by deed; estoppel *in pais* (or estoppel by representation) and promissory estoppel. The last two are of most immediate application. Their effect may be summarised thus: where a person has made to another either (1) a clear and unequivocal representation of fact either with knowledge of its falsehood or with the intention that it should be acted upon (estoppel *in pais*); or (2) a clear and unequivocal promise or assurance intended to affect the legal relations between them and to be acted on accordingly (promissory estoppel); then, in both cases, if the other person has acted on the representation or promise (and, in the case of estoppel *in pais*, altered his position to his detriment) an estoppel arises against the first party preventing him from going back on his word. A particular application of the doctrine of estoppel *in pais* arises in the case of agency: a principal who holds out and represents his agent as having authority (*i.e.* ostensible authority) to enter into a transaction may not subsequently deny the absence of express authority.

(b) Estoppel and planning authorities

It is clear that the doctrine of estoppel extends to local authorities, and that in general they may be held to representations and promises made by

---

[64] *Moorgate Mercantile Co. Ltd.* v. *Twitchings* [1976] Q.B. 225 at 241; and *cf. Crabb* v. *Arun D.C.* [1976] Ch. 179 at 188, *per* Lord Denning M.R., and 193, *per* Scarman L.J.

[65] *Campbell Discount Co. Ltd.* v. *Bridge* [1961] 1 Q.B. 445 at 459; and see too the highly restrictive rule drawn from *Crabb* v. *Arun D.C. (supra)* by a differently constituted Court of Appeal in *Western Fish Products Ltd.* v. *Penwith D.C.* (1978) 38 P. & C.R. 7 at 25–27; and the trenchant criticisms of the broad formulations of the rule by Lord Denning M.R. and Scarman L.J. in *Crabb*, in Spencer Bower and Turner, *Estoppel by Representation* (3rd. ed. 1977), para. 308.

[66] Halsbury's *Laws of England* (4th ed.), paras. 1501–1506; and see the leading works, Spencer Bower and Turner, *Estoppel by Representation* (3rd. ed., 1977) and Spencer Bower and Turner, *Res Judicata* (2nd ed., 1969).

them.[67] Equally, though, it is clear that an authority may not, at least as a general rule, be estopped from carrying out their statutory *duties*.[68] The rationale is straightforward. No public body may escape its duties by contracting out of them, and it would be anomalous to permit estoppel to have the same effect. It follows, too, that as the fettering of a statutory *discretion* by contract is also impermissible,[69] then equally, so is fettering by estoppel.[70]

At first glance, to hold a planning authority to representations made by their officers as to the need for planning permission would always infringe that rule, by fettering the authority's discretion subsequently to take enforcement action. But that is nowadays too bland an assumption, and any understanding of the application of the estoppel rules to planning authorities calls for a more detailed analysis.

Analysis, unfortunately, takes place against a mobile backcloth. There have been sharp conflicts in judicial opinion as to the proper scope of estoppel in planning; conflicts which reflect the uncertainty of the scope of estoppel itself. The recent decision of the Court of Appeal in *Western Fish Products Ltd.* v. *Penwith District Council*[71] has signalled, at least for the time being, an end to further development of the doctrine. But there is sufficient ambiguity and uncertainty in the single judgement handed down by the Court to ensure that the debate will continue.

An understanding of the present state of play calls for an analysis that goes back to first principles. The essential preliminary distinction to draw is that between representations of authorities which are expressly or effectively statutory decisions, and those which are not.

(i) Formal determinations. Where there has been a formal application to the authority for permission or for a section 53 determination as to whether permission is necessary for a proposed development, their decision is clearly binding upon them and is irrevocable. It is an answer to any enforcement action in respect of the development. The position is the same in the case of an established use certificate. In none of these cases is estoppel involved at all. It is unnecessary, because the decision is binding as a statutory decision.[72] That is true whether the decision is taken by the full council or is delegated to a committee or an officer. Their decision is the decision of the authority.

---

[67] See, *e.g. Crabb* v. *Arun D.C.* [1976] Ch. 179 (council estopped from denying plaintiff a right of access); *Salvation Army Trustees Co. Ltd.* v. *West Yorkshire C.C.* (1980) 130 New L.J. 880 (council estopped from resiling from their intention to acquire the plaintiff's land).

[68] See. *e.g. Maritime Electric Co. Ltd.* v. *General Dairies Ltd.* [1937] A.C. 610, *North Western Gas Board* v. *Manchester Corporation* [1964] 1 W.L.R. 64.

[69] Though see, for a possible exception in the case of planning agreements under s. 52 of the 1971 Act, *Royal Borough of Windsor and Maidenhead* v. *Brandrose Investments Ltd.* [1981] J.P.L. 668: *ante*, p. 368.

[70] *Southend-on-Sea Corporation* v. *Hodgson (Wickford) Ltd.* [1962] 1 Q.B. 416.

[71] (1978) 38 P. & C.R. 7.

[72] If the decision is invalid for any reason, it may not in general be saved by estoppel even though the defect is the fault of the authority themselves: see, *e.g. Rhyl U.D.C.* v. *Rhyl Amusements Ltd.* [1959] 1 W.L.R. 465; and the Northern Ireland case of *Morelli* v. *Department of the Environment* [1976] N.I. 159. Exceptions are technical breaches waived by the authority at the time, and actions under ostensible authority, discussed below.

(ii) **Informal determinations.** It is apparently accepted that the same consequences may flow from an informally made determination under section 53. At one time the rule was broadly cast. It was said that the authority were entitled to waive any legal formalities or technicalities governing section 53 applications and to issue decisions in whatever form and on whatever material they might have. That broad principle was accepted by Lord Denning M.R. in *Wells* v. *Minister of Housing and Local Government*[73] and it offered a useful basis for holding authorities to their representations. An exchange of letters might suffice, even though neither inquiry nor response made mention of section 53.[74] And in *Lever Finance Ltd.* v. *Westminster City Council*[75] Sachs L.J. was prepared even to go so far as to suggest that a telephone conversation between a developer's architect and the planning officer would suffice.

But the Court of Appeal in the *Western Fish Products* case have cut down the broad principle. They drew from *Wells* a narrower conclusion: that it should be open to an authority to treat an application for planning permission as containing an invitation to give a determination under section 53.[76] In short, the authority ought to be able to tell an applicant that permission is not in fact required, and he should be able to act upon that reply.

Although the Court were prepared to uphold this aspect of *Wells,* and, indeed believed themselves bound to follow it, it is clear that they entertained serious misgivings.[77] Counsel for the Secretary of State and for the planning authority reserved the right to argue elsewhere that *Wells* had been wrongly decided,[78] and the Court noted the "powerful" dissenting judgement of Russell L.J. in *Wells.*[79] They also observed that the requirements of the General Development Order for section 53 applications indicated a high degree of formality. In fact, however, they were mistakenly looking at a different Order from that upon which the *Wells* decision was based. Further amendments to the Order had been made in 1969[80] following that case, prescribing in greater detail than before the requirements for an application under section 53. Those changes might just have provided the Court with the material they needed to depart from *Wells* altogether.

For the moment the rule remains. An authority may be held to their decision that permission is not required, however wrong it may be, and even though not issued specifically as a section 53 determination, provided it is a

---

[73] [1967] 1 W.L.R. 1000. The point had been rejected without hesitation, incidentally, in *Southend-on-Sea Corp.* v. *Hodgson* [1962] 1 Q.B. 416 at 425, *per* Lord Parker L.J., though without hearing detailed argument on it. *Cf. Re L.(A.C.)(an infant)* [1971] 3 All E.R. 743 at 752, where the waiver principle was applied in child care proceedings involving a local authority.

[74] See, *e.g. English-Speaking Union of the Commonwealth* v. *Westminster L.B.C.* (1973) 26 P. & C.R. 575. Although not binding on the Court of Appeal, it is curious that this decision is not at least touched upon in the *Western Fish Products* decision.

[75] [1971] 1 Q.B. 222 at 234.

[76] (1978) 38 P. & C.R. 7 at 35.

[77] *Ibid.* at 34–36.

[78] *Ibid.* at 31.

[79] *Ibid.* at 35.

[80] By the Town and Country Planning General Development (Amendment) Order 1969 (S.I. 1969 No. 276), art. 2(c). The Court of Appeal were instead referred to the 1973 Order which incorporated the 1969 amendments: *op. cit.* pp. 34–35.

"positive, written determination"[81] issued in response to a planning application. It is the equivalent of a formal determination, with the consequences discussed under the first heading above. Estoppel prevents the authority from asserting that the determination is invalid by reason of their own non-compliance with formalities, though it may still be invalid on other grounds. In particular, its validity will be governed by the substantive provisions of section 53, which confer no jurisdiction to pronounce upon the lawfulness of proposals already carried out, those intended to be carried out by some third party or the scope or validity of any existing permission.[82] But the determination is otherwise irrevocable and binding, at least once it has been acted upon.[83] The Court of Appeal in *Western Fish Products* were careful to confine the doctrine to section 53, ruling that the degree of formality required for the issuance of established use certificates precluded any possibility of informal determinations.[84]

(iii) Determinations made under ostensible authority. A statutory determination or decision made by an officer with delegated powers is, of course, as good as one made by the authority themselves. But the courts are prepared also to extend that status to those made by an officer who acts without or beyond formal authority. In *Lever Finance Ltd.* v. *Westminster City Council*[85] a planning officer mistakenly represented to the developer's architect in the course of a telephone conversation that his proposed alterations to approved plans were immaterial and required no permission. The Court of Appeal upheld the declaration granted at first instance that there was a valid permission for the modifications, finding that the sanctioning of modifications in this way was a common practice within planning authorities. It was therefore within the officer's ostensible authority, and the council could not go back on his representation.

Like the *Wells* case, the *Lever* case has been roundly criticised. It is wise therefore to draw a narrow rule from it. The key to reconciliation with established principle is perhaps to regard the ostensible authority doctrine as making good a defect in the formal line of authorisation for the making of a statutory decision. Provided the decision is not otherwise *ultra vires* the authority, it will have effect as if it were a valid decision by them. A developer should not have always to inquire whether the officer who has made a statutory decision actually has the delegated power to do so. But the scope of the doctrine remains limited. Lord Denning's broad assertion that

---

[81] See, *e.g. Wells* v. *M.H.L.G.* [1967] 1 W.L.R. 1000 where part of the case was based upon the issuance of a form of by-law consent on which the printed advice that planning permission would also be necessary had been struck out: held, insufficient; and *cf. Brooks and Burton Ltd.* v. *S.O.S.E.* (1976) 75 L.G.R. 285 (reversed) [1977] 1 W.L.R. 1294, C.A.), oral consultations leading to "encouraging noises" from the planning officers insufficient; *Western Fish Products Ltd.* v. *Penwith D.C.* (1978) 38 P. & C.R. 7 at 35, inconclusively worded letter from planning authority; and *Chris Foreign Foods (Wholesalers) Ltd.* v. *M.H.L.G.* (1969) 213 E.G. 1015: written assurance as to past use of land, but estoppel not apparently argued.
[82] *Ante*, p. 210
[83] This requirement is based upon the assumption that estoppel is unnecessary where no party has acted upon the representation, but in none of the cases has the issue arisen for decision and there are broad statements in *Western Fish Products* which omit the requirement: see, *e.g.* pp. 31 and 35.
[84] *Op. cit.* p. 36.
[85] [1971] 1 Q.B. 222.

any person dealing with an officer "is entitled to assume that all necessary resolutions have been passed,"[86] was swept aside in the *Western Fish Products* case. The Court of Appeal there insisted that there must always be some evidence justifying the developer in assuming the officer has power to bind his authority. Holding an office, however senior, would not suffice.[87]

If the decision which has been issued is *ultra vires* the authority for reasons other than simply the lack of formal authority of the officer, it follows that it cannot be saved by the doctrine of ostensible authority.[88] An authority may not by estoppel gain greater powers than those conferred by statute.

(iv) Representations other than statutory decisions. It is clear law that an authority may be held through estoppel to their representations, much as they may be held to their formal contracts. But it is in this context that the most difficult issues of public policy arise. The issuing of a statutory decision granting planning permission or determining that it is not required does not constitute a fettering of any statutory discretion. But an informal representation to the same effect may well have a fettering effect. For example, an authority may be concerned that an unauthorised development should not be stopped, but that the site should be tidied up. One method of achieving this is to entertain a planning application and grant permission subject to conditions. That will be binding upon them for the future. But another course might be to write to the developer and to indicate that provided the site is tidied and maintained in a tidy condition for the future, no enforcement action will be taken. May they subsequently turn around and serve a notice if the terms have all been complied with? Or may they, in another case, overturn a representation made by their officers (other than in response to a formal application) that no permission is required? There are no clear answers, and much depends upon how far some of the broad judicial statements in *Lever* and *Wells* may be thought to have survived the *Western Fish Products* case. But all the indications are that there is no longer any scope for estoppel in this residual area. There are four main reasons for this view.

First, the present trend is strongly against further extension of estoppel in planning cases. In *Brooks and Burton Ltd.* v. *Secretary of State for the Environment*[89] Lord Widgery C.J. stressed that it was "extremely important," in his view that:

" . . . local government officers should feel free to help applicants who come and ask them questions without all the time having the shadow of estoppel hanging over them and without the possibility of their immobilising their authorities by some careless remark which produces such an estoppel."

---

[86] *Ibid.* at 231.

[87] (1978) 38 P. & C.R. 7 at 30.

[88] See, *e.g. Co-operative Retail Services Ltd.* v. *Taff-Ely B.C.* (1979) 39 P. & C.R. 223 where planning permission had been issued by the clerk to the council quite without authority, and after they had become functus officio by reason of having formed the opinion that a "county matter" was involved.

[89] (1976) 35 P. & C.R. 27 at 40; and see also *Bedfordia Plant Ltd.* v. *S.O.S.E.* [1981] J.P.L. 122.

And those sentiments were expressly endorsed by the Court of Appeal in the *Western Fish Products* case.[90]

Secondly, the courts are opposed to estoppel for the further reason that the "public interest" ought not to be shut out through estoppel. Estoppel may prevent injustice to an individual applicant, but in turn cause injustice to the public, such as in the *Lever Finance* case where neighbours had to live with the consequences of the planning officer's "wrong and careless" decision.[91] Such broad assertions of the public's disadvantage deserve to be regarded with caution, however. The public would equally have suffered had the same decision been made on an express application and without necessarily any greater rights of involvement or participation. The approval of reserved matters outstanding from an outline permission, for example, frequently involves similarly significant third party interests, but the matter need not be advertised or notified.[92] Further, the fact remains that there is a discretion whether or not to take enforcement action, and there is no provision for public involvement in its exercise. The authority may decide not to proceed, or the opportunity may simply be lost through expiry of time. Neighbours must live with the consequences.

Third, since judicial policy is so clearly against allowing careless and unauthorised representations by planning officers to bind authorities, it follows that an authority will not be held to a representation which involves something outside their own powers; and also that the scope of ostensible authority of unauthorised officers to bind them to matters within the council's powers will be narrowly drawn. The doctrine is clearly seen by the courts as having application to representations generally, but there is no case yet where it has been relied upon to uphold representations other than those involving a statutory decision.[93] But where an officer's representations are fully authorised, the objection does not apply and estoppel presumably will run. Authorised representations should be as capable of binding, provided the ingredients of estoppel are present, as authorised contracts.

Finally, a point which has been considered in none of the cases is the possibility of enforcement action being taken by an authority other than the one which has made the representation relied upon. The county, for example, may take the view that it is a "county matter," or the Secretary of State may intervene. Both would be bound by a statutory decision, but not by a representation made by the district authority. That is a factor which makes even more anomalous the application to statutory bodies, in the exercise of their statutory powers, of principles devised to achieve justice between private individuals.

(v) Estoppel by conduct. Only estoppel by representations is capable of binding an authority. It is insufficient that they might have encouraged or

---

[90] *Ibid.* at 32.
[91] *Western Fish Products Ltd.* v. *Penwith D.C.* (1978) 38 P. & C.R. 7 at 32.
[92] See further *ante*, p. 203.
[93] Though where an authority had resolved to refuse permission but by mistake the developers were sent a notification that permission had been granted, the Divisional Court appeared to accept that it might have bound the authority had the developer acted upon it to his detriment: see *Norfolk C.C.* v. *S.O.S.E.* [1973] 1 W.L.R. 1400. It is doubtful whether the members of the Court of Appeal in *Western Fish Products* would have arrived at a similar conclusion.

led on a developer to carry out works in the belief or expectation that permission was unnecessary or would be granted. Estoppel by acquiescence, or "proprietary estoppel," is capable of binding authorities generally,[94] but the essence of the claim is that it rests upon the expectation that a right will be created in respect of the land of the representing party. It is therefore inapplicable where the expected right is a planning permission or other decision in respect of land belonging to the developer.[95]

(c) An alternative remedy?

The attempted extension of the estoppel doctrine to planning authorities is understandable, in the absence of any other remedy. But it is quite anomalous except as a means of backing up statutory decisions which might otherwise be vulnerable for want of "technical" formality. Financial compensation for negligent misstatement may yet provide a better alternative remedy, although the effect of a properly developed doctrine might be to hold authorities even more firmly to officers' unauthorised statements, ultimately by declining to take enforcement action, because of the costs of doing anything else. The risk would be that discretion would be very much more effectively fettered in practice by financial considerations than by estoppel. It is true that the opportunity exists now for an authority to buy its way out of an unwelcome binding decision by revocation proceedings. But the power extends only to unimplemented grants of permission, and not to determinations and certificates under sections 53 and 94 (though authorised uses may be extinguished under section 51). Neither course is likely to prove attractive to an authority unless the circumstances are particularly pressing.

C. Enforcement notices

1. *Introduction*

The purpose of enforcement notices is primarily remedial. The procedure is designed to offer the developer an opportunity to make good his breach. The notice must specify the remedial steps required by the authority, and allow a reasonable period for compliance. Criminal liability ensues only when that period has elapsed without the notice being complied with. There is a right of appeal, and broad powers for the Secretary of State to resolve conflicts of law and fact.

But enforcement is the sharp end of planning, and the relationship between the enforcers and the enforcees understandably tends to be combative and ridden with litigation. In consequence, there has emerged a great body of case law governing the minimum legal requirements of enforcement notices. Some of the cases date from before the reforms of 1960, and their relevance to the subsequent legislation is a matter of some doubt. They were fought and decided in the era of strict constructionism, but the modern view is that:

---

[94] See, *e.g. Crabb* v. *Arun D.C.* [1976] Ch. 179.
[95] *Western Fish Products Ltd.* v. *Penwith D.C.* (1978) 38 P. & C.R. 7 at 25–27.

"A good deal of water has flowed under the bridge since then. . . . Formalities were being used to defeat the public good. So we no longer favour them."[96]

Unfortunately, however, the 1960 Act did not itself sweep aside the old cases. It provided a new procedure but not a comprehensive code,[97] and the old cases have had therefore to be expressly overruled in cases where they have been thought to be at odds with the new philosophy. Many still remain, but there is necessarily some uncertainty as to their long-term prospects of survival.

The effect of the 1960 Act was to alter the procedure for challenging enforcement notices, by routing to the Secretary of State certain types of challenge which formerly might have been determined by the magistrates. This was achieved by prescribing a number of grounds upon which an appeal could be based, backed up by a privative clause which prohibited any challenge in the courts on some (since the 1981 Act, all) of those grounds. But the Act made no specific provision for challenge in the case of a notice so defective as to constitute a nullity; that is, a notice which fell so far short of the Act's requirements as to be worthless.

The consequence today is that there are four main categories of challenge: first, challenge on the basis that the notice is a nullity, which may be pursued in the courts (by way of action for declaration or by way of defence to a prosecution, for example); or the notice may simply be ignored, albeit at the recipient's risk that his view may not be shared by the courts in a subsequent prosecution. Although the Secretary of State has no jurisdiction to entertain an appeal, the most practicable course is to lodge a protective appeal, which may then be set aside by the Secretary of State if he takes the view that the notice is a nullity. Second, a notice may not be a nullity on the face of it, but be invalid for reasons (such as a misuse of power by the planning authority) which are not exclusively within the Secretary of State's jurisdiction to review. Third, there are several grounds of challenge which may be pursued only by way of appeal to the Secretary of State, but which, if made out, lead to the invalidity of the notice, with an obligation upon the Secretary of State to quash. Fourth, there are those grounds where challenge is again only by way of appeal, but where the Secretary of State has discretion to vary or correct the notice where he is satisfied that it can be done without injustice.

The alternative routes of challenge to the validity of an enforcement notice are set out in Table 15.

There has traditionally been a sharp distinction drawn between nullity and invalidity in the case of enforcement notices, which is followed in the analysis in the next few pages although it is perhaps no longer reflected in all administrative law. It is true that the courts have been less prepared in recent years to accept such rigid classifications. Instead, there has been a preference for viewing the possible consequences of unauthorised administrative action as, "not so much a stark choice of alternatives but a spectrum of possibilities in which one compartment or description falls gradually into another."[98]

---

[96] *Munnich v. Godstone R.D.C.* [1966] 1 W.L.R. 427 at 435, *per* Lord Denning M.R.

[97] *Miller-Mead v. M.H.L.G.* [1963] 2 Q.B. 196 at 220–221, *per* Lord Denning M.R., 232–233, *per* Upjohn L.J. and 239, *per* Diplock L.J.

[98] *London & Clydeside Estates Ltd. v. Aberdeen D.C.* [1979] 3 All E.R. 876 at 883, *per* Lord Hailsham L.C.

Table 15
Enforcement Notices: Challenges to Validity

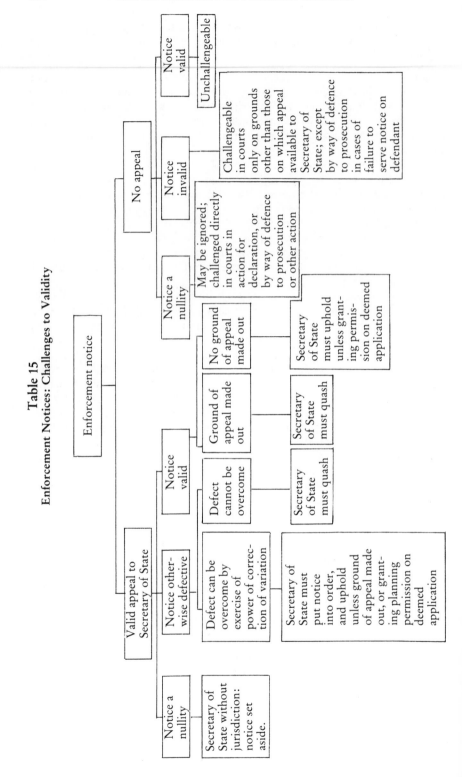

The traditional analysis still prevails in planning enforcement, however, and it offers some degree of certainty in this technical area. Reform is certainly overdue, but only thorough-going legislative change is likely to achieve the necessary improvements of certainty and simplicity.

A remarkably high proportion of appeals succeed every year already because of defects in enforcement notices, despite the publication by the Department of a model form of notice and accompanying advice.[99] That may be partly the product of planning authorities' inadequacy of resources and expertise in enforcement, but it is also a reflection of the technicality of the subject.

2. Contents of an Enforcement Notice

The Act[1] requires that an enforcement notice should "specify" six different matters:

(1) the matters alleged to constitute a breach of planning control; and
(2) the steps required by the authority to be taken in order to remedy the breach; and
(3) any other steps required by them to be taken to make the development comply with planning permission or for removing or alleviating an injury to amenity; and
(4) the date on which the notice is to take effect; and
(5) the period in which any step is to be taken; and
(6) such additional matters as may be prescribed by regulations. The Town and Country Planning (Enforcement Notices and Appeals) Regulations 1981 (S.I. 1981 No. 1742) require that a notice should also specify:
(a) the reasons why the local planning authority consider it expedient to issue a notice; and
(b) the precise boundaries of the land to which the notice relates, whether by reference to a plan or otherwise.

The notice must also require the breach to be remedied.

The obligation to "specify" these matters has two elements. It means that the matters must be identified with precision and with accuracy. The terms of the notice may be so vague as to fall short of the requirement that they be specified; or the notice may be based upon false assumptions of fact. Failure to achieve a sufficiently high standard of accuracy or precision may render a notice a nullity, or invalid.

The generally accepted test for adequacy is that propounded by Upjohn

---

[99] Or perhaps because of it. The form and the instructions for its completion are complex: see now D.O.E. Circular 38/81 (formerly D.O.E. Circular 109/77, Appendix). As to the consequences of failure to strike out the necessary alternatives on the form, see *Hawkey* v. *S.O.S.E.* (1971) 22 P. & C.R. 611 (Secretary of State may make necessary minor amendments on appeal). The T.C.P. (Enforcement Notices and Appeals) Regulations 1981 (S.I. 1981 No. 1742), reg. 4, now require that each notice should be accompanied by an explanatory note of the statutory rights of appeal.
[1] T.C.P.A. 1971, s. 87.

L.J. in *Miller-Mead* v. *Minister of Housing and Local Government*[2]; "does the notice tell [the recipient] fairly what he has done wrong and what he must do to remedy it?"

3. Defective Notices: Nullities

Failure to specify any of the above matters altogether, or with sufficient clarity, is liable to render the notice a nullity. What standard of precision is required by the courts?

(a) The matters alleged to constitute the breach of planning control

To allege matters constituting a breach it is insufficient for a notice to specify nothing more than the facts as they appear to the authority.[3] It must additionally specify the alleged breach in terms that distinguish between the two limbs of the breach of control definition: that is, between the carrying out of development without planning permission on the one hand, and breach of a condition or limitation on the other.[4] The notice need not express the distinction in exactly those terms, and it is sufficient if it is clear from reading it as a whole which is being alleged.[5]

The requirement is apparently based upon the statutory pre-condition that the authority should have directed their minds to this distinction in order for it to have "appeared" to them that a breach of planning control had occurred.[6] But it is a hangover from the earlier days of planning control, and may well yet be set aside by the courts[7] if not by legislation.[8] It can have quite artificial consequences. In *Copeland Borough Council* v. *Secretary of State for the Environment*,[9] for example, the authority wished simply to require a developer who had built a house with the wrong type of roof tiles, to remove them and replace them with the tiles approved by the planning

---

[2] [1963] 2 Q.B. at 232; specifically endorsed by the Court of Appeal in *Munnich* v. *Godstone R.D.C.* [1966] 1 W.L.R. 427 and followed in numerous cases since, including *Mansi* v. *Elstree R.D.C.* (1964) 16 P. & C.R. 153, *Hawkey* v. *S.O.S.E.* (1971) 22 P. & C.R. 610, and *Eldon Garages Ltd.* v. *Kingston-upon-Hull Corporation* [1974] 1 W.L.R. 276.

[3] *Eldon Garages Ltd.* v. *Kingston-upon-Hull Corporation* [1974] 1 W.L.R. 276 at 280–281.

[4] *Ibid.* at 281; and see *East Riding C.C.* v. *Park Estate (Bridlington) Ltd.* [1957] A.C. 223 ("contravention of planning control" insufficient); *Miller-Mead* v. *M.H.L.G.* [1963] 2 Q.B. 196 at 219, *per* Lord Denning M.R. and 225, *per* Upjohn L.J., and *Copeland B.C.* v. *S.O.S.E.* (1976) 31 P. & C.R. 403 at 410.

[5] See, *e.g. Eldon Garages (supra)* where a notice alleging simply that land was being used in contravention of the planning Acts was upheld by Templeman J., on the ground that in the absence of any mention of conditions or limitations it was clear overall that it was directed to breach by development without permission. And *cf. Clarke* v. *M.H.L.G.* (1966) 64 L.G.R. 346: not essential that notice should specify former and present use, though there may be cases where it is necessary to ensure fairness to the occupier.

[6] T.C.P.A. 1971, s. 87(1).

[7] The rule has been criticised and the prospect of review held out: see *Garland* v. *M.H.L.G.* (1968) 20 P. & C.R. 93 at 101, *per* Lord Denning M.R.; *Pilkington* v. *S.O.S.E.* [1973] 1 W.L.R. 1527 at 1533, *per* Lord Widgery C.J.

[8] The Department of Environment had indeed assumed that this had already occurred through the redrafting exercise in the 1968 Act which introduced the concept of "breach of planning control" (see *Enforcement and Allied Appeals* (H.M.S.O., 1976), section 5, para. 2); but they were defeated by the judgement of Templeman J. in *Eldon Garages Ltd.* v. *Kingston-upon-Hull C.B.C.* [1974] 1 W.L.R. 276.

[9] (1975) 31 P. & C.R. 403.

permission. Their notice alleged only that the roof had been constructed without permission. But the Divisional Court held that the real breach was the whole building operation.[10] The notice was therefore invalid for failing to identify the breach properly, notwithstanding that all concerned were fully aware of what was the substance of the authority's allegations. They should, it seems, have required the whole house to be demolished, or at least have based their notice upon that possibility. There is, however, no requirement that a notice should go further and distinguish between breach of condition or limitation,[11] or between material change in use and operational development.[12]

A notice is not a nullity, however, if it gets the distinction wrong and alleges one variety of breach when it ought to have alleged another, provided it makes some distinction.[13] It is not then defective on the face of it, although if the Secretary of State finds on appeal that the wrong choice has been made he must quash the notice.[14] An appeal to him will be necessary to have it set aside.

Nor is a notice a nullity if there are minor errors,[15] or if the facts contained in it turn out to be false: they need, after all, be no more than allegations by the authority, and it may be that no development has taken place at all,[16] or the development turns out to be authorised by a permission or under the General Development Order.[17] But the consequence is that failure to exercise the right of appeal may result in criminal liability for breaching the terms of the notice, by doing something not otherwise unauthorised.

By the same token it is not essential to validity that the "matters" be specified in great detail or particularity.[18] A general description will suffice, and it need not, for example, identify the proper planning unit.[19] A notice which is too vague or is unintelligible on the face of it will be a nullity and may not be saved by reference to extrinsic evidence,[20] but otherwise the test is one of reasonably general communication: the details may be supplied by the Secretary of State by variation to the notice on appeal.

---

[10] Presumably, though, if the permission had contained a condition calling for strict compliance with the approved plans, the authority could have chosen either limb for enforcement.

[11] T.C.P.A. 1971, s. 243(5).

[12] Although curiously the Secretary of State has asserted that the distinction is important, (*Enforcement and Allied Appeals*, section 5, para. 2) his view appears to read too much into the *Eldon Garages* case, and *Francis* v. *Yiewsley & West Drayton U.D.C.* [1958] 1 Q.B. 478. The better view is that if the notice does distinguish, but gets it wrong, it may be a matter which can be put right on appeal by varying the notice: see *post*, p. 410–411.

[13] *Miller-Mead* v. *M.H.L.G.* [1963] 2 Q.B. 196 at 221.

[14] *Post*, p. 409.

[15] See, *e.g. Patel* v. *Betts* [1978] J.P.L. 109: minor clerical errors, which could have been corrected by the Secretary of State on appeal.

[16] See, *e.g. Jeary* v. *Chailey R.D.C.* (1973) 26 P. & C.R. 280.

[17] See, *e.g. Tidswell* v. *S.O.S.E.* (1976) 34 P. & C.R. 152; but *cf. Findlow* v. *Lewis* [1963] Q.B. 151: suggestion that false recital of fact may result in nullity, though that view must now be read in light of Upjohn L.J.'s analysis in *Miller-Mead* v. *M.H.L.G.* [1963] 2 Q.B. 196 at 232.

[18] See, *e.g. Bristol Stadium Ltd.* v. *Brown* [1980] J.P.L. 107: sufficient to describe the general activity complained of.

[19] *Hawkey* v. *S.O.S.E.* (1971) 22 P. & C.R. 611; *Joyce Shopfitters Ltd.* v. *S.O.S.E.* (1975) 237 E.G. 576; *Morris* v. *S.O.S.E.* (1975) 237 E.G. 649.

[20] *Miller-Mead* v. *M.H.L.G.* [1963] 2 Q.B. 196 at 234, *per* Upjohn L.J.

(b) The steps required

The notice must specify the steps to be taken. These must be steps for the purpose of restoring land to its condition before the development took place or (according to the particular circumstances of the breach) of securing compliance with the conditions or limitations subject to which planning permission was granted.[21] They may include the demolition of any buildings or works, the discontinuance of any use of land or the carrying out of any building or other operations.[22] But to specify them, means to prescribe them with certainty. The inclusion of vague or open-ended requirements, such as "to comply or seek compliance" with a condition requiring the demolition of a building[23]; to stop using land "as a paddock"[24] or to install "satisfactory sound proofing" and "take all possible action to minimise the effects created by the use of acrylic paint"[25] will render the notice a nullity.

Vague language may sometimes have to suffice because there is no more precise requirement available. A common example is in the case of material changes of use involving intensification, where it may be possible to do no more than require a return to pre-1964 levels of activity, however uncertain they may be.[26]

Provided there is certainty, it is of no relevance to whether the notice is a nullity that the steps required are excessive, irrelevant or inadequate (though see below for an analysis of the extent to which an authority may elect to under-enforce).[27] Specific power is conferred on the Secretary of State on appeal to vary the requirements of a notice, and that was seen by Lord Denning M.R. in the *Miller-Mead* case as disposing of the possibility of technical objections on this point.[28]

Further, the privative clause formerly did not extend to challenges based upon this ground. That fact led, or misled, the Divisional Court[29] to assume

---

[21] T.C.P.A. 1971, s. 87.

[22] *Ibid.* and the 1981 Act has introduced a new power to require steps to be taken for the purpose of making the development comply with planning permission or removing or alleviating any injury to amenity: see further *post*, p. 412.

[23] *Hounslow L.B.C.* v. *S.O.S.E.* [1981] J.P.L. 510.

[24] *Sykes* v. *S.O.S.E.* [1981] J.P.L. 285; where the Divisional Court accepted the argument that "paddock" was a concept of enclosure rather than use, and that land was not used as a paddock—it either was or was not a paddock.

[25] *Metallic Protectives Ltd.* v. *S.O.S.E.* [1976] J.P.L. 166. As to the possibility of leaving requirements for precise determination in a scheme to be agreed, see *Murfitt* v. *S.O.S.E.* [1980] J.P.L. 598 where the Divisional Court upheld a variation made by the Secretary of State providing for agreement on a scheme of restoration, with provision for determination by the Secretary of State in default. But it must be doubtful that that arrangement, even if capable of operating effectively under a notice varied on appeal, could form the basis for a valid original notice.

[26] See, *e.g. Trevors Warehouses Ltd.* v. *S.O.S.E.* (1972) 23 P. & C.R. 215. In an appeal decision at [1979] J.P.L. 633 the Secretary of State took the view that it was insufficient simply to require such steps to be taken "as are necessary to remedy the alleged breach." But in an appeal from a subsequent prosecution on the stop notice the Divisional Court apparently disagreed: see *Bristol Stadium Ltd.* v. *Brown* [1980] J.P.L. 107.

[27] *Post*, p. 412.

[28] [1963] 2 Q.B. 196 at 221; referring to the former power to vary a notice "in favour of the appellant." The power now is one to vary the notice where the Secretary of State is satisfied that it can be done "without injustice." T.C.P.A. 1971, s. 88A(2).

[29] *Smith* v. *King* (1969) 21 P. & C.R. 560; followed in *Hutchinson* v. *Firetto* [1974] J.P.L. 314; *Redbridge L.B.C.* v. *Perry* (1976) 53 P. & C.R. 176, *Rochdale M.B.C.* v. *Simmonds* [1981] J.P.L. 191.

that as the matter was not precluded from judicial examination, it was open to magistrates in any prosecution to declare the requirements of a notice to be excessive as being unreasonable. The effect of that ruling was to allow magistrates to treat the whole notice as a nullity, for they had no power to amend the notice.[30] But the 1981 Act has overridden the Divisional Court ruling, by bringing within the preclusive clause all grounds upon which challenge may be made by way of appeal to the Secretary of State, and thus depriving the courts of jurisdiction.[31]

(c) The time periods

A notice will be a nullity if it fails to specify the date (at least 28 days following service) on which it is to come into effect,[32] and the period allowed for compliance. The reasonableness of the latter period may, however, be reviewed by the Secretary of State on appeal.[33] Both requirements are straightforward enough, but difficulties formerly arose if the time periods were fixed in the notice by reference to the date of service rather than to an actual date. Service upon different affected parties at different times, even if only a day or two apart, might then result in there being a variety of different periods specified for different recipients of the same notice, and in the notice being pronounced a nullity.[34] But the Act now requires that a fixed date be specified in the notice when it is issued,[35] which will then be the same for all persons on whom copies of the notice are served.

At one time it was accepted that a notice might be regarded as a nullity if there were no proof of service at all,[36] because knowledge of the date of service was a vital factor in assessing whether the 28 day minimum period had been observed. But that was shown to offer too wide a loophole, particularly in the case of postal service, and amendments were made in 1968 to close it. It is now instead a ground of appeal to the Secretary of State that the notice has not been served in accordance with the Act,[37] and the privative clause extends to this ground, though with an exception. Challenge to a notice may still be made in defence to a prosecution by any person who should have been served but was not, and who satisfies the court that he had no actual or constructive knowledge of the notice and that failure to serve him with it has substantially prejudiced his interests.[38]

---

[30] It is ironical to note that formerly they did have that power, by virtue of T.C.P.A. 1947, s. 23(4)(*b*). But that was taken away in 1960, presumably because it was assumed that jurisdiction now rested solely with the Secretary of State.

[31] See now T.C.P.A. 1971, s. 243(1)(*a*).

[32] See, *e.g. Burgess* v. *Jarvis and Sevenoaks R.D.C.* (1952) 2 P. & C.R. 377. The practical importance of the period is that it sets the time within which any appeal must be lodged.

[33] *Post*, p. 416.

[34] *Bambury* v. *Hounslow L.B.C.* [1966] 2 Q.B. 204; *Stevens* v. *Bromley L.B.C.* [1972] 1 Ch. 39 (Plowman J.); 400 (C.A.). The Court of Appeal in *Stevens* expressly left the point open for future reconsideration, however, although subsequent legislative reform has now overcome some of the problems.

[35] T.C.P.A. 1971, s. 87(13)

[36] See, *e.g. Caravans and Automobiles Ltd.* v. *Southall B.C.* [1963] 1 W.L.R. 690; *Munnich* v. *Godstone R.D.C.* [1966] 1 W.L.R. 436.

[37] T.C.P.A. 1971, s. 88(2)(*f*). Under s. 88A(3) the fact that a person has not been served may be disregarded by the Secretary of State if there has been no substantial prejudice.

[38] *Ibid.* ss. 243(2), 88(5), 88(4)(*a*)

4. Defective notices: invalidity

A notice is a nullity only if it is defective on the face of it. But a notice may also be shown to be defective, or "invalid," once it has been looked at against the true facts. It may be that there has been no unauthorised development at all; or the notice may have been issued without the necessary authorisation by the planning authority. A notice which is not a nullity stands until it is quashed by the Secretary of State or the court. It is the scheme of the legislation that most challenges to validity may be made only by way of statutory appeal to the Secretary of State, and if no appeal is lodged within the prescribed time the right to challenge is lost.

There are some grounds of challenge, however, which may be taken directly to the courts. These include challenge on the basis of misuse or absence of power. The recipient of a notice may seek to establish that the authority acted manifestly unreasonably in issuing it, for example, or that they were estopped from doing so. The Secretary of State also has jurisdiction to inquire into such allegations, but it is not in these circumstances an exclusive jurisdiction.

The grounds upon which the Secretary of State must quash a notice are considered below. But they must nowadays be balanced against his powers on appeal to correct or vary the terms of a notice. These are important, because they may be used to save a notice, at least from challenge on purely technical grounds. There were formerly two separate powers. First, the terms of a notice might be varied, provided the variation was made in favour of the appellant. Secondly, the Secretary of State had jurisdiction to "correct any informality, defect or error in the enforcement notice if he is satisfied that the informality, defect or error is not material." The main scope for exercise of the first power was in recasting, in the appellant's favour, the requirements of a notice for the taking of remedial steps, or for extending the period allowed for compliance. But the second power went beyond that, because it was not limited to corrections only in favour of the appellant, provided they were not "material." That was a limitation which the courts chose to rephrase, by asking whether the error in respect of which correction was necessary was one going to the substance of the matter.[39] If it was not, and could be corrected without injustice to the appellant or the local planning authority, then to correct it was a proper exercise of the power.

The 1981 Act has taken the old formula and recast it in a way which reflects that judicial interpretation. The Secretary of State now has power to "correct any informality, defect or error in the enforcement notice, or give directions for varying its terms, if he is satisfied that the correction or variation can be made without injustice to the appellant or to the local planning authority."[40] So far as corrections are concerned, the test has now been reformulated to accord with the judicial interpretation; but by assimilating the test for "variation" to the same criteria, the Act has allowed for the making of a variation which goes against the interests of the appellant, provided it can be made without injustice.[41] "Injustice" is not

---

[39] *Miller-Mead* v. *M.H.L.G.* [1963] 2 Q.B. 196 at 221, *per* Lord Denning M.R.

[40] T.C.P.A. 1971, s. 88A(2).

[41] It also overcomes the problem of selecting between the right label of "correction" or "variation:" see, *e.g. Morris* v. *S.O.S.E.* (1975) 31 P. & C.R. 216, where the Divisional Court were able to uphold as a "variation" an amendment which had purportedly been made as a "correction."

easily definable in this context: no doubt a variation which radically altered the terms of the notice would cause injustice because it would alter the whole basis upon which the enforcement appeal had been brought; but a variation which went against the appellant's interests would not necessarily be one which caused him injustice.

The power of correction and variation therefore allows the Secretary of State to put an enforcement notice into proper shape, and to overcome defects which formerly might have invalidated it. It amounts to more than power to correct inadvertent slips, and it means that a notice may be amended so as to reflect the facts established in the course of the appeal. But it does not go so far as to allow the Secretary of State to undertake material amendments so as to accommodate a complete change of mind on the part of the planning authority. There are some defects which remain beyond the power of the Secretary of State to correct, and these may now be examined:

(a) Nullities

The Secretary of State has no power to entertain an appeal against a notice that is a nullity, and although it is a wise precaution to lodge a protective appeal in order to leave open any other alternative grounds upon which challenge may be sought, the Secretary of State's practice is to decline to take any further steps once he has taken the view that the notice is a nullity.

(b) The breach of planning control alleged by the notice has not taken place

It is clear that a notice must be quashed by the Secretary of State on appeal if its factual allegations turn out to be groundless. The 1981 Act has made this an express ground of appeal to the Secretary of State,[42] and it follows that such an appeal is the only means of challenging the factual basis of the notice. The power to correct or vary the terms of the notice allows the Secretary of State some flexibility, however, where there has been some error in the recital of the facts, such as an inaccurate description of a past or present use.[43]

(c) The wrong breach of planning control is alleged

It has been seen that a notice is a *nullity* if it fails to distinguish adequately between development without permission and breach of condition.[44] It will be *invalid* if, having made the distinction, it has selected the wrong limb. That is a defect which is apparently incapable of correction by the Secretary of State, on the basis that the necessary amendment would *always* be "material."[45] Similarly a notice may be invalid if, having selected the right limb it has nonetheless identified the wrong breach. Thus in *Copeland Borough Council* v. *Secretary of State for the Environment*[46] the "wrong

---

[42] T.C.P.A. 1971, s. 88(2)(*c*)

[43] See further *post*, pp. 410–411.

[44] *Ante*, p. 405.

[45] *Eldon Garages Ltd.* v. *Kingston-upon-Hull Corporation* [1974] 1 W.L.R. 276; and *cf. Garland* v. *M.H.L.G.* (1968) 20 P. & C.R. 93; *Rochdale M.B.C.* v. *Simmonds* [1981] J.P.L. 191.

[46] (1976) 31 P. & C.R. 403; *post*, p. 404.

tiles" case, where the Divisional Court held the real breach was the whole operation (the erection of a dwelling-house without permission), to have amended the recitals of the enforcement notice, with consequential amendments to its requirements, might have resulted in the appellant being now required not simply to replace the roof tiles, but to demolish the whole house. That would necessarily have been a "material" alteration.

(d) The matters alleged by the notice do not constitute a breach of control

This is a statutory ground of appeal.[47] If the matters alleged in the notice are true, then the substance of the appellant's claim under this ground is that no breach of planning control has taken place. He may show that permission exists, or is not required. Or he may assert that the condition alleged to have been breached is in fact invalid. But the ground is curiously worded: it suggests that if the allegations are not accurate it may nonetheless be sufficient for the appellant simply to accept them and to show, perhaps by pointing to the General Development Order or an express permission, that no breach is disclosed by them, notwithstanding that he may in some other way on the true facts be in breach of control.

(e) The breach of control is immune from enforcement

A notice must be quashed by the Secretary of State if he is satisfied that the development is immune. There are alternative statutory grounds of appeal according to whether the breach of control alleged is governed by the four year rule or not.[48]

(f) The allegations in the notice do not correspond to the facts

This is nowadays a ground for quashing the notice only where the allegations are unsupported at all by the facts. Otherwise it is the facts themselves that should govern the notice, and the power to correct the notice may be used to cut down the allegations to fit the facts "provided that some facts are proved to support a charge of the kind specified."[49] This means, for example that the Secretary of State may recast the labels used in the notice so that it will more accurately describe the breach.[50]

But what is, or is not, a material defect and incapable of correction is often little more than a matter of impression, or, to adopt the accepted terminology, a matter of fact and degree. For example, there is no formal requirement that a notice must distinguish between breaches consisting of

---

[47] T.C.P.A. 1971, s. 88(2)(b).

[48] Ibid. s. 88(d) and (e).

[49] Miller-Mead v. M.H.L.G. [1963] 2 Q.B. 196 at 240, per Diplock L.J.; and cf Francis v. Yiewsley & West Drayton U.D.C. [1958] 1 Q.B. 478: enforcement notice quashed because it proceeded on wholly false basis of fact.

[50] See, e.g. Hammersmith L.B.C. v. S.O.S.E. (1975) 30 P. & C.R. 19 where the Divisional Court overturned the Secretary of State's ruling that the label "guest house" used in a notice was inappropriate and a material defect. The Court held the label could be changed to "lodging house" or "hostel" without injustice. Similarly, Lloyd-Jones v. M.H.L.G. (1967) 204 E.G. 1200: "shop" to "shop or market."

material change of use and those involving operational development.[51] If the notice does draw the distinction but does it wrongly, that again is not necessarily a material defect. It may be, however, that it cannot be corrected without injustice. The error may have misled an appellant into basing his appeal on the four year rule only to find himself required to answer a materially different allegation on appeal. It is, of course, a highly subjective question whether an appellant actually has been misled. There is the risk that the more care he puts into the preparation of his case the less likely is he to be thought to have been misled, whilst the "tactically blinkered" appellant may succeed.

But it will necessarily be a material defect, on the other hand, if it goes "to the substance of the matter[52];" if, for example, the wrong allegation is quite unsupported by the facts. Thus, if the allegation is that the use of a building has been materially changed to use for industrial purposes and that turns out to be untrue but it transpires in the course of the inquiry that the building itself has been erected without permission, the notice cannot then be amended to catch the different breach.[53]

The presence of a material defect in the allegations need not always lead to the quashing of the notice. The power of "variation" may instead be used and the notice varied in favour of the appellant by deleting the defective part. The remainder may then stand with the scope of the allegations reduced.[54]

(g) The notice has not been properly served

This is a statutory ground of challenge,[55] but one which has now been closely circumscribed by the Act.

(h) Estoppel

Although an authority may, under the principles discussed earlier in this chapter, be estopped from denying the validity of a planning permission or a section 53 determination in certain limited cases, it does not follow that they are thereby estopped from taking enforcement action in respect of it. The estoppel does not act as a fetter on the enforcement power. Instead, it allows an appeal to be made against the notice on the grounds that permission exists for the development (ground (b) above) or is not required (ground (d) above).

The power to serve an enforcement notice could be fettered only by a representation by the authority that they would not take enforcement action.

[51] See, *e.g. Eldon Garages Ltd.* v. *Kingston-upon-Hull Corporation* [1974] 1 W.L.R. 276, where a simple notice making no specific distinction was upheld; though see *ante,* p. 405, footnote 12.
[52] *Miller-Mead* v. *M.H.L.G.* [1963] 2 Q.B. 196, at 221, *per* Lord Denning M.R.
[53] In one particularly cautious decision, an inspector (acting under the transferred jurisdiction arrangements) has refused to amend a notice alleging change to office use, upon finding that the new use was in fact a composite use of offices and residential which he thought materially different from that alleged: [1979] J.P.L. 786.
[54] See, *e.g.* appeal decisions reported at [1974] J.P.L. 159 and 353 (deletion of part of site covered by notice); [1974] J.P.L. 677 (deletion of materially defective allegation). But *cf.* [1979] J.P.L. 188 (relevant buildings not included in defined enforcement area: material error and not capable of correction.)
[55] T.C.P.A. 1971, s. 87(6)(*b*)

5. *"Under-enforcement"*

It frequently happens that an authority are concerned only about one element of a particular unauthorised development, and it makes sense that they should be able to tailor the requirements of their enforcement notice so as to allow the retention of the unobjectionable. But the legislation has always insisted that the notice should require the breach of planning control to be "remedied," and that it should specify the steps required by the authority to be taken to restore the land or make the development comply with the conditions or limitations subject to which planning permission was granted for it. Those formulae both suggest that nothing less than full remedy may be required, and that an authority have no power to seek anything less. The Secretary of State on appeal may allow something less, by granting permission for part of the unauthorised development; but such a power can be read into the local planning authority's obligations only if the phrase "the steps which are required by the authority to be taken" can be read as conferring a discretion as to how far to enforce. That interpretation has found some favour with the courts,[56] but has also encountered some questioning[57] and an insistence that the notice still correctly identify the breach[58]; and the ability of authorities to under-enforce remains in doubt.

It may have been the intention of the draftsmen of the 1981 Act to remove those doubts, because the new provisions require that a notice now should specify:

> "(*a*) any steps which are required by the authority to be taken in order to remedy the breach;
>
> (*b*) any such steps as are referred to in subsection (10) of this section and are required by the authority to be taken."[59]

Subsection (10) in turn authorises a requirement that steps be taken to make the development comply with planning permission, or to remove or alleviate any injury to amenity. The most logical interpretation of the provisions is that they allow an authority to underenforce in one of two ways. Thus, in a case such as the *Copeland*[60] case, involving a development in breach of a planning permission (or, like the *Garland*[61] case, in excess of a General Development Order limitation), the authority may simply require steps to be taken to bring the development into line with what is permitted, and need not seek the demolition of the whole. Alternatively, they may require steps to be taken to alleviate or remove injury to amenity, such as a landscaping scheme intended to shield the unauthorised development from view.[62]

---

[56] See, *e.g. Iddenden* v. *S.O.S.E.* [1972] 1 W.L.R. 1433 where the Divisional Court and Court of Appeal were both unanimous that underenforcement should be permitted, although Lord Denning's leading judgement in the Court of Appeal was based primarily on the ground that no permission had been needed for the works.

[57] See, *e.g. Kerrier D.C.* v. *S.O.S.E.* [1981] J.P.L. 193 at 195, *per* Lord Lane C.J.

[58] *Copeland B.C.* v. *S.O.S.E.* (1975) 31 P. & C.R. 403, where however Lord Widgery C.J. at 407 preferred, despite the Court of Appeal's opinion in *Iddenden* (and despite his own judgement in the Divisional Court in that case) to reserve for future consideration the whole question of under-enforcement.

[59] T.C.P.A. 1971, s. 87(7)

[60] *Copeland B.C.* v. *S.O.S.E.* (1975) 31 P. & C.R. 403.

[61] *Garland* v. *M.H.L.G.* (1968) 20 P. & C.R. 93.

[62] This is the interpretation apparently favoured by the Secretary of State, in D.O.E. Circular 26/81, Annex, para. 8.

Although that may be the logical interpretation, it is still difficult to square with the language of the Act. An enforcement notice must still require the breach to be "remedied,"[63] and the Act defines the phrase "steps to be taken in order to remedy the breach" as meaning steps for the purpose of restoring the land to its earlier condition or for securing compliance with planning permission.[64] In short, the scheme of the Act is to regard nothing short of restoration as amounting to a "remedy" of a breach. Moreover, the new requirements are not expressed as alternatives, and to read into them a power to under-enforce requires either reading in the word "or" (so as to allow the authority to require either the taking of steps to remedy the breach, or the steps described in subsection (10)); or accepting that each requirement is discretionary in itself, and that "any steps required by the authority to be taken" allows them to require only such steps as they think fit, and to achieve something less than complete restoration.

Moreover, if the requirements are not alternatives, they must be cumulative. But they do not fit together easily as cumulative requirements, unless the above interpretation is also adopted. There is little point in allowing an authority to insist both that the land be fully restored to its former condition *and* that steps be taken to remove or alleviate injury to amenity. The provisions make sense only if they are to be read as wholly alternative, or at least as partially alternative, thus allowing an authority to require complete restoration in respect of part of the site, perhaps, and steps to be taken for the alleviation of injury to amenity on another part.

There must also be uncertainty as to the scope of the Secretary of State's power of variation in this context. He would seldom be able to increase the burden on the applicant by, for example, requiring complete restoration rather than the steps for amenity protection required by the authority, without causing injustice. Yet if he finds the steps required by them to be taken to be impracticable, and takes the view that no such steps are capable of removing or alleviating the damage, he may have no choice but to quash the notice altogether. It would not be surprising, therefore, if authorities continued as a matter of course to require complete restoration in their enforcement notices, so as to leave broad discretion to the Secretary of State on appeal either to alter the requirements or to grant permission for all or part of the unauthorised development.[65]

If the requirements of the new provisions are indeed alternative, they offer the facility of allowing an authority to grant a permission on an application for all or part of the unauthorised development, and then to serve an enforcement notice as a means of giving effect to the permission and requiring the developer to bring the development into line with the new permission. But the new provisions still do not go so far as to allow the authority unilaterally to impose a permission on the developer, and the arrangements are therefore dependent still upon his agreeing to submit an application.

[63] T.C.P.A. 1971, s. 87(1).
[64] *Ibid.* s. 87(9)
[65] This is because an appeal to the Secretary of State is deemed to constitute an application for planning permission (whether or not it is a ground of appeal that permission should be granted for the unauthorised development), allowing him to grant permission for all or part of it and thus, under s. 92 of the 1971 Act, taking it outside the penal provisions of the Act altogether: see, *e.g. Dudley B.C.* v. *S.O.S.E.* [1980] J.P.L. 181.

6. *Withdrawal of a Notice*

An enforcement notice may be withdrawn by the authority at any time before it takes effect.[66] Since the effect of a notice is suspended once an appeal is lodged,[67] this allows the authority to reassess the position upon examination of the grounds of appeal and before the matter goes any further. Withdrawal is without prejudice to service of another notice.[68] Once a notice has taken effect, however, withdrawal is not possible and the only way of overriding it is by granting planning permission for the breach of control alleged.[69]

D. Appeals

1. *Introduction*

It can be seen from the foregoing analysis of the technicalities that still surround enforcement notices, that the right of appeal is an essential safeguard. It is also a convenient means for suspending the effect of enforcement notices. So enforcement appeals are popular. By appealing, a developer is given a breathing space not only to continue with the unauthorised development (which in some cases the authority may override by serving a stop notice), but to assess the strength of the enforcement notice. An enforcement notice may take effect after 28 days following service, although the period is customarily extended by a week or two to take account of the perennial difficulties of postal service. Any appeal must be lodged before the notice takes effect, and many of the possible grounds of challenge may be pursued only through appeal. And so appeals are often lodged simply as a holding device. A substantial proportion are subsequently withdrawn, usually following negotiation between planning authority and appellant.

2. *The Right of Appeal and the Statutory Grounds*

The appeals machinery is structured so as to allow an assessment of both the form and the merits of enforcement action. The right to appeal was formerly conferred upon any person actually served with the notice,[70] but has now been restricted by the 1981 Act to persons having an interest in the land (whether or not served with a copy of the notice). The Act, in subsection (2) of section 88, specifies eight grounds of appeal:

"(*a*) that planning permission ought to be granted for the development to which the notice relates or, as the case may be, that a condition

---

[66] T.C.P.A. 1971, s. 87(14). The authority must forthwith give notice of withdrawal to every person served with the notice.

[67] *Ibid.* s. 88(10).

[68] *Ibid.* s. 87(14).

[69] *Ibid.* s. 92.

[70] This had been held by the Secretary of State to include even a person to whom a copy of the notice was sent accompanied by a letter explaining that the authority thought service on him unnecessary. They had still arguably "served" it: see [1977] J.P.L. 465. The authority did not pursue the point in their subsequent appeal: *Camden L.B.C.* v. *S.O.S.E.* [1980] J.P.L. 31.

or limitation alleged in the enforcement notice not to have been complied with ought to be discharged."

This allows the Secretary of State to review the planning merits of enforcement and to quash the notice if he is satisfied that authorisation should be given to the contravening development. Every appeal is deemed to include an application for planning permission, whether or not this ground of appeal is expressly relied on.[71] But it is a limited jurisdiction. The Secretary of State may only grant permission for the development to which the notice relates[72] or discharge the particular condition or limitation alleged to have been infringed. In the latter case he may substitute another condition or limitation, whether more or less onerous.[73] And the scope of the deemed application is necessarily confined to the site defined by the enforcement notice. In some cases it may be that the best planning solution requires a broader view which only a broader formal application can authorise. Further, and particularly where ground (a) is not relied upon, there may be inadequate material available to the Secretary of State upon which to make a proper planning assessment.[74]

Otherwise, the Secretary of State's powers resemble those applicable to ordinary planning appeals. There is power to grant permission subject to such conditions as he thinks fit, and to authorise the retention or completion of any buildings or works.[75]

"(b) that the matters alleged in the notice do not constitute a breach of planning control."

If there has been no breach, there can be no enforcement; and there is no alternative but to quash the notice if this ground is made out by the appellant. It may be that the activities alleged by the authority to have occurred do not constitute development requiring planning permission, or that they fall within the terms of an express or deemed permission.

"(c) that the breach of planning control alleged in the notice has not taken place."

This ground was introduced by the 1981 Act, perhaps in response to the surprise voiced by Lord Widgery C.J. in *Hammersmith London Borough Council* v. *Secretary of State for the Environment*[76] that there was no separate ground upon which the argument could be raised that the breach alleged by the notice had not in fact occurred. But the courts had already accepted that this ground should be regarded as incorporated into ground (b) above, in that it necessarily required a dual inquiry as to whether the development had been carried out and whether it required permission.[77] The new provisions are therefore declaratory of the former law.

[71] T.C.P.A. 1971, s. 88(3)
[72] *Richmond-upon-Thames L.B.C.* v. *S.O.S.E.* (1972) 224 E.G. 1555: decision quashed because permission granted for parking of motor vehicles when notice concerned only with parking of motor coaches.
[73] T.C.P.A. 1971, s. 88B(2)
[74] See, *e.g. Hansford* v. *M.H.L.G.* (1969) 213 E.G. 637: no material on which limited permission could be based.
[75] T.C.P.A. 1971, s. 88B(1).
[76] (1975) 30 P. & C.R. 19 at 21.
[77] *Jeary* v. *Chailey R.D.C.* (1973) 26 P. & C.R. 280 (C.A.).

"(d) in the case of a notice which, by virtue of section 87(4) of this Act, may be served only within the period of four years from the date of the breach of planning control to which the notice relates, that that period had elapsed at the date when the notice was issued."

"(e) in the case of a notice not falling within paragraph (d) of this subsection, that the breach of planning control alleged by the notice occurred before the beginning of 1964."

The two grounds are logically alternative, but there may be rare occasions when both must be pleaded. The notice may be unclear whether the authority regard it as a case to which the four-year rule applies, or they may themselves have got the rules round the wrong way.

"(f) that copies of the enforcement notice were not served as required by section 87(5) of this Act."

Ineffective service is now a matter for the Secretary of State and his power to quash is discretionary. The details of his jurisdiction have already been discussed.[78]

"(g) that the steps required by the notice to be taken exceed what is necessary to remedy any breach of planning control or to achieve a purpose specified in section 87(10) of this Act."

This ground and the following one are of some significance. The test of what is necessary is one not simply of reasonableness but of legal entitlement. The requirements of a notice may be such as to override former use rights, for example, and under the doctrine in *Mansi* v. *Elstree R.D.C.*[79] discussed below it is necessary for the Secretary of State to ensure that they are protected. He may do so, whether or not the appeal is based on this ground.[80]

"(h) that the specified period for compliance with the notice falls short of what should reasonably be allowed."

This is essentially a matter for discretion, and the Secretary of State is entitled to take a realistic approach looking at the whole history of the site and taking previous delays and prevarications into account.[81]

Those are the statutory grounds of appeal, but it will always be possible for an appellant additionally to assert that the notice is a nullity or invalid for some other reason. It is clearly within the Secretary of State's jurisdiction to consider such submissions, and of course he is able to proceed no further if he finds the complaint established. But an assertion of nullity will not in itself constitute a valid appeal in the absence of reliance upon any of the statutory grounds, because it is essentially an invitation to the Secretary of State to disregard the notice entirely, rather than accept it as a basis for appeal.

---

[78] *Ante*, p. 408.
[79] (1964) 16 P. & C.R. 153; *post*, p. 000
[80] *Camden L.B.C.* v. *S.O.S.E.* [1980] J.P.L. 311.
[81] *Mercer* v. *Uckfield R.D.C.* (1962) 60 L.G.R. 226.

3. *Lodging an Appeal*

The rules for lodging an enforcement appeal are strict. There is a limited time. The appeal must be received by the Department before the notice takes effect,[82] and there is no power to grant an extension of time.[83] Failure to appeal in time means that the notice will take effect and that many of the possible grounds of challenge will have been lost.

The Act requires that the appeal be made by notice in writing, and that the appellant should submit to the Secretary of State, either when giving notice of appeal or within a time to be prescribed thereafter, a statement in writing specifying the grounds of appeal and giving such further information as may be prescribed.[84] These requirements were introduced by the Act of 1981, but are intended to provide an administrative framework for the implementation of the Court of Appeal's decision in *Howard* v. *Secretary of State for the Environment*.[85] That case had determined that it was sufficient compliance with the legislation, as it then stood, for a notice of appeal to be lodged in the first instance within the limited time, and for details of the grounds of appeal and supporting facts to be supplied subsequently. The Court took the view that failure to supply them after being requested to do so would entitle the Secretary of State to dismiss the appeal summarily.[86] The new provisions sharpen up that requirement, by authorising the Secretary of State to dismiss an appeal summarily and without notice if the appellant should fail to supply the further details within a time to be prescribed; and also authorising him to allow an appeal if the local planning authority should fail to comply with a requirement (see below) to submit within a prescribed time a statement indicating the matters they propose to put forward on the appeal.[87]

There appears still to be sufficient flexibility for the Secretary of State to accept late amendments and additions to appeal statements, though if submitted at too late a stage it may be necessary to offer further opportunity to the local authority for consideration, by postponing or adjourning an inquiry.[88] There is no jurisdiction otherwise for the Secretary of State to make interim or preliminary decisions,[89] and if he should decline to proceed with an appeal because he believes there to have been no adequate notice of

---

[82] T.C.P.A. 1971, s. 88(1). The Secretary of State will, however, accept a notice of appeal which is posted within the period, even although it is delivered late: *Selected Enforcement and Allied Appeals*, p. 3. Where, under the old law, the notice specifies a period running from the date of service rather than a specific date for taking effect, the period is to be measured in clear days disregarding the day of service: *R.* v. *Melton & Belvoir Justices, ex parte Tynan* (1977) 75 L.G.R. 544.

[83] *Howard* v. *S.O.S.E.* [1975] Q.B. 235.

[84] T.C.P.A. 1971, s. 88(3) and (4). The T.C.P. (Enforcement Notices and Appeals) Regulations 1981 (S.I. 1981 No. 1742) reg. 5, require the appellant to submit, either with the notice of appeal or within 28 days of being required by the Secretary of State to do so, a statement specifying the grounds of appeal and stating briefly the facts on which he proposes to rely in support of each of those grounds. A statement of facts is necessary even where the appeal is based on questions of law: see, *P.A.D. Entertainment Ltd.* v. *S.O.S.E. The Times*, May 11, 1982.

[85] [1975] Q.B. 235.

[86] *Ibid.* at 245, *per* Roskill L.J.

[87] T.C.P.A. 1971, s. 88(6)

[88] See further, *Selected Enforcement and Allied Appeals*, p. 4.

[89] *R.* v. *Melton and Belvoir Justices, ex parte Tynan* (1977) 75 L.G.R. 544 at 548.

appeal, that is a final decision which is capable of being challenged directly in the High Court.[90]

4. Fees for Enforcement Appeals

When fees were introduced for planning applications by the Local Government, Planning and Land Act 1980, the Government agreed that they should not, as a general principle, be payable in respect of appeals to the Secretary of State because developers might otherwise be inhibited from seeking relief against local planning authority decisions. But in the case of enforcement appeals there is a deemed application for planning permission, and if no fee were to be charged for the appeal there would be an incentive for some developers to avoid liability altogether by the simple expedient of not seeking permission from the local planning authority before commencing work. There is therefore provision for the payment of fees for enforcement appeals on the same basis as for an application for planning permission for the contravening development.[91] The fee is payable by every person who appeals against the notice, but it is refundable upon the withdrawal of the appeal, or the withdrawal of the enforcement notice, the dismissing or allowing of the appeal on the grounds that the appellant or the authority failed to comply with the procedural requirements, or in the event of the Secretary of State allowing the appeal on any of the grounds (b) to (f) discussed above.[92]

5. Suspension of the Effect of the Notice

Where an appeal is brought the effect of the enforcement notice is suspended "pending the final determination or the withdrawal of the appeal."[93] Since there is a right of appeal from the Secretary of State's decision, that is not necessarily the "final determination." The notice does not therefore take effect immediately a decision is issued upholding it. The suspension continues until the time for making an appeal to the High Court has expired without an appeal being lodged, and similarly through the next tier if a further appeal is lodged.[94] When the appropriate stage is reached the notice takes effect, and the possibility that leave may yet be given out of time for appeal may safely be disregarded.[95]

These provisions apply equally where a purported appeal is rejected as ineffective by the Secretary of State. If his view is right, then the suspension provisions are of no effect; but even if he is wrong and the appeal was in fact valid, suspension will continue for the 28 days from his decision in which an

---

[90] *Button v. Jenkins* [1975] 3 All E.R. 585; *Wain v. S.O.S.E.* (1978) 39 P. & C.R. 82.
[91] T.C.P. (Fees for Applications and Deemed Applications) Regulations 1981 (S.I. 1981 No. 369), reg. 8 (as amended by S.I. 1982 No. 716). The fee is payable whether the appeal relates to unauthorised development, or breach of limitation or condition (by virtue of T.C.P.A. 1971, s. 32(2)); but no fee is payable if the appellant had applied for planning permission before the issuance of the enforcement notice and paid the appropriate fee, and the application remained undetermined when the notice was issued: reg. 8(4A).
[92] *Ibid.* reg. 8. There is no refund on this ground, however, in the case of a notice relating to use of land as a caravan site.
[93] T.C.P.A. 1971, s. 88(3).
[94] *Garland v. Westminster L.B.C.* (1970) 21 P. & C.R. 555.
[95] *Ibid.* at 557.

appeal to the court should be lodged, but will then cease unless an appeal is actually lodged.[96] The suspension provisions are capable of being overridden in urgent cases by the service of a stop notice. The details are discussed later in this chapter.

6. The Authority's Response to an Appeal

Since early 1982, an obligation has been imposed on the local planning authority to respond to an enforcement appeal by serving on the appellant and the Secretary of State, not later than 28 days before the date fixed for the inquiry (or, if the appeal is to be determined by written representations, the date the Secretary of State requests the statement), a statement indicating the submissions which they propose to put forward on the appeal and including (a) a summary of their response to each of the grounds of appeal relied on and (b) a statement whether they would be prepared to grant planning permission in respect of the breach of control and the conditions, if any, they would wish to impose.[97] The statement not only provides the appellant with notice of the authority's case, but is also capable of providing the basis for negotiation on the scope of any possible planning permission. But it is no more than a statement of intention by the authority, and not an open-ended undertaking by them to grant permission. Any application for permission made in response to the statement would still need to be notified, advertised and determined in the usual way.

7. Appeals Procedure

The appeals procedure resembles closely that for ordinary planning appeals. The written representations procedures may be used,[98] or there may be an inquiry (and must be one if either party insists). The Inquiries Procedure Rules formerly did not apply, but the Secretary of State had undertaken that they would be observed in practice.[99] The Act of 1981 conferred power to make rules and the Town and Country Planning (Enforcement) (Inquiries Procedure) Rules 1981 (S.I. 1981 No. 1743) came into operation on January 11, 1982. The Rules are modelled closely on the 1974 Rules governing planning appeals (see further Chapter 13).

Inquiry procedure is therefore much the same as for other planning

---

[96] *Button* v. *Jenkins* [1975] 3 All E.R. 585; *Wain* v. *S.O.S.E.* (1978) 39 P. & C.R. 82.

[97] T.C.P. (Enforcement Notices and Appeals) Regulations 1981, reg. 6.

[98] See generally D.O.E. Circular 38/81, Part II. Costs may be awarded in enforcement cases dealt with by way of written representations, though the power in other cases exists only in respect of inquiries. The enabling provision, s. 110(1), refers not to "inquiries" but "proceedings."

[99] *Memorandum*, D.O.E. Circular 109/77, para. 6; and *Warnock* v. *S.O.S.E.* [1980] J.P.L. 590 where application had in fact been made to quash on the basis of breach of the Rules, but counsel for the Secretary of State raised no objection and accepted they should be complied with. In *Pollock* v. *S.O.S.E.* [1979] J.P.L. 680 the Divisional Court wrongly assumed that the Inquiries Procedure Rules were applicable, and proceeded to quash a decision of the Secretary of State for breaching them. On appeal, the Court of Appeal welcomed the Secretary of State's concession that he accepted the post-inquiry provisions of the Rules as applicable: [1981] J.P.L. 420.

inquiries whether the matter is for determination by the Inspector[1] or the Secretary of State, with two practical exceptions. The first is that it is customary to take evidence on oath in appeals based on grounds (d) and (e), because there is frequently conflicting factual evidence as to the date of occurrence of the alleged breach. Second, there has become established a doctrine of burden of proof in enforcement appeals, again due largely to problems of resolving conflicts of fact. It is for the authority to prove the substance of the allegations in their notice, but the burden of proof otherwise is on the appellant to make good his grounds of appeal.[2] The justification for this is clear enough. It should not fall to the authority, for example, to have to prove that permission should *not* be granted; and further, as Lord Widgery has pointed out,"where development takes place behind closed doors, it is the developer who knows precisely when the development occurs, and the local planning authority may have only the most nebulous idea as to the precise date of change."[3]

8. *Protecting existing rights: the Mansi doctrine*

It is axiomatic that enforcement is limited to making good any breach of planning control. It may not be used additionally as a means of cutting down established rights enjoyed by virtue of a permission or which are immune from enforcement. But it is easy for the requirements in an enforcement notice inadvertently to have this effect. They may, for example, seek the discontinuance altogether of a particular use when the substance of the notice is not the use itself but its intensification. Or a notice requiring the cessation of an admittedly unauthorised use may have the effect of prohibiting a legitimate exercise of the use as ancillary to the primary use of the land: an undertaker may be stopped from making and selling furniture from his premises, but to require him to cease all carpentry and sales activities would be to destroy an essential ancillary use.

The courts have recognised the dangers, and have insisted that it is incumbent on the Secretary of State to use his power of variation of notices in favour of appellants to ensure that established rights are not cut down. In the leading case of *Mansi* v. *Elstree R.D.C.*[4] the Divisional Court remitted to the Minister a notice which required the discontinuance of sales of any goods from certain premises, though the evidence showed there was an old established use for retail sales of produce from a garden nursery. The

---

[1] Transferred jurisdiction in enforcement appeals was extended in 1977. Formerly the pleading of legal appeal grounds meant that the case was reserved for Secretary of State's determination: but now it is a matter for recovery of jurisdiction by him in cases raising "very complex legal issues" (D.O.E. Circular 30/77, para. 30). Otherwise all appeals, except for those involving the operational land of statutory undertakers, are now transferred: see *post*, p. 568.

[2] *Nelsolvil Ltd.* v. *M.H.L.G.* [1962] 1 W.L.R. 404; *Britt* v. *Buckinghamshire C.C.* (1962) 60 L.G.R. 430; *Allen* v. *Hounslow L.B.C.* (1971) 222 E.G. 453; *Small Pressure Castings Ltd.* v. *S.O.S.E.* (1972) 223 E.G. 1099.

[3] *Nelsolvil Ltd.* v. *M.H.L.G.* [1962] 1 W.L.R. 404 at 408.

[4] (1964) 16 P. & C.R. 153.

doctrine has been applied in numerous cases since.[5] It is applicable solely to cases involving change in use. In the case of operational development the authority are able to enforce against the whole operation, and they are not required to dissect a building, for example, into parts that have immunity under the four year rules and those that have not.[6] And the Divisional Court has in recent years come to insist that the *Mansi* doctrine should not be taken too far, and that obvious ancillary uses need not be given any special attention.[7]

9. *Appeal to the High Court*

There is a further appeal to the High Court on a point of law from any decision, direction or order of the Secretary of State.[8] It is available to the appellant, the planning authority, and any other person upon whom the notice was served, whether or not they took part in the appeal. The Court has no power to quash the notice if the appeal is allowed. They must instead remit it to the Secretary of State for reconsideration.[9] An examination of the Court's powers is contained in Chapter 14.

E. The Consequences of Enforcement

1. *Reversion to Former Use*

The effect of an enforcement notice is not necessarily to leave the land without any authorised use. No permission is needed to revert to the former lawful use.[10] But if the former use was itself unlawful in the sense of being unauthorised under the Act, the exemption does not apply, even although the use may previously have been immune from enforcement.[11] The site may therefore be left with a nil use, and be totally dependent upon the grant of permission for lawful use for any purpose except, perhaps, agriculture or forestry.[12] There will be some cases, however, where enforcement has

---

[5] See, *e.g. Clare & Ridgeway Ltd.* v. *M.H.L.G.* (1970) 217 E.G. 873 (ancillary use) *Decorative and Caravan Paints Ltd.* v. *M.H.L.G.* (1970) 214 E.G. 1355 (ancillary rights); *Ipswich C.B.C.* v. *S.O.S.E.* (1972) 225 E.G. 797 (existing use rights); *Trevors Warehouses Ltd.* v. *S.O.S.E.* (1972) 23 P. & C.R. 215 (restriction of sale of goods to extent carried on before 1964 cut down levels that had been achieved by intensification not constituting development up to 1970, before the material change occurred which was the subject of the notice); *Hilliard* v. *S.O.S.E.* (1977) 34 P. & C.R. 193 (intensification, but new building erected with permission had already destroyed existing rights); *Day and Mid-Warwickshire Motors Ltd.* v. *S.O.S.E.* [1979] J.P.L. 538 (protection of rights conferred by Use Classes Order upon reversion to former use); *Newport* v. *S.O.S.E.* [1980] J.P.L. 596 (pre-1964 use).
[6] *Ewen Developments Ltd.* v. *S.O.S.E.* [1980] J.P.L. 404.
[7] See, *e.g. Cord* v. *S.O.S.E.* [1981] J.P.L. 40, where the Court declined to rule that a notice which prohibited, *inter alia*, "the parking and storage of commercial vehicles," should be amended so as to protect such rights as might be ancillary to the use of the dwelling house on the land; *North Sea Land Equipment* v. *S.O.S.E.* [1982] J.P.L. 384.
[8] T.C.P.A. 1971, s. 246.
[9] *Ibid.* s. 246(3)(*a*); R.S.C. Ord. 94, r. 12.
[10] T.C.P.A. 1971, s. 23(9)
[11] *L.T.S.S. Print and Supply Services Ltd.* v. *Hackney L.B.C.* [1976] 1 Q.B. 663 (C.A.), effectively overruling *W.T. Lamb & Sons Ltd.* v. *S.O.S.E.* [1975] 2 All E.R. 1117 where the Divisional Court had held that a use could be regarded as unlawful only if prohibited by an enforcement notice.
[12] Due to the curious wording of T.C.P.A. 1971, s. 22(2)(*e*), *ante*, p. 193.

attached to a smaller planning unit than the unit of occupation but where steps taken in compliance with the notice have meant that it is no longer identifiable as such, and has been absorbed into the larger unit.

The problems of determining what the lawful use may be following enforcement has led to the conferral of a special power on the Secretary of State to make such a determination on appeal.[13] This allows the issue to be settled without recourse to further proceedings, and the effect of such a determination is similar to that of a section 53 determination. But there is no duty upon him to issue the ruling, and in practice he will do so only where requested to by one of the parties and where sufficient evidence is available.[14]

2. Offences of Non-Compliance

The Act prescribes two main offences for non-compliance. The first is in respect only of owners of the land at the time the notice was served. It is the owner's obligation to ensure that the steps required by the notice to be taken are taken within the time allowed for compliance. If any have not been taken he is liable on summary conviction to a fine not exceeding £1,000, and on conviction on indictment to an unlimited fine.[15] But if he has ceased to be the owner before the expiry of the period allowed for compliance he may insist on having his successor brought before the court and attaching the blame to him.[16] The subsequent owner may be convicted if he is wholly or partly to blame; and the original owner acquitted if he proves he took all reasonable steps to secure compliance with the notice.[17] Conviction is not, of course, the end of the matter. Failure by the convicted person "as soon as practicable to do everything in his power to secure compliance" is a further offence.[18]

The second offence, which carries the same penalties, is directed at any person contravening the provisions of an effective notice by using the land for a use required to be discontinued, by infringing a condition or limitation required to be complied with, or by "causing or permitting" either of those.[19] Such requirements in a notice are of permanent effect[20] unless permission is granted for the development.[21] The provision allows action to be taken against "any person," so that although a landowner may be liable under the first offence even although he may be unable to take steps on land physically occupied by tenants of his, the second offence will catch the tenants themselves. The landowner will not be liable for "causing or permitting" their contravention if he lacks power to prevent it.[22] An offence

---

[13] T.C.P.A. 1971, s. 88(5)(*b*)

[14] *Selected Enforcement and Allied Appeals*, p. 62.

[15] T.C.P.A. 1971, s. 89(1). This is a once and for all offence, committed at the end of the period: *St. Albans D.C.* v. *Norman Harper Autosales Ltd.* (1977) 35 P. & C.R. 70. The former requirement that prosecution should be commenced within 6 months was abolished by the Criminal Law Act 1977, s. 18(1) (see now Magistrates' Court Act 1980, s. 127).

[16] *Ibid.* s. 89(2).

[17] *Ibid.* s. 89(3).

[18] *Ibid.* s. 89(4).

[19] *Ibid.* s. 89(5). Unauthorised reinstatement of works or buildings is a separate offence under s. 93(5).

[20] *Ibid.* s. 93.

[21] *Ibid.* s. 92.

[22] *Redbridge L.B.C.* v. *Perry* (1976) 33 P. & C.R. 176.

under this provision is a continuing offence from day to day, and hence unless an information is confined to a specified date it will be alleging more than one offence and be void for duplicity.[23]

3. Execution of Works by Planning Authority

Where the requirements of an enforcement notice (other than the discontinuance of a use of land) have not been complied with within the time allowed, the authority may themselves enter the land and do the work.[24] The costs are recoverable from the owner. If the breach was committed by some other person he may in turn recover those costs as well as any of his own in complying with the notice, from the person who committed the breach of control.[25]

F. Stop Notices

1. Introduction

The stop notice procedure allows authorities to take swift and effective action. They are able to obtain the equivalent of an effective enforcement notice in as little as three days. But its misuse may involve them in liability to pay compensation, and there is an understandable hesitation to use the procedure. The provisions were introduced as recently as 1968 but were initially confined to cases of operational development. But in 1977[26] they were extended to cover most cases of change of use as well.

Ironically, it was the lengthening delay in handling enforcement appeals which led to demands for the procedure and particularly for its extension. Developers were able openly and profitably to flout planning control for periods of months and even years, often producing a *fait accompli* where the required restorative work could no longer adequately remedy the breach, or might be regarded by the Secretary of State as excessive in the changed circumstances.

2. Circumstances of Use

A stop notice is parasitic. It attaches to an enforcement notice, and its purpose is to give the enforcement notice almost immediate interim effect, notwithstanding that the time specified by the notice may not have expired nor that an appeal may have been lodged. There is no appeal against a stop notice. It stands or falls with the enforcement notice.

A stop notice may be served in any case where an enforcement notice has been served requiring a breach of planning control to be remedied, and where the authority consider it "expedient"[27] to prevent, before the

---

[23] *Parry* v. *Forest of Dean D.C.* (1977) 34 P. & C.R. 209.

[24] T.C.P.A. 1971, s. 91(1). It is open to the authority to do less than the full requirement imposed by the notice: *Arcam Demolition Construction Co. Ltd.* v. *Worcestershire C.C.* [1964] 1. W.L.R. 661.

[25] *Ibid.* s. 91(2).

[26] Town and Country Planning (Amendment) Act 1977. A circular issued on that Act contains detailed advice on the use of stop notices: D.O.E. Circular 82/77.

[27] The need to act circumspectly and the relevant considerations to be taken into account in forming their judgment are examined in D.O.E. Circular 82/77, para. 3.

enforcement notice can take effect, the carrying out of any activity which is, or is included in, a matter alleged by the notice to constitute the breach.[28] The use of the word "activity," which is nowhere defined, implies that the authority may select any one or more constituent parts of the breach for prohibition, whether or not the part constitutes development in itself. They may not, however, prohibit the use of any building as a dwelling house, or the use of land as a site for a caravan occupied by any person as his only or main residence, or the taking of any of the remedial steps required by the enforcement notice.[29] And there is a further exemption. No notice may be served in respect of "activities" on land which have continued for more than twelve months.[30] The exemption stems from the 1977 legislation which brought change of use within the provisions, and it is apparently based upon the assumption that if an authority have allowed a year to elapse before taking action, the breach cannot be serious or urgent enough to warrant stop notice treatment. A particular difficulty, however, is that the Act nowhere requires that the 12 month user should have been unauthorised, and the Court of Appeal have refused to imply such a limitation into it.[31] The consequence is that a formerly authorised use under a time-limited planning permission will also qualify, and may deprive the authority of the power to serve a notice if the use continues beyond the permitted period.

3. Procedure

The service of a stop notice follows, and is a separate act from the service of the enforcement notice. It must be served before the enforcement notice takes effect, and itself takes effect on a date specified by it being not earlier than 3 days and not later than 28 days from the day on which it is first served on any person.[32] Since the effect of an enforcement notice is suspended when an appeal is lodged against it, a stop notice may be served some considerable time after the original enforcement notice. The notice refers to, and has annexed to it a copy of the relevant enforcement notice,[33] and it may be served upon any person appearing to the authority to have an interest in the land or to be engaged in any activity prohibited by the notice. The authority must also display a site notice.[34] Liability under a stop notice which has taken effect is not limited to persons upon whom it has been served, and it commences as soon as a site notice is displayed, or otherwise, in the case of a person actually served, two days after service; and there is provision for unlimited fine on indictment (£1,000 on summary conviction) for any person contravening, or causing or permitting the contravention of, the notice.[35] A notice may be withdrawn at any time[36] (without prejudice to

---

[28] T.C.P.A. 1971, s. 90(1) as amended.
[29] *Ibid.* s. 90(2).
[30] *Ibid.* s. 90(2). The twelve-month rule does not apply to any activity "which is, or is incidental to, building, engineering, mining or other operations or the deposit of refuse or waste materials."
[31] *Scott Markets Ltd.* v. *Waltham Forest L.B.C.* (1979) 38 P. & C.R. 597.
[32] T.C.P.A. 1971, s. 90(3).
[33] *Ibid.* s. 90(1). Recourse may therefore legitimately be had to the enforcement notice in interpreting the stop notice: *Bristol Stadium Ltd.* v. *Brown* [1980] J.P.L. 107.
[34] *Ibid.* s. 90(5).
[35] *Ibid.* s. 90(7).
[36] *Ibid.* s. 90(6).

the service of another, though with liability to compensate); and it ceases to have effect if the enforcement notice is quashed or withdrawn, or once the period for compliance with the requirements of the enforcement notice has expired, and the enforcement notice itself takes full effect.[37]

4. *Compensation*

Use of stop notice procedure may be expensive. Compensation may be claimed by any person owning an interest in or occupying the land when the notice is first served,[38] in the following circumstances:

(*a*) where the enforcement notice is quashed on grounds other than those mentioned in section 88(2)(*(a)*); other, that is, than in accordance with the grant of permission by the Secretary of State.[39] This includes, therefore, cases where no permission was in fact required or where enforcement action was taken out of time. But whether it includes cases where the notice was a nullity is left in doubt by the Act. Technically, a nullity need not, indeed cannot, be quashed. But to apply so technical an analysis to these provisions would be to deprive a claimant of compensation in the most extreme cases of misuse of the enforcement power, and it is little consolation that a developer may be in as good a position as the authority to recognise the notice to be a nullity, and to mitigate his loss by ignoring it.

(*b*) where the enforcement notice has been varied otherwise than in accordance with the grant of permission so that matters alleged to constitute a breach of planning control cease to include one or more of the activities prohibited by the stop notice[40];

(*c*) where the enforcement notice is withdrawn by the authority otherwise than in accordance with the grant by them of permission legitimising the breach[41]; and

(*d*) where the stop notice is withdrawn.[42]

Compensation is awarded for the "loss or damage directly attributable to the prohibition contained in the notice"[43] and its quantum is a matter for determination ultimately by the Lands Tribunal.[44]

G. Enforcement by Injunction

The carrying out of development without the necessary permission is unlawful, but it carries no direct sanctions. Criminal liability attaches to instances of non-compliance with an enforcement notice or stop notice. There is, however, an established jurisdiction for the courts by injunction to uphold a public right. May this be used to provide extra-statutory

---

[37] *Ibid.* s. 90(4).
[38] *Ibid.* s. 177(1). Compensation might not therefore be payable direct to a contractor, but the owner is entitled to claim also in respect of a breach of contract caused by the taking of action necessary to comply with the prohibition: subs. (5).
[39] *Ibid.* s. 177(2)(*a*).
[40] *Ibid.* subs. (2)(*b*).
[41] *Ibid.* subs. (2)(*c*).
[42] *Ibid.* subs. (2)(*d*).
[43] *Ibid.* s. 177(1).
[44] No cases have yet been reported, but see, for a guide to the relevant principles, Corfield and Carnworth, *Compulsory Acquisition and Compensation* (Butterworths, 1978), pp. 441–46.

supplementation to the ordinary procedures? It has been clear for some years that it may, so long as the action was brought by the Attorney-General at the relation of the planning authority. The courts have held, indeed, that they should refuse the injunction only in exceptional cases provided there is a clear breach,[45] and they have indicated that it is unnecessary that the statutory remedies should first have been exhausted. In the words of Lord Goddard C.J.:

> " . . . if a defendant shows by his conduct that he intends to avoid the Act and act in breach of it so far as he can and for as long as he can, then the Attorney-General is entitled to an injunction. . . . "[46]

Thus, the injunction need not be confined to a particular site. It may be in terms of a prohibition against breaches of planning control for the whole of the planning authority's area.[47]

Although local authorities since 1933 have had power themselves to bring proceedings "for the promotion or protection of the interests of the inhabitants of their area," the courts were originally reluctant to accept that this might confer upon them a "public interest" right equivalent to that of the Attorney-General.[48] But when the Local Government Act 1972 re-enacted the earlier power it added an authorisation for authorities to institute civil proceedings in their own name,[49] and this has since been held to have overcome the earlier objections.[50]

Thus, it seems, a planning authority may sue for an injunction in a case where there has been a deliberate and flagrant flouting of the planning Act.[51] Much remains uncertain, however. There has been no suggestion in the post-1972 cases that an authority ought, like the Attorney-General, to have their injunction in all but exceptional cases, and instead it is likely that the remedy will issue in only the clearest cases. Thus, although statutory remedies need not necessarily first have been exhausted and proved inadequate, in many cases it may only be then that an inference of deliberate and flagrant breach can clearly be drawn.[52] Insistence that statutory enforcement proceedings should first have been undertaken is therefore an important safeguard against arbitrary use of the injunction procedure.

Flagrant and deliberate breaches of a stop notice or effective enforcement notice would clearly offer grounds for injunctive relief, notwithstanding that

---

[45] *Attorney-General* v. *Bastow* [1957] 1 Q.B. 514 (persistent breaches and failure to pay fines).
[46] *Attorney-General* v. *Smith* [1958] 2 Q.B. 173, at 186 (persistent breaches, and caravans shifted from site to site).
[47] See, *e.g. Attorney-General* v. *Smith (supra)* (injunction restraining use of any land within the U.D.C. boundaries as unauthorised caravan site); *Attorney-General* v. *Morris* (1973) 227 E.G. 991 (county-wide injunction against unauthorised caravan sites).
[48] *Prestatyn U.D.C.* v. *Prestatyn Raceway Ltd.* [1970] 1 W.L.R. 33; *Hampshire C.C.* v. *Shonleigh Nominees Ltd.* [1970] 1 W.L.R. 865.
[49] L.G.A. 1972, s. 222.
[50] *Solihull M.B.C.* v. *Maxfern Ltd.* [1977] 1 W.L.R. 127; *Stafford B.C.* v. *Elkenford Ltd.* [1977] 1 W.L.R. 324; *Kent C.C.* v. *Batchelor (No.2)* [1979] 1 W.L.R. 213; and *cf Hammersmith L.B.C.* v. *Magnum Automated Forecourts Ltd.* [1978] 1 W.L.R. 50 (action under Control of Pollution Act 1974).
[51] See, *e.g. Stafford B.C.* v. *Elkenford Ltd.* [1977] 1 W.L.R. 324 at 329, *per* Lord Denning M.R., 330, *per* Bridge L.J. (although the injunction in that case was sought, not for breach of planning control, but for breach of the Shops Act 1950); *Westminster C.C.* v. *Jones* [1981] J.P.L. 750 (flagrant breach of a stop notice.)
[52] *Ibid.* at 330, *per* Bridge L.J.

no prosecution had been undertaken[53] and even though the prohibition sought through the injunction is broader, as in the case of a county-wide injunction, than that obtained through the statutory system. There is in those cases at least an established criminal liability.

But in a case where no action has been taken at all under the statutory procedures, or where the effect of an enforcement notice has been suspended pending the outcome of an appeal, the case for granting an injunction must be very much weaker. This is particularly the case in the era of the stop notice and its guarantee of compensation in the case of misuse. But the jurisdiction is flexible, and cases may even then occur when it is appropriate to call upon the High Court's "jurisdiction to ensure obedience to the law wherever it is just and convenient to do so[54];" but they will be most rare. The procedures and safeguards now provided by the legislation ought not lightly to be overridden.

H. Challenging Enforcement in the Courts: the Privative Clause

Provisions governing the statutory right of appeal to the High Court, and the Court's general jurisdiction in planning, are discussed in chapter 14. But there have been a number of problems in the context of enforcement, arising particularly from the distinction between nullity and invalidity, which call for further comment here.

The scheme of the 1960 legislation was to route challenges to enforcement notices to the Minister, and the general jurisdiction of the courts to review was excluded by a privative clause, which now provides that "the validity of an enforcement notice shall not, except by way of an appeal under Part V of this Act, be questioned in any proceedings whatsoever on any of the grounds on which such an appeal may be brought."[55]

That is an exclusion which clearly applies equally to the questioning of validity by way of defence to prosecution[56] as it does to actions for judicial review. But it is limited to challenges based upon the prescribed grounds of appeal. It does not, therefore, preclude challenge on any other grounds, such as that the enforcement notice was issued in bad faith and nor does it preclude challenge based on nullity.[57] Further, it clearly remains possible for a landowner or authority to seek a declaration as to the proper interpretation of a notice,[58] or the scope of a planning permission where dispute has arisen between authority and developer. In many cases the privative clause is irrelevant, but in others where enforcement action has already been taken or is threatened, proceedings by way of declaration have sometimes been used as a means of raising issues relating directly or indirectly to the validity of an enforcement notice, without the effect of the privative clause having

---

[53] Thus in *Kent C.C.* v. *Batchelor (No.2)* [1979] 1 W.L.R. 213 where the county had been awarded an interlocutory injunction restraining B. from cutting down or damaging trees subject to a tree preservation order, they had at no stage prosecuted him for breach of the orders, and indeed gave an undertaking to the court that they proposed not to.

[54] *Attorney-General* v. *Chaudry* [1971] 1 W.L.R. 1614 at 1624, *per* Lord Denning M.R.

[55] T.C.P.A. 1971, s. 243(1).

[56] Though there is an exception under subs. (2) in the case of any owner not served with his notice, not knowing of it and substantially prejudiced by the failure to serve.

[57] See, *e.g. Ormston* v. *Horsham R.D.C.* (1965) 63 L.G.R. 293, *Jeary* v. *Chailey R.D.C.* (1973) 26 P. & C.R. 280 at 284.

[58] See, *e.g. Fordham* v. *Elstree R.D.C.* (1968) 207 E.G. 893.

apparently been considered.[59] Much depends upon timing. An action seeking a declaration as to the validity or scope of a planning permission, where there is no threat of enforcement, is clearly not caught by the clause. But if the authority have already served an enforcement notice in respect of the same issue, then to allow the action to proceed is effectively to permit challenge to be made to the validity of the notice on a ground falling within section 88(2)(b), and thus is caught by the privative clause. In *Square Meals Frozen Foods Ltd.* v. *Dunstable Borough Council*[60] the Court of Appeal were prepared to go further, holding that where proceedings were commenced in anticipation of the service of an enforcement notice, and such a notice was subsequently served, the proceedings were barred by the privative clause. And even if that were not so, the Court held that they ought nonetheless to stay the proceedings, because the statutory appeals system provided a more satisfactory means of determining the issue.

The result is that an authority may, by serving an enforcement notice relating to the central point at issue in declaratory proceedings, bring the privative clause into play. In *Lever Finance Ltd.* v. *Westminster City Council*,[61] for example, where it was the Council's resolution to take enforcement action which triggered off the developers' action, service of the enforcement notice could, under the *Square Meals* ruling, have swiftly brought the High Court proceedings to a halt.

It is remarkable that in *Western Fish Products Ltd.* v. *Penwith District Council*[62] the Court of Appeal found it unnecessary to consider the scope of the privative clause. In that case, enforcement notices and stop notices had already been served, and the time for appeal had expired. So there was an effective enforcement notice and the clause operated to prevent any challenge to its validity. But much of the declaratory relief sought by the plaintiffs and the issues raised by them went directly to the validity of the notice. They sought, for example, a declaration that they were entitled to established user rights under Class IX of the Use Classes Order. But that, except to the extent that it sought the granting of an established use certificate, was an issue falling directly within section 88(2)(b); and the certificate would have been ineffective against an enforcement notice which had taken effect.

The privative clause is limited, however, to the prescribed grounds of appeal to the Secretary of State. Proceedings may still be brought on other grounds,[63] but if the issues overlap substantially with the statutory grounds the court may nonetheless wish to exercise its discretion to stay proceedings pending the outcome of an appeal to the Secretary of State.[64] That is not

---

[59] See, *e.g. Cookham R.D.C.* v. *Bull* (1972) 225 E.G. 2104, action for declaration that authority entitled to enter and restore land; real concern with validity of the enforcement notice.

[60] [1974] 1 W.L.R. 59; followed in Scotland in *James Barrie (Sand and Gravel) Ltd.* v. *Lanark D.C.* 1979 S.L.T. 14, where the authority had done no more than threaten the service of a notice, and the proceedings were brought to prevent them from doing so.

[61] [1971] 1 Q.B. 222.

[62] (1978) 30 P. & C.R. 7.

[63] See, *e.g. Flashman* v. *Camden L.B.C.* (1979) 130 New L.J. 885 where the Court of Appeal, distinguishing the *Square Meals* case, held that where the grounds of action went outside s. 243, or there was at least an arguable question as to how far that section afforded a defence to the plaintiff's claims, the action should be allowed to proceed.

[64] *Square Meals Frozen Foods Ltd.* v. *Dunstable B.C.* [1974] 1 W.L.R. 59.

relevant where the right has already been unsuccessfully exercised, or lost, but the proceedings must then be confined to issues not covered by the privative clause.

CHAPTER 10

PLANNING AND ENVIRONMENTAL CONTROL

A. Environment, amenity and the planning system

1. *Relationships between Systems of Control*

"Environment" and "amenity" are both powerful words, describing very broad and elusive concepts. "Amenity" was the catchword of all early planning legislation, and it was used to signify an ideal which was difficult to capture in more precise language. "Amenity" was to be the opposite of what the congested cities had become. It was an expression that hinted at well designed and well laid out development, with fresh air, trees and parks, churches and schools and convenient shopping facilities all near at hand. It meant "pleasant circumstances or features, advantages,"[1] or "those qualities and conditions in an area which contribute to the pleasantness, harmony, and coherence of the environment and to its better enjoyment."[2] Though incapable of precise definition, the pursuit and enhancement of "amenity" was and is a central feature of planning ideology.

"Environment" too is a catchword, but its modern significance stems more from the rise in public consciousness and concern at the growing extent of ecological destruction and the unrestrained exploitation of natural resources. "Environment" therefore is used as an all-embracing term, without the urban settlement connotations of "amenity;" and the tasks of environmental protection and resource conservation have come to be seen as increasingly important priorities for modern governments.

There has therefore been an impetus to introduce new and further legal controls and restrictions in the interests of environmental preservation, but in Britain this process has caused something of a dilemma for the land use planning system. It already offers an existing system of comprehensive control over new development, vested in democratically accountable authorities, on to which further criteria, controls and prohibitions can be comparatively readily grafted. This has been the pattern adopted in the case of a wide range of supplementary amenity controls, in instances where the basic machinery has been found to be in need of strengthening. Examples include the control of outdoor advertising, and the preservation and conservation of historic buildings and areas of interest. These and other controls which have been harnessed to the planning system are examined in the following chapter.

In the field of environmental protection, however, there has developed a variety of statutory powers based initially primarily upon non-planning considerations, such as public health and industrial safety, and they have been administered by other agencies. Further provision for environmental

---

[1] The classic statement by Scrutton L.J. in *Re Ellis and Ruislip-Northwood U.D.C.* [1920] 1 K.B. 343 at 370.
[2] Town and Country Planning Act (N.Z.) 1977, s. 2(1).

protection in recent years has been concentrated largely upon reviewing and extending those powers, rather than upon developing the planning power. That, in many ways, has been a perfectly rational choice. There are obvious difficulties in attempting to control environmental pollution, for example, through the planning system. Development control concentrates for the most part solely on new development. Powers exercisable against already authorised development generally involve lengthy procedures and the payment of compensation. The broad exemptions of the Use Classes Order and the General Development Order mean that changes may be made in the use of, and in processes carried on in existing premises without any need for planning permission. And the enforcement system for breaches of planning control has never been sufficiently strong to allow for the swift and effective detection, remedy and punishment thought necessary for a pollution policing system.

New environmental powers have therefore tended to develop as separate codes, administered by different central and regional agencies, with a strong back-up of criminal sanctions and with no, or at best minimal, provision for compensation to be paid for the exercise of power. Lessons have been learned from the planning system, and in some of the codes there are closely comparable provisions for consents, conditions, appeals and the like. But there remains, in each subject area of environmental control, an ill-defined area of overlap between the planning system and the other statutory code. Even where strict and comprehensive controls exist elsewhere, development control is seen as offering a valuable early warning system, and a means of influencing the location, layout and design of new development in such a way as to ensure minimal detriment to the environment. Use of the planning power in this way can reduce the subsequent enforcement difficulties of the other agencies; and even although powerful sanctions may exist to control subsequent pollution, early consultation and cooperation in design can reduce waste and lessen the possible pressure by the operators of an authorised development for subsequent relaxation of pollution quality standards. And where the risk of pollution from new development cannot be readily reduced to an acceptable level, planning permission may be refused; environmental considerations are clearly material considerations in the control of new development.

But there are operational and legal difficulties. How far, for example, should planning authorities attempt to seek continuing control through the imposition of conditions over matters falling squarely within the jurisdiction of another agency such as the water authority or the Alkali Inspectorate? And how far should there be provision for formal input of views into development control, and even powers of veto, from that other agency? These are questions of balance and of co-ordination. Surprisingly little provision is currently made in the General Development Order, but the gap has been filled in practice through a variety of informal consultative arrangements which have gradually developed between the responsible agencies.

This chapter examines the impact upon the planning system of the developing environmental protection codes, but it is by no means a comprehensive survey. The aim has been largely to describe and illustrate the way in which the provisions tie into and supplement the planning system, and to indicate the formal and informal links between them.

2. Assessment of Environmental Impact

So far as new development is concerned, the broad powers of planning authorities in development control are a significant means of preventing development which may have an adverse environmental impact. Authorities may take into account the extent to which the proposed development is likely to cause environmental damage: it may be likely to injure precious flora or fauna, for example, or to give rise to undesirable noise levels or the emission of noxious substances. A decision may be taken to refuse permission on these grounds; or an attempt made to limit the damage through conditions or planning agreements. The flexibility of development control and the breadth of the "other material considerations" discretion has meant that planning authorities have been able to increase their scrutiny of environmental impact in response to public pressure, without need for further legislation.

But there is a strong case for arguing that a more formalised procedure ought to be built into development control to encourage special weight in decision making to be attached to environmental damage. The model most commonly cited is that of the United States' National Environmental Policy Act of 1969. The Act established a Council for Environmental Quality to be appointed by the President, with a general supervisory and monitoring role; and it placed an obligation on all agencies of Federal Government to include in every recommendation or report on proposals for legislation or other major Federal actions "significantly affecting the quality of the human environment," a detailed statement of the environmental impact of the proposed action and possible alternatives. Additionally, many state governments have adopted parallel provisions governing their own major development proposals.

The common procedure adopted requires that an environmental impact statement be prepared prior to the undertaking of potentially environmentally damaging development. Statements must be produced in draft form, and under the Federal Act must be made available to the public for 90 days before action is initiated. Various limitations to the effectiveness of the system are apparent. The Federal Act applies only to Federal agencies, and although the state legislation has extended the principles to state government developments, development by the private sector remains outside the scope of all legislation except where it is federally assisted or licensed. Further, there is no formal approval or rejection procedure; and the consequence is that the task of overseeing compliance with the procedure has fallen to the courts. Members of the public and public interest groups have been able to commence proceedings, and the intensity of the resultant judicial scrutiny has meant that the government development agencies have predictably attempted to produce statements which will be "judge proof" rather than designed to stimulate public discussion. Technical objection and delay flowing from judicial scrutiny have become respectively sought and avoided by objectors and the government developers.[3]

The American experience cannot therefore be easily translated directly into the British context, nor is it likely that the British judiciary would

---

[3] National Environmental Policy Act 1969, s. 2, For a useful study of the Act, see Garner, *Environmental Impact Statements in the U.S. and Britain* (1979).

embrace such a role with enthusiasm. There is also a significant difference between the planning systems of the two countries, and environmental impact assessment in the United States is practically a substitute for, rather than an aid to, a national planning system. But American experience has pointed the way to a method of scientifically structured environmental impact analysis which might readily enough be grafted onto the existing British planning system. A Study commissioned by the Department of the Environment, published in 1976, concluded that for the most part the existing planning system allowed authorities to deal sufficiently rigorously already with planning applications for new development; but that a sufficient number of projects, between 25–50, came up every year of such a large scale and involving such complex environmental impact that a systematic process of analysis using specialist skills was needed.[4] The Study recommended that responsibility in these cases should vest with the county councils for deciding whether an analysis was necessary in respect of any private sector development, and for setting it up.[5] In the case of public sector development the procedure should be kept as flexible as possible, and the initiative should vest with the initiating body though with fullest co-operation with the planning authority.

Although the British Government remained unconvinced by the need to introduce special legislation, the European Community had been working for some years under the Environment Action Programme[6] on a Directive intended to introduce environmental impact analysis in all Member States. The basis of the Community's proposals is the view that a significant disparity between measures presently in force in the various Member States "may create unfavourable competitive trading conditions and thereby directly affect the functioning of the common market;" and the Directive is therefore regarded by the Community as falling within the duty under Article 100 of the EEC Treaty to undertake the "approximation" or harmonisation, of laws of Member States.

A Draft Directive was published by the Commission in 1980,[7] following a lengthy period of consultation during which it had progressed through no fewer than 21 drafts. The Draft Directive proposes environmental impact assessment of two forms. First, there would be a general duty to ensure that before any planning permission is given, projects likely to have "a significant effect on the environment by virtue of their nature, size and/or location" should be made subject to an "appropriate assessment" of those effects.[8] The assessment would be required to take into account the effects of the project on:

"— human beings, fauna and flora;
— soil, water, air, climatic factors;
— material assets, including the cultural heritage, and the landscape;

---

[4] J. Catlow and C.G. Thirlwall, *Environmental Impact Analysis*, D.O.E. 1976.
[5] George Dobry Q.C. had also favoured a system of impact statements for specially significant proposals, and proposed that the burden of preparation should fall upon the applicant: *Final Report* paras. 7.61—7.67.
[6] See further *ante*, p. 66.
[7] European Communities Document No. 7972/80 (published in the Official Journal, No. C. 169/14 (July 9, 1980.) Amendments to that Draft were approved by the European Parliament on February 2, 1982, and published by the Commission as Com. (82) 158 Final.
[8] *Ibid.* Arts. 2 and 3.

— natural resources;
— the ecological balance."

That duty is expressed in such general terms as to be capable of being undertaken within existing legislation, and indeed a number of experiments have already been undertaken in Britain with impact analysis harnessed to normal development control procedures.[9] Even in the case of development whose scale of impact does not call for a detailed analysis, it is true that general environmental assessment is now implicit in the planning system of this country; although doubts remain as to how far the power to require an applicant to supply further information (under article 5 of the General Development Order) entitles a local planning authority to insist on the submission of any formal analysis.

The more controversial proposal of the Draft Directive is one which would require a specific assessment to be carried out by the developer and submitted to the planning authority with the planning application. There are two groups of projects to which such a duty would apply. The first includes a list of industrial and engineering projects, classified by type rather than size.[10] In this case, the duty to prepare an environmental assessment is mandatory, and exemption from the duty is possible only in "exceptional cases unlikely to have any significant effect on the environment," and then only with the consent of the Commission.[11] The second group includes a further list of industrial, manufacturing and engineering projects, and also extends to a number of agricultural projects. The agricultural class includes, amongst other matters, drainage and irrigation schemes and intensive livestock rearing units. In the second group (and in the case of modifications to existing projects included in the first group) the "competent authority" are to have power to establish the criteria and thresholds to determine which projects should be subject to the duty to prepare impact assessments.[12] The criteria and thresholds are to be reported to the Commission, who would have the duty of carrying out regular reviews with a view to ensuring consistency between Member States.

These proposals do have important implications for the present planning system. First, they remove an element of discretion, and they substitute for it a necessarily arbitrary classification system. Although the projects listed in the first group may have a significant impact, it does not necessarily follow simply from the type of the operation involved in each case that it will do so; and many of the individual categories are only vaguely defined. Yet planning authorities would not be permitted to exercise their own judgement as to whether an impact assessment should be made. The arbitrariness is also demonstrated by the requirement that "competent authorities" should set their own criteria and thresholds for projects in the second group.[13]

[9] Including over 25 studies carried out in Scotland, largely in connection with off-shore oil development, and studies for the Belvoir and Park coal fields and various other studies undertaken for reservoir proposals, water extraction and pipelines, and motorway proposals.
[10] Draft Directive, Annex 1.
[11] *Ibid.* Art. 4(1).
[12] *Ibid.* Art. 4(2). The authority are also required to examine other projects likely to have a significant effect on the environment, especially those on environmentally sensitive sites, with a view to requiring an impact assessment to be undertaken: Art. 4(3).
[13] Art. 4(2). The thresholds and criteria established may also indicate that a "simplified form of assessment" should be undertaken rather than the full assessment otherwise required, but the Draft Directive leaves it to the authority to determine what form this might take.

"Threshold" implies a limitation set by reference to some objective measurement, perhaps in terms of size or value of the project. But neither relates directly to the likely environmental impact of the project. This substitution of rules for discretion which the Draft Directive proposes lies at the heart of British objections to it. The Department of the Environment's view is that:

> "We do not consider that it is feasible to prepare in advance a sensible and non-arbitrary list of projects requiring assessment, or to consider a single or absolute set of thresholds and criteria for the whole of Europe."[14]

That objection found favour with the European Communities Committee of the House of Lords in 1981, who suggested instead that more subjective criteria should be employed and that these should include references to the existing planning framework for the area.[15]

The second major implication for present British practice is the inclusion of agricultural projects within the assessment requirements. All agricultural land-use change, together with most "requisite" operational development, is outside the scope of development control, and thus outside the net of environmental assessment. Areas that are environmentally sensitive are instead protected to some extent from damaging agricultural development by protective ownerships and special designations, such as sites of special scientific interest. The requirements of the Draft Directive go well beyond this.

The burden of preparing the assessment would fall on the developer, with the assistance of the competent authority where necessary; and the Draft Directive envisages that it will be a detailed document. The most important parts of the assessment would be those directed to an analysis of the likely significant environmental effects of the project; the measures envisaged to eliminate, reduce or compensate for adverse effects; the relationship between the project and existing land-use plans for the area and, in the case of "significant" environmental effects, an explanation of the reasons for the choice of site and design of the project compared with alternative solutions which might have less adverse effects.[16] The assessment is also required to include a non-technical summary of these matters.

The assessment would then be submitted with the planning application, and the planning authority would undertake consultation with the public and with government agencies on it. In many cases the application would no doubt be called-in for central government decision, and the contents and adequacy of the impact statement would be a factor in deciding whether to exercise the call-in power.

The effect of introducing environmental impact assessment, whether in terms of the Draft Directive or in another form, would be to direct increased attention to protection of the environment in development, and also to require developers to take environmental factors into account at an earlier stage in planning a project. To require the assessment to be undertaken

---

[14] *Eleventh Report from the European Communities Committee* 1980–81, Evidence, p. 133.

[15] *Ibid.* para. 55.

[16] Draft Directive, Art. 6. The detailed data required may be supplied at the outset, or "at the appropriate stages of the planning procedure."

before the application is formally submitted means that it may form part of early project assessment rather than be seen purely as an additional requirement arising in the later stages of project planning. The European Communities Committee of the House of Lords, in endorsing the general principles of the Draft Directive, maintained that a systematic approach to early assessment could avoid rather than create excessive delay, and would not be a high cost to the developer compared with the total cost of the project.[17] But the Government's view, later endorsed by the First Standing Committee on European Documents (of the House of Commons), was that mandatory assessment should be avoided, and that instead its use should be encouraged within the existing statutory framework.[18]

Whatever the final form of the Community's requirements, it is apparent that the use of systematic environmental impact assessment in Britain will grow. It will necessarily involve considerable further development in scientific technique in assessing and measuring impact, and in devising methods of minimising harmful effects of development. And it will add more weight to environmental considerations against economic, technological and social considerations in planning decisions.

B. The Control of Environmental Pollution

1. *The Control of Pollution Act 1974*

The evolution of controls over environmental pollution in Britain, outside the planning system, has been a process of pragmatic response to pressing problems. Different measures have been introduced from time to time on a largely ad hoc basis to deal with problems of noise, water pollution and atmospheric pollution. Although they had a common base in that all were rooted in considerations of public health, the controls developed along quite different lines and were enforced by a variety of different agencies. But the upsurge in environmental consciousness of the late sixties and early seventies led to demands that these separate problems be seen as one of overall environmental control, and the Control of Pollution Act 1974 was introduced as a step towards a more integrated environmental policy.

The Act was based upon a number of reports by expert committees, including the Royal Commission on Environmental Pollution[19] and other committees which had examined problems of the collection, storage and disposal of refuse[20] and solid toxic wastes,[21] sewage disposal,[22] noise[23] and

---

[17] *Op. cit.* para. 84. The British Gas Corporation claimed to the Committee that they had saved around £30m. over 10 years by using environmental assessment, mainly because of time saved on determining planning applications; but they opposed the Draft Directive because of the potential for further delay from a mandatory procedure: para. 102.

[18] Official Report, First Standing Committee of European Community Documents, June 9, 1981. That view is also taken in the Report by the Commission on Energy and the Environment, *Coal and the Environment* (H.M.S.O., 1981), p. 203.

[19] See, *e.g.* the first four Reports by the Royal Commission on Environmental Pollution, Cmnd. 4585 (1971); Cmnd. 4894 (1972); Cmnd. 5054 (1972) and Cmnd. 5780 (1974).

[20] *Report of the Working Party on Refuse Disposal* (H.M.S.O., 1971); and see the Consultation Document, *Waste Disposal. Proposals for a new Framework* D.O.E. (1973).

[21] *Report of the Technical Committee on the Disposal of Solid Toxic Wastes* (H.M.S.O., 1970).

[22] *Report of the Working Party on Sewage Disposal* (H.M.S.O., 1970).

[23] *Neighbourhood Noise* Report by the working Group on the Noise Abatement Act (H.M.S.O., 1971); and see also *Final Report of the Committee on the Problem of Noise*, Cmnd. 2056 (1963).

atmospheric pollution.[24] It drew together and extended a variety of existing pollution controls. But it was by no means comprehensive, and many supplementary controls remain still outside the Act. Further, the Act contained surprisingly little by way of a common basis between the different controls it established. It offered no general uniformity in approach to questions of standards, means of control and procedures for enforcement, nor in its choice of implementing agencies. And so the law relating to pollution control remains piece-meal, with little by way of cohesive concept or procedure to draw its ends together. Although much of the Act came into force within two years of its enactment, Part II which contains a new regime for control over pollution of water has been held back for implementation because of its expenditure implications.

The general pragmatism of approach is further reflected by the reluctance of central government to prescribe detailed and uniform standards in any of the specific areas of pollution control. The setting of standards and their enforcement has been a matter primarily of discretion. Opposition to uniform standards is based on two main grounds. First, that they tend to be set at low levels, which often then become acceptable minima to industrialists, and revising them to higher levels is made more difficult. Secondly, the system is rooted in discretion, and in a pragmatic approach to setting realistic standards on a site-by-site or factory-by-factory basis, in the light of technical advance, economic implications and changing environmental needs. "Realistic" in this context involves an economic test because the cost of meeting improved standards is imposed primarily on the polluter; and standards set for individual firms inevitably reflect a compromise between the goals sought by the pollution agency and the economic ability of the polluter to adjust. As with the planning system, negotiation and advice are important elements in the control relationship. But whereas planning control is largely exerted against new development, the main thrust of pollution control is against established industry; and improvements in standards tend to be measured to a greater extent in terms of the competitiveness and employment implications of the industry concerned.

What follows inevitably from a system of discretionary control based upon persuasion and negotiation is a lack of openness and public involvement, leading to problems of accountability. The work of the Alkali Inspectorate in supervising industrial atmospheric emissions has come in for increasing criticism on this score, and the management of industrial discharges into rivers has also been characterised by secrecy. Little is publicly known of the standards imposed, the reasons for them or the extent to which they are adhered to; and prosecutions for breaches are rare.

2. Waste Disposal

The disposal of waste is governed both by planning legislation and by special site licensing controls under the Control of Pollution Act. Planning control

---

[24] *Information about Industrial Emissions to the Atmosphere.* Report by a Working Party of the Clean Air Council (H.M.S.O. 1973).

is relevant, because over 90 per cent. of waste in Britain is disposed of by landfill, and most of it is untreated waste.[25] Most of the remainder is incinerated, but the residue is also disposed of primarily by landfill. The unit cost of landfill disposal is dramatically lower than any other method of disposal, and it is thus economic to transport waste by road or rail for considerable distances to dispose of it. The planning implications of waste disposal thus spread far beyond the individual sites involved. In the case of mining and quarrying waste, which is produced in far greater quantities than all other waste, there is generally no alternative to returning it to the land, but it is for the most part innocuous and is governed by separate legislation.[26]

The site licensing controls now cover many matters which were formerly dealt with by conditions on planning permissions, and the formal relationship between the two systems is contained in the requirement that no licence may be granted where a site requires planning permission, until permission has been granted.[27] Permission is necessary where the disposal of waste constitutes a material change in the use of the land,[28] and that includes most new tipping sites. But there may be cases where the deposit of waste material forms part of an overall building or engineering operation rather than a use in its own right and will thus be ancillary to the primary development. On agricultural land, there is deemed permission for engineering operations requisite for agricultural purposes, and the deposit of waste materials so as to render a field suitable for cropping, for example, may not therefore require permission.[29]

The concern of planning control is now mainly with matters of amenity and access rather than detailed site management, which falls under the licensing provisions. There is inevitably some overlap, because the way in which disposal is carried out frequently raises amenity issues. But conditions imposed on a site licence are a more flexible means of control than planning conditions because they can be up-dated, usually without compensation liability, and because they impose direct criminal liability and thus avoid the lengthy enforcement procedures prescribed under planning legislation. Development involving the use of land for the deposit of refuse or waste materials and associated operational development is now, (except in Wales),

---

[25] A detailed breakdown of waste disposal practice and cost is contained in *Digest of Environmental Statistics*, D.O.E. (1976), pp. 72–74; and in Waste Management Paper 22, *Local Authority Waste Disposal Statistics 1974/75 to 1977/78*, Appendix 5. Despite increased efforts the proportion of waste reclaimed accounts for less than 1 per cent. of the total in terms of tonnage, and is made up largely of ferrous metals.

[26] Mines and Quarries (Tips) Act 1969; and the Mines and Quarries (Tips) Regulations 1971 (S.I. 1971 No. 1377), Mines and Quarries (Tipping Plans) Rules 1971 (S.I. 1971 No. 1378).

[27] C.O.P.A. 1974, s. 5. The prohibition is against the granting of a licence rather than excluding jurisdiction to entertain an application and the two may therefore be considered together by the authority. A supplementary provision in s. 5(2) which authorised the Secretary of State to make regulations regulating this was repealed by the L.G.P.L.A. 1980, s. 1 and Sched. 2, para. 8.

[28] T.C.P.A. 1971, s. 22(3)(b); and see also *R v. Derbyshire C.C., ex p. North East Derbyshire D.C.* (1979) 77 L.G.R. 389 at 385, *per* Bridge L.J.; *Northavon D.C. v. S.O.S.E.* (1980) 40 P. & C.R. 33.

[29] *Northavon D.C. v. S.O.S.E.* (1980) 40 P. & C.R. 332; and see *ante*, p. 194.

a "county matter,"[30] largely because of the role of county authorities as disposal authorities under the Control of Pollution Act, (except in Wales) with responsibility for site licensing, and also because of their interest as mineral planning authorities in many of the sites to be used for landfill disposal.[31] Landfill is widely used in the restoration of sites following mineral extraction.

The site licensing provisions have been in force since June 14, 1976 and county authorities (as site licensing authorities) have also been under a duty since July 1, 1978 to prepare comprehensive waste disposal plans.[32] The provisions make it an offence for any person to deposit household, industrial or commercial waste (known as "controlled waste"), or knowingly to permit waste to be deposited, on any land unless that land is occupied by the holder of a licence and the deposit is in accordance with the terms of the licence.[33]

The only grounds upon which an application for a site licence may be refused are water pollution and danger to public health.[34] If the water authority objects or disagrees with the conditions proposed by the disposal authority, a licence may be issued only after the matter has been referred by either of them to the Secretary of State and in accordance with his decision.[35] Although the criteria for granting or refusing licences are limited, the power to impose conditions on a licence is broad. The Act specifically authorises conditions relating to kinds and quantities of waste and other operational matters, and also conditions relating to steps to be taken "with a view to facilitating compliance with" any conditions on the relevant planning permission.[36] Planning conditions may therefore be incorporated as site licensing conditions and come under the more direct enforcement provisions of the Act, and authorities have also been advised that where no express planning permission exists they may pursue planning ends through site licences so long as the effect would not be to nullify the benefit of an existing

[30] T.C.P. (Prescription of County Matters) Regulations 1980 (S.I. 1980 No. 2010): the class includes not only operational development and change of use involved in the deposit of material, but also "the erection of any building, plant or machinery designed to be used wholly or mainly for purposes of treating, storing, processing or disposing of refuse or waste materials." The disposal of mineral waste is also a county matter by virtue of L.G.A. 1972, Sched. 16, para. 32 (c). In Wales, district councils are disposal authorities, and the "county matter" designation does not apply.

[31] The "mineral planning authority" designation is made by the Town and Country Planning (Minerals) Act 1981: see further *post*, p. 490.

[32] C.O.P.A. 1974, s. 5. The procedures for plan preparation mirror those governing local planning under the 1971 Act, including broad consultation and publicity requirements; but there is no requirement for plans to be submitted to or approved by the Secretary of State. Advice on the preparation of waste disposal plans was given by Waste Management Paper 3, *Guidelines for the Preparation of a Waste Disposal Plan* (H.M.S.O., 1976).

[33] C.O.P.A. 1974, s. 3. Allowance is made by subs. (4) for four specific defences to prosecution; and a wide range of excepted cases is prescribed by the Control of Pollution (Licensing of Waste Disposal) Regulations 1976 (S.I. 1976 No. 732), reg. 4. It is not necessary for the prosecution to establish that the defendant knowingly permitted the alleged breach of condition in addition to proving that he knowingly permitted the deposit of controlled waste: *Ashcroft* v. *Cambro Waste Products Ltd.* [1981] 3 All E.R. 699.

[34] C.O.P.A. 1974, s. 5(3). These limitations are specifically imposed only in respect of sites with planning permission, and arguably do not apply to established use sites.

[35] *Ibid.* s. 5(4).

[36] *Ibid.* s. 6(1) and (2). Guidance as to the imposition of conditions under this power is contained in Waste Management Paper 4, *The Licensing of Waste Disposal Sites* (H.M.S.O., 1976); and there is a model set of conditions in Table 1 to Chap. 5 of that report.

or deemed planning consent.[37] Site licence conditions are effective only for the life of the licence, and longer term issues such as restoration and aftercare are better dealt with by planning conditions or agreements.

Conditions may be subsequently varied, either on the application of the licence holder or unilaterally by the authority, to any extent which is in their opinion desirable and unlikely to require unreasonable expenditure by the licence holder.[38] There is a right of appeal to the Secretary of State against such a modification, as well as against a refusal or conditional grant of a licence.[39] Where an appeal is lodged against a modification, the modification has effect pending the decision on appeal only where the disposal authority certify that in their opinion it is necessary for the purpose of preventing water pollution or danger to public health.[40] If the Secretary of State then finds that they acted unreasonably in so doing, compensation is payable to the licence holder for loss attributable to the interim prohibition.[41] But otherwise, the modification of conditions does not carry compensation, and the right of appeal is the only check on the economic question raised by the test that modification should not involve "unreasonable expenditure."

The disposal authority are under a further duty to revoke a licence where they believe that modification of its terms would not avoid the water pollution, danger to public health or serious detriment to amenities that continued use of the site would cause.[42] Revocation (and also modification) are thus possible on a ground—serious detriment to amenity—which is not a factor for the authority to take into account in granting the licence; and this machinery provides a back-up to planning control over waste disposal. Revocation is also available as a means of enforcing compliance with conditions,[43] and disposal authorities are under a duty to ensure that conditions are complied with and may themselves carry out emergency works on the land and recover the costs from the licence holder.[44]

A disposal licence is a personal right, and breach of its terms is punishable by prosecution of the licence holder. But there is a limited right of transfer by the holder to any other person, subject to a right of veto on the part of the disposal authority within eight weeks of notification to them of transfer.[45]

New regulations,[46] effective from March 16, 1981, impose special requirements governing the disposal of hazardous wastes, superseding the Deposit of Poisonous Wastes Act 1972. Although the detailed regulation of kinds of waste and methods of disposal will be governed by the site licence, the Regulations impose additional requirements as to the notification of the disposal authority upon the receipt of consignments of hazardous waste and

---

[37] *The Licensing of Waste Disposal Sites*, pp. 11–12. See also D.O.E. Circular 55/76, paras. 43–48.

[38] C.O.P.A. 1974, s. 7. There is a duty to modify a licence for ensuring that the activities to which it relates do not cause water pollution, danger to public health or become seriously detrimental to the amenities of the area: ss. 7(2); 9(1)(a).

[39] C.O.P.A. 1974, s. 10.

[40] *Ibid.* ss. 7 and 10(3).

[41] *Ibid.* s. 10(3).

[42] *Ibid.* s. 7(4).

[43] *Ibid.* s. 9(4).

[44] *Ibid.* s. 9(1), (2) and (3).

[45] *Ibid.* s. 8(1): if the power of veto is exercised the licence ceases to have effect 10 weeks after receipt by the authority of the notification.

[46] Control of Pollution (Special Waste) Regulations 1980 (S.I. 1980 No. 1709).

the keeping of site registers and detailed records. The hazardous wastes within the requirements are defined by the regulations in some detail in terms of their flammability, carcinogenicity, corrosivity and toxicity.[47]

3. Water Pollution

The Control of Pollution Act 1974 also brought together and strengthened a range of controls over water pollution. But implementation of the new provisions has been seriously delayed. It had been expected that they would be brought into force by the end of 1979, but further cut-backs in public expenditure meant that water authorities would have been unable to meet the new demands imposed upon them, and they and the National Water Council urged the Government to defer implemetation again.[48] The majority of provisions contained in Part II of the Act, which relates to water pollution, had still to be brought into force at the time of going to press.

Under existing legislation, control is exercised primarily through the provisions of the Public Health Act 1936, and under the discharge consent procedure of the Rivers (Preventation of Pollution) Act 1951, as extended by the Clean Rivers (Estuaries and Tidal Waters) Act 1960 (which brought new or altered discharges into most estuaries under the controls) and the Rivers (Prevention of Pollution) Act 1961 (which brought under control the pre-1951 discharges for which consent had not been required under the 1951 Act).

(i) Existing legislation

The Public Health Act 1936 regulates the discharge of material into public sewers. Although any person has a right to connect to a public sewer and hence to discharge matter into it,[49] there are two major exceptions. The first is that of dangerous substances. The Act makes it an offence to discharge any matter (including steam or liquid at a temperature exceeding 110 degrees F and petroleum spirit) likely to damage the sewer or the treatment process.[50] Secondly, the discharge of trade effluent is controlled under a consents procedure.[51] Trade effluent may be discharged only after the service of a trade effluent notice on the water authority, and then only in accordance with such conditions as they may prescribe. The authority may prohibit the discharge, or agree to accept it only if treated first by the discharger; or they may accept it untreated. The water authority have power to impose conditions tailored to individual requirements, and there are no national standards; but in practice there is substantial uniformity within authorities, partly because of the wish to achieve equality of treatment and partly because of their lack of resources to operate a more individualised system.[52] The Control of Pollution Act 1974 retains these controls, and has

---

[47] Detailed advice on implementation of the Regulations is contained in Waste Management Paper 23, *Special Wastes* (H.M.S.O., 1981), and D.O.E. Circular 4/81.
[48] See, *e.g. Annual Report of the National Water Council 1978/79*, p. 20.
[49] Public Health Act 1936, s.34.
[50] *Ibid.* s. 27.
[51] Public Health (Drainage of Trade Premises) Act 1937.
[52] For a detailed discussion, see Richardson and Ogus, "The Regulatory Approach to Environmental Control" (1979) 2 *Urban Law and Policy* 337.

strengthened them by extending control to the "prescriptive," pre-1937 discharges to which the 1936 Act did not extend.[53]

Regulation of discharges into rivers under the 1951–61 Acts is by means of a consents procedure. The 1951 Act prohibited the construction of any new or altered outlets for discharge of industrial or agricultural effluents into streams, and the making of new discharges, without the consent of the authority.[54] The authority may refuse consent, or grant it subject to conditions regulating the quality and quantity of discharge permitted. The conditions must be reviewed periodically by the authority,[55] and there is a right of appeal against conditions or refusal of consent to the Secretary of State. Compliance with the standards imposed through conditions generally requires that the discharge be treated by the discharger, and that adequate safeguards are employed against accidental discharges. Performance is monitored by sampling, and contravention of the conditions of discharge is an offence.

But although the regulatory machinery bears a number of resemblances to development control machinery, there is one major distinguishing factor, which is that regulation is not a public operation. And although the controls have had some marked success in improving water quality (and in preventing further deterioration), there has been considerable anxiety that the close relationship between enforcers and dischargers has inhibited the quest for improved standards. The setting of standards and their enforcement has been a matter based more upon bargaining than upon open regulation, and prosecutions for breach of conditions have been rare.

(ii) The Control of Pollution Act

The 1974 Act therefore proposes substantial changes, by requiring water authorities to set up public registers of consents and discharges to rivers, and of tests of related samples.[56] It extends the scope of control to include any discharges of trade or sewage effluent to rivers, streams, the sea and to specified underground waters, and renders unauthorised discharge an offence.[57] Applications for consent are required by the Act to specify the place, nature, quantity and rate of the proposed discharge and its composition and temperature.[58] Unless the authority take the view that the discharge will have no appreciable effect on the water into which it is proposed to be made, they will be obliged to advertise the application, to send copies to the relevant local authorites and government departments and

---

[53] Control of Pollution Act 1974, s. 43 (brought into force from December 12, 1974 by Commencement Order No. 1 (S.I. 1974 No. 2039)). The provisions allow an old consent to be cancelled and a new consent to be granted subject to new conditions. There is a right of appeal to the Secretary of State, governed by the Control of Pollution (Discharges into Sewers) Regulations 1976 (S.I. 1976 No. 958).

[54] Rivers (Prevention of Pollution) Act 1951, ss. 2 and 7.

[55] Rivers (Prevention of Pollution) Act 1961, s. 5, although under s. 42 the Secretary of State may exempt applications from the publicity requirements on the grounds of trade secrecy or public interest, and none of the details may then be entered in the register.

[56] Control of Pollution Act 1974, s. 41. Water authorities were required by s. 7(7) of the 1951 Act to maintain registers of conditions imposed on discharges in their areas, but inspection was open only to persons "interested" in the outlet, land or premises concerned. That test has been narrowly construed, and public access denied.

[57] Control of Pollution Act 1974, s. 32.

[58] *Ibid.* s. 34(1).

to consider any consequent written representations.[59] There is to be a three month decision period, at the end of which (unless a longer period has been agreed) the consent is deemed to be refused.[60] There is also provision for the calling-in of applications by the Secretary of State[61]; and the usual rights of appeal against conditions or refusal of consent to the Secretary of State are preserved.[62]

Public involvement in the new system is enhanced by a requirement that where representations have been received by the water authority in response to the advertisement of an application, they may not give consent without first serving notice on any person who has made representations, and that person may then request the Secretary of State to call-in the application.[63] If notice of that request is served on the authority within 21 days of the service by them of notification to the person making the representations, they are prohibited from proceeding to grant consent until the Secretary of State notifies them that he proposes not to exercise the call-in power. The three month period for their issuing a decision is suspended in the interim.

The Act also makes it possible for prosecutions for contravention to be brought by private individuals, except in the case of certain types of condition which the Secretary of State may prescribe by regulations and where prosecution will be able to be brought only with the consent of the Director of Public Prosecutions or by the water authority which gave the consent.[64] One consequence of the new provisions is that water authorities will become liable themselves for prosecution for non-complying discharges from sewage treatment plant. Discharge consents given for their own discharges are supervised at present by the Secretary of State through a notification procedure,[65] but water authorites are otherwise subject to the Act.[66] A substantial proportion of sewage effluent is still unsatisfactory in terms of the consents under which it is discharged, and a major barrier to water quality improvement in the past has been the lack of funding available' to water authorities to improve their own plant.

The Act lays down no new minimum quality standards, and implementation is still therefore a matter primarily within the discretion of the water authorities. The standard commonly employed in the past has been that recommended by a Royal Commission as long ago as 1912,[67] expressed in terms of biochemical oxygen demand (BOD)(which is a measure of the rate at which the oxygen in the water is used up in the breaking down of organic pollutants) and suspended solids (SS). They proposed a 30:20 effluent

[59] *Ibid.* s. 36(1) and (4).
[60] *Ibid.* s. 34(2).
[61] *Ibid.* s. 35.
[62] *Ibid.* s. 39.
[63] *Ibid.* s. 36(6).
[64] *Ibid.* ss. 31, 36(9). Under the old provisions the consent of the Attorney General was required to a private prosecution: Rivers (Prevention of Pollution) Act 1961, s.11.
[65] Water Authorities (Control of Outlets and Discharges) Regulations 1975 (S.I. 1980 No. 450).
[66] Control of Pollution Act 1974, s. 55; although the Act may be modified in relation to water authorities by regulation, and subs. (2) of s. 55 envisages continuing supervision by the Secretary of State.
[67] Royal Commission on Sewage Disposal (1898–1915), *Eighth Report*, Cmd. 6464 (1912). The Jeger Committee in 1970 *Taken for Granted. Report of the Working Party on Sewage Disposal* (H.M.S.O., 1970), para. 39 thought the recommended standard still a useful minimum standard provided it was adapted to the needs of the particular river.

standard, comprising not more than 30mg/litre of suspended solids and 20mg/litre BOD (that is, it should not take up, at 18.3 degrees C, more than 20 parts per million of dissolved oxygen in 5 days). But the Royal Commission had envisaged that effluent would be diluted with 8 volumes of clean river water with a BOD of 2 mg./litre, and that amount of dilution is not always available today.

In a paper issued in 1978, *River Water Quality: The Next Stage* the National Water Council urged water authorities to start work on an extensive review of existing discharge consents, based not upon the automatic appliction of the Royal Commission standards but upon river quality objectives set by the authority for the short term and long term improvement of river quality. The revision exercise was not necessarily to be one of raising the standards previously imposed, because many had been set as long term targets rather than immediate requirements and the new public right to institute prosecution meant, in the words of the *Review* "if inherited consent conditions were not reviewed this could leave dischargers open to prosecution at random."

The *Review* recommended that authorities should proceed to classify the rivers in their areas according to their existing and potential use, and that quality objectives and discharge consents should be set accordingly. The five levels of classification proposed are:

Class 1A: water of high quality suitable for potable supply abstractions and for all other abstractions; game and high class fisheries and high amenity value.

Class 1B: water of less high quality than class 1A, but usable for substantially the same purposes.

Class 2: waters suitable for potable supply after advanced treatment, supporting reasonably good coarse fisheries and of moderate amenity value.

Class 3: waters which are polluted to an extent that fish are absent or only sporadically present. May be used for low grade industrial abstraction purposes. Considerable potential for further use if cleaned up.

Class 4: waters which are grossly polluted and are likely to cause nuisance.

Class X: insignificant water courses and ditches not usable, where the objective is simply to prevent nuisance developing.

An important instrument in securing improvement in standards over future years will be the conditional consent, and the flexibility built in for future variation. The Act authorises water authorities to impose "reasonable" conditions,[68] and it allows these to be varied subsequently unilaterally, or consent to be revoked, by the authority after an initial stable period to be prescribed by the consent, but not less than two years.[69] Similarly, there must ordinarily be a period of stability before any further modification may be made or any consent revoked.[70] Modification or revocation within the stable period may involve the authority in the payment of compensation.[71]

[68] Control of Pollution Act 1974, s. 34(4).
[69] *Ibid.* ss. 37 and 38.
[70] *Ibid.* s. 38(2).
[71] *Ibid.* s. 38(3) and (4).

The Act builds in a further safeguard against unauthorised pollution by a means which allows authorities to bind an offender through the consent system. Where they believe that a contravention has occurred and further contravention is likely they may serve an instrument on the polluter granting consent, subject to any conditions, for any future discharges specified in the instrument.[72] The procedure offers the authority a more flexible means of using its powers in a remedial and regulatory manner, rather than having to resort to prosecution immediately as a means of bringing contravention under general control.

Causing, or knowingly permitting, the discharge of trade or sewage effluent, and the breach of any terms of a consent, are offences.[73] So, too, are individual acts of pollution: the Act extends beyond "discharges," which signifies a continuing process, to "causing or knowingly permitting" the entry to any streams, controlled waters or specified underground waters, of any poisonous, noxious or polluting matter.[74] Exceptions include instances where the entry falls within the terms of a discharge consent or waste disposal licence, emergency cases where the action was taken in order to avoid danger to the public, and entries following some act or omission in accordance with good agricultural practice.[75]

The water pollution code is not designed to tie in formally with the planning system. It is not a prerequisite for the granting of a discharge consent, for example, that the land use giving rise to the discharge should have planning permission. But the possibility of water pollution is clearly a factor to which planning authorities may have regard in considering an application for new development, and the consultation provisions of the General Development Order[76] require that they seek the views of the water authority in certain specified cases. This allows the water authority to be brought in at an early stage of the design of new development. For the most part the preferable course will be for the planning authority to allow detailed pollution control to be undertaken by the water authority, and rarely if ever would they be justified in using planning conditions to regulate effluent discharge. But there are limited overlapping issues of principle between the two codes. The planning authority would be justified, for example, in refusing permission for new development where sewage treatment facilities were already over-committed in the area: but their objective in so doing is to protect the authority from new demand for sewage treatment capacity rather than to prevent water pollution as such.

---

[72] *Ibid.* s. 34(3).
[73] *Ibid.* s. 34(1). The approach of the courts in interpretation of the closely similar provisions of the earlier Rivers (Prevention of Pollution) Act 1951, s. 2(1), has been to regard the particular wording as giving rise to two separate offences: knowingly permitting pollution, involving a failure to prevent it, accompanied by knowledge; and causing pollution, which involves some positive act, or some chain of operations leading to pollution: *Alphacell Ltd.* v. *Woodward* [1972] A.C. 824, *Price* v. *Cormack* [1975] 1 W.L.R. 988.
[74] Control of Pollution Act 1974, s. 31. Further sanctions exist under Salmon and Freshwater Fisheries Act 1975 against putting any liquid or solid matter into any waters containing fish, to such an extent as to be poisonous or injurious to fish or their spawning grounds, spawn or food; and under the Prevention of Oil Pollution Act 1971.
[75] *Ibid.* s. 31(2). The agricultural practice exemption may be limited by the Secretary of State, upon application by the water authority, in respect of particular sites: s. 51.
[76] General Development Order 1977, art. 15(1)(f).

4. *Atmospheric pollution*

Pollution of the atmosphere was not brought within the Control of Pollution Act, although there are some supplementary provisions there. Legal controls are still to be found mainly in the Alkali, etc. Works Regulation Act 1906[77] (although much of the original has since been repealed), and in the Clean Air Acts of 1956 and 1968. A great deal has been achieved under these provisions: for example, the emission of smoke from industrial processes in the United Kingdom has been reduced by 96 per cent. over the period 1956–73.[78] But there have been problems in developing an integrated approach to control of atmospheric pollution. Responsibility for control is currently split between the national Alkali and Clean Air Inspectorate, (now an agency of the Health and Safety Executive), in respect of works wherein processes registered under the Alkali Act are carried out; and the local authorities in respect of non-registered processes and domestic emissions, although it has been proposed by the Health and Safety Executive that local authority powers should be removed.[79] The Alkali Inspectorate is a small and specialised body, whose approach traditionally has been based upon close relationships with industry, and a preference for persuasion rather than prosecution. They have enjoyed a broad area of autonomy in the past, although there has been greater public criticism in recent years of their approach and their isolation. The local authorities for their part have implemented a broad range of controls, usually through environmental health departments. The controls are designed to regulate the emission of smoke, dust and fumes and they are backed by criminal sanctions.[80] They are strengthened within areas designated by local authorities[81] or the Secretary of State[82] as smoke control areas, where smoke emission from any building and the use of unauthorised fuels are offences.[83]

All these measures clearly impinge upon the planning system, but the split of responsibility has too often been found to cause problems in achieving a

---

[77] As amended by the Alkali etc. Works Orders 1966 (S.I. 1966 No. 1143) and 1971 (S.I. 1971 No. 960); and the Control of Pollution Act 1974. The Act contains a schedule of "registrable" works, and the controls are exercisable against air pollution, defined in terms of "noxious or offensive gases" which include smoke, grit and dust, hydrochloric acid gas, acid forming oxides of nitrogen, fumes containing a wide range of common and trace elements, carbon monoxide and sulphur oxides. The basis of legislative control is that the "best practicable means" are to be used to prevent emissions and to render harmless all that which is emitted: Act of 1906, s.7.

[78] For a statistical breakdown, see *National Survey of Air Pollution 1961–1971* (H.M.S.O., 1972–76).

[79] *Hansard*, H.C.Debs., Vol. 990, cols. 510–511 (August 8, 1980).

[80] The main offences are: emission of dark smoke from chimneys (Clean Air Act 1956, s. 1; Clean Air Act 1968, s. 1); installation of new industrial furnace which is not, so far as practicable, smokeless (Clean Air Act 1956, s. 3); use of certain furnaces without plant for arresting grit and dust (*ibid.*, s.6 and Clean Air Act 1968, ss. 3 and 4) and the emission of grit and dust (Clean Air Act 1968, s.2); and the acquisition and sale of unauthorised fuel in a smoke control area (Clean Air Act 1968, s. 9). There are numerous prescribed exemptions and defences to the offences. A supplementary duty is prescribed by the Health and Safety at Work Act 1974 s. 5 to use the best practicable means to prevent noxious and offensive emissions from prescribed premises, and to render harmless and inoffensive any substances emitted. For details of the local authority role, see D.O.E. Circular 11/81.

[81] Clean Air Act 1956, s. 11.

[82] Clean Air Act 1968, s. 8.

[83] Clean Air Act 1956, s. 11(2); Clean Air Act 1968, s. 9.

close working relationship. The Royal Commission on Environmental Pollution has been critical of the failure of planning authorities to take atmospheric pollution implications into account sufficiently fully in development control, and has pointed to instances where authorities have allowed the building of hospitals, housing and schools too near to polluting industry.[84] And there has not always been close cooperation in the case of applications involving new polluting industry, or extensions to existing factories.

The Royal Commission recommended that long-term pollution policies based on air quality guidelines should be drawn up in consultation with the relevant authorities and departments, as a guide in development control decision making.[85] But their recommendations have not yet been implemented, at least on any national scale; nor is there yet any formal consultation requirement on planning applications involving development of, or adjacent to, polluting industry.[86] Planning authorities are left to their own risk assessment, though supported from internal input from their environmental health departments and on an informal basis from the Alkali Inspectorate.

One particular planning tool commended by the Royal Commission was the establishment of "buffer zones" around polluting industry. This would be a designation designed, like the green belt, to restrict development in the area. Such designation is already possible on an informal basis, provided it is not used simply as a means of rubber-stamped refusal of planning applications in the area.[87] But there are other considerations which would weigh heavily with a planning authority, such as the need not to sterilise land which might be needed for housing, and the possible unfairness of imposing upon adjoining landowners part of what should be either the polluter's costs, or a general, shared, social cost. The alternative would be a requirement that the polluter should himself establish the buffer zone, through ownership or restrictive covenant.

In line with the improved provisions for public information and involvement in decision making on water pollution, the Control of Pollution Act 1974 introduced a scheme for the dissemination of information relating to local levels of atmospheric pollution. Local authorities are authorised to require information from industrialists and others, and to publish the information.[88] The authority may make arrangements for measurements of emissions to be carried out by them or by the occupier of the premises; and they may by notice demand that certain information be supplied to them.[89] They are obliged from time to time to carry out consultations with local

[84] *Fifth Report (Air Pollution Control: An Integrated Approach)* Cmnd. 6371 (1976), Chap. XI.
[85] *Ibid.* paras. 167–178; 338–341.
[86] The Royal Commission found that existing informal arrangements were inadequate, not only between planning authorities and the Alkali Inspectorate, but also between the planning and environmental health departments of the same authorities: *op.cit.*, paras. 345–50.
[87] See, *e.g. Stringer* v. *M.H.L.G.* [1970] 1 W.L.R. 1281 (establishment of buffer protective zone around Jodrell Bank telescope).
[88] Control of Pollution Act 1974, s. 79.
[89] The types of information which may be required are prescribed by the Control of Atmospheric Pollution (Research and Publicity) Regulations 1977 (S.I. 1977 No. 19). By virtue of the Control of Atmospheric Pollution (Exempted Premises) Regulations 1977 (S.I. 1977 No. 18) the reqirements extend to Crown premises except those specifically exempted.

industry and industrial organisations and persons appearing "to be conversant with problems of air pollution"[90] and the Secretary of State has advised[91] that this would best be done through local clean air committees established along the lines recommended by the Report of the Working Party of the Clean Air Council in 1973.[92] The occupier of the premises has a right of appeal against an information notice, on the grounds that public disclosure of the information would prejudice a trade secret or be contrary to the public interest, or that the information could not be provided except at undue expense.[93] Any information obtained by the authority under these provisions is required to be kept in a publicly accessible register.[94]

5. *Noise pollution*

Controls over noise levels have in the past been introduced through a variety of means to serve different purposes. There have been, for example, the measures designed to reduce industrial noise levels in order to protect workers' hearing, measures based upon the statutory nuisance provisions of the Public Health Acts, measures introduced on a broader scale through legislation initially promoted by the Noise Abatement Society and measures aimed at specific types of site and particular types of objects, such as airports and highways, and cars and machinery.

The Control of Pollution Act incorporates and expands upon some of these measures. The provisions are aimed primarily at the abatement and restriction of noise levels, wherever they emanate from, and with special powers to control noise from construction sites,[95] in streets[96] and in designated noise abatement zones.[97] The general provision adopts the Public Health Acts' approach, but substitutes broader powers and a streamlined procedure for those formerly available under the statutory nuisance provisions. It allows an authority to serve a notice on the person responsible or the owner or occupier of the premises where they are satisfied that a noise

[90] Control of Pollution Act 1974, s. 79(8); consultation is required not less than twice in each financial year: subs. (9).
[91] D.O.E. Circular 2/77, para. 4.
[92] *Information About Industrial Emissions to the Atmosphere* (H.M.S.O., 1973).
[93] Appeals are regulated by the Control of Atmospheric Pollution (Appeals) Regulations 1977 (S.I. 1977 No. 17); and the authority are obliged in any event in publishing information to ensure that no information relating to a trade secret is disclosed, except with the consent in writing of a person entitled to disclose it, or of the Secretary of State: Control of Pollution Act 1974, s. 79(5).
[94] Control of Pollution Act 1974, s. 79; Control of Atmospheric Pollution (Research and Publicity) Regulations 1977, reg. 6.
[95] Control of Pollution Act 1974, ss. 60 and 61: these new powers allow local authorities to specify working hours and noise levels and restrict usage of types of plant and machinery on construction sites, which includes buildings, structures and roads. A Code of Practice prepared by the British Standards Institution (B.S. 5228: 1975) has been approved under the Control of Noise (Code of Practice for Construction Sites) Order 1975 (S.I. 1975 No. 2115).
[96] Control of Pollution Act 1974, s. 62: the section restricts the use of loudspeakers in streets.
[97] *Ibid.* s. 63: designation is by way of order, confirmed by the Secretary of State. There is no obligation upon the authority to make any formal inspection of the area before exercising this power: *Morganite Special Carbons Ltd.* v. *S.O.S.E.* (1980) 256 E.G.1105. The authority thereafter are obliged to measure noise levels from premises in the zone and record them in a public register (s. 64); and those levels may not subsequently be exceeded without the authority's written consent (s. 65). The authority may also require the reduction of noise levels (s. 66).

amounting to a nuisance either exists, or is likely to occur or recur.[98] The notice may require the abatement of the nuisance and may include terms restricting or prohibiting its occurrence or reoccurrence. There is a right of appeal to the magistrates' court within 21 days. Alternatively, action may be taken by a private individual, on a complaint to the court that he is, in his capacity as an occupier of premises, aggrieved by noise amounting to a nuisance.[99]

These are remedies which provide a useful means of controlling individual noise nuisances in everyday life, but they are not a complete approach to the noise problem. Reduction in noise levels and amelioration of their effects may also be attempted through noise insulation of buildings and through the segregation of noisy and noise-sensitive land uses. It is in these areas that the planning power is of particular value, because of its preventative potential in connection with new development.

In a comprehensive circular[1] on planning and noise the Department of Environment has suggested that there should be a strong presumption against permitting residential development in areas which are, or are expected to become, subject to excessive noise. In particular, the effects of traffic and road noise are matters which will be taken into account both in the siting of new roads[2] and in the location of noise sensitive development. But where close vicinity is unavoidable, efforts will normally be made through controls over siting and design of buildings, including noise insulation, to minimise the effects of noise.

The planning powers can also be of importance in providing controls over new development likely to give rise to noise pollution, not only in guiding locational choice and in controlling siting and the provision of areas of open space as insulation, but also through conditions restricting levels of noise emission and limiting working hours.[3] The recommended procedure is that applicants should at the outset be required to provide predictions of corrected noise levels on the boundaries of the site, which will be referred to the environmental health department for assessment and advice.[4]

---

[98] *Ibid.* s. 58. There has been a large increase in the number of notices served by local authorities under this section since 1974: for details see *Local Government Trends* C.I.P.F.A. (1980) Table. 6.5. The procedure on appeal to the magistrates' court is governed by the Control of Noise (Appeals) Regulations 1975 (S.I. 1975 No. 2116), Part II. Under reg. 10(2)(*b*) the authority are authorised to insist in certain circumstances that the effect of the notice should not be stayed pending appeal, and they may be awarded an injunction under the inherent powers of the court if the breach continues nonetheless: see *Hammersmith L.B.C.* v. *Magnum Automated Forecourts Ltd.* [1978] 1 All E.R. 401.

[99] *Ibid.* s. 59.

[1] D.O.E. Circular 10/73.

[2] Particularly following the recommendations of the Urban Motorways Committee in their Report on Urban Motorways, *New Roads in Towns* (H.M.S.O. 1972). For a detailed study of noise evaluation see *Report of the Urban Motorways Project Team to the Urban Motorways Committee* (H.M.S.O. 1973), Part II.

[3] It will also be possible upon an application to extend existing premises, for the authority to consider overall noise levels from the premises; they are not necessarily restricted simply to an assessment of the impact of the new development: *Penwith D.C.* v. *S.O.S.E.* (1977) 34 P. & C.R. 269. Intensification of noise from existing development, and noise arising from temporary uses of land such as sports or entertainment, are both problems which the planning system is ineffective to prevent: see further Noise Advisory Council, *Noise in Public Places* (H.M.S.O. 1974), Chap. 4.

[4] D.O.E. Circular 10/73, Appendix 4.

6. Private law

Environmental protection and land use planning have been brought squarely into the public law field over the past half century, but there remain two main private law remedies which are independently exercisable. First, restrictions may be achieved through contract, translatable in the case of adjoining property owners into restrictive covenants enforceable against subsequent land owners. Second, and of greater significance in environmental protection, is the common law action of nuisance. It has enabled individuals to secure through the courts remedies such as damages and injunctions where their enjoyment of their land has been unduly interfered with. A defendant may be liable for such types of emission as smells[5] and noise,[6] and the pollution of rivers and streams.[7]

The provisions of the common law have been supplemented by the introduction by the Public Health Acts[8] of a concept of statutory nuisance, which extends to a variety of things which are prejudicial to health or a nuisance,[9] including the state of any premises, the keeping of animals, accumulations and deposits,[10] and any dust or effluvia caused by any trade, business manufacture or process. The purpose of these provisions is to offer summary remedy. The local authority may require the abatement of the nuisance, failing which an abatement order may be sought through the magistrates' court.[11] Alternatively, any "person aggrieved" by the nuisance may proceed by way of complaint to the court, and the court may make an abatement order or may direct the local authority to abate the nuisance.[12]

The two functions of pollution control by public agency and action by private individuals through the courts are complementary, but their relationship is not necessarily harmonious. This has been the case particularly in respect of pollution by public sector agencies, where stealthy attempts to remove some individual rights of action[13] have been strongly and successfully opposed. With the establishment of the water authorites the conflict of function between sewage disposal and water quality control is perpetuated, and although new provision is made in the legislation for greater public scrutiny of decisions and standards, the discretionary nature of the consents system ensures that the resolution of policy conflicts remains primarily a political matter. The continuance of private law remedies ensures

---

[5] See, e.g. Bainbridge v. Chertsey U.D.C. (1915) 84 L.J. Ch. 626 (sewage farm) and cf. Shoreham-by-Sea U.D.C. v. Dolphin Canadian Proteins Ltd. (1972) 71 L.G.R. 1973 (proceedings by a local authority to restrain a public nuisance); Halsey v. Esso Petroleum Co. Ltd. [1961] 1 W.L.R. 683.

[6] See, e.g. Halsey v. Esso Petroleum Co. Ltd. [1961] 1 W.L.R. 683.

[7] At the suit of a riparian proprietor: Pride of Derby and Derbyshire Angling Association Ltd. v. British Celanese Ltd. [1953] Ch. 149.

[8] Public Health Act 1936, s. 92.

[9] That is, in the common law sense of having harmful effects beyond the boundaries of the particular site: National Coal Board v. Neath B.C. [1976] 2 All E.R. 478; setting aside Betts v. Penge U.D.C. [1942] 2 K.B. 154.

[10] But not inert matter: Coventry C.C. v. Cartwright [1975] 2 All E.R. 99.

[11] Public Health Act 1936, ss. 93–98.

[12] Ibid. s. 99. The courts have been at pains to stress the flexibility which the magistrates have in framing abatement orders, in terms particularly of time limits for compliance: see, e.g. Nottingham D.C. v. Newton [1974] 2 All E.R. 760, and Salford C.C. v. McNally [1975] 2 All E.R. 860.

[13] See further G.W. Newsom, Water Pollution (1975), Chap. 1.

at least that individuals may enforce through the courts observance of some minimal environmental standards, but the phenomenon of environmental interest group suits, now common in the United States of America and some Commonwealth countries, has not yet emerged in Britain.

7. Environment and Safety: Hazardous Uses

Safety has always been an important consideration in development control, but its significance has been heightened in recent years in the context of particularly hazardous land uses. Attention has been focused upon the problem, and upon the role of planning law in offering safeguards, in well-known instances such as the Flixborough explosion,[14] the investigation into safety on Canvey Island,[15] and the Windscale Inquiry.[16] How far the planning system should be employed as a primary mechanism in controlling hazardous land use, and how far it should be supplemented or even substituted by a more rigid code administered by other authorities are issues which are still being worked out. The design and location of new development are important factors in reducing and confining hazards, and the approach in recent years has been to try to feed a safety input into development control based upon informal arrangements with the Factory Inspectorate. Planning authorities have been urged to take into account all safety factors on applications for development involving a major hazard, unless safety aspects were already adequately dealt with under other legislation, and to consult with the Health and Safety Executive, particularly in cases where the proposals involved the storage of large quantities of prescribed chemicals and other materials.[17] The Inspectorate will advise on siting and layout, and may recommend that conditions be attached to any permission in the interests of safety. One such condition which they are anxious to see imposed on all industrial emmissions would prohibit the introduction of any notifiable hazard on the site without specific consent. And there is agreement that the Inspectorate will make a witness available, to answer questions on the advice given, at any public inquiry following refusal of permission or the imposition of conditions.

But the arrangements are informal, and concern has been expressed by the Advisory Committee on Major Hazards at their weakness.[18] The Committee has urged that consultation with the Health and Safety Executive should be mandatory in all cases of applications involving, affecting or affected by, a notifiable installation. The Committee has also sought to tighten control in instances where an authority may not wish to follow the Executive's advice,

[14] *The Flixborough Disaster*, Report of the Court of Inquiry. (H.M.S.O. 1975).
[15] The Report, *Canvey: An Investigation of Potential Hazards from Operations in the Canvey Island/Thurrock Area* (H.M.S.O., 1978) had been sought in a joint request to the Health and Safety Commission from the Secretaries of State for Employment and Environment, following a public inquiry into proposals for the revocation of planning permission granted in 1973 for the construction of an oil refinery on Canvey Island. The Report was supplemented and up-dated in 1981 by *Canvey. A second report* (H.M.S.O., 1981).
[16] See further *post*, p. 453.
[17] D.O.E. Circulars 1/72, 97/74. The assumption in the second circular seemed to be that the arrangements would need to be operative only pending the introduction of comprehensive safety control under the Health and Safety at Work Act 1974, but they have remained in force.
[18] *Advisory Committee on Major Hazards: First Report* (H.M.S.O. 1976), Chap. 5.

by seeking the introduction of a procedure whereby the Executive would be notified of an authority's intention to grant permission and would then be able to urge the Secretary of State to call in the application for decision.[19]

Tighter control generally over installations involving hazardous uses has been sought by the Health and Safety Commission, whereby the operators of installations having significant quantities of hazardous materials would be required to carry out detailed hazard surveys to provide a basis for enforcement action, if necessary, under the Health and Safety at Work Act 1974.[20]

But a major area of unregulated activity remains, which highlights the inadequacy of reliance purely upon existing planning controls to regulate hazardous uses. Once an industry has become established it may introduce new hazardous operations or intensify existing operations, or bring new notifiable material onto the site without breaching planning control. The new activity may not amount to "development" at all; or it may be permitted development under the broad permission conferred by Class VIII of the General Development Order 1977. New plant and machinery may be installed and buildings extended or altered without permission, and subject to limitations expressed in terms only of size or location rather than the purpose to which it is to be put. Continuing control by the planning authority is then possible only through a condition imposed on the permission, or a planning agreement, or through the procedures for discontinuance of use or modification of the planning permission. The notification condition recommended by the Advisory Committee on Major Hazards would aid an authority in maintaining future control, and a more complex scheme might be regulated by a planning agreement, but the other courses carry liability to compensation.

The Advisory Committee's *Second Report*[21] proposed that control through the planning system should therefore be extended, by specifically bringing within the definition of "development" the introduction of a notifiable activity to a site. That would mean that an application for planning permission would be required before that activity could be undertaken, but the broad conceptual structure of the existing definition could not readily be adapted in the way the Committee propose. It would need to be established whether it was to be operational development or deemed to constitute a material change of use, and whether there would be a four year time limit for enforcement. In short, it is not a matter which fits easily into a land-use planning system, and a more specialised licensing system administered by the Health and Safety Executive (upon whose advice the planning authority would in any event be heavily dependent) might be a preferable arrangement. But the Committee were strong in their preference for the matter to be governed by planning controls, because only through that system could the community be given the opportunity of deciding whether they were prepared to accept the introduction of the hazard.[22] An alternative course might be to limit the General Development Order permission so as to

[19] *Ibid.* para. 17.

[20] Health and Safety Executive, *Consultative Document: Hazardous Installation (Notification and Survey) Regulations 1978* (H.M.S.O., 1978). The regulations were prepared in draft form for consultation, but none have yet been formally approved.

[21] *Advisory Committee on Major Hazards: Second Report* (H.M.S.O. 1979), Chap. 4.

[22] *Ibid.* pp. 29–30.

exclude plant or machinery intended to be used for the purposes of a notifiable activity, which the Committee thought a less preferable course. Or a notification and approval condition might be imposed by statute to bring all existing industry in line with the terms now proposed to be imposed on new conditions. But the true weaknesses of the planning system to regulate major hazards become apparent in the case of established hazards, and where intervention is possible only upon the payment of compensation, which, in the case of any industrial development, is liable to be substantial.

Nuclear installations and the reprocessing and disposal of radioactive waste are obvious major hazards, but until the Windscale Inquiry of 1978 issues of safety had been seldom taken into account within the planning framework. The siting of nuclear reactors tended to be dictated by the need to be on a coast so that hot water discharges would not be made into rivers or streams or unsightly cooling towers erected; and by a wish to be well away from major centres of population.[23] The chief planning issues were thus the choice of precise location against a backcloth of coastline preservation policies, protective ownerships, and national park and "area of outstanding natural beauty" designations. Safety fell within the scope of detailed controls under the Radioactive Substances Act 1960 and the Nuclear Installations Act 1965. But the terms of reference of the Windscale Inquiry were far more widely drawn, reflecting the public concern at the general issues of public safety in the proposed reprocessing of nuclear fuel. The questions posed by the Inspector for consideration at the inquiry went to the essential preliminary issues of whether oxide fuel from United Kingdom reactors should be reprocessed in this country at all, and if so whether the reprocessing-plant should be constructed with spare capacity to allow also the reprocessing of foreign fuels.[24]

---

[23] See further the *Sixth Report of the Royal Commission on Environmental Pollution: Nuclear Power and the Environment* Cmnd. 6618 (1976), paras. 293–6, and Health and Safety Executive, *Some Aspects of the Safety of Nuclear Installations in Great Britain* (H.M.S.O., 1977).
[24] *The Windscale Inquiry* (H.M.S.O., 1978).

CHAPTER 11

PLANNING, AMENITY AND CONSERVATION

A. The structure and purpose of the amenity controls

In this chapter there is an examination of the many additional controls which have developed in supplementation of ordinary development control. In some cases they have existed from the earliest days of comprehensive planning control, based on a realisation that in dealing with some specific problems stronger controls would be needed. Examples include the control of outdoor advertising and tree preservation. Other measures have been introduced subsequently to overcome unforeseen weaknesses and to deal with unforeseen problems: the licensing of caravan sites, and the introduction of new controls over mineral workings are examples.

The range of different purposes underlying these various powers helps explain the lack of any uniformity in their design. Some are based squarely upon development control, others are almost self-contained codes and often highly complex. But they all operate within the general planning framework and have a direct impact upon development control.

B. Discontinuance orders

The scheme of planning legislation is that the statutory powers are generally exercisable only against proposed urban change. They do not, in general, authorise any interference with existing land uses. These, provided they have permission or are otherwise authorised as "established," may continue free from control and subject only to observance of any planning conditions. Land use rights may of course be lost as a consequence of the implementation of a subsequent planning permission, and authorities will often seek expressly through planning conditions or agreements when granting a permission to limit or forbid the exercise of existing use rights.

But the only statutory power that otherwise authorises intervention is that conferred by section 51 of the 1971 Act, which allows an authority to order the discontinuance of any use or the imposition of conditions upon its continuance; or to require steps to be taken for the alteration or removal of any works. The power is exercisable whether the use enjoys established user status or has express planning permission; and thus in the latter case is supplementary to the power to revoke or modify a permission, which is exercisable only up to the time a permission is implemented.[1] There are two limbs to the section. The first authorises discontinuance of a "use" of land, but it does not extend to action against operational development. Although the Court of Appeal has been prepared to interpret the power broadly to encompass any form of land use which does not involve any physical alteration in the land,[2] a project of continuing operational development such

[1] *Ante*, p. 270.
[2] *Parkes* v. *S.O.S.E.* [1978] 1 W.L.R. 1308, where the Court upheld an order requiring discontinuance of a use of land for the purpose of storing, sorting and processing of scrap machinery and scrap materials.

as building or engineering is outside its scope. Mining operations are a special case, and new provisions regulating their discontinuance are analysed later in this chapter. Under the second limb an authority may require the removal or alteration of any building or works, and thus although the carrying out of operational development itself may be beyond the scope of the section, its results may be acted against. The two limbs are independent: neither is subordinate to the other.[3]

The circumstances in which the power may be exercised are, on the face of it, very broad. It may be used where it appears to the authority to be "expedient in the interests of the proper planning of their area (including the interests of amenity), regard being had to the development plan and to any other material considerations." And "amenity" is not limited to "present amenity:" the authority are entitled to have regard to possible future detriment.[4] But there are two major safeguards. The order may take effect only once it has been confirmed by the Secretary of State[5]; and compensation is payable in respect of any exercise of the power. Confirmation must be preceded by an inquiry if objection is lodged to the order by any person affected by it and on whom a copy has been served.[6] The Secretary of State may reject, confirm or modify the order, and may include in it, as may the local authority in drafting it,[7] a grant of planning permission for the development of any of the land to which the order relates.[8] The permission may be for the retention of buildings or works on the land or for the continuance of a use instituted on it; and the power is therefore able to be used to except some part of the activity on the land from the general prohibition contained in the order. But it need not be confined to authorising an existing activity, and may relate to "any development of the land." The power may be used therefore, to mitigate the authority's compensation liability by conferring permission for an acceptable yet beneficial use of the land.

The compensation liability is the major practical limitation on the use of the discontinuance power. Compensation is payable under three heads: for any depreciation of value in the claimant's interest in the land, for disturbance in his enjoyment of the land and for the expense of carrying out any works in compliance with the order.[9] It is therefore a comprehensive liability, under which all the costs incurred are imposed upon the local authority. The expense of exercising the power has been a major inhibition in its use in practice, and authorites have tended to limit it to instances of most serious injury to amenity, and to the imposition of limited controls which will restrict the activity to more reasonable hours of working, or to

[3] *Re Lamplugh* (1967) 19 P. & C.R. 125.
[4] *Ibid.* at 134, *per* Roskill J.
[5] In relation to operational land of statutory undertakers confirmation is by the Secretary of State and the "appropriate minister" jointly: T.C.P.A. 1971, s. 228.
[6] T.C.P.A. 1971, s. 51(6). If there is no objection to the making of an order, a more economical procedure would be an agreement under s. 52.
[7] *Ibid.* s. 51(2). The power to impose a conditional planning permission is additional to the power to impose conditions upon the continuance of the use (s. 51(1)), and the effect is not quite the same. Breach of the order imposing conditions is an offence, whilst breach of the conditions of an imposed permission will simply render the offender liable to enforcement action.
[8] *Ibid.* s. 51(5)(*b*)
[9] *Ibid.* s. 170; and see further *post*, p. 662.

part only of a site. The only exception to general compensation liability is in the case of mineral extractions where in certain circumstances a proportion of the cost is imposed on the operator.[10]

Breach of the terms of a discontinuance order is an offence, and liability is direct and not dependent upon the taking of enforcement action. Any person who uses the land for a purpose prohibited by the order, or in breach of conditions imposed upon the continuance of a use of the land, or who causes or permits the land to be so used, is guilty of an offence.[11] It is thus a more direct power than the power to modify or revoke a planning permission, which may need to be backed by enforcement action to be made effective. There is a further power to enforce positive terms contained in the order by the authority entering upon the land, taking the required steps and recovering the cost from the owner.[12] The effect of a confirmed discontinuance order is thus akin to that of an effective enforcement notice, and in a case where there is some doubt as to the lawfulness of a use of land which the authority wish to see discontinued, the two powers may be used in tandem. There is no reason why the discontinuance power should not be used as an alternative to enforcement action, since it is clearly effective against both authorised and unauthorised uses. But its use in the latter case would still render an authority liable to compensate for disturbance and for the carrying out of any required works; although it is doubtful whether compensation would be required for the loss in value of an interest in land which had been enhanced by the carrying out of an unlawful activity.[13]

C. Trees

1. *Introduction*

The importance of trees in town and country landscapes and the need for special legal controls over their preservation has become increasingly apparent in recent years. Changing agricultural practices have led to the loss of many traditional tree features such as hedgerows and woods, and trees have also been lost as a result of Dutch elm disease and the belief shared by many developers that efficiency and hence profitability in site development is dependent upon the land having first been completely cleared.

The lopping or felling of a tree does not constitute "development," unless, perhaps, it could only be done by means of an elaborate engineering

---

[10] See further *post*, p. 496.

[11] T.C.P.A. 1971, s. 108(1). The section is repealed and re-enacted in amended form by the Town and Country Planning (Minerals) Act 1981, s.11, from a date to be appointed. In addition to extending its provisions to the new minerals discontinuance orders under that Act, the amendments introduce a defence to prosecution under the section where the person charged proves that "he took all reasonable measures and exercised all due diligence to avoid commission of the offence by himself or by any person under his control." Reliance on that defence which involves an allegation that the fault lay with another is dependent upon prior notice being given to the prosecution of the details relating to that other person. A confirmed order is registrable as a "planning charge" in the Local Land Charges Register, under the Local Land Charges Rules 1977 (S.I. 1977 No. 985).

[12] T.C.P.A. 1971, s. 108(2); subs (4) of the new s. 108.

[13] Such an element of value is specifically excluded in the case of the compulsory acquisition of an interest in land, under the Land Compensation Act 1961, s. 5, rule 4, but those rules do not extend directly to valuations of depreciation. As to compensation and its assessment generally, see Chap. 15, *post*.

operation. It does not, therefore, require planning permission. But even if it did, the consequences under the normal planning machinery would be inadequate to secure any effective means of preservation; the enforcement notice requirement to remedy the breach is impossible to achieve in full; and the only feasible partial fulfilment, replanting, is a long way short of full remedy. And so provision has been made for a separate code for the protection of trees, under which special controls backed by direct penal sanctions are now extended to trees in conservation areas, and to trees subject to tree preservation orders made by the local planning authority. And a great deal of emphasis has come to be placed upon the importance of ensuring the planting and maintenance of new trees, particularly when new development is undertaken. The most common mechanism is by way of a landscaping condition, which may be imposed upon an outline permission or a full permission, and which typically reserves a discretion to the authority to approve and supervise a suitable landscaping scheme.

2. Tree Preservation Orders

The idea of establishing a system of protection for selected trees and woodlands first emerged in the 1932 Act,[14] but was given more force by the Town and Country Planning (Interim Development) Act 1943,[15] which for the first time conferred general powers which were not confined to local planning schemes, and which provided for penal sanctions. Those provisions were then carried through to the 1947 Act,[16] and have been strengthened by the Civic Amenities Act 1967 and the Town and Country Amenities Act 1974.

The power to make tree preservation orders was formerly exercisable by both county and district authorities, and was subject to supervision by the Secretary of State. The 1980 Act altered this allocation of functions, however, by reducing county involvement and taking away the requirement of Secretary of State's confirmation. A county authority has power to make tree preservation orders now only in connection with the grant of a planning permission, or in respect of land not lying wholly within the area of a single district authority, land in which the county hold an interest or land in a National Park.[17] Tree preservation orders are otherwise a matter entirely for district authorities, unless there has been a reallocation of function by agreement between the two tiers.

A tree preservation order is made by the local planning authority in a prescribed form,[18] in respect of any specified trees, groups of trees or woodlands. That formula is broad, and it was held in *Bullock* v. *Secretary of State for the Environment*[19] to authorise the making of an order in respect of

---

[14] T.C.P.A. 1932, s. 46.

[15] s. 8.

[16] T.C.P.A. 1947, s. 28.

[17] T.C.P.A. 1971, s. 60(1A); inserted by L.G.P.L.A. 1980, Sched. 15, para. 13.

[18] The standard form of order is presented in the Schedule to the Town and Country Planning (Tree Preservation Order) Regulations 1969; and authorities are required to comply with it substantially (reg. 4(1)) and to include a map defining the position of the trees, groups of trees or woodlands to which the order relates. General criteria and extensive guidance for making orders and advice on trees generally is contained in D.O.E. Circular 36/78.

[19] (1980) 40 P. & C.R. 246.

a coppice, notwithstanding that the purpose of a coppice is to provide timber for periodical cutting and that it is therefore a crop whose harvesting may be prevented by the order. The court rejected the submission that preservation was inconsistent with the purpose of a coppice, and accepted that a practical scheme of management could be drawn up under the consents procedure which would satisfy both requirements.

The tree preservation order will prevent the "cutting down, topping, lopping, uprooting, wilful damage, or wilful destruction"[20] of the trees, without the consent of the authority, and their consent may be conditional.[21] The Act contains no definition of "tree," and there has been some difficulty in applying the general prohibition in the case of woodlands orders. Clearly it does not extend to all growth in the woodland, such as scrub or bushes; and Lord Denning has suggested that a distinction ought to be drawn between mature trees and saplings, with only trees having a greater diameter than 7 inches—8 inches being protected under a woodland order.[22] But the suggested distinction is arbitrary, and it was expressly rejected by Phillips J. in the *Bullock* case, where he preferred to let "tree" bear its ordinary meaning and to allow programmes of selective thinning to be undertaken under general consents issued under the preservation order.

An order is made by the authority first in draft, and has no effect until confirmed by them unless it is specifically made as a provisional order with effect from such date as they may specify.[23] This procedure, which would be appropriate in a case where there existed a present threat of felling, allows an order to be made with immediate effect which will continue in force until either it is confirmed in the usual way by the authority, or a period of six months has expired without confirmation. Confirmation was formerly a matter for the Secretary of State unless there were no objections to the making of the order, but the Act of 1980 has conferred the function of confirmation of the order on the local planning authority themselves. Having made the order, they are required to place it on deposit for public inspection, to serve copies on owners and occupiers of land affected by it (and on persons with rights of mineral extraction and tree felling) and to send a copy to the Conservator of Forests and the District Valuer.[24]

There is a right of objection, exercisable within 28 days, and the authority are obliged to take into account any objections and representations duly

---

[20] T.C.P.A. 1971, s. 60(1)(*a*). It is lawful also for the order to prohibit a person from "causing or permitting" the felling or other activity: *R.* v. *Bournemouth J.J.*, *ex parte Bournemouth Corporation* (1970) 68 L.G.R. 261. There are exceptions in Schedule 2 to the Model order in respect of trees subject to forestry dedication orders, cultivated fruit trees in an orchard or garden, where the action is taken by certain public authorities, and where authorised development of the site is imminent. A further exemption exists in the Act (s. 60(6)) in respect of trees which are dying or dead or have bcome dangerous, or the action is necessary to comply with any Act of Parliament or for the prevention or abatement of a nuisance. Direct action by local authorities in respect of dangerous trees is authorised by Local Government (Miscellaneous Provisions) Act 1976, ss. 23 and 24.

[21] By art 4. of the Model order, the authority may impose such conditions as they think fit, including conditions requiring the replacement of any tree by one or more trees on the site or in the immediate vicinity thereof. There is a special enforcement procedure in T.C.P.A. 1971, s. 103 for such conditions.

[22] *Kent C.C.* v. *Batchelor* (1976) 33 P. & C.R. 185 at 189.

[23] T.C.P.A. 1971, s. 61A. The order is given provisional effect by including in it a direction that s. 61 applies to it.

[24] T.C.P. (Tree Preservation Order) Regulations 1969, reg. 5.

made before deciding to confirm the order.[25] But they are inevitably cast in the position of acting as judges in their own cause, and the procedure offers objectors no independent evaluation of the merits of making an order. The opportunity of review is offered through the consents procedure, and by way of appeal to the Secretary of State against a refusal of consent by the local planning authority to the felling or lopping of the trees.[26] But the question at issue in those proceedings is quite different from the initial question of whether protection of the particular trees was justified, and turns instead on the question of whether a case can be made out for the felling or lopping or other action for which consent is sought.

(a) Breach of the order

Breach of an order in wilful cutting down, uprooting, or destruction or through wilful damage by topping or lopping a tree in such a manner as to be likely to destroy it, is an offence punished more severely[27] than other breaches of an order.[28] The offence of wilful destruction is not confined to instances of actual felling. A tree may be regarded as having been destroyed when as a result of some injury inflicted upon it, it ceases to have any further use as "amenity"—as something worth preserving.[29] The offence is one of strict liability.[30] And authorities have succeeded in reinforcing the statutory penalties and remedies by taking action in the High Court for an injunction to restrain threatened or further breaches of an order, even where no prosecution for breach of the order has been instituted.[31] The penalty for breach of the injunction is fine or imprisonment for contempt of court, although because it is a criminal matter the court will wish to be satisfied of the breach beyond reasonable doubt.[32]

---

[25] *Ibid.* reg. 8.

[26] The procedure on appeals against the refusal of consent or conditions imposed, is regulated by the Third Schedule to the Model Order under the 1969 Regulations, and by the Inquiries Procedure Rules (see further Chap. 13, *ante*).

[27] T.C.P.A. 1971, s. 102(1): on summary conviction the offender will be liable to a fine of £1,000 or "twice the sum which appears to the court to be the value of the tree, whichever is greater," and on indictment to a fine, the amount of which is to be determined "having regard to any financial benefit accruing or appearing likely to accrue from the offence."

[28] Other breaches are punishable upon summary conviction by a fine not exceeding £200: T.C.P.A. 1971, s. 102(2).

[29] *Barnet L.B.C.* v. *Eastern Electricity Board* [1973] 1 W.L.R. 430.

[30] *Maidstone B.C.* v. *Mortimer* [1981] J.P.L. 112, where the Divisional Court set aside the acquittal of a tree feller who had been warned of the possibility that an order was in force but continued regardless in reliance on the owner's assurance that consent had been granted. Park J. insisted that "plainly it is of the utmost public importance that such trees should be preserved. The risk to their continued existence in these days of extensive building operations, which encroach further and further into rural areas, is very great. It is not a difficult task for any member of the public wishing to interfere with the shape, size or continued existence of a tree to obtain from the local authority reliable information on the question whether the tree is the subject of a preservation order and, if so, to seek the authority's consent to the operation proposed."

[31] *Barnet L.B.C.* v. *Eastern Electricity Board* [1973] 1 W.L.R. 430. The effect of the Local Government Act 1972, s. 222, has been to authorise local authorities to commence "public interest" proceedings in pursuance of their duty to protect public amenities, without any longer requiring the Attorney-General's fiat: *Kent C.C.* v. *Batchelor (No. 2)* [1978] 3 All E.R. 980.

[32] *Kent C.C.* v. *Batchelor (No. 1)* (1976) 33 P. & C.R. 185, and *cf. Attorney-General* v. *Melville Construction Co. Ltd.* (1968) 20 P. & C.R. 131.

Consent to action which would otherwise be in breach of an order may be granted by the planning authority conditionally or unconditionally, and there is provision for appeal to the Secretary of State against refusal of consent and against any conditions imposed. And compensation is payable to any person suffering loss or damage in consequence of refusal or conditional grant of consent.[33]

(b) Control by the Forestry Commission

There is an overlap between the controls exercised by local planning authorities through tree preservation orders, and the control exercised by the Forestry Commission over the felling of trees, under the Forestry Act 1967. That Act prohibits the felling of any tree without a felling licence granted by the Commission, except in the case of:

(a) the felling of trees with a diameter not exceeding 8 centimetres, or in the case of a coppice or underwood, with a diameter not exceeding 15 centimetres;

(b) the felling of fruit trees or trees standing or growing on land comprised in an orchard, garden, churchyard or public open space;

(c) the topping or lopping of trees or the trimming or laying of hedges.[34]

Other exceptions include trees covered by an approved plan of operations under a Forestry Commission Dedication Scheme[35]; and there is a general permission for up to 30 cubic metres of timber to be felled in any quarter, although not more than 5.5 cubic metres of this may be sold.[36]

The Forestry Act controls were introduced originally to maintain a supply of timber and to build up a strategic reserve of standing timber as part of a national forestry policy, but the concept of a strategic reserve has now gone and the controls are exercised almost wholly in the interests of amenity, landscape and nature conservation. The controls are, however, exercised by the Forestry Commission rather than the local planning authority, except where a tree preservation order is also in force. In that case, the Commissioners may either refer the appliction for a felling licence to the authority for determination or may notify them that they propose to grant a felling licence.[37] If the authority object, the application is to be referred to the Secretary of State for determination. These arrangements supplant the

---

[33] T.C.P.A. 1971, s. 174. Provision is made for claims by the Model order, arts. 9–12; but compensation is excluded in cases where the authority certify when making their decision that it is made in the interests of good forestry, or that the trees (other than woodland trees) have an outstanding or special amenity value.

[34] Forestry Act 1967, s. 9(2).

[35] *Ibid.* s. 14, which requires that the Commissioners shall not in such a case refuse a felling licence unless the Minister certifies that, "by reason of Act of God or other emergency which has taken place or arisen since the approval of the plan, the granting of a felling licence in respect of those trees, or in respect of trees of any class which comprises those trees, would be detrimental to the national interest."

[36] *Ibid.* s. 9(3). The Act also authorises felling for the prevention of danger or nuisance, compliance with statutory obligation, at the instance of an Electricity Board in the case of obstructive or interfering trees and felling immediately required for the purpose of carrying out development authorised by planning permission.

[37] *Ibid.* s. 15(1).

usual consent procedures under the tree preservation order wherever a felling licence is required.[38]

The Forestry Commission announced in a consultative paper in 1980 that they proposed to withdraw from close involvement in felling control.[39] The thinning of trees in woodlands for silvicultural purposes will be exempted from felling licensing, and other administrative changes made. New legislation will be required to implement the changes.

(c) Trees in conservation areas

Special provision for the preservation of trees in conservation areas was introduced in 1974, and it takes the form of an early warning system. Although the effect of the legislation is to extend preservation order control to all trees (although there is a range of excepted acts in conservation areas[40]) liability may be avoided by serving notice of intention on the local planning authority before proceeding to injure the tree.[41] If consent is given, or a six week period expires without a preservation order being made, the work may proceed without liability, provided it is done within two years.[42]

(d) Trees and new development

None of the protective devices discussed above has effect where the destruction or injury of trees is immediately required for the purposes of carrying out development permitted by planning permission on the land.[43] There is thus a need to give special consideration to tree preservation in development control, and the Act imposes an unequivocal duty on authorities to ensure that adequate provision is made through planning conditions and further preservation orders when granting permission for development.[44] The planting of new trees where appropriate is a common requirement as a means of enhancing (or hiding) new development, and is enforceable through conditions. The normal arrangement is to provide for a landscaping scheme to be agreed with the authority, and for there to be a

---

[38] *Ibid.* s. 15(5); Sched. 3. The consequence is that a felling licence is sufficient authorisation also for the purposes of the tree preservation order.

[39] *Private Forestry* Consultative Paper on the Administration of Felling Control and Grant Aid (1980), para. 6. The Government announced in 1982 (*Hansard*, Vol. 18 H.C.Deb. col. *419*, May 27, 1982) that it had decided not to proceed with proposals in the consultative paper (i) to exclude detached woodlands of less than 0.25 ha. from felling licensing, (ii) to remove the restriction on sale of the licence-free quota of timber and (iii) to introduce fees for licence applications.

[40] Including, in addition to those applicable to trees protected by orders, the cutting down, uprooting, topping or lopping of trees on land in the occupation of the authority itself and with its consent, and of trees of diameter (at a point 1.5m above ground level) not exceeding 75mm: see further Town and Country Planning (Tree Preservation Order)(Amendment) and (Trees in Conservation Areas)(Exempted Cases) Regulations 1975, reg. 3.

[41] T.C.P.A. 1971, s. 61A(3).

[42] *Ibid.*

[43] Model Order, Sched. 3; Forestry Act 1967, s. 9(4)(*d*) The Order refers to permission granted or deemed to be granted on an application, and it may be that the exemption is therefore inapplicable to development for which permission is granted by development order or for which no permission is for any other reason required. The Forestry Act, however, includes any permission granted or deemed to be granted.

[44] T.C.P.A. 1971, s. 59.

requirement that trees diseased, damaged, or removed within a year or two of planting should be replaced.[45]

D. Listed Buildings

1. *The Listing Process and its Financial Effects*

Legal controls designed to prevent the destruction of buildings which have some special architectural or historic interest are as old as planning itself. The absence of any general control over the demolition of buildings has meant that a separate selective control has had to be devised. The essence of the scheme is that a ban is imposed against the demolition or alteration, without consent, of those buildings which have been selected for inclusion in a special list maintained by the Department of the Environment. Once a building has been listed the owner is required to seek listed building consent before carrying out any works of demolition, alteration or extension.

It is a straightforward enough system but it operates often in the context of great financial pressures. The redevelopment value of a town centre site may be reduced enormously if consent is not forthcoming for the demolition of a listed building covering part or all of the site, and the financial incentive is great to demolish in breach of the law, or in anticipation of a possible listing; or simply by neglect to allow the building to deteriorate in the knowledge that ultimately demolition will be the only practicable course. These pressures have led to a significant strengthening of the controls in recent years, and to the development of some subsidiary measures.

They are reflected, too, in the highly informal procedures through which buildings are added to the list. There is no preliminary notification to the owner and hence no opportunity for the making of formal representations. Listing is regarded as a purely administrative act, and the justification for the procedure is the prevention of anticipatory demolition.[46] The right to challenge the listing is provided for, in effect, through the procedure for seeking listed building consent. Further, a building may be excluded from the list at any time, and it is open to an owner to make representations to the Secretary of State seeking exclusion. But it is undeniable that these alternatives provide only limited remedy. From the time of listing there operates a general presumption that the building should be preserved, and the burden of displacing the presumption rests with the owner.

In some instances the listing of a building may prove of financial benefit to an owner, enhancing the value of the property to a potential purchaser. But in many cases, particularly where site redevelopment is likely, the converse

---

[45] The landscaping scheme may be made a reserved matter on an outline permission; and there are model conditions relevant to detailed permissions set out in Appendix 4 to D.O.E. Circular 36/78.

[46] In *Amalgamated Investment and Property Co. Ltd.* v. *John Walker & Sons Ltd.* [1977] 1 W.L.R. 164 the Court of Appeal expressed misgivings about the fairness of the procedure, particularly when the civil servant whose responsibility it was to determine what properties should go into the list disclaimed in the witness box any capacity to make a professional judgement. But as between the vendor and purchaser of a building which had been listed two days after its sale for redevelopment the Court held that listing was an inherent and not unforeseeable risk accepted by the purchaser, against whom the sale contract therefore remained enforceable.

is true, and the consequence of listing may be to impose upon an individual owner in the interest of general amenity a heavy economic disadvantage. This rather arbitrary distribution of costs and benefits is by no means unusual in planning, but it has become particularly apparent in this context, especially in the light of the limited public money available to aid owners and as the lists have come to include more recent buildings, whose listing might not have been reasonably foreseeable at the time of their acquisition and whose priority for grant aid is low.

These factors have been recognised and highlighted in the United States of America, where attempts have been made through state and municipal legislation to require the preservation of historic buildings. But they have necessarily been constrained by the Fifth Amendment to the Constitution which forbids the "taking" of property for public use without "just compensation," and under which the courts have had to draw the line between planning costs that should be funded by the state, and those which may be imposed upon private landowners. The provisions have therefore paid closer regard than the British system to the financial consequences of the listing or designation of individual buildings, and have generally attempted to ensure that owners should still be able to achieve a reasonable return on their properties. In a majority ruling in 1978 the United States Supreme Court upheld the constitutionality of New York City's historic building designation scheme, finding that the restriction it imposed upon air space development above the existing building, (the Grand Central Railway Terminal) although operating to the financial disadvantage of the owners, did not do so to the extent necessary to constitute a "taking" of "property" from them.[47] A particular feature of the New York law was that it allowed the transference and exploitation of development rights from the designated site to another nearby site in the company's ownership, which in the circumstances was a valuable benefit: it provided some limited compensation in the form of increased capital value of the other site. No similar provision exists under British legislation, and although comparative costings of rehabilitation and redevelopment are relevant considerations on an application for listed building consent, the issue is primarily whether further use of the building is an economic possibility, rather than whether listing has imposed an unfair cost upon the owner.

But many authorities in Britain have been prepared to accept preservation and conservation as legitimate planning gains in connection with new development, and to negotiate with the developer for a larger commercial element in a redevelopment scheme or a higher plot density ratio than would otherwise be permitted, in return for the developer undertaking to carry out necessary preservation works on a listed building on part of the site, or even (though with less legitimacy) on a different but adjacent site.[48]

2. The Listing Criteria

Two main classifications are employed in listing buildings. Grade I buildings are those of exceptional interest, and only about 1 per cent of all listed

---

[47] *Penn Central Transportation Co.* v. *City of New York* (1978) 438 U.S. 104.
[48] And *cf. Brighton B.C.* v. *S.O.S.E.* [1979] J.P.L. 173 (need for funds to rehabilitate a listed school building a material consideration in determining to grant permission for residential development on unused playing fields belonging to the school.)

buildings appear on this list. Grade II buildings are those of special interest, which warrant every effort being made to preserve them: some particularly important buildings on the list are distinguished as Grade II*.[49] The current criteria[50] for listing provide for the inclusion of:

(i) all buildings built before 1700 which survive in anything like their original condition;
(ii) most buildings built between 1700 and 1840, although selection is necessary;
(iii) buildings of definite quality built between 1840–1914, where the selection is designed to include the principal works of the principal architects;
(iv) a few buildings built between 1914–39.[51]

In choosing buildings, particular attention is paid to:

"Special value within certain types, either for architectural or planning reasons or as illustrating social and economic history (for instance, industrial buildings, railway stations, schools, hospitals, theatres, town halls, markets, exchanges, almshouses prisons, lock-ups, mills).

Technological innovation or virtuosity (for instance, cast iron, prefabrication or the early use of concrete).

Association with well known characters or events.

Group value, especially as examples of town planning (for instance, squares, terraces or model villages)."[52]

The Secretary of State is not confined to considering the merits of a building in isolation: he may have regard to its contribution to a group of buildings, and to any man-made structures or objects fixed to the building or part of the land within the curtilage.[53]

Around 250,000 buildings are currently listed, but it is estimated that perhaps double that number of buildings presently satisfy the listing criteria. Gradual revision of the original lists is being undertaken, but only 8,000

---

[49] Lists compiled before 1970 include a third category, Grade III, of buildings not qualifying for the statutory list but still of some significance. Many of these are being added to the statutory lists in the course of their revision.

[50] The criteria appear in full as Appendix 4 to the comprehensive D.O.E. Circular 23/77, *Historic Buildings and Conservation Areas – Policy and Procedure.*

[51] D.O.E. Circular 12/81 announced that the range of buildings of this era qualifying for listing was to be widened very substantially so as to represent three main building styles (modern, classical and vernacular) and nine categories of building types: (*a*) Churches, chapels and other places of public worship (*b*) Cinemas, theatres, hotels and other places of public entertainment (*c*) Commercial and industrial premises including shops and offices (*d*) Schools, colleges and educational buildings (*e*) Flats (*f*) Houses and housing estates (*g*) Municipal and other public buildings (*h*) Railway stations, airport terminals and other places associated with public transport (*i*) Miscellaneous. In addition, selection is to include the work of the principal architects of the period.

[52] D.O.E. Circular 23/77, Appendix I.

[53] T.C.P.A. 1971, 5. 54(2), confirming *Corthorn Land and Timber Co. Ltd.* v. *M.H.L.G.* (1965) 63 L.G.R. 490 where the Court had refused to quash an order which had extended to fixtures such as wood panelling, portrait panels, carved figures and a staircase. In *Att.-Gen.* v. *Calderdale B.C.* (unreported, 1981) the Divisional Court held that protection extended to other buildings within the curtilage of a listed mill building; but in the absence of any reference to ancillary buildings in the list, that doctrine would stretch protection farther than is contemplated by s. 54.

buildings were added in 1977–78 and complete up-dating may take 20 years or more.[54] This slow rate of progress has led to an increase in the practice of "spot listing," whereby individual properties may be listed as a result of representations made to the Secretary of State, usually prompted by the announcement of plans for development. Over one-third of additions to the lists in 1977–78 were spot listings. But the system is capable of abuse. Listing may be done without any adequate survey of the property, and the policy of spot listing only where there is some real threat to the building usually means that a ban is imposed upon demolition at a late stage in the preparation of plans, when an earlier decision might have influenced a different approach from the beginning. The unsatisfactory nature of these arrangements led to the introduction of a new procedure in the 1980 Act, which allows a developer (or any other person) to seek from the Secretary of State a certificate to the effect that he does not propose to list the building.[55] There must first be an application for planning permission for development involving the alteration, extension or demolition of the building, or a grant of permission (which may be a deemed permission under the General Development Order). The effect of a certificate of non-intention to list is to provide the developer with a five year guarantee against listing, thereby providing a certain basis for the preparation of redevelopment plans. A positive certificate not only precludes listing by the Secretary of State, but it also prevents the local planning authority from serving a building preservation notice. It does not, however, overcome the requirement of consent to demolition for a building located in a conservation area.

The Historic Buildings Council has recently recommended that responsibility for listing Grade II buildings should be conferred on the local authorities, given their increasing involvement in local conservation; with the intended consequence that revision of the lists might be completed as quickly as possible and the need for spot listing overcome.[56] No legislation would be required, as any revisions could still be promulgated by the Secretary of State on the basis of the local authority research.

3. Building Preservation Notices

Local authorities have supplementary power to extend listed building protection provisionally to a building not actually on the list, where it appears to them "that it is of special architectural or historic interest and is in danger of demolition or of alteration in such a way as to affect its character as such."[57] The control operates through the service of building preservation notice on both the owner and occupier of the building (or, in urgent cases,

---

[54] See further *Annual Report of the Historic Buildings Council for England 1977–78* (H.M.S.O., 1979), p. 2.

[55] T.C.P.A. 1971, s. 54A (added by L.G.P.L.A. 1980, Sched. 15, para. 5). Advice on the use of the procedure is contained in D.O.E. Circular 12/81, which asks that applications be made to the Department Urban Conservation and Historic Buildings Division, Room 114, 25 Savile Row, London, W.1. together with a plan showing the position of the building(s) involved, photographs of each elevation and of any notable interior features, details about the approximate date of its construction, the architect (if known) and any available information about the architectural or historic interest of the building(s).

[56] *Annual Report of the Historic Buildings Council for England 1977–78*, p.2.

[57] T.C.P.A. 1971, s. 58.

by fixing it conspicuously to some object on the building),[58] which has immediate effect in extending listed building control to the building for six months, or until either the building is included on the statutory list or the Secretary of State notifies the authority that he does not intend to list it.[59]

But use of this procedure can involve the authority in liability to pay compensation if the building does not become listed before the notice ceases to have effect.[60]

4. Buildings in Conservation Areas

Control of demolition in conservation areas has now also been achieved through a blanket extension of the listed building provisions.[61] There are exceptions, including buildings with a cubic content less than 155 cubic metres, some buildings whose erection would constitute permitted development under the General Development Order, and buildings whose demolition is required by a discontinuance order, section 52 agreement, enforcement notice, Housing Act demolition order or planning condition, or which are within a housing clearance area.[62]

5. Exempted buildings

Buildings owned by the Crown may be listed,[63] and although the consent provisions are not formally binding it has been agreed that the normal Crown development consultation provisions should apply.[64] Ecclesiastical buildings may also be listed, but there is a broad exemption from the requirement to obtain listed building consent in the case of works for the demolition, alteration or extension of such a building "which is for the time being used for ecclesiastical purposes or would be so used but for the works."[65] The exemption does not extend to any building used wholly or mainly as a residence by a minister of religion,[66] nor does it extend to the total demolition of any ecclesiastical building, since there could then be no question of its continued use for ecclesiastical purposes.[67] The exemption is

---

[58] *Ibid.* s. 58(6).

[59] *Ibid.* s. 58(3).

[60] *Ibid.* s. 173: compensation is payable for "any loss or damage directly attributable to the effect of the notice" including any sum payable in respect of a breach of contract through being required to countermand or discontinue any works to the building on account of the notice.

[61] Through the Town and Country Amenities Act 1974 which introduced s. 277A to the Act of 1971. It had formerly been possible under powers conferred by the T.C.P. (Amendment) Act 1972, s. 8, to extend demolition control by order to selected conservation areas. The control extends only to actual demolition, and not to works of alteration or extension: Town and Country Planning (Listed Buildings and Buildings in Conservation Areas) Regulations 1977, reg. 10 and Sched. 3.

[62] The exceptions are prescribed by a Direction made under s. 277A(4), published as para. 71 of D.O.E. Circular 23/77. They are in addition to the listed buildings exemptions discussed below.

[63] T.C.P.A. 1971, s. 266(1)(*c*)

[64] D.O.E. Circular 7/77, paras. 21–23.

[65] T.C.P.A. 1971, s. 56(1)(*a*). The Government have agreed that the ecclesiastical exemption should be reviewed in 1982: *Hansard* H.C. Debs., Vol. 980, col. *155* (March 4, 1980).

[66] T.C.P.A. 1971, s. 56(1).

[67] *Attorney-General, ex. rel. Bedfordshire C.C.* v. *Howard United Reformed Church Trustees, Bedford* [1976] A.C. 363.

not limited to the Church of England, but whether it extends to the buildings of non-Christian sects is an open question.[68] Further exemption in respect of partial or total demolition of a redundant church building is extended, although to the Church of England alone, where the works are in pursuance of a pastoral or redundancy scheme within the meaning of the Pastoral Measure 1968.[69]

Other exempted buildings are scheduled monuments,[70] for which alternative legal controls exist elsewhere.[71]

6. Listed building consent

Consent to the demolition, alteration or extension of a building which is listed or subject to a building preservation order, or to the demolition of a building within a conservation area, may be sought from the local planning authority. For listed building consent for their own buildings, however, local planning authorities are now required to apply to the Secretary of State.[72]

The procedure for obtaining consent resembles closely the procedure for obtaining planning permission. Regulations govern the making of applications,[73] notification of owners,[74] the advertisement of applications,[75] and appeals.[76] An authority may not grant consent in the case of listed buildings without having first notified the Secretary of State,[77] (in the case of London boroughs, via the Greater London Council[78]) of the application and either having had no response within 28 days, or having been notified that the matter would not be called in.[79] In the case of unlisted buildings in conservation areas application for consent could formerly be included in an application for planning permission, but consent was not taken to be granted

---

[68] See, e.g. Phillips v. M.H.L.G. [1965] 1 Q.B. 156 at 162 per Roskill J.; and Attorney-General, ex rel. Bedfordshire C.C. v. Howard United Reformed Church Trustees, Bedford [1976] A.C. 363 at 376, per Lord Cross; but cf. the narrow definition of "ecclesiastical property" adopted for another purpose in the 1971 Act: s. 274(5).

[69] Redundant Churches and other Religious Buildings Act 1969, s.2.

[70] T.C.P.A. 1971, s. 56(1)(b). It is not uncommon for an ancient monument to be listed as a holding measure pending its inclusion in the schedule of monuments.

[71] Now primarily under the Ancient Monuments and Archaeological Areas Act 1979; see further post p. 477.

[72] Town and Country Planning (Listed Buildings and Buildings in Conservation Areas) Regulations 1977, reg. 11; T.C.P. General Regulations 1976, reg. 11.

[73] Ibid. reg. 3. Responsibility rests with district councils (Local Government Act 1972, Sched. 16, para. 25) and the London boroughs.

[74] Ibid. reg. 5.

[75] Ibid. reg. 4: advertisement (including a site notice) is necessary in all cases except where the proposed works will affect only the interior of a Grade II building (not Grade II*).

[76] Ibid. reg. 6.

[77] T.C.P.A. 1971, Sched. 11, para. 5. The 28 day-period may be extended by notice served by the Secretary of State within the period.

[78] T.C.P.A. 1971, Sched. 11, para. 6. Notification is not however required of an application involving works of alteration or extension of a Grade II (unstarred) building, unless a grant has been made or applied for: D.O.E. Circular 23/77, para. 55.

[79] In London the Secretary of State is notified by the G.L.C., who, subject to the calling-in power, have power to authorise or direct the manner in which the borough may determine the application: Sched. 11, para. 6. In the case of unlisted buildings in conservation areas the G.L.C. is notified, and any representations made by them within 21 days must be taken into account by the borough: Sched. 11, para. 6 as modified by the T.C.P. (Listed Buildings and Buildings in Conservation Areas) Regulations 1977, reg. 10 and Sched. 3.

unless the permission specifically provided for it. Similarly, in other cases, consent might be granted by planning permission for the alteration or extension of a listed building, again provided the permission was framed so as to authorise the works expressly. But those provisions were repealed by the 1980 Act, and separate applications and approvals are now required in all cases for planning permission and listed building consent.[80]

Table 16

Listed Building Consent: Secretary of State's Criteria

(a) the importance of the building, both intrinsically and relatively bearing in mind the number of other buildings of special architectural or historic interest in the neighbourhood. In some cases a building may be important because there are only a few of its type in the neighbourhood or because it has a fine interior, while in other cases its importance may be enhanced because it forms part of a group or series. Attention should also be paid to the contribution to the local scene made by a building, particularly if it is in a conservation area; but the absence of such a contribution is not a reason for demolition or alteration;

(b) in assessing the importance of the building, attention should be paid to both its architectural merit and to its historical interest. This includes not only historical associations but also the way the design, plan, materials or location of the building illustrates the character of a past age; or the development of a particular skill, style or technology;

(c) the condition of the building, the cost of repairing and maintaining it in relation to its importance, and whether it has already received or been promised grants from public funds. In estimating cost, however, due regard should be paid to the economic value of the building when repaired and to any saving through not having to provide alternative accommodation in a new building. Old buildings generally suffer from some defects but the effects of these can easily be exaggerated;

(d) the importance of any alternative use for the site, and in particular whether the use of the site for some public purpose would make it possible to enhance the environment and especially other listed buildings in the area; or whether, in a rundown area, a limited redevelopment might bring new life and make the other listed buildings economically viable.

Source: D.O.E. Circular 23/77, para. 63

In considering applications for consent, authorities are required to "have special regard to the desirability of preserving the building or its setting or any features of special architectural or historic interest which it possesses."[81] The Secretary of State has indicated the general criteria which should in his opinion be taken into account, and these are set out in Table 16. In addition, local authorities are warned to be particularly vigilant and to set an example to others in respect of listed buildings owned by themselves.[82] The presumption in favour of preservation has been strengthened by advice contained in the Department's Circular 12/81, which indicates that the Secretary of State:

---

[80] L.G.P.L.A. 1980, Sched. 15, paras. 7 and 26(2).
[81] T.C.P.A. 1971, s. 56(3).
[82] D.O.E. Circular 23/77, para. 65; reinforced by D.O.E. Circular 12/81, para. 3 which urges authorities to make a diligent search for new uses for their buildings and if necessary a new owner, such as a building preservation trust, before seeking consent to demolish.

" . . . will not be prepared to grant listed building consent for the demolition of a listed building unless he is satisfied that every possible effort has been made to continue the present use or to find a suitable alternative use for the building. He would normally expect to see evidence that the freehold of the building had been offered for sale on the open market. There would need to be exceptional circumstances to justify the offer of a lease or the imposition of restrictive covenants which would unreasonably limit the chance of finding a new use for the building."[83]

These are brave words, but the strength of the presumption in favour of preservation of buildings is made necessary by the financial pressures in favour of demolition. Listed building consent applications bring planning authorities directly up against the financial implications of their decisions, not necessarily in the sense of weighing up the profitability of redevelopment (although this may be a factor weighing in favour of a mixed scheme of part rehabilitation and part redevelopment), but of assessing the financial reasonableness of insisting that the building should remain. The questions have to be considered in the light of the very limited government financial assistance available to owners, and against a number of factors whose effect or relationship can be assessed only tenuously: the possible future of the building if consent is refused, for example, or the importance of retaining it weighed against the likely economic impact upon the area of permitting redevelopment. The real objection to granting consent may in fact be an objection to the proposed scheme of redevelopment,[84] with the authority aware that their ability to resist an undesirable proposal is likely to be diminished substantially if listed building consent is granted. But the authority are without power to insist that an appliction for consent be accompanied by an application for planning permission for redevelopment; and even if such power existed there could be no guarantee, save perhaps through a planning agreement, that the particular plans which might influence the decision would be implemented. Once the building is gone, the question of redevelopment raises quite different issues: any scheme may be better than a vacant site.

7. Conditional Consent

Listed building consent may be granted subject to conditions, including conditions in respect of the preservation of particular features of the building, making good any damage after the works are completed, or requiring its reconstruction wholly or in part using original materials so far as possible.[85] Further, there is specific power to impose a condition that the building should not be demolished before a contract for the carrying out of the works of redevelopment of the site has been made, and planning

---

[83] D.O.E. Circular 12/81, para. 3.
[84] The Secretary of State originally took the view that the quality of proposed redevelopment could not be a material consideration, but the question was left open by Phillips J. in *Kent Messenger Ltd.* v. *S.O.S.E.* [1976] J.P.L. 372, who observed that another appeal to the court was pending on that point. The appeal was subsequently withdrawn. In many cases the application will be accompanied by an application for permission for redevelopment, and the two will necessarily be considered together.
[85] T.C.P.A. 1971, s. 56(4A).

permission granted for the redevelopment.[86] Every consent now granted is also subject to a condition limiting its operation to a period of five years from the date of the consent, or such other period as the authority may specify.[87] If the works authorised by the consent are not carried out within the specified period, the consent will lapse and fresh authorisation will be required.[88]

8. Appeals

There is a right of appeal to the Secretary of State against the refusal of listed building consent, or the imposition of any condition (including a time-limit condition) on the grant of consent.[89] An appeal may also be made where the authority have failed to issue any decision within the prescribed eight week period (or such longer period as may have been agreed).[90] Notice of appeal is required to be served within 28 days of the decision or the expiry of the prescribed period, and one of the grounds of appeal is that the building is not of special architectural or historic interest and ought to be removed from the list.[91] The Secretary of State is required to afford the parties an opportunity to be heard should either require it,[92] and the procedure is governed by the Inquiries Procedure Rules.[93] Although there is power for jurisdiction to be transferred to inspectors,[94] it has not been exercised and all listed building consent appeals continue to be determined by the Secretary of State. There is a right of appeal to the High Court against his decision on law, but its validity is otherwise unchallengeable.[95]

9. Demolition or other works without consent

It is an offence to execute without consent any works of demolition on a listed building or a building which is subject to a building preservation notice, or any works for its alteration or extension in any manner which would affect its character as a building of special architectural or historic merit.[96] The offence is not limited to acts which would constitute

---

[86] *Ibid.* s. 56(5).

[87] *Ibid.* s. 56A, added by L.G.P.L.A. 1980, Sched. 15, para. 11. The condition is also extended to past consents, and those granted before January 1, 1978 will expire on November 13, 1983; whilst those granted since January 1, 1978 but before the new provisions came into force on November 13, 1980, will expire on November 13, 1985: s. 56A(3) and (4).

[88] The Act curiously makes no express provision for the expiry of consent, (*cf.* the comparable requirements in respect of planning permission in s. 43(7)) and the condition is simply one requiring the commencement of the works within the specified period. But if the works have not begun within the period, their subsequent execution would be unauthorised and an offence under s. 55, because they would not be in compliance with the consent condition.

[89] T.C.P.A. 1971, Sched. 11, para. 8; as extended to control over demolition of unlisted buildings in conservation areas, by T.C.P. (Listed Buildings and Buildings in Conservation Areas) Regulations 1977, reg.10.

[90] T.C.P.A. 1971, Sched. 11, para. 9.

[91] Except in the case of unlisted buildings in conservation areas: reg. 10 and Sched. 3 to the 1977 Regulations.

[92] T.C.P.A. 1971, Sched. 11, para. 8(4).

[93] See further Chap. 13, *post.*

[94] T.C.P.A. 1971, Sched. 11, para. 8(9).

[95] *Ibid.* ss. 242(3)(*k*); 245; and see further *post*, p. 617.

[96] T.C.P.A. 1971, s. 55(1). By s. 55(2) it is necessary also to notify the Royal Commission on Historical Monuments of any proposal to demolish a listed building, and to allow them reasonable access for at least one month before demolition for the purpose of recording the building, before the demolition is "authorised" for these purposes.

"development" under the Act: alterations to the interior of the building, for example, may affect its special character. And "demolition" need not involve total demolition, since a "building" is defined by the Act as including parts of a building.[97] The unauthorised demolition of a building in a conservation area is also an offence.[98] The penalties for the offences include imprisonment. There is liability to 3 months imprisonment on summary conviction or a fine not exceeding £1,000, or both; and to 12 months imprisonment or an unlimited fine or both on conviction on indictment.[99] In fixing the fine the court is required in particular to have regard to the financial benefit to the offender from commission of the offence.[1] Breach of a condition subject to which consent has been granted is also an offence.[2]

It is a defence to prosecution for the above offences that the works were urgently necessary in the interests of safety or health or for the preservation of the building, and that written notice of the need for the works had been given to the authority as soon as reasonably practicable.[3] That defence is not available in prosecutions brought under section 57 of the Act, however, which makes it an offence to cause "damage" intentionally to a listed building except in accordance with consent.

The criminal sanctions are backed up by a special enforcement system which is separate from, but similar to, the usual enforcement procedures.[4] A listed building enforcement notice may be issued and served in respect of works contravening the Act, specifying the alleged contravention and requiring restoration of the building within a specified period.[5] An appeal may be lodged, and the notice is then suspended pending its final outcome or its withdrawal. Eleven grounds of appeal are prescribed, and these are reproduced in Table 17. The procedures are modelled closely on those regulating enforcement of general planning control, and the amendments made in that context by the Local Government and Planning (Amendment)

---

[97] T.C.P.A. 1971, s. 290(1). and see *R.* v. *North Hertfordshire D.C., ex parte Sullivan* [1981] J.P.L. 752.
[98] T.C.P.A. 1971, s. 55(1) as modified by Town and Country Planning (Listed Buildings and Buildings in Conservation Areas) Regulations 1977, reg. 10 and Sched. 3.
[99] T.C.P.A. 1971, s. 55(5).
[1] *Ibid.*
[2] *Ibid.* s. 55(4).
[3] T.C.P.A. 1971, s. 55(6). The authority should not react to advance notice under this sub-section as if demolition were a fait accompli, but should give consideration to using their powers under ss. 101 or 115 of the 1971 Act so as to preserve the building: *R.* v. *Stroud D.C., ex parte Goodenough* [1982] J.P.L. 246.
[4] *Ibid.* ss. 96–99. The procedures were reformed by the Local Government and Planning (Amendment) Act 1981, which introduced new ss. 96, 97, 97A, 99A and 100. Enforcement procedures are available not only in respect of listed buildings, but also in respect of the demolition of unlisted buildings in conservation areas (though subject to minor amendment by virtue of the T.C.P. (Listed Buildings and Buildings in Conservation Areas) Regulations 1977, reg. 10 and Sched. 3), and to breaches of building preservation notices (by virtue of T.C.P.A. 1971, s. 58(4).)
[5] T.C.P.A. 1971, s. 96(1). Appeals procedure is governed by the T.C.P. (Enforcement Notices and Appeals) Regulations 1981, Part III; and the T.C.P. (Enforcement) (Inquiries Procedure) Rules 1981. The authority may require that the building be restored to its former state, or to the state in which it would have been if the conditions of listed building consent had been complied with; or, if restoration to the former state is not reasonably practicable, they may require works to be carried out to alleviate the effect of the unauthorised works.

Act 1981 have been carried through to the listed building provisions. There is thus now power for the Secretary of State to dismiss an appeal for failure by the appellant to specify the grounds of appeal, or to allow the appeal if the authority fail to comply with the procedural obligations.[6]

Breach of the terms of an effective listed building enforcement notice is an offence, and the authority have supplementary powers to enter the land and carry out the required works in default of the owner and at his expense.[7] The notice remains effective unless and so far as listed building consent is granted for the retention of the works or the discharge of the condition to which it relates.[8]

Table 17

Listed Building Enforcement Notices: Grounds of Appeal

(a) that the building is not of special architectural or historic interest;

(b) that the matters alleged to constitute a contravention of section 55 of this Act do not involve such a contravention;

(c) that the contravention of that section alleged in the notice has not taken place;

(d) that the works were urgently necessary in the interests of safety or health or for the preservation of the building;

(e) that listed building consent ought to be granted for the works, or that any relevant condition of such consent which has been granted ought to be discharged, or different conditions substituted;

(f) that copies of the notice were not served as required by section 96 (3) of this Act;

(g) except in relation to such a requirement as is mentioned in section 96 (1) (b) (ii) or (iii) of this Act, the requirements of the notice exceed what is necessary for restoring the building to its condition before the works were carried out;

(h) that the period specified in the notice as the period within which any step required thereby is to be taken falls short of what should reasonably be allowed;

(i) that the steps required by the notice for the purpose of restoring the character of the building to its former state would not serve that purpose;

(j) that steps required to be taken by virtue of section 96 (1) (b) (ii) of this Act exceed what is necessary to alleviate the effect of the works executed to the building;

(k) that steps required to be taken by virtue of section 96 (1) (b) (iii) of this Act exceed what is necessary to bring the building to the state in which it would have been if the terms and conditions of the listed building consent of had been complied with.

Source: T.C.P.A. 1971, s. 97(1).

10. *Buildings in Disrepair*

The enforcement and prosecution provisions examined above extend only to deliberate acts. They do not provide for the situation where a building has been permitted, deliberately or otherwise, to fall into a state of disrepair. There is no duty upon the owner of a listed building to maintain it in a state

[6] T.C.P.A. 1971, s. 97(5).
[7] *Ibid.* s. 98 and 99.
[8] *Ibid.* s. 99A.

of repair. But there is an assembly of surprisingly complex powers through which local authorities may intervene to forestall dereliction.

The first is by serving an "urgent repairs" notice, in respect of an unoccupied listed building where it appears that works are urgently necessary for its preservation.[9] The purpose is to give the owner at least seven days notice of the authority's intention to execute the necessary works, and they may thereafter recover from him the cost of doing so. The owner may make representations to the Secretary of State that the amount claimed from him is unreasonable, or that the works were unnecessary; and the Secretary of State has indicated that as a precondition of recovery against an owner there should first have been a precise notice specifying the works to be done, and that the cost sought to be recovered should be attributable solely to those specified works.[10] That view has been upheld by the Divisional Court, where it was also accepted that the section did not enable an authority to recover a recurring cost, such as a hire charge for scaffolding used to support a building.[11]

The second procedure is through compulsory purchase. Compulsory purchase is authorised under these powers only where it appears to the Secretary of State that reasonable steps are not being taken for properly preserving a listed building (including buildings subject to a building preservation notice, but not unlisted buildings in conservation areas).[12] An essential preliminary step is the service of a repairs notice more than two months previously, specifying the works considered reasonably necessary for the proper preservation of the building.[13] And within 28 days of the service of a compulsory purchase order the owner may apply to the magistrates' court for an order staying the purchase proceedings on the ground that reasonable steps have been taken for properly preserving the building.[14]

Compensation for compulsory purchase is based upon the normal planning assumptions, but with two important exceptions. In making the assessment it may be assumed that listed building consent would have been granted for any works for the alteration or extension of the building, but not (except so far as might have been permitted for the purpose of any Schedule 8 development) for its demolition.[15] Second, in the case of a listed building which has been deliberately allowed to fall into disrepair for the purpose of justifying its demolition and the development or re-development of the site or any adjoining site, the authority may seek as part of the compulsory purchase order a direction that minimum compensation only should be

---

[9] *Ibid.* s. 101. A notice may be served by the Secretary of State; but the power will be exercised sparingly and only where the building is of exceptional interest or the conservation area of national significance: D.O.E. Circular 23/77, para. 98.

[10] [1978] J.P.L. 637; and see detailed criteria at D.O.E. Circular 23/77, para. 99.

[11] *R.* v. *S.O.S.E., ex parte Hampshire C.C.* [1981] J.P.L. 47.

[12] T.C.P.A. 1971, s. 114. There is broad power under T.C.P.A. 1971, s. 119(2) and (3) to purchase any listed building by agreement, together with contiguous or adjacent land; and, under s. 126, to make appropriate arrangements for the management, use or disposal of listed buildings acquired compulsorily or by agreement.

[13] *Ibid.* s. 115.

[14] *Ibid.* s. 114(6).

[15] *Ibid.* s. 116, as amended by the Town and Country Amenities Act 1974, s. 6. As to 8th Schedule development, see *post,* p. 651.

payable.[16] The effect of such a direction is that the building is valued as having no redevelopment value except in respect of development or works necessary for restoring it to and maintaining it in a proper state of repair.[17] Challenge to such a direction is by way of application to the magistrates' court within 28 days of service of the draft compulsory purchase order in which the direction is included.[18]

The procedures are cumbersome and slow, and significant reforms have been proposed in a Private Member's Bill which was before the House of Lords at the time of going to press.

11. *Finance for Preservation and Conservation*

Preservation and conservation are liable to be expensive tasks, not simply in terms of the opportunity costs imposed by the inability to demolish and redevelop, but also in real terms. The most satisfactory method of financing is normally through putting the building to some beneficial use, sufficiently profitable to render preservation an economic proposition.[19] It may involve the making of a change in use which might not otherwise have been permitted, such as permitting conversion to office use of residential premises; and it may require the waiving of strict planning and building regulations requirements which have been designed with new building in mind.

But finding a new use is not always possible, and the economic recession has made the prospects of conversion more difficult. The Annual Report of the Historic Buildings Council for England for 1979/80 has painted a gloomy picture, pointing out in particular the problems in Northern England where the chances of finding a good alternative use for an historic building have become slim.[20] The Council have urged that there should be a review of the impact of fiscal policy on preservation, and an attempt to design a system of incentives for the task which would encourage private capital to be applied to it at small public sector cost. In the opinion of the Council, tax allowances for the conversion of empty listed buildings would result in a negligible loss of revenue, but would concentrate efforts on important decaying buildings. They have also pointed to the anomaly which arises with value added tax, payable on repairs but not new construction, which distorts the economic choice for developers in favour of demolition rather than preservation.

The alternative to tax incentive, however, is direct grant-aid, and there exist a number of powers and funds administered by a variety of agencies. But the available funds are thinly spread, and tend to be concentrated on the most important buildings. Further grant-aid is directed specifically to conservation areas, and is discussed further below.

---

[16] *Ibid.* s. 117.
[17] *Ibid.* s. 117(4).
[18] *Ibid.* s. 117(5).
[19] See further, *Aspects of Conservation – New Life for Old Buildings* (H.M.S.O. 1971); *A Critical Bibliography of Building Conservation* (Mansell, 1978); *New Uses for Older Buildings in Scotland*, (H.M.S.O. 1981).
[20] *Historic Buildings Council for England Report 1979/80* (H.C. 289)(H.M.S.O., 1981), p.1.

(a) Local authority grants

Local authorities have power to make grants available for preservation of buildings of architectural or historic interest, under the Local Authorities (Historic Buildings) Act 1962.[21] Alternatively, funds may be made available by way of loans at favourable interest rates.[22] Grant-aid (but not loans) may be conditional upon the owner agreeing to give a right of public access to the property at such times and for such a period as the agreement may provide.[23] And grant-aid or loans under these provisions may be tied in with improvement and repair grants under the Housing Act 1974, in the case of works on dwelling houses.

(b) Grants by the Secretary of State

The Secretary of State has power to make grants, under the Historic Buildings and Ancient Monuments Act 1953, but they are restricted to the repair of buildings which either individually or as part of a group are of outstanding historic or architectural interest.[24]

(c) The National Heritage Fund

The National Heritage Act 1980 confers power on the Trustees of the National Heritage Fund to make grants or loans towards the acquisition, maintenance or preservation of any land, building, structure, object or group of objects which in their opinion is of outstanding scenic, historic, aesthetic, architectural or scientific interest.[25]

E. Conservation Areas

The listed building procedure necessarily concentrates primarily upon individual buildings. But their attraction and the impetus for their preservation often stems as much from their setting as from their individual merits. In recognition of the need to adopt a broader approach both to building preservation and to the enhancement of selected urban areas, the "conservation area" designation was introduced in the Civic Amenities Act 1967.[26] The idea was that authorities should designate areas "of special architectural or historic interest the character or appearance of which it is desirable to preserve or enhance." Progress in designation was slow to start with, but by 1980 over 4,800 areas had been declared in England and Wales, a number far in excess of the expectations of the architects of the early legislation.[27] Since 1974 there has been a further duty upon authorities to

---

[21] It is not a pre-requisite that the building should be listed, but it would be rare for funds to be applied to buildings which were not recognised by the Secretary of State as being of special interest.

[22] By virtue of s. 1(2) the authority may grant an interest free loan, and may at any time renounce repayment of capital or interest.

[23] Local Authorities (Historic Buildings) Act 1962, s. 1(3).

[24] S.4. Recovery of aid is possible under s.4A (inserted by the Ancient Monuments and Archaeological Areas Act 1979) if any condition attached to the grant is not complied with.

[25] National Heritage Act 1980, s. 3.

[26] See now T.C.P.A. 1971, s. 277(1).

[27] For details, see the *Annual Report of the Historic Buildings Council for England 1979/80*, p. 10. The Council note that during the first 10 years of the scheme designation was orientated more towards historic towns, but that the emphasis is now shifting to villages.

review their use of the power, and to consider whether any more areas should be designated.[28] Designation is a formal process, to be preceded by consultation between the two tiers of local government when the proposal is made by a county authority[29] (the power being exercisable concurrently)[30]; and to be followed by notice to the Secretary of State,[31] newspaper advertisement and notice in the London Gazette,[32] and by registration as a local land charge.[33]

Some of the consequences of designation have been considered earlier in this chapter, including the tree preservation provisions[34] and control of the demolition of buildings.[35] And there are two positive duties stemming from designation: a duty to pay special attention to the desirability of preserving or enhancing the character or appearance of the area in the exercise of powers under the Act of 1971,[36] and a duty to formulate and publish proposals for preservation and enhancement to be submitted for considera-tion to a public meeting in the area to which they relate.[37] The proposals may be prepared on a purely informal basis, or they may be incorporated into a local plan.

Around 550 conservation areas have been recognised by the Secretary of State as "outstanding," a supplementary designation which formerly was a precondition to grant-aid. That designation is less important since the financial reforms of the 1980 Act, but it is clear that funds will still be concentrated upon the most significant areas. There are two main sources of financial aid for works of repair to buildings in conservation areas.

(a) Town schemes

A town scheme is an arrangement under which a fund is made up annually for the making of grants towards repair costs, from joint contributions by the local authority and the Department of the Environment. The local authority contribution may be split between the two tiers of local government. The arrangement was originally operated on a non-statutory basis under the general powers conferred by the Historic Buildings and Ancient Monuments Act 1953, which tied it to "outstanding" areas, but separate legislative backing now exists in section 10B of the Town and Country Planning (Amendment) Act 1972.[38] But the Department have advised authorities that still there will be required a "high standard of cohesive townscape quality" as well as a need for a comprehensive programme of repairs before a town scheme may be established.[39] The area must first be a conservation area, and it must also be included on a town

---

[28] T.C.P.A. 1971, s. 277(2). Although there was originally power for the Secretary of State to direct that the review be carried out within a specified period, he has declined to make any direction and the power was repealed by the L.G.P.L.A. 1980, Sched. 15, para. 26.

[29] *Ibid.* s. 277(5).

[30] *Ibid.* s. 277(10). The Secretary of State may also designate an area after consultation: s. 277(4).

[31] *Ibid.* s. 277(6).

[32] *Ibid.* s. 277(7).

[33] *Ibid.* s. 277(9).

[34] *Ante*, p. 461.

[35] *Ante*, p. 466.

[36] T.C.P.A. 1971, s. 277(8).

[37] *Ibid.* s. 277B.

[38] Inserted by L.G.P.L.A. 1980, Sched. 15, para. 28.

[39] D.O.E. Circular 12/81, para. 41.

scheme list or shown on a town scheme map, compiled by the Department of the Environment and the local authority after consultation with the Historic Buildings Council.[40] The authority and the Department then enter into a "repair grant agreement" which records the sums of money to be devoted to the scheme over a specified period of years. The purpose of the town scheme is to concentrate money on restoring the character of an historic area, and by underwriting a programme of repairs, to encourage other owners to carry out repairs as property values in the area rise.

(b) Grants by the Secretary of State

The Secretary of State has power to make grants or loans from funds allocated by Parliament in any case where in his opinion "the expenditure in question has made or will make a significant contribution towards preserving or enhancing the character or appearance" of a conservation area or part of an area.[41] Except in cases of urgency, there is a requirement that he consult with the Historic Buildings Council before incurring expenditure.[42] It is again no longer necessary that the conservation area be "outstanding," and aid is now available in respect of any conservation area. But the policy in its administration is to favour a concentration of aid on a small area, such as a terrace, square or a street, rather than that it should be spread across properties scattered throughout the conservation area. Guidelines adopted by the Department indicate that an application should fall into one of the following categories[43]:

(a) It is for works to a building in a conservation area of particular architectural or historic interest, for which the local authority have been invited by the Department to submit a programme of conservation work.

(b) There is a town scheme in operation in the conservation area concerned.

(c) It is for a scheme of conservation work prepared by local authorities, amenity societies, preservation trusts or a group of private owners, for example a scheme for the restoration of buildings in a particular square, terrace, street or village. The individual grants sought could be for relatively small sums provided that they are part of a scheme.

Grants may be made subject to conditions,[44] and the Secretary of State has discretion to recover a grant paid, if the property is sold within a certain time or the terms on which it has been paid have not been complied with.[45]

F. Ancient Monuments and Archaeological Areas

1. *Introduction*

The preservation of ancient monuments is a function primarily of central government, under a system of controls administered by the Secretary of

---

[40] T.C.P. (Amendment) Act 1972, s. 10B(2).
[41] *Ibid.* s. 10(1), as amended by L.G.P.L.A. 1980, Sched. 15, para. 27.
[42] T.C.P. (Amendment) Act 1972, s. 10(4).
[43] D.O.E. Circular 12/81, para. 35.
[44] T.C.P. (Amendment) Act 1972, s. 10(2).
[45] *Ibid.* s. 10A, inserted by the Ancient Monuments and Archaeological Areas Act 1979, s. 48.

State. The controls date back to the Ancient Monuments Protection Act 1882, and were drawn together and strengthened by the Ancient Monuments Consolidation and Amendment Act 1913. That Act, together with the Ancient Monuments Act 1931, has now been repealed and its provisions consolidated in the Ancient Monuments and Archaeological Areas Act 1979. The provisions of Parts I and III of the Act were brought into force in October 1981, and Part II, which deals with the designation of areas or archaeological importance, was brought into force on April 14, 1982.[46]

2. Scheduling of Monuments

The most important control over the preservation of ancient monuments is through the scheduling procedures, akin to the listing of buildings of special historic or architectural interest. The Secretary of State is required to maintain a Schedule of ancient monuments, and may include in it any monument which appears to him to be of national importance.[47] He is advised by the Ancient Monuments Board in exercising this function, and in determining whether to delete or amend entries in the Schedule. Scheduling is a continuing process, and 249 further monuments were scheduled in 1980, including burial grounds, megalithic monuments, camps, ritual ceremonial sites, settlements, Roman and Saxon Remains, ecclesiastical monuments, castles and fortifications and industrial monuments.[48] The main practical distinction between buildings which are designated as monuments and those which are listed under the 1971 Act is that the former generally have no present beneficial use.

The effect of scheduling is to introduce immediate protection from damage. It becomes an offence to carry out, without authorisation, any works resulting in the demolition or destruction of or any damage to the monument, any works of removal, repair, alterations or additions and any flooding or tipping operations on the land.[49] Works are authorised only if they were urgently necessary or they have scheduled monument consent, and are carried out in accordance with the terms of the consent. There is deemed consent for a range of works, granted by the Ancient Monuments (Class Consents) Order 1981,[50] the terms of which are reproduced in Table 18. Other works require specific consent, obtained by way of an application to the Secretary of State.[51] He is obliged before determining the application, to cause a public local inquiry to be held or to afford the applicant, and any

---

[46] S.I. 1981 No. 1300; S.I. 1982 No. 362.

[47] Ancient Monuments and Archaeological Areas Act 1979, s. 1.

[48] *Ancient Monuments Board for England 27th Annual Report 1980* (H.C. 414)(H.M.S.O., 1981).

[49] A.M.A.A.A. 1979, s. 2. The consent procedures are new, and replace a system under which the owner or occupier was required to give three months' notice of intention to carry out works, and the Secretary of State was thereupon empowered to serve an Interim Preservation Notice if the monument was in danger of destruction or damage. The Notice would lapse after 21 months, but in the interim period a preservation order could be placed on the monument, putting it under permanent protection.

[50] S.I. 1981 No. 1302. The consent may be withdrawn by direction in particular cases or classes of case: A.M.A.A.A. 1979, s. 3(3).

[51] The form of application is prescribed by the Ancient Monuments (Applications for Scheduled Monument Consent) Regulations 1981 (S.I. 1301). Applications are required to be accompanied by an ownership or notification certificate: A.M.A.A.A. 1979, Sched. 1, para. 2.

other person to whom it appears to him expedient, an opportunity of appearing before and being heard by a person appointed for the purpose.[52]

Table 18

Ancient Monuments: The General Consent

CLASSES OR DESCRIPTIONS OF WORKS FOR THE EXECUTION OF WHICH CONSENT IS GRANTED BY ARTICLE 2 OF THIS ORDER

Class I Agricultural, horticultural or forestry works, being works of the same kind as works previously executed in the same field or location during the period of five years immediately preceding the coming into operation of this order but not including subsoiling, drainage works, the planting or uprooting of trees, hedges or shrubs, or any other works likely to disturb the soil below the maximum depth affected by normal ploughing.

Class II Works executed more than ten metres below ground level by the National Coal Board, or any person acting pursuant to a licence granted by the said Board under section 36(2) of the Coal Industry Nationalisation Act 1946.

Class III Works executed by the British Waterways Board in relation to land owned or occupied by them, being—
   (a) works of repair or maintenance not involving a material alteration to a monument;
   (b) works which are essential for the purpose of ensuring the functioning of a canal.

Class IV Works for the repair or maintenance of machinery, being works which do not involve a material alteration to a monument.

Class V Works which are essential for the purposes of health or safety.

Source: Ancient Monuments (Class Consents) Order 1981 (S.I. 1302), art. 2 and Schedule.

If scheduled monument consent is refused, or conditions are imposed, there is an entitlement to compensation under provisions which achieve some sharing of cost between owner and the state. It is limited to loss or damage sustained or expenditure incurred as the result of the refusal or conditional grant of consent to carry out works:

(a) which are reasonably necessary for development authorised by express planning permission granted before the scheduling of the monument, though limited to the amount of loss due to the extent that the works could not now be carried out; or

(b) which do not constitute development, or have deemed permission, but not works which would or might result in the total or partial demolition or destruction of the monument unless they are solely agricultural or forestry operations incidental to the use of the site for those purposes; or

(c) which are reasonably necessary for the continuation of the existing use of the monument, though limited in the case of conditional grant of

[52] A.M.A.A.A. 1979, Sched. 1, para. 3(2).

consent to instances where compliance with the conditions would make it impossible to continue the use.[53]

3. *Acquisition of Monuments*

The Secretary of State and any local authority may acquire any ancient monument by agreement or gift.[54] And the Secretary of State has compulsory powers to acquire any ancient monument "for the purpose of securing its preservation."[55] In such a case, compensation is limited, if the monument is scheduled, through a valuation assumption that scheduled monument consent would not be granted for any works "which would or might result in the demolition, destruction or removal of the monument or any part of it."[56] There are further powers to acquire land, or easements and similar rights, in the vicinity of an ancient monument, for purposes of maintenance, control and access.[57]

4. *Guardianship*

The fee simple owner of an ancient monument (which need not be scheduled)[58] or a person having a life interest in it or a leasehold interest exceeding 45 years, may with the consent of the Secretary of State or the local authority, constitute them guardians of the monument.[59] The principal effect of this arrangement is to pass the maintenance burden onto the Secretary of State or the local authority.[60] It was formerly possible for guardianship to be imposed compulsorily, but those provisions have been overtaken by the compulsory purchase powers, and guardianship is now purely a voluntary arrangement. It imposes no acquisition costs on the authority or the Secretary of State, but it confers upon them broad powers in relation to the monument without excluding the true owner.[61]

5. *Management Agreements*

An alternative mechanism for securing preservation is provided by management agreements, which may be entered into between the occupier of a monument and the Secretary of State or local authority.[62] The

---

[53] *Ibid.* s. 7(2), as qualified by subs. (3), (4) and (5). Any compensation paid is recoverable if scheduled monument consent is subsequently granted for the works.
[54] A.M.A.A.A. 1979, s. 11.
[55] *Ibid.* s. 10(1).
[56] *Ibid.* s. 10(4).
[57] *Ibid.* ss. 15 and 16.
[58] An "ancient monument" for the purposes of the Act includes not only scheduled monuments but also "any other monument which in the opinion of the Secretary of State is of public interest by reason of the historic, architectural, traditional, artistic or archaeological interest attaching to it.": A.M.A.A.A. 1979, s. 61(12).
[59] A.M.A.A.A. 1979, s. 12.
[60] By virtue of s. 13(1) of the Act a duty is imposed upon the guardian to maintain the monument, and subs.(2) confers on them "full control and management" of it.
[61] Including, under s. 13, a right of access at all reasonable times, right to do all things necessary for the maintenance, management and control of the monument and power to carry out excavations and even remove the whole or any part for the purposes of preserving it. These powers may be varied by provisions in the guardianship deed.
[62] A.M.A.A.A. 1979, s. 17.

agreement may cover a range of matters relating to the maintenance and preservation of the monument, and it is normally supported by financial provisions. Payment may be made towards the costs of carrying out works provided for under the agreement, or simply as consideration for the restrictions accepted by the occupier under the agreement. Management and control remains with the owner or occupier, and no maintenance obligation is imposed on the Secretary of State or local authority.

6. Archaeological Areas

The 1979 Act introduced a further protective designation in the interests of rescue archaeology, designed to give statutory backing to what has become a common practice in some areas, of permitting the archaeological excavation and investigation of sites prior to the commencement of major development projects. Not all development necessarily destroys buried archaelogical sites, but the large scale redevelopment of city centre sites over the past 30 years has involved deep excavations in order to take the foundations of high buildings, and a great amount of archaeological material has been destroyed completely.

Over the past decade, however, access has often been permitted by developers for archaeological investigation before development, usually on a voluntary basis, and perhaps supported by a condition imposed on the planning permission:

> "Archaeologists and developers in general now appear to understand each other's needs, and local agreements which permit archaeological investigation before development have been produced in respect of many sites. These agreements are flexible, cheap and efficient and often remove any need for central government or local authority intervention."[63]

The new Act confers broader statutory powers which will allow archaeological access as of right prior to development in certain designated areas of archaeological importance; and the provisions extend beyond operations constituting development and thus falling under planning control.

Designation of archaeological areas may be undertaken by either the Secretary of State or a local authority of either tier.[64] The Government propose that it should be limited to a few areas of highest archaeological importance, where it appears unlikely that co-operation from developers to enable archaeological access or excavation would otherwise be forthcoming.[65] The Government have not accepted any liability for devoting further resources to rescue archaeology, and this is a further factor limiting

---

[63] *Areas of Archaeological Importance* D.O.E. Discussion Paper (1981), para. 18.
[64] A.M.A.A.A. 1979, Part II. The procedure for designation is prescribed by Sched. 2, and requires that the order is first made in draft and placed on public deposit for six weeks. In the case of an order made by the Secretary of State, it may then be made in final form, with or without modifications. In the case of an order made by a local authority, it is required to be submitted to the Secretary of State for confirmation, whether or not any objections have been made to it. In neither case does the order come into force before six months from the date of the Secretary of State's decision or confirmation.
[65] *Hansard*, H.C.Deb., Vol. 983, col. 496 (April 14, 1980).

implementation of the new powers. Selective designation means that it is not necessarily the most important areas which will be designated, since the powers will not be used where voluntary arrangements already are working satisfactorily. The Department have suggested also that designation ought not to be necessary for agricultural land, where the occasional threats to important archaeological remains can be met by negotiation or scheduling; nor to mineral bearing land, where a voluntary scheme has been agreed between the Department and the Confederation of British Industry, and nor to urban and sub-urban areas capable of protection through scheduling or negotiation.[66]

The effect of designation of an area is to bring into effect a procedure under which developers are required to give six weeks' notice (an "operations notice") to the local authority of their intention to carry out any:

(a) operations which disturb the ground;
(b) flooding operations (covering the land with water or any other liquid or partially liquid substance); or
(c) tipping operations (tipping soil or spoil or depositing building or other materials or matter, including waste materials or refuse, on any land.)[67]

There is an exemption in the case of operations to which the investigating authority consent, and further exemptions may be made by regulations, which are expected to cover such activities as normal agricultural or horticultural operations, burials and emergency works.[68]

Upon the service of an operations notice by a developer, a specially designated investigating authority[69] have a right of entry for the purpose of investigating the site to determine whether it would be desirable to carry out any archaeological excavations, and to observe any operations carried out there with a view to examining and recording material of archaeological or historical interest.[70] The investigating authority may secure the right to excavate the site, by serving within four weeks of the operations notice, a notice of intention to excavate.[71] The developer is then obliged to allow excavation to be undertaken over the period of four months and two weeks following the initial six week notification period.[72] Alternatively, if the operations specified in the operations notice are to be carried out after the clearance of the site, the period runs from the date of notification by the developer of the clearance of the site.[73] Where there is a gap between those

---

[66] D.O.E. Discussion Paper, op. cit. para. 22.
[67] A.M.A.A.A. 1979, ss. 35(2); 61.
[68] Ibid. s. 37.
[69] The Secretary of State is empowered to appoint as "investigating authority" any person whom he considers to be competent to undertake archaeological investigations (s. 34), and the Discussion Paper indicates that the practice will be to appoint archaeological units, perhaps attached to or part of a local authority or university, or independently constituted: op. cit. para. 11.
[70] A.M.A.A.A. 1979, s. 38(1).
[71] Ibid. s. 38(2). Notice is required to be served on the developer and on the Secretary of State and any council served with the operations notice. The Secretary of State may intervene at any time by way of a direction issued under s. 38(8).
[72] Ibid. s. 38(4)(a).
[73] Ibid. s. 38(4)(b).

two periods, the investigating authority have the right to carry out excavations in the interim but only if they do not thereby obstruct the clearance operations or other operations not within the controls of the Act.[74]

The purpose of the provisions is not to act as a barrier to new development on archaeological sites, but simply as a means of enabling archaeological recording before the opportunity is lost for the further lengthy period of the life of a new building.

G. Control of Advertising

The control of outdoor advertising was of high priority in immediate post-war planning. There had been earlier controls, but they had proved largely ineffective, and members of Parliament feared strongly that the countryside would soon become completely disfigured by billboards and garish signs unless fresh powers were conferred: some, indeed, would have supported a ban on all advertising.[75]

The outcome was a detailed code of considerable complexity. But its application has proved remarkably successful, and its provisions today give rise to little practical difficulty. Many authorities have developed links with representatives of the advertising industry and with major individual advertisers such as the petroleum companies, allowing general agreement to be reached on control policies. Further, local authorities are now among the main landowners of sites suitable for roadside advertising (around 35 to 40 per cent. ownership), and of many town centre sites as a result of their participation in town centre redevelopment.[76]

The scheme of the advertisement regulations is, first, that some advertisements[77] may be displayed without restriction. They include election advertisements (provided they are removed within 14 days of the poll), statutory advertisements and authorised traffic signs.[78] Other advertisements may be displayed without express consent, but their discontinuance may be ordered by the authority.[79] They include advertisements which were being displayed on August 1st, 1948,[80] indoor advertisements,[81]

---

[74] *Ibid.* s. 38(5).
[75] See e.g. the introductory comments of the Rt. Hon. Lewis Silkin M.P. at 432 H.C. Deb., cols. 964–967 (January 29, 1947).
[76] See further the *Report of the Monopolies and Mergers Commission into Outdoor Advertising* (H.M.S.O. 1981), paras. 2.20–2.22.
[77] "Advertisement" is broadly defined as meaning "any word, letter, model, sign, placard, board, notice, device or representation, whether illuminated or not, in the nature of, and employed wholly or partly for the purposes of advertisement, announcement or direction . . . and . . . includes any hoarding or similar structure used, or adapted for use, for the display of advertisements. . . . :" Town and Country Planning (Control of Advertisements) Regulations 1969, reg. 2(1); T.C.P.A. 1971, s. 290(1).
[78] Town and Country Planning (Control of Advertisements) Regulations 1969, reg. 9.
[79] *Ibid.* reg. 16: a discontinuance notice may require the discontinuance of the display of an advertisement other than one within reg. 9 or subject to a current express consent. There is a right of appeal. In the case of an advertisement displayed on August 1, 1948, compensation is payable for exercise of the power: T.C.P.A. 1971, s. 176.
[80] *Ibid.* reg. 11. Alteration of the advertisement is lawful, provided it is not "substantial," and neither a change in the method nor a change in the product advertised necessarily is substantial: *Mills & Allen Ltd.* v. *Glasgow D.C.* [1980] J.P.L. 409.
[81] *Ibid.* reg. 12.

advertisements displayed by the local planning authority themselves,[82] advertisements still on display following the expiry of an express consent,[83] and a wide range of advertisements falling within "the specified classes."[84] These include certain business, temporary and miscellaneous advertisements and there are detailed conditions governing size and location. The Secretary of State has power to restrict their display in specified areas by special direction.[85] Display of all advertisements is subject to standard conditions requiring that the land be kept in a clean and tidy condition, that the structure of the advertisement be kept safe and that where removal is required, it should be carried out to the reasonable satisfaction of the planning authority.[86]

The display of other advertisements requires the express consent of the district planning authority, but the Act and Regulations are explicit that only two criteria are relevant in granting or refusing it: considerations of amenity and of public safety.[87] An authority may not under these powers censor an advertisement that it finds misleading or offensive, or otherwise undesirable. Consent is normally granted for no longer than five years,[88] and is subject to the standard conditions[89] together with any other the authority may think fit to impose.[90] There is provision for appeal to the Secretary of State.[91]

More detailed control is possible in an "area of special control," which may be designated by an order prepared by the planning authority and approved by the Secretary of State.[92] The designation may be used in respect of rural areas, or other areas appearing to require special protection on grounds of amenity.[93] Much of the open countryside has already been designated and it is intended to bring most of it within special control.[94] The additional control is also useful in non-rural areas, particularly conservation areas; but some additional justification is sought by the Secretary of State before approval.[95] The effect of designation is that the range of "deemed consent" advertisements is reduced[96]; that the power of the planning authority to grant express consent is restricted,[97] and that existing advertisements which are no longer authorised must be removed.[98]

[82] *Ibid.* reg. 10.
[83] *Ibid.* reg. 13.
[84] *Ibid.* reg. 14.
[85] *Ibid.* reg. 15.
[86] *Ibid.* reg. 7 and Sched. 1.
[87] *Ibid.* reg. 5(1); T.C.P.A. 1971, s. 63(1).
[88] *Ibid.* reg. 20.
[89] *Ibid.* regs. 7, 19(1) and (2), Sched. 1.
[90] *Ibid.* reg. 19.
[91] *Ibid.* reg. 22. Appeal is almost always by way of written representations, and advice on procedure is contained in M.H.L.G. Circular 96/69, para. 24.
[92] *Ibid.* reg. 26; Sched. 2. Designations may be by either tier of planning authority, and are to be reviewed by the authority at least every five years with a view to revocation or modification.
[93] *Ibid.* reg. 26(2).
[94] M.H.L.G. Circular 96/69, paras. 11 and 12.
[95] *Ibid.* para. 11. The Act was, however, amended by the Town and Country Amenities Act 1974 to allow regulations to be made dealing separately with conservation areas, but none have yet been made.
[96] Town and Country Planning (Control of Advertisements) Regulations 1969, reg. 27(1); and there is a further restriction on size of lettering which may be used in "specified classes" advertisements: reg. 14(2)(*a*).
[97] *Ibid.* reg. 27(2).
[98] *Ibid.* reg. 27(4): display for a further 6 month period is authorised, followed by a 2 month period to allow for removal.

Contravention of the Regulations is an offence carrying liability to a fine of £100 on summary conviction, and a further £5 per day for a continuing offence.[99] But breach of a condition is not an offence in respect of any person who is only deemed to be displaying an advertisement, unless he has failed to comply with the condition within 28 days (or such longer period as may be specified) of being served with notice by the planning authority.[1]

H. Wasteland and Derelict Land

The reverence with which planning legislation regards existing and established users is nowhere more clearly reflected than in the limited powers available to authorities to require the abatement of lawful but unsightly land use. The judges have been forthright enough in their approach to interpretation, as witness Harman L.J.'s trenchant dismissal of counsel's arguments in one celebrated case:

> "It is said that the man who is told to abate an eyesore ought to be compensated for it. That seems to me to be a most astonishing doctrine, I must say. I can see no reason why this man, who has for years made the country hideous by his goings-on, should not be made to put his house in order, and no reason at all why he should be paid by the public for doing it."[2]

But the powers are limited, particularly when compared with the abatement powers that occur in public health legislation. Section 65 of the 1971 Act permits an authority to serve an abatement notice on the owner and occupier of land, where it appears to them that "the amenity of any part of their area, or of any adjoining area, is seriously injured by the condition of any garden, vacant site or other open land in their area."[3] The notice will specify the steps required to be taken to abate the injury to amenity, but at any time before it is to take effect (which must be not less than 28 days from service)[4] the person upon whom it has been served may appeal to the magistrates' court.[5] The grounds of appeal are broadly stated. They allow the court to review whether the prescribed criteria for use of the power are satisfied: to consider, for example, whether the injury to amenity is serious, or whether the land is in fact a garden, vacant site or other open land.[6] If they find that this is not the case, the notice may be quashed; and it may also be quashed where the appellant shows that the condition of the land "is attributable to, and such as results in the ordinary course of events from, the carrying-on of

---

[99] *Ibid.* reg. 8(1). The replacement of an offending advertisement after its initial removal following conviction is not a continuing offence, but a fresh offence: *Kensington and Chelsea Royal L.B.C.* v. *Elmton Ltd.* (1978) 246 E.G. 1011.

[1] *Ibid.* reg. 8(2); T.C.P.A. 1971, s. 109. It is a defence under s. 109(3) that the advertisement was displayed without the knowledge or consent of the accused.

[2] *Britt* v. *Buckinghamshire C.C.* [1964] 1 Q.B. 77 at 88.

[3] T.C.P.A. 1971, s. 65(1). The power is exercisable by district authorities and London boroughs.

[4] *Ibid.* s. 65(2).

[5] *Ibid.* s. 105.

[6] *Ibid.* s. 105(1)(*a*) and (*c*). The Court of Appeal in *Stephens* v. C kfield R.D.C. [1964] 2 Q.B. 373 cautiously avoided offering any more precise formulation o. the statutory test, but in fact adopted a narrow interpretation, refusing to accept as "open land" a car breakers' yard which was open to the air and unbuilt upon, but fenced.

operations or use of land which is not in contravention" of planning control.[7] The effect of this provision is that the power is not available against the reasonable consequences of authorised development, although development commenced unlawfully but which is now immune from enforcement action will not be protected. The reference to "the carrying-on of operations" confirms, too, that the "condition" of the land is not limited to "passive condition;" and the power may be used even where its effect might be to force the cessation of a business.[8] Nor is the section confined, as the side-note to it suggests, to "wasteland:" land may be in a condition seriously injurious to amenity without being wasteland, a word which appears nowhere in the section itself.

A notice may be varied by the magistrates so as to correct any immaterial informality, defect or error,[9] and so as to alter, in the appellant's favour, the requirements of the notice and the time permitted for compliance.[10] Where the notice is upheld, or no appeal is lodged within the specified time, its terms become binding. Enforcement then is by prosecution in the magistrates' court, but the power was formerly curiously circumscribed. Not only had the prosecution to establish that any of the steps required by the notice had not been taken, but they had also to establish that the accused had done "anything which has the effect of continuing or aggravating the injury caused by the condition of the land to which the notice relates." The wording suggested that to do nothing at all in response to a section 65 notice was sufficient to avoid penal liability, and this interpretation was upheld in 1980 by the Divisional Court, in *Red House Farms (Thorndon) Ltd.* v. *Mid Suffolk District Council.*[11] New provisions were therefore substituted by the Local Government and Planning (Amendment) Act 1981, which renders it an offence "if any owner or occupier of the land on whom the notice was served fails to take any steps required by the notice within the period specified in it for compliance with it."[12]

There is a supplementary power for the authority itself to enter the land and take the steps required by the notice and to charge the person who caused or permitted the land to be in such a condition.[13] Unlike the position with discontinuance orders, with which there may often be some overlap, the use of abatement orders imposes no compensation liability upon the planning authority.

There is a further set of powers which allow local authorities to take steps to bring neglected land back into use or to improve its appearance. Under section 89 of the National Parks and Access to the Countryside Act 1949 an authority may carry out works at their own expense and with the owner's

---

[7] *Ibid.* s. 105(1)(*b*).
[8] Thus confirming *Britt* v. *Buckinghamshire C.C.* [1964] 1 Q.B. 77 which had been decided under the 1947 Act, and independently of the appeal provisions first introduced by the Caravan Sites and Control of Development Acts 1960, Sched. 3.
[9] T.C.P.A. 1971, s. 105(4).
[10] *Ibid.* s. 107(5). The variation power is not expressly limited to these matters and might conceivably be employable in response to the other three grounds of appeal discussed above. They, however, raise preconditions to the validity of a notice (as is recognised by s. 243(4) and (5)) and if established must therefore result in the notice being quashed.
[11] (1980) 40 P. & C.R. 119.
[12] T.C.P.A. 1971, s. 104, as amended by L.G.P.(A.)A. 1981, Sched., para. 13.
[13] T.C.P.A. 1971, s. 108.

consent on land appearing to them to be derelict, neglected or unsightly.[14] The power is of general application, and is not restricted to land in national parks or in the countryside. Where no consent is forthcoming from the owner, the land may be compulsorily purchased, although the Secretary of State may confirm a compulsory purchase order only where he is satisfied that the land is derelict, or that "by reason of neglect following the abandonment of the previous use of the land, the condition of the land is, and is likely to continue to be, such that it is desirable in the public interest that the land should be acquired . . . for the said purpose."[15]

Finally, there is an extensive system of grant aid administered by central government for the reclamation or improvement of derelict land. The grants are now payable not only to local authorities but to any persons, in respect of land "which is derelict, neglected or unsightly land requiring reclamation or improvement," or land required for connected purposes.[16] The main purpose of the scheme is to tackle areas of widespread industrial dereliction and obsolescence, and in respect of land in development areas and intermediate areas grant is payable at the rate of 100 per cent. Outside those areas, the rate is 50 per cent. of notional loan charges incurred on the expenditure over a 60-year period. At the time of going to press, the Derelict Land Bill, which consolidates and extends the earlier legislation, was before Parliament.

I. Planning Controls over Mineral Working

1. Minerals and Planning Control

A number of reforms in the nature of the control exercised through the planning system over mineral workings have been made by the Town and Country Planning (Minerals) Act 1981. Mineral workings, like other development, have in the past fallen within the general scope of development control under the 1971 Act, although certain of its provisions have been specially modified by the Town and Country Planning (Minerals) Regulations 1971.[17] But mineral working is quite unlike other land uses and development, and the legislation has never adequately accommodated the basic distinctions. Most important is the fact that mineral extraction is, in land development terms, an entirely destructive process. Other land development is undertaken to improve land or increase its profitability; it is the process through which land changes from one state to another. But with mineral working the "development" is an end in itself, to which the earlier and later uses of the land are largely irrelevant. Mineral workings have a progressive, long term and irreversible effect, and they are capable of causing considerable environmental harm.

Development control under planning legislation has proved to be incapable of providing adequate safeguards against the adverse consequences of mineral working, largely because it is designed as a "once and forever"

[14] National Parks and Access to the Countryside Act 1949, s. 89(2) and (3).
[15] Ibid. s. 89(5), as qualified by the Local Authorities (Land) Act 1963, s. 6. Alternatively, the "planning purposes" powers of acquisition under T.C.P.A. 1971, s. 112, may be appropriate.
[16] Local Government Act 1966, s. 9, as amended by L.G.P.L.A. 1980, s. 117(1); Local Employment Act 1972, s. 8, as amended by L.G.P.L.A. 1980, s. 117(2).
[17] S.I. 1971, No. 756.

system of control. With most development carried out under a grant of planning permission, the time span between the grant of permission and the completion of the development is sufficently short for the permission itself to provide a sufficient basis for control. But the far greater time span of mineral working means that planning and environmental standards may change considerably during the life of a permission. This problem has become particularly acute in recent years because of the rudimentary (and, by today's standards, quite inadequate) standards sought by local planning authorities in the early years of comprehensive planning. Extraction is still being undertaken from sites where permission was freely granted in the early post-war years, sometimes subject to no conditions at all. Mineral permissions granted today are detailed and sophisticated by comparison, and impose onerous requirements governing not only the carrying out of the operations but also the restoration of the land once extraction has been completed. So there is a widening gap between the standards required by the older, and by the more recent, permissions; and increasing concern with the breadth of licence enjoyed and the irreversible damage done by many operators with long term permissions.

2. The Stevens Committee and the Verney Committee

The Stevens Committee were appointed in 1972 in response to concern on the part of planning authorities and the public at the phenomenon of largely uncontrollable extraction and despoliation; and equally, the concern felt by the extraction industry at what they believed to be a negative and short-sighted stance by planning authorities. The Committee's remit was to examine the operation of the present planning controls over mineral working and to consider whether the existing provisions needed to be amended or supplemented. Their Report, *Planning Control over Mineral Working*[18] was an exhaustive study of the problems encountered in practice, and it contained over 100 recommendations for reform. Its publication coincided with the publication of the report of the Advisory Committee on Aggregates appointed in 1972 under the chairmanship of Sir Ralph Verney. Their Report, *Aggregates: The Way Ahead*[19] although it overlaps with the *Stevens Report,* deals with the problems of only one sector of the minerals industry. It is an important sector, however, since around two-thirds of the 6,000 acres of land in respect of which permission is granted each year for mineral working is for sand and gravel. Although sand and gravel extraction tends to be short-lived and shallow by comparison with other minerals, it raises similar problems of restoration and after-care. On this problem the Verney Committee were in general agreement with the recommendations of the Stevens Committee, and the main thrust of their own Report was directed towards the need for long term planning for aggregate extraction in an era of sharpening conflict between extraction requirements and environmental damage. The committee forecast that by the early 1990s almost all of the gravel-bearing land in the South East which is not agriculturally valuable or environmentally precious will have been worked out. Although there was

---

[18] Report of the Committee under the Chairmanship of Sir Roger Stevens G.C.M.G., (H.M.S.O., 1976).
[19] H.M.S.O. 1976.

no acceptable alternative in the short term to the releasing of more land for extraction, a longer term solution would be required.

The Stevens Committee's *Report* focused mainly on shortfalls in the planning system. Although they had no wish to see control over mineral working removed from the scheme of the 1971 Act, they urged that a special, separate regime should be established with its own provisions for mineral applications and mineral permissions; and that authorities should have power to regulate existing workings and to require the industry at its own cost to meet new environmental standards. The Government rejected the notion of a special regime, but the statement[20] by the Secretary of State for the Environment on the Report accepted most of the Committee's other recommendations. The Government accepted that those relating to the review of existing permissions were "of first significance," and promised early legislation. Conferring the necessary additional powers to review permissions and to impose further conditions could be expected to be comparatively uncontroversial; the most difficult problem was to be that of devising a formula for the assessment of compensation at a level which would enable authorities to exercise their new powers effectively, yet not penalise operators or lessen substantially the viability of the extraction.

3. *The Package of Reform*

The 1981 Act was the first measure in a programme of four reforms to be carried out in implementing selected recommendations of the Stevens Committee, and its provisions had been foreshadowed in the Local Government, Planning and Land Act 1980 which strengthened the control by county planning authorities over mineral matters by broadening the category of applications over which they had jurisdiction, to the exclusion of district authorities.

The Secretary of State has undertaken[21] that the Act will be followed by:

(1) changes to the General Development Order: the new Act extends the definition of "development" to include the removal of material from mineral waste tips, but it is proposed to amend the Order so as to grant permission in certain circumstances.

(2) revision of the "Green Book:" the Government's memorandum, *The Control of Mineral Working* provides a detailed code of guidance for planning authorities and operators, but it is now substantially out of date. It contains much valuable material on the general effect of the legislation and includes detailed guidance on the use of conditions on minerals permissions. A new edition is to be prepared, and when published will be the principal policy document on the implementation of the Act.

(3) It is proposed also to develop and publish a series of regional guidelines for aggregate minerals production in England and Wales, in line with the recommendation by the Verney Committee that national policies should be formulated for individual minerals. One purpose of the guidelines will be to ensure that national demands for aggregates are met, and that shortfalls in some regions can be met by inter-regional flow arrangements. The *Guidelines* have now been published in D.O.E. Circular 21/82.

[20] Published as the Annex to D.O.E. Circular 58/78.
[21] *Hansard* H.L. Deb., Vol. 416, cols. 497–98 (January 22, 1981).

4. *Mineral Planning Authorities: Powers and Duties*

All the powers conferred by the 1981 Act are exercisable only by mineral planning authorities, which are the county planning authorities[22] and, in London, the Greater London Council (in respect of mineral extraction from sites exceeding two hectares other than in the City) and otherwise the London boroughs.[23] The Act also transfers all enforcement powers to mineral planning authorities in relation to mineral matters, and district authority jurisdiction is excluded.[24]

The Act imposes a general duty on mineral planning authorities to review all mineral sites in their areas.[25] Although the timing of reviews is left to the authorities' discretion, the purpose of the duty is to ensure that authorities will exercise the new powers conferred upon them against existing mineral workings on a systematic basis, rather than ad hoc. Since the duty includes a duty to review operations that have been carried out over the preceding five years, and since five year intervals must in general elapse between the use of the new powers if the special compensation provisions are to be taken advantage of by authorities,[26] it is likely that five years will be the normal frequency of review. Review will in most cases take place in accordance with a rolling programme, rather than as a recurrent event.

The new powers conferred by the Act are directed to the environmental problems of mineral extraction, and in particular, to securing the restoration of sites after extraction has been completed. They are intended to be used not only in the case of new permissions for mineral working, but also in the case of workings which are presently under way and those in respect of which there are outstanding permissions. The principal instruments available to mineral planning authorities under the Act are:

(i) Aftercare conditions. Effective post-extraction restoration of land is dependent upon long term positive care, in order to put the land back to a beneficial use rather than allow it to become derelict and unused. The Act authorises the imposition of aftercare conditions by mineral planning authorities, intended to impose upon operators a five year obligation, after the land has been restored, to carry out a programme to bring the land up to the necessary standard for agricultural, forestry or amenity use. The details are considered further below.

(ii) Time-limiting conditions. Every mineral permission will for the

---

[22] T.C.P.A. 1971, s. 1(2B), inserted by the Town and Country Planning (Minerals) Act 1981, s. 2(1). The arrangements had been foreshadowed by the rearrangement of development control functions in the Local Government, Planning and Land Act 1980, which retained and strengthened the "county matter" jurisdiction in relation to minerals.

[23] T.C.P.A. 1971, Sched. 3, para. 4B, added by T.C.P.(M).A. 1981, s. 2(3); T.C.P. (Local Planning Authorities in Greater London) Regulations 1980, reg. 3(*b*).

[24] L.G.A. 1972, Sched. 16, para. 24, as amended by T.C.P.(M).A. 1981, s. 2(4).

[25] T.C.P.A. 1971, s. 264A, inserted by T.C.P.(M.)A. 1981, s. 3.

[26] See further, *post* p. 497.

future be limited to a 60-year life, and that limitation is extended to existing permissions from the date of the Act coming into force.[27]

(iii) **Revocation and discontinuance orders.** The powers under the 1971 Act to make revocation and modification orders in respect of existing planning permissions, and discontinuance orders in respect of existing uses of land, are extended by the new Act to include powers to impose restoration and aftercare conditions.[28] The authority are therefore empowered to seek higher environmental standards in respect of development already under way or having permission, and to bring past permissions into line with modern requirements. Compensation is payable for the exercise of the powers, but on a basis which imposes part of the cost of the industry. The details are considered further below.

(iv) **Prohibition and suspension orders.** The cessation of mineral extraction before the mineral resources at a site have been fully exhausted has posed a major problem for planning authorities in the past. If it is temporary cessation, to seek restoration of the site is futile; and in the case of permanent cessation restoration conditions were often ineffective because they were designed to take effect only upon "completion" of operations or the exhaustion of the site. The new Act therefore empowers authorites to require that works be carried out upon the cessation of extraction, and that these should be works of amenity and protection in the case of temporary cessation, and full restoration and aftercare in the case of permanent cessation. The details are considered further below. Again, compensation is payable for the exercise of these powers, but subject to special modifications under which part of the expense may be shifted to operators.

At the time of going to press, the provisions relating to revocation, discontinuance, prohibition and suspension orders, and the new compensation arrangements, had still to be brought into force.

5. Aftercare Conditions

It has always been possible for planning authorities to impose conditions requiring restoration, although enforcement of even the minimal requirements to restore topsoil and subsoil has often proved difficult once the site is no longer of economic attraction to the operator.[29] Where restoration has

---

[27] T.C.P.A. 1971, s. 44A, inserted by T.C.P.(M.)A. 1981, s. 7. The period of 60 years was recommended by the Stevens Committee as striking the best balance, for three reasons:
(a) It should not in any case be necessary to allow a longer peri od than 60 years for the amortization of capital investment, and in many cases a shorter period will be appropriate.
(b) sixty years is an an appreciable period in terms of the changing attitudes and needs of society.
(c) normal valuation practice regards a reversion after 60 years as equivalent to being subject to a tenancy in perpetuity; the assessed present value of the right to extract minerals beyond the 60 years will be negligible, and the limitation should therefore have no appreciable financial consequences at the time it is imposed." (*Report*, para. 7.13)
[28] T.C.P.A. 1971, s. 45(6), added by T.C.P.(M).A. 1981, s. 8; T.C.P.A. 1971, s. 51(1A)–(1G), added by T.C.P.(M).A. 1981, s. 9. The new provisions deem development consisting of the winning and working of minerals to constitute a use of land, rather than operational development, for the purpose of making discontinuance orders.
[29] The most effective means in the past of securing restoration has been by imposing a scheme of progressive restoration, under which the site is progressively worked and restored and future working is dependent upon past restoration.

been properly carried out, however, the work may still be undone by a failure to treat and manage the land subsequently. There has been no effective means in the past of insisting upon the after-care of restored workings, because an after-care programme is undertaken after the land has come into its new use and may no longer be governed by the original minerals permission and its conditions. The Stevens Committee heard evidence which "conclusively attests to the need for aftercare," and urged that special powers should be given to impose the necessary conditions.[30] The 1981 Act implements their recommendation, and in the words of Lord Bellwin introducing the second reading of the Bill in the House of Lords, it represents "a major attempt to achieve better restoration of old mineral workings for agriculture or forestry so that the land achieves a higher quality and greater potential for future productive use."[31]

An after-care condition may be imposed upon the grant of planning permission for new mineral operations, provided that a restoration condition has also been imposed. After-care conditions may also be imposed against existing workings, though in this case involving potential liability to compensation, under the new extended powers to modify a planning permission to order the discontinuance of a use or to prohibit the resumption of extraction.

In each case there is a preliminary two-stage consultation process.[32] The Minister of Agriculture, Fisheries and Food and the Forestry Commission must be consulted before the authority impose an after-care condition, as to whether it is appropriate to specify a use respectively for agriculture or for forestry; and having determined which should be specified, the authority must consult again with regard to the steps to be specified, whether the steps required should be specified in the condition itself or left for determination in an after-care scheme, and before approval of any after-care scheme.

An after-care condition must specify two things. First, the use to which the land is to be put following restoration. The choice is between agriculture or forestry (subject to the necessary consultations with the Minister or the Forestry Commission) or amenity. "Amenity" is not defined, but the "required standard" prescribed for it is in terms of suitability for sustaining trees, shrubs or plants, and suggests a decorative rather than a positive use.[33] An after-care condition may not specify any other future use, although it would be open to an authority and the surface landowner to make alternative arrangements by way of a planning agreement for bringing the land to a state fit for use for other purposes.

Second, the condition must either specify the steps to be taken to bring land to the required standard for the specified use; or require that the steps be taken in accordance with a scheme to be approved subsequently. The steps required may extend to planting, cultivation, fertilising, watering, draining or otherwise treating the land[34]; and the period in which any step is to be taken may also be specified by the condition (provided it is within the after-care period). Thus the authority have the choice, subject to consulta-

---

[30] *Report, op.cit.,* para. 9.22.
[31] Hansard, H.L.Deb., Vol. 416 cols. 499–500 (January 22, 1981).
[32] T.C.P.A. 1971, s. 30A, inserted by T.C.P.(M).A. 1981, s. 5.
[33] *Ibid.* s. 30A(12).
[34] *Ibid.* s. 30A(5).

tion, of imposing a detailed after-care condition at the outset, or of reserving the details for approval in an after-care scheme. The latter procedure allows the operator himself to prepare a scheme, and to submit it for the authority's approval at any time. The authority may approve the scheme as submitted or modify it.[35] The normal rights of appeal to the Secretary of State against the authority's decision to impose an after care condition and its terms, and against their rejection or conditional approval of a submitted aftercare scheme, are preserved by the new Act.

The maximum period over which after-care steps may be required to be taken is five years, although there is power for the Secretary of State by regulations to prescribe a longer period.[36] Five years is the period recommended by Stevens and accepted initially by the Government but it was raised to ten years by an amendment to the Bill at Committee stage in the Commons. Representatives of the industry were strongly opposed to the increase, and the Ministry of Agriculture advised that agricultural and afforestation uses could be satisfactorily catered for in the shorter period. And so the Government agreed to an amendment at Report stage restoring the period to five years. The period runs from the time of completion of the restoration works, and not simply from the completion of the extraction operations.

Enforcement of after-care conditions raises important issues about the adequacy of the enforcement machinery, and the possibility that exists for evasion of the requirements. Except in the case where an after-care condition has been imposed by way of a discontinuance order or by a prohibition order, where there is direct criminal liability,[37] the only sanctions behind a condition are those available through the normal planning enforcement machinery.

The procedures work best where it is sought to enforce conditions which are negative in nature, and the positive terms of an after-care condition may cause difficulties in enforcement. The Act avoids some of the problems by itself prescribing "the required standard" for the alternative after-uses, but to be readily enforceable the steps required by the condition or after-care scheme will need to be specified in detail and unambiguously.

There is a risk, too, that effective enforcement may be undermined by deliberate evasion. Except in the case of progressive extraction and restoration schemes the operator usually has no economic incentive to undertake satisfactory restoration and after-care, and may even seek to avoid liability altogether by deliberately transferrring the operation to a subsidiary company with no assets from which to meet the liability. The surface landowner remains liable, and although he may recover his expenditure incurred in complying with the condition from the operator,[38] that remedy may also be rendered nugatory by the liquidation of the company.

The Stevens Committee studied in great detail the possibility of devising a bonding or funding scheme which might guarantee compliance, but concluded that the evidence did not support the view that a major cause of past dereliction was the avoidance by operators of their obligations by

[35] *Ibid.* s. 30A(4).
[36] *Ibid.* s. 30A(6)–(8).
[37] Under T.C.P.A. 1971, s. 108, as re-enacted by T.C.P.(M).A. 1981, s. 11.
[38] T.C.P.A. 1971, s. 30A(18).

resorting to bankruptcy or liquidation.[39] They hesitated to reject bonding or funding altogether but suggested that the matter should be kept for further review after 10 years. Their recommendation was accepted by the Government, but subject to the caveat that if the industry should fail to demonstrate that statutory arrangements were unnecessary further action might be taken before 10 years had expired.[40]

Any person with an interest in land may seek a certificate from the mineral planning authority that an after-care condition has been complied with.[41] It does not extend to restoration conditions, and the purpose of the procedure is to record whether the authority are satisfied that the necessary steps have been taken within the after-care period. But it is an isolated provision which stands apart from other planning procedures. There is no provision made for appeals against refusal to issue a certificate, nor is there any indication of the legal effect a certificate is to have. An established use certificate issued under section 94 of the 1971 Act is deemed "conclusive" evidence in any subsequent enforcement proceedings,[42] but that is not the case with the aftercare certificate. It may indeed be used as evidence of the authority's opinion if they should subsequently change their mind and issue enforcement proceedings, but the Secretary of State on appeal may nonetheless conclude that a breach of planning control has occurred.

6. Permanent Cessation of Working: Prohibition Orders

The cesssation of operations may be permanent or temporary, and in the latter case the future of the site may remain uncertain for years, untidy, derelict and an eyesore. The Stevens Committee found that suspended working could result from:

> "(a) changes in costs of production and supply, selling price of the mineral concerned or demand for that mineral, rendering further extraction uneconomic unless and until these market conditions improve;
> (b) rationalisation of activity following company mergers or takeover;
> (c) attempts to defer liability to restore;
> (d) financial difficulties associated with the particular operator rather than with the viability of the working;
> (e) deliberate action to keep a mineral permission alive."[43]

The mineral planning authority's new powers in the case of permanent cessation allow them to prohibit the resumption of development and to impose any of a range of requirements, including restoration and after-care requirements; steps for the alteration or removal of plant or machinery or for the purpose of removing or alleviating injury to amenity caused by the mining and working of minerals; and a requirement seeking compliance with any planning condition imposed in respect of the operations.[44]

[39] Op.cit. Chap. 9.
[40] D.O.E. Circular 58/78, Annex, para. 19.9.
[41] T.C.P.A. 1971, s. 30A(17).
[42] Ibid. s. 94(7).
[43] Op. cit. para. 10.1.
[44] T.C.P.A. 1971, s. 51A, inserted by T.C.P.(M).A. 1981, s. 10.

Permanent cessation may only be assumed where no mineral development has been carried out "to any substantial extent" for a period of at least two years, and where it appears to the authority that resumption of the development is unlikely.[45] The wording "to any substantial extent" indicates that operations which are *de minimis* or insubstantial, undertaken perhaps with the sole purpose of preventing action from being taken by the authority, may be ignored; but the question of what is substantial and what is not is one of fact, and there are no precise guidelines for its determination.

The critical time for the making by the authority of their decision as to the likelihood of future resumption is the time of the making of the order, and provided their decision is properly made upon the evidence then available to them the validity of the order will not be defeated by the subsequent resumption of operations. Should the authority wish to avail themselves of the reduced compensation arrangements, they will need to have carried out preliminary "special consultations"[46] about the making and the terms of the order with persons owning interests in the land and in the minerals, and with the other-tier local planning authority for the area. If they then conclude that resumption of operations is likely, they may still have recourse to their powers under section 51B, discussed below, to make suspension orders.

The order is made in draft, and it requires confirmation by the Secretary of State, with or without modification, before coming into effect.[47]

The effect of a confirmed order is that:

(1) any planning permission for the development to which the order relates ceases to have effect (without prejudice to the power of the authority to revoke the order and grant further permission subsequently)[48];

(2) it becomes an offence to resume, or cause or permit to be resumed, development consisting of the winning and working of minerals where that has been prohibited by the order; and to contravene any requirement specified in the order.[49]

7. Temporary cessation: Suspension Orders and Supplementary Suspension Orders

The environmental problems presented by temporary cessation of mineral development are not substantially different from those presented by permanent cessation, but the machinery for dealing with them has to be different, because of the futility in requiring full restoration and after-care where further extraction may yet take place. If the mineral planning authority wish to prevent any further extraction, they may resort to the powers of revocation of the planning permission under section 45 of the 1971 Act, or order discontinuance of the minerals use of the land under section 51 of the 1971 Act.

The powers under the new section 51B allow them to regulate the interim use and management of the site by means of a "suspension order" pending the resumption of mineral operations, without preventing the resumption

[45] *Ibid.* s. 51A(2).
[46] *Post* p. 498.
[47] The procedure is prescribed by T.C.P.A. 1971, s. 51A(8)–(10).
[48] T.C.P.A. 1971, s. 51A(11).
[49] *Ibid.* s. 108.

(although notice of intention to resume following a suspension order must first be given to the authority). A suspension order is in the nature of a holding operation. It may not, therefore, be used to impose restoration and after-care requirements, but it may require the taking of certain "steps for the protection of the environment."[50]

A suspension order may be served only where no mineral development has been carried out to a substantial extent anywhere on the whole site (and not just on the area of land concerned) for at least twelve months, and where it appears to the authority "on evidence available to them at the time when they make the order" that resumption is likely.[51] The most important evidence available will normally be the representations made by the operator and owners, pursuant to the carrying out of the "special consultations" by the authority which are a prerequisite to their being able to reduce their compensation liability.

The making of a suspension order is not a once and for all means of regulation, and there is specific provision for an authority to make a supplementary suspension order, either adding to the steps previously required to be taken, or revoking the suspension order or any supplementry suspension order.[52]

Enforcement of suspension orders and supplementary orders is through the penal provisions of section 108 of the 1971 Act, which make it an offence to contravene any requirement of such orders, or to cause or permit any requirement to be contravened.

It is not the intention that suspension and supplementary orders should inhibit the recommencement of mineral development. Their function is purely an interim one. But the value of the scheme could easily be lost if the lifting of the orders followed automatically upon the resumption of development, because there would be a strong incentive for operators to circumvent the requirements of an order by undertaking a purely token recommencement of development. And so the Act makes allowance for a trial period following recommencement. The operator is obliged to notify the authority of his intention to recommence specifying the date of recommencement.[53] If the authority do not revoke the order within two months of the date specified by the operator, he may apply to the Secretary of State for revocation. He, if satisfied (following a public local inquiry should the parties desire it) that the development has recommenced to a substantial extent, is obliged to revoke the order.

8. *Compensation*

Compensation lies at the heart of the new legislation. The objectives of the Act call for frequent reviews and modifications to be made by planning authorities, but the cost of implementation under the usual provisions would

---

[50] As defined by s. 51B(3), these include steps for preserving the amenities of the area while working is suspended, for protecting the area from damage during that period and for preventing any deterioration in the condition of the land during the period of suspension.

[51] T.C.P.A. 1971, s. 51B(2).

[52] T.C.P.A. 1971, s. 51B(5). Both suspension orders and supplementary suspension orders require the confirmation of the Secretary of State before taking effect; both are local land charges (s.51D); and there is a duty on the authority to review their operation at not less than five yearly intervals (s.51E).

[53] T.C.P.A. 1971, s. 51F.

render effective implementation impossible. The Stevens Committee had foreseen this problem, and had recommended that a special compensation code should be devised under which the operator himself would be required to bear a certain proportion of the cost of works required for protecting the environment. Their view was that the industry should be prepared to absorb reasonable additional costs arising from changes in conditions, and that compensation should not be payable at all unless the cost incurred by the operator was substantial. The principle was accepted by both the industry and the Government, but there proved to be some difficulty in devising a formula which would strike a workable balance between the industry and planning authority; be fair as between small and large scale operators, and between operators engaged in different types of operation; and which yet would offer a clear-cut basis from which calculations might easily be made in advance of intervention. It was the need to secure a straightforward valuation base that led the Stevens Committee to reject proposals based upon the written down value of the mineral asset at the site and other forms of capital valuation, and instead to choose as a starting point the annual value of the right to work the mineral. Annual value is already used in the preparation of valuation lists as the basis for rating assessments, although the lists are presently many years out of date.

The Government accepted this base, and the Act contains special provisions allowing authorities to reduce their compensation liability in certain circumstances (where "mineral compensation requirements" are met) by an amount calculated in accordance with the following formula:

$$\text{Reduction in compensation} = AV \times y \times CF \times 10 \text{ per cent.}$$

where AV is the annual value; y is an updating figure to bring the 1973 valuation lists more up to date (a multiplier of 4x is currently envisaged); CF is a capitalisation factor, to take account of the estimated future life of the working, proposed to be based on an $8\frac{1}{4}$ per cent. simple rate (though a scale will be prescribed by Regulations); and the 10 per cent. figure is the proportion of the notional value so calculated which the industry will be required to bear, with a proposed minimum in every case of £2,500. Opposition attempts in both Houses to have the percentages raised to 20 per cent. so as to strengthen the hand of the planning authorities failed in light of strong resistance from the extraction industries.

The details are to be prescribed by Regulations and the Act contains only the framework for assessment; but on the basis of the above assumptions the Government have calculated on the basis of a 10 per cent. sample of all mineral working hereditaments, that the impact of the provisions for reduced compensation will be distributed as indicated by Table 19.

Reduced compensation is to apply only where certain preconditions are met. In general, five years must elapse between the granting of the planning permission and the making of any of the orders discussed above; and further periods of five years must elapse before further orders are made.[54] Orders may lawfully be made more frequently than this, but compensation is then

---

[54] *Ibid.* ss. 164A, 170A, 170B(5)(*a*). The sections were inserted by T.C.P.(M).A. 1981, ss. 13 and 15.

Table 19
Mineral compensation estimates

Scale of value of site	Amount of reduction
Bottom 35%	£2,500–4,000
next 15%	4,000–8,000
next 20%	8,000–20,000
top 10%	20,000–100,000

Source: H.C. Official Report, Standing Committee G. May 21, 1981, cols. 41–42.

payable at the full rate. An exception to the five year rule arises in the case of orders imposing only after-care conditions in respect of permissions granted before the coming into effect of section 5 of the 1981 Act.[55]

A further precondition to reliance upon the reduced compensation provisions is that the making of the orders must have been preceded by "special consultations" by the planning authority with any persons owning an interest in the land or the minerals (so far as they can be traced by the taking of reasonable steps); and with the other-tier local planning authority.[56]

Finally, in the case of orders for the modification of an existing mineral permission, and for the discontinuance of the use of land for mining operations, the reduced compensation provisions apply only if the order does not impose any restriction on the winning and working of the minerals, or modify or replace any such restriction that may already have been imposed.[57] The provisions for reduced compensation are based upon the principle that the industry should itself meet part of the cost of environmental improvement; not that it should accept without compensation any reduction in the scope of what has already been permitted by way of the winning or working of minerals itself.

It will remain open to authorities to continue to make orders for modification or discontinuance which do not satisfy these requirements, but in such a case compensation would be payable at the full rate. Orders which restrict the winning or working of minerals, (other than those which prohibit the resumption of operations after permanent cessation, which is a special case), and orders made within the five year period will therefore cast a more substantial compensation burden upon the planning authority.

But even the reduced compensation provisions leave a substantial proportion of the burden of seeking improved environmental standards in respect of existing workings with the authority; and the result is likely to be that the powers will be used rarely, or only in respect of minor works on each occasion. Implementation of the Act carries no commitment of further central government funds to its objectives, and in the present economic climate local authorities have limited resources to apply to them.

[55] *Ibid.* s. 164A(2) and (3).
[56] *Ibid.* s. 178B.
[57] As defined in s. 178C.

CHAPTER 12

POSITIVE PLANNING

A. Introduction

1. *The Concept of Positive Planning*

Development control is primarily a regulatory function. Positive planning is primarily interventionist. It may take a variety of forms. The classic examples of positive planning by central government have been the new towns programmes and the regional economic strategy, which have both concentrated upon promoting new development to attract industrial growth and population dispersal. At local government level, examples include town centre redevelopment schemes, partnership arrangements with private sector developers, site assembly and land supply schemes and area based strategies such as slum clearance and initiatives to stem inner city decay. The common theme in all cases is that of public sector intervention in areas of the economy which have traditionally remained largely unregulated, in particular, the market in development land. Public ownership of development land is a key issue in positive planning, and the rules governing its acquisition, management and disposal are examined later in this chapter.

Broad power to undertake positive planning has rested with planning authorities since 1944,[1] when it was foreseeable that only the public sector was likely to have the resources and the powers to deal with war time damage and with the problems of urban congestion and housing shortage that it had exacerbated. The technical attractions of positive planning have always been clear. As the Pilcher Committee have pointed out, it includes " . . . the power to carry out or to ensure that others carry out (necessary development and redevelopment) in the right places, at the right time and to the right standards."[2] These are not aims which can easily be attained by a purely regulatory system of planning. Even in an area of high demand, neither the allocation of sites in a development plan nor even the granting of permission will guarantee that the land will actually be made available for development. The timing normally depends upon assessments of optimum profitability by both landowner and developer, and the urge to realise profit immediately through sale or development may be offset by other factors, including uncertainty as to future events. The incidence of tax, the possibility of a change of government, interest rates and long term development prospects are all relevant factors. Whilst a planning authority may resist development which it considers premature, the regulatory system offers no means of hastening development considered immediately neces-

---

[1] Town and Country Planning Act 1944, Part I; especially ss. 9 and 10 (purchase of land for planning purposes).
[2] *Report of the Advisory Group on Commercial Property* (H.M.S.O., 1976), para. 3.10. There are echoes in that definition of the wording of the Government's definition of the purposes of the Land Commission: "to secure that the right land is available at the right time for the implementation of national, regional and local plans" (Cmnd. 2771, para. 7); and of the community land scheme: "to enable the community to control the development of land in accordance with its needs and priorities" (Cmnd. 5730, para. 16).

sary. Not only is this liable to lead to inefficient use of publicly funded infrastructure, but it often also leads to pressure by developers on authorities to release further, less suitable, sites for development. The planning authority are often left following, rather than leading, the private market. In the case of redevelopment, the arguments are even more persuasive. Piecing together a suitably sized site from a multiplicity of different ownerships and bearing the risks of an expensive scheme are burdens which are unattractive to the private sector.

The technical case for positive planning is powerful, but in practice has proved almost continuously controversial, for three main reasons. There is first the political debate. Positive planning constitutes public sector intervention in a private economy, and the desirable scope of such intervention and of the mixed economy is one of the key ideological issues in Britain today. It is also highly dependent upon public ownership of land, acquired compulsorily if necessary, and that is a further critical political issue. Second, there is the financial aspect. Positive planning requires substantial investment, and it may not be profitable. Should loss-making schemes nonetheless be encouraged, and how should financial control be exercised? Third, there is the issue of the ability, and indeed the suitability, of local authorities as entrepreneurs, and the extent to which the commercial ends of positive planning can be reconciled with its planning aims. The committee basis of the local government decision making process is well enough suited to regulatory functions such as development control, but it denies authorities the flexibility required for commercial competition. And how far ought local authorities, even in a mixed economy, to compete in the market place, and to supplement their traditional role as suppliers of services with a municipal trading function? And how also should they be supervised so as to minimise the ever present risks of personal corruption? The three issues overlap quite substantially particularly because the responses likely to be made on the last two depend very much on the first. There are few areas in modern government where ideological differences have so often led to dramatic legislative changes by alternative administrations.

2. The Political Debate

There has been no major difference between the main political parties as to the *principle* of positive planning. Both have agreed that there should be some scope for government intervention. But there is a clear difference as to the *function*, and consequently the extent, of the intervention. Conservative philosophy has generally seen positive planning as an enabling function, as a means of allowing or encouraging private enterprise to undertake development which would otherwise be difficult or unattractive. The public sector should play only a complementary role. This might involve bringing land forward for development by acquiring it compulsorily from an unwilling landowner, or piecing together sites from different ownerships. If an authority should profit financially as a result, then so much the better, but that should not be the primary purpose. A public authority ought not to undertake positive planning with the purpose of competing in the market, nor with the aim of controlling it.

Socialist ideology, on the other hand, has viewed public ownership of development land not simply as a key to better planning, but as a desirable end in itself. This is partly a nationalisation argument, but it is also based on the clear financial and planning advantages that public ownership is capable of bringing to the community.

The financial aspects of development land ownership have played a particularly significant part in the debate, because positive planning is in practice linked closely with the problem of land values. Thus it is generally recognised that the impact of planning is felt directly by the market through land value redistribution. Favourable planning decisions make some sites more attractive for development than others, and therefore increase their value to a prospective developer. Conservative ideology has traditionally held that gains reaped through planning by landowners, no matter how adventitiously, should not be recouped from them save through the normal taxing provisions. Socialist philosophy, on the other hand, regards such profits as having arisen from actions taken not by the landowner but by the general community through its elected decision-makers, and thus belonging to the community and recoupable from the landowner. It recoils at the idea that a local authority purchasing land for positive planning purposes, should have to pay a price which reflects the value to the owner of other decisions taken by them as a planning authority. And so socialist ideology has favoured public land ownership as a means of containing land prices, or for exploiting for the community the difference between the value of land in its current use and its possible development value to the benefit of the state. The Community Land scheme, for example, was designed to allow authorities eventually to purchase their land at no more than current use value, and then to resell it to developers at full market value.

Ideological differences between the two main political parties have brought sharp swings in legislative policy on each change in government since the war. The details of the financial provisions of the 1947 Act (and their dismantling in 1951); the establishment of the Land Commission in 1967 and its dissolution in 1970, and the Community Land Act 1975 and its repeal in 1980 have been discussed already in Chapter 1. In practice, though, whilst each step has been highly controversial, its impact upon positive planning by local authorities has been surprisingly small. The reason is that authorities have never lacked adequate statutory powers to undertake positive planning: what has been lacking has been adequate finance. The necessity of relying largely on private sector finance, and their limited ability to do so, has tempered authorities' enthusiasm for wholesale intervention.

3. Positive Planning in Practice

The character of positive planning by authorities today is partly the product of the legislative powers and finance available to them, but it is equally the result of experience gained over the past 40 years. Some authorities have avoided positive planning altogether, while in other cases whole towns and cities have been transformed through the use of the powers.

In the immediate post-war era many local planning authorities needed urgently to clear areas of bomb damage and to promote redevelopment. A pattern emerged whereby sites came to be acquired by the authority, using compulsory powers where necessary. Then a lease would be granted, by tender or negotiation, to a private developer who, with financial backing from a financial institution such as a bank or insurance company, would undertake a development to the authority's requirements.[3] Individual units in the development could then be sub-let to retailers and other users. The authority through their freehold ownership retained close legal control over the use of the property, and also, provided they had the benefit of rent revision clauses in their lease, they could share in the subsequent profitability of the development.

Clearance of areas of slum housing and site redevelopment was also a major local authority task in the 1950s. In some cases the land was used for further housebuilding, usually for council housing. In other cases the land might be used for light industrial use, or for new commercial building in order to allow for further expansion of the central business district. A duty to rehouse displaced residents meant that clearance was almost always tied in with new council house building programmes (though often some distance away) and in some authorities was seen simply as a housing and public health function related only peripherally to planning.

By the end of the 1950s many other authorities were becoming interested in promoting town centre redevelopment, no longer to deal with war damage so much as to display civic pride. They were encouraged by the commercial success of the early schemes and anxious to obtain modern and comprehensive facilities. The Ministry of Housing and Local Government encouraged redevelopment, and offered detailed advice on planning, land acquisition and management techniques.[4] In 1963 legislation conferred new acquisition and land development powers on authorities, allowing them to buy land generally in advance of requirements and to promote private sector development by advancing money to developers against land sold by the authority to them, and even against building agreements entered into with them.[5] The consequence was that the rate of local authorities' speculative land purchases soared. By 1966 their expenditure on land "for planning purposes" alone was running at £50m. per annum, of which £19m. was for land "in advance of requirements," and central government was forced to intervene through stricter application of loan sanction controls.[6] The Labour Government's new Land Commission had positive planning as one of its main objectives, but it had little time in which to become established.

The property boom period of the early 1970s brought new problems for planning authorities, particularly those in major growth areas. It became increasingly difficult for them not to intervene in the market, where action was often needed to overcome land supply problems. Authorities were exhorted by central government to act swiftly to acquire land for resale, and a special loan sanction of £80m. was offered for the purpose.[7] The property boom also marked the widespread emergence of planning gain as a tool in

---

[3] The best account of these schemes is in O. Marriott, *The Property Boom* (Hamish Hamilton, 1967), Chaps. 4 and 5. Marriott stresses that in the early years only one or two developers undertook such work, and that most of those in the real estate business were unsure what to make of the new relationship between local authorities and developers. (*Ibid.*, at 62).

[4] See, *e.g.* Planning Bulletins No. 1, *Town Centres. Approach to Renewal* (1962) and No. 3, *Town Centres. Cost and Control of Redevelopment* (1963); M.H.L.G. Circular 50/66 and *Development Control Policy Note No. 5* (1969).

[5] Local Authorities (Land) Act 1963.

[6] The details were contained in M.H.L.G. Circular 50/66 which expressed concern at the number of "grandiose" and "over optimistic" building schemes proposed. Details of annual expenditure are set out in H.C.Deb., Vol. 738, cols. 35–37 (December 12, 1966).

[7] D.O.E. Circular 102/72, especially paras. 16–31, D.O.E. Circular 122/73, Annexes A and B.

development control. The great pressure for sites suitable for development and the huge profits able to be made by developers encouraged authorities to barter, and to seek positive gains in return for the grant of planning permission. Developers were frequently prepared to enter into partnership arrangements and to alter their plans so as to accommodate or include some facility sought by the planning authority, if that was to be the price of gaining permission.

The scope for positive planning was theoretically greatly strengthened by the Community Land Act 1975, which conferred broad powers of land acquisition and resale upon authorities and established separate key sector borrowing arrangements for funding. But as we have seen, the extent of such activity undertaken following the Act was small, and some authorities found that the scheme actually inhibited their positive planning, because of the scope and rigidity of the central government control it introduced.

The 1980 Act has restored the pre-1975 position, except in Wales, and except also that it has altered the powers conferred upon authorities to purchase land compulsorily for "planning purposes." But positive planning will no longer be a separately budgeted item of public expenditure and there is likely to be little finance to underwrite the new powers.

4. *Positive Planning in Population Distribution and Dispersal Policy*

Attention so far has been focused solely on positive planning by local government, and much of the rest of this chapter also concentrates on the local level. But the picture would not be complete without an examination of centrally initiated positive planning. Central government effort has been directed primarily towards national and regional objectives, and the strongest calls for central action have come from the congested cities and the economically depressed areas. The main policy for relief of congestion has been one of population dispersal, pursued through the building of new towns and through the expansion of existing towns in order to accommodate population "overspill" from the cities.

(a) The new towns

The new town programme was established separately from the land use planning system in 1946, but it shared the same visionary ideals. Lord Silkin was to write, many years later, that the new towns:

> "set out to show that we in Britain could do something better than the soulless suburbia, ribbon development, single industry towns, and one class housing estates of the '30's; that our big cities need not forever go on expanding until all their people were engulfed in a sea of bricks and mortar, cut off from the open countryside; that our obsolete, overcrowded, slum-ridden and bomb-stricken towns could be thinned out and transformed from their Victorian squalor into decent centres of living of which we need no longer be ashamed. The new towns were part of a much wider vision of which as yet we have barely touched the fringe."[8]

---

[8] Foreword to Frank Schaffer, *The New Town Story* (Paladin, 1972).

The new towns were to be "an essay in civilisation,"[9] and broad powers were needed to make them work. The New Towns Act 1946[10] conferred them. It allowed the Minister to designate areas for new town development, and to appoint a corporation for the development of each. Subject to planning and financial controls retained by the Minister, the corporation had broad powers to borrow money and to acquire, develop and dispose of land.

Some 32 new towns have been designated since 1946 and over one million people have gone to live in them. The details are contained in Table 20. The total is made up of 21 towns in England (of which 8 are in the outer Metropolitan area), 5 in Scotland, 2 in Wales and 4 in Northern Ireland. As the Table shows, there has been substantial variation between the sizes and proposed growth rates of the towns. The last new town was designated in 1970, and no more are planned in the immediate future. Plans for a further new town at Stonehouse in Scotland were halted in 1976 pending a review of overall new town strategy. That review has resulted in a reduction in new town goals, and the long term population targets of the six most recently designated English towns have been reduced by 380,000. Proposals have also been approved for the winding up of a further 11 development corporations, in addition to four whose tasks had been largely completed in the 1960s and had been wound up then. The 1980 Act has conferred power on the Secretary of State to require development corporations to pay money to him[11] and facilitate the disposal by them of their landholdings in order to comply with such a requirement.[12] It also authorises him to reduce, by order, the size of any designated area.[13]

The downward revision of the new town programme is the product not simply of ideological opposition to the idea of substantial public ownership, but also of the general fall in rate of population growth and pressures from the older cities where evidence of the decay that set in as population levels declined suggested that perhaps the dispersal policies had been too successful. Further, as the House of Commons Expenditure Committee[14] had pointed out in 1974, there had never been any comprehensive public study of new town policy, and there was a need in particular to monitor and reconsider the towns' social and economic objectives as well as the rate of physical development.

Planning within new towns is undertaken through different machinery from that generally applicable. Forward planning is by means of a non-statutory master plan prepared by the development corporation.[15] This is a strategic document, and its approval by the Secretary of State is normally preceded by a public inquiry. Whilst the plan is under preparation, the corporation usually begin the task of land assembly. Prices are held generally to current use level,[16] and development value need be paid only where there

---

[9] *Interim Report of the New Towns Committee,* Cmd. 6759, para. 1(7)(1946).
[10] Since repealed, and now consolidated with later amendments in the New Towns Act 1981.
[11] L.G.P.L.A. 1980, s.126; see now New Towns Act 1981, ss.63–66.
[12] *Ibid.* s.127; see now New Towns Act 1981, s. 64.
[13] *Ibid.* s.128; see now New Towns Act 1981, s.2.
[14] *Thirteenth Report from the Expenditure Committee* (Session 1974–75), Vol. 1. The Report is accompanied by three large volumes of minutes of evidence presented to the Committee, which constitute an important source of background material on new towns.
[15] See further Memorandum, D.O.E. Circular 4/79, para. 4.13–4.28.
[16] By virtue of Land Compensation Act 1961, ss.6 and 7 and Sched. 1.

Table 20
New Towns: England, Scotland and Wales

	Date designated	Area (acres)	Population (thousands)		
			Original	Proposed[1]	As at 31.12.78
A. London ring					
Basildon	1949	7,818	25.0	103.6	95.7
Bracknell	1949	3,303	5.1	60.0	49.5
Crawley	1947	5,920	9.1	85.0	75.0
Harlow	1947	6,395	4.5	—	79.5
Hatfield	1948	2,340	8.5	25.0	26.0
Hemel Hempstead	1947	5,910	21.0	65.0	79.0
Stevenage	1946	6,256	6.7	74.0	73.5
Welwyn Garden City	1948	4,317	18.5	42.0	41.0
B. Others in England					
Aycliffe	1947	3,103	.06	—	27.5
Central Lancashire	1970	35,255	234.5	285.0	251.0
Corby	1950	4,423	15.7	70.0	54.0
Milton Keynes	1967	22,000	40.0	150.0	85.0
Northampton	1968	19,966	133.0	173.0	150.0
Peterborough	1967	15,940	81.0	150.0	115.0
Peterlee	1948	2,979	.2	30.0	25.5
Redditch	1964	7,180	32.0	69.4	59.5
Runcorn	1964	7,234	28.5	71.0	61.6
Skelmersdale	1961	4,124	10.0	52.0	39.5
Telford	1968	19,300	70.0	130.0	101.3
Warrington	1968	18,612	122.3	161.5	135.4
Washington	1964	5,610	20.0	65.0	49.9
C. Wales					
Cwmbran	1949	3,160	12.0	55.0	43.5
Mid-Wales (Newtown)	1967	1,497	5.0	11.5	8.5
D. Scotland					
Cumbernauld	1955	7,788	3.0	49.0	8.2
East Kilbride	1947	10,250	2.4	76.5	15.8
Glenrothes	1948	5,765	1.1	35.4	8.9
Irvine	1966	12,440	34.6	58.0	15.0
Livingston	1962	6,692	2.1	35.0	6.6

Source: Town and Country Planning, *Vol. XLVII, pp. 138–139 (1979).*

Note: (1) the proposed population in most cases is that envisaged in consequence of planned inward migration. In most cases continued natural growth is expected to lead to limited expansion beyond these figures.

would have been demand for the land for development of the type proposed by the corporation irrespective of the new town proposals.[17] There are broad powers of compulsory purchase,[18] and it has been common practice for up to 80 per cent. of the designated area to be acquired by the development corporation.

[17] *Myers v. Milton Keynes Development Corporation* [1974] 1 W.L.R. 696.
[18] New Towns Act 1981, s.10 and Sched. 4.

Following approval of the master plan the corporation prepare general phasing proposals for development and detailed development proposals. The detailed proposals require statutory approval,[19] but once that has been given planning permission follows by virtue of a special development order.[20] The permission extends to development by the corporation and to authorised development by others on land held or formerly held by the corporation.[21] Those provisions suffice in practice to cover almost all the new development, but the Planning Acts are not otherwise excluded and thus power is retained by the local planning authorities to approve applications in respect of unapproved development in the normal way.

(b) Town development schemes

Town expansion under the Town Development Act 1952 has played a function similar to that of the new towns in population dispersal, but with the important distinctions that the schemes have been initiated by local authorities acting jointly rather than by central government, and that they have generally been on a smaller scale than the new towns. The aim has been to build upon existing settlements, rather than the creation of new communities. The Act authorises voluntary agreements between urban authorities with problems of congestion and town authorities willing to accept people and industry from the cities in order to promote their own expansion.[22] To date, provision has been made in England alone to accommodate over 300,000 people through 70 different schemes, of which 30 relate to London. Over half are now completed, but the future of the "overspill" programme has been put in doubt because of the same policy considerations that have affected the new towns. The two main "exporting" authorities, Greater London and Glasgow, have each resolved to enter into no further agreements and the Greater London Council have sought to renegotiate or terminate their existing agreements. The voluntary nature of the agreements has left the G.L.C. powerless to impose fresh terms, but a termination scheme has been prepared,[23] and has strong Government support.[24]

The town development schemes involve no separate development corporations, and their planning is a matter for the local planning authorities.[25] There are, however, supplementary powers of compulsory purchase which have allowed authorities to acquire land even though not designated for acquisition in the old development plans.[26]

---

[19] *Ibid.* s. 7(1).
[20] Town and Country Planning (New Towns Special Development) Order 1977, art. 3.
[21] *Ibid.* art. 3(2).
[22] Town Development Act 1952, s.8.
[23] *The Future of Town Development Schemes associated with the G.L.C.* D.O.E. Consultation Document, 1978.
[24] The terms of the new Government's statement appear at H.C.Deb., Vol. 975, cols. *814–816* (December 14, 1979). The Government announced in 1981 that they intended to proceed with termination on the terms announced, and to bring six schemes to an end forthwith, and to allow a transitional 5-year period for termination in the case of 16 other schemes: *Hansard* H.C.Deb., Vol. 5, cols. *328–329* (June 2, 1981). The power to enter into further agreements was taken away from county councils by L.G.P.L.A. 1980, s. 124.
[25] Town Development Act 1952, s.21.
[26] *Ibid.* s.6.

(c) Regional policy

All post-war British governments have pursued regional economic strategies, designed to mitigate the economic imbalance between regions that had been so clearly identified in the Barlow report in 1942.[27] The regional problem stems largely from the long term decline of regionally concentrated industries, such as shipbuilding, coal, steel and textiles and their local associated and supplying industries. The consequence has been disproportionate concentrations of unemployment in the declining regions, and associated land use problems of industrial dereliction and general physical decay. Government policy has been directed to promoting new industrial growth to the regions and for the most part the strategy has been economic. Industries wishing to relocate have been offered government grants, tax reliefs, employment subsidies and assistance with the recruitment and training of staff.

The true costs of regional policy are difficult to calculate, since they include not only the direct grant-aid and indirect subsidisation by central government, but also costs imposed upon other regions outside the designated development and special development areas. Similarly, the effects of regional policy are incapable of being analysed precisely, because it is but one factor in the economy, and but one factor in an industrialist's locational and expansion decisions. The Department of Industry have attempted to assess and analyse the impact of the policy, but have been able to glean only very generalised answers:

> "When present methodologies are used to examine the pattern of events in the regions over the past decades, it seems highly probable that positive regional policies have had a positive effect in the regions to which those policies have been applied. What we cannot obtain from the methods which have been applied is a precise indication of the nature or scale of these effects, or of the costs which may have been imposed elsewhere. . . . On a conceptual level the problem is that there is no unambiguous answer to the question of how worthwhile in national terms a set of regional policy measures may be. . . . Decisions about the type of policy to be pursued have necessarily to take account of the changing nature of the U.K.'s economic problems. But they are also concerned with such questions as the weight to be attached to improvements in welfare in particular regions, and the contribution of regional well-being to the unity of the United Kingdom and the costs which it is permissible to impose to achieve these ends. . . . In the final analysis, the allocation of resources to the objectives of regional policy is essentially a political decision to provide the amount of economic aid which it is believed the country can afford to the economically and socially disadvantaged areas of the United Kingdom."[28]

There has been no power to direct industry to the regions, but the industrial development certificate procedures have been used to guide industry by restricting growth elsewhere.[29] New towns and expanding

---

[27] Cmnd. 6513 (1940).
[28] *Fifth Report from the Committee of Public Accounts* (Session 1980–81, H.C. 206), pp. 3–4.
[29] See further *ante*, pp. 216–218.

towns schemes have also been used as a means of promoting new
development and attracting industry to declining regions. Development
corporations and local authorities have been able to offer industrialists green
field sites for new industrial development, or prebuilt factory units, coupled
with financial incentives (such as rent free periods) and readily available
housing for key workers.

For the most part regional economic policy is centrally directed, though it
ties in with local physical planning through the regional physical planning
system discussed in Chapter 3. The statutory plans of local planning
authorities in the assisted areas are prepared generally with the regional
economic problem as a major priority, and with a view to encouraging
industrial regeneration. Some authorities have attempted also to build upon
the national regional strategy by taking initiatives in local economic
planning, by assisting industry with grants and loans, and by acquiring joint
shareholdings in industrial companies, for example; and through positive
physical planning. In some cases, as with the establishment of industrial
improvement areas, special powers have been taken under local legislation.
Broader powers have now been conferred by general legislation and their
effects are considered further below.

B. Public Land Ownership

1. *Introduction*

Public land ownership is the cornerstone of most positive planning, because
only actual ownership guarantees an authority full control over the
development of land. For that reason it has remained a central concept in
new town development where it has been customary for development
corporations to acquire as much as 80 per cent. of the land; and it was also
the chief mechanism envisaged for the Land Commission and the
community land scheme. Ownership by a local planning authority of
development land allows them to release sites or withhold them from the
market in accordance with their planning priorities, and it also gives them a
closer control over the actual development through their proprietary
interest. Except in the case of residential development, leasehold has been
the normal form of disposal, and covenants inserted in the lease to secure
adherence to planning standards have been enforceable through the
landlord/tenant relationship. But it does not follow that land ownership has
the effect of freeing an authority from the influence of market forces.
Substantial holdings of development land may allow individual authorites to
influence or even largely control their local market, but it does not give them
a free hand in price fixing. The price of land sold by them is necessarily fixed
by market demand for it, and in that calculation the value of the site for
development is usually the decisive factor. Restrictions imposed to achieve
planning goals, such perhaps as reduced densities and the provision of public
facilities, reduce the profitability of the development and hence the
authority's financial gain.

Positive planning, therefore, takes place within the market and the
achievement of planning objectives needs to be balanced against their
viability in financial terms. There will be cases where the planning objective
is of such high priority that public money, in the form of grants and

subsidies, should be put towards it. But the conflict between planning and finance underlies all positive planning. In the case of positive planning by local planning authorities that conflict is almost always internalised. The authority have the dual role of planner and developer, and the balance between the two may depend upon nothing more than the respective strengths within the authority of the planning committee on the one hand, and the policy and resources or finance committee on the other. Further, the financial success of an authority's positive planning is liable to turn upon the extent to which it can undertake the entrepreneurial role required for effective market participation. But the hallmarks of that role, such as swift decision making and the ability to maintain secrecy in commercial negotiations, are completely opposed to the requirements of a locally elected and democratically accountable body.

Positive planning has therefore proved highly controversial in practice, particularly with the growth of public participation. It is difficult to convince objectors that their views will be considered when the decision maker is fulfilling two roles, and when the confidentiality required to achieve optimum market advantage usually rules out unrestricted consultation.

The need for safeguards against arbitrary conduct by authorities is reflected in the rules governing the ownership and development of land held by them. They have, however, been relaxed substantially since 1944, and the 1980 Act continues that trend. The land-holding powers of local authorities are described in the following pages.

2. Land Acquisition by Agreement

Local authorities generally have power to buy land only for their specific statutory functions. Once acquired, land is held by them for the purpose for which it was acquired. It may be used for another purpose temporarily, but a permanent change of purpose requires that the land first be "appropriated" to the new purpose. There is no power to appropriate without statutory authority, and although broad powers have now been conferred there are certain safeguards.

Land-holding by authorities is thus a comparatively formalised affair and most land that is acquired is in practice bought and used for specific purposes such as roads, schools and playing fields, under various specific statutory powers. Authorities have a variety of powers to buy land compulsorily for most of their purposes, and the compulsory powers in each case usually encompass a power to buy land for the purpose by agreement. Broader powers to buy by agreement are also conferred upon authorities by the Local Government Act 1972, and by the Town and Country Planning Act 1971 in respect of land required for "planning purposes."

By virtue of section 120 of the Local Government Act authorities may acquire land by agreement for any of their functions, and also for the "benefit, improvement or development" of their area.[30] The powers extend to land outside their area as well as within it, and there is no need to obtain

---

[30] The latter power was first introduced by the Local Authorities (Land) Act 1963, and it may be exercised only by agreement: it has no corresponding compulsory power. Before the 1963 Act many authorities had taken similar powers under local Acts.

ministerial consent. Nor is it necessary that the land be immediately required for the purposes proposed: it may be acquired in advance of requirements and used in the interim for the purposes of any of the authority's functions.[31]

The power to acquire by agreement "for planning purposes" is narrower, and its provisions are largely encompassed by the broader local Government Act powers.[32] It authorises purchase for any planning purpose for which the authority may be authorised to acquire compulsorily, and the 1980 Act has removed the former requirement of prior ministerial consent to certain acquisitions. The power is exercisable by all planning authorities (though there are restrictions on the G.L.C.),[33] and the 1980 Act has also extended the powers to the Special Planning Boards.[34]

Between them the provisions confer largely unfettered power on authorities to acquire land, even speculatively, for positive planning. The real constraints are financial rather than legal, and the necessity in the past of obtaining loan sanction approval has often meant that there was detailed ministerial supervision of many agreement purchases.

3. Compulsory Acquisition

Compulsory purchase is more tightly controlled. The powers are more narrowly conferred, and, in the case of any objection to an authority's draft compulsory purchase order, they must establish a case for the acquisition to the satisfaction of the Secretary of State.

There is no power to purchase land compulsorily simply for the "benefit, improvement or development" of an authority's area, and the only general planning purposes power now is that conferred by section 112 of the 1971 Act. The Community Land Act 1975 had conferred very broad power indeed. Authorities could purchase any land which, in their opinion, was suitable for development.[35] On the repeal of the Act in 1980 it was initially proposed that authorities should continue to have that power, and the Bill as originally drafted included a clause couched in similarly subjective terms, which would have widened section 112 considerably. A Government amendment proposed and accepted in the third reading debate,[36] however, has had the effect of narrowing not only the initial proposal but also, curiously, the provisions of section 112 as it formerly stood.

Under the new Act a local authority may, with the Secretary of State's authorisation, acquire compulsorily land which is in their area, and which "is suitable for and is required in order to secure the carrying out of one or more of the following activities, namely development, redevelopment and improvement"; or which "is required for a purpose which it is necessary to

---

[31] L.G.A. 1972, s.120(2).

[32] The section does, however, confer additional powers to acquire buildings appearing to the authority to be of special architectural or historic interest (though not necessarily listed) and certain other land required in connection with the acquisition: s.119(1)(*b*) and (*c*)

[33] Generally the G.L.C. require the consent of the borough concerned or the Secretary of State: s.119(4).

[34] L.G.P.L.A. 1980, s.119. The Boards, not being "principal councils" under the 1972 Act, do not have the powers conferred by that Act.

[35] Community Land Act 1975, s.15(1).

[36] For details of the debate, see H.C.Deb., Vol. 988, cols.*460–467* (July 8, 1980).

achieve in the interests of the proper planning of an area in which the land is situated."[37]

Under the first power the land must be both "suitable" for, and "required" for, the purposes proposed. By virtue of a new subsection, 112(1A), suitability is to be considered in terms of the provisions of the development plan, so far as material; whether planning permission for any development on the land is in force, and any other considerations material to the development of the land. The purpose of these provisions is to require authorities to establish a planning case for their acquisitions, and where planning backing is available in the development plan the Secretary of State is able to disregard objections which amount to objections to the plan's provisions.[38] To be "required" for the purposes proposed, does not mean that acquisition of the land need be "essential": the courts have held that it is sufficient that the acquiring authority and the Secretary of State should think it desirable.[39]

The second power is not confined to proposals for development, redevelopment or improvement, and thus would permit a purchase designed to retain the status quo in the form of an existing use or building. It would similarly allow an authority to overcome problems such as access to a development site where the land to be acquired was not itself to be developed.

Neither power extends to land outside an authority's area, but it is possible for it to be so extended. The precondition is that it must be land which an authority for the area concerned could have been authorised to acquire,[40] and that the authority and any other relevant authority have been consulted.[41]

The "planning purposes" powers have been widely used in past years, though they have been progressively supplemented by more specific provisions in support of particular initiatives, such as in the various area based strategies considered below. In some cases, as with large scale redevelopment, their main usefulness is often as a back-up, enabling authorities to acquire land not already held by them under other powers, such as slum clearance or highways. But their major significance is that they allow land to be brought onto the market. The new Act makes clear that the question of who it is who is to carry out the purposes proposed is immaterial to the compulsory purchase[42]; and the normal course is for the acquired land, or an interest in it, to be transferred to private developers. The various partnership and other arrangements are considered further below.

---

[37] T.C.P.A. 1971, s.112(1)(as amended by L.G.P.L.A. 1980, s.91). A subsidiary power is conferred by subs.(1B) to acquire adjoining land, and land required for the purposes of exchange for common land, open space or allotment land acquired. The procedure for compulsory purchase is prescribed by the Acquisition of Land Act 1981.

[38] T.C.P.A. 1971, s.132(1).

[39] *Errington* v. *Metropolitan District Railway Co. Ltd.* (1882) 19 Ch.D. 559; *Company Developments (Property) Ltd.* v. *S.O.S.E.* [1978] J.P.L. 107.

[40] T.C.P.A. 1971, s.112(2).

[41] *Ibid.* subs.(2) and (3).

[42] *Ibid.* s.112(1B)(as inserted by L.G.P.L.A. 1980, s.91).

4. *Acquisition by Gift*

Acquisition of land by gift is the converse of compulsory acquisition. It is sanctioned, not by the agreement purchase provisions (for which the acquisition must be for money or money's worth)[43] but by section 139 of the Local Government Act 1972. That allows authorities to "accept, hold and administer" gifts, including land, made for the purpose of their functions or for the benefit of inhabitants of their area. The section extends only to genuine gifts, and not, for example, to contributions sought by an authority as an inducement to their granting planning permission.[44]

Special provisions, however, authorise authorities to accept responsibility for land dedicated to public use; examples include land for the purposes of providing public open space[45] or for use as a public highway.[46]

5. *Appropriation of Land*

It is a basic principle that no land held by an authority may be appropriated by them to a purpose other than that for which it was acquired without statutory authority.[47] The purpose of the rule is to guard against misuse of the acquisition powers, particularly in the case of compulsory purchase. But it has now been largely excluded by broad statutory authorisation. Even the former rule, that required ministerial consent to any appropriation of land within ten years of its acquisition through direct or indirect use of compulsory powers, has now been swept away by the 1980 Act.[48]

The general rule now is that any authority may appropriate land for any purpose for which they are authorised to acquire land by agreement, provided it belongs to them and is no longer required for the purpose for which it has been held.[49] The question of whether land is or is not any longer required for the former purpose is a matter entirely for the authority, and in the absence of bad faith their decision is unchallengeable.[50] The general rule does not extend to land held for planning purposes,[51] but similar provisions have now been introduced. Their effect is the same except so far as common land is concerned, which is considered below. General safeguards now exist in the case of any proposed appropriation of open space, commons and allotments.

(a) Open space

Any proposed appropriation of open space should first be advertised in two consecutive weeks in a newspaper circulating in the area in which the

---

[43] L.G.A. 1972, s.120(5).
[44] *County and District Properties Ltd.* v. *Horsham U.D.C.* (1970) 215 E.G. 1399.
[45] Open Spaces Act 1906, s.9.
[46] Highways Act 1980, s.38.
[47] *Attorney-General* v. *Harwell U.D.C.* [1900] 2 Ch. 377.
[48] L.G.P.L.A. 1980, Sched. 23, para. 14.
[49] L.G.A. 1972, s.122(1).
[50] *Attorney-General* v. *Manchester Corporation* [1931] 1 Ch. 254; *Dowty Boulton Paul Ltd.* v. *Wolverhampton Corporation (No. 2)* [1973] Ch. 94 (Plowman J.); [1976] Ch. 13 (C.A.). In the Court of Appeal Russell L.J. took the view that "not required" should be interpreted as meaning "not needed in the public interest of the locality" for the original purpose, rather than in terms of the private interests of the plaintiffs who were users of the land (p. 26).
[51] T.C.P.A. 1971, s.122(5).

land is situated, and any objections to the proposal must be considered by the authority.[52] There are, however no provisions as to the time or form within which objections must be lodged. The effect of appropriation is now automatically to free the authority from any duties and restrictions imposed in respect of the open space land under the Public Health Act 1875 and the Open Spaces Act 1906.[53] It does not, however, of itself override any private rights in respect of the land nor any charitable trust upon which the land is held.[54]

Where land has been appropriated to planning purposes and development is proposed in accordance with a planning permission, then it is possible to override private rights over the land, subject to liability for the payment of compensation.[55]

(b) Commons and allotments

Appropriation of land which is or forms part of a common, fuel allotment or garden allotment requires ministerial approval, through the confirmation of an order made by the authority.[56] There is an exception, however, in respect of small amounts of land. These may be appropriated by an authority under their general power, provided the total appropriated in any particular common or allotment does not in the aggregate exceed 250 square yards, and that before appropriating the land the authority have advertised their intention and considered objections in the same way as for open space appropriations.[57]

(c) Common land held for planning purposes

Any land held for planning purposes may be appropriated for another purpose in the same way as other land held by an authority, except for common land, for which ministerial consent is required.[58] It is not, however, as formal a process as that required for commons and allotments held for other purposes, and the Secretary of State is empowered to grant general consents.[59]

6. Development on Acquired Land

Statutes authorising the acquisition of land for specific purposes normally also authorise the carrying out of development on the land for those purposes. Planning permission, though, is still required for all local

---

[52] L.G.A. 1972, s.122(2A)(as inserted by L.G.P.L.A. 1980, Sched. 23, para. 12). "Open space" is defined as "any land laid out as a public garden, or used for the purposes of public recreation, or land which is a disused burial ground:" T.C.P.A. 1971, s.290(1) as applied by L.G.A. 1972, s.270(1)(added by L.G.P.L.A. 1980, Sched. 23, para. 20). It is capable therefore of extending to land used as *de facto* open space by members of the public, perhaps whilst awaiting development, although not formally dedicated to that use.
[53] *Ibid.* s.122(2B).
[54] See, *e.g. Hauxwell* v. *Barton-upon-Humber U.D.C.* [1974] Ch. 432.
[55] T.C.P.A. 1971, s.127(1).
[56] *Ibid.* s.121.
[57] L.G.A. 1972, s.122(2).
[58] T.C.P.A. 1971, s.122(1).
[59] *Ibid.* s.122(2).

authority development in the same way as for private sector development, except that it is obtained under the "deemed permission" provisions discussed in Chapter 5.

Further powers for land development, more general than the "specific purpose" powers, are contained in the Local Authorities (Land) Act 1963 and in Part VI of the 1971 Act. The 1963 Act permits authorities to "erect any building and construct or carry out works on land," provided that this is done "for the benefit or improvement of their area."[60] The 1971 Act is in similar terms, but there is no requirement that the work should be for benefit or improvement of the area, and the power is available only in respect of land acquired or appropriated for planning purposes.[61] It does not avail an authority where a specific power exists under an alternative enactment for the development proposed by them. Formerly neither power could be exercised without the Secretary of State's consent, but that requirement was lifted altogether in 1974.[62] The advantage of the "planning purposes" power is that it allows the authority to override existing private rights over the land including easements and restrictive covenants, provided the development undertaken by them has planning permission.[63] Compensation then becomes payable, however, as if the right had been compulsorily acquired. Where land is held by them upon a so-called "public trust," that is, subject to the restrictions imposed upon pleasure grounds and open spaces by the Public Health Act 1875 and the Open Spaces Act 1906 respectively, the trusts may be abrogated through appropriation or disposal of the land under the new procedures.[64] And any open space, once acquired or appropriated for planning purposes, may be developed in accordance with planning permission[65]; as may consecrated land and burial grounds provided prescribed requirements have been met.[66]

The most significant constraints over exercise of the broad development powers are financial. Central government controls over borrowing by local authorities mean that resources for large scale development are scarce, and authorities have for the most part instead encouraged private sector development using private capital, retaining sufficient control through their terms for disposal of the land to ensure adherence to their planning standards.

---

[60] Local Authorities (Land) Act 1963, s.2.

[61] T.C.P.A. 1971, s.124.

[62] Local Government Act 1974, Sched. 6, paras.14 and 25(9); Sched. 8.

[63] T.C.P.A. 1971, s.127; and see *Dowty Boulton Paul Ltd.* v. *Wolverhampton Corporation (No. 2)* [1973] Ch. 94, [1976] Ch. 13 (C.A.).

[64] L.G.A. 1972, ss.122(2A) and 123(2A) as inserted by L.G.P.L.A. 1980, Sched. 19, paras.11 and 13. Otherwise the authority are limited to uses reasonably necessary to the public enjoyment of the land as open space: see *e.g. Attorney-General* v. *Poole Corporation* [1938] Ch. 23; and *Attorney-General* v. *Southampton Corporation* (1969) 21 P. & C.R. 281. There is also a general prohibition against the construction of non-ancillary buildings on metropolitan green belt land except with the consent of the Minister and every contributing local authority: Green Belt (London and Home Counties) Act 1938, s.10.

[65] T.C.P.A. 1971, ss.129 and 133(3).

[66] *Ibid.* s.128, although some limited relaxations are made by the Disused Burial Grounds (Amendment) Act 1981.

7. Disposal of Land

The 1980 Act has made two major changes in the laws governing local authority land disposal. First, it has repealed the requirement imposed by the Community Land Act that ministerial consent should be obtained for all disposals. Although a general consent had been granted, specific consents were still needed until late 1979 for freehold disposals of commercial and industrial land, and for leasehold disposals for more than 99 years.[67] The purpose of these limitations was to ensure that authorities would generally retain long term ownership and control over the land. Second, the new Act gives the Secretary of State power to intervene where he believes that local authorities and other public bodies have surplus land-holdings. He may prepare public registers of their land-holdings, and direct them to take steps to dispose of them.

There is now a general power to dispose of land, or of any interest in land without ministerial consent.[68] But there are some important exceptions.

(a) Open space

Formerly, the consent of the Secretary of State was specifically required for the disposal of open space, and no disposal of "public trust" land was permitted except where it was of less than 250 square yards and the disposal had been advertised. The new procedure requires that as with appropriation, the intention to dispose of any land in either category should first be advertised and any representations considered.[69] But there are no longer any limitations upon the quantity of "public trust" land that may be disposed of, and the disposal itself frees the land of any public trust obligation.[70] It does not, however, authorise the authority to breach any other trust, covenant or agreement.[71]

(b) Disposals at less than best consideration

Ministerial consent is still required for any disposal for a "consideration less than the best that can reasonably be obtained,"[72] though the requirement does not extend to short-term leasehold disposal or assignment.[73] Often the most significant factor in calculating the "best

---

[67] Under the terms of the consent contained in D.O.E. Circular 26/76. The incoming Government in 1979 abolished these restrictions. The requirement to obtain consent was lifted by the repeal of L.G.A. 1972, s.123A, by L.G.P.L.A. 1980, Sched. 23, para. 16.

[68] L.G.A. 1972, s.123 (as amended by L.G.P.L.A. 1980, Sched. 23, para. 14). There remains a limited number of controls over disposal of land held for specific purposes, to which the general consent does not extend: see L.G.A. 1972, s.131(1)(b) and (2).

[69] L.G.A. 1972, s.123(2A)(as inserted by L.G.P.L.A. 1980, Sched. 23, para. 14). For the definition of "open space," see note 52 above.

[70] Ibid. s.123(2B); inserted by L.G.P.L.A. 1980 in order to overcome the rulings in Laverstoke Property Co. Ltd. v. Peterborough Corporation [1972] 1 W.L.R. 1400, and its sequel, Third Greytown Properties Ltd. v. Peterborough Corporation [1973] 3 All E.R. 731.

[71] Ibid. s.131(1)(a); and see Earl of Leicester v. Wells-next-the-sea U.D.C. [1973] Ch. 110 where an authority were restrained from disposing of land for housing purposes, having covenanted when acquiring it 25 years earlier to confine its use to smallholdings and allotments.

[72] L.G.A. 1972, s.123(2).

[73] Defined on the grant of a term not exceeding seven years, or the assignment of a term with less than seven years to run: L.G.A. 1972, s.123(7).

consideration" is the development potential of the site, but the section by no means obliges an authority to ensure that land to be disposed of should be able to be put to the most profitable use possible. The "best consideration" for the land will necessarily be measured by a purchaser against the planning constraints upon its use, and an authority may clearly choose for planning reasons to restrict development, and hence profitability, without seeking ministerial consent provided their decision is not arbitrary. But where land is disposed of at nominal or diminished consideration in order to subsidise a purchaser, the transaction will require ministerial consent. Failure to obtain consent will not act to the prejudice of the purchaser,[74] and there is no obligation upon him to ensure that consent has been granted or, as the case may be, that the disposal has been advertised and objections considered.[75] The adequacy of any consideration is, however, professionally certified either by a valuer employed by the authority, or by the District Valuer. Under arrangements introduced in 1976, the District Valuer also maintained a selective supervision over internal certification,[76] but that scheme has since been abandoned in favour of informal liaison between him and local authority valuers. There is no longer any duty for a report to be made to the District Valuer on completed transactions.[77]

(c) Land held for planning purposes

The general disposal consent does not extend to land held for planning purposes,[78] but similar freedom of disposal now exists in respect of such land, and authorities are given broad powers on disposal to ensure that the land is put to its best use, and that any buildings and works needed for the proper planning of the area will be erected or carried out thereon, whether by themselves or by any other person. The consent of the Secretary of State is now required only for disposals at less than best consideration, and for disposals of land which presently or formerly was common land and which is held or managed by the authority in accordance with a local Act.[79]

There is a general duty upon the authority and upon the Secretary of State to ensure that their powers are exercised so as to secure that persons formerly living or carrying on business on acquired land should have an opportunity to obtain suitable accommodation there again, on terms settled "with due regard to the price at which any such land has been acquired from them."[80] But it is an obligation which is broadly cast. It has been largely overtaken in the case of residential occupiers by the rehousing provisions of the 1973 Land Compensation Act. So far as business occupancy is concerned, the section imposes no duty to offer new accommodation at a low rent, and the small shopkeepers typically displaced by redevelopment schemes can seldom afford the high rents demanded for the new facilities. The duty to have regard to the price paid to them for their former interest

---

[74] L.G.A. 1972, s.128(2)(*a*)

[75] *Ibid.* s.128(2)(*b*)

[76] See further D.O.E. Circular 48/76 on the *Implementation of the Borner Report* (Cmnd. 5518).

[77] Under D.O.E. Circular 18/80.

[78] By reason of T.C.P.A. 1971, s.123(9).

[79] *Ibid.* s.123(2)(as amended by L.G.P.L.A. 1980, Sched. 23, para. 11).

[80] *Ibid.* s.123(7).

when settling reletting terms has been held to be a relic from the era when authorities were able to acquire land below market value, and of no relevance today save in exceptional circumstances.[81]

8. Land Disposal Procedures

There are no prescribed statutory procedures for land disposal by local authorities, and nor do authorities' own standing orders usually extend to land disposal. There is therefore a choice between several different methods, ranging from private negotiation to public auction. Public auction most visibly satisfies the requirements of public and impartial conduct, but there are occasions when it works against an authority. In the case of "planning purposes" disposals, for example, it is the development which is to be undertaken on the site which is all-important, and an authority are usually anxious to ensure that the choice between developers should be made on the basis of more than purely financial criteria. They may have difficulty in attracting reliable developers in open competition, and may prefer to negotiate privately with no more than one or two developers, selected on the basis of their past work and their general reputation. In some cases there may be an obligation to dispose to a particular developer, as where the purpose of the transaction is to vest the freehold of the site in the authority in return for a long lease back to the developer.

Local authority schemes have not always been attractive to private developers, because of the financial risks and the public controversy they so often involve. But the processes of private negotiation upon which developers may insist as a precondition of their participation are open to the objection that they may encourage corruption, and that the adequacy of the consideration agreed by the authority becomes difficult to assess. The Pilcher Committee have therefore recommended that where disposals proceed through negotiations with a single developer the terms should be agreed by an independent assessor,[82] though that recommendation has not yet received legislative backing. They were unable, however, to recommend that confidentiality should be removed from the negotiations themselves: it should suffice that the broad terms of a deal should be made public once a bargain had been struck.[83]

In practice, land disposal for positive planning purposes is often preceded by the preparation of a development brief. This is a non-statutory document whose purpose is usually partly promotional. It typically describes the site and the factors affecting its development, the nature of the development proposed for it by the authority, and the terms upon which they propose to dispose of it. The general view is that the brief should leave developers with sufficient flexibility to prepare their own design and development

---

[81] A. Crabtree & Co. Ltd. v. M.H.L.G. (1965) 64 L.G.R. 104 at 110. It is curious, therefore, that it has now been extended to land disposals by the new urban development corporations: L.G.P.L.A. 1980, s.118.

[82] First Report of the Advisory Group on Commercial Property Development (H.M.S.O., 1975), para. 6.29. A special code of land disposal procedure has been prepared by the Chief Inspector of Audit and recommended for adoption by authorities: see further Report of the Chief Inspector of Audit for year ended 31st March 1980 (D.O.E., 1980) paras. 158–161.

[83] Ibid. para. 6.27.

standards,[84] and that although the land will often be made available with planning permission for the proposed development, the permission will normally be in outline form only. Legal effect may be given to other conditions required by the authority through planning agreements and the other legal relationships considered further below. Developers most commonly compete for the site, whether on an open or selective tendering basis, in terms of price. But an alternative approach is for the authority to fix a price for the land and to invite competition in terms of design.

There are no longer any restrictions on disposal of freeholds, or on leasehold disposal for terms greater than 99 years, which had previously been imposed under the community land scheme. Authorities are also free to choose between the various methods of leasehold disposals, particularly between granting a lease at a premium with provision thereafter for only nominal ground rent; or granting it instead at a rack rent, with provision for regular reviews. There are many possible intermediate variations.

9. Land Disposal by Requirement of Central Government

Surprisingly little is known of the extent of local authorities' land-holdings. Central statistics are kept only of the amounts of land that have been compulsorily acquired, but there are no figures for acquisitions by agreement, and the amounts purchased compulsorily may represent only the tip of the iceberg. More significantly, perhaps, little is known of the extent to which land which has been acquired has actually been put to beneficial use by authorities. Much acquisition has been speculative, and other properties have been bought in pursuance of statutory functions such as slum clearance, but left vacant after site clearance because of inadequate funds to proceed with redevelopment. Uncertainty in financial planning, particularly during eras of cutbacks in public expenditure, has often made it difficult for authorities to match their land acquisitions to their capital programmes. In recent years there has been mounting criticism of the amounts of vacant land held by local authorities and by the nationalised industries and other public bodies. The bulk of it is located either at the urban fringe, or in central areas of towns and cities, often at the edge of the central business district. The land is held against eventual development requirements, and the true land holding costs have been disguised by public sector accounting techniques. Authorities have been reluctant to dispose of the land to the private sector, partly because disposal in many cases would be at a value below original acquisition and clearance costs, and partly because of the possible need to reacquire the land or search for new sites once the resources for development become available.

But the extent of vacant and derelict urban land has grown significantly to the point where it has been identified as a major planning problem. Planning authorities have been criticised for bringing more and more agricultural land into urban development instead of concentrating upon existing vacant urban

---

[84] Advice on the preparation of development briefs is contained in Planning Bulletin 3: *Town Centres. Cost and Control of Redevelopment* (M.H.L.G. 1963), paras.74–79 and Appendix B; and in *Development Advice Note No. 1* (D.O.E., 1976); but their form and content is entirely a matter for the authority concerned. See further *ante*, p.301.

sites[85]; and the unsightliness and dereliction of empty, boarded up sites has had a blighting effect on neighbourhoods and seriously damaged the amenity of the residents.[86] Not all the vacant land is publicly owned, but the proportion is often 50 per cent. or more. Nor is vacancy necessarily a long term problem. Recent research conducted in South Wales based upon a systematic survey of vacant sites found that the majority of sites were progressing through the pre-development stages.[87] Some 20 per cent. were the subject of some form of conflict at the planning stage, 20 per cent. had development hindered by physical difficulties relating to the site, 20 per cent. were hindered by poor access or problems associated with the development of an adjoining site and 33 per cent. had difficulties associated with ownership (including land assembly problems and lengthy negotiations for acquisition).

The research results do not necessarily hold true for all cities, nor do they necessarily present a true picture in the case of publicly owned land where sites are often held against long term projects, such as the building of a new electricity generating station, which are dependent upon uncertain future energy demands and government policies, and development for which authorities are unlikely to have the necessary resources for many years.[88] And so the Government took powers in the 1980 Act to "privatise" publicly owned vacant land, authorising the Secretary of State to prepare and maintain registers of sites, and conferring power on him to order their disposal.

The provisions of the Act must first be brought into effect by statutory instrument, and the Government first conducted an experiment by introducing the provisions only in a limited number of areas. Some 37 district and borough areas were designated,[89] and the first 32 registers prepared identified some 8,000 hectares of land on over 2,000 sites. On the basis of that experiment, it was resolved to introduce the provisions for all local authority areas in England.[90] Following designation, the Secretary of State is authorised to compile and maintain a register of land in the area or land adjoining such land of which a leasehold or freehold interest is owned by one of the prescribed bodies or its subsidiaries,[91] and which, in his opinion, is "not being used or not being sufficiently used for the purposes of

---

[85] See, e.g. A. Coleman, "Land use Planning—Success or Failure?" in Vol. 165 *Architects Journal* (January 19, 1977).

[86] See further the criticisms contained in the detailed analysis of vacant land in London in Nabarro and Richards, *Wasteland* (Thames T.V. Report, 1980).

[87] Bruton and Gore, "Vacant Urban Land" *The Planner* (1981) 34.

[88] In Liverpool, for example, the Inner Area Study team calculated that over 11 per cent. of land in the inner city area was vacant, and that over three-quarters of it was owned by the city council. About half had remained vacant for two years or more; and some 1,250 acres, mainly owned by the city and county councils, were unlikely to be developed in any way within five years: *Change or Decay* (H.M.S.O., 1977), pp. 174–175.

[89] Under L.G.P.L.A. 1980 Commencement Orders Nos. 1 (S.I. 1980 No. 1871); 4 (S.I. 1981 No. 194) and 6 (S.I. 1981 No. 1251).

[90] L.G.P.L.A. 1980 (Commencement No. 7) Order 1981 (S.I. 1981 No. 1618).

[91] The prescribed bodies are listed in Sched. 16 to the Act, and include the local authorities, development corporations, statutory undertakers and various nationalised industries: the list may be altered by the Secretary of State under s.93.

the body's functions or of carrying on their undertaking."[92] The criteria by which this assessment is carried out have not been published.

A copy of the register may then be sent to the council of the district or London borough, who are obliged to make it available for public inspection and to incorporate in it any subsequent amendments made by the Secretary of State.[93] These steps may in themselves encourage the authorities and public bodies to offer the listed sites for sale, but the Secretary of State has a further power to direct them to take steps for the disposal of their interest in any land. The direction may specify what steps are to be taken, and the terms and conditions on which an offer to dispose is to be made.[94]

There is, however, a requirement that the Secretary of State should first consult with the body affected, who may make representations.[95] In the case of local authorities and other bodies for which the Secretary of State has responsibility or is the "appropriate minister," he may not proceed to make a direction against their representations unless he is satisfied that disposal could proceed without serious detriment to the performance of their functions or the carrying on of their undertaking.[96] For other public bodies, the consent of the "appropriate minister" is required before a direction may be made against their wishes.[97]

10. *Land Transactions of Other Authorities*

The powers to acquire, appropriate and dispose of land that have been described in the preceding pages are exercisable by all county and district councils, and by the Greater London Council and the London boroughs. The 1980 Act has also extended the various "planning purposes" powers to the Peak Park Joint Planning Board and the Lake District Special Planning Board.[98]

Parish and community councils have power to acquire land by agreement for the purposes of their functions and for the "benefit, improvement or development of their area," whether within or outside their area.[99] But they have no power of compulsory purchase, which must instead be undertaken on their behalf by the district council.[1] Appropriation and disposal of land is governed by the same rules as for county and district authorities.[2]

Land acquisition, including compulsory acquisition, by Ministers of the

---

[92] L.G.P.L.A. 1980, s.95(2). There is no obligation under the section to list all the land satisfying the conditions; and the Secretary of State is also free to enter Crown land in the register, though there is no power to order its disposal. Section 91 confers a supplementary power to require public bodies to supply the Secretary of State with the necessary information.

[93] *Ibid.* s.96.

[94] *Ibid.* s.98.

[95] *Ibid.* s.99(1); a period of 42 days is allowed for the making of representations.

[96] *Ibid.* s.99(4). The "appropriate minister" is defined by the Public Bodies (Appropriate Ministers) Order 1981 (S.I. 1981 No. 15).

[97] *Ibid.* s.99(5).

[98] *Ibid.* s.119.

[99] L.G.A. 1972, s.124.

[1] *Ibid.* s.125: the district council first hold a local inquiry themselves, before preparing a draft order for confirmation by the Secretary of State. Where the district authority refuse to act, the parish or community council may petition the Secretary of State.

[2] *Ibid.* ss.126 and 127 (as amended by L.G.P.L.A. 1980, Sched. 23, paras.17–19).

Crown has frequently been specifically authorised for their statutory purposes, and there is also a general power for the Secretary of State to acquire any land "necessary for the public service."[3] That power has been broadened by the 1980 Act (re-enacting with modifications provisions originally contained in the Community Land Act) so as to authorise acquisitions:

"(a) to meet the interests of proper planning of the area, or
(b) to secure the best, or most economic, development or use of land."[4]

The power also extends to acquisitions for the benefit of international organisations and foreign powers.[5]

11. *Positive Planning in Wales*

Local authorities in Wales enjoy the same positive planning powers as their English counterparts, but there is also a special Land Authority for Wales, established originally under the Community Land Act. Its success in undertaking the functions conferred on it by that Act has enabled it to survive the repeal of the Act itself and to continue to buy and sell development land. Its function now is that of "acquiring land in Wales which in its opinion needs to be made available for development, and of disposing of it to other persons (for development by them) at a time which is in the Authority's opinion appropriate to meet the need."[6] That is the clearest and least restrictive legislative authorisation for positive planning that now exists. The Authority have broad powers to acquire land which in their opinion is suitable for development, subject to their being under a duty first to consider the likelihood of the site otherwise becoming available for development, its planning position and the general needs of the community including those engaged in building, agriculture, and forestry. Pending the disposal of any land they are required to manage it and turn it to account; and they may with the consent of the Secretary of State for Wales, carry out necessary servicing of the land for development, before disposal.[7]

Two factors in particular contributed to the Authority's success under the 1975 Act, and prevented their abolition. First, they are a single purpose authority, and, unlike the local planning authorities of England and Scotland, were able, and indeed required, to pursue positive planning as their first priority. Second, the Authority are not themselves a planning authority. They operate within the confines of the planning policies administered by the Welsh local planning authorities, and, where their planning applications are refused they have the usual right of appeal to the Secretary of State for Wales. They have managed therefore to avoid the suspicion of conflict of interest which has often attached to the positive planning efforts of local planning authorities. In practice they have also assisted Welsh local

---

[3] *Ibid.* s.113(1) as construed in accordance with L.G.P.L.A. 1980, s.122(1).
[4] *Ibid.* s.113(1) as construed in accordance with L.G.P.L.A. 1980, s.122(2).
[5] L.G.P.L.A. 1980, s.122(3).
[6] *Ibid.* ss.103(1) and 104(1).
[7] *Ibid.* s.103(3).

authorities in land availability studies and with advice on land disposal for development.[8]

In their first three years the Authority succeeded in making substantial profits on land disposals, due partly to the benefits of the net of tax purchasing arrangements under the Development Land Tax Act 1976 (which had accounted for around one-third of their profit by April 1978); and due partly also to favourable movements in the development land market during those years. By 1979 the Authority's land bank in residential land represented no less than one-third of the annual land requirements for house-building in the Principality. And their strong financial position allowed them to turn to longer term projects involving expensive site clearance and major infrastructure works necessary to achieve regeneration and renewal.

The tax advantages exist no longer, and the likely financial success of the Authority for the future is difficult to assess. Their past performance is perhaps the nearest any public authority outside the new towns has ever come to the ideal of positive planning since the 1947 Act. But their new financial structure will force upon them a more commercial role and a reduced capacity to apply profits to socially needed development. The *Land Strategy and Programme* published by the Authority in 1981 concentrates on land trading, and adopts a strategy of building up a land bank of between two and three years' supply of residential land during periods of low market demand, obtaining planning consents and designing and providing infrastructure, and then disposing of the serviced land using development briefs when the market is buoyant.[9] Depending upon the amount of land acquired, the strategy in itself will achieve some stability in the market. They anticipate their main role in commercial development as one of resolving problems of multiple ownerships by site assembly and disposal; whilst in relation to industrial development, the large scale of government and other public agency involvement means that the Authority will act largely in partnership with them.

C. Local Authority/Private Enterprise Partnership Schemes

1. *Introduction*

Positive planning is seldom a purely public sector activity. Planning authorities have broad powers to buy and sell land as a means of promoting development, but they have seldom had either the resources or the expertise to carry out the subsequent development itself on a commercial basis. There have been some notable exceptions, particularly in the case of direct development of small industrial units over the past few years, but the more common pattern has been for authorities to secure development objectives through arrangements with private developers and financial institutions. A variety of different arrangements have been used, and an authority's choice between them in each instance depends usually upon two factors: the extent

---

[8] General information on the Authority's activities is contained in their *Land Policy Statement and Rolling Programmes,* 1978 and 1979; and see further, Grant, "Britain's Community Land Act: A Post-Mortem," in *Urban Law & Policy* 1979, Vol. 2, p.359.

[9] L.A.W., *Strategy and Programme 1981–86,* paras.2.1.1–2.1.4.

to which they may wish to exert any continuing control over the development, and the extent to which they may wish to participate in profits made from it. With smaller developments there is often no need for any arrangements at all, and an authority may confine themselves to control through their normal planning powers.

There has, however, been a trend towards closer and more frequent partnership between local authorities and private enterprise in recent years which is likely to continue as inner city and land supply initiatives gather momentum. Authorities are increasingly entering into additional legal arrangements with private developers, both where the development proposed is for land acquired by the authority as a product of positive planning, and also arising from negotiations with developers in the normal course of development control. In the latter case, for example, a developer might agree to vest in the authority the freehold of a site acquired by him in return for the grant of a long leasehold, often as part of a more complex deal involving adjoining sites already owned by the authority or by other developers. Or a developer may reach an agreement with the authority with regard to the phasing of development in accordance with the rate of provision of infrastructure, to the cost of which he may agree to contribute. It is to be expected that arrangements of this nature will become more common in future with further cutbacks in public sector funding for infrastructure, and as authorities become more aware of their ability to use planning powers in a promotional way.

The legal basis for arrangements between developers and planning authorities is usually contractual. Authorities have broad powers to enter into contracts in furtherance of any of their functions, and they are able in some cases to register the terms of their planning agreements against the land itself, ensuring enforceability against any subsequent purchasers. These agreements are considered in more detail in Chapter 8.

2. Development Agreements

Planning agreements are a useful aid in positive planning, but they offer only a limited basis for partnership, particularly for profit sharing. This is partly because of problems in enforceability against third parties of terms which are of a purely financial character, and partly also because an authority will often wish to enter into an arrangement with a developer before he or they have acquired any of the site at all. In these cases it is common for them to agree that the developer will undertake site assembly (with back-up through the authority's compulsory powers if necessary), and vest the freehold in the authority. Subsequently, in the case of commercial development, and often industrial as well, the authority agree to grant a long lease of the whole site either to the developer or to the financial institution funding the development. The purpose of including the financial institution in the leasehold chain is to allow them to participate in the profits accruing from the development. Instead of simply receiving interest on the capital advanced, they are able to take their share by way of a "rent" under their sub-lease to the developer and to have the benefit of regular rent reviews. Equity participation by the financial institutions has become more popular in recent years, and there have been a number of instances recently where they have dispensed with the developer altogether, and have undertaken development directly themselves.[10]

Development agreements containing provisions as to site assembly, allocating responsibility for any necessary road closures and planning permissions and setting out the heads of agreement for subsequent leasehold disposal, have been widely used. In many cases authorities took special statutory powers under local Acts, but the agreements have now been held to fall within the general powers of local planning authorities without the need for any specific statutory authority.[11] Further, the courts have dismissed the contention that such agreements would necessarily constitute a fetter on the statutory discretion of the authority, or of the Secretary of State in confirming any compulsory order made pursuant to them.[12]

But much depends upon the terms of the agreement, and there is clearly a potential conflict of interest between the planning and the commercial elements of the development where the authority propose to participate in it themselves. Unless the development agreement clearly distinguishes between the contractual obligations of the authority as participants and their role as planning authority, there is a possibility that it may be found to have acted as a fetter. Thus in *Steeples* v. *Derbyshire County Council*,[13] the council had bound themselves by a development agreement "to take all reasonable steps to obtain the grant of outline planning permission for such part or parts of the development area as may be necessary to enable the development to be completed as provided in this agreement and to obtain all other necessary outline consents for the development." If the council failed to use its best endeavours to procure the grant of permission it was liable to pay £117,000 to the developers as liquidated damages.

The obligations would have been unremarkable in an agreement between individuals, but the special status of the council to planning authority placed a different interpretation upon the formula used: it suggested that "best endeavours" might extend not only to the submission of an application for permission but also to the way it was determined. That suggestion is commonly negatived in local authority agreements by a clause which formally saves the authority's powers as planning authority (although it may be little more than a formality). But in the *Steeples* case the potential liability of the authority and the rapid way in which they processed and determined the application was held to have vitiated their grant of permission. It was such as to give the impression that they had fettered their discretion.

3. *Leasehold as a Basis of Partnership*

An important advantage to planning authorities of leasehold disposal of sites lies in their ability to use the landlord/tenant relationship as a means of enforcing planning requirements. Conditions may be inserted as covenants

---

[10] A sample survey carried out for the Property Advisory Group in 1979 showed that as many as 29 per cent. of pension funds were prepared to undertake direct development, and that the trend had been followed among other financial institutions: *Structure and Activity of the Development Industry* (H.M.S.O., 1980), para. 3.13.

[11] *Jones* v. *Secretary of State for Wales* (1974) 28 P. & C.R. 280.

[12] *A. Crabtree & Co. Ltd.* v. *M.H.L.G.* (1965) 64 L.G.R. 104 at 108.

[13] [1981] J.P.L. 582.

in the lease, and enforced directly in the courts by means of actions for damages and injunctions rather than through the less immediate and inadequate statutory enforcement mechanisms. Further, retaining freehold ownership reserves power to the authority to control the eventual redevelopment of the site, whether during the term of the lease or after it has fallen in.

But an additional advantage of leasehold disposal, which now is coming increasingly to be understood by authorities, is the opportunity it provides for profit sharing by the authority. Traditionally authorities have provided land and infrastructure for partnership development in exchange for a fixed premium at the outset, equal usually to the freehold value of the site; or they have settled for a relatively fixed long term income in the form of a ground rent. But the pattern increasingly is for the authority to negotiate also a proportion of future rents from the completed development. There is a variety of methods by which the profits may be shared, and there is a choice of "vertical" or "horizontal" sharing or a combination of the two.[14] "Vertical" sharing involves a splitting of actual net rack rents on the completed development according to an equity sharing ratio (or "gearing") fixed either at the outset, or according to some formula such as the relationship the ground rent bears to the total net rack rents at some defined time in the future. "Horizontal" sharing places a prior claim on total profits to the developer up to a predetermined amount. The authority then participate, normally through a vertical sharing arrangement, in profits above the fixed amount. If the authority are entitled to all the profits after the developer's slice has been taken, the arrangement is known as the "two slice" method. A variant is the "three slice" method, where the local authority take an initial slice by way of a delayed premium for the site, the developer takes the second slice to recover his costs, and the third slice is shared. And there is a "four slice" arrangement, where the developer takes a second slice after recovering his costs, in respect of a predetermined amount of profit, with the fourth slice either going to the authority (in which case the arrangement is one of wholly horizontal division) or shared between the parties.

The local authority/developer arrangements discussed above do not include the separate division of profit between developer and funding institution, which again is commonly achieved through leasehold arrangements. The funding institution will enter into a lease/leaseback arrangement with the developer in respect of his own leasehold interest in the land, or alternatively take the head lease direct from the authority (although there may be difficulties in such a case because of the lack of privity of estate between authority and developer). In return for funding the development, the institution then require a rent from the developer with provision for regular reviews in order to share in development profits. Alternatively, they may simply enter into a forward purchase agreement, undertaking to buy the developer's interest once the development is completed and fully let.

---

[14] See further, Ratcliffe, *Urban Land Management* (Estates Gazette (1978)), Chap. 13; Barrett and Boddy, *Local Authority/Private Sector Industrial Development Partnerships* (School for Advanced Urban Studies, 1981); Bows, "Development Agreements with Funding Institutions" in *Law Society's Gazette* (1980) 464; Cadman and Austin-Crowe, *Property Development* (Spon. 1978), Chap. 7.

Their acquisition may be at a predetermined value, or it may include an element of profit sharing.

As a recent Report by the Government's Advisory Group on Property Development points out, authorities participating in these ways in the profits of development are required also to share in the risks.[15] In return for future profits, they accept a lower amount by way of premium or ground rent, and may only recoup the difference over a long term. But in a well designed scheme the long term returns will often be substantially greater than those from straightforward freehold disposal. And the leasehold structure gives the parties interests which are independently marketable.

Leasehold arrangements are also regularly employed in other ways so as to finance or underwrite development. The lease/leaseback, or sale/leaseback, for example, is a form of borrowing rather than partnership in the true sense, although it is adaptable to profit sharing. The usual arrangement is that the authority grant a lease of land to a financial institution at a capital premium, and then take a lease back at a rent. The authority have thus realised a capital sum on which "interest" is payable in the form of rent. Such an arrangement may be used to finance direct development by authorities, and would rarely involve a private developer. They carry an element of risk which falls wholly on the authority, however, until the rack rents from the completed development exceed their liabilities under the leaseback, or they are able to "sell on" their interest. Leasebacks were formerly attractive to authorities because they involved no borrowing and fell outside central government loan sanction controls. But the new capital expenditure controls introduced by the Local Government, Planning and Land Act 1980 require that the leaseback should now count against the authority's expenditure entitlement at full freehold value,[16] and the arrangement no longer has significant advantages to authorities.

The final variant on the lease as a basis of partnership comes in the form of headleasing schemes, but in these arrangements the authority are underwriting rather than profit sharing. Headleasing is used as a way of attracting developers to undertake development which the authority wish to promote, particularly small industrial units. The developer is offered a guarantee by the authority's undertaking to take a head lease of the completed development at a pre-determined rent, and thus assume the liability themselves of letting off the individual units. This arrangement has similarly been brought within the new capital controls; but as the individual units are let by the authority their freehold value is credited to the expenditure allocation, and a quick turnover therefore costs them little in terms of lost allocation.

[15] *Structure and Activity of the Development Industry*, para. 4.13.
[16] L.G.P.L.A. 1980, s.80(4); further, by subs.(5) and (6) if the authority acquire a leasehold interest in land on which it is intended that some other person shall erect a building for them, the authority are taken to have made annually a payment equal to the value of the works carried out each year. There is a limited exception in respect of the acquisition of leaseholds where there is no intention that some person should erect a building for the authority, under the Local Government (Prescribed Expenditure) Regulations 1981 (S.I. 1981 No. 348), Sched. 3, para. 3; but it extends only to interests for 20 years or less.

4. *Corporate Relationships*

A further potential partnership mechanism is through the limited company structure. By promoting a private company a developer and an authority are able to achieve a relationship based on company law, in which a variety of corporate variations in terms of shareholding, voting rights, directorship appointments and debenture funding are possible. An example is provided by the arrangements entered into by Norwich City Council in 1972 which involved the formation of two private companies between them and a development firm for the development (and its funding) of a 3 acre site owned by the council near the city centre.[17] Both parties held 50 per cent. of the shares in each company, and nominated 4 of the 9 directors; the chairman was independent. Short-term finance came to the company from a commercial bank, and the borrowing was backed by a council guarantee. A different model was adopted by Hampshire County Council in 1972 in an attempt to finance land assembly schemes in two areas likely to be identified for major growth. The county arranged with a merchant bank for the establishment of a company, to which it had power to appoint the directors, and with which it then entered into a complex series of agreements. Their general effect was that land was purchased by the company on terms negotiated with the owners by the council. The company then granted an option to the council to purchase the land at any time up to an agreed date, in consideration of payment of an annual option fee representing interest accruing on the capital advanced for the purchase of the land. The fees could, if the county wished, be capitalised instead and added to the purchase price. The county would then buy the land at the original price including fees, together with capitalised interest charges. The intention was that the land should have increased in value as it was brought forward for development, at a rate greater than the compounded interest payable on its purchase price.

In that particular case, however, the arrangements proved seriously disadvantageous to the authority. Land prices slumped while interest rates rose; and, additionally, a substantial proportion of the land purchased originally at a price reflecting the prospect of development, or "hope value," was later deleted from the proposed allocations in the authority's statutory plans. The financial loss to the authority eventually exceeded £3.5m.

There are other difficulties as well, such as the ethical problems of "insider trading" between company and authority, which might, for example, result in a company acquiring land in advance of the publication by the authority of a draft plan allocating the site for development. In short, although the corporate basis for partnership is usually legally sustainable,[18] there may be serious disadvantages. From the parties' point of view, two particular disadvantages are that the taxation position may be unfavourable to the authority, and that shares, unlike leasehold interests, are not easily marketable.[19] These factors may continue to limit the value of companies for straightforward partnerships, but they need not affect the willingness of

---

[17] See further Minns and Thornley, *State Shareholding* London. Macmillan (1978); and the *Report of the Working Party on Local Authority/Private Enterprise Partnership Schemes* (H.M.S.O., 1972), Annex N.
[18] See further the discussion *post*, p. 551.
[19] *Structure and Activity of the Development Industry*, para. 6.7.

authorities to participate in non-profit making companies which may then in turn enter into arrangements with private developers. A number of authorities have recently been involved in the setting up of companies for the promotion of economic development in their areas; and these arrangements are discussed along with other economic development measures in a later section of this chapter.

D. Area Strategies and Urban Renewal

1. *Introduction*

There can be no doubt that the most important task calling for the exercise of positive planning powers in the future is that of urban renewal, and in particular, the regeneration of inner city areas. British cities contain many areas of worn-out housing, and abandoned and derelict industrial buildings. They are the product of blight and of economic decline, and they have become the centres of social deprivation, characteristically populated by underprivileged groups living in sub-standard housing, with high levels of unemployment and urban crime. These are problems which go far beyond planning: they raise broad issues of economic balance and of the distribution of resources within contemporary society. But there probably is general agreement that the unforeseen or unavoidable consequences of some planning decisions have too often contributed to rather than alleviated, the problems of inner areas. The obvious villains are planning blight, arising often from uncertainty as to proposed public sector schemes, particularly new roads; and the inflexible application of planning policies which may, for example, lead an authority to view an application for expansion by a small factory simply as the extension of a non-conforming use and therefore undesirable, rather than as the opportunity to provide more local employment and thus to be encouraged. And there has been the strong post-war emphasis upon dispersal, which has concentrated resources upon new towns and expanded towns and drawn skilled and semi-skilled labour from the older urban areas, without any balancing policies for their regeneration.

Conventional land use planning can do little on its own to secure inner area regeneration. Private developers are unwilling to bring new development to a declining area unless it can be guaranteed that their investment will be backed by other substantial private and public sector investment in the area. Also there is the difficulty that land and development costs tend to be very much higher than for green field sites. The land must first be cleared, and old infrastructure renewed. Development control powers can achieve little where the market is sluggish, and new development plans can make little impression unless backed by sufficient public sector investment commitment to restore development confidence.

The need for public sector intervention to create the right conditions for urban regeneration has been apparent for many years. During the 1950s and 1960s the most widely used strategy was that of straightforward slum clearance, using the powers conferred by Part III of the Housing Act 1957. But in more recent years there have been attempts towards more flexible approaches. In particular, government thinking has turned more towards the rehabilitation of areas of older housing coupled with general environmental improvements, and that strategy is now in turn being applied to industrial areas.

These are all initiatives that are capable of being taken by local authorities, but there have been repeated complaints that authorities are administratively unsuited to the tasks. Democratic accountability tends to slow down decision making, particularly when the area concerned falls within the areas of two or more authorities. Public participation is an important factor, because the decisions to be taken may involve substantial disruption to the lives of people living in the area. Further, policies of intervention necessarily cut across traditional departmental lines within authorities, and co-ordination has proved far from easy. One approach has been that of area management, that is, of setting up a small management team with representation on it from the authority's departments and with responsibility for all or many of the authority's functions in the area. But that has not always succeeded in cutting down delays or in bringing local government closer to the people.

Dissatisfaction with what has been achieved to date has led the legislature to introduce two more radical strategies in the 1980 Act. The first is that of urban development corporations, intended to take over from local authorities in areas of particularly acute decay. The second is the creation of enterprise zones, where fiscal and other advantages will be available to attract private entrepreneurs to establish businesses and to undertake redevelopment.

It is far from easy to create a satisfactory legal structure for urban renewal. Radical change often requires apparently arbitrary and individually harmful decisions; yet only radical change is likely to stem the rate of decline. The law needs therefore to ensure that, whatever strategies are adopted, there is preserved an opportunity for different viewpoints to be heard, for conflicts of interest to be openly resolved where possible and for adequate redress to be made available to those liable to be adversely affected. It is at best questionable whether these criteria have been satisfied in the past, and there is no guarantee that they will in the future.

These are issues which are increasingly important as policy makers turn more and more to area based strategies, whose attraction is that they allow authorities to set priorities and to concentrate resources upon achieving rapid and visible change. But they are policies of positive discrimination designed to promote the interests of specific areas, and there is always the risk that where the lines of discrimination are too sharply drawn, they may have unfair consequences. Discriminatory policies in favour of one area too frequently drain resources from another area, often one adjoining the first. Equally, discriminatory subsidies may distort an industrial market sufficiently to promote the interests of one firm and its employees in a favoured area at the expense of another in a different locality, perhaps to the point of destroying jobs overall by a policy intended to create them.

These are not matters which lend themselves to easy legislative regulation, however, and the course which has usually been followed has been to establish a broad statutory framework, and to leave central government free to set the detailed terms upon which local authorities may operate.

2. Slum Clearance

Slum clearance fits uneasily into a discussion of positive planning, because it is in itself an entirely destructive operation. Its purpose is simply to bring about the demolition of houses no longer fit for human habitation. But it is of course a strategy that has important planning implications, and extensive slum clearance programmes have changed the face of many British cities since the war. Slum clearance activity in England and Wales rose from immediate post-war levels of around 2,500 houses per year to peaks of over 50,000 in the late 1960s. There was a slight slump in the early 1970s but following a brief resurgence of activity in 1972 levels of clearance have since dropped dramatically. Areas declared in 1978 and 1979 contained fewer houses than at any time since 1955.[20] Clearance today involves two major planning decisions, the choice between clearance and rehabilitation, and the decision as to the ultimate re-use of cleared land. The procedures, however, continue to be based primarily on public health criteria, and attempts to broaden authorities' practical approach have had only limited success.

(a) The clearance resolution

Slum clearance is initiated by a resolution by the housing authority declaring an area to be a slum clearance area.[21] This is a purely administrative act, and they are under no obligation first to consult with residents of the area.[22] They must, however, first be satisfied either that the houses in the area are unfit for human habitation; or that they are "by reason of their bad arrangement, or the narrowness or bad arrangement of the streets, dangerous or injurious to the health of the inhabitants of the area, and that the other buildings, if any, in the area are for a like reason dangerous or injurious to the health of the said inhabitants."[23] Fitness for human habitation is not specifically defined, but the Act does indicate the criteria by which fitness must be assessed. They are physical criteria, relating to the state of repair, stability, freedom from damp, internal arrangement natural lighting, ventilation, water supply, drainage and sanitary conveniences and facilities for preparation and cooking of food and for the disposal of waste water.[24] If a house is "so far defective" in one or more of those respects, it is unfit. There is no duty upon an authority to undertake clearance wherever such conditions are present, although they may take action under Part II of the Act in respect of individual dwellings to secure their repair (where satisfied that the dwelling can be rendered fit at reasonable expense), or their closing or demolition.

Before passing a clearance resolution, the authority must also be satisfied that clearance is the most satisfactory method of dealing with the conditions in the area.[25] Their opinion on that point may need to be justified by them at

---

[20] Detailed figures may be found in the Government's *Housing and Construction Statistics*, in particular the summary tables contained in Volumes 6, IX (1967); 16, III (1970) and 32, VI (1980).

[21] Housing Act 1957, s.42. Under s.49 the authority may include in the declaration any land already belonging to them, and thereafter it will be affected by the same provisions of the Act as other land in the area.

[22] *Fredman* v. *Minister of Health* (1935) 154 L.T. 240. The Government's view is that it would be difficult and "probably undesirable" for an authority to publicise their intentions before they actually pass the declaration: see M.H.L.G. Circular 54/55, para. 5.

[23] Housing Act 1957, s.42(1)(*a*)

[24] *Ibid.* s.4.

[25] *Ibid.* s.42(1)(*b*).

the public inquiry into any subsequent compulsory purchase orders, and it raises directly the question of the most satisfactory strategy to adopt. The comparative costs of clearance and redevelopment on the one hand, and of rehabilitation and improvement on the other, are relevant issues[26], although there are difficulties in establishing clear bases for comparison. Much depends upon estimates of anticipated life of rehabilitated and new dwellings; and on the likely availability of funds for the works. Further, a policy of rehabilitation requires the support and intervention of the local authority, and probably the backing of a housing action area or general improvement area designation. But neither of these can be imposed by the Secretary of State, and if the authority are firmly opposed to rehabilitation and unlikely to support it, it cannot easily be argued to be the "most satisfactory method of dealing with conditions in the area," because the prospect is then one of continuing decline.[27]

Two further matters must be considered by authorities, and these are also issues which go to the validity of their resolution. They must be satisfied that suitable accommodation is, or will be, available for the persons to be displaced; and that the resources of the authority are sufficient for the purposes of carrying the resolution into effect.[28] But they need not have specific figures on which to base that decision,[29] and indeed it may be difficult sometimes to make more than an honest estimate given the lengthy time-span of large-scale clearance and the uncertainty of local authority long-term financial planning. Similarly, in assessing the availability of suitable accommodation, the authority need not strive to preserve the existing community, even although this may involve them in substantial disruption. Thus in *Savoury* v. *Secretary of State for Wales*[30] Cantley J. observed that the residents of the area were:

" . . . a particularly close knit community with a strong community spirit. The ages of many of the residents are between 60 and 80 years and some of them have lived in [the two streets] all their lives. Some of the elderly receive practical help and moral support from kind neighbours, on whom they are thus to some extent dependent."

Yet the Act conferred such broad powers upon local authorities that unless it could be shown that their decision was capricious or based on no evidence, it could not be challenged in the courts. In such an action the residents will often be hampered by lack of information[31] and the inference from the formal documents that an authority have acted reasonably and properly is far from easy to rebut.

---

[26] *Eckersley* v. *S.O.S.E.* (1977) 34 P. & C.R. 124.
[27] See, *e.g. Parker* v. *S.O.S.E.* (1980) 257 E.G. 718. Private rehabilitation initiative may also be frustrated by the refusal of grant-aid. By virtue of the Housing Act 1974, s.61(3)(d) an authority may pay an improvement grant only where satisfied that the dwelling is likely to provide satisfactory housing accommodation for 30 years (reduceable to 10 years under subs.(5) where the authority think it reasonable).
[28] Housing Act 1957, s.42(1).
[29] *Goddard* v. *M.H.L.G.* [1958] 1 W.L.R. 1151.
[30] (1974) 31 P. & C.R. 344 at 345.
[31] See further, *ibid.* at 352.

(b) Purchase of land

The passing of a clearance resolution places a duty on authorities to proceed to secure clearance of the land by purchasing it and clearing it.[32] This may be done by agreement, or by the use of compulsory powers. The Act authorises also the purchase of so-called "added lands" or "grey lands,"[33] that is, land which is *surrounded* by the clearance area and the acquisition of which is reasonably necessary for the purpose of securing a cleared area of convenient shape and dimensions, and any *adjoining* land the acquisition of which is reasonably necessary for the satisfactory development or use of the cleared area.[34]

Where compulsory purchase is necessary, it was formerly essential to submit the draft order for confirmation within six months of the clearance resolution, (or 12 months in the case of surrounded or adjoining land) but that requirement has now been lifted by the Housing Act 1980[35] and authorities are free to proceed at their own pace.

Once land is acquired by them, however, they come under a further duty as "soon as may be" to cause every building on it to be vacated and secure its demolition.[36] There is an exception in the case of houses which in their opinion are, or may be rendered, capable of providing accommodation of a standard which is adequate for the time being. These may be retained temporarily for that purpose as short-life accommodation[37]; but the Act offers authorities no exemptions from any express or implied contractual liability to repair,[38] nor from the statutory nuisance provisions of the Public Health Act 1936.[39]

(c) Objections to compulsory purchase

Because there is not generally any formal opportunity for public consultation prior to the declaration of an area, the public inquiry held prior to confirmation of compulsory purchase orders has developed into the main mechanism for participation. It is not a planning inquiry, and although authorities are required to indicate in broad terms the future use they propose for the land,[40] the planning merits of that use are not within the Inspector's remit. The central policy issue is whether clearance is the most satisfactory means of dealing with the present conditions in the area,

---

[32] Housing Act 1957, s.43(1)(*b*). It was possible until 1974 to choose instead to require the owner, by means of a clearance order, to demolish the property himself and that procedure was widely used. It was abolished by the Housing Act 1974, s.130(4) and Sched. 15.

[33] In the maps prepared for compulsory purchase, surrounded and adjoined land is shown as "grey land," unfit houses are shown as "pink land," and lands included because of the bad arrangement of their buildings as "pink hatched yellow:" such are the requirements of Form 24, of the Housing (Prescribed Forms) Regulations 1972 (S.I. 1972 No. 228).

[34] Housing Act 1957, s.43(2).

[35] Housing Act 1980, s.147 and Sched. 25.

[36] Housing Act 1957, s.47(1).

[37] *Ibid.* s.48(1). It is also possible under s.48(3) for the authority to retain houses within an area for purposes of support or for other special reasons.

[38] Although this may generally be excluded through the use of possessory licences rather than leases.

[39] *Salford City Council* v. *McNally* [1976] A.C. 379.

[40] M.H.L.G. Circular 44/56, para. 6; and see *Coleen Properties Ltd.* v. *M.H.L.G.* [1971] 1 W.L.R. 433.

irrespective of how they may have arisen.[41] The Secretary of State may take the view that rehabilitation is a more satisfactory alternative, but there is the obstacle in such a case that he has no power to direct an authority to take positive steps to achieve it.

Rejection of a compulsory purchase order made in respect of the whole of a clearance area necessarily has the practical effect of overturning the authority's clearance resolution, although there is no specific provision in the Act in respect of this.[42] The resolution is not statutorily irrevocable, however, and may therefore be revoked at any time before confirmation, by an authority in accordance with their standing orders should they decide to pursue an alternative strategy. But following confirmation by the Secretary of State the authority are obliged to proceed with requisition and clearance, and their ability to change course in favour of rehabilitation is lost.[43]

Objection to a compulsory purchase order may be made by any person upon whom it is required to be served. These are every owner, lessee and occupier (except tenants for a month or a less period than a month) and, so far as ascertainable, every mortgagee, of any land to which the order relates.[44] These so-called "statutory objectors," provided their objections have not been withdrawn, have the right to appear and be heard by an Inspector at an inquiry.[45] There are no detailed procedural rules prescribed for inquiries, but Inspectors follow a uniform procedure of first hearing the authority's case in support of the order and then hearing objections, with mutual and often wide ranging cross-examination by the opposing parties. The Secretary of State is not obliged to accept the Inspector's recommendations, and there is a right of appeal by any person aggrieved to the High Court within six weeks of advertisement of the confirmation of the order.[46] The court has no power to remit an order for reconsideration, and a decision to quash the order means that the procedure must start again. If the vitiating factor is the clearance resolution itself, then the authority must start again from the beginning should they still wish to press for clearance; but otherwise it is the compulsory purchase order alone which will fall.

The ability of statutory objectors to challenge an order at a public inquiry and subsequently in the courts is thus a potentially powerful right. It has been widely used, not the least because it offers the only formal means for residents to challenge clearance policies, often after many years of blight and uncertainty. But the powers of authorities are so broad, and the ability and willingness of the courts to review their exercise so limited, that the right of

---

[41] Thus in *Attorney-General ex. rel. Rivers-Moore* v. *Portsmouth C.C.* (1978) 36 P. & C.R. 416 the Court refused to intervene to prevent demolition by the council of houses owned by them in a clearance area prior to the public inquiry, holding that the authority had no choice but to treat the conditions in the area as they found them.

[42] But see *R.* v. *S.O.S.E., ex parte Wellingborough B.C.* [1982] J.P.L. 241, where the Divisional Court held that the effect of the Secretary of State's refusal to confirm a compulsory purchase order was that the land was excluded from the clearance area.

[43] *Wahiwala* v. *S.O.S.E.* [1977] J.P.L. 511 at 513.

[44] Housing Act 1957, Sched. 3, para. 2(1)(*a*). There is no obligation to serve notice upon persons occupying as statutory tenants under the Rent Acts (para. 2(3)); nor presumably upon persons in unauthorised occupation as squatters: see, *e.g. Woodcock* v. *South Western Electricity Board* [1975] 1 W.L.R. 983.

[45] *Ibid.* para. 3(3). An inquiry need not be held, however, into objections relating solely to matters of compensation: para. 3(6).

[46] *Ibid.* Sched. 4, para. 1.

High Court challenge has often been exercised as much for its ability to delay proceedings and to act as a background to further negotiations, as for the hope of any substantive remedy.

(d) Compensation

An important feature of slum clearance is that it allows authorities as a general rule to acquire land at its site value.[47] The exceptions are in the case of houses which are not unfit (and many objections to compulsory purchase orders are challenges not to the principle of purchase or clearance so much as to the classification of affected properties as unfit)[48]; and houses which although unfit, have nonetheless been well maintained by their owners/ occupiers or other prescribed persons.[49]

These provisions do not mean, however, that land is able to be acquired cheaply by authorities: clearance and preliminary redevelopment costs are often too great to be borne without subsidy.[50]

3. Housing Improvement and Rehabilitation

By the late 1960s there was developing a general reaction against the wide-reaching clearance and redevelopment programmes of the post-war era. It found legislative expression in the Housing Act 1969, which gave authorities new powers to promote general improvement areas (G.I.A.'s), in which older housing would be improved rather than demolished. These provisions were added to by the Housing Act 1974, which introduced the further area strategies of housing action areas (H.A.A.'s) and priority neighbourhoods (P.N.'s). H.A.A.'s were to be areas of acute housing stress where substantial public sector intervention was likely to be necessary in the form of subsidy, acquisition of properties and improvements to relieve the stress. The idea was that there should be a concentrated five-year programme intended to improve living conditions in the area. Priority neighbourhoods were to be fringe areas, but the idea remained dormant, and the powers were repealed by the Housing Act 1980, which also reduced the Secretary of State's supervisory controls over the declaration of G.I.A.'s and H.A.A.'s by local authorities.

(a) General improvement areas

G.I.A.'s were introduced somewhat tentatively in 1969. The Government's accompanying advice stressed that experience of area improvement was very limited, and that much remained to be learnt about the assessment

---

[47] Ibid. s.59.
[48] Where objection is lodged against an unfitness classification the authority are obliged to give written notice more than 14 days before the inquiry to the objector of the facts they allege as their principal grounds for being satisfied that the building is unfit; and the objector is further entitled, on making a written request, to be furnished by the Secretary of State with a written statement of reasons for deciding that the building is unfit: Sched. 3, paras.(4) and (5).
[49] See generally Housing Act 1957, s.60 and Sched. 2, Part I.
[50] For a detailed analysis, see New Houses in the Cities (The Role of the Private Developer in Urban Renewal in England and Wales) (H.M.S.O., 1971). Slum clearance subsidy from central government is broadly 75 per cent. of the loss incurred on clearance: Slum Clearance Subsidy Regulations 1974.

of economic advantage as between renewal and rehabilitation, the wider social effects of improving whole areas, and the check of improvement upon land values and on patterns of demand.[51] But by 1975 the Government were convinced that large-scale slum clearance should be drawing to a close, and that the area rehabilitation approach, despite a disappointing start under the 1969 Act, should be taking over.[52] An important objective of rehabilitation policy is that it should prevent, or at least substantially postpone, clearance and redevelopment.

A housing authority may now by resolution declare a G.I.A. in respect of any predominantly residential area where it appears to them, on the basis of a report prepared by suitably qualified persons, that living conditions in the area "can most appropriately be improved by the improvement of the amenities of the area of the dwellings therein or both and that such an improvement may be effected or assisted" by the exercise of their powers under the Act.[53] There is no longer any need for the submission of such resolutions to the Secretary of State, and power no longer exists for him to terminate G.I.A. status.

Authorities are advised to employ G.I.A. strategy for areas of fundamentally sound houses capable of providing good living conditions for many years to come.[54] High levels of owner occupation or of local authority ownership are necessary, because voluntary improvement is the key to the strategy, and this is often far from easy to achieve in the case of privately rented properties. It follows that public participation is a necessary pre-condition of G.I.A. declaration and to its effective subsequent operation. Detailed advice has been given to authorities on encouraging participation,[55] and experience has generally been considerably more encouraging than with broader participation in planning. The issues are local, the benefits of improvement policy apparent to all residents, and money is made available for programmes of general environmental improvement selected in consultation with the residents.[56]

Experience of G.I.A. treatment has shown marked variations between authorities. By 1976 over 1,000 areas containing more than 300,000 houses had been declared in England and Wales, and around 75,000 dwellings had been improved with grant-aid.[57] Research evidence suggests that the take-up of grants has been low, notwithstanding that the 1974 Act extended more favourable grant terms to G.I.A. dwellings[58] and that the remaining proportion of improvement cost contributed by the owner has generally

---

[51] M.H.L.G. Circular 65/69, para. 4.

[52] D.O.E. Circular 13/75, para. 4 & 5.

[53] Housing Act 1969, s.28 as re-enacted in amended form by Housing Act 1980, s.109 and Sched. 13, para. 1(1).

[54] D.O.E. Circular 13/75, para. 18; and see generally Memorandum C, D.O.E. Circular 14/75.

[55] Memorandum C, D.O.E. Circular 14/75, paras.31–35, and see Area Improvement Note 8: *Public Participation in G.I.A.'s* (H.M.S.O., 1973).

[56] Housing Act 1969, s.37, as substituted by Housing Act 1980, s.108 and Sched. 13 para. 5.

[57] The figure is an estimate based on the D.O.E.'s research figures published in 1978: see further D.O.E. Circular 63/78. The survey shows a substantially higher rate of improvement for local authority owned dwellings than for private sector. Further research findings are discussed by Grove, "The Rise and Fall of the G.I.A." *The Planner* (1979), pp. 35–37.

[58] Housing Act 1974, s.59(1)(b) which raised from 50 per cent. to 60 per cent. the maximum percentage of grant aid towards improvement costs.

been well covered by consequent capital value increases.[59] There has too often been inflexibility and delays in administering the grants system and in administering environmental programmes, and some authorities have failed to generate any noticeable increase at all in home improvements.

(b) Housing action areas

Housing action areas are quite different from the planning action areas provided for under the 1971 Act. Their purpose is to preserve an area's residential quality, but to bring about radical improvements in the living conditions within it. The Act requires a five-year programme, and declaration of an H.A.A. expires after five years unless especially extended for a further two-year period with the assent of the Secretary of State.[60] H.A.A.'s are to be areas where physical and social factors combine to create housing stress,[61] and authorities are subject to detailed central government supervision over their powers to declare areas.[62] They are obliged by the Act to have regard to guidance given by the Secretary of State on selection of areas,[63] and the detailed criteria prescribed require them to consider not only the extent of the adverse physical and social conditions, but also the extent to which they interact and the adequacy of resources available for undertaking the programme.[64] Housing conditions will generally be poorer than in the case of a G.I.A., though not so bad as to be likely to require early clearance.[65]

Within an H.A.A. there are more generous improvement grant provisions,[66] broad compulsory purchase powers tied in to H.A.A. objectives,[67] and some limited assistance towards environmental works.[68]

Experience gained in the early H.A.A.'s declared indicates that achievement of substantial improvement within the five-year period is a near impossible task, and that greater financial and manpower resources have been needed than authorities have been able to command.[69] Administrative difficulties are almost inevitably greater than in G.I.A.'s, and often exacerbated by transient populations and absentee landlords. And there have been problems of low grant take-up coupled with an unwillingness by building societies to advance monies for purchase and improvement. The likely consequence is that authorities may revert increasingly again in the future to clearance, perhaps using H.A.A. declarations as a holding operation to forestall blight in the interim period.

---

[59] D.O.E. Circular 63/78, Annex 1, para. 6.
[60] Housing Act 1974, s.39.
[61] *Ibid.* s.36(1).
[62] Housing Act 1974, s.37, which allows the Secretary of State to disallow an H.A.A. declaration.
[63] *Ibid.* s.36(3).
[64] Memorandum A, D.O.E. Circular 14/75, paras.11–19.
[65] *Ibid.* para. 18.
[66] Housing Act 1974, s.59(1)(*a*), which authorises grants of 75 per cent. of eligible expenditure; rising to 90 per cent. under subs.(3) in cases of hardship.
[67] *Ibid.* s.43.
[68] *Ibid.* s.45.
[69] "Housing in Action Areas" in *Roof* (1979), pp. 151–153.

4. *Industrial and Commercial Improvement Areas*

Some local authorities have experimented with extending their housing rehabilitation experience to industrial and commercial areas. One highly successful example was that of the Metropolitan Borough of Rochdale, who set about a programme of industrial improvement in 1974, implementing it through persuasion and co-operation with private industrialists and without any additional statutory powers or subsidies.[70] Other authorities were anxious to expand the concept, and, after one county succeeded in obtaining local Act powers for the declaration of industrial improvement areas (based closely upon the Housing Act provisions),[71] general powers were extended to all the specially designated authorities under the Inner Urban Areas Act 1978.[72] It is a strategy intended to operate primarily upon persuasion, promotion and co-ordination of private sector activity, concentrating attention and resources on the area with a view to restoring confidence in its future. Rochdale's primary aim was environmental improvement rather than economic growth, but the experiment succeeded also in encouraging investment and making land available for new industrial development.

The 1978 Act additionally enables authorities to make grants and loans available for the carrying out of specified improvement works,[73] and to offer improvement grants for the conversion or improvement of buildings. The maximum amount of improvement grant was originally specifically tied in to the job creation potential of the scheme involved, and up to £1,000 could be offered for each job likely to be created or preserved up to a ceiling of 50 per cent. of the cost of carrying out the works. The 1980 Act has removed the job creation requirement, however, and simply set a 50 per cent. ceiling.[74]

Declaration and termination of an I.I.A. are matters for the authority concerned, but there is power for the Secretary of State to disallow a declaration in whole or in part at any time.[75] Central government controls are present because a high proportion of the funding is centrally provided through the urban programme.

5. *Inner Cities: the Urban Programme*

The fate of the inner cities has rapidly become the key planning issue of the day, and there has recently been a surge of legislative activity and a

---

[70] A study of the project has now been published as *Time for Industry* (H.M.S.O., 1979).
[71] Tyne and Wear Act 1976, ss.53–56. The Act offered only limited powers to authorities to promote improvement by others and to carry out works.
[72] Inner Urban Areas Act 1978, ss.4–6. As to the designated authorities, see *post*, p. 539.
[73] *Ibid.* s.5. The accompanying circular, D.O.E. Circular 68/78, emphasises that the power is to be used for the benefit of the I.I.A., rather than just an individual firm, and that the money is not intended to be used simply for routine external maintenance: Annex 1, para. 11.
[74] *Ibid.* s.6 (as amended by L.G.P.L.A. 1980, s.191). Details of criteria for assessment, and background financial arrangements are contained in D.O.E. Circular 68/78, Annex 1, section 6; and Annexes 3 and 4. Details of all assistance approved up to 1980 are set out in Hansard, H.C. Deb., Vol. 977, col. 759., January 31, 1980.
[75] *Ibid.* s.4 and Schedule. Amendments introduced by the L.G.P.L.A. 1980, s.191(2) allow the Secretary of State to exclude from an I.I.A. any land included in any urban development area. Urban development corporations are given powers to declare I.I.A.S. themselves: L.G.P.L.A. 1980, s.162(4).

substantial reallocation of financial resources intended to overcome the problems and restore confidence to the inner areas. The most recent initiatives have been the introduction of "programme,""partnership" and "designated" authority status under the 1978 Act, and the enterprise zones and urban development corporations promoted by the 1980 Act. But the beginnings of a separate inner cities policy go back further than this. The longest running initiative has been the urban programme established under the Local Government Grants (Social Needs) Act 1969, which conferred a remarkably broad power upon the Secretary of State to pay grants to any local authorities "who in his opinion are required in the exercise of any of their functions to incur expenditure by reason of the existence in any urban area of special social need."[76] No provisions prescribed the amount, purposes or conditions of aid, and the broad discretion that vested therefore in the Secretary of State has meant that the programme has been able to accommodate some substantial changes in purpose since its inception. In the early years the programme concentrated upon specifically social subjects. Prominent amongst these was the community development programme established under the aegis of the Home Office, and designed to encourage the establishment of special community facilities in areas of "social need," though not necessarily inner city areas. Central government provided 75 per cent. of the cost of projects, and local authorities the remainder. The bulk of the money went in fact to local authority projects, but in the view of the Government the grants also played a useful part in stimulating innovation and self-help, and allowed money to be channelled through local authorities to voluntary bodies and ethnic minorities.[77]

But the programme was recast in 1977 and extended to cover industrial, environmental and recreational projects as well, with substantially increased funding.[78] These changes were made in anticipation of the Inner Urban Areas Act 1978, the first specific legislative response to the problems of inner city decay. Its background was the commissioning of three inner area studies by the Department of the Environment in 1972, in Lambeth, Birmingham and Liverpool. The reports on those studies each painted a clear picture of inner area deprivation and stressed the need for new initiatives, pointing to industrial investment as the key to economic growth and future prosperity.[79] They also raised questions of the roles of central and local government, and of levels of government funding and subsidies.

The 1978 Act made provision for the designation of inner area authorities at two levels of priority. A broad power authorised the Secretary of State to designate any district where satisfied of the existence of special social need in an inner urban area within it which might be alleviated by the use of the

[76] S. 1.

[77] *Policy for the Inner Cities*, Cmnd. 6845 (H.M.S.O., 1977), para. 63.

[78] *Ibid.* para. 64. The original programme remains in operation, however, and the criteria for the award of grant-aid are set out in D.O.E. Circular 15/80.

[79] *Unequal City* (Birmingham I.A.S.)(H.M.S.O., 1977); *Change or Decay* (Liverpool I.A.S.)(H.M.S.O., 1977) and *Inner London: Policies for Dispersal and Balance* (Lambeth I.A.S.)(H.M.S.O., 1977).

Act's powers.[80] County and district authorities for the area then enjoyed new powers to make grants and loans available and to declare industrial improvement areas.[81] More extensive powers are reserved by the Act for areas designated as "special areas," (the so-called "partnership areas") where a "concerted effort" is needed to alleviate the conditions.[82] Provision had already been made for partnership arrangements between central government and the local authorities for areas of particularly severe deprivation, and the Act has built upon these. There are further powers for authorities in these special areas to lend money for site preparation,[83] and to make grants towards rental payments to encourage new industrial and commercial firms[84] and towards loan interest for small firms.[85] Much of the funding for these new arrangements comes from the recast urban programme.

A number of authorities have also been selected as "programme" authorities, which is not a statutory designation but represents informal recognition of a priority for action falling between the two statutory' designations. Like the partnership authorities, they are invited to draw up inner area programmes, though not in partnership with central government.

The strategy of the 1978 Act, therefore, is one of area-based action. It offers a means of assessing priorities and concentrating resources, and it relies primarily upon local authorities as the agents of change. It required of them a change in urban management technique: the programmes were to be corporate plans, intended to lead to a unified approach between and within authorities in dealing with the problems of the inner areas.[86] There have, however, been delays in practice, and criticisms have emerged of failures to achieve the planned-for co-ordination in practice, of failures to engage public participation in programme preparation and of the top-heavy and bureaucratic central/local partnership arrangements.

6. Urban Development Corporations

Criticisms of the limited achievements of the earlier initiatives led the Government to introduce the two new area strategies contained in the 1980 Act: urban development corporations and enterprise zones. The two are quite separate concepts, though they may be used simultaneously for any area.

Urban development corporations represent a break with the idea that urban regeneration should be a matter for local authorities. It is proposed instead to transplant the model of the new town development corporations

---

[80] Inner Urban Areas Act 1978, s.1. The basic data by which the assessment of need in the districts which were selected for designation is set out in *Hansard*, H.C.Debs., Vol. 951, cols. *468–478* (June 13, 1978); and an updated assessment appears in *Hansard* H.C. Debs., Vol. 4, cols. *324–330* (May 14, 1981). Following a review based on the new data, the Government decided to make no changes in the authorities with partnership or programme status or designated under the Act: *Hansard* H.C.Debs., Vol. 998, cols. *603–610* (February 9, 1981).
[81] *Ibid.* ss.1–6.
[82] *Ibid.* s.7.
[83] *Ibid.* s.9.
[84] *Ibid.* s.10.
[85] *Ibid.* s.11.
[86] A detailed assessment of the inner area programmes is contained in R. Nabarro, "Inner City Partnerships" in *Town Planning Review* (1980) Vol. 51, p. 25.

into the inner cities. An urban development corporation is to be a single function agency, whose task is "to secure the regeneration of its area."[87] This objective will be achieved "by bringing land and buildings into effective use, encouraging the development of existing and new industry and commerce, creating an attractive environment and ensuring that housing and social facilities are available to encourage people to live and work in the area."[88] The objectives and powers are deliberately broad, and the Secretary of State has equally broad powers to determine where and when corporations should be established, and what their powers should be. In short, these are exceptional powers.

(a) Declaration of urban development areas

An urban development area, for which a U.D.C. will be established, may be designated by the Secretary of State if he is of the opinion that it is "expedient in the national interest"[89] to do so. On the assumption that that wording conferred a quite unfettered discretion the Government arranged the appointment of key members for two shadow U.D.C.'s some months in advance of the enactment of the 1980 Act. Corporations are proposed initially only for the London and Merseyside docklands, although power remains to designate other areas subsequently.

Designation is by way of statutory instrument. There is no requirement for preliminary consultation with local authorities in the areas, or for a local public inquiry. Any order must first be approved by resolution of each House of Parliament, however,[90] and the Parliamentary procedures to be followed offer the chance for public opinion to be heard at this stage. This is because designation orders fall to be considered as hybrid measures, and are therefore scrutinised in a different manner from general legislation. An initial technical scrutiny is undertaken by the Joint Committee on Statutory Instruments, then the order is referred to the Hybrid Instruments Committee of the House of Lords.[91] A petition to the House not to affirm the order may be made by any person within 14 days of the report of the Chairman of Committees declaring the order in his opinion to be hybrid. The Hybrid Instruments Committee considers any written representations, and if they think fit may hear the petitioners, in order first to decide whether they have *locus standi*. If they so decide, the Committee report to the House whether there ought to be a further inquiry by select committee into all or any of the matters complained of. If so, the House may refer all or any of the matters to a Select Committee consisting of five Lords, and the Committee has the usual general powers to receive evidence, to call and examine witnesses and to report to the House.

The procedures for designation are thus quite substantially different from those for new towns. Although no objection was sustained against the

---

[87] L.G.P.L.A. 1980, s. 124(1).
[88] *Ibid.* s. 124(2).
[89] *Ibid.* s. 122(1).
[90] *Ibid.* ss. 122(2)(declaration of area); 123(3) (establishment of U.D.C.). Both orders may be made at the same time: s. 123(2).
[91] A summary of the procedures was given in the Standing Committee debate (Official Report Standing Committee D Cols. 741–742)(May 1, 1980); and is also contained in *Erskine May's Parliamentary Practice* (19th ed. Butterworths, 1976), pp. 583–585.

Merseyside Development Corporation Order,[92] a number of petitions were lodged against the Order for the London Docklands Development Corporation when it was made in 1981, and the Select Committee procedure was put to the test. All petitioners were held to have sufficient *locus standi* with the exception of the National Association of Local Government Officers (NALGO), and both public bodies and community groups were therefore able to call evidence. The task for the Select Committee was one of considering whether the Government's proposals for the area were justified, and this assessment was carried out in light of the various targets set and the progress made over past years, particularly during the era of the existing body (believed by the London Boroughs involved to be the best alternative organisation to be entrusted with regeneration), the London Joint Docklands Committee. But even bearing in mind that the early targets for the area, based partly on the Travers Morgan Study[93] (and later translated into the *London Docklands Strategic Plan*[94]) were overly optimistic and had been rendered more unrealistic by the deepening recession (8,500 jobs had been lost over the preceding five years in the area, against the *L.D.S.P.* projection of 10,000–12,000 new jobs), the Joint Committee's prospects for achieving long term regeneration were thought to be not as strong as those of the proposed corporation.[95]

The Committee therefore upheld the creation of a new development corporation, and also supported the proposal to transfer development control functions in the area from the London Boroughs to the Corporation, although taking the view that this was not a step easily to be justified.[96] The Committee expressed strong doubts about the suitability of the Select Committee procedure for the task imposed upon them, which had involved 50 days of hearings and argument; and they urged that alternative machinery be considered for the next occasion.[97]

Whether another such occasion will ever arise for the designation of whole new urban development areas is matter purely for speculation at this stage, but the same procedures have been followed again in the case of further subordinate legislation relating to the Docklands Corporation. Orders providing for the vesting of land owned by other public bodies in the area directly in the Corporation have been petitioned against, although in each case the Select Committee have found that the main grounds of objection have been those already taken into account in the main Report, and have recommended acceptance of the Order.[98]

The vetting procedure exercised through the Hybrid Instruments Committee and the resulting Select Committee was something of an

---

[92] An initial objection by the National Association of Local Government Officers was later withdrawn following negotiations.

[93] *Docklands. Redevelopment Proposals for East London. Report to the Greater London Council and the Department of the Environment by the London Dockland Study Team* (G.L.C., 1973).

[94] *London Dockland Strategic Plan* (Dockland Joint Committee, 1976).

[95] *Report from the Select Committee of the House of Lords on the London Docklands Development Corporation (Area and Constitution) Order 1980* (H.L. 198)(H.M.S.O., 1981).

[96] *Ibid.* para. 8.8.

[97] *Ibid.* para. 10.1 and 10.2.

[98] See, *e.g.* Session 1980–81, H.L. 216 (Port of London Authority); H.L. 260 (Newnham London Borough Council).

unforseen event, and despite the detailed scrutiny of the Government's case which the Committee undertook, their function differed from that of a conventional planning inquiry. The focus of debate was different, for a start: it was a debate about the capacity of vying institutions to bring about the desired urban regeneration rather than about the principle or location of regeneration in itself. And the Committee's function was not merely that of reporting to a minister, but of reporting to Parliament, which gave it an independent status. But the Committee's purpose is probably best regarded as a long-stop safeguard against the quite unjustified use of the extensive powers vested in the Secretary of State, rather than as one of balancing the more difficult policy issues surrounding the likely performance (and the criteria by which it might be measured) of a proposed urban development corporation.

An urban development corporation's members are appointed wholly by the Secretary of State, to whom the Act reserves a great deal of power in defining their functions and directing their day to day activities.[99] Funding is by way of borrowing, backed up by Treasury grants, and the direct costs of grants and loans in the early years are expected to be around £100m. per annum.

There are exceptionally broad powers for the acquisition of land by the corporations, including compulsory powers. Land may be acquired compulsorily if it is within the urban development area[1]: there is no further test of suitability for redevelopment or the like, and although the Secretary of State may require further evidence as to this before confirming an order for compulsory purchase the language of the Act is unconstrained. These powers are supplemented by a power conferred on the Secretary of State to order the vesting in the Corporation of any specified land held by any local authority or other public body in the area.[2] Such a compulsory transfer requires nothing more than the making of an order. There is no direct provision for objections by the dispossessed authorities to be heard, although the hybrid nature of these orders means that challenge may be made under the procedures outlined above. Further, the orders are subject to positive confirmation procedure in both Houses of Parliament, and may be further debated there following the Select Committee's report on them.

(b) Planning in urban development areas

In both the urban development areas, the development corporations have been given broad planning powers in place of the usual local planning authorities. First there are powers similar to those conferred on new town corporations, of preparing and submitting to the Secretary of State proposals for the development of the land in the area. He may, after consultation by him with the local planning authority for the area and any other local authority, approve the proposals. The proposals may be submitted in a loose and broad brush form, and there are none of the requirements of the usual

---

[99] L.G.P.L.A. 1980, s. 135, Sched. 26, para. 2.

[1] *Ibid.* s. 142.

[2] *Ibid.* s. 141. The following orders have been made under these provisions: Merseyside, S.I. 1981, Nos. 999, 1000, 1001, 1002, 1003; London Docklands S.I. 1981, Nos. 941, 942, 1145, 1146.

forward planning system of surveys, consultation and public participation. But upon approval, planning permission is granted without more for development in accordance with the approved proposals, by virtue of a special development order.[3] The permission extends to development to be carried out by the Corporation or by any other person, although in the latter case the Corporation retain power of approval over details of "the siting, design, external appearance, means of access, provision for vehicle parking and for loading, unloading and storage of vehicles and containers, storage of materials in the open and landscaping of the site."[4] There is a five-year time limit on the commencement of development following the Secretary of State's approval; and the Corporation are obliged to carry out consultations with the usual agencies prescribed by the General Development Order before undertaking any approved development themselves, or granting detailed consent to others.[5]

The second set of planning powers exercisable by the development corporations relate to general development control. The existing local planning authorities in the development areas have been stripped of their development control powers, and full power vested in the corporations.[6] Although the authorities retain forward planning powers, these are effectively overridden as well because all the powers required for plan implementation are conferred on the corporations. The development corporations have been given exclusive powers in relation not only to determining planning applications (as well as their own development proposals) but also to enforcement, tree preservation, conservation areas, advertisements, wasteland and listed building controls.[7]

The major uncertainty which remains over the two urban development corporations is the extent to which large scale injections of public money can succeed in attracting private sector investment to the areas. In this respect, the London Docklands area has greater obvious potential because of its locational advantages, particularly once communications infrastructure is improved. Greater planning flexibility may be an attraction to private investors, enhanced in the case of the Docklands by an enterprise zone (see below) in the Isle of Dogs; but the major consequence in planning terms of the reorganisation of planning functions is that the new corporations subsume all the powers formerly exercised by the various authorities for the area at borough and district, and strategic level. That in itself at least provides for a unified approach to policy and a slimmed down administrative structure capable of swift response to development proposals; but whether that aim in itself can justify overriding the familiar democratic basis of local planning can only be assessed against the long term achievements of the corporations and the extent to which they succeed in harnessing local support.

---

[3] The Town and Country Planning (Mersey Urban Development Area) Special Development Order 1981 (S.I. 1981 No. 560); Town and Country Planning (London Docklands Urban Development Area) Special Development Order 1981 (S.I. 1981 No. 1082).

[4] *Ibid.* art. 3 (in each case).

[5] *Ibid.* art. 7 (in each case).

[6] By virtue of the Merseyside Development Corporation (Planning Functions) Order 1981 (S.I. 1981 No. 561); London Docklands Development Corporation (Planning Functions) Order 1981 (S.I. 1981 No. 1081).

[7] *Ibid.* art. 3 and Sched. 1 (in each case).

7. Enterprise Zones

Enterprise zones were a comparatively late addition to the 1980 Act, and the provisions regulating them appear therefore only in a late schedule to the Act.[8] Like the urban development corporation, their purpose is to secure urban regeneration, but in this case the strategy is deliberately to reduce the role of the public sector rather than the setting up of a specific public sector agency. The original vision was that enterprise zones would be government "no go" areas, or "mini Hong Kongs:" that is, areas dedicated entirely to the principles of a free market, where entrepreneurs, released from the bonds of state controls, would be eager to establish businesses and create new prosperity. They would be free from all fiscal controls including taxes and rates, and customs and excise controls; free to exploit and to prosper, and thus to achieve indirectly an upturn in the fortunes of the areas selected for their operations.

The provisions which were eventually enacted were considerably diluted from the original. Instead of the economic piracy initially sought, there emerged a package of fiscal and bureaucratic exemptions intended to make the designated areas attractive to new and expanding businesses. Freedom from planning control is one of the exemptions offered, and the enterprise zones revert instead to a zoning-based control system. At the heart of the new system is the enterprise zone scheme.

(a) Enterprise zone schemes

The Act makes it clear that the zones may not, unlike the urban development corporations, be imposed upon unwilling authorities (except that an enterprise zone may subsequently be declared in respect of all or part of an urban development area). Instead, authorities may be invited by the Secretary of State to prepare a scheme for the development of an area, with a view to its becoming an enterprise zone.[9] It is thus a matter for them, subject to the terms of the invitation, what planning concessions should be offered. Should they accept the invitation, they may prepare a scheme in draft, and then must secure that adequate publicity is given to its contents; that persons who may be expected to want to make representations on it are made aware of their entitlement to do so; that they are given an adequate opportunity and that the representations are considered by the authority.[10] Representations need only be considered, however, if they are made within the prescribed time, and if they are made on the ground that "all or part of the development specified in the scheme should not be granted planning permission in accordance with the terms of the scheme."[11]

The authority may then, after considering representations, adopt the scheme, modified if necessary to take account of representations (though not so as to make it inconsistent with the original invitation).[12] The validity of the scheme may be challenged within six weeks of publication of the notice of adoption, but otherwise may not be questioned in any legal proceedings

---

[8] L.G.P.L.A. 1980, Sched. 32.
[9] *Ibid.* Sched. 32, paras. 1 and 2.
[10] *Ibid.* para. 2(2).
[11] *Ibid.* para. 2(3).
[12] *Ibid.* para. 3.

whatsoever.[13] The Secretary of State may, after the expiry of the six-week period, then designate the area to which the scheme relates as an enterprise zone.[14] Although the procedures are modelled closely upon those governing the preparation of statutory plans, there is no obligation on either the Secretary of State or the promoting authority to hold a local public inquiry at any stage. There is no independent assessment of the strength and validity of objections lodged by residents and occupiers of land excluded from the scheme, and there is no obligation upon the authority to comply with any existing statutory plans in preparing it.[15]

Details of the 11 zones which have now been selected and designated in England and Wales are given in Table 21. Although there proved to be no shortage of authorities willing to participate in the experiment, drawing the boundaries of the designated areas proved difficult and controversial. In some areas there was already a high proportion of public land ownership, and enterprise zone designation meant that the local authority were in a particularly advantageous position to promote development. But in other areas where there was primarily private sector ownership, the drawing of zone boundaries immediately distorted established trading patterns. One firm, fortunate enough to be located within the new zone, would enjoy the ten year rates holiday and other fiscal advantages conferred by the new status, whilst another competing firm located nearby would not. Such an arbitrary distribution of benefits is inevitable in any precise, area-based scheme, but it has added to the difficulties of determining sensible and fair boundaries. A further difficulty has been that comparatively few of the cities selected for enterprise zone treatment contained single areas of land of sufficient size to be separately designated; and instead it has been necessary to piece together two or three neighbouring areas.

(b) Planning in enterprise zones

The order designating the zone has the effect of granting planning permission for development specified in the scheme.[16] In effect, the procedure allows local authorities to prepare the equivalent of a special development order for the area. Permission may be specific or may relate to particular classes of development; and it may be conditional or subject to limitations.[17] The Secretary of State also has power in the designation order to confer upon the enterprise zone authority (the authority who have prepared the scheme) some or all of the powers of the local planning authority for the area,[18] and this has the effect of supplanting, to the extent provided, any other planning authority.[19] That would normally be the

---

[13] *Ibid.* para. 4.

[14] *Ibid.* para. 5. Designation is by statutory instrument, which requires Treasury consent and is subject to negative resolution procedure in either House of Parliament. A list of orders appears in Table 21.

[15] Instead, the statutory plans are required to yield to the enterprise zone, and there is a duty on authorities to review any structure plan or local plan for the area, and to prepare any necessary alterations: Sched. 32, para. 23.

[16] Sched. 32, para. 17(1).

[17] *Ibid.* para. 17(3).

[18] *Ibid.* para. 5(7). No such provision has been made in respect of any enterprise zones designated to date.

[19] *Ibid.* para. 20(1).

Table 21

Enterprise Zones: England and Wales

Location	Designated EZ authority	S.I. No. 1981 No.	Date of coming into operation
Swansea	Swansea City Council	757	June 11, 1981
Corby	Corby		June 22, 1981
Dudley	Dudley Borough Council	825	July 10, 1981
Longthwaite Grange (Wakefield)	Wakefield Borough Council	950	July 31, 1981
Salford (3 zones)	Salford City Council	1024	August 12, 1981
Trafford (3 zones)	Trafford Borough Council	1025	August 12, 1981
Gateshead (3 zones)	Gateshead Municipal Borough Council	1070	August 25, 1981
Newcastle	Newcastle upon Tyne City Council	1071	August 25, 1981
Speke (Liverpool)	Liverpool City Council	1072	August 25, 1981
Hartlepool (3 zones)	Hartlepool Borough Council	1378	October 10, 1981
Isle of Dogs (London)	London Docklands Development Corporation	1982 No. 462	April 26, 1982

All the designations listed in the Table have been made for a period of ten years from the date of their coming into operation. Two further enterprise zones are proposed in Scotland (Clydebank) and Northern Ireland (Belfast).

county authority, or, in the case of schemes prepared by new town or urban development corporations, the district and county authorities.

A scheme may override the policies of existing structure and local plans, and the Act requires planning authorities to review their plans following a designation order and to prepare such alterations for approval or adoption as they consider necessary to take account of the scheme.[20]

There has been considerable variation between authorities in their specification of the type and scale of development to be permitted in the enterprise zones. The Swansea scheme granted a broad permission for the development "of general and light industrial projects, of wholesale and storage warehouses, of commercial offices, of hotels and motels and of retailing projects of up to 45,000 square feet," subject to a short list of standard conditions regulating land coverage and height of buildings, access and loading, and noise and atmospheric emissions.[21] Other enterprise zone authorities have attempted to confine development rights more narrowly, particularly in the case of retailing where there has often been strong pressure from existing nearby retailing centres to ban retail uses in the zones altogether.[22]

[20] *Ibid.* para. 23
[21] *Enterprise Zone Scheme. Lower Swansea Valley* Swansea C.C. (1981).
[22] See further Jones, "Enterprise Zones. The Prospect for Retailing" in (1981) 259 E.G. 1037.

How far these open planning permissions and the fiscal advantages supporting them will succeed in revitalising the selected areas cannot yet be estimated; and nor can the costs which are likely to be imposed on other areas. A proportion, at least, of firms coming to the zones will simply have moved from another location within the same area, and their transfer will not necessarily have created any new employment and may have left vacant premises elsewhere. Much relocation may be expected from the "collar" zone surrounding the enterprise zone, with a gradual decline in the perimeter areas. Firms coming to the zones may find that the fiscal advantages of the zones have been leeched away by rent increases and land price rises, destroying the sought-for stimulus to growth, although in those zones where there is a high proportion of public ownership it may be possible to control this. In short, there are many imponderables, and it will require detailed research to establish whether, over a long term period, the experiment will achieve revitalisation at a socially acceptable cost.

(c) Fiscal and administrative benefits

The administrative benefits offered within enterprise zones, which include swifter planning decisions on applications requiring consent and fewer requests by Government departments for information, are comparatively insignificant compared with the fiscal benefits. These include:

Exemption from rates. There is a general exemption from the payment of rates for the whole period for which the area remains an enterprise zone,[23] which is to be 10 years at least. The exemption does not extend to dwelling houses, private garages or private storage premises, or to certain premises of public utilities; but it is otherwise all embracing, and the revenue loss to the local authorities affected is to be made up in full by central government. The impact of the rates exemption can be expected to vary as between different types of firm, but many manufacturing firms already face rates bills exceeding the amount which they pay by way of corporation tax; and for warehousing and distribution firms with comparatively low employment levels, rates liability is a substantial proportion of operational expenses.

Exemption from development land tax. This exemption, which was introduced by the Finance Act 1980,[24] is intended to lift any fiscal inhibition on the release of sites in the enterprise zones.

Capital allowances on industrial and commercial buildings. The Finance Act 1980 also introduced 100 per cent capital allowances on buildings in enterprise zones, and the significant attraction of these is that they extend not only to industrial development, for which extensive allowances were already available, but also to commercial buildings.[25] They may therefore prove attractive to firms proposing office retail, hotel and other commercial development in the zones.

Exemption from industrial training levies. Exemption from the levies was introduced by the Employment and Training Act 1981, although the effect is to cast the burden onto the remaining sectors of industry.

[23] Sched. 32, para. 27.
[24] Finance Act 1980, s. 110.
[25] Capital Allowances Act 1968, as extended by Finance Act 1980, s. 74(4).

Exemption was also conferred from the requirement to obtain industrial development certificates in enterprise zones,[26] but that has since been overtaken by the Government's decision to suspend the certification system altogether.[27]

E. Economic Development by Local Authorities

1. *Introduction*

The deepening economic recession of the past five years has seen a substantially broadened economic role being assumed by many local authorities, particularly in the more economically depressed areas. They have acted in an attempt to alleviate unemployment in their areas by intervening in the local economy to support firms in difficulties and to promote new industrial development and new employment. These activities are "positive planning" in its broadest sense, but they also embrace the more conventional activities of land acquisition and disposal, direct development for industrial purposes and private sector/public sector partnerships. Although many authorities have now set up special and separate economic development committees to supervise and promote these operations, there is still a substantial land-use planning input.

The main activity undertaken by authorities to date has been the provision of serviced sites for industrial development and the erection of industrial nursery units and small factories, filling a market gap left by the private sector industrial developers. In some cases authorities have undertaken direct development, but in others there have been partnership schemes with private developers, perhaps with the authority underwriting the scheme through head-leasing arrangements or rent guarantees. Similarly, there has been some attention paid to carrying out the conversion of large scale industrial premises in order to provide smaller units, with the added "planning gain" of bringing vacant property back into use.[28]

These are activities which are able to be undertaken within the powers discussed earlier in this chapter, and they are in practice coupled with a more employment-oriented use of development control powers so as to encourage new development and to tolerate non-conforming and even unauthorised development where it has employment implications.

But the more controversial aspect of local economic development is that of direct grant aid and other forms of subsidy to firms. The distinction between subsidised and unsubsidised intervention by local authorities is often impossible to draw clearly, even in the case of land supply and partnership development. An inducement to a firm to take on a lease of a new industrial unit, in the form of an offer of a period of reduced rent, for example, may be a necessary marketing technique in order to let the

---

[26] Town and Country Planning (Industrial Development Certificates) Regulations 1980 (S.I. 1980 No. 867) reg. 2.

[27] Town and Country Planning (Industrial Development Certificates) (Prescribed Classes of Building) Regulations 1981 (S.I. 1981 No. 1826).

[28] For a general survey of these activities, see Barrett and Boddy, *Local Government Involvement in the Industrial Development Process* School for Advanced Urban Studies Working Paper 6 (1979) and *Local Authority/Private Sector Industrial Development Partnerships* S.A.U.S. Working Paper 18 (1980).

property. Many authorities have therefore been willing to offer direct and indirect financial assistance to industry, in the form of grants, loans and rent free lettings periods in order to attract new industrial growth; and some have have also invested in firms by taking shareholdings to prevent liquidation and loss of jobs.

These forms of financial aid to industry create special problems. First, without special government aid the costs of intervention are inevitably cast in part upon the ratepayers of the area, at a level which may in turn threaten existing firms. Second, local economic activity is essentially parochial, and it results in competition between adjoining areas to attract new growth. An employment gain in one area is not necessarily the consequence of growth which would not otherwise have occurred at all; it is equally possible that it represents no more than a locational change, either from an existing location or from a proposed alternative location. The gain therefore is also a loss imposed upon the other location. If the other location is an economically better-off area, the loss represents at least a step in the direction of national regional policy, intended to secure a better economic balance between the regions. But it may be a loss inflicted instead upon a less well off area, and local economic policy can therefore cut directly across national policy for the regions. Thirdly, assessment of the cost effectiveness of local economic activity is at best uncertain, particularly once it goes beyond pump-priming and promotion and into more long term support for ailing firms. It is not a problem simply of measuring financial input against potential job loss, but also of assessing costs imposed elsewhere by discriminatory financial policies.

Fourthly, Britain's membership of the European Community imposes upon it the treaty obligation not to grant aid "which distorts, or threatens to distort competition . . . insofar as it affects trade between Member States."[29] Any programme of substantial aid to industry is liable to breach the Treaty; and it may also distort internal markets to the disadvantage of established firms.

2. Powers to Aid and Promote Industry and Industrial Development

The difficulties outlined above have inhibited attempts to mark out the boundaries of a proper economic role which might be played by local authorities, and the result is that the powers under which authorities have been acting have been largely either temporary or indirect. The temporary powers are those conferred by local Acts of Parliament, and their purpose in general has been to expand upon the powers available to authorities under two general Acts, the Local Authorities (Land) Act 1963, and the Inner Urban Areas Act 1978. Under section 3 of the 1963 Act, authorities are permitted to make loans for the erection of buildings on land sold or let by the authority (and some have rather deviously extended the power to other land by entering into sale and leaseback or lease/leaseback agreements with industrialists on their own sites). The maximum advance that may be made is 75 per cent. of the mortgage security, and the interest rate is one-quarter per cent. above the prevailing Treasury rate. Those powers are extended in respect of designated areas under the Inner Urban Areas Act 1978, which

[29] Art. 92 of the Treaty of Rome.

permits the making of long term loans of up to 90 per cent. of site value for land acquisition, or for the carrying out of works, again limited to 90 per cent. of the value which it is estimated the security will bear when the works are completed.

Those general powers have been supplemented in many areas by special local Act powers, authorising loans for the erection and improvement of buildings and the acquisition of land, rent guarantees and general industrial assistance. But those powers have now lapsed in Metropolitan areas, and are due to lapse elsewhere by the end of 1984. Further, the 1984 deadline has been accepted where additional local economic powers have been taken in local legislation enacted since 1974. Unless new general legislation is brought forward, therefore, the powers of many authorities will after 1984 be more restrictive than they have been in the past for engaging in programmes of support for industry.

3. The Section 137 Power

Section 137 of the Local Government Act 1972 confers a general power on local authorities to incur expenditure "which in their opinion is in the interests of the inhabitants of their area or any part of it or all or some of its inhabitants." The section is the successor to the old "free penny rate" provisions of the 1963 Local Government Act, and its purpose is to give authorities an elastic but limited reserve power of expenditure. The limits are twofold. First, annual expenditure under the section is limited to the product of a two-penny rate for the authority's area.[30] For county authorities the sums involved are therefore substantially greater than for districts, but the section has come to be used increasingly by both tiers as authorising economic activity. Second, the power is to be invoked only where no other power exists for the purpose. The authority may not incur any expenditure "for a purpose for which they are, either unconditionally or subject to any limitation or to the satisfaction of any condition, authorised or required to make any payment by or by virtue of any other enactment."[31] This limitation restricts the use of the power to that of a reserve power: it may not be used to supplement any existing power or to overcome any statutory limitation or condition. But it raises important problems of interpretation, hinging on the breadth of meaning to be given to the word "purpose." If positive planning is already a purpose for which an authority are able to make payments, the section 137 power would be excluded. But "purpose" is perhaps a narrower term than "function," and it is arguable that a "purpose for which they are . . . authorised or required to make any payment" refers only to a specific authorisation, and that the section 137 power may be used to support other functions of the authority where specific financial power is lacking. The powers of the Inner Urban Areas Act 1978 are expressly stated to be without prejudice to section 137, and therefore the only conflict of purpose which arises on this narrower interpretation is with the specific local Act powers enjoyed by some authorities. Steps were taken in the Local

---

[30] Local Government Act 1972, s. 137(4). The rate product for the purposes of the section is calculated in accordance with the special provisions of the Rate Product Rules 1981 (S.I. 1981 No. 327).
[31] L.G.A. 1972, s. 137(1).

Government (Miscellaneous) Provisions) Act 1982 to resolve the doubts about the scope of section 137, and the Act inserted new subsections (2A) and (2B) which declare that the provisions include power to incur expenditure to give financial assistance to persons carrying on industrial or commercial undertakings, and that the assistance may be by way of lending, guarantee or grant-aid.

Section 137 money has therefore come to play an important role in local economic intervention, and although the powers were never designed with such a purpose in mind, it has become their main and even sole use by a number of authorities, particularly in the metropolitan areas.[32] Although its conversion to this role has been somewhat fortuitous, it is an attractive model for intervention powers which combines overall financial limits with maximum local flexibility.

The Government proposed in early 1982 to restrict the finding which might be used for industrial assistance under section 137 (outside the designated areas under the Inner Urban Areas Act 1978) to the product of a half-penny rate,[33] but the proposal was strongly opposed by the local authority associations and was abandoned (at least for the interim) in favour of the restructuring of section 137 mentioned above.

4. Local Authority Economic Development Companies

Several local authorities have participated in the formation of private companies intended to carry out an economic development role. The advantage of using this indirect route is that the company is a separate legal entity from the authority, and funds may be transferred to it from the authority under section 137 powers. A number of companies, indeed, were established shortly before the end of the 1980–81 financial year with a view to transferring funds out of the authorities before the coming into force of the new capital expenditure limits introduced by the 1980 Act. In some cases, the company is formed by officers or members of the authority acting in a private capacity; whilst other authorities have taken the view that the formation or acquisition of a company as a vehicle for the implementation of economic functions is incidental or conducive to their general positive planning function, or alternatively to their exercise of their powers under section 137 and thus within the general power of section 111 of the Local Government Act 1972.[34] Typically, the company's objects are limited to

---

[32] This was the finding of the Burns Committee in their report *Review of Local Authority Assistance to Industry and Commerce* (unpublished, 1980), although they found considerable variation between authorities in their interpretation of the section, and suggested reform in terms of a broader redrafting of the section and/or the enactment of a package of specific powers.

[33] Consultation Paper, *Local Authority Powers to Assist Industry and Commerce* (D.O.E., 1982).

[34] Thus *cf. Manchester City Council* v. *Greater Manchester County Council* (1979) 78 L.G.R. 71 (C.A.); (1980) 78 L.G.R. 560 (H.L.) where the court upheld the submission that a trust set up by the county for educational purposes under s.137 (being purposes which were otherwise *ultra vires* the authority) could be regarded as a vehicle for the implementation of the county's policy, and its formation as reasonably incidental to, or consequential on, their power to spend the money for the pupose proposed. Despite the lawfulness of direct participation, however, many authorities have preferred to avoid it in order to establish a genuinely independent, or at least more visibly separate body, so as to minimise the risk of any lifting of the veil of incorporation by the courts.

purposes *intra vires* the authority, although there is no reason why the company should not have a broader brief provided that the terms upon which it is funded by the authority are tied to *intra vires* purposes.

It is also common for economic development companies to be limited by guarantee, and for there to be an express prohibition against distribution of profits. The company may thereby be established as a body "which provides any public service in the United Kingdom otherwise than for the purpose of gain," within subsection (3) of section 137, to whose funds contributions may be made by the authority (and, for that matter, by other authorities in the area) without being subject to the limitation of subsection (1) that precludes payments under that subsection being used to supplement the resources allocated to existing functions of the authority.

The companies established to date display a wide variety in approach to the functions of local economic development. In some cases the function is primarily one of positive planning and development promotion, in which the company engages with the private sector in land assembly and underwriting new development. In others, the primary purpose is one of providing venture capital for new or existing industries in the locality, with investment by the company being undertaken with a view to long term growth rather than short term profitability, and designed to achieve job retention and job creation. The total resource available under section 137 is dwarfed by the scale of the economic recession, but the companies may yet succeed in attracting additional institutional investment to their areas, including local pension funds, with a potentially substantial role as local merchant bank.

CHAPTER 13

APPEALS AND INQUIRIES

A. Structure and Functions of the Appeals System

1. *Introduction*

The right of appeal to the Secretary of State against adverse decisions taken by local planning authorities is a fundamental right. When George Dobry Q.C. in 1973 tentatively questioned whether it might, in the interests of administrative efficiency, be taken away in respect of minor applications, he found instead that there was "considerable support" for retaining it intact and some suggestion that its scope should be broadened.[1] But the procedures of appeals and inquiries have caused more than their share of controversy. The system serves three often contradictory purposes. First, it provides a means for challenging local planning authority decisions. It offers applicants for planning permission the opportunity to go over the head of the planning authority, and it gives them an important safeguard against arbitrary decision making at local level. Second, it provides a forum for public participation through the procedures of the local public inquiry, with an opportunity to question the assumptions and arguments of the main protagonists and to put forward alternative points of view. Third, it provides the Secretary of State with the means to supervise the development control functions of local planning authorities and to reassert national policy.

Thousands of appeals are lodged every year against refusals of planning

Table 22
Planning Appeals under ss.36 and 53 of the 1971 Act

Year	Total decided	Secretary of State cases			Inspectors' cases		
		% of total	% allowed	% by written representations	% of total	% allowed	% by written representations
1969	6,557	88.3	29.4	47.7	11.7	26.0	64.4
1970	5,786	56.7	30.5	38.3	43.3	23.0	60.6
1971	5,828	44.8	28.1	31.0	55.2	17.9	59.9
1972	6,216	33.4	30.2	32.6	66.6	22.0	64.5
1973	11,409	22.5	29.2	43.0	77.5	19.7	76.2
1974–5	13,159	22.0	21.5	51.0	78.0	22.8	79.8
1975–6	11,739	24.6	26.8	47.9	75.4	26.7	79.8
1976–7	9,238	23.9	31.1	47.8	76.1	29.1	76.3
1977–8	8,970	19.4	32.4	49.7	80.6	28.2	80.4
1978–9	9,598	17.6	31.4	45.4	82.4	27.0	79.7

Source: adapted from Development Control Statistics 1978/79 (*D.O.E., 1980*), *Tables 27–29.*

[1] G. Dobry, *Review of the Development Control System. Interim Report* (1974) pp. 72–73; *Final Report* (1975), p. 122.

permission, against conditions imposed by authorities on permissions granted by them and against the failure of authorities to issue a decision within the prescribed time. The Secretary of State is, at least statistically, the single most prolific decision maker in the land. The figures in Table 22 show the annual fluctuations in numbers of appeals, and in particular the substantial swell in applications and appeals during the "boom" years of 1971–73. The figures are for England only, and they do not include the wide range of other matters coming to the Secretary of State for decision, including enforcement appeals, and a variety of orders requiring confirmation by him such as revocation and modification orders, discontinuance orders and compulsory purchase orders.

The single most important consequence of this heavy workload is delay. Programming decision making is a complex task, and over the period from 1960 the length of time between the lodging of an appeal and the issuing of a final decision has gradually lengthened, until delays of a year or more became commonplace. Combatting delay has become a high priority in the past few years, however, and the steps taken to achieve this have been more than purely administrative. The cumulative effect has been nothing less than the dismantling of the traditional departmental decision making structures. It has been a quiet revolution, and its impact has not yet been fully appreciated. Reform has proceeded on two fronts. First, there has been a progressive handing over of power to inspectors themselves to hear and determine appeals without reference back to the Secretary of State. New Regulations issued in 1981 convert that transfer from a matter of exception to the general principle, into being the principle itself to which only a limited number of exceptions remain. Second, there has been a progressive moving away from the public local inquiry as the primary means of hearing appeals. Parties have instead been encouraged systematically to present their cases by way of written representations. In the great majority of written representation cases the decision is taken by the inspector himself, although on some matters jurisdiction remains with the Secretary of State.

The consequences of these reforms are wide reaching. In 1960 all decisions were taken by the Secretary of State, and the role of inspectors was limited to hearing representations and reporting, with their recommendations, to him. Today, jurisdiction to decide is transferred to inspectors in approximately 95 per cent. of cases, although certain important matters (including decisions on called-in applications) remain still solely within the Secretary of State's jurisdiction. Similarly, in 1960 only a handful of appeals were determined by way of written representations. Today, over 80 per cent. are determined in that way.

It is only partly true that this change in procedures stems from a wish to speed up appellate decision making. There are, of course, obvious advantages in simplifying procedures and in dispensing with inquiries. As Table 23 illustrates, by way of a flow chart for each of the four different methods now pursued, the steps involved are considerably compressed where jurisdiction rests with the inspector; and the time scales indicated in the Table have been further reduced as a result of administrative changes since 1980. But the transfer of jurisdiction is also partly the result of the progressive judicialisation of planning appeals following the report of the Franks Committee in 1957, which is discussed further below. Much of the traditional freedom of the Secretary of State to take an independent course from his inspector has been eroded by the post-inquiry procedures first introduced by the Inquiries Procedure Rules in 1962, and by the manner of the courts' interpretation of them.

In this context the expression "Secretary of State" is used to encompass decision making within the Department, and comparatively few decisions ever rise as far as ministerial level in the departmental hierarchy. The late Richard Crossman confided to his Diary a few weeks after taking office as Minister in 1964 that:

> "Ever since I've been Minister I've noticed that each morning the papers carry news of a planning decision I have taken, usually stating that I've considered it sympathetically before turning it down. So there is a whole mass of stuff in the press about what the Minister has been doing and feeling where in fact the Minister hasn't been consulted at all."[2]

In some legal metaphysical sense, the Secretary of State is his Department, and they are he. He alone in constitutional theory is accountable to Parliament for decisions taken by his Department, and the corporate fiction offers a convenient shorthand for legislators and political analysts. But in an era of increasing pressure for more open government, the custom of decision making by anonymous officials who are not personally accountable cannot expect to attract great public popularity. That too has been a certain, if indirect, factor in the steady transference of decision making powers to inspectors.

Yet the retention of the Secretary of State as the nominal decider of appeals helps to underpin the political basis of planning, and there have been many cases where the personal imprint of individual ministers, and in some instances the Cabinet itself, has been clearly visible in the decision.

2. Appeals, Applications and Objections

There is a variety of cases under the Act where the Secretary of State's intervention or review powers are relevant, and the same basic procedures are applicable to each. In addition to ordinary planning appeals and enforcement appeals, which are in practice the most common, there are three main categories. The first is that of "called-in" applications, where the Secretary of State has directed an authority to refer an application to him for determination. This normally occurs where the authority are minded to grant the application, but the Secretary of State wishes first to have a detailed examination of the issues. The original applicant therefore becomes the appellant, and because of the circumstances in which the power is used, is often supported rather than opposed by the planning authority.

The second category is that of cases where action has been initiated by the planning authority against individual rights, such as for the revocation or modification of a permission, for the discontinuance of an existing use or for the compulsory purchase of land. In these cases the general procedure is that an order is first prepared in draft form by the authority, published and served on those affected, and submitted to the Secretary of State for

---

[2] *The Diaries of a Cabinet Minister* (1975), Vol. 1, pp. 66–67.

Table 23
Procedural Stages of an Appeal

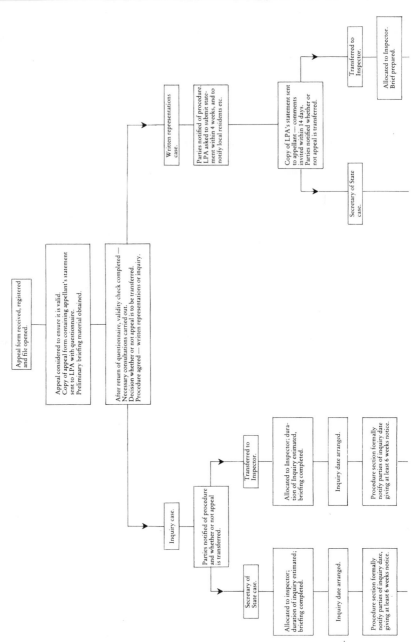

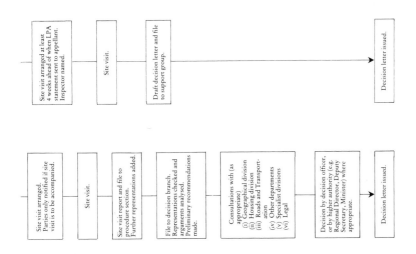

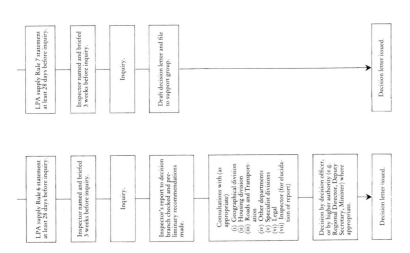

Source: adapted from Review of the Development Control System
HMSO 1973, Appendix III.

confirmation. There is provision for the making of objections, and for the hearing of objections at a public local inquiry.

The final category to which the same basic procedures extend is that of proposals initiated by the Secretary of State himself, or by some other Government Department. Examples include highways proposals and ministerial compulsory purchase. The major difference is that the draft order is prepared by the Department concerned, and that it is their function rather than that of the local planning authority to defend it or justify it at inquiry.

Whilst this chapter deals primarily with ordinary planning appeals, many of the principles discussed are equally applicable to the other categories of case. Major differences are set out in the final section of the chapter.

3. The Quasi-Judicial Role

Defining the proper role of the Secretary of State and his inspectors in appellate decision making has proved one of the perennial controversies of planning law. It is a function which falls awkwardly between two traditional and familiar models of decision making. On the one hand, there is the administrative, or political model. Planning is, after all, a political function concerned with the making and implementation of policy, and planning appeals are an important means of supervising the interpretation and application of policy by local planning authorities. This involves a purposive approach to decision making. The wish to maintain a particular policy may dictate that a planning appeal should fail, notwithstanding that, in forensic terms at least, the appellant may have emerged as the clear victor from the inquiry. Above all, it is not a system of justice: it is discriminatory, demanding the subjugation of private interests to a greater public good.

The other traditional model is that of judicial decision making. In comparison with the politician, the judge is blinkered. The British judge hears only those things that the parties to the dispute put to him, and he makes his decision by applying the rules to the facts as established by the evidence. The procedure is adversarial rather than inquisitorial. He observes strict procedural formalities, designed to ensure that each party has the right to present his case and to hear and be able to comment upon all the submissions of the other prarties. These are the safeguards of natural justice, or procedural due process, which require that decisions should not be taken without the parties having been properly heard; that is, heard by an impartial adjudicator and with adequate notice of the hearing and adequate opportunity to participate.

The rules of natural justice are, ex facie, as directly applicable to ministerial decision making as they are to judicial decision making. The analogy is sometimes very close: there is often a simple dispute between two parties, a lis inter partes, and a clear statement of rules whether in the development plan or elsewhere. But the analogy is never exact. There is a "policy" element involved in every planning case, and the greater the policy element the more illusory becomes the guarantee offered by elaborate procedural safeguards. The appeals procedure becomes part of a more broadly political function. The arguments of the parties directly concerned become simply a facet of the overall administrative process.

And so neither the purely political model nor the purely judicial model satisfies the needs of planning decision making. It is necessarily a compromise between the two, as the label "quasi-judicial" recognises. What has emerged is a process of which part, the hearing or inquiry, is fairly closely modelled along judicial lines, and the rest, particularly the post-inquiry procedure, is more flexible. Subject to certain safeguards, the Secretary of State may consult within and outside his Department, seek further evidence and take into account further policy considerations before coming to a decision.

But the two models pull in different directions and the practical reconciliation of their requirements is far from easy. Back in 1932, it was possible for the Donoughmore Committee to argue that it was largely an intellectual, if not a metamorphical, matter: their view was that "at some stage in his mental operations before his action takes final shape [the Minister] passes from the judge into the administrator."[3] That is, he is bound in coming to his decision, to act in good faith and listen fairly to both sides, "for that is a duty lying upon everyone who decides anything."[4] But thereafter, his political function supersedes his judicial role. It is a convenient but unsatisfying analysis. How should the balance be set? How far should the policies of government be susceptible to the influence of parties in individual cases? How far should it be possible for the expectations of fairness which arise from observance of quasi-judicial rules, to be defeated by the less than open and impartial considerations of political expediency?

The courts in the early part of this century were particularly sensitive to the claims of administrative efficiency, and anxious to ensure that courtroom rules of fair procedure should not automatically be imposed upon ministers. The classic statement of this position is that of Lord Shaw of Dunfermline, in *Local Government Board* v. *Arlidge:*

> " . . . that the judiciary should presume to impose its own methods on administrative or executive officers is a usurpation. And the assumption that the methods of natural justice are ex necessitate those of Courts of justice is wholly unfounded. This is expressly applicable to steps of procedure or forms of pleading. In so far as the term "natural justice" means that a result or process should be just, it is a harmless though it may be a high-sounding expression; in so far as it attempts to reflect the old jus naturale it is a confused and unwarranted transfer into the ethical sphere of a term employed for other distinctions; and, in so far as it is resorted to for other purposes, it is vacuous."[5]

The background reasons for this judicial restraint require further examination. It had become the practice of the legislature in the early years of the twentieth century to confer powers of decision making upon ministers and governmental boards which would formerly have vested in the courts. The departmental inquiry had proved a swifter, cheaper and less formal forum for the settlement of disputes. If the courts had then insisted upon the observance by ministers of judicial-style procedural rules, those advantages would have been defeated. Further, although no rules had been made governing the conduct of departmental inquiries, there was a comparatively

---

[3] *Report of the Committee on Ministers' Powers*, Cmd. 4060, p. 78.
[4] *Board of Education* v. *Rice* [1911] A.C. 179 at 182, *per* Lord Loreburn L.C.
[5] [1915] A.C. 120 at 138. There are echoes still to be found of these sentiments in the judgments of the House of Lords in the recent highways inquiries case of *Bushell* v. *S.O.S.E.* [1980] 3 W.L.R. 22, especially at 27–29, *per* Lord Diplock.

well established, if secretive, procedure. By successively extending the range of matters allocated to ministerial decision under twentieth century social legislation, the legislature must be taken to have endorsed the procedures as they stood.

Whatever the reasons, the tradition of judicial non-intervention has remained, and the courts have remained largely unmoved by pleas for greater openness and more visible fair play in decision making. Change has had to come instead through political and legislative action. There has long been pressure for the introduction of further safeguards to ensure greater fairness: in effect, to break down the discretionary power of the Minister. The most obvious cases have been those matters, like motorway inquiries, where the Secretary of State is both promoter of the scheme and decision maker. No matter how fair the procedure may actually be, it must always bear the stamp of unfairness if objectors are to be invited "to a proceeding which has all the trappings of a judicial inquiry, and to let them find when they get there that prosecutor, judge and jury all appear to be wearing the same uniform, and to draw their pay from the same master."[6] In these cases the prime question is that of the distribution of power: should the Minister be able to override objection to his motorway policies, no matter how convincingly presented at an inquiry and no matter what view is taken by his inspector? Violence and disruptive behaviour at recent motorway inquiries are symptons of public dissatisfaction with a legal structure which permits government ministers to act in that way.

Equally, the courts' early endorsement of ministerial procedures was mainly in the context of broad scale planning decisions such as slum clearance, war damage clearance and new town development, where the legislation itself reflected a strong will to achieve radical urban change, notwithstanding the strength and sincerity of individual objections. But as McAuslan[7] has pointed out, the broad procedures have not coped so well with the very different situation in practice of "a multiplicity of small-scale appeals in which the policy content seemed small and the effect on an otherwise blameless land-owner seemed large." In these cases, he suggests, there was bound to be conflict between the public officials who saw the public inquiry as nothing more than a step in a total process of administrative decision making, and the appellant or objector who saw it as the sole instrument of his participation and influence.

4. The Franks Committee

That was a factor which weighed heavily with the Franks Committee, appointed in 1956 following the infamous Crichel Down affair, which had demonstrated the capacity of the departmental inquiry to allow the truth to be disguised and the public misled. Their remit was to review the workings of tribunals, and to examine procedures for inquiries and hearings held by, or on behalf of, ministers. Most of the evidence presented to the Committee, other than by Government departments, supported a move towards greater "judicialisation" of inquiry procedure.[8] The evidence suggested "that

[6] Outer Circle Policy Unit, *The Big Public Inquiry* (1979), p. 5.
[7] *The Ideologies of Planning Law* (Pergamon Press, 1980), p. 46.
[8] *Report of the Committee on Administrative Tribunals and Enquiries*, Cmd. 218 (1957), para. 275.

present procedures, either in regard to actual law or to practice, do not sufficiently reflect the essentially adjudicative nature of the process."[9] It was perhaps predictable, therefore, that the Committee's quest for a "reasonable balance" between the administrative and the judicial model, should have involved a clear shift towards the latter. Their recommendations were designed to secure greater independence for the inspectorate (by placing them under the control of the Lord Chancellor)[10] and more openness before, during and after the inquiry. In particular, they recommended that inspectors' reports should be in a standard form and should be published,[11] and that the Minister should not be permitted to take into account any factual evidence, including expert evidence, after the inquiry without first submitting it to the parties for their comments.[12] They proposed also that there should be statutory codes of procedure for inquiries,[13] and that a Council on Tribunals should be established to keep tribunals and inquiry procedures under review.[14]

Most of the recommendations were accepted by the Government and implemented. And the Report itself has continued to operate as a guide to good practice, particularly as a basis for the Council on Tribunals' continuing scrutiny of inquiry procedure.

New inquiry procedure rules were made in 1962 under the Tribunals and Inquiries Act 1958, after consultation with the Council on Tribunals, and their form has remained basically the same, though with some modifications, since then. The rules do not extend to all planning inquiries, and their emphasis is primarily upon pre-inquiry and post-inquiry procedures rather than upon the actual conduct of inquiries themselves. That remains largely a matter for the inspector. But their effect has been to tilt the balance generally in ministerial decision making towards a more judicialised style, and that impression was substantially reinforced when legislation in 1968 introduced the new powers for inspectors themselves to take the decisions rather than merely to report. The inspector had become the judge.

The growth of public participation over the past 15 years has led to new pressures for greater judicialisation, and to a re-opening of the debate. Comparatively little of the legislation governing participation actually confers rights upon third parties. For the most part, the extent to which authorities involve the public in their decision making is a matter for their own discretion. But planning appeals offer virtually an open forum for environmental debate, and objectors, who have often sought to present detailed and sophisticated cases at inquiries, have also pressed for legal guarantees that their influence will be felt by the Minister. In particular, where the public inquiry has followed the calling in of an application which the planning authority are minded to grant, it is often the third party objectors who alone provide the necessary ammunition for effective assessment of the proposal. Yet their arguments fall still to be considered by

---

[9] *Ibid.* para. 275.

[10] *Ibid.* para. 303.

[11] *Ibid.* paras. 327–346.

[12] *Ibid.* para. 350.

[13] *Ibid.* paras. 310, 312.

[14] *Ibid.* para. 43. The Council has had frequently in the course of its life to deal with planning inquiry problems, and its Annual Reports are a useful source of background information on the internal departmental procedures and policies.

the Secretary of State in the light of government policy. It may be an issue upon which there is a clear split between the major political parties, perhaps even a commitment in the election manifesto. It is a matter for the Secretary of State whether that should prevail against, perhaps, the recommendations of his inspector following a possibly lengthy public inquiry. Further judicialisation of the process in a way which would bind him to the latter course is seen as an important step in strengthening the role of planning inquiries as a vehicle for public participation.

Further judicialisation is not, however, a universally accepted goal. The more detailed the rules, the greater the scope for inadvertent breach. One of the consequences of implementation of the Franks Committee's recommendations has been that more effort has been applied by officials to making decisions "lawyer proof:"

> "For the Ministry the rules to be observed are now substantially more complicated and, at points, more difficult of interpretation; and the time taken to reach decisions has inevitably lengthened. . . . The quasi-judicial work is now potentially explosive; and unless the responsible branch feels able simply to endorse the inspector's report, cases go to a senior officer before decision, and often to a Minister, with consequent clogging of the works."[15]

As well as the problem of increased delay, (which is to a large extent no more than a manpower and resources issue) there is the further risk that decisions may be taken not so much on the planning merits as on legalistic grounds; or that the true reasons for decision will be dressed up in meaningless but safe lawyers' catchphrases, such as "matter of fact and degree," or "no substantial reason to depart from established policy." Rules intended to reinforce rationality and openness in decision making may instead have induced a more guarded and less open style.

Further, pressure for increased judicialisation of the procedure is based largely upon the assumption that the issues to be resolved are qualitatively comparable to those determined in courts of law. But the reasoning process is not the logical judicial style of applying or extending established rules, but the policy purposive style of considering the extent to which possible alternative decisions may advance or hinder the attainment of the aims which the relevant policies are intended to achieve. The issues are often aesthetic, or speculative; requiring the balancing of alternatives against long-term and short-term gains and losses, comparing risks and forecasts, and weighing imponderables such as, for example, the balance to be struck between undesirable environmental intrusion on the one hand, and desirable job creation on the other. The issues often go far beyond the interests of the parties represented at the inquiry, and there is seldom a clear-cut "right" or "wrong" answer.

Judicial analogies are therefore often unhelpful in coping with the substance of the decisions; or to put it another way, the issues are not readily justiciable. The parties may choose to confine their dispute to one aspect of the whole issue which concerns the Secretary of State; or they may have produced quite inadequate evidence on a point which he feels requires

---

[15] E. Sharp, *The Ministry of Housing and Local Government* (G. Allen and Unwin, 1969), pp. 36–37.

independent assessment. Techniques designed to bring out truth do not always succeed in providing a basis for sophisticated policy evaluation. But that is not to say that judicial type procedures are necessarily irrelevant, or that the forensic techniques of oral evidence and cross-examination cannot be employed to advantage. The problem lies in devising means for their most effective use, and in developing supplementary procedures where traditional ones are demonstrably inadequate. These needs are clearest in the case of decisions with a high policy content, such as Windscale and the perennial search for a site for the third London Airport. Steps that have been taken to meet the demands for more effective scrutiny of large-scale public sector development are considered subsequently in this chapter.

B. Preliminary

1. *Introduction*

The legislation governing appeals is complex, and is distributed between a variety of Acts and statutory instruments. In addition to those provisions of the 1971 Act which authorise the lodging of appeals and objections against planning decisions, reference must also be made to the procedural provisions of the General Development Order (G.D.O.), and there is a choice between two sets of procedural rules according to whether the decision is one to be taken by the Secretary of State (in which case the procedure is prescribed by the Town and Country Planning (Inquiries Procedure) Rules 1974, (hereafter the I.P.R.) or by an inspector (who is governed by the Town and Country Planning Appeals (Determination by Appointed Persons) (Inquiries Procedure) Rules 1974, (hereafter the A.P.R.). The issue of which set of rules is applicable is itself governed by Schedule 9 to the 1971 Act and by the Town and Country Planning (Determination of appeals by appointed persons) (Prescribed Classes) Regulations, 1981. Enforcement appeals, listed building enforcement appeals and established use certificate appeals are governed by the Town and Country Planning (Enforcement) (Inquiries Procedure) Rules 1981 (hereafter the E.I.P.R.) which extend both to Secretary of State and inspectors' cases.

The inquiries procedure rules do not apply in all cases, however. They do not extend at all to cases determined by way of written representations, nor to objections to revocation and discontinuance orders, where there are no rules whatever prescribed beyond the basic statutory provisions creating the right to object. As a matter of practice, however, similar procedures are followed, under the general discretionary power of the Secretary of State and the inspector to regulate the proceedings as they think best.

2. *Pre-Appeal Negotiations*

Once a planning decision has been issued by a local planning authority, their jurisdiction is spent and they are *functus officio*. They lack the power to revoke or vary the decision otherwise than through the statutory procedures, even with the consent of the applicant. What they may do, however, is to entertain a fresh application, and this means that there is always room for negotiation between them and the developer. This is particularly the case where the grounds of refusal, or the reasons for imposing an unfavourable condition, relate only to some technical matter, such as the inadequacy of sightlines or insufficient provision for car-parking. But a negotiated settlement may also be possible of some objection in principle to the development, by preparing a revised and less obtrusive scheme, for example, which might allow the proposal to be brought within an exception to the general policy which formerly dictated its refusal. It has been Government policy consistently to encourage negotiations of this sort,[16] and a refusal on the part of either party to negotiate at the request of the other is liable to be met by an order for costs.[17]

Negotiations may not succeed in disposing of an appeal altogether, but they often lead to partial agreement as to what should be the scope of the appeal, and as to how technical matters may be dealt with should the appeal succeed. In the latter case the parties may choose to enter into a planning agreement, making its effect conditional upon permission being granted. This not only leaves the inspector free to consider broader objections of principle to the development, but it also often allows the authority to retain closer control over the development through their agreement than might be possible through any conditions which might otherwise be imposed by the Secretary of State should he grant permission. An unexecuted agreement may in itself be of little value to the Secretary of State,[18] although if it relates to a central issue and planning permission would be forthcoming if it were executed, he may postpone giving a decision to give the parties time to negotiate, and there is no reason why an agreement might not be concluded between the parties after the appeal has been heard, and then taken into consideration by the Secretary of State in reaching the actual decision.[19] The lodging of an appeal does not at law affect the negotiating capacity of the parties. The *sub judice* rule is inapplicable, and negotiations may therefore continue right up to the inquiry date, and even beyond. There is no obligation upon the Secretary of State to accept the terms negotiated by the parties, however, and unless the appeal is withdrawn he may proceed to determine it. But their agreed terms would be a material consideration.[20]

---

[16] Thus even before the first appointed day in 1948 authorities were being urged to "display a willingness to discuss the matter further with the applicant," and to undertake "helpful and sympathetic handling of applications at an early stage to avoid an appeal:" M.T.C.P. Circular 69/47. For more recent echoes of these sentiments see D.O.E. Circulars 22/80 and 38/81.

[17] M.H.L.G. Circular 73/65, and the *Report of the Council on Tribunals on the Award of Costs at Statutory Inquiries*, Cmnd. 2471, para. 27(iii); and see further *post*, p. 600.

[18] *Tarmac Properties Ltd.* v. *Secretary of State for Wales* (1976) 33 P. & C.R. 103. Note that although that decision was subsequently reversed by the Court of Appeal, (noted at (1977) 39 P. & C.R. 601), it was apparently done in highly unusual circumstances as a formality rather than on the merits of the first instance judgment: see the explanation appearing at [1977] J.P.L. 409. As to the proper course for an inspector to take when an unexecuted agreement is in issue, see *McLaren* v. *S.O.S.E.* [1981] J.P.L. 423.

[19] Thus in the *Tarmac* case the Inspector had been aware of continuing post-inquiry negotiations between appellant and planning authority and had delayed the submission of his report. If an agreement had then been concluded, that would have been a material consideration, though it might have been necessary to obtain the views of other parties before taking it into account.

[20] In *Robert Hitchens Builders Ltd.* v. *S.O.S.E.* [1979] J.P.L. 534 the Court of Appeal held that it would be an error of law for the Secretary of State to refuse an appeal automatically where he believed that the terms agreed by the parties went beyond his powers to impose by way of conditions: he was still obliged to consider other courses, such as whether permission could be granted without the conditions.

3. *The Nature of a Planning Appeal*

It is now possible to appeal against any decision of a local planning authority made on an application:

"(*a*) for planning permission;
(*b*) for any consent, agreement or approval of that authority required by a condition imposed on a grant of planning permission; or
(*c*) for any approval of that authority required under a development order;"

either refusing agreement, consent or permission or granting it subject to conditions.[21] Item (*b*) was added by the 1980 Act, and introduces a long needed control over the use by authorities, outside the conventional context of outline permissions, of conditions reserving matters for their subsequent approval. Item (*c*) includes applications for approval of reserved matters under an outline planning permission.

Further, for the purposes of the Act, the failure of an authority to issue any of the above decisions within a period of eight weeks from the application (or such longer period as may have been agreed in writing) entitles the applicant to appeal as if permission had been refused.[22] The procedures are therefore the same. Similarly, the basic provisions are extended to cases of unfavourable determinations under section 53, or the failure to issue any determination under that section within the prescribed time.[23]

4. *Capacity to Lodge an Appeal*

An appeal may be lodged only by the original applicant for permission.[24] The right is not therefore exercisable by the owner of the land unless he is a party to the application.

Nor is there any provision for appeals by third parties against the grant of permission. Their influence is therefore limited to persuading the authority to refuse permission, or persuading the Secretary of State to call the application in for decision or direct the authority to refuse it. Once permission has been granted their options are effectively limited to seeking revocation. This absence of any third party appeal is a substantial gap in the legislation, and there have been repeated requests, dating back at least as far as the Scott Committee in 1942,[25] for such a right to be created in at least some types of case. The early assumption was that the development plan framework under the 1947 Act would hold authorities closely to their approved plans, and that further formal public involvement in development control was therefore superfluous and unnecessary. It was to prove to be a groundless assumption, and decision making in development control has regularly ranged beyond the confines of approved plans with only limited

[21] T.C.P.A. 1971, s. 36 (as amended by L.G.P.L.A. 1980, Sched. 15. para. 4(2))).
[22] *Ibid.* s. 37.
[23] *Ibid.* s. 53(2).
[24] *Ibid.* s. 36(1).
[25] *Report of the Committee on Land Utilisation in Rural Areas*, Cmd. 6378, para. 235.

overview through the "departure" procedures. A remarkably high proportion of new development in the past 30 years has taken place on land which was never formally allocated for it. There is threfore good reason to reconsider the position. It would be administratively difficult to handle the large number of appeals which might ensue, but that is an objection of expedience rather than principle. The real fear is that the power could, if conferred without adequate safeguards, too readily be used simply as a weapon for delay. One answer might be for the Secretary of State to be more responsive in considering requests from the public for applications to be called-in for decision, but that would involve reversing the trend of the past 20 years towards less direct central government intervention in local planning.

5. Lodging an Appeal

A planning appeal must be lodged within six months of the date of decision or determination of the authority (or, in the case of an appeal in default of any decision, from the expiry of the prescribed time), or within such longer time as the Secretary of State may at any time allow.[26] There is no prescribed form for appeals against section 53 determinations, but forms are prescribed for other planning appeals and are obtainable from the Secretary of State.[27] The applicant is obliged also to forward a copy of the application and all relevant plans and documents submitted with it, the notice of the decision or determination by the authority and all other relevant correspondence with them.[28] The grounds of appeal may be shortly stated and will normally relate to the reasons for refusal. There is good reason for providing a comprehensive statement of grounds of appeal where the matter is to be dealt with by way of written representations, however, because the appeal document is then treated as the appellant's statement of his case.

There is a supplementary power for the Secretary of State to require the applicant to submit a detailed statement of his case before the inquiry.[29] The power is presently exercised only in exceptional circumstances.

The legislation[30] also requires that the formalities under section 27 of the 1971 Act, requiring notification by the appellant of the owners of the land, should be undertaken again so as to ensure that the appeal is made known to them. Notification of other interested parties is undertaken by the local planning authority as required by the Secretary of State.

6. Acceptance of an Appeal and Interim Rulings

There is no legislative requirement that the Secretary of State should formally accept or reject jurisdiction when an appeal is lodged, but such a decision and its notification are probably implicit in the Inquiries Procedure

---

[26] G.D.O., art 20(1).
[27] Ibid.
[28] Ibid. art. 20(2). This includes copies of any notices and certificates provided under s. 26 (unneighbourly development) and s. 27 (ownership certificates).
[29] See further post, p. 578.
[30] T.C.P.A. 1971, s. 36(5).

Rules.[31] An appeal may be rejected by him for a variety of reasons: because it is late, for example, or is formally defective or outside his jurisdiction. His discretionary power to extend the time for lodging an appeal[32] allows him to confer an additional period of grace in suitable cases, and to give an appellant a further opportunity to put his appeal properly. Rejection of an appeal at this stage does not, however, mean that the appellant has lost forever the right of challenge. It remains open to him to submit a fresh application to the planning authority, and then to appeal if their decision remains the same. Alternatively, he may choose to take the risk of developing without permission or in breach of a condition, and await enforcement proceedings. The jurisdiction of the Secretary of State in an enforcement appeal is broad enough to allow him to consider all the planning issues and, should he wish, to grant permission for the development.

So far as jurisdiction is concerned, the Act confers specific power on the Secretary of State to decline, at any time before or during the determination, to proceed with a planning appeal if he forms the opinion that planning permission could not have been granted at all by the local planning authority or could only have been granted subject to the conditions actually imposed by them.[33] The power has never apparently been used, because the view has been taken that its purpose when originally conferred in 1947 was to allow the Minister to refuse to entertain appeals in cases where the planning authority's decision was in clear compliance with the development plan.[34] But the rigid degree of plan compliance that the draftsman foresaw failed ever to eventuate, and the power could not be used.

That justification is not altogether satisfying. The subsection clearly extends also to cases where the Secretary of State takes the view, perhaps not until after the inquiry has concluded, that an industrial development certificate or some other necessary preliminary authorisation should have been obtained. He may then, under the section, decline to proceed; although there is the alternative analysis that he lacks the power to proceed because an application without the necessary certificate is a nullity, and the express statutory power is therefore unnecessary.

The fact that there may be some legal defect in the decision being appealed against does not necessarily vitiate the appeal, however. Provided the application itself is valid, the Secretary of State has power to determine it *de novo*, and the fact that the planning authority's decision may be a nullity is irrelevant.[35]

7. Withdrawal of an Appeal

There are no specific provisions governing the withdrawal of appeals,[36] but as a matter of practice withdrawal is possible by notification to the Secretary

---

[31] See, *e.g.* I.P.R. r. 4(1) which obliges the Secretary of State to notify the local planning authority of his intention to proceed with consideration of the appeal.

[32] G.D.O., art 20(1).

[33] T.C.P.A. 1971, s. 36(5).

[34] See further G. Dobry, *Review of the Development Control System* Final Report, para. 11.14.

[35] *Stringer* v. *M.H.L.G.* [1970] 1 W.L.R. 1281.

[36] Though in *Slough Estates Ltd.* v. *Slough B.C.* [1968] Ch. 299 there was implicit acceptance by Ungoed-Thomas J. that an appellant might withdraw as of right.

of State. Around 25 per cent. of appeals are withdrawn each year. Where withdrawal is attempted at too late a stage to avoid holding a public inquiry, however, the appellant may be liable for the planning authority's costs.[37] Where there is a prospect of successful negotiation, therefore, it is a useful precaution to ask the Department in advance to hold back inquiry arrangements pending the outcome.

8. Powers of the Secretary of State on Appeal

The whole of the decision of the local planning authority is open to review on appeal. The Act confers original jurisdiction on the Secretary of State: he is empowered to deal with the application as if it had been made to him in the first instance.[38] As well as being able to dismiss or allow the appeal, he may reverse or vary any part of the decision of the local planning authority, whether or not the appeal itself relates to that part.[39] This power allows him to range beyond the alternatives presented to him by the parties.[40] It allows him, for example, to overturn a grant of permission altogether although the appeal relates only to some condition imposed upon it; or to impose yet further conditions upon it. It is a power which must, however, be exercised fairly, and it would be prima facie unfair to use it so as to remove or limit an existing right without first at least notifying the applicant of the proposal and taking into account his representations on it.[41]

C. Transferred Jurisdiction

1. Introduction

Until 1968 all decisions on planning appeals were taken by the Secretary of State, or in his name, following consideration of the inspector's report. But legislation introduced that year, belatedly implementing a recommendation of the Franks Committee,[42] allowed responsibility for the decision to be shifted to the inspector himself in a limited number of cases. The rationale was clear: in only a small proportion of cases did the Secretary of State ever overrule the inspector (and the Franks Committee's recommendations had made it increasingly difficult to do so), and to keep a proportion of cases outside the Department would result in a considerable streamlining of case work.

Since then the trend has been to confer increasingly broad powers upon inspectors, and the consequences in terms of case allocation are shown in Table 22 (ante, p. 553).

The limits to transferred jurisdiction were initially narrowly confined. Inspectors had power to determine only applications involving residential

---

[37] Post, p. 600.

[38] T.C.P.A. 1971, s. 36(3) and (5).

[39] Ibid. s. 36(3).

[40] See, e.g. Robert Hitchens Builders Ltd. v. S.O.S.E. [1980] J.P.L. 534.

[41] The appeal may be restricted to the condition itself only where it forms part of an enforcement appeal relating to breach of that condition, or where the appeal relates to refusal of the authority to modify or discharge the condition on a subsequent application under s. 32(2).

[42] Report of the Franks Committee, paras. 392–394.

development of up to 10 dwelling houses. But by 1977 the category of transferred cases had expanded to include all planning and enforcement appeals involving residential development of up to 60 dwellings (or covering up to two hectares where no number of dwellings was specified in the application), as well as industrial development (up to 1,500 square metres) and a variety of operational and ancillary development.[43] There were some important exceptions, including cases of development by local planning authorities and statutory undertakers, and cases where the original decision had been made by the authority in accordance with views expressed in consultation by a government department or new town corporation, or in accordance with a direction by the Secretary of State. By 1980 the proportion of appeals determined by the Secretary of State had fallen to around 15 per cent., and the arbitrary way in which the transfers were defined meant that this group did not necessarily contain the more important appeals. Many were relatively minor, and even in the cases where the Secretary of State had recovered jurisdiction from an Inspector, it was often for purely technical reasons. But in cases where an inquiry was held, the involvement of the Secretary of State would add on average a further 12 weeks to the process, and even in written representation cases a further eight weeks. An additional factor was the time and care involved in making a full report for the Secretary of State so that he would have, and be seen to have, all the relevant material before him. Inspectors' own decision letters could be more rapidly drafted, because there was no need to rehearse all the evidence in order to demonstrate that it had been fully taken into account.

The 1977 Regulations also transferred the majority of enforcement appeals to Inspectors, and the Secretary of State announced that he would recover jurisdiction only where it was clear at the outset that a particular appeal was likely to raise very complicated legal issues.

A Consultation Paper issued in 1980 by the Department proposed therefore that jurisdiction should be transferred in all cases as a matter of principle, and that the Secretary of State's jurisdiction should be retained only for a limited number of cases. Those proposals were given effect by the Town and Country Planning (Determination of appeals by appointed persons)(Prescribed Classes) Regulations 1981. All planning and enforcement appeals now fall to be determined by inspectors except where they relate to the operational land of statutory undertakers, where the Act requires that the decision be made jointly by the Secretary of State and the "appropriate minister" for the purposes of the undertaking.[44]

There is no power for called-in applications to be transferred to inspectors, since these are by definition cases where the local planning authority are themselves being denied jurisdiction and where there is normally an issue of national policy at stake. And although power to transfer jurisdiction exists in respect of other types of cases including listed building consent and tree preservation consent,[45] it has not yet been exercised.

---

[43] Under the Town and Country Planning (Determination of appeals by appointed persons)(Prescribed Classes) Regulations 1972, as amended.
[44] T.C.P.A. 1971, s. 225(3).
[45] Power exists to transfer jurisdiction in established use certificate appeals (s. 95(7)); listed building enforcement appeals (s.97(7)); appeals under tree preservation orders (s. 103(4)) and listed building consent appeals (Sched. 11, para.8).

2. Recovery of Jurisdiction by the Secretary of State

In those cases where jurisdiction is transferred to inspectors, the inspector has, with any necessary modifications, all the powers and duties of the Secretary of State.[46] But the Secretary of State has power to recover jurisdiction, in two ways. First, he may direct that any class of case should come to him for decision.[47] The purpose might be to ensure that some proposal under consideration in the Department, such as a possible new town, or a local plan called in for decision,[48] should not be prejudiced and that the decision on appeal should be taken against a full understanding of the outstanding policy issues. Second, he may recover jurisdiction in particular cases, by making a direction to that effect (which must include a statement of his reasons), which must then be served on the parties and on third parties.[49] The Government's Consultation Paper indicates that this power will be used sparingly for the future:

> "The general criterion should be that he would recover jurisdiction only when there is good reason for it—for instance the scale of the development, the complexity of the issues or the involvement of another Government department in a case which involves Government policy considerations."[50]

Jurisdiction may be taken over by the Secretary of State even after a particular inspector has been appointed,[51] and will often indeed be done at his request. This is likely where particularly difficult legal issues have arisen, for example, (although inspectors still retain access to the Secretary of State's legal advisors) or where, as a case progresses, it becomes clear that there is a large element of technical evidence or government policy involved. An alternative course may be to transfer jurisdiction to another inspector[52] or to appoint an assessor to advise the original inspector.

There is no power for the parties to an appeal to require the Secretary of State to assume jurisdiction. Nor does the machinery operate the other way to allow the Secretary of State to transfer jurisdiction in cases which are reserved for his own decision. The categories are firmly drawn. It is not possible to challenge the validity of a decision taken by an inspector on the ground that it should have been taken by the Secretary of State, except where challenge has been made to the inspector's jurisdiction before the determination has been made.[53] But, curiously, there is no comparable deemed validity in the converse case of any decision which ought to have been taken by an inspector but has, otherwise than pursuant to a direction under the Act, been taken by the Secretary of State.

---

[46] T.C.P.A. 1971, Sched. 9, para. 2(1).

[47] *Ibid.* para. 1(1). Reg. 5 of the 1981 Regulations empowers the Secretary of State to direct the authority affected by the direction to publicise any direction made under these provisions.

[48] These examples were advanced by the Minister in the course of the Standing Committee debate on the 1968 Act: *Official Report,* Vol. IX, col. 497 (March 21, 1968), although the prospect of further new town designations is somewhat remote under present Government policy: see further *ante*, p. 504.

[49] T.C.P.A. 1971, Sched. 9, para. 3(1) and (2).

[50] *Consultation Paper on Planning Appeals,* D.O.E. 1980, para. 11.

[51] T.C.P.A. 1971, Sched. 9, para. 3(2).

[52] *Ibid.* para. 4.

[53] *Ibid.* para. 2(3).

Although the transference of jurisdiction to inspectors gives them a large measure of autonomy, they work nonetheless within the policies adopted by the Secretary of State, and they are still not entirely freed from Departmental supervision. The reports and decisions of some inspectors are scrutinised by the Department and suggestions made with a view to improving the quality of the decision and to ensure consistent application of national and local policy. The Council on Tribunals has investigated the practice, and found it unobjectionable.[54]

D. Written Representations

1. *Introduction*

There has been a dramatic increase over the past 10 years in the proportion of planning appeals which are determined without a public inquiry. Over 70 per cent. of all appeals are now handled by way of written representations, and the proportion has risen to over 80 per cent. in the case of appeals where jurisdiction is transferred to an inspector.[55] The advantage of this procedure is that it is notably swifter, and it is almost always cheaper for an appellant, particularly when it saves him the cost of professional representation at an inquiry. It has always been highly popular for advertisement appeals, but its use has now been encouraged in all cases of appeal.[56]

There is a statutory right for both the planning authority and the appellant to appear before, and be heard by, an inspector, if they so desire.[57] Written representations procedure is therefore a voluntary alternative which requires the consent of both parties, and the concurrence of the Secretary of State. Departmental policy is to encourage the procedure, however, and parties are invited to consider proceeding by written representations wherever the method "is not clearly unsuitable."[58]

2. *The Procedures*

Written representation procedures are (except in enforcement cases) entirely non-statutory. There is, however, a reasonably precise administrative timetable.[59] Parties are asked to indicate on the appeal form whether they consent to written representations. If both sides agree, the authority are then invited to submit, within four weeks of notification of the appeal, a statement in response to the appellant's grounds of appeal.[60] This is sent to the appellant who will be invited to comment on it within two weeks. A copy of those comments is sent to the authority. That is normally the end of

---

[54] *Annual Report 1974/75*, paras. 93–94.
[55] For a detailed breakdown of cases see *Development Control Statistics 1978/79* D.O.E. 1980, and Table 22, *ante*, p. 553.
[56] D.O.E. Circular 38/81, Part I.
[57] T.C.P.A. 1971, s. 36(4); Sched. 9, para. 2(2).
[58] D.O.E. Circular 142/73, para. 14. D.O.E. Circular 38/81, para. 10, now urges parties to opt for an inquiry only when it is "essential."
[59] New arrangements were announced in D.O.E. Circular 38/81, superseding those formerly contained in M.H.L.G. Circular 32/65. Table 2 of the new Circular contains a target timetable for handling representations.
[60] The form to be followed for presenting the authority's statement is set out as Table 1 in D.O.E. Circular 38/81.

the exchange, although further representations may be made and exchanged if desired. A site visit is usual, but not essential if the area has recently been inspected.

The decision is then notified to the parties. Unlike the situation where decision follows a planning inquiry, the duty to give reasons arises only where a request has been made by one of the parties.[61] Reasons are always given, however, as a matter of good practice and if they should indicate any errors of law in arriving at the decision they may be used as a basis for legal challenge in the same way as if they had been statutorily required.[62]

3. Third parties

Written representations procedure works best simply as a bilateral arrangement in largely straightforward cases. If there is any substantial local objection an inquiry is a better means of considering the appeal, and authorities have been asked to indicate to the Secretary of State when that is likely to be the case.[63] Less powerful third party interest can always be fed into written representations procedure, however, provided there is adequate notification to affected persons, both that the appeal is taking place and that any written statement of their views will be taken into account.[64]

4. Shortfalls in the Procedures

The essence of this procedure, and its greatest weakness, is that the interaction between the various parties is limited to commenting on the other's submissions. Because the procedure is non-statutory, there are no supplementary powers to require the production of particular documents by any party. Thus the local authority who choose to suppress the report and recommendation of their chief planning officer, for example, may do so.[65] It is for them to choose what material to put forward, although the inspector may draw his own conclusions from their actions. Argument through written submissions is quite a different matter from oral cross-examination, and there is thus a limit to the depth at which the issues may be probed through this procedure.

A further consequence of the lack of statutory rules is that there is no effective means of enforcing compliance with the Secretary of State's timetable, while the obligation, in the interests of fairness, to forward copies of successive submissions to all parties for comment before making any determination means that one party may delay a decision interminably simply by continuing to submit further documents.[66] Nor may deliberately

---

[61] Tribunals and Inquiries Act 1971, s. 12.
[62] *Elmbridge B.C. v. S.O.S.E.* [1980] J.P.L. 463.
[63] D.O.E. Circular 71/73, para. 20.
[64] As to the informal publicity requirements, see D.O.E. Circular 71/73, para. 21.
[65] A limitation regarded by the Council on Tribunals in their *Annual Report for 1978/79* (para. 6.24) as not completely satisfactory, but not calling for any further action on their part.
[66] The Council on Tribunals have asked the Department of the Environment to consider ways and means of overcoming this problem: *1978/79 Annual Report,* para. 6.32, but the Department have already rejected the recommendation of the *Dobry Report* for a statutory timetable, which "would be difficult to enforce:" D.O.E. Circular 113/75, para. 8.

unreasonable conduct be recognised by an award of costs in favour of the other party: the power to make such an order extends only to cases where an inquiry has been held.

5. Revocation of Consent to Procedure

Since the parties are entitled to insist upon an inquiry should they desire one, their agreement to written representations procedure is entirely voluntary. It constitutes the waiver of a statutory right. As it is made otherwise than for consideration, it is normally revocable. Prima facie, therefore, a party to the appeal (other than a third party), if dissatisfied with what transpired in the course of written representations, could at any time prior to determination of the appeal reassert his desire to appear before, and be heard by, an inspector. In the case of appeals falling to be determined by an inspector, however, the wording of the Act suggests that once the election has been made it may not be revoked; but in Secretary of State cases the inquiry may be dispensed with only if neither party expresses a wish to be heard by the inspector.[67] That formula suggests that an initial consent may be withdrawn by the later expression of a wish to be heard.

There is, however, a possible constraint through the doctrine of promissory estoppel. There is no clear authority on the point, and the principles are far from easy to discern. But it has been held that the relationship between each of the parties and the Secretary of State is a sufficient base upon which to found an estoppel[68]; and, applying similar principles, such a sufficient legal relationship no doubt exists between the appellant and the planning authority as well. It is arguable therefore that a party may be estopped from revoking his waiver of the right to appear before an inspector if either of the other parties has acted upon it. At one time, it might have been necessary to show that the party had in reliance upon the waiver altered his position detrimentally, or to the extent that he could not resume his original position without injustice.[69] He might, for example, have destroyed documents or taken other irretrievable steps in the belief an inquiry would not be held. But more recent dicta in the Court of Appeal suggest that the courts are moving to a more flexible approach, and may be more willing than formerly to hold people to a unilateral waiver of their legal rights simply where they have led others to act upon them.[70] Under that test, it would presumably be sufficient simply that another party had been put to the expense of undertaking written representations procedure. An order for costs may be made against a resiling party, but the scope of the order is limited to expenditure incurred at the inquiry, and does not extend to abortive expenditure incurred in fruitless pursuit of written representations procedure.[71]

[67] Cf. T.C.P.A. 1971, Sched. 9, para. 2(2)(a)(inspectors' cases) and s. 36(4)(Secretary of State cases).
[68] Augier v. S.O.S.E. (1978) 38 P. & C.R. 219.
[69] See, e.g. Ajayi v. R.T. Briscoe (Nigeria) Ltd. [1964] 3 All E.R. 556 at 559, per Lord Hodson.
[70] Crabb v. Arun D.C. [1976] Ch. 179.
[71] T.C.P.A. 1971, s. 290; L.G.A. 1972, s. 250(5); see further post, p. 600.

E. Inquiries

1. *Introduction*

The public local inquiry is firmly established as an instrument of British administrative procedure. It has even been suggested[72] that it has its roots in the surveys undertaken for the Domesday Book. The evolvement of the present form of procedure has taken place largely since the mid-nineteenth century when private Acts began to give way to provisional orders, which required the holding of a public local inquiry, as a means of extending powers to local authorities. Planning inquiries date back to the Housing, Town Planning, etc. Act 1909,[73] although the primary mechanism for resolution of disputes under the Act was by way of arbitration through the Local Government Board.

The essence of an inquiry is that it is the judicial or quasi-judicial part of a process of administrative decision making. It is this factor which distinguishes an inquiry from a tribunal (although there are also, confusingly enough, tribunals of inquiry, which really are inquiries); and it remains a distinguishing factor even in cases where jurisdiction is transferred to an inspector. But there remains, as has already been considered, an inevitable tension between the judicial and administrative elements. The rules which are examined in the following pages reflect that tension. They are intended to secure a fair and efficient dispatch of business, and to establish a relationship between inquiry and decision that will be sufficiently loose to allow considerations of general policy to be weighed and balanced, yet direct enough to ensure that the major arguments advanced at the inquiry will not be rejected without rational explanation.

2. *The Duty to Hold an Inquiry*

The duty imposed upon the Secretary of State in planning appeals is simply one of allowing the appellant and the local planning authority an opportunity of appearing before, and being heard by, a person appointed for that purpose. The Act does not, therefore, specify that an "inquiry" should be held, and at one time the Ministry sometimes preferred to arrange for a "hearing" instead, which was not open to the public. But following widespread criticism of that procedure, "hearings" as opposed to "inquiries" are now held only exceptionally, and only in the case of purchase notice confirmation proceedings and certain advertisement appeals.[74] In all other cases the Secretary of State exercises his power under the Local Government Act 1972 to direct that a local inquiry should be held.[75] The

---

[72] R.E. Wraith and G.B. Lamb, *Public Inquiries as an Instrument of Government* (George Allen and Unwin, 1971), p. 17. The book, which is the classic work on the subject, contains in Chap. 2 a detailed history of inquiries.

[73] See, *e.g.* s. 61 and Sched. 5, para. 2(c)

[74] D.O.E. Circular 113/75, para. 8. With some modifications, the Inquiries Procedure Rules apply equally to hearings as to inquiries, however.

[75] L.G.A. 1972, s. 250, which confers powers to order inquiries authorised under T.C.P.A. 1971, s. 282(1), and supplants the supplementary powers formerly conferred by s. 282(2) incorporating s. 290 of the Local Government Act 1933 (now repealed).

legislation does not, curiously, use the phrase *"public* local inquiry," although that is the term in common usage. It is, however, implicit in the provisions of the Regulations protecting the rights of third parties that an inquiry must always be a public event, subject to the inspector's power to exclude persons for disruptive conduct or other reason.[76]

Inquiries are also sometimes held on a non-statutory basis, either because the matter involved does not relate to any specific statutory function for which a statutory inquiry could be ordered, or because it is desired to adopt a different format from the statutory inquiry. The best known examples are the Crichel Down inquiry, and the first Stansted inquiry into the siting of a third London airport. There is no power in such cases, nor in the case where a "hearing" is directed, to summons witnesses, take evidence on oath or order the payment of costs; and the proceedings fall outside the supervisory remit of the Council on Tribunals. A public inquiry may also be held at the instance of a local authority, but this again (except in the case of an inquiry into a statutory local plan) is necessarily non-statutory.[77]

3. The Inquiries Procedure Rules and the Duty to Act Fairly

The Inquiries Procedure Rules apply only to five classes of planning appeal:[78]

(1) appeals against the refusal or conditional grant of planning permission;
(2) "called-in" applications;
(3) appeals under tree preservation orders;
(4) advertisement appeals, and
(5) listed building consent appeals, including appeals in respect of unlisted buildings in conservation areas and applications (such as those made by local planning authorities themselves) referred to the Secretary of State for determination.

Further, the Rules apply only to appeals in which an inquiry or hearing is to be held, and not to cases disposed of by way of written representations. There are two sets of Rules, applicable respectively to cases where the decision is to be taken by the Secretary of State,[79] and where jurisdiction is transferred to an inspector.[80] But the general provisions of each are similar.

The contents of the Rules are a clear recognition of the quasi-judicial nature of planning inquiries. So far as they go, they are an embodiment of the applicable natural justice principles, and they set the standards by which "fairness" may be assessed, even in inquiries to which they do not formally extend. But they are not exhaustive. There may be some action taken by the

---

[76] As to the hearing of evidence in camera, see *post*, p. 584.
[77] Classic examples include the Bognor Regis Inquiry held by Ramsey Willis Q.C. in 1967; and see generally *Ad Hoc Inquiries in Local Government*, S.O.L.A.C.E. (1978).
[78] I.P.R., r. 3(1); A.P.R., r. 3(1). The Rules apply equally to inquiries relating to land within Greater London, but with some modifications: see I.P.R., r.16; A.P.R., r.19.
[79] The Town and Country Planning (Inquiries Procedure) Rules 1974 (S.I. 1974 No. 419), herein the I.P.R. Enforcement appeals are now governed by the Town and Country Planning (Enforcement) (Inquiries Procedure) Rules 1981: see further *post*, p. 599.
[80] The Town and Country Planning Appeals (Determination by Appointed Persons) (Inquiries Procedure) Rules 1974 (S.I. 1974 No. 420), herein the A.P.R.

inspector in the conduct of the inquiry or by the Secretary of State in coming to his decision which is not in breach of the Rules, yet still offends the doctrines of natural justice. A refusal to allow adjournment or cross-examination at the inquiry is an example. This does not mean that the courts will go far beyond the Rules and require proceedings to be conducted as if they were a trial. In the words of Lord Moulton, speaking of the old Local Government Board, a duty to act "fairly" or "judicially" means no more than that "it must preserve a judicial temper and perform its duties conscientiously, with a proper feeling of responsibility, in view of the fact that its acts affect the property and rights of individuals."[81]

And compliance with the Rules does not, of course, prevent a decision from being challenged on other grounds. The reasoning may disclose an error of law, for example, or show that an irrelevant consideration has been permitted to influence the decision. These grounds of challenge are examined further in the next chapter.

4. Pre-Inquiry Procedure

(a) Notification

The first step following the lodging of an appeal and its acknowledgement, is formal notification by the Department of the Environment to the local planning authority of their intention to proceed. The authority are then required to notify the applicant of the names and addresses of every section 29 party, that is, of those persons who have been statutorily notified of the appeal and have made written representations to the Secretary of State, or to the planning authority whether in consequence of the original application or the appeal.[82]

If the authority's decision has followed a direction issued by the Secretary of State, or an unfavourable representation by a government department or local authority, it is necessary next that they should be notified by the planning authority of the appeal. They are then under a duty forthwith to furnish to the authority a statement in writing of the reasons for the direction or expression of opinion.[83] There is no duty at this stage for the information to be conveyed to the applicant, though it must be subsequently incorporated into the authority's Rule 6 statement.[84] The purpose of the procedure is to allow the authority to prepare a full preliminary statement.

The next step is the fixing of a date, time and place for the holding of the inquiry. This is fixed, and may be varied, by the Secretary of State. Not less than 42 days' notice to all parties, including section 29 parties, is required by the Rules, though a shorter period may be agreed with the applicant and the planning authority.[85] The authority may be required to publish notice of the inquiry by means of newspaper advertisement, by service on persons or classes of persons specified by the Secretary of State and notices posted near the site[86]; and the applicant, where the land is under his control, may also be

---

[81] *Local Government Board* v. *Arlidge* [1915] A.C. 120, at 150.
[82] I.P.R.,r. 4(1); A.P.R., r. 4(1).
[83] *Ibid.* r. 4(2).
[84] *Post,* p. 578.
[85] I.P.R., r. 5(1); A.P.R., r.5(1).
[86] *Ibid.* r. 5(2).

required to post a site notice.[87] It is a matter for the Secretary of State's discretion in each case what publicity should be given, and no rules have been laid down. Third parties upon whom notice of the inquiry has been served have a right to appear at the inquiry.[88] Where jurisdiction to determine the appeal has been transferred to an inspector, the parties will also be notified of his or her name.[89]

(b) Application for postponement

An inquiry may be postponed before it has opened, or, once opened, may be adjourned. In the former case the power vests with the Secretary of State,[90] although in transferred jurisdiction cases it may be exercised by the inspector.[91] Adjournment of an inquiry which has been opened, on the other hand, is a matter entirely for the inspector, and is considered later in this chapter. Refusal to postpone an inquiry is challengeable by means of an application for judicial review, but not by way of statutory application under the 1971 Act because the decision is not one "disposing" of an appeal[92]; rather, its effect is to insist that the appeal should proceed.

The courts have declined to extend to decision making in this area the criteria applicable to ordinary civil or criminal litigation.[93] Where there are a number of parties involved, arranging for a postponement to a date suitable for all is obviously considerably more cumbersome than in more straightforward cases. The fairness accorded to one party in acceding to a request for postponement may be set off by unfairness to other parties in rescheduling the inquiry. An alternative solution might be for a party who is unable to be present to submit written representations, or to be represented in his absence, or to be heard separately on a later occasion. These are possibilities which are less likely to be fair, however, where it is the appellant in a planning or enforcement appeal, as opposed to a third party or an objector, who is unable to be present, because the burden of presenting the appeal rests upon him. Whether or not the interests of fairness require postponement must therefore rest on the facts of each case, such as the reason for the request (serious illness, for example, would generally be a stronger reason than a failure simply to have prepared a case in time), the possibility of delaying tactics being used[94] and the timing of the request. It is not necessary that it should have been made before any date has been fixed for the inquiry,[95] but an early rescheduling is likely to cause less general inconvenience than a last minute postponement. It is also an important factor that a decision to refuse postponement is not necessarily final, in that

---

[87] *Ibid.* r. 5(3).
[88] I.P.R., r. 7(1)(j); A.P.R., r.9(1)(j)
[89] A.P.R., r.6.
[90] I.P.R., r. 5(1); A.P.R., r. 5(1).
[91] A.P.R., r. 8.
[92] *Co-operative Retail Services Ltd.* v. *S.O.S.E.* (1979) 39 P. & C.R. 428; and see further *post*, pp. 617–618.
[93] *Ostreicher* v. *S.O.S.E.* (1978) 37 P. & C.R. 9, a slum clearance case where an objector maintained that the date fixed for inquiry was unsuitable for religious reasons.
[94] See, *e.g. Jolliffe* v. *S.O.S.E.* (1971) 218 E.G. 565 (an enforcement case, where the appellant stood to benefit from lengthy delay).
[95] *Ostreicher* v. *S.O.S.E.* (*supra*) at 18, *per* Waller L.J. expressly disagreeing with the view expressed on that point by the trial judge.

an application may subsequently be made to the inspector once the inquiry has been opened, for an adjournment.[96]

(c) Rule 6 statements

Under Rule 6 of the Inquiries Procedure Rules the local planning authority and, if the Secretary of State so directs, the appellant, are required to provide a written statement of the submissions they propose to put forward at the inquiry.[97] The statement must also list any documents (including maps and plans) they propose to refer to, and these must be made available for inspection and copying by the other parties, including section 29 parties.[98] The local planning authority's statement must also include, where appropriate, a statement of the reasons for any direction or unfavourable expression of view given by a government department or local authority.[99] Their Rule 6 statement must be served on the parties not less than 28 days before the date fixed for the inquiry, and a copy forwarded to the Secretary of State.[1]

The purpose of the procedure is to give appellants a clear indication of the case they will have to meet at the inquiry, recognising that the reasons given by the authority for refusal of permission or for imposing conditions are often in themselves inadequate for the purpose.[2] The authority are not confined to those reasons in preparing their statement: the Secretary of State has jurisdiction to consider the application *de novo,* and is under a duty to look at all the relevant considerations. The Rule 6 procedure is therefore considerably less strict than pleadings in civil litigation. The power to require appellants to submit statements is rarely used in view of the fact the authority already have the original application and a statement of grounds of appeal.[3] And authorities are not confined rigidly at the inquiry to the submissions contained in their Rule 6 statements. They may be allowed by the inspector to alter or add to their submissions or to their list of documents "so far as may be necessary for determining the questions in controversy between the parties."[4] The inspector is then required, however, to give the other parties, if they object,[5] an adequate opportunity of considering any fresh submission or document, if necessary by adjourning the inquiry.[6]

The inspector's power to adjourn is an important element in securing fairness in inquiry procedure, because it offers the only apparent sanction for compliance by an authority with the terms of Rule 6. Failure by an

---

[96] See further *Co-operative Retail Services Ltd.* v. *S.O.S.E.* (1979) 39 P. & C.R. 428.
[97] The relevant Rule of the A.P.R. is in fact Rule 7, but the expression "Rule 6 statement" has become embedded in planning jargon, and for convenience is retained in the text.
[98] I.P.R., r. 6(3); A.P.R., r. 7(3).
[99] *Ibid.* rr. 6(2) and 7(2) respectively.
[1] *Ibid.* rr. 6(1) and 7(1) respectively.
[2] This factor was among the reasons given by the Franks Committee for their recommendation which led to the procedure: *op. cit.* para. 280.
[3] The power is likely to be used only in major cases raising difficult and complex issues, such as where detailed statistical evidence is likely to be produced: D.O.E. Circular 142/73, para. 18.
[4] I.P.R., r. 11(5); A.P.R., r. 12(5).
[5] It is not incumbent upon the inspector at his own initiative to check every document and every submission against the r. 6 statement: *Behrman* v. *S.O.S.E.* [1979] J.P.L. 667.
[6] *Ibid.* The Rules specifically authorise the inspector to make a recommendation to the Secretary of State as to costs occasioned by any such adjournment.

authority to submit their statement in time, or actually to make copies of documents available, is not a ground upon which the Secretary of State's decision may subsequently be quashed.[7] The Court of Appeal has therefore pointed to the need to exercise the adjournment power so as to ensure fairness. In *Performance Cars Ltd.* v. *Secretary of State for the Environment*[8] they quashed a decision where the planning authority had declined, until the morning of the inquiry, to provide the applicant with copies of a bundle of documents they proposed to put in and which had long before been requested by him; and where the inspector had declined his request for an adjournment of 30 days to consider the material, offering instead nothing more than an extended lunch-break. Despite the fact that no further adjournment had been sought by the applicant after perusing the documents, the Court agreed that the procedure had been unfair.

In the case of called-in applications there are similar requirements, but in this case the duty falls on the Secretary of State to issue a written statement of the reasons for the calling-in, and of the points which seem to him to be likely to be relevant to his consideration of the application.[9] The effect of his statement is thus to set the terms of reference for the inquiry, which he may do as broadly or as narrowly as he thinks necessary.

(d) Securing attendance by witnesses

There is a general power, exercisable only by the inspector, to summons any witness to give evidence or to produce relevant documents.[10] An obligation to obey the summons only arises if the necessary expenses of attendance are paid or tendered to the witness, but subject to that, failure to comply is an offence.[11] The power is rarely used in planning inquiries, largely because it is seldom that any matters of importance turn on conflicts of fact. Its exercise might be justified however, if, for example, a witness who had given evidence failed to remain or to attend for cross-examination by a party entitled under the Rules to cross-examine.

A more specific, and more commonly used, power arises where the original decision has been taken by the local planning authority pursuant to a direction or unfavourable expression of views by a government department or another local authority. In this case the applicant is entitled to insist that a representative of the department or the authority should attend the inquiry, by making written application to the effect to the Secretary of State not less than 14 days before the date of the inquiry.[12] He is not entitled under these

---

[7] This is because under T.C.P.A. 1971, ss. 242 and 245 only procedural breaches by the Secretary of State provide a basis for challenge: see further the observations of Browne L.J. in *Performance Cars Ltd.* v. *S.O.S.E.* (1977) 37 P. & C.R. 92 at 98. Although Sir Douglas Frank Q.C. appears to have assumed otherwise in *Davies* v. *Secretary of State for Wales* [1977] J.P.L. 102 his decision predates *Performance Cars* and the point seems not to have been taken before him.

[8] (1977) 37 P. & C.R. 92; but *cf. Grant* v. *M.H.L.G.* (1967) 204 E.G. 579, a clearance case where council had failed to make documents available before inquiry, but had offered to recall any witnesses: held, no unfairness.

[9] I.P.R., r. 6(1). Called-in applications are not transferred to inspectors for decision.

[10] Local Government Act 1972, s. 250.

[11] *Ibid.* s. 250(2) and (3).

[12] I.P.R., rr. 8 and 9; A.P.R., rr. 10 and 11. As to attendance by G.L.C. representatives at inquiries in London, see rr. 9A and 11A respectively (as inserted by rr. 16 and 19 respectively).

provisions to insist upon the attendance of any individual named by him: the obligation is simply to provide a "representative."[13] Nor may he use the provisions to call representatives of the local planning authority itself. The primary purpose of the procedure is to allow the appellant to hear and examine the reasons for the action taken by the department or other authority. Arrangements are usually made in any event by the planning authority for the attendance of such a representative, although there is no power for them actually to insist upon it. The representative, except in the case of called-in applications,[14] is called as a witness by the local planning authority and is subject to cross-examination (except, in the case of government representatives, on matters going to the merits of government policy)[15] in the same manner as any other witness.[16]

(e) Appointment of assessors

The inspector appointed for an inquiry may be assisted, in a case raising complex technical issues, by an assessor. His task is to act as a specialist adviser, examining evidence on matters beyond the knowledge of the inspector. As the Council on Tribunals have pointed out, he has no general function independent of the inspector, and his evaluation is only a factor to be weighed by the inspector with other considerations.[17] Nonetheless, the Council have expressed concern at the departmental practice of appointing technical advisers from the department concerned to act as assessors, and have recommended that outside assessors be used.[18]

5. *Inquiry procedure*

(a) The inspector's discretion

Subject to the Rules, the procedure to be followed at the inquiry is at the discretion of the inspector.[19] There is, however, a fairly standard form for straightforward inquiries, and it resembles trial procedure. Following the inspector's formal opening remarks and his taking of appearances, the appellant has the right to commence presentation of his case. He has also the right of final reply, and neither of those may be changed by the inspector without the appellant's consent.[20] The evidence of the appellant is subject to cross-examination by the representative of the planning authority (who may be their clerk or any other officer, or a barrister or solicitor),[21] by the section 29 parties, and, at the inspector's discretion, by other parties. The inspector may himself then put questions, and witnesses may be re-examined.

---

[13] See, *e.g. Ghafoor* v. *Secretary of State for Wales* [1976] J.P.L. 95. Despite the comment appended to that report, there is no reason why the procedures should not apply, as in that case, to appeals in default of decision. The only essential condition is that there should have been a direction or expression of views.

[14] I.P.R., r. 8(3).

[15] *Ibid.* r. 8(5); A.P.R. r. 10(4). And see further *post*, p. 587.

[16] I.P.R., rr. 8(4) and 9(3); A.P.R., rr. 10(3) and 11(3).

[17] Annual Report 1975–76, para. 97.

[18] *Ibid.* para. 95.

[19] I.P.R., r. 10(1); A.P.R., r. 12(1).

[20] *Ibid.* rr. 10(2) and 12(2) respectively.

[21] *Ibid.* rr. 7(3) and 9(3) respectively.

The local planning authority will normally follow and their evidence is similarly liable to cross-examination. They will normally be required to present their summing-up at the end of their evidence, although with the inspector's consent this may be postponed until other parties have been heard. Section 29 parties then have the right to call evidence, but other parties may do so only to the extent permitted by the inspector.[22] Finally, the appellant has his right of reply.

The order of appearances is essentially a matter for the inspector, however, and special arrangements are often made, to accommodate witnesses who are unable to attend at certain times, for example. In the case of large-scale inquiries it has become common to hold a pre-inquiry meeting between the inspector and the parties to establish a programme for the presentation of evidence. Where the inquiry is involved with a local authority application or draft order, the authority first present their case and objectors are then heard, with the authority having the right of reply.

The breadth of the inspector's discretion means that the character of any inquiry in practice owes much to the personality of the person appointed. In some instances the atmosphere may be friendly and informal, in others it is often formal and modelled closely on courtroom procedure. An inquiry is not a court however, and in particular there is no application to inquiries of the rules of contempt of court.[23] This means that there is no bar to free and critical discussion in the news media of the issues involved in an inquiry. It also means that the inspector has no sanction against unruly or disruptive conduct in the course of an inquiry except for the power to exclude parties from the proceedings.

(b) The position of third parties

The key participants in a planning inquiry are the applicant and the local planning authority. But inquiries have increasingly become vehicles for broader public involvement, and participation by so-called "third" parties has been encouraged, initially simply by administrative concession, but more recently through legislative provision. At one time the underlying philosophy was tolerantly patronising: inquiries gave members of the public an opportunity to "blow off steam."[24] But that opportunity has developed, for some participants at least, into a legal right.

So far as the Rules are concerned, third parties fall into three categories with differing legal consequences.

(i) **Section 29 parties.** In planning appeals this category includes only those persons who are owners or agricultural tenants of any of the land to which the aplication relates, notification of whom will have been a prerequisite to the validity of both the original application and the appeal.[25] Only those who have submitted representations to the authority or the Secretary of State within the prescribed time are included. In called-in cases,

---

[22] *Ibid.* rr. 10(3) and 12(3) respectively.
[23] *Attorney-General* v. *B.B.C.* [1980] 3 W.L.R. 109, where the House of Lords refused to interpret R.S.C. Ord. 52, r. 1 in such a way as to bring administrative tribunals and inquiries within the contempt jurisdiction of the Divisional Court.
[24] See further *Nicholson* v. *Secretary of State for Energy* (1977) 76 L.G.R. 693 at 700.
[25] I.P.R., r. 3; A.P.R., r. 3.

however, the category is extended so as also to include any persons who may have made representations within the prescribed time where the application has been advertised under section 26 of the 1971 Act, as "unneighbourly" development.[26]

Section 29 parties have the right to full participation at the inquiry; including rights to call witnesses and to cross-examine witnesses called by the other parties.[27]

(ii) Other parties entitled to appear. A right to appear at an inquiry is conferred not only upon the applicant, the authority and section 29 parties, but also upon[28] (i) the other relevant planning authority for the area (district or county as the case may be)[29]; (ii) the National Park Committee if not the planning authority, where the land is situated in a national park; (iii) any joint planning board or new town development corporation where the land is situated in their area; (iv) the parish or community council, if they have made representations in the prescribed manner, and (v) any other persons upon whom the Secretary of State has required notice of the inquiry to be served.

The position of parties "entitled to appear" is ambiguous. Their right of appearance implies a right to be heard and to make representations, and to have their representations properly considered.[30] Under the Rules their ability to go further, and to call evidence and cross-examine witnesses, is a matter for the inspector's discretion.[31] It is, however, also a matter of natural justice, and the discretion is not therefore unfettered. Its purpose is to allow the inspector to control the flow of irrelevant or repetitive material, but not to deprive the party of the right to be heard properly, which his entitlement to appear at the inquiry implies.[32]

(iii) Other parties. Any other person may appear at an inquiry at the discretion of the inspector.[33] Until that discretion has been exercised in his favour, he has no right to participate in the proceedings. But once it has, he becomes a "person permitted to appear." At one time the view was taken that persons in this category were second-class participants, and that their representations might be made without any guarantee that they would be considered by the Secretary of State within the terms of the statute and Rules. But that approach was rejected decisively in the High Court in 1973. In *Turner* v. *Secretary of State for the Environment*,[34] Ackner J. refused to differentiate at all between any person who appeared at an inquiry as of right, and one who appeared by permission of the inspector.

Although the point in issue in that case was the right of permitted parties to challenge decisions in the High Court, the ruling effectively assimilates the two categories of "entitled" parties and "permitted" parties for all

---

[26] *Ibid.*
[27] I.P.R., r. 10(3); A.P.R., r. 12(3).
[28] I.P.R., r. 7(1); A.P.R., r. 9(1).
[29] Special provisions in respect of London are contained in I.P.R., r. 16(*d*); A.P.R., r. 19(iv).
[30] *Buxton* v. *M.H.L.G.* [1961] 1 Q.B. 278 at 285, *per* Salmon J.
[31] I.P.R., r. 10(3); A.P.R., r. 12(3).
[32] Matters of evidence and cross-examination at inquiries are considered further below.
[33] I.P.R., r. 7(2); A.P.R., r. 9(2).
[34] (1973) 28 P. & C.R. 123 at 134–139.

purposes of the inquiry, save only that in the latter case permission may presumably be withdrawn by the inspector at any time during the course of the inquiry.

Entitlement or permission to appear at an inquiry implies the right to attend all sessions, although the inspector is specifically authorised in his discretion to proceed in the absence of any party. It is clear, though, that any party may be ejected from the inquiry for noisy or disruptive behaviour, and that the inquiry may then continue without infringing the rules of natural justice.[35]

(c) Evidence

It has become customary for evidence at inquiries to be given by way of a prepared written proof, copies of which are made available to the inspector and other parties and which is read out by the witness. It is a convenient procedure, but it is by no means obligatory. There is power for the inspector to require evidence to be given under oath,[36] but this is rarely exercised in the case of planning appeals. It is common, however, in certain enforcement appeals and established use certificate appeals where much will often turn upon disputed questions of fact. Admission of evidence is at the discretion of the inspector, subject to a duty to exclude any evidence which would be contrary to the public interest.[37] The discretion has traditionally been tolerantly exercised, although a departmental circular asserts that "Inspectors have now been asked to encourage all parties to be brief as well as relevant and in particular to confine evidence, cross-examination of witnesses and comments on evidence to essential points."[38] There is an assurance, however, that inspectors "will take care to ensure that the saving of time at inquiries is not done at the expense of giving everyone concerned the opportunity to put forward all of the points and evidence which are relevant to his case."[39]

There are no strict rules of evidence. Documentary evidence and hearsay evidence may be admitted and taken into account provided it can fairly be regarded as reliable.[40] It is not a prerequisite of reliability that the evidence should first have been tested by cross-examination: natural justice may be satisfied by allowing the parties to comment upon it and to contradict it.[41]

The Rules also authorise the inspector to take into account any written

[35] *Lovelock v. Secretary of State for Transport* [1979] R.T.R. 250.
[36] Local Government Act 1972, s. 250.
[37] I.P.R., r. 10(4); A.P.R., r. 12(4).
[38] D.O.E. Circular 142/73, para. 19
[39] *Ibid.*
[40] Subject, in the case of documentary evidence submitted by the planning authority, to its inclusion in their rule 6 statement, or the inspector's consent to adding to the statement. The suggestion by Ackner L.J. in *Blackpool B.C. v. S.O.S.E.* (1980) 40 P. & C.R. 104 at 107 that an inspector is entitled to refuse to admit affidavit evidence where there is no justifiable reason for the appellant's non-appearance, though represented, overlooks the essential difference between court room and inquiry procedure, and the inherent discretion of the inspector to attach such weight as he thinks fit to the evidence.
[41] *T.A. Miller Ltd. v. M.H.L.G.* [1968] 1 W.L.R. 992. The inspector may direct that documentary evidence admitted at the inquiry may be inspected by any party and that facilities be afforded him to take or obtain copies: I.P.R., r. 10(4); A.P.R., r. 12(4).

representations or statements received by him before the inquiry from any person.[42] He is, however, obliged to "disclose" them at the inquiry, and although that does not means that he must read them out, it implies at least that the documents should be made available for inspection by the parties so that they should have the opportunity to comment upon them.

(d) Evidence in camera

It is of the essence of an inquiry that it should be a public event, and that all evidence should be heard in public. At one time, however, inspectors were prepared in exceptional cases to hear evidence in camera. Following disquiet over one particular case in 1967 where the public had been excluded for the hearing of evidence relating to a confidential commercial process,[43] the Council on Tribunals sought the preparation of detailed rules to govern such cases.[44] The Government declined, and instead announced that it was to be "Government policy that inspectors should in future not accede to requests that they should hear evidence in private at planning inquiries."[45] The question was reopened by the Stevens Committee in 1976 in their Report on *Planning Control over Mineral Working*.[46] They foresaw the possibility that confidential evidence of a commercially sensitive nature might be important in a planning inquiry. It might, for example, relate to the extent and nature of the mineral resources at the site or nearby, or to a new extraction or treatment process. The Committee recommended that provision should be made for evidence to be taken in camera in a suitable case, but that elaborate safeguards should be applied to ensure that the practice was limited to exceptional cases. Any party wishing to avail themselves of the procedure would first be required to obtain an order of the High Court, and the Court would need to be satisfied that public disclosure would result in a disadvantage to the applicant which would, by comparison with the advantage to the public of that disclosure, be unwarranted. The test would be extremely difficult to apply without any clearer indication of how the balance could be struck, and the Government rejected the recommendation.[47] They held open, however, the possibility of adopting an ad hoc procedure in the future in consultation with the Council on Tribunals if a "most exceptional" case requiring confidentiality should arise.

Those events have now been overtaken by the Planning Inquiries (Attendance of Public) Act 1982, the result of a private Member's Bill introduced by the M.P. who had led the protests at the action taken in the 1967 inquiry. The Act establishes the principle that oral evidence at planning inquiries must be heard in public, and that documentary evidence shall be open to public inspection. The only exception is where the Secretary of State directs that evidence shall be restricted. A direction may be given only where

---

[42] I.P.R., r. 10(7); A.P.R., r. 12(7).
[43] Details of the case are set out in the Second Report of the Parliamentary Commissioner for Administration, session 1969–70, pp. 55–58, who found the procedure unobjectionable on the particular facts.
[44] See further their *Annual Reports* for 1969–70 (para. 80) and 1972–73 (paras. 100–102).
[45] *Hansard*, H.C.Deb., Vol. 836, *col. 199* (May 4, 1972).
[46] H.M.S.O. (1976), pp. 167–168.
[47] D.O.E. Circular 58/78, Annex. para. 19.16(c).

he is satisfied that public disclosure of information relating to national security or to the security of any premises or property would be likely to result from the giving of the evidence, and that public disclosure would be contrary to the national interest.

(e) Cross-examination

(i) **Entitlement.** The right to cross-examine witnesses is a central feature of the common law tradition of adversarial proceedings. It is the means through which issue is joined, and conflicts of evidence scrutinized. That tradition is carried over into planning appeals through the provision of the Rules which confers a right of cross-examination upon the applicant, the planning authority and section 29 parties.[48] That is a general right, though it is subject to the inspector's power to confine proceedings to the issues in dispute, and to disallow repetitive and irrelevant questioning.

Other parties, however, may cross-examine only to the extent permitted by the inspector.[49] That discretion must, of course, be exercised fairly, but it has seldom been easy to discern from decisions of the courts how far a right to cross-examine could be considered to be a requirement of natural justice. As a matter of practice, inspectors have tended to exercise their discretion broadly and have generally permitted cross-examination by all parties except where some special factor has indicated that they should not. It is often the case that a party has difficulty in formulating questions, or seeks to cross-examine on irrelevant or immaterial points.

The case for a right of cross-examination by third parties was strengthened by the decision of Sir Douglas Frank Q.C. (sitting as a deputy judge of the High Court) in *Nicholson* v. *Secretary of State for Energy*[50] where he ruled that objectors at an inquiry into a proposal for opencast coal mining ought not to have been refused the right to cross-examine material witnesses. The court held that the refusal had infringed the rules of natural justice, in the sense that "a reasonable person viewing the matter objectively would consider that there was a risk that injustice or unfairness would result if a person considering himself to be injuriously affected by a proposal was denied cross-examination of a witness who had given evidence contrary to his case."[51]

But in the more recent highways case *Bushell* v. *Secretary of State for the Environment*[52] a majority in the House of Lords took a more restrictive view. Their approach placed greater emphasis upon the likely utility to the inspector of a proposed cross-examination than on possible feelings of unfairness to an objector. Lord Diplock insisted that a refusal to permit cross-examination was not *per se* unfair,[53] and indicated that the relevant criteria by which fairness should be assessed, where the issue in dispute is one of expert opinion on a technical matter, included:

---

[48] I.P.R., r. 10(3); A.P.R., r. 12(3).
[49] *Ibid.*
[50] (1977) 76 L.G.R. 693.
[51] *Ibid.* 701.
[52] [1980] 3 W.L.R. 22.
[53] *Ibid.* p. 29; Lord Lane (at 52–53) expressly concurred on this point, and Lord Fraser of Tullybelton (at 49) expressed general agreement with both.

"the nature of the topic on which the opinion is expressed, the qualifications of the maker of the statement to deal with that topic, the forensic competence of the proposed cross-examiner, and, most important, the inspector's own views as to whether the likelihood that cross-examination will enable him to make a report which will be more useful to the minister in reaching his decision than it otherwise would be is sufficient to justify any expense and inconvenience to other parties to the inquiry which would be caused by any resulting prolongation of it."[54]

Those criteria may not be relevant to every case, but they indicate the breadth of the inspector's discretion. They also imply that a blanket refusal by an inspector to permit cross-examination by third parties would be unfair, and that the issue must be fairly determined on each occasion.

What is clear, however, is that as a matter of law it is no part of the inspector's function to formulate questions on behalf of unrepresented parties who have difficulty in adjusting to the procedures.[55] As a matter of practice, however, that may sometimes be the only fair way of ensuring that important points are properly examined. In an informal inquiry where there is no legal representation, for example, an inspector might be expected to adopt a more inquisitorial role than that usually appropriate. But it is difficult for him to conduct anything approaching a searching cross-examination without discarding all appearance of impartiality, and thus in practice the "inquisitorial" function is confined to straightforward questioning on points of information.

(ii) **Professional planning evidence.** A perennial problem at planning inquiries has been the status of the local authority's planning officer as a witness. There are two views. Either he appears in his capacity as servant of his authority with the task of explaining and defending their policies and decision, or he appears as a professional planner with an independent stance. The conflict between the two views becomes apparent in cases where the authority have acted contrary to their planning officer's advice. The Royal Town Planning Institute, not unsurprisingly, stress the professional role of their members. They insist that evidence given in the form of professional opinion must be the officer's own opinion, and that he must not, if challenged in cross-examination, conceal any difference between him and his authority, or between him and his superior officers.[56] Where there is a difference of opinion between the chief planning officer and his committee, the Institute's advice is that the committee chairman instead should be called as witness.

(iii) **Requiring answers.** There is, in general, no obligation on any witness to answer questions put in cross-examination. Failure to respond may, of course, seriously damage a party's case, but it does not mean that the Secretary of State will have breached any requirements of the statute if he

---

[54] *Ibid.* at 30.
[55] *Snow* v. *S.O.S.E.* (1976) 33 P. & C.R. 81.
[56] *R.T.P.I. Practice Advice Note No. 1,* published in *The Planner* (1979) 89. The Note is a rewritten version of earlier advice published at [1961] J.P.L. 94.

nonetheless upholds that case.[57] The only way in which a witness may by law be required to answer is through the issuance of a summons under section 250 of the Local Government Act 1972.

(iv) Matters of government policy. Government policy is an important factor in many planning appeals, and its significance is particularly great in cases involving government sponsored projects. Where it is firm government policy that there should be a national motorway network, or a third London airport or a further new town, it is clear from the outset that any statutory decision taken pursuant to a public inquiry will be taken within the context of that policy. Policies are the product of politics, and the traditional view is that governments and ministers should be accountable to Parliament alone for their policies. It follows that there should be no obligation for a minister to defend his policy at a public local inquiry. The purpose of an inquiry, at least in the case of government schemes, is to provide the minister with sufficient information to ensure that he is in a position to weigh the harm to local interests and private persons who may be adversely affected by the scheme, against the broader public interest represented by pursuing the policy.

Adopting this formulation, the courts have been prepared to rule that government policy is not a matter which it is appropriate to examine at an inquiry.[58] The argument is that policy-making is dependent upon a broader range of considerations than those liable to be presented at an inquiry. As Lord Diplock[59] has pointed out, the decision to construct a nationwide network of motorways is one of broad policy, and any decision to alter it is appropriate for Parliamentary debate, but not for separate investigation before individual inspectors up and down the country upon whatever material happens to be presented to them.

The special immunity of government policy is reinforced in the case of planning appeals by the Inquiries Procedure Rules, which require the inspector to disallow any question put to a departmental witness and directed to the merits of government policy.[60] The rule does not prevent parties from cross-examining on the factual basis of government policy or from leading evidence of their own directed to questioning government policy, which may be cross-examined; nor does it forbid a departmental witness from discussing or explaining government policy otherwise than in response to questioning; nor does it affect the conduct of inquiries where no departmental representative appears. But the question of relevance remains, and it is a matter for the discretion of the inspector how far he should hear evidence on matters which are beyond his investigative competence. Clearly, natural justice does not require that he should do so. The Secretary of State is in any event entitled to take into account any government policy, whether

---

[57] Thus see *Accountancy Tuition Centre* v. *S.O.S.E.* [1977] J.P.L. 799 where the conduct of a planning officer who refused to answer any questions going beyond the content of his proof of evidence was described as "deplorable," and the suggestion was made that it was not for the witness to determine the proper scope of his answers, although the advocate who called him might object to improper questions.

[58] *Bushell* v. *S.O.S.E.* [1980] 3 W.L.R. 22.

[59] *Ibid.* at 30.

[60] I.P.R., r. 8(5); A.P.R., r. 10(4).

emanating from his own or other departments and whether or not discussed at the inquiry.[61]

The privileged status that is accorded government policy is clearly in accordance with tradition, but it has given rise to serious misgivings in many quarters. First, there comes a point at which the statutory decision is effectively predetermined by the adoption of a policy, and where the opportunity presented by an inquiry to influence the Secretary of State is little more than an empty ritual. Lord Denning M.R. has pointed to the danger that objectors may be brushed off with the remark "It is government policy" by departments who come to inquiries with their minds made up.[62] Second, the more "appropriate" forum of Parliamentary debate is far from perfect. There is seldom an adequate opportunity for specific debate on the floor of the House, and the procedure is unsuited to the detailed scrutiny of policy assumptions. Policies and policy shifts are not automatically brought to or debated in the House, although arrangements have now been made, following adverse criticism, for roads programmes to be announced annually in a white paper.[63]

Third, there remains some confusion as to what actually constitutes government policy. There is no definition in the Rules. Policy is necessarily amorphous and evolutionary: there is no fixed reference book of operative government policy. It need not be published. The announcement by the Secretary of State or his representative before or during an inquiry that a given matter is government policy therefore carries considerable weight. But should the Secretary of State himself be free to determine what is, and what is not, immune from questioning at an inquiry? In the *Bushell* case, much turned in the Court of Appeal on definitions of policy and the distinction between policy and facts. Thus, Lord Denning M.R., speaking of the Department's "Red Book" of methodology for undertaking traffic forecasts, insisted that:

> "For myself, I do not regard these traffic forecasts as Government policy at all. They are the predictions by the Department's experts about the future. They are as much matters of fact as the evidence of a medical man as to the prognosis of a disease."[64]

But a majority in the House of Lords was prepared to offer far broader immunity. Lord Diplock's approach was to couch the question in terms of the function of the inquiry, and to ask simply whether the material was suitable for investigation at individual local inquiries.[65] If a relevant statement or document relied upon by the Department raises issues of national application, then under Lord Diplock's test it is inappropriate for local investigation and is therefore "government policy in the relevant sense." But equally, a document or statement of intention could not qualify for immunity, even though purporting to be government policy, if it was directed solely to issues arising in the particular case.

---

[61] See further *post*, pp. 592–594.
[62] In *Bushell* v. *S.O.S.E.* (1979) 78 L.G.R. 10 at 15 (C.A.).
[63] *Post*, p. 599.
[64] 78 L.G.R., 10 at 16.
[65] [1980] 3 W.L.R. 22 at 32.

(f) Sittings and adjournments

The arrangements for sittings are a matter for the inspector, and special arrangements may be made by him, for example, for late sittings to get through evidence more expeditiously, or for evening or weekend sessions for the convenience of parties unable to attend during the normal working day.

Similarly, the inspector has power to adjourn proceedings.[66] Adjournment may be necessary in the interests of fairness to give a party an opportunity to consider some new point raised late in the proceedings by another party, and perhaps to find a witness to deal with it. There is a difference between adjournment of an inquiry that has been opened and the postponement of one that is yet to commence, and the Court of Appeal have indicated that a more generous approach may be needed in the former case than in the case of postponement in the interests of securing fairness.[67] The inspector is bound to consider adjournment when the authority (or, where appropriate, another party) seek to go beyond their rule 6 statement, and he may also make recommendations as to the award of costs in such cases.[68] If it is possible to announce a date, time and place for the adjourned inquiry before the adjournment, no further notice is necessary.[69]

(g) Informal inquiries and rapid decisions

Among the proposals advanced by the Government's *Consultation Paper* in 1980 was the idea of informal inquiries, which would presumably be intended to bridge the gap between written representations and the full formal inquiry. Parties would be invited in advance by the inspector to allow him to conduct the inquiry as an informal meeting, with the inspector in the chair and with any cross-questioning being conducted through the chair. There would be scope, therefore, for the inspector to adopt a more inquisitorial role, and the procedure has advantages for unrepresented appellants by reducing the importance of legal representation and professional evidence. It is in essence a retreat from the formality which has followed the implementation of the Franks Committee's recommendations, but it involves yet a further move towards conferring greater adjudicatory powers on inspectors, and if it is to be effective would require either protective legislation insulating decisions from judicial review, or a correspondingly tolerant attitude on the part of the judiciary towards any procedural irregularities arising.

A less well founded proposal in the *Consultation Paper* was that which proposed that inspectors should, in suitable cases, give instant decisions. The idea that the inspector might give an *ex tempore* decision immediately at the close of the inquiry was rejected (so as to ensure his safe exit from the

---

[66] I.P.R., r. 10(8); A.P.R., r. 12(8).
[67] *Co-operative Retail Services Ltd.* v. *S.O.S.E.* [1980] 1 All E.R. 449 at 453, *per* Stephenson L.J.; and *cf. Gill & Co. Ltd.* v. *S.O.S.E.* [1978] J.P.L. 373 where a compulsory purchase order under Part III of the Housing Act 1957 was quashed for failure by the inspector to allow an adjournment, which had not been opposed by any other party and the expense of which could readily have been met by an order for costs.
[68] I.P.R., r. 10(5); A.P.R., r. 12(5).
[69] *Ibid.* rr. 10(8) and 12(8) respectively.

inquiry room), but instead it was proposed that he would send to the parties on the following day an advance notice of his decision, and forward a fully reasoned decision at a later date. The procedure has a superficial attractiveness, but it is unlikely to operate effectively in practice in any but the most straightforward cases. The immediate impressions formed by the inspector are not always those which remain with him after a careful review of the evidence, and if a speedier decision process is desired it would be preferable by far to arrange for the swift dispatch of the reasoned decision. Early notification of the decision itself without the reasons for it may do little to dispel the uncertainty felt by the parties, particularly if the decision is to grant permission subject to unspecified conditions.

(h) Site inspection

The site itself is sometimes the most important piece of evidence at an inquiry, and the inspector is expressly entitled to view it at any time without informing the parties of his intentions.[70] But where requested to do so by either the authority or the appellant he is obliged to undertake an accompanied inspection after the close of the inquiry.[71] They and any section 29 parties are entitled to accompany the inspector, but it is not the purpose of the inspection to continue the inquiry "on location." The inspector may not hear any further representations from the parties nor consult the neighbours for their views,[72] and there is even a limit to the extent to which he may use any knowledge gained purely visually by him at the inspection. If he bases his decision or recommendations upon something seen by him on the site but not discussed at the inquiry he may have infringed the natural justice rules.[73] The best course is for the inquiry to be re-opened, and the matter pursued further in the presence of the parties. On the other hand, if the matter is one which has been discussed at the inquiry and is by way of an issue of opinion rather than fact, such as the standard of architecture of an existing building for example, there is no denial of natural justice in failing to offer a party the opportunity to call expert evidence to counter the inspector's impressions.[74] The dividing line between the two is far from easy to draw.

The duty to carry out an inspection extends only to "the land," which the Rules define as being "the land (including trees and buildings) to which the inquiry relates."[75] The inspector is not, therefore, obliged to visit other sites, such as any possible alternative sites to which reference may have been made at the inquiry, or neighbouring sites whose amenities may be affected if the development is permitted. But it obviously is good practice for the inspector to do so, at least as far as it is physically possible.

---

[70] *Ibid.* rr. 11(1) and 13(1) respectively.
[71] *Ibid.* rr. 11(2) and 13(2) respectively.
[72] *Hibernian Property Co. Ltd.* v. *S.O.S.E.* (1973) 27 P. & C.R. 197.
[73] See, *e.g. Fairmount Investments Ltd.* v. *S.O.S.E.*[1976] 1 W.L.R. 1255 where the inspector following a clearance inquiry formed the view on inspection that the foundations of a house were unstable on evidence—a broken "tell tale"—which had not been discussed at the inquiry. The House of Lords upheld the quashing of the decision.
[74] See, *e.g. Winchester C.C.* v. *S.O.S.E.* (1979) 39 P. & C.R. 1.
[75] I.P.R., r. 3(1); A.P.R., r. 3(1).

6. *Post-Inquiry Procedure*

It is the post-inquiry stage of ministerial decision making which has traditionally departed most substantially from the judicial model. In the early days of inquiries the inspector's report was nothing more than an aid to internal departmental decision making. Officials were free to engage in further consultations with government departments and others and to draw widely upon their own expertise and wisdom. But following the Franks Report, that free-wheeling administrative world has disappeared. Inspectors' reports are now required to be published, and although the Secretary of State remains under no duty to accept their recommendations, he must record valid reasons for overriding them. If he proposes to rely upon fresh information or on matters not in issue at the inquiry, he must in certain circumstances allow the parties an opportunity to make further comment, if necessary by re-opening the inquiry. Further, the courts have been prepared to insist that, whilst matters of planning policy and judgment must remain entirely within the province of the Secretary of State, the validity of his decisions is dependent upon the adequacy of the reasons given by him.

These various requirements are partly contained in the Inquiries Procedure Rules, and partly the product of judicial development of the natural justice concept within the context of the Rules. The Rules are not exhaustive, and the Secretary of State may still fall foul of the requirements of fairness though acting in compliance with the Rules. The analysis contained in the following pages therefore needs to be read alongside the examination contained in the next chapter of judicial review of planning decisions. Access to the courts to challenge decisions is limited, and it is not every instance of breach of the Rules which will lead automatically to the quashing of a decision. In particular, the Act provides that the courts may quash for failure to comply with procedural requirements only where satisfied that the interests of the applicant have been substantially prejudiced thereby.[76]

The Rules make different provision for post-inquiry procedure according to whether the decision is one for the Secretary of State, or has been transferred to an inspector.

(a) Secretary of State's decisions

(i) **The inspector's report.** The starting point in the case of Secretary of State's decisions is the inspector's report. The Rules require that it should be submitted in writing, and that it should include the inspector's findings of fact and his recommendations (or, if none, his reasons for making no recommendations).[77] The wording of the Rules reflects the Franks Committee's recommendation[78] that reports should be prepared in two parts, the first reporting the facts and inferences of fact based thereon, and the second recording recommendations. But, except in Scotland, their further recommendation[79] that the first part should be distributed to parties

---

[76] T.C.P.A. 1971, s. 245(4); and see *post*, pp. 621–623.
[77] I.P.R., r. 12(1). The Franks Committee recognised that it might be difficult for an inspector to make recommendations in cases involving a large policy element: *op. cit.* para. 328.
[78] *Ibid.* para. 328.
[79] *Ibid.* para. 345.

for factual correction before the decision was made has not been accepted.

The inspector's duty in writing his report is to give the Secretary of State a fair account of the evidence on which he has made findings of fact and recommendations.[80] This means too that he must record details of legal argument and cases cited to him in so far as they are relevant in the sense of being necessary to record an intelligible account of the case presented to him. But he must necessarily be selective, and mere failure to exclude some peripheral point or passing comment is no breach of the duty.[81] He must deal properly with the major points at issue. If he omits to include any point the court may look behind his report to evidence of what transpired at the inquiry,[82] especially where both sides are agreed that there has been an omission though they dispute its importance.[83] Whilst the courts are not concerned to examine minutely the basis upon which the inspector has included or rejected material,[84] it is clear that they will be prepared to quash the Secretary of State's decision if satisfied that a major point which might have affected his decision has not been properly reported to him.[85] In order to make that judgement the court necessarily is involved not only in weighing the evidence and assessing its relevance, but also in judging from the documents whether it has been adequately reported to the Secretary of State and properly taken into account by him. Unsurprisingly, the authorities are often difficult to reconcile, because so much is dependent upon inference and suggestion.[86]

The inspector's conclusions and recommendations similarly must flow from the facts reported by him, and this will be a ground for review of the decision in cases where the Secretary of State has relied upon them, such as where he has expressly adopted and incorporated them as part of the reasoning of his decision letter.

(ii) **Disputed facts.** The Rules provide that where the Secretary of State differs from the inspector on a finding of fact, and for that reason is disposed to disagree with one of his recommendations, he must first notify the applicant, the local planning authority and any section 29 party who appeared at the inquiry, giving his reasons.[87] They then have the opportunity to make representations within 21 days. The Secretary of State may also, if he thinks fit, re-open the inquiry to allow the matter to be re-examined.[88]

The practical difficulty in operating the Rule is that of distinguishing matters of "fact" in an inspector's report from its other contents. The usual

---

[80] *North Surrey Water Co.* v. *S.O.S.E.* (1976) 34 P. & C.R. 140.

[81] *A.B. Motor Co. of Hull Ltd.* v. *M.H.L.G.* (1969) 67 L.G.R. 689.

[82] See, *e.g. East Hants D.C.* v. *S.O.S.E.* [1978] J.P.L. 182; and see further *post*, p. 620.

[83] *Preston D.C.* v. *S.O.S.E.* [1978] J.P.L. 548.

[84] *North Surrey Water Co.* v. *S.O.S.E.* (1976) 34 P. & C.R. 140.

[85] *East Hampshire D.C.* v. *S.O.S.E.* [1979] J.P.L. 533 (C.A.).

[86] See, *e.g. London Welsh Association Ltd.* v. *S.O.S.E.* where Forbes J. at first instance ([1979] J.P.L. 464) was prepared to quash a compulsory purchase order because the Minister had failed to deal specifically with an alternative development proposal advanced at the inquiry by the appellants. But the Court of Appeal ((1980) 255 E.G. 1095) unanimously held that it was sufficient that the Secretary of State should simply have accepted his inspector's recommendations on the point.

[87] I.P.R., r. 12(2)(*a*)

[88] I.P.R., r. 12(3).

division of a report into "findings of fact," "conclusions" and "recommendations" is of some assistance but not necessarily conclusive.

In *Luke* v. *Minister of Housing and Local Government*[89] the Court of Appeal, reversing the decision at first instance, adopted a narrow construction of the phrase "finding of fact." The Court insisted that "facts" should be distinguished from "opinions," and that the Minister should be able to come to a different view on the planning merits of the case without referring the matter back to the parties. If he could not, then the Rules should have required that the parties be consulted on every occasion he proposed not to accept an inspector's recommendation. The distinction is clear enough in theory. The Secretary of State may accept all the facts as found by the inspector, but take the contrary view from him as to their planning consequences. His inspector may think that the appellant has established a case for making an exception to green belt policy, for example. The Secretary of State may disagree. He need not refer the issue back to the parties. His disagreement is on a question of policy judgment. Similarly, it is a matter of planning judgment whether a proposed development would, "far from harming the countryside, add to the existing charm of its setting;"[90] or "would not have an adverse impact on the countryside;"[91] that a proposed supermarket would not have a detrimental effect on an existing town centre,[92] or that with landscaping and the council's supervision and control a caravan site should not be either "unduly obtrusive or damaging."[93] These are matters of opinion, or inference, and even of pure speculation; but not of fact. But they are none of them questions of policy, and it is far from easy to understand why it should be thought that a decision made by a civil servant who has not seen the site should be preferred to the opinion of the inspector who has.

On the other hand, if the Secretary of State should form a different view from his inspector as to the recorded facts or the inferences of *fact* rather than planning *opinion* to be drawn from them, he must seek the views of the parties. Examples include cases where the Secretary of State has rejected the inspector's classification of the primary and ancillary uses on a site,[94] his classification of a firm as a "local" firm,[95] his view that acquisition of a property was not "reasonably necessary,"[96] and his opinion that a listed building when rehabilitated would have a value exceeding the cost of

---

[89] [1968] 1 Q.B. 172.

[90] *Ibid.*

[91] *Vale Estates (Acton) Ltd.* v. *S.O.S.E.* (1970) 69 L.G.R. 543, and *cf. J. Murphy & Sons Ltd.* v. *S.O.S.E.* [1973] 2 All E.R. 26 (balancing exceptional housing need against site unsuitability in terms of noise levels); and *Sunley Homes Ltd.* v. *S.O.S.E.* (1974) 233 E.G. 57.

[92] *J. Sainsbury Ltd.* v. *S.O.S.E.* [1978] J.P.L. 379.

[93] *Brown* v. *S.O.S.E.* (1978) 40 P. & C.R. 285 at 293.

[94] *Pollock* v. *S.O.S.E.* (1979) 252 E.G. 914 (though wrongly decided on the assumption that the Rules applied to enforcement appeals, which they did not: see the Court of Appeal decision at [1981] J.P.L. 420). See also the criticism of the Divisional Court's distinction, which was not overruled by the Court of Appeal, in *S.J.D. Properties Ltd.* v. *S.O.S.E.* [1981] J.P.L. 673.

[95] *Pyrford Properties Ltd.* v. *S.O.S.E.* (1977) 36 P. & C.R. 28; and *cf. Merevale Builders Ltd.* v. *S.O.S.E.* (1978) 36 P. & C.R. 87.

[96] *Coleen Properties Ltd.* v. *M.H.L.G.* [1971] 1 All E.R. 1049; though strictly a slum clearance case to which the Rules did not apply, and *cf. Islington B.C.* v. *S.O.S.E.* (1980) 43 P. & C.R. 300 (prophesy as to likelihood of future event an issue of opinion and not fact).

repairs.[97] In each of those cases there was no aesthetic or other "planning" judgment involved in the Secretary of State's disagreement. Although none involved a challenge to the primary facts as found by the inspector, there was a difference of view at the second stage of decision-making, that of drawing conclusions or inferences of fact from primary facts.

The distinction is fine, but in practice interpretation is tempered by the limitation on the court's power to quash for breach of the Rule, to cases where the applicant has been "substantially prejudiced." The effect is to turn the question around, and to ask what further representations the applicant could reasonably have made on the issue, had it been referred back to him. He is more likely to have been prejudiced by being denied the opportunity to make representations on a factual dispute which might be resolved by further evidence, than on a more subjective, evaluative issue.

As it stands at present, the distinction is confusing and creates considerable practical difficulties. In one remarkable case, involving the controversial development by E.M.I. Ltd., in London's Tottenham Court Road, the Secretary of State was prepared to concede in court that he had indeed breached the rule, only to have both the first instance judge and the Court of Appeal rule that he had not.[98]

(iii) Fresh evidence and new issues of fact. A similar procedure also applies where the Secretary of State proposes to take new evidence into account or to pursue new issues of fact, only in this case he is under a duty to re-open the inquiry should either of the parties insist.[99] "New evidence" is defined as including any new expert opinion on a matter of fact, and the implication is that the Secretary of State is able to seek further expert opinion should he wish, provided he refers the matter back if necessary. Similarly, he is not bound to accept the issues as framed by the parties and examined at the inquiry, and his duty under section 29 to take into account all material considerations may require him to consider additional questions of fact. The matter will again need to be referred back to the parties, unless (1) the issue is not properly one of fact at all, or is not "new"[1]; or (2) his conclusion is that he should not disturb any of the inspector's recommendations, (the new issue of fact or fresh evidence may instead be used to reinforce his inspector's conclusions); or (3) the new issue of fact is a matter of government policy.

The Rules are not conclusive, and it may be that natural justice may impose additional requirements. But the courts have accepted that there is inevitably a heavy burden upon a complainant in attempting to establish a breach of natural justice when Rules designed to secure justice have been

---

[97] *Thanet D.C.* v. *S.O.S.E.* (1977) 246 E.G. 229. *Ibid.* 230 per Sir Douglas Frank Q.C.; and *cf. Copthall Holdings Ltd.* v. *S.O.S.E.* (1973) 228 E.G. 925.

[98] *Camden L.B.C.* v. *S.O.S.E.* (1975) 235 E.G. 375. *Camden L.B.C.* v. *S.O.S.E.* [1975] J.P.L. 661 (C.A.): the Court took the view that the Inspector's conclusion that the company's electronic expertise enabled them to disperse their staff and that they had failed to show the need for one single office, was merely conjecture as to what was feasible, and not a finding of fact at all.

[99] I.P.R., r. 12(3).

[1] *Webb* v. *S.O.S.E.* (1972) 224 E.G. 869, where the court was prepared to look to the authority's Rule 6 statement as well as to the inspector's report to examine whether the issue had been canvassed at inquiry; and see *Warnock* v. *S.O.S.E.* [1980] J.P.L. 590 (not a new issue of fact for inspector to select a planning urit different from that agreed by the parties).

complied with.[2] Further, there is no ipso facto breach of natural justice in the mere receipt by the Secretary of State of further representations after the close of an inquiry and failure to circulate them to the parties.[3]

The problems of defining "government policy" have already been touched upon. The provision continues the right recognised at common law[4] for the Secretary of State to consult other departments and to take their views and policies into account,[5] and have regard to the policy of his own department. Nor does natural justice require that any new policy or change in old policies be disclosed to the parties in advance for their views,[6] though the courts will be prepared to review the validity and relevance of any policy employed.[7]

(b) Inspector's decisions

In cases of transferred jurisdiction the position is slightly different, because there is no question of a recommendation being overridden by the Secretary of State. The Rules instead require that the inspector should not take into consideration any new evidence (including expert opinion on a matter of fact) or any new issue of fact (not being a matter of government policy) which was not raised at the inquiry and which he considers to be material to his decision without first notifying the parties.[8] The parties may respond by way of written representations, or may require that inquiry be re-opened.[9] The Rules are supplementary to the rules of natural justice, so that the broad discretion suggested by the words "which he considers material to his decision" is tempered by the fact that all material information not produced or examined at the inquiry ought to be disclosed. Thus, where an inspector refused to grant permission for a casino on the extraordinary ground which had certainly not been taken at the inquiry, that it might lead to an increase in robberies in the vicinity, the court was prepared to quash the decision with the agreement of the Secretary of State.[10]

7. Decisions on Appeal and Reasons

There is a duty to notify the decision to the applicant, the local planning authority, the section 29 parties and any other person who has appeared at

[2] See, e.g. Lake District Special Planning Board v. S.O.S.E. (1975) 236 E.G. 417.
[3] Ibid., 419; and cf. Local Government Board v. Arlidge [1915] A.C. 120, Maxwell v. Department of Trade and Industry [1974] Q.B. 523.
[4] See, e.g. Summers v. Minister of Health [1947] 1 All E.R. 395, Darlassis v. Minister of Education (1954) 4 P. & C.R. 281.
[5] See, e.g. Kent C.C. v. S.O.S.E. (1976) 33 P. & C.R. 70 at 78–9 (parliamentary statement by Energy Secretary); Hyndburn B.C. v. S.O.S.E. (1979) 251 E.G. 473 (government circular). A decision may be quashed, however, if the Secretary of State effectively fetters his own discretion and acts at the direction of another department: H. Lavender and Sons Ltd. v. M.H.L.G. [1970] 1 W.L.R. 1231.
[6] See, e.g. Enfield L.B.C. v. S.O.S.E. (1974) 233 E.G. 53 (review of metropolitan green belt).
[7] See, e.g. Peak Park Joint Planning Board v. S.O.S.E. [1979] J.P.L. 618 where the Court held that a ministerial policy in M.H.L.G. Circular 17/69 of favouring re-applications after expiry of old unimplemented permissions was not "planning policy" at all but "administrative policy" and irrelevant to a planning decision.
[8] A.P.R., r. 14(1).
[9] Ibid. r. 14(2).
[10] Ellinas v. S.O.S.E. [1977] J.P.L. 249; and cf. Wontner Smith & Co. Ltd. v. S.O.S.E. [1977] J.P.L. 103.

the inquiry and has asked to be notified.[11] In the case of Secretary of State's decisions, a copy of the inspector's report must either accompany the decision, or be forwarded to any party upon written application made within one month of the date of decision.[12]

There is no general rule of fairness or natural justice that requires reasons to be given for decisions, but that deficiency has been cured by legislation in the case of planning inquiries.[13] And the courts have built upon the legislative requirement by requiring full, clear and precise reasons. That, in turn, has provided them with a valuable basis for judicial review. They are provided with an unusually comprehensive record of evidence and reasoning which lays bare the whole decision process, and from which they may assess whether the Secretary of State has gone wrong in law. He may have misdirected himself in law, by asking himself the wrong question or taking into account irrelevant considerations or overlooking material considerations; or he may have breached the natural justice requirements. These grounds for review are examined in greater detail in the next chapter.

The requirement to give reasons applies equally to decisions by the Secretary of State and those taken by inspectors. In the case of inspectors' decisions, there is no equivalent to the report of the inquiry which is otherwise prepared for the Secretary of State, and all that is issued is a decision letter to the parties. Its purpose is therefore different: there need not be an elaborate report of the inquiry,[14] but reasons must be given which, though not necessarily elaborate,[15] must nonetheless be adequate and intelligible.[16]

In the case both of inspectors' decisions and Secretary of State's decisions, the courts have taken seriously the duty to give reasons. Whilst repeatedly professing that decision letters and inspectors' reports should not be perused too minutely, "hypercritically" or with the "eye of a schoolman," their scrutiny has nonetheless been detailed and critical. The effect of their review may be summarised under two main heads:

(a) Intelligibility of reasons

The duty to give reasons has been interpreted as one of "the setting forth with reasonable precision and clarity of matters which are relevant and indicating and explaining, positively or negatively, the reasons for the Minister's decision."[17] The duty is breached if the reasoning is so obscure as to leave "in the mind of the informed reader . . . real and substantial doubt as

---

[11] I.P.R., r. 13(1); A.P.R., r. 16(1).

[12] I.P.R., r. 13(2); documentary evidence need not be forwarded, but an opportunity must be made for inspection if requested.

[13] Tribunals and Inquiries Act 1971, s. 12 (which is applicable to all cases, but which strictly imposes a duty only where a party has asked before or during the hearing for a reasoned decision); and I.P.R., r. 13(1); A.P.R., r. 16(1) which are of narrower application, but impose an absolute duty.

[14] See, e.g. D.F.P. (Midlands) Ltd. v. S.O.S.E. [1978] J.P.L. 319; Grainger v. S.O.S.E. [1978] J.P.L. 631.

[15] Ellis v. S.O.S.E. (1974) 31 P. & C.R. 130.

[16] Hope v. S.O.S.E. (1975) 31 P. & C.R. 120. And in a case where there has been no inquiry it is not sufficient for him merely to say "I have considered the written representations;" Shepperton Builders Ltd. v. S.O.S.E. [1979] J.P.L. 102

[17] Givaudan & Co. Ltd. v. M.H.L.G. [1967] 1 W.L.R. 250 at 259; and see further post pp. 634–636.

to the reasons."[18] Minor or trivial errors or obscurity, or glaringly obvious clerical mistakes[19] will not suffice. The courts are prepared to read the decision as a whole and to try to reconcile ambiguities and construe obscure statements in their overall context.[20]

(b) Relating the decision to the evidence

Where the decision is taken by the Secretary of State it is customary to incorporate by reference into the decision letter the conclusions of the inspector. That then necessarily becomes part of the reasoning,[21] and it will be necessary to ensure that the conclusions are based on the evidence summarised by the inspector, and that the decision relates to those conclusions. Whilst the weight to be attached to the evidence and the planning judgments made on it are matters solely for the Secretary of State, the courts will quash his decision if his reasons reveal no evidence at all upon which he could have acted.[22] Similarly, the inspector's conclusions and recommendations must flow from the evidence. Where, on the other hand, the Secretary of State has rejected such a recommendation by his inspector, he must show good reason for doing so.[23]

In general his reasons must deal with the main points raised at the inquiry and be based upon them. A major point may not simply be ignored in the decision.[24] But there are two major qualifications. The first is that of reasons based on matters of opinion, for which it clearly would be impracticable to demand detailed factual support.[25] The second arises from the fact that the Secretary of State's duty is to have regard to all "material considerations" and not merely the issues as presented by the parties at the inquiry.[26] He is not therefore bound to accept uncontested evidence presented at the inquiry,[27] nor is he bound by agreement between the parties on any issue.[28] But in each case he will be obliged whether by the Rules or by natural justice, to refer the matter back before reaching an adverse decision (unless

---

[18] *Ibid.* at 258. *Cf. W.H. Gibbs Ltd.* v. *S.O.S.E.* (1973) 229 E.G. 103, where the report of an inspector following a compulsory purchase inquiry was held to be so lacking in precision and intelligibility as to have been of no real value to the Secretary of State.

[19] *Elmbridge B.C.* v. *S.O.S.E.* [1980] J.P.L. 463 (distance between proposed new house and existing house stated to be 400 feet instead of 170 feet, but obvious that inspector knew from his site visit the true dimensions and that this was an "obvious silly mistake"). Although Cooke J. in *Essex Construction Co. Ltd.* v. *East Ham B.C.* (1963) 61 L.G.R. 452 took the view that the Secretary of State might have inherent jurisdiction to amend errors in his decision letter, except where there was substantial prejudice, other judges have rejected the "slip rule" in favour of the view that once the letter is issued, the Secretary of State is functus officio: see, *e.g. Miller* v. *Weymouth and Mounsdon B.C.* (1974) 27 P. & C.R. 488; *Gosling* v. *S.O.S.E.* (1974) 234 E.G. 531; *Preston B.C.* v. *S.O.S.E.* [1978] J.P.L. 547.

[20] See, *e.g. Iveagh* v. *M.H.L.G.* [1964] 2 Q.B. 295 at 410, *per* Lord Denning M.R.

[21] *Givaudan & Co. Ltd.* v. *M.H.L.G.* [1967] 1 W.L.R. 250.

[22] See, *e.g. Banks Horticultural Products Ltd.* v. *S.O.S.E.* [1980] J.P.L. 33; and *cf. Wontner Smith & Co. Ltd.* v. *S.O.S.E.* [1977] J.P.L. 103.

[23] See, *e.g. French Kier Developments Ltd.* v. *S.O.S.E.* [1977] 1 All E.R. 296.

[24] See, *e.g. Camden L.B.C.* v. *S.O.S.E.* [1980] J.P.L. 31 (failure to advert to the likely consequences of granting permission, which had been a substantial issue at the inquiry).

[25] *Wholesale Mail Order Supplies Ltd.* v. *S.O.S.E.* [1976] J.P.L. 163.

[26] T.C.P.A. 1971, s. 29(1), as applied by s. 36(5).

[27] *Burwoods (Caterers) Ltd.* v. *S.O.S.E.* (1972) 224 E.G. 2021.

[28] *Lewis Thirkell Ltd.* v. *S.O.S.E.* [1978] J.P.L. 844. See, *e.g. Grangewalk Properties Ltd.* v. *M.H.L.G.* (1969) 213 E.G. 133.

his disagreement is on a matter of opinion or professional expertise); and similarly where he includes in his reasons a matter not canvassed at the inquiry.[29] If there has been conflicting evidence at the inquiry he is entitled to prefer one piece of evidence to another though he must have valid reasons for doing so,[30] and may, if disagreeing with his inspector's recommendation, need to refer the matter back.

8. *Other Inquiries*

The procedures examined in the foregoing pages all apply to straightforward planning appeals. There are some variations, however, in the case of other matters also covered by the Inquiry Procedure Rules, and various other sets of rules govern procedures at other inquiries, notably highways and compulsory purchase inquiries. Finally, there are still a number of areas where no Rules have yet been made. A brief summary of all these variations is necessary.

(a) Called-in applications

These are governed by the Rules (except that there is no provision for transferred jurisdiction to inspectors), modified so as to secure a broader class of section 29 parties,[31] and so as to require the production by the Secretary of State of a modified Rule 6 statement giving his reasons for directing the referral of the application to him, and the points which seem to him to be likely to be relevant.[32]

(b) Tree preservation consent appeals

The Rules apply, but are modified so as to exclude section 29 parties and to dispense with some of the pre-inquiry notification procedures.[33]

(c) Listed building consent appeals

The Rules apply, and extend to cases involving the demolition of unlisted buildings in conservation areas. References in the Rules to "development" and "permission" are changed to "works of demolition, alteration or extension" (as the case may be) and "consent" respectively.[34]

(d) Advertisement consent appeals

The Rules apply but are modified in the same way as for tree preservation consent appeals, and with references to "development" construed as references to the "display of advertisements."[35]

---

[29] See, *e.g. Blankney* v. *M.H.L.G.* (1967) 205 E.G. 109; *Webb* v. *S.O.S.E.* (1972) 224 E.G. 869; *Sabey, H. & Co. Ltd.* v. *S.O.S.E.* (1977) 245 E.G. 397.
[30] *Seddon Properties Ltd.* v. *S.O.S.E.* (1978) 248 E.G. 949.
[31] I.P.R. rr. 2(1)(*a*) and 3(1) (see *ante*, p. 581.) The Rules also extend to referred applications in respect of tree preservation orders, listed buildings and advertisements.
[32] *Ibid.* r. 6(1).
[33] I.P.R., r. 2(1)(*b*); A.P.R., r. 2(1)(*b*).
[34] *Ibid.* r. 2(1)(*c*) in each case.
[35] *Ibid.* r. 2(1)(*d*) in each case.

(e) Highways inquiries

These are governed by Rules made in 1976,[36] which contain roughly equivalent provisions governing pre-inquiry statements, attendance by representatives of government departments[37] and post-inquiry procedures, but modified to take account of different circumstances. Instead of section 29 parties there are "statutory objectors"[38] who may appear as of right; and other persons may be heard at the discretion of the inspector. Highway inquiries have been at the forefront of public criticism of inquiry procedure in recent years, and this has led to efforts by the Departments of Transport and Environment to restore confidence in the system. New arrangements have been made for, *inter alia,* the independent appointment of inspectors, for supplying better information to objectors, broadening the possibility of re-opening an inquiry and for distributing the inspector's factual summary to the parties for correction before its submission to the Secretary of State.[39]

(f) Compulsory purchase inquiries

Special Rules have also been made governing inquiry procedure for compulsory purchase by local authorities under the Acquisition of Land Act 1981[40] and by ministers.[41] The procedures are, broadly speaking, similar to those discussed above.

(g) Enforcement and established use certificate appeals

Enforcement (including listed building enforcement) and established use certificate appeals are now governed by the Town and Country Planning (Enforcement) (Inquiries Procedure) Rules 1981.[42] The Rules are modelled closely on the 1974 Rules, but with three important modifications. First, there is no provision for a Rule 6 statement in the case of enforcement (and listed building enforcement) appeals, because of the similar requirements imposed by regulation 6 of the Town and Country Planning (Enforcement Notices and Appeals) Regulations 1981. Secondly, the provisions relating to the expression of views by government departments and other local

---

[36] Highways (Inquiries Procedure) Rules 1976.

[37] *Ibid.* rr. 6 and 7: attendance is to be automatic, and not dependent upon any party's request.

[38] Defined by r. 3(1). Broadly speaking the categories include only local authorities, navigation authorities, water authorities and owners and occupiers of property likely to be affected by the proposals in the sense of being likely to lose their land or to be entitled to claim compensation under Part I of the Land Compensation Act 1973 in respect of the use of the highway.

[39] The details are contained in the Report on the *Review of Highway Inquiry Procedures,* Cmnd. 7133 (1978), which followed the influential Leitch Report (*Report of the Advisory Committee on Trunk Road Assessment,* H.M.S.O., 1978) and was accompanied by the first of the new series of roads policy white papers intended to be presented annually to Parliament, *Policy for Roads: England 1978,* Cmnd. 7132, 1978.

[40] Compulsory Purchase by Public Authorities (Inquiries Procedure) Rules 1976. The Rules extend only to acquisitions using the 1981 Act's procedures, and not, therefore, to acquisitions where the procedure is prescribed by other legislation, such as slum clearance acquisition under the Housing Act 1957.

[41] Compulsory Purchase by Ministers (Inquiries Procedure) Rules 1967.

[42] S.I. 1981 No. 1743.

authorities are modified to take account of the different circumstances of enforcement and established use certification. Thirdly, there are no section 29 parties, and although the list of third parties entitled to attend the inquiry is broadened to include urban development corporations and enterprise zone authorities (where they are not the local planning authority) and any persons on whom the Secretary of State has caused notice of the inquiry to be served, only the appellant and the local planning authority are entitled under the Rules to call evidence and cross-examine witnesses. Other parties may do so only to the extent permitted by the inspector.

There are various special provisions governing the lodging of enforcement appeals, the grounds of appeal and the Secretary of State's powers. These are examined in Chapter 9.

(h) Slum clearance

No Rules have been made, but the compulsory purchase Rules are followed in practice, and the courts have shown a willingness to rely on them as indicating the general requirements of fairness.[43]

(i) Other appeals and applications

There are similarly no Rules governing inquiries held for other planning purposes, such as in respect of orders for the revocation or modification of planning permission or the discontinuance of existing uses; but new Rules were made in 1981 governing applications for consent for the construction and extension of electricity generating stations and the erection of overhead electric lines.[44]

F. Costs

The power to award costs in connection with public inquiries is conferred by section 250 of the Local Government Act 1972. It arises only in the case of inquiries, and does not extend to decisions taken on written representations. The Act prescribes neither criteria nor limits. There are two conflicting views about the way in which the power should be exercised. One is that it should be used frequently, as a way of cutting down delays and avoiding inquiries, by penalising parties who misjudge their prospects or act inefficiently or unreasonably.[45] The other view, which is current policy, is that the power should be used sparingly. Inquiries should remain as accessible and informal as possible, and parties should feel free to participate without fear of financial penalty. The criteria by which costs are awarded therefore are restrictive, and they are generally based not upon ideas of success or failure as in civil litigation, but upon the conduct of the parties.

---

[43] See, *e.g. Fairmount Investments Ltd.* v. *S.O.S.E.* [1976] 1 W.L.R. 1255 at 1258, *per* Viscount Dilhorne.

[44] The Electricity Generating Stations and Overhead Lines (Inquiries Procedure) Rules 1981 (S.I. 1981 No. 1841), which came into operation on February 2, 1982.

[45] See, *e.g.* Eighth Report from the Expenditure Committee, paras. 64 and 65; and George Dobry's *Review of the Development Control System* (1975) in which he unsuccessfully urged the adoption of a new comprehensive code for costs: paras. 11.96–11.103.

The policy is contained in Circular 73/65, which in turn incorporates guidelines suggested by the Council on Tribunals in 1965.[46] The policy leaves considerable scope for discretion, although the various rules are followed closely in practice.[47] In planning appeals the main categories of occasions where costs may be awarded are (1) where postponement or adjournment of an inquiry has been made necessary by the fault of any party (including any third party) and (2) in exceptional cases of unreasonable behaviour. An indication is given that this will cover cases where an inquiry could have been avoided, (a) because it was clear from earlier decisions on the site, or from other comparable decisions or policy statements what the decision would be; or (b) where a party has refused to discuss the matter or to disclose information when that could have avoided an appeal; or (c) where the authority have been unable to support their decision or their failure to give one by any substantial evidence or have clearly been motivated by irrelevant considerations. Other grounds are where an inquiry may have been prolonged by mishandling procedure by introducing new reasons or grounds of appeal at a late stage or where an authority have failed to cooperate in supplying relevant information beforehand. The Department accepts that it is reasonable to accept a higher standard of conduct from planning authorities than from applicants.

Third parties are not mentioned expressly in the Circular, but the recommendation of the Council on Tribunals was that costs should be awarded in favour of or against third parties only in exceptional cases. Adjournment or postponement by fault or default is given as an illustration of a case where such costs might be awarded, whether for or against.

At inquiries where parties appear as objectors, such as highways, compulsory purchase and revocation orders, an award of costs is usually made only to successful statutory objectors. This rule is considerably less rational than the others, not only because it rests on the idea of costs following the event which is largely irrelevant to decisions containing large elements of policy, but also because the various categories of statutory objectors are so narrowly drawn. But it has survived all attempts at reform.[48]

G. Large Scale Development and the Public Inquiry System

1. The Problems of Large Scale Development

The appellate machinery of central government, harnessed to the public local inquiry system, works best in the case of development raising only issues of local concern. The area of disagreement is narrow and can be contained and accommodated within the usual inquiry procedure. The Secretary of State is sufficiently remote from the issues at stake to be seen as genuinely independent in exercising his judgment. The questions arising are largely of

[46] *Report of the Council on Tribunals on the Award of Costs at Statutory Inquiries,* Cmnd. 2471. The Report in turn incorporates guidelines suggested to the Council initially by the Ministry, which may explain their readiness to adopt them!
[47] In *R. v. S.O.S.E., ex parte Reinisch* (1971) 22 P. & C.R. 1022 the Divisional Court unhesitatingly rejected claims that the Circular and the Minister's reliance upon it in that case constituted an unlawful fettering of his discretion.
[48] Including representations made in the course of the review of highways procedures: see further Cmnd. 7133, para. 51.

fact and opinion, to be weighed against site specific considerations and local policies.

But large scale development which raises issues of regional and national concern places strains on the inquiry system and the quasi-judicial functions of the Secretary of State. Seldom is it a matter of applying recognised policies to an individual site. The forward planning system more often than not provides no guidance other than in very general terms to questions such as the location of major new infrastructure works, including motorways, airports, electricity generating establishments and the like. The public local inquiry becomes, therefore, the focus of policy making, and in matters ranging beyond purely local significance. Objectors are anxious to question not only the local impact of the development, but also to suggest alternative locations, alternative forms of development, and ultimately, to question the need for the proposal at all. Questions of need, in turn raise issues of national policy. Whether there is a need for a motorway between points A and B is, in national terms, part of a wider question of the need for new motorways at all. That in turn spills over into the question of whether alternative forms of surface transport which cause less environmental damage and consume less energy should be pursued by Government. Similarly, for applications for nuclear energy establishments the issues arising go well beyond traditionally narrow land use considerations to the point of questioning the whole of future energy policy and the technical adequacy of nuclear development.

The public local inquiry is a hopelessly inadequate mechanism for the determination of these wide ranging issues. It is site specific, in that it is concerned only with the site which is the subject of the particular planning application in question. And the procedures of evidence and cross examination, whilst highly effective in resolving differences of fact and pursuing verifiable truths, are poorly suited to the examination of broader issues. They do not necessarily provide the inspector with the best or broadest information base from which to proceed, because the terms of reference are determined by what the parties choose to bring before him. He lacks any independent investigatory power. Any questions of policy are ultimately value judgments, not readily susceptible to adversarial examination. The court room techniques tend to be long-winded and inefficient routes to truth, and unsuited to the balancing of values.

One answer to these problems lies in defining the terms of reference of the inquiry closely, and the means by which this is most commonly done in practice is through the concept of "government policy." As discussed above,[49] government policy is regarded by the courts as being outside the scope of a local public inquiry because of the very unsuitability of a locally directed mechanism to look at broader issues; and this demarcation is built into the Inquiry Procedure Rules. But it is not entirely satisfactory, because by limiting the scope of the inquiry its effect is to force objectors and the inspector to accept, as given doctrine, various assumptions which are by their nature based more on subjective policy than objective fact.

The more specific the national policy involved, the greater the burden on local objectors to pursue their objections; and the more illusory become the elaborate procedural safeguards built into the public inquiry system. The

[49] *Ante*, p. 587.

sense of disillusionment naturally increases where it is a policy to which central government is strongly committed, and where the agency promoting the development is a government department or a related governmental agency. Strong commitment to a policy necessarily implies a bias in decision making towards the result which will advance the policy. It is here that the demands of administration and justice collide. Planning *policy* is not "just" in the sense that planning *procedures* may be; but it ought to be responsive.

There are therefore two main issues arising from the functioning of the planning system in relation to large scale development. The first is technical, in the sense that it questions the adequacy of the traditional planning inquiry to cope with the fact-gathering and evaluative processes required; and the second is to do with the distribution of power.

2. The Roskill Inquiry into the Third London Airport

The perennial quest for a site for the third London airport demonstrates clearly the complexity of the relationship between national planning and local planning. No other development has so widespread and detrimental effect over an area than a large international airport. Its environmental impact spreads far further than the immediate locality in which it is sited. When the Government in the mid-1960s determined, as a matter of national policy, that provision should be made for a third London airport in anticipation of increased demand for air travel, they chose a new method of assessing the most suitable location for it.[50] Instead of there being a planning application for a pre-selected site which would then be examined at a public local inquiry, the Government set up a non-statutory inquiry under 11 Commissioners, chaired by Lord Justice Roskill. The Commission was given both investigative and quasi-adjudicative powers under a five part procedure. First, the Commission were to examine a range of possible sites, and narrow the range to a number of sites which they thought required further investigation. Second, they were to hear evidence of a local character about those sites. Third, they were to carry out their own evaluation of relevant matters, such as air traffic patterns, surface transport and regional planning policy. Fourthly, they were to consider the material arising from the two earlier stages; and, finally, to provide an opportunity for interested parties to be heard on the material.[51]

But the crucial question, which in fact subsequently determined the action taken by the Government, was excluded from the Commission's terms of reference. It was the question of the need for the airport at all. The Commission were to assume that such a need existed, and their function was limited to evaluating the various disadvantages and advantages of the sites identified by them. To do this, they relied heavily on cost benefit analysis. This was an attempt to make the evaluation as objectively rational as possible, and more in the nature of a technical exercise than a political balance of social advantage and detriment. But it involved the placing of

---

[50] For an account of the work of the Roskill Commission and the earlier investigations, see Ganz, *Administrative Procedures* London (Sweet and Maxwell (1974)), Chap. 4.
[51] *Hansard* H.C. Deb. Vol. 765, cols. *32–40* (May 20, 1968); *Report of the Commission on the Third London Airport* H.M.S.O. 1971.

monetary values on such abstract concepts as quality of life, and in doing so disguised a variety of highly subjective assumptions.[52]

The procedure adopted at least had the advantage over conventional procedures that it involved a positive, investigatory role and not merely a passive role of reporting representations to Government, and the operational defects of the particular experiment should not be permitted to obscure the benefits of the procedure.

3. The Planning Inquiry Commission

At the same time as they were setting up the Roskill experiment, the Government introduced in the Town and Country Planning Act 1968 a new general procedure for use in similar future cases. Planning Inquiry Commissions were to be an alternative means of determining planning applications or proposals where:

> "(a) there are considerations of national or regional importance which are relevant to the determination of that question [whether the proposed development should be permitted] and require evaluation, but a proper evaluation thereof cannot be made unless there is a special inquiry for the purpose;
>
> (b) the technical or scientific aspects of the proposed development are of so unfamiliar a character as to jeopardise a proper determination of that question unless there is a special inquiry for the purpose."[53]

The procedure prescribed has two stages. First, the Commission are required to carry out an investigation. Their duty is to identify and investigate the considerations relevant to, or the technical or scientific aspects relevant to the development and to assess the importance to be attached to them. Secondly, the Commission are required to give the applicant,[54] the local planning authority and persons whose representations the local planning authority are required to take into account, an opportunity of appearing before and being heard by one or more members of the Commission at a local public inquiry.[55]

The procedure thus differs substantially from that adopted for the Roskill Commission. Most significantly, it is triggered by a site-specific development proposal, so that the site-comparison exercise conducted by Roskill does not fall to the Planning Inquiry Commission[56]; and it also means that the proposal must have reached a comparatively advanced stage of preparation and carry a degree of commitment on the part of its proposers which will make it more difficult for alternatives to be accepted by them. There is also the fact that the Commission must inevitably have reached

---

[52] For a powerful critique of the Commission's methodology, see P. Self "Nonsense on Stilts: Cost Benefit Analysis and the Roskill Commission," in (1970) 41 Political Quarterly; Econocrats and the Policy Process (1975).

[53] Now contained in T.C.P.A. 1971, s. 48(2).

[54] T.C.P.A. 1971, s. 48(6). Subs (7) confers power for a commission to arrange for the carrying out of research, subject to the approval of (and at the expense of) the Secretary of State.

[55] T.C.P.A. 1971, ss. 48(6), 49(3).

[56] Although two or more applications or proposals may be referred to the same Commission if they relate to development for similar purposes on different sites.

certain conclusions, however tentative, as a result of their first stage investigations and assessment. Their views may or may not be known to those participating in the second stage, but they will necessarily influence the final decision.

The Planning Inquiry Commission has never been used, although there have been a number of occasions over the years since 1968 when the statutory criteria were capable of being met. The Government's reluctance to use the procedure has never been explained, and it has been suggested that it may have been unfairly tarnished by reason of the failure of the Roskill Commission, notwithstanding that quite different procedures are prescribed.[57] The then Secretary of State, Mr. Peter Shore, indicated in 1978 that he believed the problem inherent in the two-stage procedure of conclusions being arrived at before the hearing of evidence was insurmountable, and this has doubtless also been a factor in not activating the procedures.[58] There is also the problem of delay. Given that the Planning Inquiry Commission introduces an additional investigatory stage into decision-making, it can be expected to be more time consuming than the conventional planning inquiry.

The local public inquiry has therefore continued to operate as the basic procedure for considering objections to major developments although widespread public dissatisfaction has led to a number of attempts to improve the model. In the case of highway inquiries, for example, the role of the Department of Transport has been substantially recast, and, whilst questions of national policy and national need for the particular highway under consideration are still outside the terms of reference, the Department have now undertaken to explain the relevance of their standards and forecasts to the scheme in its local setting, and to answer questions on that subject.[59] Similarly, attempts have been made to extend the usefulness of the public local inquiry in particular cases by extending its terms of reference. This is really possible only in "called-in" cases, where the Secretary of State is obliged to serve on the parties a preliminary written statement of his reasons for directing the call-in, "and of any points which seem to him to be likely to be relevant to his consideration of the application."[60] In the case of the Windscale inquiry, this power was used to determine a frame of reference for the inquiry that was so broad as to go well beyond conventional land-use considerations. The inquiry was invited to consider "the implications of the proposed development for the safety of the public and for other aspects of the national interest," as well as the environmental impact of the construction and operation of the proposed nuclear reprocessing plant, and the more predictable areas of inquiry such as the effect on amenities, traffic movements, local employment and housing demand.[61]

But the broadening of the terms of reference did nothing to overcome the problems arising from reliance upon primarily adversarial techniques in the

---

[57] Edwards and Rowan-Robinson "Whatever Happened to the Planning Inquiry Commission?" [1980] J.P.L. 307.
[58] The Speech is reported in [1978] J.P.L. 731.
[59] Report on the Review of Highway Inquiry Procedures, Cmnd. 7133 (1978), para. 26.
[60] T.C.P. (Inquiries Procedure) Rules 1974, r. 6(1).
[61] See further The Windscale Inquiry Report by Hon Mr. Justice Parker (H.M.S.O. 1978).

assessment of technologically complex issues, and although the inspector was aided by two expert assessors, their role was not investigative.[62]

4. *Alternatives to the Planning Inquiry Commission*

Two alternative models for decision making in large and complex cases have been advanced in an attempt to overcome the problems arising from the Planning Inquiry Commission and the conventional inquiry. The first was proposed by Mr. Peter Shore in his 1978 speech.[63] He suggested a three stage process, in which the first stage would be a public examination by an independent body, such as a Committee or Commission, to examine the background and need for the proposal. It would presumably be an investigatory function, and it would be pursued outside the inquiry system. Their report would then be published. The second stage would consist of the making of a special development order in draft for the proposal, and this would then be the subject of a wide ranging inquiry against the background of the report. The inquiry would be site-specific, and would be conducted by an inspector and assessors. But it would not, unlike the Planning Inquiry Commission, be conducted by members of the commission responsible for the first stage. The report of the inquiry would also be open to public discussion, and the special development order in its final form would then, if the report so recommended, be laid before Parliament and be subject to debate on a motion to annul.

The significance of this procedure is not only that it seeks to overcome some of the technical difficulties of the public local inquiry, by supplementing its function through the first stage investigation; but also that it reduces the role of central government in the decision making. Questions of need for the proposal are not to be excluded by reason of Government policy; instead they are, presumably, to be investigated in the first stage and perhaps also in the second. And the transfer of power directly to Parliament to assume final responsibility is more than a pure formality. It suggests that the Department's role is intended to be substantially altered.

A second alternative, similar in many respects to that outlined above but more fully developed, was proposed by the Outer Circle Policy Unit in 1979.[64] The O.C.P.U. proposal is for a Project Inquiry in cases where there is a controversial project which has substantial and complex national or international implications which are not obviously foreseeable, especially where the proponent is a public authority. The Inquiry would be set up by the Secretary of State on a non-statutory basis before the making of any planning application, but once the proposal had become sufficiently advanced to make it likely that a planning application would be forthcoming. The function of the Inquiry would be "to investigate, impartially, thoroughly and in public, all the forseeable economic, social and environmental implications and repercussions of the project including its benefits, and its costs and risks of all kinds."[65] They would be required to investigate

---

[62] For a detailed study, see Pearce *et al, Decision Making for Energy Futures: A Case Study of the Windscale Inquiry* (1979) Macmillan, Chaps. 6–8.

[63] [1978] J.P.L. 731.

[64] *The Big Public Inquiry* London O.C.P.U. (1979).

[65] *Ibid.* at p. 10.

alternatives, and the question of the need for the project would be expressly included in their terms of reference.

There would be two stages to the Inquiry's deliberations. The first would be investigative, but it would not be a closed investigation. It would involve the exchange of information between parties and some public meetings. The second stage will be an inquiry, but it would differ from the conventional model because it would not be evidence-based. The relevant "evidence" will already have been put in by the parties during the first stage, and oral evidence would only be permitted if the Commission thought it the best way of investigating an issue. So the inquiry would be more a forum for discussion and argument, at which the parties would be able to address the Commission on the inferences they would seek to draw from the available material. The O.C.P.U. report envisages that it would be rare that the Commission would be able to offer a firm conclusion on the project, and that its recommendations to Government would more likely be in the form of conditional or contingent proposals, clarifying and identifying a set of policy options.

The final decision is reserved for Government and Parliament, either by way of a decision by Government which is then laid before the House, or by first testing the reaction of the House to it. Like Mr. Shore's proposal, therefore, the O.C.P.U. Project Inquiry places the whole issue in the hands of a Commission, and gives the final decision to Parliament. But it creates a far closer link between the two stages of investigation and inquiry and thereby offers a means of overcoming the shortfalls of the conventional inquiry model in dealing with highly technical evidence through adversarial techniques. But in so doing, it deliberately subordinates the participating function of the public inquiry to the preliminary technical investigation, and despite the Report's protestations to the contrary it reduces effective public involvement.

No reforms have yet been made along the lines suggested either by Mr. Shore of the O.C.P.U., and there is indeed sufficient flexibility for either course to be followed on an ad hoc extra-statutory basis without any general amending legislation.[66]

It is mistaken to see the issue involved, however, as being purely one of getting the procedures "right," as if that were a largely politically neutral process. What all the reform proposals are directed towards is a better system of participatory democracy, and a scheme for decision making on vital issues which will allow the public voice to be heard. In some respects it is purely coincidental that the voice should be heard through the planning system, because the issues raised in the types of cases which are suitable for these special procedures go far beyond issues of land-use planning concern. But it is the fact that the planning system, unlike most government systems, has built into it, in the form of the public local inquiry, a mechanism of participation which is capable of being stretched to accommodate wider issues, which is why it has come to play this extended role.

---

[66] There has been some experimentation within existing procedures with determining together applications for similar development on different sites, including the new search for a site for the Third London Airport. Joint and linked inquiries have also been used to consider applications for hypermarket development, but with mixed results: see further Couper and Barker, "Joint and Linked Enquiries" [1981] J.P.L. 63.

CHAPTER 14

APPEALS AND APPLICATIONS TO THE HIGH COURT

A. Introduction

The supervision exerted by the courts over the planning process has a profound influence upon the way it operates. Access to the courts is expressly preserved by the Act of 1971 by way of application or appeal from decisions of the Secretary of State, and these provisions are supplemented by the prerogative supervisory powers of the High Court. The function of the courts is twofold. The source of power underlying British land use planning is parliamentary legislation, and the resolution of disputes as to its interpretation is a matter ultimately for the courts. Further, the administration of planning is vested in public agencies of central and local government, and they are susceptible to the supervision of the High Court in their exercise of statutory powers under broad administrative law principles. For the most part the two functions overlap, and although there are occasions when the courts are asked to interpret provisions of planning legislation otherwise than in the context of the exercise of power—such as in a dispute between two private citizens—questions of interpretation are usually closely connected with questions of the validity of the action taken. In short, statutory interpretation in planning law is concerned primarily with assessing the limits to the powers conferred by the legislation. If the local planning authority or Secretary of State can be shown to have gone outside the power conferred by the Act, as interpreted by the court, then their action may be struck down as unauthorised.

It would be wrong to see judicial supervision as a purely mechanical interpretative process, however. Not only are the powers themselves so broadly drawn as to allow a range of interpretation, but the grounds upon which challenge is permitted and the criteria devised by the courts for assessing the validity of decisions are similarly broad. In the way they exercise their discretion on a case by case basis the courts establish the boundaries of power in a flexible and thus often uncertain way, tending to avoid general statements of principle in favour of ad hoc responses to individual fact situations. It is unsurprising that there have been occasions when sharply conflicting judicial views have emerged. One such has been in the case of attempting to determine the scope of the "material considerations" formula which governs the matters to which the statutory authorities may have regard in development control. The question of whether financial considerations, including the resources of the developer actually to undertake the development, could ever be "material" for example, has evoked a variety of conflicting responses. The original firm view of Ackner J. in *J. Murphy and Sons Ltd.* v. *Secretary of State for the Environment,*[1] that it could not, was later equally firmly rejected by Forbes J. in *Sovmots Investments Ltd.* v. *Secretary of State for the Environment.*[2] Of this conflict of opinion Professor McAuslan[3] has commented:

[1] [1973] 1 W.L.R. 560.
[2] [1977] Q.B. 411.
[3] *The Ideologies of Planning Law*, p. 174.

"The private intra-departmental reactions to this revelation that Ackner J. was not, after all, correct will, fortunately no doubt for the self esteem of the judiciary, be kept from public knowledge until after the start of the next century, but the view of this commentator is that it is a sad reflection on the understanding and knowledge about planning of the judiciary that two such diametrically opposed views about material considerations could be held and illustrates in a most pertinent way the contribution the law and lawyers make to the general lack of certainty over the purpose and function of development control."

But that criticism itself confuses the function of the courts and overlooks the strengths of the pragmatic approach to interpretation which the judiciary has been prepared to adopt. The hint of adverse "private intra-departmental reactions" to a conflict of judicial opinion is supremely irrelevant, and a more realistic criticism of the two decisions is that the judges were prepared to accept and determine a question posed in such broad and artificial terms.[4] But is it so fundamental a defect in the judiciary that it should display a conflict of opinion, when opinion on the point at issue was equally split within and outside the Department? And is it not surprising that official views of the second decision should have been expressions of dismay (at the inconsistency) rather than delight at the broadened and more progressive approach taken in it? The more fundamental point made by McAuslan and also by Professor J. Griffith,[5] is that in their review of planning and other administrative decisions, judges have been caught between the two competing ideologies of private property and public interest, and have leaned in favour of the former and away from a participative model of public interest.

It is true that the incremental approach leads to uncertainty and to a degree of unpredictability in judicial decision making, but it is an uncertainty which is inherent in the open texture of the legislation itself. Whilst the ultimate interpretative function rests with the courts, it cannot realistically be carried out in isolation from the perceptions of those whose function it is to administer the system and those whose rights are at stake. There has been a considerable change in approach in the past 30 years. In 1958, for example, the Court of Appeal was insistent that in the construction of a statute, practice notes prepared by the Central Land Board should be regarded not only as unhelpful but as inadmissible even in argument, because "their use might well result in the court being influenced by official opinion, albeit unconsciously, on questions of construction, the decision on which properly rested on the court alone."[6] But in recent years departmental circulars containing not only policy advice and guidance on the practical operation of legislation, but also ministerial interpretation of it, has come to play an increasingly influential part in seeking an interpretation which will accord with accepted practice.[7]

---

[4] See further ante, pp. 290–294.

[5] J.A.G. Griffith, The Politics of the Judiciary (Fontana, 1977).

[6] London C.C. v. Central Land Board (1958) 10 P. & C.R.1 at 5, per Jenkins L.J.

[7] Perhaps the most striking example was the willingness of members of the House of Lords in Coleshill and District Investment Co. Ltd. v. M.H.L.G. [1969] 2 All E.R. 525 to take into account ministerial advice on whether demolition might constitute "development," which, Lord Wilberforce accepted, had "acquired vitality and strength" through its application in practice over a long period (p. 538).

This interrelationship between the courts and the Secretary of State, and the point at which the line between their respective functions should be drawn, is the most persistently controversial and uncertain area in judicial review. The established demarcation is that policy making and its implementation are matters solely for the Secretary of State and for local planning authorities, and that jurisdiction of the courts is limited to checking any excess or abuse of power by them. That distinction prevailed in 1947 and prevails today, but over the intervening period the extent of judicial review has developed dramatically. The draughtsmen of the 1947 legislation clearly anticipated little judicial intervention. No provision was made for appeals or applications to the High Court, except in the case of challenges to the validity of development plans where a preclusive clause was added at a late stage at the wish of the Minister, though he remained unconvinced of the necessity for it.[8] Otherwise, the use of highly subjective formulae in the wording of the discretionary powers, such as "if the Minister is satisfied" or "if the Minister deems it expedient," and deeming his decision to be "final," was thought sufficient to carve out a broad area of unfettered discretionary power. Except in the special case of enforcement, where the provisions were unhappily drafted, that assumption remained largely true for the ensuing 12 years.

The dramatic change in approach which developed over the 20 years that then followed is attributable to two main factors. First, there was the Report of the Franks Committee,[9] and the consequences of its implementation for the planning system. Three of the Committee's recommendations were to have a wide ranging impact: their proposals that there should be a statutory right of appeal on a point of law to the High Court from ministerial decisions (given effect by the Town and Country Planning Act 1959 and the Caravan Sites and Control of Development Act 1960); that there should be a code of procedure governing statutory inquiries (given effect by the Town and Country Planning Act 1959 and the Inquiries Procedure Rules 1962) and that reasons should be given for administrative decisions (given effect for planning in the Inquiries Procedures Rules 1962). The cumulative effect of these reforms was that a great deal of ministerial decision making became subject to detailed legal rules, the scope of which was often—as with the duty to supply reasons—quite uncertain, and yet compliance with which was often a precondition to the making of a valid decision.

The new provisions did not extend to all areas of statutory planning, and in particular they did not directly affect the greater part of decision making by local planning authorities. But the impetus which they were to give to expanding the scope of judicial supervision of planning was matched, over the same period, by a remarkable development of general administrative law principles by the courts under their inherent powers of judicial review, which not only extended to those categories of decision outside the direct access provisions of the new legislation, but also informed the interpretation of those provisions. With some adroitness[10] the courts came to incorporate these principles within the terms of the statutory criteria for challenge established by the post-Franks legislation, and the result is that although the traditional policy/law demarcation remains intact, the dividing line has been

[8] See further *ante*, p. 133.
[9] *Report of the Committee on Administrative Tribunals & Inquiries*, Cmnd. 217 (1957).
[10] *Post*, p. 633.

redrawn at a point which allows a significantly greater area of judicial review over the quality of decision making in planning.

In quantitative terms, High Court litigation is peripheral. It follows in only a tiny fraction of all the decisions taken by local planning authorities and the Secretary of State, but it has nonetheless a highly significant impact on the way in which decisions are taken. The incidence of judicial review means that it is insufficient that a planning decision be manifestly correct on its merits; it must also manifestly be correct in law and in its observance of prescribed procedures. There is a danger in too strict an overview that decision making will become characterised by ritualistic observance of empty formalities, and that the efforts made to make decisions judge-proof will result in delays and in poorer quality decisions.

The grounds of challenge in the High Court to planning decisions, the status of an applicant to make a challenge and the procedures through which challenge is made, vary according to the type of decision. The reasons for the distinctions are largely historical, resulting from the fact that direct access to the courts was conferred at different times in respect of different areas of decision making, but although the courts have tended to assimilate the different criteria and to relate them to those applicable in general administrative law, some significant areas of difference remain. The four available procedures may be summarised as follows:

1. Challenges to the Validity of Development Plans and Certain Other Orders

A right of application to the High Court in such cases to quash the plan or order was conferred originally by the 1947 Act, and it is coupled with a privative provision which prevents the questioning of the validity of the plan or order except by way of the statutory procedure and within the six-week period allowed for challenge.

2. Enforcement Appeals and Decisions on Section 53 Determinations

A right of appeal to the Secretary of State on a point of law in enforcement appeals was introduced by the Caravan Sites and Control of Development Act 1960. The Court's powers on appeal are limited to remitting the decision to the Secretary of State for reconsideration. A similar right exists in respect of determinations by the Secretary of State under section 53 of the 1971 Act.

3. Challenges to Other Decisions or Action Taken by the Secretary of State

This category extends to all planning appeals apart from enforcement appeals, and the procedure is by way of application to the High Court to quash the decision or action complained of, rather than a right of appeal as such.

4. Challenges in Respect of Decisions or Action not Within the Statutory Categories Above

In this case, challenge may be possible under the prerogative powers of the High Court by way of an application for judicial review, or for an injunction or declaration otherwise than through the application procedure. Judicial review does not extend automatically to all decisions or action outside the categories above, but it is available in respect of certain residual decisions of the Secretary of State, and it is the only procedure applicable to most decision making by local planning authorities. Nor is there a right of direct access to the court. Instead there is a requirement that leave of the court be first obtained to the making of an appliction, and regard is had at that stage to the prima facie merits of the application and the applicant's interest in the matter to wich it relates. There is no need to obtain leave where an injunction or declaration is sought by way of civil action rather than by application for judicial review, but more restrictive "standing" provisions apply.

Each of the three statutory procedures is backed up by a privative clause which limits the right of challenge to a specific period, and which precludes the questioning otherwise of the validity of the action complained of in any legal proceedings whatsoever. This means that the prerogative jurisdiction under category (4) above is excluded in each case, but there remain some types of decision and, in the case of enforcement appeals, some grounds of challenge, to which the preclusive provisions do not apply.

The procedures prescribed for each category are examined in greater detail in the following pages, and the later sections of this chapter contain an analysis of the grounds of challenge and the scope of the privative provisions.

B. Procedures for High Court Challenge

1. *Challenges to the Validity of Development Plans and Other Orders*

(a) Scope of the provisions

This category encompasses the questioning of the validity of any statutory plan (or an alteration, repeal or replacement), whether before or after it has been adopted or approved; and any order under section 214(1)(*a*) of the 1971 Act (extinguishment of public right of way over land) or section 235 (relief of statutory undertakers from impracticable obligations).[11] The procedure has been rarely used, even in the case of statutory plans, because the powers under which the function of plan approval has been undertaken in the past have been widely drawn.[12] Now that ministerial supervision has been lifted in the case of local plans, it may be that challenge may be made more frequently.

(b) Standing

Challenge may be made only by "any person aggrieved" by the plan, or the alteration, repeal or replacement.[13] The formula is discussed further

---

[11] T.C.P.A. 1971, s.244(1). This procedure is also prescribed as the means for challenge to orders made by the Secretrary of State for the stopping up, diversion and conversion of highways, and the extinguishment of rights of way, under ss.209–214 of the Act; and the privative provisions of s.242 preclude other challenge in all these cases except orders under s.214(1)(*a*) for the extinguishment of a public right of way.

[12] See further *ante*, p. 133; and *Bradley (E.H.) Ltd.* v. *S.O.S.E., The Times*, August 4, 1982.

[13] T.C.P.A. 1971, s.244(1).

below.[14] There is no express extension of it in this instance, although there is in the case of enforcement appeals, to include the local planning authority.

(c) Procedure

The application is made by way of originating motion and the grounds of the application are required to be stated in the notice of motion.[15] Notice of motion is required to be entered at the Crown Office (even in the case of challenge to a local plan adopted by a local planning authority without ministerial intervention), and served on the appropriate Minister or government department (where applicable)[16] and the local planning authority who prepared the plan.[17] Jurisdiction is exercisable by a single judge of the Queen's Bench Division.[18]

(d) Evidence

Evidence at the hearing of the motion is by affidavit.[19] Affidavits in support of the motion are required to be filed by the applicant in the Crown Office within 14 days of service of the notice of motion, and copies served on the respondent. The respondent then has 21 days to file any affidavit in opposition to the motion, which must also be served on the applicant.[20]

(e) Grounds of challenge

Challenge to validity is limited to the grounds that the order, plan, alteration, repeal or replacement is not within the powers conferred by Part II of the 1971 Act,[21] or that any requirement of Part II or of any regulations made thereunder has not been complied with in relation to its approval or adoption.[22] It does not, therefore, extend to breaches of the purely non-statutory codes adopted for the examination in public of structure plans and for public local inquiries into local plans, although these may be relevant in determining the appropriate standards of the duty of fairness or natural justice owed to objectors in considering objections.

(f) Powers of the court

There is power for the court by interim order to suspend wholly or in part the operation of the plan, alteration, repeal or replacement either generally or insofar as it affects the applicant's property,[23] but the forward planning framework is now so flexible and the immediate impact of a new plan in itself so small, that it would be a rare case in which use of the interim

---

[14] *Post*, p.618.
[15] Rules of the Supreme Court (R.S.C.) Ord. 94, r.1.
[16] *Ibid.* r. 2(3).
[17] *Ibid.* r. 2.
[18] *Ibid.* r. 1.
[19] *Ibid.* r. 3; but subject to the power of the court under Ord. 38 to order that evidence be given at the trial.
[20] *Ibid.* Ord. 94, r. 3(3).
[21] In the case of orders the provisions are subject to "necessary modifications" (s.244(3)–(5)), and thus a reference to the appropriate Part of the Act should be substituted.
[22] T.C.P.A. 1971, s.244(1).
[23] *Ibid.* s.244(2)(*a*)

suspension power would be justified. It would not prevent an authority from having regard to the suspended provisions in development control as material considerations, and nor would it normally lift any blighting effect of the plan's provisions. The power available to the court upon a final determination of the proceedings is to quash the plan, alteration, repeal or replacement, either generally or insofar as it affects the property of the applicant.[24] It is, curiously, a power to quash the plan itself rather than the decision to adopt or approve it, which suggests that the planning authority may be required, as in the case of the quashing of a compulsory purchase order, to start all over again. But the power to quash is exercisable only where the court is satisfied that the plan is wholly or to any extent outside the powers conferred by the Act, or that the interests of the applicant have been substantially prejudiced by the failure to comply with any requirements of the Act or the regulations. This apparent distinction between substantive and procedural *ultra vires*, with a requirement of substantial prejudice in the latter case, is made also in the case of applications falling under category (2) below, and is discussed further below. Given the flexibility of the new forward planning system and its indirect impact on other planning powers, "substantial prejudice" may prove a more difficult matter to establish than in the case of decisions or orders of direct impact.

2. Enforcement Appeals and Section 53 Determinations

(a) Scope of the provisions

Challenge in these instances takes the form of a right of appeal to the High Court,[25] against a decision given in proceedings by the Secretary of State on an appeal against an enforcement notice, a listed building enforcement notice, or a notice under section 103 of the 1971 Act (relating to tree planting requirements); or a decision on a section 53 determination (as to whether planning permission is required for a proposal). In that last instance, the right does not extend to challenge in respect of any application for planning permission of which the application for a section 53 determination forms part, and such a challenge would need to be made under the provisions discussed in category (3) below.[26] Similarly, to the extent that a challenge is made to the Secretary of State's decision to grant planning permssion (but not where he refuses to do so) on the deemed application in an enforcement appeal, it must be made by way of originating motion under category (3) below.[27] The wording of the legislation is broad enough to extend to any decision given in the course of the proceedings before the Secretary of State, such as on an application for adjournment or a ruling rejecting an appeal for failure to supply the necesssary facts[28]; except in the case of section 53 determinations where the narrower wording "any decision . . . on an

---

[24] *Ibid.* s. 244(2)(*b*).
[25] *Ibid.* ss.246 and 247. There is provision in both sections allowing the parties alternatively to require the Secretary of State to state a case for the opinion of the court, but effect has never been given to the procedure by amendment to the Rules of the Supreme Court, and it remains therefore unavailable: *Hoser* v. *M.H.L.G.* [1963] Ch. 428.
[26] T.C.P.A. 1971, s.247(3).
[27] *Ibid.* s.242(3)(*f*) and 245(3); and see *Broxbourne B.C.* v. *S.O.S.E.* [1980] Q.B.1 at 9.
[28] *Button* v. *Jenkins* [1975] 3 All E.R. 585; *Horsham D.C.* v. *Fisher* [1977] J.P.L. 178.

appeal" suggests that only a final determination of the appeal is challenge-able under these provisions.[29]

(b) Standing

The right of appeal in these instances is limited. In the case of enforcement appeals, it extends only to the appellant, the local planning authority and any other person having an interest in the land to which the notice relates.[30] The right of appeal formally extended to all persons served with the notice, but their right was taken away by the Local Government and Planning (Amendment) Act 1981, except in the case of tree replacement orders under section 103. Appeal against the Secretary of State's decision on a section 53 determination is limited to the person who made the application and the local planning authority.[31] In none of these cases, therefore, is there reckoned to be any legitimate third party interest calling for a broader right of appeal. But the strictness of the limitation is mitigated somewhat in the case of enforcement appeals by the fact that the privative provisions are not absolute. They allow for a limited exception in the case of persons prosecuted where there has been a failure to serve them with a copy of the notice[32]; and the grounds of challenge protected by the provisions are not exhaustive. An enforcement notice may still therefore be challenged in the courts on grounds other than those prescribed as possible grounds of appeal to the Secretary of State, by any person having adequate *locus standi*, under the procedure of category (4) below.

(c) Procedure

Appeal to the High Court is by way of originating motion,[33] notice of which must be served and the appeal entered, within 28 days after the date of the decision against which the appeal is brought.[34] Although the Rules require that the period should be calculated from the time that "notice of the decision was given to the appellant,"[35] the Divisional Court has felt obliged by earlier authority to hold that the formula refers to the date the decision letter is posted to the applicants rather than the date it is received.[36] There is, however, jurisdiction for the Court to extend the time for appeal.[37] Notice of the originating motion is required to be served on the Secretary of State, the local planning authority (or, as the case may be, the appellant or applicant in the proceedings before the Secretary of State) and any other person on whom the notice to which those proceedings related was served.[38] The court having jurisdiction was formerly the Divisional Court, but the

---

[29] *Cf. Co-operative Retail Services Ltd.* v. *S.O.S.E.* [1980] 1 W.L.R. 271, where the Court of Appeal accepted a restricted interpretation of the almost identical formula in s.242(3)(*b*)
[30] T.C.P.A. 1971, s.246(1); as amended by L.G.P.(A)A. 1981, s.1 and Sched. 1.
[31] *Ibid.* s.247(1).
[32] *Ibid.* s.243(2).
[33] R.S.C. Ord. 94, r. 12.
[34] *Ibid.* Ord. 55, r. 4.
[35] *Ibid.* Ord. 55, r. 4(4).
[36] *Ringroad Investments Ltd.* v. *S.O.S.E.* (1979) 40 P. & C.R. 99. Doubt has since been cast on that ruling by the Court of Appeal in *Griffiths* v. *S.O.S.E., The Times,* January 30, 1982.
[37] R.S.C. Ord. 3, r. 5.
[38] *Ibid.* Ord. 94, r.12(3).

function is now exercisable by a single judge unless the court otherwise directs,[39] and further appeal to the Court of Appeal requires leave of either the Divisional Court or the Court of Appeal.[40]

(d) Evidence

The main document before the court will be the decision letter of the Secretary of State and the inspector's report or decision (if applicable). There is power for the court to receive further evidence on questions of fact, and the evidence may be given either by affidavit or by oral evidence in court.[41] Or the court may remit the matter to the Secretary of State for him to provide such further information as the court may direct.[42] But the appeal is confined to points of law, and although new evidence may be admissible in that context on a point of jurisdiction or procedure, there is no power for the court to engage in a rehearing on the primary facts.[43]

(e) Grounds of challenge

Appeal is on a point of law, but is otherwise unlimited.[44] It is thus open to the appellant to establish that the Secretary of State has erred in law or procedure, and in the latter case the general principles discussed below[45] are applicable.

(f) Powers of the court

The powers of the court in these cases are limited to remitting the matter to the Secretary of State for rehearing and redetermination by him.[46] There is thus no power to quash a decision or to set aside an enforcement notice, and the intention is that the Secretary of State should be able to correct any error without the necessity of starting afresh provided the enforcement notice itself is valid. His amended decision is itself amenable to appeal, and may again be remitted by the court for reconsideration.[47] In some cases, however, the decision of the court is equivalent to a decision to quash the enforcement notice, because it identifies a fundamental defect which is incapable of remedy by redetermination. There is no burden upon the appellant under these provisions to establish that his interests have been

---

[39] *Ibid.* Ord. 94, r.12(2A), as substituted by S.I. 1980 No. 2000.

[40] T.C.P.A. 1971, ss.246(4) and 247(5).

[41] Or by deposition taken before an examiner or in any other manner: R.S.C. Ord. 55, r.7(2).

[42] R.S.C. Ord. 94, r.12(4). Alternatively, the appellant may apply to the inspector under Ord. 55, r. 7(4) for a signed copy of any note of proceedings made by him, but in *Forkhurst Ltd.* v. *S.O.S.E.* [1982] J.P.L. 448 it was suggested that this procedure should be restricted to where the appellant wishes to take place before the court all the material that was before the inspector either because the decision letter did not itself contain a record of the evidence, or a ground of appeal related to the inaccuracy of the inspector's report.

[43] *Green* v. *M.H.L.G.* [1967] 2 Q.B. 606. As to the exercise of this discretion in cases falling under category 3 below, see *post*, p.620.

[44] T.C.P.A. 1971, ss.246(1) and 247(1).

[45] *Post*, p.621.

[46] R.S.C. Ord. 94, r.12(5). The power under Ord. 55, r.7(5) to give any other judgment or decision is expressly excluded by Ord. 94, r.12(6); and the reference to such a power in *Price Brothers (Rode Heath) Ltd.* v. *Department of the Environment* (1978) 38 P. & C.R. 579 at 590 is mistaken.

[47] See, *e.g. Emma Hotels Ltd.* v. *S.O.S.E.* (1980) 41 P. & C.R. 255.

substantially prejudiced, and the view has been expressed that the matter should be remitted to the Secretary of State if there is any possibility that he was influenced by the error, however slight.[48]

3. Challenges to Other Decisions or Other Action Taken by the Secretary of State

(a) Scope of the provisions

An application may be made under section 245 of the 1971 Act to quash certain orders (whether made by the local planning authority or the Secretary of State) or actions of the Secretary of State. This is a residual category, which extends to most (but not all) types of ministerial decision not encompassed by the two other statutory procedures, including the most common case of ordinary planning appeals. The list of decisions and orders which are challengeable under these provisions is:[49]

(i) any decision of the Secretary of State on a planning appeal (including not only an application for planning permission but also an application for approval of reserved matters, or for any consent, approval or agreement required by condition on a planning permission)[50]; or on an application referred to (or "called-in" by) him, although in this case, presumably by oversight, only actual planning applications are included.[51] A decision on a called-in application for approval of reserved matters would be susceptible to challenge under the prerogative powers of review, however, under category (4) above.

(ii) any decision to grant (but not a decision to refuse) planning permission on an enforcement appeal.

(iii) any decision to confirm or not to confirm a purchase notice.

(iv) any decision to confirm (but not a decision not to confirm) a completion notice.

(v) any decision relating to an application for consent or any certificate or direction under a tree preservation order or under the Regulations.

(vi) any decision on an established use certificate.

(vii) any decision on a listed building appeal or reference, or a decision to grant consent or planning permission in listed building enforcement proceedings.

(viii) the following orders, whether made by the Secretary of State or a local planning authority: orders for the revocation or modification of planning permission or listed building consent, discontinuance orders, tree preservation orders and orders defining areas of special control for advertisement display.

---

[48] *L.T.S.S. Print and Supply Services Ltd.* v. *Hackney L.B.C.* [1975] 1 W.L.R. 138 at 142 *per* Lord Widgery C.J. (D.C.); [1976] Q.B. 663 at 681–2 *per* Goff L.J. (C.A.).

[49] The categories are prescribed by T.C.P.A. 1971, s.242(2) and (3), as incorporated by s.245(3). Decisions taken by inspectors themselves are deemed to be taken by the Secretary of State, and references to anything done by the Secretary of State in connection with such an appeal are to be taken as references to his inspector: *Ibid.* Sched. 9, para. 2(3) and (4).

[50] T.C.P.A. 1971, s.36(1).

[51] *Turner* v. *S.O.S.E.* (1973) 28 P. & C.R. 123.

The wording of the different categories varies, so that in some cases the provisions extend to any decision *relating to* an application, whilst in others it is limited to any decision *on* the application. The Court of Appeal in *Co-operative Retail Services Ltd.* v. *Secretary of State for the Environment*[52] has taken the view that the distinction is significant, and that a decision *on* an application is a decision which is at least made in the disposing of the appeal and in the course of coming to a final decision on it. A refusal to grant an adjournment of an inquiry was held in that case not to be such a decision, and doubt remains as to whether a refusal to entertain an appeal at all would qualify.[53] The Act expressly reserves the right of an applicant to proceed against the Secretary of State, by mandamus or otherwise, in respect of any refusal or failure to take any of the decisions in the above categories,[54] and there is therefore no need to stretch the language of the Act to cover such a case.

Except in the case of orders falling within (viii) above, only action by the Secretary of State is challengeable under these provisions, so that the bulk of decision making by local planning authorities falls outside the statutory machinery for challenge. So too does action by a local planning authority in the course of proceedings before the Secretary of State, such as a failure by the authority to comply with the Inquiries Procedure Rules.[55] But in either case a remedy may exist through the non-statute based procedures under category (4) below.

(b) Standing

The right of challenge is conferred on any "person aggrieved," and on the authority "directly concerned" with the order or decision.[56] Few statutory formulae have caused greater conceptual difficulty than the phrase "person aggrieved." On the face of it, it extends standing to any person seeking to challenge the decision or action, without imposing any preconditions as to proprietary status or indeed any other link between the applicant and the decision. But in the course of interpretation over a lengthy period, and in a variety of different statutory contexts, the courts have restricted its ambit substantially. In *Buxton* v. *Minister of Housing and Local Government*[57] the question arose whether those restrictive interpretations should as a matter of principle be carried across to planning law, where the right to challenge under these provisions had then been only recently introduced. The applicant was certainly aggrieved in the broader sense of the word, because the Minister had overruled his inspector's recommendation against granting

---

[52] [1980] 1 W.L.R. 271.

[53] The view of Slynn J. in *Chalgray Ltd.* v. *S.O.S.E.* (1977) 33 P. & C.R. 10 that a refusal to entertain an appeal was challengeable under these provisions was expressly doubted by the Court of Appeal in the *Co-operative Retail Services* case.

[54] T.C.P.A. 1971, s.242(4); and see *R.* v. *S.O.S.E., ex parte Percy Bilton Industrial Properties Ltd.* (1975) 31 P. & C.R. 154.

[55] *Davies* v. *Secretary of State for Wales* (1976) 33 P. & C.R. 330; *Performance Cars Ltd.* v. *S.O.S.E.* (1977) 34 P. & C.R. 92 at 97 *per* Browne L.J.

[56] *Ibid.* s.245(1) and (2). By virtue of subs.(7) the authority directly concerned is the local planning authority who were involved in the matter or who are named in the order or notice made by the Secretary of State.

[57] [1961] 1 Q.B. 278.

permission for development on adjoining land, which had been made on the primary ground that the applicant's amenity would be seriously interfered with. But Salmon J. proceeded to take a remarkably narrow view of the legislation. The formula had been held in other contexts to include only persons with a legal grievance, that is, those whose legal rights had been infringed. Planning law, he insisted, conferred no new rights on individual members of the public, but sought only to restrict development for the benefit of the public at large. There was thus no right of the applicant infringed by the decision, and thus no basis upon which he might claim to be a person aggrieved by it.

The artificially restrictive approach of the *Buxton* decision was out of line with the then emerging concept of land use planning as a broadly based political process, involving more than a process of restriction of private property in the neutral public interest. And it is certainly substantially out of line with the steps taken towards effective public participation since the late 1960s, and the contemporary concept of planning as a basic and important environmental control. The decision was criticised,[58] especially in light of a broader interpretation of the formula accepted by the Privy Council in an appeal from Gambia,[59] where it was held to include any person "who has a genuine grievance because an order has been made which prejudicially affects his interests."

The breakthrough to a broader approach in planning came in *Turner Secretary of State for the Environment*,[60] where counsel for Secretary of State challenged the standing of the applicant, the chairman of a local preservation society which had appeared at the public local inquiry by permission of the inspector. In upholding the status of the applicant, Ackner J. distinguished the *Buxton* case on the narrow ground that the Inquiries Procedure Rules, which had been made since that case had been decided, conferred procedural rights on third parties appearing at inquiries. These included the right to have their representations considered by the Secretary of State, and thus impliedly the right to insist that he should comply with the relevant requirements of the statute and the Rules in doing so. But there was a broader principle underlying these arguments, which was that access to the courts to challenge a decision which is *ex hypothesi* bad in law should not, as a matter of general principle, be blocked by a restrictive interpretation of the formula. The new extended category of entitlement established by the case includes all persons appearing at an inquiry whether as of right or at the inspector's discretion, and it is probably broad enough to include most genuinely aggrieved persons on an ordinary planning appeal.

But there is a more general principle at stake. In line with the liberalisation of access to the courts for judicial review which is discussed in a later section of this chapter,[61] it is now likely that entitlement will also in appropriate cases extend to persons who have made representations but not participated in inquiries, and certainly so in cases where there has been no inquiry, such as appeals under written representation procedures and orders made and confirmed by local planning authorities.

[58] See, *e.g. Maurice* v. *London C.C.* [1964] 2 Q.B. 362.
[59] *Attorney-General of the Gambia* v. *N'Jie* [1961] A.C. 617 at 634.
[60] (1973) 28 P. & C.R. 123; followed in *Bizony* v. *S.O.S.E.* [1976] J.P.L. 306.
[61] *Post,* pp. 626–629.

(c) Procedure

Challenge is by way of originating motion, notice of which is required to be served on the Secretary of State and on the authority directly concerned; or, if the authority are the applicant, on every person who would, if he were aggrieved by the decision, be entitled himself to apply to the court.[62]

(d) Evidence

Evidence is by affidavit,[63] supported by the power of the court to order the attendance for cross-examination of any person making such an affidavit.[64] There is no power otherwise for the court to receive oral or other evidence.[65] The power to permit cross-examination is rarely used, and the Court of Appeal has sought to restrict it to exceptional cases.[66] It might be permitted where the affidavits of one party are so unsatisfactory that although they cannot be regarded as worthless evidence, they cannot be confidently accepted as evidence of fact without cross-examination.[67] But the courts have taken the view that it is undesirable that the inspector should be cross-examined, or the applicant; and have pointed to the danger, in allowing cross-examination, of parties taking advantage of the opportunity to undermine the findings of fact.[68] That fear also underlies the reluctance of the courts to admit fresh evidence by affidavit. The powers of the court are limited to a review of questions of law and procedure and fresh evidence going to the merits of the case is not admissible, even in relation to facts which were not known to the parties at the time of the Secretary of State's determination. It is a rule which is capable of causing some curious results, because it subordinates the true facts to the state of knowledge of the parties which prevailed at the time of the inquiry. In *Glover* v. *Secretary of State for the Environment*,[69] for example, an inspector had granted permssion for a car-park near a country club, for a period concurrent with that of the club's liquor licence. It later transpired that, unknown to the parties, the licence had been revoked some two months before the inquiry and the permission was thus apparently without effect, but the court declined to remit the matter for rehearing. The only two recognised exceptions to the ban on fresh

---

[62] R.S.C. Ord. 94, r. 1(*d*). Application must be made within six weeks from the date on which the action is taken, which is the date when the Secretary of State's decision letter is put in the post rather than when it is received: *Griffiths* v. *S.O.S.E. The Times*, January 30, 1982. Applications are entered in the Special Paper List administered by the Head Clerk of the Crown office, and since they affect third parties the court has adopted a vigorous policy of dismissing applications which are not pursued after notice: see *Biggins* v. *S.O.S.E.* [1981] 1 All E.R. 1200.

[63] *Ibid.* Ord. 94, r. 3(1).

[64] *Ibid.* Ord. 38, r. 2(3).

[65] The power to receive further evidence under Ord. 55, r.7, extends only to appeals, and not to applications by way of originating motion, and the implication in *Glover* v. *S.O.S.E.* [1981] J.P.L. 110 that the powers are applicable cannot be supported.

[66] *George* v. *S.O.S.E.* (1979) 77 L.G.R. 689.

[67] *Ibid.* at 698 *per* Cumming-Bruce L.J.; but *cf.* Lord Denning's observation that the affidavits in that case were so untrustworthy as *not* to require cross-examination.

[68] *Ibid.* at 693 *per* Lord Denning M.R., and *cf. Behrman* v. *S.O.S.E.* [1979] J.P.L. 677, where the court declined to review a conflict of fact which would have required cross-examination of the inspector for its resolution.

[69] [1981] J.P.L. 110.

evidence are in the case of a particular matter of real importance which was before the inspector, but had been wholly omitted from his report to the Secretary of State, or completely misunderstood or put in an entirely wrong or misleading way[70]; or the converse, that there was no evidence before him upon which he could properly have come to the conclusion he has.[71] Those are all instances of errors of law, in that their effect is that either the right of a party to be heard has been denied, or the inspector or Secretary of State has failed to have regard to a material consideration.

(e) Grounds of challenge

A decision or order, or other action by the Secretary of State falling within the category above, may be challenged on the grounds either that it is not within the powers of the Act, or that any of the "relevant requirements" have not been complied with.[72] "Relevant requirements" means any requirements of the Act of 1971 or of the Tribunal and Inquiries Act 1971, or of any order, regulations or rules made under either Act.[73] Thus failure by the Secretary of State to comply with, for example, the Inquiries Procedure Rules, is expressly made a ground for challenge, though subject to the "substantial prejudice" rule discussed in the next paragraph below. The courts have construed the statutory provisions broadly, however, so as to encompass the general administrative law principles of review such as the doctrine of natural justice and the requirement that the Secretary of State should neither have taken into account irrelevant considerations nor failed to have regard to relevant considerations. The requirement to give reasons for decisions has provided a basis for a detailed system of review, and the principles are discussed more fully in Part C of this chapter.

(f) Powers of the court

The powers of the court are formulated in the same way as in the case of challenge to development plans, to include a power to make interim orders (except in the case of tree preservation orders, where a temporary suspension of the order might amount to an invitation to fell the tree at once).[74] The power to quash the decision or order on final determination arises only where the court is satisfied that it is not within the powers of the Act; or, in the case of non-compliance with the "relevant requirements," that the interests of the appellant have been substantially prejudiced by the failure to comply.[75] The Act therefore draws a distinction between decisions outside the powers of the Act and those arrived at in breach of the requirements of the Act and the subordinate legislation, but there is no such sharp line of

---

[70] *East Hampshire D.C.* v. *S.O.S.E.* [1978] J.P.L. 182; and *cf. Chichester D.C.* v. *S.O.S.E.* [1981] J.P.L. 591 where evidence was admitted to explain discrepancies between the inspector's report and the decision letter.

[71] *Ashbridge Investments Ltd.* v. *M.H.L.G.* [1965] 3 All E.R. 371 at 374, *per* Lord Denning M.R.; *H. Sabey & Co. Ltd.* v. *S.O.S.E.* [1978] 1 All E.R. 586.

[72] T.C.P.A. 1971, s.245(1).

[73] *Ibid.* subs.(7). There is a specific bar to challenge on the ground of lack of jurisdiction of an inspector to determine an appeal in place of the Secretary of State, unless his powers have been challenged before his decision on the appeal was given: *Ibid.* Sched. 9, para. 2(3)(*b*).

[74] *Ibid.* subss.(2)(*a*) and (3).

[75] *Ibid.* subs.(2)(*b*).

distinction in modern administrative law. A failure to allow an applicant to be heard before coming to a decision, for example, is more than simply a failure to comply with the "relevant requirements," because it is regarded by the courts as an error going to the powers of the Secretary of State to make the decision. This blurring and overlapping of concept has made it "difficult, if not impossible, to formulate exhaustively how the distinction between these two limbs is to be drawn."[76] The consequence is that the courts have attempted to minimise the differences between their powers under each limb. They have held, for example, that even in cases falling clearly within the first category, they have a discretion as to whether to quash, similar to their discretion in granting certiorari which had been superseded by the Act. That discretion will be exercised against the applicants unless they are entitled to have the decision quashed *ex debito justitiae*. Thus in *Miller* v. *Weymouth and Melcombe Regis Corporation*[77] the court declined to quash a discontinuance order where the Secretary of State's decision letter contained a clerical error which had caused the applicants no prejudice. And similarly in *Kent County Council* v. *Secretary of State for the Environment*[78] the court found that the error complained of by the applicants was an amendment which, far from being prejudicial to them, had been made in order to meet one of their major objections. There was therefore no entitlement to have the decision quashed *ex debito justitiae*. There is, therefore, at least a residual discretion under the first head, even although the general rule must be that the decision should be quashed unless the point is purely technical or there is no possible detriment to the applicant.[79]

Conversely, in cases falling more obviously under the second limb as instances of non-compliance with the "relevant requirements," such as a failure to give adequate reasons, the approach has been to find "substantial prejudice" in most cases where an error other than a mere technicality has occurred. That is particularly so where the finding as to whether there has been an instance of non-compliance involves a question not only of principle but of degree. A finding that there has been a failure to give "adequate" reasons relating to all important parts of the case, for example, contains the implicit assumption that the error is more than purely technical, and there is likely therefore always to be a substantial prejudice to the parties in such a case.[80] Moreover, such a finding frequently implies that the Secretary of State has failed to have regard to a material consideration, and that is an error which brings the case under the first limb and entitles the applicant to have the decision quashed save in the limited circumstances discussed above.[81] In

[76] *Miller* v. *Weymouth and Melcombe Regis Corporation* (1974) 27 P. & C.R. 468, at 478–79, *per* Kerr J.
[77] (1974) 27 P. & C.R. 468.
[78] (1976) 33 P. & C.R. 70.
[79] *Peak Park Joint Planning Board* v. *Secretary of State for the Environment* (1979) 39 P. & C.R. 361 at 385.
[80] See, *e.g. Preston B.C.* v. *S.O.S.E.* [1978] J.P.L. 548; *Seddon Properties Ltd.* v. *S.O.S.E.* [1978] J.P.L. 835; *Rogelen Building Group Ltd.* v. *S.O.S.E.* [1981] J.P.L. 506. The same is true of a finding that there has been a breach of the rules of natural justice, and the Court of Appeal have accepted that one should not find that there has been such a breach unless there has been substantial prejudice: *George* v. *S.O.S.E.* (1979) 38 P. & C.R. 609.
[81] See, *e.g. Seddon Properties Ltd.* v. *S.O.S.E.* [1978] J.P.L. 835; *Brown and Gilston Estates Ltd.* v. *S.O.S.E.* [1979] J.P.L. 454; and *cf. Ellinas* v. *S.O.S.E.* [1977] J.P.L. 249 (breach of natural justice regarded as coming under either category).

short, the courts have in practice drawn together the two limbs of discretion, and they have been reluctant to allow entitlement to relief to turn on fine conceptual distinctions between errors going to power and procedural breaches.

The effect of quashing a *decision* by the Secretary of State is normally that the matter is remitted to him for reconsideration[82]; but in the case of an *order* under these provisions it is the order itself, rather than simply the decision on it, which is quashed, and this would necessarily involve setting it aside altogether. Where a decision is quashed, however, the appeal may be regarded as still standing, and the Secretary of State is empowered to come to a fresh decision upon it in accordance with the ruling of the court. This does not mean that the matter need always be completely reopened. It may require no more than that the applicants be permitted to present evidence on the points found by the court to have been overlooked, or to make representations on a point of law found by the court to have been wrongly determined.[83] In the case of inadequate or unintelligible reasons, the Secretry of State may need to do no more than issue a fresh decision making the reasons clear.[84] But the Secretary of State is not obliged to overlook events in the real world since his previous determination, and may take into account any material consideration that affects the matter up to the date of the fresh decision. In doing so, however, he would remain subject to the post-inquiry provisions of the Inquiries Procedure Rules, where applicable, and thus be obliged to solicit further representations and reopen the inquiry if necessary in order to re-examine any new issue or difference of fact.[85]

4. Applications for Judicial Review

(a) Introduction

The rights of statutory challenge discussed in the preceding pages cut across the inherent powers of the High Court to review official action, but they do not supplant them altogether. They provide an exclusive remedy in respect of the decisions and orders that fall within their scope, but they do not extend to all action by the Secretary of State, and the bulk of local planning authority action is completely outside their scope. Recourse may therefore continue to be had in those cases to the old remedies by way of certiorari, declaration, injunction, prohibition and mandamus, so far as they are available to review such action. But, unlike the statutory remedies, there is no fixed or automatic entitlement to seek relief. The decision or action complained of must first be shown to be one to which the remedy sought is appropriate, and different grounds of challenge and different criteria for assessing the standing of the applicant apply in respect of different remedies.

---

[82] *Hartnell* v. *M.H.L.G.* [1963] 1 W.L.R. 1141, *per* Sachs J.; *Price Brothers (Rode Heath) Ltd.* v. *Department of the Environment* (1978) 38 P. & C.R. 579.

[83] *H. Sabey & Co. Ltd.* v. *S.O.S.E.* [1977] J.P.L. 661.

[84] *Price Brothers (supra)* at 592–593, *per* Forbes J.; *Rogelen Building Group Ltd.* v. *S.O.S.E.* [1981] J.P.L. 506.

[85] In *Niarchos (London) Ltd.* v. *S.O.S.E.* (No.2) [1981] J.P.L. 118 the Secretary of State had proposed to re-open the inquiry although this had not been required by the parties.The Court of Appeal ruled the decision to be perverse on the reasons advanced by him and granted mandamus requiring him to determine the appeal forthwith.

Some of the long-standing technicality and confusion arising from these distinctions was overcome by procedural reforms in 1977, which marshalled together the remedies behind a new application for judicial review.[86] An application for the prerogative orders of mandamus, prohibition or certiorari may now be made only by way of an application for judicial review, whilst an application for a declaration or injunction may be made either in that way or under ordinary civil law. On an application for judicial review the court has complete discretion to select and grant the appropriate remedy; and may grant a declaration or injunction instead of, or in addition to, a prerogative order where to do so would be just and convenient.[87]

The availability of the remedies is dependent upon the nature of relief sought, the type of decision or action challenged, the standing of the applicant and the discretionary power of the court to withhold relief.

(i) **Certiorari.** Of the three prerogative orders, certiorari is the most commonly employed, and it is the model upon which the statutory provisions discussed above are based. It is an order, directed to the body concerned, for the purpose of quashing the decision or action complained of. Its scope has been expanded considerably by the courts in recent years, following the ruling by the House of Lords in *Ridge* v. *Baldwin*,[88] which lifted the requirement which had been thought to flow from *R.* v. *Electricity Commissioners, ex parte London Electricity Joint Committee Co. (1920) Ltd.*,[89] that only bodies under a duty to act "judicially" were subject to certiorari. It is sufficient now that the function be one involving the determination of "questions affecting the rights of subjects."[90] This liberalisation of doctrine has allowed certiorari to go against resolutions of local planning authorities, such as to quash planning permission[91] or listed building consent,[92] where there is no obvious quasi-judicial element yet issues of great significance involved. Its full impact has yet to be felt, because the obvious remedy so far as a disappointed applicant is concerned is to appeal to the Secretary of State. In most cases that will provide a more effective and more convenient remedy, and certiorari will be withheld.[93]

That alternative remedy is not available to third parties, however, and certiorari is therefore the primary means through which they may seek to overturn decisions by local planning authorities which err in law, and the recent relaxation by the courts of "standing" requirements (discussed below) may be expected to increase the future popularity of the procedure.

Certiorari will also go to the Secretary of State in cases under the Act involving the determination by him of matters affecting the rights of subjects, to which the statutory rights of challenge do not extend. Examples

---

[86] See now R.S.C. Ord. 53, as substituted by S.I. 1977 No. 1955, and amended by S.I. 1980 No.2000.

[87] *Ibid.* Ord. 53, r.1(2).

[88] [1964] A.C. 40.

[89] [1924] 1 K.B. 171.

[90] *Ibid.* at 205 *per* Atkin L.J.

[91] *R.* v. *Hillingdon L.B.C., ex parte Royco Homes Ltd.* [1974] Q.B. 720; *R.* v. *Sheffield C.C., ex parte Mansfield* (1978) 37 P. & C.R. 1; *Covent Garden Community Association Ltd.* v. *G.L.C.* [1981] J.P.L. 183.

[92] *R.* v. *North Hertfordshire D.C., ex parte Sullivan* [1981] J.P.L. 752.

[93] See further the observations of Lord Widgery C.J. in *R.* v. *Hillingdon L.B.C. ante* at 728; and Bridge J.'s comment at 732 that certiorari should only be granted in "a clear case."

include decisions on the extent to which an owner should bear the costs of urgent works carried out on his listed building by the local planning authority,[94] and interlocutory decisions in some planning appeals.[95]

(ii) Mandamus. The purpose of the order of mandamus is to require compliance with a statutory duty. The right to seek the order is expressly preserved in the case of the statutory remedies available under the Act of 1971,[96] so that although the validity of any action falling within those provisions may not be questioned except through the prescribed procedures, mandamus remains available where the Secretary of State has refused to take any decision at all, such as by declining jurisdiction in an appeal.[97] Mandamus is of limited availability against local planning authorities, because in most cases of failure to decide there is instead a default entitlement to appeal to the Secretary of State.[98]

(iii) Prohibition. This order, which has rarely been used in planning, is available to restrain an excess of jurisdiction in the course of determining an issue. Like certiorari, it is available in respect of functions involving questions affecting rights, and would equally in an appropriate case extend to decisions proposed to be taken by local planning authorities where no other convenient remedy existed.[99]

(iv) Declaration. A declaration may be sought either as a public law remedy as part of an application for judicial review, or in civil proceedings between the parties. The former course would be more suitable in a case where it is sought to question a determination by the Secretary of State or a local planning authority, and where evidence might readily enough be given by affidavit. The Court of Appeal has also urged that the procedure of application for judicial review be used if it is available, because of the greater expertise of the Divisional Court in such matters by comparison with the Chancery Division,[1] but that point loses its strength where originating proceedings are commenced in the Queen's Bench Division rather than the Chancery Division because of the powers now exercisable by single judges under the statutory challenge procedures described above.[2] Declaratory proceedings may be brought by way of ordinary action, therefore, where it is desired to call oral evidence and to have provision for cross-examination, although the consequence is that the court may be called upon to determine at first instance matters usually within the jurisdiction of the Secretary of State.[3] It may also be used in order to obtain a ruling on interpretation of a document, such as a planning permission, for which no convenient

---

[94] Under T.C.P.A. 1971, s.101: see, *e.g. R. v. S.O.S.E., ex parte Hampshire C.C.* [1981] J.P.L. 47; and *cf. R. v. S.O.S.E., ex parte Powis* (1980) 258 E.G. 57.

[95] *Co-operative Retail Services Ltd. v. S.O.S.E.* [1980] 1 W.L.R. 271.

[96] T.C.P.A. 1971, s.242(4).

[97] See, *e.g. R. v. S.O.S.E., ex parte Percy Bilton Industrial Properties Ltd.* (1975) 31 P. & C.R. 154.

[98] *Ante*, p. 565.

[99] See, *e.g. Allen v. City of London Corporation* [1981] J.P.L. 685, where on the facts no order was made.

[1] *Uppal* v. *Home Office* (1978) 123 S.J. 17.

[2] *Price Brothers (Rode Heath) Ltd.* v. *Department of the Environment* (1978) 38 P. & C.R. 579, at 595–96. A civil action for a declaration is in most cases commenced in the Chancery Division, but may be commenced in any division.

[3] See, *e.g. Marshall* v. *Nottingham Corporation* [1960] 1 W.L.R. 707.

machinery is provided by the legislation.[4] The declaration also offers a means of testing the validity of action taken, provided it is sought on grounds not precluded by the Act,[5] and it has been used not only by individual applicants but also by local planning authorities.[6]

(v) **Injunction.** An injunction may also be sought either in an application for judicial review or in civil proceedings. It is commonly sought in conjunction with declaratory relief as a means of giving effect to the declaration. An interim injunction may be sought, as an anticipatory or pre-emptive procedure, restraining the taking of any further action pending the outcome of the proceedings.[7] The main use of the injunction in planning, however, has been by planning authorities themselves, in civil proceedings, as a means of supplementing their enforcement powers.[8]

(b) Standing

The necessary status for seeking the remedies is governed not by statutory formula but by judge made rules. Those rules have developed differently over many years for the different remedies, but the general trend over the past 30 years has undoubtedly been towards a more liberal approach. The courts have proved increasingly reluctant to exclude an applicant from relief against unlawful action solely on the ground of his inadequate status assessed in terms of property, statutory or other rights. The progressive shedding of technical limitations was taken a step further by the procedural reforms of 1977 which allowed all or any of the remedies to be sought in an application for judicial review. Under the new rules the court may not give leave for an application to be made unless it considers "that the applicant has a sufficient interest in the matter to which the application relates. . . . "[9] One interpretation of the new formula was that it supplanted the old distinctions entirely. Lord Diplock in *Inland Revenue Commissioners* v. *National Federation of Self-Employed and Small Businesses Ltd.*[10] argued that the question of *locus standi* was one of practice rather than jurisdiction, and that the effect of the new rules was to leave to the court "an unfettered discretion to decide what in its own good judgement it considers to be a "sufficient interest" on the part of an applicant in the particular circumstances of the case before it."[11] Although that approach was rejected by the majority of the Lords, all recognised that the progressive relaxation of the earlier rules was carried further by the reforms. Thus Lord Wilberforce, whilst accepting that

---

[4] It is available, for example, in cases where a section 53 determination is not: see *e.g. Edgwarebury Park Investments Ltd.* v. *M.H.L.G.* [1963] 2 Q.B. 408.

[5] In enforcement cases the preclusive provisions extend only to the grounds upon which an appeal may be made to the Secretary of State, and that the issue of the power of the authority to serve the notice may be reviewable in proceedings for a declaration: see *e.g. Western Fish Products Ltd.* v. *Penwith D.C.* [1981] 2 All E.R. 204, where, however, the Court of Appeal found it unnecessary to determine the scope of the residual jurisdiction.

[6] See, *e.g. Cookham R.D.C.* v. *Bull* (1972) 222 E.G. 1014; 225 E.G. 2155 (authority awarded declaration that enforcement notices valid and effective, and injunction restraining defendant from interfering with or obstructing demolition works).

[7] R.S.C. Ord. 29, r. 1.

[8] See further *ante,* pp. 425–427.

[9] R.S.C. Ord. 53, r. 3(5).

[10] [1981] 2 All E.R. 93.

[11] *Ibid.* p. 105.

the new test of "sufficient interest" applied to all relief sought by way of application for judicial review, maintained that the question was still a mixed decision of fact and law and not purely of discretion, and that the same test might not apply in the case of each remedy.[12] But that was not a matter of technical distinction: it derived from the different character of the remedies themselves. For example, "sufficient interest" in the case of an applicant seeking to compel an authority by mandamus to carry out a duty, might be different from that where the complaint is that a judicial or administrative body had exceeded their powers, to the applicant's detriment. The class of persons affected and the manner in which they are affected in each case is likely to be different. But beyond such tentative drawing of distinctions the Lords were reluctant to go, insisting instead that the primary consideration in each case was the sufficiency of the relationship between the applicant and the issues at stake. For that reason the question of *locus standi* ought not to be subjected to abstract analysis divorced from the merits of the application.

The link between the applicant and the decision complained of in planning matters may be direct, in the sense that some proprietary or other right is affected by the decision. Where an application for permission had been made by a person other than the owner, for example, the owner would presumably be sufficiently interested, on the basis of his proprietary interest in the decision, to have standing. Similarly in a case where the authority are obliged to take into account representations made by certain individuals or by members of the public at large, there would be "sufficient interest" on the part of those responding to complain that the duty owed to them had not been complied with. Both instances are examples of decisions affecting legally recognised rights, but the liberalising effect of the 1977 reforms has encouraged the courts to go beyond these relationships, and to accept as sufficient an interest based solely upon more general environmental grounds. In this they have come at last to lay the legal basis for an effective system of public participation at local level, and the implications are potentially far-reaching. For the reasons outlined above, the value of the prerogative orders is confined almost entirely to third parties, and to action against local planning authorities. In *Covent Garden Community Association Ltd.* v. *Greater London Council*[13] the court had no hesitation in holding that the company, which had been formed expressly to represent the interests of the residents of the Covent Garden area, had sufficient interest to challenge the validity of a resolution of the Council granting themselves deemed planning permission. In *R.* v. *North Hertfordshire D.C., ex parte Sullivan*[14] the court granted an order of certiorari to a neighbour to quash a grant of planning permission and listed building consent for development which would have intruded on her privacy and to which she had objected. In that case, the neighbour's interest in the matter was apparently assumed without argument to be sufficient.[15]

In the case of mandamus the test of *locus standi* was originally stricter than

---

[12] *Ibid.* p. 91.
[13] [1981] J.P.L. 183.
[14] [1981] J.P.L. 752.
[15] Nor does any question of standing appear to have arisen in *Allen* v. *City of London Corporation* [1981] J.P.L. 685 or *Davies* v. *Hammersmith and Fulham L.B.C.* [1981] J.P.L. 682, although no remedy was granted upon the final determination of each.

for certiorari, and an applicant would be required to show that he had a specific legal right to ask for the interference of the court. The House of Lords in the *Federation of Self-Employed* case were unanimous in holding that such a requirement no longer prevailed, and they agreed that in gauging the sufficiency of an interest, regard should be had both to the nature of the duty sought to be enforced and its implictions for the applicant. But they demonstrated the uncertainty and subjectivity of that formula by dividing 3:2 on the question of whether the applicants in the case actually had sufficient interest to seek mandamus against the Inland Revenue Commissioners.[16]

Nothing in the procedural reforms of 1977 affects the *locus standi* requirements in the case of actions for declarations and injunctions other than by way of application for judicial review. These are instances of use of essentially private law remedies in the public law arena, and it is because they lack an exclusively public law basis and because there is therefore no requirement that leave should first be obtained from the court, that the judges have expressed reservations about applying a similarly relaxed test of standing. The precondition of leave establishes a filter against the anticipated horde of "busybodies and cranks"[17] who might besiege the courts with complaints against public authorities, and the ability of those failing to qualify in their own right to seek to join the Attorney-General in a relator action means that a remedy is not necessarily excluded by a higher test of standing. The traditional approach was to require the plaintiff to show the infringement of some legal right. The classic case in planning law is *Gregory* v. *Camden London Borough Council*[18] where a neighbour sought a declaration that a grant of planning permission for an extension to a private school was *ultra vires* because of an admitted failure to notify the Minister of the proposal as a departure from the development plan. Whilst agreeing that on the assumed facts the grant was unlawful, Paull J. declined to award a declaration on the ground that there had been no infringement of the plaintiff's legal rights.

Now that a declaration may be sought in an application for judicial review, and under a liberalised conception of standing which is capable of including neighbours, the ruling in the *Gregory* case no longer rations relief against local planning authorities as tightly as it formerly did, but whether the rule for civil proceedings should now be relaxed, whether or not to the extent of bringing it into line with the exclusively public law rules, continues to be debated. Two recent decisions of the High Court have taken divergent approaches. In *Steeples* v. *Derbyshire County Council*,[19] Webster J. took the view that the criteria should now be brought together, and that any difference in substance between the two forms of proceeding could if necessary be given effect to when exercising the discretion as to the relief to be given. That

[16] Thus Lords Diplock and Scarman [1981] 2 All E.R. 93 at 106–7 and 114 respectively) agreed that had the Federation succeeded in establishing a breach of duty, they would have had sufficient interest to seek relief; Lords Fraser and Roskill (at 108 and 121) were clear that no sufficient interest existed, and Lord Wilberforce (at 99) expressed the view that on a matter of general principle the Federation could have no sufficient interest, although exceptions might exist.
[17] *Barrs* v. *Bethell, The Times,* July 14, 1981, *per* Warner J.
[18] [1966] 1 W.L.R. 899.
[19] [1981] J.P.L. 582.

opinion was expressed *obiter*, however, since he had already concluded that the plaintiff enjoyed *locus standi* by reason both of the interference by the proposed development with his private rights (because a small part of his land would be required so as to create a visibility splay), and because, to the extent that public rights were involved, the loss of view and other amenity likely to be suffered by him was a special damage conferring the necessary status.

In *Barrs* v. *Bethell*,[20] however, Warner J. declined to accept that *locus standi* existed in the case of a group of ratepayers unable to show any such interference with proprietary rights or special damage arising from a local authority's financial policies. In particular, he rejected the argument that the judicial review test should be applied to civil proceedings, maintaining that the filter of obtaining leave was a crucial distinction, and that the court's discretion as to relief did not in itself protect the potential defendant from the burden of litigation or the risk of costs.

The principle that must be regarded as remaining intact, therefore, is that where a declaration or injunction is sought by way of civil proceedings rather than judicial review, the applicant will be required to demonstrate that some private right of his is at stake, or that he has suffered special damage from the infringement of a public right. That latter ground is capable, as interpreted in the *Steeples* case, of extending the scope of the concept beyond instances of purely physical property interference, and the interference with amenity which was held there to suffice would no doubt equally qualify the plaintiff in *Gregory* v. *Camden London Borough Council* if that case were redecided today. But groups and individuals representing broader interests will by definition have greater difficulty in demonstrating special damage. That need not disqualify them from seeking judicial review, but it will prevent a civil action for declaration or injunction.

To maintain a distinction between the two is difficult to justify, except as a safeguard against irresponsible litigation, and it may inhibit the bringing of proceedings by civil action in cases where that may be the better course because of a substantial conflict of fact. The alternative is to seek the consent of the Attorney-General to the bringing of a relator action, in his capacity as guardian of the public interest. His discretion whether to grant or refuse consent is unfettered and his decision unchallengeable,[21] but there are two normal preconditions. The first is that the plaintiff will be required to give the Attorney-General an indemnity as to costs.[22] Second, he will not assent unless it can be shown that the plaintiff has no *locus standi* in his own right. In the *Barrs* v. *Bethell* case, for example, the Attorney-General refused to assent until the court had determined that no *locus standi* existed in the plaintiffs, but undertook to give urgent consideration to an application in that event.

---

[20] *The Times*, July 14, 1981.
[21] For a full discussion of the relator action and the Attorney-General's function see *Gouriet* v. *Union of Post Office Workers* [1978] A.C. 435.
[22] In *Covent Garden Community Association Ltd.* v. *G.L.C.* [1981] J.P.L. 183 the Association had chosen to discontinue declaratory proceedings and apply instead for judicial review because of their inability to provide the required indemnity.

(c) Procedure

An application for judicial review is made in two stages. There is first an application for leave, made *ex parte* to a single judge. The application may be determined in private and without a hearing unless one is requested, but if leave is refused or granted on terms the application may be renewed in open court.[23] The requirement that leave should be obtained operates as a filter, not only in respect of applications which disclose no merits, but also for cases where the court considers that the applicant has "no sufficient interest in the matter to which the application relates."[24] At this preliminary stage there may be no clear answer to that question, particularly in view of the insistence of the House of Lords in *Inland Revenue Commissioners* v. *National Federation of Self-Employed and Small Businesses Ltd.*[25] that the sufficiency of the applicants' interest could only be determined once the "matter" to which the application relates had been clearly identified. At the preliminary stages it is therefore a threshold requirement, and the only realistic approach is that suggested by Lord Diplock in that case:

> "If on a quick perusal of the material then available, the court thinks that it discloses what might on further consideration turn out to be an arguable case in favour of granting to the applicant the relief claimed, it ought, in the exercise of a judicial discretion, to give him leave to apply for that relief."[26]

The second stage, if leave is granted, is the application for judicial review itself. The time limit for applications was substantially reduced in 1981, and the requirement now is that the application be made " . . . promptly, and in any event within three months from the date when the grounds for the application first arose."[27] That date, in the case of certiorari, is the date of the order or proceeding which it is sought to have quashed.[28] The court has discretion to extend the time if it considers there to be good reason, and although the exercise of that discretion is no longer governed expressly by the consideration of whether a late application might be "detrimental to good administration," that will doubtless remain a factor in practice, particularly where a planning permission or other decision has been acted upon.

. The application for judicial review is no longer made in all cases to the Divisional Court, but instead to a single judge in open court by way of originating motion, unless the court otherwise directs.[29]

Where a declaration or injunction is sought instead through civil proceedings, there is no preliminary requirement as to leave. The action is commenced either by writ or originating summons, but the latter course is indicated by the Rules of the Supreme Court as being appropriate where the

---

[23] R.S.C. Ord. 53, r.3.
[24] *Ibid.* r. 3(7).
[25] [1981] 2 All E.R. 93.
[26] *Ibid.* at 106.
[27] R.S.C. Ord. 53, r.4 (as substituted by S.I. 1980 No. 2000, with effect from January 12, 1981).
[28] *Ibid.* r. 4(2).
[29] *Ibid.* r. 5(2).

sole or principal question is likely to be one of construction or law, and there is unlikely to be any substantial dispute of fact.[30]

(d) Evidence

Evidence on an application for judicial review is by affidavit,[31] and the courts have in general adopted the same approach to the admission of fresh evidence as in the case of statutory applications to quash. In *R. v. Secretary of State for the Environment, ex parte Powis*[32] the Court of Appeal ruled that fresh evidence should be admissible in judicial review only where it is needed to show what material was before the Minister or body making the decision; to determine challenges on questions of procedural error or jurisdictional fact, and in cases of proceedings tainted by misconduct such as bias, or fraud or perjury by one of the parties.

Those restrictions do not apply as such in the case of other proceedings brought for declaration of injunction, where the question arising may be one of interpretation or construction which has not already been before an inferior tribunal.[33] But the rationale for the fresh evidence rule in judicial review—that the courts will not reopen the merits of any decision taken—extends equally to these proceedings.

(e) Grounds of challenge

The grounds of challenge in proceedings for judicial review are discussed in the following section of this chapter.

(f) Powers of the court

The reforms of 1977 have conferred considerably greater flexibility in applications for judicial review. The application is no longer liable to be defeated on the ground that the wrong remedy has been sought, and the court has power to select the appropriate remedy. Further, where the court issues certiorari it may also remit the matter to the authority concerned with a direction to reconsider and reach a decision in accordance with the findings of the court.[34]

C. The Principles of Judicial Review

1. *Introduction*

Town and country planning is not a function which Parliament has vested in judges. Theirs is a supervisory, and not an executive role, concerned with issues not of policy but of law. Judicial review goes to questions of the

---

[30] *Ibid.* Ord. 5, r. 4(2). As to procedure generally in such cases, see Ords.4, 5 and 28. There is no provision for notification to the Secretary of State of declaratory proceedings to which he is not a party, and he may therefore be unaware of litigation touching on matters relevant to planning administration. He may be joined as respondent in an appropriate case if he has been apprised of the litigation: see, *e.g. Western Fish Products Ltd.* v. *Penwith D.C.* (1978) 38 P. & C.R. 7, 22.

[31] *Ibid.* Ord. 53, r. 6.

[32] (1980) 42 P. & C.R. 73.

[33] Evidence in such cases is governed generally by R.S.C. Ord. 38.

[34] R.S.C. Ord. 53, r. 9(4).

quality of the process of decision making, rather than the quality of the actual decisions arrived at. Whether or not a particular development should be permitted in a green belt, for example, is a question purely of policy and one entirely for the local planning authority and, if necessary, the Secretary of State. A judge may personally disagree with the decision and take the view that the impact of the proposal would be so great as to breach the whole concept of green belts. But that would not give him jurisdiction to set it aside. It would be a matter of merits rather than law. His intervention might be justified only where some defect appeared in the way the decision was reached. The Secretary of State's decision might, for example, have been based upon an incorrect understanding of his inspector's report, or the inspector may have misrecorded an important item of evidence.

This distinction between law and policy is a fundamental doctrine of judicial review. It is a well understood demarcation of power and responsibility. It is expressly incorporated into the legislation in the instances where a right of appeal or challenge is conferred. Thus, the scope of the reviewing powers of the High Court, in considering a challenge to the Secretary of State's decision on a planning appeal, is limited to questioning the validity of the decision on the grounds that the order is not within the powers of the Act, or that any of the relevant procedural requirements have not been complied with.[35] It is a formula which suggests a process of largely mechanical review of limited ambit.

But the reality is that the fundamental distinctions are neither precise nor immutable. The courts have over the past twenty years proceeded to carve out a broad area of jurisdiction for review. One aspect of this phenomenon, which has been touched upon already, has been the substantial extension of the "standing" rules so as to confer a power to challenge upon persons whose legal or proprietary rights are not necessarily at stake. In the accepted rhetoric, the standing rules have been "liberalised," and that expression has been used also to describe the broadening of the grounds of review. The movement towards increased judicial intervention tends to be portrayed as a progressive trend, and as a popular response to public uneasiness about large, unaccountable, bureaucratic structures. But little is understood about the impact of judicial scrutiny on the quality of government and administration. There is a danger that, as the different processes of government are opened up to public scrutiny, the forms of effective power shifts away from them and decisions continue to be taken away from the limelight. The steps in the process which have been exposed then tend to become empty formalities, carefully observed but meaningless. Time and effort may be required to make decisions "judge proof," without improving the quality of either the decision or the administrative justice involved.

It is equally true, however, that the official defence of traditional administrative methods has often been overstated and official fears have been proved unfounded in practice. Thus Dame Evelyn Sharp's arguments to the Franks Committee against publication of inspectors' reports were almost entirely based upon the wish to avoid any prospect of embarrassment. It would, she maintained, "make government impossible" if officials' recommendations were published.[36] But government continues, and although the

---

[35] T.C.P.A. 1971, s.245(1).
[36] *Evidence before the Committee on Administrative Tribunals and Inquiries* February 22, 23 1956; paras.616–618.

publication of inspectors' reports may have made it more difficult for the Secretary of State to justify taking an independent line on policy grounds, there are no signs that either he or the inspectorate have been embarrassed by any differences of opinion. What has happened instead is that the constitutional norm has altered, and political embarrassment is no longer the inevitable consequence of departmental disagreement.

The reforms which followed the Franks Committee's report have already been identified as establishing a strong new foundation for judicial review in planning.[37] They have been carried further by broad judicial interpretation, and two instances of this trend—interpretation of the statutory formula for challenge, and the requirement to give reasons—deserve further comment.

2. The Statutory Grounds of Challenge and the Ashbridge Doctrine

The formulae by which the powers of the court are defined in the case of statutory appeals and applications have been set out in the earlier pages of this chapter. In essence, on appeal from an enforcement notice determination or a determination under section 53, the appellant is limited to a "point of law"; whilst in the case of an application to quash a development plan or other orders, decisions or actions, the formula is twofold: whether the action is within the powers of the Act, or whether any of the relevant requirements of the Act or regulations have not been complied with.

The courts were initially hesitant in their interpretation of these grounds. Three members of the House of Lords in *Smith* v. *East Elloe Rural District Council*,[38] which involved a similar formula in the Acquisition of Land (Authorisation Procedure) Act 1946, took the view that to check whether action was "within the powers of the Act" involved an examination of whether, on the face of it, it went beyond what was authorised. The applicant might be permitted to show, for example, that the wrong procedure had been adopted or that some express statutory limitation had been breached. But he would not be permitted to go further, and to seek to show that there had been an underlying misuse of discretionary power, in the sense that the authority or the Minister had taken into account irrelevant considerations or been actuated by improper motives. Lord Reid thought that it would be a "strained and unnatural reading" of the language of the Act to extend it to review on these grounds.[39]

Nine years later, Lord Denning M.R. proceeded to reject the narrow construction and to embrace an interpretation which would allow the courts full scope under the statutory formulae in reviewing decision making. In *Webb* v. *Minister of Housing and Local Government*[40] he maintained that there had been "differing voices" in the House of Lords in the *East Elloe* case:

> "So differing that they give no clear guidance, or, at any rate, no guidance that binds us."

---

[37] *Ante*, p. 560.
[38] [1956] A.C. 736.
[39] *Ibid.* 763. Lords Morton of Henryton at 755 and Somervell at 772 agreed that there was no jurisdiction to intervene on the ground of bad faith under the statutory formula.
[40] [1965] 1 W.L.R. 775 at 770.

A few months later, in *Ashbridge Investments Ltd.* v. *Minister of Housing and Local Government*[41] he took the opportunity to break altogether with the narrow view, and offered an analysis of the scope of the statutory formula which has become the modern *locus classicus:*

> "The court can only interfere on the ground that the Minister has gone outside the powers of the Act or that any requirement of the Act has not been complied with. Under this section it seems to me that the court can interfere with the Minister's decision if he has acted on no evidence; or if he has come to a conclusion to which on the evidence he could not reasonably come; or if he has given a wrong interpretation to the words of the statute; or if he has taken into consideration matters which he ought not to have taken into account, or vice versa. It is identical with the position when the Court has power to interfere with the decision of a lower tribunal which has erred in point of law."

This reformulation derived not from any analysis of past decisions, but, as it later transpired, from a concession made by counsel for the Minister in the course of argument.[42] And although it has been adopted and followed in a number of subsequent cases, Lord Denning has continued to seek to confer greater legitimacy upon it. Thus in *R.* v. *Secretary of State for the Environment, ex parte Ostler*[43] he said of the *Ashbridge* doctrine:

> " . . . the Minister did not dispute it. It has been repeatedly followed in this Court ever since and never disputed by any Minister. So it is the accepted interpretation."

The different heads of review contained in the *Ashbridge* formula are analysed in greater detail below, but it is necessary first to consider the other major foundation of judicial review in planning, the duty to give reasons for decisions.

3. *The Duty to Give Reasons*

A formal duty to supply reasons for his decisions is imposed upon the Secretary of State by the Inquiries Procedure Rules.[44] It extends equally to decisions taken by inspectors in cases falling under the Rules,[45] but not to decisions made by written representations without the holding of an inquiry. Nor does it extend to inquiries not covered by the Rules. There is in those two instances, however, a duty to furnish a statement of reasons if so requested on or before the giving or notification of the decsion,[46] and it is

---

[41] [1965] 1 W.L.R. 1320 at 1326.

[42] It was, in Lord Denning's own (extra judicial) words, a "remarkable turn of events." "The one who did it—strange to relate—was the Minister himself, through his mouthpiece—the Treasury Devil;" Lord Denning, *The Discipline of Law* (Butterworths, 1979), p. 106.

[43] [1977] 1 Q.B. 122 at 133–134. Lord Denning's formulation in the *Ashbridge* case has since been adopted consistently in a number of cases at first instance (*Howard* v. *M.H.L.G.* (1967) 65 L.G.R. 257, *British Dredging Services Ltd.* v. *Secretary of State for Wales* [1975] 1 W.L.R. 687, *Seddon Properties Ltd.* v. *S.O.S.E.* (1978) 42 P. & C.R. 26 and by the Court of Appeal in *Coleen Properties Ltd.* v. *M.H.L.G.* [1971] 1 W.L.R. 433; *Gordondale Investments Ltd.* v. *S.O.S.E.* (1971) 23 P. & C.R. 334, *Eckersley* v. *S.O.S.E.* (1977) 34 P. & C.R. 124).

[44] T.C.P. (Inquiries Procedure) Rules 1974 (S.I. 1974 No. 419) r. 13(1).

[45] T.C.P. Appeals (Determination by Appointed Persons)(Inquiries Procedure) Rules 1974 (S.I. 420) r. 16(1).

[46] Tribunals and Inquiries Act 1971, s.12(1).

standard practice for the Secretary of State to provide reasons automatically.[47]

The duty to provide reasons is simple and unqualified. There is no express statement of the adequacy or cogency required, and the breadth of the formula has thus left to the courts a substantial area for interpretation. From the beginning they insisted that the requirement was something more than purely procedural, and that it imported a qualitative element. In *Givaudan & Co. Ltd.* v. *Minister of Housing and Local Government*[48] in 1966, the court quashed a decision where the Minister's decision letter had failed to identify clearly the "conclusions" it purported to adopt from the inspector's report, and had summarised parts of the report selectively and clumsily. The letter was therefore "so obscure, and would leave in the mind of an informed reader such real and substantial doubt as to the reasons for his decision and as to the matters which he did and did not take into account,"[49] that it did not comply with the duty to provide reasons.

The test of "real and substantial doubt" implies that a decision is not to be quashed for inadequate reasons if its inadequacies are capable of being overcome by some reasonable construction or deduction. It is not to be assumed, for example, that simply because some immaterial point is touched upon in the letter, that it necessarily influenced the decision. Nor, it is commonly asserted, is the decision letter to be read strictly, "like a statute or philosophical treatise"[50] or "hypercritically,"[51] but "fairly and tolerantly."[52] But supervision of the duty to give reasons is necessarily an exercise in inference and conjecture which requires the courts, under the guise of pursuing a point of law, to step further than ever into the arena of policy and fact. The question of the weight to be attached to a particular policy or fact, for example, is undoubtedly a matter for the inspector or Secretary of State alone. But if the decision letter shows that an "important" point of policy or fact has been overlooked, or misunderstood, or inadequately related to the decision taken then the courts may quash the decision. In doing so they have undoubtedly to consider points going to the adequacy of the material before the Secretary of State and his handling of it, in a way which raises issues of policy and merits. To require that the reasons should show that the Secretary of State has grappled with the "main" issues and dealt "adequately" with them[53] is to reserve to the courts the function of identifying what are and what are not the issues of importance, and how adequately they should be covered.

---

[47] In which case the reasons are reviewable as if they had been supplied pursuant to the statutory duty.

[48] [1967] 1 W.L.R. 250.

[49] *Ibid.* at 258, *per* Megaw J.

[50] *French Kier Developments Ltd.* v. *S.O.S.E.* [1977] J.P.L. 30, *per* Willis J.; and see further, in the context of planning appeals, *ante*, p. 596.

[51] *Sears Blok and Co.* v. *S.O.S.E.* (1980) 254 E.G. 1195 Lloyd J.; and *cf.* the comment by Forbes J. in *Millard* v. *S.O.S.E.* (1979) 254 E.G. 733: "There were moments during the argument in this case when I could see the shadow of angels dancing on pinpoints. But it is plain to me that that type of analytical examination of the Secretary of State's letter is alien to the procedure in the special paper on cases of this kind."

[52] *Preston B.C.* v. *S.O.S.E.* [1978] J.P.L. 548 at 551 *per* Slynn J.

[53] Applying the formula enunciated by Forbes J. in *French Kier Developments Ltd.* v. *S.O.S.E.* [1977] J.P.L. 311 at 313.

An example of the extent of judicial intervention under this head in recent years is *Thornville Properties Ltd.* v. *Secretary of State for the Environment*,[54] where the Secretary of State had overturned his inspector's recommendation that permission be granted, because he took the view that the inspector had "given insufficient consideration to the effect which the granting of planning permission now might have on the preparation of the district plan." That was, of course, a perfectly proper consideration to be taken into account, and as the decision letter indicated, the plan under preparation had still to go through further statutory stages, and modifications were possible. But in the High Court the decision was quashed. The Secretary of State, it was held, ought to have gone further and specified in what way the local plan would be prejudiced; and he should have said what it was in the local plan which might vitiate the inspector's conclusions, and more particularly, why. The effect of this ruling was to impose on the Secretary of State a duty to justify what was essentially a balance of policy, as to whether the grant of permission should precede the formal allocation of the site by the statutory plan and thereby pre-empt the debate on the plan.

The danger of pursuing too detailed an account of the Secretary of State's reasoning processes lies not ony in the obvious risk of the usurpation by the courts of his policy role, but also in the highly subjective nature of much planning decision making. The more subjective the decision itself, the more subjective tends to be the courts' analysis of the adequacy of the reasons advanced for it. It is often no more than a matter of overall impression whether adequate reasons have been given, and different judges often tend to have quite different impressions. The most outspoken disagreement between judges on the adequacy of ministerial reasons appears in *Bell and Colvill Ltd.* v. *Secretary of State for the Environment*[55] where Forbes J. announced that he "profoundly disagreed" with Sir Douglas Frank's interpretation of the Secretary of State's decision letter in *Niarchos (London) Ltd.* v *Secretary of State for the Environment*,[56] and suggested that "even a cursory glance" at the letter would have made it clear that the Secretary of State had taken into account the issue which the judge had held to have been overlooked.

The failure to give adequate reasons is in itself a ground for quashing a planning decision of the Secretary of State, but it is used just as frequently as a springboard for review under one of the traditional heads, such as the failure to have regard to a material consideration. There is a degree of overlap. If no mention of a particular consideration which appears to the court to have been material can be found in the decision letter, then either the Secretary of State has failed to have regard to it, or he has failed to give reasons for thinking it to be not material.

The main heads of review under the *Ashbridge* formula may now be analysed in greater detail.

4. The Grounds of Review

The grounds of review identified by Lord Denning in the *Ashbridge* formula were, in summary, that there should be at least some evidence to justify the

---

[54] [1981] J.P.L. 116.
[55] [1980] J.P.L. 823.
[56] (1978) 35 P. & C.R. 259.

Secretary of State's decision, that he should not act perversely, that he should not have misinterpreted the words of the statute and that he should not have overlooked any material considerations nor taken into account any immaterial considerations.[57] To that list there may be added the ground of the adequacy of compliance with the procedural requirements of the Act and regulations, and with the rules of natural justice (so far as applicable). The deliberate broadening, in the *Ashbridge* case, of the bare statutory grounds, brings the right of statutory challenge into line with those instances where the legislation confers a right of appeal on a "point of law," such as with enforcement appeals and section 53 appeals.

It also brings it largely into accord with the grounds for applications for judicial review by way of certiorari, although some anamalous differences remain.[58] The House of Lords decision in *Anisminic* v. *Foreign Compensation Commission*[59] in 1969 went some distance towards broadening the scope of certiorari by extending it to all errors of law, and not merely jurisdictional errors appearing on the face of the record. That development took some time to become fully appreciated, but it has survived two recent rulings by the Privy Council[60] and House of Lords.[61] Although they both restricted its applicability to inferior courts, the old distinction between jurisdictional and non-jurisdictional errors no longer governs judicial review of decisions by tribunals and public authorities. The impact of the *Anisminic* decision has been that:

" . . . the old distinction . . . was for practical purposes abolished. Any error of law that could be shown to have been made by them in the course of reaching their decision on matters of fact or of administrative policy would result in their having asked themselves the wrong question with the result that the decision they reached would be a nullity."[62]

There is therefore now also a broad area of review on applications for certiorari, and the courts have come to apply the same principles across the board in relation to ministerial decision making.[63]

In principle, the same criteria extend also to decision making by local planning authorities under their statutory discretionary powers. What is different is the machinery of decision making. There is no requirement to state the reasons for decisions, except in the case of a decision adverse to the applicant (who has in any event a statutory right of appeal)[64]; and there is therefore generally no carefully compiled "record" of the decision to grant or refuse planning permission, nor is it a decision necessarily based on

---

[57] For the full statement of the formula, see *ante*, p. 634.
[58] See generally de Smith's *Judicial Review of Administrative Action* (Sweet and Maxwell, 4th ed., 1980), pp. 404–408.
[59] [1969] 2 A.C. 147.
[60] *South East Asia Fire Bricks Sdn. Bhd.* v. *Non-Metallic Mineral Products Manufacturing Employees Union* [1981] A.C. 363.
[61] *In re A Company Ltd. (sub. nom. In re Racal Communications Ltd.* [1981] A.C. 374.
[62] *Ibid.* at 383, *per* Lord Diplock.
[63] See, *e.g. R.* v. *S.O.S.E., ex parte Hampshire C.C.* [1981] J.P.L. 47; *R.* v. *S.O.S.E., ex parte Powis* (1980) 42 P. & C.R. 73.
[64] Thereby normally excluding judicial review; but see *R.* v. *Hillingdon L.B.C., ex parte Royco Homes Ltd.* [1974] Q.B. 720, and *ante*, p. 624.

"evidence." Although there has been little direct judicial review as yet of local planning authority decisions, the courts have not apparently found this lack of formal and detailed documentation a barrier to review. Decisions have been questioned for error of law and for non-compliance with procedure, and regard has been had to committee resolutions and officers' reports in piecing together the background to the decision.[65]

(a) The no evidence rule

The first heading of the *Ashbridge* formula is the requirement that the decision of the inspector or the Secretary of State should have been based on at least some evidence. It is a requirement which ties in with the rule that he should not act perversely, and it also overlaps with the procedural requirements which confine him to the evidence adduced by the parties or on which they have had an opportunity to make representations. In *Wontner Smith and Co.* v. *Secretary of State for the Environment,*[66] for example, the inspector had refused permission for change of use to office premises from a warehouse use on the ground that the building could be used for light industry. Not only had neither of the parties relied on this ground, but there was no evidence upon which the inspector's decision could have been based.

Alternatively, the Secretary of State may have misdirected himself on the issues by, for example, selecting the wrong planning unit, and thereby coming to a conclusion which was not based upon sufficient evidence.[67] The question then is whether there is sufficient material before him and on which he could, directing himself properly in law, reach the conclusion which he did reach.

One area in which the rule plays an important part is where the inspector's recommendation is overturned by the Secretary of State. The post-inquiry procedure is governed by the Inquiries Procedure Rules which require that where there is a difference on a finding of fact or any new evidence or issue of fact leading the Secretary of State to disagree with an inspector's recommendation, it must be referred back to the parties.[68] The converse is that the matter need not be referred back in a case where the inspector's recommendation is overruled but the difference is one of government policy or planning opinion, or a different interpretation by the Secretary of State of the facts as found by the inspector. In that latter case the courts will insist that some evidence should exist to support the Secretary of State's decision. In *Coleen Properties Ltd.* v. *Minister of Housing and Local Government*[69] the Minister had overruled the inspector's recommendation that compulsory acquisition of a certain new building was not reasonably necessary for the satisfactory development of a clearance area. It was a question of fact, not of

---

[65] See, *e.g. R.* v. *North Hertfordshire D.C., ex parte Sullivan* [1981] J.P.L. 752 (error of law: no need to show that no reasonable authority could have reached the decision); *R.* v. *Hammersmith and Fulham L.B.C., ex parte People Before Profit Ltd.* [1981] J.P.L. 869.

[66] [1977] J.P.L. 103; and *cf Banks Horticultural Products Ltd.* v. *S.O.S.E.* [1980] J.P.L. 33 where with the agreement of the parties the inspector had sought further information on a central issue after the inquiry, but had not obtained the evidence necessary to support the conclusion he had come to.

[67] *Snook* v. *S.O.S.E.* (1975) 33 P. & C.R. 1; *Hilliard* v. *S.O.S.E.* [1978] J.P.L. 840.

[68] See further *ante*, pp. 592–595.

[69] [1971] 1 W.L.R. 433.

planning policy, and there was no evidence other than the opinion of the local authority, and nothing to indicate what kind of development would be "satisfactory development" of the area.

The rule has limited applicability to local planning authorities, because of their more loosely structured decision making procedures. They are not confined to the consideration of "evidence" as such, and it would be a difficult task to establish that no material existed, in any form to which the members of an authority could legitimately have regard, to support their decision. Such a case would more obviously fall under the second rule below, that the authority had acted perversely.

(b) Acting perversely

There is no power in the courts to quash decisions on the ground of unreasonableness, because that would involve a substantial usurpation of the executive function of government. The point may be reached, however, where a decision may be described as being so manifestly unreasonable, arbitrary, or perverse as to be outside the powers conferred by the Act. It is a rare case in which the substance of a decision will be so categorised by the courts, because it implies a condemnation of the action of the Secretary of State or the local planning authority going beyond that of a mere error of law.[70] It was said by Lord Greene M.R. in *Associated Provincial Picture Houses Ltd.* v. *Wednesbury Corporation*[71] to require "something overwhelming" to prove a case of that kind, but that qualification has not found full acceptance since. Instead, Lord Greene's comment that "if a decision on a competent matter is so unreasonable that no reasonable authority could ever have come to it, then the courts can interfere"[72] has been translated into the form of:

> " . . . if the court considers that no reasonable person in the position of the Secretary of State, properly directing himself on the relevant material, could have reached the decision that he did reach, the decision may be overturned."[73]

But the fact that the test still calls for a qualitative assessment, and that it is a question more of degree than of principle, means that it is more commonly employed as a longstop rather than as a primary ground of challenge.[74]

---

[70] A rare example is provided by *Backhouse* v. *Lambeth L.B.C.* (1972) 116 S.J. 802, where the authority in purported compliance with the requirement under the Housing Finance Act 1972 to achieve through rent increases a balance in their housing revenue account, raised the rent of a single vacant dwelling from £7 to over £18,000 per week.

[71] [1948] 1 K.B. 223, 230.

[72] *Ibid.*

[73] *Seddon Properties Ltd.* v. *S.O.S.E.* (1978) 42 P. & C.R. 26, *per* Forbes J.; and *cf. Emma Hotels Ltd.* v. *S.O.S.E.* [1979] J.P.L. 390; [1981] J.P.L. 283 where the Divisional Court twice disagreed with the Secretary of State's conclusions on the facts.

[74] In *Niarchos (London) Ltd.* v. *S.O.S.E.* (1978) 35 P. & C.R. 259 Sir Douglas Frank Q.C. (sitting as a deputy judge) ostensibly set aside a decision on the grounds of unreasonableness, but it is clear from a reading of the judgment that the true ground was that he believed the Secretary of State to have misdirected himself. In a subsequent instalment, *Niarchos (London) Ltd.* v. *S.O.S.E. (No.2)* [1981] J.P.L. 118 the Court of Appeal held the Secretary of State's decision to re-open the inquiry following the first judgment to be perverse on the facts before him, there being no sensible purpose which could be served in so doing.

(c) Misinterpretation

Error by the Secretary of State or local authority in interpreting the scope of their powers under the Act is a further ground of review. Again, there is substantial overlap. The error may have led to an unwarranted assumption of power, or conversely to a fettering of discretion; or it may have led to the taking into account of non-material considerations or have resulted in procedural error.

(d) Material and non-material considerations

The principle that planning decisions should be based upon "material considerations" is enshrined in the 1971 Act, but it is also a broader principle of administrative law that the exercise of a statutory discretion should be guided only by material considerations, and that all material considerations should be taken into account and all non-material considerations discarded. "Materiality" is by no means a fixed quantity, given the broad scope and imprecision of the Act, and there is considerable room for judicial intervention under this head.[75] But the courts have hesitated to be dogmatic, and for good reason. Their assessment of what has or has not influenced the taking of a particular decision and the extent of the influence is often purely inferential, and unless a decision can be said to be clearly based upon an irrelevant factor or has been taken in ignorance of some important factor, review under this head carries an aura of artificiality. Further, too rigid and generalised a classification of considerations into those which are capable of being material and those which are not is artificial. An example is the question of the relevance of the planning history of a site on an application for planning permission. The fact that permission already exists for some development on the site is clearly a relevant consideration in determining the new application, because the compatability of the two proposals is a matter of importance.[76] That question does not, however, arise if the former permission has expired at the time the new application is made. But it must be wrong to conclude from that, as did Sir Douglas Frank Q.C. in *Peak Park Joint Planning Board* v. *Secretary of State for the Environment*,[77] that the expired permission can no longer be a relevant consideration. It is a factor in the planning history of the site, and it indicates the development which the authority were previously prepared to permit there. Certainly, it ought not to carry the same weight and its legal implications ought not to be confused with those of an extant permission, but those are different questions from the issue of its "materiality," and there is a risk that by too ready a reliance upon this test the courts will intrude too far into questions of policy and the balance of relevant considerations.

(e) Procedural error and natural justice

The grounds upon which a decision may be challenged under sections 242 (development plans and orders) and 245 (other decisions and orders) of the

---

[75] See further *ante*, p. 282.
[76] See, *e.g. Spackman* v. *S.O.S.E.* [1977] 1 All E.R. 257; *Millard* v. *S.O.S.E.* (1979) 254 E.G. 733.
[77] [1979] J.P.L. 618. For other criticisms of this decision, see *ante*, p. 207 and also *South Oxfordshire D.C.* v. *S.O.S.E.* [1981] J.P.L. 359

1971 Act expressly include non-compliance with any requirement of the Act or regulations made under it, although in such a case the court may grant relief only if satisfied that the applicant's interests have been "substantially prejudiced."[78] In short, it must be a procedural error causing injustice. That is the essence, also, of a breach of the principles of natural justice. Although much of the procedure governing decision making by inspectors and by the Secretary of State is now prescribed in some detail by the Inquiries Procedure Rules, the rules of natural justice are not automatically excluded. Not only do they extend to those types of decision which are not yet regulated by Rules (where, in applying them, the courts are closely influenced by the procedural models of the Rules)[79]; but there are also some aspects of procedure which are touched upon only in very general terms by the Rules. On issues of procedure at an inquiry itself, for example, the courts have been prepared to identify additional requirements and safeguards under the rules of natural justice, including rights of cross-examination[80] and to inspection of documents.[81] "Substantial prejudice" is approached differently, in the sense that it is implicit in a finding that there has been a breach of the rules of natural justice that the applicant has been prejudiced, and the courts have therefore rejected the notion of a "technical" breach of the rules.[82]

(f) Conclusions

Although judicial review of the administration of planning is indirect, in the sense of being a supervisory rather than appellate function, there is greater scope for intervention than is often assumed. The criteria for review are flexible and subjective and they intermesh and overlap. The area of discretionary power remaining beyond the purview of the courts has diminished dramatically in the past 15 years, and the focus of judicial attention is now being shifted to the activities of local planning authorities as the standing of third parties to seek relief comes to be accepted. Historically, Professor McAuslan[83] is right to point to the competing ideologies which informed judicial review in planning as the forces of private property and the legitimacy of the "public interest." In the manner of its evolutionary development, and as evidenced by the legislation by which it is established, planning is a process of regulation of private property in the public interest. For the first 20 years or so of judicial review of planning, practically all the disputes adjudicated upon were between landowners and the local and central government agencies. There was no alternative expression of the public interest. But in more recent years those agencies have lost their

---

[78] See further *ante*, pp. 621–623.

[79] See, *e.g. Pollock* v. *S.O.S.E.* [1981] J.P.L. 420 (enforcement appeals procedure).

[80] See, *e.g. Nicholson* v. *Secretary of State for Energy* (1977) 76 L.G.R. 693; *Bushell* v. *S.O.S.E.* [1981] A.C. 75; although in neither case was the inquiry actually governed by any of the Inquiries Procedure Rules.

[81] *Performance Cars Ltd.* v. *S.O.S.E.* (1977) 34 P. & C.R. 92. And see, on post-inquiry procedure, *Thanet D.C.* v. *S.O.S.E.* [1978] J.P.L. 250; *Fairmount Investments Ltd.* v. *S.O.S.E.* [1976] 1 W.L.R. 1255.

[82] See, *e.g. Lake District Special Planning Board* v. *S.O.S.E.* [1975] J.P.L. 220; *George* v. *S.O.S.E.* (1979) 38 P. & C.R. 609.

[83] *The Ideologies of Planning Law, passim.*

monopoly, partly because of the move towards greater public participation in planning and partly because of the proliferation of well organised interest groups concerned with advancing particular causes or the interests of the inhabitants of an area. Representative democracy as the embodiment of the public interest has been partly supplanted, and it is this populist movement which has also helped strengthen the hand of the judiciary in reviewing governmental action. It has also altered the focus of review, which has moved from the arena of the property rights/public interest conflict to a debate as to the required standard of public administration owed to those affected, in the broadest sense, by planning decisions.

D. Late Challenge and the Privative Provisions

The primary remedy in British administrative law is the setting aside by the courts of the administrative action complained of as invalid, rather than the award of financial compensation. The timing of challenge is therefore critical, because more is at stake than potential monetary liability. Works may have been commenced, properties acquired and people displaced before any invalidating defect has been discovered. And so Parliament has sought to confer a status of unimpeachable validity on many planning decisions, by requiring that each of the three forms of statutory challenge available under the Act should be commenced only within a prescribed time, and that the validity of the decision may not "be questioned in any legal proceedings whatsoever."[84]

In the case of challenge to development plans and other orders, the prescribed period is six weeks from the date of the publication of the first notice of the approval or adoption of the plan or order.[85] The relevant provisions are examined in Chapter 3.[86] In enforcement cases, the exclusion is partial. The jurisdiction of the courts is supplanted by the powers vested in the Secretary of State but no further,[87] and there is a right to appeal on a point of law from the Secretary of State's decision within 28 days.[88] The scope of these provisions is examined in Chapter 9.[89]

In respect of the other decisions and action taken by the Secretary of State and falling within section 245 of the 1971 Act, the prescribed period is six weeks from the date on which the order is confirmed or the action taken, as the case may be.[90] Finally, in respect of challenge by way of application for judicial review, there is now a requirement that the application be made " . . . promptly, and in any event within three months from the date when the grounds for the application first arose."[91] In this case, however, unlike in the case of the statutory rights of challenge, there is power for the court to extend the time for good cause.

---

[84] T.C.P.A. 1971, ss.242(1), 243(1) (though note that in that case, enforcement notices, the word "legal" is omitted).
[85] *Ibid.* s.244(1),(3) and (4).
[86] *Ante,* pp.132–137, and see as to the scope of ss.242 and 244 *ante,* pp.612–614.
[87] *Ante,* p.614.
[88] T.C.P.A. 1971, s.246; R.S.C. Ord. 94, r.1; and see *ante,* p.615.
[89] *Ante,* pp.427–429.
[90] T.C.P.A. 1971, s.245(1).
[91] R.S.C. Ord. 53, r.4.

The absence of such a power under the legislative provisions means that relief is automatically and irretrievably excluded once the time has expired without challenge being made. In 1956 the House of Lords in *Smith* v. *East Elloe Rural District Council*[92] ruled that the provisions were effective even to prevent an action alleging bad faith on the part of the authority. The far-reaching later decision of the house of Lords in *Anisminic* v. *Foreign Compensation Commission*[93] was widely believed to have sabotaged statutory preclusive clauses altogether, by holding that a provision which prevented the questioning of validity of a determination of the Commission did not extend to a purported determination which was in fact a nullity. But there was arguably just sufficient by way of distinction between the two to allow the claims of administrative certainty to continue to prevail in planning and compulsory purchase cases. The Foreign Compensation Commission was a judicial rather than an administrative body, and the provision preventing the questioning of its decisions was absolute.

But the preclusive provisions under planning and other similar legislation relate to an administrative function with implications going beyond the interests simply of the parties directly involved; and the prohibition is partial rather than absolute. The courts have held, therefore, that the arguments in favour of securing long term certainty should prevail.

In *R.* v. *Secretary of State for the Environment, ex parte Ostler*,[94] the applicant alleged that a compulsory purchase order had been made and confirmed on the basis of a collusive agreement between the Department and a neighbouring landowner, which had come to his knowledge only some years later. The Court of Appeal distinguished the *Anisminic* decision and rejected his claim. Their decision is doubtless pragmatically correct, but it is doctrinally confusing in the light of *Anisminic.* All three members of the Court appeared to reserve the question of whether an order or decision amounting to a nullity, because of lack of jurisdiction on the part of the authority, might still be questioned outside time, but failed apparently to appreciate the breadth of the nullity concept as enunciated in *Anisminic.* The better view is the pragmatic one that all challenge outside the prescribed period should be regarded as statute barred, even though the consequence is that a nullity is converted into a valid and unimpeachable decision or order. In some cases where such a rule would cause injustice, it may be possible to mitigate it administratively by agreement or through the Parliamentary or Local Commissioners; or by seeking to revoke a grant of planning permission or ordering the discontinuance of an authorised use. But unless there is established a broader compensation entitlement for administrative malfeasance, there is no other prospect of late redress.

The preclusive provisions prevent only the questioning of the validity of decisions and orders, but they leave untouched the jurisdiction of the courts to interpret them and to determine their legal effect. The governing doctrine is that enunciated by Viscount Simonds in *Pyx Granite Ltd.* v. *Minister of Housing and Local Government*,[95] that:

[92] [1956] A.C. 736.
[93] [1969] 2 A.C. 147.
[94] [1977] Q.B. 122; and *cf Routh* v. *Reading Corporation* (1970) 217 E.G. 1337 and *Hamilton* v. *Secretary of State for Scotland*, 1972 S.L.T. 233.
[95] [1960] A.C. 260 at 286.

"It is a principle not by any means to be whittled down that the subject's recourse to Her Majesty's courts for the determination of his rights is not to be excluded except by clear words."

The House of Lords held in that case that there was jurisdiction in the courts to determine the question of whether planning permission was required for proposed development. Although the Act provided an alternative means of determining the question by way of (what is now) a section 53 determination, the jurisdiction of the courts to grant declaratory relief was not thereby restricted. That ruling remains effective today, despite the introduction of the direct right of appeal to the High Court against the Secretary of State's decision on a section 53 determination and the associated preclusive clause, because the two procedures are independent of each other. The only exemption to the liberal right of access to the courts carved out by *Pyx Granite* must be where declaratory proceedings are brought in an attempt directly or indirectly to circumvent the privative clause, by raising questions going to the validity of decisions already taken, or proposed to be taken in enforcement proceedings.[96]

---

[96] See, *e.g. Square Meals Frozen Foods Ltd.* v. *Dunstable B.C.* [1974] 1 W.L.R. 59, and see further *ante*, p.428.

Chapter 15

PLANNING, FINANCE AND COMPENSATION

A. Introduction

There is no more complex set of relationships in planning than those between planning control, finance and compensation. Regulation of land-use imposes costs on both the public and private sectors of the economy, but little is known of how those costs are distributed between the two sectors, or how they fall on landowners and developers. Apart from the administrative costs of the planning system, there are the costs of development delay occasioned by planning, and the costs to owners refused permission for development or prevented by planning intervention from continuing an existing use of their land. How far those costs should be left where they fall, and how far they should be recouped from compensation payments by the State is a dilemma that is central to every land-use planning system.

To insist that the State should compensate for every private cost occasioned by planning without allowing recoupment in turn through a betterment scheme, is to paralyse effective planning. That is evidenced by the experience in Britain under the pre-war legislation, which imposed heavy compensation liabilities on local authorities wishing to restrict development. The major advance made by the 1947 Act was to free the control of development from direct liability to compensate, and that principle remains largely intact today despite the dismantling in 1953 of the £300m. fund set up to meet compensation claims nationally and on a once-and-for-all basis.

The fundamental principle of British planning, therefore, is that no compensation is payable to landowners for planning restrictions imposed on the development of their land. To that rule there are some limited and largely anomalous exceptions, but the general idea that the costs of regulation of new development should fall where they are imposed has found general acceptance, largely because over a period the market has adjusted according-ly and without causing excessive hardship. Planning assumptions and expectations now govern land prices, and the unpredictability of a discretionary planning system has come to be seen as a risk inherent in land investment.

But the dividing line between regulation and compensation is drawn at the existing use of land. Restrictions may in general be imposed upon the carrying out of development without compensation, but not against the continuance of the existing use. Intervention by way of the modification or revocation of a planning permission, or by requiring the discontinuance of an existing use, carries with it liability to compensate. There has also been acceptance of the principle that the State should bear some of the costs imposed on private landowners by public sector development ("injurious affection") and the depreciatory effects of development proposals (planning blight).

In summary, the occasions on which compensation is now payable in respect of planning decisions is limited to three categories of case:

(1) Compensation payable in respect of planning restrictions limiting development: the cases falling under this head, which create an extremely restricted entitlement, are (a) claims in respect of unexpended development value, (b) loss of Eighth Schedule development rights and (c) purchase notices.

(2) Compensation payable in respect of direct intervention against a lawful use, or right of use, of land, such as the revocation or modification of a planning permission or other planning consent, the making of a discontinuance order or compulsory purchase order, or the unjustified service of a stop notice.

(3) Compensation payable in respect of the depreciatory effect, on the value of any interest in land, of public sector development proposals or the carrying out or use of public sector development on nearby land.

The details of these compensation entitlements are discussed in the following pages. In the majority of cases the procedures allow for the making of a straightforward claim to the local planning authority or public agency concerned, assessed in terms of the extent of the depreciation of the claimant's interest in land; or the value of the rights which are rendered unexercisable, plus, in the case of direct intervention entitlements, a sum in respect of any loss or damage occasioned by the intervention. In two cases, however, those of purchase notices and blight notices, compensation is secured indirectly by conferring on the claimant an entitlement to require the acquisition of his interest by the appropriate public authority, at a value which will normally be at least its current market value (in which case the procedures provide no compensation as such) but is often in excess of that value and sometimes by a substantial margin. This is because the compensation payable is that which is payable upon the compulsory acquisition of land, governed by the rules, including certain hypothetical assumptions as to development potential, of the Land Compensation Act 1961.

Overall, the compensation rules are poorly designed, and uneven in their application. Some are the unnecessary hangover from the original regulation/compensation structure of the 1947 Act, and have little practical relevance to the land market conditions of today. The impact of the compensation code on planning decisions is little understood, and there are defects in the administration of the provisions which require reform. Five main preliminary points call for further comment:

(1) Compensation entitlement is often uneven and arbitrary. In the case of blight notices and purchase notices, for example, entitlement is restricted in such a way as to ensure that the costs of regulation should fall on the landowner up to the point where that would cause undue hardship. That point is measured, in the case of purchase notice procedure, by the formula that the land must have become incapable of any reasonably beneficial use; and in the case of blight notices, that the owner should have been unable to sell except at a price substantially below unblighted value. Once that point of hardship is reached (and in each case the burden is on the claimant to establish that it has been reached) compensation is payable in full for the land at a value which may impose no cost at all on the claimant.

(2) Local authorities have rarely been in a position to buy environmental improvements by using the powers of direct intervention, and have often sought to minimise their compensation liability by reversing planning

decisions or bargaining with claimants in planning terms. They may grant planning permission for a development to which they object on planning terms, because of potential liability to a purchase notice if they refuse. Or they may grant permission for development on one site in return for agreement that a use on another site will be discontinued. Restrictions on public expenditure are liable to force authorities further into the market in this way.

(3) Except in cases involving the actual acquisition by the authority of a claimant's interest, the compensation provisions ignore entirely the impact of inflation on entitlements. The Lands Tribunal has held repeatedly that it has no power to award interest on compensation back to the date of claim but only from the date of its decision, and it has rejected attempts to disguise such claims as claims for the loss of use of the money or for interest on borrowing incurred by the claimant pending settlement.There are frequently lengthy delays in settling claims, and this is capable of diminishing substantially the real value of the compensation remedy.

(4) The provisions in general place the burden upon the claimant to establish entitlement to compensation and restrict entitlement to property owners. The only exception is in the case of the more recent entitlements under the Land Compensation Act 1973 where there has developed, with the assistance of the central and local ombudsmen, what is almost a fixed duty on the part of the responsible authority to notify individuals likely to be able to claim of their entitlement to do so.

(5) There is no direct relationship between the compensation (or "worsenment") provisions of the Act, and the land value taxation (or "betterment") provisions of the Development Land Tax Act 1976. The link between these two concepts was fundamental to the 1947 Act, but was severed by the Town and Country Planning Acts of 1953 and 1954. The consequence is that whilst the landowner who is refused permission for development has, in general, no compensation entitlement, the landowner who obtains permission is entitled to retain the enhanced development values accruing to the land except to the extent that they are liable to taxation. The redistributive effect of planning control is uneven and, by market criteria, arbitrary. Moreover, whilst development land tax is a national tax payable to the Exchequer, planning compensation is primarily a local liability, and there is thus no direct recoupment for compensation from the tax.

B. Compensation for Planning Restrictions

Compensation is payable for planning restrictions imposed upon land development in only three circumstances, which must today for various reasons be regarded as largely anachronistic. They have been overtaken by the passage of time, by inflation and by changes in the forward planning system, but they still have some impact. The three cases, in ascending order of practical importance, are:

(a) compensation in respect of the unexpended balance of development value of land;
(b) compensation for "non-new" development under the Eighth Schedule to the 1971 Act; and

(c) purchase notices in respect of land rendered incapable of any reasonably beneficial use.

1. *Compensation in Respect of the Unexpended Balance of Development Value*

The availability of compensation under this head is a hangover from the dismantling in 1953 of the financial machinery of the 1947 Act. The Town and Country Planning Act 1953 had restored development values in land by repealing the development charge formerly payable to the Central Land Board. Except in the case of land acquisition by local authorities, landowners able to develop were to be entitled to retain realised development values in full. It ought perhaps to have followed in the interests of equal treatment that landowners who were deprived of development rights should have been entitled to compensation for that loss, but the obvious consequence of such an entitlement would have been to paralyse effective development control in precisely the way planning authorities acting under the 1932 Act had been paralysed. That might have been avoided by meeting compensation claims nationally rather than locally, but the amounts likely to be involved were too substantial for the Government to contemplate.

A compromise resulted. Although the £300m. fund was to be disbanded, claims which had been lodged against the fund and accepted by the Central Land Board would be met, not by way of the once-and-for-all distribution originally proposed, but as a means of recompensing those claimants who subsequently were refused planning permission for development or had it granted subject to conditions. As Davies[1] has described it:

> "To have asked for one thing was now to be made the qualification for getting something different. The claims had been made on the central government, and it is true that they would still have to be met (if at all) by the central government. But they had been made in the light of development potentialities in 1948, yet would be met in respect of planning situations arising at any time in the future after 1954. They had been made in respect of the loss suffered by owners of land, yet would be met in respect of the value of the land itself. . . . [Compensation] is payable in accordance with the claim (if any) that the owner of the land saw fit to make in relation to the state of affairs which existed in 1948, to the way in which that claim was handled by him or on his behalf and by the Central Land Board, and to the Market values then prevailing."

The rough justice effected by the 1954 Act has diminished in importance with time, and although an entitlement to seek compensation remains in some cases, the disparity between today's development values and those of 1948 mean that the *quantum* of compensation payable is seldom likely to bear any relation to actual losses. Much of the land which had development potential in 1948 has now been developed and no compensation rights remain; and in the case of land which for planning reasons has not been developed, claims have in the majority of cases long since been submitted

---

[1] K. Davies, *Law of Compulsory Purchase and Compensation* (Butterworths, 3rd ed., 1978), p.325 and see also on this topic, Corfield and Carnwath, *Compulsory Acquisition and Compensation* (Butterworths 1978), Chap. 10.

and determined. Even in the remaining cases there may often be a better remedy available under the purchase notice procedures analysed later in this chapter.

The machinery for seeking compensation under this head need therefore be only broadly described. The general principle is that the owner of an interest in land is entitled to compensation in respect of a planning decision refusing planning permission for the carrying out of new development, or granting it conditionally,[2] but only if:

(a) the value of that interest is depreciated by that decision[3] (which implies that the decision must have defeated a legitimate expectation that development would be permitted);

(b) the refusal of permission does not relate to material change of use nor to advertisements[4];

(c) in the case of conditional permission, the conditions must be in respect of matters other than those relating to the conventional matters of design, layout, densities or access[5];

(d) the refusal of permission is not based on the ground of prematurity by reason of an existing deficiency in sewerage or water supply services (although a second refusal more than seven years later will qualify),[6] or unsuitability of the land due to liability to flooding or subsidence[7];

(e) there is no other planning permission available, nor an undertaking by the Secretary of State to grant permission, for any development of a residential, commercial or industrial character[8];

(f) there is in respect of the land an unexpended balance of established development value.[9]

The amount of original unexpended balance, if any, is ascertainable by application to the Secretary of State, who is obliged to supply a certificate.[10] The certificate may also indicate what subsequent events have served to reduce the original amount, which may include former payments of compensation,[11] increase in actual land value following the initiation of new development thereon,[12] or the compulsory acquisition of the land at some time since 1958 (in some cases earlier), which has the effect of extinguishing the compensation right.[13]

2. Compensation for "existing use" Development Restrictions

Compensation payable under this head is also explicable only in terms of the history of the financial provisions of the planning Acts. The Act of 1947

---

[2] T.C.P.A. 1971, s.146.
[3] Ibid. s.146(b).
[4] Ibid. s.147(1). In the case of advertisements, conditional grant of permission is also excluded.
[5] Ibid. s.147(2).
[6] Ibid. s.147(4).
[7] Ibid. s.147(5).
[8] Ibid. s.148.
[9] Ibid. s.146(a)
[10] Ibid. s.145.
[11] Ibid. s.140.
[12] Ibid. s.141.
[13] Ibid. ss.142, 143.

established a set of exemptions from the development charge, designed in terms of development tolerances. Development up to certain limits was deemed not to involve "development" at all for compensation and development charge purposes.[14] It was regarded as falling within the existing use of the land, but it still required planning permission unless deemed permission existed under the General Development Order. Refusal or conditional grant of permission could involve the planning authority in liability to compensate, because it constituted an interference with the existing use right. Although the development charge has long since been abolished, the distinction is preserved in the 1971 Act.

The situation now is that compensation is payable in respect of the refusal or imposition of conditions on a planning permission for any development prescribed by Part II of Schedule 8 to the 1971 Act (set out in Table 24), but the decision must be a decision of the Secretary of State on appeal or on the reference of the application to him, and not simply a first instance decision of the local planning authority.[15] If the Secretary of State has simply confirmed the planning authority's decision, the Act requires that the decision be treated as a decision of the local planning authority.[16] Much of the development in the Schedule is already permitted development under the General Development Order and no compensation is therefore payable, although where the permission had been taken away by an Article 4 Direction,[17] and an application later refused or granted conditionally, compensation would be available under these provisions. There is also a range of development in the Schedule which is not permitted development, such as the enlargement, improvement or alteration of *any* type of building (and not just dwelling-houses or factories) by up to one tenth. Unlike the development in Part I of the Schedule, the development does not extend to the rebuilding of an existing building. The owner is entitled, however, to have the value of the prospective development rights under both Part I and Part II of the Schedule reflected in the compensation payable upon the compulsory acquisition of his land,[18] and this includes inverse compulsory acquisition under a purchase notice.[19] This means that there may be a right to compensation upon the refusal or conditional grant of permission for rebuilding, where that decision renders the land incapable of any reasonably beneficial use; but there is no right to compensation under both heads.[20]

There is power for the Secretary of State, in granting conditional permission, to direct that any of the conditions regulating the design or external appearance of buildings, or the size or height of buildings, should be disregarded in whole or in part for the purposes of assessing compensation.[21] Such a direction, which may have the effect of destroying compensation entitlement altogether, is to be issued "having regard to the

---

[14] T.C.P.A. 1947, s.69 and Sched. 3.

[15] T.C.P.A. 1971, s.169(1).

[16] *Ibid.* s.290(4); though the sub-section is concerned only with references to "planning decisions," a term used only in the marginal note to s.169.

[17] *Ante*, p.179.

[18] Land Compensation Act 1961, s.15(3).

[19] *Post*, p.653.

[20] By virtue of s.169(8), no compensation is payable under that section where a purchase notice has served in respect of the interest concerned.

[21] T.C.P.A. 1971, s.169(4).

Table 24

Eighth Schedule Development

DEVELOPMENT NOT CONSTITUTING NEW DEVELOPMENT

PART I

DEVELOPMENT NOT RANKING FOR COMPENSATION UNDER S. 169

1. The carrying out of any of the following works, that is to say—
    (*a*) the rebuilding, as often as occasion may require, of any building which was in existence on the appointed day, or of any building which was in existence before that day but was destroyed or demolished after 7th January 1937, including the making good of war damage sustained by any such building;
    (*b*) the rebuilding, as often as occasion may require, of any building erected after the appointed day which was in existence at a material date;
    (*c*) the carrying out of works for the maintenance, improvement or other alteration of any building, being works which affect only the interior of the building, or which do not materially affect the external appearance of the building and (in either case) are works for making good war damage,
so long as (in the case of works falling within any of the preceding sub-paragraphs) the cubic content of the original building is not exceeded—
    (i) in the case of a dwellinghouse, by more than one-tenth or 1,750 cubic feet, whichever is the greater; and
    (ii) in any other case, by more than one-tenth.
2. The use as two or more separate dwellinghouses of any building which at a material date was used as a single dwellinghouse.

PART II

DEVELOPMENT RANKING FOR COMPENSATION UNDER S. 169

3. The enlargement, improvement or other alteration, as often as occasion may require, of any such building as is mentioned in paragraph 1 (*a*) or (*b*) of this Schedule, or any building substituted for such a building by the carrying out of any such operations as are mentioned in that paragraph, so long as the cubic content of the original building is not increased or exceeded—
    (*a*) in the case of a dwellinghouse, by more than one-tenth or 1,750 cubic feet, whichever is the greater; and
    (*b*) in any other case, by more than one-tenth.
4. The carrying out, on land which was used for the purposes of agriculture or forestry at a material date, of any building or other operations required for the purposes of that use, other than operations for the erection, enlargement, improvement or alteration of dwellinghouses or of buildings used for the purposes of market gardens, nursery grounds or timber yards or for other purposes not connected with general farming operations or with the cultivation or felling of trees.
5. The winning and working, on land held or occupied with land used for the purposes of agriculture, of any minerals reasonably required for the purposes of that use, including the fertilisation of the land so used and the maintenance, improvement or alteration of buildings or works thereon which are occupied or used for those purposes.
6. In the case of a building or other land which, at a material date, was used for a purpose falling within any general class specified in the Town and Country Planning

(Use Classes for Third Schedule Purposes) Order 1948, or which having been unoccupied on and at all times since the appointed day, was last used (otherwise than before 7th January 1937) for any such purpose, the use of that building or land for any other purpose falling within the same general class.

7. In the case of any building or other land which, at a material date, was in the occupation of a person by whom it was used as to part only for a particular purpose, the use for that purpose of any additional part of the building or land not exceeding one-tenth of the cubic content of the part of the building used for that purpose on the appointed day, or on the day thereafter when the building began to be so used, or, as the case may be, one-tenth of the area of the land so used on that day.

8. The deposit of waste materials or refuse in connection with the working of minerals, on any land comprised in a site which at a material date was being used for that purpose, so far as may be reasonably required in connection with the working of those minerals.

Note: Part III of the Schedule, which contains provisions governing its interpretation, is not reproduced here.

Source: Town and Country Planning Act 1971, Schedule 8

local circumstances," and the implication perhaps is that its purpose is to limit compensation payment in respect of conditions of a type required by local circumstances or commonly imposed in the area, such as the use of certain building materials in national parks, for example.

The compensation payable is the difference in value of the claimant's interest in land and the value if the permission had been granted, or had been granted unconditionally, as the case may be.[22] In assessing the value, regard must be had to any undertaking given by the Secretary of State to grant permission for some other development of the land in the event of an application being made in that behalf.[23] The power to give such an undertaking must be regarded as an exception to the general rule that the Secretary of State may not fetter the future exercise of a statutory discretion, but the dangers in terms of policy of committing himself in advance to approve a proposal which has not been advertised or considered by the local planning authority are obvious. The procedures are capable of overriding the safeguards in the handling and determination of applictions, many of which have evolved since the original enactment of the compensation provisions. An alternative course is for the Secretary of State actually to grant permission for development of a different type on the original application by reviewing the decision following the making of the claim for compensation, or alternatively at that stage issuing an undertaking to grant planning permission.[24] In this case, however, there is a requirement that the Secretary of State first notify his proposed direction to the claimant and the local planning authority, and if so required by either of them, afford them an opportunity to appear before and be heard by a person appointed by him for the purpose.[25]

---

[22] *Ibid.* s.169(2). The amount may be purely nominal: see, *e.g. Rendall* v. *Ealing L.B.C.* [1982] R.V.R. 162.
[23] *Ibid.* s.169(3)(*b*).
[24] *Ibid.* s.38.
[25] *Ibid.* s.39.

Compensation entitlement is also limited by restrictions introduced by the Town and Country Planning Act 1963, in response to fears that local planning authorities were issuing permissions for redevelopment proposals to which they were opposed on planning grounds, because of the potential compensation liability which a refusal might attract under the then compensation provisions. Modern building methods had made it possible for developers to exploit the ten per cent. cubic tolerance so as to provide an additional 40 per cent. or more of floor space,[26] thus overriding substantially the authority's plot ratio standards for the area. The effect of the 1963 Act, whose provisions are now incorporated into the 1971 Act,[27] was to introduce as a valuation assumption a gross floor space limit of eleven-tenths the gross floor space available in the original building[28]; and in the case of a building erected or rebuilt since July 1, 1948, again purely as a valuation assumption, to remove the ten per cent. cubic content tolerance and preclude the extension of a use of part of the building to a further part thereof (under para. 7 of the Schedule).[29]

Claims for compensation under these provisions are lodged with the local planning authority from whom the appeal or the reference was made and are payable by them, although they may be entitled to reimbursement from another authority if the Secretary of State so directs.[30]

3. *Purchase Notices*

The purchase notice procedure provides an indirect means of securing compensation for planning restrictions, by allowing the landowner to require the planning authority to acquire his interest in the land. It thus operates as a compensatory device only where the value that the authority are required to pay exceeds the market value of the site. This may occur because the planning assumptions upon which compensation assessment is based include the assumption that planning permission would be granted for Eighth Schedule development, and for development for which the land is allocated in the development plan. It is where the authority are not in fact prepared to permit such development to take place, and the land is "incapable of reasonably beneficial use in its existing state," that the purchase notice procedure becomes available.

(a) Background

The relevant provisions of the legislation are not only obscurely drafted, but difficult to apply rationally in modern market conditions. A brief explanation of their history is therefore required. The original purpose of the procedure was probably to provide a remedy to landowners whose land was identified in a development plan as needed by the local authority for a

---

[26] See further *London Employment, Housing: Land,* Cmnd. 1952 (1963); and *ante,* p.324; and O. Marriott, *The Property Boom* (1967) Chap. 4.

[27] T.C.P.A. 1971, s.278 and Sched. 18.

[28] *Ibid.* Sched. 18.

[29] *Ibid.* s.278(2).

[30] Local Government Act 1972, Sched. 16, para. 34 (as to London, see T.C.P.A. 1971, Sched. 3).

specific purpose.[31] The Government envisaged that there would be cases where permission for development and redevelopment would be refused by the authority because of the future proposals. The owner would have no right to require advance acquisition by the authority on that ground alone ("blight" notices were not introduced until 1959), and the land might still be capable of profitable use, unaffected by the authority's proposals. But the purchase notice procedure was to be available if the land had become "incapable of reasonably beneficial use," a phrase which an early draft of the legislation had qualified with the words "whether by reason of deterioration or obsolescence of buildings or the occurrence of war damage or otherwise."[32] Although the qualification was dropped, the original purpose of purchase notices is clear enough: they were precursors of blight notices, intended primarily to allow an owner to advance the acquisition of his land for the public purpose which was blocking his own development proposals required to secure a "beneficial" use for the land. The early ministerial decisions on purchase notices were concerned largely with war damaged premises, where permission had been refused on the ground that a larger scheme of comprehensive development was proposed.[33]

But two events changed the original purpose. First, the introduction of blight notice procedure in 1959, and the subsequent extension by the Land Compensation Act 1973 of the categories of land to which the procedures extended, meant that there was a more obvious remedy available in respect of plan reservations, and one under which the owner was not required to establish that the land was incapable of reasonably beneficial use. The economic test for blight notices was simply that the owner had been unable to sell his interest except "at a price substantially lower" than that which might have been available but for the plan designation.

Second, the restoration of development value in land in 1953, and the subsequent inflation in development value, has made the question of capability for reasonably beneficial use far more difficult and subjective to assess in economic terms. The new economic equation has meant that purchase notices are liable to be used today not only as a supplement to blight notices (in respect of sites and premises of a type or value which fall outside the blight notice descriptions) but also as a means of shifting the burden of an uneconomic site onto the local authority and where possible securing a high value for it, whether or not the condition of the land is the fault of the authority.

The planning assumptions which govern compensation assessment indicate that the use of the purchase notice procedure as a means of obtaining compensation is more valuable in three main cases:

[31] Site reservation was clearly the major purpose envisaged by the Minister in the Committee debate on the Bill in the House of Commons: *Official Report* Standing Committee D, cols.321–338 (March 11, 1947); and the earlier provisions of the 1932 Act were limited to land required for public open space: see further *Epsom and Ewell Corp.* v. *Streatham Property Co. Ltd.* [1949] Ch. 40.

[32] In the first draft of the Town and Country Planning (Scotland) Bill, but later amended in the House of Commons: *Hansard*, Vol. 439, cols.1925–1927 (July 7, 1947).

[33] See, *e.g.* ministerial decisions at [1952] J.P.L. 289 (imminent redevelopment of the area, which planning authority anxious not to prejudice: notice upheld); [1953] J.P.L. 643 (land allocated for public open space, and permanent storage usage not suitable: notice upheld); and *cf* [1967] J.P.L. 730 (war damaged houses, and redevelopment imminent: notice upheld), [1969] J.P.L. 239 (road proposals, land with uncertain future: notice upheld), [1976] J.P.L. 651 (two dilapidated lock-up garages, long term redevelopment proposals for the area).

1. Where the development proposed for the land falls within Schedule 8 (*ante*, p.651). This may be the case, for example, with a proposal to rebuild a property which has been destroyed or has deteriorated, because the value of such a right is deemed to be included in the value of the existing use of the property.[34] The valuation would therefore reflect the value of the land for that development, which may be substantially greater than, say, purely agricultural value in the case of a derelict country cottage.

2. Where the land is allocated for a beneficial use in the development plan, but the authority decline to grant permission for that use, perhaps by reason of the unsuitability of the particular site. The development plan assumption governs the compensation assessment.[35]

3. Where the land has a negative value by reason of some continuing liability, such as a liability to maintain an area of open space, and the landowner seeks to avoid liability by shifting the maintenance burden to the authority by means of a purchase notice.[36]

The list is by no means comprehensive, but it serves to illustrate the influences behind the use of purchase notices in the modern land market.

(b) "Reasonably beneficial use"

A purchase notice may be served where on an application[37] planning permission has been refused or granted conditionally, and the owner[38] of the land[39] claims that (1) the land has become incapable of reasonably beneficial use in its existing state; and (2) that, in the case of conditional permission, it cannot be rendered capable of reasonably beneficial use by the carrying out of development subject to these conditions; and (3) that in any case the land cannot be so rendered by the carrying out of any other development for which planning permission has been granted or for which the local planning authority or the Secretary of State has undertaken to grant permission.[40]

In determining the question of what is, or would be, a reasonably beneficial use, no account may be taken of any prospectve use which would involve the carrying out of new development[41] (that is, development not within the "existing use" development of Schedule 8). Development within the Schedule must be taken into account provided it can be undertaken without planning permission because it is part of the "existing state" of the land,[42]

---

[34] Land Compensation Act 1961, s.15(3).

[35] *Ibid.* ss.16–18.

[36] See, *e.g. Adams and Wade Ltd.* v. *M.H.L.G.* (1965) 18 P. & C.R. 60; though the case was partly superseded by later legislation: see further *post,* p.657.

[37] Thus a conditional deemed permission under a development order would not suffice.

[38] Which may be a freeholder, or under a building lease, a tenant: see the detailed analysis in the ministerial decision at [1980] J.P.L. 53. The Lands Tribunal has shown reluctance, for compensation purposes, to lift the corporate veil and to accept ownership by a subsidiary or associated company as sufficient, given that in these proceedings the claimants are the initiators of the compulsory purchase and in a position to put their house in order before serving a notice: *Rakusen Properties Ltd.* v. *Leeds C.C.* (1978) 37 P. & C.R. 315 L.T.

[39] That is, all the land which was the subject of the planning application: *Smart and Courtenay Dale Ltd.* v. *Dover R.D.C.* (1968) 19 P. & C.R. 408; *Wain* v. *Secretary of State for the Environment* [1981] J.P.L. 678.

[40] T.C.P.A. 1971, s.180(1). All the land included in the notice must be incapable of reasonably beneficial use: *Wain* v. *S.O.S.E.* [1982] J.P.L. 244 (C.A.).

[41] *Ibid.* s.180(2).

[42] *Brookdene Investments Ltd.* v. *M.H.L.G.* (1969) 21 P. & C.R. 545.

but excluding any prospect of increasing cubic capacity or floor space, or of extending the use of any part of the building under para. 7 of the Schedule.[43] Otherwise the extent to which Eighth Schedule rights may be taken into account in assessing reasonable capability for beneficial use is a matter of discretion for the Secretary of State.[44] Conditions imposed limiting the life of a planning permission if unimplemented and those deriving from office or industrial development certificates are to be disregarded.[45]

Apart from these points, the Act offers no guidance on interpretation of the formula, and its content is surprisingly vague. It is not, at the one extreme, a requirement that the land be quite incapable of any beneficial use; nor, at the other, is it a question simply of whether the land is of less use or substantially less use in its present state than if developed.[46] The question is one partly of economics, and partly of development expectations, and other considerations such as the past history of the site and its future prospects may set the economic context. The fact that the land may be worth £2,000 per acre in its present agricultural use, and £80,000 with permission for housing, is not a reason for saying that it is no longer capable of reasonably beneficial agricultural use; but it may be if, as a result of housing development in the area, the land is now too awkward in shape and cut off from other agricultural units to be able to be worked beneficially.[47] The land may be able to be rendered capable of beneficial use by investment in improvements, such as works of rehabilitation on buildings not requiring planning permission, or the setting up of a more intensive method of agriculture.[48] But the scale of investment required would need to be related to the likely profitability of the use, and also to the short term future of the land.

The problem in applying these criteria in practice is that the assessments are often necessarily arbitrary. Decisions of the Secretary of State show a willingness to allow decisions to be influenced by the different economic circumstances of individual owners,[49] and he has insisted generally that the previous history of the site is irrelevant to the question of its capability in its present state. He has taken the view that it is not incumbent on the owner of the land to show that it is the refusal of planning permission[50] that has caused the land to become incapable of reasonably beneficial use, and it may

---

[43] T.C.P.A. 1971, s.180(3), Sched. 18.

[44] *Brookdene Investments Ltd.* v. *M.H.L.G. (Supra).* The Secretary of State does not now, as a matter of policy, have regard to such development unless there is an actual permission, whether granted before or after the service of the purchase notice (see, *e.g.* [1981] J.P.L. 762), or an unequivocal undertaking to grant permission: see decisions at [1978] J.P.L. 194, 197 and 485; and M.H.L.G. Circular 26/69 Appendix 1, para. 6.

[45] T.C.P.A. 1971, s.180(4).

[46] *R.* v. *M.H.L.G., ex p. Chichester R.D.C.* [1960] 1 W.L.R. 587.

[47] See, *e.g.* decisions at [1967] J.P.L. 730 (site reserved as private open space: notice upheld); [1976] J.P.L. 647 (site physically unsuitable for agricultural use: notice upheld); [1973] J.P.L. 604 (no reasonable access available to owners, though being used by others for unauthorised grazing: notice upheld); but *cf.* [1977] J.P.L. 256 (wedges of agricultural land between residential sites, capable of beneficial use despite difficulties of topography and proximity of urban development); and [1976] J.P.L. 189 (land suitable for grazing capable of reasonably beneficial use).

[48] See, *e.g.* [1978] J.P.L. 486.

[49] See, *e.g.* [1978] J.P.L. 486, although not, in the event, upholding the notice.

[50] See, *e.g.* [1958] J.P.L. 897.

be no more than the owner's past neglect,[51] or his failure to plan his building scheme properly.[52]

The Secretary of State has identified the relevant factors as being:

" . . . the physical state of the land, its size, shape and surroundings, and the general pattern of uses in the area. A use of relatively low value may be reasonably beneficial if such a use is common for similar land in the neighbourhood: it may be possible for a small area of land in certain circumstances to be rendered capable of reasonably beneficial use by being used in conjunction with a wider area, provided, in most cases, that the wider area is owned by the owner or prospective owner of the purchase notice land. Profit may be a useful test in certain circumstances but the absence of profit is not necessarily material: the notion of reasonably beneficial use is not specifically identifiable with profit. It should be noted that a use which is reasonably beneficial to someone other than the owner or prospective owner of the land to which a purchase notice relates cannot be taken into account."[53]

But despite the apparent decisiveness of the criteria, their practical application is often quite uncertain. It is often fortuitous whether the server of the purchase notice owns or does not own other adjoining land,[54] or whether an adjoining owner has shown any interest in purchasing the land to use along with his holding.[55]

The extent to which the system might be used so as to impose land on authorities where development had been refused for good reason, is demonstrated by *Adams and Wade Ltd.* v. *Minister of Housing and Local Government*,[56] where developers succeeded in their attempt to require an authority to acquire land which had been deliberately preserved as amenity land for the developers' own housing estate. That ruling was overturned by legislation in 1968, but the new provisions have been given a restricted interpretation. They impose no restriction upon the service of a purchase notice in these circumstances, but they give the Secretary of State discretion to refuse to confirm a notice where the land has a restricted use by reason of a previous permission granted for a larger area, either on an application

---

[51] See, *e.g.* [1967] J.P.L. 491; and *cf. Leominster B.C.* v. *M.H.L.G.* (1971) 218 E.G. 1419. But the test is not satisfied if the condition of the land is due to unlawful activity, such as the carrying out of unauthorised development; *Purbeck D.C.* v. *S.O.S.E.* (1982) 263 E.G. 261.

[52] See, *e.g.* [1967] J.P.L. 299; upheld in *West Bromwich C.B.C.* v. *M.H.L.G.* (1968) 206 E.G. 1085.

[53] M.H.L.G. Circular 26/69, Appendix 1, para. 4.

[54] See, *e.g.* [1977] J.P.L. 749 (extent to which land could be used with other adjoining land had varied considerably since notice served, so to be considered on its own): [1972] J.P.L. 523 (land capable of being worked with adjoining land in same ownership).

[55] See, *e.g.* [1977] J.P.L. 750 (owner of adjoining property had offered to buy: notice not upheld); [1977] J.P.L. 44 (garden land capable of being used in conjunction with adjoining land, owner had made no attempt to sell: notice not upheld). In *Adams and Wade Ltd.* v. *M.H.L.G.* (1965) 18 P. & C.R. 60, Widgery J. expressed the view that "owner" might include prospective owners, but held that the Minister was not entitled to have regard to purely theoretical possibilities.

[56] (1965) 18 P. & C.R. 60. And *cf.* decision at [1969] J.P.L. 659: authority required to acquire a former clay pit filled to about 5 feet short of the general level of surrounding houses, where owners had failed to comply with condition requiring it to be landscaped and maintained as open space.

which contemplated that the part should not be developed or should be preserved or laid out in a particular way as amenity land, or granted subject to a condition to that effect.[57]

But three important limitations have emerged. First, the High Court in *Plymouth Corporation* v. *Secretary of State for the Environment*[58] insisted that the power arises only where all the land to which the purchase notice relates is land which has a restricted use by reason of the previous planning permission. The Court was unmoved by the suggestion that the provisions might now be avoided completely by a developer who deliberately omits land from his first application but includes it in the second. Next, the Secretary of State has taken the view that the power arises only where the restriction was imposed by the original planning permission, and not merely upon the approval of details.[59] This limitation is based upon too narrow a view of the function of outline permissions, and if the correct view is that the approval of details amounts to no more than the filling of gaps in the outline permission,[60] then the limitation cannot be supported. Its effect is to force local planning authorities to require an increasing amount of detail on an outline application in order to avoid later being required to take on and maintain the amenity land on an estate.

The third limitation is that the permission must have been implemented to the extent necessary to bring the relevant amenity land condition into play. In *Sheppard* v. *Secretary of State for the Environment*[61] a condition was capable of being interpreted as attaching to one part only of the development permitted, and there was no possibility now that that part would be carried out. It was held to be ineffective for the purposes of the Secretary of State's powers to decline to confirm a notice.

(c) Purchase notice procedure

Upon the service of a purchase notice,[62] the council are obliged within three months to notify the server either that they or another authority have agreed to comply with the notice, or that they are not willing to do so, for the reasons specified by them, and that they have transmitted a copy to the Secretary of State.[63] In such a case, the Secretary of State first exercises a preliminary jurisdiction, and considers whether to confirm the notice. His proposal is then notified to the parties,[64] and an opportunity given to them, if they wish, to appear before, and be heard by, a person appointed for the purpose. It is customary for the format of a "hearing," rather than a public local inquiry, to be employed in purchase notice cases; and the consequences

---

[57] T.C.P.A. 1971, s.184.

[58] [1972] 1 W.L.R. 1347; and *cf.* decision at [1978] J.P.L. 394.

[59] See, *e.g.* [1974] J.P.L. 38.

[60] *Inverclyde D.C.* v. *Secretary of State for Scotland* 1981 S.L.T. 26.

[61] (1974) 233 E.G. 1167.

[62] Which must be within 12 months of the decision to which it relates: Town and Country Planning General Regulations 1976 (S.I. 1976 No. 1419) reg. 14.

[63] T.C.P.A. 1971, s.181(1).

[64] There is a strict timetable by virtue of T.C.P.A. 1971, s.186, which requires that the notice shall be deemed to be confirmed unless the Secretary of State has granted, or directed the grant of, planning permission within nine months of the date of service of the notice, or six months from the date of receipt by him if that is sooner. The provisions do not apply, however, if his preliminary decision is not to confirm the notice and that is notified within the period: *Sheppard* v. *S.O.S.E.* (1974) 233 E.G. 1167.

are that the hearing need not be in public and that no orders as to costs may be made.

The only power available to the Secretary of State if he is not satisfied that the land is incapable of reasonably beneficial use, is to refuse to confirm the notice. If he is satisfied, however, there is a choice of powers:

(1) he may confirm the purchase notice without modification; or

(2) he may substitute another local authority or statutory undertaker as acquiring authority; for which the criterion is the "probable ultimate use of the land."[65] The power is exercised therefore only where the land is to be used for the functions of the other authority[66]; or

(3) he may, in lieu of confirming the purchase notice, grant planning permission for the development proposed in the application, or revoke or amend the relevant conditions so as to enable the land to be rendered capable of reasonably beneficial use[67]; or he may direct that permission be granted for other development in the event of an appliction being made in that behalf, so as to render the land, or any part of it, capable of reasonably beneficial use within a reasonable time.[68] The power to direct that permission be granted in respect of part only of the land confers on the Secretary of State a discretion to confirm the purchase notice in respect of part only of the land, and direct the grant of permission for the remainder. But before the discretion arises, he must be satisfied that all the land is incapable of reasonably beneficial use, and not merely rely upon this power to confirm the notice in part where part only of the land satisfies the test[69]; or

(4) he may decline to confirm the notice where the land has a restricted use as amenity land by virtue of a previous planning permission, and it appears to him that the land ought to remain undeveloped or preserved or laid out as amenity land in accordance with that previous permission.[70] The limits subsequently established to this power to decline to confirm a notice have already been noted,[71] and it should be noted also that it is a discretionary provision.[72]

Upon the confirmation of a purchase notice, or its acceptance by the local authority, the authority are deemed to be authorised to acquire the owner's interest compulsorily, and to have served a notice to treat.[73] That relationship does not mean that there is a binding contract of sale between the parties,[74] but it allows either side to require that compensation be

---

[65] *Ibid.* s.183(4). He may not make such a substitution without first offering a hearing to the other authority: *Ealing B.C.* v. *M.H.L.G.* [1952] Ch. 856.

[66] M.H.L.G. Circular 26/69, Appendix 1, para. 11.

[67] T.C.P.A. 1971, s.183(2).

[68] *Ibid.* s.183(3).

[69] *Wain* v. *S.O.S.E.* [1982] J.P.L. 244 (C.A.). *Cf.* the express power to confirm in part only in the case of listed building purchase notices: T.C.P.A. 1971, Sched. 19, para. 2(1).

[70] T.C.P.A. 1971, s.184. The provisions do not apply to a purchase notice served before the 1968 Act: *Hoddesdon R.D.C.* v. *S.O.S.E.* (1971) 115 S.J. 187.

[71] *Ante*, p.657.

[72] See, *e.g.* decision at [1974] J.P.L. 158, where the Secretary of State confirmed a notice despite being satisfied of the grounds under s.184, because the land was required for future highway use.

[73] T.C.P.A. 1971, s.181(2)(notice to treat as at date council notify owner of acceptance of notice); s.186(1)(as at date specified by Secretary of State).

[74] *I.R.C.* v. *Metrolands (Property Finance) Ltd.* [1981] 1 W.L.R. 637; [1982] 1 W.L.R. 341 (H.L.).

determined and thus create a contract of sale.[75] The deemed notice to treat may not be withdrawn by the authority.[76]

(d) Valuation and compensation

Compensation under a purchase notice is paid in respect of the value of the land as assessed in accordance with the Land Compensation Act 1961, rather than directly as compensation for the depreciation of the value of the owner's interest in the land. The valuation rules of the 1961 Act establish market value as the basis for compensation, but allow that amount to be increased or decreased in certain cases. Their effect on purchase notice acquisitions may broadly be summarised as follows. Where the purpose to which the land is devoted is one for which there is no general demand or market, compensation may be assessed instead on the basis of the reasonable cost of equivalent reinstatement.[77] And where the value of the land is diminished by reason of the scheme underlying the acquisition, that decrease is to be ignored.[78] A planning condition on a previous permission reserving land for some future purpose does not amount to a "scheme" for these purposes,[79] but redevelopment proposals for the area may. The benefit of planning permission for development may be assumed in respect of development for which the land is allocated in a development plan[80]; or, if there is no appropriate allocation, for development certified by the authority as being appropriate for the land if it were not being acquired.[81] Finally, the benefit of permission for Eighth Schedule development may be assumed.[82]

(e) Purchase notices in special cases

A purchase notice may also be served where the owner claims that his land has become incapable of reasonably beneficial use because of the service of an order revoking or modifying an existing planning permission[83]; a discontinuance order[84]; an order revoking or modifying a listed building consent,[85] or a refusal or conditional grant of listed building consent.[86] The use of the procedure in the first three cases is uncommon, because there is provision already for the payment of compensation in respect of abortive expenditure and other loss or damage directly attributable to the making of the relevant orders, or depreciation and disturbance compensation in the case of discontinuance orders.[87] In the case of refusal or conditional grant of

---

[75] Under the Compulsory Purchase Act 1965, ss.5 and 6.

[76] T.C.P.A. 1971, s.208.

[77] Land Compensation Act 1961, s.5, r. 6. For a discussion of the valuation principles, see *M.E.P.C. Housing Limited* v. *East Sussex C.C.* [1982] R.V.R. 158.

[78] *Pointe Gourde Quarrying and Transport Co. Ltd.* v. *Sub-Intendent of Crown Lands* [1947] A.C. 565.

[79] *Birmingham D.C.* v. *Morris and Jacombs Ltd.* (1976) 33 P. & C.R. 27.

[80] Land Compensation Act 1961, s.16.

[81] *Ibid.* s.17; and see *Hoveringham Gravels Ltd.* v. *Chiltern D.C.* (1977) 76 L.G.R. 533.

[82] *Ibid.* s.15(3), though subject to certain exceptions in subs.(4). The right must be one which would be actually exercisable and not abandoned or overtaken by other permission: Vol. 4 *Lands Tribunal Cases*, case 10 (1976).

[83] T.C.P.A. 1971, s.188.

[84] *Ibid.* s.189.

[85] *Ibid.* s.190(1); Sched. 11.

[86] *Ibid.* s.190(1).

[87] *Ibid.* ss.164, 170 and 172.

listed building consent,[88] (including where such consent is required for non-listed buildings in conservation areas),[89] use of the purchase notice procedure is more common, and the assumption that listed building consent would be granted for works other than those for which consent has already been refused,[90] may involve the authority in compensation liability exceeding market value. Moreover, the usual provisions allowing a local planning authority to seek a direction for minimum compensation in the case of a building deliberately left derelict do not apply to purchase notice procedure, which supersedes the earlier compulsory purchase stages at which such a direction may be made.[91] But if a repairs notice in respect of the listed building has already been served by the local planning authority, no purchase notice may be served within the following three months.[92] If the authority have commenced compulsory purchase proceedings in that time, the bar continues until their discontinuance.

A listed building purchase notice must be served on the district planning authority (or London Borough) within twelve months of the date of the decision it relates to.[93]

C. Compensation in respect of direct intervention

The costs of compensation mean that the powers of direct intervention against existing uses have been seldom used in practice. Authorities have been forced to secure environmental improvements largely through their controls over new development, and taking advantage of their powers to obtain fortuitous improvements on existing uses by way of planning conditions or negotiated agreements, as and when applications for related development are made.

The burden of compensation in minerals cases in particular has caused difficulties, because of the pressing need to prescribe improved environmental standards for long term extraction taking place often under permissions granted many years ago in the most rudimentary form. Acceptance by the extraction industry of the Stevens Committee's[94] recommendation that a proportion of such costs should be borne by operators themselves has now been reflected in the Town and Country Planning (Minerals) Act 1981. The Act modifies the usual compensation provisions in respect of minerals orders, and these provisions are discussed separately in Chapter 11.[95]

---

[88] Compensation is payable under s.171 only for refusal or conditional consent in respect of works not constituting development or enjoying deemed permission, but still requiring listed building consent

[89] By virtue of T.C.P.A. 1971, s.277A(8).

[90] T.C.P.A. 1971, s.116. Since the Town and Country Amenities Act 1974, s.6, the assumption no longer extends to the demolition of the building, except for the purposes of Eighth Schedule development.

[91] T.C.P.A., s.190, Sched. 19, para. 1(2), by virtue of which confirmation or acceptance of a listed building purchase notice is deemed to authorise the acquisition compulsorily under s.114, and there is deemed notice to treat from that time. Under s.114 a direction for minimum compensation may be made only at the earlier stage of making the compulsory purchase order.

[92] T.C.P.A., s.180(5) and (6).

[93] Town and Country Planning (Listed Buildings and Buildings in Conservation Areas) Regulations 1977 (S.I. 1977 No. 228) reg. 7.

[94] *Planning Control over Mineral Working* (H.M.S.O., 1976).

[95] *Ante,* p.496.

The main cases of compensation for direct intervention are considered below. Contingent compensation for the use of stop notices, which generally becomes payable only in the event of the enforcement notice allegations proving false or the procedures defective, is discussed in Chapter 9 above.[96]

1. *Modification or Revocation of Planning Permission*

The formula for compensation assessment in the case of revocation and modification orders has two limbs. Compensation is payable to any person interested in the land in respect of any expenditure incurred in carrying out work which is rendered abortive by the revocation or modification, which includes the preparation of plans for the purposes of any work and other similar preparatory matters.[97] Otherwise no work carried out before the grant of the planning permission may be included in the claim.[98] The second limb encompasses any other loss or expenditure sustained which is directly attributable to the revocation or modificaion. That formula is broad enough to include depreciation in the value of land,[99] whenever occurring, and any other loss or damage provided it does not arise out of anything done or omitted to be done before the grant of the permission.[1] "Directly attributable" suggests a close causal link, but provided it is established the measure of loss may include loss of anticipated future business profits likely under a specific contract, subject to any appropriate deferment.[2] But anticipated profits of a business yet to be established are too remote a head of claim.[3] In assessing compensation the Lands Tribunal have declined to award any sum in respect of interest pre-dating the date of award, on the grounds that this would constitute a loss arising not from the order itself but from the failure to pay compensation money immediately.[4]

Notice of any compensation paid under these provisions is registrable as a local land charge,[5] and the compensation may subsequently be repayable, to the extent that it is awarded in respect of depreciation of the value of an interest in the land, if new development is carried out on the land.[6]

---

[96] *Ante*, p.425.

[97] T.C.P.A. 1971, s. 164(1)(*a*) and (2). In *Pennine Raceway Ltd.* v. *Kirklees M.B.C., The Times*, June 9, 1982, the Court of Appeal held that a company who had rights as licensee rather than as owners of an interest in the land, were nonetheless "interested" and entitled to claim compensation.

[98] *Ibid.* s.164(3).

[99] And the Lands Tribunal has expressed the view that the *Pointe Gourde* principle (*supra*, note 78) is applicable to such a claim: *Loromah Estates Ltd.* v. *Haringey L.B.C.* (1978) 38 P. & C.R. 234. In calculating the extent of depreciation, it is to be assumed that planning permission would be granted for Schedule 8 development (s.164(4)), and that is "an exclusive definition" of what assumption is to be made, overriding the fact that the building has been listed since the granting of the permission: *Burlin* v. *Manchester C.C.* (1976) Vol. 4 of the *Lands Tribunal Cases*, case 11.

[1] *Ibid.* s.164(1)(*b*) and (3).

[2] *Hobbs (Quarries) Ltd.* v. *Somerset C.C.* (1975) 30 P. & C.R. 286 (L.T.): loss of profits of £0.25m. on motorway contract which would almost certainly have been awarded to the claimants, reduced to take account of corporation tax liability on lost profits.

[3] *Hanford* v. *Oxfordshire C.C.* (1952) 2 P. & C.R. 358; *Evans* v. *Cheshire C.C.* (1952) 3 P. & C.R. 50.

[4] *Loromah Estates Ltd.* v. *Haringey L.B.C.* (1978) 38 P. & C.R. 234.

[5] T.C.P.A. 1971, s.158 as applied by s.166(5) in respect of compensation exceeding £20.

[6] *Ibid.* ss.159 and 160, as applied by s.168.

The compensation liability rests with the local planning authority who made the order, except that in the case of revocation or modification of a permission by the Secretary of State the liability rests with the local planning authority who granted the permission concerned.[7] There is in these arrangements a potential financial sanction which may be used against district planning authorities who are determined to grant planning permission in breach of structure plan policy and against the representations of the county authority.

2. Discontinuance Orders

Compensation in the case of discontinuance orders is assessed according to a different formula. It is payable not only to persons who have suffered damage by depreciation of the value of an interest in the land to which they are entitled, but also to "any person" for damage in consequence of being disturbed in his enjoyment of the land.[8] Further, any person who carries out any works in compliance with the order is entitled to recover expenses reasonably incurred by him in doing so.[9] Compensation is not therefore in this case limited to those whose occupation is by virtue of ownership of an interest.

A use which is required to be discontinued, or continued subject to conditions, under an order to which these provisions relate, may be lawful or unlawful; and if the latter, may be either immune or still liable to enforcement action. There is no distinction drawn between these categories for the purposes of compensation assessment, (unlike where land has been compulsorily acquired, where the value of an unlawful use may have to be disregarded)[10] except to the extent that the different status may be reflected in the land value. The fact that a use may be unlawful but immune should not in itself preclude the payment of compensation, because the benefit of such immunity is capable of enjoyment by successors in title, and therefore of influencing the value of the land.[11] But it would be a curious result if an authority were to be required to pay compensation in respect of a use against which enforcement action might still be taken. Compensation may reflect commitment entered into by the claimant after the service of the order but before its confirmation[12]; but there is no claim in respect of loss of use of the compensation money from the date of confirmation.[13]

3. Refusal or Conditional Grant of Listed Building Consent

The listing of a building has an immediate effect upon the existing rights of the owner, in that there he may no longer carry out works not requiring

---

[7] Local Government Act 1972, Sched. 16, para. 34.

[8] T.C.P.A. 1971, s.170(1).

[9] *Ibid.* s.170(2). By virtue of subs.(3), compensation is to be reduced by the value to the claimant of any timber, apparatus or other materials removed for the purpose of complying with the order. The purpose, presumably, is to prevent double compensation payment.

[10] Land Compensation Act 1961, s.5, rule 4.

[11] *K. & B. Metals Ltd.* v. *Birmingham C.C.* (1976) 33 P. & C.R. 135 (L.T.).

[12] *Hobbs (Quarries) Ltd.* v. *Somerset C.C.* (1975) 30 P. & C.R. 286 (L.T.).

[13] Uncertainty as to the true scope of established user rights, which would depress the price a purchaser would be prepared to pay, may reduce the *quantum* of compensation: *Blow* v. *Norfolk C.C.* [1967] 1 W.L.R. 1280.

planning permission if listed building consent would be required. If listed building consent for alteration or extension is then refused or granted conditionally, by the Secretary of State on appeal or on reference, there is an entitlement to compensation to the extent of the difference between the value of the interest in the land and its value if consent had been granted, or granted unconditionally, as the case may be.[14] But no compensation is available where consent is refused for demolition, and the provisions do not therefore extend to non-listed buildings in conservation areas, where control is limited to demolition.[15]

Where the listing of a building has been preceded by the service of a building preservation notice, the refusal or conditional grant of listed building consent during the period of the notice may form the basis for a claim under the above provisions, once the listing has taken place.[16] But if the building is not then listed, compensation is payable by the authority whether or not any application for listed building consent was made, "in respect of any loss or damage directly attributable to the effect of the notice."[17]

4. Tree Preservation

Compensation is payable, under the terms of the prescribed Model Tree Preservation Order, in respect of loss or damage suffered in consequence of any refusal (including revocation or modification), or conditional grant, of consent under the Order,[18] except in the case of trees where the authority certify that they are satisfied that the refusal or condition is in the interests of good forestry, or that the trees (other than woodlands) have an outstanding or special amenity value.[19]

There is also entitlement to compensation in respect of any direction issued under a tree preservation order, by a local planning authority or the Secretary of State, for the replanting of all or any part of a woodland area felled in the course of forestry operations permitted by or under the Order.[20] Liability to compensate arises where the Forestry Commissioners decide not to make any advance for replanting, on the grounds that the direction frustrates the use of the woodland area for the growing of timber or other forest products for commercial purposes and in accordance with good forestry practice.[21]

5. Advertisements

Compensation for advertisement control is limited to cases where the local planning authority require the removal of any advertisement which was

---

[14] T.C.P.A. 1971, s.171.
[15] T.C.P.A. 1971, s.277A.
[16] T.C.P.A. 1971, s.173(2).
[17] *Ibid.* s.173(3). By subs.(4), entitlement is extended to include any sum payable in respect of a breach of contract, caused by the need to countermand or discontinue works to the building.
[18] Town and Country Planning (Tree Preservation Order) Regulations 1969 (S.I. 1969 No. 17), Schedule, art.9.
[19] *Ibid.* art 5.
[20] T.C.P.A., s.175.
[21] *Ibid.* s.175(2).

being displayed on August 1, 1948, or the discontinuance of that use on a site used for that purpose at that date.[22]

D. Compensation for the depreciatory effects of public sector development proposals: Planning Blight

1. *Introduction*

Planning blight is the product of uncertainty and delay in decision making, and in plan implementation. Proposals for public sector development or redevelopment, even at a tentative stage, tend to lead quickly to a withdrawal of private sector investment in the area. Land and premises become unsaleable, except at a much reduced price, because few purchasers are interested in acquiring an interest of uncertain duration. The prospect of compulsory purchase and demolition is a disincentive to investment in improvement and maintenance of buildings, and the consequence is that there is an acceleration of the physical decline of the area. As more and more buildings become vacant and dilapidated, so the prophecy of comprehensive redevelopment becomes self-fulfilling as the only possible cure for the prevailing conditions, and market values for existing uses plunge further. Planning permission for individual development and grant-aid for housing improvement are both likely to be refused by the local authority, and land becomes sterilised until the implementation of the plan can commence. Delays in implementation are in turn liable to be exacerbated by uncertainty in long term public expenditure planning.

The introduction of the post-war planning system increased substantially the problem of planning blight, because for the first time authorities were required to identify in their development plans the sites to be reserved for future public sector requirements. The early Development Plan Regulations required, in particular, precise details to be shown on special designation maps of land allocated for the purposes of any functions of a Minister, local authority or statutory undertaker, and of land comprised in, or contiguous or adjacent to, a comprehensive development area.[23]

These designations in turn were subject to challenge and argument at development plan inquiries, and uncertainty about the future of the area might continue for several years before any final planning decision was taken. The problem had been partially foreseen in the 1947 Act, and provision was made for landowners to serve a purchase notice on the planning authority requiring them to acquire land where planning permission was not forthcoming for development. But the statutory criterion was narrow. The land had to have become incapable of reasonably beneficial use,[24] and it was insufficient merely that its market value had declined as a result of blight.

By 1959, the public costs which were being imposed on private owners by planning blight had been recognised, and the Town and Country Planning

---

[22] *Ibid.* s.176. As to compensation for the revocation or modification of consent to display advertisements, see Town and Country Planning (Control of Advertisements) Regulations 1969 (S.I. 1969 No. 1532), reg. 24.

[23] Town and Country Planning (Development Plans) Regulations 1948 (S.I. 1948 No. 1767) reg. 8 and Sched. 1, Pt.V.

[24] *Ante*, p.655.

Act of that year introduced a new blight notice procedure, modelled on the purchase notice provisions but broader in scope. The entitlement provisions were further broadened by the Land Compensation Act 1973, in response to the recommendations of the Urban Motorways Committee[25] that more of the burden of environmental cost of highways development should be shifted from private landowners to the public sector.

The purpose of the blight notice procedure is to enable certain categories of landowner to advance the acquisition of their property by requiring authorities to purchase it. The procedure is that a blight notice is served on the appropriate authority[26] (being the body by whom the land is liable to be acquired),[27] who may then within two months object on one or more prescribed grounds by serving a counter-notice.[28] The claimant may then, within two months, require the authority's objection to be referred to the Lands Tribunal for determination.[29] If the notice is upheld, or if no counter notice has been served, the authority are deemed to be authorised to acquire compulsorily the claimant's interest, and to have served a notice to treat.[30] The categories of entitlement to serve blight notices, and the prescribed grounds of objection, are analysed below.

It can be seen that the blight notice procedures offer no remedy to the phenomenon of planning blight, except indirectly by forcing authorities to accept financial responsibility at an earlier stage for their proposals. The purpose is to relieve individual cases of hardship rather than to lift the blight, and the effect of advance acquisitions often is to promote further decay as buildings are vacated and demolished on a piecemeal basis. The precision formerly required of development plan allocations has now gone, however, and one of the reasons for adopting purely diagrammatic maps in structure plans was the wish to avoid planning blight. In preparing local plans, authorities have been urged to restrict site-specific development proposals to those which they reasonably expect will be started within a reasonable period, normally not more than ten years away.[31]

But despite these changes, blight remains an inevitable consequence in a planning system which properly provides for public and accountable decision making, and which not only discourages but often actually prevents any development or improvement from taking place in the area in the interim period.

2. Persons Entitled to Serve a Blight Notice

The right to serve a blight notice is limited to the owner-occupiers of certain categories of land (see under 3 below) and their personal representatives.[32]

---

[25] New Roads in Towns.Report by the Urban Motorways Committee, (H.M.S.O., 1971); and see also the Report of the Urban Motorways Project Team (H.M.S.O., 1973) Pt. IV. The Government's proposals behind the 1973 Act are sketched out in the White Paper, Development and Compensation—Putting People First, Cmnd. 5124 H.M.S.O. (1972).

[26] T.C.P.A. 1971, s.193. The forms for notices are prescribed by the Town and Country Planning General Regulations 1976 (S.I. 1976 No. 1419).

[27] Ibid. s.205.   [29] Ibid. s.195.

[28] Ibid. s.194.   [30] Ibid. s.196.

[31] Memorandum, D.O.E. Circular 4/79, para. 3.35.

[32] Land Compensation Act 1973 (hereafter L.C.A. 1973), s.78. The pre-conditions are that the deceased person should have been entitled to an interest in the land at his death, qualifying for blight notice protection; that the personal representative has made reasonable endeavours to sell it but has failed to find a price other than one substantially below "unblighted" value, and that one or more persons are beneficially entitled to the interest.

In the case of dwelling-houses, they must be *resident* owner-occupiers of the hereditament concerned[33]; and, in the case of business premises, owner-occupiers of premises with an annual value not exceeding £2,250.[34] Qualifying interests in agricultural units are also only those of owner-occupier.[35] Entitlement is also extended to mortgagees exercising their power of sale.[36]

From the outset the Government have proved reluctant to extend entitlement to the whole range of investment properties and to the more valuable commercial and industrial properties, because of the assumed capacity of larger organisations to bear the costs of blight without hardship and a reluctance to give "owners of commercial and industrial properties, regardless of hardship, a statutory right to unload onto local authorities at any time they thought fit."[37]

3. *Qualifying Land*

It is a prerequisite to the service of a blight notice that the land should have been identified in some way as being likely to be affected by public sector proposals. The provisions were initially restricted to instances where proposals had been formally approved, as in an approved structure plan or local plan. But delays in plan approval could mean that several years lapsed between the initial identification and the final approval, and that blight might then be well advanced. The Minister of Housing and Local Government in 1970 had urged authorities to be aware of the hardship which might exist, and to be prepared to acquire land at an earlier stage in certain cases.[38] The Land Compensation Act 1973 then gave statutory effect to that request, by advancing the entitlement date to the point where plans had reached some preliminary stage in preparation, but short of final approval. The 1973 Act amends the 1971 Act in a clumsy fashion, but the combined effect of the two measures on blight procedure entitlement may be summarised under five headings:

(a) Planning requirements

This category includes, first, land which is "indicated" as land which may be required for the purposes of any functions of a government department, local authority, statutory undertaker or the National Coal Board (or

---

[33] T.C.P.A. 1971, s.192(3) and (4). By virtue of s.203(3), a "resident owner-occupier" must be an individual (not a company) who has occupied the whole or a substantial part of the hereditament as a private dwelling in right of an owner's interest therein for the preceding six months; or for the whole of a six-month period ending not more than 12 months before service of the notice and the property has remained unoccupied since.

[34] *Ibid.* s.192(4)(a); Town and Country Planning (Limit of Annual Value) Order 1973 (S.I. 1973 No. 425). By virtue of s.203(1) an "owner-occupier" means a "person" who occupied the whole or a substantial part of the hereditament in the same way as for a "resident owner-occupier" (see preceding note), and so the definition is broad enough to encompass corporate occupation.

[35] *Ibid.* s.192(5). Special provisions relating to the severance of agricultural units are contained in L.C.A. 1973, ss.79–81.

[36] *Ibid.* s.201.

[37] *Hansard* H.C. Debs., Vol. 595 col. 593 (Mr. J.R. Bevins M.P., Parliamentary Undersecretary to the M.H.L.G.)(November 15, 1958).

[38] M.H.L.G. Circular 46/70.

proposed for inclusion in an action area) in any *structure plan*, whether approved or submitted for approval, and in any submitted proposals for alteration or any Secretary of State's proposed modifications.[39] Similarly, the category includes land which is "allocated" by any *local plan* (including a deposited plan, proposals for alterations and proposed modifications) for those purposes, or which is defined as the site of proposed development for the purposes of any such functions.[40] Third, the category includes land allocated in an *old-style development plan* (or proposals for alterations or Secretary of State's modifications).[41] In the case of proposals not yet approved, the authority are entitled subsequently to issue a different counter-notice upon the approval or rejection of the proposals.[42] Finally, there is also an entitlement in respect of proposals in any *non-statutory plan* of an authority, provided it has been approved by a resolution of the authority[43]; and also in respect of land which the authority have resolved to safeguard for development for any of the functions mentioned above, or in respect of which they have been directed by the Secretary of State to restrict the grant of planning permission to safeguard it for such development.[44]

In all the cases, the requirement is that the land be allocated as needed for public sector development. A proposal for development which can be expected to be carried out by the private sector, or through private/public sector partnership, does not qualify.[45] The effect of that allocation is often an enhancement rather than a diminution of land values.

(b) Highways requirements

Proposals for new highways and for road widening schemes are a principal source of blight, due both to the number of properties that may be affected and the lengthy timescale of road planning. The functional split since 1974 between county-level local highway authorities, and district council responsibility in development control has not assisted in coordinating planning and highway requirements, and highways blight is a maliase which local planners may be largely powerless to prevent. The categories of land in respect of which a blight notice in highways cases may be served are, first, land indicated in a development plan (otherwise than in the manner which would qualify it as a "planning" requirement above) as land on which a highway is proposed to be constructed or land to be included in a highway as proposed to be improved or altered.[46] Second, the qualification extends to land shown on plans approved by a resolution of a local highway authority

---

[39] T.C.P.A. 1971, s.192(1)(*a*); L.C.A. 1973, s.68(1). By virtue of T.C.P.A. 1971, s.192(2), the structure plan indication is superseded for the purposes of these provisions once a local plan has come into force allocating or defining land in "the district" for the relevant functions.

[40] T.C.P.A. 1971, s.192(1)(*b*); L.C.A. 1973, s.68(2).

[41] T.C.P.A. 1971, Sched. 24, para. 58; L.C.A. 1973, s.68(3).

[42] L.C.A. 1973, s.68(6).

[43] L.C.A. 1973, s.71. Approval in principle by the authority's engineer will not suffice, unless he has power to exercise this function on behalf of the authority: *Page* v. *Gillingham B.C.* (1970) 21 P. & C.R. 973 (L.T.).

[44] L.C.A. 1973, s.71.

[45] *Bolton Corporation* v. *Owen* [1962] 1 Q.B. 470 (area listed in the development plan as one to be cleared and redeveloped: Lands Tribunal not entitled to draw inference from scale of the clearance that local authority powers would have to be used).

[46] T.C.P.A. 1971, s.192(1)(*c*).

as land comprised in the site of a highway as proposed to be constructed, improved or altered by them.[47] It does not, however, extend to plans approved informally by the highways engineer[48] (unless he has power to exercise the approval function on behalf of the authority), and there is a suspicion that some highway authorities have in the past deliberately resorted to such a method of approving plans, especially for improvement lines, as a means of avoiding blight notice liability. The third category is that of land on or adjacent to the line of highways works as indicated in an order or scheme under Part II of the Highways Act 1980 relating to trunk roads, special roads or classified roads.[49] Fourthly is land on which the Secretary of State proposes to provide a trunk road or special road and of which he has notified the local planning authority.[50] The final category of highways requirements is the case of land affected by new street orders.[51]

(c) Housing requirements

Land may be indicated as required for specifically public sector housing functions, including clearance and redevelopment, in a development plan, and thus within category (a) above. Other cases covered separately are where land is indicated by information published in accordance with proposals for a general improvement area as land the authority propose to acquire[52]; and land within a declared slum clearance area, or surrounded by or adjoining such an area and which the authority have determined to purchase.[53]

(d) New town and urban development areas

This category includes land within the area of a proposed new town or urban development area, or a designated site for a new town or urban development area.[54]

(e) Other compulsory purchase requirements

A blight notice may be served in respect of land where there is a compulsory purchase order in force in respect of the land,[55] or in respect of rights over the land,[56] but the authority have yet to serve a notice to treat; and also where land is authorised to be acquired by a special enactment.[57]

---

[47] Ibid. s.192(1)(e).
[48] See, e.g. Page v. Gillingham B.C. (1970) 21 P. & C.R. 973 (L.T.); Fogg v. Birkenhead C.B.C. (1970) 22 P. & C.R. 208 (L.T.).
[49] T.C.P.A. 1971, s.192(1)(d) (as amended by the Highways Act 1980, Sched. 24, para. 20). The category extends to any order or scheme submitted for confirmation to, or prepared in draft by, the Secretary of State: L.C.A. 1973, s.69 (as amended by the Highways Act 1980, Sched. 24, para. 23).
[50] T.C.P.A. 1971, s.192(1)(f).
[51] L.C.A. 1973, s.76.
[52] T.C.P.A. 1971, s.192(1)(h).
[53] L.C.A. 1973, s.73.
[54] Ibid. s.72 (new towns); L.G.P.L.A. 1980, s.147 (urban development).
[55] T.C.P.A. 1971, s.192(1)(j). By L.C.A. 1973, s.20, this category is extended to include a compulsory order submitted to, or prepared in draft by, a Minister, though not yet confirmed.
[56] Ibid. s.192(1)(g)(as amended by L.C.A. 1973, s.75).
[57] Ibid. s.192(1)(i).

4. *The Requirement to Make Reasonable Endeavours to Sell*

It is a precondition to the service of a blight notice that the claimant should have made reasonable endeavours to sell his interest in the property, but in consequence of the fact that the land fell into one of the above categories he has been unable to sell "except at a price substantially lower than that for which it might reasonably have been expected to sell" if it were not so affected.[58] The Lands Tribunal have accepted that the claimant must in all cases actually put his interest on the market, no matter that he is advised by the agent that it is impossible to sell it,[59] but that in appropriate circumstances an advertisement displayed by the claimant in the window of the premises rather than through the usual agency channels may suffice.[60] The main principle is that the attempt to sell should be genuine. In *Glodwick Mutual Institute and Social Club* v. *Oldham Metropolitan Borough Council*,[61] for example, the Tribunal declined to accept the Club's endeavours as reasonable where they had informed people responding to their advertisements of the authority's compulsory purchase order, but failed to inform them that the borough solicitor had formally disclaimed any intention to proceed with the acquisition.

5. *The Authority's Counter-Notice*

The authority may object to a blight notice on any one or more of seven prescribed grounds, set out in Table 25, although not all are available in respect of every category of land. Different consequences attach to different grounds, and, most importantly, the burden of proof if the matter is referred to the Lands Tribunal is cast differently in the case of different objections. The general rule is that, unless it is shown to the satisfaction of the Tribunal that the objection is not well founded, the Tribunal must uphold the objection.[62] The effect is to cast the onus on the claimant to prove the objection to be not well founded.[63] It is his duty, for example, to show that the land comes within one of the categories listed above, and that he has made reasonable endeavours to sell. But in the case of objections on grounds (b), (c) or (d) (no intention to acquire all or any of the land, or to acquire it within 15 years), the objection must be made out to the satisfaction of the Tribunal before it may be upheld.[64]

The latter grounds of objection arise where the authority have either abandoned their proposals altogether, or have postponed them for 15 years or more. Grounds (b) and (c) are not available in the case of a blight notice relating to a slum clearance area.[65] The effect of successfully relying upon grounds (b) (abandonment) or (d) (postponement for 15 years or more) is

---

[58] *Ibid.* s.193(1).
[59] *Parkins* v. *West Wiltshire D.C.* (1975) 31 P. & C.R. 427.
[60] *Lade* v. *Brighton Corporation* (1970) 22 P. & C.R. 737.
[61] (1979) 19 R.V.R. 197.
[62] T.C.P.A. 1971, s.195(2).
[63] *Bolton Corporation* v. *Owen* [1962] 1 Q.B. 470.
[64] T.C.P.A. 1971, s.195(3). The 15 year ground is available only in respect of long term planning or highways proposals (structure plan indications and highways proposals no further advanced than an indication in the development plan).
[65] L.C.A. 1973, s.73(2).

Table 25

Grounds of Objection to a Blight Notice

(a) that no part of the hereditament or agricultural unit to which the notice relates is comprised in land of any of the specified descriptions;

(b) that the appropriate authority (unless compelled to do so by virtue of these provisions) do not propose to acquire any part of the hereditament, or (in the case of an agricultural unit) any part of the affected area, in the exercise of any relevant powers;

(c) that the appropriate authority propose in the exercise of relevant powers to acquire a part of the hereditament or (in the case of an agricultural unit) a part of the affected area specified in the counter-notice, but (unless compelled to do so by virtue of these provisions) do not propose to acquire any other part of that hereditament or area in the exercise of any such powers;

(d) that (in the case of land falling within paragraph (a) or (c) but not (d), (e) or (f) of section 192 (1) of this Act) [*i.e., land indicated or allocated by a structure plan or local plan, but not for highways purposes*] the appropriate authority (unless compelled to do so by virtue of these provisions) do not propose to acquire in the exercise of any relevant powers any part of the hereditament or (in the case of an agricultural unit) any part of the affected area during the period of fifteen years from the date of the counter-notice or such longer period from that date as may be specified in the counter-notice;

(e) that, on the date of service of the notice under section 193 of this Act, the claimant was not entitled to an interest in any part of the hereditament or agricultural unit to which the notice relates;

(f) that (for reasons specified in the counter-notice) the interest of the claimant is not an interest qualifying for protection under these provisions;

(g) that the conditions specified in paragraph (c) and (d) of section 193 (1) of this Act are not fulfilled [*i.e., the requirements as to having made reasonable endeavours to sell*].

Source: Town and Country Planning Act 1971, s. 194 (2).

that any compulsory purchase order which has been made under the appropriate enactment, and any authorisation under a local Act, ceases to have effect[66]; but there is no other general sterilisation for the future of powers of acquisition. Successful reliance upon ground (c) (intention to acquire part only) has a similar consequence in respect of land not proposed to be acquired,[67] but it may still be possible for the claimant to require the acquisition of the whole area under the usual compulsory purchase rules, and the Tribunal in considering an objection under this ground are obliged to consider whether part of the land can be taken without material detriment to the house, building or manufactory (or, in the case of a park or garden belonging to a house, without seriously affecting the amenity or convenience of the house).[68]

[66] T.C.P.A. 1971, s.199(1) and (2).
[67] *Ibid.* s.199(3) and (4).
[68] *Ibid.* s.202(2).

6. *Compensation*

Compensation is assessed generally according to the normal rules for compulsory acquisition, and thus any effect upon the value of the interest attributable to the scheme underlying the acquisition,[69] or to the fact that an indication has been given that the land is, or is likely to be, acquired by an authority possessing compulsory purchase powers,[70] is to be disregarded. It is through this principle that the value of the blight notice procedure as a compensatory remedy is secured, although since its availability is limited to those who have been quite unable to sell on the open market, or only at a price substantially below unblighted value, not all the costs of planning blight are yet imposed upon public authorities. Further, an authority's successful objection on the grounds of abandonment or postponement of their acquisition too often fails to lift the blight on a property, because it comes too late, at a time when the area may already have suffered serious decline with little prospect of early self-regeneration.

There are three exceptions to the usual compensation rules. The first is that the special compensation provisions applicable to listed buildings are carried through to blighted properties.[71] Secondly, the special compensation code relating to slum clearance properties applies also to advance acquisitions under the blight notice procedures.[72] Third, there is no right to a "home loss"[73] payment or "farm loss"[74] payment where acquisition is pursuant to a blight notice.

7. *Discretionary Acquisition*

The statutory provisions, following their broadening by the 1973 Act, extend now to most instances of blight. But cases are still liable to arise of badly blighted properties which do not fall within the prescribed categories, and of types of ownership which do not qualify. There is no entitlement in such cases to require advance acquisition, but there is a discretion. Authorities have been urged by the Secretary of State to exercise that discretion as sympathetically as possible.[75] If a proposal is so uncertain that there is little chance of its being implemented in the foreseeable future, they have been asked to say so clearly. If, on the other hand, there is a reasonable likelihood that the proposal will go ahead, and consequential difficulty in selling the property is causing hardship, the authority is urged to treat a request to acquire in substantially the same way as if a formal blight notice were served.

---

[69] *Pointe Gourde Quarrying and Transport Co. Ltd.* v. *Sub-Intendent of Crown Lands* [1947] A.C. 565; L.C.A. 1961, s.6 and Sched. 1.
[70] L.C.A. 1961, s.9.
[71] T.C.P.A. 1971, s.197.
[72] L.C.A. 1973, s.73(4) and (5); T.C.P.A. 1971, s.197(*b*)
[73] *Ibid.* s.29(5).
[74] *Ibid.* s.34(6).
[75] See generally M.H.L.G. Circulars 48/59, paras.63 and 64; and 15/69, para. 26. By virtue of D.O.E. Circular 73/73, para. 74 the advice remains effective following the passing of the 1973 Act.

E. Compensation for the depreciatory effects of public sector development

1. *Introduction*

Much of the development carried out by public agencies, including government departments, statutory undertakers and local authorities, is, because of its scale and purpose, obtrusive and unattractive. It imposes a cost upon adjoining land, which loses value because of the inconvenience caused by the development. In some cases, such as with a large airport, the depreciatory impact spreads over a wide area. In other cases, the effect is more localised, and beyond the area of immediate impact the effect of the development may be to enhance land values.

These interactions are in many respects identical to those between private land uses, and as such are generally accepted as risks inherent in land ownership. But in one important respect there has long been a significant difference. Whilst the common law action for nuisance was available against a private owner in respect of the external effects of his use of land, it would not lie against a use carried on under statutory authorisation. In *Hammersmith and City Railway Co.* v. *Brand*[76] the House of Lords held that a statutory authorisation to carry out a particular function, in that case the construction of a railway, implicitly extended to authorise any nuisance arising from its use if that was the unavoidable consequence of carrying out the function.

This principle of implicit statutory immunity was narrowed to some extent as a result of robust judicial interpretation of the Land Clauses Consolidation Act 1845, section 68, which provided a procedure for determining claims for compensation for land "injuriously affected" by the execution of works, "if any party shall be entitled to any compensation" in respect of the land. This formula the courts managed to convert into an *entitlement* to compensation in respect of land which had not been held along with land taken for the carrying out of the works (for which there was clear entitlement for such compensation).[77] It was:

> " . . . an interpretation which fixes upon it a meaning having little perceptible relation to the words used. This represents a century of judicial effort to keep the primitive wording—which itself has an earlier history—in some sort of accord with the realities of the industrial age."[78]

But the remedy failed to fill the vacuum left by the immunity from the common law action in nuisance. It was limited to the injurious effects of the execution of works, and did not extend to the use of the works once

---

[76] (1869) L.R.4 H.L. 171.

[77] Under the Land Clauses Consolidation Act 1845, s.63, although this had been given an unnecessarily narrow interpretation in *Edwards* v. *Minister of Transport* [1964] 2 Q.B. 134 limiting it to injury resulting from use of the former land of the claimant, and excluding use of land acquired from others. That ruling has since been reversed by L.C.A. 1973, s.44.

[78] *Argyle Motors (Birkenhead) Ltd.* v. *Birkenhead Corporation* [1975] A.C. 99 at 127, *per* Lord Wilberforce. This interpretation has since been given legislative blessing by the Compulsory Purchase Act 1965, s.10(2), which endorses "the right which section 68 of the Land Clauses Consolidation Act, 1845, has been construed as affording."

construction was complete.[79] Further, it was limited by reference to injury to the value of the land, or the interest in the land. No claim could therefore be made out for injury to purely personal and not proprietary rights, nor in respect of damage such as loss of profits or goodwill, except to the extent that they depreciated the value of the claimant's interest in land.[80]

The effect of these limitations was that the external costs of public development were imposed upon the market arbitrarily and with only limited relief. For many types of modern development, including highways and airports, it is the nuisance arising from the use, far more than the construction, which damages the surrounding environment. The arbitrariness of the rules had attracted much criticism by the late 1960s from *Justice* and the land-related professional bodies,[81] and the Government eventually introduced reforming legislation in 1973. The purpose of the legislation was not simply that of rectifying past anomalies, but of shifting a very much greater proportion of the cost of public sector development onto the community as a whole. That objective has been reflected not only in the new remedies introduced by the Act, but also in the measures taken to inform landowners of their new rights and to encourage the making of claims.

The Land Compensation Act 1973 introduced three major new remedies. First, a new entitlement to compensation for depreciation caused by the use of public works; secondly, provisions for the mitigation of the effects of the use of public works, including the sound-proofing of buildings, and thirdly, additional benefits for persons displaced from their land as a consequence of public works. All three remedies necessarily increase the costs of major public sector development proposals, and by explicitly becoming a factor in the design costs may be expected to influence the design of future public development so as to minimise compensatable environmental impact. Discussion of the third remedy, which includes home loss payments, farm loss payments, rights to rehousing and extended provisions for disturbance payments, is outside the scope of this book,[82] but the first two have specific implications for land use planning and require further discussion.

2. Preconditions for Depreciation Compensation

Where land which was formerly held with land that has been taken for statutorily authorised development is injuriously affected by the use of the development, compensation is payable for the resulting depreciation in value of the affected land.[83] That entitlement is no longer limited to injury arising

---

[79] Although in borderline cases the distinction between the two tended to be drawn by the courts in favour of allowing the claimant some remedy: see *e.g. Fletcher* v. *Birkenhead Corporation* [1907] 1 K.B. 205.

[80] In *Argyle Motors (Birkenhead) Ltd.* v. *Birkenhead Corporation* [1975] A.C. 99 the House of Lords declined to overthrow this limitation, and dismissed a claim for the loss of profits suffered by a car dealing business when access to their premises was obstructed temporarily during the construction of an approach road to the Mersey Tunnel, and permanently upon the completion of the works.

[81] Justice, *Compensation for Compulsory Acquisition and Remedies for Planning Restrictions* (1969) and *Supplemental Report* (1972); Chartered Land Societies Committee, *Compensation for Compulsory Acquisition and Planning Restrictions* (1968); the Law Society, *Memorandum on Compensation and Planning Blight* (1971).

[82] See generally the *Encyclopaedia of Compulsory Purchase* (Sweet and Maxwell), Vol. 1; and Corfield and Carnwath, *Compulsory Acquisition and Compensation*, pp. 372–392.

[83] Land Clauses Consolidation Act 1845, s.63.

from the use of the land actually taken, but extends to the use of the whole of the works.[84]

Where no land has been taken from the claimant, the former limited rights to compensation for execution of the works have been extended by the Act of 1973 to include an entitlement to compensation for depreciation of the value of an interest in land by "physical factors" caused by the use of new public works.[85] The physical factors prescribed are noise, vibration, smell, fumes, smoke and artificial lighting and the discharge on to the claimant's land of any solid or liquid substance.[86] By confining the provisions to the effects of physical factors, the legislation deliberately excludes non-physical factors such as loss of amenity, privacy or view.[87] Also excluded, because it does not qualify as an effect of the "use of public works," is the effect of traffic management measures such as one-way street diversions and kerbside parking restrictions which may have a substantial impact upon the property values and trading profits of the neighbouring area.

The "public works" to which the provisions extend include any works or land provided or used in the exercise of statutory powers, including highways (for which "physical factors" excludes accidents involving vehicles) and aerodromes (for which "physical factors" includes those caused by aircraft arriving at or departing, but not aircraft accidents).[88] The works must also be such, except in the case of highways, as to be immune from actions for nuisance,[89] and the provisions have effect only in relation to works which were first used after completion after October 17, 1969.[90] Alterations to existing public works are also included where they have been reconstructed, excluded or otherwise altered, or their use has been changed.[91]

As with blight notices, entitlement to claim is restricted to owner-occupiers of premises, and in the case of dwelling-houses the right to claim is restricted to the fee simple owner or tenant under a fixed term tenancy with more than three years unexpired term, occupying the dwelling as his residence if the interest carries the right of occupation, at the time of the claim.[92] In other cases the right is limited to owner-occupiers' interests[93] in

---

[84] L.C.A. 1973, s.44.

[85] *Ibid.* s.1.

[86] *Ibid.* s.1(2).

[87] And *cf. Shepherd* v. *Lancashire C.C.* (1976) 33 P. & C.R. 296 (mere proximity to refuse tip insufficient in absence of physical factors).

[88] *Ibid.* s.1(2) and (7).

[89] *Ibid.* s.1(6). Where the responsible authority avoid compensation liability by contending that there is no immunity, no immunity will then extend to a subsequent action in nuisance on the same claim: s.17.

[90] *Ibid.* s.1(8) and (9). In the case of a highway, the relevant date is the date on which it was first open to public traffic.

[91] *Ibid.* s.9(1). The change of use provisions do not extend to aerodromes or highways (subs.(1)(c)), nor to mere intensification of use (subs.(7)). Only runway or apron alterations (as defined by subs.(6)) suffice in the case of physical factors caused by aircraft. In the case of highways, only alterations where (a) the location, width or level of the carriageway is altered (otherwise than by resurfacing) or (b) an additional carriageway for the highway is provided beside, above or below an existing one (subs.(5)).

[92] *Ibid.* s.2(2).

[93] *Ibid.* s.2(3), (4) and (5). An "owner-occupier" in this case is a person who occupies the whole or a substantial part of the land in right of an owner's interest (fee simple or fixed term tenancy with more than three years unexpired). For an agricultural unit the claimant must occupy the whole unit, and be entitled to an owner's interest in the whole or any part.

whole or part of either an agricultural unit or a hereditament with an annual value of no more than £2,500.[94]

There is a settling-in period of 12 months after the works first come to be used (the "relevant date"), and claims may not be made until after the expiry of that period except in the case of land sold during the period.[95] There was formerly a two year limit for the lodging of claims, but following disquiet at the failure by authorities to advertise extensively the right to claim compensation, the limit was lifted by the Local Government, Planning and Land Act 1980 and replaced by a general limitation period of six years,[96] and provision made for the retrospective acceptance of late claims in highways cases where the Minister is satisfied "that the publicity given to the right to claim compensation in respect of those works and to the period within which and the events before which claims should be made was not such as to make potential claimants sufficiently aware of those matters."[97]

3. Assessment of Compensation

Compensation for depreciation under these provisions is based upon prices current on the "first claim day" (the day following the expiry of the 12 month settling-in period); and account is required to be taken of the level of use then prevailing and any intensification that can then be reasonably expected.[98] Any building, or improvement or extension of a building on the land first occupied after the relevant date is to be ignored, along with any change of use made before then.[99] The benefit of any works carried out in mitigation of the effect of the works under the provisions discussed below under heading (4), is to be taken into account[1]; although their effect on the value of the interest may often be substantially less than their actual cost, and may even be negative.

The value of the interest is required to be assessed as at the date of service of the notice of claim,[2] and the planning assumptions to be made include an assumption that permission would be granted for any Eighth Schedule development, except to the extent that compensation has already been paid under section 169 (unexpended balance of development value) or has become payable under a discontinuance order relating to any building or use to which the Eighth Schedule would otherwise apply.[3] It is to be assumed that permission would not be granted for any other development (even if it has in fact been granted)[4] and there is provision for set off where the land or other land of the claimant is benefited by the public works.[5]

Despite the elaborate valuation assumptions, the assessment is often necessarily highly subjective and arbitrary. Three main factors in practice

---

[94] *Ibid.* s.2(6); Town and Country Planning (Limit of Annual Value) Order 1973 (S.I. 1973 No. 425).
[95] *Ibid.* s.3(2).
[96] Now L.C.A. 1973, s.19(2A); and see now Limitation Act 1980, s.9.
[97] L.G.P.L.A. 1980, s.113(1)(c).
[98] L.C.A. 1973, s.4(1) and (2).
[99] *Ibid.* s.4(5).
[1] *Ibid.* s.4(3).
[2] *Ibid.* s.4(4).
[3] *Ibid.* s.5(2) and (3).
[4] *Ibid.* s.5(4).
[5] *Ibid.* s.6.

contribute to this. The first is that of inflation. The "before and after" comparison which is required to assess depreciation works best in a relatively steady market. It is a wholly artificial comparison in an era of high inflation in land values, especially where the valuation is being undertaken on the basis of a claim made some years after the first claim date. In absolute terms, inflationary increases over the intervening period will often have exceeded the depreciatory effects of the public works as the first claim date by a substantial margin. Even in real terms, an interest which was affected by the public works may have nonetheless increased in value due to inflation, and the compensation payable becomes something of an additional bonus.

Second, the time lag involved in the various stages between the planning of new public works (and their potential blighting effect), their execution and their completion means that the benefit of compensation does not necessarily go to those who have borne the loss. The landowner who sells during the period from the planning of the works through to their completion is liable to find the price depressed because of the works and uncertainty as to their potential effect, but be unable to serve a blight notice as a means of obtaining unblighted value because the land is not actually intended to be acquired. If he sells (or enters into a contract for sale) during the 12 month settling-in period, he is entitled to lodge a claim under the 1973 Act,[6] and so recoup as far as possible his loss on the sale. Following that period he has the right to claim irrespective of any intention to sell. Theoretically, the prospect of making a compensation claim should prevent market values from becoming substantially depressed during planning and execution stages, but in practice the effect has not been particularly marked, and the benefit of the new provisions is thus unevenly spread. Some, but not all, of the depreciatory effect of public works are now recoverable, but to a different extent depending upon timing.

Third, in assessing the impact of the prescribed physical factors on land values, there is little to guide the valuers. There are seldom any true "market" comparables for the location, because prices for comparably affected properties may have in turn been affected by the availability of mitigating works, and the gap between depreciated values and undepreciated values eroded by inflation. In consequence, resort has been had, in practice, to comparatively arbitrary rules of thumb, expressed as a percentage of capital value. Allowances for noise from new highways, for example, have tended to range from between 2½ to 15 per cent., based ultimately upon the levels of settlement achieved by the district valuer on other comparable claims.[7]

4. Mitigating Works

An important feature of the 1973 legislation is the provision of non-pecuniary rights to have sound-insulation works carried out to mitigate the

[6] *Ibid.* s.3(3). Compensation does not actually become payable, however, until after the first claim day.
[7] See, *e.g. Barb* v. *Secretary of State for Transport* (1978) vol. 6 of the *Lands Tribunal Cases*, case 18 (7½ per cent. of capital value in respect of property some 730 metres from the highway); *Marchant* v. *Secretary of State for Transport* (1979) 19 R.V.R. 113 (bungalow situated 582 metres from motorway; Lands Tribunal accepted that the level of sound would have affected a prospective purchaser's bid, who would have expected to find a peaceful and rural, if not idyllic situation).

injurious effects of the public development.[8] The right exists in respect of dwellings and other buildings within 300 metres of the carriageway, identified as being likely to experience certain prescribed levels of noise, by means of a map or list drawn up by the highway authority in accordance with a technical memorandum issued by the Government.[9] The works include the double-glazing of certain windows and doors, and the provision of sound-attenuated ventilation equipment, in accordance with detailed specifications prescribed by Regulations.[10] The specifications are remarkably inflexible, and their effect may be to force an owner to accept disfiguring works without modification at risk of losing all entitlement. For the purpose of assessing compensation under the other provisions of the 1973 Act discussed above, the benefit of the sound-proofing works is to be assumed whether or not the owner has availed himself of them.[11]

Control over aircraft noise can be maintained to some extent by prescribing flight paths and limiting operational hours under powers conferred by the Civil Aviation Act 1982. Power to carry out mitigating works on dwellings and other buildings affected by aircraft noise was conferred originally by the Airports Authority Act 1965, and is now contained in the Civil Aviation Act 1982.[12] The machinery is that the Secretary of State is empowered by statutory instrument to establish grant-aiding schemes for noise insulation, limited to such buildings and to such areas as may be specified in the scheme.[13]

[8] L.C.A. 1973, s.20.
[9] Noise Insulation Regulations 1975 (S.I. 1975 No. 1763), regs.6 and 7. The methodology is contained in *Calculation of Road Traffic Noise* (H.M.S.O., 1975).
[10] Noise Insulation Regulations 1975, Sched. 1.
[11] L.C.A. 1973, s.4(3).
[12] Sections 78–80.
[13] See, *e.g.* the Heathrow Airport-London Noise Insulation Grants Scheme 1980 (No. 153); Gatwick Airport-London Noise Insulation Grants Scheme 1980 (No. 154); Heathrow Airport-London Noise Insulation Grants (Schools) Scheme 1977 (No. 1319).

APPENDICES

APPENDIX A

STRUCTURE PLANS AND LOCAL PLANS (AS AT JUNE 1, 1982)

I. STRUCTURE PLANS

A. England

1. Approved plans

((A) = Alteration or replacement)

	Operative		Operative
Bedfordshire	11.1.80	Leicestershire (excl Rutland)	27.5.76
Berkshire (Central)	14.4.80	Leicestershire (excl Rutland)	
Berkshire (East)	14.4.80	(Transport) (A)	7.2.80
Berkshire (West)	26.2.79	Leicestershire (Rutland)	7.12.79
Buckinghamshire	5.12.79	Lincolnshire	17.12.81
Cambridgeshire	6.8.80	Merseyside	27.11.80
Cheshire	9.7.79	Norfolk	6.12.79
Cleveland—East Cleveland	31.10.77	Norfolk (Norwich Area Shopping)	
Cleveland—East Cleveland		(A)	2.11.81
(Housing) (A)	28.12.79	Northamptonshire	21.1.80
Cleveland—Hartlepool	27.3.80	Northumberland	25.9.80
Cleveland—Teesside	31.10.77	North Yorkshire	26.11.80
Cleveland—Teesside (Industry)		Nottinghamshire	22.7.80
(A)	28.12.79	Oxfordshire	26.2.79
Cleveland—West Cleveland	31.10.77	Peak District NP	5.12.79
Cleveland—West Cleveland		Shropshire (Salop)	28.2.80
(Housing) (A)	29.12.79	Somerset	22.2.82
Cornwall	14.8.81	South Yorkshire	19.12.79
Derbyshire	2.7.80	Staffordshire	23.5.78
Devon	1.5.81	Staffordshire—Burton upon Trent	23.5.78
Dorset (South East)	5.2.80	Staffordshire—Stoke on Trent	23.5.78
Durham—County	28.1.81	Staffordshire (N Staffs Transport	
Durham—Darlington (Reg. 8)	28.1.81	Review) (A)	13.12.79
East Sussex	17.5.78	Suffolk	10.8.79
East Sussex—First Alteration (A)	26.9.80	Surrey	14.4.80
Essex	26.4.82	Tyne and Wear	5.10.81
Gloucestershire	21.10.81	Warwickshire	28.7.75
Greater London Development		Warwickshire—Nuneaton &	
Plan	6.76	Bedworth (Reg 8)	10.8.79
Greater Manchester	26.3.81	Warwickshire—Warwick	
Hampshire (Mid)	30.9.80	Leamington & Kenilworth (Reg	
Hampshire (North East)	20.10.80	8)	10.8.79
Hampshire (South)	11.3.77	Warwickshire—Rugby (Reg 8)	10.8.79
Hereford &		Warwickshire (Transport) (A)	10.8.79
Worcester—Herefordshire	26.1.76	Warwickshire (Popn. Empl. etc.)	
Hereford &		(A)	10.8.79
Worcester—Worcestershire	28.7.75	West Midlands—Birmingham	17.5.78
Hereford &		West Midlands—Coventry CB	6.5.75
Worcester—Worcester City	27.3.80	West Midlands—Coventry (Land	
Hereford & Worcester—Worcs		Review) (A)	10.8.79
(Area adj Worcester City) (A)	27.3.80	West Midlands—Dudley	17.5.78
Hertfordshire	21.9.79	West Midlands—Solihull CB	6.5.75
Humberside	19.3.79	West Midlands—Walsall	17.5.78
Isle of Wight	8.2.79	West Midlands—Warley	17.5.78
Kent	31.3.80	West Midlands—West Bromwich	17.5.78
Lancashire (North East)	12.11.79	West Midlands—Wolverhampton	17.5.78

West Midlands—Replacement (A)	16.4.82	Wiltshire (South)	31.7.80
West Sussex	13.6.80	Wiltshire (West)	10.6.81
West Yorkshire	8.7.80	Wiltshire (North-East)	10.12.81

2. *Submitted plans*

Buckinghamshire—1st Alteration (A)	Kent—1st Alteration (A)
Buckinghamshire—2nd Alteration (A)	Lancashire (Central/North)
Cambria/Lake District NP—Joint	Norfolk—Gt. Yarmouth Housing
Dorset (end. S.E.)	Guidelines (A)
East Sussex—2nd Alteration (A)	Norfolk—Popn. & Housing (A)
Lancashire (Central/North)	Oxfordshire (Minerals) (A)
Hampshire (South West)	Staffordshire—Replacement
Hertfordshire—First Alteration (A)	Warwickshire—3rd Alteration
Isles of Scilly	Warwickshire—Stratford-upon-Avon (Reg 8)

B. Wales

1. *Approved plans*

Gwent	23.4.81	South Glamorgan	14.1.80
Gwynedd	29.7.77	West Glamorgan	11.9.80
Mid Glamorgan	11.3.82		

2. *Submitted plans*

Clwyed	Dyfed
Powys	

II. LOCAL PLANS

A. England

1. *Local plans adopted*

(DP = District Plan: SP = Subject
Plan: AA = Action Area Plan)

		Date of Adoption
Birmingham City	Sutton Coldfield DP	24.4.78
Blaby DC	Glenfield DP	23.5.78
Bolton MBC	Farnworth DP	16.6.81
Brent LB	Willesden Green DP	13.12.80
Brent LB	Harlesden Modified DP	4.2.82
Bromsgrove DC	Belbroughton DP	1.11.80
Camden LB	Borough Plan DP	15.11.78
Camden LB	Camden Town AA	15.11.78
Charnwood BC	Rothley Mountsorrel AA	10.3.80
Cherwell DC	Banbury Town DP	3.11.80
City of London	Smithfield DP	2.4.81
Cleethorpes BC	Laceby Village Plan (DP)	24.11.80
Cleveland CC	River Tees Plan for Recreation &	
	Amenity (SP)	14.1.81
Coventry City	Eagle Street AA	8.2.77
Coventry City	Eden Street AA	9.12.75
Coventry City	Longford AA	27.12.78
Croydon LB	Croydon DP	18.4.82
Derwentside DC	Green Street AA	1.9.81
East Hertfordshire DC	East Hertfordshire DP	1.11.81
East Northants DC	Irthlingborough DP	30.11.81
Eastleigh BC	Eastleigh Town Centre AA	21.6.69
Gillingham BC	Gillingham Town Centre DP	15.12.81
Glanford DC	Messingham DP	21.5.81
GLC	Covent Garden AA	25.1.78
Hammersmith and Fulham LB	Borough Plan DP	15.7.81
	1st alteration	18.3.82
Hampshire CC	Fareham Western Wards AA	19.3.79
Hampshire CC	Totton DP	24.11.80
Hampshire CC	Chandlersford DP	26.10.81

Harborough DC	Broughton Astley Central Area DP	16.12.81
Haringey LB	Haringey Central Area AA	20.7.81
Haringey LB	Haringey DP	19.4.82
Harrow LB	Harrow Town Centre AA	16.9.81
Havant BC	Havant Town Centre AA	1.7.80
Hinckley & Bosworth BC	Groby DP	23.6.78
Hinckley & Bosworth BC	Markfield DP	14.8.79
Hinckley & Bosworth BC	Ratby DP	16.10.79
Horsham DC	Horsham Area DP	24.2.82
Hove BC	Brunswick Town DP	2.10.80
Humberside CC	Coastal Caravans and Camping SP	28.7.81
Hyndburn BC	Church DP	14.7.81
Ipswich BC	Ipswich Central Area	9.12.81
Lambeth LB	Waterloo DP	19.9.77
Leicester City	Abbey DP	28.9.78
Leicester City	Central Leicester DP	25.3.82
Leominster DC	Kington DP	15.4.81
Lewes DC	Town of Lewes DP	27.8.79
Lichfield DC	Northern Area DP	28.10.80
Malvern Hills DC	Kempsey DP	26.3.80
Merton LB	Mitcham AA	14.12.81
New Forest DC	Totton Town Centre AA	18.2.81
Newbury DC	Newbury and Thatcham DP	17.11.81
Newcastle-under-Lyme BC	Audley DP	17.6.80
Newcastle-under-Lyme BC	Red Street AA	20.12.78
Newham LB	Beckton DP	4.3.80
North Warwickshire DC	Atherstone DP	20.5.81
North West Leics DC	Coleorton DP	4.10.77
North West Leics DC	Coalville Area DP	10.3.81
North West Leics DC	Bardon Industrial AA	5.1.82
North West Leics DC	Ashby Woulds Area DP	5.1.82
Nottingham City	Basford, Forest Fields, Radford DP	11.3.81
Nuneaton BC	Galley Common DP	11.4.79
Nuneaton BC	Nuneaton Town Centre DP	8.7.81
Oadby and Wigston DC	Oadby DP	2.2.82
Peak Park Jt.P.B.	Bakewell	23.4.82
Portsmouth City	Portsmouth City Airport DP	19.9.79
Redbridge LB	Ilford Town Centre AA	17.4.80
Redditch DC	Feckenham DP	14.11.79
Ribble Valley DC	Clitheroe DP	4.3.82
Richmond-upon-Thames LB	Richmond Town Centre AA	9.3.82
Rochdale MBC	Rochdale Town Centre DP	8.10.80
Rossendale BC	Rossendale DP	28.4.82
Salford City	Brunswick DP	21.3.80
Sandwell MBC	Oldbury with Langley DP	16.12.80
Scunthorpe BC	Skippingdale AA	15.10.79
Shepway DC	Folkestone and Hythe DP	19.12.81
Solihull MBC	Elmdon Heath/Lugtrout Lane/Wheryetts Lane AA	5.10.77
Solihull MBC	Solihull Green Belt SP	5.10.77
South Staffordshire DC	South Staffordshire DP No 1	22.7.80
South Staffordshire DC	South Staffordshire DP No 2	1.1.82
Stafford BC	North West Stafford DP No 3	4.3.80
Stafford BC	Stone DP	30.9.80
Stafford BC	South West Stafford DP No 2	10.3.81
Staffordshire Moorlands DC	Leek DP	7.2.81
St. Helens B.C.	Newton-le-Willows DP	21.4.82
Stratford-upon-Avon DC	Bishops Itchington DP	25.10.78
Stratford-Upon-Avon DC	Leisure in the Avon Valley SP	14.4.80
Stratford-Upon-Avon DC	Southam DP	5.1.79
Sutton LB	South Sutton DP	10.12.79
Sutton LB	Wrythe and Hackbridge DP	22.10.79

Sutton LB	Sutton DP	12.1.81
Vale Royal DC	Frodsham and Helsby DP	22.5.81
Vale Royal DC	Northwich DP	22.5.81
Vale Royal DC	Winsford DP	25.1.82
Walsall MBC	Darlaston DP	16.6.80
Waltham Forest LB	Waltham Forest DP	17.4.80
Warrington BC	Rixton Brickworks SP	31.10.80
Warrington BC	Walton Park SP	30.3.82
Warrington BC	Stretton Airfield SP	18.5.82
Warwick DC	Lapworth DP	17.3.80
Watford BC	Watford DP	11.5.81
Wealdon DC	Crowborough DP	26.4.82
West Oxfordshire DC	Eynsham DP	24.2.82
Worcester City	Recreation SP	2.2.82
Wychavon DC	Fladbury DP	16.10.79

2. *Local plans on deposit*

Alnwick DC	Alnwick Town Centre DP
Amber Valley DC	Belper – Kilburn DP
Ashford BC	Ashford DP
Babergh DC	Hadleigh DP
Babergh DC	Sudbury DP
Barnsley MBC	Penistone DP
Barnsley MBC	Dearne Towns DP
Berkshire CC	Minerals SP
Bexley LB	Bexleyheath Town Centre AA
Bexley LB	Borough (excl. Bexleyheath TC) DP
Birmingham City	Harborne District Centre DP
Blaby DC	Enderby/Narborough DP
Blaby DC	Blaby, Glen Parva and Whetstone DP
Blackburn BC	Darwen DP
Blackburn BC	Blackburn DP
Bolsover DC	Shirebrook Centre DP
Boothferry BC	Swinefleet DP
Boothferry BC	Gilbardyke/Newport DP
Bracknell DC	Eastern Bracknell DP
Bracknell DC	Crowthorne Central DP
Brighton BC	Brighton Central Area DP
Broxbourne BC	Broxbourne DP
Buckinghamshire CC	Minerals SP
Bury MBC	Tottington Area DP
Bury MBC	West Bury DP
Bury MBC	Unsworth Area DP
Calderdale MBC	Todmorden DP
Cambridge City	Newnham & West Cambridge DP
Charnwood DC	Quorn DP
Cheshire CC	South Cheshire Green Belt SP
Chester City	Greater Chester DP
Chichester DC	Chichester and Downland DP
Chiltern DC	Chesham Town Centre and Waterside DP
Coventry City	Foleshill DP
Crawley BC	Crawley Borough DP
Croydon LB	Croydon DP
Cumbria CC	Sedbergh DP
Dacorum DC	Dacorum DP
Daventry DC	Woodford Hales DP
Derby City	Chellaston DP
Derby City	Oakwood DP
Derby City	City Centre DP

Derbyshire CC	South and South East Derbyshire Green Belts SP
Derwentside DC	Annfield Plain DP
Doncaster MBC	Mexborough/Conisbrough DP
Doncaster MBC	Armthorpe, Edenthorpe, Kirk Sandall, Barnby Dun and Adjoining Area DP
Durham CC	Waste Disposal SP
East Hants DC	Alton Area DP
East Northants DC	Thrapston DP
East Yorkshire BC	Market Weighton DP
East Sussex CC	Combe Haven Valley DP
Enfield LB	Borough Plan DP
Glanford BC	Barton-upon-Humber DP
Gloucester City	City of Gloucester DP
Greater Manchester CC	Green Belt SP
GMC/Oldham/Manchester City/Tameside	Medlock Valley SP
Greenwich LB	Woolwich AA
Hammersmith and Fulham LB	Fulham Town Centre Inset Plan
Harborough DC	Lutterworth and Bitteswell DP
Haringey LB	Haringey DP
Havant BC	Elmsworth Town Centre DP
Hertsmere DC	Hertsmere DP
Hillingdon LB	Northwood DP
Hillingdon LB	Ickeham DP
Horsham DC	Crawley Western Fringe DP
Hounslow LB	Brentford DP
Humberside CC	Intensive Livestock Units SP
Islington LB	Islington DP
Kensington and Chelsea RB	RB Kensington and Chelsea DP
Kent CC	Dungeness Countryside Plan SP
Kent CC	Kent Countryside Plan SP
Kent CC	Minerals (sand, gravel & flagstone) SP
Kent CC	Stour Valley Countryside SP
Knowsley MBC	Prescot Town Centre AA
Lambeth LB	Norwood Industrial AA
Lambeth LB	Borough (excl. Waterloo) Plan DP
Leeds City	Central Business Area DP
Leeds City	Wetherby DP
Leeds City	Rothwell DP
Lewes DC	Newhaven DP
Lewisham LB	Catford DP
Lewisham LB	Catford AA
Lewisham LB	Deptford DP
Lichfield DC	Burntwood Area DP
Lichfield DC	Fradley Area DP
Luton BC	Chapel Langley DP
Macclesfield BC	Macclesfield DP
Malvern Hills DC	Upon-upon-Severn DP
Merseyside CC	Green Belt SP
Merton LB	Borough Plan DP
Mid Bedfordshire DC	Sandy, Biggleswade and Potton End DP
Mole Valley DC	Dorking Area DP
New Forest DC	Copythorne - Netley Marsh DP
Newbury DC	West Berks Rural Area DP
Newcastle-upon-Tyne City	Little Benton Area DP
Newcastle-upon-Tyne City	Shields Road Area DP
Newham LB	Stratford and Canning Town DP
North Beds BC	Kempston DP
North East Derbys DC	Dronfield Town Centre DP

North East Derbys DC	Clay Cross/North Wingfield DP
North Hertfordshire DC	North Hertfordshire DP
North West Leics DC	Kegworth DP
North Wiltshire DC	Malmesbury DP
Nottinghamshire CC	Sand and Gravel SP
Peak Park PB	Bakewell DP
Penwith DC	Hayle DP
Purbeck DC	Lytchett Maltravers DP
Restormel DC	St. Austell Area DP
Richmond-upon-Thames LB	Richmond Town Centre AA
Rossendale BC	Rossendale DP
Rushcliffe BC	Wilford-Clifton-Ruddington DP
St. Albans City	St. Albans DP
St. Helens BC	Newton-le-Willows DP
St. Helens BC	Sutton DP
Salford City	Worsley and Boothstown DP
Salford City	Walkden and Little Hulton DP
Salford City	Eccles DP
Salford City	Central Salford DP
Salford City	Great Cheatham Street DP
Sandwell MBC	Owen Street, Tipton AA
Sandwell MBC	Oldbury District Centre AA
Scarborough BC	Whitby DP
Scunthorpe BC	Town Centre DP
Sedgefield DC	Aycliffe Village DP
Sedgefield DC	Bishop Middleham DP
Selby DC	Sherburn in Elmet DP
Sevenoaks DC	West Kingsdown DP
Sheffield City	Stocksbridge DP
Sheffield City	Lower Don Valley DP
Sheffield City	Green Belt SP
Shepway DC	Folkestone and Hythe DP
Shropshire CC	Severn Gorge DP
Shropshire CC	Mineral Extraction on Wenlock Edge SP
Somerset CC	Lynton and Lynmouth DP
South Beds DC	Houghton Regis DP
South Northants DC	Towcester DP
South Wight BC	West Wight DP
Southwark LB	North Southwark DP
St. Helens BC	Newton-le-Willows DP
Staffordshire CC	North Staffordshire Green Belt SP
Stevenage BC	Stevenage DP
Surrey CC	North West Surrey Minerals SP
Swale BD	Faversham DP
Tamworth BC	Tamworth DP
Teignbridge DC	Newton Abbot DP
Teignbridge DC	Bovey Tracey DP
Test Valley BC	Romsey Town Centre DP
Tewkesbury DC	Gloucester Northern Environs DP
Thamesdown BC	Swindon Central Area DP
Three Rivers DC	Three Rivers DP
Tonbridge and Malling DC	Borough Green and Platt DP
Tunbridge Wells and Maidstone Joint	Paddock Wood DP
Tyne and Wear CC	Ryton Greenside Quarries SP
Tynedale DC	Hexham Town Centre DP
Vale of White Horse DC	Farringdon DP
Vale Royal DC	Tarporley DP
Wandsworth LB	Wandsworth DP
Wansbeck DC	Ashington Town Centre DP
Warrington BC	Stretton Airfield SP
Warrington BC	Warrington Town Centre DP

Warwick DC	Leamington Town Centre DP
Warwickshire CC	Green Belt SP
Wealden DC	Crowborough DP
Welwyn Hatfield DC	Welwyn Hatfield DP
West Midlands CC	Barr Beacon and Sandwell Valley Countryside and Recreation SP
Westminster City	City of Westminster DP
Wigan MBC	Ince and Platt Bridge DP
Wimborne DC	Wimborne and Colehill DP
Winchester City	Denmead DP
Worcester City	St. Peter the Great DP
Wrekin DC	Wrekin Rural Area DP
Wyre Forest DC	Stourport-on-Severn Town Centre DP

B. Wales

1. Local plans adopted

Local Planning Authority	Plan	Date of adoption
Gwent CC	Brynmawr DP	2.7.80
Cardiff City	East Moors DP	2.12.80
Gwynedd CC and Dwyfor BC	Porthmadog-Ffestiniog DP	12.7.79
Gwynedd CC	Touring Caravans and Tents SP	28.4.80
Cardiff City	South Butetown DP	28.10.81
Cardiff City	North Butetown DP	26.11.81
Aberconwy BC	Llandudno-Conwy DP	11.3.82
Islwyn BC	Trinant and Pentwyn DP	7.4.82

2. Local plans on Deposit

Local Planning Authority	Plan
Gwynedd CC	Ardudwy DP
Cardiff City	Lisvane DP
Gwynedd CC	Llanelltyd DP
Cardiff City	Radyr/Morganstown DP
Afan BC	Upper Afan Valley DP
Cardiff City	West Ely/St. Fagans DP
Gwynedd CC, Arfon BC and Ynys Mon BC	Menai Strait DP
Torfaen BC	South East Pontypool DP
Vale of Glamorgan BC	Barry DP
Vale of Glamorgan BC	Barry-Penarth Coastal DP

APPENDIX B

Town and Country Planning General Development Order 1977

(S.I. 1977 No. 289)

Dated February 22, 1977, made by the Secretary of State for the Environment under the Town and Country Planning Act 1971 and Local Government Act 1972

ARTICLE

3. Permitted development.

٭   ٭   ٭   ٭   ٭

8. Notice under section 26.

٭   ٭   ٭   ٭   ٭

Schedule 1

PERMITTED DEVELOPMENT

CLASS

  I. Development within the curtilage of a dwelling house.
  II Sundry minor operations.
  III. Changes of use.
  IV. Temporary buildings and uses.
  V. Uses by members of recreational organisations.
  VI. Agricultural buildings, works and uses.
  VII. Forestry buildings and works.
  VIII. Development for industrial purposes.
  IX. Repairs to unadopted streets and private ways.
  X. Repairs to services.
  XI. War damaged buildings, works and plant.
  XII. Development under local or private Acts, or orders.
  XIII. Development by local authorities.
  XIV. Development by local highway authorities or the Greater London Council.
  XV. Development by drainage authorities.
  XVI. Development by Water authorities.
  XVII. Development for sewerage and sewage disposal.
  XVIII. Development by statutory undertakers.
  XIX. Development by mineral undertakers.
  XX. Development by the National Coal Board.
  XXI. Uses of aerodrome buildings.
  XXII. Use as a caravan site.
  XXIII. Development on licensed caravan sites.

٭   ٭   ٭   ٭   ٭

Permitted development

3.—(1) Subject to the subsequent provisions of this order, development of any class specified in Schedule 1 to this order is permitted by this order and may be undertaken upon land to which this order applies, without the permission of the local planning authority or of the Secretary of State:

Provided that the permission granted by this order in respect of any such class of development shall be defined by any limitation and be subject to any condition imposed in the said Schedule 1 in relation to that class.

(2) Nothing in this article or in Schedule 1 to this Order shall operate so as to permit any development contrary to a condition imposed in any permission granted or deemed to be granted under Part III of the Act otherwise than by this order.

(3) The permission granted by this article and Schedule 1 to this order shall not, except in relation to development permitted by classes IX, XII or XIV in the said Schedule, authorise any development which requires of involves the formation, laying out or material widening of a means of access to an existing highway which is a trunk or classified road, or creates an obstruction to the view of persons using any highway used by vehicular traffic at or near any bend, corner, junction or intersection so as to be likely to cause danger to such persons.

(4) Any development of class XII authorised by an Act or order subject to the grant of any consent or approval shall not be deemed for the purposes of this order to be so authorised unless and until that consent or approval is obtained; and in relation to any development of class XII authorised by any Act passed or order made after 1st July 1948 the foregoing provisions of this article shall have effect subject to any provision to the contrary contained in the Act or order.

*   *   *   *   *

Notice under section 26

8.—(1) The following classes of development are designated for the purposes of section 26 of the Act:—

(*a*) construction of buildings for use as public conveniences;

(*b*) construction of buildings or other operations, or use of land, for the disposal of refuse or waste materials or as a scrap yard or coal yard or for the winning or working of minerals;

(*c*) construction of buildings or other operations (other than the laying of sewers, the construction of pumphouses in a line of sewers, the construction of septic tanks and cesspools serving single dwelling-houses or single buildings in which not more than ten people will normally reside, work or congregate, and works ancillary thereto) or use of land, for the purpose of retention, treatment or disposal of sewage, trade waste or sludge;

(*d*) construction of buildings to a height exceeding 20 metres;

(*e*) construction of buildings or use of land for the purposes of a slaughter-house or knacker's yard, or for killing or plucking poultry;

(*f*) construction of buildings and use of buildings for any of the following purposes, namely, as a casino, a funfair or a bingo hall, a theatre, a cinema, a music hall, a dance hall, a skating rink, a swimming bath or gymnasium (not forming part of a school, college or university), or a Turkish or other vapour or foam bath;

(*g*) construction of buildings and use of buildings or land as a zoo or for the business of boarding or breeding cats or dogs;

(*h*) construction of buildings and use of land for motor car or motor-cycle racing;

(*i*) use of land as a cemetery.

(2) The form of notice required to be published under section 26(2) of the Act shall be that set out in Part I of Schedule 3 hereto, and the copy of the notice accompanying the application shall be certified by or on behalf of the applicant as having been published in a named newspaper on a date specified in the certificate.

(3) Certificates issued for the purposes of section 26(2) of the Act shall be in the forms set out in Part II of Schedule 3 hereto.

(4) The form of notice required by section 26(3) of the Act to be posted on the land shall be that set out in Part III of Schedule 3 hereto.

SCHEDULE 1

The following development is permitted under Article 3 of this order subject to the limitations contained in the description of that development in column (1) and subject to the conditions set out opposite that description in column (2).

Column (1)	Column (2)
Description of Development	Conditions

Class I.—Development within the curtilage of a dwellinghouse

¹[1. The enlargement, improvement or other alteration of a dwellinghouse so long as:

(*a*) the cubic content of the original dwellinghouse (as ascertained by external measurement) is not exceeded by more than—

---

¹ Substituted by S.I. 1981 No. 245 as from April 1, 1981. In its application to land which on April 1, 1981, is within a National Park, Area of Outstanding Natural Beauty or Conservation Area, the following limitations apply in place of those specified in Class I.1 of this Order: see S.I. 1981 No. 246, *post*:

(*a*) the cubic content of the original dwellinghouse (as ascertained by external measurement) is not exceeded by more than 50 cubic metres of ten per cent., whichever is the greater, subject to a maximum of 115 cubic metres;

(*b*) the height of the building as so enlarged, improved or altered does not exceed the height of the highest part of the roof of the original dwellinghouse;

(*c*) no part of the building as so enlarged, improved or altered projects beyond the forwardmost part of any wall of the original dwellinghouse which fronts on a highway;

(*d*) no part of the building (as so enlarged, improved or altered) which lies within a distance of two metres from any boundary of the curtilage of the dwellinghouse has, as a result of the development, a height exceeding four metres;

(*e*) the area of ground covered by buildings within the curtilage of the dwellinghouse (other than the original dwellinghouse) does not thereby exceed fifty per cent. of the total area of the curtilage excluding the ground area of the original dwellinghouse:

Provided that:—

(*a*) the erection of a garage, stable, loosebox or coachhouse within the curtilage of the dwellinghouse shall be treated as the enlargement of the dwellinghouse for all purposes of this permission (including calculation of cubic content);

(*b*) for the purposes of this permission the extent to which the cubic content of the original dwellinghouse is exceeded shall be ascertained by deducting the amount of the cubic content of the original dwellinghouse from the amount of the cubic content of the dwellinghouse as enlarged, improved or altered (whether such enlargement, improvement or alteration was carried out in pursuance of this permission or otherwise); and

Column (1)   Column (2)

Description of Development   Conditions

(i) in the case of a terrace house, 50 cubic metres or ten per cent., whichever is the greater; or

(ii) in any other case, 70 cubic metres or fifteen per cent., whichever is the greater, subject (in either case) to a maximum of 115 cubic metres;

(b) the height of the building as so enlarged, improved or altered does not exceed the height of the highest part of the roof of the original dwellinghouse;

(c) no part of the building as so enlarged improved or altered projects beyond the forwardmost part of any wall of the original dwellinghouse which fronts on a highway;

(d) no part of the building (as so enlarged, improved or altered) which lies within a distance of two metres from any boundary of the curtilage of the dwellinghouse has, as a result of the development, a height exceeding four metres;

(e) the area of ground covered by buildings within the curtilage (other than the original dwellinghouse) does not thereby exceed fifty per cent. of the total area of the curtilage excluding the ground area of the original dwellinghouse:

Provided that:—

(a) the erection of a garage or coachhouse within the curtilage of the dwellinghouse shall be treated as the enlargement of the dwellinghouse for all purposes of this permission (including the calculation of cubic content) if any part of that building lies within a distance of five metres from any part of the dwellinghouse;

(b) the erection of a stable or loose-box anywhere within the curtilage of the dwellinghouse shall be treated as the enlargement of the dwellinghouse for all purposes of this permission (including the calculation of cubic content);

(c) for the purposes of this permission the extent to which the cubic content of the original dwellinghouse is exceeded shall be ascertained by deducting the amount of the cubic content of the original dwellinghouse from the amount of the cubic content of the dwelling-

(c) the limitation contained in subparagraph (d) above shall not apply to development consisting of:—

(i) the insertion of a window (including a dormer window) into a wall or the roof of the original dwellinghouse, or the alteration or enlargement of an existing window; or

(ii) any other alterations to any part of the roof of the original dwellinghouse.

Column (1)	Column (2)
Description of Development	Conditions

house as enlarged, improved or altered (whether such enlargement, improvement or alteration was carried out in pursuance of this permission or otherwise);

(d) where any part of the dwellinghouse will, as a result of the development, lie within a distance of five metres from an existing garage or coachhouse, that building shall (for the purpose of the calculation of cubic content) be treated as forming part of the dwellinghouse as enlarged, improved or altered; and

(e) the limitation contained in subparagraph (d) above shall not apply to development consisting of:—

    (i) the insertion of a window (including a dormer window) into a wall or the roof of the original dwellinghouse, or the alteration or enlargement of an existing window; or

    (ii) any other alterations to any part of the roof of the original dwellinghouse.]

2. The erection or construction of a porch outside any external door of a dwellinghouse so long as:

(a) the floor area does not exceed 2 square metres;

(b) no part of the structure is more than 3 metres above the level of the ground;

(c) no part of the structure is less than 2 metres from any boundary of the curtilage which fronts on a highway.

[2][3. The erection, construction or placing, and the maintenance, improvement or other alteration, within the curtilage of a dwellinghouse, of any building or enclosure (other than a dwelling, stable or loose-box) required for a purpose incidental to the enjoyment of the dwellinghouse as such including the keeping of poultry, bees, pet animals, birds or other livestock for the domestic needs or personal enjoyment of the occupants of the dwellinghouse, so long as:

(a) no part of such building or enclosure projects beyond the forwardmost part of any wall of the original dwellinghouse which fronts on a highway;

(b) in the case of a garage or coachhouse, no part of the building is within a distance of five metres from any part of the dwellinghouse;

(c) the height does not exceed, in the case of a

[2] Substituted by S.I. 1981 No. 245 as from April 1, 1981. In its application to land which on April 1, 1981, is within a National Park, Area of Outstanding Natural Beauty or Conservation Area this class does not include development consisting of the erection, construction or placing, or the maintenance, improvement or other alteration, of garages and coachhouses.

Column (1)   Column (2)

Description of Development   Conditions

building with a ridged roof, 4 metres, or in any other case, 3 metres;

(d) the area of ground covered by buildings within the curtilage (other than the original dwellinghouse) does not thereby exceed fifty per cent. of the total area of the curtilage excluding the ground area of the original dwellinghouse.]

4. The construction within the curtilage of a dwellinghouse of a hardstanding for vehicles for a purpose incidental to the enjoyment of the dwellinghouse as such.

5. The erection or placing within the curtilage of a dwellinghouse of a tank for the storage of oil for domestic heating so long as:

(a) the capacity of the tank does not exceed 3500 litres;

(b) no part of the tank is more than 3 metres above the level of the ground;

(c) no part of the tank projects beyond the forwardmost part of any wall of the original dwellinghouse which fronts on a highway.

Class II.—Sundry minor operations

1. The erection or construction of gates, fences, walls or other means of enclosure not exceeding 1 metre in height where abutting on a highway used by vehicular traffic or 2 metres in height in any other case, and the maintenance, improvement or other alteration of any gates, fences, walls or other means of enclosure: so long as such improvement or alteration does not increase the height above the height appropriate for a new means of enclosure.

2. The formation, laying out and construction of a means of access to a highway not being a trunk or classified road, where required in connection with development permitted by article 3 of and Schedule I to this order (other than under this class).

3. The painting of the exterior of any building or work otherwise than for the purpose of advertisement, announcement or direction.

[3]Class III.—Changes of use

[Development consisting of a change of use:—

(a) to use as a light industrial building as defined

[3] Substituted by S.I. 1981 No. 245 as from April 1, 1981. In its application to land which on April 1, 1981, was within a National Park, Area of Outstanding Natural Beauty or Conservation Area, the limitations on the cubic content and the aggregate floor space of buildings extended or altered pursuant to sub-paragraph (iv) are that:

(i) the cubic content of the original building (as ascertained by external measurement) is not exceeded by more than 10 per cent.; and

(ii) the aggregate floor space of the original building is not exceeded by more than 500 square metres.

Column (1)	Column (2)
Description of Development	Conditions

by the Use Classes Order from use as a general industrial building as so defined;

(b) to use as a light industrial building as defined by the Use Classes Order from use for any purpose included in class X referred to in the Schedule to the Use Classes Order;

(c) to use for any purposes included in class X referred to in the Schedule to the Use Classes Order from use as a light industrial building or from use as a general industrial building (as defined respectively by the Use Classes order);

(d) to use as a shop for any purpose included in class I refered to in the Schedule to the Use Classes Order from use as:—

   (i) a shop for the sale of hot food;
   (ii) a tripe shop;
   (iii) a shop for the sale of pet animals or birds;
   (iv) a cat's meat shop; or
   (v) a shop for the sale of motor vehicles:

Provided that paragraphs (b) and (c) above apply only where the total amount of floor space in the building used for the purposes of the undertaking does not exceed 235 square metres.]

Class IV.—Temporary buildings and uses

1. The erection or construction on land in, on, over or under which operations other than mining operations are being or are about to be carried out (being operations for which planning permission has been granted or is deemed to have been granted under Part III of the Act, or for which planning permission is not required), or on land adjoining such land, of buildings, works, plant or machinery needed temporarily in connection with the said operations, for the period of such operations.

Such buildings, works, plant or machinery shall be removed at the expiration of the period of such operations and where they were sited on any such adjoining land, that land shall be forthwith reinstated.

2. The use of land (other than a building or the curtilage of a building) for any purpose or purposes except as a caravan site on not more than 28 days in total in any calendar year (of which not more than 14 days in total may be devoted to use for the purpose of motor car or motor-cycle racing or for the purpose of the holding of markets), and the erection or placing of moveable structures on the land for the purposes of that use:

Provided that for the purpose of the limitation imposed on the number of days on which land may be used for motor car or motor-cycle racing, account shall be taken only of those days on which races are held or practising takes place.

Column (1)	Column (2)
Description of Development	Conditions

Class V.—Uses by members of recreational organisations

The use of land, other than buildings and not within the curtilage of a dwellinghouse, for the purposes of recreation or instruction by members of an organisation which holds a certificate of exemption granted under section 269 of the Public Health Act 1936, and the erection or placing of tents on the land for the purposes of that use.

Class VI.—Agricultural buildings, works and uses

1. The carrying out on agricultural land having an area of more than one acre and comprised in an agricultural unit of building or engineering operations requisite for the use of that land for the purposes of agriculture (other than the placing on land of structures not designed for those purposes or the provision and alteration of dwellings), so long as:—

(a) the ground area covered by a building erected pursuant to this permission does not, either by itself or after the addition thereto of the ground area covered by any existing building or buildings (other than a dwellinghouse) within the same unit erected or in course of erection within the preceding two years and wholly or partly within 90 metres of the nearest part of the said building, exceed 465 square metres;

(b) the height of any buildings or works does not exceed 3 metres in the case of a building or works within 3 kilometres of the perimeter of an aerodrome, nor 12 metres in any other case;

(c) no part of any buildings (other than moveable structures) or works is within 25 metres of the metalled portion of a trunk or classified road.

2. The erection or construction and the maintenance, improvement or other alteration of roadside stands for milk churns, except where they would abut on any trunk or classified road.

3. The winning and working, on land held or occupied with land used for the purposes of agriculture, of any minerals reasonably required for the purposes of that use, including—

(i) the fertilisation of the land so used, and

(ii) the maintenance, improvement or alteration of buildings or works thereon which are occupied or used for the purposes aforesaid,

so long as no excavation is made within 25 metres of the metalled portion of a trunk or classified road.

Column (1)   Column (2)

Description of Development   Conditions

Class VII.—Forestry buildings and works

The carrying out on land used for the purposes of forestry (including afforestation) of building and other operations (other than the provision or alteration of dwellings) requisite for the carrying on of those purposes, and the formation, alteration and maintenance of private ways on such land, so long as:—

(*a*) the height of any buildings or works within 3 kilometres of the perimeter of an aerodrome does not exceed 3 metres;

(*b*) no part of any buildings (other than moveable structures) or works is within 25 metres of the metalled portion of a trunk or classified road.

Class VIII.—Development for industrial purposes

[4][1. Development of the following descriptions, carried out by an industrial undertaker on land used (otherwise than (i) in contravention of previous planning control or (ii) without planning permission granted or deemed to be granted under Part III of the Act) for the carrying out of any industrial process, and for the purposes of such process, or on land used (otherwise than as aforesaid) as a dock, harbour or quay for the purposes of an industrial undertaking:—

(i) the provision, rearrangement or replacement of private ways or private railways, sidings or conveyors;

(ii) the provision or rearrangement of sewers, mains, pipes, cables or other apparatus;

(iii) the installation or erection, by way of addition or replacement, of plant or machinery, or structures or erections of the nature of plant or machinery, not exceeding 15 metres in height or the height of the plant, machinery, structure or erection so replaced, whichever is the greater;

(iv) the extension or alteration of buildings (whether erected before or after 1st July 1948) so long as the height of the original building is not exceeded and the cubic content of the original building (as ascertained by external measurement) is not exceeded by more than twenty per cent. nor the aggregate floor space thereof by more than 750 square metres;

so long as:—

(*a*) in the case of operations carried out under sub-paragraphs (iii) or (iv) the external

[4] Substituted by S.I. 1981 No. 245.

Column (1)	Column (2)
Description of Development	Conditions

appearance of the premises of the undertaking is not materially affected;

(*b*) in the case of operations carried out under sub-paragraph (iv), no part of the building is, as a result of the development, within a distance of five metres from any boundary of the curtilage of the premises; and

(*c*) in the case of operations carried out under sub-paragraph (iv) no certificate would be required under section 67 of the Act if an application for planning permission for the development in question were made:

Provided that the erection on land within the curtilage of any such building of an additional building to be used in connection with the original building shall be treated as an extension of the original building, and where any two or more original buildings comprised in the same curtilage are used as one unit for the purposes of the undertaking, the reference in this permission to the cubic content shall be construed as a reference to the aggregate cubic content of those buildings, and the reference to the aggregate floor space as a reference to the total floor space of those buildings.]

2. The deposit by an industrial undertaker of waste material or refuse resulting from an industrial process on any land comprised in a site which was used for such deposit on 1st July 1948, whether or not the superficial area or the height of the deposit is thereby extended.

Class IX.—*Repairs to unadopted streets and private ways*

The carrying out of works required for the maintenance or improvement of an unadopted street or private way, being works carried out on land within the boundaries of the street or way.

Class X.—*Repairs to services*

The carrying out of any works for the purpose of inspecting, repairing or renewing sewers, mains, pipes, cables, or other apparatus, including the breaking open of any land for that purpose.

Class XI.—*War damaged building, works and plant*

The rebuilding, restoration or replacement of buildings, works or plant which have sustained war damage, so long as:—

Column (1)	Column (2)
Description of Development	Conditions

(a) the cubic content of the building or of the works or plant immediately before the occurrence of such damage is not increased by more than such amount (if any) as is permitted under Class I or Class VIII;

(b) there is no material alteration from the external appearance immediately before the occurrence of such damage except with the approval of the local planning authority.

Class XII.—Development under local or private Acts, or orders

Development authorised (i) by any local or private Act of Parliament or (ii) by any order approved by both Houses of Parliament or (iii) by any order made under section 14 or section 16 of the Harbours Act 1964 being, in any such case, a local or private Act, or an order, which designates specifically both the nature of the development thereby authorised and the land upon which it may be carried out:

Provided that where the development consists of or includes the erection, construction, alteration or extension of any building (which expression shall include any bridge, aqueduct, pier or dam, but not any other structure or erection), or the formation, laying out or alteration of a means of access to any highway used by vehicular traffic this permission shall be exercisable in respect of such building or access as the case may be only if the prior approval of (a) the district planning authority (except in Greater London or a National Park); (b) in Greater London, the local planning authority, or (c) in a National Park, the county planning authority is obtained for the detailed plans and specifications thereof; but that authority shall not refuse to grant approval, or impose conditions on the grant thereof, unless they are satisfied that it is expedient so to do on the ground that:—

(a) the design, or external appearance of such building, bridge, aqueduct, pier or dam would injure the amenity of the neighbourhood and is reasonably capable of modification so as to conform with such amenity; or

(b) in the case of a building, bridge, aqueduct, pier or means of access, the erection, construction, formation, laying out, alteration or extension, ought to be and could reasonably be carried out elsewhere on the land.

Column (1)   Column (2)

Description of Development   Conditions

Class XIII.—Development by local authorities

1. The erection or construction and the maintenance, improvement or other alteration by local
authority of:—

   (i) such small ancillary buildings, works and
      equipment as are required on land belonging
      to or maintained by them, for the purposes of
      any functions exercised by them on that land
      otherwise than as statutory undertakers;

  (ii) lamp standards, information kiosks, passenger
      shelters, public shelters and seats, telephone
      boxes, fire alarms, public drinking fountains,
      horse-troughs, refuse bins or baskets, barriers
      for the control of persons waiting to enter
      public vehicles, and such similar structures or
      works as may be required in connection with
      the operation of any public service adminis-
      tered by them.

2. The deposit by a local authority of waste
material or refuse on any land comprised in a site
which was used for that purpose on 1st July 1948,
whether or not the superficial area or the height of
the deposit is thereby extended.

Class XIV.—Development by local highway authorities or the Greater London Council

The carrying out by a local highway authority or
the Greater London Council of any works required
for or incidental to the maintenance or improvement
of existing highways being works carried out on land
outside but abutting on the boundary of the highway.

Class XV.—Development by drainage authorities

Any development by a drainage authority within
the meaning of the Land Drainage Act 1930, in, on or
under any watercourse or drainage works, in connection with the improvement or maintenance of such
watercourse or drainage works.

Class XVI.—Development by water authorities

Development of any of the following descriptions
by a water authority established under the Water Act
1973:—

  (a) the laying underground of mains, pipes or
     other apparatus;

  (b) the improvement, maintenance or repair of
     watercourse or land drainage works;

  (c) the erection, construction or placing of build-
     ings, plant, or apparatus on land or the

On completion of the
survey or investigation, or

Column (1)	Column (2)
Description of Development	Conditions

carrying out of engineering operations in, on, over or under land, for the purpose of surveys or investigations. | at the end of 6 months from the commencement of the development permitted by this class, whichever is the sooner, all such operations shall cease and all such buildings, plant or apparatus shall be removed and the land restored to its former condition.

Class XVII.—Development for sewerage and sewage disposal

Any development by or on behalf of a water authority (established under the Water Act 1973), or by a Development Corporation authorised under section 34 of the New Towns Act 1965 to exercise powers relating to sewerage or sewage disposal, being development not above ground level required in connection with the provision, improvement or maintenance of sewers.

Class XVIII.—Development by statutory undertakers

A. Railway or light railway undertakings.
   Development by the undertakers of operational land of the undertaking, being development which is required in connection with the movement of traffic by rail, other than:
   (i) the construction of railways;
   (ii) the construction or erection, or the reconstruction or alteration so as materially to affect the design or external appearance thereof, of—
      (a) any railway station or bridge;
      (b) any hotel;
      (c) any residential or educational building, office, or building to be used for manufacturing or repairing work which is not situate wholly within the interior of a railway station;
      (d) any car park, shop, restaurant, garage, petrol filling station or other building or structure provided in pursuance of the powers contained in section 14(1)(d of the Transport Act 1962 or section 10(1)(x) of the Transport Act 1968 which is not situate wholly within the interior of a railway station.

Column (1)

Description of Development

Column (2)

Conditions

B. Dock, pier, harbour, water transport, canal or inland navigation undertakings.

1. Development by the undertakers or their lessees of operational land of the undertaking, being development which is required for the purpose of shipping, or in connection with the embarking, disembarking, loading, discharging or transport of passengers, livestock or goods at a dock, pier or harbour, or the movement of traffic by canal or inland navigation, or by any railway forming part of the undertaking, other than the construction or erection, or the reconstruction or alteration so as materially to affect the design or external appearance thereof, of:—

(a) any bridge or other building not required in connection with the handling of traffic;

(b) any hotel;

(c) any educational building not situate wholly within the limits of a dock, pier or harbour;

(d) any car park, shop, restaurant, garage, petrol filling station or other building not situate wholly within the limits of a dock, pier or harbour, provided in pursuance of the powers contained in any of the following enactments:—

    the Transport Act 1962
      section 14(1)(d);
    the Transport Act 1968
      section 10(1)(x);
    the Transport Act 1968
      section 50(6).

2. The improvement, maintenance or repair of any inland waterway to which section 104 of the Transport Act 1968 applies which is not a commercial waterway or a cruising waterway, and the repair or maintenance of culverts, weirs, locks, aqueducts, sluices, reservoirs, let-off valves or other works used in connection with the control and operation of such waterways.

3. The use of any land for the spreading of dredgings.

C. Water or hydraulic power undertakings.

Development required for the purposes of the undertakings of any of the following descriptions, that is to say:—

(i) the laying underground of mains, pipes, or other apparatus;

(ii) the improvement, maintenance or repair of watercourses or land drainage works;

(iii) the maintenance or repair or works for measuring the flow in any watercourse or

Column (1)	Column (2)
Description of Development	Conditions

channel or the improvement of any such works (otherwise than by the erection or installation, by way of addition or replacement, of any structures of the nature of buildings or of any plant or machinery);

(iv) the installation in a water distribution system of booster stations, meter or switch gear houses, not exceeding (except where constructed underground elsewhere than under a highway) 29 cubic metres in capacity;

(v) the erection, construction or placing of buildings, plant or apparatus on land, or the carrying out of engineering operations, in, on, over or under land, for the purpose of surveys or investigations.

On completion of the survey or investigation or at the expiration of six months from the commencement of the development the subject of this permission, whichever is the sooner, all such operations shall cease and all such buildings, plant or apparatus shall be removed and the land restored to its former condition.

(vi) any other development carried out in, on, over or under the operational land of the undertaking except:—

   (a) the erection, or the reconstruction or alteration so as materially to affect the design or external appearance thereof, of buildings;

   (b) the installation or erection, by way of addition or replacement, of any plant or machinery, or structure or erections of the nature of plant or machinery, exceeding 15 metres in height or the height of the plant, machinery, structure or erection so replaced, whichever is the greater.

D. Gas undertakings.

Development required for the purposes of the undertaking of any of the following descriptions, that is to say:—

   (i) the laying underground of mains, pipes, or other apparatus;

   (ii) the installation in a gas distribution system of apparatus for measuring, recording, controlling or varying the pressure flow or volume of gas, and structures for housing such apparatus not exceeding (exept where constructed underground elsewhere than under a highway) 29 cubic metres in capacity;

   (iii) the construction, in any storage area or protective area specified in an order made

Column (1)

Column (2)

Description of Development

Conditions

under section 4 of the Gas Act 1965 of boreholes, other than those shown in the order as approved by the Secretary of State for Energy for the purpose of subsection (6) of the said section 4, and the erection or construction, in any such area, of any plant or machinery, or structure or erections in the nature of plant or machinery, not exceeding 6 metres in height which is required in connection with the construction of any such borehole;

(iv) the placing and storage on land of pipe and other apparatus needed for inclusion in a main or pipe which is being or is about to be laid or constructed in pursuance of a planning permission granted or deemed to be granted under Part III of the Act;

On completion of the laying or construction of the main or pipe, or at the expiration of nine months from the commencement of the development, the subject of this permission, whichever is the sooner, such pipe and apparatus shall be removed and the land shall be restored to its condition before the development took place.

(v) the erection on operational land of the undertaking, solely for the protection of plant or machinery, or structures or erections of the nature of plant or machinery, of buildings not exceeding 15 metres in height;

Approval of the details of the design and external appearance of the buildings shall be obtained from (a) the district planning authority (except in Greater London or a National Park), (b) in Greater London, the local planning authority, or (c) in a National Park, the county planning authority before the erection of the building has begun.

(vi) any other development carried out in, on, over or under operational land of the undertaking except:—

(a) the erection, or the reconstruction or alteration so as materially to affect the design or external appearance thereof, of buildings;

(b) the installation of any plant or machinery, or structures or erections of the nature of plant or machinery, exceeding 15 metres in height, or capable, without addition, of being extended to a height exceeding 15 metres;

(c) the replacement of any plant or machinery, or structures or erections of the

Column (1)	Column (2)
Description of Development	Conditions

nature of plant or machinery, to a height exceeding 15 metres or the height of the plant, machinery, structure or erection so replaced, whichever is the greater.

E. Electricity undertakings.

Development required for the purpose of the undertaking of any of the following descriptions, that is to say:—

    (i) the laying underground of pipes, cables or any other apparatus, and the construction of such shafts and tunnels as may be necessary in connection therewith;

   (ii) the installation in an electric line of feeder or service pillars, or transforming or switching stations or chambers not exceeding (except when constructed underground elsewhere than under a highway) 29 cubic metres in capacity;

  (iii) the installation of service lines to individual consumers from an electric line;

  (iv) the extension or alteration of buildings on operational land as long as the height of the original building is not exceeded and the cubic content of the original building (as ascertained by external measurement) is not exceeded by more than one-tenth nor the aggregate floor space thereof by more than 500 square metres;

   (v) the sinking of any boreholes for the purpose of ascertaining the nature of the sub-soil, and the installation of any plant or machinery, or structures or erections of the nature of plant or machinery, as may be necessary in connection therewith;

On completion of the development or at the expiration of six months from the commencement of the development the subject of this permission, whichever is the sooner, such plant or machinery or structures or erections shall be removed and the land shall be restored to its condition before the development took place.

  (vi) the erection on operational land of the undertaking, solely for the protection of plant or machinery, or structures or erections of the nature of plant or machinery, of buildings not exceeding 15 metres in height;

Approval of the details of the design and external appearance of the buildings shall be obtained from (a) the district planning authority (except in Greater London or a National Park), (b) in Greater London, the local planning authority, or (c) in a National Park, the county planning authority, before the erection of the building has begun.

Column (1)	Column (2)
Description of Development	Conditions

(vii) any other development carried out on, in or under the operational land of the undertaking except:—

    (a) the erection, or the reconstruction so as materially to affect the design or external appearance thereof, of buildings; or

    (b) the installation or erection, by way of addition or replacement, of any plant or machinery, or structures or erections of the nature of plant or machinery, exceeding 15 metres in height or the height of the plant, machinery, structure or erection so replaced, whichever is the greater.

F. Tramway or road transport undertakings.

Development required for the purposes of the undertaking of any of the following descriptions, that is to say:—

    (i) the installation of posts, overhead wires, underground cables, feeder pillars, or transformer boxes not exceeding 17 cubic metres in capacity in, on, over or adjacent to a highway for the purpose of supplying current to public vehicles;

    (ii) the installation of tramway tracks; conduits and drains and pipes in connection therewith for the working of tramways;

    (iii) the installation of telephone cables and apparatus, huts, step posts and signs required in connection with the operation of public vehicles;

    (iv) the erection or construction, and the maintenance, improvement or other alteration of passenger shelters and barriers for the control of persons waiting to enter public vehicles;

    (v) any other development of operational land of the undertaking, other than:—

        (a) the erection, or the reconstruction or alteration so as materially to affect the design or external appearance thereof, of buildings;

        (b) the installation or erection, by way of addition or replacement, of any plant or machinery, or structures or erections of the nature of plant or machinery, exceeding 15 metres in height, or the height of the plant, machinery, structure or erection so replaced, whichever is the greater;

        (c) development, not wholly within the interior of an omnibus or tramway station, in pursuance of the powers contained in

Column (1)	Column (2)
Description of Development	Conditions

section 14(1)(i)(*d*) of the Transport Act 1962 or section 10(1)(*x*) of the Transport Act 1968.

G. Lighthouse Undertakings

Development required for the purposes of the functions of a general or local lighthouse authority under the Merchant Shipping Act 1894 and any other statutory provisions made with respect to a local lighthouse authority, or in the exercise by a local lighthouse authority of rights, powers or duties acquired by usage prior to the Merchant Shipping Act 1894, except the erection, or the reconstruction or alteration so as materially to affect the design or external appearance thereof, of offices.

H. The British Airports Authority.

Development by the Authority of operational land of the undertaking, being development which is required in connection with the provision by the Authority of services and facilities necessary or desirable for the operation of an aerodrome, other than:—

    (i) the construction or erection, or the reconstruction or alteration so as materially to affect the design or external appearance thereof, of:—

        (*a*) any hotel;

        (*b*) any building (not being a building required in connection with the movement or maintenance of aircraft or with the embarking, disembarking, loading, discharge or transport of passengers, livestock or goods at an aerodrome); and

    (ii) the construction or extension of runways.

I. Post Office.

Development required for the purposes of the undertaking of any of the following descriptions, that is to say:—

    (i) the installation of public call offices (telephone kiosks), posting boxes or self-service postal machines;

    (ii) the placing of any telegraphic line as defined in the Telegraph Act 1878 in the exercise of an easement or other right compulsorily acquired under section 55 of the Post Office Act 1969;

    (iii) the use of land in case of emergency for the stationing and operation of movable apparatus required for the replacement of telephone exchanges, telephone repeater stations and

           At the expiration of the period of use all such apparatus shall be removed and the land shall be restored to

Column (1)	Column (2)
Description of Development	Conditions

radio stations and generators which have become unserviceable, for a period not exceeding six months;

(iv) any other development carried out in, on, over or under the operational land of the undertaking except:—

   (a) the erection, or the reconstruction or alteration so as materially to affect the design or external appearance thereof, of buildings;

   (b) the installation or erection, by way of addition or replacement, of any plant or machinery, or structures or erections of the nature of plant or machinery, exceeding 15 metres in height or the height of the plant, machinery, structure or erection so replaced, whichever is the greater.

its condition before the development took place.

Class XIX.—Development by mineral undertakers

1. Where mining operations have been carried out in any land at any time on or after 1st January 1946 and before 1st July 1948

   (a) in conformity with the provisions of a planning scheme or of permission granted thereunder or in accordance with permission granted at any time before 22nd July 1943 by or under an interim development order and in force immediately before 1st July 1948, or

   (b) under article 4 of the Town and Country Planning (General Interim Development) Order 1946.

and an application for permission to continue those mining operations in adjoining land was made during the period of six months from 1st July 1948 or was treated by virtue of paragraph 1 of Schedule 10 to the Town and Country Planning Act 1947 as having been made under that Act, the continuation of those operations until the application (or any appeal in respect thereof) has been dealt with.

2. The erection, alteration or extension by mineral undertakers on land in or adjacent to and belonging to a quarry or mine comprised in their undertaking of any building, plant or machinery, or structure or erection of the nature of plant or machinery, which is required in connection with the winning or working of minerals, including coal won or worked by virtue of section 36(1) of the Coal Industry Nationalisation Act 1946, but not any other coal, in pursuance of permission granted or deemed to be granted under Part III of the Act, or which is required in connection with the treatment or disposal of such minerals:

Column (1)	Column (2)
Description of Development	Conditions

Provided that where the development consists of or includes the erection, alteration or extension of a building, this permission shall be exercisable in respect of such building only if the prior approval of the local planning authority, in Greater London, and elsewhere the county planning authority is obtained for the detailed plans and specifications of the building; but that authority shall not refuse to grant approval, or impose conditions on the grant thereof, unless they are satisfied that it is expedient so to do on the ground that:—

    (*a*) the erection, alteration or extension of such building would injure the amenity of the neighbourhood and modifications can reasonably be made or conditions can reasonably be imposed in order to avoid or reduce the injury;
    or
    (*b*) the proposed building or extension ought to be, and can reasonably be, sited elsewhere.

3. The deposit of refuse or waste materials by, or by licence of, a mineral undertaker in excavations made by such undertaker and already lawfully used for that purpose so long as the height of such deposit does not exceed the level of the land adjoining any such excavation.

Class XX.—Development by the National Coal Board

Development of any of the following descriptions carried out by the National Coal Board, or their lessees or licensees, that is to say:—

    (i) the winning and working underground, in a mine commenced before 1st July 1948, of coal or other minerals mentioned in paragraph 1 of Schedule 1 to the Coal Industry Nationalisation Act 1946, and any underground development incidental thereto,
    (ii) any development required in connection with coal industry activities as defined in section 63 of the Coal Industry Nationalisation Act 1946 and carried out in the immediate vicinity of a pithead.

Provided that where the development consists of or includes the erection, alteration or extension of a building this permission shall be exercisable in respect of such building only if the prior approval of the county planning authority is obtained for the detailed plans and specifications of the building, but the county planning authority shall not refuse to grant approval, or impose conditions on the grant

Column (1)	Column (2)
Description of Development	Conditions

thereof unless they are satisfied that it is expedient so to do on the ground that:—

(a) the erection, alteration or extension of such building would injure the amenity of the neighbourhood and modifications can reasonably be made or conditions can reasonably be imposed in order to avoid or reduce the injury;
or
(b) the proposed building or extension ought to be, and can reasonably be, sited elsewhere;

(iii) the deposit of waste materials or refuse resulting from colliery production activities as defined by paragraph 2 of Schedule 1 to the Coal Industry Nationalisation Act 1946 on land comprised in a site used for the deposit of waste materials or refuse on 1st July 1948, whether or not the superficial area or the height of the deposit is thereby extended;

1. If the County planning authority so require, the Board shall, within such period as the authority may specify (not being less than three months from the date when the requirement is made) submit to them for approval a scheme making provision for the manner in which the depositing of waste materials or refuse is to be carried out and for the carrying out of operations in relation thereto (including, where appropriate the stripping and storage of surface soil and the after-treatment of the deposit) for the preservation of amenity, such scheme to relate only to the depositing and after-treatment of waste materials or refuse deposited after 1st April 1974.

2. Where a scheme submitted in accordance with condition 1 has been approved the depositing of waste materials or refuse and their after-treatment shall be carried out in accordance with the scheme, or in accordance with the scheme as modified by conditions imposed on the grant of approval, as the case may be.

(iv) development by the National Coal Board consisting of the temporary use of land for the purpose of prospecting for coal workable by

1. No development shall be begun until after the expiration of 42 days from

Column (1)   Column (2)

Description of Development   Conditions

opencast methods and the carrying out of any   the date of service of notice
operations requisite for that purpose.   in writing on the county
                                                      planning authority, indicat-
                                                      ing the nature, extent and
                                                      probable duration of the
                                                      prospecting.
                                                          2. At the expiration of the
                                                      period of prospecting, any
                                                      buildings, plant or machin-
                                                      ery and any waste materials
                                                      shall be removed and any
                                                      boreholes shall be properly
                                                      and sufficiently sealed and
                                                      other excavations filled in
                                                      and levelled, any topsoil re-
                                                      moved being replaced as the
                                                      uppermost layer.

Class XXI.—Uses of aerodrome buildings

The use of buildings on an aerodrome which is
vested in or under the control of the British Airports
Authority for purposes connected with the air
transport services or other flying activities at such
aerodrome.

Class XXII.—Use as a caravan site

The use of land, other than a building, as a caravan   The use shall be discon-
site in any of the circumstances specified in para-   tinued when the said cir-
graphs 2 to 9 (inclusive) of Schedule 1 to the Caravan cumstances cease to exist,
Sites and Control of Development Act 1960 or in the   and all caravans on the site
circumstances (other than those relating to winter   shall then be removed.
quarters) specified in paragraph 10 of the said
Schedule.

Class XXIII.—Development on licensed caravan sites

Development required by the conditions of a site
licence for the time being in force under Part I of the
Caravan Sites and Control of Development Act 1960.

APPENDIX C

Town and Country Planning (Use Classes) Order 1972

(S.I. 1972 No. 1385)

Dated September 11, 1972, *made by the Secretary of State for the Environment under s.22 of the Town and Country Planning Act* 1971.

Citation and commencement

1.—This order may be cited as the Town and Country Planning (Use Classes) Order 1972 and shall come into operation on October 28, 1972.

Interpretation

2.—(1) The Interpretation Act 1889 shall apply to the interpretation of this order as it applies to the interpretation of an Act of Parliament.

(2) In this order—

"the Act" means the Town and Country Planning Act 1971;

"shop" means a building used for the carrying on of any retail trade or retail business wherein the primary purpose is the selling of goods by retail, and includes a building used for the purposes of a hairdresser, undertaker, travel agency, ticket agency or post office or for the reception of goods to be washed, cleaned or repaired, or for any other purpose appropriate to a shopping area, but does not include a building used as a fun-fair, amusement arcade, pin-table saloon, garage, launderette, petrol filling station, office, betting office, hotel, restaurant, snackbar or café or premises licensed for the sale of intoxicating liquors for consumption on the premises;

"office" includes a bank and premises occupied by an estate agency, building society or employment agency, or (for office purposes only) for the business of car hire or driving instruction but does not include a post office or betting office;

"post office" does not include any building used primarily for the sorting or preparation for delivery of mail or for the purposes of Post Office administration;

"betting office" means any building in respect of which there is for the time being in force a betting office licence pursuant to the provisions of the Betting and Gaming Act 1960;

"launderette" includes any building used for the purpose of washing or cleaning clothes or fabrics in coin-operated machines;

"industrial building" means a building (other than a building in or adjacent to and belonging to a quarry or mine and other than a shop) used for the carrying on of any process for or incidental to any of the following purposes, namely:—

(*a*) the making of any article or of part of any article, or

(*b*) the altering, repairing, ornamenting, finishing, cleaning, washing, packing or canning, or adapting for sale, or breaking up or demolition of any article, or

(*c*) without prejudice to the foregoing paragraphs, the getting, dressing or treatment of minerals,

being a process carried on in the course of trade or business other than

711

agriculture, and for the purposes of this definition the expression "article" means an article of any description, including a ship or vessel;

"light industrial building" means an industrial building (not being a special industrial building) in which the processes carried on or the machinery installed are such as could be carried on or installed in any residential area without detriment to the amenity of that area by reason of noise, vibration, smell, fumes, smoke, soot, ash, dust or grit;

"general industrial building" means an industrial building other than a light industrial building or a special industrial building;

"special industrial building" means an industrial building used for one or more of the purposes specified in Classes V, VI, VII, VIII and IX referred to in the Schedule to this order;

"motor vehicle" means any motor vehicle for the purposes of the Road Traffic Act 1960.

(3) Reference in this order to a building may, except where otherwise provided, include references to land occupied therewith and used for the same purposes.

Use Classes

3.—(1) Where a building or other land is used for a purpose of any class specified in the Schedule to this order, the use of such building or other land for any other purpose of the same class shall not be deemed for the purposes of the Act to involve development of the land.

(2) Where a group of contiguous or adjacent buildings used as parts of a single undertaking includes industrial buildings used for purposes falling within two or more of the classes specified in the Schedule to this order as Classes III to IX inclusive, those particular two or more classes may, in relation to that group of buildings, and so long as the area occupied in that group by either general or special industrial buildings is not substantially increased thereby, be treated as a single class for the purposes of this order.

(3) A use which is ordinarily incidental to and included in any use specificed in the Schedule to this order is not excluded from that use as an incident thereto merely by reason of its specification in the said Schedule as a separate use.

Revocation

4.—The Town and Country Planning (Use Classes) Order 1963 and the Town and Country Planning (Use Classes) (Amendment) Order 1965 are hereby revoked.

Schedule

Class I.—Use as a shop for any purpose except as:—
  (i) a shop for the sale of hot food;
  (ii) a tripe shop;
  (iii) a shop for the sale of pet animals or birds;
  (iv) a cats-meat shop;
  (v) a shop for the sale of motor vehicles.

Class II.—Use as an office for any purpose.

Class III.—Use as a light industrial building for any purpose.

Class IV.—Use as a general industrial building for any purpose.

Class V. (*Special Industrial Group B*)—Use for any work which is registrable under the Alkali &c Works Regulation Act 1906, as extended by the Alkali &c Works Orders 1966 and 1971 and which is not included in any of Classes VI, VII, VIII or IX of this Schedule.

Class VI. (*Special Industrial Group B*)—Use for any of the following processes, except a process ancillary to the getting, dressing or treatment of minerals which is carried on in or adjacent to a quarry or mine:—

    (i) smelting, calcining, sintering or reduction of ores, minerals, concentrates or mattes;

    (ii) converting, refining, re-heating, annealing, hardening, melting, carburising, forging or casting of metals or alloys, other than pressure die-casting;

    (iii) recovery of metal from scrap or drosses or ashes;

    (iv) galvanising;

    (v) pickling or treatment of metal in acid;

    (vi) chromium plating.

Class VII. (*Special Industrial Group C*)—Use for any of the following processes except a process ancillary to the getting, dressing or treatment of minerals which is carried on in or adjacent to a quarry or mine:—

    (i) burning of bricks or pipes;

    (ii) lime or dolomite burning;

    (iii) production of zinc oxide, cement or alumina;

    (iv) foaming, crushing, screening or heating of minerals or slag;

    (v) processing by heat of pulverized fuel ash;

    (vi) production of carbonate of lime and hydrated lime;

    (vii) production of inorganic pigments by calcining, roasting or grinding.

Class VIII. (*Special Industrial Group D*)—Use for any of the following purposes:—

    (i) distilling, refining or blending of oils (other than petroleum or petroleum products);

    (ii) production or employment of cellulose and employment of other pressure sprayed metal finishes (other than the employment of any such finishes in vehicle repair workshops in connection with minor repairs, and the application of plastic powder by the use of fluidised bed and electrostatic spray techniques);

    (iii) boiling of linseed oil and the running of gum;

    (iv) processes involving the use of hot pitch or bitumen (except the use of bitumen in the manufacture of roofing felt at temperatures not exceeding 2200°C and also the manufacture of coated roadstone);

    (v) stoving of enamelled ware;

    (vi) production of aliphatic esters of the lower fatty acids, butyric acid, caramel, hexamine, iodoform, napthols, resin products (excluding plastic moulding or extrusion operations and production of plastic sheets, rods, tubes, filaments, fibres or optical components produced by casting, calendering, moulding, shaping or extrusion), salicylic acid or sulphonated organic compounds;

    (vii) production of rubber from scrap;

    (viii) chemical processes in which chlorphenols or chlorcresols are used as intermediates;

    (ix) manufacture of acetylene from calcium carbide;

    (x) manufacture, recovery or use of pyridine or picolines, any methyl or ethylamine or acrylates.

Class IX. (*Special Industrial Group E*)—Use for carrying on any of the following industries, businesses or trades:—

Animal charcoal manufacturer.

Animal hair cleanser, adapter or treater.

Blood albumen maker.

Blood boiler.

Bone boiler or steamer.

Bone burner.

Bone grinder.

Breeder of maggots from putrescible animal matter.

Candle maker.

Catgut manufacturer.

Chitterling or nettlings boiler.

Dealer in rags or bones (including receiving, storing, sorting or manipulating rags
in or likely to become in an offensive condition, or any bones, rabbitskins, fat
or putrescible animal products of a like nature).

Fat melter or fat extractor.

Fellmonger.

Fish curer.

Fish oil manufacturer.

Fish skin dresser or scraper.

Glue maker.

Gut scraper or gut cleaner.

Maker of feeding stuff for animals or poultry from any meat, fish, blood, bone,
feathers, fat or animal offal, either in an offensive condition or subjected to
any process causing noxious or injurious effluvia.

Manufacture of manure from bones, fish, offal, blood, spent hops, beans or other
putrescible animal or vegetable matter.

Size maker.

Skin drier.

Soap boiler.

Tallow melter or refiner.

Tripe boiler or cleaner.

Class X.—Use as a wholesale warehouse or repository for any purpose.

Class XI.—Use as a boarding or guest house, or an hotel providing sleeping
accomodation.

Class XII.—Use as a residential or boarding school or a residential college.

Class XIII.—Use as a building for public worship or religious instruction or for
the social or recreational activities of the religious body using the building.

Class XIV.—Use as a home or institution providing for the boarding, care and
maintenance of children, old people or persons under disability, a convalescent
home, a nursing home, a sanatorium or a hospital.

Class XV.—Use (other than residentially) as a health centre, a school treatment
centre, a clinic, a creche, a day nursery or a dispensary, or use as a consulting room or
surgery unattached to the residence of the consultant or practitioner.

Class XVI.—Use as an art gallery (other than for business purposes), a museum, a
public library or reading room, a public hall, or an exhibition hall,

Class XVII.—Use as a theatre, cinema, music hall or concert hall.

Class XVIII.—Use as a dance hall, skating rink, swimming bath, Turkish or other
vapour or foam bath, or as a gymnasium or sports hall.

Scale of Fees for Planning Applications

Outline applications (all types)	£44 per 0·1 ha. (or part thereof) of site area. Maximum fee £1,100 for sites of 2·5 ha. or more.

Full applications and applications for approval of reserved matters

Alterations or extensions to existing dwellings	£22 per dwellinghouse. Maximum fee of £44 per site.
Erection of dwellings	£44 per dwelling created by development. Maximum fee £2,200 for 50 or more dwellings.
Erection of buildings (other than dwellings or plant and machinery) (Subtract 465 sq. m. from the floorspace of agricultural buildings for fees purposes)	Works not creating more than 40 sq. m. of additional floorspace—£22. Works creating more than 40 sq. m. but not more than 75 sq. m. of additional floorspace—£44. Each additional 75 sq. m. (or part thereof) of floorspace—£44. Maximum fee £2,200 for 3,750 sq. m. or more.
Erection, alteration or replacement of plant and machinery	£44 or 0·1 ha. (or part thereof) of site area. Maximum fee £2,200 for 5 ha. or more.
Applications for approval of reserved matters not including design and external appearance, where design and external appearance have also been reserved	£44.

Applications for works other than building works

Winning and working of minerals	£22 per 0·1 ha. (or part thereof) of site area. Maximum fee £3,300 for 15 ha. or more.
Waste disposal	£22 per 0·1 ha. (or part thereof) of site area. Maximum fee £3,300 for 15 ha. or more.
Car parks, service roads or other accesses for existing uses	£22.
Playing fields (for sports clubs or other non-profit-making recreational bodies)	£44.
Other operations on land	£22 per 0·1 ha. (or part thereof) of site area. Maximum fee £220 for 1 ha. or more.

Other applications

Variation or removal of a condition	£44.
Change of use of a building to dwellings	£44 per additional dwelling created, subject to a maximum of £2,200.
Other changes of use	£44.

Advertisements

—relating to the business on the premises	£11.
—advanced signs directing the public to a business	£11.
—other advertisements	£44.

Concessionary fees and exemptions

Extensions and alterations to a disabled person's dwellinghouse to improve access, safety, health or comfort	No fee.
Applications required by reason of an Article 4 direction	No fee.
Applications required because of the removal of permitted development rights by a condition attached to a planning permission	No fee.
Revised application for development of the same character or description within 12 months of refusal, or of the making of the earlier application if withdrawn, or within 12 months of expiry of the statutory 8 week period, where the applicant has appealed to the Secretary of State on the grounds of non-determination	No fee.
Duplicate applications made by the same applicant within 28 days	Full fee for the first application and one-quarter of the full fee for the second application.
Renewal of temporary permission	No fee.

Source: D.O.E. Circular 14/82 (Welsh Office Circular 25/82), Appendix 3.

INDEX